Fourth Edition

THE LIFE SPAN

Human Development for Helping Professionals

PATRICIA C. BRODERICK
Penn State Prevention Research Center

PAMELA BLEWITT
Villanova University

PEARSON

Boston   Columbus   Indianapolis   New York   San Francisco   Upper Saddle River
Amsterdam   Cape Town   Dubai   London   Madrid   Milan   Munich   Paris   Montreal   Toronto
Delhi   Mexico City   São Paulo   Sydney   Hong Kong   Seoul   Singapore   Taipei   Tokyo

Vice President and Editorial Director: Jeffery W. Johnston
Vice President and Publisher: Kevin M. Davis
Editorial Assistant: Caitlin Griscom
Development Editor: Gail Gottfried
Director of Marketing: Margaret Waples
Marketing Manager: Joanna Sabella
Senior Managing Editor: Pamela Bennett
Project Manager: Lauren Carlson
Procurement Specialist: Michelle Klein
Senior Art Director: Diane Lorenzo
Text Designer: S4Carlisle Publishing Services
Cover Designer: Studio Montage
Cover Art: Kathy Collins/Getty Images
Media Project Manager: Noelle Chun
Full-Service Project Management: Christian Holdener, S4Carlisle Publishing Services
Composition: S4Carlisle Publishing Services
Printer/Binder: LSC Communications
Cover Printer: LSC Communications
Text Font: ITC Garamond Std

Credits and acknowledgments for material borrowed from other sources and reproduced, with permission, in this textbook appear on the appropriate page within the text.

Every effort has been made to provide accurate and current Internet information in this book. However, the Internet and information posted on it are constantly changing, so it is inevitable that some of the Internet addresses listed in this textbook will change.

Library of Congress Cataloging-in-Publication Data
Broderick, Patricia C.
    The life span : human development for helping professionals / Patricia C. Broderick, Pamela Blewitt. — Fourth edition.
        pages cm
    Includes bibliographical references and index.
    ISBN-13: 978-0-13-294288-1
    ISBN-10: 0-13-294288-7
1. Developmental psychology.   I. Blewitt, Pamela.   II. Title.
    BF713.B755 2015
    155—dc23
                                                        2013037511

9   18

ISBN 10:   0-13-294288-7
ISBN 13: 978-0-13-294288-1

Preface

What's New in This Edition?

The first developmental textbook written specifically for helping professionals, *The Life Span: Human Development for Helping Professionals* is now in its fourth edition. The following are just a few of the improvements and additions to this revision:

- Good empirical research about culture and ethnicity is increasingly available and has been fully integrated into this edition.
- Updated biological and neuropsychological underpinnings of development are presented in keeping with recent cutting edge advances in the developmental sciences.
- Expanded attention has been given to the effects of poverty and other adverse childhood experiences on development relative to cognitive, emotional, and health-related outcomes.
- New figures and tables give students efficient means for accessing a great deal of information. For example, Chapter 1 presents a timeline that gives the student an historical context for contemporary research within the field of developmental psychology.
- Linkages have been made between research in early and late-life cognition, in particular with regard to executive functioning.
- New boxes provide in-depth exploration of current developmental issues, such as the special challenges facing the children of immigrant families.
- Research and applications to practice are updated in all chapters.

The Conceptual Framework of This Book

The study of human development over the life span reveals the fascinating story of human beings and how they change over time. The story is both universal and uniquely personal, because it speaks to us about ourselves and the people who are important in our lives. Besides being intrinsically interesting, knowledge about development has obvious relevance for professionals engaged in psychology, counseling, education, social work, and other helping and health-related fields. We believe that in order to understand the strengths and challenges of our clients or students, we must see them in context. One important context is developmental history. As helping professionals, we must take into account the threads of continuity and change in people's lives that bring them to their present point in development. This text provides the background and the tools to enable professionals to view their clients from a developmental perspective.

This text also reflects the contemporary view that life span development is a process deeply embedded within and inseparable from the context of family, social network, and culture. People do not progress through life in isolation; rather, their developmental course influences and is influenced by other people and systems. Some of these forces are related to the cultural differences that exist in a world of increasing diversity. We recognize the importance of these factors in understanding human development and emphasize cultural and systemic influences on human growth and change throughout the book.

We would also be remiss if we neglected to emphasize the rapidly growing body of knowledge from neuroscience that is refining our appreciation of how biology and context interact. The marriage of "nature and nurture" and our greater awareness of how they interrelate contribute significantly to a more fully informed understanding of how people change over the life course. This emphasis, which has been strengthened in this new edition, provides an overarching template for practitioners to use in understanding development and in applying developmental knowledge to their work.

Research and applications within the field of human development are becoming more and more interdisciplinary with expanding links to health, social processes, well-being, and so forth. This can make it exceptionally difficult to summarize this dynamic field. Presumably, every author of a book of this nature needs to make some choices about what to include. This particular text is configured to emphasize selected theories and research that have useful applications for helping professionals. A main purpose of this book is to provide students in the helping professions with information that can be translated into professional "best practice" applications. To this end, we have tried to use the most current research available to summarize domains of knowledge that remain, essentially, fields "under investigation." Science by its very nature continually evolves in its efforts to reveal the nature of human experience. Thus, one of the assumptions we continue to emphasize in this edition is the importance of reflective practice for helping professionals.

Reflective practice involves "active, persistent, and careful consideration of any belief or supposed form of knowledge in light of the grounds that support it and the further conclusions to which it leads" (Dewey, 1933/1998, p. 9). Our primary vehicle for accomplishing this goal is twofold: (1) encouraging the reader to reflect on personal experience and assumptions about development, and (2) communicating the value of research-based knowledge as a means of understanding human development. Our particular orientation intentionally emphasizes the significance of developmental research to the work of the professional helper. We attempt to integrate various lines of developmental research into a useful whole that has practical value for helpers in applied settings. This book bears witness to the enormous amount of work done by developmental researchers, particularly in the last several decades. Without their groundbreaking contributions, helping professionals' efforts to improve people's lives would be greatly impoverished. It has been a challenge and an honor to record their contributions in this book.

Coverage and Organization

The opening chapters establish the theme of the text and introduce broad issues in development. Chapter 1 begins with an examination of the role of developmental knowledge in reflective practice. Students are introduced to classic and contemporary theoretical models and to issues that appear and reappear throughout the text. They are encouraged to reflect on their own theoretical assumptions about development and on the impact those assumptions could have in practice. Students are introduced to developmental psychopathology in a focus feature, and they can learn about prevention science and its connection to developmental research in a box feature.

Chapter 2 takes a close look at the coaction of genetic and environmental factors in the development of all aspects of the human organism. Students are introduced to genetic mechanisms in the context of epigenesis, the control of genetic expression by forces beyond the genes themselves. Sections on atypical early developments and on early brain development highlight the coaction of many genetic and environmental factors in prenatal and early postnatal development. Students are also introduced to the concept of development as adaptation and to the critical stress and adaptation system. Students emerge with an understanding of how biology and experience together craft this system and determine healthy and unhealthy outcomes.

The remaining chapters follow a chronological sequence, covering a full range of critical topics in physical, cognitive, social, and emotional development. In Chapters 3 through 5, the infancy and preschool periods are the focus. Among the topics covered are the many aspects of early cognitive growth, such as the development of representational thought and memory, executive functions, early "theory of mind" or naive psychology, the early understanding of symbols and of language, and more. Coverage of early social development includes the emergence of emotions, emotion regulation, attachment processes, early self-development, temperament, and the role of parental disciplinary style in the growth of self-regulation.

Chapters 6, 7, and 8 examine important developments in middle childhood and in the transition to adolescence, including the growth of logical thinking, the expanding capacity to process and remember information, perspective-taking skills and friendship development, influences on cognitive functioning, such as formal schooling, influences on the developing self-concept, developments in moral thinking, influences on the emergence of prosocial and antisocial behavior, sex-role development, and peer relationships. The impact of culture and context for many of these developments, such as self-concept, are considered.

Adolescence is the subject of Chapters 9 and 10, covering pubertal change, advances in logical and metacognitive skill, changes to the brain and stress system, identity development, sexual orientation, risk taking, and the influences of biology, peers, parents, school, media, and culture on adolescent behavior. Chapters 11 and 12 describe the young adult period, or what has been called "emerging adulthood," and include a close look at the way thinking changes as adulthood looms and at the progress of work, career, and intimate relationships.

Chapters 13, 14, and 15 describe developmental processes in middle and late adulthood. Chapter 13 focuses on changes in physical, cognitive, and social functioning during the middle adult years. Chapter 14 considers the questions that all middle adults face: What constitutes a well-lived life, and how do normally functioning adults cope with the enormous demands, progress, and setbacks that adult life brings? Finally, Chapter 15 reviews the challenges and developmental processes involved in late adulthood and end-of-life experiences. These chapters examine the many kinds of change that adults experience and the maintenance of well-being in the face of loss. Among the key developmental tasks discussed are marriage and its discontents, the experience of child rearing, spirituality, coping and health, the role of wisdom, stereotypes about aging, facing death and bereavement, and many more.

Features and Highlights

- **Depth of coverage:** Because the book is designed for graduate students, most topics, especially those that have special relevance to helping professionals, are covered in greater depth than in a typical life span text. The expanded coverage of research in specific areas will enhance students' understanding of the scientific basis for applications.
- **Applications:** Blending empirically supported information about treatments with the issues covered in each chapter, these revised sections offer more extensive discussion of how developmental science can inform practice. Applications sections include new and expanded topics such as adolescent health and well-being, new interventions for promoting secure infant attachments, encouraging learning through play, helping parents avoid corporal punishment, and mindfulness-based practices, among many others.
- **Focus on Developmental Psychopathology:** In many chapters, sections on psychopathology trace the developmental roots of disorders such as autism, disorganized attachment, conduct problems, depression, eating disorders, and PTSD. These specific disorders were selected because each represents an example of how developmental processes interact to produce psychopathology.

Linkages between normal and abnormal pathways of development are explained. A review of basic concepts of developmental psychopathology and prevention science is also included.

- **Boxed features:** In many chapters, boxes highlight special topics and provide opportunities for in-depth coverage of research. These may be the biographies of influential theorists or detailed examinations of issues such as how adversity alters child outcomes, children's credibility as eyewitnesses, children of immigrant families, the effects of divorce on children, the criminal culpability of juveniles, identity processes in multiracial individuals, gay and lesbian couples and their families, leadership development in women and men, the burden of caring for elderly relatives, cross-cultural differences in funeral rituals, and many others.

- **Culture and gender:** In every chapter, cross-cultural and cross-gender issues are discussed wherever relevant developmental research is available. Several new tables that examine cultural differences, such as in parenting and in coping, add to the increased coverage of culture in this edition.

- **Chapter summaries:** Every chapter ends with a summary of the major topics covered in that chapter, providing yet another study tool for students and a planning tool for instructors.

- **Case studies and case study discussion questions:** Case studies and questions at the end of each chapter are another set of pedagogical tools for helping students think about the clinical implications of the developmental facts and theories they have learned.

- **Journal questions:** Journal questions at the end of each chapter help students reflect on the issues they have read about, encouraging them to consider the relevance of these issues in their own development.

- **Key concepts:** Throughout the text, new or technical terms are printed in **bold** and defined. At the end of each chapter, a list of these key terms is provided as a study tool.

- **Glossary:** A glossary at the end of the text provides students with a handy reference for key terms.

- **Appendix:** An appendix helps students understand how developmental processes are studied scientifically and how scientifically established information can be useful in practice.

- **Writing style:** The writing style is conversational in tone and is aimed at making even complex material accessible. To avoid sexist language use and yet still have the luxury of using the singular pronouns "she" and "he," we use the feminine pronoun in odd-numbered chapters and the masculine pronoun in even-numbered chapters.

Supplemental Materials

Two online supplements are available for instructors at **www.pearsonhighered .com/educator**. Simply enter the author, title, or ISBN and select this textbook. Click on the "Resources" tab to view and download the available supplements.

- **Online Instructor's Manual and Test Bank:** A new Online Instructor's Manual and Test Bank (ISBN: 0-13-294297-6) has been developed with an average of 30 multiple-choice test items and 3 to 5 essay-style questions per chapter. Carefully scrutinized for accuracy, the multiple-choice questions in the Test Bank include both lower-level and higher-level questions. The lower-level questions expect students to access content knowledge and comprehension; the higher-level questions assess students' ability to synthesize, compare and contrast, and apply their knowledge to problem solving.

- **Online PowerPoint® Slides:** The Online PowerPoint® slides (ISBN: 0-13-294298-4) include key concept summaries, outlines, and other graphic aids to enhance learning. These slides are designed to help students understand, organize, and remember concepts and developmental theories.

Acknowledgments

We want to express our deep appreciation to Kevin Davis, our publisher, who has nurtured this project with his expertise and encouragement since we proposed the first edition. We also want to thank Lauren Carlson for her gentle guidance and support throughout this project. Thanks also to Christian Holdener, our project manager. He is wonderfully efficient and organized, and he has coordinated the production process with good-natured patience throughout. We especially appreciate Marcia Craig, our expert copy editor, whose careful reading of the manuscript truly improved it. Thanks go as well to Tania Zamora, Janet Woods, and Renae Hortsman, who have worked closely with us on permissions, and to the entire editorial and marketing staff who have contributed to the success of this project. We also are grateful to those who developed the excellent supplementary materials that accompany this text. We also wish to thank the following reviewers: Rina Chittooran, Saint Louis University; Kathryn Cooper, University of Northern Colorado; Rosalie Rohm, Ball State University; and Bridget Walsh, University of Nevada, Reno. Finally, our deepest gratitude goes to our families for their love and ongoing support.

Brief Contents

Contents

Chapter 10 The Social World of Adolescence 368

Chapter 11 Physical and Cognitive Development in Young Adulthood 408

Chapter 12 Socioemotional and Vocational Development in Young Adulthood 438

THE LIFE SPAN

CHAPTER 1

Organizing Themes in Development

What importance do difficulties in getting along with others have for a 6-year-old youngster? Is she just "passing through a stage"? How do parenting practices affect a child's developing self-concept? How much freedom should be given to adolescents? Does the experience of sex discrimination affect a teenage girl's identity formation? What implications do social problems with friends and coworkers suggest for a 22-year-old male? Does stereotype threat (such as expecting to be judged on the basis of race) alter the course of development? How significant is it for a married couple to experience increased conflicts following the births of their children? Does divorce cause lasting emotional damage to the children involved in a family breakup? What kind of day care experience is best for young children? Do we normally lose many intellectual abilities as we age? What factors enable a person to overcome early unfavorable circumstances and become a successful, healthy adult?

These intriguing questions represent a sampling of the kinds of topics that developmental scientists tackle. Their goal is to understand **life span development**: human behavioral change from conception to death. "Behavioral" change refers broadly to change in both observable activity (e.g., from crawling to walking) and mental activity (e.g., from disorganized to logical thinking). More specifically, developmental science seeks to

- describe people's behavioral characteristics at different ages,
- identify how people are likely to respond to life's experiences at different ages,
- formulate theories that explain how and why we see the typical characteristics and responses that we do, and
- understand what factors contribute to developmental differences from one person to another.

Using an array of scientific tools designed to obtain objective (unbiased) information, developmentalists make careful observations and measurements, and they test theoretical explanations empirically. See the Appendix for *A Practitioner's Guide to the Methods of Developmental Science.*

Developmental science is not a remote or esoteric body of knowledge. Rather, it has much to offer the helping professional both professionally and personally.

As you study developmental science, you will build a knowledge base of information about age-related behaviors and about causal theories that help organize and make sense of these behaviors. These tools will help you better understand client concerns that are rooted in shared human experience. And when you think about clients' problems from a developmental perspective, you will increase the range of problem solving strategies that you can offer. Finally, studying development can facilitate personal growth by providing a foundation for reflecting on your own life.

REFLECTION AND ACTION

Despite strong support for a comprehensive academic grounding in scientific developmental knowledge for helping professionals (e.g., Van Hesteren & Ivey, 1990), there has been a somewhat uneasy alliance between practitioners, such as mental health professionals, and those with a more empirical bent, such as behavioral scientists. The clinical fields have depended on research from developmental psychology to inform their practice. Yet in the past, overreliance on traditional experimental methodologies sometimes resulted in researchers' neglect of important issues that could not be studied using these rigorous methods (Hetherington, 1998). Consequently, there was a tendency for clinicians to perceive some behavioral science literature as irrelevant to real-world concerns (Turner, 1986). Clearly, the gap between science and practice is not unique to the mental health professions. Medicine, education, and law have all struggled with the problems involved in preparing students to grapple with the complex demands of the workplace. Contemporary debate on this issue has led to the development of serious alternative paradigms for the training of practitioners.

One of the most promising of these alternatives for helping professionals is the concept of **reflective practice**. The idea of "reflectivity" derives from Dewey's (1933/1998) view of education, which emphasized careful consideration of one's beliefs and forms of knowledge as a precursor to practice. Donald Schon (1987), a modern pioneer in the field of reflective practice, describes the problem this way:

> In the varied topography of professional practice, there is a high, hard ground overlooking a swamp. On the high ground, manageable problems lend themselves to solution through the application of research-based theory and technique. In the swampy lowland, messy confusing problems defy technical solutions. The irony of this situation is that the problems of the high ground tend to be relatively unimportant to individuals or society at large, however great their technical interest may be, while in the swamp lie the problems of greatest human concern. (p. 3)

The Gap Between Science and Practice

Traditionally, the modern, university-based educational process has been driven by the belief that problems can be solved best by applying objective, technical, or scientific information amassed from laboratory investigations. Implicit in this assumption is that human nature operates according to universal principles that, if known and understood, will enable us to predict behavior. For example, if I understand the principles of conditioning and reinforcement, I can apply a contingency contract to modify my client's inappropriate behavior. Postmodern critics have pointed out the many difficulties associated with this approach. Sometimes a "problem" behavior is related to, or maintained by, neurological, systemic, or cultural conditions. Sometimes the very existence of a problem may be a cultural construction. Unless a problem is viewed within its larger context, a problem-solving strategy may prove ineffective.

Most of the situations helpers face are confusing, complex, ill-defined, and often unresponsive to the application of a simple, specific set of scientific principles. Thus, the training of helping professionals often involves a "dual curriculum."

The first is more formal and may be presented as a conglomeration of research-based facts, whereas the second, often learned in a practicum, field placement or first job, covers the curriculum of "what is really done" when working with clients. The antidote to this dichotomous pedagogy, Schon (1987) and his followers suggest, is reflective practice. This is a creative method of thinking about practice in which the helper masters the knowledge and skills base pertinent to the profession but is encouraged to go beyond rote technical applications to generate new kinds of understanding and strategies of action. Rather than relying solely on objective technical applications to determine ways of operating in a given situation, the reflective practitioner constructs solutions to problems by engaging in personal hypothesis generating and hypothesis testing.

How can one use the knowledge of developmental science in a meaningful and reflective way? What place does it have in the process of reflective construction? Consideration of another important line of research, namely, that of characteristics of expert problem solvers, will help us answer this question. Research studies on expert–novice differences in many areas such as teaching, science, and athletics all support the contention that experts have a great store of knowledge and skill in a particular area. Expertise is domain specific. When compared to novices in any given field, experts possess well-organized and integrated stores of information that they draw on, almost automatically, when faced with novel challenges. Because this knowledge is well practiced, truly a "working body" of information, retrieval is relatively easy (Lewandowsky & Thomas, 2009). Progress in problem solving is closely self-monitored. Problems are analyzed and broken down into smaller units, which can be handled more efficiently.

If we apply this information to the reflective practice model, we can see some connections. One core condition of reflective practice is that practitioners use theory as a "partial lens through which to consider a problem" (Nelson & Neufelt, 1998). Practitioners also use another partial lens: their professional and other life experience. In reflective practice, theory-driven hypotheses about client and system problems are generated and tested for goodness of fit. A rich supply of problem-solving strategies depends on a deep understanding of and thorough grounding in fundamental knowledge germane to the field. Notice that there is a sequence to reflective practice. Schon (1987), for example, argues against putting the cart before the horse. He states that true reflectivity depends on the ability to "recognize and apply standard rules, facts and operations; then to reason from general rules to problematic cases in ways characteristic of the profession; and only then to develop and test new forms of understanding and action where familiar categories and ways of thinking fail" (p. 40). In other words, background knowledge is important, but it is most useful in a dynamic interaction with contextual applications (Hoshman & Polkinghorne, 1992). A working knowledge of human development supplies the helping professional with a firm base from which to proceed.

Given the relevance of background knowledge to expertise in helping and to reflective practice, we hope we have made a sufficiently convincing case for the study of developmental science. However, it is obvious that students approaching this study are not "blank slates." You already have many ideas and theories about the ways that people grow and change. These implicit theories have been constructed over time, partly from personal experience, observation, and your own cultural "take" on situations. Dweck and her colleagues have demonstrated that reliably different interpretations of situations can be predicted based on individual differences in people's implicit beliefs about certain human attributes, such as intelligence or personality (see Dweck & Elliott-Moskwa, 2010). Take the case of intelligence. If you happen to hold the implicit belief that a person's intellectual capacity can change and improve over time, you might be more inclined to take a skill-building approach to some presenting problem involving knowledge or ability. However, if you espouse the belief that a person's intelligence is fixed and not amenable to incremental improvement, possibly because of genetic inheritance, you might be more likely to encourage a client to cope with and adjust to cognitive limitations. For helping professionals, the implicit theoretical lens that shapes their worldview can have important implications for their clients.

We are often reluctant to give up our personal theories even in the face of evidence that these theories are incorrect (Gardner, 1991; Kuhn, 2005). The best antidote to misapplication of our personal views is self-monitoring: being aware of what our theories are and recognizing that they are only one of a set of possibilities. (See Chapter 11 for a more extensive discussion of this issue.) Before we discuss some specific beliefs about the nature of development, take a few minutes to consider what you think about the questions posed in Box 1.1.

Box 1.1: Questionnaire

Examine Your Beliefs About Development

Rate yourself using the forced-choice format for each of the following items.

1. Physical characteristics such as eye color, height, and weight are primarily inherited.

❏	❏	❏	❏
Strongly Disagree	Moderately Disagree	Moderately Agree	Strongly Agree

2. Intelligence is primarily inherited.

❏	❏	❏	❏
Strongly Disagree	Moderately Disagree	Moderately Agree	Strongly Agree

3. Personality is primarily inherited.

❏	❏	❏	❏
Strongly Disagree	Moderately Disagree	Moderately Agree	Strongly Agree

4. Events in the first 3 years of life have permanent effects on a person's psychological development.

❏	❏	❏	❏
Strongly Disagree	Moderately Disagree	Moderately Agree	Strongly Agree

5. People's personalities do not change very much over their lifetimes.

❏	❏	❏	❏
Strongly Disagree	Moderately Disagree	Moderately Agree	Strongly Agree

6. People all go through the same stages in their lives.

❏	❏	❏	❏
Strongly Disagree	Moderately Disagree	Moderately Agree	Strongly Agree

7. Parents have a somewhat limited impact on their children's development.

❏	❏	❏	❏
Strongly Disagree	Moderately Disagree	Moderately Agree	Strongly Agree

8. The cultural context in which the individual lives has a primary effect upon the psychological development of that person.

❏	❏	❏	❏
Strongly Disagree	Moderately Disagree	Moderately Agree	Strongly Agree

9. Common sense is a better guide to child rearing than is scientific knowledge.

❏	❏	❏	❏
Strongly Disagree	Moderately Disagree	Moderately Agree	Strongly Agree

A HISTORICAL PERSPECTIVE ON DEVELOPMENTAL THEORIES

Now that you have examined some of your own developmental assumptions, let's consider the theoretical views that influence developmentalists, with special attention to how these views have evolved through the history of developmental science. Later, we will examine how different theoretical approaches might affect the helping process.

Like you, developmental scientists bring to their studies theoretical assumptions that help to structure their understanding of known facts. These assumptions also guide their research and shape how they interpret new findings. Scientists tend to develop theories that are consistent with their own cultural background and experience; no one operates in a vacuum. A core value of Western scientific method is a pursuit of objectivity, so that scientists are committed to continuously evaluating their theories in light of evidence. As a consequence, scientific theories change over time.

Throughout this text, you will be introduced to many developmental theories. Some are broad and sweeping in their coverage of whole areas of development, such as Freud's theory of personality development (see Chapters 7 and 8) or Piaget's theory of cognitive development (see Chapters 3, 6, and 9); some are narrower in scope, focusing on a particular issue, such as Vygotsky's theory of the enculturation of knowledge (see Chapter 3) or Bowlby's attachment theory (see Chapters 4 and 12). You will see that newer theories usually incorporate empirically verified ideas from older theories, but they also reflect changing cultural needs, such as the need to understand successful aging in a longer-lived population. Newer theories also draw from advances in many disciplines, such as biology. Scientific theories of human development began to emerge in Europe and America in the 19th century. They had their roots in philosophical inquiry, in the emergence of biological science, and in the growth of mass education that accompanied industrialization. Through medieval times in European societies, children and adults of all ages seem to have been viewed and treated in very similar ways (Aries, 1960). Only infants and preschoolers were free of adult responsibilities, although they were not always given the special protections and nurture that they are today. At age 6 or 7, children took on adult roles, doing farmwork or learning a trade, often leaving their families to become apprentices. As the Industrial Revolution advanced, children worked beside adults in mines and factories. People generally seemed "indifferent to children's special characteristics" (Crain, 2005, p. 2), and there was no real study of children or how they change.

The notion that children only gradually develop the cognitive and personality structures that will characterize them as adults first appeared in the writings of 17th- and 18th-century philosophers, such as John Locke in Great Britain and Jean-Jacques Rousseau in France. In the 19th century, Charles Darwin's theory of the evolution of species and the growth of biological science helped to foster scholarly interest in children. The assumption grew that a close examination of how children change might help advance our understanding of the human species. Darwin himself introduced an early approach to child study, the "baby biography," writing a richly detailed account of his young son's daily changes in language and behavior. By the 18th and 19th centuries, the Industrial Revolution led to the growth of "middle-class" occupations (e.g., merchandizing) that required an academic education: training in reading, writing, and math. The need to educate large numbers of children sharpened the public's interest in understanding how children change with age.

The first academic departments devoted to child study began to appear on American college campuses in the late 19th and early 20th centuries. The idea that development continues even in adulthood was a 20th-century concept and a natural outgrowth of the study of children. If children's mental and behavioral processes change over time, perhaps such processes continue to evolve beyond childhood. Interest in adult development was also piqued by dramatic increases in life expectancy in the 19th and 20th centuries, as well as cultural changes in how people live. Instead of single households combining three or four generations of family members, grandparents and other relatives began to live apart from "nuclear families," so that understanding the special needs and experiences of each age group took on greater importance. As you will see in the following discussion of classic developmental theories, in the 1950s Erik Erikson first proposed that personality development is a lifelong process, and by the 1960s cognitive theorists began to argue that adult thinking also changes systematically over time.

Most classic developmental theories emerged during the early and middle decades of the twentieth century. After you learn about some of the classic developmental theories, you will be introduced to contemporary theories. You will see that the newest theories integrate ideas from many classic theories, as well as from disciplines ranging from modern genetics, neuroscience, cognitive science, and psycholinguistics, to social and cultural psychology and anthropology. They acknowledge that human development is a complex synthesis of diverse processes at multiple levels of functioning. Because they embrace complexity, contemporary developmental theories can be especially useful to helping professionals. See the Timeline in Figure 1.1 for a graphic summary of some of the key theories and ideas in the history of developmental science.

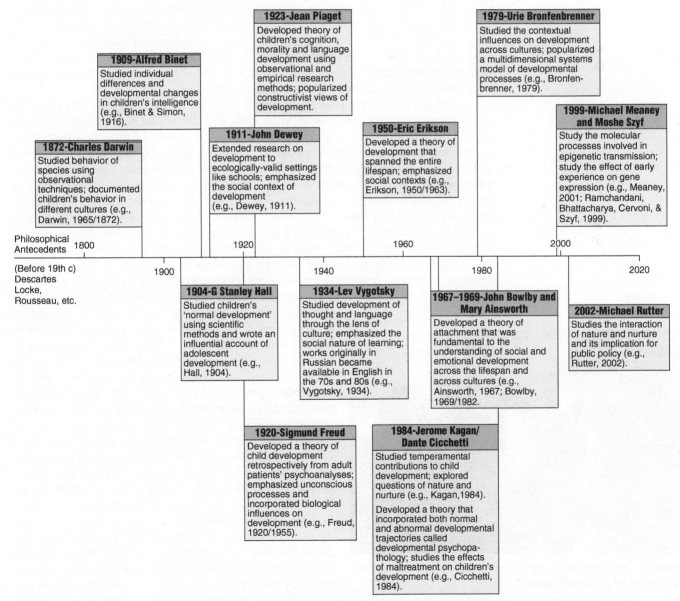

FIGURE 1.1   **Timeline of selected influences on developmental science with dates of representative works.**

Emphasizing Discontinuity: Classic Stage Theories

Some of the most influential early theories of development described human change as occurring in stages. Imagine a girl when she is 4 months old and then again when she is 4 years old. If your sense is that these two versions of the same child are fundamentally different in kind, with different intellectual capacities, different emotional structures, or different ways of perceiving others, you are thinking like a stage theorist. A **stage** is a period of time, perhaps several years, during which a person's activities (at least in one broad domain) have certain characteristics in common. For example, we could say that in language development, the 4-month-old girl is in a preverbal stage: Among other things, her communications share in common the fact that they do not include talking. As a person moves to a different stage, the common characteristics of behavior change. In other words, a person's activities have similar qualities within stages but different qualities across stages. Also, after long periods of stability, qualitative shifts in behavior seem to happen relatively quickly. For example, the change from not talking to talking seems abrupt or discontinuous. It tends to happen between 12 and 18 months of age, and once it starts, language use seems to advance very rapidly. A 4-year-old is someone who communicates primarily by talking; she is clearly in a verbal stage.

The preverbal to verbal example illustrates two features of stage theories. First, they describe development as qualitative or transformational change, like the emergence of a tree from a seed. At each new stage, new forms of behavioral organization are both different from and more complex than the ones at previous stages. Increasing complexity suggests that development has "directionality." There is a kind of unfolding or emergence of behavioral organization.

Second, they imply periods of relative stability (within stages) and periods of rapid transition (between stages). Metaphorically, development is a staircase. Each new stage lifts a person to a new plateau for some period of time, and then there is another steep rise to another plateau. There seems to be discontinuity in these changes rather than change being a gradual, incremental process. One person might progress through a stage more quickly or slowly than another, but the sequence of stages is usually seen as the same across cultures and contexts, that is, universal. Also, despite the emphasis on qualitative discontinuities between stages, stage theorists argue for functional continuities across stages. That is, the same processes drive the shifts from stage to stage, such as brain maturation and social experience.

Sigmund Freud's theory of personality development began to have an influence on developmental science in the early 1900s and was among the first to include a description of stages (e.g., Freud, 1905/1989, 1949/1969). Freud's theory no longer takes center stage in the interpretations favored by most helpers or by developmental scientists. First, there is little evidence for some of the specific proposals in Freud's theory (Loevinger, 1976). Second, his theory has been criticized for incorporating the gender biases of early 20th-century Austrian culture. Yet, some of Freud's broad insights are routinely accepted and incorporated into other theories, such as his emphasis on the importance of early family relationships to infants' emotional life, his notion that some behavior is unconsciously motivated, and his view that internal conflicts can play a primary role in social functioning. Several currently influential theories, like those of Erik Erikson and John Bowlby, incorporated some aspects of Freud's theories or were developed to contrast with Freud's ideas. For these reasons, it is important to understand Freud's theory. Also, his ideas have permeated popular culture, and they influence many of our assumptions about the

Helping professionals need to understand the needs of clients of different ages.

development of behavior. If we are to make our own implicit assumptions about development explicit, we must understand where they originated and how well the theories that spawned them stand up in the light of scientific investigation.

Freud's Personality Theory

Sigmund Freud's **psychoanalytic theory** both describes the complex functioning of the adult personality and offers an explanation of the processes and progress of its development throughout childhood. To understand any given stage it helps to understand Freud's view of the fully developed adult.

Id, Ego, and Superego.   According to Freud, the adult personality functions as if there were actually three personalities, or aspects of personality, all potentially in conflict with one another. The first, the **id**, is the biological self, the source of all psychic energy. Babies are born with an id; the other two aspects of personality develop later. The id blindly pursues the fulfillment of physical needs or "instincts," such as the hunger drive and the sex drive. It is irrational, driven by the **pleasure principle**, that is, by the pursuit of gratification. Its function is to keep the individual, and the species, alive, although Freud also proposed that there are inborn aggressive, destructive instincts served by the id.

The **ego** begins to develop as cognitive and physical skills emerge. In Freud's view, some psychic energy is invested in these skills, and a rational, realistic self begins to take shape. The id still presses for fulfillment of bodily needs, but the rational ego seeks to meet these needs in sensible ways that take into account all aspects of a situation. For example, if you were hungry, and you saw a child with an ice cream cone, your id might press you to grab the cone away from the child—an instance of blind, immediate pleasure seeking. Of course, stealing ice cream from a child could have negative consequences if someone else saw you do it or if the child reported you to authorities. Unlike your id, your ego would operate on the **reality principle**, garnering your understanding of the world and of behavioral consequences to devise a more sensible and self-protective approach, such as waiting until you arrive at the ice cream store yourself and paying for an ice cream cone.

The **superego** is the last of the three aspects of personality to emerge. Psychic energy is invested in this "internalized parent" during the preschool period as children begin to feel guilty if they behave in ways that are inconsistent with parental restrictions. With the superego in place, the ego must now take account not only of instinctual pressures from the id, and of external realities, but also of the superego's constraints. It must meet the needs of the id without upsetting the superego to avoid the unpleasant anxiety of guilt. In this view, when you choose against stealing a child's ice cream cone to meet your immediate hunger, your ego is taking account not only of the realistic problems of getting caught but also of the unpleasant feelings that would be generated by the superego.

The Psychosexual Stages.   In Freud's view, the complexities of the relationships and conflicts that arise among the id, the ego, and the superego are the result of the individual's experiences during five developmental stages. Freud called these **psychosexual stages** because he believed that changes in the id and its energy levels initiated each new stage. The term *sexual* here applies to all biological instincts or drives and their satisfaction, and it can be broadly defined as "sensual."

For each stage, Freud posited that a disproportionate amount of id energy is invested in drives satisfied through one part of the body. As a result, the pleasure experienced through that body part is especially great during that stage. Children's experiences satisfying the especially strong needs that emerge at a given stage can influence the development of personality characteristics throughout life. Freud also thought that parents typically play a pivotal role in helping children achieve the satisfaction they need. For example, in the **oral stage**, corresponding to the first year of life, Freud argued that the mouth is the body part that provides babies with the most pleasure. Eating, drinking and even nonnutritive sucking are presumably more satisfying than at other times of life. A baby's experiences with feeding and other parenting behaviors are likely to affect her oral pleasure, and could influence how much energy she invests in seeking oral pleasure in the future. Suppose that a mother in the early 20th century believed the parenting advice of "experts" who claimed that nonnutritive sucking is bad for babies. To prevent her baby from sucking her thumb, the mother might tie the baby's hands to the sides of the crib at night—a practice recommended by the same experts! Freudian theory would predict that such extreme denial of oral pleasure could cause an **oral fixation**: The girl might grow up to need oral pleasures more than most adults, perhaps leading to overeating, to being especially talkative, or to being a chain smoker. The grown woman might also exhibit this fixation in more subtle ways, maintaining behaviors or feelings in adulthood that are particularly characteristic of babies, such as crying easily or experiencing overwhelming feelings of helplessness. According to Freud, fixations at any stage could be the result of either denial of a child's needs, as in this example, or overindulgence of those needs. Specific defense mechanisms, such as "reaction formation" or "repression," can also be associated with the conflicts that arise at a particular stage.

In Table 1.1, you will find a summary of the basic characteristics of Freud's five psychosexual stages. Some of these stages will be described in more detail in later chapters. Freud's stages have many of the properties of **critical (or sensitive) periods** for personality development. That is, they are time frames during which certain developments must occur. Freud's third stage, for example, provides an opportunity for sex typing and moral processes to emerge (see Table 1.1). Notice that Freud assumed that much of personality development occurs before age 5, during the first three stages. This is one of the many ideas from Freud's theory that has made its way into popular culture, even though modern research clearly does not support this position.

By the mid-1900s, two other major stage theories began to significantly impact the progress of developmental science. The first, by Erik Erikson, was focused on

TABLE 1.1 Freud's Psychosexual Stages of Development

STAGE	APPROXIMATE AGE	DESCRIPTION
Oral	Birth to 1 year	Infants develop special relationships with caregivers. Mouth is the source of greatest pleasure. Too much or too little oral satisfaction can cause an "oral fixation," leading to traits that actively (smoking) or symbolically (overdependency) are oral or infantile.
Anal	1 to 3 years	Anal area is the source of greatest pleasure. Harsh or overly indulgent toilet training can cause an "anal fixation," leading to later adult traits that recall this stage, such as being greedy or messy.
Phallic	3 to 5 or 6 years	Genitalia are the source of greatest pleasure. Sexual desire directed toward the opposite-sex parent makes the same-sex parent a rival. Fear of angering the same-sex parent is resolved by identifying with that parent, which explains how children acquire both sex-typed behaviors and moral values. If a child has trouble resolving the emotional upheaval of this stage through identification, sex role development may be deviant or moral character may be weak.
Latency	6 years to puberty	Relatively quiescent period of personality development. Sexual desires are repressed after the turmoil of the last stage. Energy is directed into work and play. There is continued consolidation of traits laid down in the first three stages.
Genital	Puberty through adulthood	At puberty, adult sexual needs become the most important motivators of behavior. The individual seeks to fulfill needs and expend energy in socially acceptable activities, such as work, and through marriage with a partner who will substitute for the early object of desire, the opposite-sex parent.

personality development, reshaping some of Freud's ideas. The second, by Jean Piaget, proposed that there are stagelike changes in cognitive processes during childhood and adolescence, especially in rational thinking and problem solving.

Erikson's Personality Theory

Erik Erikson studied psychoanalytic theory with Anna Freud, Sigmund's daughter, and later proposed his own theory of personality development (e.g., Erikson, 1950/1963). Like many "neo-Freudians," Erikson deemphasized the id as the driving force behind all behavior, and he emphasized the more rational processes of the ego. His theory is focused on explaining the psychosocial aspects of behavior: attitudes and feelings toward the self and toward others. Erikson described eight **psychosocial stages**. The first five correspond to the age periods laid out in Freud's psychosexual stages, but the last three are adult life stages, reflecting Erikson's view that personal identity and interpersonal attitudes are continually evolving from birth to death.

The "Eight Stages of Man."   In each stage, the individual faces a different "crisis" or developmental task (see Chapter 9 for a detailed discussion of Erikson's concept of crisis). The crisis is initiated, on one hand, by changing characteristics of the person—biological maturation or decline, cognitive changes, advancing (or deteriorating) motor skills—and, on the other hand, by corresponding changes in others' attitudes, behaviors, and expectations. As in all stage theories, people qualitatively change from stage to stage, and so do the crises or tasks that they confront. In the first stage, infants must resolve the crisis of **trust versus mistrust** (see Chapter 4). Infants, in their relative helplessness, are "incorporative." They "take in" what is offered, including not only nourishment but also stimulation, information, affection, and attention. If infants' needs for such input are met by responsive caregivers, babies begin to trust others, to feel valued and valuable, and to view the world as a safe place. If caregivers are not consistently responsive, infants will fail to establish basic trust or to feel valuable, carrying mistrust with them into the next stage of development, when the 1- to 3-year-old toddler faces the crisis of **autonomy versus shame and doubt**. Mistrust in others and self will make it more difficult to successfully achieve a sense of autonomy.

The new stage is initiated by the child's maturing muscular control and emerging cognitive and language skills. Unlike helpless infants, toddlers can learn not only to control their elimination but also to feed and dress themselves, to express their desires with some precision, and to move around the environment without help. The new capacities bring a strong need to practice and perfect the skills that make children feel in control of their own destinies. Caregivers must be sensitive to the child's need for independence and yet must exercise enough control to keep the child safe and to help the child learn self-control. Failure to strike the right balance may rob children of feelings of autonomy—a sense that "I can do it myself"—and can promote instead either shame or self-doubt.

These first two stages illustrate features of all of Erikson's stages (see Table 1.2 for a description of all eight stages). First, others' sensitivity and responsiveness to the individual's needs create a context for positive psychosocial development. Second, attitudes toward self and toward others emerge together. For example, developing trust in others also means valuing (or trusting) the self. Third, every psychosocial crisis or task involves finding the right balance between positive and negative feelings, with the positive outweighing the negative. Finally, the successful resolution of a crisis at one stage helps smooth the way for successful resolutions of future crises. Unsuccessful resolution at an earlier stage may stall progress and make maladaptive behavior more likely.

Erikson's personality theory is often more appealing to helping professionals than Freud's theory. Erikson's emphasis on the psychosocial aspects of personality focuses attention on precisely the issues that helpers feel they are most often called

The children in this preschool classroom are preparing for their lunch. As you watch, note the ways that the children demonstrate a developed sense of autonomy and an emerging sense of initiative.

TABLE 1.2   Erikson's Psychosocial Stages of Development

STAGE OR PSYCHOSOCIAL "CRISIS"	APPROXIMATE AGE	SIGNIFICANT EVENTS	POSITIVE OUTCOME OR VIRTUE DEVELOPED	NEGATIVE OUTCOME
Trust vs. Mistrust	Birth to 1 year	Child develops a sense that the world is a safe and reliable place because of sensitive caregiving.	Hope	Fear and mistrust of others
Autonomy vs. Shame & Doubt	1 to 3 years	Child develops a sense of independence tied to use of new mental and motor skills.	Willpower	Self-doubt
Initiative vs. Guilt	3 to 5 or 6 years	Child tries to behave in ways that involve more "grown-up" responsibility and experiments with grown-up roles.	Purpose	Guilt over thought and action
Industry vs. Inferiority	6 to 12 years	Child needs to learn important academic skills and compare favorably with peers in school.	Competence	Lack of competence
Identity vs. Role Confusion	12 to 20 years	Adolescent must move toward adulthood by making choices about values, vocational goals, etc.	Fidelity	Inability to establish sense of self
Intimacy vs. Isolation	Young adulthood	Adult becomes willing to share identity with others and to commit to affiliations and partnerships.	Love	Fear of intimacy, distancing
Generativity vs. Stagnation	Middle adulthood	Adult wishes to make a contribution to the next generation, to produce, mentor, create something of lasting value, as in the rearing of children or community services or expert work.	Care	Self-absorption
Ego Integrity vs. Despair	Late adulthood	Adult comes to terms with life's successes, failures, and missed opportunities and realizes the dignity of own life.	Wisdom	Regret

on to address: feelings and attitudes about self and about others. Also, Erikson assumed that the child or adult is an active, self-organizing individual who needs only the right social context to move in a positive direction. Further, Erikson was himself an optimistic therapist who believed that poorly resolved crises could be resolved more adequately in later stages if the right conditions prevailed. Erikson was sensitive to cultural differences in behavioral development. Finally, developmental researchers frequently find Eriksonian interpretations of behavior useful. Studies of attachment, self-concept, self-esteem, and adolescent identity, among other topics addressed in subsequent chapters, have produced results compatible with some of Erikson's ideas. (See Chapter 4, Box 4.2 for a biographical sketch of Erikson.)

Piaget's Cognitive Development Theory

In Jean Piaget's **cognitive development theory**, we see the influence of 18th-century philosopher Jean-Jacques Rousseau (e.g., 1762/1948), who argued that children's reasoning and understanding emerges naturally in stages and that parents and educators can help most by allowing children freedom to explore their environments and by giving them learning experiences that are consistent with their level of ability. Similarly, Piaget outlined stages in the development of cognition, especially logical thinking which he referred to as operational thought (e.g., Inhelder & Piaget, 1955/1958, 1964; Piaget, 1952, 1954). He assumed that normal adults are capable of thinking logically about both concrete and abstract contents but that this capacity evolves in four stages through childhood. Briefly, the first **sensorimotor stage**, lasting for about 2 years, is characterized by an absence of representational thought (see Chapter 3). Although babies are busy taking in the sensory world, organizing it on the basis of inborn reflexes or patterns, and then responding to their sensations, Piaget believed that they cannot yet symbolically represent their experiences, and so they cannot really reflect on them. This means that young infants do not form mental images or store memories symbolically, and they do not plan their behavior or intentionally act. These capacities emerge between 18 and 24 months, launching the next stage.

Piaget's second, third, and fourth stages roughly correspond to the preschool, elementary school, and the adolescent-adult years. These stages are named for the kinds of thinking that Piaget believed possible for these age groups. Table 1.3 summarizes each stage briefly, and we will describe the stages more fully in subsequent chapters.

Piaget's theory is another classic stage model. First, cognitive abilities are qualitatively similar within stages. If we know how a child approaches one kind of task, we should be able to predict her approaches to other kinds of tasks as well. Piaget acknowledged that children might be advanced in one cognitive domain or lag behind in another. For example, an adolescent might show more abstract reasoning about math than about interpersonal matters. These within-stage variations he called **décalages**. But generally, Piaget expected that a child's thinking would be organized in similar ways across most domains. Second, even though progress through the stages could move more or less quickly depending on many individual and contextual factors, the stages unfold in an invariant sequence, regardless of context or culture. The simpler patterns of physical or mental activity at one stage become integrated into more complex organizational systems at the next stage (**hierarchical integration**). Finally, despite the qualitative differences across stages, there are functional similarities or continuities from stage to stage in the ways in which children's cognitive development proceeds. According to Piaget, developmental progress depends on children's active engagement with the environment. This active process, which will be described in more detail in Chapter 3, suggests that children (and adults) build knowledge and understanding in a **self-organizing** way. They interpret new experiences and information in ways that fit their current ways of understanding even as they make some adjustments to their ways of understanding in the process. Children do not just passively receive information from without and store it "as is." And, knowledge does not just emerge from within as though preformed. Instead, children actively build their knowledge, using both existing knowledge and new information. This is a **constructivist** view of development.

TABLE 1.3 Piaget's Cognitive Stages of Development

STAGE	APPROXIMATE AGE	DESCRIPTION
Sensorimotor	Birth to 2 years	Through six substages, the source of infants' organized actions gradually shifts. At first, all organized behavior is reflexive—automatically triggered by particular stimuli. By the end of this stage, behavior is guided more by representational thought.
Preoperational	2 to 6 or 7 years	Early representational thought tends to be slow. Thought is "centered," usually focused on one salient piece of information, or aspect of an event, at a time. As a result, thinking is usually not yet logical.
Concrete operational	7 to 11 or 12 years	Thinking has gradually become more rapid and efficient, allowing children to now "decenter," or think about more than one thing at a time. This also allows them to discover logical relationships between/among pieces of information. Their logical thinking is best about information that can be demonstrated in the concrete world.
Formal operational	12 years through adulthood	Logical thinking extends now to "formal" or abstract material. Young adolescents can think logically about hypothetical situations, for example.

Piaget's ideas about cognitive development were first translated into English in the 1960s, and they swept American developmental researchers off their feet. His theory filled the need for an explanation that acknowledged complex qualitative changes in children's abilities over time, and it launched an era of unprecedented research on all aspects of children's intellectual functioning that continues today. Although some of the specifics of Piaget's theory have been challenged by research findings, many researchers, educators, and other helping professionals still find the broad outlines of this theory very useful for organizing their thinking about the kinds of understandings that children of different ages can bring to a problem or social situation. Piaget's theory also inspired some modern views of cognitive change in adulthood. As you will see in Chapter 11, post-Piagetians have proposed additional stages in the development of logical thinking, hypothesizing that the abstract thinking of the adolescent is transformed during adulthood into a more relativistic kind of logical thinking, partly as a function of adults' practical experience with the complexity of real-world problems.

Emphasizing Continuity: Incremental Change

Unlike stage theories, some theoretical approaches characterize development as a more continuous process. Change tends to be incremental, metaphorically resembling not a staircase but a steadily rising mountainside. Again, picture a 4-month-old girl, and the same girl when she is 4 years old. If you tend to "see" her evolving in small steps from a smiling, attentive infant to a smiling, eager toddler, to a smiling, mischievous preschooler, always noting in your observations threads of sameness as well as differences, your own theoretical assumptions about development may be more compatible with one of these **incremental models**. Like stage models, they can be very different in the types and breadth of behaviors they attempt to explain. They also differ in the kinds of processes they assume to underlie psychological change, such as the kinds of processes involved in learning. But they all agree that developmental change is not marked by major, sweeping reorganizations that affect many behaviors at once, as in stage theories. Rather, change is steady and specific to particular behaviors or behavioral domains. Incremental theorists, like stage theorists, tend to see "change for the better" as a key feature of development. So, adding words to your vocabulary over time would be a typical developmental change, but forgetting previously learned information might not. Social learning theory and most information processing theories are among the many incremental models available to explain development.

Learning Theories

Learning theories, in what is called the **behaviorist tradition**, have a distinguished history in American psychology, having been the most widely accepted class of theories through much of the 20th century, influenced by many thinkers from John B. Watson (e.g., 1913) to B. F. Skinner (e.g., 1938) to Albert Bandura (e.g., 1974). These theories trace their philosophical roots from ancient Greece and the writings of Aristotle through John Locke and the British empiricists of the 17th and 18th centuries. In this philosophical tradition, knowledge and skill are thought to accumulate as the result of each person's individual experiences. The environment gradually leaves its imprint on one's behavior and mind, a mind that in infancy is like a blank slate. Locke described several simple processes—association, repetition, imitation, reward, and punishment—by which the environment can have an impact. Many of the processes Locke described were incorporated into behaviorist approaches to development.

Some learning theories explain behavioral change as a function of chains of specific environmental events, such as those that occur in **classical** and **operant conditioning**. In these processes, change in behavior takes place because environmental events (stimuli) are paired with certain behaviors. Let's begin with classical conditioning, also called **respondent conditioning** (Vargas, 2009). A **respondent** is an automatic response to a stimulus. For example, when you hear an unexpected loud noise you will automatically produce a startle response. This stimulus/response association is unconditioned, built-in to your biological system. But the response can be conditioned to a new, neutral stimulus. Suppose a child calmly watches a dog approach her. For now, sight of the dog is a neutral stimulus. But the dog suddenly barks loudly, causing the child to automatically startle and pull back. Suppose that the next time the child sees the dog, it does not bark. Even so, just the sight of the dog triggers the same response as loud barking would: The child automatically startles and pulls back. The child has learned a new response, because the formerly neutral event (sight of dog) has been paired with an event (loud barking) that automatically causes a startle. Perhaps the startle reaction is also accompanied by feelings of fear. If so, the child has learned to fear this dog and will likely generalize that fear to other, similar dogs. When a neutral event or stimulus is associated with a stimulus that causes an automatic response, the neutral stimulus can become a **conditioned stimulus**, meaning that it can cause the person to make the same automatic response in the future, called a **conditioned response**. This is classical conditioning.

Operant conditioning is different. First, a person performs some behavior. The behavior is an **operant**, any act with potential to lead to consequences in the environment (that is, to "operate" on the environment). Immediately after the operant occurs, there is a "reinforcing event," or **reinforcement**, something that is experienced by the person as pleasurable or rewarding. For example, suppose that a young child happens to babble "da" just as a dog appears in the child's line of sight, and the child's mother excitedly claps and kisses the child. (The mother has mistakenly assumed that the child has tried to say "dog.") The mother's reaction serves as a reinforcement for the child, who will repeat the "da" sound the next time a dog comes into view. In operant conditioning, the child learns to produce a spontaneous behavior or operant (e.g., "da") in response to a cue (e.g., the appearance of a dog) because the behavior was previously reinforced in that situation. A reinforcement is a consequence of the operant behavior that maintains or increases the likelihood of that behavior when the cue occurs again (Sparzo, 2011). The mother's approving reaction is an example of a **positive reinforcement**: Something pleasurable is presented after the operant occurs. There are also rewarding consequences that are called **negative reinforcements**: An aversive experience *stops* or is removed after the operant occurs. If your brother releases you from a painful hammer-hold when you yell "Uncle," you have been negatively reinforced for saying "Uncle" (the operant) in that situation.

Social learning theories, which have focused specifically on how children acquire personality characteristics and social skills, consider conditioning processes part of the story, but they also emphasize "observational learning," or **modeling**. In this kind of learning, one person (the learner) observes another (the model) performing some behavior, and just from close observation, learns to do it too. The observer may or may not imitate the modeled behavior, immediately or in the future, depending on many factors, such as whether the observer expects a reward for the behavior, whether the model is perceived as nurturing or competent, and even whether the observer believes that the performance will meet the observer's own performance standards. Current versions of social learning theory emphasize many similar cognitive, self-regulated determiners of performance and suggest that they too are often learned from models (e.g., Bandura, 1974, 1999).

Whatever the learning processes that are emphasized in a particular learning theory, the story of development is one in which behaviors or beliefs or feelings change in response to specific experiences, one experience at a time. Broader changes can occur by **generalization**. If new events are experienced that are very similar to events in the original learning context, the learned behaviors may be extended to these new events. For example, the child who learns to say "da" when a particular dog appears may do the same when other dogs appear, or even in the presence of other four-legged animals. Or a child who observes a model sharing candy with a friend may later share toys with a sibling. But these extensions of

 Modeling is a particularly effective teaching strategy with young children, who can observe and replicate the behavior better than they can understand complicated instructions for how to do a task.

learned activities are narrow in scope compared to the sweeping changes hypothesized by stage theorists. While these processes explain changes in discrete behaviors or patterns of behavior, learning theories do not explain developmental reorganizations and adaptations in the ways that classic stage theories do.

Information Processing Theories

Since the introduction of computing technologies in the middle of the 20th century, some theorists have likened human cognitive functioning to computer processing of information. Not all **information processing theories** can be strictly classified as incremental theories, but many can. Like learning theories, these do not hypothesize broad stages, but emphasize incremental changes in narrow domains of behavior or thought. The mind works on information—attending to it, holding it in a temporary store or "working memory," putting it into long-term storage, using strategies to organize it or to draw conclusions from it, and so on. How the information is processed depends on general characteristics of the human computer, such as how much information can be accessed, or made available for our attention, at one time. These characteristics can change to some degree over time. For example, children's attentional capacity increases gradually with age. Yet most changes with age are quite specific to particular domains of knowledge, such as changes in the strategies children use to solve certain kinds of problems.

Furthermore, processing changes are not stagelike; they do not extend beyond the particular situation or problem space in which they occur. For example, Siegler and his colleagues (e.g., Siegler, 1996, 2007; Siegler & Svetina, 2006) describe changes in the ways that children do arithmetic, read, solve problems of various kinds, and perform many other tasks and skills. Siegler analyzes very particular changes in the kinds of strategies that children use when they attempt these tasks. Although there can be similarities across tasks in the ways that strategies change (e.g., they become more automatic with practice, they generalize to similar problems, etc.), usually the specific strategies used in one kind of task fail to apply to another, and changes are not coordinated across tasks. To illustrate, a kindergartner trying to solve an addition problem might use the strategy of "counting from one". "[T]his typically involves putting up fingers on one hand to represent the first addend, putting up fingers on the other hand to represent the second addend, and then counting the raised fingers on both hands" (Siegler, 1998, p. 93). This strategy is characteristic of early addition efforts, but would play no role in tasks such as reading or spelling. Overall, then, cognitive development in this kind of model is like social development in social learning theories: It results from the accrual of independent changes in many different domains of thought and skill. Development involves change for the better, but it does not lead to major organizational shifts across domains.

Classic Theories and the Major Issues They Raise

Classic theories of development have typically addressed a set of core issues. In our brief review you have been introduced to just a few of these. Is developmental change qualitative (e.g., stagelike) or quantitative (e.g., incremental)? Are some developments restricted to certain critical periods in the life cycle or are changes in brain and behavior possible at any time given the appropriate opportunities? Are there important continuities across the life span (in characteristics or change processes) or is everything in flux? Are people actively influencing the course and nature of their own development (self-organizing), or are they passive products of other forces? Which is more important in causing developmental change, nature (heredity) or nurture (environment)? Are there universal developmental trajectories, processes, and changes that are the same in all cultures and historical periods, or is development more specific to place and time?

Classic theorists usually took a stand on one side or the other of these issues, framing them as "either-or" possibilities. However, taking an extreme position does not fit the data we now have available. Contemporary theorists propose that human development is best described by a synthesis of the extremes. The best answer to all of the questions just posed appears to be "Both."

CONTEMPORARY MULTIDIMENSIONAL OR SYSTEMS THEORIES: EMBRACING THE COMPLEXITY OF DEVELOPMENT

Throughout this text you will find evidence that development is the result of the relationships among many causal components, interacting in complex ways. Modern developmental theories, which we refer to as **multidimensional** or **systems theories**, explain and describe the enormous complexity of interrelated causal processes in development. They generally assume that in all behavioral domains, from cognition to personality, there are layers, or levels, of interacting causes for change: physical/molecular, biological, psychological, social, and cultural. What happens at one level both causes and is caused by what happens at other levels. That is, the relationships among causes are reciprocal or **bidirectional processes**. For example, increased testosterone levels at puberty (biological change) might help influence a boy to pursue an aggressive sport, like wrestling. The boy's success at wrestling may cause his status and social dominance to rise among his male friends (social change), and this social change can reciprocally influence his biological functioning. Specifically, it can lead to additional increases in his testosterone levels (Cacioppo & Berntson, 1992).

These theories acknowledge and incorporate many kinds of change: qualitative, transforming changes, both great (stagelike) and small (such as strategy changes within a particular problem-solving domain), as well as continuous, incremental variations that can even be reversible, such as learning and then forgetting new information (e.g., Overton, 1990). This is one example of how contemporary theories integrate features of many classic theories of development.

Think again about a girl who is 4 months old, and then later 4 years old. Do you perceive so many changes that she is transformed into a different sort of creature, and yet, at the same time, do you see enduring qualities that characterize her at both ages? Does your sense of the forces that have changed her include influences such as her family, community, and culture? Do you also recognize that she has played a significant role in her own change and in modifying those other forces? If so, your implicit assumptions about development may be more consistent with multidimensional models than with either stage or incremental theories alone.

Multidimensional theories portray the developing person metaphorically as a vine growing through a thick forest (Kagan, 1994). In doing so, the vine is propelled by its own inner processes, but its path, even its form, is in part created by the forest it inhabits. There is continuous growth, but there are changes in structure too—in its form and direction—as the vine wends its way through the forest. Finally, its presence in the forest changes the forest itself, affecting the growth of the trees and other plants, which reciprocally influence the growth of the vine.

Many multidimensional theories have been proposed, but they are remarkably similar in their fundamental assumptions and characteristics. They are typically different in which aspects of development they provide most detail about. They include transactional theory (e.g., Sameroff & Chandler, 1975), relational theory (e.g., Lerner, 1998), dialectical theory (e.g., Sameroff, 2012), bioecological theory (e.g., Bronfenbrenner & Ceci, 1994), bio-social-ecological theory (e.g., Cole & Packer, 2011), epigenetic theory (e.g., Gottlieb, 1992), life course theory (Elder & Shanahan, 2006), life span developmental theory (e.g., Baltes, 1997; Baltes, Lindenberger, & Staudinger, 2006), dynamic systems theory (e.g., Thelen & Smith, 1998), and several others. Figure 1.2 provides one illustration of the multiple, interacting forces that

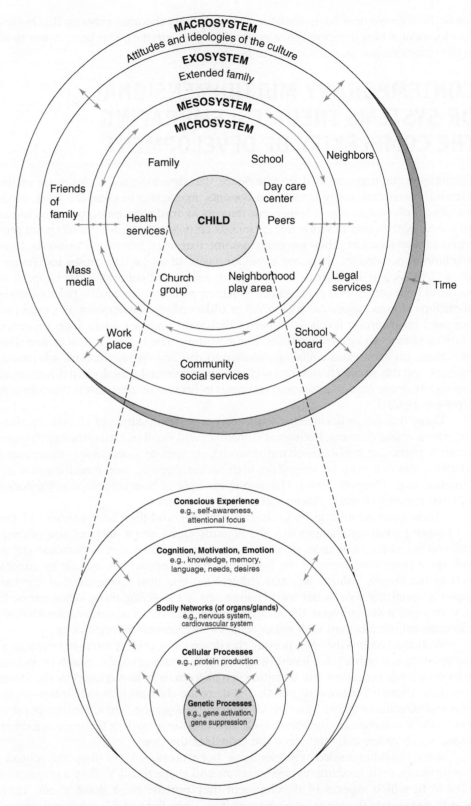

FIGURE 1.2 **A multidimensional (systems) model of development.** This figure illustrates the external influences described in Bronfenbrenner's bioecological theory along with internal influences on the developing child over time. Two-way arrows show bidirectional causality between all adjacent levels and between different parts of the same level. Proximal processes occur at the interface between the child and her microsystems.
SOURCE: Based on Berger, K. S. (2004). *The developing person through the lifespan.* New York, NY: Worth, p. 3.

these theories identify. Two examples of multidimensional models will help flesh out the typical characteristics of many of these theories.

Bronfenbrenner's Bioecological Theory

In Urie Bronfenbrenner's **bioecological theory**, he and his colleagues (e.g., Bronfenbrenner & Ceci, 1994; Bronfenbrenner & Morris, 1998, 2006) described all developments—including personality and cognitive change—as a function of **proximal processes**. These are reciprocal interactions between an "active, evolving biopsychological human organism and the persons, objects and symbols in its immediate external environment" (Bronfenbrenner & Morris, 1998, p. 996). In other words, proximal processes refer to a person's immediate interactions with people or with the physical environment or with informational sources (such as books or movies). These proximal processes are modified by more **distal processes**. Some of these are within the organism—such as genes. Others are outside the immediate environment—such as features of the educational system or of the broader culture. Proximal processes are truly interactive: The organism both influences and is influenced by the immediate environment.

The quality and effectiveness of the immediate environment—its responsiveness to the individual's particular needs and characteristics and the opportunities it provides—depend on the larger context. For example, parental monitoring of children's homework benefits children's academic performance. But monitoring is more effective if parents are knowledgeable about the child's work. A parent who insists that his child do her algebra homework may have less effect if the parent cannot be a resource who guides and explains the work. Thus, the parent's own educational background affects the usefulness of the monitoring (Bronfenbrenner & Ceci, 1994).

An individual's characteristics also influence the effectiveness of the environment. For example, motivations affect the impact of learning opportunities in a given context. A man interested in gambling may learn to reason in very complex ways about horses and their relative probability of winning at the track, but he may not display such complex reasoning in other contexts (Ceci & Liker, 1986). Other important individual qualities include **demand characteristics**, behavioral tendencies that often either encourage or discourage certain kinds of reactions from others. A child who is shy and inhibited, a trait that appears to have some biological roots (Kagan & Fox, 2006), may often fail to elicit attention from others, and may receive less support when she needs it, than a child who is open and outgoing (Bell & Chapman, 1986; see also Chapters 4 and 5).

Changes in the organism can be emergent, stagelike, qualitative changes, such as a shift from preoperational to concrete operational thought (see Table 1.3), or they can be more continuous, graded changes, such as shifts in academic interest or involvement in athletics. Both kinds of change are the result of proximal processes, influenced by more distal internal and external causes. Once changes occur, the individual brings new resources to these proximal processes. For example, when a child begins to demonstrate concrete operational thought, she will be given different tasks to do at home or at school than before, and she will learn things from those experiences that she would not have learned earlier. This is a good example of the bidirectionality of proximal processes: Change in the child fosters change in the environment leading to more change in the child and so on.

In earlier versions of his theory, Bronfenbrenner characterized in detail the many levels of environment that influence a person's development. He referred to the immediate environment, where proximal processes are played out, as the **microsystem**. Babies interact primarily with family members, but as children get older, other microsystems, such as the school, the neighborhood, or a local playground and its inhabitants, become part of their lives. Relations among these microsystems—referred to as the **mesosystem**—modify each of them. For example, a child's interactions with teachers affect interactions with parents. The next level of the environment, the **exosystem**, includes settings that children may not directly interact with but that influence the child nonetheless. For example, a teacher's family

As he describes what he does when he is not in school, this young boy discusses primarily proximal processes. What are some of the more distal processes that also have an effect on his development?

life will influence the teacher and thereby the child. Or a child's socioeconomic status influences where her family lives, affecting the school the child will attend, and thus affecting the kinds of experiences the child has with teachers. Finally, there is the **macrosystem**, including the customs and character of the larger culture that help shape the microsystems. For example, cultural attitudes and laws regarding the education of exceptional students influence the operation of a school and therefore a child's interactions with teachers.

The environment, then, is like "a set of nested structures, each inside the next, like a set of Russian dolls" (Bronfenbrenner, 1979). In newer versions of his theory, Bronfenbrenner gives equal attention to the nested internal levels of the organism. As we have seen, a person brings to proximal processes a set of dispositions, resources (preexisting abilities, experiences, knowledge, and skills), and demand characteristics. These, in turn, are influenced by biological and physical levels of functioning that include the genes. Bronfenbrenner also emphasizes, as other multidimensional theorists do, the bidirectional effects of each level on the adjacent levels. For example, proximal psychological processes playing out in the immediate context are both influenced by, and influencing, physiological processes (Bronfenbrenner & Morris, 1998, 2006; Ceci, Rosenblum, de Bruyn, & Lee, 1997). Finally, these interactions continue and change across time.

Life Span Developmental Theory

In **life span developmental theories**, the same developmental processes that produce the transformation of infants into children, and children into adults, are thought to continue throughout adulthood until death. Developmental change is part of what it means to be alive. Adaptation continues from conception to death, with proximal interactions between the organism and the immediate context modified by more distal processes both within the individual and in the environment. Life span theorists like Paul Baltes (e.g., 1997; Baltes, Lindenberger, & Staudinger, 2006) refer to the interacting web of influences on development as the "architecture" of biological and cultural supports. Baltes proposes that successful adaptation is benefited more by biological supports in childhood than in adulthood. Cultural supports are important in childhood, but if not optimal, most children have biological supports (we could think of them as a complex of biological protective factors) that have evolved to optimize development in most environments. For adults, successful adaptation is more heavily dependent on cultural supports or protective factors. "The older individuals are, the more they are in need of culture-based resources (material, social, economic, psychological) to generate and maintain high levels of functioning" (Baltes, Lindenberger, & Staudinger, 1998, p. 1038). We will have more to say about life span developmental theories in Chapter 13.

Applying Theory to Practice

We have described both classic theoretical approaches to development and the more integrative and complex multidimensional theories that contemporary developmentalists favor. Preferring one of these paradigms can influence the way helping professionals assess and interpret client concerns. Let's consider how various theoretical orientations to development might apply to a counseling situation:

Juliana is a 26-year-old Latina female who was raised in an intact, middle-class family. Her father was a teacher and her mother a housewife who occasionally worked in a neighborhood preschool as a teacher's aide. Juliana was the second child in the family, which included an older brother and a younger sister. She attended parochial schools from kindergarten through 12th grade, where she worked very hard to achieve average and sometimes above-average grades. During her early years in school, Juliana had reading difficulties and received remedial instruction. At home, her parents stressed the value of education and kept a close watch on the children. The children were well behaved, respectful, and devoted to the family.

Most of their spare time was spent with their close relatives, who lived nearby. Despite Juliana's interest in dating during high school, her parents did not permit her to spend time with boyfriends. They told her that she needed to concentrate on her schoolwork so that she could be a nurse when she grew up. After graduation, Juliana entered a small local college and enrolled in a program designed to prepare her for a career in nursing. She lived at home and commuted to school on a daily basis. Life proceeded as it had for most of her high school years. Her course work, however, became increasingly more difficult for her. She also felt isolated from most of her classmates, many of whom were working and living on their own. She tried to participate in some of the college's social events, but without much satisfaction or success. To pass her science courses, Juliana had to spend most of her time studying. By the middle of her academic program, it was clear that she was in danger of failing. She felt frustrated and angry. At this point, she became romantically involved with Bill, a young White man who worked at the college. She dropped out of school and moved in with him, hoping their relationship would lead to marriage. Her family was shocked and upset with her decision and put pressure on her to come home. Eventually, the relationship with Bill ended, and Juliana, unwilling to return home, moved in with a group of young students who were looking for someone to share the rent. She found a low-wage job, changed her style of dress to look more like the younger students, and quickly became involved in a series of other romantic relationships. Juliana grew increasingly despondent about her inability to maintain a relationship that would lead to marriage and a family. In addition, she felt some distress about not completing her college degree. She enrolled in a night-school program at a local community college to retake her science courses. Once again, she experienced confusion, problems fitting in, and academic difficulty. She went to the college counseling center to ask for help.

Take a minute to think about how you would respond to Juliana. Do any of your views about development enter into your appraisal of her situation? If you tend to be a stage theorist, you might consider Juliana's problems to be based on Erikson's crisis of intimacy in early adulthood (see Table 1.2). She does seem to have difficulties with intimacy, and she is just at the age when these issues are supposed to become central to psychosocial development. But a rigid assumption of age–stage correspondence could prevent you from considering other possibilities, such as an unresolved identity crisis.

If you tend to be an incremental theorist, perhaps favoring social learning explanations, you might perceive Juliana's situation quite differently. You may see Juliana as having problems in her intimate relationships that are similar to her difficulties with school. In both domains she is apparently "delayed," perhaps because she has had insufficient opportunities to learn social and academic skills or perhaps because she has been reinforced for behaviors that are ineffective in more challenging contexts. Although this may be a useful way of construing Juliana's dilemma, any stage issues contributing to her distress may be missed. Also, there could be factors in her social environment, such as cultural expectations, that might not be considered.

If you take a more multidimensional approach, as we do, you will try to remain alert to multiple influences, both proximal and distal, on Juliana's development. The roles of her biological status, her individual capabilities, her stage of development, her earlier experiences, her family, and her culture will all be considered as possible influences and points of intervention. One disadvantage could be that the complexity of the interacting factors is so great that you may find it difficult to sort out the most effective place to begin. Another disadvantage is that macrosystem influences, such as cultural expectations about appropriate roles for women, may be quite resistant to intervention. However, one of the advantages of a multidimensional view is that it *does* highlight many possible avenues of intervention, and if you can identify one or a few that are amenable to change, you may have a positive influence on Juliana's future.

Helping professionals with different developmental assumptions would be likely to choose different approaches and strategies in working with Juliana. In a sense, any set of theoretical biases is like a set of blinders. It will focus your attention on some aspects of the situation and reduce the visibility of other aspects. Taking a multidimensional or systems view has the advantage of minimizing the constraints of those blinders. In any case, knowing your own biases can help you avoid the pitfalls of overreliance on one way of viewing development.

A NEW LOOK AT THREE DEVELOPMENTAL ISSUES

In the following sections, we examine three classic developmental issues that have garnered a great deal of attention in recent years. As you read about these issues from the viewpoint of contemporary research, you will begin to see why modern developmental theories take a multidimensional approach. Notice whether any of the new information causes you to reexamine your own assumptions about development.

Nature *and* Nurture

How did you respond to the first three items of the questionnaire in Box 1.1? Did you say that physical traits are primarily inherited? Did you say that intelligence or personality is inherited? Your opinions on these matters are likely to be influenced by your cultural background. For example, North Americans have traditionally seen intelligence as mostly hereditary, but Japanese tend to disregard the notion of "native ability" and to consider intellectual achievements as a function of opportunity and hard work (Stevenson, Chen, & Lee, 1993). Alternatively, North Americans usually view personality and social adjustment as a result of environmental experiences, especially parents' nurturance and socialization practices, but Japanese traditionally see these qualities as mostly unalterable, native traits.

Developmental researchers acknowledge that both nature and nurture influence most behavioral outcomes, but in the past they have often focused primarily on one or the other, partly because a research enterprise that examines multiple causes at the same time tends to be a massive undertaking. So, based on personal interest, theoretical bias, and practical limitations, developmental researchers have often systematically investigated one kind of cause, setting aside examination of other causes of behavior. Interestingly, what these limited research approaches have accomplished is to establish impressive bodies of evidence, *both* for the importance of genes *and* for the importance of the environment!

What theorists and researchers face now is the difficult task of specifying how the two sets of causes work together: Do they have separate effects that "add up," for example, or do they qualitatively modify each other, creating together, in unique combinations, unique outcomes? Modern multidimensional theories make the latter assumption and evidence is quickly accumulating to support this view. Heredity and environment are interdependent: The same genes operate differently in different environments, and the same environments are experienced differently by individuals with different genetic characteristics. Developmental outcomes are always a function of interplay between genes and environment, and the operation of one cannot even be described adequately without reference to the other. The study of **epigenetics**, the alteration of gene expression by the environment, has led to a radically new understanding of some mechanisms of gene-environment interaction. Epigenetic changes have long-term, important effects on development, and some epigenetic changes can even be transmitted transgenerationally (Skinner, 2011). In Chapter 2 you will find many examples of this complex interdependence.

Enriched and stimulating environments provide long-term benefits for children's functioning "especially during periods of maximum sensitivity."

Neuroplasticity *and* Critical (Sensitive) Periods

Neuroplasticity refers to changes in the brain that occur as a result of some practice or experience. Neurons, the basic cells of the nervous system, get reorganized as a result of such practice, resulting in new learning and memory. The realization that our brains continue to change throughout life has revolutionized the way scientists regard the brain. Not only do these changes primarily occur in infancy and early childhood, as had been proposed in the past. Contemporary neuroscientists recognize that "there is no period when the brain and its functions are static; changes are continuous throughout the lifespan. The nature, extent and the rates of change vary by region and function assessed and are influenced by genetic as well as environmental factors" (Pascual-Leone & Taylor, 2011, p. 183). As we have seen, modern multidisciplinary theories incorporate descriptions of relative life-long plasticity.

The time-related "variation by region and function" noted above is at the heart of the classic question about *critical (sensitive) periods*. Although the brain exhibits plasticity throughout life, do some changes, such as first language learning, occur more easily and more effectively at certain ages and stages? Or, is the organism able to develop or learn any new skill at any time with the right opportunities? There is little doubt that there are some behavioral developments that usually take place within a particular period. In many ways, language acquisition is nearly complete by the age of 5 or 6, for example. But is it possible to acquire a language at another point in the life cycle if this usual time is somehow "missed"? Pinker (1994) reviewed several findings that led him to conclude that although language can be learned at other times, it is never learned as well or as effortlessly as it would have been in the critical period from about 1 to 5 years. One interesting example from Pinker's review concerns the learning of sign language by deaf individuals. American Sign Language (ASL) is a "real" symbolic language, with a complex grammar. Often, however, American deaf children are not given the opportunity to learn ASL in their early years, sometimes because of a belief that deaf children should learn to read lips and speak English (the "oralist" tradition). As a result, many deaf children simply do not learn any language. When these individuals are introduced to ASL in late childhood or adolescence, they often fail to acquire the same degree of facility with the grammar that children who learn ASL as preschoolers achieve.

If findings like these mean that a sensitive period has been missed, what could be the cause of such time-dependent learning? It is usually assumed that the end of a sensitive period is due to brain changes that make learning more difficult after the change. The environmental conditions that are likely to support the new learning may also be less favorable at certain times. As we have seen, the explanation is likely to be complex. For example, total immersion in a language may be just the right arrangement for a preschooler who knows no other communicative system. Older learners, even deaf children or adults who have learned no formal language early in life, may always filter a new language through previously established communication methods, such as an idiosyncratic set of hand signals. If so, for an older child or adult, total immersion may be less effective than a learning environment that can make correspondences between the new language and the old one. In later chapters, we will examine this issue as it relates to several developments, such as the emergence of sexual identity (Chapter 8) and the formation of bonds between mothers and infants (Chapter 4). In each case, the evidence indicates that time-dependent, region-specific windows of opportunity for rapid neural reorganization exist alongside continuing plasticity.

Universality *and* Specificity: The Role of Culture

Developmental science is concerned with explaining the nature and characteristics of change. Are developmental changes universal, having the same qualities across ethnic, racial, or socioeconomic status groups, between genders, and from one historical period to another? Or does development depend entirely on the specific group or time within which it occurs? Many classic developmental theories have posited basic similarities in development across different groups and historical periods. Stage theories, like Freud's theory in particular, often specify invariant sequences in personality or cognitive outcomes that are thought to apply to everyone, regardless of culture, group, or historical time. Yet even classic stage theories do incorporate sociocultural influences.

In Erikson's psychosocial stage theory, for example, all adolescents confront the task of formulating an adult identity. But the nature of that identity will certainly differ across groups. How complex and arduous a struggle the adolescent might face in forming an identity could vary dramatically depending on her context. Erikson's studies of identity development in two Native American groups, the Sioux in South Dakota and the Yurok on the Pacific coast, and of mainstream White culture revealed different struggles and different outcomes in each (Erikson, 1950/1963).

Some **sociocultural theories**, which trace their roots to the work of Lev Vygotsky (e.g., 1934, 1978; see Chapter 3), argue that cognitive developments may be qualitatively different in different cultures (e.g., Rogoff, 1998, 2003; Sternberg, 2004). For example, in Western cultures, classifying objects by functional associations (birds with nests) is a trademark of preschoolers' sorting behavior. Hierarchically organized taxonomic classification (e.g., collies and dachshunds grouped as kinds of dogs, dogs and birds grouped as animals) is more typical of elementary-school-age children. Piaget regarded taxonomic sorting to be an indicator of the logical thinking that emerges in middle childhood. But in some ethnic groups, such as the African Kpelle tribe, even adults do not sort objects taxonomically. They use functionally based schemes, perhaps because these are more meaningful in their everyday lives, and they would probably consider such schemes more sophisticated than a taxonomic one (Cole, 1998). Bronfenbrenner (1979) explained how culture could influence behavior through proximal processes, the daily give and take with others in one's social networks that he considered the primary engines of development. Other early pioneers, such as anthropologist Margaret Mead, began the process of growing a multicultural knowledge base (see Mead, 1928; Whiting & Whiting, 1975).

In general, however, the bulk of social science research has been done on a relatively narrow sample of WEIRD (Western, Educated, Industrialized, Rich, and Democratic) people (Henrich, Heine, & Norenzayan, 2010) and developmental research is no exception (Fernald, 2010). Researchers are now acutely aware of the need to discover how developmental processes play out among other groups both within and outside North America to answer questions about universal versus specific developmental trajectories. To this end, culture, race and ethnicity have greater prominence in research than in the past, even though these constructs have proven somewhat difficult to define (Corbie-Smith et al., 2008).

Formerly, differences among **racial groups**, like Blacks, Whites, and Asians, were considered to be due to heredity, identifiable by variations in hair, skin color, bone structure, or other physiological markers. But apparent differences among racial groups are not greater than the range of differences within groups, and genetic indicators of race have not been found (Bamshad & Olson, 2003). Racial groupings may be no more than a social construction, founded on shifting and superficial characteristics, so reliance on this term may be misleading (Afshari, Bhopal & Afshari, 2002). **Ethnicity** is sometimes used interchangeably with race, although this too is problematic. Shared ancestry, language, a common place of origin and a sense of belonging to the group are elements commonly used to describe membership in an ethnic group.

Adding to the complexity, **culture**, which can also include shared values, rituals, psychological processes, behavioral norms and practices (Fiske, Kitayama, Markus, & Nisbett, 1998) is frequently used as a proxy for ethnicity. Early studies often represented culture as a kind of "social address" (Bronfenbrenner, 1979) with gender, race, religion, age, language, ethnic heritage and socioeconomic status as labels signifying some cultural group membership. Think of your own status in relation to the items on this list. Then consider the status of another person you know. How similar or different from you is this other person? Is there one category that stands out for you when you try to describe her social/cultural address? For someone you consider to be culturally similar to you, do all the labels overlap? Just a little reflection gives you a taste of the dizzying complexity of such distinctions.

Some research demonstrates that shared values might not be the most reliable indicator of culture. For example, a recent study of values drawn from approximately 169,000 participants from 6 continents revealed broad agreement in values, contrary to what one might expect. Autonomy, relatedness, and competence were highly ranked across all cultures although some differences were observed for the value of conformity (Fischer & Schwartz, 2011). This finding questions the assumption that cultures are reliably different in their value systems. People in the same cultural group may be too diverse to justify painting with a broad brush. Some individuals may even have multiple ethnic/cultural identities (Sedikides & Brewer, 2001), so these terms are among the hardest for social scientists to define. Currently, there is a tendency to move away from static conceptualizations of what constitutes ethnic/cultural group membership toward more dynamic, process-oriented definitions for these important variables (Brubaker, 2009).

In particular, researchers are concerned about disaggregating social class, or **socioeconomic status (SES)**, from race and ethnic/cultural distinctions. *Socioeconomic status* is based on social standing or power, and is defined by characteristics of the adults in a household, including educational background, income, and occupation. Frequently, variables of race/ethnicity and SES are conflated in research, leading to questionable findings. A good example of why disaggregation is important comes from a study of preschool children's everyday activities in four cultural communities (Black and White in the United States, Luo in Kenya, and European descent in Porto Allegre, Brazil). Tudge and his colleagues (2006) observed everyday behaviors of preschool children, hypothesizing that each culture provides its young with the kinds of opportunities (e.g., school or work-related activities) deemed important for successful participation in their culture. Equal numbers of high and low SES children within each culture were included to study the intersection of culture and class. The Brazilian children engaged in fewer academic activities compared to White and Kenyan groups. Nonetheless, middle class Brazilian children were involved in more academic lessons than their working class counterparts. Kenyan children participated in significantly more work-related activities than all other groups. However, the working class Kenyan children engaged in twice as much work as those from all other groups, including middle-class Kenyan children.

Let's examine some other ways of looking at the effects of culture on development. From a process-oriented perspective, individuals participate in modes of interacting (such as scripted interchanges) that differ from one cultural group to another (Cole, 1996). One promising approach to understanding the role of culture in development is to ask whether exposure to such systematic cultural differences affects individual development. If so, are the effects only at a superficial level (e.g., learning different behaviors, manners, customs), or are there effects on more fundamental processes, such as information processing and developing brain structures (Fiske, 2009; Kitayama & Park, 2010)? This is precisely the kind of question that experimenters in the field of cultural psychology have taken on (Miller, 1999).

Consider, for example, the often-cited distinction between the holistic (interdependent) modes of interacting in cultures of the Eastern hemisphere and the analytic (independent) modes in cultures of the Western hemisphere. A body of research now supports the existence of reliable differences beyond just superficial behavioral ones. First, differences have been identified in information processing (attention, understanding cause and effect, memory, and categorization) between people from Eastern and Western cultures (Nisbett & Masuda, 2003). Some analysts have speculated that the historical-cultural antecedents of these processing differences may be ancient ways of viewing the world common to Chinese and Greek societies respectively (Nisbett, Peng, Choi, & Norenzayan, 2001). In turn, each of these ways may have been shaped by the respective economies of those societies (large-scale farming vs. hunting and trading) along with their different physical environments (open plain vs. seaside mountains). Freed from the interdependence required for massive farming and irrigation projects, ancient Greeks, the forebears of Western societies, came to view the world by focusing on central objects. In other words, the ancient Greeks inhabited a world where objects were typically perceived as relatively unchanging and detached from their context. The objects' features (size, shape, color, etc.) were investigated so as to understand their operating rules and to predict and control their operations. Logic and scientific empiricism are related to this perspective on the world.

Needing to pay attention to the larger context in order to thrive, members of Eastern societies such as China focused more holistically on interrelationships, paying as much attention to the field wherein objects existed as to the objects themselves. Understanding the world from this perspective was more likely to incorporate figure-ground relationships and to hold the dialectic of opposing points of view in balance (Nisbett & Masuda, 2003). It could be that these fundamental differences in Greek and Chinese social organization and cognition, based upon geographical constraints and the exigencies of survival, continued to affect the development of people and societies that followed in their wake.

Any study of cultural differences embodies a fundamental wish to see the world as others do. Imagine that you could literally see what people pay attention to as a way of gaining knowledge about their perspective. Seeing the world through the eyes of people who live in the Eastern and Western regions of the globe could be a fruitful place to start because any differences that evolved from long histories of practice might be more obvious. Recent studies of attention and visual processing comparing these two cultural groups, made possible by the development of eye-movement tracking technology, have indeed proved fruitful.

Results of many studies have demonstrated a greater tendency among Eastern participants to attend to context when compared to Western participants who are more likely to attend to central objects (e.g., in photos of animals in complex environments; Boduroglu, Shah, & Nisbett, 2009; Kitayama, Duffy, Kawamura, & Larsen, 2003; Masuda & Nisbett, 2001, 2006). Eastern research subjects also process groups of items in relationship to each other rather than by category (e.g., linking a cow and grass instead of a cow and chicken; Chiu, 1972; Ji, Zhang, & Nisbett, 2004). The Eastern emphasis on field also extends to making causal attributions for events. When Westerners were asked to explain the reasons for outcomes in athletic competitions or the causes of criminal events, they emphasized internal traits as causal, whereas Easterners gave more contextualized explanations for outcomes (Choi, Nisbett, & Norenzayan, 1999).

In an ingenious study demonstrating the interrelated effects of culture, development, and neuroplasticity, Goh et al. (2007) show that what you pay attention to makes a subtle yet enduring difference in your brain over time. Repeated practice results in changes in the brain that become our preferred modes of thought and action. The cultural shaping of visual processing in the brain was explored in groups of young and old North Americans and East Asians from Singapore. Researchers studied the visual ventral cortex, a complex of brain structures responsible for identifying what is being processed visually (Farah, Rabinowitz, & Quinn, 2000). Some parts of this complex process object information and other parts process background information (see Park & Huang, 2010). The inclusion of older individuals in this study allowed researchers to analyze whether sustained cultural experience with analytic (central object) versus holistic (background/context) processing

Young Westerners   **Young East Asians**

Old Westerners   **Old East Asians**

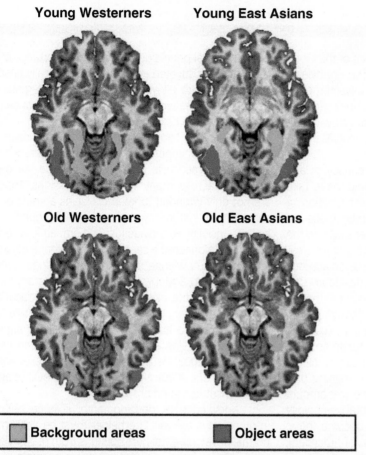

Background areas	Object areas

FIGURE 1.3 **East/West differences in visual processing of younger and older individuals.** Colored areas show brain areas that are active when processing central objects (blue) and background (orange) visual information. Younger Easterners and Westerners show brain activity for visual processing in both central object and background areas. Older Western participants show activity for visual processing of background and reduced processing for central objects. Older Eastern participants show activity in background processing areas but no activity in central object processing areas.
SOURCE: Goh, J. O., & Park, D. C., J. Y. Chiao (Ed.) (2009). Culture sculpts the perceptual brain, *Progress in Brain Research, 178*, 95–111. Sage Publications. Reprinted by Permission of SAGE Publications.

sculpted the brain in unique ways over time. During experimental sessions utilizing an adapted functional magnetic resonance imaging (fMR-A) paradigm (see Chapter 2), which shows which parts of the brain are in use during different tasks, all participants viewed pictures of objects in scenes. As you can see in Figure 1.3, young Westerners' and Easterners' brains were similar in where and to what extent they processed objects versus backgrounds. Older participants from both cultures showed reduced processing of objects relative to backgrounds compared to younger participants. But there was an East/West difference in the older participants: The older Asian participants showed much more of a reduction than older Western participants in object processing. These older Asians did not lose their ability to focus on central objects, but they needed to be prompted to do so. For them, holistic processing had become the default mode, suggesting a lifetime cultural habit of attention to context.

APPLICATIONS

In this chapter, we have discussed the importance of the study of development and introduced you to some of the worldviews and issues central to the field. The value of developmental knowledge to practitioners of the helping professions cannot be underestimated, as is underscored by a consensus growing out of a number of different theoretical orientations (e.g., Fisher & Lerner, 1994; Noam, 1992, 1998).

These developmental approaches to counseling and therapy, for the most part, have encouraged clinicians to take into account the developmental features of client functioning as a critical part of assessing and treating problems. These approaches share a number of commonalities: a sensitivity to the fact that persons grow and change over time and that their capacities and concerns also shift over the life course; an appreciation for the knowledge that scientific studies of developmental change can provide for clinicians; and a commitment to the application of this knowledge to improving the lives of individuals, families, and society as a whole. Instead of asking clinicians to choose a therapeutic approach from a set of treatment modalities, each with its own bounded theoretical tradition, Noam (1998) argues for a developmental viewpoint in training programs, which can help new clinicians organize the vast amount of information they need to master. "Developmental psychology and developmental psychopathology need to become 'basic sciences' for the mental health field" (Rolf, Masten, Cicchetti, Neuchterlein, & Weintraub, 1990). We would add to this list of basic requirements a working knowledge of biologically based and culturally relevant information. Use of such broadened developmental knowledge as a kind of metatheory helps clinicians integrate the problems presented by the "person-in-situation" and can help reduce the confusion often felt by helpers exposed to a heterogeneous array of treatments for isolated problems.

Efforts are underway to make diagnostic taxonomies like the Diagnostic and Statistical Manual of Mental Disorders (DSM-V) and the International Classification of Diseases-11 (ICD-11) more developmentally and culturally sensitive (Kupfer, Regier, & Kuhl, 2008). Because good treatment begins with an in-depth understanding of causes, current diagnostic systems need to move beyond superficial descriptions of symptoms. Instead of providing just a "book of names," Jensen and Hoagwood (1997) argue that diagnostic classification systems need to include a comprehensive understanding of the way people grow and adapt, for better or for worse, to their changing circumstances. One system, proposed by Sadler and Hulgus (1994), would incorporate three levels of symptom assessment into treatment planning. Examples of these three levels include syndromes related to personal history (such as early parental deprivation), syndromes related to interpersonal environments (such as victimization or divorce), and syndromes related to extrapersonal environments (such as job loss or systemic discrimination). What these approaches share is the desire to shift the prevailing theoretical paradigm from a model of pathology "within the individual" to a more integrative model that incorporates critical developmental principles such as the importance of contextual features. Sophisticated advances in biologically based research in mental health allow professionals to integrate knowledge about syndromes with clearer understanding of causal mechanisms (Cannon & Keller, 2006).

Integrative approaches to mental health treatment emphasize the importance of cultural differences. Culturally competent practice is now considered the standard for performance across many helping professions. These changes are not only intended to keep clinicians abreast of current research about cultural variations. They are grounded in the ethical responsibility to provide just and empathic care for all. Early advocates pioneered a set of guidelines that addressed cultural awareness, knowledge, and skills (Arredondo & Perez, 2006; Sue, Arredondo, & McDavis, 1992), and now many helping fields, including medicine, psychology, social work, education, nursing, and so on, have incorporated similar aspects within their professional practice guidelines. Table 1.4 shows standards from psychology, nursing and social work (American Psychological Association, 2003; Douglas et al., 2011; National Association of Social Workers, 2000). Notice the general level of agreement in what constitutes good practice.

Knowledge of developmental science helps clinicians in other ways as well. The helper must be able to distinguish normal developmental perturbations from real deviations in development to intervene wisely. A prime example of this occurs in adolescence, which Freud described as a period of "normal psychopathology." Understanding some of the issues typical of this time of life can inform a clinician's guidance, advocacy, and support. Moreover, using a developmental focus can allow the helper to consider ways to support developmental transitions (Lerner, 1996) to later life stages by taking steps to promote a caring network.

Some Rules of Thumb

In this chapter, we have introduced you to some of the classic paradigms and issues in the field of human development and have specified ways in which knowledge of development is fundamental to practitioners. We now suggest a few general guidelines for the application of developmental research to the work of the helping professional.

1. Keep abreast of new and reliable developments in the field. It is important to sort out the worthwhile information in this ever-expanding field of study to help clients more effectively.
2. Take a multidimensional view of developmental processes. Awareness of the interacting contributions of genetics and environment can allow helpers to take a more reasoned and accurate view of problems. The competent helper understands that biologically based research contributes to understanding development, personality, and psychopathology by clarifying the complex mechanisms underlying these processes, ultimately setting

TABLE 1.4 Standards for Cultural Competence Across Three Helping Professions

CATEGORY	PSYCHOLOGY (APA)	NURSING (DOUGLAS ET AL., 2011)	SOCIAL WORK (NASW)
Self-Awareness	Understand that one's beliefs and values might be different from clients, become aware of personal attitudes, and work to increase contacts with diverse groups.	Critically reflect on personal beliefs and values as they affect practice.	(1) Recognize how personal values might conflict with needs of diverse clients in professional practice. (2) Develop understanding of personal values and beliefs.
Sensitivity to/Gaining Knowledge About Other Cultures	Increase knowledge about others' worldviews, including the effects of stigmatization. Become knowledgeable about social policies that affect other cultures.	Recognize and gain knowledge about the specifics of other cultures.	Continue to develop knowledge about cultural differences.
Professional Training	Infuse multicultural information into professional training and include it in coursework in psychology in general.	(1) Work toward a multicultural workforce through education, retention and recruitment policies. (2) Provide training and continuing education in culturally congruent care and global health issues.	(1) Participate in training and continuing education in cultural competence. (2) Support and advocate for professional diversity through recruitment, admissions and hiring, and retention efforts.
Research	Conduct culturally sensitive, ethical research. Ethnic, racial, and linguistic differences should be considered in research design, analysis, interpretation, and assessment.		
Skills for Practice	Apply culturally appropriate clinical skills in practice by focusing on the client within his or her cultural context, using culturally appropriate assessment tools, and having a broad repertoire of interventions.	(1) Engage in culturally competent practice. (2) Employ culturally relevant verbal and nonverbal communication skills. (3) Base interventions on those with evidence to support effectiveness with diverse groups.	(1) Utilize culturally appropriate skills and techniques and understand what role culture plays in the helping process. (2) Develop understanding of community and societal resources to make appropriate referrals. (3) Advocate for language-appropriate materials and services.
Operations of Organizations and Systems; Social Justice Advocacy	Apply culturally informed organizational practices and expand professional role to change agent.	(1) Ensure that health care organizations provide the structure and resources necessary to evaluate and meet the cultural and language needs of their diverse clients. (2) Advocate for inclusion of patient's cultural beliefs in all aspects of health care. (3) Advocate for social justice and develop leadership skills to support social justice. (4) Demonstrate leadership to influence individuals, groups, and systems to achieve outcomes of culturally competent care. (5) Advocate for culturally competent care through establishment of policies for professional organizations.	(1) Be aware of the effect of social policies and programs on diverse client populations and advocate for them whenever appropriate. (2) Demonstrate leadership in communicating information about diverse groups to others.

the stage for more effective prevention and intervention (Beauchaine, Neuhaus, Brenner, & Gatzke-Kopp, 2008).

3. The contemporary helper's tool kit needs to include information about culture. Awareness of ourselves and others as deeply embedded in our own cultural frames can open our eyes to areas of difference. But it can also help professionals strengthen our empathy and allow us to realize

the "connection that is attributed to shared humanness" (Browning & Artelt, 2012, p. 227).

4. Interpret stage sequences as guidelines for development. It helps to bear in mind that the various theoretical models or metaphors for developmental growth that we have presented should not be applied rigidly. One size never fits everyone. Nonetheless, views that abandon all sense

of developmental stage progressions may prove unwieldy for the helper who needs to construct a developmental map of the client. What is the answer? As usual, an informed middle ground may be the best alternative. Stages of psychosocial development are not entirely dependent on chronological age and maturational attainments. However, they are not independent of these achievements, either. The skilled clinician must consider a number of possibilities at the same time and, like the reflective thinker described earlier, work to find the best fit.

5. Keep in mind the scientific meaning of *theory*. The term *theory* is often used differently in science than it is in everyday language. In science, a theory frequently represents a synthesis of hypotheses that have been tested and supported by careful research, such as the theory of relativity or evolution. In everyday use, a theory can mean one's personal opinion, such as one's opinion about the best way to educate or counsel children or one's guess about what causes marriages to fail. Scientific theories are not immutable; they can evolve or be disproved with the accumulation of evidence. Although evaluating theories in light of evidence is by no means the only way we learn about life, this approach offers many strengths that set it apart from everyday speculation. Consequently,

skilled clinicians should keep themselves well informed about current research findings, but they must also avoid overgeneralizing from single studies.

6. Be selective about your sources of information. Clinicians should be cautious about the sources of information they accept. As with any scientific endeavor, knowledge builds relatively slowly and is buttressed by repeated observations of similar results. A simplistic approach to developmental issues typically will miss the mark by ignoring the complexities of interacting factors, including contextual and historical influences. Additionally, the kinds of direct causal connections between experiences and outcomes that would make prediction much easier for therapists and consultants are, unfortunately, almost impossible to obtain.

7. Be committed to ongoing education in the field. If we are to pursue the best possible outcomes for our clients, we need to be committed to advancing our professional knowledge. We will try in this book to present the best available information that applies to helpers; however, it is important to be aware that the field of developmental science is itself continually developing. Helpers and others need to keep an open mind and continually work to accommodate new information as they practice reflection in action.

FOCUS ON DEVELOPMENTAL PSYCHOPATHOLOGY

In several chapters of this text, you will find sections titled **Focus on Developmental Psychopathology**, which highlight developmental approaches to specific behavioral disorders. These sections emphasize work in the relatively new field of **developmental psychopathology**, offering clinicians a unique perspective on dysfunctional behavior by integrating work from many disciplines, including developmental, clinical, and abnormal psychology. This field takes a life span perspective on disturbed behavior by assuming that it is an outgrowth of complex but lawful developmental processes (e.g., Rutter & Sroufe, 2000). Unhealthy social, emotional, and behavioral processes, like depression or conduct disorder, emerge in the same way that healthy ones do: as a function of the individual's attempts to adapt to her environment. Behaviors or coping strategies that are adaptive in one developmental circumstance can be maladaptive in other concurrent contexts or they may establish a trajectory that can result in maladaptive outcomes later. "In contrast to the often dichotomous world of mental disorder/nondisorder depicted in psychiatry, a developmental psychopathology perspective recognizes that normality often fades into abnormality, adaptive and maladaptive may take on differing definitions depending on whether one's time referent is immediate circumstances or long-term development, and processes within the individual can be characterized as having shades or degrees of psychopathology" (Cicchetti & Toth, 2006, p. 498).

Developmental psychopathology is largely guided by multidimensional or systems theories of development (e.g., Cicchetti & Sroufe, 2000; Cicchetti & Toth, 2006; Rutter & Sroufe, 2000;

Sameroff, 2000; Sameroff & MacKenzie, 2003). Every individual is seen as an active organism, influenced by multiple levels of internal processes, and continuously adapting to multiple embedded contexts. Abnormality results from the same proximal processes that produce more normative patterns: As the individual transacts with the environment, she attempts to meet her needs and to adjust to environmental inputs and demands. She brings both strengths and vulnerabilities to these transactions, and the environment contributes both stressors and supports. Both the individual and the environment are somewhat altered by each transaction, reciprocally influencing each other. That is, the change processes are bidirectional. The individual's strengths and vulnerabilities as well as environmental stressors and supports are all variables or factors that impact the overall development of the individual. Both healthy and unhealthy outcomes are the result of the interplay of the individual's characteristics *and* her experiences across time. "Single factors can be potent in destroying systems . . . a gunshot can destroy a child. But single factors cannot *create* a child or any other living system" (Sameroff, 2000, p. 37).

The individual's strengths and the environment's supports are **protective factors**, helping to promote healthy outcomes; the individual's vulnerabilities and the environmental stressors she experiences are **risk factors** that can interfere with healthy development (see Box 1.2 for a fuller discussion of such factors). Among the individual's characteristics that may matter are various genetic and other biological factors, temperamental traits, cognitive capacities, social skills, attitudes, beliefs, and so on. Among the environmental factors are socioeconomic status, safety of the neighborhood, quality of the schools, family history and culture, parental nurturing and monitoring, peer attitudes, friendships, marital and community supports, cultural dynamics including racial and ethnic processes, and so on.

Work in developmental psychopathology has brought into focus the importance of both *mediating* and *moderating* relationships between variables or factors in development. Let's begin with **mediating variables**. Suppose that one factor appears to be a cause of some behavioral outcome. For example, when a child experiences early, pervasive poverty, she is at higher risk than other children for developing mental health problems and medical diseases in adulthood, from depression to cardiovascular disease to some cancers (Chen, 2004). Even if children's economic circumstances improve in later childhood or adulthood, the increased risk of adult problems persists. One mediating variable that links early poverty to later health vulnerability is a compromised immune system. Specifically, poor children are more prone to inflammation. Changes in the functioning of certain genes cause this "pro-inflammatory profile," which lasts into adulthood and can contribute to poor health, including some mental health problems like depression (Chen, Miller, Kobor, & Cole, 2011).

Moderating variables are those that affect the strength of the relationship between other variables (Baron & Kenny, 1986). They interact with causal factors, altering and sometimes even eliminating their effects on outcome variables. For example, researchers have found that not all adults exposed to early poverty are characterized by a "pro-inflammatory profile" (Chen, Miller, Kobor, & Cole, 2011). Adults who suffered chronic early poverty but who report having a warm, supportive relationship with their mothers in childhood often have normal immune system functioning. Warm mothering appears to be a protective factor that *moderates* the impact of early poverty, a risk factor. See Figure 1.4 for a graphic illustration of both mediating and moderating factors related to early poverty's effects.

Recent research in psychopathology has focused on the role of **endophenotypes** as mediators and moderators. *Endophenotypes* are biobehavioral processes that can be traced to genes. These processes serve as intermediary links between the actual genes that contribute to disorders and their expressed behavioral manifestations. The "pro-inflammatory profile" that serves as a mediator between early childhood poverty and later

mental and physical health problems is an example of an endophenotype, because it has been found to result from epigenetic processes (Chen et al., 2011). Lenroot and Giedd (2011) artfully describe endophenotypes as "bridges between molecules and behavior" (p. 429). Study of these intermediary links can help us better understand the processes by which genetic information exerts influence on observable behavior (Gottesman & Gould, 2003).

Because so many interacting factors are involved, there is no such thing as perfect prediction of who will have healthy outcomes, who will not, when problems may arise, and how they will evolve. A rough guideline for prediction is that the more risk factors and the fewer protective factors there are, the more likely an individual is to have adjustment problems. Developmental psychopathology also recognizes two axiomatic principles: *multifinality* and *equifinality* (e.g., Cicchetti & Rogosch, 1996). The **principle of multifinality** is that individual pathways of development may result in a wide range of possible outcomes. For example, children exhibiting conduct-disordered behavior in the elementary school years may as adults display one or more of several different disorders, including antisocial personality, depression, substance abuse, and so on. The complementary **principle of equifinality** specifies that different early developmental pathways can produce similar outcomes. For example, Sroufe (1989) has demonstrated two pathways, one primarily biological and one primarily related to parenting style, that lead to attention deficit hyperactivity disorder (ADHD). Using these ideas from systems theory allows for the study of multiple subgroups and multiple pathways to disorders. Most important, it allows for a more realistic look at the problems people face (Cicchetti & Toth, 1994).

Here again, biobehavioral research is taking us a step closer to making better predictions about who will be affected by disorders and who will have more healthy outcomes. It may also help us unravel the mystery of multifinality. For example, why do some emotionally abused children become depressed as they age while others develop substance abuse disorders? Research on transdiagnostic risk factors (Nolen-Hoeksema & Watson, 2011), which are conceptually similar to endophenotypes, takes a close look at how risk factors other than the target one (e.g., history of emotional abuse) may moderate the effects of the target factor. Assessment of the moderating impact of different risk factors on each other is aimed at explaining

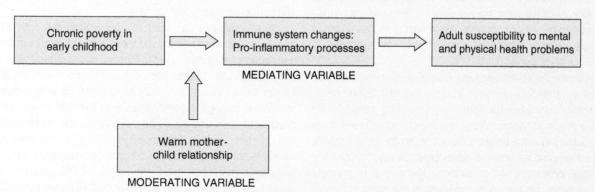

FIGURE 1.4 **Example of mediating and moderating variables.** The effects of chronic poverty on adult susceptibility to health problems are *mediated* by immune system changes and can be *moderated* by warm mother-child relationships.

"divergent trajectories": how different disorders evolve from the same target risk factors. Careful explication of these intervening sequences supports the fundamental goals of these new scientific fields.

Two primary goals of developmental psychopathology are to increase the probability of successfully predicting problematic outcomes and to find ways of preventing them. Developmental psychopathology is therefore closely linked to the field of **prevention science**, which aims at designing and testing prevention and intervention techniques for promoting healthy development in at-risk groups (see Box 1.2). Developmental psychopathologists also emphasize the value of studying individuals at the extremes of disordered behavior, for the purpose of enlightening us about how developmental processes work for everyone. Consider one example: Typically developing children eventually form a coherent and relatively realistic notion of self, so that they distinguish the self from others, they differentiate the real from the imagined, they form integrated memories of what they have done and experienced, and so on (see Chapters 5 and 7). Our understanding of when and how a coherent sense of self emerges in normal development has benefited from studies of maltreated children whose sense of self is often disorganized. In one study comparing maltreated with non-maltreated preschoolers, maltreated children showed substantially more dissociative behaviors, such as talking to imaginary playmates, being forgetful or confused about things the child should know, and lying to deny misbehavior even when the evidence is clear (Macfie, Cicchetti, & Toth, 2001). Note that all of these kinds of behaviors are typical of preschoolers *sometimes*. But finding that non-maltreated preschoolers are less likely to engage in these behaviors than maltreated youngsters helps substantiate two things: First,

relationships with caregivers are important to the development of a coherent self-system, and second, typically developing preschoolers are beginning to form a cohesive self-system even though the process is not complete.

The field of developmental psychopathology has several practical implications for clinical practice. First, interventions and treatments need to be developmentally appropriate to be effective. One approach will not fit all situations or age groups. For example, maltreated preschoolers showing signs of excessive dissociative behavior can be helped to form a more coherent self-system if helpers intervene with primary caregivers to increase their positivity, sensitivity, and responsivity (see Chapters 4 and 5); interventions with adults who suffer from dissociative behaviors would require other approaches. Second, periods throughout the life span marked by disequilibrium or disorganization with resultant reorganization may be considered points at which individuals might be most receptive to change. Developmental psychopathologists suggest that at these sensitive periods, interventions may be most effective because the individual can incorporate treatment into newly emerging levels of cognitive, emotional, and behavioral organization. Thus, the issue of timing of interventions is one of great interest to this field. In addition, the wide variety of possible pathways and outcomes involved in the development of psychopathology is an argument for the use of multiple means of intervention and treatment. However, interventions should be carefully considered and based on a thoughtful assessment of a person's developmental level and her quality of adaptation, the contexts that she must function within, as well as the availability of external supports. Because this field is relatively new, much more research is needed to establish these principles with greater certainty. However, this discipline's ideas and research findings hold out great promise for helpers.

Box 1.2: Prevention Science

There is a clear connection between developmental knowledge and prevention. Indeed, it is hard to imagine a more compelling reason for studying human growth and development than to be able to use this knowledge to prevent problems from occurring. Thinking developmentally about prevention automatically leads a helper to consider why problems occur, the nature of the forces acting on individuals that lead to certain endpoints, the strengths and weaknesses that are part of personal histories, and the functions that maladaptive behaviors might serve.

The relatively new and evolving discipline of *prevention science* takes an empirical approach to designing and testing effective intervention strategies for limiting or eliminating mental health problems. It draws on the knowledge and experience of researchers and practitioners in many different disciplines to do this effectively, including developmental science, developmental psychopathology, epidemiology, education, and criminology. The goal is to promote positive outcomes for everyone, especially those most at risk of developing social, emotional, and behavioral problems. Coie and his associates (1993) state that the primary objective of this new field

is to "trace the links between generic risk factors and specific clinical disorders and to moderate the pervasive effects of risk factors. If generic risks can be identified and altered in a population, this can have a positive effect on a range of mental health problems, as well as job productivity, and can reduce the need for many health, social, and correctional services" (p. 1014).

To effectively design and test interventions, it is critical for prevention scientists to understand the role of risk factors in the origin and sequencing of disordered outcomes, to understand what protective factors may mitigate such outcomes, and which risk and protective factors can most readily be targeted for intervention. Thus, prevention science is closely allied with the field of developmental psychopathology (see *Focus on Developmental Psychopathology*, this chapter). Together, they model relationships among risk and protective factors, specify ways to detect early warning signs of disorder, and then construct strategic approaches for disrupting a downward spiral. Scientific testing of the effectiveness of prevention techniques is a key contribution of prevention science to this process (e.g., Botvin & Griffin, 2005). The beauty of this discipline is that it has the potential to provide a coherent, community-based approach to intervention that is focused, effective, and developmentally appropriate. It draws on the knowledge and experience of researchers and practitioners across many related disciplines (e.g., those in social and psychological services, medicine, law enforcement, and education) and typically addresses problems at multiple levels by encouraging interdisciplinary collaboration to implement and test programs. For the helper who is concerned about best practice, prevention science can help her to select and support effective interventions.

Prevention has been a part of community efforts to improve health and human functioning for over a century in the United States (Spaulding & Balch, 1983). However, the science of preventing mental health problems has only recently been taken seriously. Documented increases in the numbers and kinds of problems affecting children and adolescents over the last several decades (Dryfoos, 1997), combined with advances in our knowledge of effective intervention techniques, have breathed new life into prevention efforts. The current enthusiasm for the promise of prevention is epitomized by the national interdepartmental initiative "Safe Schools/Healthy Students" (SS/HS), launched by the U.S. Departments of Education, Health and Human Services, and Justice in 1999 to fund the implementation and testing of effective programs for preventing violence and drug abuse in schools and communities across the United States.

What might a helping professional need to know about effective prevention and the science that supports it? We have attempted to address that query in a question-and-answer format.

Q & A About Prevention

How Is Prevention Defined?

Historically, clinicians interested in community-based mental health programs differentiated between primary, secondary, and tertiary prevention. **Primary prevention** is an attempt to forestall the development of problems by promoting health and wellness in the general population through group-oriented interventions. Requiring mandatory vaccinations for children or providing developmental guidance activities in schools might constitute primary prevention activities. **Secondary prevention** is an attempt to reduce the incidence of disorders among those who are at high risk or to provide treatment to forestall the development of more serious psychopathology in cases that are already established. Programs developed to identify students at risk for dropping out of school and to provide them with remedial programs might be examples of secondary-level prevention. In this case, a selected sample, rather than the general population, receives services. **Tertiary prevention** is directed toward rehabilitating persons with established disorders.

Because of the need to distinguish between the concepts of tertiary prevention and treatment, another way of categorizing types of prevention was suggested by the Institute of Medicine report (Institute of Medicine, 1994): universal, selective, and indicated. These three levels of prevention are clearly differentiated from treatment, which in this model is similar to tertiary prevention. **Universal prevention** is directed to the general population. **Selective prevention** targets individuals at some epidemiological risk, such as low-birth-weight babies. **Indicated prevention** addresses individuals who show subclinical symptoms of disorders, such as children whose behavioral problems are not yet serious enough to warrant a diagnosis of conduct disorder.

Some debate about how best to define the concept of prevention is focused on whether it should be seen strictly as problem prevention for high-risk individuals, or whether it should be expanded to include promotion of social and intellectual competency in all individuals. The American Psychological Association's Task Force on Prevention: Promoting Strength, Resilience, and Health in Young People, launched in 1998, took the position that the dual goals of reducing problems *and* generally enhancing social competence and health could not easily be separated and should both be seen as part of prevention efforts (Weissberg, Kumpfer, & Seligman, 2003).

What Are Risk and Protective Factors?

As defined by developmental psychopathology (see **Focus on Developmental Psychopathology**), *risk factors* are those variables in a person's life that compromise healthy development, whereas *protective factors* are those things that promote healthy development and/or moderate the negative effects of risk. Both kinds of factors may be internal to the individual, or part of the individual's developmental history, or part of the individual's environment. Examples of risk factors include, but are not limited to, certain genes, sensory or organic disabilities, low levels of intelligence, academic failure, family conflict, poverty, emotional undercontrol, and peer rejection. Protective factors include positive temperamental characteristics, intelligence, parental support and monitoring, good schools and community environments, and positive relationships with competent adults.

Risk and protective factors seem to have both cumulative and interactive effects on development. Negative outcomes are affected by a combination of elements: the number of risk factors present in a person's life, the severity of each, the duration of their effects, and the dearth of protective factors that lessen their ill effects. The presence of several risk factors exponentially increases the probability of a disorder. A good example of this phenomenon was reported by Zagar and his associates in their study of what puts adolescent boys at risk of committing murder (Zagar, Arbit, Sylvies, & Busch, 1991). The probability of murdering someone was doubled for boys with the following four risk factors: history of criminal violence in the family, history of being abused, gang membership, and abuse of illegal substances. The chances of committing murder were three times as great if these additional risk factors were present as well: prior arrest, possession and use of a weapon, neurological problems affecting cognition and affect, and school difficulties, including truancy.

You may recognize that many of these risks seem to fit together. As Garbarino (1999) points out, many children "fall victim to the unfortunate synchronicity between the demons inhabiting their own internal world and the corrupting influences of modern American culture" (p. 23). So not only do risks gain power as they accumulate, but they also operate in clusters that serve as "correlated constraints" (Cairns & Cairns, 1994). In other words, they reinforce each other by their redundancy and work together to shape the developmental trajectory. As a result, although altering one or just a few risk factors *can* have a positive impact on behavior and outcomes, sometimes such limited changes have little effect because the other related risks maintain the status quo.

(Box 1.2 continued)

Box 1.2 *Continued*

Certain risks, as well as certain protections, become more important at different points in development. For example, the protection offered by prosocial peers and the risks associated with exposure to deviant ones are particularly powerful as children approach adolescence but less so in early childhood (Bolger & Patterson, 2003). On the other hand, some protections, such as authoritative parenting, retain their power throughout childhood and adolescence (see Chapters 5 and 10). Some risk factors are common to many disorders. Deficits in perspective taking or problems with peer relationships may be related to the development of conduct disorder or depression.

How Do Risk and Protective Factors Operate to Produce Developmental Outcomes?

Risk and protective factors are conceptualized as independent, not just opposite ends of a risk-protection continuum. In other words, it is possible to have many risk factors as well as many protective factors operating in a person's life. Researchers are interested in protective factors because they are so closely intertwined with the concept of resilience, that quality that permits developmental success for some individuals despite grave setbacks or early adversity. For example, Hauser (1999), reporting on a retrospective analysis of young adults who had experienced severe trauma in adolescence, found that the ones who made the best adjustment had the highest levels of protection despite their early risks. Those who fared less well in adulthood had less support and greater risk.

Researchers have hypothesized that protective factors can work in two ways. They can improve life-course outcomes *directly* by their presence so that regardless of whether or not a child is exposed to one or more risks, she will experience some benefit from such a factor. Or, they can operate more *indirectly*, as *moderating variables*, altering the effects of risk factors. Gutman, Sameroff, and Eccles (2002) looked at how academic performance by African American adolescents was affected by risk factors that had been identified in other studies. These included maternal depression, low family income, father absence, low parent education, and so on. Participants in their sample ranged from low risk (zero to one or two risk factors) to high risk (seven or more risk factors). They also looked at possible protective factors, like parents' positive involvement with their children and supportive peers. They found that some factors, like parental school involvement, benefited children directly. For all adolescents, regardless of whether they were exposed to any risks, parental school involvement was associated with better academic performance. But other factors did operate more as moderating variables, specifically changing the impact of risks. Peer support for academics really made a positive difference for the academic achievement of high-risk adolescents, especially in math, but it was not especially important for low-risk kids. More research is needed to identify and explain these relationships with greater precision.

Does Prevention Really Work?

Based on a rapidly growing body of research findings, the answer is yes. Prevention scientists have provided evidence that well-designed and well-implemented preventive programs can reduce the incidence of problem behaviors such as aggressiveness, violence, and drug abuse as well as increase positive outcomes, such as academic achievement and social competence. We include examples of such programs in later chapters (Barrera & Sandler, 2006).

What Kinds of Prevention Efforts Work Best?

There is an increasing consensus among researchers, practitioners, and policy makers about criteria for successful prevention efforts. First, good prevention is based on developmentally appropriate, empirically valid approaches. Ideally, programs should show evidence that the positive effects have been maintained over a period of time before being implemented widely. Obviously, this implies the need for high-quality program evaluation research.

Second, successful programs take a multidimensional approach to problem prevention, enhancing protective factors while reducing risks (Reynolds & Suh-Ruu, 2003; Weissberg et al., 2003). They therefore include components directed to many levels of the system. In other words, clinicians, teachers, parents, health care providers, community leaders, policy makers, and others need to work together to get the job done. The challenge of combining forces given the spectrum of political, cultural, economic, and social diversity that exists in society is formidable indeed. But it can be done. Programs such as the Midwestern Prevention Project (MPP; Johnson et al., 1990; Pentz et al., 1990) have used school-based, parent, and community efforts to reduce substance abuse in young adolescents. This ambitious project combined in-school social skills training exercises, homework assignments to be completed with parents, community intervention such as TV and radio messages, and community policy changes as part of a comprehensive approach. Results after several years of evaluation indicated lower prevalence of substance use for students exposed to the program (see Chapter 10).

Third, good programs are sensitive to cultural differences in the application of strategies and in their delivery of messages. Adapting programs to make them relevant and effective is an increasingly important goal as our cultural landscape becomes ever more diverse. However, the best way to accomplish this is not yet entirely clear. Various methods are possible, including developing unique programs for diverse populations based on established theoretical frameworks, adapting empirically supported programs to make them culturally relevant and engaging for diverse populations, or building programs on the existing practices of indigenous communities (Barrera, Castro, & Holleran-Steiker, 2011).

Adaptations to empirically based prevention programs can be a shared task, with community members, professional researchers and clinicians each bringing a critical skill set to the table. Community members have first-hand knowledge of concerns, and they know what is most important to the health and well-being of the community. Youth, in particular, are experts in their own youth culture. Community members assist in disseminating and evaluating efforts whereas researchers can provide theoretical grounding and research capacity.

One such project, "Keepin' it real" (Kulis, et al., 2005), used community based paricipatory research (CBPR; Wallerstein & Duran, 2002) to address drug abuse among Mexican/Mexican American youth in Arizona. A complimentary program for parents was also developed. The school-based program supported cultural identification issues, such as respect and family, along with drug resistance skills. Videos created for the program featured local students in recognizable locations demonstrating adolescent-relevant ways to resist drugs. Materials were available in English and Spanish, and supplemental projects, school assemblies, and local media supported the effort.

Three versions of the program were tested: a Latino version, a generically multicultural version, and a non-Latino version. Students who completed either the Latino or multicultural versions showed significant reductions in drug use and improved resistance skills compared to controls, although the Latino version showed a somewhat wider array of benefits. The researchers concluded that it may not be necessary to adapt interventions to a specific cultural or ethnic group to be effective, provided programs possess culturally relevant messages. However, it may be useful to make adaptations based on local norms even when ethnicities are the same. For example, when the Arizona-based Latino program was implemented in Texas with a similar group of Mexican/Mexican American youth, both video and workbook adaptations were made by the local youth to ground it in their Texas culture (Holleran Steiker, 2008).

Fourth, they focus more on general problem-solving skills rather than on providing didactic information to participants, and they are interactive in nature. Fifth, programs are greatly strengthened by the use of peer-oriented strategies, especially for substance abuse prevention (Tobler, 1992). Finally, programs that operate over several years and that are sensitive to the developmental transitions that participants experience are more successful than briefer programs.

The failure of prevention programs has been widely attributed to the fact that programs are not fully implemented in accordance with the empirical model or are shortened before they have a chance to work. Commonly observed institutional problems, such as lack of funding for services, inadequate training for service providers, lack of effective leadership, and failure to cooperate with "outsiders" who represent various levels or components of the system, plague prevention efforts (Gottfredson, Fink, Skroban, Gottfredson, & Weissberg, 1997). Ideally, good prevention should be executed with fidelity, be targeted to multiple levels of functioning, have cross-generational linkages, and be kept in place for a sufficient length of time to ease developmental transitions. "To be effective, lifelines that are extended must be kept in place long enough to become opportunities for a lifetime" (Cairns & Cairns, 1994, p. 273).

SUMMARY

Reflection and Action

1. The fields of counseling and human development have long been linked. Counselors are dedicated to the enhancement of human development, and researchers in human development provide counselors with theories and data that can contribute to therapeutic practice. In the approach to counseling called reflective practice, developmental research and theory are among the resources counselors use to generate hypotheses about appropriate problem solutions, which the counselor will then test and revise in practice. The more extensive and well organized the counselor's knowledge of basic developmental issues, the more able the counselor will be to retrieve developmental information that is useful to problem solving.

A Historical Perspective on Contemporary Developmental Theories

2. Scientific theories of human development began to emerge in the 19th century, tracing their roots to the writings of 17th- and 18th-century philosophers, and were influenced by Darwin's theory of evolution and by the growth of universal education. Traditional theories of human development either emphasized discontinuity

(stage theories) or continuity (incremental change theories). In stage theories, a person's activities share some common characteristics during the period called a stage; these characteristics change qualitatively as the person moves from one stage to another. Stages occur in a fixed sequence, though different individuals may progress through the stages at different rates.

3. In Freud's theory of psychosexual stages, personality develops in childhood through five periods: the oral, the anal, the phallic, the latency, and, finally, the genital stages. A child moves from one stage to another as the biological self, or id, changes. At each stage, the child's experiences of need fulfillment play a critical role in the formation and further development of the other aspects of personality—the ego and the superego. Although there is little evidence to support Freud's developmental theory, it has influenced other theories, and Freud's ideas are so widely known that they are a part of our culture.

4. In Erikson's eight psychosocial stages of development, personal identity and interpersonal attitudes are expanded and reworked throughout the life span. At each stage, changes in the individual's needs or abilities or changes in societal expectations create new challenges or crises. As each crisis is faced, a new aspect of

self-concept emerges, along with feelings or attitudes toward others. If others are sensitive and responsive to the individual's needs during a given stage, positive feelings will result. If the individual's needs are not adequately met, predominantly negative feelings toward self or others may be the consequence. Erikson's emphasis on explaining the development of feelings about self and other has been appealing to helping professionals, and many of his ideas are compatible with findings from developmental research on issues such as attachment formation and the development of self-esteem.

5. Piaget's cognitive developmental theory describes changes in children's logical thinking skills through four stages. Infants in the sensorimotor stage do not yet have the capacity for representational thought. Children in the stage of preoperational thought, from 2 to 7 years of age, can think, but their thinking is not yet logical. In the concrete operational stage, 7- to 11-year-olds think logically, but they do so most effectively if what they are thinking about can be directly related to the concrete, real world. By the formal operational stage, however, young adolescents begin to be able to think logically about abstract contents. Although many details of Piaget's theory are no longer considered correct, his general characterizations of children's abilities at different ages are widely seen as useful descriptions.

6. Incremental theories of development come in many different forms, but they all characterize behavioral change as a gradual, step-by-step process. Learning theories, for example, emphasize that behavior changes as children learn responses through the processes of classical and operant conditioning. Social learning theories stress one more learning process: modeling, or observational learning. All learning theories portray any change in behavior as a result of specific experiences, affecting specific behaviors. Development results from many independent changes in many different behaviors or mental processes.

7. Among incremental models are many information-processing theories. As the mind attends to, analyzes, and stores information, there are gradual changes in the amount of information stored, in the availability of strategies to process information or solve problems, in the links established between or among pieces of information, and perhaps in the size of one's attentional capacity. Most of these changes are limited to whatever kind of information is being processed, so that, for example, acquiring a new strategy for adding or subtracting numbers does not affect the strategies a child might use in reading. Thus, development involves the accrual of small changes within specific domains of knowledge rather than broad, sweeping changes that affect many domains at once.

8. Classic theories have typically addressed a set of core issues in their attempts to characterize development, such as: Are developmental changes qualitative or quantitative? Contemporary theories of development acknowledge that the answer to any such question is "Both."

Contemporary Multidimensional or Systems Theories: Embracing the Complexity of Development

9. Contemporary theories incorporate the complexity of interacting and divergent causal processes in development. There are many of these multidimensional or systems theories, but they are quite similar in the assumptions about and descriptions of developmental process. They are broad in scope, explaining both cognitive and social developments. Changes in behavior are the result of causes both within the organism and in the environment. These causes mutually influence one another as well as behavior. In Bronfenbrenner's bioecological model, for example, all developments are seen as the result of proximal processes—reciprocal interactions between an active organism and its immediate environment. More distal processes modify proximal processes and include aspects of the organism, such as genetic functioning, and aspects of the environment, such as family structure or cultural institutions. Proximal processes, such as a child's particular interactions with peers or adults, also influence distal processes, such as the child's internal physiological functioning or the dynamic structure of the child's family. In life span developmental theories, these same complex processes continue to influence change throughout adulthood.

10. Applying a particular developmental model to the assessment of a client's needs can help a helping professional organize what she knows about a client and gain insight into how to intervene. But our theories also provide a set of blinders, focusing our attention on some aspects of a situation and reducing the visibility of other aspects. Maintaining an awareness of our own theoretical biases can help us avoid the problems of a narrowed perspective.

A Contemporary Look at Three Developmental Issues

11. Among the core issues that classic developmental theorists often addressed is whether nature (genes) or nurture (environment) is more important in development. Although specific theories often focus attention on the importance of just one type of cause, research has established that for most behavioral developments, genetic and environmental processes interact, mutually affecting each other and the behavior in question. Modern multidimensional theories take into account the complexity of this interdependency.

12. Another core issue addresses the question of whether some behaviors can develop only at certain crucial times in the life span (critical/sensitive periods) or whether the brain and behavior can change at any time (neuroplasticity). Some have argued, for example, that learning language is best accomplished in the preschool years. If critical periods for the development of behaviors like language exist, a further question (which may have

different answers depending on the behavior) concerns whether developmental changes in the brain could be the source of time-limited opportunities for learning or whether favorable environmental conditions are simply more likely to exist in some developmental periods than in others.

13. A third core issue is whether some aspects of development (e.g., cognitive stages) are universal or whether some or all developments are specific to the individual's cultural context. In the past, much of developmental research focused on Western, middle-class samples, based on the assumption that fundamental developmental processes work the same way across all groups. But modern researchers more often investigate cultural, racial, ethnic, gender, and socioeconomic variations in developmental processes and outcomes. Multidimensional theories recognize the importance of context as causal in development, and current research supports the conclusion the effects of factors such as culture are more than skin deep: they can change brain functioning over time.

CASE STUDY

Anna is a 9-year-old third-grade student in a public school on the outskirts of a large industrial city. She is the oldest of three children who live in an apartment with their mother, a 29-year-old White woman recently diagnosed with rheumatoid arthritis. Despite her young age, Anna's past history is complicated. Anna's biological father, Walter, is a 37-year-old man who emigrated from Eastern Europe when he was in his early 20s. He married Anna's mother, Karen, when she was 19 years old. The couple married hastily and had a child, Anna, but Walter abandoned the family shortly after Anna's birth. Walter and Karen had fought constantly about his problems with alcohol. Karen was particularly upset about Walter's behavior because her own father, now deceased, had suffered from alcoholism and left her mother without sufficient resources to care for herself.

Alone with a child to support and only a high school degree, Karen went to work in the office of a small family-owned business. There she met Frank, one of the drivers who worked sporadically for the company. They married within a few months of meeting and, within another year, had a son named John. Karen, with Frank's grudging consent, decided not to tell Anna about her biological father. She reasoned that Anna deserved to believe that Frank, who filled the role of father to both children, was her real parent. Anna was developing normally and seemed to be attached to Frank. But, unknown to Karen, Frank had some problems of his own. He had been incarcerated for theft as a young man and had an inconsistent employment history. The family struggled to stay together through many ups and downs. When Anna was 6, Karen became pregnant again. Frank wanted Karen to have an abortion because he didn't think the family's finances could support another child. Karen refused, saying that she would take on another job once the new baby was born. Ultimately, the marriage did not survive the many stresses the couple faced, and Karen and Frank were divorced when Anna was 7.

Karen's situation at work is tenuous because of her medical condition. Her employer balks at making accommodations for her, and she fears she might be let go. After the divorce, Karen filed for child support, and Frank was directed to pay a certain amount each month for the three children, but Frank was outraged that he should have to pay for Anna's care because she was not his biological child. During a particularly difficult conversation, Frank told Anna the "truth" that he was not her "real" father. Karen, still unable to deal with this issue, insisted to Anna that Frank *was* her biological parent. Karen could not bring herself to mention Walter, whose existence had never been mentioned to the children before. Karen desperately needed the money for Anna's support, especially because she had amassed substantial credit card debt. She felt her only pleasure was watching shopping shows on TV and ordering items for her children.

In school, Anna is struggling to keep up with her peers. Her academic performance is a full grade level behind, and her teachers are concerned. The school Anna attends has high academic standards and pressures for achievement are intense. Anna behaves in immature ways with peers and adults, alternating between excessive shyness and overly affectionate behavior. She does not appear to have any friendships within the class.

Discussion Questions

1. Consider Anna's development with regard to the following issues or concepts: contributions of nature; contributions of nurture; interaction of nature and nurture, proximal processes; distal processes.
2. Can you predict outcomes? Consider issues of continuity and change.
3. What are the strengths and weaknesses of each of the family members?
4. What environmental modifications would be helpful to promote healthy developmental outcomes? Be specific about each family member.

JOURNAL QUESTIONS

1. The long-standing debate on the value of empirically based knowledge versus applied knowledge can be applied to a course such as this. Empirically based knowledge is often explanatory, providing explanations that answer the question "Why does this happen?" Applied knowledge provides solutions and answers the question "What should I do about this?" As a helping professional, and as an educated person, what are your views on this debate?

2. What do you hope to gain from this course? What are your specific learning goals?

3. How open are you to revising your assumptions about the way development works? How might this influence your practice?

KEY CONCEPTS

life span development (p. 2)
reflective practice (p. 3)
stage (p. 8)
psychoanalytic theory (p. 9)
id (p. 9)
pleasure principle (p. 9)
ego (p. 9)
reality principle (p. 9)
superego (p. 9)
Freud's psychosexual stages (p. 9)
oral stage (p. 9)
oral fixation (p. 10)
critical (sensitive) period (p. 10)
anal stage (p. 10)
phallic stage (p. 10)
latency stage (p. 10)
genital stage (p. 10)
Erikson's psychosocial stages (p. 11)
trust versus mistrust (p. 11)
autonomy versus shame and doubt (p. 11)
Piaget's cognitive development theory (p. 12)
sensorimotor stage (p. 13)
décalages (p. 13)
hierarchical integration (p. 13)
self-organizing (p. 13)
constructivist (p. 13)

preoperational stage (p. 13)
concrete operational stage (p. 13)
formal operational stage (p. 13)
incremental models (p. 14)
behaviorist tradition (p. 14)
classical (respondent) conditioning (p. 14)
operant conditioning (p. 14)
respondent (p. 14)
conditioned stimulus (p. 15)
conditioned response (p. 15)
operant (p. 15)
reinforcement (p. 15)
positive reinforcement (p. 15)
negative reinforcement (p. 15)
social learning theories (p. 15)
modeling (p. 15)
generalization (p. 15)
information processing theories (p. 16)
multidimensional (systems) theories (p. 17)
bidirectional processes (p. 17)
Bronfenbrenner's bioecological theory (p. 19)
proximal processes (p. 19)
distal processes (p. 19)
demand characteristics (p. 19)
microsystem (p. 19)
mesosystem (p. 19)

exosystem (p. 19)
macrosystem (p. 20)
life span developmental theories (p. 20)
epigenetics (p. 22)
neuroplasticity (p. 23)
sociocultural theories (p. 24)
racial group (p. 24)
ethnicity (p. 24)
culture (p. 24)
socioeconomic status (SES) (p. 25)
developmental psychopathology (p. 30)
protective factors (p. 30)
risk factors (p. 30)
mediating variables (p. 31)
moderating variables (p. 31)
endophenotypes (p. 31)
principle of multifinality (p. 31)
principle of equifinality (p. 31)
prevention science (p. 32)
primary prevention (p. 33)
secondary prevention (p. 33)
tertiary prevention (p. 33)
universal prevention (p. 33)
selective prevention (p. 33)
indicated prevention (p. 33)
resilience (p. 34)

CHAPTER 2

Epigenesis and the Brain: The Fundamentals of Behavioral Development

THE NATURE–NURTURE ILLUSION

Look at the image in Figure 2.1 Do you see two faces or a vase? If the figure that you focus on is the vase, the other parts of the image fade into the background or become the "ground." If you change your focus, the two faces will become the "figure" and the rest background. It is virtually impossible to maintain both perspectives simultaneously.

Images like this one have been used by Gestalt psychologists to illustrate a perceptual phenomenon known as figure-ground, but we introduce it here because it provides a useful model for understanding the nature–nurture debate. No one would dispute that both heredity and environment influence human development, but when we focus on information about one of these contributors, the other seems to fade into the background. Evidence from both sides is compelling, and the clinician may be persuaded to attend to one side of the argument to the exclusion of the other. The challenge is to guard against taking such a one-sided perspective, which allows for consideration of only half of the story. The most effective way that we know to avoid this kind of oversimplification is to understand the fundamentals of how gene-environment interactions function. The "take away" message, as you will see, is that genes can do nothing without environmental input—and that environmental effects are shaped by

FIGURE 2.1 **Head-to-head optical illusion.**
SOURCE: *Ye Liew/Fotolia*.

genetic constraints. For helping professionals, learning about these intricate transactions makes clear that there is little value in placing "blame" for problematic outcomes (Fruzzetti, Shenk, & Hoffman, 2005). This knowledge also improves a helper's ability to fashion for clients therapeutic interventions that are realistic and valid, and to help both clients and the general public to understand the complex interplay of heredity and environment in physical and behavioral outcomes (Dick & Rose, 2002). In this chapter, we will consider the fundamental processes that determine who we are, both physically and psychologically.

EPIGENESIS AND COACTION

Identical twins will help us tell the story of heredity and environment. They are called "identical" because they carry the same biological inheritance. Often, identical twins are remarkably alike—with traits so similar that even friends may have trouble telling them apart. But their parents can usually tell you who is who; one has a slightly different shape to his face or one is a bit taller or the tone of voice is slightly different between them. They may be very similar behaviorally, but again, those who know them well will recognize clear differences, in interpersonal style or anxiety levels or problem solving skill. You may assume that twins' great similarity is due to their identical heredity—and that their differences must be somehow due to their environments. But what does that really mean? How can environments make a difference in traits such as the shape of a face? In fact, the similarities *and* the differences are the outcome of both heredity and environment. Neither heredity nor environment can work alone.

Conception and Early Growth

You probably know that the inheritance of traits begins with conception, when a man's sperm fertilizes a woman's egg, called an **ovum**. Fertile women usually release an ovum from one of their ovaries into a fallopian tube during every menstrual cycle. The human ovum is a giant cell with a nucleus containing 23 **chromosomes**, the physical structures that are the vehicles of inheritance from the mother. The sperm, in contrast, is a tiny cell, but it too carries 23 chromosomes: the father's contribution to inheritance. The ovum's nucleus is surrounded by a great deal of cellular material called **cytoplasm**; the cytoplasm is loaded with a vast array of chemicals. During fertilization, the tiny sperm penetrates the outer membrane of the ovum and makes the long journey through the ovum's cytoplasm to finally penetrate the nucleus, where the sperm's outer structure disintegrates. The sperm's chromosomes become part of the nuclear material in the fertilized ovum, which is called a **zygote**.

The zygote contains 46 chromosomes, or more accurately, 23 pairs of chromosomes; one member of each pair came from the mother (ovum) and one from the father (sperm). Twenty-two of these pairs are matched and are called **autosomes**. In autosome pairs, the two chromosomes look and function alike. The chromosomes of the 23rd pair are called **sex chromosomes**, because they have an important role to play in sex determination. In female zygotes, the 23rd pair consists of two matched chromosomes, called **X chromosomes**, but male zygotes have a mismatched pair. They have an X chromosome from their mothers but a much smaller **Y chromosome** from their fathers. Figure 2.2 presents two **karyotypes**, one from a male and one from a female. A *karyotype* displays the actual chromosomes from human body cells, photographed under a microscope and laid out in matching pairs. Notice the 23rd pair is matched in the female example but not in the male example. (See Chapter 8 for a fuller description of the role of sex chromosomes in human development.)

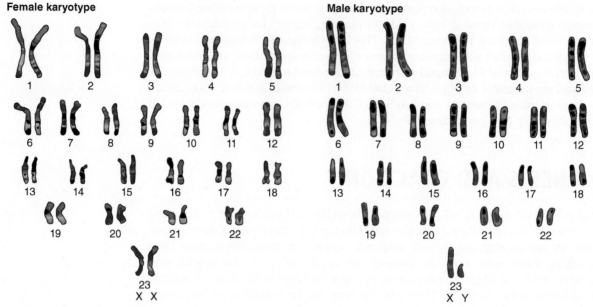

FIGURE 2.2   Human karyotypes.

Chromosomes for a karyotype can be taken from cells anywhere in a person's body, such as the skin, the liver, or the brain. That's because a duplicate copy of the original set of 46 chromosomes from the zygote are found in nearly every body cell. How did they get there? The chromosomes in a zygote begin to divide within hours after conception, replicating themselves. The duplicate chromosomes pull apart, to opposite sides of the nucleus. The nucleus then divides along with the rest of the cell, producing two new cells, which are essentially identical to the original zygote.

This cell division process is called **mitosis** (see Figure 2.3). Most importantly, mitosis produces two new cells each of which contains a duplicate set of chromosomes. The new cells quickly divide to produce four cells, the four cells divide to become eight cells, and so on. The cell divisions continue in quick succession, and before long there is a cluster of identical cells, each containing a duplicate set of the original 46 chromosomes. Over a period of about two weeks, the growing organism migrates down the mother's fallopian tube, into the uterus, and may succeed in **implantation**, attaching itself to the uterine lining, which makes further growth and development possible. Now it is called an **embryo**.

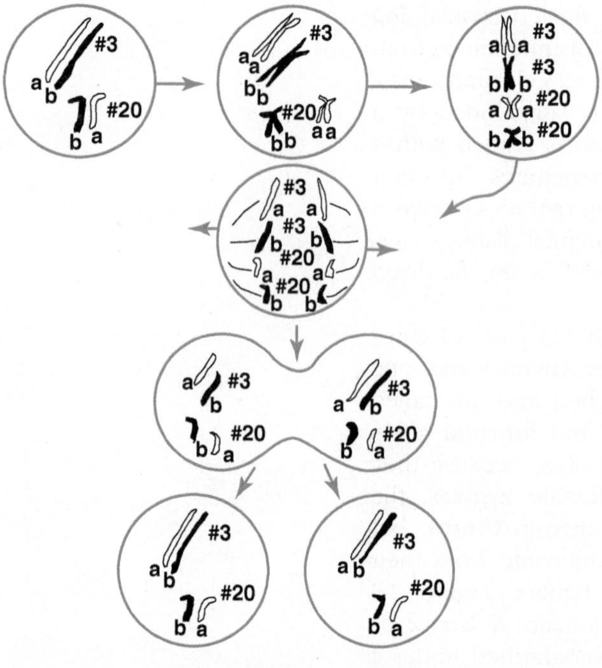

Defining Epigenesis and Coaction

If every new cell contains a duplicate set of the chromosomes from the zygote, and chromosomes are the carriers of heredity, then it would seem that every cell would develop in the same way. Yet cells differentiate during prenatal development and become specialized. They develop different structures and functions, depending on their surrounding environments. For example, cells located in the anterior portion of an embryo develop into parts of the head, whereas cells located in the embryo's lateral portion develop into parts of the back, and so on. Apparently, in different cells, different aspects of heredity are being expressed. The lesson is

FIGURE 2.3   Cell dividing by mitosis. (Only 2 of the 23 pairs of chromosomes—pairs #3 and #20—are depicted for illustration.)

clear: Something in each cell's environment must interact with hereditary material to direct the cell's developmental outcome, making specialization possible.

Biologists have long recognized that cell specialization must mean that hereditary mechanisms are not unilaterally in charge of development. Biologists first used the term **epigenesis** just to describe the emergence of specialized cells and systems of cells (like the nervous system or the digestive system) from an undifferentiated zygote. It was a term to describe the emergence of different outcomes from the same hereditary material, which all seemed rather mysterious (Francis, 2011). The term has evolved as biology has advanced. Biologists now define *epigenesis* more specifically as the set of processes by which factors outside of hereditary material itself can influence how hereditary material functions. These "factors" are environmental. These include the chemicals in the cytoplasm of the cell (which constitute the immediate environment surrounding the chromosomes) to factors in the cells and tissues adjacent to the cell, to factors beyond the body itself, such as heat, light, and even social interaction. The **epigenome** is the full set of factors, from the cell to the outside world, that controls the expression of hereditary material. "The activity of the genes can be affected through the cytoplasm of the cell by events originating at any other level in the system, including the external environment" (Gottlieb, 2003, p. 7).

But, as you will see, the chemicals in the cytoplasm of the cell are themselves partly determined by the hereditary material in the chromosomes. These chemicals can move beyond a cell to influence adjacent cells and ultimately to influence behavior in the outside environment. Heredity and environment are engaged from the very beginning in an intricate dance, a process called **coaction**, so that neither one ever causes any outcome on its own. Gottlieb (e.g., 1992, 2003) emphasizes coaction in his **epigenetic model** of development, a multidimensional theory. He expands the concept of epigenesis, describing it as the emergence of structural and functional properties and competencies as a function of the *coaction* of hereditary and environmental factors, with these factors having *reciprocal effects*, "meaning they can influence each other" (p. 161). Figure 2.4 gives you a flavor of such reciprocal effects.

The Cell as the Scene of the Action

Understanding epigenesis starts with the cell. The chromosomes in the nucleus of the cell are made of a remarkable organic chemical called **deoxyribonucleic acid** or **DNA**. Long strands of DNA are combined with proteins called **histones**, wrapped and compacted to make up the chromosomes that we can see under a microscope. Chromosomes can reproduce themselves, because DNA has the extraordinary property of self-replication. **Genes** are functional units or sections of DNA, and they are often called "coded" sections of DNA. For each member of a pair of chromosomes, the number and location of genes are the same. So genes, like chromosomes, come in matched pairs, half from the mother (ovum) and half from the father (sperm).

You may have read reports in the popular press of genetic "breakthroughs" suggesting that scientists have identified a gene for a trait or condition, such as

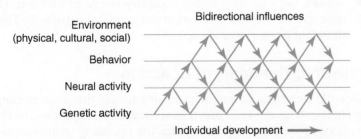

FIGURE 2.4 Gottlieb's epigenetic model of gene/environment coaction.
SOURCE: Gottlieb, G. (1992). *Individual development and evolution: The genesis of novel behavior.* p. 186. Used by permission of the Gottlieb Estate, Nora W. Gottlieb.

depression or obesity. These reports are extremely misleading. Genes provide a code that a cell is capable of "reading" and using to help construct a **protein**, a complex organic chemical, made up of smaller molecules called amino acids. Proteins in many forms and combinations influence physical and psychological characteristics and processes by affecting cell processes.

First, let's consider the multistage process by which a gene's code affects protein production. The complexity of this process can be a bit overwhelming to those of us not schooled in biochemistry, so we will only examine it closely enough to get a sense of how genes and environment coact. The DNA code is a long sequence of molecules of four bases (that is, basic chemicals, not acids): adenine, cytosine, guanine, and thymine, identified as A, C, G, and T. In a process called **transcription**, intertwined strands of DNA separate, and one of the strands acts as a template for the synthesis of a new, single strand of **messenger ribonucleic acid** or **mRNA**. In effect, the sequence of bases (the "code") is replicated in the mRNA. Different sections of a gene's code can be combined in different ways in the mRNA it produces, so that a single gene can actually result in several different forms of mRNA. In a second step, called **translation**, the cell "reads" the mRNA code and produces a protoprotein, a substance that with a little tweaking (e.g., folding here, snipping there) can become a protein. Here again, the cell can produce several protein variations from the same protoprotein. Different cell climates (combinations of chemicals) can induce different protein outcomes. One example will help here. A gene labeled the "POMC" gene is eventually translated into a protoprotein called "proopiomelanocortin" (thus the POMC abbreviation). This protein can be broken up into several different types of proteins. Cells in different parts of the body, with their different chemical workforces, do just that. In one lobe of the pituitary gland (a small gland in the brain), POMC becomes adrenocorticotropic hormone (ACTH), an important substance in the stress reaction of the body, as you will see later in this chapter. In another lobe of the pituitary gland, the cells' chemical environments convert POMC into an opiate, called β-endorphin. In skin cells, POMC becomes a protein that promotes the production of melanin, a pigment (Francis, 2011).

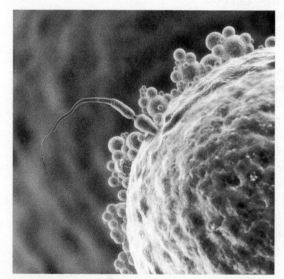

The moment of conception: Sperm and ovum unite to create a new organism.

You can see that the chemical environment of the cell affects the production of proteins at several points in the transcription and translation of coded genes. The entire transcription through translation process is referred to as **gene expression**. Whether or not genes will be expressed, and how often, is influenced by the environment of the cell. Most genes do not function full-time. Also, genes may be turned "on" in some cells and not in others. When a gene is on, transcription occurs and the cell manufactures the coded product or products. To understand how this works, let's begin by noting that coded genes make up only a small portion (2% to 3%) of the DNA in a chromosome; the rest is called "intergenic" DNA. How and when a gene's code will be transcribed is partially regulated by sections of intergenic DNA, sometimes referred to as **noncoded genes**, because they do not code for protein production. They function to either initiate or prevent the gene's transcription. This process is called **gene regulation**.

Gene Regulation: The Heart of Coaction

What provokes the gene regulation mechanisms to get the transcription process going? Some chemicals in the cells are **transcription factors**; they bind with the regulatory portions of the DNA, which initiates the uncoiling of the strands of DNA at the gene location. This allows mRNA production to begin. Of course, it is more complicated than that. For example, transcription factors cannot bind to the regulatory DNA unless they first bind to another chemical called a **receptor**. Each kind of transcription factor binds to one or only a few receptors. Some receptors are found on the surface of a cell, binding with transcription factors coming from outside the cell. Other receptors are located inside the cell.

Let's follow the functioning of one transcription factor to illustrate how gene regulation works. Hormones, like testosterone and estrogen, are transcription factors. We'll focus on testosterone, produced in larger quantities by males than females. Testosterone is primarily produced in the testes, and then it circulates widely through the body via the blood. Only cells in some parts of the body, such as the skin, skeletal muscles, the testes themselves, and some parts of the brain, have receptors for testosterone. In each of these locations, testosterone binds with a different receptor. As a result, testosterone turns on different genes in different parts of the body. In a skeletal muscle, it triggers protein production that affects the growth of muscle fibers; in the testes, it turns on genes that influence sperm production.

Notice the bidirectionality of the processes we have been describing. Genes in the testes must be turned on by cellular chemicals (transcription factors and receptors) to lead to testosterone production. Then testosterone acts as a transcription factor turning on several different genes in different parts of the body where testosterone-friendly receptors are also produced. The cell's chemical makeup directs the activity of the genes, and the genes affect the chemical makeup of the cell. What makes all of this much more complex is that many influences beyond the cell moderate these bidirectional processes.

How can factors outside of the cell, even outside the organism, influence gene regulation? Here again, the biochemistry of complex sequences of events can be daunting to follow, but let's consider a few fundamental mechanisms at the cellular level. One epigenetic change that can affect the expression of a gene is **methylation**, the addition of a methyl group (an organic molecule) to DNA, either to the coded gene or to regulatory DNA (e.g., Bird, 2002). Such methylation makes transcription of the gene more difficult. Heavy methylation may even turn off a gene for good. Methylation is persistent, and it is passed on when chromosomes duplicate during cell division, although some events can cause **demethylation**. That is, methyl groups may detach from DNA. In this case, gene transcription is likely to increase. Another class of epigenetic changes affects histones, the proteins that bind with DNA to make up the chromosomes. How tightly bound histones are to DNA affects how likely it is that a coded gene will be transcribed, with looser binding resulting in more transcription. A variety of biochemicals can attach to, or detach from, histones, such as methyl groups (methylation and demethylation) and acetyl groups (**acetylation** and **deacetylation**) (e.g., Grunstein, 1997). Each of these can affect how tightly histones and DNA are bound together. Methylation causes tighter binding and reduces gene transcription, demethylation causes looser binding and more transcription. Acetylation loosens the binding, typically increasing gene transcription, and deacetylation, tends to tighten the bonds again. Methylation, acetylation, and their reverse processes are common modifications of histones, but there are many others as well, each of them having some effect on the likelihood that a gene will be transcribed (Meaney, 2010).

When the environment outside the organism alters gene regulation, its effects on the body must eventually influence processes like methylation or acetylation inside cells, so that certain genes in these cells become either more or less active. Let's consider one example that demonstrates the impact that the social environment can have on cellular processes in the development of rat pups. There is reason to suspect that somewhat analogous processes may occur in primates as well, including humans.

Rat mothers differ in the care they give their pups, specifically, in how much licking and grooming (LG) they do. In a series of studies, Michael Meaney and his colleagues (see Meaney, 2010; Kaffman & Meaney, 2007, for summaries) discovered that variations in mothers' care during the first postnatal week alters the development of a rat pup's hippocampus. The hippocampus is a part of the brain with a central role to play in reactions to stress. The offspring of "high LG" mothers grow up to be more mellow—less reactive to stressful events—than the offspring of "low LG" mothers. Of course, these differences could simply indicate that the "high LG" mothers pass on to their offspring genes that influence low stress reactivity. But Meaney and colleagues were able to show that it is actually the mothers' care that makes the difference. They did a series of **cross-fostering studies**: They gave the offspring of high LG mothers to low LG mothers to rear, and they gave the offspring of low LG mothers to high LG mothers to rear. Rat pups reared by high LG foster mothers grew up to be more mellow than rat pups reared by low LG foster mothers. When Meaney and others studied the biochemistry of the rats' response to stress, they found that pups who receive extra maternal care respond to stress hormones (glucocorticoids) differently than other rats. (See later sections of this chapter for a description of the stress response in mammals, including humans). Ordinarily, when glucocorticoids are produced, the body has been aroused for immediate action—fight or flight. But the body also launches a recovery from this arousal, reacting to *reduce* the further production of stress hormones. The hippocampus is the part of the brain that initiates the recovery. In rats that experience high LG as pups, just a tiny quantity of glucocorticoids is sufficient for the hippocampus to trigger a rapid reduction in the production of more stress hormones, resulting in a minimal behavioral response to stress.

Now you will see the importance of epigenesis. A mother rat's external stimulation of her pup causes changes in the regulatory DNA of the pup's hippocampus. One of the changes is that the affected DNA is demethylated. Because of this demethylation, regulatory DNA turns on a gene that produces a stress hormone receptor in hippocampus cells. With larger amounts of the stress hormone receptor, the hippocampus becomes more sensitive, reacting quickly to small amounts of stress hormone, which makes the rat pup recover quickly from stressful events, which makes it a mellow rat. So maternal rearing, an environmental factor, changes the activity of the rat pup's DNA by demethylating it, which changes the pup's brain, affecting its behavioral response to stress. This change is permanent after the first week of life. What is truly remarkable is that this cascade of changes has consequences for the next generation of rat pups. Mellow female rats (who have experienced extra mothering as pups) grow up to be mothers who give *their* pups extra grooming and licking. And so their pups are also mellow—for life.

Epigenesis is one reason that identical twins can have the same **genotype** (the full complement of an organism's genes), but not have identical **phenotypes** (physical and behavioral traits). Their genotype is exactly the same because they come from a single zygote. Usually after a zygote divides for the first time, the two new cells "stick together" and continue the cell division process, leading to a multicelled organism. But in identical twinning, after the first cell division, the two new cells fail to adhere, and each of the new cells continues the cell division process separately. Each of the two clusters of cells can develop into a complete organism, producing identical, or **monozygotic** twins. Yet, even though they have the same genotypes, their environments may diverge, even prenatally (e.g., Ollikainen et al., 2010; Wong, Gottesman, & Petronis, 2005). Different experiences in their physical and social environments throughout their lifetimes can affect the cellular environments of the twins, and these effects can cause differences in how, and how often, some genes are expressed. As a result, as they age twins tend to diverge more and more both physically and behaviorally.

A large, longitudinal study of both monozygotic and **dizygotic** twins illustrates how variable epigenetic effects can be at the cellular level. *Dizygotic twins,* often called **fraternal twins**, are conceived when a mother releases two ova in the same menstrual cycle, and each ovum is fertilized by a separate sperm. Thus, these twins develop from two separate zygotes, and like any two siblings, they share about 50% of their genes on average. Wong, Caspi and their colleagues (Wong et al., 2010) studied a large number of both kinds of twins, taking cell samples when the children were 5 and 10 years old. For each child, the researchers measured the methylation of the regulatory DNA of three genes that affect brain function and behavior. You might expect a great deal of **concordance** (similarity between members of a pair of twins) in methylation, given that the members of each pair were exactly the same age and were growing up in the same families. Yet, the differences in the twins' experiences were enough to lead to substantial **discordance** (differences between members of a pair of twins) in methylation for both monozygotic and dizygotic twins. The investigators also found that gene methylation tended to change for individual children from age 5 to age 10. These changes sometimes involved increased methylation and sometimes involved decreased methylation. Differences between twins, and changes with age within each child, could partly be a result of random processes. But much of this variation is likely to be caused by the impact that differences in life experience have on the functioning of each child's cells.

More About Genes

What significance is there to having matched pairs of genes, one from each parent? One important effect is that it increases hereditary diversity. The genes at matching locations on a pair of chromosomes often are identical, with exactly the same code, but they can also be slightly different forms of the same gene, providing somewhat different messages to the cell. These slightly different varieties of genes at the same location or locus on the chromosome are called **alleles**. For example, Tom has a "widow's peak," a distinct point in the hairline at the center of the forehead. He inherited from one parent an allele that would usually result in a widow's peak, but he inherited an allele that usually results in a straight hairline from the other parent. These two alleles respresent Tom's *genotype* for hairline shape.

This example illustrates that two alleles of the same gene can have a **dominant-recessive relationship**, with only the first affecting the phenotype. In this case, the impact of the second gene allele is essentially overpowered by the impact of the first allele, so that the phenotype does not reflect all aspects of the genotype. Tom is a **carrier** of a recessive gene that could "surface" in the phenotype of one of his off-spring. If a child receives two recessive alleles, one from each parent, the child will have the recessive trait. For instance, in Table 2.1, a mother and a father both have a widow's peak. Each of the parents has one dominant gene allele for a widow's peak and one recessive allele for a straight hairline, so they are both carriers of the straight hairline trait. On the average, three out of four children born to these parents will inherit at least one widow's peak allele. Even if they also inherit a straight hairline allele, they are likely to have a widow's peak. But one child out of four, on average, will inherit two straight hairline alleles, one from each parent. Without a widow's peak allele to suppress the effects of the straight hairline allele, such a child is likely to have a straight hairline, probably much to the surprise of the parents if they were unaware that they were carriers of the straight hairline trait!

TABLE 2.1 Intergenerational Transmission of Recessive Traits (by parents who are carriers)

		MOTHER	FATHER	
	Genotype:	Ww	Ww	
	Phenotype:	Widow's peak	Widow's peak	
	CHILD$_1$	**CHILD$_2$**	**CHILD$_3$**	**CHILD$_4$**
Genotype:	WW	Ww	Ww	ww
Phenotype:	Widow's peak	Widow's peak	Widow's peak	Straight hairline*

*On average, one child in four will have the recessive trait if both parents are carriers.

NOTE: *W* stands for the dominant widow's peak allele; *w* stands for the recessive straight hairline allele.

Two different alleles will not necessarily have a dominant-recessive relationship. Sometimes alleles exhibit **codominance**, producing a blended or *additive* outcome. For example, Type A blood is the result of one gene allele; Type B blood is the result of a different allele. If a child inherits a Type A allele from one parent and a Type B allele from the other parent, the outcome will be a blend—Type AB blood.

Gene alleles at a single gene location can heavily influence some traits, as you have seen with hairline shape and blood type. But most traits are influenced by the protein products of many different gene pairs. These genes may even be located on different chromosomes. Such **polygenic** influences make the prediction of traits from one generation to another very difficult and suggest that any one pair of gene alleles has only a modest influence on phenotypic outcomes. Height, skin color, and a host of other physical traits are polygenic, and most genetic influences on intelligence, personality, psychopathology, and behavior appear to be of this kind as well. Twelve or more genes have been implicated in the development of schizophrenia, for example (Straub & Weinberger, 2006).

Do not lose sight of the importance of epigenesis in any of the gene effects we have been describing. Regulation of genes by the cellular environment, influenced by environments outside the cell, can trump dominance-recessive or codominance relationships between alleles. For example, if cellular events lead to heavy methylation of a dominant allele, so that it is not expressed, a carrier of a recessive allele may develop the recessive trait. The phenomenon of **genomic imprinting** provides a special example of how methylation can change outcomes (e.g., Jaenisch, 1997; Reik et al., 2001). In this process, a gene allele is deactivated by heavy methylation even before conception, in the sperm or the ovum. Imprinted gene alleles cannot influence the phenotype of the offspring, regardless of whether they are dominant or recessive. Some gene alleles are imprinted in ova, but not in sperm, and so can only be expressed if inherited from the father. Others are imprinted in sperm but not in ova, and so can only be expressed if inherited from the mother. Imprinting occurs at a relatively small number of gene locations (about 1%); for most gene locations, if one allele is transcribed, so is the other one. But for a small number of gene locations, imprinting alters the process of genetic expression, such that "parent of origin" becomes an important factor in whether a gene will influence development.

ATYPICAL DEVELOPMENT

Typical prenatal development is an amazing story of orderly and continuous progress from a single fertilized cell to a highly differentiated organism with many interconnected and efficiently functioning systems. The 9-month gestational period spans the **period of the zygote** (about 2 weeks), from fertilization to implantation; the **period of the embryo** (from about the 3rd to 8th week), when most of the body's organ systems and structures are forming; and finally, the **period of the fetus** (from the 9th week until birth), when the reproductive system forms, gains in body weight occur, and the brain and nervous system continue to develop dramatically. (Figure 2.5 illustrates major developments during the periods of prenatal development.)

Typical development depends on the *genome* to code for the products that the body needs to grow and function normally; and it depends on the *environment* to provide a normal range of inputs, from nutrients to social interactions, in order for gene expression to be properly timed and regulated. The principle of coaction operates at every level of the developmental drama—with genes and environment in constant communication.

What role does the gene/environment dance play in atypical development? Deviations in *either* the genome *or* the environment can push the developing organism off course. In this section you will learn about genetic and chromosomal deviations as well as environmental distortions that can alter development as early as the period of the zygote. But remember: Neither ever works alone. The effects

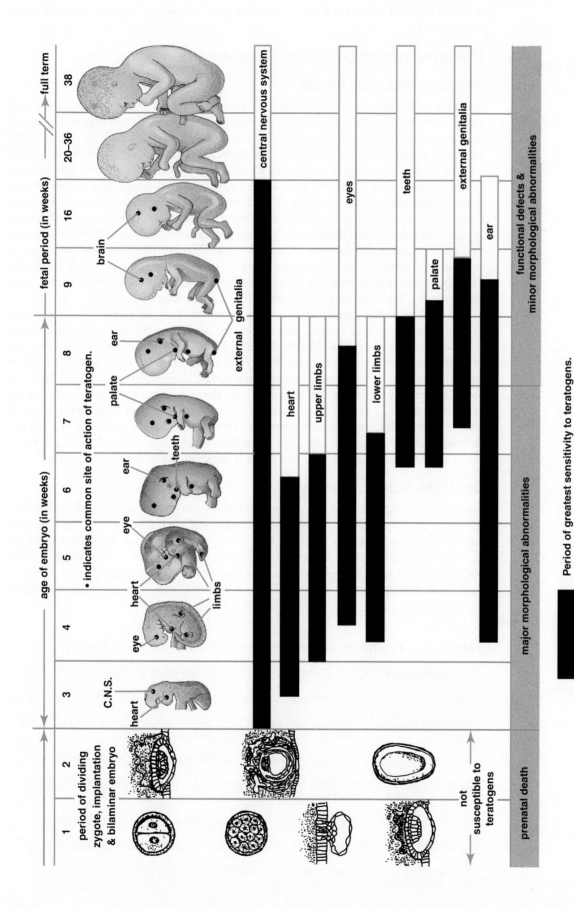

FIGURE 2.5 Fetal development.

SOURCE: Moore, K. L., & Persaud, T. V. N. (1984). *Before we are born: Basic embryology and birth defects* (3rd ed.). Philadelphia, PA: Saunders.

of the genome depend on the environment and vice versa. Watch for indicators of this coaction.

The Influence of Defective Gene Alleles

Recessive, Defective Alleles

In **sickle-cell anemia**, the red blood cells are abnormally shaped, more like a half moon than the usual, round shape. The abnormal cells are not as efficient as normal cells in carrying oxygen to the tissues. Victims of this disorder have breathing problems and a host of other difficulties that typically lead to organ malfunctions and without treatment, to early death. Fortunately, modern treatments can substantially prolong life span. A recessive gene allele causes the malformed blood cells. If one normal gene allele is present, it will be dominant, and the individual will not have sickle-cell anemia. Many hereditary disorders are caused by such recessive, defective alleles, and it is estimated that most people are carriers of three to five such alleles. Yet, most of these illnesses are rare because to develop them an individual has to be unlucky enough to have both parents be carriers of the same defective allele and then to be the one in four (on average) offspring to get the recessive alleles from both parents. Table 2.2 lists some examples of these illnesses.

Some recessive, defective genes are more common in certain ethnic or geographic groups than in others. The sickle-cell anemia gene, for example, is most common among people of African descent. For some of these disorders, tests are available that can identify carriers. Prospective parents who have family members with the disorder or who come from groups with a higher than average incidence of the disorder may choose to be tested to help them determine the probable risk for their own offspring. **Genetic counselors** help screen candidates for such testing, as well as provide information and support to prospective parents, helping them to understand genetic processes and cope with the choices that confront them—choices about testing, childbearing, and parenting (Coughlin, 2009; Resta et al., 2006).

Dominant, Defective Alleles

Some genetic disorders are caused by dominant gene alleles, so that only one defective gene need be present. There are no carriers of such disorders—someone who has the defective gene will probably have the problem it causes, because the effects of a dominant gene allele overpower the effects of a recessive allele. Suppose that such an illness causes an early death, before puberty. Then, the defective, dominant allele that causes the illness will die with the victim because no offspring are

TABLE 2.2 Some Disorders Caused by Recessive Gene Alleles

DISORDER	DESCRIPTION
Cystic fibrosis	Inadequate mucus production; breathing and digestive problems; early death.
Phenylketonuria (PKU)	Metabolism of phenylalanines in food is insufficient; gradually compromises the nervous system, causing mental retardation.
Sickle-cell anemia	Blood cells have an unusual "sickle" shape; causes heart and kidney problems.
Tay-Sachs disease	Enzyme disease; causes degeneration of the nervous system and death in the first few years of life.
Thalassemia	Blood cells abnormal; low energy, paleness, poor resistance to infection.
Hemophilia	Blood-clotting factor not produced; vulnerable to death by bleeding.
Duchenne's muscular dystrophy	Wasting of muscles produces gradual weakness, eventual death.

produced. When these alleles occur in some future generation, it must be through **mutation**, a change in the chemical structure of an existing gene. Sometimes mutations occur spontaneously, and sometimes they are due to environmental influences, like exposure to radiation or toxic chemicals (Strachan & Read, 2000). For example, **progeria** is a fatal disorder that causes rapid aging, so that by late childhood its victims are dying of "old age." Progeria sufferers usually do not survive long enough to reproduce. When the disease occurs, it is caused by a genetic mutation during the embryonic period of prenatal development, so that while it is precipitated by a genetic defect, it does not run in families.

Some disorders caused by dominant, defective alleles do not kill their victims in childhood, and thus can be passed on from one generation to another. When one parent has the disease, each child has a 50% chance of inheriting the dominant, defective gene from that parent. Some of these disorders are quite mild in their effects, such as farsightedness. Others unleash lethal effects late in life. Among the most famous is **Huntington's disease**, which causes the nervous system to deteriorate, usually beginning between 30 and 40 years of age. Symptoms include uncontrolled movements and increasingly disordered psychological functioning, eventually ending in death. In recent years the gene responsible for Huntington's disease has been identified, and a test is now available that will allow early detection, before symptoms appear. Unfortunately, there is no cure. The offspring of victims face a difficult set of dilemmas, including whether to have the test and, if they choose to do so and find they have the gene, how to plan for the future. Again, genetic counselors may play a critical role in this process (Hines, McCarthy Veach, & LeRoy, 2010).

Often, having a dominant defective allele, or two recessive, defective alleles, seems like a bullet in the heart: If you have the defective gene or genes you will develop the associated disorder. Yet epigenetic effects can alter the course of events. The disorder may not develop if epigenetic processes prevent the transcription of defective alleles. These could be processes such as methylation of the coded gene or the regulatory DNA for that gene. Research on the role of epigenesis in the expression of defective genes is in its infancy (Heijmans & Mill, 2012; Mazzio & Soliman, 2012). Yet it promises to help solve some medical mysteries, such as, why occasionally one monozygotic twin develops a hereditary disease but the other does not, or why some people have milder forms of a disease than others (e.g., Ollikainen et al., 2010; Wong et al., 2005).

These outcomes illustrate that coaction is always in play. This is true for behavioral disorders as well. For example, Caspi and his colleagues (2002) studied people with a range of variations in the "MAOA" gene. This gene provides the cell with a template for production of the MAOA enzyme, a protein that metabolizes a number of important brain chemicals called neurotransmitters, like serotonin and dopamine. (You'll learn more about neurotransmitters later in this chapter.) Its effect is to inactivate these neurotransmitters, a normal process in neurological functioning. Apparently, while these neurotransmitters are critical to normal brain function, too much of them is a problem. Animals become extremely aggressive if the MAOA gene is deleted so that the enzyme cannot be produced. In humans, variations in the MAOA gene (different alleles) result in different amounts of MAOA enzyme production. Could alleles that lead to low levels of production contribute to increased aggression and antisocial behavior in humans? Most research has suggested no such relationship. But Caspi et al. hypothesized that child rearing environment might affect how different gene alleles function. Specifically, they hypothesized that early abusive environments might make some MAOA alleles more likely to have negative effects on development. They studied a sample of New Zealand residents who had been followed from birth through age 26. They identified each person's MAOA alleles and looked at four indicators of antisocial, aggressive behavior, such as convictions for violent crimes in adulthood. Finally, they looked at each person's child-rearing history. Caspi et al. did find a link between gene alleles that result in low levels of MAOA enzyme production and aggression, but only when the individual carrying such an allele had experienced abuse as a child. For people who had normal childhoods, with no history of abuse, variations in the MAOA gene were not related to adult aggressive behavior. This appears to be epigenesis in action. We do not yet know how child-rearing environments modify the influence of the DNA at a biochemical level, as we do in some research with animals, but we clearly see that factors beyond the genetic code can change the impact of that code (see also Edwards et al., 2010; Weder et al., 2009).

Polygenic Influences

As with most normal characteristics, many inherited disorders seem to be related to more than one gene, such that some combination of defective alleles at several chromosomal sites predispose the victim to the illness. Like all polygenic traits, these disorders run in families, but they cannot be predicted with the precision of disorders caused by genes at a single chromosomal location. Most forms of muscular dystrophy are disorders of this type. Polygenic influences have also been implicated in diabetes, clubfoot, some forms of Alzheimer's disease, and multiple sclerosis, to name just a few. As we noted earlier, genetic effects on behavioral traits are usually polygenic. This appears to be true for many mental illnesses and behavioral disorders as well, such as alcoholism, criminality, schizophrenia, and clinical depression (e.g., Charney & Nestler, 2009).

The Influence of Chromosomal Abnormalities

Occasionally, a zygote will form containing too many chromosomes, or too few, usually because of problems in the production of either the ovum or the sperm. Such zygotes often do not survive. When they do, the individuals usually have multiple physical or mental problems. Among the most common and well known of these disorders is **Down syndrome** (also called **trisomy 21**), caused by an extra copy of chromosome number 21. Children with Down syndrome experience some degree of mental retardation, although educational interventions can have a big impact on the severity of intellectual impairment. In addition, they are likely to have several distinctive characteristics, such as a flattening of facial features, poor muscle tone, and heart problems. The causes of chromosomal abnormalities are not well understood. Either the mother or the father could be the source, and ordinarily, the older the parent, the more likely that an ovum or sperm will contain a chromosomal abnormality. Oddly enough, however, with Down syndrome, the increased risk with parental age holds only for mothers. Older fathers are actually less likely than younger fathers to produce sperm carrying an extra chromosome number 21 (Merewood, 1991).

Teratogenic Influences

From conception, the environment is an equal partner with genes in human development. What constitutes the earliest environment beyond the cell? It is the mother's womb, of course, but it is also everything outside of the womb—every level of the physical and social and cultural context. For example, if a mother is stressed by marital conflict, her developing fetus is likely to be influenced by the impact that her distress has on the biochemical environment of the uterus. (For simplicity, we will use the term *fetus* to refer to the prenatal organism in this section, even though technically it might be a zygote or an embryo.) Even the ancient Greeks, like Hippocrates who wrote 2,500 years ago, recognized that ingestion of certain drugs particularly during the early stages of pregnancy could "weaken" the fetus and cause it to be misshapen. Environmental substances and agents that can harm the developing fetus are called **teratogens**. The name comes from the Greek and literally means "monstrosity making."

The fetus is surrounded by a **placenta**, an organ that develops from the zygote along with the embryo; it exchanges blood products with the baby through the umbilical cord. The placenta allows nutrients from the mother's blood to pass into the baby's blood and allows waste to be removed by the mother's blood, but otherwise

Cigarette smoking during pregnancy can have teratogenic effects on the developing fetus, from slow growth to cleft palate.

it keeps the two circulatory systems separate. Teratogens can cross the placental barrier. They include some drugs and other chemicals, certain disease organisms, and radioactivity. The list of known teratogens is quite lengthy, so we have presented in Table 2.3 a summary of the main characteristics of a few of the most well-researched agents. A few principles are helpful to understand in guiding your thinking about the operation of these causes of birth defects. Generally, the potential for harm is impossible to determine with absolute precision. Rather, what happens to the developing organism depends on several principles (Wilson, 1973).

The first principle is that the kind of damage done is related to the stage of development during which the mother is exposed to the teratogen (refer again to Figure 2.5). If, for example, exposure to some harmful substance occurs during the fourth or fifth week of gestation when the major organ systems are being laid down, the result may be major structural malformation. If the mother is exposed to the same teratogen during the last month of her pregnancy, possible neurobehavioral rather than gross structural deficits may occur. If the mother contracts rubella, or German measles, during the first trimester of pregnancy, the virus can cross the placental barrier and produce blindness, deafness, heart defects, and intellectual deficits in the fetus. However, if the infection occurs during the second trimester, less severe problems involving vision and hearing may result. It is important to note that although prenatal development is divided into three periods for the sake of convenience, development is orderly and continuous throughout gestation. "At any time in the total span of development, these ongoing processes can be subtly deflected, severely perturbed, or abruptly halted, resulting in death or abnormal development" (Stratton, Howe, & Battaglia, 1996, p. 37).

TABLE 2.3 Selected Teratogens

	EFFECTS ON FETUS	SAFE DOSAGE	REFERENCES
Legal and illegal drugs			
Alcohol	Great variability in outcome. May include distinct facial structure, cardiac, skeletal, and urogenital abnormalities; dental abnormalities, growth deficiencies, metacognitive deficits, attentional problems, social perception problems, language deficits, and other learning problems.	No safe dosage during pregnancy	Riley, Infante, & Warren, (2011)
Tobacco	Low birth weight due to constricted blood flow and reduced nutrition; prematurity; respiratory problems, cleft palate; learning problems, hyperactivity, disruptive behavior.	No safe dosage during pregnancy	Abbott & Winzer-Serhan (2012)
Cocaine	Prematurity or stillbirth, low birth weight; drug withdrawal after birth including irritability, restlessness, tremors; medically and psychologically fragile; higher rates of later learning problems and ADHD.	No safe dosage during pregnancy	Bateman, Ng, Hansen, & Heagarty (1993)
Marijuana	Less well studied; some data to link its use to neurological effects; low birth weight, learning problems, etc.	No safe dosage during pregnancy	Hayatbakhsh et al. (2012)
Infections			
AIDS	Transmitted through contact with maternal blood via the placenta or at delivery. Causes damage to immune system, facial abnormalities, growth problems, brain disorders, developmental delays; usually fatal.		Nozyce et al. (1994)
Environmental hazards			
Lead	Prematurity, low birth weight, brain damage, mental retardation, physical deformities.		Dye-White (1986)
PCBs (Polychlorinated biphenyls)	Low birth weight, cognitive impairments.		Majidi, Bouchard, Gosselin, & Carrier (2012)

A second principle is that teratogenic effects are a function of the coaction of genes and environment. Not all developing organisms are equally susceptible to teratogenic effects. Both the mother's and the baby's genes play a role in sensitivity or resistance to a teratogen. A teratogen that is harmful to one individual may produce different outcomes or no outcome in another individual. For example, there is some evidence that male fetuses are more susceptible than female fetuses to the effects of teratogens (e.g., Otero & Kelly, 2012). Such differences appear to be related to genetically influenced variations in factors such as metabolism rates or placental structure. Streissguth and Dehaene (1993) report that monozygotic (identical) twins, who are alike genetically, show more similar patterns of alcohol-related birth defects than dizygotic (fraternal) twins, who share only about half of their genes. Researchers have even begun to identify specific genes, and gene alleles, that can modify the effects of teratogens such as nicotine (Price, Grosser, Plomin, & Jaffee, 2010).

A third principle is that adverse outcomes also depend on dosage amount. Larger amounts of a teratogenic agent over longer periods of time generally have more potent effects than smaller doses over shorter periods. For example, babies who are exposed to alcohol prenatally may be born with **fetal alcohol syndrome (FAS)**, which is identifiable in its victims by virtue of their unique facial configuration (small head, widely spaced eyes, flattened nose, and so on). These children are also characterized by growth retardation, either pre- or postnatally, both in weight and length. Many organ systems can be affected (see Table 2.3) but the most vulnerable seems to be the central nervous system. Children with FAS are likely to suffer from mental retardation and behavior problems. Children exposed to smaller amounts of alcohol prenatally do not necessarily have to meet the diagnostic criteria of FAS to exhibit deficits. Such children are said to exhibit **fetal alcohol effects (FAE)**. Significant learning impairments are often found in children who have been prenatally exposed to alcohol even when they do not have the physical features or growth deficiencies of FAS children. The absence of physical symptoms or structural malformations does not rule out serious cognitive limitations from prenatal alcohol exposure (Lebel, Roussotte, & Sowell, 2011; Welch-Carre, 2005).

The possible toxic effects of a teratogen such as alcohol can be construed to range along a continuum from no observable effect to one that is lethal. The impact of a pregnant mother's alcohol consumption helps illustrate the range. If the amount of alcohol exceeds that of the **no observable effect level**, the fetus will experience some functional impairment (**lowest observable adverse effect level**) but may sustain structural malformations only as dosage is increased. This hypothetical dose–response relationship presumes that the effects of alcohol ingestion on the fetus are always more potent than they are on the mother. In other words, the fetus may have crossed the toxic threshold even if the mother experiences few or very mild alcohol-related effects (Stratton et al., 1996). Consequently, as the U.S. Surgeon General has warned, there is no safe level of alcohol consumption during pregnancy (2005).

A final principle regarding the effects of teratogens is that their negative effects can be amplified if the fetus or infant is exposed to more than one risk factor (e.g., Bailey, McCook, Hodge, & McGrady, 2012). For example, mothers who take cocaine typically use other drugs such as alcohol, marijuana, tobacco, and heroin and have poorer nutrition. They may also experience more poverty and stress during and after pregnancy than other women. Drug effects are therefore confounded by, and can be amplified by, the effects of the maternal lifestyle, and the results of these interacting risk factors are not yet well understood (Lester, Freier, & LaGasse, 1995). Generally, babies born to cocaine-abusing mothers are at increased risk for poor developmental outcomes. Bendersky and Lewis (1998) found that infants exposed to cocaine prenatally showed less enjoyment during playful interactions with their mothers and had more difficulty calming themselves after they sustained a period of maternal nonresponsiveness. The result was still significant when other variables (such as abuse of other drugs, bad environmental conditions) were controlled. This evidence points to cocaine's negative impact on regulation of arousal, which can have an impact on the child's social interactions. Needless to say, the presence of other deleterious factors, such as nonresponsive parenting, can only exacerbate the situation. Thus, babies who were prenatally exposed to cocaine benefit from a stabilizing environment, and their postnatal risks are reduced.

Exposure to teratogens clearly can change the course of prenatal development, but what mechanisms account for these effects? One possibility is that teratogens actually alter coded genes, that is, that they instigate mutations. Evidence for this kind of "mutagenic" activity has been found for some known teratogens, including some of the chemicals in cigarette smoke (Bishop, Witt, & Sloane, 1997). A second possibility, suspected for many and perhaps even most teratogens, is that they alter gene expression (Csoka & Szyf, 2009). Many drugs appear to have such epigenetic effects. For example, isotretinoin, a prescription drug used to treat chronic, severe acne, is a powerful teratogen. Even one dose can be catastrophic for the developing fetus. It can cause severe physical malformations, often resulting in prenatal death. Isotretinoin is believed to have such extreme effects because it can alter the expression of more than 500 genes!

Nutritional Influences

Teratogens are problematic because they add something to the ordinary fetal environment, intruding on the developing system and driving it off course. But what happens when contextual factors that *belong* in the ordinary fetal environment are missing or in short supply? When food sources are short on protein or essential vitamins and minerals during prenatal and early postnatal development, an infant's physical, socioemotional, and intellectual development can be compromised (e.g., Eysenck & Schoenthaler, 1997; Lenroot & Giedd, 2011), and epigenetic alterations seem to be at the root of these developmental problems.

Rush, Stein, and Susser (1980) provided nutritional supplements to pregnant women whose socioeconomic circumstances indicated that they were likely to experience inadequate diets. At age 1, the babies whose mothers received a protein supplement during pregnancy performed better on measures of play behavior and perceptual habituation (which is correlated with later intelligence) than those whose mothers received a high-calorie liquid or no supplement at all.

Are there longer-term behavioral consequences of inadequate prenatal nutrition? Some research does reveal enduring effects. When the fetus is unable to build adequate stores of iron, for example, the infant is likely to show signs of anemia by 4 to 6 months of age, and even if corrected, a history of anemia has been shown to affect later school performance. One large longitudinal study demonstrates the many long-term effects that famine can have on the developing fetus. During World War II, people in the western part of The Netherlands experienced a serious food shortage as a result of a food embargo imposed by Germany over the winter of 1944–45. Since the war ended in 1945, scientists have studied the cohort of babies born to pregnant women who experienced the famine, comparing them either to siblings who were not born during the famine, or to another sample of Dutch people who were born in the same period, but who were not exposed to the famine (e.g., Lumey et al., 2007). Among the many long-term consequences of prenatal exposure to the famine are: higher rates of obesity by young adulthood; increased risk of schizophrenia and mood disorders, such as depression; more high blood pressure, coronary artery disease, and type II diabetes by age 50; and the list goes on (see Francis, 2011, for a summary). These long-term consequences appear to result from epigenetic changes at the cellular level. For example, one group of investigators found significant demethylation of a gene that codes for "insulin-like growth factor II" (IGF2) in individuals exposed to the famine very early in gestation, when methylation of this particular gene usually occurs (Heijmans et al., 2008). In another study, methylation and demethylation changes in six genes were identified. The kind of change depended on the gene, the gender of the individual, and the timing of fetal exposure to the famine (Tobi et al., 2009).

It is not surprising that prenatal nutrition has such effects, given what we have learned about the effects of postnatal nutrition on children's functioning.

Good prenatal and postnatal nutrition is essential for children to reach their full cognitive potential.

We have known for decades that children who suffer severe protein and calorie shortages at any age may develop **kwashiorkor**, characterized by stunted growth, a protuberant belly, and extreme apathy (Williams, 1933; see Lui et al., 2001, for instances of kwashiorkor in the United States). Therapeutic diets can eliminate the apathy of kwashiorkor, but cognitive impairments are likely to persist (e.g., Yatkin & McClaren, 1970). Some research indicates that even much less severe nutritional deficits may have impacts on children's cognitive functioning. An intriguing study of changes in the food supplied to New York City schools provides a strong illustration (Schoenthaler, Doraz, & Wakefield, 1986). In a three-stage process, from 1978 to 1983, many food additives and foods high in sugar (sucrose) were eliminated from school meals, so that children's consumption of "empty calories" was reduced, and, presumably, their intake of foods with a higher nutrient-to-calorie ratio increased. With each stage of this process, average achievement test scores increased in New York City schools, with improvements occurring primarily among the children who were performing worst academically.

Findings such as these suggest that children whose prenatal and postnatal environments are short on protein and other essential nutrients may not achieve the levels of behavioral functioning that they could have with adequate diets. But the long-range impact of early diet, like the effects of teratogens, is altered by the presence or absence of other risk and protective factors. Some studies have found, for example, that economically advantaged children subjected to early malnutrition due to illness or to the privations of war are not as likely to show long-term cognitive or behavioral deficits as children from less affluent families (Pollitt, Gorman, Engle, Martorell, & Rivera, 1993; Stein, Susser, Saenger, & Marolla, 1975). Apparently, social, educational, and medical advantages help moderate the effects of early food deprivation. As we saw in Chapter 1, any single developmental risk factor, either biological or environmental, often has its effects lessened by other more benign influences. It is in combination that risk factors do the most harm. One heartening consequence is that when we intervene to reduce one risk factor, such as malnutrition, we may actually reduce the impact of other negative influences on development as well.

THE DEVELOPING BRAIN

Now that you have a sense of the genetic and epigenetic processes at work in development, we can begin to examine behavioral change over time. We will first focus on the physical system that underlies behavior: the central nervous system and, especially, the brain. Helping professionals can better understand how their clients think, feel, and learn if they give some attention to the workings of this marvelously complex system. We will guide you through the story of prenatal and immediate postnatal brain development. Then we will examine in depth a key process mediated by the brain: the stress and adaptation system. As you will see throughout this text, stress, and individual differences in the response to stress, are at the core of what helpers must understand about human development.

Early Prenatal Brain Development

When you were just a 2-week-old embryo, your very existence still unknown to your parents, cells from the embryo's upper surface began to form a sheet that rearranged itself by turning inward and curling into a **neural tube**. This phenomenon, called **neurulation**, signaled the beginning of your central nervous system's development. Once formed, this structure was covered over by another sheet of cells, to become your skin, and was moved inside you so that the rest of your body could develop around it. Around the 25th day of your gestational life, your neural tube began to take on a pronounced curved shape. At the top of your "C-shaped" embryonic self, three distinct bulges appeared, which eventually became your hindbrain, midbrain, and forebrain. (See Figure 2.6.)

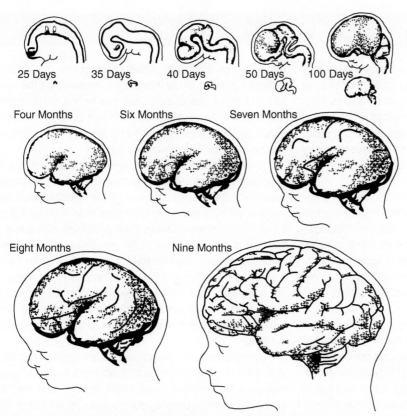

25 Days   35 Days   40 Days   50 Days   100 Days

Four Months   Six Months   Seven Months

Eight Months   Nine Months

FIGURE 2.6 **Stages of brain development.** The developing human brain viewed from the side in a succession of embryonic and fetal stages. The small figures beneath the first five embryonic stages are in proper relative proportion to the last five figures.
SOURCE: Cowan, W. M. (1979). The development of the brain. In R. R. Llinas (Ed.). *The workings of the brain* (p. 41). *Scientific American* (Sept. 1979), p. 166. Illustration by Tom Prentiss. Reproduced with permission. Copyright © (1979) Scientific American, Inc. All rights reserved.

Within the primitive neural tube, important events were occurring. Cells from the interior surface of the neural tube reproduced to form **neurons**, or nerve cells, that would become the building blocks of your brain. From about the 40th day, or 5th week, of gestation, your neurons began to increase at a staggering rate—one quarter of a million per minute for 9 months—to create the 100 billion neurons that make up a baby's brain at birth. At least half would be destroyed later either because they were unnecessary or were not used. We will have more to say about this loss of neurons later.

Your neurons began to migrate outward from their place of birth rather like filaments extending from the neural tube to various sites in your still incomplete brain. Supporting cells called **glial cells**, stretching from the inside of the neural tube to its outside, provided a type of scaffolding for your neurons, guiding them as they ventured out on their way to their final destinations. Those neurons that developed first migrated only a short distance from your neural tube and were destined to become the **hindbrain**. Those that developed later traveled a little farther and ultimately formed the **midbrain**. Those that developed last migrated the farthest to populate the **cerebral cortex** of the **forebrain**. This development always progressed from the inside out, so that cells traveling the farthest had to migrate through several other already formed layers to reach their proper location. To build the six layers of your cortex, epigenetic processes pushed each neuron toward its ultimate address, moving through the bottom layers that had been already built up before it could get to the outside layer. (See Box 2.1 and Figures 2.7 and 2.8.)

Box 2.1: The Major Structures of the Brain

Multidimensional models of mental health and psychopathology now incorporate genetics and brain processes into their conceptual frameworks. Thus, a working knowledge of the brain and its functioning should be part of a contemporary helper's toolkit. Consumers of research also need this background to understand studies that increasingly include brain-related measures. Here we present a very short introduction to some important brain areas and describe their related functions.

The complex human brain can be partitioned in various ways. One popular way identifies three main areas that track evolutionary history: hindbrain, midbrain, and forebrain. Bear in mind, however, that brain areas are highly interconnected by neural circuitry despite attempts to partition them by structure or function. In general, the more complex, higher-order cognitive functions are served by higher-level structures while lower-level structures control basic functions like respiration and circulation.

Beginning at the most ancient evolutionary level, the hindbrain structures of medulla, pons, cerebellum, and the reticular formation regulate autonomic functions that are outside our conscious control. The *medulla* contains nuclei that control basic survival functions, such as heart rate, blood pressure, and respiration. Damage to this area of the brain can be fatal. The *pons*, situated above the medulla, is involved in the regulation of the sleep–wake cycle. Individuals with sleep disturbances can sometimes have abnormal activity in this area. The medulla and the pons are also especially sensitive to an overdose of drugs or alcohol. Drug effects on these structures can cause suffocation and death. The pons transmits nerve impulses to the *cerebellum*, a structure that looks like a smaller version of the brain itself. The cerebellum is involved in the planning, coordination, and smoothness of complex motor activities such as hitting a tennis ball or dancing, in addition to other sensorimotor functions.

Within the core of the brainstem (medulla, pons, and midbrain) is a bundle of neural tissue called the reticular formation that runs up through the midbrain. This, together with smaller groups of neurons called nuclei, forms the reticular activating system, that part of the brain that alerts the higher structures to "pay attention" to incoming stimuli. This system also filters out the extraneous stimuli that we perceive at any point in time. For example, it is possible for workers who share an office to tune out the speech, music, or general background hum going on around them when they are involved in important telephone conversations. However, they can easily "perk up" and attend if a coworker calls their name.

The midbrain also consists of several small structures (superior colliculi, inferior colliculi, and substantia nigra) that are involved in vision, hearing, and consciousness. These parts of the brain receive sensory input from the eyes and ears and are instrumental in controlling eye movement.

The forebrain is the largest part of the brain and includes the cerebrum, thalamus, hypothalamus, and limbic system structures. The *thalamus* is a primary way station for handling neural communication, something like "information central." It receives information from the sensory and limbic areas and sends these messages to their appropriate destinations. For example, the thalamus projects visual information, received via the optic nerve, to the occipital lobe of the cortex (see below). On both sides of the thalamus are structures called the basal ganglia. These structures, especially the nucleus accumbens, are involved in motivation and approach behavior (Galvan et al., 2006).

The *hypothalamus*, situated below the thalamus, is a small but important area that regulates hunger, thirst, body temperature, and breathing rate. Lesions in areas of the hypothalamus have been found to produce eating abnormalities in animals, including obesity (Leibowitz, Hammer, & Chang, 1981) or starvation (Anand & Brobeck, 1951). It is also important in the regulation of emotional, stress-related responses. The hypothalamus functions as an intermediary, translating the emotional messages received from the cortex and the amygdala into a command to the endocrine system to release stress hormones in preparation for fight or flight. We will discuss the hypothalamus in more detail in the section on the body's stress systems.

Limbic structures (hippocampus, amygdala, septum, and cingulate cortex) are connected by a system of nerve pathways (limbic system) to the cerebral cortex. Often referred to as the "emotional brain," the limbic system supports social and emotional functioning and works with the frontal lobes of the cortex to help us think and reason. The *amygdala* rapidly assesses the emotional significance of environmental events, assigns them a threat value, and conveys this information to parts of the brain that regulate neurochemical functions. The structures of the limbic system have direct connections with neurons from the olfactory bulb, which is responsible for our sense of smell. It has been noted that pheromones, a particular kind of hormonal substance secreted by animals and humans, can trigger particular reactions that affect emotional responsiveness below the level of conscious awareness. We will have more to say about the workings of the emotional brain and its ties to several emotional disorders in Chapter 4.

Other limbic structures, notably the *hippocampus*, are critical for learning and memory formation. The hippocampus is especially important in processing the emotional context of experience and sensitive to the effects of stress (Fink, 2009). Under prolonged stress, hippocampal neurons shrink and new neurons are not produced (Sapolsky, 1984). The hippocampus and the amygdala are anatomically connected, and together they regulate the working of the HPA axis (described later in this chapter). In general, the amygdala activates this stress response system while the hippocampus inhibits it (McEwen & Gianaros, 2010).

The most recognizable aspect of the forebrain is the *cerebrum*, which comprises two thirds of the total mass. A crevice, or fissure, divides the cerebrum into two halves, like the halves of a walnut. Information is transferred between the two halves by a network of fibers comprising the corpus callosum. These halves are referred to as the left and right hemispheres. Research on hemispheric specialization (also called lateralization), pioneered by Sperry (1964), demonstrated that the left hemisphere controls functioning of the right side of the body and vice versa. Language functions such as vocabulary knowledge and speech are usually localized in the left hemisphere, and visual–spatial skills are localized on the right. Recently, this research was introduced to lay readers through a rash of popular books about left brain–right brain differences. Overall, many of these publications have distorted the facts and oversimplified the findings. Generally the hemispheres work together, sharing information via the corpus callosum and cooperating with each other in the execution of most tasks (Geschwind, 1990). There is no reliable evidence that underlying modes of thinking, personality traits, or cultural differences can be traced exclusively to hemispheric specialization.

Each hemisphere of the cerebral cortex can be further divided into lobes, or areas of functional specialization (see Figure 2.8). The occipital lobe, located at the back of the head, handles visual information. The temporal lobe, found on the sides of each hemisphere, is responsible for auditory processing. At the top of each hemisphere, behind a fissure called the central sulcus, is the parietal lobe. This area is responsible for the processing of somatosensory information such as touch, temperature, and pain. Finally, the frontal lobe, situated at the top front part of each hemisphere, controls voluntary muscle movements and higher level cognitive functions.

The prefrontal cortex (PFC) is that part of the frontal lobe that occupies the front or anterior portion. This area is involved in processes like sustained attention, working memory, planning, decision-making and emotion-regulation. Generally, the PFC plays a role in regulation and can moderate an overactive amygdala as well as the activity of the HPA axis. Another important regulatory pathway involves the anterior cingulate cortex (ACC), a structure in the middle of the brain above the corpus callosum. The ACC mediates cognition and affect. Impaired connections between the ACC and the amygdala are related to higher levels of anxiety and neuroticism, and lower ACC volume has been found in depressed patients (Lopez-Munoz & Alamo, 2011). The size of the various brain regions and the integrity of their circuitry play a role in individuals' cognition, affect, and behavior.

Hindbrain, Midbrain, and Forebrain

This is a picture of the brain from the left side. Beneath the cortex are three parts of the brain: the hindbrain, the midbrain, and the forebrain. The hindbrain controls some basic processes necessary for life. The midbrain is a relay station to the brain. The forebrain is where complex thoughts, motives, and emotions are stored and processed.

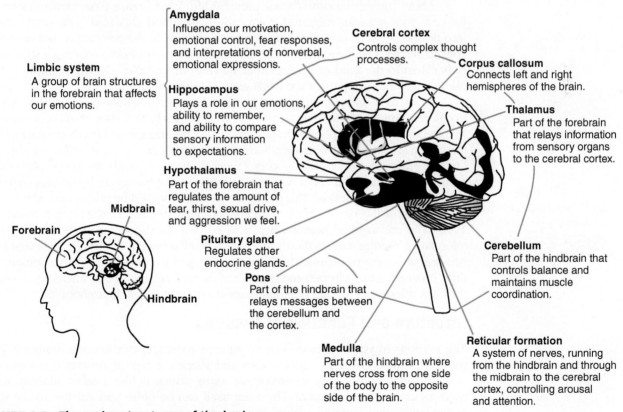

FIGURE 2.7 **The major structures of the brain.**

SOURCE: Uba, L. & Huang, K. (1999). *Psychology*. Reprinted by permission of Laura Uba.

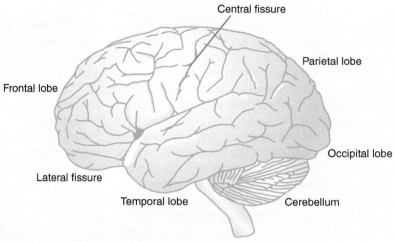

FIGURE 2.8 **The cerebral cortex.**

Scientists have discovered that neurons sometimes need to find their destinations (for example, on the part of the cortex specialized for vision) before that part of the cortex develops. It's a little like traveling in outer space. Or as Davis (1997) has suggested, "It's a bit like an arrow reaching the space where the bull's-eye will be before anyone has even set up the target" (pp. 54–55). Certain cells behave like signposts, providing the traveling neurons with way stations as they progress on their journey. Neurons may also respond to the presence of certain chemicals that guide their movements in a particular direction.

About the 4th month of your prenatal life, your brain's basic structures were formed. Your neurons migrated in an orderly way and clustered with similar cells into distinct sections or regions in your brain, such as in the cerebral cortex or in the specific nuclei. The term **nucleus** here refers to a cluster of cells creating a structure, rather than to the kind of nucleus that is found in a single cell. An example is the nucleus accumbens, part of the basal ganglia in the brain's interior.

As we have seen, one important question concerns just how specialization of cells in different regions of the brain occurs and what directs it. This issue is still controversial and extraordinarily complicated to research. However, most available evidence supports the view that cortical differentiation is an epigenetic process, primarily influenced by the kinds of environmental inputs the cortex receives. In other words, the geography of the cortex is not rigidly built in but responds to activity and experiences by making changes in its structural organization. This principle was demonstrated by researchers who transplanted part of the visual cortex of an animal to its parietal lobe (O'Leary & Stanfield, 1989). The transplanted neurons began to process somatosensory rather than visual information. Studies such as these have shown that the brain is amazingly malleable and demonstrates great **neuroplasticity**, particularly during early stages of development. In time, however, most cells become specialized for their activity, and it is harder to reverse their operation even though neuroplasticity continues to exist throughout life.

Structure and Function of Neurons

The neurons in your brain are one of nature's most fantastic accomplishments. Although neurons come in various sizes and shapes, a typical neuron is composed of a cell body with a long extension, or **axon**, which is like a cable attached to a piece of electronic equipment. The axon itself can be quite long relative to the size of the cell's other structures because it needs to connect or "wire" various parts of the brain, such as the visual thalamus to the visual cortex. At the end of the axon are the **axon terminals**, which contain tiny sacs of chemical substances called

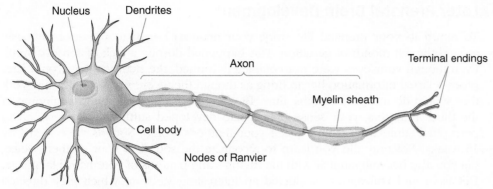

FIGURE 2.9 **Structure of a neuron.**

neurotransmitters. Growing out from the cell body are smaller projections, called **dendrites**, resembling little branches, which receive messages or transmissions from other neurons. The unique structure of the neuron equips it to do its job very effectively. (See Figure 2.9.)

So how do brain cells "talk" to each other? Even though we speak of wiring or connecting, each neuron does not actually make physical contact with other neurons but remains separate. Communication is a process of sending and receiving electrochemical messages. Simply put, when a neuron responds to some excitation, or when it "fires," an electrical impulse, or message, travels down the axon to the axon terminals. The sacs in the axon terminals containing neurotransmitters burst and release their contents into the space between the neurons called the **synaptic gap**. About a hundred different neurotransmitters have been identified, and many more are likely to be. Among those that have been widely studied are **serotonin**, **acetylcholine**, **glutamate**, **gamma-amino butyric acid (GABA)**, **epinephrine (adrenaline)**, **norepinephrine (noradrenaline)**, and **dopamine**. Some of these are more common in specific parts of the brain than in others. They are literally chemical messengers that stimulate the dendrites, cell body, or axon of a neighboring neuron to either fire (excitation) or stop firing (inhibition). For example, glutamate is an excitatory transmitter that's important for transmission in the retina of the eye; GABA is an inhibitory transmitter that is found throughout the brain.

If the message is to fire, the speed of the resulting electrical impulse is increased when glial cells wrap themselves around the axon, thus facilitating conduction. This phenomenon, called **myelination**, begins prenatally for neurons in the sensorimotor areas of the brain but happens later in other areas. This brain maturation process continues throughout much of the lifespan. With the aid of advanced technologies, researchers have demonstrated developmental changes in white matter functioning up to age 30 in areas involving decision-making and emotion regulation (Giedd et al., 2006). Overall, the peak of white matter volume occurs around age 50 (Westlye et al., 2010). The term **white matter** mainly refers to bundles of myelinated axons while **grey matter** refers to bundles of cell bodies, dendrites, and unmyelinated neurons.

Neurons are not "wired together" randomly. Rather, they are joined via their synaptic connections into groups called **circuits**. Circuits are part of larger organizations of neurons, called systems, such as the visual and olfactory systems. Two main types of neurons populate these systems, **projection neurons**, which have axons that extend far away from the cell body, and **interneurons**, which branch out closer to the local area (see Katz & Shatz, 1996). The intricate neural fireworks described earlier are going on all the time in your brain. Perhaps as you read this chapter, you are also listening to music and drinking a cup of coffee. Or you may be distracted by thoughts of a telephone conversation that you had earlier. The neuronal circuitry in your brain is processing all these stimuli, allowing your experiences to be perceived and comprehended.

Later Prenatal Brain Development

To return to your prenatal life story, your neurons began to fire spontaneously around the 4th month of gestation. This happened despite a lack of sensory input. Even though your eyes were not completely formed, the neurons that would later process visual information began firing as though they were preparing for the work they would do in a few months' time. By the end of the second and beginning of the third trimesters, your sense organs had developed sufficiently to respond to perceptual stimulation from outside your mother's womb. Sounds were heard by 15 weeks. Not only did you learn to recognize the sound of your mother's voice, but you also became familiar with the rhythms and patterns of your native language. DeCasper and colleagues conducted an interesting study in which they directed pregnant women to recite a child's nursery rhyme out loud each day from the 33rd to the 37th week of pregnancy (DeCasper, Lecaneut, Busnel, Granier-Deferre, & Maugeais, 1994). During the 38th week, the women were asked to listen to a recording of either the familiar rhyme or an unfamiliar one while their fetuses' heart rates were being measured. The fetal heart rates dropped for the group who heard the familiar rhyme, signifying attention, but did not change for the group who heard the unfamiliar one. This result suggests that the fetus can attend to and discriminate the cadence of the rhyme. Studies such as this one should not be misinterpreted to mean that the fetus can "learn" as the term is commonly used. No one has suggested that the fetus can understand the poem. However, what this and other similar studies do indicate is an early responsivity to experience that begins to shape the contours of the brain by establishing patterns of neural or synaptic connections.

By your 25th week, you could open and close your eyes. You could see light then rather like the way you see things now when you turn toward a bright light with your eyes closed. At this point in development a fetus turns her head toward a light source, providing her visual system with light stimulation that probably promotes further brain development. Sensory experience has been found to be critical for healthy brain development after birth, and vision provides a good example of this principle. The interplay between neurons and visual experience was documented dramatically by Wiesel and Hubel (1965), who, in a series of experiments with kittens for which they won the Nobel Prize, showed that early visual deprivation has permanent deleterious effects. They sewed shut one of each kitten's eyes at birth so that only one eye was exposed to visual input. Several weeks later when the eyes were reopened, the kittens were found to be permanently blinded in the eye that had been deprived of stimulation. No amount of intervention or aggressive treatment could repair the damage. The neurons needed visual stimulation to make the proper connections for sight; in the absence of stimulation, the connections were never made, and blindness resulted. The existence of a critical or sensitive period for visual development was established. This research prompted surgeons to remove infant cataracts very shortly after birth so that permanent damage to sight could be avoided, instead of waiting several years.

Sensory systems, such as the auditory and visual systems, influence each other so that their eventual development is a function of their interrelationships. The integration of these systems seems to serve the baby well in making sense of her world. So, for example, when a 4-month-old sees an object she also has some sense of how it feels.

The amount of stimulation is also important. A series of studies lends support to the idea that there is an optimal range of sensory input that is necessary for proper development. Too much stimulation or too little can cause disturbances in the sensory systems at birth. Moreover, from birth and perhaps even before, babies partially control how much or how little sensory stimulation they experience. Lewkowicz and Turkewitz (1980, 1981) showed that young infants attend to high- or low-arousing visual and auditory stimuli depending upon their own level of arousal. For example, if they are hungry they pay less attention to highly arousing external stimuli. We shall have more to say about this question in our discussion of stress processes later in this chapter.

Postnatal Brain Development

After your birth, your neurons continued to reproduce at a rapid pace, finally slowing down around 12 months of age (Huttenlocher, 1994). For many years it was assumed that neurons do not reproduce after early infancy. Recent research, however, has definitively documented the growth of new neurons throughout the lifespan (Eriksson et al., 1998). These adult **neural stem cells** (NSCs, Gage, 2000) are generated throughout adulthood in two principal brain areas, the **subventricular zone (SVZ)** located near the ventricles and in part of the hippocampus called the **subgranular zone**. SVZ neurons migrate to the olfactory bulb where they appear to maintain its functioning by generating interneurons. New hippocampal neurons appear to integrate into existing networks that involve learning and memory. The location, migration patterns, and the ways adult neural stem cells integrate with existing neural networks are subjects of intense current investigation given the potential contribution this knowledge can make to disease prevention and remediation (Curtis, Kam, & Faull, 2011).

Brain growth after birth is also due to the formation of **synapses**, new connections among neurons. The growth spurt in synapses reflects the vast amount of learning that typically occurred for you and for most babies in the early months of postnatal life. Some areas of your developing brain experienced periods of rapid synaptic growth after birth, such as in the visual and auditory cortices, which increased dramatically between 3 and 4 months. In contrast, the synapses in your prefrontal cortex developed more slowly and reached their maximum density around 12 months. As you will see in the following sections, infants make rapid strides in cognitive development at the end of the first year, at about the time when prefrontal synapses have reached their peak density.

The growth of these connections was the product of both internal and external factors. Certain chemical substances within your brain, such as **nerve growth factor**, were absorbed by the neurons and aided in the production of synapses. Your own prenatal actions, such as turning, sucking your thumb, and kicking, as well as the other sensory stimulation you experienced, such as sound, light, and pressure, all contributed to synaptic development. However, as we noted earlier, the major work of **synaptogenesis**, the generation of synapses, took place after birth, when much more sensory stimulation became available.

You arrived in the world with many more neurons than you would ever need. Over the next 12 years or so, through a process known as **neural pruning**, many neurons would die off and many synaptic connections would be selectively discarded. Some of these neurons migrated incorrectly and failed to make the proper connections, rendering them useless. Some of the synaptic connections were never established or were rarely used, so they ultimately disappeared as well. What counts most after birth is not the sheer number of neurons, but the number and strength of the interconnections. Those branching points of contact that remained to constitute your brain would be a unique reflection of your genetics and epigenetics, the conditions of your prenatal period, the nutrition you received, and your postnatal experience and environment. This rich network of connections makes your thinking, feeling brain, and its structure depends heavily upon what happens to you both before and after your birth.

You may be wondering how to account for the simultaneous processes of synaptogenesis and pruning, which seem to be acting at cross-purposes. What is the point of making new synaptic connections if many neurons and connections will just be culled eventually? Greenough and Black (1992) offer an explanation for the apparent contradiction. They argue that **synaptic overproduction** occurs when it is highly likely that nature will provide the appropriate experience to structure the development of a particular system. For example, many animal species, as well as humans, go through a predictable sequence of activities designed to provide information for the brain to use in the development of vision. These include opening eyes, reaching for and grasping objects, and so on. This type of development depends upon environmental input that is **experience-expectant** because it is experience that is part of the evolutionary history of the organism and that occurs reliably in most situations. Hence, it is "expected." Lack of such experience results in developmental abnormalities, as we saw in the kitten experiments performed by Wiesel and Hubel. The timing of this particular kind of experience for nervous system growth is typically very important; that is, there is a critical period for such experience-expectant development. Nature may provide for an overabundance of synapses because it then can select only those that work best, pruning out the rest.

In contrast to overproducing synapses in anticipation of later experience, some synaptic growth occurs as a direct result of exposure to more individualized kinds of environmental events. This type of neural growth is called **experience-dependent**. The quality of the synaptic growth "depends" upon variations in environmental opportunities. Stimulating and complex environments promote such growth in rat pups and other mammals (e.g., Kolb, Gibb, & Robinson, 2003). It seems likely that the same is true for infants and children. Imagine what might be the differences in synaptic development between children raised by parents who speak two different languages in their home and children raised by those who speak only one. Or imagine the synaptic growth of an infant raised in impoverished conditions with very little verbal interaction from adults, and very little chance to explore the environment, as compared to that of an infant reared in an environment rich in adult attention and opportunities for engagement with interesting objects. Experience-dependent processes do not seem to be limited to sensitive periods but can occur throughout the life span. Connections that remain active become stabilized, whereas those that are not used die out. This type of experientially responsive synaptic growth and the concomitant changes in brain structure it induces have been linked to learning and the formation of some kinds of memory. This process fine-tunes the quality of brain structure and function and individualizes the brain to produce the best person-environment fit (Paus, Keshavan, & Giedd, 2004).

Clearly, your early experiences played a vital role in the functional and structural development of your brain. Your experiences helped stimulate the duplication of neurons in some parts of your brain, and it prompted synaptogenesis and pruning. These processes contribute to the plasticity of brain development, which can be quite remarkable. Suppose, for example, that you had suffered an injury to your left cerebral cortex during infancy. You can see in Box 2.1 that ordinarily, the left cerebral cortex serves language functions. Yet when the left hemisphere is damaged in infancy, the right hemisphere is very likely to take over language functions. Your language acquisition might have been delayed by an early left hemisphere injury, but by 5 or 6 years old, you would most likely have caught up with other children's language development. Adult brains also exhibit some plasticity after brain injury, but nothing as dramatic as we see in children (e.g., Kolb & Wishaw, 2006; Stiles, 2001).

Understanding of postnatal brain development has improved dramatically over the last few decades, spurred by modern technologies. In Table 2.4, we describe several of the newer approaches that are recurrently mentioned in this and later chapters.

TABLE 2.4 Studying the Developing Brain

TECHNIQUES	PROCEDURES AND PRODUCTS
Electroencephalography	Electrodes attached to the scalp can allow recording of the electrical (EEG) activity of the cerebral cortex. Recordings from the electrodes graph the frequency and amplitude of brain waves. Event related potentials (ERPs), which are specific brain wave changes in response to sights, sounds, or other experiences, can be recorded as well, helping to identify areas of cortex that process the type of input used.
Functional magnetic resonance imaging (fMRI)	A computerized system for recording activity anywhere in the brain by imaging responses to input to input. Stimulation causes the affected areas of the brain to increase blood flow and metabolism. A magnetic scanner detects these changes and sends the information to a computer, which produces an image that shows the differential activity of brain areas. fMRI is one of several MRI technologies, generally referred to, along with PET techniques, as "brain imaging."
Positron emission tomography (PET)	Like the fMRI, a type of brain scan that detects changes in blood flow and metabolism in any part of the brain, and produces an image that shows the differential activity of brain areas. Requires either injection or inhalation of radioactive material.

THE DEVELOPING STRESS AND ADAPTATION SYSTEM

From that single cell onward, development may be viewed as progressive adaptation across multiple levels of functioning. We adapt to the ebb and flow of daily shifts like sleeping and waking, to predictable developmental transitions like adolescence, and to unexpected events like trauma. Now that you've considered epigenetic processes and brain development, you understand that experience has had a hand in shaping biological and psychological adaptations, not only in your early years but also throughout your lifespan. An interesting scientific narrative has evolved to explain how humans and other organisms manage these adaptations to life. One especially promising way to unpack the mysteries is to focus on the development of stress processes, because stressors pose a clear opportunity for the organism to adapt. A burgeoning literature on stress is uncovering how biology and experience cooperate to produce healthy and unhealthy developmental outcomes. When we consider the word *stress* in this current formulation, we need to think broadly. Let's review a bit of history about stress to help us understand the broader conceptualization of this term.

Classic and Contemporary Views of Stress and Adaptation

Early views of adaptation to stress (Cannon, 1929) emphasized the body's capacity to regulate internal physiology primarily through systems that exert reciprocal control. Adaptive processes were seen as functioning like a thermostat to maintaine internal balance. This view, called **homeostasis**, has been a prominent model in research and thinking about human adaptation and stress. Homeostatic views describe reflexive, physiological feedback loops, primarily controlled by lower-level brain areas, that balance internal systems around a fixed set-point. Researchers have come to realize that this set-point model cannot account for all the dynamic adaptations organisms make. Blood pressure, for example, does not have a fixed set point but varies normally depending upon times of the day, sleep-wake cycles, and response to challenge.

Selye (1956) expanded the discussion from regulation of internal states to include how we adapt to demands posed by external threats. He proposed a characteristic way of responding to **stress**, a term he adopted from physics and later came to regret. Selye's use of the word *stress*, which almost immediately gained worldwide popularity, is best defined as a nonspecific response to any demand (i.e., adaptation). Thus, stress can be noxious as well as positive, something he called "eustress" or positive stress. According to Selye, stress is a demand for adaptation, regardless of the specific nature of the situation (Fink, 2009).

Selye observed that there was a generic way that organisms responded to threats to their well-being. Calling it the **general adaptation syndrome (GAS)**, he proposed three phases. The first is the alarm phase, when a threat is first recognized and when the body prepares for flight or fight. The second is the resistance phase, during which the body's stress response is active as it continues to resist the effects of the stressor. The third and final stage is exhaustion, which occurs if the struggle persists to the point of complete resource depletion. Depression, illness, or even death can occur after severe, prolonged stress.

When faced with acute stress, physical systems that are less important for survival are temporarily sidelined. Once the stress has ended, processes like digestion and reproduction come back on-line. Selye's GAS served as a helpful model for severe stress but has been superseded by more current ways of measuring and understanding stress processes (Fink, 2009). Selye (1950) did recognize, however, that there was an intermediate step that linked the stressor to the physiological responses, although this step was not defined in his model.

It soon became clear that the need to incorporate individual cognitive and affective responses to experience played a critical part in predicting stress-related effects.

Stress, to some degree, is in the eye of the beholder. While most people would agree that certain situations are more traumatic than others, individual differences in appraisal of what is stressful are influenced by prior learning, memories, internalized expectations, and perceptions about one's ability to cope. For example, a marathon runner puts her body under a lot of stress, but crossing the finish line in record time can make it a jubilant experience. Psychosocial factors certainly influence psychological and physiological processes in important ways (e.g., Lazarus & Folkman, 1984; Wheaton, 1985).

Recently, more complex models have arisen to incorporate and extend basic tenets of older theories. An integrated view of physiological and psychological adaptation processes that incorporates higher-level brain functions was needed to adequately explain such complex phenomena. Sterling and Eyer (1988) offered a decidedly more intricate explanation of stress processes in their model of **allostasis**, which proposed that central nervous system (CNS) control over multiple interacting regulatory processes maintains "balance through adaptation." *Allostasis* allows for adjustments to be made within a range of possibilities across a variety of systems to suit the circumstances. Instead of returning to a fixed set point, the best balance for each specific challenge is found, a dynamic process called **allostatic accommodation** (Ganzel et al., 2010). Nervous, immune, and endocrine systems are the primary interconnected networks that mediate this adaptive response.

The allostatic model privileges the brain with a primary role because it is the organ that determines the nature of the demand: dangerous threat or interesting challenge? The brain is the top-down manager. It is uniquely able to incorporate anticipation of threat, memories of past experiences, appraisal of coping resources, and other psychological contributions into its oversight of peripheral physiological processes and behavior (McEwen, 2004). This contemporary view of adaptation and stress management moves the fields of biological and behavioral sciences closer together by providing physiological evidence for psychological processes like coping and resilience that are important to helpers.

The Architecture of the Stress Response

Let's review what generally happens when a person perceives or anticipates stress. This process is quite complicated and relies on a network of lower brain, limbic, and higher order cortical areas. Certain structures, notably the amygdala and basal ganglia, are primarily tasked with emotion processing (LeDoux, 1996; Wager, Phan, Liberzon, & Taylor, 2003). However, they are closely connected to other areas (hippocampus, hypothalamus, and prefrontal cortex) that also have important roles to play in emotion (and thereby allostatic) processing (e.g., Ganzel, Morris, & Wethington, 2010). Some play a major role in activating (amygdala) or inhibiting (hippocampus) the **hypothalamic-pituitary-adrenal (HPA) axis**, which is a major stress managing apparatus.

Davidson and colleagues (2004) note that emotional stimuli have unique status given that the brain recruits so many of its processing resources to attend to emotion-related stimuli. Overall, core emotional areas of the brain are primarily involved in stress responding and are most affected by the wear and tear of chronic stress, called **allostatic load** (McEwen & Stellar, 1993). Allostatic load or overload is the cost of accommodation, the cumulative burden on systems that need to adjust constantly to psychological or environmental demands. Let's once again use the simple example of blood pressure. When confronted with an emergency at work, blood pressure may rise temporarily to accommodate the challenge until the problem is resolved and things go back to normal. When work challenges are unremitting, high blood pressure can become maladaptive, creating allostatic load. Wear and tear on emotional systems in the brain can also have serious implications for mental health.

The stressor is first detected via an interconnected network of sensory areas in the cortex, thalamus, and amygdala, the brain's specialist in threat detection

(LeDoux, 2000). The amygdala is involved in virtually all fear conditioning and works to jumpstart stress-related networks peripheral to the central nervous system. Two major peripheral systems subject to this central control are the **sympathetic nervous system (SNS)** and the HPA axis (Gray & McNaughton, 2000). The *SNS* releases important chemicals such as epinephrine (adrenaline) and norepinephrine (noradrenalin) that send a burst of energy to those organs necessary for fight or flight (e.g., heart, lungs) while diverting energy from less necessary systems (e.g., growth, reproduction). Adrenaline is instrumental in causing the well-known effects of arousal, such as racing heart and sweaty palms. Under normal conditions, the **parasympathetic nervous system (PNS)** counteracts the sympathetic system's effects and down-regulates its activity once the threat has passed.

A second system initiated by the amygdala involves activating the hypothalamus. The hypothalamus subsequently communicates the danger message to the **pituitary gland** by means of the chemical messenger **corticotropin releasing factor (CRF)**. The message is read by the pituitary as a sign to release **adrenocorticotropic hormone (ACTH)**, into the bloodstream. Both CRF and ACTH production can be permanently affected by early trauma, and abnormalities in these chemical messengers have been shown to be markers for later depression. The early experience of stress may confer a lifetime disadvantage, rendering the individual sensitized to stress by means of altered functioning of the HPA axis (Gillespie & Nemeroff, 2007).

ACTH then makes its way to the **adrenal glands**, situated atop the kidneys, which receive the message to release cortisol. **Cortisol** is a key **glucocorticoid** hormone produced by humans. Some of these so-called stress hormones (particularly cortisol) then travel back to the brain and bind to receptors on the amygdala and the hippocampus. Both glucocorticoid and mineralocorticoid receptors in the brain receive information from these stress hormones (Reul & de Kloet, 1985). In normal circumstances, sufficient glucocorticoid receptors exist to terminate the system effectively. An inadequate system of glucocorticoid receptors is a key reason for hyperactive stress system. As we describe elsewhere in greater detail, rat pups who receive inadequate maternal care during a sensitive period of HPA development show fewer hippocampal glucocorticoid receptors and less ability to turn off their chronically stressed physiology (e.g., Meaney et al., 2000).

Under normal circumstances, cortisol levels in the bloodstream show a regular daily pattern of morning elevation and afternoon decline. In contrast, highly stressed individuals show elevated cortisol levels throughout the day or disrupted diurnal variations (e.g., high afternoon levels). Maltreated children, for example, show generally elevated cortisol levels compared to non-maltreated children (Cicchetti & Rogosh, 2001). Another dysregulated cortisol pattern involves a blunted, reduced level of hormone production throughout the day with no highs or lows. This abnormal pattern may be a compensatory adjustment that the system makes to chronic activation in certain individuals with certain types of psychopathology. Some research suggests that different kinds of HPA patterns are associated with different emotional problems. **Atypical depression**, for example, has been linked to blunted cortisol functions whereas **melancholic depression** is associated with elevated cortisol levels (Gold & Chrousos, 2002). Children who experience sexual abuse before the age of 5 often have blunted cortisol responses compared to children whose abuse occurs after age 5 (Cicchetti, Rogosch, Gunnar, & Toth, 2010).

Other systems also interface with the HPA axis in a concerted effort to adapt to threat (e.g., Sapolsky, 2004). Cortisol acts to increase glucose levels in the bloodstream providing an energy boost. When stress is chronic, this process goes awry and can contribute to metabolic problems and diabetes. The immune system reads the glucocorticoid message as a signal to activate its own operations. After providing a short-term immunity boost, cortisol eventually suppresses immune function, compromising its capacity to fight infection and ward off disease.

Chemical messengers of the immune system, called **cytokines**, are produced during the immune response. These proteins can be either pro-inflammatory or anti-inflammatory in nature. Inflammation, it should be noted, is the body's protective response to infection or injury. When appropriate, inflammation is adaptive; however, when inflammatory processes persist unremittingly, mental and physical diseases can result. Overproduction of pro-inflammatory cytokines, which occurs when the stress-response system is chronically active, has been linked to depression and other mood disorders. Cytokines pass through the blood-brain barrier to affect brain areas related to emotion (Wilson & Warise, 2008).

Recall that the hippocampus can serve an inhibiting role with regard to HPA activity through a negative feedback loop. Feedback to the hippocampus enables it to downregulate the stress response. When the feedback loop is impaired, systems are chronically on duty, putting a great deal of wear and tear on the body and especially the emotional areas of the brain that are on the front line of the efforts to adapt. Studies have also found damaged or shrunken nerve cells in the hippocampus of humans and animals exposed to traumatic or social stressors. For example, McEwen and Sapolsky (1995) reported that the hippocampi of veterans with posttraumatic stress disorder (PTSD) were 25% smaller than those of a control group, causing those veterans significant problems in memory formation and retrieval despite the fact that they had otherwise normal brains. It is not yet clear whether such effects are due to an excess of cortisol, pumped in from the agitated adrenals, or to a highly sensitized cortisol-response system, but it is clear from studies such as these that a negative relationship exists between excessive stress and memory function.

Chronic HPA activation is important for other cognitive and behavioral reasons as well. Because stress remodels the circuits in the hippocampus and reduces synaptic branching, the ability to learn new information is compromised. Because the prefrontal cortex is important for cognitive functions and highly interconnected with the emotional systems, stress disrupts functions like ability to shift and sustain attention (Liston, McEwen, & Casey, 2009). Highly stressed individuals are less able to think clearly about their challenges and less likely to plan and execute effective ways to cope.

Some general points about allostasis, allostatic load, and brain-HPA activity are important to keep in mind. The relationship between exposure to stress and adaptive outcomes can be portrayed as an inverted U-shaped curve (McEwen & Seeman, 1999). Up to a certain point, challenges like exercise and appropriate stimulation are brain-enhancing in that they promote neuron growth (Kempermann, Kuhn, & Gage, 1998; Colcombe et al., 2003). Past the tipping point, when stress is chronic and/or intense, the costs of allostatic load mount up, leading to a host of mental and physical problems mediated through the HPA axis (McEwen, 1998).

There is some evidence that both number and timing of stressor exposure matter. We present some information about the impact of numbers of adverse events in Box 2.2. Their timing may also be important because critical periods of development, by definition, are highly receptive to environmental experience. When neural circuits are developing, epigenetic mechanisms can influence their course in profound ways. Deleterious effects of early maltreatment, neglect, and separation have been amply demonstrated (Andersen et al., 2008; De Bellis, Baum, Birmaher, Keshavan, & Ryan, 1999; De Bellis et al., 1999; Levine, 2000; Spinelli et al., 2009; Tottenham & Sheridan, 2010; Vazquez et al., 2006), yet some research indicates effects differ depending upon the timing of adverse experience. To investigate this question, Kaplan and Widom (2007) examined the effects of early adversity among children who experienced it continuously (prenatal to age 11), among those who experienced adversity before age 6, and among those whose adversity began later in childhood (6–11). They followed individuals with documented cases of physical and sexual abuse and neglect until adulthood (approximately age 40). Results showed a higher risk of depression and anxiety disorders in adulthood among those who suffered early abuse (before age 6). However, behavioral disorders (antisocial personality disorder, dropping out of school, alcohol abuse) were associated with the experience of abuse in later childhood. Such effects may demonstrate the phenomenon of multifinality. Early sculpting of stress sensitive systems lays an important foundation for later developmental health or illness, and we shall return to this topic in subsequent chapters. In other words, "it is not just that skill begets skills (i.e., history matters), but that allostatic accommodation in one period will serve as the foundation for accommodation in subsequent periods" (Ganzell & Morris, 2011, p. 969).

APPLICATIONS

In this chapter, we present some breakthroughs in research on nature and nurture and their complicated yet fascinating interdependence. It may be relatively intuitive to understand that different kinds and levels of exposure to environmental substances, like alcohol or toxins, in combination with different genetic combinations interact to produce varying effects on a developing organism. For example, two hypothetical unrelated individuals, whose mothers were exposed to the same level of a toxin during pregnancy, might show greater or lesser effects depending upon genetic makeup, timing of exposure and other contextual circumstances. This is just one possible scenario that illustrates gene by environment interactions. However, it's clearly more mystifying to contemplate *how* other levels of environmental experience, like caregiving, produce genetic differences. Caregiving is not a substance, like a drug, an x-ray, or a vitamin. Yet, as we have seen, nonrandom variations in caregiving have been shown to produce observable genetic modifications. The epigenome, which literally translates as "above the genome," has a way of exerting its influence via chemical changes to genetic material. Methylation, one major way of accomplishing the job, is like a signature that your environment writes on your DNA. These genetic signatures replicate throughout life and often across generations, although sometimes they can be reversed by environmental supports or chemical means. This is a striking discovery, and it brings us to a whole new level of discussion about nature and nurture. "From an epigenetic perspective, divisions between genes, brain, and behavior are artificial, as the environment becomes embodied in the genome. It is the epigenomic-modified DNA sequence that results in protein synthesis, which, in turn, canalizes development. In fact, to a large extent *nature is nurture*" (van Izjendoorn, Bakermans-Kranenburg, & Ebstein, 2011, p. 309).

A second major realization is the exquisite sensitivity of the stress system to experience. Current research shows that epigenetic programming, beginning in utero and continuing throughout life, affects genes related to functioning of the hippocampus and other brain systems central to stress management (Meaney, 2010). The experience of prenatal and early life stress can alter their operations, programming the settings like those of a thermostat to be more or less stress-reactive.

It should be noted that knowledge about epigenetic influences on development will most likely continue to increase, given improvements in methods of genomic analysis. The effects and connections we are able to describe at this point in time may only be the proverbial tip of the iceberg. We stand to learn a lot more about the subtleties of these processes. Even so, we are gaining a much better look at the mechanisms through which stress processes affect normal and abnormal development. We also see clear evidence of the importance of early experience in programming lifetime HPA pathways. This work is particularly relevant to helpers because it has the potential to explain the highly significant relationship between adverse early life experience and disorders. It can also lead the way to better methods of treatment and prevention of pathology. Because so many physical and mental disorders are strongly associated with chronic activation of the stress system, this is news we can use to inform our work, particularly in the area of infant mental health and caregiving.

Szyf (2011) points out that epigenetic changes occur subsequent to neural signaling, once again pointing to the brain's central perceptual role. The basic model posits that we anticipate and adapt to cues in our environments. For an infant, signals transmitted through caregiver behavior trigger complex chemical sequences, especially those involving serotonin and glucocorticoid receptors. Therapy and environmental enrichment may influence this process by beginning upstream before pathways are shaped. For older individuals, therapies such as mindfulness-based approaches that alter the experience of stress have been recommended to reduce allostatic load and readjust stress-related set points (Ganzell & Morris, 2011). We will discuss these approaches in more detail in later chapters.

Healthy Baby Guidelines

As you have read in this chapter, certain practices really do promote healthy prenatal development and others put the fetus's well-being at substantial risk.

1. One of the most well-established recommendations offered to pregnant women is to eat a healthy diet that includes a variety of foods. To prevent the risk of brain and spinal birth defects, foods high in folic acid should be eaten regularly and supplemented by a multivitamin.
2. Because alcohol is such a powerful teratogen, its consumption during pregnancy should be completely eliminated. Drugs, both legal and illegal, and cigarettes should be avoided as well because of their potential to damage the fetus. The spouses or partners of pregnant women should also avoid dangerous substances, both to provide support for their partners and to reduce the availability of the substance in the home. If a woman must take prescription medication for preexisting conditions such as epilepsy, bipolar disorder, cancer, or thyroid dysfunction, she should inform her physician, if possible, when she

Box 2.2: Do Numbers Matter? The Relationship Between Early Stress and Later Adversity

No doubt about it, early experience matters. In this chapter, we describe some of the processes that explain how adverse experiences exert harm. During pregnancy, high levels of maternal stress hormones can pass through the placenta to calibrate the child's developing stress systems in harmful ways (DiPietro, 2004). This knowledge raises serious concerns for practitioners. Do the harmful effects of prenatal stress affect every developing fetus? Is there a tolerable level of stress for children? If so, how much stress is too much? At first glance, these questions seem impossible to answer. Each individual possesses a unique blend of strengths and vulnerabilities making exact prediction unlikely. Nonetheless, some large-scale epidemiological investigations of this question could provide useful guidance for clinicians and public health experts.

Several longitudinal investigations have looked at numbers of stressful experiences in children's lives and their subsequent relationship to health or adversity. A western Australian study (Robinson et al., 2011) followed a group of 2,868 pregnant women from 16 weeks gestation (updated at 34 weeks gestation) until their children were adolescents. During their pregnancies, mothers were asked about the number and types of stressors they experienced. Stressors included financial difficulties, job loss, deaths of relatives, residential moves, marital difficulties, separation, or divorce. The researchers controlled for maternal SES, age, ethnic status, smoking, drinking, education, and history of emotional problems. Child variables, including gestational age, birth weight, and histories of breastfeeding, were also controlled. Assessments of children's physical, emotional and behavioral functions were made at ages 1, 2, 3, 5, 8, 10, and 14.

Results showed that offspring of mothers who reported zero to two stressors during pregnancy did not differ significantly on measures of internalizing and externalizing child problems. However, children whose mothers experienced three or more stressful events during their pregnancies exhibited significantly higher levels of internalizing and externalizing problems at every assessment period across the prospective study compared to the group with fewer stressors. Externalizing problems were more pronounced in children whose mothers experienced four events compared to children of mothers reporting no stress. If mothers experienced five or more events, higher rates of child internalizing disorders were observed even after controlling for many other possible contributions to depression and anxiety. Maternal stressors experienced at 16 weeks gestation were more strongly related to later problems than those experienced at 34 weeks. Overall, the results of this study support a dose-response relationship between numbers of prenatal stressors and later maladaptive outcomes. This means that lower levels of stressors predicted lower symptom levels. Symptoms increased with each additional stressor exposure in a stepwise fashion. It's important to keep in mind, however, that the nature of some stressors (e.g., low SES, financial difficulty) can exert an ongoing influence on development in addition to having prenatal impact. Conditions of low SES can provide a context for ongoing development in which adverse consequences accumulate (Duncan & Brooks-Gunn, 1997).

A similar epidemiological approach was taken in California, the site of a study of early stress and health outcomes. This study was designed to examine the effects of early abuse and maladaptive rearing conditions on the problem of chronic illness. Chronic diseases like cancer, heart disease, and diabetes account for 70% of deaths in the United States (The Centers for Disease Control [CDC], 2012). To a large degree, these diseases are related to unhealthy behaviors like smoking, overeating, drinking, lack of exercise, and so on. Because such behaviors are modifiable, efforts to understand the factors underlying unhealthy behaviors can improve public health, reduce mortality, and potentially decrease national health expenditures. Two waves of patient data from San Diego's Kaiser Permanente Medical System were collected for the Adverse Childhood Experiences (ACE) study (Felitti et al., 1998). Respondents (N = 17,421) reported their early experiences of adversity in the following categories: emotional abuse, physical abuse, sexual abuse, exposure to substance abuse in the home, mental illness of parent or household member, witnessing violence directed to mother or stepmother, incarceration of a household member, parental divorce or separation. Over 50% of the sample reported having experienced at least one of the adverse categories. Over 6% reported four or more, and rates of comorbidity were high. The most common adverse experience was substance abuse in the home. Findings showed a similar pattern to that observed in the Australian study. Adult incidence of smoking, depressed mood, suicide attempts,

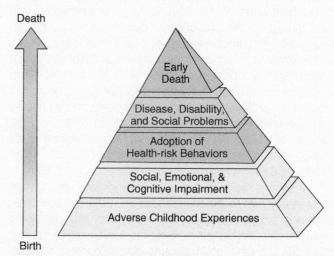

FIGURE 2.10 Potential influences throughout the lifespan of adverse childhood experiences. Adverse experiences in childhood add to the risk of physical, social and emotional problems throughout the lifespan.
SOURCE: Felitti, V. J., Anda, R. F., Nordenberg, D., Williamson, D. F., Spitz, A. M., Edwards, V., Koss, M. P., & Marks, J. S. (1998). Relationship of childhood abuse and dysfunction to many of the leading causes of death in adults. *American Journal of Preventive Medicine, 14,* 245–258. Used with permission from Elsevier.

panic disorders, memory problems, sleep disorders, drug and alcohol use, sexually transmitted diseases, unintended pregnancies, involvement in teen pregnancies (males), physical inactivity, and severe obesity increased in a stepwise fashion proportional to the number of their early adverse experiences (Anda et al., 2006). Some risk behaviors, like smoking, may serve a stress management function early on. Over time, smoking to relieve stress becomes maladaptive and can lead to emphysema, cardiovascular disease, or malignancy. Another analysis of the data showed that prescription rates for psychotropic medications also increased in a dose-response relationship to increasing ACE scores, even after excluding family history of mental illness in the analyses (Anda et al., 2007). This linear relationship was found for antidepressant and antianxiety medication for the entire sample (18 to 80 years of age). Prescription rates for mood-stabilizing and antipsychotic medications reflected the same pattern for younger and middle aged (18–64) adults but not for the oldest (65–89) group. The use of actual prescription data, in place of self-reports, supports the overall findings observed in other studies.

Researchers involved in these large-scale studies conclude that early adverse experiences contribute to the etiology of later illness through developmental, biologically based stress mechanisms (see Figure 2.10). If this is what's actually happening, you would expect that the effect would be present regardless of changing social attitudes about reporting mental illness, medication use, and so on. In other words, the biologically based changes attendant upon adversity would be fundamental. Analyses of ACEs in four patient cohorts from 1900 to 1978 provided supportive results (Dube, Felitti, Dong, Giles, & Anda, 2003). The strength of the dose-response association between ACEs and health outcomes was observed within each successive cohort, even though the prevalence of risk behaviors varied across decades. For example, changes in attitudes about smoking and variations in smoking behavior have occurred over the 78 years included in this analysis. Nevertheless, the relationship between ACE and smoking remained consistent. This evidence suggests that early adverse experiences contribute to multiple health problems by means of "inherent biological effects of traumatic stressors (ACEs) on the developing nervous systems of children" (Dube et al., 2003, p. 274).

is considering a pregnancy and certainly if she suspects she is pregnant. No over-the-counter medication should be taken without the advice of a physician. Even the innocuous aspirin tablet, if taken in excess during the last trimester, can prolong labor and cause excessive bleeding. Herbal supplements should be taken only with the approval of a health care provider. Exposure to toxic chemicals like lead, solvents, mercury, paint, paint thinners, and so on should be avoided.

3. Good medical care is one of the most important elements in a healthy pregnancy and delivery. Research has shown that it is significantly associated with fewer birth complications and lower rates of infant mortality (Kotch, Blakely, Brown, & Wong, 1992). Pregnant women should see their health care provider early in the pregnancy and frequently thereafter.

4. Stress, particularly if chronic and serious, can be detrimental to a healthy pregnancy. Every effort should be made to provide social support and to reduce ongoing interpersonal conflict during this time. Fathers and extended family members are likely support-system candidates. When they are not available, the helper must use creative means to provide for contacts (support groups, church members, agency contacts, etc.) who will lend a listening ear and a helping hand to mothers-to-be experiencing the emotional upheaval of pregnancy.

Recently, the American Academy of Pediatrics (AAP) published a policy statement for its practitioners that translates research from multiple research areas on toxic stress into practices that can be applied in the real world (AAP, 2011). First, the document advocates that practitioners adopt an **ecobiodevelopmental (EBD)** approach to health and illness. In other words, psychosocial problems affect functioning of mind and body, and thus should not be viewed as substantially different from other biological impairments. Second, it advocates that information about consequences of toxic stress on the developing brain and its impact on lifelong functioning should be part of education for all current and future physicians. Third, the policy calls for taking a leadership role in education and advocacy to prevent stress-related developmental problems. Fourth, it supports research, development and implementation of evidence-based practices to protect children from adverse experiences and reduce their harmful effects. Finally, it calls for active screening of patients on issues related to stress in the home, development of community resources for prevention and treatment of children at risk, and provision of guidance to families about positive parenting practices. This statement serves as a model for those who work with pregnant women, parents and young children because it takes seriously what we know about development and translates this information into usable guidelines for action.

Helping the Most Vulnerable: Preterm and Low-Birth-Weight (LBW) Babies

For some populations, primarily women who live in poverty, who abuse drugs and alcohol, who are unmarried or teenagers, or who live in highly stressful circumstances, the stakes are higher during pregnancy. Poverty, teratogens, insufficient prenatal care, and inadequate health insurance are all associated with the risk of delivering an infant preterm (less than 37 weeks gestation) or of low birth weight (less than 5 pounds, 8 ounces). From 2000 to 2001, approximately 16% of infants in the United States were born with disorders related to prematurity and LBW, the leading cause of death for neonates—from birth through 28 days (Anderson & Smith, 2003). Preterm and LBW infants who survive are much more likely to suffer from a number of chronic medical problems such as respiratory infections; delays in achievement of developmental milestones; behavioral problems; feeding problems; and low IQ and related academic consequences, such as grade retention, dropping out of high school, and increased need for special education services for learning disabilities and ADHD (Conley & Bennett, 2002; Wallace & McCarton, 1997). LBW has also been associated with developing anxiety disorders over the lifespan (Vasiliadis, Buka, Martin, & Gilman, 2010). The price of prevention seems eminently reasonable, given the huge burden associated with preterm and LBW births both in human and economic terms.

The Healing Touch

Touch has long been recognized as one of the primary forms of human communication, bonding, and healing (Hertenstein, 2002), and it appears to be the infant's best developed sense at birth (Reisman, 1987). Field and her associates have applied the power of touch to enhance the development of preterm and LBW infants by developing a standard infant massage therapy protocol. Outcome studies of this intervention demonstrate that massage is effective for increasing weight gain (Field et al., 1986; Scafidi, Field, & Schanberg, 1993); social responsiveness (Field, Scafidi, & Schanberg, 1987); bone growth and development (Moyer-Mileur, Brubstetter, McNaught, Gill, & Chan, 2000); and for decreasing cortisol levels, crying, and sleep disturbances (Acolet et al., 1993). Improvements in weight gain and reductions in stress after massage therapy have also been found for infants exposed to cocaine and HIV (Field, Hernandez-Reif, & Freedman, 2004; Wheedon et al., 1993).

Because it has been demonstrated that touch can be excessively arousing and disorganizing to extremely fragile infants who have great difficulty regulating tactile stimulation (Als, 1986), infant massage therapy is indicated for preterm and LBW infants who are considered medically stable and who need to gain weight. It is important that professionals consider the infant's medical condition and vulnerabilities so as to adjust the therapeutic regimen accordingly. More research is needed in this area to clarify just how treatments should be individualized for the most vulnerable infants.

What Is Massage Therapy?

The massage therapy protocol used in research and practice involves three standardized segments of massage, each lasting 5 minutes. Stroking of the infant's body using moderate pressure from the top of the head to the feet in a systematic way comprises the first and third segments. During the middle segment, the infant's limbs are gently flexed and extended. The beneficial outcomes obtained in research studies have resulted from a fairly brief course of therapy—three sessions per day for 5 to 10 days—offering a potentially cost-effective way to improve health and shorten hospitalizations for these babies. Mothers suffering from postpartum depression who were trained to use massage therapy for one 15-minute period two times a week for 6 weeks were able to reduce infant crying and improve their infants' sleep. The mothers also reported less depression themselves (Field, et al., 1996). Based on these findings, it appears

that massage can be a useful skill to teach parents and grandparents because it helps reduce stress both for the one who gives and the one who receives.

Beyond Massage Therapy

As we have noted, prevention efforts that are comprehensive in their scope are most successful. For women in at-risk groups (with diabetes, chronic hypertension, or who have experienced preterm labor), the health of their infants might be further enhanced by a combination of services and continuity of care. In an experimental study that investigated the effectiveness of such a program, Brooten and associates (2001) were able to reduce the rate of infant mortality, preterm deliveries, and infant rehospitalizations for high-risk women by providing prenatal medical care, education, and counseling (partly in the women's homes), frequent telephone contact and daily telephone availability, and postpartum visits by nurse specialists. The rate of infant mortality was over four times as high ($n = 9$) in the control group of 88 mothers when compared to the rate ($n = 2$) in the treatment group of 85 mothers. This result suggests that consistency of care and ongoing relationships with caregivers offer clinicians a good chance of supporting a healthy start for infants at high risk of prematurity and LBW. Similar principles have been applied to programs for pregnant teenagers, who often face multiple risks as well. Teen pregnancy represents a particular challenge to the helper because the normal tasks of adolescent development (see Chapters 9, 10, and 11) are overlaid on the issues of pregnancy and parenthood. Whereas rates of teenage births have stabilized or have declined slightly in recent years (National Campaign to Prevent Teen Pregnancy, 1999), the numbers are still unacceptably high. Studies have demonstrated that children of teenage mothers are likely to face a grim future that includes poverty, academic failure, high rates of family violence, unemployment, contact with the criminal justice system, and the likelihood of becoming teenage parents themselves. Pregnant teens experience more health problems, have higher rates of birth complications due to poor prenatal care, and tend to drop out of school, risking under- or unemployment in the future (Furstenberg, Brooks-Gunn, & Chase-Lansdale, 1989; Hayes, 1987).

For a multifaceted and cyclical problem such as this, interventions need to be embedded in the social and cultural system of the teenager, and most effective programs address concerns of parenthood and adolescent development together. Although evidence is somewhat scanty, the best approaches appear to involve coordination of school and clinic services. In other words, programs that target multiple issues, providing support and information on birth control, pregnancy, and child care, academic and vocational education, and the social and emotional concerns of the teenager hold out the promise of greater success than do programs that address single issues alone (Cowen et al., 1996). Programs for pregnant teens should also provide coordinated services for the new mothers, their babies, and the grandmothers who often play a central role in the caretaking functions. To break the repetitive cycle of early pregnancy, children of teenage mothers should be the target of preventive efforts as they approach adolescence themselves (Chase-Lansdale & Brooks-Gunn, 1994).

SUMMARY

The Nature–Nurture Illusion

1. Both heredity and environment influence human development, but when we focus our attention on one of these causes the other seems to fade into the background. It is an especially important challenge for the helper to avoid taking a one-sided perspective.

Epigenesis and Coaction

2. Ova (eggs) in females and sperm in males, contain only one member of each chromosome pair, or 23 chromosomes altogether. When a sperm fertilizes an ovum, the resulting zygote contains 46 chromosomes. Thus, mother's ovum and father's sperm each contribute one member of every chromosome pair to their offspring.

3. The 46 chromosomes in each body cell consist of 22 structurally and functionally matched pairs or autosomes, and one pair of sex chromosomes which are matched in females (2 X chromosomes), but mismatched in males (1 X and 1 Y chromosome). Growth is made possible by mitosis, or cell division, and each new cell contains a duplicate set of the original 46 from the zygote.

4. Epigenesis is the set of processes by which factors outside of hereditary material itself can influence how hereditary material functions. For example, cells specialize (becoming liver or brain or skin cells) because chromosomal material is influenced by the environment surrounding the cell. Coaction describes the fact that all physical and behavioral developments are the result of environment acting on heredity and vice versa.

5. Chromosomes are made of DNA, and sections of DNA called genes are coded by the sequences of four basic chemicals that comprise them. The cellular processes of transcription and translation of genetic codes ends with the production of proteins.

6. Because cellular environments vary in different parts of the body, transcription and translation of the same gene can produce different proteins in different cells. The environment of the cell is affected by genes and by the environment outside the cell, including the social environment.

7. A variety of epigenetic changes, such as methylation and acetylation, can affect whether, when and how much a gene will be transcribed. For example, if rat mothers groom their newborn pups a great deal, a gene that affects development of the pups' stress response is permanently "demethylated," causing brain changes that make the pups quicker to recover from stressful events.

8. As a result of epigenesis, even monozygotic twins with identical heredity can show discordant physical and behavioral characteristics, because different experiences cause changes in cellular processes that affect gene expression.

9. Genes, like chromosomes, come in matched pairs, one from the mother, one from the father. Matching genes can come in slightly different forms, called alleles, presenting cells with slightly different blueprints to follow. Different alleles of the same gene can have a dominant-recessive relationship such that one has a larger influence on the phenotype. In this situation, a person is a carrier of an unexpressed trait, which can be passed on to the next generation. Sometimes two different alleles have a codominance relationship and together produce a blended trait.

Atypical Development

10. Hereditary diseases can occur either as a function of defective genes or because an ovum or a sperm contains the wrong number of chromosomes. Some disorders are caused by a single pair of genes. In this case, defective gene alleles can be recessive, so that a victim must have two of them to have the disorder, or a defective allele can be dominant, causing the disorder in anyone who has one of the defective genes. Many hereditary diseases, including many mental illnesses and behavioral disorders, are polygenic. Finally, some hereditary disorders result when a zygote forms containing too many chromosomes or too few. Genetic counselors can help parents and prospective parents who may be at risk of passing on hereditary diseases.

11. Teratogens are environmental agents, including many disease organisms and drugs that can have negative effects on the developing fetus. Their effects depend on when they are introduced, the mother's and baby's genes, and the amount of exposure or dosage the fetus experiences. For example, the effects of prenatal exposure to alcohol can range from subtle learning and behavior problems to fetal alcohol syndrome, which includes physical abnormalities, mental retardation, and behavioral problems. The number of risk factors to which a child is exposed, both prenatally and postnatally, can also influence how severe the long-term effects of teratogens will be. Teratogens may sometimes have their effects by causing genetic mutations in the fetus, but are most likely to alter gene expression through epigenetic processes.

12. Inadequate protein, vitamins, and minerals in the prenatal or early postnatal diet can have long-term consequences for children's physical, social and cognitive development and health. Epigenetic changes at the cellular level seem to be a primary reason for the long-term effects of poor early nutrition. But like other risk factors, poor pre- or postnatal nutrition is more problematic the more risks a child experiences. Social, educational, and medical advantages during childhood can moderate the impact of early food deprivation.

The Developing Brain

13. The embryo begins to form a neural tube at about 2 weeks of gestation. By birth there are 100 billion of neurons. Until about 4 months of gestation much of brain development involves neuron migration. The first neurons produced at the interior surface of the neural tube migrate the shortest distance and form the hindbrain. Later developing neurons travel farther to form the midbrain, and the last neurons to be produced travel farthest and form the forebrain or cerebrum and its cortex. Neurons in different parts of the brain later specialize for certain functions. Specialization is influenced by the context or environment of the cell, that is, by epigenetic processes. Neurons from one part of the cortex will re-specialize if transplanted to another part of the cortex.

14. A neuron has one long extension called an axon, and may have many shorter extensions called dendrites. Electrical impulses begin when dendrites or cell bodies pick up a message from another cell. The impulse then passes through the axon to the axon terminals, where chemicals called neurotransmitters are released into the gap—or synapse—between neurons. The neurotransmitters carry the message to the next cell, causing it to fire or to stop firing. Myelination, formation of an insulating substance around axons, promotes efficient conduction of electrical impulses. Myelination occurs prenatally and throughout childhood and adolescence. Neurons begin firing spontaneously at about 4 months of gestation. Before birth, sensory neurons are beginning to be functional. A fetus will turn toward a light source by 25 weeks of gestation, and she can begin to recognize some aspects of sounds, like her mother's voice, in the later weeks of pregnancy. Availability of appropriate stimulation appears to be critical in the late prenatal and early postnatal period for normal sensory functioning to develop. There is an optimal range of stimulation—too much as well as too little may be problematic. Different sensory systems influence one another's development.

15. Rapid neuron reproduction continues after birth until the end of the 1st year. Although some neurons can reproduce even in adulthood, most nerve cell reproduction seems to end in infancy. The formation of synapses is ongoing throughout childhood and adolescence, and perhaps even into adulthood, and seems to be linked to cognitive advances. Many more synapses are formed than will be needed, and brain development postnatally involves synapse formation and neural pruning. Experience-expectant synapses are formed in anticipation of typical experiences. Experience shapes the pruning process—synapses that are used remain, and those that are not may be discarded. Experience-dependent synapses are formed as a result of exposure to certain kinds of experience and may be pruned if they do not remain active.

The Developing Stress and Adaptation System

16. A contemporary view of the individual's response to stress, the allostatic model, suggests that the central nervous system controls multiple regulatory processes, making adjustments to a variety of systems to create an adaptive balance among them that depends on the particular challenge that is confronted. The brain is the "top down" manager of the stress response.

17. The primary stress management apparatus is the hypothalamic-pituitary-adrenal (HPA) axis. The initial response to stressful challenges, executed through the sympathetic nervous system, releases epinephrine and norepinephrine, which activate some bodily systems preparing for "fight or flight." The heart beats faster increasing activation in places like the heart and lungs, but decreasing activation in less necessary parts, such as the reproductive system. When the threat is reduced, the parasympathetic nervous system reverses these effects.

18. Part of the stress response involves the release of glucocorticoids (primarily cortisol) by the adrenal glands. Receptors in the amygdala and hippocampus bind to the glucocorticoids, leading to an end to the stress response that originated in the HPA. The more receptors that are present, the faster the stress response will end. A hyperactive stress system is one with an inadequate system of glucocorticoid receptors. The early experience of high stress levels resulting from, for example, early sexual abuse, can lead to a hyperactive stress system. Chronically high levels of cortisol can lead to many problems, because cortisol has many effects, such as increasing glucose levels and triggering and then suppressing immune responses. Related disorders include a range of emotional, cognitive, and physical problems. The number and timing of exposure to stress during development is important for the kinds of disorders that chronic stress may induce.

CASE STUDY

Jennifer and Jianshe Li have been married for 10 years. Jennifer is a White, 37-year-old woman who is an associate in a law firm in a medium-sized, midwestern city. Her husband, Jianshe, a 36-year-old Chinese American man, is a software developer employed by a large locally based company. The couple met while they were in graduate school and married shortly thereafter. They have no children. They own a home in one of the newly developed suburban areas just outside the city. Jennifer was adopted as an infant and maintains close ties with her adoptive parents. She is their only child. There has been no contact between Jennifer and her biological parents, and she has never attempted to learn their names or find out where they live. Jianshe's parents, two brothers, and one sister live on the U.S. West Coast, and all the family members try to get together for visits several times a year. Jennifer and Jianshe are active in a few local community organizations. They enjoy the company of many friends and often spend what leisure time they have hiking and camping.

The Lis have been unsuccessful in conceiving a child even though they have tried for the past 4 years. Both husband and wife have undergone testing. Jennifer has had infertility treatment for the past 3 years but without success. The treatments have been lengthy, expensive, and emotionally stressful. Approximately a year ago, Jennifer began to experience some mild symptoms of dizziness and dimmed vision. At first, she disregarded the symptoms, attributing them to overwork. However, they persisted for several weeks, and she consulted her physician. He thought that they might be a side effect of the medication she had been taking to increase fertility. Jennifer's treatment protocol was changed, and shortly afterward, much to the couple's delight, Jennifer became pregnant.

Unfortunately, the symptoms she had experienced earlier began to worsen, and she noticed some mild tremors in her arms and legs as well. Jennifer's physician referred her to a specialist, who tentatively diagnosed a progressive disease of the central nervous system that has a suspected genetic link and is marked by an unpredictable course. The Lis were devastated by the news. They were very concerned about the risks of the pregnancy to Jennifer's health. They also worried about the possible transmission of the disease to the new baby whom they had wanted for such a long time. In great distress, they sought counseling to help them deal with some of these concerns.

Discussion Questions

1. As a helper, what are some of the issues you would need to be prepared to discuss with this couple? What information or training do you think you would need to deal effectively with this family?
2. List the possible problems faced by this couple as well as the supports available to them. What are the options available to Jennifer and Jianshe?
3. As a genetic counselor, how would you help them in the decision-making process?

JOURNAL QUESTIONS

1. Consider one feature of your own development (a trait, talent, behavior). Discuss the development of this feature using the idea of nature–nurture coaction. How has this particular feature of your personality influenced and been influenced by other people?
2. Interview your mother or father, if possible, about your prenatal developmental period. What can you learn about this important period of your development?
3. How has increased knowledge about prenatal development changed the behaviors of pregnant women? Are there any beliefs specific to your particular cultural background that shaped the way your mother viewed her pregnancy or acted during her pregnancy? Ask a member of a different culture about the ways that culture views pregnancy.
4. Discuss the chronic stress in your life. How might it be affecting your health and well-being?

KEY CONCEPTS

ovum (p. 41)
chromosome (p. 41)
cytoplasm (p. 41)
zygote (p. 41)
autosomes (p. 41)
sex chromosomes (p. 41)
X chromosome (p. 41)
Y chromosome (p. 41)
karyotype (p. 41)
mitosis (p. 42)
implantation (p. 42)
embryo (p. 42)
epigenesis (p. 43)
epigenome (p. 43)
coaction (p. 43)
epigenetic model (p. 43)
deoxyribonucleic acid (DNA) (p. 43)

histones (p. 43)
gene (p. 43)
protein (p. 44)
transcription (p. 44)
messenger ribonucleic acid (mRNA) (p. 44)
translation (p. 44)
gene expression (p. 44)
noncoded genes (p. 44)
gene regulation (p. 44)
transcription factor (p. 44)
receptor (p. 44)
methylation (p. 45)
demethylation (p. 45)
acetylation (p. 45)
deacetylation (p. 45)
cross-fostering study (p. 46)
genotype (p. 46)

phenotype (p. 46)
monozygotic (identical) twins (p. 46)
dizygotic twins (fraternal) twins (p. 46)
concordance (p. 47)
discordance (p. 47)
allele (p. 47)
dominant-recessive relationship (p. 47)
carrier (p. 47)
codominance (p. 48)
polygenic (p. 48)
genomic imprinting (p. 48)
period of the zygote (p. 48)
period of the embryo (p. 48)
period of the fetus (p. 48)
sickle-cell anemia (p. 50)
genetic counselor (p. 50)
mutation (p. 51)

progeria (p. 51)
Huntington's disease (p. 51)
Down syndrome (trisomy 21) (p. 52)
teratogen (p. 52)
placenta (p. 52)
fetal alcohol syndrome (FAS) (p. 54)
fetal alcohol effects (FAE) (p. 54)
no observable effect level (p. 54)
lowest observable adverse effect
     level (p. 54)
kwashiorkor (p. 56)
neural tube (p. 56)
neurulation (p. 56)
neuron (p. 57)
glial cell (p. 57)
hindbrain (p. 57)
midbrain (p. 57)
cerebral cortex (p. 57)
forebrain (p. 57)
medulla (p. 58)
pons (p. 58)
cerebellum (p. 58)
reticular formation (p. 58)
autonomic functions (p. 58)
nuclei (p. 58)
reticular activating system (p. 58)
superior colliculi (p. 58)
inferior colliculi (p. 58)
substantia nigra (p. 58)
cerebrum (p. 58)
thalamus (p. 58)
hypothalamus (p. 58)
limbic system (p. 58)
basal ganglia (p. 58)

nucleus accumbens (p. 58)
limbic structures (p. 58)
hippocampus (p. 58)
amygdala (p. 58)
septum (p. 58)
cingulate cortex (p. 58)
corpus callosum (p. 58)
hemispheric specialization (lateralization)
     (p. 58)
occipital lobe (p. 59)
temporal lobe (p. 59)
central sulcus (p. 59)
parietal lobe (p. 59)
frontal lobe (p. 59)
prefrontal cortex (PFC) (p. 59)
anterior cingulate cortex (ACC) (p. 59)
nucleus (p. 60)
neuroplasticity (p. 60)
axon (p. 60)
axon terminals (p. 61)
neurotransmitters (p. 61)
dendrites (p. 61)
synaptic gap (p. 61)
serotonin (p. 61)
acetylcholine (p. 61)
glutamate (p. 61)
gamma-amino butyric acid (GABA) (p. 61)
epinephrine (adrenalin) (p. 61)
norepinephrine (noradrenalin) (p. 61)
dopamine (p. 61)
myelination (p. 61)
white matter (p. 61)
grey matter (p. 61)
circuits (p. 61)

projection neurons (p. 61)
interneurons (p. 61)
neural stem cells (p. 63)
subventricular zone (SVZ) (p. 63)
subgranular zone (p. 63)
synapses (p. 63)
nerve growth factor (p. 63)
synaptogenesis (p. 63)
neural pruning (p. 63)
synaptic overproduction (p. 63)
experience-expectant (p. 64)
experience-dependent (p. 63)
homeostasis (p. 65)
stress (p. 65)
general adaptation syndrome (GAS) (p. 65)
allostasis (p. 66)
allostatic accommodation (p. 66)
hypothalamic-pituitary-adrenal (HPA) axis
     (p. 66)
allostatic load (p. 66)
sympathetic nervous system (SNS) (p. 67)
parasympathetic nervous system (PNS) (p. 67)
pituitary gland (p. 67)
corticotropin releasing factor (CRF) (p. 67)
adrenocorticotropic hormone (ACTH) (p. 67)
adrenal glands (p. 67)
cortisol (p. 67)
glucocorticoid (p. 67)
atypical depression (p. 67)
melancholic depression (p. 67)
cytokines (p. 67)
dose-response relationship (p. 70)
ecobiodevelopmental (EBD) (p. 71)

CHAPTER **3**

Cognitive Development in the Early Years

Is there any value for helping professionals in learning the details of infant and pre-school development? The benefits are obvious if you work primarily with infants, preschoolers, and their parents, but what if the majority of your clients are older children, adolescents, and adults? As you have already seen, developments at these later ages cannot be divorced from earlier events. Skills, abilities, and tendencies that develop in the early years of life establish trajectories that influence the progress and direction of later developments. To put it simply, who a person will become is at least partially channeled even before birth.

Perhaps you are wondering why understanding early cognitive processes should be an important part of your concern given that many helping professionals work with their clients on emotional and social issues. The fundamental reason is that cognitive, emotional, and social processes are so intimately interconnected that you can have little understanding of any one of these processes without some knowledge of all of them. For example, cognitive processes affect social functioning, and social experiences have important impacts on cognitive development, as you will readily see in this chapter. In fact, realms that seem discreet, like emotion and logic, are typically two different aspects of one global process. In the next chapter, where you will learn more about emotional development, you will find that logic without emotion turns out to be rather illogical!

If you had to guess, would you say that more intellectual growth occurs in the first few years of life or in some later period, such as adolescence? John Flavell, a noted cognitive researcher, has argued that "the brief span from young infancy to young childhood is marked by a momentous transformation of the cognitive system unparalleled by any other period of life" (Flavell, Miller, & Miller, 1993). In this chapter, we look first at how Jean Piaget described the vast changes that occur in these early years. Then, we examine what modern researchers are learning about the many intellectual changes that take place from earliest infancy through the preschool years, with an eye to evaluating how Piaget's theory accounts for these changes. Finally, we take a look at another major theory of cognitive development, that of Lev S. Vygotsky, whose ideas and findings were compatible with Piaget's in many ways but who added a special emphasis on the importance of culture and social experience to the story of intellectual change in childhood.

PIAGET'S CONSTRUCTIVIST THEORY

Debbie, age 10, and Mark, age 4, are overheard discussing their mother's pregnancy. Their parents have read them children's books about how babies are conceived and born, and the topic has been discussed openly in the family. The children have the following conversation:

Debbie: Do you know how the baby got there?
Mark: Sure. Mommy got a duck.
Debbie: A duck?
Mark: Yeah, they just get a duck or rabbit and it grows a little more and it turns into a baby.
Debbie: A duck will turn into a baby?
Mark: Sure. They give them some food, people food, and they grow into a baby.
Debbie: Where did you get that idea?
Mark: I saw it in a book and Mommy and Daddy told me.
Debbie: They told you that ducks turn into babies?
Mark: Yeah!

(Based on Cowan, P. A. (1978). *Piaget with feeling: Cognitive, social and emotional dimensions.* New York: Holt, Rinehart & Winston and Bernstein, A. C., & Cowan, P. A. (1975). Children's concepts of how people get babies. *Child Development*, 46, 77–91).

This anecdote a fundamental feature of learning, knowing, and understanding according to Piaget's theory: that the human mind constructs its knowledge. When infants and children are presented with new stimuli or pieces of information, what is learned or stored is not just a "true" reflection of what comes from the environment. That is, new information is not simply written on a blank slate, as John Locke and other empiricists assumed. Rather, children learn by a process of **adaptation**. First, they interpret new stimulation in ways that fit with what they already know, sometimes distorting it as a result. This aspect of adaptation is called **assimilation**. As the new information is assimilated, the child's existing knowledge may be modified somewhat, providing a better match or fit to what is new. The latter process is called **accommodation**. Assimilation and accommodation are complementary activities involved in every interaction with the environment. To accommodate (learn), children must be able to assimilate. In other words, they cannot learn something that they cannot make some sense out of already. Assimilation often means that new information is distorted or changed so that sense can be made of it! A child's understandings are gradually changed as a result of interactions with the environment, although what a child will learn in any single step is always shaped by what the child already knows, and the new "understanding" may not be a completely accurate reflection of reality. In Mark's case, his parents' explanations, which apparently included comparing human reproduction to ducks laying eggs, far outstripped Mark's knowledge structures, and Mark's assimilation and accommodation of his parents' elaborate explanations produced a charmingly naive linear progression: Ducks turn into people.

Piaget spent a lifetime doing intensive research on the development of knowledge; he wrote dozens of books on his findings and hundreds of articles (see Box 3.1). His own ideas evolved and changed as new work was completed, discussed, and challenged by scientists around the world. Since his death, developmental researchers have followed up on his pioneering work, and, naturally, the field has moved on. Not all of his ideas have been corroborated, but in a remarkable number of areas, his research has been the starting point for more expanded, clarifying work, and his theoretical explanations have informed newer theories.

The idea that knowledge is constructed by the developing child (and adult.) is a Piagetian view that

These children, while studying tadpoles, are learning something new about growth. They can assimilate the idea that the tadpole grows legs, but they need to accommodate their concept of growth to understand why the tadpole's tail gets smaller.

Piaget was one of the first theorists to propose that children actively construct their knowledge.

Box 3.1: Biographical Sketch: Jean Piaget

Jean Piaget (1896–1980) was remarkably precocious as a child, publishing his first scholarly paper at the age of 10. At 14, after producing a series of scientific reports, he was offered a position as curator of a museum of natural history—an offer promptly withdrawn when his age was discovered. Piaget completed a bachelor's degree by age 18 and a PhD by 22, despite spending a year away from school when he suffered a nervous breakdown (which he later attributed to his study of philosophy). His early education, research, and writing ranged widely from biological science (his first published article reported his observations of an albino sparrow), to mathematics and logic, to experimental psychology, to psychoanalysis, to psychopathology. He even wrote a philosophical novel! He found a way to integrate many of his interests when he was hired by Henri Simon, an early developer of IQ tests, to standardize an English test with French children. Piaget soon lost interest in the task he was assigned—asking children test questions, recording their responses, and specifying whether they were right or wrong for the purposes of quantifying intelligence. But he was intrigued by the qualitative features of children's answers. Even children's wrong answers often seemed to reveal an underlying structure or pattern of thought. While studying psychopathology, Piaget had learned to conduct clinical interviews with mental patients. Now, he began to combine clinical interview techniques with the use of standardized questions in an effort to reveal the nature of children's knowledge and reasoning. After publishing several articles on his findings, Piaget was invited to become the director of studies in the Institute Jean-Jacques Rousseau in Geneva, a center for scientific child study and teacher training. At the age of 25, his life's work had begun. Until his death at 84, Piaget wrote prolifically on the development of children's knowledge, reporting an endless stream of studies, and constructing a wide-ranging, coherent theory. His empirical methods combined observations of children's hands-on problem solving with the probing, clinical interview technique that he pioneered in Simon's laboratory. He originated a remarkable array of problem tasks that are easy for adults to solve but not for children, revealing what appeared to be astonishing age changes in our reasoning about the world. As Piaget put it, "Just as the tadpole already breathes, though with different organs from those of the frog, so the child acts like the adult, but employing a mentality whose structure varies according to the stages of its development" (Piaget, 1970, p. 153).

It is rare today to find any subject in cognitive development, from perception to mathematical reasoning to memory to social perspective taking, for which Piaget did not pose key questions and design provocative, ingenious research tasks. Given the breadth, depth, and complexity of Piaget's work, it is not surprising that others often oversimplify it in their effort to understand. For example, Piaget has been described as a nativist by some, as an empiricist by others. In fact, Piaget was a true interactionist. He, like modern systems theorists, viewed development as taking place at the proximal interface between the organism and the environment. Biological and psychological systems affect how the knower acts on the environment, and the environment "feeds" the knower. What the environment provides is absorbed and changed by the organism, but the environment also shapes and changes the organism's knowledge.

Educators have been especially affected by Piaget's work, although again, they have sometimes misinterpreted its implications. Piaget saw schooling as an opportunity to provide children with food for their naturally occurring "mental digestion." He warned teachers, however, that children will either memorize new information by rote or ignore it if it is beyond their current level of understanding. But if information is at least partially comprehensible to them or moderately novel, children will actively and eagerly explore and absorb it. Unfortunately, educators have sometimes misinterpreted Piaget's emphasis on children's active exploration as a recommendation that children simply be provided with lots of interesting and fun "stuff" and then left on their own to learn. Instead, Piaget encouraged educators to plan the presentation of learning opportunities carefully, being especially sensitive to children's current level of functioning in introducing tasks and allowing children to actively explore and discover but recognizing that an orchestrated, if flexible, presentation of tasks aimed at the child's level of understanding can promote development (e.g., 1970).

Interestingly, although Piaget recognized the advantage of teachers' carefully crafting a program of learning opportunities to optimize a child's progress, he was somewhat exasperated by what he referred to as "the American question": "How can we speed up children's development?" He once remarked that kittens have been found to go through some developments in 3 months that take human babies 9 to 12 months to achieve. But "the kitten is not going to go much further. The child has taken longer, but he is capable of going further so it seems to me that the nine months were not for nothing" (as quoted in Elkind, 1968). Respect, appreciation of children's cognitive pace, and an enormous empathy may be what made Piaget so successful in uncovering the mysteries of cognitive development in general.

SOURCE: Patricia Broderick & Pamela Blewitt.

has become an underlying assumption of much of the current research on cognitive development and educational practice (e.g., American Psychological Association's [APA] Board of Educational Affairs, 1995). This constructivist stance takes the child to be an active participant in the learning process, constantly seeking out and trying to make sense of new information. In other words, children are intrinsically motivated to learn—another idea that is widely accepted by modern developmental scientists. Piaget also considered a child's active exploration to be organized and organizing. When children assimilate new information to what they already know they are fitting the new information into an organized way of thinking—some sort of knowledge structure. When they accommodate their knowledge structures to fit what is new in the environment, the organization is changing. (We will have more to say about knowledge structures in later chapters.) The ideas that mental activity is organized and that the organization evolves in response to the environment are further Piagetian notions that seem to be taken for granted by many modern researchers.

Thus, many widely accepted assumptions about cognitive development are derived from Piaget. But some of his fundamental ideas are particularly controversial. Among these is the idea that cognitive development can be characterized by stages (see Chapter 1). Although Piaget saw cognitive change as the result of small, gradual reorganizations of knowledge structures, he described periods of time in which all of a child's mental structures can be expected to have some organizational properties in common. For example, the infancy and preschool periods covered in this chapter were divided by Piaget into two stages, the sensorimotor stage (from birth to about age 2) and the preoperational stage (between ages 2 and 7). Each of these stages was further divided into substages. The notion of stages implies that children's understandings within a stage (or a substage) about many different things will have some general similarities. So, for example, in the early preoperational stage, whether we are examining a child's understanding of number or causality, we should be able to detect some similarities in the ways in which children organize their thinking about these concepts.

Although Piaget did find many such similarities, more recent research, using different kinds of tasks, often finds less support for the notion of overarching stages. In particular, newer work suggests that infants and preschoolers sometimes show signs of understandings that Piaget believed to be possible only for much older children. And children's progress in understanding concepts from different domains of knowledge is not always organized or structured in the same ways at the same time. In fact, an important addition to cognitive-developmental work since Piaget is the idea that progress is often **domain specific**. That is, development can proceed at different rates in different domains. Domains that have been studied in detail include number concepts, morality, biological versus physical realities, and so on. For example, if we want to learn about children's understanding of causality, we may need to look at it within particular domains of knowledge. Children's understanding of physical causality (e.g., how objects move) may progress differently from their understanding of human or animal agency (e.g., how animate organisms move). We should note that Piaget, in his later years, continued to revise his theory. Recent translations of his later work show that he put less emphasis on stages and more on the dynamic quality of repeated assimilation and accommodation in the context of feedback from the environment (e.g., Piaget, 1975/1985).

Nonetheless, most developmental scientists, clinicians, and educators still find Piaget's stage divisions to be useful for many purposes. On the whole, for example, infants' understandings of many different concepts are more similar to one another's than to those of a 5-year-old. For this reason, in this chapter and in other discussions of cognitive development in this book, we will use Piaget's stage divisions as an aid in describing children's cognitive progress.

INFANT COGNITION: THE SENSORIMOTOR STAGE

Infants' cognitive functioning seems more mysterious than that of older children and adults because infants do not talk. We cannot ask them to describe what they can see or how many objects are in front of them or to tell us their solutions to a problem. Most efforts to probe cognition at all other age levels depend on giving verbal instructions, and they usually also require at least some verbal responses from study participants.

How then can we understand what a baby knows, thinks, or even feels? Piaget's research with infants, done primarily with his own three children, focused on detailed analyses of babies' motor interactions with the environment. A newborn's reflexive responses to sensory stimuli—like looking and following when a visual stimulus moves across the visual field, head turning in the direction of a sound, grasping at a touch to the palm, and sucking at a touch to the lips—were examined under many different stimulus conditions. Piaget carefully noted how these sensorimotor patterns functioned and, especially, how they changed with time and experience. From such observations, Piaget inferred what babies might actually understand or be capable of learning.

Careful observation of infants' reactions to environmental events is still at the heart of infant research, but today we have strategies that take advantage of technology to make these observations more precise. Among these strategies, for example, is the **habituation paradigm**, which takes advantage of a baby's tendency to orient to new stimulation and to habituate to repeated or old stimulation. Suppose, for example, that a baby is propped up in an infant seat in a darkened room in front of a large, blank video screen. Suddenly, a picture of a green circle flashes on the screen. The baby is likely to produce an **orienting response** to this new stimulus. She will look longer at the picture than she had at the blank screen. She will suck more vigorously on the pacifier in her mouth, and her blood pressure and her heart rate are likely to decrease from their previous base rate. If we repeatedly present the green circle, after a time the baby will seem to grow bored with the stimulus. Perhaps it now seems familiar, even "old." We call this response **habituation**, and it is indicated by shorter looking times, less vigorous sucking, and a return to base rate for heartbeat and blood pressure. With the help of video cameras and computers, all of these subtle response changes can be closely monitored. Now, suppose we flash a new picture on the screen, a picture of a yellow circle. We are looking for a **dishabituation** response, that is, a renewed orienting response, which we will take to mean that the baby has noticed the difference between the first circle and the second, and her interest is renewed. If the baby is a newborn, we will be disappointed. Newborns show no sign of being able to tell the difference between green and yellow: They do not dishabituate to yellow after becoming habituated to green. But if the baby is 3 months old, she probably will dishabituate to the yellow stimulus, indicating to us that she can discriminate between the two colors. Thus, we have learned that newborns cannot perceive differences between most colors, but that babies differentiate major color groups by 3 months old, and that their color discrimination is as nuanced as an adult's by 4 months old (Kellman & Arterberry, 2006).

Another strategy for studying infants' abilities is to determine what they prefer to look at or listen to or taste, and so on, using what are called **preferential response paradigms**, in which multiple stimuli are presented to the infant and we record which the baby seems to respond to most. In the *preferential looking paradigm*, for instance, we present a baby with two visual stimuli, side by side, on a screen. Suppose one is a circle with black and white stripes, and the other is an entirely gray circle of the same size. Using video cameras focused on the baby's eyes, a computer can track the baby's looks to each circle. Babies tend to look more at patterns than at solid stimuli, and so our baby is likely to look more at the striped circle than the solid gray circle. Now we can use this preference to measure the baby's **visual acuity**, that is, to find the level of detail the baby can see. We can vary the stripe width for the striped circle, using finer and finer (narrower and narrower) stripes, until the baby shows no preference for the striped pattern. Because babies consistently prefer patterns, "no preference" suggests that the baby can no longer see the difference between the striped circle and the solid color circle. We have learned from such studies that newborns have substantially less visual acuity than adults (their vision is blurrier) but that by 8 months old, babies' visual acuity is adult-like. See Table 3.1 for more detailed information about infants' visual and auditory capacities and the kinds of motor abilities that correspond to these sensory developments.

TABLE 3.1 Major Milestones in Normally Developing Motor, Visual, and Auditory Processes

| AGE | MOTOR DEVELOPMENT | | VISUAL DEVELOPMENT | AUDITORY DEVELOPMENT |
	GROSS MOTOR	FINE MOTOR		
1 Month	Lifts head	Holds things placed in hands	Visual acuity: 20/600; scans edges of figures and visual objects	Alert to sounds; prefers sound of mother's voice
2 Months			Visual acuity: 20/300; shows preference for faces over objects; discriminates basic colors	
3 Months			Faces (especially mother's face) perceived as attractive; scans interiors of faces and objects	Locates where sounds come from
4 Months	Sits with support; rolls over from front to back	Visually guided reaching	Visual acuity: 20/160; smooth tracking of slowly moving objects; development of *stereopsis,* or ability to perceive depth based upon information from both left and right eyes	
5 Months				
6 Months				Coordination of vision and hearing; turns eyes to nearby sounds smoothly
7 Months	Sits without support	Transfers objects from hand to hand; plays with simple toys		
8 Months			Visual acuity: 20/20	
9 Months	Crawls	Pincer grasp	Interprets others' facial expressions	
10 Months	Stands holding on; drops and throws things			
11 Months				
12 Months	Walks holding on	Scribbles with crayon		
12–18 Months	Walks alone			
18–23 Months		Draws lines; constructs simple tower; drinks from cup using one hand		
2–3 Years	Runs, jumps, climbs; balance improves; kicks ball forward Stands on one foot briefly	Pours milk; dressing and feeding improves; builds towers of 6 blocks; turns pages in book	Oldest age at which surgical correction of crossed eyes for depth perception can be successful	
3–4 Years	Walks up stairs alternating feet; walks on tiptoes; throwing improves; buttons clothing; eats with spoon and fork	Completes simple puzzles; uses art materials, scissors; more careful in execution of art and drawing projects	Continued integration of visual-motor systems	
4–5 Years	Ties knots; dresses and undresses easily	More skillful with scissors		

SOURCE: Broderick, Patricia C. (2010). *The life span: Human development for helping professionals* (3rd ed.). Upper Saddle River, NJ: Pearson Education, Inc.

Research using habituation and preferential response paradigms has provided us with much of what we know about the infant's perceptual abilities, especially what they can see and hear. But researchers also use these methods to make inferences about what babies can understand and how they think, as you will see. Modern researchers do not always agree about what inferences to draw from such data (e.g., Cohen & Cashon, 2006), but their work has certainly stimulated a great deal of interest in looking more closely at infant development, and it has led to several challenges of Piaget's ideas. Let's consider now three interesting and important cognitive developments in infancy, combining data from both older and newer approaches.

Understanding Objects

There would be little that you and I would understand about the physical or social world if we did not have a fundamental understanding that there are objects (including human objects, such as ourselves!) with substance and constancy, occupying locations in a spatial field. To become attached to a parent and to begin the process of healthy emotional development, a baby must have some conception of the parent as a permanent, substantive object in her world. (See Chapter 4 for an account of the infant's ability to conceptualize the parent as a separate being.)

What must infants understand to "know" about objects—that is, to have an **object concept**? First, they need to know that objects have properties that can stimulate all of their senses: vision, hearing, taste, smell, and touch. For example, what they feel in their mouths as they suck a pacifier is the same as what they see when Mom or Dad holds the pacifier up in front of them. When can they make such connections? It appears that they have some capacity to do so as early as the 1st month of life. In a classic study, Meltzoff and Borton (1979) gave 1-month-olds an opportunity to suck on either a smooth pacifier or a bumpy one, without letting the infants see the pacifiers. Then, the researchers used the preferential looking paradigm to explore whether the babies had learned anything about the visual characteristics of the pacifiers that they had sucked on but had never seen. The babies looked at a split video screen. On one side was a picture of the smooth pacifier, on the other side a picture of the bumpy pacifier. A camera recorded the infants' eye movements. The babies spent more time looking at whichever pacifier they had previously sucked—suggesting that they were capable of identifying the appearance of the pacifier from their tactile experience of it. Findings like this one indicate that when young babies perceive an object in one way, they can construct some notion of the object's other perceptual characteristics. This quality of **intersensory integration** (also referred to as cross-modal matching or **intermodal perception**) is not surprising given what we now know about prenatal brain development. The development of one sensory system is influenced by the development of other systems (see the discussion of the brain in Chapter 2). Piaget (1954), without the benefit of today's research methods, assumed that intersensory integration appeared later in infancy, after babies have learned to coordinate their reflexive responses to stimulation. For example, not until about 6 weeks do babies reach up to grasp an object that they are sucking; and not until 4 to 6 months do they smoothly coordinate grasping and looking, allowing easy exploration of objects through visually guided reaching. Surely, these motor coordinations enrich a baby's understanding of objects as "packages" of perceptual characteristics, but such understanding is initiated earlier than Piaget realized.

What else must infants know to have an understanding of objects? Piaget pointed out that adults realize that objects have a separate existence from the perceiver. Think for a moment about something that is out of sight, like the sink in your bathroom. Despite your inability to see the sink at this moment, you realize that it still exists. Your perceptual processes or actions on the object are not necessary to its continuation. This quality of objects is referred to as **object permanence**: They exist apart from the perceiver.

It can be argued that to understand the permanence of objects, a child must have at least a rudimentary capacity to keep the object in mind when it is not present. To put it another way, the child must have a mental representation of the object, like your mental image of the bathroom sink. The capacity to think about things or events that are not currently stimulating our senses is called **representational thought**. Thus, if we could find out when a baby understands object permanence, we would not only know something about her object concept, but we would also know that she was capable of representational thought. Piaget invented the **hidden object test** to assess object permanence. An interesting object, like a small toy, is placed in front of a baby, within her reach. As the baby watches, we cover the object with a cloth, so that it is out of sight. What we want to know is, will the baby search for the object under the cloth, or does the baby act as if the object's disappearance means that the object no longer exists? Studies using the hidden object test, beginning with Piaget's own studies, have consistently found that infants younger than 8 to 12 months fail to search for the object, even though they have the motor skills they need to succeed much earlier (e.g., they engage in visually guided reaching by about 4 months, and they can sit without support by about 6 months). Piaget concluded that understanding object permanence has its rudimentary beginnings late in the 1st year of life and gradually improves thereafter. He also inferred that representational thought—the ability to form mental representations, such as images—is a skill that begins to develop only in the late months of the 1st year of life. Piaget's work demonstrated that representational ability improves through the 2nd year of life, until, by the end of the sensorimotor period, children not only think about objects but can mentally plan their actions, solve simple problems "all in their heads," remember past experiences, and so on. In other words, they have developed a broad capacity for thinking.

In recent years, studies using procedures such as the habituation paradigm have indicated that babies may have some understanding of object permanence, and therefore, perhaps, some representational thinking skills, much earlier in infancy. For example, Aguiar and Baillargeon (1999, 2002) showed infants a display with a doll standing to the left of one screen (see Figure 3.1). To the right of the screen was a space and then another screen. Babies watched as the doll moved toward the first screen and disappeared behind it. Even 2½-month-olds acted surprised if the doll reappeared to the right of the second screen, without ever being visible

 Infants across cultures develop an understanding of object permanence at approximately the same age, beginning around the end of the first year of life.

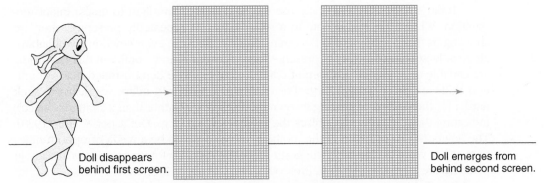

Doll disappears behind first screen.

Doll emerges from behind second screen.

FIGURE 3.1   Stimuli for a test of object permanence by Aguiar and Baillargeon.
SOURCE: Aguiar, A., & Baillargeon, R. (1999). 2.5-month-old infants' reasoning about when objects should and should not be occluded. *Cognitive Psychology*, 39, 116–157. Used with permission from Elsevier.

in the space between the screens. You and I would be surprised as well, expecting the doll to follow a normal trajectory, emerging from behind the first screen, continuing to move to the right before disappearing again behind the second screen, and then emerging at the far right. If 2½-month-olds expect hidden objects to follow that trajectory as well, perhaps young babies understand that objects continue to exist when they cannot be seen.

Studies by Baillargeon and her colleagues (see Baillargeon, 2000), as well as other infancy researchers, have created lively controversy about just when representational thinking begins (see discussions by Haith & Benson, 1998; Kagan, 2002; Mandler, 2004) and about what aspects of objects young babies are likely to represent (e.g., Kibbe & Leslie, 2011; Wilcox, Haslup, & Boas, 2010). Nonetheless, there is general agreement that thinking, and conceptual developments that are dependent on thinking, such as object permanence, gradually improve through the 1st and 2nd years of life and beyond (see Cohen & Cashon, 2006). In the next section, we will see that studies of infant memory and of babies' abilities to plan their actions indicate the same kind of gradual development.

Remembering

New research on infant memory is becoming available at a very rapid rate, stimulated by the availability of methods such as the habituation and preferential response paradigms and by the special interest of researchers who favor information processing theories of cognitive development (see Chapter 1). Storage of information, duration of storage, retrieval of stored information—these are the centerpieces of cognitive functioning from the point of view of scientists who think about the human cognitive system as akin in some ways to a computer processor. Their special interest has provided us with a much better picture today of what infants can learn and remember than we had 20 years ago. What follows is only a sampling of what we are discovering about infant memory, that is, the ability to learn and to store information.

First, memory is not just one mental function. There are different kinds of memory. Here we will describe two: **recognition** and **recall**. Recognition memory is the ability to differentiate between experiences that are new and experiences that we have had before. When you see a face across a room and say to yourself, "I've seen that person before," you are demonstrating recognition. Piaget (1952) guessed from the way babies use their reflexes that at least a primitive form of recognition is possible in earliest infancy. Babies will suck anything that touches their lips, but if they are hungry, they continue to suck only objects that have become associated with nourishment, like nipples. Thus, they show a kind of motor recognition of the nipple through their sucking.

Today's researchers typically use the habituation paradigm to assess infant recognition. When babies habituate to a stimulus that is repeatedly presented, they are showing us that the stimulus is becoming familiar. Because even newborns will habituate to at least some repeatedly presented stimuli, we are now confident that newborns are capable of recognition. Operant conditioning has also demonstrated that recognition skills are present from birth. For example, a 3-day-old infant will learn to suck harder for the reward of hearing its own mother's voice (rather than a stranger's voice), indicating that the baby recognizes the mother's voice (e.g., DeCasper & Fifer, 1980). The newborn's recognition of the mother's voice seems to be a result of opportunities to hear her voice before birth, suggesting that the capacity for recognition is already in place before birth (DeCasper & Prescott, 1984; DeCasper & Spence, 1986).

Recognition improves throughout infancy. In many instances, recognition in the newborn period fades after a few minutes or even seconds, although some studies have found much longer durations (e.g., DeCasper & Spence, 1986). If infants are 3 months old or older when they are exposed to a stimulus, they sometimes recognize it after several months of nonexposure, especially if it is a moving stimulus (e.g., Bahrick & Pickens, 1995).

Not only does the duration of recognition increase with age, but the speed with which babies habituate increases as well. Younger babies need more exposures to a stimulus than older babies before they show signs of recognition. But there are also individual differences among babies of the same age. Interestingly, how quickly babies habituate to a new stimulus is one of the few measures of infant functioning that has been found to correlate with later intelligence test performance. Apparently, recognition speed is an early indicator of the efficiency with which a child may later process information (Bornstein & Colombo, 2010).

In contrast to the early and rapid development of recognition memory, recall seems to emerge later in infancy. Recall is the ability to bring to mind an experience that has happened in the past. It is different from recognition because the to-be-remembered experience is not presently occurring, but must be mentally represented. In other words, thinking that involves mental representation, such as forming mental images, is necessary for recall. One indicator of recall is **deferred imitation**, in which children observe the actions of another on one occasion, and then imitate those actions sometime later. We should note that babies imitate some *immediate* actions as early as the newborn period. For example, if you stick out your tongue at a newborn, you are likely to see the baby's tongue protrude as well (Meltzoff & Moore, 1977), an action that is often interpreted as a reflexive response to a looming stimulus (e.g., Mandler, 2004). But soon babies will imitate other actions. If you clap your hands at a 4-month-old, she may clap her hands as well (Piaget, 1951). It seems that babies slowly work out the correspondences between their own and other people's body parts, and as they do, they extend their range of imitation. (See Box 3.2 for a possible brain mechanism that supports this process.) But immediate imitation does not indicate recall. Only if there is a time delay between the observed action and the baby's imitation of it can we say that representations in memory were necessary for the imitation.

Based on observations of his own children's behavior, Piaget believed that deferred imitation begins around the middle of the baby's 2nd year. At 16 months, for example, his daughter Jacqueline watched a visiting boy have a temper tantrum, screaming and stamping his feet in a playpen. The next day, Jacqueline did the same, only she was smiling and her foot stamping was gentle. She was not actually having a temper tantrum, but was imitating her little friend's fascinating performance (Piaget, 1962). More recent research demonstrates that infants from about 9 months of age will recall, and later imitate, actions that they have witnessed. For example, Meltzoff (1988) showed babies an interesting box, then demonstrated that pushing a button on the box would produce a beep. The next day, the babies were given the opportunity to play with the box themselves for the first time. Nine-month-old babies who had watched the button pushing the previous day were much more likely to push the button themselves than were babies who had not previously observed the action. On the whole, available research suggests that deferred imitation can begin late in the 1st year but that it does improve dramatically over the next year, both in duration and in the complexity of what can be recalled. For example, 11-month-old babies will imitate a simple action as long as 3 months later, but 20-month-olds can imitate more elaborate sequences as long as 12 months later (see Bauer, 2006). Deferred imitation is, of course, what makes observational learning, or modeling, possible (see Chapter 1). Once children can mentally represent and thus recall the actions of others, they have a cognitive skill that is critical for social learning. A toddler who has watched his big sister painting pictures might on his own open a jar of paint, dip a paintbrush into it, and then sweep the paintbrush across some available surface. His proficiency at each of these actions will be limited, but the sequence will be executed more or less correctly because he recalls his big sister's past actions.

Searching for a hidden object, which begins at about 8 months of age, can be seen as a sign not only that a child believes in the object's permanence but that the child recalls the object. A particularly important sign of such recall is the beginning of **separation anxiety**. When parents leave a young baby with another caregiver,

Box 3.2: Brain and Behavior: Mirror Neurons and Early Development

Suppose we offered a monkey a piece of food and the monkey reached out to grasp it. And suppose that at the same time, we were recording the activity of individual neurons in the monkey's motor cortex via tiny electrodes implanted in those neurons. If we were recording in the right location, we would find that certain neurons fire when the monkey executes the grasping action. Using this kind of single-cell recording technique, a team of Italian researchers discovered a remarkable group of brain cells they called mirror neurons (e.g., Rizzolatti, Fadiga, Fogassi, & Gallese, 1996). These neurons, located primarily in motor cortex, were activated (fired) not only when a monkey performed a particular action, like grasping, but also when the monkey saw someone else, a person or a monkey, perform that action on an object. These neurons appear to help monkeys understand the actions of others. Rizzolatti and Craighero (2004) explain it this way:

> Each time an individual sees an action done by another individual, neurons that represent that action are activated in the observer's premotor cortex. This automatically induced, motor representation of the observed action corresponds to that which is spontaneously generated during active action and whose outcome is known to the acting individual. Thus, the mirror system transforms visual information into knowledge (p. 172).

Do people also have mirror neurons that help them understand the actions of others? Single-cell recording is too invasive a procedure to use with healthy people, but electroencephalography and other psychophysiological techniques, such as brain imaging, can safely measure the activation of broader areas of the brain. Many studies using these methods demonstrate that parts of human motor cortex, which is activated when someone performs an action, are also activated when the individual observes someone else performing the same action. So humans, too, have mirror neurons, and they probably do for

humans what they do for monkeys. That is, they help us to understand the actions of others. But in human brains the mirror neuron system appears to be much more extensive than in monkeys (Molenberghs, Cunnington, & Mattingly, 2012), and it contributes to some capacities that are more uniquely human, such as our ability to learn how to do things by imitating the actions of others (Ferrari & Fogassi, 2012).

How could mirror neurons support the ability to imitate? It may work something like this. If you observe someone else performing an action, aspects of that experience are recorded in a group of mirror neurons. Mirror neurons can also trigger action—they have motor properties—so if these neurons encode the observed action, they can initiate our own, similar action, or help us plan such an action. Sometimes mirror neurons activate our own muscles at a minimal level even when we do not enact the full motion. For example, have you ever noticed that when you watch someone make a sad or happy face, your own facial muscles seem primed to mimic that expression?

In addition to imitation, mirror neurons appear to facilitate other skills that begin in infancy and early childhood, such as the development of gaze following, intention understanding, language, and empathy (see Rizzolatti & Craighero, 2004; Triesch, Jasso, & Deak, 2007). Their special property of both recording others' actions and participating in the observer's own actions can provide neural support to all of these skills. Interestingly, the abilities that mirror neurons may facilitate are often the ones that are poorly developed in children with autism spectrum disorders (see *Focus on Developmental Psychopathology* in Chapter 2), and some studies suggest that neuronal abnormalities in autistic children do include the development of fewer or less active mirror neurons (Enticott et al., 2012; Oberman & Ramachandran, 2007). Research on mirror neurons is truly in its infancy, but it promises to open a window on the development of both typical and atypical development of social and cognitive skills (see Ferrari & Fogassi, 2012; Glenberg, 2011).

the baby typically does not seem to miss the absent parents or to mourn their loss while they are gone. When they are out of sight, they seem to be out of mind. But in the second half of the 1st year, at about 8 months for most babies, leaving a child with another caregiver may be more difficult. The baby may continue for some time to watch for the missing parents, to cry or fuss, and to generally act distressed. Bouts of separation anxiety are usually of fairly short duration at first, but tend to increase in length, suggesting that the child's ability to recall the parents is increasing in duration. An 18- to 24-month-old left with a babysitter might show signs of anxiety repeatedly throughout the parents' absence. Of course, many factors contribute to separation anxiety: the familiarity of the alternate caregiver and of the surroundings, the quality of the infant's relationship to the parents, the infant's temperament (see Chapter 4), and so on. But the consistency with which babies around the world begin showing separation distress at about 8 months is attributable to advances in basic cognitive skills such as recall and object permanence (Kagan, Kearsley, & Zelazo, 1978; McBride & DiCero, 1990).

Such related cognitive and social developments in the second half of the infant's first year also correspond to important brain developments. Rapid myelination of axons increases the efficiency of several brain areas, especially in the frontal lobes, which support thought processes like planning; in the hippocampus, which is important for memory; and in the cerebellum, which helps control movement and balance (e.g., Bell & Fox, 1992; Pujol et al., 2006; Richmond & Nelson, 2007). As a result, while representational processes like recall improve, so do motor skills, advancing the infant's capacity to explore the environment and to enrich her understanding of objects. Thus, biological, cognitive, motor and social developments are intricately interdependent.

Having and Inferring Intentions

If we intentionally act, choosing to pick up a fork rather than a spoon, searching through a closet for just the right outfit to wear, or planning a presentation at work, we are thinking about what we do before we do it. Very little conscious effort may be involved in some intentional acts, but at least some thought is required. Like the other cognitive skills we have examined, the ability to intend to do something has important consequences not just for intellectual performance but for social interactions as well. A child who can choose whether to cry to call for attention, for example, is likely to be treated differently than one who can only reflexively cry in response to discomfort. Obviously, the development of intentional action is related to the development of self-control and decision making, which we will discuss at greater length later in this and other chapters.

Having Intentions

When does intentional action begin? Piaget (1952) assumed that infants' earliest behaviors are entirely unintentional and are typically based on reflexive responses to incoming stimulation and on the need to act, that is, to repetitively exercise one's reflexes. By 4 to 8 months, infants' behaviors have expanded as a result of constant differentiation and integration of the original reflexes, according to Piaget, and now a baby has a large repertoire of behavioral responses to stimuli. If one of these behaviors accidentally produces an interesting event, a child is likely to notice the effect and repeat the action, as if she were hoping to repeat the effect. Piaget called this **making interesting sights last**. He did not consider it to be intentional behavior, but a precursor of intentional behavior. In fact, it appears to be simple operant conditioning. After a behavior occurs, there is a reinforcing event, and the behavior is likely to be repeated. But there is a twist. Piaget described infants as appearing somewhat reflective, as if they had noticed the connection between their action and the outcome, and they were trying to make it happen again. Modern researchers have observed similar sequences in infants as young as 3 months old (Rovee-Collier & Barr, 2001). When a mobile hanging over a baby's crib is tied to a baby's foot, the child will soon learn to shake her foot to make the mobile move. At some point, the baby appears to notice the connection, as if she were having an insight, and the baby shakes her foot more vigorously afterward.

From these first inklings of intentional behavior, infants move to more clearly intentional action in that magical time, the last several months of the 1st year. By 8 to 12 months, Piaget reported that babies will engage in **means–end behavior**: They will divert their attention from a goal, such as grasping a toy, to produce another action that will help achieve the goal. For example, a baby might try to grasp a rattle that is behind a clear Plexiglas screen. When her hand touches the screen, the baby redirects her attention to the screen, perhaps pushing it aside, before focusing again on the rattle. Younger babies simply keep reaching for the rattle and failing. Their behavior seems more controlled by the stimulus of the rattle than by their own plans. Thus, again, it appears that a behavior that requires mental representation, planning, begins in the 8- to 12-month period. Newer studies also indicate that infants may do some fairly complex sizing up of such situations. Willatts (1989) found that 9-month-olds would put aside a barrier and then pull a cloth to get an out-of-reach toy resting on the cloth. But when the toy was not on the cloth, babies tended to simply play with the barrier, as though they realized there was no point in pulling on the cloth.

More sophisticated intentional control of behavior emerges in the 2nd year. Whereas a 10-month-old typically will use only previously practiced actions as means to an end, 12- to 18-month-olds begin to actively invent new variations on their actions to fit the situation, trying out one variation after another. By 24 months, toddlers' control of their mental representations is advanced enough that they will mentally invent new means to an end. Rather than trying this and trying that, sometimes they solve a problem by quietly studying the situation first, and producing a useful means to an end on the first try.

The beginning of intentional behavior by the end of the 1st year is evident in babies' communicative behaviors. When a younger baby repeats an action that has attracted attention in the past, such as patting Mommy's cheek, the child may be doing no more than "making interesting sights last." But by 8 to 12 months, most babies are using some of their behaviors, including some vocalizations, not just to attract attention but as a communicative means to an end. For example, a typical 12-month-old might make a wailing sound while intently looking at her father. When he looks in her direction, she extends her hand in an urgent reach, apparently indicating a toy that she would like retrieved. It is difficult not to interpret such complex means–end behavior as intentional communication (Golinkoff, 1983).

Intentionally controlling our own behavior and thought—setting goals, determining what we will pay attention to, and choosing to make one response rather than another—are among a set of cognitive processes that researchers today refer to as **executive functions (EFs)** (see Box 3.3). These functions heavily engage areas of the prefrontal cortex, which as we noted earlier, shows maturational gains late in the first year.

Inferring Others' Intentions

As babies are developing intentions of their own, what do they understand about the intentions of others? Researchers make a distinction between a child's understanding of human **agency** and of human **intention**. *Agency* refers to the ability to act without an external trigger. People and animals have agency because they can act without being pushed or "launched" by some other force, whereas objects require launching. *Intention* is an internal mental state, such as a plan or a desire, that is the source of an action. Infants begin to understand agency by the end of the 1st year. Just trying to get other people to do things for her, like the baby described in the last paragraph, suggests that a baby has some sense that others are agents. Understanding that other people have intentions, desires, feelings, and so on, and inferring what those intentions might be, appear to be much more difficult achievements. As you will see in the discussion of the preoperational stage, understanding intentions is part of developing a **theory of mind**, and it is a complex and long-term process (e.g., Sodian, 2011).

Yet, as with other cognitive skills, there appear to be preliminary developments in the understanding of intentions by the end of the 1st year. Using a habituation task, Woodward (1998) found some apparent awareness of the goal-directedness (intentionality) of human action even in babies as young as 6 months. In her study, babies saw an actor's arm reach for one of two toys that were side-by-side on a platform. Say, for example, that the arm reached for the toy on the left. The sequence was repeated until the babies habituated. Then, the position of the toys was switched, so that the toy that had been on the left was now on the right. The babies now witnessed one of two events. In the first event, the actor reached for the same toy as before, but the actor's arm had to reach in a different direction (to the right in our example) because the toys had been switched. In other words, the actor's goal remained the same—to pick up the same toy. In the second event, the actor reached for a new toy that was now in the original location (on the left in our example). Babies dishabituated more to the second event, as though they were surprised by the change in goal. The change in the direction of movement in the

Box 3.3: The Development of Executive Functions: The Mind in Charge

Suppose you see this word: *Green*. And suppose I ask you to tell me what the word says. Your response would be immediate: You would automatically read the word. Now suppose that I ask you to tell me the color of the ink the word is printed in. Your response in this case would probably be a little slower and would require more effort. Most people feel that they have to inhibit the automatic tendency to read the color named by the word in order to name the color of the ink. This kind of voluntary inhibition of a dominant response is an example of *executive functions (EFs)* at work. EFs are ". . . a set of abilities required to effortfully guide behavior toward a goal, especially in nonroutine situations" (Banich, 2009, p. 89). In other words, they are the cognitive skills that allow us to control and regulate our attention and behavior, making cognitive tasks such as planning and problem solving possible (see Zelazo, Muller, Frye, & Marcovitch, 2003; Fuhs & Day, 2011).

The three fundamental skills most often described as EFs are **working memory**, **self-regulation** (or inhibitory control), and **cognitive flexibility**. The color naming task above, which is a version of the widely used "Stroop Task," requires all of these skills. First, in order to name the color of the ink, you must hold in mind the goal. *Working memory* is the part of our cognitive system that holds information that we are actively thinking about at the moment. You can also think of it as "short-term memory." Consider Piaget's claim that a preschooler's thinking is initially "centered," tending to focus on one thought at a time. A modern version of this idea re-interprets centering as a working memory limitation: A preschooler's working memory has a very limited capacity (e.g., Case, 1985). A simple way to test working memory capacity is to use a digit span test: Present a series of digits and ask a child to say the digits back in the correct order. Four-year-olds can generally recall 2 to 3 digits correctly, 12-year-olds about 6 digits, and average adults about 7 digits. Estimates for younger children are harder to validate, but 2-year-olds seem to be able to hold in mind only about 1 digit (e.g., Cowan, 2001; Gathercole, 1998). Infants and toddlers do seem to be somewhat handicapped by the limitations of their working memories.

The Stroop Test clearly requires *self–regulation* or inhibitory control: the ability to prevent yourself from making a dominant or automatic response and/or to make yourself perform a nondominant response (Cameron Ponitz et al., 2008; Rueda et al., 2005). Choosing to pay attention to the color of the ink requires you to deliberately ignore distractions and inhibit the tendency to read the word. Finally, the Stroop Test makes you purposefully shift your goals or attention from what you are accustomed to, those dominant expectations and responses, to different ones, which is the hallmark of *cognitive flexibility* (e.g., McClelland & Cameron, 2012).

The three aspects of executive functioning we have described are difficult to separate (see Zhou, Chen, & Main, 2012). Taking charge of your own behavior in a goal directed way seems to require all three at once. As a result, tasks that researchers use to test any one of these skills in children typically involve the others to some degree, just like the Stroop Test. For example, do you remember the game "Simon Says?" To play, one person acts as a guide, and everyone else is supposed to do what the guide says (e.g., "touch your elbow") but ONLY if the instruction is preceded by "Simon says." More complex versions of this game are often used to assess self-regulation, but they also tap working memory and cognitive flexibility. In one version, "Head, Shoulders, Knees, Toes" (Cameron Ponitz et al., 2008) children follow the directions of the guide as in Simon Says, but the rules require that children do the opposite of what the guide says. When the guide says touch your head, the rule is to touch your toes and vice versa. When the guide says touch your shoulders, the rule is to touch your knees and vice versa. For children to be successful, their working memories must keep the rules available; children must inhibit their dominant responses (to do what the words actually say to do) in order to follow the rules; and they must be cognitively flexible just to pay attention to the directions while following the rules (McClelland & Cameron, 2012).

Executive functions typically improve substantially from ages 2 to 5, and studies in several countries, including the United States, Taiwan, China, and South Korea, find that preschoolers' performance on tests of executive functioning predicts their later academic progress (see McClelland & Cameron, 2012). The improvement of executive functions during the preschool years seems to be important for the development of many other social and cognitive skills, such as theory of mind skills (e.g., Carlson, Moses, & Claxton, 2004). But the causal influences seem to work both ways: Other developments in these years help improve executive functioning. For example, as children gain skill at using language, their self-regulation skills also advance. Vygotsky and others have argued that language in the form of private speech is especially important for the development of self-control (Vygotsky & Luria, 1930; see *Vygotsky's Sociocultural Theory*, this chapter).

Remember that influences on development are often bidirectional. Inter-relationships among causal processes make development very complex, but they can also provide a special benefit to helping professionals. It is often possible to make improvements in multiple skill areas by focusing on one or two areas that are intimately tied to all of the rest. So, for example, in the *Applications* section of this chapter, you will read about an intervention called "Tools of the Mind" that uses teacher-guided role play (focusing on theory of mind skills and language practice) to improve children's executive functions. This intervention helps children make gains in self-regulation, cognitive flexibility, and problem solving in general.

first event did not seem to be experienced as particularly new or important. Rather, it was the change in goal that the babies noticed. The same study done with an inanimate rod "reaching" toward the toys did not produce the same results. The babies seemed to expect goal-directedness from humans, but they did not expect it from an inanimate rod. The results of Woodward's study suggest that although full understanding of human intentions may take a long time, babies appear to have a rudimentary sense that there are significant differences between humans and other objects as early as 6 months.

PRESCHOOLERS' COGNITION: THE PREOPERATIONAL STAGE

By the age of 2, children have moved beyond the limits of sensorimotor activity to become thinkers. Instead of responding to the world primarily by connecting sensation to action, constantly exercising and adapting reflexive patterns of behavior, children can engage the world on the plane of thought. They understand that objects exist apart from their own perceptions and actions. They can call to mind previously experienced events. They can plan and execute complex behaviors, even behaviors they have not tried before, and they know that humans, unlike objects, are agents of action whose behavior is goal directed. Whereas there are precursors to most or all of these skills even in early infancy, and scientists argue about when the earliest representations actually occur (e.g., Cohen & Cashon, 2006), the flowering of thinking in the 2nd year of life is indisputable. Among the abilities that toddlers' thinking permits is the use of **symbols** (Piaget, 1962). *Symbols* are stand-ins for other things. Words are symbols; so are the props used in pretend play when they stand for something else, the way a broom stands for a horse when a child gallops around "riding" the broom. To use and understand such symbols, children must be able to mentally represent the things being symbolized. As babies' representational skills grow, especially over the 2nd year, language skill and pretend play begin to blossom.

This toddler is learning to use symbols, connecting words and pictures that represent objects in his world.

In this section, we will highlight some of the cognitive developments of the preschool years that are launched as the infancy period ends. You will find that Piaget, although celebrating the accomplishments of what he called the "preoperational" or prelogical years, also identified many limitations of children's early thought. You will also learn that in recent years developmental scientists have focused heavily on exploring the limitations that Piaget identified. Sometimes, the newer data suggest that preschoolers possess greater skill than Piaget may have realized, and some of the newer findings have helped us to specify step-by-step changes in some of the abilities that Piaget first described. You will also see that many significant changes in cognitive functioning through the preschool years are conceptualized by modern researchers as grounded in the development of executive functions (see Box 3.3).

Understanding Numbers

Piaget (1952) launched the systematic study of children's number skills by inventing the **number conservation task**. A set of discrete items, let's say five candies, is laid out in a neatly spaced line. Below the first set is a second set, laid out the same way, with the candies in each row matched one to one. A child is asked if the two rows have the same number or whether one or the other has more candies. Typically, 3- and 4-year-olds recognize that the two rows have the same number of candies. But when the researcher then changes the appearance of the second row by spreading out the candies, preschoolers usually think that the number has changed along with the appearance of the row. Most frequently, they say that the longer row now has more candy. Even if they count the candies and report that each has five, they believe that the longer row has more. Do they really believe that? They seem to. If you ask them which row they would rather have to eat, they will choose the longer row!

Endless debate has swirled around the meaning of preschoolers' failure on this number conservation task. Piaget felt that children were revealing some fundamental characteristics of preoperational thought. Most important, preoperational thought tends to be centered or focused on one salient feature of an experience or event at a time, a characteristic referred to as **centration**. In a sense, young thinkers can think about only one thing at a time. In the number conservation task, when they look at the rows of candies, preschoolers focus on the differences in length, but they ignore the differences in density. If they noticed both, especially the transformations that occurred in both as the second row was reconfigured, they might recognize that as the length of the row increased, the density of the row decreased, so that the number of candies stayed the same despite the increased length. Because their thought is centered, Piaget argued, preoperational children tend to link observations in serial order, rather than discovering and representing the more complex relationships among them. In the number conservation task, even when children notice both the change in length and the change in density of the second row, they observe these changes serially, and they do not recognize the reciprocal relationship between them. All in all, the contents of preoperational thought tend to be limited to the most salient perceptual characteristics. Young children have trouble recognizing "underlying realities" (Flavell et al., 1993). For example, children fail to realize that the number of candies is conserved even when they are moved around, because they do not take into account all the relevant observations at one time. As a result, young children do not discover the relationships among the facts, and they draw conclusions that to adults are quite illogical.

Piaget argued that as children interact with the world and practice representing the events they observe, their thinking becomes more efficient, and eventually they are able to decenter, that is, to take into account multiple pieces of information simultaneously, a process referred to as **decentration**. As a result, important relationships among their observations can be discovered and represented, and their thinking becomes more logical and sensible from an adult's point of view. Piaget found that improvements in children's thinking moved forward rapidly in the years from 5 to 7, so that most children were successful on tasks such as number conservation by about age 7.

Newer research on children's understanding of numbers emphasizes how much preschoolers do know about numbers, even though they still fail Piaget's number conservation task. Even newborns appear to discriminate differences between small numbers; they will habituate to displays of two items, but then dishabituate to a display of three items (Antell & Keating, 1983). Five-month-olds may even have some implicit understanding of simple addition and subtraction. If they watch one doll placed behind a screen, and then a second doll placed behind the same screen, babies seem surprised if there is only one doll there when the screen is removed. They are not surprised if there are two dolls (e.g., Wynn, 1992).

In exploring the number skills of preschoolers, Gelman and her colleagues (e.g., Gelman & Gallistel, 1978; see also Gelman, 1982; Gelman & Williams, 1998) found that 2- to 3-year-olds have at least implicit understanding of many fundamental counting principles. For example, they know that counting requires the "one-to-one" principle: one number for one item. Such young children sometimes do mistakenly recount items, but they seem to realize that recounting is not really acceptable. Between 3 and 5 years, children can count the same set of items in versatile order, starting once with the item on the left, another time with the item on the right, and so forth. Gelman calls this the "order-irrelevance principle." She has even found that children as young as 3 can sometimes remain focused on number despite changes in the length and density of rows.

In a series of studies using "magic number games," Gelman showed children two plates, each with a row of toy mice, two mice on one plate, and three mice on the other. For some children, the rows of mice were of equal length but of unequal density; for other children, the rows of mice were of unequal length but equal density. First, the children were trained to pick the "winner" plate (the one with three mice) by giving them lots of trials and telling them whether they were right or wrong. Once they had learned to pick the correct plate without error, the researcher surreptitiously changed the appearance of the plates. For example, if the rows of mice had been of equal length, they were changed to be of equal density. Children tended to register surprise when the changed plates were revealed, but they still correctly picked the winners. Thus, it was clear that they had learned to select the correct plate on the basis of number, not on the basis of length or density differences. It appears that under the right circumstances, young children can pay attention to "underlying realities," although their ability to do so is quite fragile and easily disrupted. The same children who succeeded in the magic number games still failed Piaget's classic number conservation tasks.

Gelman's magic number games are characteristic of many of the tasks that modern researchers have designed to explore the apparent limitations of preschoolers' thinking. They are different from Piaget's tasks in that they provide simple instructions, and they often do not require verbal responses or explanations. They also establish different criteria for granting children some knowledge or skill. Piaget's criteria were conservative. He wanted children to demonstrate that they had complete mastery of a skill or concept, such as the concept of number, so that it could not be disrupted by countersuggestions or by superficial transformation, before he granted that the skill was present. He often required that children be able to give sensible explanations of their right answers before he credited them with true understanding (Haith & Benson, 1998). Modern researchers tend to make minimal demands on children and to grant them the presence of a skill even when children's success can be easily disrupted by increased demands. The data are not in dispute, but the interpretation of the data is (see Geary, 2006). One approach to resolving the dispute is to assume that concepts such as number are understood by children in ever-increasing depth and breadth. What today's researchers often focus on is specifying what those levels of understanding are, and what kinds of experience help children to advance from one level to another (Bidell & Fischer, 1997; Blewitt, 1994; Haith & Benson, 1998).

Studies by Siegler and Ramani (2008; Ramani & Siegler, 2008) are good examples of research that focuses on how experience influences change in preschoolers' number understanding. They began by noting that at the beginning of first grade children are very different with regard to how much they know about numbers. For example, some children (especially higher SES children) can do a good job on "number line estimation." That just means that if we draw a line, and mark one end with a "1" and the other end with a "10," these children can figure out approximately where a 7 should go on the line. To do this right, a child has to have some implicit knowledge of the relative size of different numbers (e.g., 4 is twice as big as 2). It's an important understanding, one that is foundational for acquiring other math skills. Lower SES children are less likely to start school with this skill than higher SES children. Siegler and Ramani hypothesized that the difference is due to how often higher versus lower SES families play counting and number games with their children, including board games that involve numbers. They developed a number board game, a little like *Chutes and Ladders,* where the object of the game is to advance along a series of 10 squares, each marked by a number. If lower SES preschoolers played the number board game repeatedly over a 2-week period, sure enough the children's "number line estimation" skills improved dramatically in comparison to children who played a similar game that did not include numbers.

The effectiveness of the Siegler and Ramani (2008) game highlights the value of play for cognitive development in early childhood. Toddlers and young preschoolers spontaneously engage in **exploratory play**. They manipulate objects, check out their properties, sort and organize them. In so doing, children learn not only about the properties of objects, but also about spatial relations, numerical relations, categorical relations, and so on. For example, Mix, Moore, and Holcomb (2011) quite elegantly demonstrated the direct benefits of children's exploratory play for learning about number equivalence. First, they tested 3-year-olds for their ability to match one set of items (e.g., 3 turtles) with an equivalent set of other items (e.g., 3 flowers). Only children who failed the original test were included in the remainder of the study. Mix et al. (2011) gave the children sets of toys to take home and play with over the course of 6 weeks, with no instructions regarding what to do with the toys.

Parents were asked to make sure the toys were continuously available and to keep a log of what children did with them. One group of children received "objects with slots" that made one-to-one correspondence play easy, such as six balls and a muffin tin—the balls fit just right into the six slots of the muffin tin. Another group of children received "objects with objects," such as six balls and six toy frogs (see Figure 3.2). Children who were given "objects with slots" engaged in much more one-to-one play as reported in parent logs, and when they were tested after 6 weeks, many of these children showed substantial improvement on the numerical equivalence matching test. Clearly, play is a medium for learning.

FIGURE 3.2 **Examples of toys for one-to-one correspondence play from Mix, Moore, & Holcomb.**
SOURCE: Mix, K. S., Moore, J. A., Holcomb, E. (2011). One-to-one play promotes numerical equivalence concepts. *Journal of Cognition and Development*, 12, 468. Used with permission from Taylor & Francis.

We have learned a great deal about children's number understanding since Piaget's early work, but many of Piaget's characterizations of the limitations of preoperational thought remain useful. Preschoolers do seem to make appearance-based conclusions, and they often miss the deeper significance of events. Also, their thinking often does seem especially affected by singular, salient dimensions of a situation. However, most researchers recognize that such limitations aptly describe young children's abilities sometimes, but not always, and that experience, especially how adults interact with young children, can be an important factor in how early abilities develop.

Understanding the Mind

Piaget (1926; Piaget & Inhelder, 1956) pioneered the investigation of children's understanding of other people's mental processes by studying perspective-taking skills in preschoolers. In his "three mountains task," a three-dimensional model of three mountains was shown to children from several different angles. Children then had to select a picture of how the scene looked to them, as well as a picture of how it looked to another observer on a different side of the display. Until about age 7, children tended to select the same picture both times, suggesting that they believed that other observers shared their perspective. Piaget believed children's poor perspective-taking skills reflected **preoperational egocentrism**. Because preschoolers can think about only one thing at a time, they are centered on their own perspective and have no awareness of the possibility of a different perspective.

Young children often appear to be egocentric in their encounters with others. A young girl may suggest that Daddy would like a dollhouse for his birthday. She assumes that he wants what she wants. When parents eagerly ask for information about what happened in nursery school, their son fails to respond, as if he cannot fathom what it is the parents do not know. If he knows what happened today, surely they do too. During a telephone conversation, when her grandmother asks a toddler what she's going to wear to her birthday party, the child responds "This!" and points to the dress she is wearing, as if her grandmother can see what she can see. These are all typical examples of a failure to take another person's perspective.

Today, researchers see perspective taking (or its failure) as aspects of one's *theory of mind* or "naive psychology," that is, the understanding that people's behavior is a function of their internal, subjective mental states—such as desires, emotions and beliefs. Such understanding is critical for developing satisfactory relationships with others. We have already seen that in the 1st year of infancy children begin to have a sense that humans are agents of action and that others' (and perhaps their own) behaviors can be goal directed (intentional). Among the earliest signs that children have some notion of the existence of mental states is their use of "mental" words. Words for emotions or desires, such as *need, feel,* and *want,* tend to occur as early as age 2, and words such as *think, forget,* and *remember* that describe cognitive functions are often used by age 3 (Huttenlocher & Smiley, 1990; Ruffman, Slade, & Crowe, 2002). What concepts underlie these words we do not really know. It is likely that they are not the same as an adult's, but clearly the young preschooler is beginning to assign some meaning to these words.

Thus, in the early preschool years, children have a sense that they and others have mental states, such as thoughts, desires, feelings, and plans. Piaget's perspective-taking work focused on what children infer those states to be, and he found that preschoolers usually assume that others' mental states match their own. Newer work has expanded the focus of research to address questions such as what do children understand about how people acquire information, when do they understand that mental states may or may not match reality, and do children correctly impute to others some mental states before other mental states. There is some dispute about these issues (see Moll & Meltzoff, 2011), but it does appear that children very gradually build such understandings. For example, as early as age 2, a child can understand that if she is looking at a picture of a cat and you are standing opposite her, looking at the back of the picture, you will not be able to see the cat. In other words, the child can figure out that even if she can see something, you may not be able to see it. This is sometimes called "Level 1 visual perspective taking," when a child knows whether an object can or cannot be seen from a particular perspective. However, suppose we place the picture of the cat on a table, face up, so that the child can see it right side up and you, sitting across from the child, see it upside down. At age 2, the child cannot understand that you have a different perspective on the cat, and she assumes that you also see it right side up. By age 4 to 5, in this simple situation, the child will be able to attribute a different visual perspective to you. She still will not be able to compute any kind of complex perspective difference, such as Piaget's three mountains task requires, but she can understand that someone else might see the *same picture* differently from herself (e.g., Masangkay et al., 1974; Moll & Tomasello, 2006). This is sometimes called "Level 2 visual perspective taking."

When children start to pass tests of Level 2 visual perspective taking, they also begin to reason more accurately about what other people may *desire, believe,* or *know,* although here again, they seem to move along gradually, making progress from about age 3½ to 5½ (Wellman, Fang, & Peterson, 2011). Middle class American children tend to understand that people have *diverse desires* sooner than they understand that they have *diverse beliefs.* And comprehending that others may have *false beliefs* is an even more difficult concept (see Table 3.2 for a description of these abilities as measured on the "ToM Scale").

TABLE 3.2 A Brief Description of Tasks in the Theory of Mind (ToM) Scale

TASK	DESCRIPTION
Diverse desires	Child judges that two persons (the child vs. someone else) have different desires about the same object
Diverse beliefs	Child judges that two persons (the child vs. someone else) have different beliefs about the same object, when the child does not know which belief is true or false
Knowledge access	Child sees what is in a box and judges (yes-no) the knowledge of another person who does not see what is in the box
Contents false belief	Child judges another person's false belief about what is in a distinctive container when child knows what is in the container
Hidden emotion	Child judges that a person can feel one thing but display a different emotion

SOURCE: Wellman, H. M., Fang, F. M., & Peterson, C. C. (2011). Sequential progressions in a theory of mind scale: Longitudinal perspectives. *Child Development, 82,* 783.

Children's performance on **false belief tasks** illustrates how difficult they find it to escape their own perspective when it comes to what they know. In such tasks, one person has correct knowledge of a situation, but another person (or the same person at another time) has incorrect knowledge, or a "false belief." Suppose a child is aware that a box of candy has been removed from its original location and is now hidden in a cabinet. The child is asked where a second person, let's call him Sam, will look for the candy. Even though the child knows Sam was not present for the hiding, the child does not attribute a false belief to Sam but assumes that Sam will search in the appropriate hiding place, as if Sam must know what the child knows to be true (e.g., Wimmer & Perner, 1983; see also Wellman, 1990; Wellman, Cross, & Watson, 2001). In fact, until age 4 or 5 children have trouble realizing that they themselves have not always known what they know now (Gopnik & Astington, 1988). If they open a candy box expecting to find candy and are surprised to find something else instead, say pencils, they will later say that they knew before they opened the box that the pencils were there.

The trouble young children have figuring out what other people know, or need to know, is reflected in their attempts to communicate and can be responsible for both the charm and sometimes the spectacular failure of their efforts. Here are some samples from children's attempts to describe their favorite recipes (Martel, 1974):

"Skabbetti":   First you decide what it will be tonight—sausages or meatballs. When your father tells you which one, then you cook. (p. 1)

"Popcorn":   Put the popcorn seeds in the popcorn bowl and plug it in the plug hold—and get the toaster out of the way. . . . If your brother takes the lid off, popcorn go zinging all over the kitchen . . . POW! POW! POW! (p. 45)

"Banilla Cake":   1 cake stuff; 2 eggs (But on "Sesame Street" they put 8 eggs in a cake. I always watch "Love American Style" after "Sesame Street"); a drop of milk; 7 of those little silver baseballs for on the top. Put every single thing you have into a mother-size pan—a little one wouldn't do. . . . Put it in the oven department of the stove. Make it as hot as a coffee pot. Pretty soon it will come popping right out! Eat it when the news comes on. (p. 34)

(*Source:* Martel, J. G. (1974). *Smashed potatoes: A kid's-eye view of the kitchen.* Boston: Houghton Mifflin. (p. 34))

Most research on children's theory of mind indicates that, on one hand, preschoolers are less egocentric than Piaget inferred based on his very complex perspective-taking task, but that on the other hand, he was on target in assuming that taking another's perspective and understanding the limits of one's own perspective are difficult, and sometimes impossible, tasks for young children. The implications for children's social development are far-reaching. For example, when toddlers want to grab a dog's tail or to chase a ball into the street, they do not understand that the adults who restrain them want something different. Disciplinary action by others is frustrating to a 2-year-old, because she does not get what she wants of course, but also because she does not understand that other people's desires are different from her own. Three-year-olds better understand that others may not share their own desires or preferences. They might accept, for example, that their parents like coffee even though they themselves do not. But when two people have different beliefs, even 3- and 4-year-olds are often mystified (Flavell, Mumme, Green, & Flavell, 1992). For example, 3-year-olds found it difficult to comprehend that a girl in a story could think a toothbrush was hers when another child thought it was his!

Finally, when children's own emotions are strongly involved, taking another's perspective seems especially difficult. Apparently the salience of one's own perspective, especially in an emotionally charged situation, can undermine the child's fragile understanding of the differences between her own mental state and that of another person. For example, one 6-year-old girl, who in many situations was quite capable of understanding that others have different feelings and motives than she, was furious whenever she lost a board game or any other competition, calling her competitor "mean." Her own desire to win was so overwhelmingly salient that she assumed that it was shared by others, and that any interference with her success was simply mean-spiritedness!

How do young children overcome their problems with perspective taking and build a more realistic theory of mind? Piaget credited two processes: first, the gradual improvement in a child's ability to hold in mind multiple ideas at the same time (decentering), and second, the continual give and take of social interaction in which a child repeatedly confronts feedback from other people, indicating that others do not always share the child's feelings, desires, or knowledge. Children find it difficult to assimilate such feedback, but gradually they accommodate their views of others until they can conceive of independent mental states.

Modern researchers have proposed other explanations. Some suggest that perspective taking is benefited by advances in executive functions (see Box 3.3). For example, the ability to intentionally inhibit a dominant response in order to perform a less salient response might help children to respond correctly on false belief tasks. Children with poor inhibitory skills might find it very difficult to suppress saying what they *know* to be true in order to report their own or another person's false belief (e.g., Sabbagh, Xu, Carlson, Moses, & Lee, 2006).

In line with Piaget, other theorists emphasize the importance of children's experience in social interactions, especially if it involves conversation about different viewpoints (see Harris, 2006). Evidence is accumulating to support this view, including cross cultural evidence. For example, children's theory of mind skills advance more quickly when mothers frequently engage them in turn-taking conversations and when they talk about mental states (e.g., "Even though you were happy and excited when we decided to go to the party, Sam was unhappy because his Mom said he couldn't stay very long.") (Ensor & Hughes, 2008; Peterson & Slaughter, 2003). Also, young children who have siblings, especially older siblings, make more rapid progress than other children (e.g., McAlister & Peterson, 2006), apparently because they frequently engage in conversation about who believes, knows, and wants what. Siblings may also be important because, like peers, they play together. Many studies have found a link between social **pretend play** and theory of mind development. Pretend play, or make believe, generally begins at about age 2. It is a kind of "as if" behavior, where objects or people may be treated as symbols, "as if" they were something or someone else (Fein, 1981). In social pretend play, children enact roles, simulating the actions or characteristics of other people and interacting with other children playing other roles. As children's language skills improve, they may spend a good deal of time planning and negotiating who will do what and when. The more young children engage in social pretend play, the more rapidly they advance on theory of mind skills (see Pellegrini, 2009; and the Applications, this chapter).

Further support for the importance of social interaction comes from cross-cultural research on how quickly children acquire theory of mind skills. Shahaeian, Peterson, Slaughter, and Wellman (2011) found that middle class children in China and Iran made somewhat slower progress on theory of mind tasks than children in Australia or the United States, even though, at least in China, children's executive functions progress a bit more quickly than in the United States (see Sabbagh et al., 2006). In China and Iran, middle class parents endorse collectivist child-rearing goals such as teaching respect for elders, teaching that children should defer to parental authority and not express opposing views and that children should curb their individual desires when they conflict with family needs. In the United States and Australia, middle class parents tend to encourage more independence in their children and are more likely to endorse discussions and negotiations of family rules. Shahaeian et al. suggest that "middle class preschoolers growing up in Iran or China may well have less chance than those being reared in Australia or the United States to be exposed to opinion diversity during family conversations or disputes," (p. 1241) perhaps making it harder to learn about differences in perspective.

Nonetheless, children in all cultures eventually achieve basic perspective taking skills. You will see in Chapter 6 that expertise in perspective taking continues to develop throughout middle childhood and continues to depend on, and to influence, the quality of social interactions.

Understanding Symbolic Artifacts

When and how do children make sense of the many symbols that humans use to communicate? A symbol, remember, stands for something other than itself. In the next section we will look at the development of language, or linguistic symbols, which are quite arbitrary (e.g., the word *elephant* bears no resemblance to the real thing that it symbolizes), but first let's consider more analogical symbols, such as pictures or maps or scale models, which DeLoache (1999; DeLoache, Miller, & Pierrovutsakos, 1998; Uttal, Liu, & DeLoache, 2006) calls **symbolic artifacts**. Because these kinds of symbols are often similar to the things they represent, one might think that children would find them easier to interpret than words, but in fact the reverse may be true. DeLoache suggests that young children have difficulty with symbolic artifacts because of their dual nature: They are both concrete objects themselves and symbols for other things. To understand a symbolic artifact, a child must mentally represent the same thing in two ways at once, and as we have already seen, young children often have difficulty holding more than one idea in mind simultaneously. Perhaps as a result, children often understand less about things such as pictures or models than adults may think. Research on children's understanding of pictures indicates that if a picture is realistic, like a photograph, 9-month-olds attempt to pick up the object in the picture. Eighteen-month-olds are indifferent to whether a picture is right side up or upside down, and even 2-year-olds often cannot pick which picture represents a real object. Beilin (1999) found that even older preschoolers sometimes attribute the qualities of the object that is depicted to the picture itself, thinking, for example, that a photograph of an ice cream cone will be cold.

Young preschoolers have similar trouble with television (e.g., Troseth & DeLoache, 1996). When children younger than age 2½ watch a doll being hidden in a room on a video screen, the children will not be able to figure out where the doll is when they search for it in the real room. These children are able to respond directly to what they see on the screen. For example, they can follow the action and imitate what the actors do. However, they have trouble understanding that what they are watching symbolizes something that is happening somewhere else, other than on the screen. Curiously, children's performance improves if the edges of the video screen are covered and children believe that they are witnessing a scene through a window into a room. Then, even a 2-year-old will be able to find a doll hidden in a room after watching the hiding "through the window"! In this situation, the child does not have to perceive the screen events as symbolic of something happening elsewhere.

Children have even more trouble with scale models. DeLoache (1987) showed children a scale model of a room. She hid a miniature doll in the scale model and explained to the children that a full-size model of the doll was hidden in the comparable location in the full-size room. Typically, not until age 3 could children use what they knew about the location of the miniature doll in the model to help them find the full-size doll in the real room. Even though 2-year-olds recognized the similarity between the rooms, they could not use one as a symbol for the other. This point was vividly revealed when researchers convinced 2-year-olds that the scale model was actually the larger room in a shrunken state (DeLoache, Miller, & Rosengren, 1997). In this situation the children did not see the scale model as a symbol of the large room. After witnessing the hiding of the miniature doll in the "shrunken" room, the children were then further duped into thinking that the scale model had been reenlarged into its full size. Now they had no trouble locating the "enlarged" hidden doll!

Although children can usually use artifacts as symbols by age 3, their understanding is fragile and easily disrupted. Even older preschoolers and elementary school children sometimes focus on the salient properties of an object and then fail to appreciate its symbolic meaning (Uttal, O'Doherty, Newland, Hand, & DeLoache, 2009). Recognizing the problems that children can have understanding symbolic artifacts has important practical implications. For example, anatomically accurate dolls are often used to question children about their experiences when sexual abuse is suspected. Such dolls are scale models of humans, and our assumption that the symbolic use of the doll is understandable to young preschoolers is highly questionable (Poole, Bruck, & Pipe, 2011). Medical personnel often use dolls to illustrate the medical or surgical procedures that young children are going to experience, but again, the chance that these approaches are effective is questionable. Emily Rapp, who was born with a congenital defect, served as a poster child for the March of Dimes. She recalls that when she was 4 years old, doctors explained the upcoming amputation of her foot by demonstrating on a doll. She still remembers being utterly confused by the illustration and completely unable to make sense of how it related to her (Rapp, 2006).

Understanding Language

Language development is a remarkable achievement of almost all young children, made even more notable by the fact that many aspects of language learning are nearly complete by the end of the preoperational stage. Volumes can, and have, been written summarizing the research on language acquisition. Here we will provide only a sampling of what is entailed when preschoolers master language.

Phonology

First, when children learn language they are learning its **phonology**, that is, the sound system of the language. Every language employs only a subset of the sounds that humans can use for language. Babies are beginning to learn something about what sounds are important for their language even before they are born. For example, soon after birth young infants show a preference for listening to voices speaking the native language of their mothers, apparently because they have heard their mothers while in the womb (Locke, 1993). One group of researchers found that by 6 months babies exposed to just one language show signs of sharpening their ability to discriminate distinctions that are important in that language, but have begun to lose the ability to perceive distinctions that are unimportant. Japanese babies, for example, start to lose the ability to distinguish *l* sounds from *r* sounds by this time (Kuhl et al., 2006). However, babies raised in bilingual environments continue to sharpen their abilities to discriminate sound distinctions that are important in both of the languages they are hearing.

Babies begin **babbling** at about 6 months, repeating consonant-vowel-consonant sequences such as *bababa* or *doodoodoo*. At first these babblings include most possible language sounds, but by 9 months babies are matching their babbling sounds to the sounds of their native language (or languages). This advance seems to depend on other people's responses: When caregivers react contingently to a baby's babbling with smiles, touch, and so forth, infants make more rapid progress in producing the speechlike sounds (e.g., Goldstein, King, & West, 2003).

Thus, phonological development begins before birth, and there are measurable advances long before babies begin to talk. Yet the full sound system may not be mastered for many years. Most adults find it difficult to understand the speech of a 2-year-old, although doting parents, tuned in to the toddler's phonological errors, can usually translate. The problem often is that 2-year-olds have not learned how, where, or when to use some of the sound distinctions that are important for their native tongue. For example, in English, we take advantage of **voicing**, using our vocal cords to make some consonant sounds but not others. The difference between the *d* sound and the *t* sound is only that the *d* is voiced and

As children's language ability advances, their social interaction becomes more complex.

TABLE 3.3 From Birth to Five: Typical Changes in Communicative/Interactive Skills

AGE	SKILL
Newborn to 1 month	Reflexively signals needs through cries, facial expressions
1 to 3 months	Coos, grunts, makes some other vocal sounds Quiets or smiles when spoken to
3 to 5 months	Smiles and shows interest in favorite people Makes wider range of vocal sounds (e.g., vowel sounds, squeals)
6 to 7 months	Babbles (consonant-vowel-consonant repetitions)
9 to 12 months	Shows, gives objects Reaches or points to indicate desired object Engages in simple interactive games, routines (e.g., peekaboo, patty-cake) Responds to simple requests (e.g., "Look at Daddy.") Produces one or two words (e.g., *bye-bye, mama*) Deaf child produces one or two signs Produces first meaningful gestures (e.g., nodding to mean "yes," waving "bye-bye")
13 to 18 months	Increases expressive vocabulary slowly, acquiring up to 50 words for familiar actions, events, and objects (e.g., *bottle, all gone, no, kiss, shoe*) Engages in simple pretend play, using self-directed acts (e.g., eating, washing, phone to ear)
18 to 24 months	Increases expressive vocabulary rapidly (3 or more words per day) Uses short (2-word) sentences, using content words (e.g., "Baby ball?" "All gone Daddy.") Engages in pretend play involving some coordination with partners (e.g., exchanges parent–baby roles with adult)
2 to 3 years	Speaks clearly enough to be understood by family members Requests labels for objects Uses sentences of 3 or more words; uses some function words (e.g., prepositions, articles, word endings) Overuses some grammatical rules—over-regularization (e.g., "I *goed* to the store.") Takes turns in conversation
3 to 4 years	Speaks clearly enough to be understood by nonfamily members Uses some complex sentences (e.g., "I think I saw the truck.") Pretends in complex, reciprocal interactions with others, engages in interactive planning for play
4 to 5 years	Produces most speech sounds correctly (continued exceptions might be *l, s, r, v, z, ch, sh, th*) Tells stories that stick to the topic, have some structure (beginning, middle, end) Coordinates conversation with multiple partners

SOURCES: American Speech-Language-Hearing Association (ASHA), 1997–2004; Bloom, 1998; Brazelton & Greenspan, 2000; Brown, 1973; Fenson et al., 1994.

the *t* is not. A toddler may not yet have caught the importance of this distinction, and when she means to say *toy* she may say *doy*. Children master most sound distinctions like these by age 3, but may continue to struggle with other aspects of phonology, such as making the *th* sound in the right places, for much longer. By age 3, most children can make themselves understood to familiar listeners. If a child's speech is still difficult for nonfamily members to follow by age 4, evaluation by a speech pathologist may be advisable. See Table 3.3 for other milestones to watch for in children's communicative development.

Semantics

Second, when children learn language they are learning which words and word parts express what meanings. This is referred to as the **semantics** of a language. Progress in producing words begins by the end of the 1st year, as already noted, and moves slowly for a time. In the first 6 months of word use, many words are produced only in limited contexts, as though tied to particular cues. For example, a child might say *daw* only when she sees the family's cocker spaniel, and then only if the dog barks.

At about the time that children can produce about 50 words, they typically go into a new phase of vocabulary learning called the **vocabulary spurt**: At about 18 to 24 months, toddlers begin learning words very rapidly, expanding their productive vocabulary from 50 to about 500 words in just a few months. Their comprehension vocabulary appears to be even larger. The child behaves as though she has had a sudden insight into the fact that anything can be labeled and thus communicated through words. Some have suggested that the vocabulary spurt marks the end of the sensorimotor period and is made possible by a fully functioning representational capacity; words are now truly being used as symbols for concepts and ideas, rather than being triggered by contextual cues. By age 5, the typical child may understand 15,000 words, so that an average of 9 or 10 words have been added every day for 3 years! The rapidity with which young children add new words to functional vocabulary after only one or two exposures is described as **fast mapping**. Working out the full details of a word's meaning usually requires multiple exposures and is described as **slow mapping** (e.g., Blewitt, Rump, Shealy, & Cook, 2009).

Using words as symbols may be a bit simpler in one respect than the use of artifactual symbols, in that words are not things themselves: They function only to represent meanings. Using them correctly probably does not require representing them in two ways at once, as children must do with artifactual symbols. Rather, a word may at first be perceived by children as more like a part of the concept to which it refers. Understanding that words are arbitrary symbols seems to be much more difficult for children than using them to make meaning. Although toddlers and preschoolers rapidly acquire vocabulary, even at age 5 children may still fail to realize that labels are arbitrary and conventionally determined. For example, if we propose to change around our words and call things by different names, like calling a dog a *cat* and vice versa, a 5-year-old is likely to object that it cannot be done. The child seems to feel that the word, in a sense, "belongs" to the thing it symbolizes and cannot be shifted (Homer, Brockmeier, Kamawar, & Olson, 2001).

It is notable that children who grow up in bilingual homes reach vocabulary milestones at about the same time as monolingual children. That is, they produce their first words at the same time, and they grow their vocabularies at about the same pace (e.g., Pettito et al., 2001). However, their vocabulary growth is split between two languages, so they are unlikely to know as many words in either language as children who are monolingual. This may be a disadvantage to growing up bilingual, but researchers have found that there are also substantial cognitive advantages. In particular, bilinguals get extensive practice suppressing one language while listening or talking in another and shifting attention depending on the language spoken. This practice appears to sharpen executive functions such as attention regulation and inhibitory control (see Box 3.3). From early childhood, bilinguals consistently perform better on tasks that assess these abilities than monolinguals do, even when they come from similar socioeconomic and ethnic backgrounds (see Bialystok, Craik, Green, & Gollan, 2009, for a summary of bilinguals' cognitive advantages).

Syntax

Third, learning language requires learning to produce sentences that make sense. The aspect of language that specifies how to link words into meaningful sentences is called the **syntax** or **grammar**. Words must be ordered in a sentence in just the right way to communicate what we mean to someone else. Linguists have found that proper ordering of words and word parts (such as prefixes and suffixes in English) is governed by a complex set of rules. One of the most baffling things about children's language acquisition is that they learn these rules with little difficulty, despite the fact that no one teaches them.

Beginning with two-word strings at about the time of the vocabulary spurt, children quickly progress, until by age 5 they can produce most sentence structures. To give you a sense of how complex the rules are that children implicitly know, consider the following "tag questions" in English:

That boy kicked the dog, didn't he?
The ceiling leaks all the time, doesn't it?
You and I are getting along well, aren't we?

Making the right question tag at the end of the sentence requires knowledge of several rules, including how to add an auxiliary (such as *did* or *does*) to a verb and how to negate a verb, for starters. To make proper tag questions requires so many rules that children are slow to learn this particular sentence form (Brown & Hanlon, 1970). Nonetheless, most English speaking children can produce tag questions effortlessly by age 5.

Here again, the development of bilingual children generally matches the pace of monolingual children. They reach milestones at about the same time (e.g., the production of two word sentences) and their grammar in both languages becomes incrementally more complex, although the details depend on which particular languages they are learning (Bialystok et al., 2009).

Pragmatics

Finally, children must learn the **pragmatics** of language use, that is, how to use language effectively to communicate. Knowing how to put together a proper sentence, or knowing the labels for things, is not enough. One must be able to craft a **narrative**, a story or event description that conveys the full sense of an experience or gets at the point of an event while taking into account what the listener needs to hear to understand. Different listeners have different needs—say a little sister versus a grandfather—and there are different conventions of address that are acceptable in different situations. All of these kinds of language-use issues must be learned in addition to the mechanics of language. Preschoolers begin to construct narratives, usually with the help of others, by about 2 or 3 years old. Initially, their narratives are sketchy and largely uninformative. A child telling about an all-day trip to the zoo, for example, might mention only that "we went" and indicate one salient experience: "We saw a lion." A listener counting on the narrative to learn where, when, and what is likely to be quite disappointed. Some aspects of developing pragmatic skill are dependent on cognitive developments in perspective taking, which helps account for the inadequacy of children's early narratives (Cameron & Wang, 1999; Uccelli, Hemphill, Pan, & Snow, 1999).

Pragmatic skill also requires making appropriate adjustments in speech depending on the listener. Most children gradually learn **code switching**, shifting from using, say, slang with friends to using more polite forms with teachers. They also learn, eventually, to distinguish between what people really mean and the literal meaning of their words. Everyday expressions such as "What do ya' know" or "That's cool" are not to be taken literally in most social exchanges. And many such expressions require similar idiomatic responses. For example, today a greeting like "What's happening?" is usually followed by "Nothing much!"

How Language Is Learned

Language consists of so many complex systems, and it is learned so early, that it is difficult to explain how children manage the task. Some psycholinguists have proposed that language is learned by special genetically programmed procedures that are unique to language learning (e.g., Chomsky, 1968; Pinker, 1994). Others contend that the general analytic capacity of the human brain is such that even complex language rules can be worked out without any innate knowledge or special language acquisition procedures (e.g., Karmiloff-Smith, 1992, 2000). Regardless of which view is correct, experience with one's native language must be critically important. Recognizing the importance of experience raises two questions: First, how much exposure to language is necessary, and second, are there particular language experiences that can facilitate the process of learning?

Researchers have only scratched the surface in addressing these questions. Two domains in which both the quantity and the quality of experience have been linked to quality of learning are semantic development in the learning of vocabulary, and pragmatic development in the production of narratives.

Cross-cultural comparisons show both universals in language development and the diversity in the environmental input that young language learners hear. In general, children around the world show similar developmental trajectories overall, although substantial individual differences, especially in vocabulary development, are also apparent.

Cross-cultural differences in vocabulary growth help demonstrate the importance of input for semantic development. Regardless of what native language children learn, vocabulary milestones tend to be reached at similar ages. However, the types of words that children learn most readily differ across language environments. Children learning many languages, including English, seem to have a "noun bias": They learn concrete nouns, like *cat* and *chair*, earlier and apparently more easily than other types of words, like verbs. Yet children learning Mandarin Chinese, Korean, and a few other languages learn verbs at least as early and as readily as they learn nouns, suggesting that characteristics of individual languages and the way that adults speak to children may be extremely important for shaping a child's vocabulary. For example, when speaking to young children, English speakers tend to begin their sentences with verbs but end them with nouns, whereas Mandarin speakers more often both begin and end their sentences with verbs (Tardif, Shatz, & Nagles, 1997). Also, the verbs Mandarin speakers use with young children often are highly imageable or highly specific in meaning, qualities that make words easier for young children to learn (see Chan et al., 2011). Such differences in child-directed speech apparently make verbs at least as easy to learn as nouns for children acquiring Mandarin and similar languages.

Within a given culture, there are substantial individual differences among children in how rapidly they grow their vocabularies. Vocabulary differences are usually related to children's home and preschool environments (e.g., Lugo-Gil & Tamis-LeMonda, 2008; Rowe, Raudenbush, & Goldin-Meadow, 2012; Senechal & LeFevre, 2002; Weizman & Snow, 2001). The amount and kind of language experience children have with adults in parent–child conversations, during mealtimes, play times, and activities like joint book reading, seem to be key. Fernald and colleagues have found that how much mothers speak to their 18-month-olds predicts not only how large their children's vocabularies will be but also how quickly the children can process familiar words at 24 months. These findings are the same whether children are reared in middle class English-speaking families or low income Spanish-speaking families (Fernald, Perfors, & Marchman, 2006; Hurtado, Marchman, & Fernald, 2008). It seems that ". . . caregiver talk not only guides . . . vocabulary learning, but also sharpens the processing skills used during real-time language comprehension" (Hurtado et al., p. F31).

But quantity of caregiver speech is not all that matters. Tamis-LeMonda and her colleagues have studied mothers' verbal responsiveness to infants and toddlers. They measure how frequently mothers make prompt, contingent, and appropriate (positive and meaningful) verbal responses to children's behaviors or vocalizations (e.g., when a baby points to a toy). They find that children make more rapid progress in vocabulary acquisition (e.g., they reach the 50-word milestone earlier) when mothers are more verbally responsive in these early years, regardless of mothers' own productive vocabularies (Tamis-LeMonda, Cristofaro, Rodriguez, & Bornstein, 2006).

One of the most compelling demonstrations of the importance of input for children's vocabulary growth is a classic study in which researchers made monthly visits for over 2 years to the homes of children whose families were either poor and on welfare, lower middle class (mostly in blue-color occupations), or upper middle class with at least one professional parent (Hart & Risley, 1992, 1995). All of the parents were actively involved with their children, playing with them, expressing affection, providing them with toys, and so on. But there were marked differences in how much the three groups of parents talked to their children right from the start. (Children were about 9 months old at the beginning of the study.) In a 100-hour week, a toddler in a professional family might hear 215,000 words on the average. in a lower-middle-class family children heard about 125,000 words, and in the poorest homes about 62,000. All of the children learned to talk on schedule, but the differences in parental input were correlated with children's vocabulary measures by age 3. Children who heard the most language performed best. The content of parents' conversations with their youngsters also differed. Those who spoke with their children most tended to ask more questions and elaborated more on topics of conversation. Parents who spoke with their children the least tended to utter more prohibitions. Even when the researchers looked within a single socioeconomic group, so that social class was not a factor, children whose parents talked with them more had the most advanced vocabularies. From this and many other studies, it appears that, regardless of social class, the quantity and quality of parent–child conversation can be a significant factor in vocabulary expansion.

Children's narrative skills may also be tied to the kinds of language opportunities that parents and other caregivers provide (see Box 3.4). Consider how different the narrative skills of two 5-year-olds in the same classroom proved to be. Both children were retelling a story they were told about a boy's trip to a grocery store. Both children were clearly familiar with all of the details of the story, having successfully acted it out with dolls and other props.

> First child: John went to the grocery store. He got a cake for his grandmother's birthday party. And he paid the clerk and ran home.
> Second Child: He got cake and he ran home. (Feagans & Farran, 1981, p. 723)
> (*Source:* Feagans, L., & Farran, D. C. (1981). How demonstrated comprehension can get muddled in production. *Developmental Psychology, 17,* 718–727.)

Several studies have found that narrative skill differences like these are connected to the way that mothers converse with their children. If they use an **elaborative style**, engaging in lengthy discussions about children's past experiences, providing lots of details, asking questions and encouraging children to provide details as well, their children's narratives tend to be more adequate and informative (e.g., Reese & Fivush, 1993). An interesting twist is that mothers who engage their children in this kind of high-quality narrative practice also have children who remember past events in their own lives better (e.g., Boland, Haden, & Ornstein, 2003; Haden, Ornstein, Eckerman, & Didow, 2001). In one study, after 3-year-olds visited a museum with their mothers they could remember *only* what they had actually talked with their mothers about during the trip (Tessler & Nelson, 1994). Discussing an event with preschoolers either before, during, or after it actually happens benefits children's later memory of it (McGuigan & Salmon, 2004). When mothers were trained to engage in this kind of "elaborative reminiscing" with their 2½-year-olds, their children were better at remembering events even a year after their mothers were trained than children of untrained mothers (Reese & Newcombe, 2007). Katherine Nelson (e.g., 2007) has proposed that narrative practice is a key ingredient in the development of autobiographical memories. We are all familiar with the phenomenon of **infantile amnesia**, the difficulty we have remembering events in our lives earlier than about our 3rd or 4th year. There are probably many factors that contribute, but perhaps one is that our early experiences occur before we have much mastery of language. Nelson argues that it is the mastery of narrative language that is particularly important. When we tell our own life experiences in conversation with others, we also learn to encode stories in language form, a form that is well suited for later recall. In a way, talking out loud about our experiences teaches us not just how to tell stories but how to remember them as well. As you will see in the next section, Nelson's view of how autobiographical memory develops is consistent with the ideas of a highly influential psychologist and educator, Lev Vygotsky, who was a contemporary of Piaget and who emphasized the importance of social experience in many aspects of cognitive development.

VYGOTSKY'S SOCIOCULTURAL THEORY

It would be virtually impossible to consider the topic of cognitive development in children without considering Piaget's contributions. His ideas have been so widely adopted that they provide the foundation for many of our beliefs about child development, and they inform our notions of developmentally appropriate practice in profound ways. As Elkind (1968) noted, he is the "giant in the nursery." However, another theorist also lays claim to widespread influence in the area of cognitive

 Head Start is an early intervention program for preschoolers from lower income families. What characteristics of a "high-quality" preschool program can you identify in this classroom?

Box 3.4: Early Childhood Education: Helping All Children Succeed

Early experiences build the brain architecture and the behavioral foundations that support children's academic, emotional and social futures. Throughout this text, you will find evidence that socioeconomic status in the United States is a key determiner of whether infants and young children will have the experiences they need to build a sturdy foundation for success. Children from low income or impoverished neighborhoods, whose family members are often undereducated and/or face significant adversity, are more likely than children from more advantaged circumstances to suffer a range of physical and mental health problems as adults. Their cognitive development is often so compromised by the end of the preschool period that they are less likely than other children to learn to read, are more likely to need special education placements, and are especially prone to dropping out of school (e.g., Brooks-Gunn, 2003, 2007; Center on the Developing Child at Harvard University, 2007; Magnuson & Duncan, 2006). Because school achievement is strongly linked to employability and income, poverty is passed on from one generation to another (e.g., Ramey & Ramey, 1998).

Can preschool education help provide low income children with the experiences they need for positive development? Parents are the adults who have the most interaction with their young children and who have the most control over their early experiences. The more education and income parents have, the more likely they are to provide all of the experiences that support the cognitive, behavioral, and social developments that predict success in school and in life. Yet even for children from upper-SES homes, time spent in a *quality* preschool can add value (e.g., Peisner-Feinberg et al., 2001). And for children from lower SES homes, high-quality preschool substantially improves school readiness, reduces a child's chances of a "special education" placement, increases chances of high school graduation, reduces crime and incarceration rates, and benefits later earnings (e.g., Barnett & Masse, 2007; Brooks-Gunn, 2003; Pianta, Barnett, Burchinal, & Thornburg, 2009; Schweinhart et al., 2005; Temple & Reynolds, 2007). These benefits have been demonstrated in several long-term experiments that followed poor children well into adulthood (e.g., the Abecedarian Project—see Barnett & Masse, 2007; the High/Scope Perry Preschool Program—see Schweinhart et al., 2005; the Chicago Child-Parent Centers—see Reynolds, 2000).

Let's consider a bit of the history of preschool education in this country, how it is evolving, what its effects are, and how we can help parents from all income levels to assess its quality.

What Is Preschool Education?

Pre-K or preschool programs and their missions are quite diverse in the United States and fall roughly into four categories (Kagan & Kauerz, 2007). Child care (or day care) programs may serve children from infancy through school age; they are traditionally considered "custodial," meaning that they protect children's health and safety while their parents are working. Early education programs have a more academic purpose; they are intended to foster children's cognitive, social, and emotional development using "developmentally appropriate curricula" (Brauner, Gordic, & Zigler, 2004). They are usually open to children starting at age 3 and are the type that is likely to be offered by public schools. Special programs that can be considered early interventions, like the federally funded, state-administered Head Start and Early Head Start programs, are designed to enrich the social and educational experiences of infants and children from low-income families or who are disabled. They combine classroom programs and family services for children who are at high risk of being unprepared for school, both cognitively and socially. Finally, there are nursery schools, which traditionally provide programs for a few hours a day, from 1 to 5 days per week. They give young children the opportunity to play with other children, to learn to get along with teachers, and to become accustomed to some classroom routines. (For fuller descriptions of some program types, see Brauner et al., 2004; Ramey & Ramey, 1998; Schweinhart, 2003). Because programs have evolved for different purposes, there is very little systematicity in the preschool world. Different kinds of programs are often regulated and/or funded by different state and federal agencies. Child care programs in some states, for example, are governed by Departments of Public Welfare, whereas early education programs and nursery schools may be under the supervision of Departments of Education. As a result, regulations and quality control within the same state may differ quite substantially from one type of program to another.

There is a social and educational movement afoot that aims to bring more uniformity of purpose and consistency of quality to preschool programs, and to use public funding to make good preschool programs accessible to all families; it is called the "universal pre-K" movement. Advocates argue that the unifying goal for all programs, no matter what other purposes they might serve, should be to promote school readiness, that is, to make it possible for every child to be prepared to learn academic skills successfully by the time they enter first grade (e.g., Brauner et al., 2004; Kagan & Kauerz, 2007; Pianta et al., 2009). The school readiness agenda is twofold. First, it is focused on maximizing each child's quality of life, in early childhood and beyond. Early education is seen as a "powerful tool" for fostering positive development (Hyson, Copple, & Jones, 2006). Second, it is one approach to helping reduce the impediments to success faced by children in poverty and to addressing a range of social and economic problems (see Bogard & Takanishi, 2005; Brauner et al., 2004; Kagan & Kauerz, 2007). It seems to be more and more difficult for poor children to "bootstrap" their way to more middle-class status through access to public education after age 5. The failure of our schools to successfully educate substantial numbers of children has created widespread concern in the business community about America's ability to maintain a qualified workforce and to sustain economic growth (Committee for Economic Development, 2006). Social policy makers also emphasize the contribution of inadequate academic achievement to problems such as crime and homelessness, and to the soaring costs of crime management and social welfare programs (e.g., Heckman, 2006; Schweinhart, 2007).

How Does Preschool Help?

A 5-year-old sits in front of a small computer screen. Beside the screen is a red button. Every 2 seconds a picture appears briefly on the screen. The pictures are familiar objects, like a butterfly or a flower. The child knows that her task is to push the red button, but *only* when a picture of a chair appears. The task continues for over 7 minutes, requiring the child to pay close attention, respond when the correct cue appears and, just as important, *not* respond to any of the wrong cues. This version of the "continuous performance task" is a test of sustained attention and inhibitory control (Rosvold, Mirsky, Sarason, Bransome, & Beck, 1956). You may recognize these now as among the cognitive skills called executive functions. Children's pre-kindergarten performance on tests of these skills is a good predictor of later academic achievement (e.g., NICHD, 2003b). So are measures of many other cognitive, behavioral, and social developments in the first 5 years, from the growth of vocabulary to the emergence of per-spective taking. From this chapter on cognitive development in the early years, and the next two on social/emotional development, you will recognize that typical development in young children involves dramatic progress in learning language, understanding the self and the physical and social world, and controlling emotions and behav-ior. Much of this progress is foundational for later academic suc-cess (e.g., Dickinson, McCabe, Anastasopoulos, Peisner-Feinberg, & Poe, 2003; Hyson et al., 2006; Snow, 2007). All of these developments are powerfully influenced by children's interpersonal experiences, especially with parents, but caring, well-trained teachers in pre-school settings provide these experiences as well.

What, for example, makes a child ready to read? We learn to read and write by matching written forms to the spoken words they symbol-ize. Not surprisingly, many parents think that "learning your letters" in the preschool years is the quintessential prereading skill (e.g., Lewit & Baker, 1995). Some even drill their children on matching written let-ters to letter names. It *is* important, eventually, to learn the alphabet, but this is a task that is made more comprehensible and manageable if it builds on other preliteracy skills, especially strong oral language abilities. Such abilities do not require memorization or drills; rather they mostly depend on conversational interactions between sensitive, responsive adults and young children. Here are some essentials:

- Growing a good vocabulary is important for reading. Prekinder-garten vocabulary size is more predictive of reading skill by the end of third grade than knowing the alphabet before kindergar-ten. And, as you have seen in this chapter, vocabulary growth is grounded in adult–child conversation during play, at mealtimes, on outings both mundane (e.g., to the grocery store) and exotic (e.g., to the zoo), and so on.
- Narrative or story telling skill is also a building block for read-ing. Reading requires that children understand that language is symbolic and decontextualized. Telling and hearing stories about past experiences or fictional situations helps children to understand that language can function to represent events and experiences that are not part of the current context. Again, adult–child conversation about shared experiences, as in elabo-rative co-narration, is key to growing narrative skill.
- Extensive and positive early experience with books is another cornerstone of later literacy (e.g., Raikes et al., 2006; Senechal & LeFevre, 2002). Adults reading to children (shared book reading)

helps children learn that books are a source of information and entertainment. Especially if enthusiastic adults engage children in conversation as they read, encouraging children to talk about the story, to discuss new words, and to make inferences that connect the story to the child's experience, language skills grow along with children's love of reading. Lots of experience with books also begins to teach children, quite naturally, about how print works: what letters look like, that print conveys meaning, that we (English readers anyway) read from left to right, that pages turn from right to left, and so on. As children become aware of what print looks like and what it conveys, they will notice it through-out their environment—on signs, on packaging, and so on. The prevalence of print creates "teachable moments," opportunities to point out the letters of the alphabet, for example.

- Phonological awareness is critical for beginning readers (e.g., Dickinson et al., 2003), which means recognizing that words are composed of separable sounds or phonemes. These phonemes, eventually, will be matched to printed letters or letter combina-tions. When adults engage children in play with language, "Let's find everything in the room that starts with the 'tuh' sound" or "What words do we know that rhyme with 'yes,'" they are direct-ing children's attention to the smaller units of sound that make up words and therefore promoting phonological awareness. Many of children's favorite storybooks highlight phonology by having fun with alliteration (repeating the same beginning con-sonant sound over and over) or using rhyme (e.g., *The Cat in the Hat* by Dr. Seuss).

What Makes a Preschool Program "High Quality"?

As you can imagine, there are different "expert" views on this subject, but longitudinal studies analyzing preschool predictors of school readiness indicate that *quality of teacher–child interactions* is critical (e.g., Mashburn et al., 2008; Montie, Xiang, & Schweinhart, 2006). Effective teacher–child interactions are marked by enthusi-asm, respect, and mutual enjoyment, without displays of anger, ag-gression, or harshness. Teachers encourage and support child–child interactions that have the same high quality. Teachers are sensitive and responsive to children's emotional cues. Their conversation is elaborative, tuned in to children's level of understanding, with feedback that helps children to more fully develop their conceptual knowledge. Most teacher–child interactions are one-to-one or with small groups. Children's interests guide these interactions, and chil-dren are directly involved in planning daily activities and longer term projects. Activities foster practical opportunities for learning letters, phonemes, numbers, and facts about science, geography, and so on *without drilling or rote practice* (see Hamre & Pianta, 2007). Play, including exploratory, pretend, and physical (rough and tumble) play, is encouraged and supported. Play is encouraged as the medium through which children naturally learn. It is not treated simply as an occasional break from didactic teaching (Hirsh-Pasek, Golinkoff, Berk, & Singer, 2009).

These kinds of proximal processes are very much like those that effective parents create with their young children. It is not always easy

(Box 3.4 continued)

Box 3.4 *Continued*

to evaluate these moment-to-moment features of quality, but there are some structural elements that parents and helpers can look for. The following suggestions are consistent with various guidelines offered by the National Association for the Education of Young Children (NAEYC) and the National Institute of Early Education Research (NIEER).

- *Teachers' education.* Teachers with bachelors' degrees and preparation in early childhood education are more likely to engage children in the kinds of conversation and activities that promote positive development than teachers with less education (e.g., Kelley & Camilli, 2007; Montie et al., 2006). Unfortunately, many states do *not* require preschool teachers to have college degrees, particularly child care programs in which teachers have traditionally been construed to be babysitters rather than educators. Partly as a consequence, child care programs in the United States are *rarely* high quality; typically they are poor to mediocre (see Brauner et al., 2003). All preschool programs should foster school readiness, whether they also serve parents' child care needs or provide additional services to families. In this regard, requiring the lead teacher in each classroom to have a college education and certification in early childhood education is an important standard to meet. Support staff should also have early childhood certification and all classroom personnel should have annual in-service training. Of course, high teacher

standards require adequate pay. Salaries equivalent to those of kindergarten and first grade teachers are recommended.

- *Teacher–child ratios.* For 3-year-olds, maximum teacher–child ratios of 9:1 are recommended, with total class size not exceeding 18. For 4-year-olds, the recommended teacher–child maximum is 10:1, with no more than 20 children per group. (See Chapter 4 for infant/toddler recommendations.)
- *A variety of equipment and materials.* Material choices provide children with a range of opportunities to develop skills and knowledge, and they make it possible for children's interests and planning to play an important role in the curriculum. Children should have access to lots of books, art and writing supplies, opportunities to play with water, sand, and other media, blocks and other building toys, as well as a range of toys and materials that support pretend play.
- *General characteristics.* Parents should be welcome to make an appointment to visit a classroom. NIEER suggests looking for "safe spaces with children comfortable and engaged in what they are doing, not easily distracted or wandering aimlessly; children seem happy, not distressed, bored or crying; adults are caring, . . . responsive to children's needs and requests, and *involved* (emphasis added) in what children are doing. . . . Children's voices dominate!" (Frede, 2008).

development and has attracted much contemporary attention. His name was Lev S. Vygotsky (see Box 3.5). Frequently, Vygotsky's ideas are presented as a counterpoint to those of Piaget, as if the two theorists were in opposing camps. Though Vygotsky did criticize some of Piaget's ideas, the criticisms need to be understood in context. Both men understood that the advancement of scientific thinking depended on the kind of dialectic that a mutual critique of ideas provides. Even though Piaget himself was slow to respond to Vygotsky's criticisms, he applauded the work of the young Russian scholar and actually came to agree with him in certain areas, such as the usefulness of egocentric speech (van der Veer, 1996; see below). The celebrated differences between the two more often than not reflect Vygotsky's differing emphases rather than any outright rejection of major Piagetian constructs. Readers need to be careful not to misinterpret the philosophy of either theorist by oversimplifying their ideas or by construing their positions as concrete "either-or" sets of beliefs. Let's examine some of the ideas for which Vygotsky is best known and consider how these two theorists compare.

Vygotsky, as did Piaget, found the question of how thinking develops in human beings an intriguing one. However, he did not identify a progression of stages that the individual child traverses on her way to logical, abstract thought. Nor did he emphasize the importance of the individual's construction of knowledge in the cognitive developmental process. Instead, he focused on themes that provide a different perspective on development. Vygotsky is arguably best known for his emphasis on the critical role that the culture or society into which one is born plays in the transmission of knowledge. Hence, his theory is called "sociocultural." He also stressed that human thinking was mediated by the tools humans use (Wertsch, 1991).

It seems quite understandable that he would take this point of view, embedded as he was in his own cultural context. Vygotsky was a Marxist who had been powerfully influenced by the writings of Marx and Engels. He was accustomed to the concept of a dialectic, that logical advancement comes from mutual examination of

Box 3.5: Biographical Sketch: Lev S. Vygotsky

Lev Semenovich Vygotsky was born in 1896 in the small Russian village of Orscha in the province of Belorussia. His parents were both well-educated, middle-class individuals of Jewish descent. Vygotsky's father, a manager for a local bank, actively supported educational causes such as the development of the local public library. Vygotsky's experience with the Russian school system began when he reached junior high school age. Prior to this time, his parents had paid for him to be educated by a private tutor.

Vygotsky was clearly an extraordinary student from a very early age. Like Piaget, he began to write while he was still a young man. His essay on *Hamlet* was written when he was 18 and was later published. He loved to study and had wide academic interests, which included the philosophy of history, literature, art, and poetry. When he entered the University of Moscow in 1913, he was a student in the medical school. During his first semester there, he decided to transfer to the law school. As if this were not challenging enough, Vygotsky simultaneously enrolled in Shaniavsky University to study history and philosophy with some of Russia's most brilliant professors of that time.

Upon graduation from Moscow University in 1917, he secured a position teaching literature in a secondary school in the province of Gomel, where his parents lived. He worked in this capacity from 1918 to early 1924, when he left the school to join the faculty of a nearby teachers' college. He also worked to complete the requirements for his doctoral degree, which was granted from Moscow University in 1925.

One of Vygotsky's responsibilities at the college was to give lectures in the area of psychology. While presenting a lecture to professionals at the Second Psychoneurological Congress in Leningrad in early 1924, he attracted the attention of a young man named Alexander Luria. Luria was the academic secretary at the Moscow Institute of Psychology and would go on to become quite famous in the area of neuropsychology. Luria was so impressed with Vygotsky that he prevailed upon his director to hire him. Toward the end of 1924, Vygotsky moved with his wife to Moscow to take this appointment.

During his career at the institute, he studied the development of human mental functioning. Many of his ideas were not available to scientists and educators in the West until quite recently because of the general ban on dissemination of information as well as problems involved in translation. Since the release of his ideas, Vygotsky has enjoyed great popularity in the West, particularly with those involved in education. During his lifetime, Vygotsky carried out many experiments on children using qualitative methods similar to those used by Piaget. His thinking was influenced by Piaget, and he actively tried to initiate a dialogue with him about certain points of disagreement. A full-fledged dialogue never developed, possibly because of the barriers of language and ideology. However, Piaget was aware of Vygotsky's ideas. In 1962, Piaget stated that he respected Vygotsky's position and noted their areas of agreement.

While at the institute, Vygotsky wrote prodigiously and traveled extensively to oversee work in clinics with children and adults suffering from neurological disorders. Throughout much of his adult life, Vygotsky himself was in poor health. Toward the end of his life, colleagues such as Luria helped him conduct research projects because Vygotsky was too weak to leave Moscow. His promising life was cut short in 1934, when he succumbed to an attack of tuberculosis. In Vygotsky, we have another example of a truly great mind whose ideas have inspired the work of many students of cognitive development.

ideas, generating point and counterpoint and, ultimately, perhaps a more adequate synthesis of ideas. He was grounded in the idea that society could be improved by the collective efforts of its members. Marxist philosophy also emphasized human mastery of the physical world by using and producing tools (Marx & Engels, 1846/1972). Vygotsky took this concept and applied it to psychological development, reasoning that cognitive growth also resulted from continuous expansion in the use and scope of **tools**. Tools, or **signs** as Vygotsky came to refer to them, meant anything that people used to help them think and learn, such as numbering or writing systems. The most important tool for Vygotsky was language.

Let's consider the simple example of a vocabulary word, *television*. Vygotsky pointed out that the child does not independently construct a definition for such a word but rather learns the meaning that her culture has ascribed to it. Understanding this shared meaning enables the child to use the "tool" to communicate. But the word can be used not only in its literal sense. It can be transformed to create a new tool or sign, like "telemarketing," which incorporates part of the original idea but is qualitatively different. Such new signs are the products of cultural and historical **mediation**. That is, the signs are shaped and developed by others. Vygotsky claimed that a child's use of such tools or signs actually transforms thinking and shapes it into new kinds of thought. The idea of **mediated learning**, so central to Vygotsky's theory, is reminiscent of Piaget's concepts of assimilation and accommodation (van Geert, 1998), although Piaget tended to emphasize the development of thinking within the child, whereas Vygotsky's focus was squarely on the "child-in-context." In his view, because children acquire and use tools that are the products of others' thinking, "the mind is no longer to be located entirely inside the head" (Cole & Wertsch, 1996, p. 253) but is part of a collective experience. We have already learned that multidimensional models of development, such as Bronfenbrenner's bioecological model, recognize the powerful influence of the individual's environment on her development. Vygotsky went a step further. He believed that the individual could never really be separated from her environment or culture.

To illustrate this point, recall that children's autobiographical memories improve when parents engage them in elaborative conversations about past experiences. This is a pattern of behavior that is fairly typical of middle-class Americans, perhaps because knowing our own stories is important for the development of self as an independent individual. But in cultures where self as an individual is not so highly valued, autobiographical knowledge and the parenting strategies that support it may not be so important. If the culture emphasizes interdependence and engaging in hierarchically defined roles, it may be more effective for parents to use nonelaborative styles with their children. Cross-cultural research is consistent with this view. In Asian cultures, like China's and Korea's, middle-class parents do not typically engage in elaborative conversations with their children, and adults' autobiographical memories are less detailed than those of Americans (e.g., Leichtman, Wang, & Pillemer, 2003).

In one study comparing Taiwanese and U.S. middle class families, when Taiwanese parents did engage in storytelling with young children, the content and orientation of their narratives were quite different from that of American parents. Taiwanese adults engaged in more didactic storytelling, often focusing on and explaining children's misdeeds (about one third of the narratives). They used the narrative frame to teach children about what they should and shouldn't do and why, emphasizing the effects on parents and family (parents will feel shame, sadness), and casting the child in the role of listener. American parents engaged in more co-narration, asking questions and elaborating on children's answers, and even when misbehavior was the topic (less than one tenth of the time) they tended to ". . . enact a child-affirming interpretive framework, erasing or downplaying children's misdeeds" (Miller, Fung, Lin, Chen, & Boldt, 2012, p. vii). It seems that not only the frequency of elaborative narration but the content and process are very much in the service of enculturation, which affects how children cognitively process (e.g., remember) information. Vygotskian theorists suggest that parenting in more interdependently oriented societies is consistent with the goal of teaching children to see themselves as "a collection of roles in a social network" rather than, first and foremost, as individuals (Cole, 2006, p. 674).

Vygotsky's notion that cognitive development is largely socially mediated introduced developmentalists to the idea that there are likely to be cognitive differences among people reared in different cultures, and you have read about several examples of such differences. Recall from Chapter 1, for example, that people in Eastern cultures attend more to context than to focal objects in scenes, whereas Westerners focus more on focal objects. Even as early as 3½ years old, Japanese and U.S. children begin to show differences in their attentional strategies, with Japanese children attending more to contextual characteristics than American children when processing information (Kuwabara, Son, & Smith, 2011).

Another theme in Vygotsky's work is that progress or improvement in thinking is both possible and desirable. The press toward more advanced levels of thinking not only pulls the individual forward but improves the society as well. Vygotsky placed great importance on the transmission of formal knowledge because he believed that learning culturally defined concepts, which he referred to as **scientific concepts**, presented the learner with an internal organizational system for ideas and allowed the learner to utilize the ideas more efficiently (Vygotsky, 1934). But how do these cognitive advances occur? Vygotsky believed that more advanced thinkers or more capable members of a culture provide novice learners with **scaffolding** (a term coined by Wood & Middleton, 1975) that enables the novices to reach higher levels of thinking. Scaffolding serves as a temporary prop until the child has mastered a task. Interestingly, Vygotsky did not apply his ideas to specific kinds of educational practice despite the obvious parallels to teaching and the widespread popularity of his ideas among educators (van der Veer & Valsiner, 1994). He did discuss education in the broad sense of the term and highlighted the important role of society in providing the tools that form the basis for thinking.

In educational circles, the concept of scaffolding has been interpreted as guidance by a more cognitively advanced individual (a teacher or peer) with prompts, cues, and other supports to reach a point where the learner can manifest in actuality what had previously only been her potential. The notion that children have a **zone of proximal development** is one of Vygotsky's most influential ideas. It describes the situation in which a learner is able to grasp a concept or perform some skill only with support or scaffolding from someone else. She would not yet be capable of the task on her own, but she can do it with assistance. Obviously, this does not mean simply telling a child an answer to a question! It means, instead, that a parent or teacher assesses the child's thinking, provides judicious support and appropriate cognitive tools, and in so doing, propels the child's development forward. Let's consider an application of this concept presented by Tharp and Gallimore (1988):

> A 6-year-old child has lost a toy and asks her father for help. The father asks where she last saw the toy: The child says, "I can't remember." He asks a series of questions: "Did you have it in your room? Outside? Next door?" To each question, the child answers, "No." When he says, "In the car?" she says, "I think so" and goes to retrieve the toy. (p. 14)
>
> (*Source:* Tharp, R. G., & Gallimore, R. (1988). *Rousing minds to life: Teaching, learning, and schooling in social context.* New York: Cambridge University Press.)

In this case, the father scaffolded the child's thinking and, in the process, helped her develop a way of remembering where her toy was. It should be noted that neither father nor daughter knew the answer to the question, "Where is the toy?" However, by encouraging the child to consider the right questions, her father was able to help his daughter to remember. The joint effort was possible because both shared certain kinds of information, such as knowledge of which toy was missing and what the layout of the house was. And both focused attention on a common goal, finding the toy. This process has been called **intersubjectivity**. From a Vygotskian point of view, the scaffolding occurred in the intermental space between parent and child.

Current research on young children's language learning, memory development, problem solving, planning, and understanding of cultural artifacts, including the symbolic artifacts described earlier in this chapter, support Vygotsky's notion of the importance of scaffolding, and you have read many examples already in this chapter. Parents and other adults often guide children's processing of new information in everyday social interactions and doing so clearly supports children's cognitive progress (e.g., Gauvain, 2001).

Vygotsky's ideas have had a major impact on education in large measure because of their applicability to the teaching–learning process. Piaget was also sensitive to the role of outside influence on the developing learner. The frequent characterizations of Piaget as concerned only with individual cognitive development and of Vygotsky as concerned only with social influences on learning are both inaccurate. Piaget noted that the relationships between the individual and her social environment are essential to cognitive development (Piaget, 1977), as we have seen in his view of the development of perspective taking. Piaget's view of the role of teachers in cognitive development is also similar to Vygotsky's (see Box 3.1). For his part, Vygotsky posited two kinds of "developmental lines" that accounted for cognitive development, one that was "sociohistorical" or cultural, and one that was "natural," coming from within the infant, much like Piaget's stage of sensorimotor development (Vygotsky, 1931/1981). Despite differences in their emphases, both Piaget and Vygotsky can be described as concerned with the interpenetration of the individual mind and society in the formation of thought.

One difference between Piaget's and Vygotsky's ideas concerns the role of **egocentric** or **private speech** in cognitive development. Piaget originally stated that the egocentric speech of the child (talking aloud to the self, with no apparent communicative function) serves no useful purpose and simply disappears with the growth of more mature language use. Vygotsky, who used the term "private speech," had a different idea. To him and his colleague Alexander Luria, private speech serves an eminently useful purpose in human development (Vygotsky & Luria, 1930). It is construed as the precursor to problem solving, planning ability, and self-regulation—what we today consider to be aspects of, or products of, executive functions (see Box 3.3). From this perspective, private speech eventually becomes internalized or transformed into **inner speech**, the kind of internal dialogue that facilitates thinking. If you happen to be someone who talks to yourself as you think something through, you can appreciate the organizing effect it can have.

Vygotsky identified three stages in the movement of private speech to inner speech. First, the child of about 3 years of age engages in running commentaries about his actions, intentions, objects of interest, and the like whether anyone is nearby to listen or not. Very often, young children manifest a kind of "parallel" conversation, playing side by side without really interacting. Children also talk themselves through problems such as "Where is my toy?" Despite the fact that they may pose the statement as a question, they act as though they do not really expect anyone to answer it. Vygotsky believed that this speech was actually directing their thoughts and keeping them focused on the task at hand. How do children come to use speech this way? Vygotsky argued that adults' verbal guidance (scaffolding) during joint activities such as problem solving, negotiating, and planning leads eventually to the child using speech to guide her own actions.

As children reach about 6 years of age, this private speech becomes more subdued and idiosyncratic, often capturing only the general sense of the idea. Children may sub-vocalize the dialogue or only move their lips. Finally, around the age of 8, children truly internalize the dialogue, and it is no longer audible. Vygotsky claimed that private speech "went underground" and became inner speech, which was maintained for its self-regulatory properties, that is, directing and executing cognitive control over behavior and thought.

How have Vygotsky's ideas about the development of private speech fared in the light of modern research? First, the stages and ages that Vygotsky described have been largely corroborated by others (Winsler, 2009). However, private speech does not always "go underground" in the elementary school years; some people use it overtly even into adulthood (e.g., Duncan & Cheyne, 2002). Second, regarding the notion that adults' verbal guidance supports the development of self-regulation, parents' verbal scaffolding of children's behavior early in the preschool years does predict children's self-regulation later (e.g., Lengua, Honorado, & Bush, 2007). Even within a single problem solving session, when an adult uses verbal scaffolding successfully, children are more likely to use private speech to solve a problem (e.g., Winsler, Diaz, & Montero, 1997). It appears that adult scaffolding affects executive functions at least partially by fostering children's private speech. Finally, private speech does seem to benefit executive functions. The use of private speech enhances children's attention and involvement when they face a challenging task (e.g., Fernyhough & Fradley, 2005); it is linked with behavioral control (Winsler, DeLeon, Wallace, Carlton, & Willson-Quayle, 2003); and it improves working memory (Al-Namlah, Fernyhough, & Meins, 2006). Interestingly, the more prone children are to use private speech, the more detailed their autobiographical memories seem to be as well (Al-Namlah, Meins, & Fernyhough, 2012). Overall, private speech is associated with a number of cognitive functions in children, including some executive functions.

Because of its potential role in what we refer to today as inhibitory control, Meichenbaum and Goodman (1971), pioneered the use of a self-talk intervention aimed at enhancing inner speech to facilitate impulse control in children. In fact, many schools of therapy, particularly cognitive-behavioral approaches, owe a debt to Vygotsky for his elucidation of the inner speech concept.

This therapist engages with the child during play therapy, but she is nonintrusive and not controlling. How does this behavior help to establish rapport and foster a supportive, trusting relationship?

APPLICATIONS

Some special skills are required of those counselors who work with young children and their families. As Shirk points out, "The process of child psychotherapy is embedded in and, at times, constrained by the process of development" (1988, p. 12). Children are not simply clients with limited vocabulary knowledge. Development brings about a series of qualitative reorganizations of competencies in cognitive, affective, behavioral, and social areas that need to be understood and respected if counseling is to be effective. Young children generally attend to things in their environment that grab their attention (centration) and react to salient perceptible features of the environment while ignoring its other more subtle aspects (concreteness). Counselors who take a "child's-eye view" are more successful in avoiding the unmodified application of adult therapy models to their work with young children. Perhaps the most important initial task for adult professionals, then, is to recognize their own cognitive egocentrism in the many ways it might present itself, from overreliance on verbal explanations, to unfounded assumptions about young children's understanding of cause and effect, to other age-inappropriate expectations.

Also critically important to the work of child psychotherapy is the need to focus on developmental processes as mediators of presenting problems. Very often, the shape of a symptom will change depending upon the cognitive and emotional resources available to the child. For example, sadness or depression in an adolescent subsequent to a family breakup may take the form of crying, ruminating, or writing long, self-absorbed diary entries. For a preschooler who lacks such verbal

Helping professionals, like parents, adjust the environment, including their own speech, to scaffold children's understanding.

and introspective capacities, reaction to the same problem might be displayed in regressive behavior (wetting the bed, having tantrums) or pronounced social difficulties (biting, hitting). Ability to profit from therapeutic techniques also depends upon what the child can understand. Whereas a mature adolescent may be intrigued by the notion of the "unconscious," a younger child lacks the understanding of mental states needed to comprehend such a concept.

Young children's egocentrism often makes it impossible for them to consider other points of view, including those of their parents, siblings, and teachers. A helper may encounter parents who punish a 15-month-old for not being toilet trained. A preschool teacher might express concern that a 3-year-old is selfish because she won't share a special toy with her playmates. In these cases, the adults fail to recognize the nature of the young child's thinking, and they attribute to the child abilities that she has not yet mastered. Sometimes these cognitive biases also indicate deep frustration, high stress levels, or limited empathy on the part of the adults. In some cases, support and understanding should be made available to the caretaker, and measures should be taken to protect the child from a potentially neglectful or abusive situation.

Sharing the Wealth: Providing Knowledge About Child Development to Caregivers

Giving information about child development to parents and caretakers, such as information about the normal fears of childhood, can also reduce adults' misinterpretations of child behavior. For example, most normal children exhibit mild to moderately intense fears over the course of childhood (Murphy, 1985). In general, the younger the child, the more their fears result from what they *see* rather than from what they *hear* (Hayes & Birnbaum, 1980). Because preoperational children do not necessarily distinguish playing from real life and because their understanding of the world is rather limited anyway, they tend to perceive what they see as reality. Therefore, younger children are more often frightened by fearful images, by ghosts, monsters, imaginary creatures, the dark, and being alone than are older, school-aged children whose fears are more often associated with some real situation like school or personal safety. A sixth grader's intense test anxiety that is provoked by hearing about a particular teacher's reputation for giving impossible exams would be lost on a 3-year-old.

Before any clinical intervention is needed, helping professionals should ask about the intensity and duration of the fears, because fears tend to wax and wane over childhood. Another very important question concerns the amount of distress the child is experiencing and the degree to which the fear is preventing the child from engaging in other activities that are important for her development. Clinical intervention for severe, persistent fears and phobias of young children can involve a number of approaches, including systematic desensitization procedures, cognitive behavioral techniques, modeling, and operant conditioning (Burns, Hoagwood, & Mrazek, 1999). For more commonplace fears, adults should resist trying to explain to young children how their fears are irrational. Research indicates that "telling yourself it's not real" is a largely ineffective intervention for young children (Cantor & Wilson, 1988). Concrete measures, such as crafting comforting rituals like bedtime routines, asking children to engage in an activity like holding onto a favorite stuffed animal or doll, and decreasing the exposure to frightening images on TV and in movies are far more helpful.

Play Therapy: Helping the Youngest Clients

Most therapies for young children emphasize play for good reason (see Axline, 1947; Landreth, 2002a; O'Connor & Braverman, 1997). Because language skills are still under construction, children reveal themselves more clearly in play than in words. For example, the ability to express complicated feelings, like love and anger toward a parent, is not available to young children, but such feelings may be acted out in play. Suppose 3½-year-old Charlotte takes a doll from the doll house and uses it to hit the baby doll lying in a bassinet. The counselor's comments "She's hitting her baby sister. I wonder if the big girl is mad?" links the act to a verbal label and gives her the option of putting feelings into words. The counselor's goal may be to understand the child's concerns, to support the child in expressing them, to help the child learn more adaptive ways to behave and express feelings, and to educate parents to better understand their child's needs. Play therapists generally advocate a nondirective, nonintrusive counseling approach with young children. This means not talking too much or being controlling. Therapists need to be patient when working with children who, by virtue of their developmental level, are less goal directed than adults. The temperament of the child and the nature of the presenting problem might signal the need for different amounts of structure, perhaps more structure for a defiant child than for an anxious one. Landreth (2002b) suggests, however, that limits be imposed only when it becomes necessary for prevention of self- or other-directed destructive behavior. At that point, therapists should acknowledge the wish or need the child is trying to express, communicate the limit, and provide an alternative outlet that is more acceptable.

Some thoughtfully chosen toys can increase the attractiveness of the play therapist's office. In general, creative toys, such as dolls, puppets, and art supplies, are preferable to highly structured games for this age group. Remember that the counselor's office can be a scary place for young children. Therefore, attempts to child-size some of its elements (chairs, tables, etc.) can help make it less threatening. For very young children, parents should stay in the room to minimize separation anxiety (see Chapter 4).

1. *Be attentive and get out of the way.* A major part of therapeutic work with young children is to assess the nature of their concerns. For that task, good observation skills are needed. Notice what the child does and does not do; what she says and doesn't say; what she looks at and how she approaches and interacts with objects in the space. How does she interact with you and what feelings does she elicit in you? Whether in the assessment or treatment phases, it is important to give children the space and time they need to express themselves while the observant counselor tunes into the multiple dimensions of child behavior. As a rule of thumb, remember that the young child's development is occurring simultaneously on many fronts and may reflect unevenness or decalage. Therefore, pay attention to each of the following areas: physical development and motor skills, cognitive and language (both receptive and expressive) development, relatedness to caregivers, primary affects and overall mood, and exploration and use of the environment (Greenspan, 1981).

2. *Maintain cooperation over time.* Young children have short attention spans and they are easily distracted by interesting stimuli in the external environment as well as internal stimuli like hunger, boredom, fear, and fatigue. The sensitive clinician is careful to note these changes, perhaps waiting a bit to see how the child copes with stress or distraction, and then changing the environment. Maintaining flexibility is an important skill in engaging the child. An abrupt shift in attention or activity, such as when a child refuses to continue playing with toys that seemed to engage her previously, might signify a self-protective move away from an area of concern (Greenspan, 1981). Enjoyable gamelike techniques that sustain cooperation and attention can be useful in counseling very young children (see Hall, Kaduson, & Schaefer, 2002 for a description of techniques).

3. *Watch your language.* Keep your language as simple and concrete as possible. Avoid complicated sentence structure. If you need to give directions, they should be simple and short. Try not to give multistep sets of directions, such as "First put your coat over there and then we'll sit at the table for a while and then I'm going to ask you to color a picture."

   Because children of this age are still constructing their understanding of cause-and-effect relationships, helpers should not assume that preschoolers can easily grasp the connection between actions and consequences except at a very simple level. Saying to a youngster "Since you hit Jimmy at day care yesterday, you won't be able to go to the playground tomorrow" will probably be ineffective if it is intended to teach the child about the consequences of her acts. Young children's sense of time is not well developed, and their memory for event sequences is rather poor. Tying tomorrow's consequences to yesterday's behavior is really asking a child to construct or detect an underlying organization or logical connection. The child has a better chance of remembering and understanding the sequence if misbehavior is linked to immediate consequences.

   Very often, children from bilingual families may be more proficient in a language other than English, a challenge to an English-speaking counselor. Obviously, all steps must be taken to ensure accuracy of communication and to reduce the chances for misinterpretations. Any interpreters that participate in counseling should be knowledgeable about the therapeutic process (Vasquez & Javier, 1991).

4. *Don't be afraid.* Sometimes in our eagerness to make clients feel good, we unconsciously ignore or gloss over the problems or conflicts they are experiencing. This may be even more true when our clients are children. Greenspan (1981) encourages counselors to take seriously the concerns of children. When the counselor notices and comments on an area of difficulty for the child, he notes that "children are often greatly relieved to know that finally they have met someone who is not frightened by what frightens them" (p. 112).

5. *Don't jump to conclusions.* Do a complete developmental interview with the parents or guardians. Knowing about early developmental milestones, prenatal and birth history, illnesses, family dynamics, cultural background, and parenting practices enriches the understanding of the child and complements what is observed in the counseling office. Behavior is multiply determined and can be the expression of multiple needs and concerns. In some respect, the child therapist is like a detective, trying to sort out from the clues provided by the child's behavior the most important issues. Parental interviews not only involve the parent in the process but add immeasurably to the clinician's assessment picture. Parental interviews are an important element of any assessment, regardless of the age of the child, because assessment should always be based upon multiple pieces of information (Sattler & Ryan, 1998). For older children and adolescents, academic and social history should be included in the interview.

Despite its popularity and intuitive appeal, play therapy suffers from lack of empirical support. Recently, professionals have addressed the need to develop more detailed accounts of mechanisms of change, well developed theoretical foundations, clear descriptions of therapeutic processes, and careful studies that would establish a firm research base (Urquiza, 2010). Although case study data (Snow, Wolff, Hudspeth, & Etheridge, 2009) exist, more research is needed in order to provide greater credibility for the field of play therapy.

When Play Is Learning and Learning Is Play

If you speak to primary grade teachers, they just might tell you that many students enter school lacking the skills necessary to learn. Clearly, they are not entirely referring to academic subjects like math or reading skills. Rather they might be referring to the capacities for paying attention, taking turns, listening to others, staying on task, regulating behavior and following classroom rules. These are the skills that provide the foundation for academic success (see Box 3.3).

As described in this chapter, such skills are called executive functions (EFs) and include working memory, self-regulation, and cognitive flexibility. EFs have been associated with better academic performance and are, in fact, better predictors of academic success than IQ (Blair, 2002; Duckworth & Seligman, 2006). How might these kinds of skills be cultivated? One good example is a comprehensive preschool-K curriculum based on Vygotsky's principles called "Tools of the Mind" (Bodrova & Leong, 2007). The *Tools* curriculum focuses on the development of self-regulation, notably through the systematic scaffolding of mature play. Play is considered the 'leading activity' of the preschool period and the means by which children learn foundational skills for later success in school. Vygotsky (1978) and his student (Elkonin, 2005) believed that play does not necessarily reach its most mature level, nor its potential to support EF, without social mediation provided by play partners (adults and peers). The *Tools* curriculum provides explicit support for play to strengthen imagination, cooperation, flexibility, imitation of adult roles, and enriched language use (Leong & Bodrova, 2012).

A useful assessment framework for play used in Tools corresponds to the acronym PROPEL. The letters stand for Plan, Roles, Props, Extended Time Frame, Language, and Scenario. A teacher can determine the level of a child's play by observing each of these elements. Doing so helps the teacher to scaffold her interactions, taking into account the child's level. For example, the teacher would know that the child is at the first or earliest stage of make-believe play if the following behaviors are observed:

1. The child does not plan during play (e.g., does not name actions prior to play) and does not demonstrate roles (e.g., teacher, policeman).
2. The child plays with objects as objects rather than as props or symbols as in creative play (e.g., a wooden block becomes a telephone).
3. The child does not appear to have a scenario in mind to enact (e.g., daddy fixing something in the garage while mommy works in the garden).
4. The child does not have an extended time frame for completing the scenario but engages instead in simple, repetitive actions. The child may explore objects but does not integrate objects into a scenario.
5. Relatively little language is used in play.

With these elements in mind, a teacher might first observe the level of children's play before scaffolding the interaction. Let's consider a teacher scaffolding play for a group of 4-year-olds who are at a more advanced stage of make-believe play. The children want to play "restaurant" in the kitchen area of their preschool playroom. A teacher might begin by asking them what role each of them wants to take. This provides an opportunity for the children to discuss the characteristics of the roles ("Restaurant servers don't cook the food") and the coordinated rules associated with the roles. Advance problem-solving promotes conflict resolution, use of language and cognitive flexibility. For example, what will the children do if there is only one stove and two children want to play chef? They may negotiate turn-taking or create another stove from a box (or similar prop). Self-regulation is strengthened as a natural consequence of participating in social roles with peers for extended periods of time. Children at the most mature levels of play spend more time planning and coordinating play sequences than actually performing them. In the *Tools* curriculum, strategies to strengthen EFs are integrated into content areas, like reading and math, as well as play activities. Research by Adele Diamond and her colleagues (2007) demonstrated that the *Tools* curriculum improved urban, low-income preschoolers' EFs in areas of cognitive flexibility, working memory, and inhibitory control. Barnett and colleagues (2008) reported similar improvements in EFs and lower levels of problem behaviors in *Tools* classrooms.

In an age of increasing pressure on students and teachers to pass tests, it's important to note that these skills, once the focus of traditional preschool curricula, are still critical for success in life. Perhaps we should take another look at the value of learning to play. As one of Vygotsky's close colleagues noted, "Optimal educational opportunities for a young child to reach his or her potential and to develop in a harmonious fashion are not created by accelerated ultra-early instruction aimed at shortening the childhood period—that would prematurely turn a toddler into a preschooler and a preschooler into a first-grader. What is needed is just the opposite—expansion and enrichment of the content in the activities that are uniquely "preschool": from play to painting to interactions with peers and adults" (Zaporozhets, 1986, p. 88).

Lessons from Piaget and Vygotsky

One of the most useful guidelines for helpers from Piaget's work is the idea that learning results from the dynamic interaction between assimilative and accommodative processes. Because much, if not all, of what transpires in any counseling or helping interaction comes under the broad rubric of learning and adaptation, these ideas can be readily translated into applications for therapeutic work with children and even adults. Piaget's ideas suggest that the helper should find ways to relate new information or insight to a client's current knowledge structures. In other words, if new knowledge, ideas, or information is too discrepant or if the individual lacks the context or experience to understand it, the new information will be ignored or discounted. On the other hand, if the new information is too similar to what the individual already knows, it will be assimilated into existing knowledge structures without any learning or cognitive change at all. To maximize learning, the helper needs to understand how clients are thinking and what meanings they have already made. Interventions or examples that build on previous knowledge allow the client the best chance of incorporating the new information into useful working knowledge.

With young children, learning new things takes time. From studies of brain development we have seen that initial connections are somewhat fragile. The new connections

involved in learning need to be reinforced regularly for them to be firmly established. Adults are sometimes dismayed by the number of times children need to hear an idea or message repeated before they can understand it. Yet, this is the essence of cognitive development. Mature thinking is constructed bit by bit, each part building on the previous one and helping to shape the next.

One of the particularly interesting legacies of Vygotskian theory for practice is his emphasis on culture in cognitive development. In this view, our ideas, including our ideas about children's development, are conditioned and shaped by our culture. It should be stressed, however, that culture is not monolithic. Within any kind of cultural group, be it ethnic, socioeconomic, gender-based, religious, or the culture of our family homes, individual differences still flourish. Indeed individuals may be more similar in beliefs, values, and practices to members of another cultural group than they are to those with whom they share a similar cultural heritage (Greenfield & Suzuki, 1998). It has been frequently stated, for example, that Eurocentric cultures place more importance on the value of individualism than do Asian cultures, which hold more communitarian ideals. Certain assumptions, such as these about individualism and collectivism, need to be refined, clarified, and carefully evaluated to avoid dualistic overgeneralizations.

Nonetheless, members of distinct cultural groups can differ systematically in certain beliefs and values (Greenfield, 1994). Therefore, when the cultural orientation of a family is different from that of the helper, professionals need to recognize and appreciate that different developmental goals can and do exist. For example, Japanese parents generally place great value on the interdependence of family members and their mutual responsibilities toward each other. This value is expressed concretely in the sleeping arrangements parents make for their infants. In the United States, infants generally sleep in a room separated from their parents (Morelli, Rogoff, Oppenheim, & Goldsmith, 1992).

Co-sleeping is the most frequently used sleeping arrangement for children in many non-Western cultures worldwide (Konner & Worthman, 1980). Unless this and other practices, such as co-bathing and care of young children by siblings, are understood contextually, the risk of misinterpreting them as harmful is a real one. Helpers need to be able to separate culturally different child-rearing practices from those that are truly abusive or neglectful.

Whereas each cultural practice has its own costs and benefits, understanding the cultural underpinnings of different child-rearing approaches can provide us with helpful information that can reduce our own culture-bound ways of thinking.

Knowledge about the outcomes of cultural variations in practice may allow helpers to consider a fuller range of options for child care and to make sensible recommendations. Our communication with parents will be more helpful and compassionate if we understand, as Vygotsky pointed out, that our own ideas and values are mediated by the culture in which we live (see Table 3.4).

TABLE 3.4 Contrasting Cultural Models of Parent–Child Relations

	DEVELOPMENTAL GOALS	
	INDEPENDENCE	**INTERDEPENDENCE**
Developmental trajectory	From dependent to independent self	From asocial to socially responsible self
Children's relations to parents	Personal choice concerning relationship to parents	Obligations to parents
Communication	Verbal emphasis	Nonverbal emphasis (empathy, observation, participation)
	Autonomous self-expression by child	Child comprehension, mother speaks for child
	Frequent parental questions to child	Frequent parental directives to child
	Frequent praise	Infrequent praise
	Child negotiation	Harmony, respect, obedience
Parenting style	Authoritative: controlling, demanding, warm, rational	Rigorous and responsible teaching, high involvement, physical closeness
Parents helping children	A matter of personal choice except under extreme need	A moral obligation under all circumstances

SOURCES: Greenfield, P. M., & Suzuki, L. K. Cultural human development. In W. Damon et al. (1998). *Handbook of Child Psychology: Vol. 4* (5th ed. pp. 1059–1109). Hoboken: NJ. Copyright © 1998. This material is used by permission of John Wiley & Sons, Inc.

FOCUS ON DEVELOPMENTAL PSYCHOPATHOLOGY

Autism Spectrum Disorders

In recent years, *autism* has received an increasing amount of attention from researchers and the popular press largely because the incidence rate of autism and autistic spectrum disorders is rising (Rutter, 2005) reportedly affecting 1 in 110 individuals (Hu, 2012). Yet, despite a huge body of research on the topic, we do not have a clear understanding of its causes. At the University of California-Davis, a long-term epidemiological investigation begun in 2002 into the causes of autism and developmental delay is underway. The study, called CHARGE (Childhood Autism Risks from Genetics and the Environment), illustrates an important lesson for students of development and developmental psychopathology (Hertz-Picciotto et al., 2006). Its strategy is to examine the interaction of genetic and environmental factors that are associated with disorders on the autism spectrum, reflecting the contemporary understanding of coaction in the development of this heterogeneous disorder.

Early Views

Leo Kanner (1943), a psychiatrist at Johns Hopkins in the 1940s first identified *early infantile autism* and influenced psychiatric conceptualizations of the disorder that persisted for decades. Based upon his work with a small, overwhelmingly white, well-educated and relatively affluent sample of families, Kanner concluded that autism developed primarily as a function of cold and distant parenting, even though he believed that some

inborn deficit was also present in autistic children. In line with the thinking of that age, mothers were primarily responsible for parenting. Kanner referred to the mothers of his autistic patients as "refrigerator mothers," because of their apparently aloof and intellectual tendencies. Austrian pediatrician Hans Asperger (1991/1944), a contemporary of Kanner's, also studied children with some autistic symptoms but whose overall functioning was more normal. In contrast to Kanner, Asperger presumed that the roots of the developmental problems he observed were essentially genetic. Unfortunately, Asperger's ideas were not to temper Kanner's until the late 1970s and 1980s when the former's works were translated. Meanwhile, another famous psychologist, Bruno Bettleheim (1967) working at the University of Chicago, used his own considerable talent to champion the theory that dysfunctional parent–child relationships caused autism. Thus, an early historical emphasis on nurture and a lack of technology to explore genetics combined to burden families of children with autism in the 1950s and 1960s with the guilt of having caused their children's disabilities.

Developmental Characteristics

Some infants demonstrate early indications of autism right from birth. In other cases, regressions can occur when children who appear to be developing normally experience a sudden setback and loss of function in areas of affective and language skills. Fifteen percent of children in the CHARGE study experienced regressions (Hansen et al., 2008). Some say that the signs for autism are present much earlier, even for this latter group. However, early reliable diagnosis will depend on the identification of more sophisticated markers, an important consideration given that early diagnosis and treatment is associated with better outcomes (Dawson, 2008). The American Academy of Pediatrics actually recommends screening all children for autism at 18 months (Johnson & Myers, 2007).

The general consensus is that disorders of the autism spectrum are neurobiological in nature and have high family concordance rates (Folstein & Rutter, 1977). Akshoomoff and colleagues (2002) provide evidence of brain growth abnormalities in young children with autism that are related to abnormal growth and pruning of synapses. These authors posit disruptions in the timing mechanisms directing neuron growth and pruning processes. Neuron "overgrowth" may account for larger than normal cerebral volume in autistic toddlers and may be mediated by neurochemicals in the brain that support cell survival and disrupt pruning. Paradoxically, other neurochemicals present in the brains of individuals with autism appear to reduce neural growth in the cerebellum, which is reportedly smaller in this population. The risk to a sibling of a child with autism is 20 to 50 times greater than to those with non-autistic siblings (O'Roak & State, 2008).

Possible contributors to the various symptoms exhibited by those on the spectrum include individual differences in the timing of brain development, genetic variation, and metabolic influences, all in combination with environmental (teratogenic) factors. Recent controversy has centered on the association between disorders on this spectrum and pediatric vaccines containing thimerosal, a preservative containing mercury. The evidence available at this point does not support a causal relationship between the two (Hornig et al., 2008; Lancet, 2010; Thompson, Price, Goodson, Shay, Benson, et al., 2007). Yet, it is important to continue to examine environmental factors for their potential impact. In the CHARGE study, factors under investigation include pesticides, metals, flame retardants found in fabric, viruses, bacteria, medical procedures and pharmaceuticals. Recent evidence from CHARGE showed a 10% rise in rates of autism for children whose families lived closer to freeways in Los Angeles (within ¼ mile) around the time of birth (Volk, Hertz-Delwiche, Lurmann, & McConnell, 2011). Because environmental pollutants are associated with immune-related abnormalities, also found more frequently in children with autism (Ashwood et al., 2011; Block & Calderón-Garcidueñas, 2009), this may be an environmental risk factor that interacts with developing physiology.

What might be at the root of the interaction? Researchers have begun to examine the role of biochemical reactions in the **mitochondria**, small organelles within cells that produce energy for the cell's metabolism and overall function. A subset of children with autism shows signs of metabolic dysfunction, which is expressed in a wide range of autistic-like symptoms (see Weissman et al., 2008). Mitochondrial dysfunction might have a genetic basis but clearly interacts with environmental influences. Research has suggested that regressions may be more common in children with underlying mitochondrial dysfunction. In these cases, events like infection and fever may precipitate the regression, suggesting that an underlying vulnerability was triggered by the environmental event. Although more research is needed in this developing area, it appears that inflammatory processes are involved in mitochondrial dysfunction and play an etiological role in at least some cases of autism (Haas, 2010).

Diagnostic Issues

Formerly with the DSM-IV-TR, five disorders constituted the spectrum: *Autism*, *Pervasive Developmental Disorder Not Otherwise Specified (PDD-NOS)*, *Asperger's Disorder (AD, or Asperger Syndrome AS)*, *Rett's Disorder*, and *Childhood Disintegrative Disorder*. The last two disorders are much rarer than the first three. Because autism, PDD-NOS, and AD share many similarities, some view these disorders as existing on a continuum of severity. The new DSM-V groups all categories into one, called **autism spectrum disorder (ASD)** because of highly overlapping symptoms and presumably related etiologies.

Approximately two-thirds of autistic children also meet criteria for mental retardation (APA, 2000) with the remaining one-third presently characterized as having *High-functioning Autism (HFA)* with IQs above 70. Between 10% and 15% of autistic children display some unusual talent (called "splinter skills"). In later adolescence, about one-quarter of autistic individuals develop epilepsy. Compared to autistic individuals and those who do not meet criteria for autism (PDD-NOS), those with AD have higher levels of cognitive and language development and more social interest. Some researchers argue that the three related disorders should be viewed as separate because of distinct brain activity and different long-term outcomes (Dawson, Klinger, Panagiotides, Lewy, & Castelloe, 1995), while still others, such as Baron-Cohen (2000), suggest that AD is more of a "difference" than a disability. Research is needed to sort out these issues.

The most prominent features of autism have early developmental roots. Difficulties in social development relate to impairments in basic skills necessary for building a theory of mind: joint attention, imitation, and the turn-taking routines needed to cement solid interpersonal relationships. Interesting studies have linked early deficits in face recognition to these social-cognitive deficits. Children with autism process human faces with a part of the brain normally used to process objects (Dawson, Carver, Meltzoff, Panagiotides, McPartland, & Webb, 2002) while older autistic individuals actually have better memory for inverted faces than for upright faces (Hobson, Ouston, & Lee, 1988).

Social interaction skill deficits may have something to do with perception of unfamiliar (versus familiar) people as threatening. Van Hecke and her colleagues (2009) report that children with autism react to videos of unfamiliar people reading a story with reduced **heart rate regulation (HRR)**. HRR (or heart-rate variability) is determined by measuring the synchrony between respiration and heart rate as mediated by the **vagus nerve**. Heart rate accelerates on the in-breath, increasing sympathetic activation, and decreases on the out-breath, enhancing para-sympathetic activation. Higher rates of heart rate variability between in and out breaths during respiration is a mark of health and efficient operation of the vagus nerve. The vagus nerve connects brainstem areas that control ancient fight, flight, or freeze responses with various organs such as larynx, heart, and intestines. Lower rates of heart-rate variability, referred to as low vagal tone, suggest a state wherein the nervous system is chronically mobilized to respond to perceived threat (Porges, 2007). In this study, children with autism demonstrated poorer heart rate regulation (low **vagal tone**) while watching the video of the unfamiliar adult as if in a state of physiological anticipation of threat. Typically developing children showed higher vagal tone, as if anticipating social engagement with interest and curiosity. When the videos changed to reveal familiar caregivers reading stories, heart rate regulation in the children with autism returned to normal. The authors point out the importance of continuity of care (e.g., from familiar teachers, therapists, etc.) for successful therapeutic interventions for individuals with autism.

Impairments in communication for autism spectrum disorders range from having no meaningful language at all to having no language delays. Even when verbal communication is present as in the case of AD/HFA, communication is typically marked by deficits in the pragmatics of language, in highly literal interpretation of meaning, and in impairments in pitch, rhythm or stress of speech (prosody). Behavioral symptoms such as "stimming" (non-sexual self-stimulating activity), self-injurious behavior (e.g., head-banging), hyperactivity, and disruptive behavior can be present in autism. Preoccupations with highly idiosyncratic interests (e.g., TV shows, trains, or weather), uncoordinated movement and physical awkwardness are characteristic symptoms of ASD. It is easy to see how pervasive the effects of these disorders can be over the course of development. Children with ASD lack the basis for many of the normal progressions expected to occur in development, especially the formation of peer relationships.

Treatment Approaches

Behavioral treatments for ASD appear to be most successful, especially treatments that begin early and are sustained over time (Tanguay, 2000). Lovaas, a pioneer in autism treatment, developed a technique called "Applied Behavior Analysis" (ABA). This approach applies learning theory principles to facilitate communicative, social, and academic performance and has been demonstrated to be effective for significant numbers of autistic children (Lovaas, 1987; McEachin, Smith, & Lovaas, 1993). ABA techniques have been incorporated into many successful treatment programs.

The "Denver Model" (Rogers, Hayden, Hepburn, Charlifue-Smith, Hall, & Hayes, 2006; Rogers & Lewis, 1989) is a comprehensive, interdisciplinary program that utilizes parents, preschool teachers, and program coordinators to provide an intensive curriculum for 2- to 5-year-old autistic children. Several hours per day of one to one teaching makes such programs labor-intensive but necessary for severely affected children. Other structured learning experiences are embedded within the routine activities of school and home to supplement the intensive one to one exercises. The structured interventions in the Denver Model are targeted to improve cognitive and communication skills, social interactions, play quality, motor skills, and adaptive behaviors that promote independence and participation in family routines.

An adapted version of this program, the "Early Start Denver Model" (Smith, Rogers, & Dawson, 2008), is designed for children from 14 months to 3 years of age. Assuming the importance of early intervention, this program is designed to take advantage of the sensitive period for developing social networks in the brain by fostering parent–child synchronistic and contingent communication and, in particular, by stimulating the parts of the brain implicated in reinforcement of social interaction through intensive practice. The principles of coaction are clearly evident in the foundations of this program. Smith and colleagues assert that "because the expression and effects of many genes are influenced by environmental factors, it is possible that early treatment can alter genetic expression, brain development, and behavioral outcome in ASD, especially if intervention can begin early during the infant period before the symptoms of autism are fully manifest" (2008, p. 781). The results of a recent randomized control trial of this two-year intervention showed significant improvements for participating children in adaptive behavior, IQ, communication, and motor skills compared to a group who received traditional community-based interventions (Dawson et al., 2010).

Some general guidelines for intervention programs for children with ASD from the Council for Children with Disabilities (Myers, Johnson, & Council on Children With Disabilities, 2007) include:

- Early entry into intervention program
- Intensive, year-round, developmentally appropriate treatment (25 hours per week minimum) with clearly identified objectives and active child participation
- Small group teacher-student ratio that allows for individual attention
- Parent training and support
- Appropriate opportunities to interact with typically developing peers
- Ongoing assessment of progress
- Incorporation of structure and lessons that address communication, social, adaptive, and school readiness skills and decrease disruptive behavior.

Embedded within these guidelines is the understanding that education and therapeutic programs should work toward generalization of skills in naturalistic settings. Combining structured sessions with real-world instruction can help maintain educational gains and is actually more effective than structured sessions alone. This combination also makes it easier for parents to work with their children in the home (Levy, Mandell, & Schultz, 2009). Families of children on the autism spectrum experience strong emotions such as loss and sadness, worries about ability to cope, and frustration and isolation in settings that appear unresponsive to their needs. In some cases, they can be overwhelmed with the responsibilities of keeping their children safe. They experience much more stress than families with normally developing children; they need the help and support of informed, compassionate professionals. Comprehensive

programs that facilitate social engagement and promote independence should not only help mitigate the effects of disorders among individuals on this spectrum, but also provide hope and support for parents, who are their children's most important teachers.

SUMMARY

Piaget's Constructivist Theory

1. Piaget saw children as active learners, intrinsically motivated to seek out and understand new information. At any age their knowledge is organized or structured and that its organization changes over time as adaptation occurs. Adaptation is the combination of assimilation (fitting new information to existing knowledge structures) and accommodation (changing knowledge structures to fit what is new). Children's understandings change only a little at a time, and the child may distort information that is completely new as she tries to assimilate it to her current knowledge structures. According to Piaget, children progress through a series of cognitive stages. Within a stage, children organize their thinking across a variety of concepts in similar ways.

Infant Cognition: The Sensorimotor Stage

2. Modern research indicates that cognitive development is often domain specific, so that understandings in different domains of knowledge are not always organized in similar ways. Although the idea of cognitive stages may not be strictly accurate, Piaget's stage divisions are broadly useful for organizing our thinking about children, their understandings, and their limitations at different ages.

3. Piaget studied infants' cognition in the sensorimotor stage (ages birth to 2) by making inferences from babies' motor interactions with the environment. Today's researchers use additional tools, such as the habituation and preferential response paradigms. Modern research techniques produce findings that challenge some of Piaget's ideas about infants.

4. The object concept requires knowing that objects can stimulate multiple senses and that objects are permanent. Piaget assumed that infants develop the first understanding at about 2 to 4 months, as they coordinate their reflexive motor responses to stimulation. The second understanding requires representational thought, and Piaget assumed it began between 8 and 12 months, when babies will search for a hidden object. Newer research indicates earlier understandings of both aspects of the object concept. Intersensory integration is apparently possible in the first weeks of life, and some early signs of object permanence have been observed in 4-month-olds.

5. Despite these findings, most memory research indicates that representational thought in infants begins in earnest in the last part of the 1st year. Recognition ability, which requires only that a stimulus can be identified as familiar,

is present by birth. However, the earliest indicator of recall, which requires representational thought, occurs at about 8 or 9 months. Two indicators of recall are deferred imitation and separation anxiety.

6. Intentional or planful action has precursors in early infancy, but means–end behavior, which seems to require some degree of representational thought, begins in the last part of the 1st year, when babies' communicative behaviors also begin to appear. At the same time, intentional infants begin to attribute to agency to others and to understand that other people have intentions. These emerging skills mark the beginning of a child's "theory of mind": an understanding of the mental underpinnings of human behavior.

Preschoolers' Cognition: The Preoperational Stage

7. By age 2, children are in Piaget's stage of preoperational (meaning prelogical) thought. By studying early cognitive abilities, such as number understanding and perspective taking skill, Piaget identified apparent limitations on children's early representational thought. Preoperational thought tends to be centered in Piaget's terminology, focused on one salient experience or event at a time. Because they cannot keep in mind all the relevant facts in a situation at one time, young children have trouble identifying the logical relationships among such facts, as indicated by children's early failure at number conservation. Modern researchers use simpler tasks and have identified some early skills that children do have. Regarding numbers, for example, they can adhere to the one-to-one principle and to the order-irrelevance principle in counting, and in very simple situations they can even recognize that a number stays the same when objects are rearranged. Modern theorists tend to view skills like number understanding as emerging gradually, with increasing breadth and depth. Researchers seek to identify the sequence of skill levels and the experiences that facilitate acquisition. Practice through play is clearly an important kind of experience.

8. Piaget pioneered the study of preschoolers' theory of mind with his perspective-taking tasks. Young children often assume that others have the same perspective that they do. Piaget argued that young children are egocentric, centered on their own perspective and therefore unaware of the possibility of another perspective. Newer work supports this idea, but identifies a gradual progression of perspective-taking skill in early childhood, such

that even 2-year-olds realize that others do not always see what they can see. By age 3, children can sometimes attribute a different visual perspective on the same object to another viewer. Between ages 4 and 5, children begin to realize that others sometimes know or believe different things. These understandings are fragile, and when a situation is emotionally charged, even older children often fall back on the assumption that another's perspective must be like their own. Advances in perspective taking depend in part on experience with social interaction.

9. Preschool children can use and understand symbols, but research with symbolic artifacts indicates that their symbolic skills progress gradually. For example, before age 3 they cannot treat a video presentation or a toy model as both the concrete objects that they are and as symbols for other things.

10. Young children seem to have less difficulty understanding the use of words as symbols, perhaps because words are not objects in themselves. Language acquisition is a complex process that requires learning several systems.

11. Children begin to learn the phonology of their native language even before birth. By 6 months, babies have begun to lose the ability to discriminate sounds that are not important in their native language, and by 9 months their babbling is limited to only the sounds of their native language. Learning how, when, and where to use those sounds can take several years.

12. The semantic system includes the words and word parts that carry meaning. First words appear by the end of the 1st year, and a vocabulary spurt begins by 18 to 24 months. Typically, children learn new words at a rapid pace, fast mapping 9 or 10 new words a day.

13. Learning the syntactic system of a language requires learning the rules for creating meaningful sentences. Children begin to produce two-word utterances about the time of the vocabulary spurt, and can produce most sentence structures by the time they are 5.

14. Pragmatics involves using language effectively to communicate: learning to construct well-organized, clear narratives; code switching; and learning to distinguish actual meaning from literal meaning.

15. Because of the complexity of language learning, some theorists argue that aspects of language learning must be innate. But no one denies the importance of language experience. For example, both the quantity and quality of adults' speech to children are related to children's vocabulary growth and narrative skill. Cross-cultural differences in adults' language and language use affect the types of words (e.g., nouns vs. verbs) children learn first.

Vygotsky's Sociocultural Theory

16. Vygotsky's theory of cognitive development is focused on the role of culture and society in children's intellectual growth. One theme is that novice learners grasp a concept or perform a skill only when others provide scaffolding. When understanding or performance requires scaffolding, it is said to be in the child's zone of proximal development.

17. Vygotsky especially emphasized language as a tool through which others convey formal knowledge, that is, scientific concepts. Language mediates learning in children and is one of the primary means by which culture and society help children's thinking to advance. Preschool children eventually come to use language as a way to mediate their own thinking. The private speech of 3-year-olds eventually becomes the inner speech of 8-year-olds. Internalization of speech is linked to attentional control, autobiographical memory, and impulse control.

CASE STUDY

Shady Grove Preschool is located in an old suburban neighborhood adjacent to a large metropolitan area. It serves infants, toddlers, and preschoolers from families with diverse cultural and ethnic backgrounds who have lower- to upper-middle-class income levels. The director of the facility, Mrs. Anthony, has decided to implement a new component, monthly group discussion sessions for parents. She has employed a counselor to facilitate the discussions and to field questions about child development from the parents who come to the sessions.

At the first meeting, the participants, primarily a group of mothers, begin with introductions and questions of a general nature. "How do I know when my toddler is ready for toilet training?" "How can I get my 6-month-old to sleep through the night?" Then the discussion becomes more animated. One mother, Mrs. Winger, a White woman, starts to raise concerns about the educational program at the school. Her son Brad, who is 4 ½, is a precocious child who enjoys learning. "I can't understand why they don't teach the children how to use computers in this school," she says. "These children need to get a head start on technological education because they will be competing with so many other students in schools for good colleges and, eventually, good jobs. We need to give them every advantage that we can."

Mrs. Winger is quick to add that she does not believe the children should be stressed. However, she clearly feels the days when children spend their time in preschool playing in a sandbox, drawing, and building with blocks should be over. She mentions that she has been reading some new information in parenting magazines about children's brain development, and she cautions the group against letting opportunities for the children's brain development to pass them by.

Mrs. Ramirez, a Latina, has a different concern. Her daughter Tina is 2½ and her 8-month-old son Nicky is in the infant program. "Tina is so jealous of her baby brother," says Mrs. Ramirez, "that she can't stand when I pay attention to him. She whines and cries when I play with him, even if I let her watch

TV when I'm doing it. She won't let him touch anything that is hers. Her father gets very upset with her behavior, too. We've talked to her about being a big girl and about sharing with her brother. We can't believe that she is so selfish." After a pause she notes, sadly, "My sister's children are the same ages and they seem to get along much better. We're too embarrassed to take her to family gatherings now, because she doesn't know how to behave and only draws attention to herself. My parents insist that we are spoiling her."

Discussion Questions

1. What are the underlying assumptions about child development in Mrs. Winger's comments? What is your assessment of her concerns based on what you know? How would you respond to her concerns?

2. Consider Mrs. Ramirez's statements. What are her beliefs about child development? How would you go about helping her resolve her problem? How have her assumptions about development affected her family relationships?

3. If you were the counselor in this situation, how would you plan a series of parent discussion sessions? What topics would you consider most important to cover? How could you present this information?

4. What is your position on accelerating development? Do you think that children can learn more than they are typically expected to? Should they be encouraged to do so?

PRACTICE USING WHAT YOU HAVE LEARNED

In the Pearson etext, apply these ideas to working with others.

Video Exercise

JOURNAL QUESTIONS

1. *Culture* is a broad concept. Identify an idea, belief, or value that you learned as a child that came from the culture of your family, one that came from the culture of your community or neighborhood, one that came from your broader cultural or ethnic background, and one that came from your religious culture.

2. Discuss why it might be easier to talk to people of your own culture(s) from the perspective of Vygotsky's notion of intersubjectivity. Give an example from your experience.

3. Visit a preschool program (or recall one you are familiar with) and describe your impressions of its quality. What things stood out as strengths? What were the weaknesses?

4. The importance of play in some schools has been decreasing given the emphasis on academics. What do you think about this trend? How might it affect children's development for better or worse?

KEY CONCEPTS

adaptation (p. 79)

assimilation (p. 79)

accommodation (p. 79)

domain specific (p. 81)

habituation paradigm (p. 82)

orienting response (p. 82)

habituation (p. 82)

dishabituation (p. 82)

preferential response paradigms (p. 82)

visual acuity (p. 82)

object concept (p. 84)

intersensory integration (intermodal perception) (p. 84)

object permanence (p. 85)

representational thought (p. 85)

hidden object test (p. 85)

recognition (p. 86)

recall (p. 86)

deferred imitation (p. 87)

separation anxiety (p. 87)

mirror neurons (p. 88)

making interesting sights last (p. 89)

means–end behavior (p. 89)

executive functions (EFs) (p. 90)

agency (p. 90)

intention (p. 90)

theory of mind (p. 90)

working memory (p. 91)

self-regulation (p. 91)

cognitive flexibility (p. 91)

symbols (p. 92)

number conservation task (p. 92)

centration (p. 92)

decentration (p. 93)

exploratory play (p. 94)

preoperational egocentrism (p. 95)

false belief tasks (p. 97)

pretend play (p. 98)

symbolic artifacts (p. 99)

phonology (p. 100)

babbling (p. 100)

voicing (p. 100)

semantics (p. 101)

vocabulary spurt (p. 101)

fast mapping (p. 102)

slow mapping (p. 102)

syntax (grammar) (p. 102)

pragmatics (p. 103)

narrative (p. 103)

code switching (p. 103)

elaborative style (p. 105)

infantile amnesia (p. 105)

tools (signs) (p. 109)

mediation (p. 109)

mediated learning (p. 109)

scientific concepts (p. 110)

scaffolding (p. 110)

zone of proximal development (p. 111)

intersubjectivity (p. 111)

egocentric or private speech (p. 112)

inner speech (p. 112)

mitochondria (p. 118)

autism spectrum disorder (ASD) (p. 118)

heart rate regulation (HRR) (p. 118)

vagus nerve (p. 118)

vagal tone (p. 119)

CHAPTER 4

Emotional Development in the Early Years

In the course of their daily work, most helpers encounter an array of human problems. Despite their different presenting features, all concerns—a young child's difficulty adjusting to school, a teenager's uncertainty about the future, a couple's recurring arguments about money, a widower's difficulty living alone— have a common aspect. They all, to a greater or lesser degree, involve human emotion. You probably could identify the emotional responses that would most likely be manifested by the hypothetical individuals in the previous examples. The child might feel lonely; the teenager, anxious; the couple, angry; and the older person, sad. Depending upon your particular theoretical orientation, you could probably suggest ways to help each individual. Yet, simply identifying the emotions and proposing techniques, as good a starting point as that may be, reveals nothing about the person's emotional development, nor does it provide you any insight as to whether your techniques might work. Are these clients' re- actions appropriate or even adaptive in light of their situations? How concerned should you be about their symptoms? What were the precursors that led to their particular level of emotional adjustment or maladjustment? What coping styles have they developed over time and how useful are they? Unless we understand the process of emotional development in its normative context, we may view our clients' emotions only clinically, as if we were looking at their snapshots, detached from context and earlier experience. Their problems might be seen as manifestations of individual differences (for example, depressed versus anxious) rather than as reflections of their development, and their diagnoses might imply only possession of a set of clinical criteria. Overall, our understanding of clients would be impoverished.

The study of emotional development is a critical link to a better understanding of emotional problems whenever they appear during the life span. Sroufe (1996) states that "emotional development is the foundation for the study of individual adaptation and psychopathology. Pursuing these fields without being fully grounded in emotional development is analogous to trying to do research in genetics with- out being grounded in biology" (p. xii). Perhaps being an interpreter of emotional messages and a forger of affective change in a therapeutic context (Strupp, 1988) is also impossible without a fundamental working knowledge of emotional development. In this chapter, we review the beginnings of emotional development, the processes involved in early bonding, and the implications of these events for later well-being.

THEORIES OF EMOTION

Before we can address the topic of emotional development, we need to concern ourselves briefly with the question of what emotions are. This fundamental dilemma has occupied the time, attention, and brainpower of many gifted writers in the fields of philosophy, psychology and psychiatry, biology, and the neurosciences. However, there are still many unanswered questions and some major controversies in this area. For example, theorists disagree about whether emotions are best defined as physiological states, action tendencies, subjectively perceived experiences, or some combination of the above. A clear, comprehensive, universally accepted theory of the nature of emotions, the way emotions develop, the function of emotionally related brain structures, and the role of emotions in psychotherapy and mental health (Greenberg & Safran, 1989; LeDoux, 2012) has not yet been fully constructed.

Many researchers agree that there is a biological or evolutionary reason for emotions in humans. Emotions are built into our nature for their survival value (Ortony & Turner, 1992). Less agreement is found on what constitutes the set of basic human emotions. Most researchers agree that babies possess an emotional repertoire; however, opinions differ on the number, nature, and names of the emotions babies display. This is partly because different researchers emphasize different aspects of the question. Some writers have focused on the physical, particularly facial, manifestations of emotions (Ekman & Oster, 1979; Izard, 1991, 2004), others on the neurological underpinnings (Damasio, 1994; Panksepp, 1982, 2008), whereas still others have centered their attention on the emergence of changes in kinds of emotional expression over the first few years of life (Sroufe, 1996).

Functions of Emotions

Emotions exist to serve many purposes for human beings. It would be hard to disagree that they provide us with a trusty arsenal of survival skills. The fear response that alerts us to a dangerous situation signals us to fight back or escape to protect ourselves. The urge to engage in sexual relations propagates the species. The disgust we experience when we encounter decaying material protects us from exposure to potentially toxic bacteria. The affection elicited by a baby's smiling face promotes the caregiving needed to ensure his continued survival. Emotional responses have ancient, evolutionary significance.

Examples of the role emotions play in survival demonstrate how powerful emotions are as motivators of behavior. The force of conscience provides a clear example of the motivational properties of emotion. Conscience is like a thermostat that is ordinarily set at the "feel good" level. If we do something we consider morally or ethically wrong, our emotional temperature changes and we may experience shame or guilt. These feelings prod us to make restitution or to change our errant ways so that we can regain the "feel good" setting. Such social emotions (see Chapter 5) can serve as powerful reinforcers of behavior.

Emotions also serve as a major means of communication. An infant's distressed facial expression and piercing cry after receiving an inoculation serve as preemptory commands to the caretaker: "Help me! I'm in pain." When helpers speak of nonverbal communication, an essential component is always the emotional message conveyed through the face, posture, and gestures (Ekman & Friesen, 1969). The view of emotion-as-communication underscores the basic social significance of the emotions and captures an essential quality of the attachment relationship, to be discussed later in this chapter. Emotions are the stepping-stones that infants use to develop reciprocity with caregivers, ultimately leading to the capacity for emotion management.

The role of emotions in cognitive functions has received notice as well. Contrary to that age-old warning to keep your feelings out of your logical decision making, Damasio (1994) has provided compelling evidence that the absence of emotion clearly impairs rather than enhances cognition. Damasio observed patients with damage to the frontal lobe region and noted that they shared a syndrome that he called the **Phineas Gage matrix**. This syndrome consists of cognitive dysfunctions such as poor planning, inadequate decision making, inability to take another's perspective, and problems in sustaining employment. These cognitive limitations go hand in hand with emotional problems such as shallow affect, lack of an enriched emotional life, lack of passion and initiative, and a diminished sense of pleasure and pain. Far from enabling us to be more "rational," the absence of emotion in our intellectual functioning leaves us sadly lacking in resourcefulness. Contemporary views of emotion emphasize the organizing role emotions play in higher-order cognitive functions like memory, decision-making, and planful behavior (see Izard, 2009).

Last, but certainly not least, emotions have a role to play in overall mental health and wellness. Affective disturbances characterize a major category of mental illness and are strongly related to many other psychopathological conditions. On the positive side, research originally done by Salovey and Mayer (1990) and popularized by Goleman (1995) has emphasized the importance of so-called **emotional intelligence** (or emotional IQ), defined as the ability to perceive emotions, to identify and understand their meaning, to integrate them with other kinds of cognition, and to manage them. Despite recent claims found in the popular press that people with high emotional IQs have strong advantages in life over those not so well endowed, the scientific research in this area is in its infancy and cannot support such claims at the present time (Mayer & Cobb, 2000; Pfeiffer, 2001). Nonetheless, available data indicate a modest yet reliable correlation between emotional intelligence and certain positive life outcomes.

A Brief History of Emotion Research and Some Current Developments

The study of emotions is now a major area of research investigation. In past decades, however, its study languished while research in cognition took center-stage (Neisser, 1967). Perhaps this happened because researchers had difficulty defining emotions. Perhaps researchers had a bias against "soft, subjective" topics in favor of those considered more objective and, therefore, more appropriate to science. The somewhat artificial split between "cognition" and "emotion" resulted in the common perception that information processing involved only higher order thinking capacities separate from emotion. This perception existed despite the fact that higher order cognitive processing is *just one kind* of information processing that the brain is able to accomplish. In any case, the study of emotions, so central to human experience and so critical to helpers, was largely left out of the cognitive revolution that started around the middle of the 20th century. In the words of LeDoux (1996), cognitive scientists seemed to view people as "souls on ice" (p. 22). Clinicians were further distanced from an appreciation of the emotional brain because traditional academic training separated students of social science and of science into different tracks, thus leaving students with clinical interests ill-prepared in the biological sciences (deCatanzaro, 1999).

This is not to say that there has been little interest in emotions. Early theorists such as William James, Carl Lange, Walter Cannon, Philip Bard, and others provided theories of emotions that held sway for many years. These theorists tended to disagree about the directionality of emotional responses and the primacy of body or brain. James believed that environmental events lead to bodily changes and behaviors, which people then interpret as particular emotions. Cannon and Bard argued that external stimuli had to be detected and evaluated by the rational brain before conscious feelings and bodily changes could be produced (see deCatanzaro, 1999, for a review of classic theories).

An important contribution to this field was made by Charles Darwin's (1872) view that certain emotions are innate and universal among humans and primates, rather like primitive instincts. He believed that facial expressions communicated underlying emotions and that these emotions were present because they were necessary for survival. Researchers (Ekman, 1994; Ekman & Friesen, 1971) found that people across a wide variety of cultures, including societies without exposure to Western ideas, fundamentally agreed on what constituted expressions of basic emotions. The standard methodology used in cross-cultural research involved asking participants from different cultures to view pictures of facial expressions and then to identify the emotions depicted in the photographs. In reviewing studies conducted during the past 50 years, Ekman (1992) concluded that certain facial expressions are interpreted as the same emotions regardless of cultural context. From American cities to the highlands of New Guinea, both industrialized and non-industrialized peoples appear to derive the same meanings from certain characteristic facial expressions.

Drawing on this Darwinian tradition, Izard (1992) focused his attention on babies and their ways of communicating emotional messages. He reasoned that infants have little time to learn social conventions and therefore will exhibit only those emotional responses that are inborn. Izard developed coding schemes that enable researchers and clinicians to identify different emotions based upon the position of the facial musculature (Izard, 1979; Izard, Dougherty, & Hembree, 1983). Infants display predictable facial expressions in certain circumstances, implying, according to Izard, the underlying presence of a comparable feeling. For example, when an infant is presented with a new and interesting picture, he will show the facial response of interest. When interacting pleasantly with a beloved caretaker, the infant's face conveys happiness or joy. (See Figure 4.1.)

Izard (1991, 2004) concluded that infant expressive behaviors are components of **basic emotions** and the direct product of the underlying neural processes related to each discrete feeling. Izard's theory, called **differential emotions theory (DET)**,

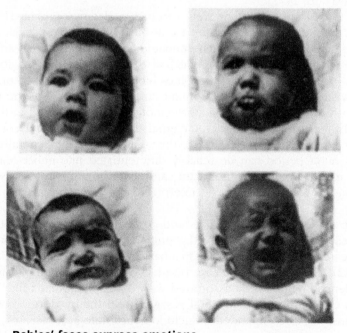

FIGURE 4.1   Babies' faces express emotions.
SOURCE: Sullivan, M. W. Expressions. 5-month-olds during reward learning and its frustration NIMT Study #061778. Rutgers School of Nursing. Used by permission of Margaret Sullivan, PhD.

posits that emotions are universal, naturally occurring phenomena mediated by evolutionarily old subcortical brain structures. Izard's (2007) list of basic emotions includes joy/happiness, interest, sadness, anger, disgust and fear. Other theorists who espouse the concept of basic emotions have closely related lists (Ekman, 1999; Tomkins, 1962). From this perspective, a sad expression implies the operation of the neural circuitry associated with sadness. If a baby looks sad, he *is* sad because babies' faces are mirrors of their felt emotions.

Our basic emotions result from a long process of human adaption. They do not depend upon learning and do not require cognitive components, such as appraisal or intent, to exist. DET distinguishes basic emotions from **emotion schemas**, which are the product of experience and culture. Emotion schemas may include memories, thoughts, images, and noncognitive elements like hormonal shifts that interact with and may amplify basic emotional experience (Izard, 1993). For example, your experience of anger (a basic emotion) might be accompanied by memories of a frustrating event, appraisals of cues as frustrating, and self-statements that reinforce anger. Such emotion schemas can become quite durable and begin to reflect a person's typical response style. Recently, Izard stated that interest and interest schemas hold a position of primacy in emotion and cognitive operations. The basic emotion of interest is profoundly connected to more overtly cognitive capacities like attention, intelligence, persistence, and goal-directed behavior (Izard, 2007; Tompkins, 1962). Interest is the driver of selective attention, from which all processing of information occurs as well as subsequent positive and negative emotions. In Chapter 14 we will discuss the foundational role of interest in adult flourishing.

Basic emotions emerge early in childhood, especially during the first 2 years of life. At birth or close to it, infants display distress (crying), contentment (smiling), disgust (avoiding bitter tastes or unpleasant odors), and interest (staring at faces and objects) (Izard & Malatesta, 1987). Anger, surprise, fear, and sadness begin to emerge from 2 months to approximately 6 months of age. So-called **self-conscious emotions** (see Chapter 5), such as pride, shame, embarrassment, empathy and guilt, depend upon self-recognition and higher levels of cognitive functioning (Lewis, 2008; Lewis & Brooks-Gunn, 1979). Emotion schema development probably depends upon later language development, when words can be used to describe feeling states (Izard, 1971).

Sroufe (1996) offers another view of emotional development. He takes the position that emotions are not fully formed at birth but that they develop from undifferentiated responses into more differentiated ones and finally into an integrated emotional repertoire. This principle is called *orthogenetic*: As behavior becomes differentiated or elaborated, it also becomes hierarchically organized or controlled by higher levels of functioning. Early infant emotional expressions are considered precursors or forerunners of more mature emotions. Emotions start in this fashion, Sroufe reasons, because infants lack the cognitive ability needed to ascribe meaning to emotional experiences. An example of this notion is that the generalized distress of the early infant period can be reliably differentiated into either fear or anger roughly at 6 months, only after the infant can recognize a threat. At this later time, the infant's facial expressions can be interpreted more reliably as communicating anger or fear.

Despite its deep theoretical roots and contemporary popularity, the field of emotion research has not yet achieved a unified point of view. Most importantly, perhaps, researchers still do not agree on a basic definition of emotion (Izard, 2006; LeDoux, 2012). This might be the case because emotions are complicated, subjectively experienced, and closely associated with other phenomena like motivation and arousal. Contemporary behavioral research and theory development, across many domains, has also expanded to include neurobiological research. While this interdisciplinary trend offers great potential, it requires scientists and helpers to accommodate new kinds of evidence, which can increase the level of complexity. Below we briefly review some of the history and contemporary work on emotions and the brain in order to complement earlier chapters and provide background for later reading.

Emotions: The View from Neuroscience

For a long time, researchers have tried to identify brain-based correlates of emotion. Several influential contributions came from James Papez (1937), who identified the structures of the limbic circuit, and Robert MacLean (1952, 1970), who proposed that the limbic system was the *visceral brain*, or the site of emotions. MacLean, building on the earlier work of Papez, concluded that the brain had evolved over millions of years to its present tripartite, or "three-brains-in-one," state. His *triune brain* included the (1) reptilian, (2) paleomammalian, or limbic, and (3) mammalian brains, each with its own particular structures and functions. All three were thought to exist in humans and in other advanced animal species. Lower level mammals had both paleomammalian and reptilian brains, whereas lower level species had only the latter.

According to MacLean's theory, each brain was distinct, represented successfully higher levels of cortical functioning, and arrived on the scene at a different time in history. The limbic brain was composed of evolutionarily "old" cortex or brain matter that was present in species that were phylogenetically older than humans. The functions served by this system—fight, flight, feeding, mating, and so on—were necessary for the survival of the species. Many early studies of anatomy supported the ties between limbic structures and emotional responses, so that the limbic system as the processor and repository of emotions was dogma for many years.

Beginning in the 1970s, however, researchers began to uncover evidence that poked holes in MacLean's theory. First, it was shown that species that are very primitive (and old in the evolutionary sense) have brain structures that function as the cerebral cortex does in more advanced species (Northcutt & Kaas, 1995). This cast doubt on the evolution of a triune brain. Furthermore, some parts of the limbic system do not deal with emotions at all, whereas parts of the cerebral cortex do. Conventional wisdom used to be that the cerebral cortex receives sensory input first before conveying such input to the limbic structures for an emotional "reading" (Schacter & Singer, 1962). Thus, the cortex was perceived as the broker of all brain activity. Much to the surprise of many researchers, LeDoux identified a neural "back alley" through which information about a fearful stimulus travels directly from the sensory systems through the thalamus to the amygdala, bypassing the cortex altogether. Information traveling via this "low road" pathway leads to quicker, more powerful, and longer lasting, but also less rational, responses than information processed first via the cortex.

Imagine that one sunny summer afternoon you are swimming alone in the ocean, off the coast of your beach resort. Out of the corner of your eye, you spot a gray triangular shape rising above the water not too far away. Your body responds in characteristically defensive ways. Your stomach tightens, your heart races, your eyes strain to see the object, and so on. The threat is transmitted to your brain's emotional centers almost instantaneously so that your body can ready itself against the danger. Now, suppose the putative shark fin turns out to be only a piece of debris. Upon closer observation, your cortex distinguishes the difference and allows you to adjust your response to one that is more appropriate. Your initial emotional reaction is only a split second ahead of your rational response. Nature has apparently given us an early warning emotional system to provide us with a survival advantage. It is the cortex's job to decide whether the response is warranted or not. Thus, high-road and low-road processing, involving both reason and emotion, work in concert.

The glitch is that low-road emotional processing could be responsible for persistent emotional responses that we don't understand. This can happen through *conditioning*, or the pairing of emotional responses to stimuli that were once neutral. If you happen to experience marked shortness of breath, heart palpitations, and tightness in your chest while riding an elevator, you may develop a strong aversion to this form of transportation, an example of fear conditioning. LeDoux believes that phobias, panic, posttraumatic stress disorder, and anxiety all arise from the operation of the brain's fear system. As helpers know, these problems and reactions can persist despite the absence of real threat. Another tricky part is that these fears do not extinguish by themselves; probably active new learning or extinction training is needed for their control. They appear to lay in wait until, under stressful conditions, they rear their ugly heads again and affect our responses. LeDoux's explication of the "fear circuit" emphasized the complex interactivity among brain areas. A great deal of modern research has focused on such networks that have reciprocal associations with cortical areas involved in higher order thinking and decision-making. Consider, Zelazo and Cunningham's (2007) important work on the development of executive functions that involve top-down and bottom-up processes. Researchers have identified the brain stem, amygdala, insula, anterior cingulate, and sectors of the prefrontal cortex as participants in the coordinated production of emotions (see Damasio, 2003).

One organizational framework supported by recent evidence proposes two major, partially separate networks related to positive and negative affect (Gray, J. A., 1990). The positive affect system (sometimes called the Behavioral Approach System or BAS) supports appetitive, approach-related behavior while the negative affect system (Behavior Inhibition System or BIS) mediates withdrawal especially under conditions of perceived threat. As you might expect, these systems also influence motivation. Think of your desire to enjoy a delicious dinner in a four-star restaurant as an example of motivated approach behavior. When you turn up your nose in disgust after noticing something moldy in the back of your refrigerator, your BIS has kicked in. The affective quality of disgust certainly doesn't motivate you to eat lest you come down with food poisoning. The same kind of thing applies to other behaviors, such as joining an interesting social group or avoiding social contacts if they happen to make you anxious.

Positive and negative affect systems are also related to laterality, or right- and left-sided differences, in various parts of the brain. Using instruments that assess electrical activity in the brain (e.g., EEG), baseline levels of left-right activation can be determined. Left-sided activation is associated with approach-related positive affect while right-sided activation is implicated in avoidance-related negative affect (Davidson, 1992; Davidson & Irwin, 1999). In depressed individuals, lower levels of left- compared to right-sided activation have been observed, possibly accounting for the dominance of negative emotional states and negative cognitions (Davidson, 2000). In these individuals, it appears that the prefrontal cortex is unable to effectively down-regulate the amygdala's activity, which is naturally on guard against potential threats. Davidson and Fox (1989) reported that 10-month old infants who displayed greater right-sided activation cried more when separated from their mothers. In toddlers with lower left-side activation, more inhibited behavior was observed. Over time, these particular patterns of emotional responding can develop into one's habitual emotional way of responding to the world, or one's affective style (Davidson, 2000, 2012).

Research provides some support for the view that interacting brain networks (rather than localized areas) are responsible for emotions (Lindquist, Wager, Kober, Bliss-Moreau, & Barrett, 2012). But which networks are important and how should they be defined? LeDoux (2012) suggests rethinking the approach that posits distinct circuits for distinct emotions. Instead, he emphasizes the circuits associated with survival. In order to survive, organisms have several jobs to do: defend against threats, maintain fluid balance and adequate nutrition for energy, regulate temperature, and reproduce. Emotions serve to organize and assist the organism in these goals via activating certain responses and inhibiting others, motivating certain behaviors depending upon circumstances, and so forth. These are functions of emotions we mentioned earlier in this chapter. All these functions are carried out by neurophysiological systems that operate in highly coordinated ways. Approached from this comprehensive perspective, emotions are not disconnected from their adaptive function: survival. By considering emotion, motivation, and arousal together as survival circuits, LeDoux offers a synthesis that incorporates multiple neurophysiological systems (like the stress system) that function to promote adaptation. This view also reduces the difficulties involved in trying to achieve agreement on specific definitions of emotions and their distinct neural underpinnings.

THE EARLY DEVELOPMENT OF EMOTION REGULATION

Emotion regulation is one of the cornerstones of emotional well-being and positive adjustment throughout the life span. It encompasses the strategies and behaviors we use to moderate our emotional experiences in order to meet the demands of different situations or to achieve our goals. For example, healthy people find ways to comfort themselves in difficult times, keeping their distress from overwhelming them. They modulate their excitement in happy times so that they can organize and plan satisfying experiences, and they rally their excitement to push onward when challenges block the way toward desirable goals (Rothbart & Sheese, 2007). How do we learn to understand, identify, and manage the power of our emotions? The emotions of the newborn are poorly regulated. Emotional states can range from contentment to intense distress within minutes. Typically, adult caregivers serve the critical function of helping to manage the newborn's affect or to modulate affective expression while scaffolding the infant's own developing emotion regulation. The specific, facilitative environmental circumstances needed for healthy emotional development to occur include supportive, responsive caregiving.

Even in the first hours after birth, mothers and other caregivers interact with infants in ways that are likely to heighten positive affect and attention or to sooth negative affect. Mothers gaze at a newborn's face, smile, affectionately touch the baby, and vocalize in a high pitched voice. And human newborns tend to respond to such behaviors. For example, if mothers touch, talk, and coo to newborns who are alertly scanning, babies become more alert (Feldman & Eidelman, 2007). In fact, interactions between young infants and their mothers soon exhibit a repetitive-rhythmic organization, a temporal coordination of nonverbal behaviors, called **synchrony**. If baby looks at mom, mom gazes back; if baby smacks her lips, mom may smack or smile. Mothers take the lead in maintaining the synchrony by responding contingently to newborns' cues in these interactions. Babies become more responsive and contribute more to the synchrony as they grow older. Consider smiling, for example. Even though newborns sometimes smile, these seem to be reactions to physiological states. They do not yet respond to other people by smiling. By 2 to 3 months, however, a baby often smiles at human faces, especially his mother's face, and especially if she is smiling at him. A 3-month-old is more responsive than a newborn in other ways as well. When his mother gazes at him, the 3-month-old gazes back and is likely to vocalize, which encourages mom's vocalizing, and so on. When mother and baby behaviors are highly synchronized in face-to-face interactions, even the mother's heart rate tends to be responsive. If the infant's heart rate either accelerates or decelerates, the mother's heart rhythm is likely to change in the same direction within 1 second (see Feldman, 2007).

It is important to note that normal caregiver–infant interactions are "messy" (Tronick & Beehgly, 2010). Only about 30% of face-to-face interactions during the 1st year are positive in the sense that the baby is calm and alert and able to respond to the mother in a synchronous way. Moment to moment observations of mothers and infants demonstrate that most mismatches are repaired in the next interactive step, and the caregiver usually instigates the repair (e.g., Chow, Haltigan, & Messinger, 2010). Thus, babies typically experience repeated interactive derailment followed by successful repair. Through this process, sensitive, responsive caregivers modify their infants' emotions, gently prodding their babies toward longer and longer periods of positive affect and interactive coordination.

In this still-face procedure, the caregiver becomes unresponsive to the infant's appeals for attention. Note the ways in which the child tries to re-engage the adult. What do you suppose happened after the video ended?

The importance of caregivers' responsiveness for infants' emotion regulation is stunningly demonstrated in a procedure called the **still-face paradigm** (introduced by Tronick, Als, Adamson, Wise, & Brazelton, 1978). A baby is placed in an infant seat directly in front of his mother. Following instructions, the mother at first interacts in a normally pleasant and playful way with her child, which usually involves lots of gazing, smiling, vocalizing, and touching. (This is the *baseline episode*). Then, in the *still-face episode*, the mother becomes unresponsive, as though she were looking at the baby but not seeing him. Finally, in the *reunion episode*, mother resumes normal behavior. Even 2- to 3-month-olds can be heartbreakingly distressed by their mothers' unresponsiveness in the still face episode. Their natural response is to intensify the behaviors that usually "work," especially gazing intently at the mother and vocalizing. When the mother fails to respond to these **other-directed coping behaviors**, the baby's distress heightens, and he will usually resort to **self-directed coping behaviors** that seem designed for self-comfort. Babies look away or may even self-stimulate by rocking, sucking, rubbing their hair, and so on. Interestingly, this effect is observed if the mother is unresponsive for only a few seconds. The baby's negative mood persists even when the mother resumes contact. Babies look at their mothers less for several minutes after this experience. And the importance of mothers' behavior for helping babies manage their negative emotions is especially clear: The more responsive and positive mothers are during the reunion episode, the less avoidance and distress babies exhibit (see Mesman, van IJzendoorn, & Bakermas-Kranenburg, 2009).

The still-face paradigm illustrates that even very young infants have some natural strategies for coping with their emotions. It also suggests that when adults promote interactive repair they are scaffolding infants' use of other-directed coping strategies. As you will see in the next section, the ultimate effects seem to be that infants come to see others as reliable sources of support and to see themselves as effective social agents. Thus, sensitive, responsive caregiving promotes positive social development in many ways. Note that the caregiver provides the experience-dependent environment in which the baby's coping strategies are practiced and further developed. Once again, the interplay of native and environmental factors is required for a successful outcome (see Mesman et al., 2009, for a review of research and theory on infants' behavior in the still face paradigm).

The evidence is clear that babies' emotion regulation typically improves with age and that caregivers play a key role in this. Babies react less strongly in the still-face paradigm by 6 months old than they did earlier (e.g., Melinder, Forbes, Tronick, Fikke, & Gredeback, 2010). And they recover (e.g., stop crying) more quickly in other kinds of distressing situations, such as after painful inoculations. In one study, researchers assessed how responsive mothers were to infants' crying as their babies were being inoculated at 2 months and 6 months old (Jahromi & Stifter, 2007). Mothers' soothing responses included kissing, hugging, patting, stroking, holding, rocking, vocalizing, distracting, looking into the baby's face, and so on. The more responsive mothers were when their babies were 2 months old, the more quickly the babies stopped crying when they were 6 months old, suggesting that early sensitive care helped the babies to improve their emotion regulation capacity by 6 months.

Sensitive adults adjust their management efforts to the needs and abilities of the infant as he grows. For example, in another study of infants' reactions to inoculations, mothers used primarily touch to soothe 2-month-olds, holding and rocking them, but they used more vocalizing and distracting efforts when their infants were 6 months old, apparently appreciating their infants' changing abilities to respond to visual and auditory stimuli (Jahromi, Putnam, & Stifter, 2004).

Caregivers' emotional messages influence babies' willingness to crawl over the edge of the visual cliff.

With older infants, the caretaker's emotional expressions can teach the child how to make sense of the world when dealing with emotionally charged situations. Experiments by Campos and his colleagues demonstrate that 10-month-old infants who are able to crawl over a "visual cliff" (a glass-covered surface that looks like a sharp "drop-off") actively seek out their mothers' responses before proceeding to crawl over the cliff (Campos, Barrett, Lamb, Goldsmith, & Sternberg, 1983). Infants whose mothers respond with fearful facial or vocal expressions do not advance, whereas those whose mothers respond with smiles or encouragement proceed to cross the surface without fear. Interestingly, infants use the emotional information provided by caregivers to help them interpret situations that are ambiguous to them, a process called **social referencing** (Carver & Vaccaro, 2007).

ATTACHMENT: EARLY SOCIAL RELATIONSHIPS

As you have seen, human infants are emotionally and behaviorally equipped to elicit responsive care and stimulation from adults. Adults, in turn, are prepared by nature to stimulate and nurture infants. The social interactions that result help an infant to expand his emotional repertoire, and they support the development of his capacity for emotion regulation. But early interpersonal interactions may have a much broader impact on the infant's development. Theorists such as John Bowlby (1969/1982, 1973, 1980) and Erik Erikson (1950/1963) have proposed that the relationships that an infant has with one or a few caregivers during the 1st year of life provide him with a working model of himself and of others. (See Box 4.1 and Box 4.2.) These emerging models play an important role in determining how secure and optimistic a child will later feel about venturing forth to explore the broader world. Thus, early relationships are said to lay the groundwork for future interactions with others, for the child's self-concept, and even for his outlook on life.

For Erikson, the characteristics of early caregiving enable a child to form his first feelings about others. When care is timely, sensitive to the infant's needs, and consistently available, he begins to establish **basic trust**, seeing others as dependable and trustworthy. As his rudimentary view of others takes shape, it influences how he begins to see himself. If others can be trusted to provide for his needs, then his needs must be important and he must be a worthy recipient of care. Feeling trust and feeling worthy emerge together, two sides of the same coin. These early attitudes toward others and toward the self create a sense of hope or optimism that experiences beyond the caregiving relationship will also be positive and are therefore worth pursuing.

Bowlby described the infant's connection with the primary caregiver (usually the mother) as his first attachment relationship. Bowlby's theory of how it changes and what it means for the child's psychosocial life is called **attachment theory**. In Bowlby's description, infant and caregiver participate in an attachment system that has evolved to serve the purpose of keeping the infant safe and assuring his survival. As we have already noted, both the infant and the adult bring to the system a set of biologically prepared behaviors. These behaviors change as the infant's repertoire of abilities changes, partly as a function of interactions with others. Early in infancy, as we have seen, infant cries and clinging bring a caregiver. Later, instead of clinging, the toddler may keep an eye on one particular adult, often the mother, keeping track of her whereabouts in case of need. Instead of crying, the toddler may call to the caregiver or communicate by reaching or pointing. When the baby does cry, the caregiver may respond differently to different cries, assessing the level and kind of need from variations in the sound, apparently recognizing that crying can serve multiple purposes for the older baby (see Thompson & Leger, 1999). Thus,

Infants depend upon their caregivers to help them manage their emotions.

Box 4.1: Two Biographical Sketches: John Bowlby and Mary D. Salter Ainsworth

In the 1950s, 7-year-old Marianne was hospitalized for a tonsillectomy. The small-town hospital where the surgery was performed had very strict policies governing visitors to its child patients: 1 hour in the afternoon, maximum of two visitors. Marianne's experiences with doctors had generally been positive up until then. In addition, her mother was a nurse, so Marianne was warmly disposed to women dressed in white from head to foot and smelling wonderfully clean, and she was, blessedly, old enough to understand what was happening to her. The first afternoon and evening, preoperatively, were a pleasant adventure, and Marianne was able to sleep without distress despite the separation from her family. But the next day, after the early morning surgery, the pain struck, and Marianne wanted her mother's cool hand and soothing voice. The hours until her mother's first visit were endless, and the end of the visit was agony. The release into her parents' care the next afternoon was a respite from hell.

Through the middle 1900s, restricted visitation to child hospital patients was standard policy, based on concerns about infection and about disruptions to medical routines. Today, parents not only are allowed complete access to their children in most hospitals but also are encouraged to stay with their children continuously and to be part of the healing and helping process. Many hospitals provide cots and even rooms for showering and changing to encourage parental involvement. It was John Bowlby's groundbreaking theorizing and research on the sometimes devastating emotional costs of mother–child separations, especially during hospitalizations, that initiated a major shift in thinking about the relative benefits of separating children from their families.

John Bowlby (1907–1990) and Mary D. Salter Ainsworth (1913–1999) were jointly responsible for a revolution in the way that parent–child relationships are perceived by researchers and clinicians. Bowlby began his professional life in England as a psychoanalyst who worked with children. In the 1930s, Bowlby's clinical work was supervised by Melanie Klein, who invented psychoanalytic play therapy. Bowlby was inclined to look for a relationship between his young patients' behavior and the kind of parenting they were receiving, but Klein discouraged his family-oriented approach, arguing that the child's "object" relations (internalized representations of relationships) were a function of fantasy, not experience in relationships. Bowlby, however, was convinced that early relationships play a large role in personality and behavioral development. He discovered in the work of ethologists, biologists who do careful observations of animal behavior in natural environments, that animals such as ducks and geese are inclined to become devoted followers of whatever they first see moving—usually their mothers, but sometimes a different animal, such as a human researcher. Such bonding, when it works "the way nature intended," promotes the survival of ducklings and goslings by keeping them close to a protective adult.

Eventually, Bowlby integrated ideas from ethology, from systems theory, from cognitive development (including the work of Piaget), and from psychoanalysis into attachment theory, arguing that some human infant behaviors, for example clinging and sucking, help keep the mother close, whereas others, for example smiling, naturally elicit maternal caregiving. Such behaviors initiate the development of an attachment system that promotes the infant's survival and creates a feeling of security. That system changes and consolidates over time as the child's skills develop. Early clinging and sucking are later replaced by other attachment behaviors, such as protesting when mother leaves or joyfully greeting her when she returns, but the system's evolutionary function remains the same. The attachment system is enhanced and developed by the responses of the environment (i.e., of the caregiver) and helps the child develop a working model of the self (e.g., I am valuable, worthy of care) and of others (e.g., others are reliable and caring).

Bowlby's theoretical work was enhanced and enriched by research into the importance of early relationships on children's behavior. For example, he and his colleagues studied the effects of hospitalization and institutionalization on 15- to 30-month-olds using the careful, detailed observational style of ethology. They documented a series of stages of distress and withdrawal that helped create the impetus for change in hospital visitation policies described earlier. But the research that captured the attention of both the scientific and the clinical community was Ainsworth's studies of mothers and babies in their own homes.

Ainsworth, who earned a Ph.D. in psychology at the University of Toronto, relinquished her own career to follow her husband to London. There she answered Bowlby's newspaper ad seeking researchers. His views of the importance of early relationships were consistent with many of her own ideas, and Ainsworth became an eager student and associate. When her husband's career took her to Uganda, she launched a study of local mothers caring for their unweaned infants. She became convinced from her observations that Bowlby was right: Babies actively help create an attachment system that protects them and provides a foundation for later developments. She also believed that the 28 Ganda babies she studied were forming attachments of different qualities, and she looked for relationships between the infants' attachment quality and the mothers' sensitivity and responsiveness.

When her husband moved again, this time to Baltimore, Ainsworth took a position at Johns Hopkins University. Eventually, she launched a more detailed and intensive study of 26 mother–infant dyads. After 18 home visits over the course of each baby's 1st year, she invented the "strange situation test" to assess the infants' feelings of security when they were 1 year old. That test is now the preeminent means for assessing attachment quality and has been used in dozens of studies since, by researchers around the world eager to test the tenets of attachment theory and to explore the precursors and consequences of an infant's first attachments. Ainsworth's careful research both enhanced the credibility of Bowlby's views and demonstrated that interpersonal relationships, not just individual behaviors, could be meaningfully investigated using scientific techniques.

SOURCE: Karen, R. (1998). *Becoming attached: First relationships and how they shape our capacity to love.* New York, NY: Oxford University Press.

the system broadens to include and accommodate the infant's more advanced physical and cognitive abilities, but it still serves the purpose of making the child secure.

In the context of this attachment system, an affectional bond develops between infant and caregiver. Bowlby argued that as a result of cognitive and emotional developments in the infancy period, the baby's connection to the caregiver emerges in stages, with a full-fledged attachment likely by about 7 or 8 months. Schaffer and Emerson (1964) followed the development of a group of infants through their first 18 months and found a sequence of attachment stages consistent with those Bowlby has described. In the first 2 months, infants signal their needs, producing behaviors such as clinging, smiling, and crying. Although we now know that even newborns have some ability to recognize their mothers' voices (e.g., DeCasper & Fifer, 1980), they show little sign of discriminating among potential caregivers or of having a social preference, so that babies cannot yet be seen as attached to anyone. Next, between about 2 and 7 or 8 months, infants gradually show stronger and stronger preferences for particular caregivers, as when a baby smiles more brightly or is more readily soothed by Mom or Dad than by Grandma or Uncle Bill. Usually by 8 months, babies behave in ways that signal a strong preference for one caregiver, most often the mother. The chief indicator of attachment is that an infant will protest being separated from the mother and will greet her happily when she returns. Along with this **separation anxiety** (see Chapter 3 for a full description) may come **stranger anxiety**: an increased tendency to be wary of strangers and to seek the comfort and protection of the primary caregiver when a stranger is present. Note that infants can recognize familiar faces and voices much earlier than 7 or 8 months, and they may show some wariness with strangers, but a more intense reaction is common once other indicators of the first attachment emerge. Stranger anxiety has not been found in some cultures, like the Nso in Camaroon, where friendliness toward strangers is a cultural practice (Keller & Otto, 2009). Finally, Schaffer and Emerson observed that soon after babies show signs of their first emotional attachment, many of them are forming other attachments as well, with their fathers, with regular babysitters, with older siblings, and with other family members. By 18 months, most of the babies in their study were attached to more than one person.

Attachment is a system, not a particular set of behaviors. The system serves three purposes: It maintains proximity between infant and caregiver, nurturing the emotional bond (called **proximity maintenance**); it provides the potential for ongoing protection (called **secure base**); and it creates a haven for the infant when distressed (called **safe haven**). Behaviors as diverse as smiling and crying all serve attachment functions, and as already noted, the particular behaviors serving these functions can change over time and circumstance. When helpers reflect on problems faced by children and families, attachment theory indicates that the proper unit of analysis is at the level of relationships. That is, a behavior (e.g., crying or clinging) must be interpreted within its social context to understand its significance.

Let's consider the notion of safe haven more specifically, for it is here that attachments serve the important function of stress management. Think back, for a moment, to the earlier discussion of emotion regulation. The infant has limited ability to regulate his episodes of physiological distress. Threats such as hunger, pain, fatigue, loneliness, or overstimulation can produce periods of dysregulation or heightened arousal. Some infants are more easily aroused than others because of individual differences in autonomic reactivity. For all infants, and especially for these more sensitive and vulnerable ones, the stressfulness of physical or emotional discomfort activates the attachment system. By crying, clinging, or showing distress in some other way, the infant signals his need for his caregiver to step in to help manage stress. Distress, triggered from within the infant or from without, activates the attachment system. The helpless infant needs a caregiver to deactivate his escalating discomfort. With time, sensitive caregiving episodes become associated with relief and love for the caregiver. The caregiver who scaffolds the child's own developing capacity to regulate his emotions also helps him form a positive social bond.

 Separation anxiety and wariness of strangers appear across cultures, although the behaviors that the children show to indicate anxiety vary across cultures. How are these behaviors necessary for the development of attachment relationships?

Box 4.2: A Biographical Sketch: Erik H. Erikson

The parents of a 4-year-old boy named Peter brought him to Erik Erikson for treatment of a frightening problem that appeared to be emotionally based. Peter retained his feces for up to a week at a time, and his colon had become enlarged. As he learned more about Peter, Erikson came to see his problem as a reaction to the way others had dealt with normal, stage-appropriate behavior. Before the problem began, Peter had entered what Erikson described as the developmental stage of initiative versus guilt, when it is common for children to intrude themselves on others in a rather aggressive way—such as trying to take over the conversation at the dinner table or, as in Peter's case, being physically aggressive and bossy with adults (see Table 1.2 in Chapter 1). Peter's aggressive style was tolerated amiably by his nanny, but his mother was disturbed by it and by the nanny's tolerance, so she fired the nanny. Peter's anal retention problem started soon afterward. Eventually, Erikson helped Peter to see that his problem was related to his distress at losing his beloved nanny. Peter, Erikson felt, was identifying with the nanny, who had told Peter that she was going to have a baby of her own, and he was trying to hold on to her by retaining his feces.

Erikson's work with Peter reflects the Freudian roots of his perspective. He saw Peter's 4-year-old aggressiveness with his nanny as having sexual overtones, a normal process for a child in Freud's phallic stage. When Peter's aggressiveness led to the painful loss of the beloved nanny, he regressed to using behaviors more typical of the anal stage: holding on to his feces. But Erikson's interpretation also reveals his innovative, psychosocial perspective, which went well beyond his Freudian training. Preschoolers need to express their bold new sense of initiative. Adults can be accepting of this need, even as they impose some constraints so that children will learn to behave in socially acceptable ways. In the process, children will learn to curb their own behavior, controlled by their own feelings of guilt. But when constraints are imposed in an abrupt, disapproving, unsupportive way, or when they are excessive, children's appropriate exuberance can be stifled, leading a child to be overly restrained and guilty about normal behavior. Just as in infancy, when children

must form basic trust, the warmth, sensitivity, and understanding of responsive adults are important ingredients in the development of positive feelings about self or others.

Erik H. Erikson (1902–1994) was the son of Danish parents; his mother was Jewish, his father, Protestant. His parents separated before he was born, and he was raised in Germany by his mother and stepfather. His undistinguished youth seems an unlikely beginning for a great developmental theorist. He was something of a misfit as a young boy. His ethnicity as a Jew coupled with his Gentile appearance caused him to experience social rejection from both his Jewish and his Gentile peers. As a young man, Erik, born Erik Homberger, changed his surname to Erikson—a clear attempt to construct his own identity. He was not much of a student, and after high school, uncertain of his goals or interests, he wandered through Europe rather than attend college. He studied art for a while, wandered again, and eventually accepted an offer to teach children at a school where Anna Freud, daughter of Sigmund, was a cofounder. Thus began his life's work as a child clinician. He studied psychoanalysis with Anna Freud, and when he and his wife, Joan, fled Europe in 1933 with the rise of Hitler, he became the first child analyst in Boston. In his career as a therapist and developmental theorist, he held faculty appointments at Yale, in the University of California system, and finally at Harvard, despite the fact that he had earned no degrees beyond high school. In his scholarly work he not only contributed to research and theory on normal personality development, including the formerly uncharted area of adult life stages, but he also pioneered exploration into cross-cultural variations in development, observing the life experiences of Sioux Indians in South Dakota and of Yurok Indians in California. Although Erikson extended his work to include adult developmental issues, he seems to have had a special concern for the vulnerability of children. In his writing on child rearing, he urged parents to recognize that the most fundamental requirement of good parenting is to provide a sense of security, to give children the benefit of calm, reliable care, starting in earliest infancy.

SOURCE: Patricia Broderick & Pamela Blewitt.

Bowlby, like Erikson, assumed that the quality of care that an infant receives will affect the nature and the eventual impact of his attachments. With responsive, sensitive care, infants come to see their primary attachment figure as a source of security, a secure base from which to explore the world (Ainsworth, Blehar, Waters, & Wall, 1978). They correspondingly feel confidence in themselves and in their ability to negotiate that world. The infant learns that his signals of distress are heard by others—that they are adaptive in helping him get needs for care and attention met. He also learns that the very expression of these needs is legitimate in that others take them seriously.

More broadly, the nature or quality of the infant's first attachments affects his expectations and behaviors in other relationships, "providing implicit decision rules for relating to others that may, for better or worse, help to confirm and perpetuate intuitive expectations about oneself" (Thompson, 1998, p. 36). In sum, early experience with a primary caregiver helps the child form his first representations of the self, of others, and of relationships. Bowlby referred to these representations as

working models—prototypes of social functioning that affect the child's expectations and behaviors in future relationships.

Bowlby's attachment theory prompted developmental researchers to explore babies' earliest relationships, seeking a better understanding of how the first attachments develop and how important they really are for psychosocial development. In the following sections, we take a look at what this research has revealed and what it might mean for the helping professions.

Attachment Quality

In a famous study, Mary Ainsworth and her colleagues found that infants form different kinds of attachments to their primary caregivers (Ainsworth et al., 1978). To measure attachment, they invented the **strange situation test**. Twelve-month-olds and their mothers were brought to a room (the strange situation) where the child experienced a series of eight 3-minute episodes, each one introducing changes in the social situation, some of which were likely to be stressful to an infant. The stress component was important, given that attachment theory assumes that infants cannot handle stress on their own. At first the mother and baby were left alone in the room; in subsequent episodes, the mother and a stranger (one of the researchers) entered and left the room in various combinations. The baby's reactions to all of these events were carefully recorded, particularly his tendency to explore the room and the toys and his reactions to his mother and the stranger. The researchers paid special attention to the baby's response to his mother when she returned after an absence.

Ainsworth and her colleagues identified three patterns of infant response, now considered indicative of three different kinds of infant attachment to an adult caregiver. Other researchers subsequently identified a fourth category (Main & Soloman, 1990). It is important to note that all of these patterns do represent attachments, as all babies seem to have needs for proximity maintenance, a secure base, and safe haven. The style of the attachment, however, varies. The following paragraphs describe all four types of attachment patterns.

Securely Attached

Most babies are found to be **securely attached** (originally described as the "B" category). They show distress when separated from the mother, often crying and trying to go after her, but they greet her happily on her return, usually reaching up to be held, sometimes molding their bodies to the mother as they seek comfort. Once reassured by her presence and her gestures, they tend to go off and explore the room. Ainsworth argued that babies in this category can use mother as a secure base from which to explore the world; perhaps they are showing the beginnings of optimism or hope, as Erikson suggested. They may also have learned to tolerate more separation because they have confidence in the mother's availability if they need her. Sixty-five percent of the 1-year-olds in the Ainsworth et al. (1978) study showed this response pattern, and in most subsequent research the majority of babies fit this description.

Anxious Ambivalent—Insecurely Attached

Babies in this and the remaining two categories are considered to be attached, in that they show signs of having a special pattern of behavior vis-à-vis their mothers, but their attachments seem insecure, often laced with high levels of anxiety, as though the infant cannot quite achieve a sense of security and ease even when mother is available. **Anxious ambivalent** babies (originally called "C" babies, comprising about 10% of many samples) often seem stressed even in the initial episode (e.g., sometimes failing to explore at all), and they are quite distressed when separated from their mothers. It is their reunion behavior, however, that distinguishes them as insecurely attached. They may act angry, alternately approaching and resisting the mother, or they may respond listlessly to her efforts to comfort. They seem preoccupied with their mothers and rarely return to exploration after a separation.

Avoidant—Insecurely Attached

Avoidant babies, about 20% of most samples, typically fail to cry when separated from their mothers. They actively avoid or ignore her when she returns, sometimes combining proximity seeking and moving away, but mostly turning away. In contrast to babies in other categories, these children often appear unemotional during the episodes of separation and reunion. However, Spangler and Grossmann (1993) found that their heart rates are elevated as much as other babies' during separations from their mothers. Unlike other infants, when they are attending to toys instead of mother as they typically do, avoidant babies do not show the heart rate drop that normally accompanies concentration and interest. Mary Main has suggested that, in response to the stress of the strange situation test, avoidant babies may direct their attention to toys as a way of defending themselves against anxiety, whereas other babies direct their attention to mother for that purpose (Main, 1996; Spangler & Grossmann, 1993).

Disorganized-Disoriented—Insecurely Attached

The category **disorganized-disoriented** (referred to as "D" babies) was first described by Main and Soloman (1986, 1990), who examined strange situation videotapes from several studies, focusing on babies who had previously been difficult to classify. These infants produced contradictory behaviors, showing both an inclination to approach the mother when stressed and a tendency to avoid her when she approached! "D" babies are more fully described in the **_Focus on Developmental Psychopathology_** later in this chapter.

As infants progress through their first year, they become attached to their primary caregiver, seeking comfort and reassurance when stressed.

Linking Maternal Care and Attachment Quality

Where do attachment types or styles originate? As we have indicated, attachment theory suggests that caregiving during the baby's 1st year is the key, and Ainsworth's early study strongly supported that claim (Ainsworth et al., 1978). All 26 babies and mothers in her study had been observed in their homes at regular intervals from the time of birth. The middle-class mothers were their infants' primary caregivers, and they did not work outside the home. Yet, they did not all provide the same quality of care. Infants who became securely attached had mothers who responded promptly and consistently to crying during the 1st year, who handled the infant with sensitivity, who held the baby tenderly and often, and whose face-to-face interactions were responsive to the baby's signals. In other words, they showed many of the features that both Bowlby and Erikson proposed to be important for infant care to create security or trust.

Babies who became insecurely attached had mothers who seemed insensitive to their infants in one way or another. The mothers of ambivalent babies were affectionate but were often awkward in holding. They were inconsistent in their responsiveness to crying. In face-to-face interactions, they often failed to respond to their babies' signals. For example, in a game of peek-a-boo, an infant might begin to seem overstimulated and turn away his gaze. A responsive mother would be likely to wait until the baby reengaged before saying or doing anything, whereas an unresponsive mother might try to force the reengagement by vocalizing or jiggling the baby.

The mothers of avoidant babies seemed to actively avoid holding their babies. They were more often rejecting and angry, and they showed less warmth and affection than other mothers. Babies in the disorganized-disoriented category of attachment were not identified in Ainsworth's study, but in research where they have been identified, this pattern has been associated with frightening and/or abusive parental behavior, as you will see in this chapter's *Focus on Developmental Psychopathology*.

Ainsworth's initial research linking mother care to infant security excited the research community and attracted the attention of helping professionals, especially those interested in developmental psychopathology. Decades of research are now available, corroborating the importance of sensitive, responsive care during infancy for attachment quality, deepening our understanding of the nature of such care, and identifying other factors that influence the formation of early attachments. In the following sections, we will explore many aspects of the available findings, beginning with a look at the biological underpinnings of attachment.

Early Social Bonding: Biology and Behavior

Attachment is complex because it involves neurophysiological, psychological, and behavioral components. It's possible to examine these processes from both maternal (caregiver) and infant perspectives as well as from their intersection. A full description of all aspects is beyond the scope of this textbook. However, let's look at few of the key biological ingredients in the bonding process and then consider how they operate in dyadic relationships. New findings in this area are directly relevant to practitioners' interest in prevention of mental and physical disorders.

During the last trimester of pregnancy, the infant's brain undergoes a growth spurt that continues after birth. New neurons are produced and synaptic connections formed at a mind-boggling rate (e.g., around 580,000 per minute, see Bruer, 1999). Since maturational processes, including axon development and myelination, generally occur in a sequence from right hemisphere to left, we can conclude that the first two years of life are crucial ones for sculpting parts of the brain specialized for interpreting nonverbal communication and processing emotional states (Borod, Koff, & Buck, 1986; Niedenthal & Brauer, 2012). From about the 6th month of pregnancy until the second year of life, the right hemisphere matures more quickly than the left hemisphere (Matsuzawa, et al., 2001; Tallal, 2004) pointing to the key task of this early developmental period: the infant's emotional development. One area, the right orbitofrontal cortex (OFC) located in the internal region of the right frontal lobe, has been identified as a primary brain region involved in social bonding and emotion regulation (Schore, 1994). In humans, the OFC is enlarged and has dense connections to the brain's emotional centers, the amygdala, hypothalamus, and brain stem.

Neuroendocrine systems also help with bonding. **Oxytocin**, a hormone that is released in the hypothalamus and modulates the transmission of impulses, is enhanced in pregnancy, labor, delivery, and lactation. It promotes physical proximity, responsive caregiving, empathy, and affection (Strathearn, 2011). It also reduces stress and helps mothers deal with the physical and emotional challenges of childbirth and childrearing (Carter, 2003). Individual differences in maternal oxytocin levels have been associated with mother's own early experiences, both in animals and humans. Mothers who report early emotional neglect have significantly lower levels of oxytocin, pointing to one potential mechanism for the transmission of attachment across generations (Heim et al., 2009). Once oxytocin is released by infant behaviors (crying, smiling, vocalizing, etc.), the subsequent release of dopamine, a neurotransmitter associated with the rewarding aspects of caregiving, may serve to reinforce attachment behaviors. Oxytocin and dopamine systems are connected. In animal studies, repeated maternal separation during infancy disrupts the dopamine system of the animals in adulthood, resulting in more elevated stress responsivity, sensitivity to psychostimulants, and propensity to addiction (Strathearn, 2011).

Recall from the discussion of epigenetics that the environment has a lot to do with how different parts of the brain develop. Schore (2012) posits that the development and reorganization of the baby's brain over the first 2 years of life are critically dependent upon the caregiver's rhythmic, sensitive responses, which help regulate the infant's uneven hormonal, autonomic, and behavioral states. Stated another way, attachment may be viewed as the environmental scaffold for right hemisphere development. The right hemisphere is more active than the left in processing threat-related stimuli and has strong anatomical links to stress-related systems like the HPA axis (Wittig, 1997). Two recent experiments demonstrate how early these brain-based threat-detecting systems come on line. Blasi and colleagues (2011) showed that the brains of 3- to 7-month-old sleeping infants responded to emotional vocalizations, particularly sad ones, in the same areas (OFC and insula) known to process emotions in adults. Cheng and colleagues (2012) found that neonates (1 to 5 days old) registered higher amplitudes on EEG to fearful sounds than to happy or neutral ones. This research suggests that emotion processing via auditory channels emerges very early in infancy.

Sensitive and Insensitive Parenting

Secure social bonds are constructed through dyadic interaction using an emerging set of skills that grow and expand over the course of the relationship. Some of the emotion regulation behaviors you learned about earlier are part of this emerging set of skills. These behaviors are supported in part by the biology just described. Parsons and colleagues (2010) describe a sequence of emerging caregiver and infant competencies (see Table 4.1), expanding on the findings of early studies like that of Schaffer and Emerson (1964). Parsons et al. also specify some of the neuroanatomical structures supporting key attachment competencies.

As you saw in Ainsworth's seminal research on secure and insecure attachments, when early relationships between infants and caregivers go awry, it's often because maternal responsiveness is compromised. Barrett and Fleming (2011) describe it in this way: "The interaction between a mother and her infant can be like a dance. There are routines, standards and missteps, there is give and take, there is unparalleled intimacy, there are often vast differences in skill level and motivation, there is learning . . . This dance can be beautiful, it can be tender, it can be awkward, it can be difficult. And sometimes it just does not occur!" (p. 368). Adverse or insensitive "dance" styles often fit into two major caregiver categories: intrusive or neglectful, although both patterns can be present in alternation. Depressed mothers show high rates of these caregiving patterns (Field, Hernandez-Reif, & Diego, 2006; Tronick & Reck, 2009).

Neglectful (withdrawn) caregivers typically show a pattern of under-stimulation marked by reduced eye contact, infrequent holding, nonresponsiveness, less positive and more negative affect. Intrusive (over-stimulating) caregivers display more anger, irritability, coerciveness, and poorly timed responses. They fail to take their cues from the baby and often interfere with infant exploration. A baby needs help regulating his emotions and learning the predictability that characterizes well-coordinated interactions that make him feel safe and loved. Unfortunately, the depressed caregiver is unable to provide the kind of help that is needed. Both patterns can thwart babies' efforts to establish predictable contact, leading to more negative emotional periods for the infant. Infants may develop increased levels of withdrawal or distress in an effort to regulate the lack of synchrony (see Field, Hernandez-Reif, & Diego, 2006).

Physiological studies have documented differences in the brain activity of infants of depressed (withdrawn) and nondepressed mothers (e.g., Dawson et al., 1999; Field et al., 1995). For example, Field and her colleagues (1995) reported asymmetrical electrical activity in the right frontal area of 3- to 4-month-old infants of depressed (withdrawn) mothers. As discussed earlier, heightened right frontal activation and lowered left frontal activation is consistent with the patterns observed in extremely fearful and inhibited children and in chronically depressed adults, suggesting the felt experience of more negative than positive emotions. Interactions frequently go unrepaired, and the infant resorts to a style of affective coping marked by escaping and turning away. By 4 months, infants of depressed mothers are less active in face-to-face interactions with their mothers than infants of nondepressed mothers, and by 5 months they do less laughing and more fussing when

TABLE 4.1 Dyadic Skills That Foster Social Bonding

SYSTEMS	MOTHER (CAREGIVER) BEHAVIORS	INFANT BEHAVIORS
Orienting system *(Present from birth.)* *Enhances proximity between infant and caregiver.*	Stays in the middle of the infant's field of vision. Makes exaggerated facial gestures (like surprise, joy) and vocalizations. Sustains eye contact.	Shows preference for human over non-human faces. Shows preference for human speech sounds. Displays "cuteness" or attractiveness to adults.
Recognition system *(Present within a few days after birth.)* *Enhances special responsiveness to each other and encourages contact.*	Recognizes own infant from cry, touch, and smell. Prefers to look at own baby's face compared to other baby's face; viewing own infant's face induces positive mood.	Shows clear preference for caregiver's voice and smell. Prefers to look at caregiver's face compared to that of a stranger.
Intuitive parenting system *(Present in early months of infant's life.)* *Enhances the attunement of communication between parent and caregiver.*	Mirrors infants behaviors. "Reads" the behavior of infant and ascribes meaning to infant behavior; responds to cues promptly and accurately. Encourages greater tolerance by allowing for time lags in between responses to infant demands. Alters speech patterns (slows down speech, exaggerates vocalizations, uses "motherese" to direct speech to infant). Soothes negative affect in infant. Builds on infants' improved motor and visual skills through object play and repetitive games.	Mirrors caregiver's behavior. Infant anticipates response but is more tolerant. Expects contingency in communication; reacts to non-communication (still-face) with distress. Experiences feelings of joy and relief; smiles more in context of caregiving relationship. Learns repetitive action sequences.
Attachment *(Approximately 5 to 6 months after birth.)* *Development of a stable preference and way of relating to caregiver in order to maintain proximity, provide security in times of stress, and serve as a base for later independent exploration.*	Shows heightened responsiveness and emotional connection to infant. Predictably soothes and comforts infant when distressed; minimizes separation. Demonstrates predictable and sensitive caregiving related to basic needs. Exhibits capacity to consider the mental state and experiences of infant (mind-mindedness).	Demonstrates preference for caregiver. Responds with distress upon separation; shows protest behaviors (cries, clings, etc.) and seeks contact when stressed. Develops sense of confidence that care will be predictable.

SOURCE: Parsons, C. E., Young, K. S., Murray, L., Stein, A., & Kringelbach, M. L. (2010). The functional neuroanatomy of the evolving parent-infant relationship. *Progress in Neurobiology, 91*, 220–241. Used with permission from Elsevier.

their mothers interact with them (Field et al., 2007a, 2007b). Intrusive mothers show higher levels of activation in the amygdala and less inhibitory functioning compared to sensitive mothers (Atzil, Hendler, & Feldman, 2011). The infants of such mothers tend to show higher rates of unmodulated and anxious behavior. Overall, such physiological markers may be useful indicators of infants who are at risk for emotional problems and who might profit from early intervention.

Clearly, extreme or intense experiences of caregiver withdrawal and/or harsh, coercive parenting constitute serious abuse. Abundant evidence documents the devastating consequences of early exposure to severe abuse and neglect (see Chapter 2 and the Focus section later in this chapter). A more recent but growing body of evidence provides support for the emergence of different social-emotional outcomes related to "normal" variations in parental responsivity. The key lesson here may be the exquisite sensitivity of infants' developing affective systems to emotional communication from caregivers.

One study (Hane & Fox, 2006) included 185 nine-month-old infants and their U.S. mothers who were videotaped at home during three periods of interaction: mother busy in the kitchen, snack time (spoon-feeding), caregiving and changing (change of clothes and applying lotion). All participating mothers (mean age of 32) were middle class, had at least a high school education, and were not considered

TABLE 4.2 Normal Variations in U.S. Caregiving: Giving the Baby a Bath

SENSITIVE	INSENSITIVE
"A highly sensitive mother identifies the components of the bath that her infant finds aversive and attenuates their negative consequences. She prepares the bath in such a way that the water is warm and sufficiently covering the body. She removes clothing and applies soap gently, so the infant is not overly stimulated. She skillfully maneuvers the necessarily invasive washing of the face, particularly around the eyes. She prepares the clothing before application by readying the sleeves and opening the neck widely, to minimize pulling and tugging. This style of maternal caregiving may be 'optimal' simply because it prevents infant discomfort, eliminating the need for the infant to mount a defensive response while being cared for. Mother is protecting the infant's comfort in nuanced, subtle, and remarkably ordinary ways." (p. 150)	"Take, for instance, undressing the infant prior to preparing the bath. This is not what most might consider an egregious parenting error. It is not abusive or neglectful. Yet, we have observed that the impact on quality of MCB can be considerable: The freshly disrobed infant is held with one arm as mother fills the bath and gathers supplies. Across this task, mother's arm becomes strained by the infant, and she shifts him awkwardly and frequently. The exposed infant is challenged by the chill of room temperature, and he squirms and cries. Mother's arm is further taxed by the aroused infant; her holding becomes less accommodating. Placement in the bath is more abrupt as mother is eager to free her arm. The infant's response to the water is more dramatic than it might have been, because his own body temperature has cooled, increasing the saliency of the water's warmth." (p. 151)

SOURCE: Hane, A. A., & Philbrook, L. E. (2012). Beyond licking and grooming: Maternal regulation of infant stress in the context of routine care. *Parenting: Science and Practice, 12,* 144–153. Used with permission from Taylor & Francis.

high risk. Approximately ⅔ of the sample was Caucasian and ⅓ African-American, Hispanic, Asian, or mixed ancestry. Mothers were assessed on sensitivity and intrusiveness, allowing researchers to identify two maternal caregiving behavior (MCB) groups based on high and low quality (see Table 4.2 for a detailed example). Infants were assessed on frontal EEG symmetry, temperament, affect, and interaction quality with their mothers. Note that both high and low quality MCB were considered to be within the "normal" range of behaviors and not abusive.

Results showed that infants in the low quality MCB group showed more negative emotions. Specifically, they showed more fearfulness, less joint attention with mother, and elevated right frontal activity compared to infants in the high quality group. These effects were not related to infant temperament but rather associated with consistent differences in the quality of "normal" caregiving behavior.

A follow-up of these infants at ages 2 and 3 revealed persistent differences. At age 2, children in the low MCB group showed increased stress reactivity, social inhibition, and more difficult and aggressive interactions with peers. Differences between groups in right frontal EEG asymmetry were observed at age 3, with low quality children showing more negative affect. Mothers in the low MCB group identified higher levels of social and behavior problems and more internalizing and externalizing disorders in their children compared to mothers in the high MCB group. Conversely, children in the high quality MCB group were better able to cope with stress and showed good social behavior. Called "hidden regulators," normal processes embedded in mother–infant transactions help regulate the intensity, levels, and patterns of infant's responses. When disrupted by lack of synchrony or separation, we see the predictable manifestations of loss, protest, and grief (Hofer, 1994). Thus, the effects of sensitive caregiving appear to extend to mundane tasks like putting on baby lotion and responding to infant fussiness when you're busy in the kitchen. Even though subtle emotional insensitivity is often invisible to outsiders, the cost may be considerable. Some studies show that it has more damaging consequences for social and emotional development and later problem behavior than physical neglect alone, especially in high-risk urban preschool children (Dubowitz, Papas, Black, & Starr, 2002). Efforts to reduce physical and emotional neglect, which occurs at an unfortunately high rate, should be a high priority for helpers (Stoltenborgh, Bakermans-Kranenburg, & van IJzendoorn, 2013).

The Child's Role in Attachment: Infant Temperament

Clearly, quality caregiving matters for an infant's emotional development and attachment formation, directly influencing both physiology and behavior. But infants do not come into the world as blank slates. A visit to a newborn nursery provides convincing demonstrations that different babies have different emotional and be-havioral characteristics, or **temperaments**, from the time they are born. Consider Ahmed and Joseph, born at the same hospital on the same day. Ahmed has been sleeping in fairly long stretches, averaging 3 hours, with about 40 minutes of wake-fulness between naps. When he is awake, he is often quiet, although like any new-born he cries when he's hungry or uncomfortable. When the nurses pick him up he calms quickly, and his breast-feeding mother says he sucks on the nipple peacefully, with moderate force. Joseph sleeps more irregularly; at 1 day old he has had two sleep periods of about 3 hours each, and many others that have ranged from 10 to 30 minutes. When he awakens, he cries lustily and is not easy to soothe. He also seems to be in constant motion, and his mother finds him squirmy and erratic in his breast-feeding attempts.

Different researchers have identified somewhat different infant traits, but they often include **fearfulness or reactivity** (the infant's proneness to cry or pull away from new stimuli), **irritability or negative emotionality** (the infant's tendency to react with fussiness to negative or frustrating events), **activity level** (the in-tensity and quantity of movement), **positive affect** (smiling and laughing, espe-cially to social stimuli), **attention-persistence** (duration of orienting or looking), and **rhythmicity** (predictability of sleep, feeding, elimination, and so on). (See reviews by Kagan & Fox, 2006; Rothbart, 2011; and Thompson, Winer, & Goodvin, 2011; for the many ways of conceptualizing such traits.) Certain individual traits tend to be correlated with each other, revealing two or three relatively uncorre-lated dimensions or domains of temperament. Although researchers do not always agree about what these dimensions are, they typically include *emotionality* (quality and intensity of mood), *control* or *self-regulatory tendencies* (such as attentional control/persistence), and *activity level* or *surgency* (see Thompson et al., 2011).

The cataloguing of infant temperament traits raises a number of intriguing questions. Are these traits stable over time, predicting personality characteristics of older children and adults? Where do temperament traits come from? How is infant temperament related to parents' caregiving? This question has several component parts: Do infant traits affect the sensitivity and responsiveness of parents' caregiving? Can caregiving affect temperament? Are babies with different temperamental traits affected differently by sensitive versus insensitive caregiving? Finally, does temperament play a role in the development of attachment security?

We will save the first question, whether infant temperament is con-tinuous with later personality characteristics, for later chapters. For now, we will focus on characterizing infant temperament, identifying its relationship to parental caregiving, and understanding its role in attachment security.

Where Do Temperament Traits Come From?

They are assumed to be biologically based reactivity patterns, and evidence is accumulating for the importance of genetic and epigenetic contributions to the physiological processes involved. For example, Jerome Kagan and his colleagues have focused on children who as infants are "high reac-tive" or "low reactive" (see Kagan & Fox, 2006; Kagan, Snidman, Kahn, & Towsley, 2007). High reactive 4-month-olds produce frequent vigorous limb activity, have high levels of muscle tension, and react irritably (e.g., crying) to sensory stimulation, such as new smells or sounds. Low reactive infants, of course, score unusually low on these kinds of measures. Early reactivity is related to later measures of **behavioral inhibition**, or shyness. For example, by 7 to 9 months, when stranger anxiety tends to peak, high reactive U.S. infants show more extreme avoidance or distress than most other infants. These infants also tend to have relatively high heart rates before birth and in some contexts after birth. Kagan has proposed that the behavioral and physiological characteristics of high reactive infants may

Infants who show behavioral inhibi-tion often become shy children requir-ing sensitive handling by adults.

indicate a lower than average threshold of excitability in parts of the brain—the amygdala and many of its associated structures—that mediate stress responses.

A number of genes appear to contribute to these differences in brain function. Some affect the production and metabolism of neurotransmitters such as dopamine and serotonin. And, as we saw in Chapter 2, nature and nurture coact to influence stress reactivity from the prenatal period onward, so that even the biological functions that underlie high and low reactivity are likely to be an outgrowth of epigenetic processes (see, for example, Field & Diego, 2008; Rothbart & Sheese, 2007). Among the environmental factors that may alter the expression of genes important for infant reactivity are the hours of daylight during prenatal development. Like all people, pregnant mothers secrete high levels of melatonin when daylight hours are decreasing, and melatonin can affect fetal brain development in several ways, binding to receptors in many locations and suppressing the release of gene products such as dopamine. If infants are conceived in the early fall in the Northern Hemisphere when hours of daylight are decreasing (February to April in the Southern Hemisphere), they are more likely to be extremely shy than if they are conceived at other times (see Kagan et al., 2007).

The biological underpinnings of other infant temperament characteristics have not been examined as intensively as high reactivity. It is not clear whether physiological correlates exist for other traits, but it seems likely that babies are born with several natural biases to react to environmental conditions in somewhat different ways.

How Is Infant Temperament Related to Parents' Caregiving?

In the landmark New York Longitudinal Study, psychiatrists Alexander Thomas and Stella Chess (1977) found that they could categorize 3-month-olds in their large sample into four "temperament types" (using a set of nine temperament traits; see Table 4.3).

TABLE 4.3   The New York Longitudinal Study: Behavioral Traits Assessed in Infancy and Their Characteristic Levels in Babies with Easy and Difficult Temperaments

TRAIT	DESCRIPTION	LEVEL OF TRAIT IN TWO TEMPERAMENT STYLES
1. Activity level	Frequency and speed of movement	*Easy:* Low *Difficult:* High
2. Rhythmicity	Biological regularity, as in sleep–wake cycles and frequency of hunger	*Easy:* High regularity *Difficult:* Low regularity
3. Approach/withdrawal	Child's immediate reaction to new experience: acceptance or rejection	*Easy:* Approaches, acceptance *Difficult:* Withdraws, rejection
4. Adaptability	When child does withdraw, does adaptation take a short, moderate, or long time?	*Easy:* Short period of adaptation *Difficult:* Long period of adaptation
5. Threshold	Minimum strength of stimulus required for child to attend or react	*Easy:* High *Difficult:* Low
6. Intensity	Energy the child expends in expressing mood	*Easy:* Low *Difficult:* High
7. Mood	Predominance of positive vs. neutral or negative mood expression	*Easy:* More positive *Difficult:* More negative
8. Distractibility	Ease with which child's attention is drawn away from an ongoing activity by a new stimulus	*Easy:* Low *Difficult:* High
9. Attention span and persistence	Length of uninterrupted attention to a single activity, and spontaneous return to a task after interruption	*Easy:* Long *Difficult:* Short

SOURCES: Chess, S., & Hassibi, M. (1978). *Principles and practice of child psychiatry.* New York, NY; Plenum Press; Chess, S., & Thomas, A. (1987). *Origins and evolution of behavior.* Cambridge, MA: Harvard University Press.

Difficult babies (about 10%), compared to the others, were more fearful, more irritable, and more active, displayed less positive affect, were more irregular, and so on—a mix of traits that made them difficult and challenging to parents. Joseph, in the above example, might fit this category. The highly reactive babies described by Kagan and his colleagues would also be likely to be categorized as difficult. **Easy babies** (about 40%) were more placid, less active, more positive, and more regular in their rhythms than most, and thus easier to care for. Ahmed seems to fit this description. **Slow-to-warm-up babies** (about 15%) were like difficult babies in their fearfulness, showing more wariness in new situations than most other babies, but their reactions in general were less intense and negative than those of difficult babies. The last category (about 35%) was more variable in their traits and did not fit well into any of the more extreme groups.

In time, some of the children showed signs of socioemotional problems. The majority of these had displayed a difficult temperament in infancy. In fact, 70% of the difficult babies eventually had some adjustment problems, ranging from learning difficulties to stealing to phobias. What differentiated the 70% with later problems from the 30% who seemed well adjusted, however, was the "goodness of fit" that the parents were able to achieve between their caregiving and the child's needs. If the parents were consistent and patient, difficult babies often became less irritable and more adaptable in time, and they were less likely to have adjustment problems as they got older.

Easy babies were not often represented in the group with later adjustment problems. Even when their parents had trouble accepting their characteristics, they usually were able to cope effectively. But when they did have later problems, caregiving seemed to be a critical ingredient—there was usually a poor fit between parental demands and the child's temperament.

The picture that emerges from the Thomas and Chess study is complex. First, it suggests that infant temperament may show some persistence into childhood and beyond. Second, it provides some indication that infant temperament affects caregiving. For example, infant temperament can make it easier or harder for a parent to be a responsive, sensitive caregiver. Third, it indicates that caregiving can change or at least moderate temperamental qualities. A parent's care influences the impact of early temperament on later adjustment. A child with difficult temperamental traits appears to be at risk for later adjustment problems, but the right caregiving can make that child much less vulnerable. Finally, it suggests that some children, especially those with easy temperaments, can tolerate a wider range of caregiving responsiveness without developing emotional or behavioral problems later. These complex relationships between temperament and parenting factors in determining child outcomes have been corroborated by many subsequent studies (see reviews by Fox, Hane, & Pine, 2007; Nigg, 2006; and Wachs, 2006).

Children with difficult temperaments may be exhibiting **genetic vulnerability** (also referred to as **diathesis-stress**), meaning that their physiological makeup (diathesis) makes them more prone to the negative effects of unsupportive parenting or other negative environmental influences (stress) than other children. It may be, however, that difficult temperamental qualities, such as high reactivity, actually make infants more susceptible to environmental influences in general (**differential susceptibility**). In that case, they would experience both more benefit from positive parenting and more harm from negative parenting than other children (Belsky, 2005; Belsky & Pluess, 2009).

 Researchers Thomas and Chess (1977) identified three consistent temperamental patterns based on a set of typical behavioral traits shown in infants. How might the effectiveness of caregiving behaviors be different for children with each temperament?

Does Temperament Play a Role in the Development of Attachment Relationships?

Thomas and Chess did not look at children's attachment security, but the **goodness of fit model** suggests that temperament and caregiving should interact in determining the quality of a child's attachment relationships. The relationship of temperament to attachment was once a contentious issue both for researchers and clinicians.

Some argued strongly that what appears to be attachment security or insecurity could be nothing but a manifestation of infant temperament. Others argued that what appear to be biologically based temperamental differences among infants could be nothing but a reflection of the sensitivity of care the infant has experienced. For example, mothers who are inconsistent and unresponsive to infant cues may create babies who find social interactions stressful and frustrating. Soon their infants begin to look more irritable and negative than other babies (see Karen, 1998).

Neither of these extreme views accounts for the full complement of research findings, however. A multidimensional view, such as Thomas and Chess's goodness of fit model, seems to best explain the available evidence: Temperament and sensitivity of care (both also influenced by other variables) interact at several levels to produce attachment security.

Let's consider what some of these complex interactive processes are. First, as we have seen, infants whose mothers are more sensitive and responsive in early infancy are likely to make better progress on emotion regulation. For infants who are highly reactive, developing emotion regulation skills is especially important and can mitigate the effects of their reactivity, helping them to be calmer overall. This in turn may help caregivers to continue to be more responsive (see Ursache, Blair, Stifter, & Voegtline, 2012). Second, however, highly reactive infants tax caregivers more. It is simply more difficult to provide sensitive, responsive care to an infant who has these temperamental traits. Caregivers of difficult infants may themselves become more distressed and unsupportive over time. Without adequate caregiver support, these infants are less likely than others to show strong development in emotion regulation, making them increasingly more challenging to care for as they grow. Imagine caring for a newborn who cries more than others or trying to manage a toddler who cannot moderate his reaction to any frustration (see Bridgett et al., 2009; Crockenberg, Leerkes, & Bárrig Jó, 2008). Third, some mothers are more likely than others to be able to respond sensitively to difficult infants. These include mothers with few other stressors to deal with, mothers with lots of external supports, mothers who are secure and adaptable (e.g., Mangelsdorf, Gunnar, Kestenbaum, Lang, & Andreas, 1990; Cassidy, Woodhouse, Sherman, Stupica, & Lejuez, 2011). Overall then, temperament traits are linked to the formation of secure versus insecure attachments by the end of the first year, but their effects are largely the result of their influence on the quality of caregiving that infants are likely to experience (Vaughn, Bost, & van IJzendoorn, 2008).

Second, specific temperamental characteristics seem to affect the kind of insecure attachment that forms. In a classic study, Kochanska (1998) measured infants' fearfulness (comparable to Kagan's behavioral inhibition) and mothers' responsiveness when babies were 8 to 10 months and when they were 13 to 15 months. She measured attachment security with the strange situation test at the later time as well. Maternal responsiveness predicted whether babies would be securely or insecurely attached. But for insecurely attached infants, fearfulness predicted the *type* of insecurity. More fearful infants tended to be ambivalent; less fearful babies were more often avoidant. Even the tone of secure attachment behavior was related to the babies' fearfulness, with more fearful babies more highly aroused in the separation and reunion episodes.

Finally, temperamental traits seem to make infants differentially susceptible to both optimal and nonoptimal care in the formation of attachments. Reactive, irritable infants seem to be both more vulnerable to low quality care, and more benefitted by supportive care, than babies with easier temperaments.

Two studies designed to improve infants' chances of forming a secure attachment illustrate many of the interactive processes at play between temperament and caregiving. van den Boom (1994) was able to demonstrate that caregiving actually plays a causal role in attachment security, especially with children at the more difficult temperamental extreme. In a U.S. sample of low-income families, van den Boom identified a group of one hundred 1- to 2-week-olds who were assessed as highly "irritable." The author assigned half of the infants to a treatment condition in which their mothers were trained to be sensitive and responsive. The remaining infant–mother pairs simply had to fend for themselves. The mothers in both groups tended to be frustrated by their fussy babies, and, without intervention, their caregiving was often insensitive and unresponsive. By 12 months, 72% of the infants whose mothers had received no training were insecurely attached. But after being given caregiving support and training, the mothers in the intervention group treated their babies more sensitively and were more responsive to their needs. Sixty-eight percent of their infants were securely attached by 12 months! This study demonstrates experimentally that sensitive caregiving does make a difference in security of attachment.

In the second study, Cassidy and her colleagues (2011) identified both very irritable and less irritable infants in a low income sample of families. As in the van den Boom study, half of the mothers were trained to be more accepting of their infants' temperaments and to provide more sensitive care, and half were part of a control condition where no such training was given. Infants whose mothers received the training were more securely attached by the end of their first year. However, there was clear evidence of differential susceptibility: Only the more irritable infants in the treatment group seemed to benefit from the more sensitive parenting; less irritable infants showed few effects. Also, the mothers' personality characteristics mattered. Only mothers who were more secure (rather than more fearful) in the treatment condition seemed to be able to profit from the training, and it was their infants who were most likely to benefit. It appears that helpers who aim to improve the trajectory of infants' early socioemotional development would be wise to be mindful of a broad range of caregiver characteristics and needs in devising family interventions.

Mothers and Fathers

Mother is usually the primary caregiver, and so infant–mother attachments tend to be the first to form and are certainly the most often studied. But we have already noted that soon babies become attached to their fathers and other significant caregivers in their lives. The existence of multiple attachments raises several questions.

First, is attachment quality uniform across caregivers? In other words, once attached to the primary caregiver, do babies extend the same kind of attachment to others? There does tend to be consistency among an infant's attachments. Fox, Kimmerly, and Schafer (1991) compared attachment quality for mothers and fathers in 11 studies and found substantial similarities. If an infant were securely attached to one parent, he was likely to be securely attached to the other, although many exceptions were found. Also, babies with secure attachments to their mothers are generally more cooperative even with strangers than babies with insecure attachments, establishing a positive interactive trajectory (see Lamb & Lewis, 2011). These findings are consistent with Bowlby's notion that an infant forms a working model of self and other from his primary attachment relationship and then extends that model to other attachments.

But does that mean that the infant's attachment is unaffected by the sensitivity of the particular caregiver? Not necessarily. Belsky and Volling (1987) found that both mothers and fathers tend to be highly involved and responsive (or not), so the similarity of caregiving quality remains a possible explanation for the consistency of an infant's attachments to his parents. Also, the fact that not all mother and father attachments are alike suggests that the father's caregiving does matter. Some studies have also found discordance (inconsistency) between infants' maternal attachments and their attachments to nonfamily caregivers (e.g., Goossens & van IJzendoorn, 1990; Sagi, Koren-Karie, Gini, Ziv, & Joels, 2002), which could mean that the quality of caregiving in each relationship does make a difference. (See Box 4.3.) A review of eight studies found that fathers' sensitivity of care predicts the security of babies' attachments to them, although the association is much weaker for fathers and babies than for mothers and babies (van IJzendoorn & deWolff, 1997).

 Both fathers and mothers help to foster infants' coping strategies and emotion regulation skills and develop strong attachment relationships with their children. Notice how Madison's father adjusts his behavior in developmentally appropriate ways in response to Madison's needs.

 Infants in nonmaternal care situations can develop secure attachments to caregivers who are responsive. In high-quality centers with a low infant-caregiver ratio, such as the one shown here, caregivers can serve as a secure base for many children at once.

Box 4.3: Does Day Care Pose a Risk to Infants?

John Bowlby (e.g., 1973) brought attention to the damage that could be done to young children's relationships if they were separated from attachment figures for long periods of time. For example, when hospitalized children are denied regular access to their mothers, their emotional distress is intense and it progresses through a worrisome series of stages. It begins with typical separation protest such as crying and searching for the lost parent, followed by "despair," which is marked by listlessness, loss of appetite, and reduced emotional vitality. Finally, after many days or weeks, the child seems to become detached, treating the mother with indifference when she visits, or attending only to the "treats" that mother brings (e.g., Robertson & Robertson, 1989).

Extrapolating from the effects of long-term separations, Bowlby also expressed concern about shorter-term separations. He worried about the daily breaks in maternal care that babies experience when their mothers are employed and leave their children with relatives or nonfamilial caregivers. Given that attachment quality is significantly related to sensitive, responsive caregiving, could regular interruptions of that caregiving impede the development of secure attachments? When there is a change in child care arrangements—when beloved nannies or day care teachers leave—does the disruption of the child's attachment to that caregiver also disrupt the child's sense of security? Bowlby felt that although there might not be definitive answers to these questions, the potential risks associated with forming insecure attachments were great enough that parents should be encouraged to avoid regular substitute care for children under age 3.

Research over several decades has examined the issues Bowlby raised, and a sense of the scope and nature of the risks in infant day care has emerged. We begin by summarizing the current status of findings on the relationship between substitute care and infant–mother attachments. Then we examine other long-term effects that researchers either have identified or are currently assessing. Over the last several decades, large longitudinal studies have been conducted in a number of different countries. One study sponsored by the National Institute of Child Health and Human Development (e.g., NICHD, 1997, 2006) included more than 1,100 U.S. babies who were followed through age 15 (e.g., Belsky et al., 2007). Another included many thousands of Israeli mother–infant pairs in the babies' first few months and continued to follow 758 pairs (e.g., Sagi et al., 2002). Other major studies have been done in Canada (e.g., Côté, Borge, Geoffroy, Rutter, & Tremblay, 2008), Australia (e.g., Harrison & Ungerer, 2002), and several other countries. This report is based on findings from these and many smaller or shorter-term studies (for relevant reviews see Erel, Oberman, & Yirmiya, 2000; Friedman & Boyle, 2008; Lamb & Ahnert, 2006; Love et al., 2003).

Mother–Infant Attachment

It appears that the majority of infants who experience nonmaternal care on a regular basis still form secure attachments to their mothers; there is little disagreement among studies or their authors on this point. There is, nonetheless, an increase in the risk of insecure attachments for infants in day care as compared to infants in full-time maternal care.

In the NICHD study, day care alone did not create an attachment risk. But there did appear to be a "dual risk" effect. Infants in poorer quality day care or in longer periods of substitute care were more likely to develop insecure attachments to their mothers, but only when these infants were also exposed to low levels of maternal sensitivity and responsiveness. In other words, when mothers were providing insensitive care themselves, infants in day care were even more likely than infants in full-time home care to develop insecure attachments. When mothers were sensitive and responsive to their infants, even low quality substitute care did not interfere with the formation of a secure infant–mother attachment.

However, in other studies, such as the Sagi et al. (2002) study of Israeli infants, poor-quality center care *alone* predicted increased mother–infant attachment problems, even when maternal care was sensitive and responsive. Love et al. (2003) combined data from the NICHD and Israeli studies, and reviewed findings from two other studies, and concluded that the quality of center care has an impact on mother–infant attachment independent of the sensitivity of mothers' care or of the amount of time infants spend in care. The best supported inference overall is that mothers and babies can, and usually do, form secure attachments, even if mothers work outside the home during the 1st year, as long as the mother provides her infant with quality care when she is with the baby *and* as long as the substitute care is also of high quality. Substitute care becomes a significant risk to mother–infant attachment when the quality of alternative care arrangements is not adequate. The dual risk of insensitive maternal care combined with less than high-quality substitute care is particularly problematic.

Fortunately, employed mothers are about as likely as unemployed mothers to be attentive to their babies and to provide sensitive care, despite the stresses of balancing family responsibilities and work. In the NICHD study, mothers of infants who were in child care 30 hours a week interacted with their infants only 12 hours less per week than mothers whose infants spent no time in child care (Booth, Clarke-Stewart, Vandell, McCartney, & Owen, 2002). Also, the quality of maternal care in these two groups of mothers did not differ. Some research even indicates that employed mothers might be more positive in their caregiving (e.g., Crockenberg & Litman, 1991). However, at least one study suggests that very early return to work (before the baby is 12 weeks old) might put a mother at risk of being a less sensitive caregiver than she might otherwise have been (Clark, Hyde, Essex, and Klein, 1997). Mothers who returned to work at 6 weeks postpartum were less sensitive to their 4-month-old babies than mothers who returned to work at 12 weeks, especially if the mothers were exposed to other risk factors, such as depressive symptoms or a baby with a difficult temperament. Very early return to work may make it more difficult for a mother to learn to read her baby's cues (Brazelton, 1986). It may also be harder to feel effective and competent as a caregiver when a mother begins work in her infant's first weeks because the baby has not yet become very socially responsive. Sensitive caregiving appears to be easier when mothers feel competent (Donovan, Leavitt, & Walsh, 1990; Teti & Gelfand, 1991).

Among the outcomes of child care is that infants can form attachments to substitute caregivers. As you have seen, a secure attachment to a caregiver other than the mother can be a protective factor for an infant, but an insecure attachment can be a risk factor, diminishing to some extent the benefits of other secure attachments. As you might expect, the greater a nonmaternal caregiver's sensitivity the more likely babies are to become securely attached. For infants, the specific care that the individual child experiences seems to be the key. General quality indicators, such as infant–caregiver ratio, may be cues to the likelihood of sensitive caregiving, but the child's individual experience is most important (e.g., Ahnert, Pinquart, & Lamb, 2006; Booth, Kelly, Spieker, & Zuckerman, 2003).

On the whole, mothers' use of substitute caregivers does not put the mother–infant attachment relationship in jeopardy. But clearly, parents are well advised to proceed cautiously in making decisions about alternative care arrangements for their infants. Substitute care is a risk when it combines with poor maternal care, and other risk factors, such as poor-quality day care, make the danger greater.

Longer Term Effects of Early Substitute Care

Parents should also recognize that attachment risk is not the only issue of concern for infants in alternative care arrangements. Development of social and cognitive skills is also related to the quality, quantity, and timing of substitute care. Recent analyses of the NICHD data indicate, for example, that although quality of maternal caregiving in the infancy period is a stronger predictor of children's later cognitive competence than measures of substitute care, amount and kind of substitute care still matter. If mothers were employed full-time (30 hours per week or more) by the time their babies were 9 months old, their children were not scoring as well on general cognitive tests at 3 years old as children whose mothers returned to the workforce later or for fewer hours per week. *These results were moderated by quality of child care:* The more sensitive the mother was, the better the home care environment, and the better the alternative care environment, the less likely it was that early maternal employment would have negative effects (Brooks-Gunn, Han, & Waldfogel, 2002). *These effects were also moderated by family income.* If children were living in poverty, infant child care was associated with significantly *better* cognitive and language outcomes by age 3 than full-time maternal care (McCartney, Dearing, Taylor, & Bub, 2007). (Note that for preschoolers, ages 3 to 5, quality child care and preschool experiences are generally beneficial to cognitive development regardless of the family's socioeconomic status; see Box 3.4 in Chapter 3.)

In addition, the NICHD study found that the more time young children spend in nonmaternal care, especially center-based care, the more aggressive and oppositional they tend to be by kindergarten age, although the effects are small (e.g., McCartney et al., 2010). Again, *these results were moderated by the quality of child care*: They were most likely to occur with low quality substitute care and when children spent a great deal of time in large groups of peers. *Infant temperament also mattered.* Children were differentially susceptible based on the quality of child care (Pluess & Belsky, 2009). Children with more difficult temperaments (higher negative emotionality) were more likely than other children to show increased behavior problems over time when day care quality was low; but

they had fewer behavior problems than other children when day care quality was high. More time in care tended to have negative effects regardless of infant temperament.

Whether infant nonmaternal care increases the likelihood of later behavior problems also depends on family risk factors (Côté et al., 2008). In a large Canadian study, infant day care was associated with fewer externalizing and internalizing problems and more social competence for children who came from high-risk families. Children from low-risk families showed the opposite pattern, although the effects of early nonmaternal care were small. Higher risk families were characterized by one or more of the following factors: poverty, poor education, high stress, conflict, single parenthood, young and inexperienced mothers, or parental psychopathology.

One of the most troubling effects of early substitute care concerns its apparent impact on stress regulation mechanisms. Gunnar and colleagues have found that many children in center-based or family day care show increases in stress levels in the course of a day as indicated by elevations in cortisol (a hormone produced in response to stress; see Chapter 2), especially if they have difficult or fearful temperaments (see Phillips, Fox, & Gunnar, 2011, for a review). What is striking is that when the same children have been tested at home with their families, their cortisol levels typically declined gradually over the course of a day. This is the normal diurnal pattern for individuals not exposed to acute stress. Cortisol increases in the child care setting have been found in about 35% of infants studied and in about 70% to 80% of older children. Toddlers (about 1 to 3 years), especially younger toddlers, show the steepest rise, suggesting that child care may be especially stressful for this age group (Dettling, Gunnar, & Donzella, 1999; Watamura, Donzella, Alwin, & Gunnar, 2003).

Children's experience of stress in child care programs is linked, not surprisingly, to the quality of the program. In one study of family-based child care, for example, stress-related increases in cortisol were unlikely if preschoolers were in high-quality programs where caregivers gave them focused attention and stimulation (Dettling, Parker, Lane, Sebanc, & Gunnar, 2000). In another study, young children's cortisol levels tended to rise during the day if they had teachers who were intrusive and over-controlling but not if their teachers were highly supportive (Gunnar, Kryzer, van Ryzin, & Phillips, 2010). And for children who had fearful, inhibited temperaments, cortisol rises at one test time were associated with increased internalizing problems and more anxious, vigilant behavior 6 months later, whereas for other children there was no increased risk of these kinds of problems (Gunnar, Kryzer, van Ryzin, & Phillips, 2011). Preschoolers who form secure attachments to their teachers are not as likely to show rising cortisol levels during a child care day, and secure attachments with mothers also appear to have a protective effect (Badanes, Dmitrieva, & Watamura, 2012).

Researchers speculate that child care environments challenge toddlers to manage peer relations when they are just beginning to develop skills for doing so. This challenge may be particularly stressful for children with fearful, inhibited temperaments. For children in high quality child care, teachers may help children manage this stress and advance their skills, but in lesser quality care situations, temperamentally vulnerable and/or insecure children may flounder (Phillips et al., 2011).

(Box 4.3 continued)

Box 4.3 *Continued*

One consequence of elevated stress levels during day care may be a reduced immune response. Watamura and her colleagues examined levels of immunoglobin A, an antibody that is present in saliva, as an indicator of children's immune functioning (Watamura, Coe, Laudenslager, & Robertson, 2010). They found that preschoolers whose cortisol rose during weekdays at day care had lower antibody levels at home on the weekends, and their parents reported more frequent child illness, especially upper respiratory symptoms, than children in day care who did not show the daily cortisol rise. Generally, children in day care do experience more infectious illnesses than those in full time maternal care, probably because of greater exposure to disease organisms. However, in the Watamura study, children whose stress levels were affected by day care were even more likely than other children in care to get sick.

Cortisol levels were not assessed in the early years of the NICHD study, but they were measured when the study participants reached 15 years old (Roisman et al., 2009). Both maternal insensitivity in infancy, and longer hours in child care during the first 3 years, were associated with atypical daily cortisol levels at age 15. Specifically, individuals with one or both of these risk factors in their histories showed lower awakening cortisol levels than average. The effects were quite small, but they do suggest that quality of early care, whether maternal or substitute, can have enduring effects on the stress reactivity of the individual.

It is obviously critical for parents to understand what constitutes quality in substitute care and to be able to weigh the risks and benefits of different care arrangements for specific children. In the Applications section of this chapter, we discuss considerations for helping parents make good infant care decisions.

Overall, there appear to be multiple processes at work. If mother is the primary caregiver, the infant's attachment to the mother may serve as a working model, influencing the infant's reaction to the father, which may in turn influence how the father cares for the infant. But the father's own caregiving proclivities are important as well, also affecting the quality of the infant's attachment to him.

What is clear is that infants become attached to their fathers. When babies are stressed they engage in the same kinds of attachment behaviors with their fathers as they do with their mothers. Whether they are stressed by fatigue or hunger or by some perceived threat such as a stranger approaching, they seek comfort and security from whichever parent is present. When both parents are present, infants are somewhat more likely to turn to the primary caregiver, who is usually the mother (Lamb & Lewis, 2011).

Cross-Cultural Influences on Infant Attachment

The broader culture is also a factor in understanding how attachment relationships evolve. Across cultures, the majority of infants studied have been categorized as securely attached to their mothers (van IJzendoorn & Sagi, 1999). In the strange situation test, they use their mothers as a secure base for exploration, they become distressed when separated from her, but are comforted and return to exploration when she returns. However, the distribution of attachment patterns varies from one country to another. For example, infants in Japan (e.g., Takahashi, 1986), Korea (Jin, Jacobvitz, Hazen, & Jung, 2012), and Israel (Sagi et al., 2002) are less likely to form avoidant attachments and more likely to form ambivalent attachments than infants in the United States, whereas German infants (e.g., Grossmann, Grossmann, Huber, & Wartner, 1981) are more often categorized as avoidant than secure. These differences may partly reflect how stressful the strange situation test is for infants with differing amounts of separation experience. The test was designed to be moderately stressful, and it appears to be for most infants in the United States. For Japanese or Korean infants, who are rarely parted from their mothers, it may be extremely stressful, whereas for many German infants who are strongly encouraged to be independent, it may not be stressful enough.

Some theorists argue that attachment theory describes only the development of relationship quality in Western cultures (Rothbaum, Weisz, Pott, Miyake, & Morelli, 2000). But the relationship between maternal sensitivity and attachment security has been replicated across cultures in most studies (e.g., Jin et al., 2012; Posada,

Carbonell, Aolzate, & Plata, 2004; Valenzuela, 1997; Vereijken, Riksen-Walraven, & Kondo-Ikemura, 1997; see van IJzendoorn & Sagi-Schwartz, 2008, for a review). The specifics of what constitutes sensitive care may vary somewhat from culture to culture (see Kondo-Ikemura, 2001; Posada et al., 2004), and the ways in which maternal insensitivity is expressed might differ across cultures. Consider the Korean concept of *maternal dew,* a belief that mothers have an invisible, powerful bond with their infants, a kind of oneness that even confers "special healing powers" (Jin et al., p. 35). For example, a mother's touch to her infant's belly is expected to help stomachaches go away. Mothers keep their babies close and their attention is constantly on the baby. Sensitive caregiving seems very likely in this context, but when problems arise Korean mothers may be ". . . likely to err on the side of showing enmeshed over-involvement. . . ," demonstrating the intrusive behavior that is associated with ambivalent attachment (Jin et al., p. 36). What seems unlikely is that mothers will be rejecting and distancing, behavior that is associated with infants' avoidant attachment.

It appears from the available research that the tenets of attachment theory apply universally. Yet differences in cultural context contribute in meaningful ways to the kinds of attachments that are likely to develop (van IJzendoorn & Sagi-Schwartz, 2008). If different degrees of dependency are valued (or devalued) in different ways in different cultures, perhaps the working models of self and other spawned by attachment relationships have different meanings and consequences in different cultures as well. For example, an ambivalent attachment pattern in Korea may be more adaptive and have more positive impact on a child's future development than it would in North America.

The Importance of Early Attachments

Secure early attachments are said to pave the way for later psychosocial developments. Erikson and Bowlby portrayed the trusting, secure infant as one who is fortified with positive attitudes toward self and others. He enters new relationships with an expectation that his needs will be respected and with a willingness to respect the needs of others. His security helps him face new challenges; he trusts in the future.

Yet, neither Erikson nor Bowlby saw the positive outlook of the secure child as immutable. Whereas secure children play a role in making their positive expectations come true by their choice of partners and through their own responses to others (Sroufe, Egeland, Carlson, & Collins, 2005), they are not all powerful. If later experiences, especially with caregivers, violate their expectations, their burgeoning ideas about self and others could be modified, incorporating more negative expectations. In sum, early attachment is said to launch processes that can have long-term consequences, but the quality of care that the child continues to receive can either strengthen or redirect those processes.

Does early attachment quality predict later psychosocial functioning? Sroufe and his colleagues followed a large sample of Minneapolis children longitudinally, beginning with two assessments of infant–mother attachment status in the strange situation at 12 and 18 months (e.g., Vaughn, Egeland, Sroufe, & Waters, 1979; see Sroufe et al., 2005). Even though attachment security was usually stable after 12 months, it did change for about ⅓ of the dyads. Most of the change was from insecure to secure, as inexperienced mothers gained confidence and skill. Mothers whose babies shifted from secure to insecure were more likely than other mothers to report significant increases in their life stresses during the intervening 6 months. Apparently, the attachment relationship can be vulnerable to events that may distract, depress, or preoccupy the mother or otherwise upset family life.

Children whose attachment status was stable from the first to the second assessment were later evaluated on a variety of interpersonal and cognitive dimensions, and differences were found between the insecurely and securely attached children on many measures. For example, when the children were 4 years old, 40 of them participated in a summer nursery school program at the University of

Minnesota (Sroufe, Fox, & Pancake, 1983). Teachers, who knew nothing about the earlier attachment ratings, ranked the children each day on characteristics related to autonomy, such as attention seeking, extreme reliance on the teacher, involvement with teachers at the expense of peers, and so on. The children who had been securely attached as toddlers were more often seen by teachers as direct and appropriate in their dependency behaviors, seeking help when they realistically needed it but functioning independently in other situations. Insecurely attached children were more likely to act helpless, to act out for attention, or in some cases to passively avoid seeking help when they genuinely needed it.

In assessments at later ages, the children in the Minneapolis project showed other continuities as well. In a summer camp at age 10, for example, securely attached children tended to be more self-confident, to have more friends, to have better social skills, and so on (Sroufe et al., 2005). By age 16, securely attached children were more likely to trust a best friend, and by age 20 to 21, they were better able to resolve conflicts with a romantic partner (Simpson, Collins, & Salvatore, 2011). Many longitudinal studies, though not all, have found similar continuities (Thompson, 2006; Lamb & Lewis, 2011).

If infant–mother attachments predict later developments, what about infant–father attachments? When infants are securely attached to both parents they seem to have the best outcomes. If they are securely attached to one parent, but not the other, their outcomes are better than if they are insecurely attached to both (Belsky, Garduque, & Hrncir, 1984; Main, Kaplan, & Cassidy, 1985; Suess, Grossmann, & Sroufe, 1992). Thus, a secure attachment relationship with a second parent adds a protective factor, perhaps helping to safeguard a child from the negative influence of an insecure attachment. Several investigators have also suggested that because fathers and mothers tend to interact differently with their infants, the attachment relationship with each parent may affect different aspects of the child's psychosocial development. For example, in North American families, mothers spend more time with infants in quiet, ritualized routines such as peekaboo games, where synchrony of eye contact, vocalizations, and facial expressions are key factors. Fathers tend to engage in more energetic, stimulating games (such as whirling the baby through the air). They are more unpredictable and exciting (MacDonald & Parke, 1986; Pecheux & Labrell, 1994). Of course, mothers and fathers also often interact with their infants in similar ways, especially when fathers are highly involved in routine infant care. Whether infant attachments to mothers versus fathers affect different aspects of later social functioning is yet to be determined. One study is suggestive, however. Pecheux and Labrell (1994) found that 18-month-olds were more playful and more inclined to smile at a stranger if their fathers were present when the new person approached than if their mothers were present. It is important to note, however, that such differences in parental effects may be highly dependent on culture. Although North American fathers spend substantial proportions of their time with infants in active play, fathers in many other cultures do not. In some cultures (e.g., in Sweden and in Israeli kibbutz families), there is little difference between fathers' and mothers' interactions with infants (see Parke, 2002).

Overall, there is little doubt that infant attachments are predictive of some later behaviors. But does the early attachment actually have long-term effects, or could more recent and current caregiving environments be responsible for the apparent continuities? In the Minneapolis study, for example, some children who had been securely attached as infants were having behavior problems by age 4. The quality of parenting during the preschool period helped account for this change. Mothers of these children were less supportive when engaging their children in educational tasks at age 3. They provided less encouragement and were less effective teachers than mothers whose children did not develop later behavior problems. Also, children who had been insecurely attached as infants but who were well adjusted at 4 years tended to have mothers who were supportive and effective in their interactions with their preschoolers (Erickson, Sroufe, & Egeland, 1985). It seems that the role of early attachments in later development can be diminished when parental acceptance, support, and responsiveness changes substantially, either rising to the challenges of the child's new developmental stage or failing to do so (Easterbrooks & Goldberg, 1990; Landry, Smith, Swank, Assel, & Vellet, 2001; Youngblade & Belsky, 1992). The importance of ongoing quality parenting for children's socioemotional development will be taken up again in Chapter 5.

What, then, is the value of getting a "good start" with a secure infant attachment? First, a primary influence of infant attachments is their tendency to perpetuate themselves. Once a relationship pattern between parent and child is established, it tends to be repeated. When it is, the older child's behavior is consistent with predictions from the early attachment. As Erikson and Bowlby proposed, in his first relationships a baby may form an incipient "working model" of what to expect from interactions. That model affects his expectations from, and his physiological and behavioral reactions to, social experiences in the future. But the model is in progress and will be reworked in the context of new interactions. Some findings suggest, however, that even if experiences after infancy modify a child's attachment pattern and working model, there may be lasting sequelae of the original pattern.

Working Models of Attachment

As we have just seen, infant attachments appear to influence the internal working model of relationships that children begin to construct. Researchers studying adult romantic relationships describe the concept of the internal working model of attachment as providing a template for adult social relationships. Investigators now study the nature and development of these models, or representations. We will examine some of this work in later chapters, as we discuss the development of self-concept and relationship capacity beyond the infancy period, but one aspect of this research bears directly on the formation of infant attachments, and we will touch on this work here.

Main and her colleagues (Main et al., 1985) evaluated mothers' and fathers' own models of attachment using a structured interview procedure called the **Adult Attachment Inventory (AAI)**. (See Chapter 12 for a full discussion; Hesse, 2008). Parents described their memories of the parenting they had received and their beliefs about whether that parenting influenced their own personalities. The "security" of their attachment representations (categorized using a procedure devised by Main & Goldwyn, 1985–1994) was related to the quality of attachment they had established with their own infants.

"Secure-autonomous" parents valued relationships and believed that their own personalities were influenced by them. They could talk openly and objectively about their early experiences, good or bad. Their ideas were coherent and showed signs of previous reflection. Not all of these adults recalled their early experiences as positive; some had even been abused. But by whatever means, these adults had apparently come to terms with their early experiences and had faith in the power of relationships. These parents tended to have secure attachments with their own infants.

"Insecure" parents showed several patterns. In one, attachment relationships were not readily recalled, not valued, and not seen as influential. Infants tended to have avoidant attachments with parents who showed this "dismissive" pattern. Another group of parents ("preoccupied-entangled") were preoccupied with their own parents, often still struggling to please, and they seemed confused, angry, or especially passive. Their infants' attachments to them were typically ambivalent. Finally, an "unresolved-disorganized" pattern characterized parents who made irrational and inconsistent comments, especially when discussing traumatic experiences. For example, they might talk about a dead parent as if he were alive. Infants whose parents showed this pattern tended to be disorganized-disoriented in the strange situation test.

A substantial correspondence between parents' and infants' attachment classifications has been found in other studies as well (see van IJzendoorn, 1995). As Main (1996, 1999) points out, this correspondence could be affected by many factors, including similarities in temperament between parent and infant. But the match in parent–infant security measures may indicate that parents' working models of attachment can influence their infant caregiving, thereby affecting their babies' attachment security. Perhaps, parents whose concepts of relationships are more coherent, or who have come to terms with past relationships, are more likely to behave consistently and sensitively with their infants, fostering a secure attachment.

Parenting Practices Versus Relationship Quality in Infant Development

It should be clear from this overview of theory and research on infant attachments that focusing attention on relationship quality in infant–caregiver interactions has proven to be a highly productive enterprise. As Mary Ainsworth noted in her earliest observations of mother–infant dyads, the specifics of parenting practices may not be very important in the long run. For example, breast-feeding versus bottle-feeding does not seem to be critical for later emotional adjustment. Rather, it is the relationship context within which such practices occur that is significant. Some parenting practices may be more conducive to, or consistent with, responsive caregiving. Breast-feeding, for example, requires that a mother hold her baby close during feeding, providing the "contact comfort" infants find soothing. When babies are bottle-fed, they can be held and soothed just as effectively, but it is also possible to "prop" a bottle or to hold a baby away from the caregiver's body when feeding, thus failing to provide contact comfort. So, both breast- and bottle-feeding can be practiced in a way that provides close, comforting interactions, but breast-feeding is more conducive to such interactions. In addition, breast-feeding affects the mother's production of hormones related to caregiving (Jansen, de Weerth, & Riksen-Walraven, 2011). For example, baby's sucking stimulates the release of oxytocin in mothers, supporting milk production. As we have seen, animal studies and some human evidence suggest that increased levels of oxytocin tend to increase maternal caregiving and its rewarding effects for the mother. In the most extensive study of maternal breast-feeding and attachment to date, mothers tended to be more sensitive in their caregiving at 3 months postpartum if they breast-fed their infants, suggesting that there is some likelihood that breast-feeding mothers will be more sensitive caregivers. But infants' attachment was not correlated with breast-feeding specifically; only the mother's sensitivity mattered (Britton, Britton, & Gronwaldt, 2006; see Jansen et al., 2008; for a review). That's good news for fathers, adoptive parents, and other non-breast-feeding caregivers.

You should note that although both breast-feeding and bottle-feeding can be done sensitively and responsively, breast-feeding has substantial advantages for healthy physical and cognitive development that bottle-feeding does not (American Academy of Pediatrics, 2012). In comparison to baby formulas, breast milk is more digestible and more adequately balanced for infant nutrition. It contains antibodies that the mother carries, and it is sterile, a particularly important benefit in countries where water may contain disease organisms. Breast milk even carries growth hormones and other substances that may affect long-term development. The World Health Organization recommends exclusive breast-feeding for the first 6 months and breast-feeding with solid food supplements through the 2nd year (Bellamy, 2005).

Ainsworth's observations of a Ugandan baby and his mother (as described in Karen, 1998) help illustrate that feeding by breast is not the critical factor in the formation of secure attachments. Muhamidi's mother kept him close most of the time, as is the custom

Helping professionals have an important role to play in communicating with parents about their children's development.

in Ugandan families. She slept with him and breast-fed him on demand. Yet by 8 months, Muhamidi seemed insecure. Not yet having invented the strange situation test, Ainsworth depended on a variety of observations to make this classification, most notably that over time he seemed to lose his vitality, to become sadder and duller. Unlike other babies whose mothers used similar infant care practices, he did not tolerate his mother's absence even when left with an older sibling. Muhamidi's mother seemed anxious and overtaxed by the demands of her large family, and Ainsworth observed that despite her nearly constant availability, the mother's care-giving responses were somewhat brusque and did not necessarily match Muhamidi's needs. For example, on one visit, she responded to Muhamidi's crying by putting him "immediately to breast, without stopping to wipe his nose, which was stream-ing, or to wipe his face, which was muddy" (Ainsworth, 1967, p. 144).

A student of social and personality development in the mid-1900s would prob-ably have read extensive discussions about the relative importance of particular child-rearing practices such as breast-feeding versus bottle-feeding. The current trend, spawned by attachment theory, is to emphasize the overall quality of infant–caregiver relationships instead. This approach seems to be bringing us much closer to an understanding of the role of infancy in later socioemotional development.

ATTACHMENT IN CONTEXT

The attachments that develop between infants and their caregivers are embedded in a system of overlapping contexts: the parents' relationship, sibling interactions, extended family processes, parents' work, extra-familial child care, the neighborhood, and the larger community. All of these contexts can affect infants' emotional well-being and their attachment security. Sometimes contextual influences are *indirect*, and their effects are filtered through parents' caregiving. For example, a father is not as likely to be a responsive caregiver, and therefore is less likely to foster a secure attachment with his infant, if he and his wife are often in conflict (whereas a mother's care is less affected by marital disharmony) (Lamb & Lewis, 2004). But factors beyond caregiv-ing can also have *direct* effects on infant emotional functioning. When the parents' marriage is characterized by lots of arguing, infants have more negative emotional reactions to novelty and can be less well regulated emotionally. The quality of parent caregiving is also an influence but it may not eliminate the effects that witnessing con-flict can have on an infant (e.g., Crockenberg, Leerkes, & Lekka, 2007).

Unfortunately, infants and children under age 5 are more likely to be exposed to negative experiences that can reduce their emotional well-being and feelings of security than any other age group (Lieberman, Chu, Van Horn, & Harris, 2011). These experiences include traumatizing events such as maltreatment, accidents, marital conflict, and family violence. Poor and minority children are especially likely to have such experiences, along with exposure to community violence and many types of deprivation, such as homelessness. Many studies document the problematic effects of childhood adversity on long-term physical and mental health, even when a child's circumstances improve after the early years (e.g., Chen, 2004; Dube, Felitti, Dong, Giles, & Anda, 2003). These effects appear to be a function of cumulative risk: The more risk factors (e.g., adverse events) to which infants and young children are exposed, the more likely they will experience negative health and behavioral consequences into adulthood.

Infants' attachment security is one of the most important protective factors for moderating the long-term impact of adversity. Infants who are securely attached have more capacity to regulate their stress reactions than those who are insecurely attached (Gunnar & Quevedo, 2007). They are also less likely to suffer long-term negative physical and behavioral health problems. For example, one study focused on adults who had experienced poor socioeconomic environments early in life. If they had warm early relationships with their mothers, they were less likely to suffer from the chronic inflammatory processes that typically plague adults from similar early life environments but who do not have the benefit of such relationships (Chen, Miller, Kobor, & Cole, 2011).

As we noted earlier, infants' attachment status can be affected by exposure to contextual adversity in both direct and indirect ways. Here again, the balance of risk and protective factors is important. Infants from poor families and/or who have been victims of trauma are more likely to develop insecure attachments than infants in better circumstances. One reason is that many adverse events (e.g., family violence, inadequate material resources) simultaneously affect both infants and their parents, making it likely that infants are more difficult to manage and comfort at the same time that parents are themselves stressed and depleted of emotional energy. Sensitive and responsive caregiving that would foster secure attachments often seem to be a casualty of this mixture.

Some adverse events, such as violence against the mother, seem to be especially traumatizing and disorganizing for infants and much more difficult to redress with quality caregiving. The long-term behavioral and emotional consequences seem to be more severe than for most other traumatic experiences (Scheeringa, Wright, Hunt, & Zeanah, 2006). Yet, even under these highly stressful circumstances, early sensitive caregiving from mothers can be a buffer. In one large-scale study of low income families, mothers reported on the levels of partner violence in their homes. Mothers' caregiving was observed at 7 months, and infants' emotional reactivity (cortisol levels) in frustrating or frightening tasks was measured at three ages (Hibel, Granger, Blair, Cox, and The Family Life Project Key Investigators, 2011). Infants from violent homes showed much higher emotional reactivity than other infants, and their reactivity showed increases with age instead of the usual declines with age. Yet if mothers in violent homes were able to remain highly sensitive in their early caregiving, their babies were less likely to show this increased reactivity.

Perhaps the most problematic traumatic experiences for young children are perpetrated by caregivers who abuse the children who are counting on them to be their safe havens. Victimization rates are highest for infants in the first year, and mothers appear to be abusers in 64% of reported cases (U.S. DHHS, 2008). As we have already seen, infants are highly likely to form insecure attachments with abusing parents, especially disorganized attachments. Indeed, across many laboratories, 80 to 90% of abused infants have been found to form disorganized attachments (see Cyr, Euser, Bakersmans-Kranenburg, & van IJzendoorn, 2010). Neither the child's temperamental characteristics nor the genetic markers that sometimes accompany them appear to have much influence when caregiving is so completely untrustworthy (Cicchetti, Rogosch, & Toth, 2011). Why do some parents abrogate the most fundamental of their parenting obligations in such ways?

Most often, abusing parents are themselves the victims of adversity and a variety of mental health problems. Many abusive parents are repeating with their children the patterns of trauma, rejection and maltreatment that shaped their own lives. This is the phenomenon of **intergenerational transmission**: When maltreated children become maltreating parents, they pass on their insecure attachment status. When parents' own early attachments are disorganized, they often seem unable to " . . . access, process, and resolve painful affect associated with past experience" (Lieberman et al., 2011, p. 401). Thus, they tend to experience high levels of dissociation, that is, a detachment from their own emotional reality. Attachment theorists have argued that victims of unresolved childhood trauma may have particular difficulty helping their infants regulate their emotions, " . . . because they curtail their conscious attention to the child's signals of need in an effort to protect themselves from re-experiencing their early trauma" (Lieberman et al., 2011, p. 401). One mother who suffered early sexual abuse, and who was participating in a therapeutic intervention so that she could avoid hurting her own child, describes her struggle against this dissociative tendency: "I couldn't identify my own emotions, much less help him identify his . . . I was definitely needing to help myself grow up in a sense and learn about myself while trying to do that for my child . . . " (Wright, Fopma-Loy, & Oberle, 2012, p. 545). A second mother in the same intervention described how difficult it was for her to empathize with her child's pain: "Or, if they get hurt somewhere, I'll go outside to see how she is but I think it's just, it's like an act for me . . . It feels like I'm standing back and watching them . . . " (Wright et al., p. 544).

Adults whose caregiving history is marked by neglect and abuse may also have had little direct experience with effective parenting, so that they have not learned strategies for managing children's emotions or behavior from competent models. The second mother quoted above provided a poignant description of her ignorance of parenting strategies: "When my daughter first went to preschool, her very first day I took her into preschool and I just left her. I didn't know . . . you kiss them and say have a good day—I didn't know you did that stuff" (Wright et al., p. 544).

Not all parents with a history of abuse go on to abuse their offspring, and not all abusive parents have a history of being abused themselves. Clearly, there are multiple interacting processes at work. Not surprisingly, many contextual factors matter. It is worth reiterating that the more contextual risk factors, and the fewer protective factors there are, the more likely there will be a problematic outcome such as infant/child maltreatment. Parents, like children, are more likely to behave in dysfunctional ways the more adversity accumulates: poverty with its deprivations and displacements, violence in the home and community, minority status, and so on (Costello, Erkanli, Copeland, & Angold, 2010; Linares et al., 2001). Relationship variables have usually been found to be important contextual factors as well. For example, intergenerational transmission is more likely if mothers feel socially isolated, that is, if they do not feel that they have other adults they can turn to for support (Berlin, Appleyard, & Dodge, 2011). Intergenerational transmission is also more likely for mothers with strong dissociative tendencies. But many mothers who suffered abuse themselves do not have such tendencies (e.g., Egeland, Bosquet, & Chung, 2002). When they do not, they often have had experiences of quality caregiving after infancy and/or in the context of adult relationships. A good marital relationship, for example, can modify an adult's attachment status and help him or her to integrate early negative experiences into a coherent self view (see Chapter 12).

APPLICATIONS

What are we to make of this information on attachment? No one has demonstrated that relatively infrequent incidents of caretaker unavailability will harm a child for life, nor are chronic interactive failures the single pathway to a depressive future. *However, it would be incorrect to assume that early interactive patterns have no influence at all on later emotional and social development.* As Tronick (1989) observed:

> The pathways leading to the varieties of normalcy and psychopathology derive from the divergent experiences infants have with success, reparation of failure, and the transformation of negative emotions to positive emotions. Typically, there is no single traumatic juncture or special moment separating these pathways, only the slowly accumulating interactive and affective experiences with different people and events in different contexts that shape the regulatory processes and representations of the infant over time. (p. 117)

If we conceptualize the infant as constructing a framework for interacting with the world, using both the tools provided by nature and the materials available in daily experience,

it is difficult to imagine that this early experience-dependent affective learning would not be important for later emotion regulation and social relationships. Outcomes, however, are rarely the result of only one early relationship. Although mothers are most often primary caretakers, fathers, siblings, grandparents, and others are also significant. It is important to resist the assumption that all the responsibility for social and emotional development rests solely on the mother's shoulders. Future outcomes also involve co-occurring and later occurring experiences that build on and reshape prior configurations.

Infant Mental Health

If the primary caregiver's own mental representations as well as current life experiences are so important to attachment quality, how can we help parents with troubled attachment histories do better for their own children? What can be done for less troubled but stressed-out families to support security of attachment? The field of infant mental health (Zeanah & Zeanah, 2001) offers us some suggestions in this area. A major assumption of this approach is that intervention must take into account the needs of the parent as well as the child. Therapies that support the parent can reap rewards for the children and are more effective than those that focus on the child alone (Blackman, 2002). Thus, helpers should consider the dyad or the family as the target of intervention because the goal is to repair or improve a *relationship*, not just one member's behavior. Some components of effective programs include the following key elements:

1. *Provide a voice for the baby.* The therapist is the one who needs to sensitively and carefully articulate the baby's "point of view." One way is to provide parents with basic knowledge about child development. We believe that this knowledge should not just be descriptive of ages and stages, but should also emphasize the needs of infants, particularly in the affective area. Sometimes parents feel that babies will be spoiled if they are picked up and held or that they should be spanked for some perceived misbehavior. Parents may view their babies as "not listening" to them or as disrespectful. Or they may believe that infants need lots of exposure to groups of children to develop good social skills, a developmental goal that is inappropriate at this age.

These misperceptions and flawed attributions are often the basis for insensitive caregiving. Therefore, the mother of an angry toddler who does not want to share his toy can be helped to understand that the child is not selfish but is asserting his will and acting as most normal toddlers do. The mother of a difficult infant might benefit from an understanding of the concept of temperament. With the professional's support, she can be given ways to understand her baby's communication and respond to it sensitively. Her baby's fussiness might signal his feeling overstimulated, or his clinging behavior might mean that he needs more "lap-time" from her. Tomlin and Viehweg (2003) suggest that clinicians take a nonjudgmental, coaching approach when "speaking for the baby" (p. 621). The helper might ask, for example, "I wonder why Devon is fussing so much. Do you think she might want to be held for a while?"

Recognizing the baby's bids for attention will be useful only if the parent also recognizes that these needs are normal and, if sufficiently met, will foster emotional security in the long run. These shifts in knowledge and attitude, as well as new skills, can bolster parent confidence in their ability to be good parents.

2. *Provide support for the parent.* Active listening skills, well known to helpers, could be used to communicate a nonjudgmental and supportive attitude toward parents. Parents have reasons for the ways they behave toward their children. Sometimes their parenting reflects their own painful history of emotional neglect or abuse. As we have seen, they can operate according to inaccurate assumptions about child development. Often they are preoccupied and may not be paying attention due to stress, depression, illness, or overwork. A supportive stance can help parents learn to be a more secure base.

3. *Learn some new skills.* Clinicians can help parents let their children be their teachers. A technique developed by Greenspan (Greenspan & Weider, 1999), called "floor time," is a good example. This approach is designed to improve parents' observational skills, to assist them in sharing experiences and meanings with a child, to teach them to communicate in a respectful give and take with the child taking the lead, and to ultimately teach recognition of emotions. Parents literally get down on the floor for approximately 30 minutes and tune into the child's world. The goal is to let the child take the lead rather than allow parents to dominate or turn the session into a "teachable moment." The tasks vary depending upon the age of the child. Parents of infants are helped to recognize their babies' signals and temperamental styles. They are asked to notice, for example, when the baby smiles, what kind of touch the baby likes or dislikes, when the child makes eye contact, and to respond fully to his bids for attention. At about 4 months of age, babies show more interest in the outside world. Parents are helped to notice what the baby is attending to, such as a kitten sleeping nearby, and to enjoy the sight together. When maternal interaction is intrusive, teaching mothers to slow down and be silent when the baby is quiet can be useful to restore synchrony (Field et al., 2006). Parents of older, more mobile infants, about 8 months and beyond, can learn to join in their child's play or movement while not trying to control the activity. Essentially, the parent is taught to notice the child's intention, mirror and expand on the child's activity, and respond to the child's words and gestures.

Helpers can also teach games or routines that practice turn-taking and sharing. Even something as simple as passing a toy back and forth, "Now it's Brandon's turn," teaches the basics of social interaction. Also important are family routines or rituals, such as bedtime and mealtime patterns. Clinicians can help busy parents identify routines that work for them and encourage parents to adopt simple ones. Predictable routines provide security for children and opportunities for parents and children to relate to each other in a calm, attentive, and loving way.

What Works?

There is a growing awareness in the minds of researchers, helping professionals, policy makers, and the general public that healthy emotional development of young children must be a priority. Recent research has confirmed the power of attachment interventions to improve security. We now have some information about what techniques and programs are effective for children and families living in a variety of circumstances. Generally, treatment goals center on improving parental sensitivity in order to foster attachment security. A recent meta-analysis of relatively brief prevention programs to improve depressed mothers' sensitivity (Kersten-Alvarez, Hosman, Riksen-Walraven, & Van Doesum, 2011) found support for some short-term approaches. Including infant massage in the intervention improved outcomes most strongly. Interestingly, including maternal psychotherapy in the intervention program reduced its effectiveness. The authors suggest that infant massage focused on a behavior shared by the dyad and helped train mothers to be attentive to their infants' signals. Psychotherapy, in contrast, focused on the individual. While therapy might be beneficial in reducing maternal depression, it had less of an influence on the development of interaction skills. Some support for adding a maternal support group was found.

Meta-analyses have also examined attachment-based interventions for families at risk of maltreatment and for those caring for maltreated children, such as those in foster care. Although specific adaptations would likely be needed for different groups, some common elements have been identified (see Bakermans-Kranenburg, van IJzendoorn, & Juffer, 2003). In general (with the exception of highly distressed families), the most effective interventions were relatively brief (fewer than 16 sessions) and were focused on the kinds of behavioral training already described (e.g., massage, play, etc.). Interventions aimed at altering mother's mental representations of her baby were less effective that those focused on actual behavior change. In effective programs, behavior change was scaffolded and supported by working with the mother–child dyad, ideally in the home environment. Just "talking about" the way parenting practices should be done was inferior to allowing the mother to engage with the child in session. Sometimes, mother–child interactions were videotaped, allowing both parent and clinician the opportunity to discuss their observations. Interventions that included a treatment manual also showed greater effectiveness than nonmanualized treatments presumably due to improved implementation fidelity. Four examples of attachment-based intervention programs with documented effectiveness for various groups are provided in Table 4.4.

The Day Care Dilemma

Helping professionals may also be called upon to help parents make important decisions about caretaking arrangements for their infants. As we have seen in Box 4.3, the child care issue is complicated. Although researchers have made great progress in clarifying some pros and cons of child care, there are questions that await further investigation. Addressing these questions is a pressing issue because so many infants and toddlers in this country are cared for in some form of nonmaternal arrangement. In the NICHD longitudinal studies, 72% of the infants in the sample experienced regular, nonparental child care during their first 12 months. Most of these babies entered day care before they were 4 months old. Many parents have few choices available to them as they struggle to care for families and maintain jobs. The high cost of infant and toddler care, the limited availability of caregiving options in some areas, the pressures of the workplace on dual-career couples, and the poor quality of too many facilities increase the stresses on families with young children. It is impossible to draw easy solutions to this problem. However, researchers in general no longer accept the argument that all nonmaternal child care initiated in the 1st year of life is risk-free. What follows are a few important factors to consider in helping parents decide about infant care.

1. *Consider the combination of age of entry and the amount of time spent in day care.* Although there are no absolutes, there appears to be a dose–response relationship between early (before 4 months), more extensive (full or almost full time), and cumulative (across many years) care that is associated with greater noncompliance, aggression, and neediness at school age. Multiple child care settings over the early childhood years seem to exacerbate the risk.

2. *Consider the quality of the day care providers.* Infants and toddlers need the experience of felt security that comes from sensitive caregiving. Do the caregivers respond quickly and sensitively to the needs of the children? Are they warm, affectionate, and patient or do they ignore the children or become easily irritated by their needs? Do they hold the children and provide physical comfort? Are they educated in child development so that their expectations for children are reasonable and age appropriate? Do they tend to remain in the facility or is there rapid staff changeover?

3. *Consider the quality of the center.* Unfortunately, reports indicate that the quality of 85% to 90% of out-of-home child care in the United States is less than high quality (Brauner et al., 2004). Before making decisions about care, parents should consider the stability and child–caregiver ratios in the facility. Is the staff stable or is there a frequent turnover of employees? Stability of caregivers, perhaps even allowing caregivers to remain with a group of babies over several years (Greenspan, 2003), is important for children in the construction of attachments. Is the caregiver–child ratio small enough to ensure enough attention and promote nurturant interactions? The optimal ratio is *up to* 3 infants to 1 adult (American Academy of Pediatrics, American Public Health Association, and National Resources Center for Health and Safety in Child Care, 2002). Greenspan (2003) suggests only two babies per caregiver. In the large scale Israeli study mentioned earlier, the infant–adult ratio was the major factor in determining security of attachment between infants in center care and those cared for by home-based providers (Sagi et al., 2002).

TABLE 4.4   Four Attachment-Based Intervention Programs

PROGRAM	REFERENCE
Attachment and Biobehavioral Catch-Up (ABC)	Bernard, K. et al., (2012). Enhancing attachment organization among maltreated children: Results of a randomized clinical trial. *Child Development, 83,* 623–636.
Child–Parent Psychotherapy (CPP)	Lieberman, A. F., & Van Horn, P. (2005). *Don't hit my mommy: A manual for Child–Parent Psychotherapy with young witnesses of family violence.* Washington: Zero to Three Press.
Video-based Intervention to Promote Positive Parenting (VIPP)	Juffer, F., Bakermans-Kranenburg, M. J., & van IJzendoorn, M. H. (2007). *Promoting positive parenting: An attachment-based intervention.* Mahwah, NJ: Lawrence Erlbaum.
Circle of Security	Marvin, R. S., Cooper, G., Hoffman, K., & Powell, B. (2002). The Circle of Security project: Attachment-based intervention with caregiver–preschool child dyads. *Attachment and Human Development, 4,* 107–124.

SOURCE: Patricia Broderick & Pamela Blewitt.

4. *Consider the uniqueness of the child.* Not every child responds to child care in the same way. Both temperament and gender appear to be related to differential outcomes. Greenspan (2003) notes that children with underreactive or overreactive sensory system thresholds (sensitivity to sounds, touch, movement, etc.) may find the experience of group care more challenging than other children. Overreactive, difficult-to-soothe children may have trouble modulating arousal and regulating emotions in a context that is noisy, possibly crowded, and filled with children whose needs compete with their own. Underreactive children risk becoming more disengaged without adults to scaffold nurturant interactions. The higher risk of insecure attachment due to low quality care is greater for boys than for girls as we have seen, and increases in internalizing behavior, which sometimes result from long hours in care, are regularly found more often for boys than for girls (Tout, deHann, Campbell, & Gunnar, 1998; Howes & Olenick, 1986). Out-of-home care insofar as it involves coping with the demands of a group situation is somewhat stressful for all young children, let alone those with temperamental sensitivities (Watamura et al., 2003). Therefore Crockenberg (2003) concludes that "professionals have an obligation to inform parents and child care providers that males and reactive children who lack adequate regulatory abilities may be adversely affected when they spend long hours in certain types of nonparental care. To do less is to deny parents information that may help them make better decisions for the family as a whole" (p. 1036).

5. *Consider the family.* Parental sensitivity is of the utmost importance to the baby's well-being. Parent training or counseling, as we have discussed, can benefit the baby by increasing caregiver sensitivity. The NICHD studies stress the importance of the "dual risk" interaction between low-quality day care and maternal insensitivity. In some cases, high-quality out-of-home care can have a positive impact on children's cognitive and social development, particularly when families are stressed or when caregivers are insensitive. Yet it is also possible that exposure to low-quality care on a regular basis may stress infants to the point that they challenge their primary caregivers' capacity for sensitive care, thus giving rise to insecure attachments (Cassidy & Berlin, 1994). Helpers should take the approach of strengthening protective factors (by facilitating secure bonds) while reducing risks as much as possible.

6. *Consider advocating for child care.* Various governmental policies related to taxes, subsidies, welfare, and so on can be shaped to help families better provide for their young children. Employers can offer more flexible schedules and alternative work assignments that allow parents more time to care for children, especially during the critical 1st year. Professional day care providers should be afforded adequate wages, education, supervision, and respect for the important contribution they make to our children's future.

Summing Up

Attachment theory provides many useful ideas for clinicians as they assess the socioemotional needs of parents and children. First, the concept of attachment as a constellation of behaviors in a goal-corrected partnership is particularly significant in helping us understand problems and motivations for behavior. This perspective emphasizes the fundamentally social nature of human development. It reminds us that all human growth and human problems occur in some relational context. Second, attachment theory provides clinicians with a new way to view behavior that might, at first glance, seem puzzling. Because the principal goal of attachment is to maintain proximity, either physical or psychological, seemingly contradictory behaviors can be interpreted as means to this end. Even avoidant behaviors, for example, can help maintain some distant relationship while minimizing psychological threat to the self. As Greenberg and Speltz (1988) have pointed out, noncompliant child behaviors can be interpreted as bids for more attention (or closer attachment).

Presumably, all behaviors are functional in that they help individuals adapt to present circumstances. Their adaptiveness may be more or less well suited to any given situation or context. For the infant who needs to reduce the risk of rejection, avoidant behaviors or withdrawal may be an effective method for adapting to negative circumstances. However, this pattern of withdrawal from close relationships, particularly when under stress, can be counterproductive in the context of close adult relationships. Even though the behavior is not suited to the new context, it certainly can be understood.

Finally, attachment theory comes as close as any psychological theory to blending developmental and clinical orientations. It highlights the truth that not only do we grow from relationships but that we suffer from them too. Noam and Fischer (1996) make the excellent observation that, inasmuch as we are all dependent upon one another, we have all experienced injuries in relationships and are beset by specific interpersonal vulnerabilities as a result of our attachment histories. They believe that developmentalists need to incorporate into their work the "periods of regression and fragmentation" that characterize development and that coexist with capacities for integration and growth. Noam and Fischer add that clinicians "need to, and have begun to, account for the adaptive nature of psychopathology, including attempts to solve complex problems, through the detour of symptom formation. Traditional medical models of mental health need to be supplanted by truly developmental, interpersonal accounts that allow for dynamic interweaving of problems and strengths" (Noam & Fischer, 1996).

FOCUS ON DEVELOPMENTAL PSYCHOPATHOLOGY

Disorganized Attachment and Reactive Attachment Disorder

Security of attachment is a robust protective factor in development, and abnormalities of attachment place children at risk for social and emotional problems throughout the lifespan. Despite this straightforward claim, empirically validated assessments, diagnoses, and treatments for attachment-related problems in infancy and childhood remain murky and misunderstood. Consider that this lack of precision about disorders co-exists with a recent bumper crop of attachment-disorder diagnoses and treatments (Hanson & Spratt, 2000). To make sense of this state of affairs, it is helpful to draw some distinctions between two contemporary constructs: disorganized attachment and **reactive attachment disorder (RAD)**.

The most scientifically sound phenomenon is disorganized (D) attachment, first described by Main and Solomon in 1986. These attachment researchers added this category based on their study of 200 cases that were not classifiable within existing A (avoidant), B (secure), and C (ambivalent) designations. The primary behavioral manifestations of disorganized attachment, noted during Strange Situation assessments, are sequential or simultaneous displays of contradictory, conflicted behaviors (approach and avoidance), misdirected movements, disorientation, "freezing in place" for a significant length of time, and fearfulness or apprehension of the parent (Main & Solomon, 1990).

Recall that the strange situation is essentially an infant stress management assessment. Under normal circumstances, securely attached infants (B) will generally seek out and welcome the comfort provided by their attachment figures upon reunion. Infants classified in nonsecure categories also reflect an organized or coherent, albeit insecure, way of managing the stress of separation, either through avoidant (A) or clinging/angry (C) behavior patterns. The bizarre behavior of D infants is considered to be a reflection of stress that goes unmanaged. It demonstrates the absence of an organized pattern of emotion regulation, hence, the term *disorganized*. The relatively high incidence of disorganized attachment in nonclinical, middle class U.S. samples (15%) and nonclinical, lower class U.S. samples (25% to 34%) is surprising (van IJzendoorn, 1999). Unlike most other disorders, disorganized attachment has not been found to be associated with genetic or constitutional factors (Bokhorst, Bakermans-Kranenburg, van IJzendoorn, Fonagy, & Schengel, 2003; Bakermans-Kranenburg & van IJzendoorn, 2004). Parental insensitivity, strongly implicated in the development of other insecure attachment patterns, is only weakly related and does not appear to be enough to provoke attachment disorganization (van IJzendoorn et al., 1999). Furthermore, there is no substantial relationship between parental depression and disorganized attachment (NICHD, 1997).

What Are the Roots of Disorganization?

There is a strong association between disorganization and child maltreatment. Studies have reported that 32% (Valenzuela, 1990) to 86% (Barnett, Ganiban, & Cicchetti, 1997) of maltreated children fall into the D category. Overall, approximately 48% of maltreated children compared to 17% of non-maltreated children show disorganized attachment (van IJzendoorn, 1999). This makes some intuitive sense given that the threatening parent, who is also the presumable source of security, presents the child with an unsolvable problem. The attachment figure is both threat and safe haven, constituting a paradox that Hesse and Main (1999a) call "fright without solution."

The lack of an organized way to handle stress seems understandable in the face of serious abuse and neglect which can overwhelm the child's resources. However, what can account for the development of disorganization in 15% to 33% of non-maltreating, low-risk samples (Abrams, Rifkin, & Hesse, 2006)? A good deal of interest has focused on disordered parental behavior that does not meet standards for abuse but which constitutes a risk factor for D classification. In their early conceptualizations of disorganization, Main and Hesse (1992) theorized that frightened or frightening (called FR) behavior by the parent could lead to infant disorganization in much the same way that maltreatment appears to do.

In fact, studies do suggest that FR parental behavior is significantly correlated with infant disorganized attachment (Schuengal, Bakermans-Kranenburg, & van IJzendoorn, 1999). FR behavior is more likely among low-risk non-maltreating mothers who themselves are classified as U/d on the Adult Attachment Inventory. It appears that parents who struggle with the ongoing and unresolved loss of their attachment figures are more likely to relate in ways that can cause significant disruption to their own children's attachments to them (Jacobvits, Leon, & Hazen, 2006; van IJzendoorn, 1995).

Main and Hesse (1998) identified six primary subtypes of FR behavior. They include parental behaviors that are (1) threatening, as in suddenly looming or abruptly coming up close to the infant's field of vision; (2) frightened, as in showing a fearful face with wide eyes and facial grimaces; (3) timid or deferential, as in acting as if the infant were in control; (4) spousal or romantic, as in sexualized or overly intimate behavior toward the infant; and (5) disorganized, as in asymmetrical and mistimed movements. A final behavioral category is (6) dissociative, which is exemplified by the parent's freezing all movements as if in a trance while the infant is actively trying to gain parental attention or speaking in a ghostly or "haunted" voice (i.e., speaking while pulling in on the diaphragm). Of all six subtypes, threatening and dissociative behaviors are most highly associated with D infant attachment in low-risk, non-maltreating samples (Abrams et al., 2006). This makes sense if we consider that threatening and dissociative behaviors can be intensely frightening and can overwhelm a child's meager capacity to regulate emotions independently. With regard to parents themselves, dissociative behavior was most likely to occur among those with a history of unresolved trauma

(Abrams et al., 2006). Some have suggested that parental marital discord is also related to disorganization in children, but further study is needed to support this claim (Owen & Cox, 1997).

Longitudinal studies show that infants classified as disorganized show elevated levels of cortisol and less resilient coping than infants in other attachment groups (Spangler & Grossman, 1993). They are at greater risk of aggression in kindergarten (Lyons-Ruth, 1996) and more vulnerable to dissociation in young adulthood (Carlson, 1998; Liotti, 1992). Although systematic treatments for disorganized attachments have not been reported, efforts to promote caregiver sensitivity appear promising (van IJzendoorn & Bakermans-Kranenburg, 2003).

What Is Reactive Attachment Disorder?

Although the term "attachment disorder" is often used to describe children with poor social relatedness and frustratingly high levels of disruptive behavior, there is actually no real "attachment disorder" diagnosis. The precise diagnostic term is Reactive Attachment Disorder or RAD (APA, 2000) which was introduced into the DSM in 1980. This disorder is characterized by highly disturbed and inappropriate social relatedness in early childhood (beginning before age 5) which is not due to other mental disorders (e.g., ADHD, ODD, or CD) or to developmental delay (e.g., MR or PDD). The disorder is presumed to result from grossly pathological early caregiving which might include extreme child abuse, severe neglect of physical and emotional needs, or frequent changes in caregivers that disrupt attachment formation. Another major diagnostic system, the International Classification of Diseases (ICD-10), requires evidence of abuse or neglect before the diagnosis of RAD can be made (Zeanah, 1996). Although attachment theory is related to RAD because of the important effects of early maltreatment, RAD has been primarily a within-person diagnosis that manifests across settings while attachment status always refers to a relationship.

Two types of RAD have been recognized (see Gleason, Fox, Drury, Smyke, Egger et al., 2011). One type is characterized by a high degree of resistance and non-responsiveness to social interaction (*emotionally withdrawn/inhibited type*) such that children fail to show attachment behaviors, either organized or disorganized. They do not seek comfort from selected adults when distressed nor do they respond to it when present. Not much research is available on these children, but their attachments to adults are presumed to be lacking or incomplete. When placed in nurturing settings, emotionally withdrawn characteristics often diminish. Another subtype (*indiscriminantly social/disinhibited type*) shows indiscriminant familiarity and attention seeking directed toward relative strangers frequently in combination with lack of selective attachments to primary caregivers. The length of time that children spent in institutions or in foster care is related to severity and persistence of indiscriminant social behavior (Rutter et al., 2007). These children may or may not form attachments to adults, but indiscriminant social behavior tends to persist regardless of circumstances. As you can see, attachments and Reactive Attachment Disorder are not overlapping constructs.

Currently, there is evidence that both RAD subtypes are separate disorders due to their distinct symptom sets and divergent outcomes (Zeanah & Smyke, 2008). A recent validation study of children from the Bucharest Early Intervention Project (BEIP) (Gleason et al., 2011) sought to differentiate both subtypes from related conditions (e.g., depression and ADHD). The children in this project had spent much of their lives in Romanian institutional care before being moved to foster homes. Results supported the conclusion that both RAD subtypes were distinct from each other and, despite some overlaps, from other related disorders. This strengthened the proposal that each subtype be considered a distinct diagnosis, which is the approach taken in the DSM-V. Presently, there are two diagnoses instead of one: Reactive Attachment Disorder and Disinhibited Social Engagement Disorder.

Despite the significant contribution of the research just described, there are still many questions that warrant further research. A recent report by the American Professional Society on the Abuse of Children (APSAC) sums up the problem by saying that RAD is "one of the least researched and most poorly understood disorders in the DSM" (Chaffin, Hanson, Saunders, Nichols, Barnett et al., 2006, p. 80). Until very recently, the field has suffered from a lack of longitudinal research limiting understanding of the course of the disorder. Much of our previous knowledge of RAD came from case study reports, but well-validated diagnostic tools that involves structured interviews or videotaping interactions are now being developed. One clinical interviewing tool, the Disturbances of Attachment Interview (Smyke, Dumitrescu, & Zeanah, 2002), is an example.

Treatment Concerns

Frequently RAD (or DSED) is ascribed to children in foster care or adoption systems, often because of disturbed behavior and adjustment and relationship difficulties. Caregivers and adoptive parents, for example, can be understandably frustrated when problems seen intractable. The generic term "attachment disorder" may also be given to older children and adolescents whose behavioral and social problems are presumed to derive from attachment failures. Depite the fact that new empirical work provides guidelines for therapy (see Applications Section), a variety of controversial techniques have been popularized.

Among the controversial and non-empirically based subset of attachment therapies are approaches variously termed rage-reduction, holding therapy, or rebirthing therapy (e.g., Cline, 1991). Several basic assumptions provide these approaches with a theoretical framework for understanding attachment problems that contradicts the more established framework we have presented in this chapter. For example, proponents of controversial attachment therapies hold that children must release or express underlying, primal rage before healthy attachments can be formed and that any defiance or protest by children signals resistance and attempted manipulation of adults. It is assumed that defiant or resistant behavior can lead to the development of sociopathy, so relatively minor infractions are perceived as ominous. "Putting off chores, incompletely executing chores, or arguing, is interpreted as a sign of an attachment disorder that must be forcibly eradicated. From this perspective, parenting a child with an attachment disorder is a battle, and winning the battle by defeating the child is paramount" (Chaffin et al., 2006, p. 79). Other parenting techniques in this category can involve physical restraint and coercion, withholding food or water, or prolonged social isolation, and have, on occasion, resulted in the deaths of several children who were being treated with "attachment therapy" (Mercer, Sarner, & Rosa, 2003).

Authors of the aforementioned APSAC report recommend that all treatments should be based on empirically supported and extant behavioral principles, which have shown effectiveness for conduct problems (see Buckner, Lopez, Dinkel, &

Joiner, 2008). Empirically-based parent training components are also useful. Core principles of attachment development, such as provision of safety and security, patience, stability, sensitivity, and nurturance should be paramount in any intervention protocol. Coercive and potentially abusive techniques should never be used to treat children. It is important to note that behavioral problems in children and adolescents can often result from acute stress, such as that experienced in residential transitions. Treatments that view children as deliberately manipulative and deceitful and which attempt to break down their defenses so as to avert impending psychopathy do not make therapeutic sense, fail to support healthy attachments, and can compound stress and maltreatment in already traumatized children.

SUMMARY

Theories of Emotions

1. Although theorists do not all agree about how to define or characterize basic emotions, they do agree that emotions have survival value. Emotions are powerful motivators of behavior, and spontaneous emotional expressions help us to communicate with one another. For infants, this communicative function helps initiate reciprocal interaction with a caregiver. Emotions enhance cognitive functioning such as planning and social perspective taking, and they play a role in mental health and wellness. More positive life outcomes are associated with higher levels of emotional intelligence.

2. The biological basis of basic emotions has been demonstrated in three lines of research. First, across cultures people agree about what expressions signal fear, sadness, happiness, anger, and surprise. Second, young infants' facial expressions appear to display basic emotions. Third, researchers have identified some specific brain systems or circuits governing the expression of some emotions.

3. Izard's differential emotions theory argues that infant emotional expressions are innate, a product of evolution, although more elaborate emotion schemas emerge as a function of experience. In Sroufe's more orthogenetic theory, early emotional expressions are precursors of more mature emotions, and the later emotions depend on cognitive developments. Emotions are differentiated over time and come under the control of higher levels of functioning.

4. Once the limbic circuit or system was identified as important in emotional functioning, MacLean argued that it is an evolutionarily old system that serves survival functions (fight or flight) for many species. Newer work debunks this idea and demonstrates that many lower and higher brain systems are involved in emotion processing.

5. LeDoux found that there is an "early warning emotional system." Some sensory information bypasses the cortex, causing fear and allowing a rapid response to stimuli that

may pose a threat. Rational processing by the cortex is a split second behind, and sometimes determines that there is no threat, allowing fear to subside. If rapid emotional responses are paired with formerly neutral stimuli, we may be conditioned to automatically respond with fear to stimuli that are not threatening, perhaps explaining phobias, panic reactions, and posttraumatic stress disorder.

6. There appear to be two major, partially separate networks related to positive and negative affect. Left brain activation is more closely associated with approach-related positive reactions and right brain activation is more associated with avoidance-related negative reactions. Depressed individuals show lower levels of left-sided activation compared to right-sided activation.

7. Emotion regulation is a cornerstone of emotional well-being and positive adjustment. Mothers and other caregivers interact with infants in ways that scaffold the development of emotion regulation. Interactions between mothers and infants often exhibit a repetitive-rhythmic organization called synchrony. When synchrony breaks down, infants tend to show distress and mothers tend to initiate repairs that regulate the infants' emotions, encouraging longer periods of positive affect. The still-face paradigm is used to study synchrony, its break down and repair. Sensitive adults adjust their emotion management behaviors to the needs and abilities of infants as they grow. And as infants get older, they engage in social-referencing, basing their own emotional reactions to ambiguous situations on their caregivers' behaviors.

Attachment: Early Social Relationships

8. Theorists such as Bowlby and Erikson have proposed that the infant's first relationships with caregivers provide him with working models of the self, of others, and of relationships. Erikson argued that consistent, sensitive care helps the infant establish basic trust in others

and feelings of worthiness, both of which contribute to optimism about future relationships. In Bowlby's attachment theory, biologically prepared behaviors bring infant and mother into a close relationship, or attachment system, that emerges in stages such that by 7 or 8 months the infant has a strong affectional bond to the primary caregiver, which leads to both separation anxiety and stranger anxiety. The attachment system serves the purpose of proximity maintenance and provides a secure base and safe haven.

9. Using the strange situation test to measure the quality of infant–mother attachments, Ainsworth and her colleagues identified three different types of attachment quality. Securely attached infants explore a new situation when mother is present, are distressed if she leaves, and are comforted and happy when she returns. They appear to use their mothers as a secure base. Anxious ambivalent babies are insecurely attached. They are most clearly different from other babies in their response to their mothers' return from an absence. They may alternately approach and resist the mother, or may respond listlessly to her, rather than taking ready comfort. Avoidant babies are also insecurely attached. They actually avoid or ignore their mothers when they return after an absence, although their heart rates reveal that they are stressed in her absence. Main and others have identified a fourth attachment category, another insecurely attached group called disorganized-disoriented. These babies react to their mothers in contradictory ways, engaging in an odd array of behaviors.

10. Maternal caregiving in the 1st year of life is correlated with infants' attachment quality at 12 months. The mothers of securely attached babies provide consistent, sensitive care to their infants. Mothers of insecurely attached babies are more likely to be insensitive in one way or another, and the mothers of disorganized-disoriented babies can be abusive.

11. In infancy, portions of the right brain hemisphere that appear to be involved in social bonding and regulation of threat responses mature more rapidly than comparable areas of the left hemisphere. In mothers, oxytocin and dopamine systems help mediate responsive caregiving, empathy and affection.

12. As early work by Ainsworth suggested, even "normal" variations in maternal responsivity and sensitivity are linked to differences in infant attachment security and emotion regulation. Adverse or insensitive maternal care tends to fit into two major categories: intrusive or neglectful. Depressed mothers show high rates of these kinds of patterns, and their infants tend to show heightened right brain activation and lower left brain activation, suggesting more negative than positive emotional experiences.

13. Infant temperament may be one influence on attachment quality. Babies have different emotional and behavioral characteristics. Such traits make up infant temperament, and for at least one of these traits, reactivity, physiological correlates have been identified, such as high heart rates before birth. Some babies have difficult temperaments: They are highly reactive and irritable and have a number of other traits that make them more difficult than average babies to care for. Easy babies have a combination of traits that make them easy to care for. A longitudinal study by Thomas and Chess included babies with different temperaments and indicates that temperament can persist beyond infancy and that it can affect caregiving, making it easier or harder for a parent to be responsive and sensitive. But this study also found that parents who adjust to their infants' temperament, creating goodness of fit between their caregiving and the needs of a particular infant, can moderate their child's temperament and influence the impact of early temperament on later adjustment.

14. Temperament and caregiving seem to interact to affect security of attachment. For example, some caregivers may react to the frustrations of caring for a difficult baby by becoming less sensitive and responsive to their baby's needs. Their unresponsive caregiving may then contribute to an insecure attachment.

15. Across social classes and across cultures, there are differences in the proportion of infants who are categorized as securely or insecurely attached. Larger numbers of insecure infant attachments are found in lower income families. It appears that increases in life stress are related to less responsive care and to increases in insecure attachments. Across cultures, the connection between sensitive caregiving and security of attachment has been corroborated.

16. Attachment quality can change over time if caregiving quality changes. It is also possible for children with reactive attachment disorder, who have been deprived of adequate adult care as infants, to later form secure attachments. Early attachment launches processes that can have long-term consequences; but the quality of care a child continues to receive can either strengthen or redirect those processes.

17. Early attachment quality has been found to predict later psychosocial functioning, including dependency, self-confidence, and social skills. Moreover, if children have secure attachments with both parents, their later functioning is more positive than if they have a secure attachment with only one parent. However, it is unclear whether the early attachment quality is the cause of later psychosocial adjustment or whether the ongoing quality of the parents' caregiving is the key predictor. The primary influence of early infant attachments may be their tendency to perpetuate themselves. Once a pattern is established between parent and child, it tends to be repeated. However, it can be changed, and if it is, the child's working

model of relationships, of self, and of others can also change.

18. Methods for assessing attachment security in adults have been devised, such as the Adult Attachment Inventory (AAI). In some studies, parents' own attachment quality has been predictive of the quality of attachment they establish with their infants.

19. The specifics of infant care—such as bottle-feeding versus breast-feeding—may be less important to child outcomes than the sensitivity of caregiving. Focusing on the quality of infant–caregiver relations, rather than the specifics of parenting practices, seems to provide a better understanding of later socioemotional development.

Attachment in Context

20. Attachments are embedded in a system of contexts including parents' relationships, extended family relationships, neighborhoods, and so on. All contexts can affect infants' emotional well-being and attachment security. Children under 5 are especially likely to be exposed to negative experiences in these contexts, including traumatizing events such as maltreatment, accidents, and marital conflict. Attachment security can be a protective factor, but children who have such experiences are also at increased risk of forming insecure attachments.

CASE STUDY

Angela is a White 17-year-old girl who is also the mother of a baby named Adam, now 11 months of age. Both Angela and her baby live with Angela's mother, Sarah, in a small rented house in a semirural community in the Midwest. Sarah, a single mother herself, works as a food server in a local restaurant. Sarah has another child, David, who is 13. Angela's father abandoned the family when she was 7 years old. Wayne, Angela's boyfriend and Adam's father, has also become estranged primarily because Sarah refuses to allow him in her house. She is angry that Angela became pregnant and views Wayne as incapable of, and uninterested in, taking on his share of the responsibility.

During her pregnancy, Angela continued to attend classes at her high school. She dropped out, however, when she was 7 months pregnant. She had grown increasingly depressed about the prospect of caring for an infant, and she found dealing with schoolwork and her pregnancy overwhelming. Following Adam's birth, Angela tried hard to be a good mother to her son. She took on most of the caretaking responsibilities by herself, which gave her some measure of satisfaction. However, she also felt deeply ambivalent. Above all, she resented the restrictions that the baby placed on her life. Adam's frequent crying for no apparent reason was particularly frustrating. According to Angela, Adam cried even when he was not hungry or wet. Sometimes she handled Adam roughly, when he wouldn't quiet down after a feeding or around bedtime. At other times, Angela was upset that Adam didn't seem to smile enough at her when she wanted to play with him. Sometimes, Adam paid no attention to her when she wanted interaction. At these times, she would raise her voice and hold his face in her hands to make him look at her. She was beginning to feel that she was not a very good mother to her son after all.

Sarah and Angela's already strained relationship grew more hostile as Adam approached his first birthday. Angela felt that her mother wasn't interested in helping her. Angela always idealized her father and believed that it was her mother's frequent outbursts of anger that led to her father's leaving home.

For her part, Sarah believed that her daughter wasn't doing enough to help herself. Angela chose not to go back to school, even though she could have access to school-based child care services. All through Angela's high school years, Sarah had expected her daughter to find a steady job after graduation and to contribute to the family financially. Instead, Sarah found herself in the role of financial provider for another child. She was very angry and hurt that Angela didn't seem to appreciate all she had done for her over the years. Whenever the mother and daughter had an argument, Angela would say that she felt her mother never really cared about her. What was even worse for Sarah was that Angela had begun seeing Wayne again, without her mother's permission. She made it clear to Angela that she and the baby would need to move out if she ever got pregnant again.

Discussion Questions

1. Comment on the quality of the attachment relationship between Angela and Adam and between Sarah and Angela. Do you think that Adam is at risk for developmental problems? Discuss.

2. Using the model of intergenerational transmission of attachment presented in this chapter, discuss the transmission sequence as it applies in this case.

3. What kinds of interventions could you suggest to help the members of this family?

PRACTICE USING WHAT YOU HAVE LEARNED

In the Pearson etext, apply these ideas to working with others.

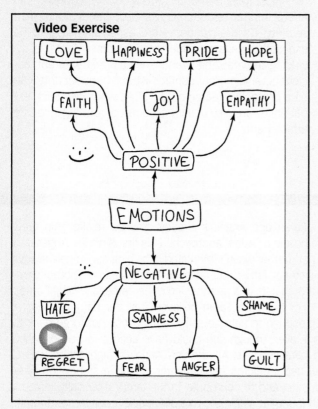

Video Exercise

JOURNAL QUESTIONS

1. Present five adjectives that describe your early childhood relationship to each parent.
   a. Why did you choose these adjectives?
   b. To which parent did you feel the closest?
   c. What did you do as a child when you were upset, hurt, or ill?
   d. What do you remember about any separation that you experienced as a child?

2. How would your parents describe your temperament as a young child? In what ways is it the same now and in what ways is it different?

3. Consider the inter-generational relationships in your family of origin (e.g., mother-grandmother). What were the qualities of your mother's (or father's) attachments to their parents? What have been the effects on your own attachment? If you have children, consider this question from their point of view.

KEY CONCEPTS

Phineas Gage matrix (p. 126)

emotional intelligence (p. 126)

basic emotions (p. 127)

differential emotions theory (DET) (p. 127)

emotion schemas (p. 128)

self-conscious emotions (p. 128)

emotion regulation (p. 131)

synchrony (p. 131)

still-face paradigm (p. 132)

other-directed coping behaviors (p. 132)

self-directed coping behaviors (p. 132)

social referencing (p. 133)

basic trust (p. 133)

attachment theory (p. 133)

ethologists (p. 134)

separation anxiety (p. 135)

stranger anxiety (p. 135)

proximity maintenance (p. 135)

secure base (p. 135)

safe haven (p. 135)

working models (p. 137)

strange situation test (p. 137)

securely attached (p. 137)

anxious ambivalent (p. 137)

avoidant babies (p. 138)

disorganized-disoriented (p. 138)

oxytocin (p. 139)

temperaments (p. 143)

fearfulness or reactivity (p. 143)

irritability or negative emotionality (p. 143)

activity level (p. 143)

positive affect (p. 143)

attention-persistence (p. 143)

rhythmicity (p. 143)

behavioral inhibition (p. 143)

difficult babies (p. 145)

easy babies (p. 145)

slow-to-warm-up babies (p. 145)

genetic vulnerability (diathesis-stress) (p. 145)

differential susceptibility (p. 145)

goodness of fit model (p. 145)

Adult Attachment Inventory (AAI) (p. 153)

intergenerational transmission (p. 156)

reactive attachment disorder (RAD) (p. 161)

CHAPTER 5

The Emerging Self and Socialization in the Early Years

"Mirror, mirror on the wall, who is the real me, after all?" Philosophers, poets, wicked stepmothers, and ordinary human beings have pondered versions of this question ever since the ancient Greeks advised, "Know thyself." The search for self embodies within it many of the profound questions at the heart of the human condition: What is the nature of human consciousness? Are we the same or different across situations and over time? How do people come to understand and accept who they are? Modern cultures, as we have noted, are not the first to express interest in these matters. Nonetheless, critics have raised concerns that the level of attention directed toward the self has increased in recent decades. Note the amount of press devoted to the ideas of self-concept, self-esteem, self-enhancement, and self-actualization, and you might agree that we have become downright self-centered!

Those of us in the helping professions are no exception to this trend. Even a cursory review of the professional literature in clinical and educational fields reveals an intense interest in topics related to the self. Therapeutic approaches that emphasize self-development are very common. Educational institutions struggle to incorporate self-development into their more traditional academic objectives. Popular magazines are saturated with advice about self-concept and self-esteem. All together, the pieces add up to a crazy quilt: part folklore, part research, part anecdote, and part good intention. Our task in this chapter is to unscramble some of this information and present the self in its developmental context.

Helpers need to understand the research findings in this critically important area lest they assume that all of our popular, contemporary notions about self-development are valid. For example, the postmodern focus on individualism might convey the idea that the self is truly independent and autonomous when, in fact, it is largely a product of social interaction. Bowlby (e.g., 1969/1982) suggested that working models of the self develop in concert with working models of attachment figures. Erikson (1950/1963) developed the idea that when others respond sensitively to their needs, children develop concepts of themselves as valuable. Cultural groups differ in their emphasis on an autonomous self. So self-development, despite our Western predilection for thinking of the self as independent, occurs in interaction with others and is influenced by culture and context. In this chapter, we will describe the earliest roots of self-development from a Western scientific perspective and emphasize the importance of parenting to this process. As we will see, the role of caretakers is of major significance in the development of many of the processes related to the self. We will also take a look at cultural approaches to specific parenting behaviors, such as discipline.

THE SELF-SYSTEM: TRADITIONAL CONCEPTIONS

The self and its development are complicated, abstract topics. Writers still grapple with the question of what constitutes a self. In their search for answers, theorists and researchers need to account for the fact that selves are multifaceted and possess elements of both stability and change. If you have ever said that you are not the same person that you were some time ago, you can understand this point. Recently, writers have begun to use the term *self-system* to replace "self," because the latter seems too unidimensional (see Damon & Hart, 1988). The **self-system** includes aspects related to the self, such as self-concept, self-regulation, and self-esteem.

The notion of an independent entity called "self" is such a deeply embedded concept in Western psychology that we tend to take it for granted. Therefore, it may be surprising to learn that the psychologies of other cultures (e.g., Buddhist psychology) take a decidedly different view. In Buddhist psychology, mind and matter change continually, and this impermanence is influenced by surrounding conditions (Bodhi, 1999). The Buddhist concept of "no-self" (anatta) does not imply that our conventional use of "self" is not helpful or that you and I are not real in some way. Rather, it emphasizes the transient nature of our phenomenological experience as human beings. The self is constantly being constructed in the moment-to-moment flow of experience. This insight is at the core of recent therapies that offer ways to alleviate the suffering that can come from our human tendency to protect and defend reified concepts about ourselves (see Olendzki, 2010). The view of "no-self" is quite different from that of classic Western psychology, which assumes a relatively permanent construct that can be studied over time.

We will begin our look at the nature of the self-system within Western psychology with a brief description of the classic work of James, Cooley, and Mead. William James (1890) made a distinction between the "I" and the "Me," a distinction that is still used productively in contemporary research about the self. That part of the self called "I" refers to the **I-Self/self-as-subject**, as active agent, or as the knower. It is that part of the self that experiences a sense of subjective self-awareness. The part called "Me" is that part of the self that is the object of self or others' observations, or in other words, the part that is known. One might think of the "Me" part of the self (Me-Self) as the **Me-Self/self-concept**.

Implicit in James's traditional construction of selfhood is the idea that the self is multidimensional. Freud (1956) once wrote that a person could be construed as a whole "cast of characters." Interestingly, this view of the multiplicity of selves was rejected by a number of influential writers in the first half of the 20th century. Gergen (1971) described the emphasis placed on the importance of maintaining a unified, coherent self by important therapists and scholars such as Horney (1950), Jung (1928), Maslow (1954), and Rogers (1951). Considerable recent evidence, however, has not supported the view of the unified self but has demonstrated that individuals vary across situations, that they may possess conflicting self-ideas that speak with different voices at different times, and that the self-concept differentiates with maturity. A basic feature of the self, then, is that it incorporates both the private and the more public sides of our nature, accommodating our ability to keep our own counsel and still be known to others by virtue of our interactions with them.

Recently, writers have developed alternative ways of categorizing the classic "I–Me" distinction. Among these are Lewis's (1994) subjective and objective self-awareness, Case's (1991) implicit and explicit self, and Neisser's (1993) ecological and remembered self. All the newer contrasts share the original distinction between the self as knower and the self as known. Furthermore, there is consensus between classic and contemporary theorists that the "I" self emerges first.

What specifically does the "I" comprise? James proposed that this is the side of the self that experiences continuity over time. Even though we all grow and change, we know we embody core elements of the same "self" throughout our lifetime. The "I" also recognizes the distinctiveness of the self as a person compared to other persons. You know where you end and the person sitting next to you begins. Finally, the "I" reflects agency or is that part of the self that engages in self-directed activity, self-control, and contemplation of the "Me." With time, these elements will be explored and further consolidated in the adolescent search for identity.

The "Me" includes all those attributes that are used to define the self and that make up the self-concept. In James's typology, these are the "material self," the "social self," and the "spiritual self," ranked in that order of importance from lowest to highest. The material self encompasses a person's physical characteristics and material possessions. The social self includes her social standing, her reputation, and those personal characteristics that are recognized by others, such as gregariousness or stubbornness. The spiritual self, viewed by James as the most precious, incorporates her qualities of character, beliefs, and personal values.

Self-concept, as defined here, is distinct from **self-esteem**. The former is a description of personal attributes. The latter is one's evaluation of these attributes, or the positive or negative valence associated with those attributes. *Valence* refers to the affective value of a characteristic, either good, bad, or neutral. James believed that self-esteem is more than just the measure of accomplishments. Rather, he believed that it depends upon the number of successes we enjoy relative to our aspirations, or, in his terminology, pretensions. Pretensions are goals that we choose to meet for ourselves because of their personal importance. For example, if it is highly important to you to be popular and socially active, the lack of a date for an important New Year's Eve party can be a real blow to your self-esteem. However, if you really care more about earning enough money to become rich at an early age, you might consider working overtime on New Year's Eve to be highly congruent with your aspirations. Your dateless condition is less damaging to your self-esteem. Failures or even successes in areas that are relatively unimportant to us may be discounted and will have less effect on self-esteem.

If James provided ideas about the structure of the self that resonate with contemporary theorizing, Charles Cooley (1902) introduced a developmental perspective that describes how interactions with others help construct the self-system. Using his now-famous metaphor of the **"looking-glass self,"** Cooley described the process of self-development as one that originates from observing the reflected appraisals of others, primarily attachment figures. Cooley hypothesized that this process consists of three steps. As we interact with others, we first imagine how we must appear to the other person on a certain dimension, such as intelligence. Then, we interpret or imagine how that other person evaluates us on that certain dimension. Finally, we experience some emotional response to that perceived evaluation. The resulting interpretation and its affective valence constitute a building block for constructing self-knowledge. So it is that our self-representations are shaped and given affective valences by the significant people in our life.

Let's consider a simplified example of a young child's display of affection for a parent. A 4-year-old girl approaches her father to give him a hug. The father, preoccupied with a pressing business matter, looks annoyed by the interruption. He gives her a quick hug and returns to his work. If this type of sequence is repeated on a regular basis across various situations, the child may come to develop a "self-idea" that she is bothersome and not important enough to interrupt her father's work. She may begin to construct a vague impression of herself as unappealing or possibly too emotionally expressive or dependent. Because the child perceives the emotion and interprets her father's response as impatient and irritated, her view of the event includes a self-appraisal—presumably that she is irritating—that is incorporated into her self-system. With repeated experience, the youngster comes to regard herself in certain ways by looking at the mirror of her parent's view of her, warped though that mirror might be. The emotional valence associated with this aspect of the child's self-image can be unpleasant or uncomfortable. This self-representation may serve as a standard for her behavior in social interactions (e.g., in her willingness to express her need for attention and affection from others) and inform her sense of right and wrong.

Now imagine this same little girl in another family. She interrupts her father to give him a hug, and he beams, expressing evident satisfaction in his daughter's affectionate nature. This child's self-concept is likely to include a positively valenced sense of being emotionally expressive. The same child and the same behavior could lead to different social responses in different families, setting the child's developing sense of self, relationships, and morality on a different pathway. Thus early attachment and parenting interactions have been viewed as instrumental in the development of individual differences in self-concept (Sroufe, 1996).

Although the development of the self is obviously influenced by many factors and is extraordinarily complex, Cooley believed that it was largely the product of social influences. Recent researchers have investigated the possibility that the sequence Cooley proposed can also operate in reverse order, namely that a positive appraisal of oneself can generate positive interpretations of others' appraisals.

George Herbert Mead (1934) expanded on Cooley's work, enlarging the scope of influence to include the role of language and society in shaping the self-system. He held that the self-idea, or self-concept, becomes internalized or "generalized" through repeated interactions with others of the same cultural group. The individual adopts the perspective of others who share the same societal perspective, producing a kind of ecological self (Neisser, 1993). An example of this phenomenon is provided by Markus and Kitayama (1991), who found cultural differences in preferred ways of viewing the self. In their study, Japanese were more likely to describe themselves by emphasizing their affiliations, such as family membership, whereas Americans used self-descriptors that emphasized their individuality. Children not only adopt descriptive information about the self from their cultural milieu, they also incorporate those standards, rules, and goals that their family and their culture have determined to be appropriate ways of behaving and thinking (Stipek, Recchia, & McClintic, 1992). Note the parallels between Mead's approach and Vygotsky's (see Chapter 3).

These classic formulations of the self as multidimensional, as influenced by the reflected appraisals of significant others, and as shaped by the cultural milieu, provide a foundation for current Western thinking about the self-system. You may have noticed that conceptions of self and of morality overlap in these models. Damon and Hart (1992) have noted:

> Children cannot know themselves without some sense of the other. Nor can they forge their self-identities without an awareness of their own values. Moreover, at all developmental periods, social activities derive from—and in turn shape—judgments about the self, other, and morality. In these and many other ways, self-understanding, social interaction, and morality are intertwined in a developing psychological system that grows and changes throughout the life span. (p. 421)

Self-understanding is one of the key building blocks of personality, social, and moral development. How does this mysterious self begin? In the next section, we will review the earliest stages of developing self-awareness.

THE EARLY DEVELOPMENT OF THE SELF-SYSTEM

The Beginnings of the "I" and the "Me"

Settling on a time that marks the beginning of the self is a difficult task because various aspects of the self emerge at different rates and may be identified differently depending upon one's theoretical viewpoint. A child's ability to describe herself as "smart" or "funny" will not be apparent until several years after birth. Does this mean there is no sense of self until the time when she can recognize and articulate her personal characteristics? Most contemporary developmentalists would disagree with this idea. In general, the development of self is viewed as a gradually unfolding process, beginning at birth and lasting throughout life. Even adults continue to grow and change, thus experiencing self-development. However, the adult sense of self is far more differentiated than that of the infant, or even that of the articulate preschooler. What are the competencies of the infant that make self-development possible? How do these competencies interact with the social relationships that ultimately give birth to the self as a manifestation of personal consciousness?

Precursors of Self-Awareness in Infancy—the "Pre-Self"

We might say that the newborn's capacities for rudimentary information processing and social bonding provide the building material out of which the self is born. For example, one early competency is the infant's capacity for imitation. As we saw in Chapter 3, babies can imitate the facial gestures of adults a few days after birth (Meltzoff, 1990). When a baby imitates an adult opening and closing his mouth, she is detecting, at least at a behavioral level, similarity between herself and the adult model. Meltzoff argues that such early imitative skills are precursors of the older child's ability to draw parallels between her own and another person's mind or feelings.

A sensitive caregiver responds to this infant's signals, allowing the child to take control of the meal. This type of behavior encourages development of a strong sense of an autonomous self.

As we saw in Chapter 4, from birth through the first half year of life, the infant is primarily engaged in the business of regulating physiological and emotional states, largely in the context of infant–caregiver interactions. Young infants have limited power to regulate a caregiver's responses, and so it is primarily the caregiver's responsibility to scaffold interactions, providing the sensitive care that allows for the establishment of routines. Meltzoff (1990) argues that from the regularity and reliability of caregiver–infant interactions babies extract notions of "self-invariance" and "other invariance," which precede self-awareness. We might say that the infant comes to possess a **pre-self**, composed of early inklings of the permanence of her body, its separateness from others, and the rhythms of interpersonal connections.

Gradually, over the second half year, the infant assumes more control in signaling the caregiver to provide for her needs. The regularity with which the caregiver is available and sensitive or unavailable and insensitive is stored in memory in what Stern (1985) calls **representations of interactions (RIGs)**. These are "procedural" representations or schemata—preverbal, unconscious, and a kind of sensorimotor memory. They are patterns generalized from the repetitive nature of caregiver–infant interactions.

When the infant's attempts to exert some control over caregiver contingencies are successful, she is thought to experience a budding sense of mastery or self-efficacy (Bandura, 1990). She takes pleasure in expressing the agentic "I." Imagine the lesson learned by an infant who, when she coos and babbles, regularly attracts the smiles and responsive vocalizations of her caregivers. This baby's world, in some small way, begins to come under her control. She might encode the message, "When I am upset or need attention, my parent responds and takes care of me." Again, the infant does not represent these ideas linguistically, but rather encodes these kinds of organized sequences as procedural models or patterns of the self-in-relationship.

Affective responses, such as feelings of love and relief, also become associated with these memories. The infant's self-system is under construction.

As the infant approaches the end of the 1st year, other cognitive and affective developments point to an increasing sense of self as separate from the caretaker. We saw in Chapter 4 that by about 8 to 10 months infants display separation anxiety, signaling the formation of an attachment to the primary caregiver. For example, they might show distress even at an impending separation from an attachment figure, perhaps by looking anxiously at the door when the babysitter arrives. Many babies cry and cling to a departing caregiver. These behaviors serve to maintain proximity, and they demonstrate the infant's recognition that the caregiver is separate from herself.

Attachment theorists like Bowlby assume that the attachment between infant and caregiver gives rise to a sense of security and optimism in an infant, what Erikson described as a burgeoning trust in others and an early sense of self-worth. From this perspective, when the 1-year-old begins to use the caregiver as a secure base from which to explore the environment, we are seeing the emergence of a kind of preliminary sense of self-worth. Once again, the infant's self-development evolves from her experience in relationships.

We also saw in the last chapter that late in the 1st year, caregivers' facial expressions influence infants' reactions to situations, such as their willingness to cross a visual cliff (Campos, Barrett, Lamb, Goldsmith, & Sternberg, 1983; Klinnert, 1984). **Social referencing**—the baby's adjustment of reactions depending on feedback provided by a caregiver—also implies recognition of the separateness of the other. This phenomenon is thought to be a source of information for the self-system, providing the baby with a context in which she begins to differentiate experience of the self from experience of the other and from the combined experience of the "we" (Emde & Buchsbaum, 1990). Social referencing demonstrates how transactional the self-development process really is. The child uses the caregiver's emotions to discern meaning in events and to intuit information about the self.

Campos, Campos, and Barrett (1989) have suggested that when caregivers communicate consistent emotional signals about environmental events, certain pervasive emotional dispositions are created. These processes can have far-reaching effects: "Can I trust other people? Is it safe to take risks?" These emotional dispositions constitute a part of the "value system" of a family or a culture. Furthermore, these authors note that emotional signaling by caregivers may affect the process of emotion regulation and emotional self-knowledge well beyond infancy. For example, a child growing up in an emotional climate marked by parental anger and blame might "read" and internalize the parents' emotional messages as shame and guilt, concluding that she is shameful (Zahn-Waxler & Kochanska, 1990).

The Emergence of Self-Awareness and Self-Concept

Certain cognitive advances in the 2nd year seem to play important roles in the development of the self-system. For example, the toddler's capacity for establishing joint reference with another supports the early development of a theory of mind. Imagine that the father of a 15-month-old girl tries to get the toddler to look at a kitten that has just walked into the room. The father points to the kitten, looks at the child, smiles broadly and says, "cat." This sequence is repeated until the child, following the direction of her father's gaze, spies the cat and looks back at him with a big grin. She and her father are sharing the same point of reference. Jointly attending to the pet, in this case, may encourage a beginning understanding of "mind," of private experience that is sometimes shared. The toddler's sense of herself as a separate person is enhanced. Note, as well, that the affective part of the experience can also be shared. The toddler and her caregiver both delight in the kitten's appearance.

A benchmark event occurs in self-development roughly around the age of 18 months, perhaps supported by an emerging capacity for mental representation (see Chapter 3). Up to this time, human infants do not show **self-recognition**

 The 12-month-old infant does not recognize himself in the mirror, but the 19-month-old shows she knows that the image is her own reflection.

This toddler recognizes that the image in the mirror is her own reflection, a milestone in self-recognition.

when they view themselves in a mirror. Self-recognition is typically manifested by the observer's display of self-directed behavior upon viewing her reflection. Reasoning that self-directed behavior signals the presence of objective self-awareness, Lewis and his colleagues used a mirror recognition technique to study infants and children (e.g., Lewis & Michalson, 1983). The researchers placed the children in front of a mirror after marking their faces with a spot of rouge. Toddlers often showed mark-directed behavior, such as touching their faces, averting their gaze, and then turning back to look again. No children younger than 15 months had this reaction, and all children in the 24-month-old group displayed it. Between 15 months and 2 years children also began to distinguish their own images from those of age mates on videotapes (see Suddendorf, Simcock, & Nielsen, 2007). Across many studies, findings suggest that self-recognition is universally acquired late in the 2nd year of life (e.g., Courage, Edison, & Howe, 2004). A recent investigation using brain imaging with toddlers indicates that its emergence is linked to maturation of one cortical area—the juncture of the parietal and temporal lobes—that is also activated in adults during self-recognition tasks (Lewis & Carmody, 2008).

The timing of self-recognition shows some variability among children from different cultures. In a study of German, Camaroon and urban and rural Indians, children from cultures that emphasized autonomous socialization goals like independence achieved mirror self-recognition a little earlier than those growing up in cultures that had more relational goals like interdependence. The authors proposed that earlier self-recognition was related to more distal face-to-face interactions with infants through which infants begin to understand themselves as independent agents. Caregivers in relational cultures tended to engage in more proximal body contact and less frequent face-to-face games. Despite these modest differences in age of acquisition, the test was found to be a good predictor of self-recognition across cultures (Kartner, Keller, Chaudhary, & Yovsi, 2012). For children whose development is delayed, as in the case of children with Down syndrome, self-recognition occurs whenever they achieve a developmental level of approximately 2 years (Kopp & Wyer, 1994). Comparison studies of maltreated and non-maltreated children show no differences in the timing of self-recognition (Schneider-Rosen & Cicchetti, 1984, 1991). These studies also suggest that self-evaluation, or self-esteem, begins to emerge along with self-recognition. Maltreated children show considerably more negative or neutral affect when seeing their faces in the mirror than do non-maltreated children, who display more positive affect.

Self-recognition is a clear signal that a child has begun to formulate a conscious concept of self. Roughly after the child's second birthday, an increase in language skills makes possible further elaboration of the self-concept or "Me-self." Children begin to describe themselves as "a boy" or "a girl" or as "big" or "little," and they begin to use appropriate personal pronouns to refer to themselves (e.g., Lewis & Ramsay, 2004). These achievements mark a watershed in the development of the self-concept, and caregivers make important contributions by virtue of the labels they apply to children. Parental statements such as "You are a big girl" can now be stored in a child's semantic memory as part of her self-knowledge (e.g., Nelson, 1993a). Caregivers' descriptions can be neutral and objective (such as the child's name or personal pronoun) or evaluative and subjective (such as "pretty" or "good"), and these appear not to be differentiated by young children according to their objectivity or subjectivity. Stipek, Gralinski, and Kopp (1990) reported that toddlers appear to believe both objective and subjective claims about themselves, apparently because the claims come from an authoritative source. In other words, young children cannot discount the negative part of the parental evaluation "bad girl" as due to parental bias or temporary bad mood. When self-description begins, maltreated children use fewer words to describe their feelings than do non-maltreated children, despite comparable performance on measures of receptive language ability (e.g., Beeghly & Cicchetti, 1994). The authors conclude that these results, together with the less-positive affective responses maltreated children display on the self-recognition task, are early indicators of poor self-esteem and of the influence of caregivers' words and deeds on children's earliest self-evaluations. In fact, maltreatment generally seems to blunt the development of self-awareness, especially children's awareness of their inner thoughts and feelings (see Harter, 2006).

As toddlers become preschoolers, their self-concepts become more and more differentiated and complex. For example, as early as 3 years of age, children can correctly identify their race, ethnicity, and skin color (Katz & Zalk, 1974). In general, children from minority groups tend to develop racial awareness faster than do nonminorities. A study by Feinman and Entwhistle (1976) demonstrated that young African American children outperform other children in their ability to discriminate colors of faces, suggesting the early influence of race on perception. Ramsey and Myers (1990) also found that race is one of the primary dimensions children refer to when describing people.

Unfortunately, many early studies of preschool children found evidence for a pro-white bias among children from minority groups (see Banks, 1976; Beuf, 1977; Spencer, 1982). Typically, these early studies involved questioning young children about their preferences for, and identification with, dolls that represent their own ethnic or racial group and that represent the majority culture (Clark & Clark, 1939). Overall, young children tended to perceive a white doll as possessing more positive attributes, and some researchers have interpreted these findings to be early predictors of identity formation problems or misidentification among minority group children. However, subsequent studies of African-American children have found that a pro-white bias may coexist with high levels of personal self-esteem (Powell, 1985). Spencer and Markstrom-Adams (1990), after reviewing this body of work, conclude that these dissonant results reflect the child's cognitive awareness of social stereotypes, but not necessarily a self-esteem deficit. In other words, young children from minority groups may be somewhat more attuned to society's valuing of white culture without necessarily devaluing themselves or their cultural heritage. A more recent computerized version of the original doll study used cartoon characters with several variations in skin tone rather than the original black- or white–skinned dolls. Preschooler participants were less likely to declare any preference for skin tone when shown the array of characters, possibly suggesting their greater exposure to individuals with many skin colors. However, when asked to select *either* a black or white character to be their "best friend," there was a trend for young African-American children to choose the white character (Jordan & Hernandez-Reif, 2009). Additional research is needed to better understand the reasons for these results.

Consistent with their level of cognitive development, preschoolers generally describe themselves in concrete, physical terms, such as "little" or "strong," whereas older children and adolescents employ more abstract words. As children mature, they become more skilled at identifying various aspects of themselves. For example, a 7-year-old might describe herself as helpful, a good soccer player, and smart in reading but not in math. As we shall see in a later chapter, the self-concept continues to become more differentiated with age.

In summary, the self-system begins to develop in earliest infancy. There are many precursors to a conscious concept of self in the 1st year, a kind of procedural knowledge of the self in action and interaction, or "pre-self." But awareness of self as a distinct entity begins with self-recognition in the 2nd year and is followed by explicit self-description in the 3rd year. Self-evaluation or self-esteem is evident as soon as toddlers show signs of self-recognition. See Table 5.1 for a summary of the early phases of self-development.

TABLE 5.1 Phases of Self-Development

AGE	DEVELOPING ASPECTS OF SELF	MANIFESTATIONS
0–6 months	Pre-Self	Beginnings of "self-invariance" and "other invariance" embedded in infant–caregiver interactions
6–12 months	Intentional or Agentic Self or "I"	Intentional signaling of caregiver; social referencing; shared referents; beginning self-efficacy; using caregiver as secure base (beginning self-worth and trust)
12–24 months	Objective Self or "Me"	Self-recognition; early self-control; early self-esteem (feelings of autonomy)
24–60 months	Self-Monitoring Self	Self-description; self-conscious emotions; self-regulation

Throughout infancy and beyond, the self-system is a joint construction of child, caregiver, and cultural and family milieu. We have described some ways in which caregiver–infant interactions seem to contribute to the development of the self. Later in this chapter, we will discuss in greater detail how parenting in the toddler and preschool years contributes to child outcomes, including the development of the self-system.

Roots of Self-Control and Self-Regulation

Up to now, we have described the emerging "I" and "Me." Now we turn our attention to another important dimension of the developing self-system, **self-control or behavior regulation** and **self-regulation**. Self-control refers to two things: first, the child's ability to stop herself from performing a proscribed act, as when a toddler can pull her hand back from the cookie jar after being told "No cookies before dinner"; and second, her ability to make herself perform an act that she may not feel much like doing, such as giving Aunt Matilda a required kiss on the cheek. According to Kopp (1982), self-regulation is a more advanced and flexible version of self-control:

> the ability to comply with a request, to initiate and cease activities according to situational demands, to modulate the intensity, frequency, and duration of verbal and motor acts in social and educational settings, to postpone acting upon a desired object or goal, and to generate socially approved behavior in the absence of external monitors. (pp. 199–200)

Professionals regularly deal with problems involving self-regulation in one form or another. The preschooler who throws tantrums in school, the rebellious adolescent who runs away from home, the young adult who repeatedly loses jobs because she fails to show up on time, all may be examples of difficulties in this area. Many other factors contribute to such adjustment problems; however, they all reflect some lack of compliance with specific requests or rules.

Obviously, achieving self-regulation is a rather formidable task for a mischievous toddler or even for a sophisticated high schooler! Even though this may sound like the accomplishment that many parents of tempestuous 2-year-olds long for, it is not realistic to expect a child to be able to master her behavior and emotions in every circumstance. The movement from dyadic emotion regulation to self-regulation of behavior and emotion, permitting harmonious interchange with the social environment, is a painstaking, complex, and long-term process (Thompson, 2006).

The Importance of Emotion Regulation

It is absolutely essential to recognize that emotion regulation underlies any ability to control behaviors. In fact, the earliest developmental task of infancy is to establish physiological balance, or control over fluctuating levels of arousal. The affective tension that the infant experiences when her homeostatic "set point" has been altered through hunger, pain, or too much stimulation motivates her to return to a more balanced state. Unable to manage this on her own, the infant signals the caregiver, whose soothing attentions function as critical ingredients in the development of the affect-regulation system. When the toddler or preschooler experiences periods of high arousal or distress, the sensitive caregiver steps in once again to help the child regain some affective control or to shore up the boundaries of the self. As we have emphasized in Chapter 4, good caregiving in infancy and beyond involves scaffolding the child's developing ability to regulate both emotional and behavioral expression.

The Early Progress of Behavior Regulation

How does behavior regulation come into being? It depends on two major cognitive and emotional advances that emerge in tandem with objective self-awareness or self-recognition: first, representational thought, and second, emotional response to wrongdoing.

Recall from our discussion of Piagetian theory that children around 18 months of age can use a symbol to stand in for an object. Toddlers hear, understand, and store structures such as "Don't jump on the furniture," which might be a manifestation of a broader value that property should not be damaged, or "Share your candy with your sister," a version of "Do unto others." This cognitive machinery allows children to construct internalized representations of standards for everyday behavior (Kopp & Wyer, 1994). These standards or rules might differ somewhat according to the child's family and culture, but every cultural group maintains them and provides sanctions for their violation (Lewis, 1993).

Along with the basic capacity for mental representation, many other cognitive skills contribute to the learning of standards: ability to focus attention, comprehension of caregiver requests, procedural knowledge of rules, and generalization of rules across situations. As these abilities are sharpened in the 2nd year, toddlers begin the process of internalizing rules and prohibitions (Emde, Biringen, Clyman, & Oppenheim, 1991). Obviously, an infant cannot comply with social conventions precisely because she has no comprehension of them. A baby may be prevented from engaging in some activity by external parental displays of control, as when a mother whisks her adventurous 10-month-old away from the edge of a swimming pool. But a 2-year-old who has the requisite level of cognitive maturity to understand and remember some rules, as well as the motivation to comply, begins to show signs of inhibiting her own behavior in such situations.

The growth of emotions often linked to violations of standards for everyday behavior appears to begin late in the 2nd year. Called social or **self-conscious emotions**, shame, embarrassment, guilt, and pride take their place in the child's emotional repertoire after objective self-awareness, or self-recognition, has been attained (Lewis, 2000). These emotions are different from the emotions of infancy because they require the ability to consider the self as separate from others and as the subject of others' judgments. Between the ages of 2 and 3, young children often display emotional responses to their wrongdoing and mistakes, suggesting that they have begun to evaluate themselves in ways that they expect to be evaluated by others (Kagan, 1981). At 18 months, a child might take notice of her rule violation but without any discernable emotional response. Consider, for example, the toddler who spills milk on the floor. She may say "Uh oh!" and giggle or point to the spill without much concern. Later, rule breaking becomes associated with some negative affect. This same youngster at 3 may experience a sense of embarrassment, evaluate herself as "bad," and try to hide the evidence (see Saarni, Campos, Camras, & Witherington, 2006).

The capacity for emotional response to wrongdoing is an important milestone, long considered to be the beginning of conscience development (Sears, Maccoby, & Levin, 1957). Although not yet a reflection of full-fledged conscience, the child's emotional responses to rule violations are linked to what she perceives her parents' reactions might be, and these perceptions shape her developing sense of morality (Emde, Johnson, & Easterbrooks, 1987). But do all social emotions produce positive moral results? Recent research on shame and guilt have shown that these social emotions can have very different consequences. Despite conventional wisdom that feeling guilty should be avoided, guilt can have adaptive consequences. Feelings of guilt have been associated with increases in other-directed empathy, positive reparative action, constructive problem solving, and low defensiveness and anger. Shame, on the other hand, is linked to hiding or denying wrongdoing, elevated levels of proinflammatory cytokines, heightened self-focus, blaming other people or situations, displaced aggression, externalizing behavior, low self-esteem, and a range of psychiatric disorders (see Tangney, Stuewig, & Mashek, 2007 for a review). As a means of making sense of transgression, children and adults who experience guilt might reason "I did a bad thing" whereas the inner script for those who experience shame might be "I am a bad person." The use of shaming as a way of disciplining children (telling child he/she should be ashamed of him/herself) has been linked to anxiety disorders in a cross-cultural study of children and parents in China, India, Italy, Kenya, Philippines, and Thailand (Gershoff, Grogan-Kaylor, Lansford, Chang, Zelli, & Deater-Deckard, 2010).

EARLY SOCIALIZATION: PARENTING AND THE DEVELOPMENT OF THE SELF-SYSTEM

Theorists from Cooley (1902) to Bowlby (e.g., 1969/1982) and Erikson (1950/1963) have assumed that many parts of the self-system grow out of our social interactions. As we saw in the last chapter, the available data do suggest that our earliest relationships create a trajectory for the development of self-concept and self-esteem. For example, when babies are securely attached to their mothers, they tend to be appropriately independent as 4-year-olds and to be self-confident and socially skilled as 10-year-olds (e.g., Sroufe, Egeland, Carlson, & Collins, 2005; see Thompson, 2006, for a review).

We know that early caregiving quality can make an important contribution to the quality of babies' attachments. Infants are likely to become securely attached to caregivers who respond promptly and consistently to crying, who react appropriately to babies' facial expressions, eye contact and other signals, who handle their infants sensitively, and who hold them often during the 1st year, providing the contact comfort that helps infants modulate their emotions. Such caregiving requires patience and a child-centered approach that can be difficult for any parent sometimes, but is especially challenging if the baby has a difficult temperament or other special needs or if the parent is stressed or depressed. But the effort and self-sacrifice required for parents to create a "good fit," as Thomas and Chess (1977) described it, between their caregiving and a baby's needs does appear to contribute to attachment quality and to the direction that self-knowledge and self-evaluation will take. This process continues after infancy, as the description of self-development in the last section indicates. In this section, we will take a close look at parent–child relationships in the toddler and preschool years. We will focus especially on the characteristics of parenting that may be most conducive to helping young children to develop positive self-esteem and adaptive self-regulatory mechanisms.

As the infant becomes a toddler, gaining cognitive, communicative, and motor skills, there are new challenges for parents trying to be sensitive and responsive, to create a good fit between their care and the child's needs. First, caregivers are faced with the need to grant some autonomy to the child. As toddlers become capable of doing more on their own, they are motivated to practice and expand their growing competencies. The strong dependency that characterizes young babies is gradually replaced by a capacity and need for independent action. Erikson theorized that toddlers' emerging feelings of worth are benefited when they can use their growing skills to function at least somewhat autonomously, whether it is by feeding themselves or by buttoning their own buttons, or more subtly, by saying "NO!"—that is, refusing to do what someone else requires (see Table 1.1 in Chapter 1). Thus, although the earliest feelings of worth grow out of an infant's trust in others to meet all her needs, those feelings of worth grow in the toddler years when the child begins to experience self-sufficiency, or autonomy, a sense that "I can do it myself."

Second, also because the child's behavioral and cognitive skills are growing, the caregiver must begin to **socialize** the child, that is, to prepare the child to be a competent member of society. This includes limiting some behaviors and demanding others, so that the child will be safe ("No, you cannot climb on the counter") and so that she will learn the standards of her culture and behave in ways that are conventionally acceptable ("You must wear clothes"). Socialization pressure requires **discipline**, when parents limit or demand behavior using techniques that either exert or require control. Parents generally impose more discipline on the child as they perceive her to be more and more capable of self-control. When parents tell a child to do, or not to do, something, they are depending on the child's ability to initiate or to stop her own actions. As we saw earlier, the only way to make an infant do, or not do, something is to rely on physically moving or restraining the child. Parents do a lot of that with infants, but they rely more and more on controlling by request or command during early childhood, as the requisite abilities (such as representational and comprehension skills) grow.

Thus, caregiver–child relationships are reorganized in the postinfancy period, with the additions of children's autonomy seeking, on one hand, and parents' imposition of discipline, on the other hand. What are the important features of this more complex relationship between parent and child? What role does the parent–child relationship play in the child's developing self-system? Let's begin by examining what research indicates are the most important dimensions or features of a parent's behavior in this relationship.

The Dimensions of Parenting Style

Studies of parenting after infancy have a long history and have produced many complicated findings. Remarkably, researchers from very different theoretical traditions have repeatedly identified two major dimensions or aspects of parents' behavior that seem to characterize the quality of parenting. These can be thought of as the primary contributors to what is called parenting style (for reviews see Baumrind, 1989, 1993; Bugental & Grusec, 2006; Darling & Steinberg, 1993; Maccoby & Martin, 1983; Parke & Buriel, 2006).

The Warmth Dimension—Parental Responsiveness

In the postinfancy period, parents continue to create an emotional climate for their children. Contributing to a positive climate is **warmth dimension (parental responsiveness)**: listening to the child, being involved and interested in the child's activities, accepting the child, making positive attributions toward the child, being "tuned in" and supportive (e.g., Baumrind, 1989; Dix, Stewart, Gershoff, & Day, 2007). In essence, high levels of warmth with toddlers and older children are comparable to high levels of responsive, sensitive care with infants. But some of the child's needs have changed. With toddlers, as we have seen, autonomy needs begin to be important, and responsive parents accept these needs, acquiescing when possible to their children's reasonable demands for autonomy (Baumrind, 1993). So, when 25-month-old Amanda begins to insist that she can dress herself, her mother tries to accommodate her by setting aside extra time for the morning dressing ritual. She also ignores the inconvenience and the sometimes strange-looking outcomes and gives Amanda positive messages about the process: "You're getting to be such a big girl to put on your own clothes!" Her attitude is **child centered**, sidelining parental needs (for time, convenience, and coordinated outfits) to meet Amanda's developmental needs.

Some parents create a more negative emotional climate. Their behavior is often **parent centered**: they show little responsiveness to their children's concerns and

 This caregiver shows both warmth and demandingness as she guides the children through the resolution of a dispute. The guidelines she provides for sharing will help the children develop their own self-control.

are unlikely to do things just to meet those concerns. They may even make hostile attributions when children's needs are out of line with their own. When 20-month-old Jessie wants to feed herself her morning cereal, for example, at first her mother ignores her. When Jessie insists, her mother attends to her demands by making negative attributions, such as "You'll just make a mess" and "Why do you always make things so hard in the morning?" When Jessie accidentally spills the milk, her mother responds in frustration, "I told you that you couldn't do it yourself!"

We have seen that sensitive, responsive mother care in infancy promotes secure attachments. Likewise, mothers' warmth and responsiveness with their toddlers help maintain secure attachments and increase the likelihood that toddlers will be cooperative when mothers place demands on them (e.g., Dix et al., 2007; National Institute of Child Health and Human Development [NICHD], 1998). For example, toddlers' compliance with their mothers has been observed in toy cleanup tasks and in a situation where mothers designate some attractive toys as "off limits." The most enthusiastically compliant toddlers are those who are securely attached to their mothers (according to a separate assessment), and whose mothers maintain a warm, positive emotional climate throughout the sessions (Kochanska, 1995; Kochanska, Aksan, & Koenig, 1995).

The Control Dimension—Parental Demandingness

The second major dimension of parenting style is the **control dimension (parental demandingness)**. If parental responsiveness means that parents sometimes acquiesce to their children's demands, parental demandingness leads parents to impose discipline. Demanding parents require their children to curb some of their behaviors and insist that they perform other behaviors that are suitable to their level of maturity (sometimes called **maturity demands**). Demanding parents impose standards and rules and enforce them. Interestingly, this dimension of parenting can be either child centered or parent centered. If the parent's concern is the development of self-control necessary for children to feel secure, to behave in ways that gain social acceptance, and to become skillful at social give and take, then discipline has a child focus. If the parents' concerns—for example, for quiet, or convenience, or orderliness, and so on—are primary, then discipline has a parent focus. Of course, parents' disciplinary motives may sometimes combine both kinds of concerns, and the same parents may shift their focus depending on the given situation. For example, Hastings and Grusec (1998) found that parents expressed more parent-centered concerns (such as wanting to be in control) when disciplining their children in public, but more child-centered concerns (such as teaching a child not to give up easily) in private interactions.

The control dimension refers to parents' *behavioral* control of their children, which as you will see, is an important element of responsible parenting. This must be distinguished from *psychological* control, which refers to a kind of intrusiveness and interference on the part of parents (e.g., Barber Stolz, & Olsen, 2005; Bugental & Grusec, 2006). The latter often involves criticizing and/or derogating the child and leaving the child without choices. Psychological control has more to do with the emotional climate a parent creates (the warmth dimension) than it does with demandingness.

Four Parenting Styles

We can describe four basic **parenting styles**, or constellations of parenting characteristics, as shown in Table 5.2, by combining and crossing the positive and negative poles of parental responsiveness and demandingness (Maccoby & Martin, 1983). As you will see, these styles are often predictive of child characteristics (e.g., Baumrind, 1989, 1993).

The Authoritative Style

Parents with an **authoritative style** are both highly responsive and highly demanding. So, they create a positive emotional climate for their children, promoting autonomy and

TABLE 5.2   Parenting Dimensions and Parenting Styles

	PARENTAL WARMTH	
	ACCEPTING, RESPONSIVE, CHILD-CENTERED	**REJECTING, UNRESPONSIVE, PARENT-CENTERED**
Parental Demandingness:		
Demanding, Controlling	*Authoritative Style*	*Authoritarian Style*
Undemanding, Not Controlling	*Permissive Style*	*Neglecting-Uninvolved Style*

SOURCE: Maccoby, E. E., & Martin, J. A. (1983). Socialization in the context of the family. In P. H. Mussin & E. M. Hetherington, *Handbook of child psychology* vol. 4 (4th ed., pp. 1–101). Copyright © 1983. Reproduced with permission of John Wiley & Sons, Inc.

supporting assertiveness and individuality. At the same time these parents accept responsibility for socializing their children by expecting mature behavior and setting and enforcing clear standards. Other qualities also tend to be part of this constellation. These parents are often openly affectionate; they encourage two-way communication with their children (that is, they genuinely listen and pay attention as well as talking themselves). Their communications about expectations and standards are usually clear and come with explanations that go beyond "You do it because I said so" to statements that help children make sense of their parents' demands. Thus, they are strong on behavioral control, but do not use psychological control.

The Authoritarian Style

Authoritarian parents are low on responsiveness, but highly demanding. Thus they do not create a positive

Parents who create a positive emotional climate promote autonomy and elicit cooperation from their children.

emotional climate nor encourage children's individualistic strivings or assertiveness, but they do tend to exercise considerable control, making maturity demands and requiring conformity to rules. In addition, other qualities tend to be characteristic of authoritarian parents. First, authoritarian parents usually communicate less effectively with their children than authoritative parents. Their communications are more one-sided ("I say what will happen; you listen"). They express less affection. And their control tends to be more restrictive, meaning that they tend to restrict their children's emotional expressiveness and other self-assertive behaviors. That is, they tend to exercise not just behavioral but also psychological control. They also are more likely to exercise control by using power assertion (see the section on parenting practices below) and are less likely to provide explanations that go beyond "Because I said so."

The Permissive Style

Permissive parents are moderately to highly responsive to their children, but low on demandingness. Thus, they exercise less behavioral control than other parents, putting fewer maturity demands on their children, especially with regard to expressions of anger and aggressive behavior. They are more nurturing and affectionate than authoritarian parents, but usually not as nurturant as authoritative parents.

The Neglecting–Uninvolved Style

Some parents are both low on responsiveness and low on demandingness, so that they actually invest little time or attention in a child and are largely parent centered in their concerns. Like permissive parents, **neglecting–uninvolved** parents seem to neglect their responsibility to socialize the child, but they also express less affection and are not likely to be responsive to their children's needs, perhaps even expressing hostility or making negative attributions to their children. When they do impose limits on their children, they tend to use power assertive techniques and little explanation.

Parenting Style and Child Outcomes

Through the long history of research on parenting, small but significant correlations have been found between parenting style, on one hand, and children's typical behaviors, on the other. Briefly, authoritative parenting has been associated with many positive outcomes in young children: adaptability, competence and achievement, good social skills and peer acceptance, and low levels of antisocial or aggressive behavior. Of particular interest to us in this chapter, authoritative parenting seems to promote positive self-development, especially high self-esteem and the capacity for self-regulation.

The children of authoritarian parents are more likely to be irritable and conflicted, showing signs of both anxiety and anger. They are conforming (self-controlled) with authority figures, but are not socially skillful and are susceptible to being bullied (e.g., Ladd & Ladd, 1998). They tend to have low self-esteem, and although they exhibit self-control with authorities, they may lack self-regulation when they believe that authorities are not monitoring them.

Permissive parents are more likely to have children who exhibit uncontrolled, impulsive behavior and low levels of self-reliance. They are low on cognitive competence and social agency, and high on aggression, especially in family interactions. In some studies they have had high self-esteem, apparently when parents exhibit high levels of warmth, but many studies suggest that warmth combined with demandingness is more certain to be associated with self-esteem (see Maccoby & Martin, 1983).

Finally, the children of neglecting/uninvolved parents are likely to be impulsive, to show high levels of both **externalizing problems** (e.g., aggressiveness) and **internalizing problems** (e.g., depression), and to have low self-esteem.

Be cautious in interpreting these relationships between parenting style and child outcomes. The strength of the associations is modest, cueing us that many factors interact with parenting and modify its effects. Researchers have begun to identify a multiplicity of interacting factors, which we will discuss in a later section of this chapter. (See Collins, Maccoby, Steinberg, Hetherington, and Bornstein, 2000, for further discussion.)

Parenting Practices: Methods of Control

Thus far, we have looked at parenting style—parents' combined responsiveness and demandingness—as a source of children's behavior and self-development. Another aspect of parenting concerns the **method of control** parents choose when they attempt to exercise control. Researchers have identified three categories of control method: **power assertion, love withdrawal,** and **induction.** Power assertion can involve physical punishment or the threat of physical punishment, ranging from spanking on the buttocks to harsh beating with objects. Or, it can involve withdrawal of privileges, from mild forms (such as time-out procedures with toddlers, see Box 5.1), to severe denial (e.g., withholding meals). Power assertion is usually effective for the immediate control of behavior. Children often show self-control when they feel threatened. But there can be unwanted side effects. Harsh or severe power assertion has been linked to high levels of anger and anxiety in children, and children whose parents use harsh, punitive practices tend to be more aggressive than other children (e.g., Baumrind, 2001; Strassberg, Pettit, Gregory, & Bates, 1994; Straus & Gelles, 1990; Straus, Sugarman, & Giles-Sims, 1997; Straus & Yodanis, 1996). New research on the effects of "milder" forms of physical discipline (e.g., spanking) will be reviewed later in this chapter.

If a child is accustomed to power assertive control, what happens when the threat is removed (e.g., Mom or Dad is not present or unlikely to find out)? Does the

The parents in this family appear to use power assertion as their method of controlling a teen that they find rebellious and difficult. Would you expect that they used a similar discipline style when the girl was younger, and that they use the same style with their younger children?

Box 5.1: Effective Ways to Use Time-Out

In many Dennis the Menace cartoons, Dennis sits in a pint-sized chair, hugging his teddy bear, facing into a corner, banished for some infraction. Dennis's parents use time-out as a disciplinary procedure: During a short span of time, Dennis is required to discontinue his involvement in ongoing activities to quietly sit somewhere apart. The technique involves mild power assertion and is suitable for use with toddlers and preschoolers. There is no pain involved, but time-out gets the attention of young children. Requiring a child to sit in a corner is one approach, but you can choose any place that separates the child from the action, while keeping her in a safe place that is within calling distance. Do not choose a spot where the child might be overwhelmed by feelings of isolation. The purpose of time-out is to eliminate the rewards of misbehavior, not to frighten a child. Indeed, it will work even if the "place apart" is in the midst of things. For example, in one day care center, the time-out chair is in the middle of a busy classroom so that the teachers can keep an eye on the offender. For the children, just being confined to the chair is sufficiently aversive to be effective.

Hamilton (1993) offers a number of pointers for using time-out effectively. To start, it helps to choose just two or three target behaviors that need to be changed. Reserve time-out for behaviors that are important to control because of safety, such as climbing on the kitchen counter, or because they are antisocial and hurtful, such as hitting or biting. Explain to the child which behaviors will lead to time-out, why they are unacceptable, and what alternative behaviors would be acceptable. It works best if children know the rules in advance so that what will lead to time-out is clear. (Don't forget to provide some positive attention for those more acceptable behaviors.) Don't use time-out for behaviors that have not been previously identified as inappropriate, and when the time-out is over, follow up with a reminder of your reasons for restricting this behavior. Remember, mild power assertion combined with induction can be very effective. Although Dennis the Menace is allowed to have a teddy bear in time-out, it is more consistent to eliminate access to toys, television, and attention from others.

Don't expect everything to go smoothly right from the start. At first a child may refuse to stay in time-out, or she may repeat the offending behavior just to test your resolve. If the child won't stay in time-out, make it very brief—a minute or so—and hold the child in place, turning your face away to create the condition of no attention. Then make eye contact and praise the child for staying in time-out. Stick it out—it will pay off. Time-out needs only to be long enough to get the point across. The younger the child, the less time is appropriate. One rule of thumb is 1 or 2 minutes for each year of age, so that the maximum time-out for a 2-year-old would be 4 minutes. Longer times are likely to become so aversive that they could defeat the purpose of simply getting the child's attention and creating an opportunity for her to think over her behavior.

Time-out when well-implemented is an effective disciplinary strategy with young children.

Time-out, like most effective discipline, requires putting aside what you are doing to attend to the misbehavior when it happens. It can be inconvenient, but *immediacy* is important to help young children make the right connection between their behavior and its consequences. Similarly, *consistency* is essential. When a parent's responses are unreliable, it is difficult for a child to learn what the rules are. Just how consistent can a parent be? There are going to be times when you simply cannot follow up on a misbehavior. But most times you can, if you make it a priority and if you are careful to use time-out for just a few important behaviors. Suppose, for example, that you are teaching your 4-year-old, Jenny, not to hit her baby brother. In the middle of your grocery shopping, sure enough Jenny hauls off and whacks him. Immediately, tell Jenny what's wrong with this picture: "Jenny, you know that hitting is not okay. It hurts and it makes people cry, and we don't hit in our family, ever! You have to go to time-out for that." Pick up the baby, grab Jenny's hand, leave the cart, and head for the car. In the car, put Jenny in the back seat and sit in the front with the baby. Say clearly, "You are in time-out," and face forward for the designated time. At the end, explain the rule again, tell Jenny that time-out is over, and head back to the shopping cart. In other words, if at all possible, improvise. (No car? Stand silently on the sidewalk for the time-out period.) There are bound to be situations that make immediate and full follow-through impossible. You could have been in the middle of checking out your groceries, for example. But if your usual response is swift and sure, your efforts will pay off.

child engage in self-regulation? In other words, will she regulate her own behavior because she is committed to an internalized set of standards? There are conflicting data on this issue. On the whole, power assertion does not seem to be particularly effective in promoting self-regulation. Interestingly, milder forms of power assertion are more effective than harsher forms. But the picture is complex and cannot be fully understood without considering other factors, such as child temperament, culture, and overall parenting style. We will return to this issue later.

Love withdrawal—such as a parent's withdrawing attention or affection, expressing disappointment or disillusionment with a child, turning away from a child, cutting off verbal or emotional contact, or enforcing separations—is rarely used alone by parents, but when it is used, it seems to generate high anxiety and is more effective in eliciting immediate compliance than any other method. As with power assertion, there is little evidence that the compliance that love withdrawal generates is anything but short term (Maccoby & Martin, 1983). Use of love withdrawal is often characteristic of parents who exercise psychological control over their children (Bugental & Grusec, 2006).

Induction refers to parents' use of explanation: giving reasons for rules ("If everybody touched the paintings they would soon be very dirty from fingerprints") and appealing to children's desires to be grown-up ("Big girls don't take toys away from babies"). "Other-oriented" explanations seem to be especially powerful in promoting empathy ("When you hit people, it hurts them and makes them sad"). Using induction seems to be the most effective way to promote the internalization of rules, so that children regulate their own behavior by the standards they have learned regardless of whether authorities are present and whether immediate consequences are likely. For example, Laible and Thompson (2002) observed mothers with their 30-month-olds in contexts where conflicts were likely to arise. These were a clean-up task and a "frustration task" where children had only a too-difficult puzzle to play with while their mothers were busy and while other more interesting toys were off-limits. The more mothers used inductive control strategies, like justification ("We can't touch those toys because they might break"), and the less they used more punitive or aggravating control strategies, like threats, teasing, and harsh commands, the more likely their children were to exercise self-control in a resistance to temptation task 6 months later.

Many studies have found that the same parents may use one practice on some occasions and another in other situations, and sometimes parents use multiple practices in the same disciplinary episode (e.g., Hastings & Grusec, 1998; Kuczynski, 1984). But most parents favor using one type of practice more than the others, and when they do, their primary practice is somewhat predictive of certain child outcomes. But, much as we found with rearing practices in infancy, such as breast versus bottle feeding, particular practices may be less important than the overall quality of the parent–child relationship. For toddlers and older children, the meaning that the child attributes to parents' practices is likely to be important and appears to be tied to the emotional climate established by parenting style (Darling & Steinberg, 1993; Grusec & Goodnow, 1994). In particular, when parents are warm and responsive, their children are more likely to comply with parental demands (e.g., NICHD, 1998).

Parenting style, then, affects how effective a parenting practice will be with a child (Darling & Steinberg, 1993). As it happens, certain practices tend to be combined with certain parenting styles. Authoritative parents, for example, are often characterized by extensive use of induction, regardless of what other practices they might sometimes use. The children of authoritative parents are likely to show higher levels of competence, self-esteem, and self-regulation than children exposed to other parenting styles. But what might happen if parents who show most of the qualities of an authoritative style—especially high responsiveness and high demandingness—were to use primarily power assertion to enforce their demands? In the next section, we will consider how parenting style interacts with practice for different children and in different cultural contexts, focusing on what we are learning about how these factors interact in the early phases of self-development, during the toddler and early preschool years. We will revisit these issues in later chapters when we describe self-regulatory and moral development in older children and adolescents.

Moderators of Parenting and Parenting Effectiveness

Authoritative parents seem to get the best results from their children, but are their behaviors really having any influence? Both developmentalists (e.g., Scarr, 1993) and popular writers (e.g., Harris, 1998) have asked whether we are wrong to assume that correlations between parenting and child outcomes imply that parenting style and practice are actually causing children's behavior. Several other possibilities exist. First, the shared biological inheritance of parents and children might account for both the parental and the child characteristics measured in these studies (Scarr, 1993, 1997). For example, the same genetic endowment that makes parents affectionate and responsive might produce children who are cooperative and good-natured. Second, children's predispositions and temperaments may actually cause parents' behaviors rather than vice versa. For example, perhaps children who are "naturally" sunny and compliant usually elicit authoritative parenting, but hostile, negative children usually elicit more authoritarian or neglectful parenting behaviors.

Overall, although controversy persists on these issues, most researchers and clinicians take a multidimensional approach to the question of direction of effects in children's social development (e.g., Bell & Chapman, 1986; Collins et al., 2000). That means that multiple causes are thought to be interacting, mutually modifying one another. As in Bronfenbrenner's bioecological model, proximal processes—reciprocal interactions between the child and the people and things that surround the child—as well as distal processes, such as genes and culture, are all playing a role (e.g., Bronfenbrenner & Morris, 2006; Lerner, Rothbaum, Boulos, & Castellino, 2002). In this section, we will consider two important factors in the multidimensional mix: the child's temperament and the broader cultural environment.

The Child's Temperament, Parenting, and Child Outcomes

Recall that in infancy, both parents and infants contribute to the quality of the caregiving relationship. It is harder for mothers to be sensitive and responsive to a baby with a difficult temperament, for example. But when mothers are highly responsive during infancy, the good fit they create between their caregiving and the baby's needs supports the development of a secure attachment even for babies with difficult temperaments. When mothers are not able to create a good fit, the type of insecure attachment that emerges often seems to be at least partly influenced by the baby's temperament (e.g., Kochanska, 1998).

With toddlers and preschoolers, temperament and other child characteristics continue to contribute to the quality of the parent–child relationship. Children's typical behaviors can affect both parenting style and the particular disciplinary practices that parents are most likely to use.

Bell and Chapman (1986) reviewed 14 studies that demonstrated the influence of children on parents. Many of these studies were at least partly experimental, with adults (usually parents) reacting to, or interacting with, children who were not their own, in situations created by the researchers. The studies examined adults' responses to children's dependence versus independence behaviors, their tendencies to be aggressive or to withdraw, and their responsiveness to adults (e.g., tendencies to smile, chat, imitate, and so on). For example, in one of these studies, Marcus (1975, 1976) showed parents videotapes of a child actor solving a puzzle. The child in the film behaved either dependently (e.g., seeking help, like, "Would this piece go better here or here?") or independently. The adults' reactions were more directive with the dependent than with the independent child. Stevens-Long (1973) examined parents' reactions to unrelated children's aggressive, uncooperative behavior or to anxious, withdrawn behavior. The adults were more likely to command or ignore the more aggressive children, but to verbally help or reward the more depressive children. Bell and Harper (1977) found that adults used more power assertive behaviors with socially unresponsive girls and more inductive behaviors with girls who were highly responsive. All of these studies demonstrate that adults' reactions are moderated by the characteristics or behaviors of the particular child with whom they are interacting.

Studies such as these, along with research on parents with their own children, began to paint a picture of a multilayered, complex interactive system between parent and child. The child's characteristics are likely to affect the parent's behavior, and the parent's style and practices affect the child's behavior. But other factors modify parents' and childrens' effects on each other. The degree to which the child affects the parent's practices and beliefs depends in part on the parent's initial attitudes toward children and child rearing, as well as the parent's emotional state and ability to manage stress. For example, parents who have child-centered rather than adult-centered concerns are able to be more supportive and responsive to their youngsters. Parents' emotional states influence how child centered they are likely to be. Depressive mothers report fewer child-oriented positive emotions and concerns than nondepressive mothers (Dix, Gershoff, Maunier, & Miller, 2004). Similarly, as we saw in the last chapter, parents' own relationship histories and their working models of attachment are likely to influence how they respond to their children and how well they adapt to their children's characteristics.

Children's Differential Susceptibility to Parenting Strategies

One illustration of the interactive complexities we have been describing is that children show **differential susceptibility** to different rearing approaches, depending on their early temperament characteristics (e.g., Belsky, 2005). Several studies now demonstrate that difficult, negatively reactive infants and toddlers are often *more* affected by parenting style—both positive and negative parenting behaviors—than children with easy temperaments (e.g., Bradley & Corwyn, 2008; van Zeijl et al., 2007; see also Kochanska, Aksan, & Joy, 2007). Let's consider the tendency to display aggressive behavior. Children who have difficult temperaments are more likely than children with easy temperaments to show inappropriate levels of aggression with peers and/or adults (Zahn-Waxler, Iannotti, Cummings, & Denham, 1990). But how aggressive they become is more closely linked to parents' disciplinary and interactive style than it is for children with easy temperaments. For youngsters with difficult temperaments, insensitive, negative parent behaviors (e.g., frowning, criticizing, yelling, being physically intrusive) appear to increase proneness to aggression, whereas sensitive, positive discipline (e.g., being affectionate, praising, using distraction) decreases proneness to aggression. For youngsters with easy temperaments, even those who seem prone to aggression, parenting differences do not have as much effect as they do for children with difficult temperaments. That is, aggressive tendencies are not moderated substantially by parenting practices (Bradley & Corwyn, 2008; van Zeijl et al., 2007; see also Rubin, Hastings, Chen, Stewart, & McNichol, 1998).

The Cultural Context, Parenting, and Child Outcomes

Just as children's characteristics can affect parenting and outcomes, cultural factors, such as the race, ethnicity, and socioeconomic class of the family, can moderate parenting practices and may even alter their effects. The preceding sections have made a strong case for the benefits of authoritative parenting, but most of the supportive research findings have come from U.S. majority samples. Does parenting differ in other parts of the world, and are these styles effective for other populations? No doubt about it, culture affects parenting. At its core, culture dynamically shapes values, self-regulation and behavior, and cultures could not continue to exist without some means of transmitting their values and worldviews to younger members. Through socialization, cultures transmit methods of coping with and adapting to specific challenges, a process that fosters resilience in children and youth (Garcia Coll, 1990).

Studying the effects of culture on parenting is a task that is nothing less than daunting. Remember that what we call "culture" is essentially embedded within the environment at every level of the ecological system, from the immediate family to the larger society and its institutions. This is culture in the broadest sense of the term, and it's sometimes difficult to avoid essentializing groups and conflating culture with geography, SES, or race. Researchers often paint with a relatively broad brush in order to capture key qualities that make one culture different from another, because, in reality, there is wide individual variation within groups (Gibbons, 1998). For example, "Hispanic" or "Latino" culture, broadly construed, reflects Mexican, Puerto-Rican, South American, Dominican, Spanish, and other group influences. "European American" culture includes British, Irish, Italian, German, French, Polish and other influences. So it's important to remember that these labels are generalizations that attempt to capture common underlying dimensions. When you consider all the labels writers have used to distinguish cultures, such as individualistic-collectivist, developing-developed, East-West, rural-metropolitan, immigrant-acculturated, native-non-native, majority-minority, and so forth, you can see what they are up against.

Despite these difficulties, some underlying cultural structures and values that are particularly salient to parenting have been identified. These structures and values may help to explain observed differences in parenting practices, such as discipline, across cultures. Table 5.3 offers several examples of traditional cultural values, reviewed by Yasui and Dishion (2007), thought to influence parenting from five major ethnic

TABLE 5.3 Parenting Values and Effects Across Five Cultures

CULTURAL GROUPS	TRADITIONAL VALUE ORIENTATION	TRADITIONALLY IMPORTANT VALUES	POSSIBLE EFFECTS ON PARENTING
African American	*Communalism*	Individualism, Importance of kinship relationships, Unity, Creativity, Cooperation, Authenticity, Awareness of racial disparities and discrimination	Authoritarian (No-nonsense) parenting; Unilateral decisions made by one parent; Egalitarian family structure
European American	Independence	Autonomy, Individualism	Authoritative; Egalitarian family structure
Latino American	Collectivism	Interdependence, *Familism, Respeto, Personalismo, Machismo, Marianismo*	Authoritarian; Patriarchal family structure; High Parental warmth
Native American	Collectivism	Interdependence, Value of Nature, Harmony, Balance, Extended Family, Respect for elders, Cooperation, Sharing	Permissive; Patriarchal and Matriarchal Structures
Asian-American	Collectivism	Interdependence; *Filial piety, Guan & Chiao shun, Amae,* Conformity, Obedience, Avoiding loss of face, Humility/Modesty	Authoritarian; Structural and managerial parental involvement; Patriarchal family structure

SOURCE: Based on Yasui, M. & Dishion, T. J. (2007). The ethnic context of child and adolescent problem behavior: Implications for child and family interventions. *Clinical Child and Family Review, 10,* 137–179.

Key:
Communalism: Emphasis on social bonds and mutual interdependence as well as individuality that contributes to the good of the group.
    SOURCE: Boykin, A. W., Ellison, C. M., Albury, A., & Jagers, R. J. (1997). Communalism: Conceptualization and measurement of an Afrocultural social orientation. *Journal of Black Studies, 27,* 409–441.

Familism: A sense of loyalty, solidarity, and identification with family and community.
    SOURCE: Marin, G. (1993). Influence of acculturation on familialism and self-identification among Hispanics. In M. E. Bernal & G. P. Knight (Eds.), *Ethnic identity: Formation and transmission among Hispanics and other minorities* (pp. 181–196). Albany, NY: SUNY.

Respeto: Respect for experience of others and deference to authority.
    SOURCE: Altarriba, J. & Bauer, L. M. (1998). Counseling the Hispanic client: Cuban Americans, Mexican Americans, and Puerto Ricans. *Journal of Counseling and Development, 76,* 389–396.

Personalismo: Preference for warm, courteous, and personal interactions with others over more formal interactions.
    SOURCE: Ojeda, L., Flores, L.Y., Meza, R.R., & Morales, A. (2011). Culturally competent qualitative research with Latino immigrants. *Hispanic Journal of Behavioral Sciences, 33,* 184–203.

Machismo: Traditional gender value for males; emphasis on the masculine role of defending, protecting, and caring for family but sometimes interpreted as dominance and sexual bravado.
    SOURCE: Torres, J. B., Solberg, S. H., & Carlstrom, M.S. (2002). The myth of sameness among Latino men and their machismo. *American Journal of Orthopsychiatry, 72,* 163–181.

Marianismo: Traditional gender value for females: emphasis on the feminine role of self-sacrifice, virtue, and caring (using the Virgin Mary as a role model).
    SOURCE: Castillo, L. G. (2010). Construction and initial validation of the Marianismo Beliefs Scale. *Counselling Psychology Quarterly, 23,* 163–175.

Filial piety: Moral obligation to respect, honor, and care for parents; considered to be a key value in intergenerational relationships.
    SOURCE: Hwang, K.-K. (1999). Filial piety and loyalty: Two types of social identification in Confucianism. *Asian Journal of Social Psychology, 2,* 163–183.

Guan and Chiao Shun: Duty to train or govern children in a loving way for their benefit.
    SOURCE: Chao, R. K. (1994). Beyond parental control and authoritarian parenting style: Understanding: Chinese parenting through the cultural notion of training. *Child Development, 65,* 1111–1120.

Amae: Characterized within a relationship by the mutual indulgence of each member's needs for love and affection; parental indulgence of children's needs to promote harmony in the relationship.
    SOURCE: Rothbaum, F., Kakinuma, M., Nagaoka, R., & Azuma, H. (2007). Attachment and amae: Parent–child closeness in the United States and Japan. *Journal of Cross-Cultural Psychology, 38,* 465–486.

groups in the United States. Definitions for less commonly used words (in italics) are provided as well.

The need for parents to set limits is a critical part of the socialization process, and different patterns of discipline have been observed across different cultural groups. European American parents who tend to employ authoritative methods often use nondirective or inductive disciplinary practices—offering suggestions, making polite requests, distracting a child, giving explanations, and so on. These practices are related to beneficial child outcomes such as empathy and prosocial behavior in their children. But some cross-cultural researchers find other patterns of associations between parents' warmth and disciplinary practices. In one study (Harwood, Schoelmerich, Schulze, and Gonzalez, 1999), no difference between Puerto Rican American and European American mothers were found in maternal warmth as they interacted with their 12- to 15-month-olds. Both European American and Puerto Rican American mothers tended to be affectionate and committed to providing a supportive emotional climate for their toddlers. But the Puerto Rican mothers were more directive and more likely to issue commands than to give children choices or opportunities to express their desires. Consistent with other research on European Americans, the Anglo mothers were more likely to let their toddlers try to do things for themselves and were more likely to make suggestions than to issue commands. These differences in mothers' behavior were consistent with their long-term goals. Puerto Rican mothers appeared to be more concerned about "sociocentric" or relational outcomes, focusing more on wanting children to recognize their obligations and their connectedness to others. The Anglo mothers appeared to emphasize "individualization" or autonomy as a long-term socialization goal, valuing assertiveness and self-reliance. In traditional cultures emphasizing interdependence (see Table 5.3), parents typically use high levels of control with children and minimize choice, placing a greater value on obedience training. This may serve the goal of teaching children to subjugate their own needs to the collective good (see Chen & French, 2008; Rudy & Grusec, 2006).

Generally, higher rates of authoritarian parenting practices, including power assertion, are found among African-American, Asian-American, and Hispanic-American groups possibly due to different parenting goals. Earlier research speculated that the authoritarian style found in these families benefitted children because it prepared them for the experience of the world they might encounter even while it was disadvantageous for European-American groups. Let's look at the way this question has evolved in research.

Disciplinary practices that involve severe physical punishments (inflicting bodily injury by beating, kicking, punching, scalding, and so on) are consistently associated with problematic child outcomes, such as aggressive behavior, emotion dysregulation, attention problems, conduct disorders, and depression (see Cicchetti & Toth, 2006) and are not considered normative, regardless of culture. While there is little disagreement about the deleterious effects of maltreatment, the issue of corporal punishment (e.g., hitting, spanking, and paddling) in schools and homes has been more contentious. Corporal punishment has been defined by Straus (1994) as "the use of physical force with the intention of causing a child to experience pain, but not injury, for the purpose of correction or control of the child's behavior" (p. 4). As research on abuse and its effects has become more refined, a growing body of evidence has accumulated to reveal the potential harm in less extreme forms of punishment. In a large early study of mother–child pairs, Straus and his colleagues (1997) asked mothers how often they had spanked their child in the last week when the children were between ages 6 and 9. The researchers measured children's antisocial behavior then and over the course of the next 2 years. More frequent spanking at the first assessment predicted increases in the children's antisocial behavior over the next 2 years. This was true regardless of the family's social class, ethnicity, the child's gender, or maternal warmth. (See Gershoff, 2002, for a meta-analytic review of similar research.)

As we have stated, however, some studies of power assertive discipline have shown culture-specific differences. In European-American samples, there is a linear relationship between amount and harshness of physical discipline and children's aggressive behavior. The more severe the punishment, the more aggressive children are likely to be. For African-American children, this relationship was found in some earlier studies (e.g., Aucoin, Frick, & Bodin, 2006), but a number of researchers either reported no association between corporal punishment and aggressiveness in children (e.g., Baumrind, 1993; Deater-Deckard, Dodge, Bates, & Pettit, 1996), or they found based on parent report that corporal punishment is related to less aggressive outcomes (Lansford, Deater-Deckard, Dodge, Bates, & Pettit, 2004).

What might account for these findings? One possibility advanced is that normativeness reduces negative impact. In other words, if children expect to be disciplined in a certain way (spanking, etc.), then they may perceive spanking as normal, and possibly even as a manifestation of parental care. A recent study (Gershoff et al., 2010) found some evidence that children's' perception of the normativeness of punishment moderated outcomes in a sample of families from China, India, Italy, Kenya, Philippines, and Thailand. Remember that a moderating influence would affect how strongly certain types of disciplinary techniques were associated with adverse outcomes. Normativeness diminished the deleterious outcomes of yelling and corporal punishment, but only by a bit. These particular forms of discipline were *always* related to greater levels of aggression in all cultural groups, despite this moderation.

Another explanation may be that the long-term effects of punishment are moderated by the warmth, affection and responsiveness of the parent who is doling out the discipline. Several large studies of American children support this idea (e.g., Aucoin et al., 2006; McLoyd & Smith, 2002). McLoyd and Smith looked at outcomes across a 6-year period in nearly 2,000 American children. Once again, for all children, African American, European American, and Hispanic, amount of spanking in the home predicted the level of children's externalizing behavior over time. But mothers' emotional support of their children moderated this link in all three groups.

You may be wondering what "spanking" means in some of these studies. Most often, data is collected on the frequency of spanking incidents, but not on how it's done. In response to Baumrind's (2002) argument that "ordinary" spanking (done with an open hand less than once a week) would not be associated with problems related to more severe discipline (e.g., frequent spanking, spanking with objects), 585 families were followed over several years to explore the effects of different forms of spanking (Lansford, Wager, Bates, Pettit, & Dodge, 2012). Some support for Baumrind's argument came from maternal self-reports indicating no differences in externalizing behavior between not-spanked and mildly (with a hand less than once per week) spanked children compared to the harshly spanked group. However, over 50% of mothers initially reporting mild spanking admitted using objects to spank later on. Findings indicated that mild spanking, compared to no-spanking, increased the probability that discipline would escalate into harsher forms in the following year by 50%. In other words, the majority of mothers who spanked continued to do so, and the majority of these mothers used objects to spank their children.

Recently, a large nationally representative sample of over 11,000 children from White/Non-Hispanic (64%), Hispanic (19%), Black/Non-Hispanic (12%), and Asian (5%) families were studied at kindergarten and again at third grade (Gershoff, 2008; Gershoff, Lansford, Sexton, Davis-Kean, & Sameroff, 2012). Two independent sources of data were provided by parents and teachers, an improvement over studies that relied solely on parents as informants. Teachers reported on children's externalizing behaviors (arguing, fighting, getting angry) and mothers responded to questions such as: *About how many times, if any, have you spanked your child over the past week*. Number of times was coded using a 0 (no spanking) or 1 (ever spanked) to 6 (five spanking incidents or more during the prior week). The research focused on spanking and excluded harsher disciplinary methods known to correlate with adverse outcomes. Overall, spanking was shown to be a popular method of discipline. At the kindergarten interview, 27% of all mothers reported spanking their children in the previous week, and 80% reported that they had used spanking at some time.

Highest rates of spanking during the previous week were reported by Black mothers at kindergarten (40%) and 3rd grade (23%) interviews. At kindergarten, spanking during the previous week was reported by 28% of Hispanic, 24% of White and 23% of Asian mothers. At third grade, spanking was reported by 23% of Black, 21% of Asian, 14% of White, and 13% of Hispanic mothers. After controlling for initial group differences in frequency, spanking was found to predict the same increases in children's externalizing behaviors for White, Black, Hispanic, and Asian American groups. In findings similar to those in the previously described study (Lansford et al., 2012), these results demonstrated a downward spiral. More spanking strengthened a pattern of coercive interaction processes in the families (see Chapter 7 for information on coercive family processes).

Associations between corporal punishment and later mental disorders were recently reported in the largest representative study to date (Afifi, Mota, Dasiewicz, MacMillan, & Sareen, 2012). Close to 35,000 U.S. adult males and females from the National Epidemiologic Survey on Alcohol and Related Conditions were interviewed by trained investigators. For purposes of analysis, a distinction was made between maltreatment and "harsh physical punishment." Maltreated individuals, defined as those who reported physical abuse (burning, injury), extreme neglect (going without clothes or food), sexual abuse or witnessing violence, were excluded from this study. Harsh physical punishment, which was the variable of interest, was defined as *either* being pushed, shoved, slapped, or hit by a parent or someone living in the home *at least once* during childhood. Findings indicated that the incidence of a lifetime mental disorder (all mood disorders, all anxiety disorders, drug abuse or dependence disorders, and several personality disorders) was significantly associated with harsh physical punishment as defined above, even after controlling for initial level of family dysfunction and other demographic variables. Interestingly, the odds of harsh physical punishment increased as families' income and educational levels increased. Although the size of the relationship was relatively modest, the implications are great when viewed from a public health perspective. The authors concluded that the rates of mental disorders could be reduced 2 to 7 percent by eliminating harsh physical punishment.

Social interactive experiences contribute to children's developing self-systems.

CONSCIENCE: THE BEGINNINGS OF A MORAL SELF

You can see that research on parenting supports the many theories of self-development that emphasize the importance of social interactive experiences in the development of the self-system. Parenting style especially has been found to correlate with children's self-esteem—how worthy and competent children feel—and it appears to be linked to self-confidence in social interaction. Children whose parents are child centered, responsive, and warm tend to show high levels of self-esteem, and they are likely to be skillful in social interaction, as evidenced by peer acceptance and teacher ratings of social competence. These findings suggest that Erikson (1950/1963) may have been on the right track when he argued that after initial feelings of worth are laid down in late infancy, these feelings will be reworked by the child as she changes. For example, as toddlers become more capable of self-sufficiency, they acquire needs, such as autonomy and control needs, that sensitive, responsive caregivers accommodate. If a toddler's needs are met in a positive, affirming way, the child

Box 5.2: Popular Views of Parenting: What Should We Believe?

Child-rearing "experts" abound in today's society, each touting his or her own set of certainties about how to raise good or happy or successful kids. Popular beliefs about effective parenting have varied from one historical era to another, and, like today, even within each era there has been wide divergence among the kinds of advice that parents could confront. Consider these two wildly different suggestions. The first is from an *Infant Care* bulletin published by the U.S. Department of Labor in 1914, a tract heavily influenced by animal studies of associationism. It seems insensitive to the emotional needs of both the child and the parent, emphasizing routine over all else:

> A properly trained baby is not allowed to learn bad habits. It is a regrettable fact that the few minutes of play that the father has when he gets home at night, which is often almost the only time he has with the child, may result in nervous disturbance of the baby and upset his regular habits . . . much of the play that is indulged in is more or less harmful. (As quoted in Lomax, Kagan, & Rosenkrantz, 1978, p. 130)

In contrast, the second example, from a *Parents Magazine* article in 1950, is based on a misinterpretation of Freudian ideas and seems remarkably overindulgent of children's emotional excesses, with no regard for control. As described in Lomax et al.:

> mothers were told that they must learn to face and accept all types of emotional outbursts on the part of their children, so that the children would not become fearful of their own feelings. . . . "we should feel suspicious of ourselves when we react strongly to something as absurdly simple, for example, as a child calling us names." (p. 66)

Ironically, as Lomax et al. note, Freud actually expected that parents *would* set limits on their children's antisocial behaviors.

Today, some self-styled "experts" advocate a "return" to authoritarian parenting from earliest childhood, reacting to what they perceive as overly permissive trends (Bolotin, 1999). These "traditionalists" encourage parents not to be child centered. John Rosemond, for example, exhorts parents to make their marriage the focus of attention. Children, he argues, acquire self-esteem from successfully facing hardship and frustration. Give them a lot of responsibility for household chores, and punish all disobedience with unpleasant, memorable consequences. He has expressed disdain for parents who place a high priority on having a "warm and fuzzy" relationship with their children (Rosemond, 1991). Gary and Anne Marie Ezzo, a former pastor and his wife, advocate "biblical principles" for families, among which they include: expecting immediate obedience to first-time directions or commands; feeding babies on a schedule and expecting them to sleep through the night when they are 8 weeks old; potty training by 18 to 24 months, with children accountable for their own cleanup of toilet "accidents" by 30 months; and the use of corporal punishment, starting with hand swatting or squeezing in infancy and moving to spanking with something that creates "a sting" by 18 months (Ezzo & Buckman, 1995, 1999). What is especially notable in the advice of these and other "traditionalists" is their lack of concern for what researchers describe as the "warmth factor": parental responsiveness to children's needs, high levels of expressed affection, and willingness to listen and explain. Their emphasis is clearly on the "control factor" alone: take care of the child's need for discipline and all else will follow. They also ignore data indicating that mild power assertion is often more effective than severe forms and that the children of parents who use physical punishment tend to be physically aggressive themselves.

What is a parent to do, and how can a helper help guide inexperienced or dissatisfied parents as they struggle to sort through the confusing array of advice? The most valuable guidance a counselor can offer is advice informed by research. From research reviewed in this and other chapters on social development, it is clear that parents have an abiding influence on their children's development, although outcomes are the product of many interacting factors, including temperament differences among children and family and cultural context. It is also clear that *both* parental warmth *and* control are important. Awareness of such information can help parents evaluate the suggestions they encounter. For example, is it true, as Rosemond argues, that self-esteem is a product of accomplishments that include overcoming hardship? It sounds sensible, but the data indicate that the picture is much more complex. Parents' responsiveness and sensitivity to children's individual and developmental needs are core elements of successful parenting. Making children do things that are too difficult for them is insensitive—in such a case, hardship seems unlikely to lead to anything but frustration and a sense of defeat or abandonment for the child. Rigid age formulas are therefore a risky business. For example, many 2-year-olds may be ready to potty train quickly, but some are not. Many 8-week-olds probably cannot sleep through the night, because they get too hungry or because their neurological systems are too immature to maintain such a routine.

But when parental demands are embedded in a context of warmth, so that they are appropriately keyed to the child's emerging skills, and when children feel safe expressing their own feelings and concerns, high levels of demandingness do indeed seem to be associated with feelings of competence and self-confidence. Authoritative, not authoritarian, parenting has the best track record.

will go beyond having global feelings of worth and will acquire more differentiated feelings of competency.

Parenting appears to contribute to other aspects of the developing self-system as well. In particular, parenting style and practice are related to children's self-regulation, including the child's ability to "generate socially approved behavior in the absence of external monitors" (Kopp, 1982, p. 200). This last ability is assumed to be a function of **internalization**, the process by which children adopt adults' standards and rules as their own. Internalization, in turn, is associated with the development of **conscience**, feelings of discomfort or distress when the violation of a rule is contemplated or carried out. Internalization and conscience formation are both aspects of the broader topic of moral development and will be discussed again in later chapters as we look at the course of moral development in older children, adolescents, and adults.

At this point, let's take a closer look at the complex connections among early parenting, the beginnings of self-regulation, and the associated processes of internalization and conscience formation. We have already noted that children can begin to learn self-control when they can understand and remember adults' behavioral commands—when statements such as "No cookies before dinner" have meaning for them—certainly during their 2nd year. At about age 2, children often begin to show signs of emotional distress if a standard is violated (see Kochanska, Gross, Lin & Nichols, 2002; Thompson, Meyer, & McGinley, 2006) and soon after they can show strong reactions if they are tempted to break a prohibition (Emde & Buchsbaum, 1990). At the same time, toddlers begin to offer comfort to others in distress (e.g., Zahn-Waxler & Radke-Yarrow, 1982).

Two aspects of parenting seem to promote these processes. First, parents' warmth and responsiveness facilitate compliance (self-control) and promote the development of concern for others (Maccoby & Martin, 1983). Sensitive, responsive parents seem to establish a cooperative, mutually responsive relationship with their toddlers—an ongoing secure attachment—and toddlers tend to be eager to maintain such relationships (e.g., Aksan, Kochanska, & Ortman, 2006). Second, children's anxiety or emotional arousal seems to play a role in their willingness to comply and in the internalization of standards (e.g., Kochanska et al., 2007). Hoffman (1983) proposed that a parent's discipline causes a child to feel **anxious arousal**. He proposed that mild arousal helps the child pay attention but is not really upsetting. When a child is aroused enough to take notice, but not to be especially fearful, she is likely to notice, to try to understand, and to remember the parent's "socialization message." She may attribute her own compliance with the rule to her acceptance of it, which is a step toward internalization of the rule. But if the child experiences intense arousal during a disciplinary episode, she may pay more attention to concerns other than the socialization message. She might notice, and later remember, how scared she is, for example, of her parent's loud and angry voice, and then attribute her compliance to these factors rather than to the standard or rule that could have been learned. Hoffman's ideas help explain why mild power assertion is more effective for long-term internalization of rules than harsh power assertion—the **minimum sufficiency principle**. His views are also consistent with findings that induction—parents' use of explanation and reasoning—is helpful for internalization. Children are more likely to remember and accept rules they can understand.

If anxious arousal is an important ingredient in how children respond to their parents' discipline, individual differences among children in how easily their anxiety is aroused should also be important. In other words, temperament differences among toddlers should influence the early development of conscience. For fearful children, gentle discipline that deemphasizes power and emphasizes requests and reasoning should be sufficiently arousing to produce optimal effects. But what about children who are not easily aroused—who seem almost fearless? Do they need harsh discipline to be sufficiently aroused to pay attention? To find out, Kochanska (1995) studied 2-year-olds' **committed compliance**, that is, their eager and enthusiastic willingness to go along with their mothers' requests. Committed compliance in 2-year-olds is predictive of measures of internalization and conscience in the later preschool period (Kochanska, Aksan, and Koenig, 1995). Kochanska found that toddlers' fearfulness is indeed an important ingredient in the effectiveness of mothers' discipline. Highly fearful children, as expected, showed the most committed compliance if their mothers used gentle discipline. Harsh discipline was not as effective. However, neither gentle nor harsh discipline was more effective in promoting compliance for the most fearless toddlers! For them, only the security of their attachment to their mothers made a difference. Securely attached, fearless toddlers tended to show committed compliance, but insecurely attached, fearless toddlers were much less likely to do so. And, as expected, committed compliance at age 2 was predictive of moral development at 4½ years (Kochanska et al., 2007). We see again that children's temperaments make them *differentially susceptible* to parenting behaviors, helping to explain why correlations between parenting behaviors and child outcomes tend to be moderate. Parenting clearly is important, but it works somewhat differently with different children.

To clarify Kochanska's findings, imagine a 2-year-old, Joel, who tends to be more fearful than the other children in his play group. For example, he holds back and ducks his head when a supervising adult offers him a turn to ride the new "race car" at the neighborhood playground, even though many of the other children are clamoring for a turn. When Joel's mother encourages him gently to participate in a cleanup session, explaining how much help it would be, he is quite cooperative. She tells an observer that she never "yells" at him because he gets so upset that it is counterproductive. José's mother, on the other hand, says that her son seems unfazed by yelling. José does not seem to be afraid of anything. He can't wait for his turn to ride the new race car, and the fact that the supervising adult is a stranger is of no concern to him. Fortunately, José and his mother seem to share a warm relationship, and José, too, cooperates enthusiastically when his mother asks him to help with the cleanup. Andrew, another toddler in the play group, seems a lot like José in his fearlessness. He is panting to ride the race car and to try all the toys on the playground, and he marches right up to the supervising adult, asking for help. But there seems to be very little warmth between him and his mother, and when she asks him to help out with cleanup, he ignores her. Even when she gives him a shove and speaks sharply to him, he only halfheartedly moves to pick up a toy and abandons the cleanup effort almost immediately.

In sum, parenting influences the development of the self-system in early childhood. Which aspects of parenting will be influential depends in part on the particular child. For the development of self-regulation, the quality of attachment, grounded in warm, responsive caregiving, may be all-important for some children. For others, particular parenting practices (methods of control) also play an important role.

APPLICATIONS

Because the stages of infancy and early childhood have long been viewed as important ones for later socioemotional development, it is worthwhile to attempt to link theories of early attachment, self-development, and parenting into a framework that provides a working knowledge for counselors. Crittendon's (1994, 1997) insightful theoretical formulation is a good starting point because it knits together these three topics and attempts to explain the effects of sensitive and insensitive parenting on children as they get older.

Building a Self Through the Attachment Relationship

In Crittendon's view, attachment classifications are linked to operant conditioning processes. Securely attached infants and toddlers receive predictable, soothing care when their physiological needs, fear, aggression, excitement, or anxiety threaten to overwhelm their capacity for homeostatic regulation. These children learn that expressions of their positive as well as their negative feelings (anxiety, distress, and anger) are acceptable because they will be tolerated by a caregiver who accepts and helps them. In other words, they are positively reinforced for expressing both positive and negative feelings. Let's consider an example that might apply to adult students. Imagine a time when you were close to despair because of all the work you had to do. You had a number of responsibilities to complete at your job, you had family obligations to attend to, and your professors were being unreasonably demanding about their assignments! On top of everything, you felt tired and on the verge of getting your annual cold. Your level of crankiness increased significantly, suggesting that you were starting to lose some emotional control. Now imagine that some loving person in your life approached you, and instead of telling you to "grow up," was able to see through the irritability to the anxieties underneath. This person offered to help shoulder some of your burdens. Emotionally you experienced what amounts to a sigh of relief. You were able to function much better with the support, and your sense of yourself as a valuable and loved person increased greatly. In this supportive context, you would probably be even more receptive to constructive suggestions about how you might schedule your time to improve your situation.

Although this example is not a strict analogy to early experience, young children have special needs for caregiver support to help them regulate their emotions and internalize positively valenced self-understanding. Crittendon believes that secure reciprocity with a caregiver allows the child to be open to both cognitive and affective experiences, gradually building procedural models of the self as competent to communicate with the caretaker, able to manage affect with the caretaker's reliable help, and able to accept and express both positive and negative parts of the self. Essentially, the positive message the secure child encodes is that she is a valuable and loved person even when she's not being particularly grown up. Crittendon believes that these repeated dyadic patterns of attachment are encoded as procedural memories that serve as precursors to the mature self.

The Emotionally Constricted Self

In contrast, insecure-avoidant infants who learn that displays of distress elicit rejection, punishment, or withdrawal become conditioned to inhibition of affect. These infants are, in fact, punished for their emotional displays, so these children come to actively avoid or block out perceptions that arouse their feelings because of the aversive consequences. Crittendon and DiLalla (1988) have reported that even very young children who have been severely abused actively block out information about their own feelings and demonstrate false affect—that is, affect that is superficially positive and incongruent with true feelings. Consistent with the general assumption of attachment theory, this pattern of avoidance is adaptive for an early nonresponsive caregiving environment but may have significantly negative consequences for later functioning. A highly defended or "false self" (Kernberg, 1976; Miller, 1981; Winnicott, 1965) may result from the inhibition of affect because the child distorts or mistrusts the evidence of her feelings. This situation effectively reduces the information that the young child can access in constructing the self. The message the child encodes is that feeling anger or distress is unacceptable and should be avoided because the expression of these feelings distances the caregiver, emotionally if not physically. The child views the self as able to communicate with caregivers only if her own emotional needs are kept in check. Positive aspects of the self may be expressed, but negative aspects, such as emotional neediness, need to be repressed.

Avoidant children who have learned that emotional expression can be dangerous take on the responsibility of their own emotion regulation without seeking caregiver help. They function defensively to keep the caregiver "close but not too close" (Crittendon, 1994, p. 95). To cope with this style of parenting, they learn a style of relating that involves repressing

emotions that might anger or distance their more authoritarian caregivers. Negative affect (feelings of distress, sadness, anger) is not well integrated into the self-system, and a false self develops that is biased in favor of its "good" parts and against its more shameful ones. These avoidant or defended children may appear self-reliant to their parents, who may not be very responsive to their children's feelings anyway. In extreme circumstances, these children may demonstrate what Bowlby called **compulsive caregiving**. This is the pattern of taking emotional care of a caregiver. A pattern of **compulsive self-sufficiency** represents an opposite yet equally unhealthy result. These children are at risk because they appear so self-possessed. A closer look reveals their self-evaluations to be based on others' negative appraisals, including shaming for their expressions of dependency or needs for closeness. Parents of these children can be helped to develop the nurturant side of authoritative parenting by using some of the attachment-related approaches described in earlier chapters.

The Emotionally Volatile Self

Insecure-anxious infants learn that their displays of distress elicit unpredictable results, sometimes positive and sometimes negative. They essentially lack a method of communicating with the caregiver that works reliably, possibly because of inconsistent or sometimes neglectful parenting. Consequently, they experience the "anxiety of unresolvable arousal in which desire for the attachment figure, distress at her absence, and aggression toward her are all felt concurrently" (Crittendon, 1994, p. 93). Their model of themselves becomes one of incompetence with respect to communicating with a caregiver. Ultimately these children learn they can trust neither their affect nor their cognitions. However, they may learn that escalation of affect often works best in getting their caregivers' attention. These children might develop highly coercive strategies (aggressiveness or tantrums) and very coy behaviors (disarming manipulation) to maintain proximity. The self incorporates messages that reflect its ineffectiveness in communicating its needs to caregivers. Their aggressive behavior threatens the caregiver ("You must

Children's sense of themselves as valuable and worthy of care is strongly shaped by the responsiveness of adults throughout the early years of development.

listen to me!"), whereas their coy behavior disarms ("Please don't get angry at me"). This pattern has been hypothesized to represent the child's attempts to cope with an unpredictable and inconsistent parental environment. Parents of these children might describe them as "out of control."

Not all noncompliant child behavior problems are due to early insecure attachments, however. Children may discover, as they become more independent and more verbal, that coercion works well in getting them what they want. Patterson (1982; see also Reid, Patterson, & Snyder, 2002), who studied the development of defiance in children, maintains that an intermittent (or inconsistent) schedule of reinforcement sustains the coercive child's behavior problems. A pattern of **negative reinforcement**, when the cessation of a stimulus increases the frequency of some behavioral response, follows the child's display of intense negativity or misbehavior. For example, a parent might tell her 4-year-old to go upstairs because it is time to go to bed. The little boy, detesting this interruption of his play time, begins to whine. The parent repeats her command several more times only to be met by continued resistance. The parent's patience begins to thin and she escalates into threats, which, according to Patterson's research, are usually not carried out. Instead, the parent appeases the child out of guilt or exasperation. The parent gives up and the child's noncompliance is reinforced. This pattern strengthens the child's coercive interaction style, which with time and repetition can become the predominant mode of communication. Ironically, Patterson believes that coercive children do not really want parents to give in. Instead, they crave the predictability that derives from knowing what their limits are and the security of knowing that parents will enforce them. Coercive children, however, need help developing a communication style that expresses their needs more directly so that caregivers will understand and respond appropriately. If left unchecked, child noncompliance can be a significant risk factor for later maladaptive outcomes, such as peer rejection and aggression. In such situations, some parent training is generally a very good idea.

Why Train Parents?

Parent training (PT; Patterson, Chamberlain, & Reid, 1982), or parent management training (PMT; Brestan & Eyberg, 1998), has the distinction of being one of a relative handful of therapies deemed efficacious for children (Kazdin, 2003). Studies have shown that PT is more effective in reducing noncompliance and promoting prosocial behavior, especially for children ages 4 through 8, than alternatives such as family therapy, relationship therapy, or play therapy (Feldman & Kazdin, 1995). The term *efficacious* is applied to therapies that have demonstrated empirical support. This is very good news, given the protective power of authoritative parenting to reduce risks for many concurrent or later disorders and its ability to greatly improve positive outcomes for children (Steinberg & Avenevoli, 2000). Authoritative parenting enhances security of attachment and provides children with a positive context in which to learn socialization skills. Difficulties with child behavior and

discipline are frequently reported referral problems for helpers. Even if these problems are a rather more intense version of normal developmental strains and even if they never materialize into more significant problems, the burdens on families who are trying to cope with them can be great. Parent training can substantially strengthen the limit-setting side of authoritativeness, improve the quality of life in the home, and reduce stress for parents who must grapple with children's noncompliance.

In some cases, an added parent management component can make a good therapeutic program even better. For example, in the case of treatments for **ADHD (attention deficit hyperactivity disorder)**, a multimodal treatment that included medication and behavioral (including parent management) treatment demonstrated an advantage over medication alone for children with comorbid conditions (anxiety or conduct problems), for children with more highly educated mothers, for members of minority groups, and for families who learned to improve their discipline techniques via this training (as cited in Arnold et al., 2004). The principles involved in parent management training have also been effectively adapted to classroom management for teachers.

Parent training is successful, no doubt, because it has a strong theoretical rationale. It draws on a set of well-established principles from operant conditioning and social learning theory that can be used in individual counseling, group counseling, psychoeducation, and consultation. The empirically supported benefits that accrue to PT, however, have been documented in outcome studies that involve sustained work with a parent or couple over the course of several sessions. Moore and Patterson (2003) note that a typical course of treatment takes an average of 20 hours of professional time. Whereas benefits of well-delivered programs can be great, they are most effective for families with young children. Given the developmental needs of older children and adolescents, training for their parents should take into consideration adolescents' need for some measure of personal control and autonomy by incorporating skills in decision making and negotiation into the counseling.

How Does Parent Training Work?

Effective parent training programs incorporate a few essential elements (Kazdin, 1991; Moore & Patterson, 2003).

1. These programs are directed toward parents or guardians; children are not directly involved in treatment. An exception to this is treatment with adolescents, which typically does require the adolescent's participation.
2. Parents are taught to observe and define their children's noncompliance in behavioral terms. They are instructed to note their own part in interaction cycles that reward and sustain noncompliance. The most problematic behaviors and their prosocial opposites are identified.
3. Basic principles of learning theory, such as reinforcement, shaping, mild punishment, generalization, and so

on, are taught to parents, used to illustrate the nature of parent–child interactions, and applied in contingent ways to achieve the goals of treatment. These principles provide the basis for therapeutic change.

4. Parents (with professional's help) put these ideas to the test at home. Target behaviors that parents wish to modify are identified, skills are practiced in sessions using role-play, modeling, therapist feedback, and discussion. These techniques are then employed in the home, and the results of the new behavior management strategies are recorded, reviewed, and further developed during subsequent sessions.

 In parent training, parents are encouraged to set limits using basic principles of learning theory, such as reinforcing desired behaviors with allowance money. This counselor encourages the parent to put the ideas to a real test, over several months and perhaps with some modification.

Parent management approaches depend upon the careful application of behavioral principles. Therefore, the therapist who uses this modality needs to understand behavioral terms correctly, must be precise about selecting and defining target behaviors, and must be able to identify contingencies that increase or decrease behavior. One method involves asking parents to identify two to four of the child's behaviors that are most problematic. This is often supplemented by the use of more formal observational assessment tools. Moore and Patterson (2003) report that a typical initial concern can be defined as "minding" versus "not minding." Once the parents are helped to notice the context wherein the "not-minding" occurs, principles like positive reinforcement (using tangible objects or the very powerful attention of parents), mild punishments (like time-out or restriction of privileges), and shaping (rewarding closer and closer approximations of "minding" with social praise) can be incorporated into some **contingency management system**. Contingency management involves presenting and withdrawing reinforcers and punishments in a systematic and consistent way to effect behavioral change. The linchpin of these approaches is the mindful use of positive reinforcement, a particularly potent response from parents when it comes in the form of warm encouragement, acceptance, and attention. A correct understanding of concepts like negative reinforcement, which is central to understanding the coercion cycle (Patterson, 1982) and which is distinct from the concept of punishment, is particularly important as well. Daily documentation of progress can be a useful part of the program, helping parents become more consistent in their use of techniques.

Recently, new interventions that address the emotional regulation and balance of the parent have been explored as a means of promoting parenting quality. We know that the presence, warmth, and listening skills of the parent are particularly important influences on the health of their relationships with their children. Parents who are stressed, distracted, or emotionally unavailable, especially when this is a chronic pattern, tend to undermine the quality of relationships and foster children's

dysregulation. Recent work in mindful parenting interventions have shown promise to improve parenting quality because of the nature of the attention they cultivate. Mindfulness practice can have an impact on relationships because it supports loving attention and helps reduce parental stress. In improving parents' own emotion regulation, all too common in distressed parent–child relationships, child behaviors can improve (Bogels, Lehtonen, & Restifo, 2010; Duncan, Coatsworth, & Greenberg, 2009). We will have more to say about mindfulness in Chapter 14.

Forewarned Is Forearmed

Higher rates of noncompliance appear to occur at certain times throughout the day (7:30 a.m., 11:30 a.m., 5:30 p.m., and 8:30 p.m.; Goodenough, 1931, as cited in Moore and Patterson, 2003). Consider this scene in the Arnold family. Mom, whose shift at work ends at 5:00 p.m., has just returned from the babysitter's house with her 6-year-old twins. Both children are hungry and tired from a long day at school. Yvonne needs help with a homework project. Kenney has a Cub Scout meeting at 6:30 and needs to find some items for the pack's activity. As their mother struggles to put together a meal, the children become more intense in their demands for her attention. Pretty soon, they are fighting with each other. She yells at them to stop, but this only makes matters worse. Yvonne ends up in tears and Kenney runs to his room. No one feels like eating dinner.

What makes scenes like this one so recognizable to so many people? The rates of noncompliance rise when several factors intersect: changes in biological states, a spike in demands for compliance, and simultaneous transitions that are occurring for all members of the system (parents and children). Because these are predictable, the use of contingency management skills, especially positive encouragement, and establishment of consistent routines can help parents navigate these flash points more successfully.

What About Spanking?

Current research is blurring what was once considered a bright line between corporal punishment and abuse, painting a picture of a slippery slope between mild corporal punishment and harsher forms of discipline (Gershoff, 2008). This may be the reality, unfortunately, because most of the corporal punishment meted out by adults is not done in a particularly calm, loving, or reflective way. The use and severity of corporal punishment tend to escalate over time, and most episodes of physical abuse occur in the context of child discipline (Durrant & Ensom, 2012). Although parents spank because they believe it is an effective way to control their children's aggressive and noncompliant behavior, the results from research clearly show the opposite to be true. While power assertion can be effective for short-term control of children's behavior, it is related to more externalizing and a higher incidence of mental disorders in the long run for all cultures studied. It also appears to have little influence on the goals that parents want most to achieve with discipline—the development of self-regulation and morality. Parents who physically punish their children "may be conveying the message that the use of force is a justifiable way in which to solve conflicts" (Bugental & Grusec, 2006, p. 402). The finding by Lansford et al. (2005) that in countries where corporal punishment is expected and accepted, children tend to score high on measures of aggression (even when they themselves have not experienced corporal punishment), suggests that typical strategies for child rearing may be read by children as indicators of acceptable behavior in other contexts.

The growing consensus from research in this area has attracted a high level of international attention. In 1989, the United Nations recognized children's right to protection from physical and psychological violence, including spanking, through the UN Convention on the Rights of the Child (United Nations, 1989). This multinational treaty has been signed and ratified by 192 countries. Currently, six countries have not ratified this document, including Somalia, Palestine, the United States, Taiwan, Western Sahara, and Vatican City (which has no child population). The United States has signed but has not yet ratified this document (endcorporalpunishment .org/). The American Academy of Pediatrics (1998) strongly advises against corporal punishment of any kind. A large group of national organizations in Canada have joined together (Durrant, Ensom, & the Coalition on Physical Punishment of Children and Youth, 2004) to promote the message that physical punishment is ineffective and only serves to threaten children's well-being.

The solution most experts advise is parent education and the provision of alternative strategies for child discipline, but this cannot occur in a vacuum. Studies have long shown that conditions of economic and social stress in families burden caregivers and undermine the quality of their parenting (Conger & Elder, 1994).

Combined efforts to support families economically and educationally may have the best chance of reducing caregiver stress and promoting more positive discipline practices. Also, efforts that educate with sensitivity to cultural context are necessary. The evidence suggests that "any efforts to reduce both spanking and externalizing behaviors would need to target Blacks, Whites, Hispanics and Asian Americans. While the approaches would likely vary by cultural group, the message would be the same—spanking children is not associated with better behavior over time" (Gershoff et al., 2012, p. 843).

The Flexible Work of Parenting

It would be incorrect to assume that the quality of the early attachment relationship will automatically be transformed into a complementary pattern of parent–child relationships in early childhood. That is, it is not necessarily the case that every securely attached baby becomes a securely attached preschooler, and so forth. But, as our discussion of parenting style in the toddler and preschool years illustrates, the elements of sensitive parenting that characterize the infancy period are not much different from those that are right for preschoolers. The specific parenting behaviors might change, but the underlying requirement to be psychologically available and sensitive to the child's developmental needs and capabilities remains the same. For the most part, messages about the self-in-relationship that the child has internalized become the foundation for more mature interactions. Cicchetti and Toth (1994) believe that the negative adolescent and adult self-views that undergird many psychological disorders stem from insults to the self experienced during childhood. Consequently, clinicians need to apply primary prevention strategies to strengthen early parent–child relationships.

As children get older, they should be provided with experiences that allow for the growth of mastery, autonomy, and self-efficacy. Parent education and discussion groups can be helpful forums for parents in which to gain support for their strengths and to learn about the developmental needs of toddlers and preschoolers. Parents sometimes construe insensitive parenting to mean actions that are mean or rejecting. But intrusive interference, such as picking up the child to give her a hug when she is absorbed in an activity, or arbitrarily restricting a child's mobility, may also be insensitive to the child's needs if done repeatedly. Of particular relevance to self-concept development is educating parents about the implications of their language when conversing with their children. Insulting or insensitive remarks, particularly those intended to shame the child, should be avoided lest they become part of the young child's self-concept.

The growth of a healthy self-system depends upon an environment that provides the child with love and limits appropriate to her developmental level. When the proximal environment is distorted, as is the environment of defended and coercive children, youngsters will make adaptations. However, their adaptations will come with a cost to the development of a child's true self. Fostering the growth of the authentic self in infancy and early childhood sets the child on a developmental pathway that will support healthy functioning at every stage thereafter.

SUMMARY

The Self-System: Traditional Western Conceptions

1. Some traditional theorists viewed the self-system as multidimensional. William James, for example, distinguished between the self-as-subject, as active agent or "I", and the self-concept, the object of our own observations and evaluations, or the "Me." The "I" is continuously experienced, is distinguished from others, and is an agent of action. The "Me" consists of personal attributes, the material (or physical), social, and spiritual characteristics of self. Self-esteem, the evaluation of one's attributes, can be good, bad, or neutral. The valence assigned to one's own attributes depends on the number of successes we enjoy relative to our aspirations.

2. James Cooley introduced a developmental perspective into theorizing about the self. Self-representations are constructed from our interactions with others, especially caregivers. We build a looking-glass self that reflects our view of how others see us.

3. George Herbert Mead added that language and society contribute to shaping the self-system. There are culturally determined differences in people's preferred ways of viewing themselves. For example, Japanese emphasize affiliations in their self-descriptions, whereas Americans emphasize more individualistic qualities.

The Early Development of the Self-System

4. The pre-self that develops in infancy begins with early inklings of one's body permanence and separateness from others that are derived from the regularity and reliability of infant–caregiver interactions. Procedural representations of interactions are established and may promote a budding sense of mastery by the second half of the 1st year, if babies' behavior controls caregiving responses. A sense of self as self-in-relationship begins to emerge. By the end of the 1st year, separation distress signals the baby's deepening understanding that the other is separate. Additional indicators include the baby's tendency to explore more readily in the presence of a familiar caregiver. If the caregiver provides a secure base, the baby in a sense has the self-worth or confidence to explore. Social referencing also implies recognition of separateness. All of these indicators of a growing sense of the self as separate emerge from and depend on the baby's relationship to others.

5. Toddlers in the second year engage in joint reference, suggesting the earliest inkling that some separate experiences are shared—the first sign of a sense of mind. Self-recognition is demonstrated as early as 15 months in tests of mirror recognition. It is a strong indicator that children are forming a self-concept, or a "Me." After the second birthday, children begin to use self-descriptive words. Self-evaluation or self-esteem advances with self-recognition, with abused children showing signs of poorer self-esteem than non-maltreated children from the beginnings of mirror recognition. Gradually, more differentiated self-descriptions emerge, with preschoolers describing more concrete characteristics, such as "little," and older children beginning to refer to more abstract, less obvious qualities, such as "funny."

6. Self-control and self-regulation are dependent on the development of the emotion regulation that begins in infancy. The attentions of a caregiver when an infant is aroused (e.g., hungry) help the baby return to a more comfortable emotional state. The interaction process gives a baby outside assistance with affective control. The caregiving relationship is the context in which the infant's own capacity for emotion regulation develops.

7. Behavior regulation begins in the 2nd year when toddlers achieve objective self-recognition. The simultaneous emergence of symbolic or representational thought and other cognitive skills allow the child to begin learning and storing rules or standards of conduct. By late in the 2nd year, self-conscious emotions emerge, such as embarrassment or guilt, emotions that require awareness of self

and of others' judgments. Between 2 and 3, children show such emotions when they realize they have broken a rule or made a mistake. Once these capacities are in place, self-regulation can begin. How its development proceeds depends on many factors, especially social-ization processes.

Early Socialization: Parenting and the Development of the Self-System

8. As the infant becomes a toddler, her needs shift from total dependency to growing independence, and the parent–child relationship reorganizes such that sensitive responsive caregiving begins to include efforts to socialize the child—to shape or control the child's autonomous action, so that she remains safe and behaves in culturally appropriate ways.

9. Two dimensions of parenting style, parents' approach to caring for and disciplining their children, are important. First is warmth or parental responsiveness, which includes affection, acceptance, involvement and interest, and so on. Second is control or parental demandingness, the degree to which parents impose and enforce standards of conduct.

10. Four parenting styles can be described, crossing the positive and negative poles of the two dimensions. Authoritative parents are high on warmth and on demandingness. Authoritarian parents are low on warmth but high on demandingness. Permissive parents are high or moderate on warmth but low on demandingness, and neglecting or uninvolved parents are low on both dimensions. Authoritative parenting is associated with the most positive outcomes in child development, including adaptability, competence, good social relations, low levels of antisocial behavior, high self-esteem, and good self-regulation. The correlations between parenting styles and outcomes are significant but moderate, indicating that such outcomes are also influenced by other factors, not just parenting style.

11. Parents use a variety of methods of control. Power assertion, which involves either physical punishment or withdrawal of privileges, tends to be effective for immediate control of behavior, but may not have longer term benefits, and harsher forms can have some negative side effects, such as increased aggressiveness in children. Love withdrawal generates high anxiety and elicits immediate compliance, but seems to have few effects on long-term self-regulation. Induction, providing explanations and emphasizing benefits to the child and to others, seems most effective for promoting internalization of rules and longer-term self-regulation.

12. Are parenting practices actually having an effect, or are there other reasons why parenting is correlated with child outcomes? For example, could it be that the correlation is the result of shared inheritance of traits between parents and children? Data support a multidimensional approach. Parenting, genetics, child temperament, and other factors all contribute to child outcomes.

13. Parenting practices are partly the result of child characteristics, such as temperament traits. For example, adults are more directive with dependent than with independent children. Also, the effectiveness of different parenting practices is partly a function of a child's temperament. For example, toddler boys with difficult temperaments respond with high levels of aggressiveness when parents use physically intrusive control methods, whereas boys with easy temperaments do not.

14. The broader cultural context seems to have an influence on parenting practices and may have an impact on their effectiveness. For example, Puerto Rican American mothers emphasize sociocentric goals with their young children, whereas European American mothers focus more on individualization. Some parenting practices may have different meaning, and therefore different outcomes, depending on ethnicity and culture. The traditional values of various cultures have shaped the ways they parent and discipline their children.

15. Corporal punishment, which inflicts pain on children in order to control behavior, has been shown to predict increases in later externalizing behavior and mental disorders. This finding generally holds up across cultural groups. When cultural influences exist, they tend to moderate the link between corporal punishments and aggression, but not change the direction of effects.

Conscience: The Beginnings of a Moral Self

16. Parenting affects the developing self-system in many ways. Children's self-esteem is related to their parents' warmth and responsiveness. Children's self-regulation is associated with parenting style and practice. A child's ability to monitor her own behavior even in the absence of authority figures is considered a function of internalization, that is, the degree to which she has adopted standards and rules as her own. Internalization is associated with conscience, feeling distress when one violates a rule.

17. Children are more cooperative and compliant when they share a warm, responsive relationship with a parent. Their compliance can also be related to anxious arousal. Hoffman argued that mild arousal can help children pay attention to a rule, but doesn't make them so anxious that they pay attention only to how afraid they are. This is consistent with the finding that mild power assertion practices are more likely to lead to children's internalization of rules and long-term compliance than strong or severe power assertion practices. Further, Hoffman's ideas help explain why children who have fearful temperaments respond best to gentle discipline, but children who are fearless are unfazed by either gentle or harsh disciplinary practices. The most important determiner of compliance for fearless children is the warmth of their relationship to the parent.

CASE STUDY

Terry and Bill, married for 5 years, are a Black couple who live in a small suburban community. Terry graduated from high school and worked as a receptionist before her marriage to Bill, a communications company manager. Because both of them believed that mothers should stay at home with young children, Terry quit her job when she had her first child, who is now an intense and active 4-year-old daughter named Dawn. Both parents were very attentive to their daughter and enjoyed caring for and playing with her when she was a baby. As Dawn got older, she became more active and assertive. When Dawn fussed, resisted, or showed frustration, Terry was patient and affectionate with her. She was able to coax Dawn out of her bad temper by making up little games that Dawn enjoyed. Both Terry and Bill liked Dawn's spirited personality. Because her parents wanted her to have access to playmates, Dawn attended a church-related program for toddlers and preschoolers three mornings a week.

When Dawn was 3 years old, Terry gave birth to the couple's second child, a son named Darren. Soon after the baby's birth, the family learned that Darren had a congenital heart problem that would require ongoing medical treatment and a specific regimen of care at home. Darren was an irritable baby. He fussed for long periods and was very difficult for Terry to soothe. Because of Darren's need for medical care and the limitations of Bill's medical insurance, the couple soon found themselves in financial difficulty. Bill began to take on overtime work at the company to subsidize some of the bills and was away from the home several nights a week and part of each weekend.

Terry found the care of two demanding young children and the worries about money to be increasingly more stressful. She was always tired and seemed to have less patience with her family. whereas she once had the leisure time to read to Dawn, to take her for walks, and to help her master tasks that proved frustrating, Terry now had to shift her attention to the care of her medically fragile infant. Because Dawn looked so grown-up compared to the vulnerable newborn, Terry began to perceive her daughter as able to do many things for herself. When Dawn demonstrated her neediness by clinging or whining, Terry became abrupt and demanded that Dawn stop. Many battles revolved around Terry's new rule that Dawn have a nap or "quiet time" each afternoon so that mother and baby could get some rest.

One day, Dawn's preschool teacher, Mrs. Adams, asked to speak with Terry. Mrs. Adams noted that Dawn's behavior was becoming a problem in the morning preschool sessions. Dawn had begun throwing toys when she became upset and often refused to cooperate in group activities. Terry was greatly embarrassed to hear about her daughter's misbehavior. Dawn was the only Black child in the small class, and her mother wondered if this was part of the problem. When Terry got home, she put her tearful, clinging daughter in her room for time-out for being bad at school. She loved Dawn, but she could not tolerate this kind of behavior, especially when Darren needed so much of her time. She began to wonder if she and Bill had spoiled their daughter. Terry feared that Dawn would have problems when it came time for her to enter kindergarten if they didn't take a strong stand with her now.

Discussion Questions

1. Explain Dawn's behavior from an attachment point of view. How would you describe Dawn's attachment history?
2. Describe Terry's parenting style. Has the style changed? What suggestions would you make to Terry and Bill about handling this problem?
3. What are some of the contextual influences on Dawn's behavior?

PRACTICE USING WHAT YOU HAVE LEARNED

In the Pearson etext, apply these ideas to working with others.

Video Exercise

Video Exercise

Exploring Impact of Past Experiences on Present Behavior

JOURNAL QUESTIONS

1. How would you describe your parents' parenting style?
2. What kinds of discipline were used in your family? What would you advise other parents about disciplining their children?
3. How would you describe the impact of cultural changes (such as the use of cellphones, texting, computers, social media, etc.) on caregiver behaviors? In your experience, does their use make it more or less difficult to pay attention to young children with full awareness, acceptance and presence?
4. Identify a cultural value from your family of origin and describe how this value was reflected in your experience as a family member. If your experience included different or contrasting values and expectations (e.g., from parents, step-parents, etc.), reflect on that as well.
5. What do you believe is the relationship between your early self-development and your later self-esteem?

KEY CONCEPTS

self-system (p. 169)

"I-self" or self-as-subject (p. 169)

"Me-self" or self-concept (p. 169)

self-esteem (p. 170)

"looking-glass self" (p. 170)

pre-self (p. 172)

representations of interactions (RIGs) (p. 172)

social referencing (p. 173)

self-recognition (p. 173)

self-control or behavior regulation (p. 176)

self-regulation (p. 176)

self-conscious emotions (p. 177)

socialize (p. 179)

discipline (p. 179)

warmth dimension (parental responsiveness) (p. 179)

child centered (p. 179)

parent centered (p. 179)

control dimension (parental demandingness) (p. 180)

maturity demands (p. 180)

parenting styles (p. 180)

authoritative style (p. 180)

authoritarian style (p. 181)

permissive style (p. 181)

neglecting–uninvolved style (p. 181)

externalizing problems (p. 182)

internalizing problems (p. 182)

method of control (p. 182)

power assertion (p. 182)

love withdrawal (p. 182)

induction (p. 182)

time-out (p. 183)

differential susceptibility (p. 186)

internalization (p. 192)

conscience (p. 192)

anxious arousal (p. 192)

minimum sufficiency principle (p. 192)

committed compliance (p. 192)

compulsive caregiving (p. 194)

compulsive self-sufficiency (p. 194)

negative reinforcement (p. 195)

ADHD (attention deficit hyperactivity disorder) (p. 195)

contingency management system (p. 196)

CHAPTER 6

Realms of Cognition in Middle Childhood

In the preceding chapters, we have described some of the major developmental tasks and achievements of infancy and the preschool years. The pace of developmental progress is quite remarkable during those periods, and much of the foundation for later achievements is laid down. Consider, for example, the qualitative difference between the skills of a newborn and those of his 6-year-old sibling. Development has been so rapid during this first 6 years that it is not uncommon for parents with a newborn second child to view their older child as having grown up, almost overnight, because of physical size, motor skills, and verbal ability. However, in middle childhood, the years spanning the elementary school period, children are still far from grown up. Their growth takes on new forms in this stage, metamorphosing into ever more highly differentiated patterns of cognitive, emotional, and social functioning.

For children at the start of the middle years, school and its peer group structure represent a new frontier. The movement into the school years ushers in a whole new set of developmental challenges for children. Many youngsters begin to spend longer periods away from home, and all children must adjust to more rigorous schedules. They must learn to control their behavior, monitor their attention, and acquire more formal and more complicated academic competencies than have been formerly attained. They must make friends and learn to navigate the schoolyard, with its greater demands for athletic prowess, social skill, and cooperative negotiation of conflicts. They must also learn the rules of the group and when to abide by them. They must learn what it means to be male or female, not to mention what it means to be themselves. So many challenges await them.

However, children at elementary school age are also more adept at almost every task when compared to their preschool-aged siblings. Observing the eagerness and energy young children exhibit in the early school years makes it easy to understand the capacity for industry that Erikson described (see Chapter 1). For most children, the challenges of school and peer group will be mastered gradually, and in many different ways. Armed with foundational skills in language, mobility, understanding of self and others, and self-control, the youngster is now poised to assume membership in a larger social network.

Clearly, the years of elementary school, as the years to follow, are marked by ups and downs. These normal fluctuations create opportunities for helpers to provide support or guidance for children, their families, and their teachers. What are the cognitive, emotional, and social needs of children at this stage? What approaches are most helpful given children's developmental level? In the next two chapters, we will attempt to provide you with information that will be useful when working with children at this point in their development. Your understanding of cognitive development, the focus of this chapter, will enable you to understand children's ways of construing the world, helping you appreciate their academic needs as well as the intellectual bases for their friendships, gender roles, moral understanding, and conflicts.

BRAIN AND BEHAVIOR

Let's begin by briefly considering the child's changing brain. Changes in brain size and organization accompany the accomplishments of middle childhood. It is tempting to assume that these brain changes are "maturational," that is, triggered by preprogrammed genetic activity. But remember the epigenetic process when you think about brain development: "it is the ongoing interaction of the organism and the environment that guides biological . . . development. Brains do not develop normally in the absence of genetic signaling, *and* they do not develop normally in the absence of essential and contingent environmental input" (emphasis added; Stiles, 2009, pp. 196–197). Put more positively, genes *and* experience dynamically interact to influence emerging brain organization. There is no simple answer to the question, "Is this brain/behavioral change genetic or determined by experience?" It is both.

Even though the brain is at 95% of its peak size by age 6, it grows measurably in middle childhood (Lenroot et al., 2007; Sowell, Thompson, & Toga, 2004; see Blakemore, 2012). One of the important contributors to this growth is that white matter increases in volume, a process that continues well into adulthood. As you learned in Chapter 2, white matter is "white" because of the fatty myelin sheaths that form around the axons, insulating them so that electrical impulses travel faster from one neuron to another. Myelination increases the speed of neural signals dramatically. Also, functional neural networks become more integrated because myelin changes the timing and synchrony of neuronal firing (Giedd & Rapoport, 2010). Overall then, increasing white matter seems to reflect increasing neural connectivity and communication between neurons and between brain areas.

For example, one important area of white matter increase is the corpus callosum. This is the system of connecting fibers (bundles of axons) between the two hemispheres of the brain. As the corpus callosum myelinates, the left and right sides of the body become more coordinated. The upshot is that children have much greater motor control, something you can appreciate if you compare the awkward full frontal running of a 3-year-old to the ducking and weaving of a 9-year-old as he avoids capture during a game of tag. Changes in the corpus callosum (along with other brain areas, like the cerebellum) influence and are influenced by the great strides school age children make in both gross motor (e.g., riding a bicycle, skating, climbing trees, jumping rope) and fine motor (e.g., cutting, drawing, writing) skills.

Much of this chapter is focused on typical or **normative** development in middle childhood, but there are many individual differences among children. Researchers are beginning to link some of these to brain development. For example, children diagnosed with **attention deficit hyperactivity disorder (ADHD)** can show atypical variations in brain development (e.g., Sowell, Thompson, et al., 2003). Between 5 and 10 percent of school-age children are diagnosed with ADHD based on one or more of a cluster of symptoms that are especially problematic for school performance: poor attentional control, restlessness or hyperactivity, and impulsivity (e.g., Kessler et al., 2005). Studies comparing structural MRIs for children with and without ADHD have found differences in several brain areas. These include the frontal lobes, where normative growth is associated with improvements in attention and other higher order cognitive processes. Other areas include the parietal lobes, basal ganglia, corpus callosum, and cerebellum (for detailed reviews see Giedd & Rapoport, 2010; Krain & Castellanos, 2006). Longitudinal research indicates that for many children the "difference" is really a delay, especially in the growth of the cerebral cortex. The middle prefrontal cortex shows the greatest delay, with growth for ADHD children lagging behind typically developing children by as much as 5 years (e.g., Shaw et al., 2007). Fortunately, about half of ADHD cases diagnosed in childhood remit by late adolescence or early adulthood. For those children, it appears that brain development follows a delayed but typical trajectory. For cases of ADHD that do not remit, researchers have found unusual, progressive loss of brain volume in some brain areas, such as the cerebellum (Mackie et al., 2007). Note that there is some disagreement about whether ADHD actually comprises more than one disorder, with different frontal brain areas more affected in one type versus another (see Diamond, 2005).

Many children *not* diagnosed with ADHD are behaviorally different from average—they have better or worse attentional control or they are more or less impulsive or active than other children their age. Giedd and Rapoport (2010) suggest that "ADHD is best considered dimensionally, lying at the extreme of a continuous distribution of symptoms and underlying cognitive impairments" (p. 730). In line with this argument, they report that for children who are considered typically developing but more active and impulsive than average, typical brain changes also take place at a slower rate. Thus, researchers are beginning to identify some neurological differences among children that align with their behavioral differences. In general, helpers need to remember that there is a significant amount of unevenness in brain development in middle childhood, both between and within children (Berninger & Hart, 1992). It is not unusual for children to show lagging performance in some skills and more rapid advances in other skills than their age mates.

COGNITIVE DEVELOPMENT

When children leave behind the preschool years, they begin to seem much more savvy to adults. They can be given fairly complex responsibilities ("Take out the dog before you go to school, and don't forget to lock the door after you leave."). They can participate in discussions of local or world events, and they often appreciate humor that would have been lost on them earlier. The cognitive developments that underlie these new capacities have been described and studied from several different theoretical traditions. We will first present Piaget's characterization of cognitive change in middle childhood.

Piaget's Stage of Concrete Operations

Since the days of Christopher Columbus, we have been teaching children that the Earth is round. Of course, it looks flat, especially if you live somewhere in the midwestern United States, such as Minnesota. How do children reconcile what they are told with what they perceive? When Vosniadou and Brewer (1992) asked Minnesota school children in grades 1 through 5 about this apparent contradiction, they got some surprising answers. Figure 6.1 illustrates a few of them. Some children said the Earth was a flat disc—like a coin. Some thought it was a ball that has a flat surface within it and a domed sky overhead. Others saw the Earth as spherical but with a flattened side

Sphere

Flattened Sphere

Hollow Sphere

(a)   (b)

Dual Earth

Disc Earth

Rectangular Earth

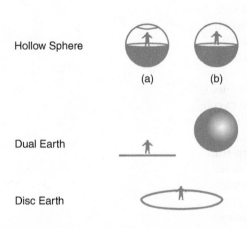

FIGURE 6.1 Children's images of a round Earth.

SOURCE: Vosniadou, S., & Brewer, N. F. (1992). Mental models of the Earth: A study of conceptual change in childhood. *Cognitive Psychology, 24,* 549. Used with permission from Elsevier.

where people live. The researchers found that the older the child, the more likely he was to represent the Earth as the sphere that scientists believe it to be. But even in fifth grade, 40% of the children still had some other idea of what it meant for the Earth to be round (see also Hayes, Goodhew, Heit, & Gillan, 2003; Vosniadou, Skopeliti, & Ikospentaki, 2004).

The inventive solutions of the Minnesota kids in the round Earth study remind us of what Jean Piaget considered the fundamental characteristics of learning and cognitive change. As we saw in Chapter 3, he stressed that knowledge is not just stamped in by experience or teaching; it is constructed. Children assimilate new information, meaning that they change it, interpreting it in ways that fit in with what they already know or with the way their thinking is structured. They also accommodate their existing knowledge structures, adjusting them somewhat. If new information is presented in ways that do not match children's current understandings, their resulting understanding probably will not be completely consistent with reality or with the information that adults mean to convey. Gradually, as new experiences are assimilated and accommodated, better approximations of reality are achieved.

You'll recall that despite the gradual construction process that Piaget described, in which knowledge structures are continually changing, he considered there to be stages of thought development, so that within a relatively broad period of time, children's thinking about many different things has some similar organizational properties. We have already discussed some of the characteristics that Piaget attributed to the sensorimotor (0 to 2 years) and preoperational (2 to 6 or 7 years) stages (see Chapter 3). In this chapter, we will consider his view of children's thinking in the *concrete operational stage*, the period spanning the elementary school years from about age 6 to 12.

To understand how Piaget described the thinking of young school-aged children, recall the limitations of the younger, preoperational thinker. Generally, preschoolers focus on one salient dimension of a situation at a time, and so they often miss the important relationships among aspects of a situation. Logical thinking is difficult to characterize, but it certainly includes the ability to recognize and take into account all of the relevant information in a problem situation and then to identify how those pieces of relevant information are related to each other. Consider the following simple problem in deductive logic: "All glippies are annoying. George is a glippy. Is George annoying?" To answer correctly, you must take into account a number of pieces of information—that there are glippies, that they are annoying, that there is an individual named George, and that George is a glippy. The important relationship you are then in a position to identify is between George and the glippies: He's one of them. From there you can infer that George is, indeed, annoying.

As we saw in Chapter 3, in very simple situations, even preschoolers can sometimes take into account more than one piece of information at a time. For example, sometimes they can solve very simple deductive inference problems (e.g., Blewitt, 1989; Smith, 1979). But more often, their thinking is centered, making it seem quite illogical. Remember the number conservation problems that Piaget invented? Let's consider another kind of conservation problem, in which children must infer that an object remains the same weight even if you change its shape. Imagine two balls of clay of identical size and shape. If we put them on a balance scale, we find their weight to be equal. Now, suppose we roll one ball into the shape of a snake so that it is long and thin. Despite its different appearance we have not adjusted its weight, so it will still be equivalent in weight to the other ball of clay. Preschoolers typically predict, however, that the weight will now be different—they often say it will be lighter than before because it's so skinny, or they might say it will be heavier because it's longer. They focus on one salient dimension and predict weight differences between the ball and the snake based on that dimension. But if they took into account both length and width, they might recognize that the changes in the two dimensions have compensated for each other, and so the weight is the same as before, even though it is differently distributed.

When children are in the concrete operational stage, they usually answer conservation questions correctly. They may look at the snake and say "it looks lighter than before" but they can logically conclude that it remains the same weight as the ball. Piaget argued that their logic is dependent on being able to see and understand the relationship between length and width changes—that one perfectly compensates for the other. Because they can decenter (think about more than one dimension of the situation at once), they can discover the relationships among those dimensions.

The compensatory relationship between the length and width of the clay snake is a kind of **reversible relationship**. In essence, one change reverses the effects of the other change. Piaget thought that being able to recognize reversible relationships is especially important for solving many kinds of logical problems, allowing children a deeper understanding of the world around them. For example, before he achieves concrete operations, a young child might learn the following two number facts: "2 + 1 = 3" and "3 − 1 = 2." But only when he recognizes reversible relationships is he likely to realize that the second fact is the inverse of the first and therefore that they are logically connected. If the first fact is true, then the second fact must be true. To put it differently, knowing the first fact allows the child to deduce the second one if he can think reversibly. When children's thinking becomes efficient enough to decenter, and thus to identify reversible relationships, children can begin to draw logical conclusions in many situations. This is the hallmark of the concrete operational child.

Piaget also identified limits to concrete operations. School-aged children seem to be most capable when the problems they are solving relate to concrete contents, and they seem to expect their solutions to map onto the real world in a straightforward way. But when a problem is disconnected from familiar, realistic content, these children have a difficult time identifying the relevant aspects of the problem and finding how those aspects are related to each other. In a classic example, Osherson and Markman (1975) asked children to say whether certain statements were true, false, or "can't tell." The experimenter made statements such as "The [poker] chip in my hand is either green or it's not green." Sometimes the poker chip was visible; at other times the chip was hidden in the experimenter's fist. If the chip were hidden, children in the elementary school years would usually say "can't tell," asking to see the chip to judge the statement. But the statement's truth was not determined by the actual color of the chip; it was determined by the linguistic elements in the sentence and the relationships between them (e.g., "either-or"). No check with the concrete world was necessary or even helpful. A chip, any chip, is either green or it's not. In other words, the abstract, formal properties of the statement, not concrete objects, were the contents of importance. Concrete operational children find it difficult to think logically about abstract contents, and they seek out concrete or realistic equivalents to think about in order to solve a problem.

Children's tendency to "hug the ground of empirical reality" (Flavell, Miller, & Miller, 1993, p. 139) is especially obvious when they need to think logically about their own thinking. Suppose for a moment that you are a child who believes that you're more likely to hit a home run playing baseball if you wear your lucky socks. To test this theory scientifically, you would need to weigh the evidence, pro and con. But before you could do this effectively, you would need to recognize that your belief about your lucky socks is really an assumption or a theory, only one of many possible theories. As such, it could be wrong. Because you already believe your theory, it will seem like a fact to you. You would need to apply careful logical thinking to your own thought processes, first to distinguish your belief from true facts or observations and then to see the relationship between your theory and those facts. However, if you are 8 or 9 years old, you have trouble thinking logically about anything abstract, and theories (or thoughts) are certainly

Although he likely understands the basics of reversible relationships, Freddie cannot yet apply that understanding to solve certain types of math problems. He solves the problem correctly when he frames it as an addition problem but is incorrect when he is asked to subtract.

abstract. So, logically evaluating any of your own beliefs or theories is not likely to be easy for you.

What we are describing is a form of egocentrism that emerges in middle childhood. The term **egocentrism** refers to some failure to recognize your own subjectivity. You fail to see things realistically because you are, in a sense, trapped in your own perspective. Preschool children often exhibit what Piaget called preoperational egocentrism (see Chapter 3). They have trouble recognizing that their own mental experiences are private and may not be shared by others. By 4 to 5 years, children's theory of mind includes knowing that people can have mental experiences that are not all the same from one person to another. So, their preoperational egocentrism recedes, and their ability to take another person's perspective begins to improve. (As you will see later in this chapter, perspective-taking skills increase in complexity and subtlety throughout childhood and adolescence.) But in middle childhood, difficulty thinking logically about abstract contents makes elementary-school-aged children vulnerable to another form of egocentrism: failure to distinguish between their own beliefs, assumptions, or theories and objective fact (see Elkind, 1981; Looft, 1972).

As a result, researchers have found that although elementary-school-aged children can think scientifically sometimes, identifying simple theories and checking them against evidence, they make a muddle of it if they already believe a certain theory (e.g., Kuhn & Franklin, 2006; Schauble, 1991). It is easy to understand why elementary school children might have difficulty believing that the Earth is really round, because they can't observe it. Children get better at evaluating their own theories as they move into adolescence and become capable of what Piaget called **formal operational thought**—logical thought about abstract contents. As you will see in Chapter 9, adolescents often extend their logical thought processes to many kinds of highly abstract contents, including their own thinking (although even adolescents and adults find this kind of abstract thinking a challenge and may fall into the same egocentric traps as concrete thinkers).

 Teachers and other helping professionals can take advantage of the fact that children generally are better problem-solvers in content areas in which they have prior knowledge.

Even though middle childhood has its cognitive limitations, Piaget was on to something in identifying it as a time when children can be expected to think logically. In every culture in the world, adults seem to recognize that somewhere between ages 5 and 7 children become more sensible, reliable problem solvers. In societies with formal schooling, kids are sent to school to work at serious tasks that will prepare them to take their place in the community of adults. In societies without formal schooling, children are given real work to do by age 6 or 7, tasks that are essential to the community (such as watching younger children, planting, or shepherding).

Piaget's description of the concrete operational child as a logical thinker about concrete contents has proved a useful one, and it seems to capture the typical cognitive characteristics of middle childhood quite well. However, as we saw in Chapter 3, newer work makes it clear that there are at best fuzzy boundaries between the stages Piaget proposed (see Halford & Andrews, 2006; Kuhn & Franklin, 2006). For example, with the right materials or simplified contexts, younger children sometimes solve problems that only older children could solve in Piaget's classic studies. In one recent study, 6- and 7-year-olds solved proportionality problems correctly with some materials (e.g., liquids) but not with others (e.g., discrete countable items; Boyer, Levine, & Huttenlocher, 2008). Proportionality is an abstract concept that generally is difficult for children to reason correctly about before age 11 or 12 (e.g., Inhelder & Piaget, 1955/1958), but with continuous materials like liquids younger children seem to have an intuitive sense of it. Logical thinking seems to emerge over an extended period of development and " . . . must be achieved at successively greater levels of complexity" (Kuhn, 2011, p. 502).

How advanced a child's thinking will be and what kinds of content a child can think logically and strategically about depend on many factors, including general knowledge (Pressley & Hilden, 2006) and quality of instruction (Schunk &

Experimental research indicates that infants show little learning from "educational videos." Human interaction works best.

Zimmerman, 2003; Vosniadou & Mason, 2012). (See Box 6.1 to examine the role that technology may play.) One important factor can be the amount of prior experience a child has had with the specific **domain of knowledge** (that is, a particular subject matter or content area) that he is thinking about. If a child has a lot of knowledge about a particular domain, say dinosaurs or chess, his ability to think logically about problems within that domain may be more advanced than in other content areas (e.g., Chi, Hutchinson, & Robin, 1989). Of course, the child may appear more logical simply because he has seen other problems of the same sort more often and can remember effective solutions, so his better problem solving may have less to do with more advanced thinking than with memory for past experiences. But it also seems to be the case that a child or adult with a lot of domain knowledge is better at identifying the important features of a problem within that domain and at identifying the relationships among those important features (see Moran & Gardner, 2006). Thus, logical thinking may be at least somewhat *domain specific* (that is, applicable to a particular area of knowledge) rather than strictly domain general and determined by one's stage of development, as Piaget's theory implies. For a child who loves experimenting with chemistry sets, reasoning about chemistry may advance more quickly than for a child whose passion is music.

In the next sections, we will consider some other ways of characterizing children's cognitive abilities in the middle years, especially the information processing approach. We will examine what we have learned about some abilities, combining research from the Piagetian, information processing, and other research traditions.

Box 6.1: Techno-Kids: Cognitive Development in a Wired World

Across from the reference desk at the local public library, Kim, Jeanine, and Serena, third-grade classmates, huddle together in front of a computer screen, looking for information for a group project. Jeanine is the only one of the three who has a computer at home; she has her hand on the mouse, and she speedily clicks, jumping from one web page to another with apparent nonchalance. The other two girls watch eagerly, but seem a little intimidated by the whole process. Besides Jeanine's comfort with the equipment, what else might be different about Jeanine as a result of her experience with computers? Are there developmental consequences to having easy access to television, video, computer games, the Internet, or any of the myriad electronic media that are part of our technologically saturated environment? Are the consequences different depending on whether access begins early or late in childhood? What practical advice should helpers give to parents who want to protect their children from harm but also to provide them with the advantages that make sense?

These are among the questions that developmental scientists are tackling, as a technological tsunami engulfs us. Let's consider some of what we have learned so far.

Infants and Toddlers

Babies automatically orient to novel stimuli. Visual electronic media like television, videos, and computer games tend to draw their attention with rapidly changing sights and sounds. There is little evidence that this attentional pull is good for very young children and some evidence that it may be harmful. In longitudinal studies of television

use, Christakis and his colleagues (e.g., Christakis, Zimmerman, DiGiuseppe, & McCarty, 2004; Zimmerman & Christakis, 2007) have found a link between infant/toddler viewing and later attention problems, even though several other sources of attention difficulties, such as low family income, were controlled in their research. In one study, the more television children watched before age 3 the more likely they were to have difficulty regulating attention at age 7. In a second study, the actual content of television programs turned out to be important. Amount of *educational* television viewing (e.g., *Barney, Sesame Street*) before age 3 *was not* a predictor of attention problems later, but children's *entertainment* television (e.g., cartoons) was. Also, the more violent the content, the more serious the later attention problems were. The researchers hypothesize that a key factor in these content differences may be the pacing of visual and auditory changes. Entertainment programming tends to have shorter scenes with more frequent changes that may "overstimulate the developing brain" (Zimmerman & Christakis, 2007, p. 990). Language use is also much more quickly paced in these programs than the slower "motherese" that young children hear in actual interaction with adults (see Chapter 3); educational programs are more likely to mimic the pacing of motherese.

While some studies implicate early video viewing as a cause of attention problems, not all researchers have found similar associations. Where links have been found there may be alternative explanations (Courage & Setliff, 2009). For example, temperament differences in infants and toddlers predict how much video viewing parents allow them to do (Brand, Hardesty, & Dixon, 2011; Brand & Dixon, 2013). Children who are difficult to sooth watch more TV, probably because parents find that it has a calming effect on them. Attention problems at 7 or 8 may be the result of these early temperament differences instead of the amount of early TV viewing children have done.

Do infants and toddlers actually learn from video that is intended to be educational? Marketers claim great educational benefits, but the evidence does not support these claims. For example, DeLoache and her colleagues (2010) tested the effectiveness of a best-selling DVD designed and marketed for infants from "12 months and up." The video shows a variety of house and yard scenes and repeatedly presents labels for household objects. Parents enthusiastically endorse the video in marketing testimonials. Yet babies who watched the video at least four times a week over 4 weeks performed no better on a test of the target words than babies who never viewed the video. In a condition where mothers were asked to teach the target words to their babies "in whatever way seems natural to you" over a 4 week period, children performed substantially better on the final word test than babies who had watched the video. Interestingly, mothers who liked the video also believed that their babies had learned a lot from it, even though they had not, which may account for some of the enthusiastic testimonials on marketing websites!

These findings are consistent with a survey of over 1,000 parents of 2- to 24-month-olds (Zimmerman, Christakis, & Meltzoff, 2007). Parents reported on the children's video viewing (including television) and completed a measure of children's language development. For 8- to 16-month-olds, viewing "educational" DVDs was actually linked to a slower pace of language development, and the more viewing the worse the language delay (even when factors such as SES were controlled; although see Ferguson & Donellan, 2013, for a different interpretation). Sometimes parents interact in positive ways with babies when they watch educational media together. When they do, children seem to learn more, but high quality interactions are much more likely when there is no TV or video playing (Simcock, Garrity, & Barr, 2011). Twelve- to 30-month-olds can learn to some degree from video—for example, they will imitate some of the actions that they see on screen—but they imitate substantially more when they witness live demonstrations of the same actions (e.g., Hayne, Herbert, & Simcock, 2003).

In sum, whether or not early use of electronic media actually causes harm (such as later attention problems) is still uncertain (see Courage & Setliff, 2009). But one thing is clear. These media *displace,* or take time away from, other activities that are more critical for positive cognitive development. Interactions with sensitive, responsive adults are central to the processes of acquiring language skills, building event and autobiographical memories, and learning about emotions, the self, and others. The "full body" exploration of objects and spaces that characterizes early play—smelling, tasting, manipulating, climbing, opening, closing, putting together, taking apart—helps babies and toddlers build a foundation of temporal, spatial, and physical knowledge that prepares them for later developments (see Chapter 3). Unfortunately, even when they are engaged in play with objects, if a television is on in the background, babies frequently turn toward the screen, reducing the length of play episodes and disrupting focused attention (Schmidt, Pempek, Kirkorian, Lund, & Anderson, 2008). Short play episodes and reduced attention

during play are "marker(s) for poor developmental outcome" (Schmidt et al., p. 1148). Concerns about brain and behavioral development have led the American Academy of Pediatrics (2011) to recommend against use of screen media (e.g., television, videos, and computer games) by children under age 2. Despite such concerns, many parents and other caregivers give infants and toddlers access to these media. For example, one startling finding from a Kaiser Foundation (Rideout & Hamel, 2006) study was that 19% of infants and 29% of 2- to 3-year-olds in America actually have televisions in their bedrooms.

Children and Adolescents

As children grow older, controlled exposure to electronic media is less problematic for perceptual and cognitive development. For example, television watching by 4- and 5-year-olds does not appear to be associated with long-term attentional problems (Stevens & Muslow, 2006; Zimmerman & Christakis, 2007), although children this age are still likely to have short-term attention difficulties after watching violent programs (Freidrich & Stein, 1973; Geist & Gibson, 2000). On the positive side, preschoolers' experience with some age-appropriate *educational* programming, such as *Sesame Street* and *Dora the Explorer,* is linked to improved school readiness, vocabulary growth and better number skills by kindergarten (Schmidt & Anderson, 2007) and with better school achievement by adolescence (e.g., Anderson, Huston, Schmitt, Linebarger, & Wright, 2001), even when other characteristics of the home environment and parenting are controlled. Among the features to look for in quality programming for young children are ". . . the use of child-directed speech, elicitation of responses, object labeling, and/or a coherent storybook-like framework throughout the show" (Bavelier, Green, & Dye, 2010, p. 693). Unfortunately, the more exposure to *entertainment* programming in the preschool and elementary school years, including child-directed programming like cartoons, the less likely children are to perform well in school. Just as we have seen with infants and toddlers, part of the problem seems to be that watching television displaces more achievement-related activities. Another problem may be that early television exposure socializes children's tastes, building preferences for superficial, rapid action, formulaic sequences and plots, and reducing the appeal of slower paced, more intellectually challenging entertainment, such as reading and puzzle solving (Comstock & Sharrer, 2006).

What are the costs and benefits when children use interactive media, such as computers and gaming devices? To begin, there is little doubt or disagreement that giving all children means and opportunity to become computer literate is an important educational goal. Learning to use basic computer software and the Internet as tools for acquiring, organizing, storing, and communicating information should be part of every child's experience. In today's world, individuals who lack computer skills are likely to be disadvantaged in many settings, especially the workplace. Also, having access to computer technology and the Internet can benefit academic performance. For example, Jackson et al. (2006) analyzed data from HomeNetToo, a longitudinal project in which low-income families were offered free computers, Internet access, and in-home technical support in return for permission to monitor each family member's Internet use. Children in these families were mostly low school achievers, but those who used the Internet more during the

(Box 6.1 continued)

Box 6.1 *Continued*

16 months of the project had higher GPAs and reading achievement scores at the end (but not at the beginning) than children who used it less. The authors suggest that surfing web pages gave children substantially more reading practice than they would otherwise have had, helping to explain the benefits. Such benefits do not seem to be limited to low-income children. In another longitudinal study, 1,000 adolescents from a range of backgrounds were surveyed in the 9th or 10th grade and then again in the 11th or 12th grade (Willoughby, 2008). Controlling for factors such as parents' education, moderate use of the Internet (about 1 to 2 hours per day) was more predictive of better school grades than either nonuse or high levels of use. It appears that nonuse is an academic liability in today's schools. Excessive use is also problematic, again perhaps because it tends to displace other important achievement-related activities.

Electronic games, whether they are played on a computer or on some other platform, such as an Xbox or Game Boy, can help develop the skills that the game uses. There is more research on these practice effects with adults than with children, but for skills that have been studied in children the same benefits apply, and they seem to be wide ranging, from improvements in vision and attention to motor skills. For example, playing action video games improves the ability to find small details in cluttered scenes or to see dim signals (Bevelier et al., 2010). Many studies indicate that electronic games can improve children's visual-spatial abilities, such as spatial rotation skill. The latter involves looking at an image of a three-dimensional object or scene and recognizing a representation of that object or scene from another perspective, a skill that many games use (see Subrahmanyam, Greenfield, Kraut, & Gross, 2001; Uttal et al., 2012) and that plays an important role in mathematical problem solving (Newcombe, 2010). Some games are designed specifically for educational purposes, such as improving math skills or vocabulary. Some are effective, some are not. Many are not substitutes for other educational experiences, but can be helpful supports. Interestingly, younger children seem to prefer educational games over games designed purely for entertainment.

Research on the cognitive benefits of interactive media for children is in its infancy. There is certainly potential not only for teaching specific knowledge or skills but also for broader cognitive impact (see Buckingham & Willett, 2006). Imagine a program that asks probing questions, encourages the child to hypothesize solutions, then to test and evaluate hypotheses, and so on. Or consider that many games have multiple levels of skill and require extended practice and intensive effort, rewarding the persistent player with the pleasure of achieving mastery at one level and the opportunity to face the challenge of a new level (e.g., Gee, 2003). These kinds of experiences seem likely to promote good problem solving and learning strategies if they generalize to other situations. But whether they do is not yet clear.

Extrapolating from decades of research on children's television viewing, it seems very likely that the *content* of a game or web page, along with the level of parent or teacher engagement in screening, explaining, and discussing that content, is more important than the electronic tool that delivers the content. What we know about television is that educational content can promote learning, and prosocial portrayals encourage prosocial behavior. Violent content can promote aggressive behavior, and, as we noted earlier, may have problematic consequences for the development of attention in very young children. Exposure to explicit sexual content and to sexism (e.g., women washing floors, men washing cars), and pervasive commercial propaganda about what is "fun" and important to own, affect children's beliefs and values about sexual behavior, gender, and what is important in life. We also know that when caring, knowledgeable adults help children to choose content, when they join children in their media use, scaffold their problem solving, and discuss and interpret media messages, children are less negatively and more positively affected (see Comstock & Scharrer, 2006; Wartella, Caplovitz, & Lee, 2004).

Guidelines for Parents

When should interactive media be introduced? Experts tend to agree that children under age 2 are better off not being "wired" at all, but opinions about access for preschoolers are much more mixed. On the one hand, organizations like the National Association for the Education of Young Children and the Fred Rogers Center for Early Learning and Children's Media (2012) are cautiously in favor of integrating "developmentally appropriate" exposure to computers and educational software into the preschool classroom. On the other hand, many researchers emphasize the dangers of preschool computer use, especially because time with electronic media displaces social interaction, pretend play, and constructive, creative problem solving in the three-dimensional world (e.g., Healy, 1998). Unfortunately, although some truly constructive computer learning games are available, much of the programming for preschoolers is focused on superficial and largely rote activities. Research on electronic books, for example, suggests that children's attention is often drawn to flashy elements—such as clicking on icons that are peripheral to the story—at the expense of attending to the story (de Jong & Bus, 2002; Parish-Morris, Hirsh-Pasek, & Maller, 2008). There are also concerns about possible health effects: muscular skeletal injuries, visual strain, and obesity due to inactivity (Alliance for Childhood, 2000). Because of such concerns, the American Academy of Pediatrics (2001) has recommended that preschoolers' *total media time* (including television) be limited to 1 to 2 hours per day.

For children older than 6 or 7, the primary concerns are that parents control content exposure, set time limits on media use so that it does not displace other important developmental experiences, monitor whom children communicate with through the Internet, scaffold children's efforts to master programs, and help children to evaluate commercial messages, which can be as ubiquitous on the Internet, for example, as they are on television. Parents and educators need to recognize that to make effective use of computers and the Internet in the classroom, teachers must be well trained in their use and how to judge the value of educational programs (e.g., Roschelle, Pea, Hoadley, Gordin, & Means, 2000). Does the teacher, for example, know how to guide children to information that comes from a reliable, objective source as opposed to a source with an agenda (commercial or cause driven)? Time and money invested in teacher training is at least as important as investments in hardware and software. "The best results from all technology use for children come accompanied by a skilled adult 'coach' who adds language, empathy, and flexibility" (Healy, 1998, p. 247).

A number of authors and organizations provide helpful guidelines and information for parents and educators, who often are not as savvy or comfortable with newer electronic media as children are. Some valuable websites are:

U.S. Department of Education (ed.gov)
The Children's Partnership (childrenspartnership.org)
Children Now (childrennow.org)
Entertainment Software Ratings Board (esrb.org)
Media Literacy Project (medialiteracyproject.org)
Center for Media Literacy (medilit.org)

An Alternative Perspective: The Information Processing Approach

Many interesting studies of middle childhood cognition—especially memory and problem solving—have been done by researchers in the information processing tradition. Information processing theories compare cognitive functioning to a computer's processing of information (see Chapter 1). The structural organization of the cognitive system is thought to be the same throughout development. A typical example of the kinds of structural components through which information is thought to "flow" during cognitive processing is presented in Figure 6.2. In this view, there are no qualitative, stagelike changes that characterize most of a child's thinking or processing. There are some changes with time, however, mostly in the amount and efficiency with which information can be processed. With increasing age, children can work with more information at once, and the strategies that children use to organize, understand, or remember information may also change. However, children apply different processing strategies to different specific contents, such as math, reading, and spatial concepts, so that strategies are not usually considered to be the

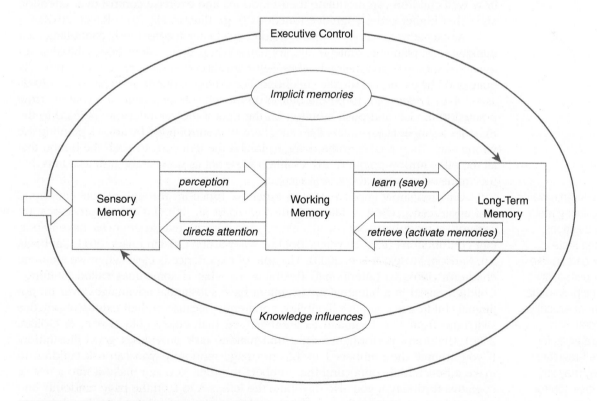

FIGURE 6.2 **The information processing system.**
SOURCE: From Woolfolk, A. (2014). *Educational psychology: Active learning edition* (12th ed.). Upper Saddle River, NJ: Pearson Education, Inc.

result of broad cognitive skills that are applied across different domains. Instead, strategies appear to be largely domain specific.

Information processing researchers focus heavily on what children do with information of particular kinds: what they pay attention to, how they encode it, what and how much information they store, what other information they link it with, how they retrieve it. In other words, information processing theories are focused on the mechanics of thinking. A Piagetian researcher might try to demonstrate that one cognitive achievement, perhaps in math, is related to another, perhaps in social perspective taking, to illustrate the global effects of some underlying stage characteristic. An information processing researcher typically tries to track the specific information handling that underlies a child's increasing mastery of a single domain.

Children spontaneously develop strategies for solving problems, including math problems.

The skills that appear to guide the flow of information are called *executive functions,* as you saw in Chapter 3 (Box 3.3). These include *working memory, self-regulation (or inhibitory control),* and *cognitive flexibility.* Improvements in the efficiency of these skills in particular may support other cognitive advances throughout childhood. Longitudinal studies find that good executive functions in childhood are related to many positive outcomes in adolescence (e.g., frustration tolerance) and adulthood (e.g., higher socioeconomic status) (Zelazo & Carlson, 2012). Interestingly, recent research indicates that some of the negative consequences of poverty on children's academic performance are related to slower development of executive functions in poor children. As you have seen in earlier chapters, many children in low income families experience chronic stress, which affects neuroendocrine pathways and the development of the body's typical reactions to stress. This in turn affects how well children can modulate their emotions and exercise control over attention and other higher order cognitive functions (e.g., Blair et al., 2011; Raver, 2012).

As executive functions improve, children get better at consciously controlling their thinking (e.g., planning, strategically problem solving), their actions (e.g., inhibiting automatic responses), and their emotions. Self-regulation or inhibitory control is typically quite good by the end of middle childhood. For example, Bunge and colleagues (2002) asked 8- to 12-year-olds to push a button on the left side of a panel if a central arrow pointed to the left and push a button on the right if the central arrow pointed to the right. It's a simple task—unless the central arrow is surrounded by arrows pointing the wrong way. Then it takes some doing to inhibit the tendency to push the button that all the other arrows point toward. Children were not as good at the task as adults, but they nonetheless were about 90% accurate.

 Preschool children have difficulty regulating their emotions and actions, and they often state that another person, like a teacher or parent, is required to help. With the development of executive control, children can articulate strategies for emotional self-regulation, although they may still sometimes lose control.

Children show improvement in executive functions through middle childhood and adolescence (Best & Miller, 2010; Zelazo et al., 2013). Genetic processes are certainly at work here, but social, cultural, and educational experiences make important contributions (e.g., Hewage, Bohlin, Wijewardena, & Lindmark, 2011; Sabbage, Xu, Carlson, Moses, & Lee, 2006). The role of experience is clear when we examine children's cognitive (attentional) flexibility, or what is sometimes called "shifting." Children raised in a bilingual environment have substantial advantages over monolingual children in cognitive flexibility, apparently because of their extensive practice switching from one language to another (see Bialystok, Craik, Green, & Gollan, 2009). Children's performance on a trail making task provides a good illustration. If you arrange the numbers 1 to 12 on a page randomly, you can ask children to make a pencil trail connecting the numbers in order. You can make it into a test of cognitive flexibility if you also distribute the letters A to L on the page randomly and ask children to alternate from numbers to letters as they make a pencil trail: from 1 to A to 2 to B, and so on. In middle childhood, bilingual children are faster on the alternation task than monolingual children, shifting back and forth with greater ease (e.g., Bialystok & Viswanathan, 2009).

Information processing theorists have traditionally paid special attention to the executive function of working memory and its role in cognitive development. This is the part of the cognitive machinery that holds information we are actively thinking about at the moment. We will take a closer look at working memory and its development in the next section.

The influence of both Piagetian and information processing approaches has fueled a rapid increase in our understanding of cognitive development, and it is not surprising that some theorists have attempted to marry the best components of both approaches. Typically known as **neoPiagetians**, these theorists explain Piaget's stages, or revise the stages, using many information processing concepts (e.g., Case, 1985, 1992; Fischer & Bidell, 2006; Halford & Andrews, 2006). For example, Case (1985) specifies four stages comparable to Piaget's, but explains the transition from one to another partly in terms of increases in the capacity of working memory. Another example, offered by Halford and colleagues (e.g., Andrews & Halford, 2002; Halford & Andrews, 2006), analyzes many of Piaget's tasks in terms of "complexity theory." Instead of assessing logical problem solving as dependent on how concrete or abstract the contents, they suggest that the difficulty children have with problems depends on the number of variables that must be related to each other, that is, the size of the "processing load." The idea being that younger children can process fewer variables at once than older children.

Let's now take a look at some of what we have learned about elementary school children's cognitive abilities. To do so, we will focus on the development of memory and attention and the many influences that help these abilities to advance.

Cognitive Improvements in Middle Childhood

Imagine a child who has just had his annual medical examination. With his parent's consent, an interviewer asks a set of questions to explore what he remembers about the experience. Some are open-ended questions, such as "Can you tell me what happened when you went to the doctor?" Others are specific yes–no questions, such as "Did she look in your nose?" A subset of the yes–no questions are strange or silly, such as "Did the doctor cut your hair?"

As you might expect, elementary-school-aged children usually answer such questions more accurately than preschoolers do. If you wait for several weeks and then ask about the doctor's exam again, a 3-year-old will forget more of what he could originally remember than a 7-year-old will. In one study, by 12 weeks after the checkup, 3-year-olds' responses to the silly questions were at chance levels of accuracy (meaning that they were saying "yes" to about half of the silly questions), but 7-year-olds averaged about 90% accuracy, despite the delay. The older children's answers had also remained relatively consistent over time, so that if they answered "yes" to a question right after the exam they tended to do so on repeated tests at later times (Gordon, Ornstein, Clubb, Nida, & Baker-Ward, 1991, as cited in Ceci & Bruck, 1998).

Almost all aspects of memory seem to improve with age, at least up through young adulthood. As you will see, developmental changes in memory are affected by many characteristics of cognitive functioning and development. In this section, we will consider several contributors to memory improvement in the school years and beyond. But before we do, let's briefly define some of the terminology that is commonly used in discussions of memory. Many of these terms were first introduced by information processing theorists, and some are included in the information processing flow model depicted in Figure 6.2.

Memory Terminology

First, we can describe memory as consisting of different memory stores. **Sensory memory** refers to a brief retention of sensory experience. For about one third of a second, when we first see a scene, we store most of the sensory information that has come in, almost as though our eyes have taken a snapshot of the whole scene. A similar phenomenon occurs with hearing. Interestingly, sensory memory capacity does not seem to change much with age. At least for visual information, even infants' sensory memory is similar to that of adults (e.g., Blaser & Kaldy, 2010).

Working memory is the next storage "unit," and in early research it was referred to as "short term store." Working memory allows us to focus attention, plan, execute problem-solving strategies, make inferences, and organize information for transfer into **long-term memory**, the almost unlimited store of knowledge. The information we pay attention to in working memory comes from our immediate sensory experience and from long-term memory. For example, suppose you are watching a movie about an African adventure, and an array of color and movement suddenly fills the screen. Your working memory combines the sensory data coming from the screen with information drawn from long-term memory to create a meaningful interpretation: It's a charging zebra. Or suppose your supervisor reminds you that your counseling approach to a client's new problem is similar to one that was not very successful in the past. Your thinking about the strategy (in working memory) combines elements of the supervisor's input with stored memories of prior interactions.

Unlike long-term memory, working memory is thought to have a limited capacity. We can pay attention to, and think about, a limited number of meaningful units of information at one time, and material is lost from working memory in 15 to 30 seconds unless we engage in **rehearsal** (i.e., unless we actually keep working with it, making an effort to pay attention, such as repeating it to ourselves). Generally, it seems that for sensory information to get into long-term memory, it must be attended to in working memory. For example, you may hear the music playing as the zebra on the screen charges, but unless you pay attention to it, you are not likely to remember it later. Or if you're mulling over another problem while your supervisor gives you feedback, you will be unlikely to profit from the comments. So, learning seems to require real work or effort. If you find you have to go back and reread a section of this chapter to commit it to memory, you are making the kind of mental effort that characterizes working memory and accounts for successful learning.

Learning, or acquiring knowledge, involves the **storage** of information. **Retrieval** is what we usually mean by remembering, that is, getting information out of storage so we can use it. In Chapter 3, we talked about two kinds of remembering or retrieval: *recognition* and *recall*. Recognition happens when the information to be remembered is immediately available to your senses. For example, you see your 9th grade gym teacher crossing the street in front of you, and you realize that you're experiencing someone who is familiar. Your sensory image elicits information about the teacher stored in long-term memory. We saw in Chapter 3 that some ability for recognition seems to be present from birth, and generally young children's recognition skills are very good, especially for visual-spatial information, such as memory for pictures. (Try playing the visual memory game "Concentration" with a 4-year-old. You might not win!) However, long-term retention of visual-spatial information does improve over the preschool years (Morgan & Hayne, 2011), and recognition of verbally presented information shows even longer-term developmental improvement (Schneider & Bjorklund, 1998).

Recall is more work. The to-be-remembered information is not present, and you must somehow draw it out of long-term memory and re-present it to yourself, as when you must answer an essay question on an exam. Or, as we described in the opening of this section, a researcher asks a child to remember what he experienced when he went to the doctor. When a child has problems with recall, it could be because he did not attend to the information in the first place, because he did not store the information in long-term memory despite having paid attention to it, or because the child does not have adequate strategies for finding the stored information. Clearly, recall depends on many processes.

One feature of human memory is that we can store different kinds of information or knowledge. Knowledge about facts and events, called **declarative knowledge**, is of two kinds. The first kind is **semantic**, which includes factual information ("the Earth is round"), rules ("red lights mean stop"), and concepts ("an elephant is a large, gray animal"). The second kind is **episodic**, which refers to our knowledge of the events that we have experienced. When researchers ask children to recall their visit to a doctor's office or when your supervisor asks you to describe a counseling session, they are asking about episodic knowledge. Episodic knowledge is organized around time and space—what happened in what order, where, and when. After we've had several experiences with one kind of event, such as being examined by a doctor, we begin to form a schematic representation of the typical features of such an event and the order in which they happen. This is called a **script**.

In addition to declarative knowledge, we have **nondeclarative knowledge**, knowledge that we cannot adequately put into words and that may not even enter our awareness. For example, you may know how to shift the gears in a standard transmission vehicle, but you might have a difficult time explaining how to do it. Many physical skills are based on this kind of unconscious, nondeclarative knowledge, which we usually call procedural. You may remember that we have used the term **procedural knowledge** to describe what infants "know" about how to do things or what to expect from interpersonal interactions (see Chapter 5). Early working models of attachment are probably a kind of procedural knowledge. Much of what infants and toddlers know seems to be nondeclarative rather than declarative.

Now that we have a vocabulary of memory terms, let's take a look at how memory seems to work in middle childhood and what improves with age.

What Improves with Development?

With age, working memory seems to expand. Like Piaget, most observers, regardless of theoretical orientation, have noted that older children usually pay attention to more pieces of information at one time than younger children. **Digit span tests** provide the standard demonstration of this change in working memory capacity. You may recognize them as a typical part of most intelligence tests. A series of digits are presented to the test participant, who must immediately repeat them in the same order. A child of 2 years can usually reproduce about two digits accurately; by the time he is 7, he will probably be able to remember a five-digit string. Adults, on average, can recall about a seven-digit string (hence, the standard telephone number; Dempster, 1981). The typical number of digits reliably increases with age up to adulthood, but the actual number of digits people can recall depends on the language of the test (Goswami, 2008). That's because number words are longer in some languages than in others. Digit span is not as great when longer words must be remembered and rehearsed. Chinese children have longer digit spans than English speaking children, because Chinese number words are shorter (Chen & Stevenson, 1988). When intelligence tests were first in use, it was thought that Welsh children were not as bright as English children because their digit span performance was not as good. However, it was only because Welsh number words are longer than their English counterparts (Ellis & Hennelley, 1980).

What accounts for increases in working memory capacity with age? There could literally be, somehow, more "room" in the older child's working memory. But many other cognitive changes seem to contribute and may actually be more important. We will consider several of these.

Although the story this 9-year-old tells sounds like an autobiographical memory, he is actually making up a story based largely on typical features of this type of event—a script.

Processing Speed. The first cognitive change that contributes to memory improvement is that children can process information more quickly as they get older. How quickly children can make a simple response (e.g., pushing a button) to a stimulus (e.g., the onset of a light on a computer screen) increases from early to middle childhood and it continues to improve until about age 15 (e.g., Kail, 1993; Luna, Garver, Urgan, Lazar, & Sweeney, 2004). Piaget attributed the decentering skill of school-aged children (their ability to pay attention to more than one thing at a time) to the speeding up of mental activities with practice, and modern research does support the idea that practice can accelerate information processing (Johnson, 2003). In addition, speed of processing can increase with physical maturation—that is, simply as a function of age (Toga et al., 2006). The upshot is that as children get older, they can do more with more information at one time (e.g., McCauley & White, 2011).

Breadth and Depth of Knowledge. The second cognitive change that affects memory improvement is that as children get older their knowledge about many things increases. They expand their **knowledge base**. Consider the study of children's recall of a medical examination mentioned earlier. One reason that a 7-year-old might have recalled information more accurately than a 3-year-old is that the older child probably knew more about medical exams. By 7, a child has formulated a script of the typical medical exam. When an interviewer asks questions about a particular exam, even many weeks after it happened, the 7-year-old may not actually remember whether the doctor cut his hair, for example, but he knows that doctors don't do that sort of thing in medical exams, and so he answers correctly. In general, older children know more about most events, and so they are more likely than younger children to be able to reconstruct accurately what probably happened in any given situation.

It should be noted that prior knowledge can also lead to false memories. For example, in a number of studies, children have been shown videos or pictures of people playing roles such as that of a doctor or a nurse. Sometimes the gender of the adult is consistent with traditional expectations—such as a man playing the role of doctor—and sometimes the person's gender and occupation are not traditionally consistent, such as a man playing the role of nurse (e.g., see Bigler & Liben, 1992). Children's preexisting beliefs about gender and work roles—that is, their gender stereotypes—influence what they will later remember about what they saw. In one particularly interesting study, Signorella and Liben (1984) found that elementary school children with strong gender stereotypes were more likely than children with less stereotyped beliefs to misremember who had played what role in the pictures they had seen when gender and occupation were not traditionally matched. So, for example, if they had seen a woman doctor, the children with strong stereotypes would be likely to remember that it was a man they had seen instead, or that the woman had been a nurse. Race stereotypes also affect children's story memory. For example, African-American children are more likely to remember that a light-skinned person in a story has a high-status job than that a dark-skinned person does (Averhart & Bigler, 1997; Williams & Davidson, 2009). (See Box 6.2 for other examples of how false memories can be induced.)

In addition to prior knowledge affecting your ability to reconstruct what you've experienced, the more you know about a particular subject, or domain of knowledge, the more easily you can learn new information in that domain and the better you will remember it later. If knowledge in most domains expands with age, then learning and retrieval of information in most domains should get better with age. But age is not what is most important—knowledge is. Suppose, for example, that you show an 8-year-old child a chessboard with chess pieces arranged as if in the middle of a chess game. Later, you ask the child to reconstruct the placement of all the pieces on an empty board—that is, to recall the layout of the pieces. If the child happens to be an "expert" chess player—someone who plays in competitions and is

Box 6.2: Children's Eyewitness Testimony

The following is an experience reported by Bill, a 4-year-old:

> My brother Colin was trying to get Blowtorch [an action figure] from me, and I wouldn't let him take it from me, so he pushed me into the woodpile where the mousetrap was. And then my finger got caught in it. And then we went to the hospital, and my mommy, daddy, and Colin [older brother] drove me there, to the hospital in our van, because it was far away. And the doctor put a bandage on this finger (indicating). (Ceci, Loftus, Leichtman, & Bruck, 1994, quoted in Ceci & Bruck, 1998, p. 749)

Bill appeared to have a clear memory of this scary event, and he was confident even about details such as where his father was at the time of the accident. But the experience Bill could describe so convincingly never happened! It was a false memory, induced by a researcher who had read brief descriptions of a set of pictures to Bill each week for 9 weeks. The description for one of the pictures had said, "Got finger caught in a mousetrap and had to go to the hospital to get the trap off." The researcher then said, "Think real hard and tell me if this ever happened to you. Do you remember going to the hospital with a mousetrap on your finger?" In the first session, Bill said he had not had such an experience. By the 10th session, as you have seen, he seemed convinced that he had.

Preschoolers can have some difficulty with reality monitoring, distinguishing fantasies from realities. Young children can tell the difference between what is real and what is not and between what it feels like to only imagine something versus to actually experience it (e.g., Flavell, Flavell, & Green, 1987), but they have more difficulty with these distinctions than older children or adults (e.g., Foley, Harris, & Hermann, 1994; Parker, 1995). In particular, if they imagine an event, they are somewhat prone to say later that it actually happened. One charming and usually harmless example occurs when a child becomes devoted to an imaginary friend. But a young child's problems with reality monitoring can make him more susceptible to suggestion than older children or adults, a serious concern when children serve as eyewitnesses. Some interviewers and therapists in child sexual abuse cases, for example, use a professional technique called guided imagery as an aid to memory. A child might be asked to pretend that an event occurred, then create a mental picture of the event and its details (Ceci & Bruck, 1998; Gilstrap, 2004). Unfortunately, if an adult encourages a child to construct a fantasy about what *might* have happened, the child may eventually come to believe that it *did* happen, even if it did not.

In considering whether children should serve as eyewitnesses, the key issue is, how valid can children's reports be expected to be? In the late 1600s, children's testimony at the witch trials in Salem, Massachusetts, led to the execution of 20 defendants. Young girls testified convincingly that they had seen defendants doing fantastic things, like flying on broomsticks. Some of the testimony was later recanted, and the whole episode created such a negative view of children's testimony that for three centuries child witnesses were not often seen in American court proceedings. Only in the 1980s did

many states end restrictions on children serving as witnesses (see Ceci & Bruck, 1998).

Modern memory research has helped increase the acceptance of children's testimony in America. Many studies indicate that what children remember *can* be accurate, although the number of details a child will recall and with what accuracy improves with age. But at any age, a witness's memory for observed events could be incomplete or distorted or simply wrong, sometimes as a result of exposure to suggestion. And the younger the child, the more susceptible he is likely to be to suggestion (e.g., Ceci, Bruck, & Battin, 2000).

We have seen that preschoolers' difficulties with reality monitoring can be a source of suggestibility, and there are several other sources as well, many of which children might encounter in the course of being interviewed by parents, police, social workers, therapists, and other court officials. When interviewers are biased, they may guide children's testimony, planting suggestions without realizing that they are doing so. So, for example, if an interviewer is already convinced that a child has been abused, she may encourage a child's admission of abuse by asking leading questions, such as "Where did he kiss you?" instead of "What did he do?" The interviewer might also ask the same question repeatedly if the child's initial answers are not consistent with the interviewer's belief. Studies of interview transcripts indicate that even the most well-meaning and concerned interviewers, including parents, use many such tactics to try to get at what they believe, or fear, is the truth (Bruck, Ceci, & Principe, 2006; Bruck & Ceci, 2012). Unfortunately, they may be planting suggestions that can lead the child to reconstruct his memory of an event.

A study by Pettit, Fegan, and Howie (1990) is just one of many that illustrates how effective such suggestions can be with young children. Two actors visited a preschool classroom. They pretended to be park rangers and talked to the children about helping a bird find a nest for her eggs. In the middle of the discussion, one "ranger" knocked a cake off the top of a piano "by accident." The cake was smashed, and there was silence for a few moments in the classroom, creating a rather distinctive event. Two weeks later, each of the children in the class was interviewed about the incident. Before the children were questioned, the researchers gave some of the interviewers an accurate account of what had happened. Others were provided with false information, and a third group was given no information at all. The interviewers' instructions were to find out what had happened from each child, but without asking leading questions. Despite the instructions, the interviewers did ask leading questions—30% of the time—and half of these were misleading. Naturally, the interviewers who had false beliefs about the event asked the most misleading questions. And the children were often misled, agreeing with 41% of the misinformation suggested to them. Apparently, interviewers biased by false beliefs can unwittingly maneuver children into providing false information (see Bruck et al., 2006, for other experimental examples).

Elementary-school-aged children are generally less suggestible than preschoolers (Ceci et al., 2000; Ceci, Papierno, & Kulkosky, 2007). For example, their reality monitoring is more adequate, and they are less affected by leading questions. But even older children

(Box 6.2 continued)

Box 6.2 *Continued*

and adults are not immune to suggestion (e.g., Ackil & Zaragoza, 1995; Loftus, 1979). Fortunately, witnesses of all ages can provide more accurate information if they are interviewed under conditions designed to minimize suggestion. Even traumatic experiences can be recalled well by young children under the right conditions (e.g., Eisen, Goodman, Qin, Davis, & Crayton, 2007; Quas & Hayakawa, 2008). Extensive reviews of research on children's eyewitness testimony reveal a number of characteristics that may reduce the influence of suggestion in interviews (Bruck et al., 2006; Bruck & Ceci, 2012). Of course, interviewers should avoid leading questions, as we have seen, and they should keep both the repetition of questions and of interviews to a minimum. The interviewer's tone should also be neutral, rather than urgent, aggressive, or accusatory. For example, an accusatory tone may be set by statements such as "Are you afraid to tell?" and "You'll feel better once you've told." In one study, when interviewers made such comments, even children who previously indicated no recall of an event sometimes agreed with questions that incorrectly suggested abuse (see Goodman & Clarke-Stewart, 1991).

Interviewers should not use inducements such as telling children they can help their friends by making disclosures. In one criminal investigation, for example, investigators said things to children such as "Boy, I'd hate having to tell your friends that you didn't want to help them" and "All the other friends I talked to told me everything that happened. . . . You don't want to be left out do you?" (quoted in Ceci & Bruck, 1998, p. 745). Such pressure might have the effect of encouraging children to produce responses even when they do not recall the events in question. Another interview strategy to be avoided involves **stereotype induction**, that is, slanting the interviewee's view of an individual. Sometimes interviewers will encourage children to make revelations by indicating that the alleged perpetrator is a bad person or does bad things. But in studies where this strategy was implemented, young children were found to produce incorrect, negative recollections of such an individual's behavior more often than children who were not exposed to the induction (see Bruck & Ceci, 2012).

As Ceci and Bruck (1998) emphasize, interviewers are motivated by concern about the welfare of the child: "[N]o interviewer sets out with the intention of tainting a child's memory" (p. 730). But even with the best of intentions, an interviewer can elicit questionable testimony. An understanding of the ways in which memory is constructed and reconstructed can help investigators to make eyewitness testimony, especially in children, more trustworthy.

highly knowledgeable about the game—his performance on this recall task will be much better than that of an average adult "novice," who knows how to play but who does not have extensive knowledge of the game. In other words, when children are more expert than adults in a domain of knowledge, they can remember more new information from that domain than adults can (e.g., Chi, 1978; Chi & Koeske, 1983). We will see later that other domains of knowledge, such as knowledge about others' perspectives and feelings, improve at this age and enhance social relationships.

Many studies suggest that as you amass knowledge of a subject, you understand new information in that domain more quickly and more completely. Some researchers describe the formation of a rich web of well-organized connections among the pieces of information in long-term store. For example, a counselor's concept of "therapy" might be part of a detailed web of stored information such as the one presented in Figure 6.3. We fit new information into this web, allowing us to retrieve it later through many routes and making it more accessible than if there were fewer connections. The processing speed for new information increases, and the depth of understanding is greater. All aspects of memory seem to be positively affected. Of course, ordinarily, the older you are, the more knowledgeable you are, and so the better you are at remembering, particularly in your area of expertise.

One advantage of a rich web of knowledge is that it allows **chunking** of information in working memory. Chunking links several pieces of information together into a single meaningful unit. For example, suppose you were given the following series of numbers in a digit span test: 149217761929. You might notice that you could divide the series into three chunks that represent famous dates in American history: 1492, 1776, and 1929 (Siegler, 1998). If so, you would be able to remember all the digits because you converted them to just three pieces of information, which would not exceed your working memory capacity. The more extensive the webs of information in your long-term memory, the more likely you are to find ways to chunk information meaningfully in working memory. When expert chess

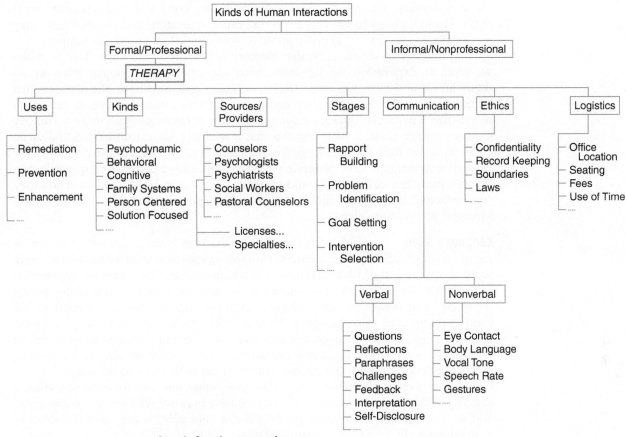

FIGURE 6.3 **A conceptual web for the term *therapy*.**

players look at a chessboard set up as if in the middle of a chess game, they see meaningfully related chunks consisting of four or five chess pieces each, allowing them to, in effect, rehearse the positions of 20 to 25 individual pieces without exceeding their working memory capacity. Novices see only individual pieces, allowing them to rehearse the positions of only about 5 to 7 pieces (Chase & Simon, 1973).

Logical Thinking Skills. A third cognitive change that contributes to memory improvement with age is advanced logical thinking. If older children can think more logically than younger children, they may have a better understanding of at least some of their experiences. Understanding better helps them to remember more about the experience later. Piaget's own research on memory improvement with age focused heavily on the contribution of logical development (see Piaget & Inhelder, 1973). In a typical study, he showed children from ages 3 to 7 an array of sticks, arranged in serial order by size. One week later, he asked children to draw what they had seen as a test of their recall. They were also given an opportunity to put a series of sticks in order according to size. This seriation task is a lot like the conservation of number task. It looks simple, but children are not usually completely successful at it until about age 7. In other words, it seems to require the logical thinking of the concrete operational stage. What Piaget found was that if children did not have the logical thinking skills needed to seriate sticks themselves, they typically could not remember the serial pattern they had been shown a week earlier. Children who could seriate the sticks (mostly 6- and 7-year-olds) showed better memory for the serial pattern. Remarkably, though, when he tested children's memory again at least 6 months later, many of the younger children were now more accurate in their memory drawings than they had been originally, depicting some aspects of the serial order. These findings have often been replicated, indicating that children's memory for some experiences can actually improve over time! How could this happen?

The key here seems to be that memory is often reconstructive. That is, when we recall an experience, we integrate "what we currently experience, what we already know, and what we infer" (Kuhn, 2000a, p. 22). You have already seen that older children may use what they know about doctor's examinations in general to reconstruct a particular doctor's examination. This helps them recall more accurately than a younger child. It also appears that if a child's logical understanding of an event improves from the time he first experiences it to the time his memory is tested, he may reconstruct it more accurately than he could have earlier. As the children in Piaget's study got older, they could understand seriation better, and so when they "remembered" the original stick array, they often inferred that the sticks had been arranged according to size.

Language Skills. A fourth cognitive change that can benefit memory with age is greater facility with language, especially improvements in **narrative skill**, the ability to tell a coherent story. Clearly, one way in which we mentally represent information is in words. As children's vocabularies grow and their skill in describing events develops, their ability to store information about experiences in coherent verbal form also improves (e.g., Tessler & Nelson, 1994). As we saw in Chapter 3, recent research suggests that this aspect of memory improvement is enhanced by narrative interactions with adults. If parents encourage their children to talk out loud about their experiences, asking questions, helping them with facts about shared events, children are better storytellers. They also have better memory for autobiographical events. On the whole, language skills such as these improve with age and experience, and so older children's memory for events can generally be expected to be better than younger children's (see Nelson & Fivush, 2004).

Memory Strategies. A fifth cognitive change that can facilitate memory improvement with age is learning to use **memory strategies**. Strategies are "potentially conscious activities a person may voluntarily carry out" to remember something (Flavell et al., 1993, p. 235). Imagine that we asked you to remember all the names of the children in your class when you were in the fifth grade. After you finished groaning, you would probably take a strategic approach to this retrieval task. That is, you would follow some plan. Maybe you would try to remember all the girls and then all the boys; or maybe all your good friends and then all your enemies; or maybe all the popular kids, then the less popular ones; or maybe you would start with the tallest kids and work your way to the shortest. Generally, adults do approach memory tasks strategically, and when they do, they remember more than if their approach is haphazard. There are a host of strategies that we can call on. Some help us encode new material that we expect to have to remember later. Others help us retrieve information that is already stored. People who are really good at remembering names and phone numbers and other details of experience are generally well practiced at applying strategies.

But what about children? Preschoolers are usually considered nonstrategic in their memory efforts. An interesting example comes from a study of 3- to 8-year-olds who were shown rows of boxes that contained either toy animals or household objects. Boxes with animals had a picture of a cage on top; boxes with household objects had a picture of a house. Children were asked to remember either the locations of the animals or the household objects. The researchers carefully observed the children's actions during a study period, and found that the younger children tended to open all the boxes, whereas the oldest children were more strategic, opening only the boxes with the items that they would have to remember later (animals or objects). In other words, older children selectively attended to the locations that they had to learn about. Younger children did not seem able to use **selective attention** to help them with the memory task (see Miller, 1994).

Selectively attending to one thing and not to another is very difficult for pre-schoolers, and so it is not a skill that 3- or 4-year-olds are likely to deploy to aid memory. But sometimes preschoolers seem to use other skills in ways that we might call "prestrategic." When they know that they will be asked to remember something later, sometimes they do things differently than they might otherwise. For example, researchers gave 4-year-olds a set of toys to play with. They told some children that later they would be asked to remember what some of the toys were. These children tended to play with the toys less and to name them more than children who were not given such instructions (Baker-Ward, Ornstein, & Holden, 1984). So, in other words, they seemed to act in ways that would help them remember.

Systematic use of strategies is much more likely in middle childhood. If you give a group of third graders the job of learning the names of all the states and their capitals, you will probably see them using rehearsal—repeating the names over and over. There are a variety of more complex strategies, but children usually do not use them spontaneously until the late elementary school years or even adolescence. For example, a child could use an **organization strategy**: sorting the items to be learned on some meaningful basis, such as grouping the names by region. Or he might use an **elaboration strategy**—finding or creating some kind of meaningful link between items. To help remember that Baton Rouge is the capital of Louisiana, he might make up a sentence like "Louise saw a bat," or he might create a mental picture, visualizing a girl named Louise with a bat on her head. At about 9 or 10, children will use organization strategies spontaneously and to good effect. Not until adolescence are they likely to use elaboration without prompting. Strategies that are particularly useful for learning textual material, such as underlining and summarizing main ideas or key points, also emerge late, during adolescence (see Schneider & Bjorklund, 1998).

Developmental progress in children's use of memory strategies is a bumpy affair. On one hand, children might at first use a strategy quite sporadically, often showing a **production deficiency**, meaning that they might fail to use it even in situations where it is ordinarily helpful. On the other hand, sometimes children use a strategy, but it does not seem to boost memory; then they are said to have a **utilization deficiency**. Although strategies usually do aid memory performance, when a child first uses a strategy spontaneously, it may be so much work that it takes up a lot of time and attention, minimizing its effectiveness for improving memory. Yet children still may use the strategy. As Siegler (1998) has argued, it's as though children intuitively understand the "law of practice"—that practice improves efficiency in the long run—even if there is no immediate profit!

We have been describing the development of children's spontaneous use of memory strategies, but effective use of strategies can be taught. Children whose parents or teachers instruct them on how to use a strategy are likely to use it on the tasks where they were taught to do so (e.g., Kurtz, Carr, Borkowski, Schneider, & Rellinger, 1990). However, they typically do not generalize the use of a strategy to new situations, and it takes considerable practice to use such strategies efficiently (Pressley & Hilden, 2006).

Metacognitive Skills.   The discussion of memory strategies leads us to a sixth, and final, cognitive change that seems to affect memory. It is the development of **metacognition**, thinking about and awareness of our own mental processes and their effects. Preschoolers have some awareness of mental processes. Four- to 5-year-olds have a theory of mind that includes understanding that their own thoughts, beliefs, and desires often differ from those of other people, as we have seen. They also have some beginning skills at judging what they know. For example, if we show a 4- or 5-year-old a classmate's picture, even if the child cannot spontaneously recall the classmate's name, he will be able to accurately judge whether he would know the name if he heard it (e.g., Cultice, Somerville, & Wellman, 1983). This kind of self-monitoring and understanding of what you can and cannot accomplish cognitively, and how to accomplish it, improves dramatically across the elementary

 Ten-year-old David shows his metacognitive awareness as he talks about and shows his skills at remembering. As he gets older, his estimate of how much he can remember will become more accurate - and with practice and elaboration, his memory strategies will improve as well.

school years. In a classic study, fifth graders understood that remembering the gist of a story is easier than remembering it word for word; only half of kindergartners understood this point. Kindergartners understood some things about memory, such as the value of writing things down if you want to remember them, but not until fifth grade did children realize that there are differences in memory ability from one person to another or from one situation to another (Kreutzer, Leonard, & Flavell, 1975). Many researchers have found that whereas preschoolers are usually overly optimistic about how much they are likely to remember about some material, such as a list of words, older children's estimates are usually much more realistic. This kind of self-knowledge continues to improve past middle childhood. Adolescents produce increasingly accurate depictions of what strategies and approaches are likely to enhance memory in given situations (Schneider & Pressley, 1997). Many theorists have argued that metacognitive awareness at least partially accounts for the increasingly effective use of strategies that develops through middle childhood into adolescence.

One aspect of memory improvement is learning to monitor your own memory and to allocate study time. This is one metacognitive skill that shows little development through elementary school, at least with challenging material. For example, elementary-school-aged children don't often use self-testing when they study. Interestingly, one of the better ways to help children in this age range use memory strategies more effectively is to train them to explicitly monitor what they have learned through techniques such as self-testing (Pressley & Hilden, 2006). In other words, teaching children to keep track of what they have learned seems to be an important element in teaching them how to learn. An important side-benefit to self-testing is that the retrieval practice it provides can actually improve later recall (e.g., Bouwmeester & Verkoeijen, 2011).

So metacognitive development involves improvement in three kinds of knowledge: declarative, or knowledge about facts, rules, or oneself as a learner; procedural, or knowledge about how to apply rules and strategies effectively; and conditional, or knowledge of when to apply the rules or strategies (Schraw & Moshman, 1995). Consider 10-year-old Amelia, who, having missed a day of school, calls a classmate to get her homework assignments. She knows that she must repeat the page numbers or write them down to remember them. She also knows how to organize her homework for each of the various assignments, for example, by showing all computations when solving math problems. She might even understand that she should do her science homework first because it takes the most time, and she may be able to judge when she has studied her spelling words sufficiently. Metacognition is the cornerstone of many clinical and educational practices that are collectively known as **self-instruction** or **self-monitoring** (Meichenbaum, 1986) and a major part of cognitive therapies for children and youth (Kendall, 1993). The general goal of such practices is to effect some behavior change (such as control of impulsivity or improvement in test-taking skills) by attending to, regulating, and sometimes changing cognitions.

This review of memory improvement through middle childhood has, of necessity, touched on many aspects of cognitive development, including advances in processing speed, growth of knowledge, development of logical thinking and language skills, growth of selective attention and other strategic skills, and metacognitive developments. It is clear that "to study memories is to study much of . . . cognition and cognitive development" (Kuhn, 2000a, p. 22). But memory is more than the product of the cognitive system. It is also influenced by affective and social developments. To illustrate the role of affective characteristics, consider the point that was made about the importance of domain knowledge in how well children learn new information in that domain. Indeed, a child will remember new information better than an adult if the child is an expert in that knowledge domain and the adult is not. But how does a child become an expert in some subject, such as chess, or dinosaurs, or baseball? Ability, such as working memory capacity is important (Hambrick & Meinz, 2011), but exceptional intelligence or talent does not determine expertise. The child's interest and motivation, supported and encouraged by training and practice opportunities, are key ingredients (Subotnik, Olszewsk-Kubilius, & Worrell, 2011). Expertise comes from long-lasting attention and practice, not typically from genius (DeLoache, Simcock, & Macari, 2007; Johnson et al., 2004).

To illustrate the role of social factors in memory, consider that adult interactions with children seem to figure critically into the development of memory skill. You have just seen that teaching children strategies for learning new material improves children's memory performance. Encouraging children to narrate their experiences helps them develop better autobiographical memories. In other words, scaffolding by adults, in the Vygotskian sense (see Chapter 3), contributes substantially to memory development and to all aspects of cognitive achievement.

Cognitive Development and Formal Schooling

You will not find it surprising that both the quantity and quality of formal education impacts children's cognitive abilities. Teachers' interactions with children are the proximal source of educational influence (e.g., Goldhaber & Hannaway, 2009; Hamre & Pianta, 2005), but these interactions are shaped partly by the school environment, by the broader community and culture, and by government policies and structures (e.g., Rindermann & Ceci, 2009). These contexts are of course affected by (and affect) many economic and social forces, from wealth and wealth distribution to degree of modernization (e.g., access to electricity, motorized forms of transportation, telecommunications, and so on; Gauvain & Munroe, 2009). In Table 6.1 you will see a list of some characteristics that researchers have repeatedly found to predict cognitive competence and academic achievement across countries and regions of the world.

TABLE 6.1 Educating Cognitively Competent Children: Some Factors Associated with Academic Achievement

Country and Cultural Factors
General educational level of adults
Access to quality preschool education
Kindergarten attendance
Valuing/training of self-regulation
Quantity of instruction per year (including after school/weekend instruction)
Achievement tests and "exit exams"
Low grade retention

School Factors
Strong leadership by principal, headmaster/mistress
Clear mission and vision shared by teachers and staff
Small class sizes
Communication with parents/encouraging parental involvement
Support and respect for multiculturalism
Consistent behavioral expectations for cooperation and courtesy
Adequate teaching materials, physical facilities
Coherent curriculum across grades
Support for teachers' preparation and training

Teacher Factors
Warmth, positive attitudes
Good behavioral management skills
High academic expectations of each child
Tailoring feedback and input to children's needs
Respect and valuing of children's ethnic differences

No single factor operates alone, including those listed in Table 6.1. Multi-dimensional processes are at work, with the impact of each moderated by several others. Student/teacher ratios are a good example. Generally, lower ratios (smaller classes) support better outcomes when other variables are well controlled (e.g., Krueger, 1999). Fewer students in a class allows more individual interactions between teachers and students, more oral participation by children, and a greater likelihood that children's learning problems or other special needs will be recognized and addressed. But the potential advantages of small class size can be reduced by poor teaching or class management. And the disadvantages of large classes can be offset as well. In many East Asian countries, where class size tends to be rather large, children perform very well academically in comparison to many other countries. The negative effects of high student/teacher ratios appear to be balanced by other characteristics, including strong cultural (and family) expectations that children will be self-disciplined and diligent in school (see Box 6.3). Also, it is often customary in East Asian countries to enroll children in private "cram schools" that offer late day and weekend classes, increasing the amount of instruction and learning time children experience. Interestingly, cram school enrollment in East Asian countries goes up as class size in public schools increases (see Rindermann & Ceci, 2009, for a summary of cross-country comparisons).

In general, educational factors that promote children's cognitive and academic growth seem to fall into three broad categories: *quantity, stimulation/engagement, and valuing*. First, there is *quantity*. More time in educational settings is valuable, especially early education in preschool and kindergarten. Another such factor is having access to extra learning opportunities, such as reading or math specialists or tutors, or cram schools. Factors that increase the amount of classroom time that is actually dedicated to instruction and learning, such as good classroom management, are also helpful.

Second, *more stimulating, engaging environments* are important, so that factors like educational level of the family and society matter. Minimal use of grade retention helps to reduce boredom, and small classes make it more likely that each child can be engaged in learning activities that meet his needs, with challenging input and individually tailored feedback. Increased amounts of instruction at school are more stimulating than doing lots of homework alone.

Finally, *valuing learning and valuing the child as learner*. Factors that fit this category include prioritizing education in the culture and the family; having high expectations of each child and believing that challenge and hard work are the keys to success (as opposed to native ability); supports for self-regulation; respecting the value of different backgrounds and interests among learners.

Let's now take a look specifically at the kinds of proximal interactions—between teachers and children—that seem to promote children's cognitive development and academic achievement. Research on children's progress in math will help us illustrate.

In the early preschool years, the typical U.S. child has several number skills. For example, he can count, he knows there is a one-to-one relationship between number word and item when he counts, and he understands that the order in which items are counted is irrelevant (e.g., Gelman, 1982; see also Chapter 3). By late preschool, he has informal arithmetic skills such as adding and subtracting small numbers by using counting strategies, like the **counting all strategy**. For example, given two red blocks and three green ones, he will probably count all the blocks to find out the sum. As children in elementary school are introduced to more formal arithmetic, with its written numbers and standard, stepwise processes (or algorithms) for computation and recording, they continue to use their informal strategies. They also devise more and more strategies, some invented, some derived from what they are taught (e.g., Siegler, 1987). For example, given a simple addition problem such as 3 + 4, they might use a strategy called **counting on**, starting with the first number and counting four more numbers from there. Soon, this strategy is likely to be modified so that the child usually "counts on" from the larger number. As children are exposed repeatedly to addition and subtraction facts, they begin to use the most efficient procedure of all: a **retrieval strategy**, pulling the answer automatically from memory.

Acquiring a store of memorized facts, or a knowledge base, is not only efficient, but it helps children advance in math problem solving. When a small set of facts in addition, subtraction, multiplication, and division is learned so well that retrieval is automatic (e.g., $2 + 2 = 4$), more complex problems become easier to solve, because little or no working memory space needs to be allocated to calculating answers to the simple problems that are always embedded in the harder problems (Willingham, 2009/10).

Some researchers in the information processing tradition have closely followed young school children's progress in discovering and utilizing math strategies. They have found interesting trends that seem to occur across cultures. First, most children use most of the strategies, sometimes using one, sometimes another. Second, children often use a particular strategy on problems where it is especially effective, and more efficient strategies gradually become more predominant. Third, however, even older school children sometimes use less efficient strategies (Siegler, 1998). Thus, it appears that cognitive development moves gradually toward greater efficiency but that less efficient strategies are not entirely abandoned. "Bumpy" progress in strategy use seems to characterize the development of many skills, as we have seen already in memory development. As in memory development, the shift toward using more adequate math strategies, more often, seems to depend partly on metacognitive development—the child's growing understanding of his own strategies and his increasing awareness of how effective those strategies are (Kuhn, 2000b).

As math learning moves beyond the simplest of problems, teachers help children acquire effective strategies by teaching them step-by-step solution procedures (e.g., in adding two digit numbers, if the sum of the first column is a two digit number, carry the tens digit from that sum to the tens column). Children might sometimes construct these more complex procedures themselves but teaching them these strategies helps children progress more efficiently (Willingham, 2009/10).

However, learning procedures is not enough. When children assimilate the procedures they are taught to a limited understanding of mathematics, they sometimes invent strategies that produce errors. In the information processing tradition, flawed strategies are referred to as "bugs." An example would be a boy who does not yet truly understand the base 10 system, but who thinks that one should always subtract the smaller from the larger number. When he is given the problem

$$\begin{array}{r} 21 \\ -\ 5 \\ \hline \end{array}$$

he subtracts the 1 from the 5 and comes up with 24 (Ginsburg, 1989).

In the Piagetian tradition, some research specifically explores developmental changes in what children understand about what they are taught about mathematics. Children's progress in understanding the base 10 system provides a good illustration of the extent to which their mathematical knowledge is constructed (e.g., Kamii, 1986, 1990). If we ask a first grader to count a set of 13 blocks and then write down the answer, he will probably be able to comply. But if we circle the "3" and then ask, "Does this part of your 13 have anything to do with how many blocks there are?" a first grader might say, "No." He thinks that only the whole number 13 tells about the number of blocks. When he's in second grade, he might say that the "3" represents a certain three blocks. When in third grade, he may talk about ones and tens, but is likely to say that the "1" in 13 represents one single item, not 10. By fourth and fifth grades, about half of children recognize that the "1" represents a 10 (example from Kamii, 1990). Thus, although a child typically hears about the base 10 system from first grade onward, he seems to assimilate it to concepts that are not correct and only gradually constructs its true meaning.

Findings such as these on children's understanding of math concepts are a reminder of an important tenet of Piaget's view of education: Teaching children facts or procedures is not sufficient for developing the kind of understanding they will need to truly advance in a subject, as was the case in the round Earth study (Vosniadou & Mason, 2012). Teachers need also to probe children's comprehension. It helps to ask questions such as "Does the '3' have anything to do with how many blocks there are?" Such questions both aid teachers in evaluating what kinds of supports a child might need to understand better and may help children begin to recognize inconsistencies in the meanings they have constructed. This kind of probing can also help teachers establish adequate placements for their students. Care should also be taken in choosing curricular materials and in structuring assessments of students' learning. Without practice and elaboration, advanced or accelerated programs of study may outstrip the abilities of many children and lead them to shallow or rote memorization of facts instead of deep conceptual understanding. Knowledge of facts without conceptual understanding is associated with slower, less accurate problem solving even in the early stages of math learning (Canobi, Reeve, & Pattison, 1998).

Thus, education in math requires, *simultaneously*, practice that promotes memorization of facts, exposure to efficient procedures or strategies, and help discovering the conceptual structure of math that makes the facts and procedures what they are (Willingham, 2009–10). You have just seen that teachers who keep track of what the child can and cannot do can then tailor instruction or suggestion to the child's "region of sensitivity" or zone of proximal development—one step beyond the level at which the child is currently performing. Effective teaching also tends to engage children in activities of many different kinds to promote the kind of conceptual understanding that's needed (e.g., McNeil, Fyfe, Petersen, Dunwiddie, & Brletic-Shipley, 2011). For example, it helps to give children many different and *familiar* examples from their experience (e.g., for fractions, sharing an apple by cutting it into equal parts). As children advance, providing familiar examples might become more difficult, but it is often possible to show them familiar situations that are *analogous* to a concept (e.g., an equation is analogous to a balance scale; if you do the same thing to each side, it stays balanced) (Willingham, 2009–10). Using familiar examples and analogous situations is important because, as Piaget argued, children build new knowledge by starting with what they already know. It is also important to understand that approaching the same concept from many different angles is not about catering to "learning styles." Researchers have found *no evidence* for the popular concept that different people learn differently (e.g., some visually, some kinesthetically, some verbally), although they might have different preferences for how information is presented (Pashler, McDaniel, Rohrer, & Bjork, 2008).

Finally, when teachers treat children with warmth, and they show respect for children's individual and cultural differences, children learn more readily. You will see evidence for the importance of this proximal factor in Box 6.3.

SOCIAL COGNITION

Just as children's knowledge about the physical world and about logical-mathematical concepts becomes more sophisticated with time, so does their understanding of the social world. This latter domain, generally referred to as **social cognition**, has been of great interest to developmentalists for many years. Although the field of social cognition is broad and encompasses many aspects of cognition, it focuses primarily on the ways people think about other people and how they reason about social relationships.

Much of what you have already learned has provided the foundation for, and can be subsumed within, social cognition. As you will recall from earlier chapters, infants and toddlers learn a great deal about social relationships within the context of the attachments they form. The discriminations infants make between objects and people, their diligent attention to caregivers, their capacity for imitation and social referencing, and their early attempts at communication presage knowledge about people and human psychology. Toddlers try to change the behaviors of others, empathize with others' distress, and use emotion words indicating that they have

Box 6.3: Children of Immigrant Families

In the middle of the school year, Elena's family arrived at their new home. On the first day at her new school, Elena's mother left her with the principal, who walked her to her second grade classroom. Her new teacher introduced her to the class, assigned her to a desk, and asked Jenna, who sat in the seat next to her, to help Elena when she had questions. Elena had just turned 8 years old. She was ordinarily shy, and in this classroom she felt nearly paralyzed. Everyone was a stranger. The classroom routine was different from that of her old school, from the order of daily activities to the books used for reading instruction. The teacher was doing a unit on plants with lessons on science and on geography that the class had been working on for 2 weeks, a topic that Elena had never confronted in school before. Only when a math worksheet was distributed with familiar addition and subtraction problems did Elena feel like she might be able to breathe.

Changing schools is hard on any child. But Elena has just arrived in the U.S. with her family from Mexico and she speaks only Spanish. Asking questions of Jenna, even if Jenna sympathizes with Elena's predicament, might not help much with the transition. Elena has become one of the 5.1 million English-language-learner (ELL) students enrolled in U.S. classrooms. The majority of these children are in grades K to 5, and they speak more than 350 different native languages (National Clearinghouse for English Language Acquisition & Language Instruction Educational Programs, 2007). Even though many are born in the U.S., they often have little exposure to English or to American culture prior to the start of school.

A child is considered to be from an immigrant family if at least one parent was born outside of the country of residence (Crosnoe & Fuligni, 2012). In the U.S., over 40% of such children are Hispanic, their parents having migrated largely from Mexico and Central America. Another 14% have parents who migrated from East or South Asia or the Pacific Islands (Jung, Fuller, & Galindo, 2012). Clearly, these children are a diverse group in many ways besides country of origin and native language. Some are the "1.5 generation," meaning they themselves have immigrated, and others are "second generation," born after their parents arrived in the host country; their parents differ in education and job training; for some, both parents have immigrated, for others only one parent; some have a history of exposure to war, famine, or other disasters in their country of origin, others do not; some have legal status in their host country, others do not.

Immigration is not unique to the U.S. It contributes most of the population growth to developed countries around the world, so the needs and developmental progress of immigrant children is a topic of international concern. Leading researchers in this field argue that "international migration is shaping the nature of child development as powerfully as it is changing the nature of the societies involved" (Crosnoe & Fuligni, 2012, p. 1475).

How do children of immigrant families fare? Are they especially vulnerable to academic or social problems because of an accumulation of risk factors (the immigrant risk model)? Or, are they relatively more successful than other children because immigrant families have strengths or protective factors that moderate the risks (the immigrant paradox model)? In fact, researchers find evidence for both models, and they are beginning to untangle the factors that contribute to vulnerability versus advantage. The circumstances that lead to migration are important. The characteristics of the country of origin and of the family (e.g., religious values, family size and structure, parents' education) are important. Finally, the family's circumstances in the host country are important, such as their socioeconomic status, job opportunities, social supports, available schools, diversity within schools and communities, and racial/ethnic tolerance and discrimination patterns. Let's consider how some of these factors relate to children's outcomes, especially their cognitive and academic outcomes.

Children's Health

Children's health is a key element in their cognitive development, so understanding whether immigrant status impacts health and health care is important. In the U.S., when children from Hispanic immigrant families are compared to native children they are often advantaged in physical and mental health, a paradoxical outcome given they are more likely to be socioeconomically disadvantaged (e.g., Markides & Coreil, 1986). Children born to immigrant Hispanic mothers in the U.S. have fewer birth problems (e.g., lower infant mortality rates, less frequent low birth weight) and fewer acute and chronic illnesses (e.g., asthma). Among the family differences that might account for these health advantages are higher rates of breast feeding among foreign born mothers, a greater tendency to fully immunize their children, and lower smoking rates (e.g., Kimbro, Lynch, & McLanahan, 2008; Jackson, Kiernan, & McLanahan, 2012). Interestingly, one study found many similar health advantages for children of immigrant families in the United Kingdom, even though they tended to migrate from different parts of the world (Jackson et al., 2012). However, in the U.S. at least, the continuing health of children varies depending on the immigration status of the parents even when comparing only low income families (Ziol-Guest & Kalil, 2012). Children of naturalized citizens tend to do quite well; children whose parents are non-naturalized (either permanent or non-permanent residents) are less likely to be in very good or excellent health as reported by their mothers. This difference corresponds to the likelihood that children are receiving regular dental or medical care. It appears that non-naturalized parents are less likely to have health insurance or to take advantage of health care programs even though their children may be entitled to them. This could happen for many reasons. Language barriers may make it difficult for parents to access information or find suitable health care providers; parents may misunderstand the consequences of seeking assistance for eligible children (e.g., worrying that it might affect their efforts to become citizens or to attain permanent residency); or if some householders do not have legal status, parents may be reluctant to call attention to themselves (Yoshikawa & Kalil, 2011).

Results are mixed on mental health. Some studies have reported better outcomes for children of low income immigrant families compared to children of low income native families (e.g., Crosnoe, 2006), but others have not. It may depend on the kind of behavioral outcomes that are examined. One study found fewer externalizing

(Box 6.3 continued)

Box 6.3 *Continued*

problems but more internalizing problems for immigrant children (Jackson et al., 2012).

Family Function

Much of what you have read in earlier chapters demonstrates that how families function, including their parenting practices, can affect every area of child development. Family functioning varies widely among immigrant families. Differences in migration and demographic history and related cultural practices are important influences. For example, among immigrants to the U.S., births to unmarried mothers are much more common for Mexicans (46% of births in 2006) than for Asians (11% in 2006). South Asian parents are more likely than Mexican parents to have completed high school and to be fluent in English. These and other differences influence the likelihood that families will live in poverty once in the U.S. Approximately 33% of Mexican families but only 8% of South Asian families live in poverty (Jung et al., 2012).

You are already aware of how problematic the stress of poverty can be for children's development in many domains. Yet immigrant families may buffer the negative effects of poverty on children in some ways. For example, "core socialization norms" in many Hispanic families emphasize "good comportment and respectful communication . . . cooperation and caring for peers . . . and the children's contribution to the collective interest of the family . . . " (Galindo & Fuller, 2010, p. 581). Immigrant Hispanic mothers also tend to describe themselves as mentally healthy (e.g., reporting low levels of depression), perhaps in part because they often feel that they have good social support (either from fathers or other family members) (Jung et al., 2012). Children from such families enter school with academically useful social competencies, such as self-control and low levels of aggressiveness. Kindergarten teachers tend to rate the social-emotional functioning of children from Hispanic immigrant families somewhat lower than children from White native families, but the differences are quite small (Galindo & Fuller, 2010). Different cultural expectations rather than problematic parenting seem to account for the slightly lower ratings. Hispanic children, who are taught not to pose questions to elders as part of respectful behavior, may seem less socially competent to U.S. teachers who value more verbal engagement and inquisitiveness.

Immigrant families are quite divergent with regard to practices that specifically prepare children for formal schooling. Country of origin makes a big difference here (e.g., Rindermann & Ceci, 2009). One large study found that Mexican immigrant mothers read to their preschool children less frequently, but Chinese mothers read more often, than native White mothers (Jung et al., 2012). Differences in parents' education might be key to this finding, because only 33% of the Mexican mothers had more than a high school education, whereas 93% of Chinese mothers did. However, even if Asian parents have very little education, their cultural beliefs and practices appear to be especially helpful for their children's academic lives. They tend to view intellectual achievements as a function of hard work, whereas many other groups (e.g., native White families) see intelligence as a fixed capacity. In Chinese and other South Asian groups, a "learning model" is typically the highest cultural value, meaning that learning is seen as bringing "honor, respect, and everything good in life" (Li, Holloway, Bempechat, & Loh, 2008, p. 12). Typically, Chinese immigrant parents with little education or income are especially focused on promoting their children's learning opportunities; for example, they may work extra jobs and longer hours so that their children can attend Chinese school on weekends. They correspondingly expect their children to work hard; commitment to academic excellence is "nonnegotiable." Interestingly, low income Chinese parents are unlikely to be involved in their children's school activities (such as helping with homework) because of long work hours and/or lack of the necessary language or academic skills, but they frequently designate an "anchor helper" for that purpose such as an older sibling or other relative. They also encourage their children to emulate peers who are academically successful, holding them up as role models. And extended family members are expected to "co-parent," reinforcing the value of school achievement, checking up on grades, offering assistance, even if they do not live nearby. As one child of Chinese immigrants said, "My grandparents call a lot; they always ask me how I'm doing in school . . . my entire family, I think they're the most concerned about grades, cause whenever they call, it's always about school . . . They call twice a week from Australia" (Li et al., 2008, p. 21). Perhaps because of the emphasis on learning in their culture, children of Chinese immigrants often perform better in school on average than native White children in the same socioeconomic circumstances.

Supporting Immigrant Children in Schools and Communities

Let's focus now specifically on the academic achievement of the children of immigrant families. You have just seen that the cultural values of the country of origin are important for children's school performance. You have also seen that parenting practices that ready children for school success, like reading to young children, are often related to parents' education. Not surprisingly, parents' education before migration is strongly related to children's academic achievement in the host country (e.g., Pong & Landale, 2012). Cultural valuing of academic success and parent education are protective factors, buffering or moderating the impact of more negative factors such as low income.

One negative factor for children of some immigrant groups is the pattern of prejudice and discrimination they might face in the host country. Discrimination is the experience of negative treatment because of group membership, and it can be from peers (e.g., teasing or exclusion), from teachers (e.g., expecting poor performance, grading unfairly, treating children as troublemakers, ignoring or isolating them), or from community members (e.g., preferring residential segregation) (Brown & Chu, 2012). Children who perceive discriminatory behavior by teachers and/or peers are often less likely to stay interested in school and to perform at their best. "Weak relations with teachers diminish students' motivation to pursue academic work, and in turn lower teachers' expectations in a self-perpetuating cycle of academic disengagement and under-achievement" (Tienda & Mitchell, 2006, p. 85). Conversely, when teachers maintain high academic expectations for *all* their students and value multiculturalism in the classroom, freely discussing cultural differences and creating an environment of respect, children perceive less discrimination not only from their teachers, but also from their peers, and they are more likely to succeed in school (e.g., Brown & Chu, 2012).

Having a strong sense of their own ethnic identity is a protective factor for children, even buffering the negative effects of perceived discrimination (Garcia, Coll, & Marks, 2009). Positive ethnic identity includes seeing your ethnicity as a central aspect of who you are and positively valuing that aspect of yourself (see Chapter 9 for a more in depth discussion). From elementary school onward, children with positive ethnic identities are more academically motivated and more likely to do well in school. This is especially important in schools where children from immigrant families are in the minority. In schools where immigrant children are in the majority, such as predominantly Hispanic schools in parts of the U.S., perceived discrimination and positive ethnic identity are not especially predictive of academic outcome (Brown & Chu, 2012; Greene, Way, & Pahl, 2006).

This brings us to a central, and contentious, factor in immigrant children's academic success: language. Many children from immigrant families are ELL students. In the U.S., they may enter school with no knowledge of English or they may have some facility in English in addition to their native language. Generally, ELL students, especially from Hispanic families, perform more poorly than native White children academically when they begin school in the U.S. Common sense

suggests that helping these children become proficient in English, the language of the classroom and of most tests, should be a high priority. But should they be immersed in all-English classes? Should their families encourage them to speak only English at home?

The most recent research suggests that ELL children are most academically successful when schools and families encourage their bilingualism, helping them to learn English while maintaining or building fluency in the family's native language. What is most effective is teaching children in both their native language and English at school, and encouraging them to use their native language at home. First, there are important cognitive advantages to bilingualism, as you have seen, including greater cognitive flexibility and better executive functioning. Second, children who continue to use their native language maintain strong connections with their families and ethnic communities, supporting a positive ethnic identity, which we have just seen is important for academic motivation. " . . . Language congruence may enhance the parent-child relationship, and, in turn . . . have great implications for children's motivation to succeed academically" (Han, 2012, p. 301). Bilingual education in schools has the best track record across immigrant groups and academic competencies in promoting ELL students' performance. One study reviewed the records of 700,000 U.S. students, comparing outcomes of ELL children in a wide range of programs (e.g., English as a Second Language [ESL] programs, pullout programs, transitional bilingual education, and so on). Four- to seven years of bilingual education and support yielded the best results by far, with early academic gaps tending to disappear and children outperforming their native English speaking peers over time (Collier & Thomas, 2004).

explicit knowledge of others' mental states (Zahn-Waxler, Radke-Yarrow, Wagner, & Chapman, 1992). These skills suggest that infants and young children are in the process of learning about social interactions almost from birth.

Studies of the young child's theory of mind focus on aspects of social cognition, addressing questions such as "When does the child come to understand that the other has a mind?" and "How does the child use information about mental states to understand people and social relationships?" We have already seen that by their fifth birthday most children realize that others often have different thoughts and beliefs from their own. For example, they now succeed on false belief tasks in which they must anticipate that a person who has not had the opportunity to see an object moved from its original hiding place to a new location might have a false belief about the object's whereabouts (e.g., Wimmer & Perner, 1983; see also Chapter 3). Success on false belief tasks has been related to reciprocal communication with peers (Slomkowski & Dunn, 1996) and to the ability to communicate about internal mental states with friends (Hughes & Dunn, 1998). Researchers are thus finding links between early cognitive social understanding and children's social relationships (see Dunn, 2004; Harris, 2006). Social cognitive research with school-aged children typically deals with the quality of children's understanding of the nature of other peoples' thoughts, feelings, and desires. Studies have examined theories of children's friendships, methods of conflict resolution, and the developing understanding of social rules and interactions that are central facets of both.

No one has to convince helping professionals that the dynamics of social relationships are important ones to understand. Although not every social relationship can be considered a friendship, it can be argued that the special relationships we have with friends teach us about human relationships in general. During the middle years, friendships take on enormous importance for children. Indeed, for school-aged children being reared in difficult circumstances, having a good friend serves as a protective factor, moderating some environmental risks. For example, in the Virginia Longitudinal Study of Child Maltreatment (see Bolger & Patterson, 2003), 107 children who were abused or neglected were identified through state social service records from a larger sample of 1,920 public school children. Most of the maltreated children were at risk in other ways as well. For example, 92% had low enough family incomes that they qualified for federal food subsidies of some kind. During the course of the study, children were asked whether they had a best friend, and their friend choices were compared to verify that they were reciprocated. Among the measures collected over time were assessments of the children's self-esteem. Using the Self-Perception Profile (Harter, 1985), children rated their own competence in a variety of domains. As you might expect, maltreated children perceived themselves as less competent than children who had no history of abuse or neglect. But maltreated children with a reciprocal friend showed substantial gains in self-esteem from grade 3 to grade 5, gains that were maintained through grade 7, and on average they were doing about as well on self-esteem as other children. Unfortunately, maltreated children who did not have a best friend showed declines in self-esteem across the years of middle childhood.

Any child's difficulties in making and keeping friends can consume much of a helping professional's time because of the far-reaching consequences of poor peer relationships and inadequate conflict resolution skills on emotional well-being, academic achievement, and behavior. What is important for helpers to understand is that the skills of friendship are not just behavioral but are heavily dependent on cognitive development. Similarly, problems in social relations may be heavily influenced by limitations in social cognitive skills. In this section, we will introduce some major theoretical approaches to friendship development that have a basis in cognitive developmental theory. In Chapter 7, the research on larger peer group interaction and peer group status will be reviewed.

Perspective Taking and Social Relationships

The idea that satisfactory social relationships are important in the overall picture of adjustment enjoys unanimous support from developmentalists of every theoretical persuasion. Social relationships are necessary for the child to gain experience in learning about others' points of view (Piaget, 1932/1965). They contribute to the child's sense of security and connectedness (Berndt, 1982), and foster the development of the self-concept (Mead, 1934). These three benefits are not as separate as they may seem but are, instead, three highly interconnected outcomes of positive social contact.

Recall for a moment what has been presented in earlier chapters about the development of the self. Self-concept has been defined by symbolic interactionist thinkers such as Mead as the individual's perception of himself that develops from the collective accumulation of social experiences. It is as if the individual proceeds through life viewing himself in the looking glass of other people's eyes. But remember as well that this process is not simply a passive reception of information. Rather, it involves the complicated consideration of the perspectives of other people. Mead believed that to define oneself, a person needs to put himself, metaphorically, in another person's shoes and then consider his own actions in the light of that alternative perspective. This uniquely human operation, which lies at the heart of self-recognition and self-knowledge, has been called **perspective taking**, and no relationship survives for very long without it.

The cognitively complex skill of perspective taking develops gradually as children mature, much in the same way that other cognitive abilities change and improve (see Miller, 2012, for a review of research). You have already read that very young children are considered egocentric insofar as they are embedded in their own perspective. In Piaget's view, the ability to decenter, meaning in this case the ability to recognize and hold in mind more than one perspective, is enhanced by repeated interactions with others. When children decenter, they understand that others have minds that are different from theirs and that minds may be coordinated in the service of mutual understanding and problem solving. Implicit in this level of awareness is the cognitive ability to engage in relationships marked by intimacy and mutuality and to solve problems in ways that consider the interests of all parties.

How does such an immensely desirable skill as perspective taking develop and improve? Some of the earliest ideas on the subject stem from Piaget's writing. He believed that about the time children enter elementary school in industrialized cultures, they are forced to consider other children's viewpoints to survive the normal give-and-take of the classroom community structure. Before then, children may have been able to rely on parents' or other family members' willingness to meet their egocentric needs and to understand their egocentric communication. Peers are typically less willing and able to do so. The child in elementary school, or even before, is forced to clarify his thoughts and adopt better communication skills in order to be accepted by peers. The major and minor conflicts that accompany this process are viewed as essential to a developing awareness of perspectives other than one's own (Flavell, 1963; Piaget, 1928).

This achievement does not mean, however, that children are now free of egocentrism altogether, as we saw earlier in this chapter. Every developmental stage has its own form of this quintessentially human weakness. Even adults are not exempt because specific forms of egocentric thinking appear to be a normal by-product of cognitive advances.

> The transition from one form of egocentrism to another takes place in a dialectical fashion in such a manner that the cognitive structures that free a child from a lower form of egocentrism are the same structures that entangle him in a higher egocentric form. (Looft, 1972, p. 77)

In fact, Looft, paraphrasing Piaget, describes egocentrism as the "central problem in the history of human affairs" (Looft, p. 73). Despite the fact that seeing the world and relationships egocentrically is an inevitable part of the human condition, maturity reduces this tendency to some degree. Friendships play a particularly significant role in this process.

Perspective Taking and Friendship Development

In one of the early theories of friendship development, Sullivan (1953) reiterated the Piagetian perspective that children need interpersonal contact in order to reduce egocentrism and promote altruism. Although very young children, in the "childhood era" according to Sullivan, primarily depend on parents for reflected appraisals of themselves, children's dependence on playmates becomes more important as they enter the "juvenile period" around age 4. However socialized some interactive behaviors (such as sharing, conformity, and expressions of sympathy) may appear at this age, these behaviors are not yet truly altruistic but are demonstrated for the egocentric purpose of gaining acceptance or building popularity in the larger peer group. A major transformation occurs around age 8, when children enter the stage Sullivan called "preadolescence." During this period, children's needs for increased interpersonal intimacy are met through the establishment of an intense, focused interest in same-sex age-mates or "chums." These relationships teach preadolescents that the needs and perspectives of other persons must be considered as carefully as their own. Seeing one's preadolescent self reflected back in the context of a "chumship" permits the validation of one's thoughts, feelings, and beliefs as well as a more

 For 8-year-old Kate, friends are not just playmates; they also provide help and support when it's needed. She points out how important it is to include a new friend in activities and to "be nice," even when they disagree.

realistic appraisal of oneself. Thus, the egocentrism of the juvenile period diminishes as the child learns to see the world through the eyes of a friend. Because the transition through early adolescence is not without its stresses and strains, attachment to a close friend or chum can function as a secure base, permitting the young person to navigate the many changes inherent in the adolescent transition without feeling totally isolated. Let's try to understand more about the primary cognitive ingredient needed for successful friendship development, perspective taking.

Many writers have documented children's maturing ability to take the perspective of their friends and to communicate this understanding in increasingly more sophisticated ways (Flavell, Botkin, Fry, Wright, & Jarvis, 1968). Possibly the most elegantly developed theory linking perspective taking with actual friendship development has been provided by Robert Selman (1980; 2008). Building on a Piagetian framework, Selman identified five stages in the development of perspective taking, beginning at preschool age and continuing though adolescence. Each level of perspective-taking skill is linked to a different level of friendship or shared experience, as well as to a different level of conflict resolution (see Table 6.2). Selman's theory highlights the tight interconnections among one's ability to understand others (perspective taking), one's needs for intimacy in relationship (friendship), one's skill in balancing personal needs without sacrificing the relationship (autonomy), and one's ability to solve conflicts (conflict resolution).

Think for a moment about your own close friendships. Regardless of how overtly agreeable or conflictual these relationships may be, there is always a tension between "what is good for me versus what is good for us" (Barr, 1997, p. 32). No friendship is immune to this underlying dynamic, which surfaces from time to time over the course of the relationship. To sustain friendships, friends must be able to coordinate both individuals' needs and resolve the inevitable conflicts that arise in ways that are mutually agreeable. Any imbalance, such as too much coercion from one partner and too little assertiveness from the other, can undermine the friendship in the long run. In other words, ineffective management of the dysynchrony between the needs of the individual and the needs of the pair puts the friendship at risk. Healthy friendships are marked by mutual give-and-take, allowing both partners to feel affirmed, understood, and respected.

If all this seems too good to be true, let us hasten to say that friendships, even in adulthood, are true "works in progress" that require mutual coordination of perspectives and ongoing balancing of needs. Imagine how short-lived a friendship would be if you typically perceived your friend's momentary insensitivity or inability to participate in some shared activity as a personal insult directed toward you. Your understanding that he might be overextended and thus under stress can help you

TABLE 6.2 Selman's Stages of Friendship and Levels of Perspective-Taking Skills

STAGE	APPROXIMATE AGES	FORMS OF SHARED EXPERIENCE	SOCIAL PERSPECTIVE TAKING	INTERPERSONAL NEGOTIATION STRATEGIES
0	3 to 6 years	Unreflective imitation or enmeshment	Undifferentiated/Egocentric	Physical force; impulsive fight or flight
1	5 to 9 years	Unreflective sharing of expressive enthusiasm	Differentiated/Subjective	One-way, unilateral power; orders or obedience
2	8 to 12 years	Reflective sharing of similar perceptions or experiences	Reciprocal/Self-Reflective	Cooperative exchange; reciprocity; persuasion or deference
3	10 to 15 years	Empathic sharing of beliefs and values	Mutual/Third-Person	Mutual compromise
4	Late teen/adulthood	Interdependent sharing of vulnerabilities and self	Intimate/In-Depth/Societal (generalized other)	Collaborative integration of relationship dynamics (commitment)

SOURCE: Selman, R. L., Watts, C. L., & Schultz, L. H. (1997). *Fostering friendship: Pair therapy for treatment and prevention.* New York, NY: Walter de Gruyter, Inc. Reprinted with permission.

take a more empathic perspective, despite your own disappointment. Children find this harder to do because they are essentially practicing their perspective-taking and other friendship skills. Hurts, betrayals, and conflicts will almost inevitably accompany their friendship development as they struggle to learn to compromise, compete, and cooperate in a civil way. Without this sometimes painful experience, however, children may not learn the intimacy and autonomy strategies they need to reap the benefits of satisfying friendships throughout their lifetimes. Helping professionals who are knowledgeable about the nature of friendship development are in a unique position to facilitate children's progress in this area.

Selman's Stages of Friendship Development

Selman (1980) provides a stagewise description of the development of children's friendship skills. As with other stage theories, the age ranges are only rough approximations. What is most important is the sequence and nature of the developmental change. Stage 0, or the "Undifferentiated/Egocentrism" stage, is typically manifested in preschool children before about age 5, when perspective-taking capacity is quite limited. Youngsters at Stage 0 have little appreciation for the thoughts and feelings of either themselves or others. Friendship is defined in very concrete terms, without an understanding of the other person's psychology. For example, a preschool child might define a friend as someone who lives next to you, who gives you gifts, who shares toys with you, or who likes you. Young children typically establish friendships with children who are like themselves in concrete ways, such as age, gender, race, and ethnicity (see Kawabata & Crick, 2008; Rubin & Coplan, 1992). Conflicts between friends are not perceived as disagreements that occur between two parties with two different and legitimate points of view but are viewed as struggles to get one's own way. Lacking much ability to consider another's perspective, children typically resort to flight ("Go away!") or fight ("I'll get you!") strategies to resolve conflicts as they seek to preserve their interests.

In Stage 1, the "Differentiated/Subjective" stage, children from about 5 to about 9 come to understand that others have viewpoints that are different from their own, but they are generally not able to coordinate these perspectives simultaneously. In other words, they can't maintain their own perspective and that of someone else at the same time. So even though they understand that their peers have different points of view, they still may act as though their own perspective or that of an "authority" is correct. They are able to understand, for example, that they can be the subject of another's thoughts, but they generally do not have the capacity to judge how their behavior is being evaluated by that other person. Dyami, for instance, might understand that his friend Kono has a viewpoint or a perspective on him, but Dyami has little insight into what Kono's view of him is really like. We might say that interpersonal perspective at this age is unilateral or one-way. Yet during this period children do become better able to infer the thoughts and feelings of others, especially when they are encouraged to reflect on them. The child's understanding of physical experience, however, is another thing altogether. In the behavioral realm, two-way reciprocity ("You hit me and I hit you back") is readily understood.

On the psychological level, friendship is still largely a one-way proposition. The child at Stage 1 may understand his own psychological perspective but may fail to do the same for his friend. In other words, friendships may be defined by the behavioral and psychological rewards they provide for the individual child and not in terms of the mutual satisfaction afforded both members of the dyad. Eight-year-old Pavla might describe a friend as someone who helps her with her homework, doesn't fight with her, and doesn't walk away from her when she's upset. Notice the mix of behavioral (homework help) and psychological (social support) characteristics that are directed toward the benefit of one person. Conflicts are also viewed as one-way propositions. The responsibility to resolve a conflict is in the hands of the person who was perceived to have initiated it. There is little understanding of problem solving by mutual consensus.

At Stage 2, the "Reciprocal/Self-Reflective" stage, older children master a critical developmental task. Between late childhood and early adolescence (about 8 to 12), they become more cognizant of the perspectives of others and learn to put themselves in another's place as a way of evaluating intentions and actions. Children can now actually assume the psychological position of another and reflect on their own behavior and motivation as perceived by someone else. Eleven-year-old Keisha, who doesn't really want to go swimming at her friend Amber's house because she'd prefer to spend the afternoon watching TV, might agree to go anyway. Keisha, seeing Amber as a person who is rather easily hurt, reasons that if she declines the invitation, Amber might think that Keisha doesn't like her or that she doesn't want to be her friend. This more sophisticated level of perspective-taking ability reflects two-way reciprocity ("I think; you think").

At this stage, children can grasp more highly differentiated patterns of motivations and emotions and make finer discriminations between thoughts and feelings. They can conceive of the fact that people, including themselves, can experience conflicting motives and feelings and can feel one thing but act in a completely different way. In our earlier example, Keisha wants to spend some time alone but she also wants to preserve her friendship with Amber. She may simultaneously feel liking and impatience toward her friend. She may decide to go swimming and cover up her true feelings of disinterest in the activity. Conflict resolution between children at this stage reflects the growing awareness that both parties must give a little to reach a solution.

At Stage 3, the "Mutual/Third-Person" stage, adolescents of about 10 to 15 learn to view each other's perspectives simultaneously and mutually. Rather than simply viewing each other's perspective in a back-and-forth approach ("first me, then you"), adolescents can mentally step back to take the perspective of a "third-party observer" even as they themselves remain a member of the pair. What this allows is a more detached view of the proceedings, somewhat like the way a disinterested spectator might construe a social interaction. Egocentrism is further reduced insofar as the adolescent can view the interchange between himself and his friend and reflect on it from the outside looking in.

Friendship at this stage is characterized by mutual support and shared intimacy and not seen just as a means of obtaining what either party desires as an individual. Consequently, conflict resolution strategies are marked by more attention to the mutuality of the relationship. There is an awareness that problems do not always reside within one of the participants but that they are the responsibility of both parties to address. Harmonious resolution of the conflicts that are inevitable in relationships is perceived to strengthen both parties' commitment to that relationship. Adolescents at this stage are more capable of understanding that a friendship could break down because "it just didn't work out between us" rather than because "she wasn't nice to me."

Finally, at Stage 4, the "Intimate/In-Depth/Societal" stage, older adolescents and adults learn to adopt the perspective of the larger society. Perspective-taking ability becomes more abstract and complex. Now the individual can assume the perspective of people beyond the limits of the dyad, namely that of a larger social group. This achievement makes possible the understanding of cultural and other group differences and the increasing appreciation of relativity—that no one person's or one group's perspective is necessarily the only correct one regardless of how deeply valued it might be. Relationships are marked by the individual's increasing ability to balance his needs for intimacy and autonomy while still preserving the friendship. With each new level of perspective-taking skill, understanding of friendship improves, interpersonal values are clarified, and social and conflict resolution skills are refined.

A Framework for Friendship

Perspective taking is an important part of social relatedness, but it is not the only determinant. We should now consider how the understanding of others' perspectives is integrated with other skills and tied to actual success in making and keeping friends. Is there a comprehensive way to look at the nature of friendship competence in children? The following friendship framework, which integrates a number of ingredients, has been proposed by Selman and his associates (Selman, Levitt, & Schultz, 1997) as one possible comprehensive model. We have chosen to describe this model in some depth because it represents a good example of a theoretical framework that lends itself to clinical applications that are developmentally sensitive. An understanding of the elements of this model can help you assess relative strengths and weaknesses in a child's social relatedness and help you choose relevant interventions.

As always, nature and nurture provide the backdrop for the child's social functioning. For example, one child's predisposition toward shyness or another child's day-to-day experience of parental discord can have some effect on the children's capacities to enter and sustain social relationships with others. In certain situations, the effects of nature or nurture are so pronounced that they make independent contributions to social functioning, as in the case of a child who lacks friends because he lives in an isolated environment. These effects are represented by dotted lines leading directly to friendship outcomes from Nature and Nurture in Figure 6.4.

What is more typical, however, is that the effects of nature and nurture are integrated with a third area of influence called **psychosocial development**. This has been defined as "the internal psychological processes of interpersonal understanding, skills, and values that comprise an individual's capacity for interpersonal relationships, including friendships" (Selman et al., 1997, p. 35). **Friendship understanding** refers to a child's changing knowledge of what friendship implies. **Friendship skills** are behavioral skills, such as appropriate assertiveness, good communication, and conflict resolution, that maintain and enhance friendships. **Friendship valuing** describes the emotional attachment or investment that the child makes in a friendship. Each of these three components is influenced and informed by developmental changes in the child's perspective-taking ability. In other

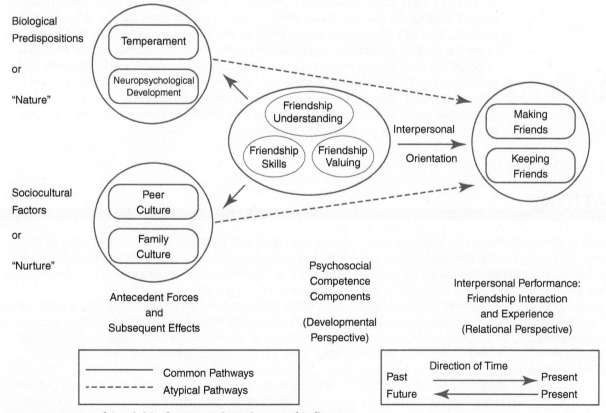

FIGURE 6.4   A friendship framework: Spheres of influence.
SOURCE: Selman, R. L., Watts, C. L., & Schultz, L. H. (1997). *Fostering friendship: Pair therapy for treatment and prevention.* New York, NY: Walter de Gruyter, Inc. Reprinted with permission.

words, competence in these three areas will be delimited by a child's cognitive understanding of interpersonal relationships.

To work effectively, helpers need to appreciate what can be reasonably expected from children at each stage of their development. Teaching appropriate social skills, such as making eye contact and communicating effectively, may be irrelevant for children whose level of friendship understanding is very egocentric or for a child who is not particularly interested in being friendly toward another member of his class. On the other hand, learning how to solve conflicts effectively may be very helpful for a child who is invested in a friendship. All three dimensions need to be considered therapeutically so that interventions can get targeted accurately.

There is one other important element in this model, linking the child's psychosocial competencies to his interpersonal performance (see Figure 6.4). This bridge is the child's **interpersonal orientation**, or the way the child characteristically interacts on a social level. The most mature interpersonal style is characterized by a flexible balance between intimacy and autonomy strivings. Less effective orientations, as identified by Selman, are **"other-transforming"** and **"self-transforming"** social interaction styles.

A child with an other-transforming style characteristically tries to dominate or coerce a friend into meeting his needs. He acts to change or transform the other and can be bullying, aggressive, or manipulative. A child with a self-transforming style typically gives in to reduce the level of tension. He changes his own behaviors or feelings to conform. Selman and Schultz (1990) found that very young children or socially immature older children tend to behave in these extreme ways. Such children are both more labile than other children, sometimes moving from victim to victimizer position depending on the relationship, and more rigid, refusing to compromise their position once established, even at the risk of losing the friendship.

What does it mean for a child to be bossy, impulsive, stubborn, passive, or shy? On its face, each label might prescribe a certain kind of intervention: self-control training for the impulsive child, assertiveness training for the shy one, and so forth. Selman's theoretical model gives us the means to go beyond this level of understanding to unpack the fundamental psychosocial competencies that the child depends on to engage in any social interaction. From this perspective, the bully and the victim can be functioning at the same developmental level of friendship knowledge, skills, and valuing, only using different personal orientations. Assessment of the fundamental properties that underlie friendship expression can be a helpful means of addressing interpersonal problems.

APPLICATIONS

The middle years of childhood are marked by major advances in reasoning, in memory, and in the comprehension of many domains, including social relationships. From infancy, the child has been navigating the social world, moving from early attachment relationships to the gradually enlarging network of peers in the school setting. There are some fundamental linkages between these early relationships and children's later social interactions. For example, caregivers' encouraging preschool children to take notice of others' perspectives has been related to empathy, good social problem solving, and perspective taking at school age (Dixon & Moore, 1990). Success in relating to others rests on having a positive internal working model for social responding, having access to peers in settings that promote mutual respect, and knowing how to resolve conflicts, among other things. And,

as we have seen in this chapter, cognitive developments contribute importantly to children's social success at this time. Children in the school years need to be successful in the classroom as well as on the playground.

Much progress has been made in understanding the ways children process, store, and retrieve information because of the explosion of research in the area of cognitive psychology. Noting a few general implications may be useful for helpers.

1. Knowledge acquisition is a constructive process, built on the foundation of prior learning and experience. Children benefit from instruction that organizes information, relates it to previously learned material, and stresses its meaningfulness. Too many children, critics have noted, are taught

in ways that reflect an emphasis on rote memorization of facts without any fundamental understanding of concepts.

2. Good instructional practice, including psychoeducational training, involves five basic elements: gaining the child's attention and motivation; activating what the child already knows about the material to be taught, such as using familiar examples or analogies; presenting the new material in many ways; providing adequate, meaningful, and interesting practice to ensure retention; and giving task-specific feedback that scaffolds the child's progress.

3. When adults teach children how to use memory strategies such as chunking, children retain more information. Children can also be encouraged to encode information both visually and verbally to capitalize on the way the mind processes material.

4. Students can also benefit from the use of techniques such as cooperative learning, if teachers or group leaders offer children opportunities to learn how to work effectively together. Encouraging children to talk over their ideas and providing them with techniques for doing so seems to be helpful. Keeping track of their progress and giving them feedback is also important. Cooperative methods should also incorporate some form of individual accountability as well as group recognition for goals achieved (Slavin, 1995).

5. Keep in mind that normal cognitive development is uneven. Theories of development have suffered, to some degree, from their emphasis on stages, because this emphasis leads to perceptions of development in terms of static, monolithic levels. In the real world, children as well as adults are much more variable. Despite the common conception that Piaget emphasized stagewise development, he also recognized that variation in skill exists within stages. Specifically, he found that logical skills were applied to some contents (such as understanding conservation of number) before other contents (such as understanding conservation of weight). This variation he called décalage. This kind of variability in skill level is clearly evident in any classroom. Some may excel in reading and language arts yet find math a chore. Others may be gifted athletes who have difficulty remembering facts in social studies. Isn't such unevenness characteristic of adults as well? Most people's panorama of abilities reflects a mix of relative strengths and weaknesses.

6. Unevenness in development may be particularly relevant to the area of special education and the concept of disability. Some authors, notably Sternberg and Grigorenko (1999), contend that virtually everyone has a disability in something. The difference is that society determines what constitutes "disability" and identifies a select group as "disabled." Within schools, weaknesses in analytical ability, an important skill for success in most academic subject areas, may be considered particularly problematic. Yet, most contemporary theories of intelligence recognize the fact that intelligence is characterized by many kinds of skills (e.g., Gardner, 1983; Sternberg, 1985).

In Sternberg's (1985) theoretical formulation, traditional analytic ability is just one part of the whole picture of intelligence. He includes creative and practical aspects of intelligence in the mix and recommends that teachers provide opportunities for students to manifest these other abilities, as a supplement to more traditional forms of teaching and assessment. For example, developing skits, creating poetry or pictures, designing experiments, establishing classroom government, or running a school store are all activities that tap creative and practical intelligence, which may be areas of relative strength or interest for students.

Tracking each child's task understanding helps teachers tailor their instruction effectively.

Assessing and Teaching Metacognitive Skills

Despite typical age-related limitations in children's abilities to reflect on their thinking, metacognitive advances do emerge during this period and open up a range of clinical possibilities. The major elements of metacognition, ability to appraise one's own thinking and ability to regulate one's own thinking, have great relevance for educational and clinical efforts to improve skills like problem-solving and perspective-taking. The role of distorted cognitions in mental health problems is also very well known to clinicians, so understanding children's self-statements can be important in this regard.

As noted above, the first component of metacognition is knowing what one is thinking. Several means of assessing cognition have been used in research, including asking people what they say to themselves while they are currently thinking about some task (called "self-talk"), asking them what they were thinking after they completed the task (called "thought-listing") or, after videotaping an activity and replaying the video, asking them to "dub" the self-talk (called "video-mediated recall"). The purpose of these techniques is to open a window on the thinking process. Lodge, Tripp, and Harte (2000) demonstrated that think-aloud and video-mediated recall, compared to thought-listing, resulted in the most productive record of self-talk among third- and fourth-grade children. A self-talk instruction might be "When you read this short paragraph [or work on this problem], just remember to say out loud all the things that come into your head." The use of self-talk can help the helper understand how the child understands a particular situation or problem, how he makes attributions about the problem, and how he goes about solving the problem.

The areas of study skills training, academic counseling, or tutoring also depend on a working knowledge of children's cognition. Counselors can attempt to appraise thinking by informal assessment of memory as described in this chapter. In the case of underachievement, students may be helped to understand the study process through prompts such as: "Do you know that studying every night will help you master the material?" (declarative knowledge); "What do you do when you study for a test?" (procedural knowledge); and "When do you think you should memorize definitions and when should you practice problems?" (conditional knowledge). Once the thoughts are revealed, helpers can clarify misconceptions and help children learn more effective study skills. Table 6.3 presents a sampling of self-monitoring questions.

Another rationale for using self-talk procedures is to help children realize the *existence* of their self-talk, its relationship to their feelings and behaviors, and the ways they can modify it to make it more adaptive. This approach is critical to many cognitive-behavioral treatments for anxiety, depression, anger control, and ADHD (see Kendall, 1991). In this latter case, the content of the self-statements is as relevant as the process of self-instruction. In other words, teaching children (and adults, for that matter) to recognize negative self-statements is a necessary first step before instruction and practice in alternatives.

Meichenbaum and Goodman (1971), who pioneered self-instruction training, began by teaching self-control to impulsive children using guided modeling and self-talk procedures. Their approach included the following steps. The helping professional models effective self-talk while doing some task or dealing with some hypothetical scenario. Next, the child is asked to repeat the same process while the adult provides overt instruction. The child is then asked to redo the activity, first talking out loud by himself and then by subvocalizing (whispering) the instructions. Finally, the child practices using private (nonvocal) self-talk.

One can imagine a situation wherein therapy involves both learning the steps of self-instruction training and modifying the content of maladaptive cognitions. For example, once self-talk assessment has identified a person's negative self-statements

("I can't do math"), training in self-instruction can strengthen the frequency of positive alternatives ("I didn't do well on this problem because I didn't spend enough time studying"). Researchers report that it is not necessary, and is actually undesirable, for people to expect to have only positive thoughts. The ratio of 2 positive thoughts to 1 negative one appears optimal for healthy adjustment (Schwartz & Garamoni, 1989). Depressed individuals, for example, show an equal 1:1 balance (Kendall, 1991). Therefore, tipping the scales in favor of more positive thoughts appears to be a clinically important goal for adults and children alike.

Focus on the second element of metacognition, self-regulation of thinking—the "how well am I thinking?" part—helps the individual translate knowledge into action. As in self-instruction approaches, this provides the basis for cognitive problem-solving techniques, used to good effect in a variety of clinical and educational settings. Typical problem-solving steps include defining the problem or goal, selecting a plan to solve the problem or meet the goal, monitoring progress toward the goal, and revising goal-directed strategies, if needed.

PATHS to Healthy Development

Therapies designed to teach problem-solving and conflict-resolution skills have figured prominently in the counseling literature for many years and have been widely used with children and adolescents (Shure & Spivak, 1988; Weissberg, Caplan, & Bennetto, 1988). One comprehensive program with demonstrated effectiveness is Promoting Alternative Thinking Strategies (PATHS), a prevention program that includes 131 lessons for children in Grades K through 5 (Greenberg & Kusche, 2002). PATHS is founded on a holistic approach to the development of emotional well-being, and like good prevention programs, reaches out to include multiple levels of the system (peers, parents, and teachers). The primary goals include the promotion of emotional literacy, self-control, and social problem-solving skills in the context of a positive school environment. The benefits of this program have extended to children from a wide range of ethnic, racial, and social class backgrounds, to children with disabilities, and to children of both genders (Conduct Problems Prevention Research Group [CPPRG], 1999; Greenberg & Kusche, 1998).

The interpersonal cognitive problem-solving portion of this program offers an example of the material we have been discussing in this chapter. This part of the curriculum includes 33 lessons (introduced in Grades 3 or 4) that are presented after the units on emotional recognition, self-control, and communicating with others have been completed. The authors note that problem-solving is not just an isolated cognitive activity but one which flows from a basic understanding of self and others. The lessons in the problem-solving unit are listed in Table 6.4. To generalize the skills and apply them to everyday life, children are encouraged to write out real problems from their life experience and put them into a "mailbox" on the teacher's desk. These problems are discussed in regular problem-solving meetings. Teachers also build problem-solving practice into other areas, such as academic subjects.

TABLE 6.3 Sample Self-Monitoring Questions

1. Why am I trying to learn this information? What is the purpose of this exercise or assignment?
2. What do I already know about this subject?
3. Do I already know any strategies that will help me learn this?
4. What is my plan of action?
5. Do I understand the steps I need to take?
6. How should I get help if I need it?
7. How should I correct my mistakes?
8. Am I accomplishing my goals? Am I being successful?
9. How will I know when I've accomplished my goals?

TABLE 6.4 Problem-Solving Unit
of the PATHS Curriculum

STOP!
1. Stop and calm down.
2. Identify the problem (collect lots of information).
3. Identify the feelings (your own and other people's).

GO SLOW!
4. Decide on a goal.
5. Think of lots of solutions.
6. Think about the consequences.
7. Choose the best solution (evaluate all of the alternatives).
8. Make a good plan (think about possible obstacles).

GO!
9. Try my plan.
10. Evaluate—How did I do?
11. If you need to, try again.

SOURCE: Based on Greenberg, M. T., Kusche, C., & Mihalic, S. F. (2002). Promoting alternative thinking strategies (PATHS). In D. S. Elliott (Series Ed.), *Blueprint for violence prevention, Book Ten* (29–30). Boulder, CO: Center for the Study and Prevention of Violence, Institute of Behavioral Science, University of Colorado. Retreived from http://www.prevention.psu.edu/projects/PATHSCurriculum.html.

Learning the Skills of Friendship

At the heart of many therapeutic approaches is a fundamental focus on teaching children how to get along with one another, which requires perspective taking. We stress the importance of learning to relate to others in elementary school, but it is clearly not a task just for children. Knowing how to get along with others is essential for people of all ages. Recent descriptions of emotional intelligence (e.g., Goleman, 1995, 1998) stress the lifelong value of having good people skills even in the adult world of work. Some define therapy as the process of building an awareness of how our actions affect other people, the very essence of perspective taking (see Pittman, 1998).

Children in the school years begin this kind of learning in earnest. Because they spend such large amounts of time in school, teachers and peers exert a strong influence on the development of social competence. Counselors often play a role by providing developmental guidance activities, social skills training programs, and other kinds of cognitive, affective, and behavioral interventions.

Selman's friendship framework (Selman et al., 1997) can be a useful and somewhat unusual guide to developing interventions, because it addresses the fundamental friendship relationship and makes practice applications that are developmentally and theoretically based. His therapeutic technique, called **pair therapy**, has been applied to both preventive and remedial work with children and adolescents. Although a comprehensive review of this approach is beyond the scope of this text, it is helpful to describe some of its basic ideas.

Children's social skills can be seen as involving both **social competence and performance**. Competence refers to the child's level of perspective-taking ability, and performance refers to the child's actual use of skills for getting along with others. Selman's research indicates that adequate competence (perspective taking) is necessary but not sufficient for good performance (social functioning). In other words, children never have high-level social skills without a commensurate level of perspective taking. However, socially unskilled children may either lack interpersonal understanding or possess it without being able to act on it. Pair therapy was designed to help both kinds of poor performers: those with low competence and low performance as well as those with high competence and low performance. This kind of therapeutic approach has been adapted for use in primary prevention efforts in schools that are intended to foster good social relationships among the whole student community. Similar approaches have also been applied at the middle and high school levels in programs to reduce racism and promote intercultural understanding (Schultz, Barr, & Selman, 2000). Table 6.5 presents a comparison of two related interventions, one for therapeutic purposes (pair therapy) and one for prevention (pairing for prevention). In pair therapy, two children with equally ineffective social styles, such as a controlling child and a fearful one, are paired. Both participants meet regularly with a helper whose job it is to encourage both children to be effectively assertive and empathic. The therapeutic material is what the children bring to the time they spend together. What they decide to do together, how they decide to do it, where it happens, and so on all become grist for the therapeutic mill. Adult helpers provide a watchful eye and a knowledge of development that facilitates the pair's movement from egocentric, unilateral understanding toward more cooperative modes of interaction. The helper must ensure the physical and emotional safety of both children while allowing for their direct experience of conflict and their increasingly more advanced efforts at resolving it collaboratively. The shy child, for example, must be helped to learn ways to articulate his needs, and the more controlling child must learn to accommodate the other instead of overwhelming him. In general, this approach provides practice in the real-life experience of friendship. The counselor functions to guide the pair toward a more even-handed balance of control and decision-making functions and nurtures them toward experiences of mutual sharing and cooperation. Within this context, children learn the tools of friendship, which include the development of a sense of personal responsibility, motivation to make the friendship work, and the ability to understand firsthand the impact of one's words and actions on another person.

Although disagreements can be painful, they can help children learn to take another's perspective.

TABLE 6.5   Pair Therapy and Pairing for Prevention

	PAIR THERAPY	PAIRING FOR PREVENTION
Context of treatment	Child guidance clinic/day treatment/residential treatment program/inpatient hospitalization (if long-term).	School-based (during or after school); community center/settlement house/Girls and Boys Clubs.
Clients	Children and adolescents with severe emotional and behavior problems. Range of psychiatric diagnoses, including cognitive and communicative disorders. Very limited peer interactions. Family trauma.	"At-risk" students with conduct and/or academic problems: may have close friends, from low-income, inner-city households; likely exposure to, and/or involvement in societal health/welfare risks. Limited social supports.
General goals	Foster personality and social development. Increase capacity to make and maintain friendships: coordinate social perspectives, communicate more effectively, resolve interpersonal conflicts, manage emotions.	Same goals as therapy but with focus on interpersonal development as vehicle for increasing capacity to make mature decisions with respect to risks. Pairs provide protective factor against risky behaviors.
Theory guiding treatment and evaluation	Primarily Psychological Orthogenetic and Structural-Developmental Model: Intimacy and autonomy as functional social management processes organized according to developmental level of perspective coordination.	Primarily Psychosocial Risk-Taking Model: Takes into account sociocultural and biological antecedents, and psychosocial dimensions (knowledge, management, and personal meaning) of risk-taking behavior. Incorporates Structural Developmental Model.
Overall treatment plan	Often in conjunction with individual psychotherapy, adjunct therapies (i.e., speech, family), and/or a therapeutic milieu.	May be only special service student receives.
Training level of providers	Supervised clinicians or residential staff, with some understanding of individual psychodynamics.	Supervised master's level students with some understanding of psychosocial development and the social system within which they are providing service.
Time frame of treatment/research focus	Long-term treatment/longitudinal study of interpersonal development (1–4 years). Process oriented basic research of both the individual and the dyad. Major focus on assessment methods: interviews and observations to assess ego development.	Focus on major transitions (elementary to middle school; middle school to high school) outcome- and process-oriented research. Focus on both individual assessment and program evaluation. Additional reliance on ethnography.
Evaluation/research	In-depth micro- and macro-level assessment of affective, cognitive, motivational, and dynamic dimensions of evolving pair relationship (nonexperimental).	Qualitative evaluation of process of change in pair's knowledge, management, and personal meaning of risk, and quantitative assessment of risk outcome in treatment group compared to control group (experimental). Additional qualitative and quantitative analysis of participant's view of prevention.

SOURCE: Selman, R. L., Watts, C. L., & Schultz, L. H. (1997). Fostering friendship: Pair therapy for treatment and prevention. New York, NY: Walter de Gruyter, Inc. Reprinted with permission.

SUMMARY

Brain and Behavior

1. Changes in the brain both enable and are affected by cognitive and motor developments. In middle childhood continuing brain growth is partially a function of ongoing myelination. Both gross motor and fine motor coordination benefit from continued myelination of the corpus callosum, connecting the left and right cortical hemispheres, and the cerebellum, as well as other brain maturation processes.

2. Some differences in cognitive and behavioral development among children are related to differences in brain development. For example, in about half of children diagnosed with ADHD brain growth is delayed, especially in the frontal lobes although most catch up by adolescence or early adulthood. Unevenness in brain development, both between and within children is to be expected.

Cognitive Development

3. In Piaget's theory, children at the concrete operational stage (6 to 12 years) can decenter, or think about more than one dimension or aspect of a situation at one time. This allows them the possibility of recognizing or constructing the relationships among the dimensions, which is important for logical thinking. Understanding reversible relationships, when one change reverses the effects of another, or one change compensates for the effects of

another, is especially important. Recognizing the nature of the relationships among features of an event makes it possible for children to infer underlying realities.

4. At the concrete operational stage, children's thinking is most logical when they are solving problems that relate to real, concrete events. They find it difficult to think logically about abstract contents, like their own thought processes. They are subject to a form of egocentrism, such that they find it difficult to distinguish between their own theories or assumptions and objective fact.

5. Logical thinking can be domain specific to some degree. When children have a great deal of experience with a specific domain of knowledge, they are more likely to think logically about problems in that domain.

6. In the information processing approach, cognition is compared to the functioning of a computer. The organization of the cognitive system stays the same across age, but there are age changes in the amount and efficiency of information flow. With increasing age, executive functions improve, including control of emotions, attention, and problem solving.

7. NeoPiagetians are theorists who try to integrate concepts from Piaget's theory and from information processing theory to explain cognitive development.

8. Two kinds of remembering or retrieval are called recognition (realizing that information being experienced now is familiar) and recall (drawing information out of long-term memory and representing it to yourself). Our memories can store declarative knowledge, both semantic (about facts and concepts) and episodic (about events we have experienced). A schematic representation of a frequently experienced event is called a script. We also store nondeclarative knowledge, which is hard to verbalize and is often referred to as procedural, which is "knowing how" rather than "knowing that." Infants' and toddlers' knowledge is largely nondeclarative.

9. Working memory (one of the executive functions) increases in capacity with age, as indicated on digit span tests. This seems to be partly a result of faster information processing, perhaps due to practice, perhaps to maturation, or to both.

10. Children's knowledge base increases with age, and that helps children reconstruct events. They "remember" more accurately because they can infer what must have happened. An expanded knowledge base also helps children learn new information more easily, perhaps because they can fit the new information into a rich web of well-organized connections. Having an expanded knowledge base also benefits chunking in working memory.

11. Advances in logical thinking can help children improve their memories. The better the child understands the original experience, the more likely he is to reconstruct it accurately.

12. Increasing facility with language helps children store memories for events in coherent verbal form and seems to improve later retrieval of those events.

13. Children also improve in the use of memory strategies with age from preschool through middle school. Rehearsal is an early strategy, with more effective strategies such as organization coming later. Children's progress in strategy use is bumpy. They may exhibit either production deficiencies or utilization deficiencies.

14. Children gradually improve their understanding of their own cognitive processes (metacognition), including memory abilities, as they approach the end of middle childhood, partly accounting for improvements in strategy use with age.

15. Memory is also influenced by affective and social developments, like motivation to learn and the amount of scaffolding available from adults.

16. Formal schooling is the context in which a great deal of adult scaffolding of cognitive development occurs. Many factors contribute to children's academic success at the country/culture level, the school level, and the proximal, teacher-child interaction level. These factors moderate each others' effects, so that some factors matter more or less depending on the presence of other factors. Overall, effective educational factors fall into three categories: *quantity (amount of instruction/practice), stimulation/ engagement, and valuing (of learning and the learner)*.

17. The kinds of proximal, teacher–child interaction processes that matter are illustrated by effective math education. Children usually begin school with informal mathematical skills, such as adopting simple counting strategies for adding and subtracting small numbers. In elementary school, they continue to invent their own strategies as well as adopting the formal procedures and strategies they are taught. Gradually, more efficient strategies win out over less efficient strategies, though again, development is bumpy.

18. Helping children build a knowledge base of memorized math facts and procedures is useful but must be accompanied by support for conceptual understanding. Children assimilate formal procedures to their own concepts, and often misunderstand. Teachers can encourage mathematical development by exploring their students' understanding; by working forward from what children already understand, such as providing familiar examples of concepts or familiar analogies to more difficult concepts.

19. Teaching is most successful when teachers treat children with warmth and create a classroom climate of mutual respect for individual interests and diversity of backgrounds.

Social Cognition

20. Learning about social interactions, including how to make and keep friends, and acquiring a theory of mind begins in early childhood and is heavily dependent on cognitive developments. For example, children's perspective taking improves as they acquire the ability to think about their own mental experiences and those of another person at the same time.

21. Theorists such as Sullivan and Selman built on Piaget's ideas and linked the gradual improvement in perspective taking with changes in the nature of friendships over age. In Selman's five-stage theory, improvements in perspective taking affect an individual's friendship understanding, influence his friendship valuing, and affect the social and conflict resolution skills (friendship skills) he develops.

22. In Selman's view, a mature interpersonal orientation balances intimacy and autonomy strivings. Less effective orientations may be other-transforming or self-transforming, and are more characteristic of very young children and of socially immature older children. Both a bully and a victim may be functioning at a similar developmental level with regard to perspective-taking skill. Assessing the properties of understanding that underlie relationship skill is a helpful approach to addressing social problems.

CASE STUDY

Alex, the second child of Ernest and Isabel Palacio, a Cuban American couple, is a fourth grader at J. F. Kennedy Elementary School. He has one older sister, Paula, who is in fifth grade, and a younger brother, Thomas, who is 4 years old. Until recently, Alex appeared to be a happy child and a good student in school. Although somewhat reserved, he interacted well with peers, was athletic, and was popular among his classmates.

During the year Alex was in third grade, the Palacios' marriage was seriously affected by Ernest's close relationship with a female coworker. Despite an attempt at counseling, the couple could not resolve their differences. During the summer before his fourth-grade year, Alex's parents separated. The children continued to live with their mother but maintained a relationship with their father, seeing him every weekend in the apartment he rented nearby.

Both parents tried hard to make this arrangement work for the sake of their children, to whom both were devoted. The fourth-grade school year began fairly smoothly for Alex, who was happy to see his friends again after the summer vacation. His teacher, Mr. Williams, was regarded as tough but usually fair, and Alex seemed to make a good initial adjustment to his class. Ernest continued his employment with an advertising agency and paid for many of the family's living costs. However, the expense of maintaining two residences quickly became burdensome. Isabel, formerly employed as a part-time library aide, needed to find a position that provided a larger income. She began a job as a secretary shortly after the children began school in September.

In December, Isabel fell ill and needed to be hospitalized. Primary care of the children fell to Isabel's mother, the children's grandmother. Ernest took over as much of the caretaking as his work schedule would permit, but he feared that if he took off too much time for family responsibilities, his job would be in jeopardy. Because of these changes in the family, all three children needed to adjust. It became much more difficult for an adult to transport the children after school to music lessons and games, so they had to drop out of some of their activities. As Isabel recuperated, she needed much more rest and general peace and quiet. She could no longer take the children on trips or allow groups of her children's friends to have sleepovers in her home.

Toward the middle of his fourth-grade year, Alex's grades started to slip, and he began to act up. Alex grew apathetic and sullen in class. Mr. Williams was a relatively young teacher in the school district. His first 2 years of teaching had been spent in the eighth grade of the district middle school. He liked teaching older students and reluctantly accepted the fourth-grade position because of his lack of seniority in the system. Mr. Williams, despite his youth, was a fairly traditional teacher. He believed in giving lots of homework and in placing high expectations for performance on his students. He ran a very disciplined classroom that was based on a system of winning and losing points for behavior. Because Alex did not participate actively in classroom exercises or turn in homework, he continually "lost points."

On one particularly difficult day, Alex and one of his friends got into an argument. Alex accused his friend of picking on him and teasing him in the lunchroom. Mr. Williams tried to intervene by taking both boys out into the hallway and listening to each version of the problem. When the disagreement got louder, Mr. Williams told both boys that they would "just have to work it out." He told them he would take away points and was sending them both to the principal's office. Alex became very agitated and said to his teacher, "Sometimes I feel like throwing my chair at you."

Mr. Williams began to see Alex as a threat and recommended to the principal that the incident be handled as a disciplinary matter. It was the teacher's belief that Alex should be suspended and then referred for special education evaluation by the school psychologist because of his "aggressiveness." He insisted that Alex not be returned to his classroom.

Discussion Questions

1. How would you assess the problem?
2. What are the different perspectives involved in this conflict?
3. What actions would you take and what recommendations would you make as a helping professional in this situation?

PRACTICE USING WHAT YOU HAVE LEARNED

In the Pearson etext, apply these ideas to working with others.

Applying Concepts

Friendship Questions
Points: 15

Name:_____
Period:_____

1. List three qualities you look for in a friend:

    a. trustworthiness

    b. funny & nice

    c. caring

2. List three qualities you would **not** want in a friend:

    a. untrustworthy

Video Exercise

JOURNAL QUESTIONS

1. If you can remember struggling with some subject or concept in school, describe the impact of this experience on your sense of competence and industry. If you were counseling a student in this situation, what advice would you have for his parents? His teachers?
2. Describe what your friendships were like in elementary school. Did you have a best friend? What characteristics did he or she possess?
3. Compare and contrast how you solved conflicts as a child in grade school and how you solve them now. How would you assess your level of perspective taking?
4. Using the "Friendship Framework" presented in this chapter, reflect on each element in light of one particular relationship that you have experienced or are experiencing. For example, what is your primary interpersonal orientation, other- or self-transforming?

KEY CONCEPTS

normative (p. 203)
attention deficit hyperactivity
    disorder (ADHD) (p. 203)
reversible relationship (p. 206)
egocentrism (p. 207)
formal operational thought (p. 207)
domain of knowledge (p. 208)
neoPiagetians (p. 213)
sensory memory (p. 213)
long-term memory (p. 214)
rehearsal (p. 214)
storage (p. 214)
retrieval (p. 214)
declarative knowledge (p. 215)
semantic memory (p. 215)
episodic memory (p. 215)
script (p. 215)
nondeclarative knowledge (p. 215)

procedural knowledge (p. 215)
digit span tests (p. 215)
knowledge base (p. 216)
reality monitoring (p. 217)
guided imagery (p. 217)
stereotype induction (p. 218)
chunking (p. 218)
narrative skill (p. 220)
memory strategies (p. 220)
selective attention (p. 220)
organization strategy (p. 221)
elaboration strategy (p. 221)
production deficiency (p. 221)
utilization deficiency (p. 221)
metacognition (p. 221)
self-instruction (p. 222)
self-monitoring (p. 222)
counting all strategy (p. 224)

counting on strategy (p. 224)
retrieval strategy (p. 225)
social cognition (p. 226)
English-language-learner (ELL) (p. 227)
immigrant family (p. 227)
immigrant risk model (p. 227)
immigrant paradox model (p. 227)
perspective taking (p. 230)
psychosocial development (p. 235)
friendship understanding (p. 235)
friendship skills (p. 235)
friendship valuing (p. 235)
interpersonal orientation (p. 236)
other-transforming (p. 236)
self-transforming (p. 236)
pair therapy (p. 239)
social competence and performance (p. 239)

CHAPTER 7

Self and Moral Development: Middle Childhood Through Early Adolescence

Honesty, dependability, kindness, fairness, respect, self-control, truthfulness, and diligence. Rare is the adult who would not agree that any one of these traits is desirable for children to attain. The advantage is very basic: Behaving in accordance with these values makes the world a better place for everyone. Certainly, individuals or groups might disagree on the particulars, such as what "being fair" may mean in a given situation. But it is truly difficult to imagine any sizable group of parents, teachers, or helpers who would promote the opposite values: meanness, laziness, dishonesty, irresponsibility, or disrespect, to name a few.

Not too long ago in the United States, there was considerable agreement that inculcating these values, virtues, or behavioral habits was perhaps the most important responsibility that adults have relative to their children. The public schools had as their express purpose the creation of good citizens—people who, for the most part, valued and practiced these virtues. Consider the advice educator Charles Davis presented in 1852 in a lecture to parents and teachers on their duties toward children:

> Education is the system of training which develops in their right direction and in their proper proportions our physical, intellectual, and moral natures. . . . The moral nature of the pupils will be, with the teacher, a subject of earnest and constant solicitude. What are the first things to be done? To establish his [the teacher's]

authority over his school—to ensure the obedience of his scholars—to win their confidence—to gain their respect, and to call into exercise their warmest affections. (Davis, 1852, pp. 6–8)

Hiram Orcutt, writing in a famous manual to parents in 1874, advises thus:

The child must establish a character of integrity and to be trained to habits of honesty, benevolence and industry or he will be lost to himself and to society. . . . We may not expect benevolence to spring up spontaneously in the heart of the child. . . . Without knowledge and experience, the child cannot appreciate the rights and wants of others, nor his own duty in regard to them. (Orcutt, 1874, pp. 72–73)

If this seems a bit quaint and outdated to you, consider the fact that even today there is evidence for broad consensus among North American parents about what they consider fundamental for children to achieve their life goals. When David R. Shaffer and his students asked young parents what they considered to be the most important aspect of a child's social development, most placed morality at the top of their lists (Shaffer, 2000). They apparently felt that acquiring a moral sense and living by its dictates were critical for self-development and central to successful adult functioning.

Perhaps this consensus is shaped by our experience of the culture we share. We are benumbed by the repetitious refrain that comes from all manner of media reporting on a world marred by violence, aggressiveness, hopelessness, underachievement, and declining civility.

Is something happening to the healthy moral and self-development we wish for our children? As you might have already guessed, the issue is complex. The world is changing in many ways at once and understanding how those changes affect our children's development is among the goals of developmental science. The answers researchers can make available have profound significance for practice, given helpers' investment in their clients' healthy development. In this chapter and the next, we will introduce the topics that are fundamental to understanding social and emotional development in middle and late childhood and provide some guidelines and suggestions for interventions. We pick up the discussion with the topic of the self.

SELF-CONCEPT

The Development of Self-Concept

Imagine that you live across the street from an empty lot. One day, you notice that workers have placed piles of building materials, bricks, lumber, and bags of concrete on the property. After some time, the frame of a large, boxlike house takes the place of the piles of materials. From your vantage point, you can see the empty beginnings of where rooms will be. With more time, the internal structure becomes clear. Walls are assembled; doors and stairways connect the parts. Each section of the new house—living, dining, bedroom, and storage areas—has multiple divisions that provide useful space dedicated to some purpose. The disparate piles have been transformed into a coherent structure, and the once simple structure has become increasingly complex. Finishing touches are made, and ongoing renovations will undoubtedly accompany the life of the home.

This image illustrates how Western science explains the development of the self concept from early childhood through adolescence and adulthood. It is important to recognize that self-concept or self-knowledge is very much like any other kind of knowledge, for the self is a cognitive construction. Therefore, knowledge of the self will be constrained by the child's general level of cognitive development and will most likely progress unevenly. As Harter (1999) has pointed out in her description of general cognitive-developmental stages, "décalage is accepted as the rule, rather than the exception; therefore, it is expected that the particular level of development at which one is functioning will vary across different domains of knowledge" (p. 30), as we noted in Chapter 6.

In addition, remember that the self-concept is multidimensional, like a house with various rooms (see Chapter 5). In many homes, rooms are added on after the initial construction. In contrast to this somewhat static analogy, the self-system is dynamic and changes throughout development. Generally, the child's self-concept proceeds from a rather undifferentiated state or simple structure to a much more organized and coherent structure in adulthood through a process of stagelike changes. Let us consider some of the developments in self-knowledge that occur as children mature.

The preschool child's rendering of herself is something like the lot filled with building materials. Self-descriptors such as "big," "girl," and "nice" are separate, uncoordinated elements in the child's self-portrait because she is cognitively unable to integrate these elements into an organized whole. We know from our discussion of cognitive development (see Chapter 3) that young children's ability to hold in mind several ideas at the same time and to integrate these in some meaningful way is quite underdeveloped. Furthermore, preschool youngsters find accommodating opposing characteristics, such as being "nice" and "mean," or opposing emotional states, such as "happy" and "sad," to be especially difficult (see Harter, 2006, 2012). Nor do young children make much use of perspective taking at this age, as we saw in Chapter 6. In failing to do so, they show limited ability to use the behaviors or perspectives of others as guides for evaluating their own conduct or performance. Stated in other words, they do not use information gleaned from observing others as a way of assessing their competencies. Consequently, the young child's self-evaluations may not conform to reality but may be overly positive (e.g., Davis-Kean, Jager, & Collins, 2009). Four-year-old Jamar might insist he has won the round of miniature golf despite hitting the ball outside the lane every time!

Gradually, the early-elementary-school-aged youngster begins to organize the characteristics of the "Me-self" into sets of categories that display some coherence. For example, the child might relate being good at drawing, at coloring, and at cutting as an indication that she is good at art. However, the child still does not accommodate sets of characteristics with opposing features (e.g., nice versus mean). Given her tendency to perceive personal qualities as good and to discount the subtlety of coexisting negative attributes, the child's thinking about herself may still have an all-or-nothing quality that is often unrealistically positive. There is little discrepancy between the "real" and the "ideal" selves. Gradual improvements in perspective-taking ability, however, allow the child to begin to evaluate her own behavior according to others' standards. The child's anticipation of another person's reaction, be it as a reward or a punishment, becomes internalized (Harter, 2012). As others' rules or standards become internalized, they become adopted as self-regulatory guidelines and form the basis for the looking-glass self.

Between middle childhood and early adolescence, the individual becomes capable of integrating opposing characteristics and begins to form more abstract traitlike concepts to describe herself. Self-assessments, such as "being smart," are bolstered by feedback from a wide variety of outside influences across many kinds of situations, and these assessments become more resistant to modification. Self-esteem tends to decline a bit during middle childhood and early adolescence because children recognize, often for the first time, how they fall short in comparison to others. Struggles to integrate abstract representations of the self characterize the period of adolescence as the young person works on defining a unique identity.

The Structure of Self-Concept

Although we continue to use the term *self-concept,* it is not a unidimensional construct, as we noted in Chapter 5. One's overall sense of self is a composite of several related, but not necessarily overlapping, elements that are evaluated by the individual to determine self-esteem, our feelings about ourselves. Although technically separate constructs, self-concept and self-esteem are closely intertwined. Shavelson, Hubner, and Stanton (1976) proposed a highly influential theoretical view of the self

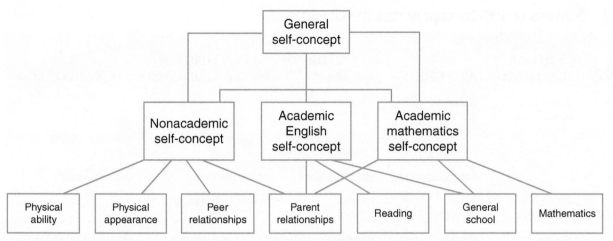

Students have many separate but sometimes related concepts of themselves. The overall sense of self appears to be divided into separate, but slightly related, self-concepts.

FIGURE 7.1 **Structure of self-concept.**
SOURCE: Marsh, H. W., & Shavelson, R. J. (1985). Self-concept: Its multifaceted, hierarchical structure. *Educational Psychologist, 20,* 114. Adapted with permission from Lawrence Erlbaum Associates, Inc. and H.W. Marsh. Used by permission of H. W. Marsh.

that has received research support (e.g., Byrne & Shavelson, 1996; Marsh, 1990). In this model (see Figure 7.1), children's general self-concept can be divided into two main domains: academic and nonacademic self-concepts. **Academic self-concept** is further divided into specific school subject areas such as math, science, English, and social studies. More recently, developmentalists have proposed the addition of other components such as artistic self-concept (Marsh & Roche, 1996; Vispoel, 1995).

The **nonacademic self-concept** is divided into social, emotional, and physical self-concepts. The last domain is further subdivided into physical ability and physical appearance. Other contemporary theories of the self (Harter, 1993; L'Ecuyer, 1992; Markus, 1977; Marsh & Hattie, 1996) also emphasize multidimensional and hierarchically arranged self-structures. Despite this general consensus, however, many researchers have retained the notion of global self-esteem within their frameworks. This appears to reflect the view that a global sense of self coexists with and shapes self-appraisals in specific domains.

By grade school, children can articulate their own assessments of their specific competencies as well as a generalized overall perception of themselves (Harter & Pike, 1984). Using her measures with individuals of different ages, Harter (1985, 1988b) has found that different domains of self-concept emerge at different points in the life span (see Table 7.1). The number of dimensions of the self that can be appraised, however, increases dramatically from early childhood through adolescence and adulthood. In middle childhood, the dimensions of importance include academic or scholastic competence, athletic competence, physical appearance, peer acceptance, and behavioral conduct.

Is any one domain more important than the others to a child's overall sense of self-esteem? Evidence from many studies reported by Harter (1999; 2012) clearly documents the powerful association between physical appearance and overall self-esteem (correlations are as high as 0.80) for older children, adolescents, college-aged students, and adults. The strength of this association holds up for special student populations such as learning disabled and academically talented groups as well. This somewhat disconcerting reality may be due to the fact that physical attractiveness is such an omnipresent, recognizable aspect of the self. It is also true that more attractive individuals receive more positive attention from others (Maccoby & Martin, 1983),

 Callie, age 7, can clearly distinguish between what activities she likes best and what activities she is best at, in a variety of domains of self.

TABLE 7.1 Domains of Self-Concept Across the Life Span

EARLY CHILDHOOD	MIDDLE TO LATE CHILDHOOD	ADOLESCENCE	COLLEGE YEARS	EARLY THROUGH MIDDLE ADULTHOOD	LATE ADULTHOOD
Cognitive competence	Scholastic competence	Scholastic competence	Scholastic competence		
			Intellectual ability Creativity	Intelligence	Cognitive abilities
		Job competence	Job competence	Job competence	Job competence
Physical competence	Athletic competence	Athletic competence	Athletic competence	Athletic competence	
Physical appearance	Physical appearance	Physical appearance	Physical appearance	Physical appearance	Physical appearance
Peer acceptance	Peer acceptance	Peer acceptance	Peer acceptance	Sociability	
		Close friendship	Close friendship	Close friendship	Relationships with friends
		Romantic relationships	Romantic relationships	Intimate relationships	
			Relationships with parents		Family relationships
Behavioral conduct	Behavioral conduct	Conduct/morality	Morality Sense of humor	Morality Sense of humor	Morality
				Nurturance Household management	Nurturance Personal, household management
				Adequacy as a provider	Adequacy as a provider
					Leisure activities Health status Life satisfaction Reminiscence
	Global self-worth	Global self-worth	Global self-worth	Global self-worth	Global self-worth

SOURCE: Harter, S. (1990). *The construction of the self: A developmental perspective.* New York, NY: Guilford Press. Used by permission of Guilford Press.

receive more affection in infancy (Langlois, Ritter, Casey, & Savin, 1995), have more good qualities ascribed to them (Dion, Berscheid, & Walster, 1972), and are generally more successful in life (Hatfield & Sprecher, 1986). Thus, physically attractive individuals may be getting a consistently larger number of positive reflected appraisals with which to construct the self than their less attractive counterparts.

It also appears that cultural emphasis on rigid and often unobtainable standards of beauty, particularly for females, contributes to observed differences in self-esteem for males and females, which we will discuss in a later section of this chapter. Beginning around early adolescence, girls report more dissatisfaction with their appearance and their bodies than do boys of the same age, but increasingly, physical appearance is becoming a central element to male self-valuing as well (Harter, 1999, 2012).

Influences on the Development of Self-Concept

We have already presented the earliest influences on the developing self of the infant, toddler, and preschooler (see Chapter 5). What can we add to the story of self-concept development that applies to older children? Are the same processes at work? What can we say about the nature of self-esteem, that evaluative dimension which colors our self-appraisals? As you might suspect, the traditional positions of James (1890) and Cooley (1902) have much to offer contemporary researchers looking for explanations. Recall that William James believed that self-esteem was dependent on the ratio of our successes to our aspirations. Harter (1990) found support for James's position. Children's, as well as adolescents' and adults', global self-esteem is heavily dependent on competence in areas of personal importance. Individuals of all ages are more able to discount weak performance if it occurs in unimportant areas. For example, if it is very important to Ashley (and to her peers and parents) to be athletically competitive, relatively weak performance in this area is likely to lower her overall self-regard. On the other hand, if Sharon's goal is to be a stellar student, a weak athletic showing is likely to have less punishing consequences to her global sense of self.

In general, Harter found that the greater the discrepancy between adequacy in some domain and importance of that domain, the greater the negative impact on self-esteem. This helps explain why some students who display low levels of competence in certain domains may still have high self-esteem overall. Evidence suggests, however, that this reality is not well understood and may even contradict conventional wisdom. Consider a survey of teachers, school administrators, and school counselors in which approximately 60% of the respondents believed poor academic performance was the major cause of low self-esteem among students (Scott, Murray, Mertens, & Dustin, 1996). This belief fails to acknowledge the diversity of attributes that are important to children (e.g., social relationships) as well as the fact that academic success may not be highly valued by everyone. Interestingly, in the same study, 69% of counselors compared to 35% of administrators believed that the self-esteem of underachieving students could be improved by more unconditional validation, a strategy we will examine more thoroughly later in the chapter.

Overall self-esteem seems to depend, at least in part, on a complicated, idiosyncratic calculation of perceived pluses and minuses factored against personally significant competencies (see Crocker & Knight, 2005). Large discrepancies, such as discrepancies between real and ideal selves as children reach adolescence, are associated with depression and anxiety (Higgins, 1991; Markus & Nurius, 1986). However, even low levels of competency in areas deemed of little personal value may not negatively alter one's general feelings about the self. High levels of competency in personally desirable behaviors, even if they are socially unacceptable (e.g., fighting, delinquent activities), may enhance self-esteem for some youth (Brynner, O'Malley, & Bachman, 1981; Cairns & Cairns, 1994).

How do children appraise their competencies in the first place? For a child at school age and beyond, there are obviously some concrete standards of performance that can be used to infer competency, such as getting good grades or being selected for a sports team. Cooley also emphasized the importance of social influences on appraisals of competence. In other words, he believed that self-perceptions can be based on the internalization of approval or disapproval of others in the social network. In one study, for example, 8- to 12-year-olds participated in an online "game" in which a jury of same-aged, anonymous peers ostensibly judged each child's "likeability" in comparison to four other "contestants" (Thomaes et al., 2010). Actually, the researchers randomly assigned a high, low, or intermediate likeability score to each participating child. The children filled out self-esteem questionnaires both before and after the "game." Receiving a low likeability score decreased their self-esteem, and receiving a high score increased their self-esteem. Children with narcissistic tendencies (that is, who had demonstrated extreme, unrealistically positive self-views) before the manipulation actually were the most vulnerable to the negative peer feedback. It does appear that, "As social beings we live with our eyes upon our reflection, but have no assurance of the tranquility of the waters in which we see it" (Cooley, 1902, p. 247).

Children put more stock in how their peers see them as they get older. For example, one study found that 6th graders' self-appraisals match those of their peers more closely than 3rd graders' self-appraisals do (e.g., Cole, Maxwell, & Martin, 1997). For both age groups, parents' and teachers' appraisals also contributed to the process. But the role of the social network involves more than just providing an accumulation of comments or responses from others that become part of the self-concept. The self-system also assimilates and accommodates evaluative data from internal ("How am I doing in reading compared to math?") and external ("How does my reading performance compare with that of my classmates?") sources in ways that involve comparison (Marsh, 1994).

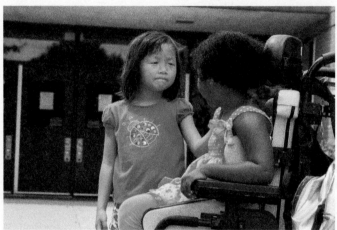

As children grow, social comparison processes contribute to the construction of the self-concept.

The process, called **social comparison** (Festinger, 1954), means that people observe the performance of others and use it as a basis for evaluating their own abilities and accomplishments. When they do this and how they do it vary somewhat depending on context and level of global self-esteem. Social comparison processes are particularly active in situations that are novel or ambiguous or when more objective standards of performance are unavailable. It is fairly obvious that classrooms provide a wealth of material for this ongoing process. Generally, children tend to make comparisons with other children who resemble them in some important ways (Suls & Miller, 1977). Most people, at least in Western cultures, are motivated to maintain moderately positive beliefs about themselves, called the **self-enhancing bias** (Taylor & Brown, 1988), which is considered a good thing in most cases.

Strategies for protecting one's self-esteem differ depending on children's level of self-esteem. When self-esteem is low, children may prefer situations that are rich in positive reinforcement. For example, Smith and Smoll (1990) reported that children with lower levels of self-esteem responded most favorably to coaches and instructors who were highly encouraging and least favorably to those who were least supportive. Children with high or moderate levels of self-esteem showed less variation in their responsiveness to adult reinforcement styles. Researchers (Pyszczynski, Greenberg, & LaPrelle, 1985) have also noted that children will make **"downward" social comparisons** by comparing themselves to less competent or less successful peers when their own self-esteem is at stake. Such comparisons protect the child from negative self-evaluations. Generally, children and adults with lower levels of self-esteem are more susceptible to the kinds of external cues that carry evaluative messages and are more reactive to social feedback (Campbell, 1990). They are reluctant to call attention to themselves and are more cautious and self-protective. Possibly they feel they have more to lose if they experience negative evaluations from others. This contrasts with individuals with high self-esteem, who demonstrate more self-enhancement strategies and are more likely to call attention to themselves (Campbell & Lavallee, 1993).

What message can we draw from research in the tradition of James and Cooley? Harter (e.g., 2006) concludes that the two theorists' positions operate in an additive way to explain the variation in self-esteem found in older children and adolescents. In other words, both competence and support contribute to the final product. The higher the level of competence in important domains and the greater the level of social support, the higher the level of self-esteem is overall.

What is the importance of self-esteem for children's development? As you might expect, positive self-esteem is not only a consequence of competence and social support, but it also has consequences for life outcomes. One longitudinal study followed participants from adolescence through old age (Orth, Robins, & Widaman, 2012). Higher self-esteem early in life predicted more positive and fewer negative emotional experiences over time, as well as more relationship and job satisfaction. Another longitudinal study began when participants were 13 years old and followed them to age 30 (Birkeland, Melkevik, Holsen, & Wold, 2012). The researchers identified three typical trajectories of global self-esteem: consistently high, chronically low, and U-shaped. In the U-shaped group, participants reported positive self-esteem when they were 13 years old and then showed a decline, reaching a low point at about 18 years old. Subsequently, their self-esteem climbed so that by their mid-20's they saw themselves much more positively again. By age 30, self-esteem trajectories appeared to have effects on life satisfaction as well as the likelihood of depressive mood, health problems, and insomnia. The importance of self-esteem is especially evident when we examine outcomes for the group that experienced an adolescent decline and subsequent rise in positive feelings (the U-shaped group). Even though by age 30 their global self-esteem was as positive as the consistently high group, they still reported more negative life outcomes.

Gender, Race, Ethnicity, and Self-Esteem Differences in North America

Gender

Much recent attention has been paid to the apparent decrease in self-esteem experienced by females around the time of their entrance to middle school. This phenomenon has been called the "loss of voice" by Gilligan and her colleagues (Brown & Gilligan, 1992), who purport that a girl experiences a gradual silencing of an authentic, imperious, and often willful self in order to identify with certain culturally prescribed roles of women as self-sacrificial and pleasing to others. Speaking one's mind, at least for women in certain contexts, can be threatening to the relationships that are such an important part of their lives. These authors argue that suppressing one's voice becomes the only possible way of maintaining important connections to others. In time, they conclude, women become disassociated from their true selves and may lose touch with their own opinions and feelings. Comparably negative claims of gender bias or silencing have been directed toward schools for "shortchanging" girls by giving them less attention than boys and for attributing their academic failure to lack of ability rather than to lack of effort (Ornstein, 1994; Sadker & Sadker, 1991). Popular accounts of these reports have contributed to the notion that the self-esteem of girls plunges precipitously around the early adolescent period, whereas that of boys remains robust (Daley, 1991).

What actually happens to girls' level of "voice" and to their views of themselves in late childhood and early adolescence? Are gender differences in self-regard real and universal? First, let's consider studies of girls' versus boys' level of voice. Harter and colleagues (Harter, Waters, Whitesell, & Kastelic, 1998) assessed level of voice by asking 9th to 11th graders to rate how able they feel to "express their opinions," "share what they are really thinking," and so on. They also asked the teens about whether others—parents, teachers, male classmates, female classmates, and close friends—listen to their opinions, respect their ideas, and show interest in their views. Finally, the researchers measured "relational self-worth" with different groups of people, asking respondents to say whether they liked or didn't like themselves the way they are around different people in their lives, such as parents or friends. The results support Gilligan's ideas about the importance of voice for self-esteem, but they do not support her notion that girls are more subject to "voice suppression" than boys, at least among today's children. Levels of voice were the same for both girls and boys with teachers, parents, and male classmates. But with female classmates and close friends, girls reported a stronger level of voice than boys did! For neither gender did level of voice decline with age, and for both genders, level of voice varied dramatically depending on whether the adolescent felt support for self-expression. For both girls and boys, feelings of self-worth varied with level of voice: In social contexts where kids felt like they could express themselves freely, they felt more self-worth.

Many studies buttress the conclusion that girls are no more likely to lose their "voice" in adolescence than boys. For example, a large-scale survey of 10- to 30-year-olds examined their reported general willingness to "go along" with peers even when they do not agree with them. Females overall reported more self-reliance: They were less likely to change their behavior to conform with peer pressure than males (Steinberg & Monahan, 2007).

Now, what about the claim that girls' overall self-worth declines in late childhood and early adolescence? Many studies of developmental change in self-esteem establish that for *both* girls and boys, self-esteem begins to decline in late childhood, levels off in late adolescence and begins a slow, moderate climb in young adulthood, peaking in the 6th decade of life and then declining again (see Robins & Trzesniewski, 2005). And, there is a gender difference. As you can see in Figure 7.2, girls' self-esteem drops more in late childhood than boys' and there is a small but significant difference between females and males until late adulthood. For example, one group of researchers looked carefully at the data from two large studies of global self-esteem, which included a combined total of 155,121 participants (Kling, Hyde, Showers, & Buswell, 1999). They found that males showed higher self-esteem. The level of difference was relatively small, however, compared to gender differences in aggressive behavior (Hyde, 1984) and activity level (Eaton & Enns, 1986). The authors concluded that the idea that girls' self-esteem plunges dramatically at adolescence relative to boys' is overstated. Other studies even indicate that gender gaps in self-esteem for specific competency areas favor girls in some domains (e.g., language arts) and boys in other domains (e.g., sports); they usually appear in early elementary school, and do not increase in magnitude at adolescence (e.g., Jacobs, Lanza, Osgood, Eccles, & Wigfield, 2002). For both girls and boys, weight and physical attractiveness are important predictors of self-esteem as early as 9 years old, but more so for girls (Harter, 2012; see Chapter 9).

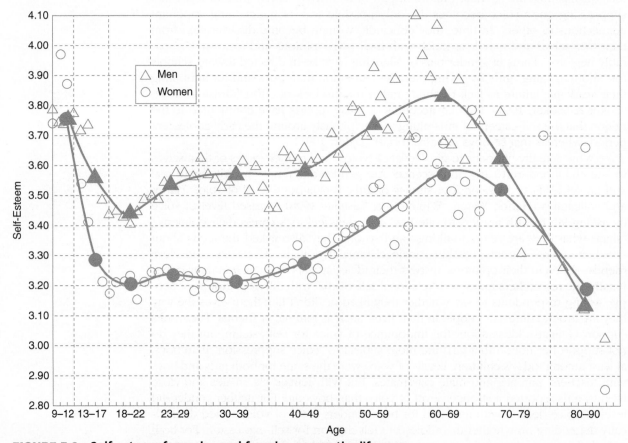

FIGURE 7.2 **Self-esteem for males and females across the life span.**

SOURCE: Robins, R. W., Trzesnlewski, K. H., Tracy, J. L., Gosling, S. D., & Potter, J. (2002). Global self-esteem across the life span. *Psychology and Aging, 17,* 428. Reprinted with permission from the American Psychological Association.

The small but stable gender difference in global self-esteem should be taken seriously, but Kling and her colleagues (1999) caution that inflating the significance of the **self-esteem slide** may create a self-fulfilling prophecy. Adults who believe that girls have lower self-esteem than boys may convey this impression to girls in subtle but powerful ways. Girls may internalize this message and alter their self-appraisals accordingly. In addition, championing the self-esteem deficits of girls may lead some to conclude that boys do not have self-esteem problems. Clearly, there are gender role strains for boys as well. For example, they are more likely than girls to feel social pressure to conform to gender stereotypes (Yunger, Carver, & Perry, 2004). Also, as noted earlier, boys are more vulnerable to peer pressure than girls (e.g., Steinberg & Monahan, 2007). Boys who are not athletically inclined can suffer greatly in social status and self-esteem relative to their peers (Kilmartin, 1994). In Chapters 8 and 9, we will examine other facets of the link between gender and self-evaluation.

Race and Ethnicity

For many years it was assumed that the self-esteem of minority group children would be lower than that of White children because of their minority status in North American culture. This interpretation was based on Cooley's idea of reflected appraisals and social comparison processes. Members of oppressed groups, for example, would be more likely than members of nonoppressed groups to internalize the discriminatory appraisals of others in constructing their sense of self (Cartwright, 1950). Similarly, social comparisons would be more negative when oppressed minorities held themselves to the standards of the majority culture (Gerth & Mills, 1953). Classic doll studies, in which investigators asked children to state their preference for dolls or pictures representing different racial groups, supported these interpretations (Clark, 1982). Preference for White dolls over Black or Brown ones was reported for all children, including those from African American (Spenser, 1970) and Native American groups (Aboud, 1977). These findings were interpreted to mean that children from oppressed minorities suffered from low self-esteem, due to the negative status accorded their racial background and their internalization of pejorative attitudes.

Current research has challenged these interpretations by demonstrating a slight but relatively consistent self-esteem advantage for Black Americans, the minority group most extensively studied, over White Americans (e.g., Gray-Little & Hafdahl, 2000; Twenge & Crocker, 2002). Several explanations have been proposed to account for this phenomenon. Crocker and Major (1989) posit that, to maintain their self-esteem, members of historically marginalized groups engage in three complementary processes. They attribute negative feedback directed toward themselves to the prejudice that exists in society. They make social comparisons to members of their own group rather than to members of the advantaged majority. Finally, they tend to enhance the importance of self-concept domains in which members of their group excel, while discounting the importance of domains in which their members do not excel.

Gray-Little and Hafdahl (2000) summarized the existing data on this subject and concluded that Blacks and other minority groups demonstrate a higher level of ethnocentrism than do Whites. In other words, racial identification is a more salient component of self-concept for members of these groups (see also Chapter 9). African Americans, in particular, benefit from this emphasis on their desirable distinctiveness within the larger society (Judd, Park, Ryan, Bauer, & Kraus, 1995). In fact, strong racial or ethnic identity correlates positively with level of global self-esteem (e.g., Harris-Britt, Valrie, Kurtz-Costes, & Rowley, 2007; Kiang, Harter, & Whitesell, 2007; Phinney, 1990).

It is important to realize, however, that these results cannot be generalized to members of all minority groups, nor even to all members within a single minority. Gray-Little and Hafdahl (2000) make the important point that race is a complex construct, confounded with socioeconomic status, culture, gender, and other important variables. Using race as a dividing criterion to compare groups is appealing because it seems so simple, but it may mask

Strong ethnic or racial identity appears to enhance self-esteem for children and adolescents who are part of a minority group.

great within-group variability. How individual differences arise within cultural/racial groups is now an important focus of research. For example, Bean, Bush, McKenny, and Wilson (2003) found that maternal support and acceptance are key factors in both academic achievement and the development of global self-esteem in African American youth, more so than paternal support. These researchers suggest that mothers play an especially central role in many African American families, and mothers' influence on youngsters' self-esteem is commensurate with that role.

Cross-Cultural Differences in the Development of the Self

As you have seen, very young children learn about themselves largely in the contexts of relationships with parents and other caregivers (Chapter 3). As children get older and their perspective taking skills improve, peer assessments, peer acceptance, and social comparisons become more and more important. The construction of self-concept is a social process, and any social process is conditioned by culture. The judgments, beliefs, values, and expectations of others—parents, teachers, and peers—are embedded in sociocultural meanings and practices. For example, parents in a culture that emphasizes individuality might value "knowing your own mind," identifying your own interests, and learning how to make your own choices. If so, their parenting practices are likely to promote independence, encouraging children to formulate and express their own opinions, interests, and needs, and to participate in family decision making. Parents from a more collectivist culture that emphasizes interdependence might place more value on conformity, respect for others, and maintaining group harmony. If so, their parenting practices might discourage children from identifying or expressing their own opinions and interests, but rather encourage them to be obedient and to concern themselves with supporting the needs of the family.

Such cultural differences suggest that the "self" that develops in one culture will be different from the self that would develop in a different culture. To illustrate, let's examine self-concept and self-esteem in individualistic as compared to collectivist cultures. Table 7.2 lists just a few of the values and expectations that characterize each of these cultural types. Western societies, and especially the United States, are typical of individualistic cultures, whereas Eastern societies, such as China and Japan, and many other regions of the world are more collectivist. Such categorizations are often overly simplistic, however, as we noted in Chapter 1. There are elements of both individualism and collectivism in all societies, and there are many shared values across cultures. For example, relationships with others are central to human functioning in all cultural environments, but the typical approaches to relating may vary. In more individualistic cultures, for example, people may feel comfortable seeking relationships with new partners, whereas in collectivist cultures, loyalty to in-group members (such as family) is often the primary path to meeting

TABLE 7.2   Individualistic and Collectivist Cultures: Differences in Values and Emphases

INDIVIDUALTISTIC	COLLECTIVIST
Becoming autonomous and self-reliant is important; this includes separating from others and following one's unique course, making choices.	Relatedness rather than autonomy is emphasized; personal choices are subordinated to the needs of the group.
Personal opinions, ideas, experiences, and feelings are important; their open, articulate expression is valued.	Perspective taking and identifying group needs is more valued than self-expression.
Social relationships serve personal goals.	Social relationships are more important than personal goals; social harmony with close others (in-group) is the ultimate value.
Achievement and competitive advantage are closely linked; they indicate ability and are self-enhancing; failure is negative.	Achievement is an indicator of both hard work and social support; failure provides information about avenues for self-improvement.

See Table 3.4 for examples related to caregiving behaviors.

relationship needs. Needs for autonomy also appear to be important across cultures, but what contributes to feelings of autonomy may differ substantially. For example, in a more collectivist context, accepting the choices that trusted others make for you may feel as "right" for the individual as making your own choices does in a more individualistic setting (see Grusec, 2011). It is also important to recognize that there are cultural differences among subgroups within countries and regions (e.g., among socioeconomic, racial or ethnic groups), and there can be substantial differences among individuals and families within groups.

When there are cultural differences in patterns of social behavior, what effects do they have on children's developing self-concepts? In more individualistic contexts, independence is a central element of the self. Separateness, personal choice, and standing out from others are part of this independent pattern (e.g., Markus & Kitayama, 2010). "Standing out" is often made possible through achievement, and having pride in one's achievements is expected. That would suggest that seeing yourself as better than others in some ways would be important and therefore seeing yourself in a positive light (high self-esteem) would also be important. Sure enough, from middle childhood onward, North Americans are more likely than people from Eastern cultures to report high self-esteem and to use self-enhancement strategies, such as downward comparisons, to help maintain their positive self-views (Heine & Hammamura, 2007). Even by age 4, Western children refer more to themselves in their narratives, and they make larger drawings of themselves, than children from more collectivist cultures (Schroder, Tõugu, Lenk, & De Gee, 2011). Western children are also more willing to express their own opinions and reactions, including emotional ones (Harter, 2012).

Children and adults in many Eastern societies are more likely than those from Western societies to incorporate the characteristics of close family and friends into their self-concepts rather than emphasizing their own uniqueness (Markus & Kitayama, 2010). A striking illustration of this comes from a study of the neural processes involved in self-representation (Zhu, Zhang, Fan, & Han, 2007). Participants judged whether traits (e.g., brave, childish) were true of themselves; true of their mothers; or true of distant others (President Clinton for U.S. participants; a former Chinese premier for Chinese participants). fMRIs indicated that when Chinese individuals made judgments about themselves the same area of the cortex was activated as when they made judgments about their mothers. Different cortical areas were activated when they judged more distant others. For U.S. participants, the cortical areas activated when they judged themselves were distinct from the areas that were activated when they made judgments about either their mothers *or* distant others.

Rather than being concerned with self-esteem as it is usually measured (e.g., rating oneself high on statements such as "I am proud of who I am"), people in Eastern cultures place more value on self-criticism and self-effacement (e.g., Diener & Diener, 2009). Negative self-evaluations are less likely to be associated with emotional problems (such as depressive tendencies) and more likely to spur self-improvement efforts (Heine et al., 2001). Hard work and achievement are important indicators of self-improvement, but they are seen as intimately related to others' efforts, not just one's own. Pride in personal accomplishments is often interpreted as arrogance; self-respect depends more on having harmonious relationships.

Overall, in Eastern cultures the concept of the self *includes* relationships with others; a person's roles in, and duties to, the in-group are part of the self. Relationships for Western children and adults are not as central to self-concept. They are more like voluntary connections that serve personal needs, and they can be given up or changed (Markus & Kitayama, 2010). Western children and adolescents may strive to be like someone else, but that kind of **identification** process (see Chapters 9 and 10) is not the same as incorporating relational processes into the self-concept. Figure 7.3 illustrates some of these differences in self-concept for developing independent and interdependent self-schemas.

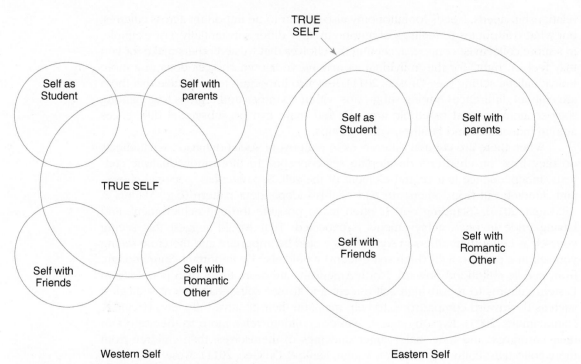

FIGURE 7.3 **Cultural differences in views of the self.**
SOURCE: Harter, S. (2011). *The construction of the self: Developmental and sociocultural foundations* (2nd Ed.). New York, NY: Guilford Press. Used by permission of Guilford Press.

THE MORAL SELF

One important ingredient in self-development is the acquisition of values. Colby and Damon (1992) found that adults who lead exemplary lives tend to have very clear beliefs about what is right, and they consider those beliefs to be a central feature of their own identities. Their self-esteem hinges on acting in responsible ways, consistent with their beliefs. As early as age 5, a child's view of herself as a moral person predicts good behavior (Kochanska, Koenig, Barry, Kim, & Yoon, 2010). For children in the middle years, behavioral conduct is an important self-concept domain that is linked to global self-esteem. Generally, moral beliefs are increasingly central to self-definition as children get older, influencing them to act in responsible ways, but as Damon (1995) points out,

> the development of the self can take many paths, and persons vary widely in the extent to which they look to their commitments and convictions in defining their personal identities. . . . For some . . . morality may always remain peripheral to who they think they are. (p. 141)

In this section, we will examine some theories and research on how the moral self develops and why for some it is more compelling than for others.

Let's begin by specifying what we mean by a moral sense, or morality. First, it is a capacity to make judgments about what is right versus what is wrong, and second, it is preferring to act in ways that are judged to be "right." In other words, morality involves both an "evaluative orientation" toward actions and events (Damon, 1988) and a sense of obligation or commitment to behave in ways that are consistent with what is right. Early on, this sense of obligation is partly influenced by rewards or punishments from parents, teachers, and other adults. Gradually, a slate of standards and principles—a *conscience*—is internalized (see discussion of self-regulation in Chapters 4 and 5) and becomes the primary guide to action, so that a moral adult could even behave in ways that are disapproved by others if she judged the behavior to be right.

It is also important to recognize that moral development and religious experience are not the same thing. Religions do, of course, address issues of morality, and they prescribe standards of conduct. But moral development is part of normal self-development in all individuals, regardless of whether they are practitioners of a religious faith or whether they receive formal religious training.

As we noted in the introduction to this chapter, it is not surprising that parents regard the development of morality as a critical concern. Even though there are cultural and historical variations in the specifics of what is construed as moral, the meaning of morality generally includes some social interactive principles or propensities that are necessary to the successful functioning of all societies and of individuals within society (see Damon, 1988; Killen & Smetana, 2008; Sachdeva, Singh, & Medin, 2011; Turiel, 2006). First, concern for others is important, as well as a willingness to act on that concern by sharing, forgiving, and other acts of benevolence. Second, a sense of justice and fairness, including a willingness to take into account the rights and needs of all parties, is part of a moral sense. Third, trustworthiness, defined primarily as honesty in dealings with others, is critical to most discussions of morality. Finally, self-control is essential. To live by standards requires a capacity and willingness to inhibit one's own selfish or aggressive impulses under some circumstances, that is, to avoid misbehavior. This is one aspect of self-control. Also, to be a useful member of society, or even to fully develop one's talents or abilities, requires effort and persistence regardless of discomfort or difficulty. This is a second aspect of self-control—a willingness to do things that are not much fun, such as work and practicing skills, even when play is more enticing. For example, there may be no exciting way to learn multiplication tables. Hard work and self-control are necessary to achieve long-term goals at any point in the life span. Research on the development of morality has largely focused on this set of fundamentals: concern for others, justice, trustworthiness or honesty, and self-control.

Elements of Morality

Morality requires a complex interweaving of three elements—emotions, cognitions, and behaviors—that do not always work together in perfect harmony. Consider the following true-life experience. Several decades ago, in a blue-collar city neighborhood, 10-year-old Carmen headed for a local grocery store to buy some items for her mother. Her family never saw her alive again. But some other folks later did see her. They were motorists, driving at high speeds on an inner-city expressway, heading home in the evening rush hour. They remembered seeing a girl who looked like Carmen, running naked along the edge of the expressway with a man following her. Apparently, she had escaped from his car when he parked along the side of the road. But none of the motorists stopped, and the man caught the girl. Her raped and beaten body was later found in a remote location.

In the days and weeks following Carmen's disappearance, first one motorist and then another either phoned police anonymously or came forward openly to describe what she or he had seen, although none had reported the incident when it happened. The city's inhabitants were horrified both by the crime and by the failure of the witnesses to help or to come forward immediately, but none were more distressed than the witnesses themselves. Their moral emotions—empathy and sympathy for the girl and her family, shame and guilt at their own failure to come to the girl's aid—were experienced by many as overwhelming. These feelings in many cases were triggered from the beginning, when they first saw the naked child. Why did their behavior not match their feelings? Many witnesses reported confusion and disbelief when they passed the strange scene, and though they felt concern for the girl and guilt at their own inaction, they reasoned that there must be a sensible explanation, one that would make them feel foolish if they made the extraordinary effort to stop. Others indicated that it was impossible to process the events—so unexpected and atypical of their ordinary experience—in the split second of decision-making, and they had only "put it all together" when they heard about Carmen's disappearance on the news. Others thought that someone else would take care of it—after all, hundreds of motorists were passing the same spot—or that the risks of helping were too great.

Most adults believe that their behavior is usually consistent with their beliefs or feelings. But the witnesses to Carmen's plight illustrate that even adults with strong moral feelings do not always think clearly about moral issues or behave in ways that are consistent with their moral sense. Some of the earliest research on children's moral development indicated that children are particularly prone to such inconsistencies. Hartshorne and May (1928–1930) observed 10,000 children between the ages of 8 and 16 in a wide variety of situations where they had opportunities to lie, cheat, or steal. For example, children could raise their scores on a test by sneaking a look at an answer key, cheat on a test of strength, pilfer some change, or tell lies that would place them in a good light. In every situation, the researchers had devised techniques to surreptitiously detect cheating, lying, or stealing. They found that children's knowledge of moral standards did not coordinate with how likely they were to cheat or to help others to cheat. They also found that children's honesty varied from one situation to another. Some children cheated in academic tasks, for example, but not on tests of athletic skill. Hartshorne and May concluded that moral conduct is usually determined by the particular situation and is not coordinated with moral reasoning or training. However, more recent research, with more adequate measures of children's emotions and cognitions, indicates that emotions, cognitions, and actions do tend to become more synchronized with age and that their interrelations are influenced by many factors, including training.

Before we consider these many factors, let's take a brief look at some classic theories of moral development with which you may be familiar, theories that emphasize either emotions or cognitions as the most important source of moral behavior. How do these theories fare in light of modern research?

Some Classic Theories of Moral Development

Freud's Psychoanalytic Theory

In Freud's (1935/1960) psychoanalytic theory of moral development, the behavior of very young children is driven by the inborn impulses of the id, which are completely self-serving desires for sustenance and release, such as hunger or the need to defecate. The superego, which emerges in the preschool period, is the source of moral emotions, such as pride in good behavior and shame or guilt about bad behavior, and once a child has a superego, it is these emotions that impel moral functioning, like an internalized system of rewards and punishments. Freud argued that the superego develops when a complex set of id-driven motives and emotions come into conflict with parental authority. Specifically, beginning at about age 3, vague sexual desire for the opposite-sex parent puts the young child in competition with the same-sex parent, who is much more powerful than the child and thus a frightening competitor. The child's solution to this no-win situation is to identify with the same-sex parent. Identification with the (imagined) aggressor is a solution for two reasons. First, by trying to be like the angry parent, a child wins the parent's approval and affection. Second, by pretending to be the parent, the child attains some vicarious satisfaction of her or his sexual longing for the other parent. The critical element of this situation for moral development is the identification process itself. Identification includes both imitation of the parent's behaviors and, most important, internalization of the parent's standards and values, creating the child's superego.

As we will see in the next chapter, the identification process described by Freud is an explanation of both moral development and sex role development in young children. Unfortunately, research fails to support its predictions. With regard to moral development, attributing moral emotions to the emergence of the superego, sometime between ages 3 and 5, is not consistent with findings that many toddlers show signs of empathy and shame as early as 18 to 24 months, beginning when they demonstrate self-recognition while looking in a mirror. By age 3, sympathy, pride, and guilt appear to be part of the emotional repertoire as well (see Chapters 4 and 5). In addition, even toddlers perform prosocial actions based on empathy (Eisenberg, Fabes, & Spinrad, 2006) and sometimes they seem eager to comply with a parent's rules, even if the parent is not around (e.g., Kochanska, Tjebkes, & Forman, 1998; Turiel, 2006). Such early signs of conscience development undermine the psycho-analytic view that early behavior is driven only by selfish impulses. Finally, and perhaps most important, Freud argued that children develop a conscience because they identify with a parent whom they fear. Yet, as we saw in Chapter 5, parents who intimidate their children are least successful in fostering the development of con-science. Rather, warmth, affection, and support are more likely to be characteristic of parents whose children exhibit signs of mature conscience formation—self-control in the absence of authority figures (e.g., Kochanska, Gross, Lin, & Nichols, 2002). We should note that psychoanalysts since Freud have increasingly explained conscience formation as linked to the bond between child and parent, that is, more as a function of the strength of attachment and the need to keep the parent close than as a func-tion of fear (e.g., Emde, Biringen, Clyman, & Oppenheim, 1987).

The Cognitive Theories of Piaget and Kohlberg

Whereas Freud focused on the impetus that emotions provide to moral behavior, cognitive theorists have emphasized the importance of changes in logical thinking as a source of moral development. To understand how children think about rules and standards of conduct, Piaget (1932/1965) presented children with moral dilemmas and asked them to both judge the behavior of the protagonists and explain what should be done. He also played marbles with children and asked them to describe and explain the rules of the game. Piaget proposed that preschoolers are **premoral** in the sense that they seem unconcerned about established rules or standards, mak-ing up their own as they go along in a game of marbles, for example, and having little regard even for their own rules. At about age 5, Piaget described children's morality as **heteronomous**. They regard rules as immutable, existing outside the self, and re-quiring strict adherence. So, 5-year-old Jasmine might argue that a rule should never be broken, even if some greater good might prevail or even if all the participants in a game agree to the change. When her older sister crosses the street without waiting for a "walk" signal, rushing to help a neighborhood toddler who has wandered into the street, Jasmine might insist that her sister should have waited for the signal no matter what. She might also judge that a boy who broke 15 cups trying to help his mother get ready for a party deserves more punishment than one who broke one cup while actually misbehaving. In heteronomous morality, the letter of the law must be followed, and failure to do so requires punishment. In fact, Jasmine might believe in **immanent justice**, expecting that misbehavior will eventually be punished, even if no one knows about it, as though some higher authority is always watching.

Piaget argued that heteronomy is based on the child's experiences in rela-tionships with parents and other authority figures, where rules seem to come from above and must be obeyed. But in middle childhood, both experience with the give-and-take of peer relationships and advances in perspective-taking skill help children to see the rules of behavior differently. As children and adolescents have more ex-perience in egalitarian relationships with their peers, their moral thinking becomes more **autonomous**, meaning that they begin to understand that rules are based on social agreements and can be changed. Advancements in perspective-taking skills, which also are benefited by interactions with peers, help young people understand that rules and standards are not just a function of authoritarian dictates but that they promote fair play and cooperation, serving to establish justice. They can also be set aside for some greater good or changed through negotiation. So, by about 9 or 10, Jasmine could support her sister's violation of their parents' rule about not cross-ing the street, recognizing the greater importance of protecting a younger child. Also, she would probably be more consistently well behaved than she was earlier, because, in Piaget's view, she has a better understanding of the value of rules and standards for social interaction.

Kohlberg (e.g., 1976, 1984) further investigated children's moral reasoning from late childhood into the adolescent and early adult years. His theory goes beyond Piaget's, offering a fine-grained analysis of changes in the older child's, adolescent's, and adult's reasoning about moral issues (see Table 7.3 for a comparison of ages and stages in Piaget's and Kohlberg's theories). Unlike Piaget's dilemmas, which focused on everyday challenges familiar in the lives of children, Kohlberg's stories were outside ordinary experience and raised broad philosophical issues. Perhaps the most famous of these is the story of Heinz, whose wife is very ill and will die without a certain medicine, which Heinz cannot afford. The druggist who makes the product refuses to sell it, though Heinz offers all the money he has managed to raise—about half of the retail cost—which would more than cover the druggist's expenses. The druggist argues that he discovered the drug and plans to make money from it. In desperation, Heinz breaks into the druggist's establishment and steals the medicine.

TABLE 7.3 Piaget's and Kohlberg's Stages of Moral Development

APPROXIMATE AGES	PIAGET'S STAGES	KOHLBERG'S STAGES
Preschool	*Premoral Period* Child is unconcerned about rules; makes up her own rules.	
		Preconventional Level
5 to 8 or 9 years	*Heteronomous Morality* Child is a *moral realist:* Rules are determined by authorities; are unalterable, moral absolutes; must be obeyed. Violations always punished.	*Stage 1: Punishment and Obedience Orientation* Child obeys to avoid punishment and because authority is assumed to be superior or right. Rules are interpreted literally; no judgment is involved.
8 or 9 to 11 or 12 years	*Autonomous Morality* Social rules are arbitrary, and promote cooperation, equality, and reciprocity; therefore, they serve justice. They can be changed by agreement or violated for a higher purpose.	*Stage 2: Concrete, Individualistic Orientation* Child follows rules to serve own interests. Others' interests may also need to be served, so follow the principle of fair exchange, e.g., "You scratch my back, I scratch yours."
		Conventional Level
13 to 16 years		*Stage 3: Social-Relational Perspective* Shared feelings and needs are more important than self-interest. Helpfulness, generosity, and forgiveness are idealized.
Late adolescents/young adults		*Stage 4: Member-of-Society Perspective* The social order is most important now. Behaviors that contribute to functioning of social system are most valued, e.g., obeying laws, hard work.
		Postconventional Level
Some adults		*Stage 5: Prior Rights and Social Contract* The social contract now is most valued. Specific laws are not most valued, but the process that they serve is, e.g., democratic principles, individual rights.
Some adults		*Stage 6: Universal Ethical Principles* Certain abstract moral principles are valued over anything else, e.g., above specific laws. Social order is also highly valued, unless it violates highest moral principles. (Theoretical; Kohlberg's subjects did not achieve this stage.)

Kohlberg was not interested in whether participants judged Heinz's behavior to be right or wrong, assuming that reasonable people might disagree. He focused instead on the reasons they gave for their judgments. He found there to be three levels of moral reasoning, each characterized by two stages. At the first level, elementary school children usually show **preconventional morality**, roughly corresponding to Piaget's heteronomous level, in which what is right is what avoids punishment, what conforms to the dictates of authority, or what serves one's personal interests. Then, young adolescents move to **conventional morality**, more consistent with Piaget's autonomous level, in which what is right depends on others' approval or on the need to maintain social order. Finally, by adulthood, some people move to **postconventional morality**, in which right is defined by universal principles or by standards of justice, not by the particular rule in question (see Table 7.3 for further elaboration of the stages within each level).

Although individuals at different levels of moral reasoning might come to the same conclusion about what is "right," their explanations reveal that they come to their decisions by different routes. Compare the "pro-stealing" decisions of Jay and Jesse when given the "Heinz" dilemma to resolve. Jay, a preconventional thinker, bases his choice on personal need:

> Heinz should take the drug, because the druggist won't really suffer, and Heinz needs to save his wife.

Jesse, a conventional thinker, bases her decision on the importance of others' agreement or approval:

> Heinz should take the drug, because nobody would blame him for wanting to keep his wife alive. They might blame him if he didn't.

There is some research support for the general trends in moral reasoning suggested in the work of Piaget and of Kohlberg. Consistent with Piaget's view, for example, when young children judge moral culpability they usually pay more attention to consequences (e.g., the number of cups broken by a child who is helping his mother prepare for a party), whereas older children pay more attention to intentions (e.g., whether the child was helping or misbehaving). Consistent with Kohlberg's view, young people around the world progress through the stages of the preconventional and conventional levels of moral reasoning in the same, invariant order. Cross-cultural differences are more likely to be found at Kohlberg's higher stages: The few who reach Stage 5 of the post-conventional level are most often Western, middle-class, urban adolescents and adults (for reviews, see Gibbs, Basinger, Grime, & Snarey, 2007; Jensen, 2008; Snarey, 1985).

Perhaps most important, the roles of perspective taking and peer interactions in the growth of moral reasoning skills, emphasized both by Piaget and by Kohlberg, have been supported. For example, advances in perspective-taking skills such as those described in Chapter 5 generally precede, although they do not guarantee, advances in moral reasoning (see Eisenberg, Fabes, et al., 2006). Also, when children discuss moral issues with their peers they are more likely to think carefully about the ideas and to advance in their reasoning than when they discuss those issues with adults (e.g., Kruger, 1992; Kruger & Tomasello, 1986). Perhaps challenges from a peer may seem less threatening and create less defensiveness than challenges from adults (Walker & Taylor, 1991). See Box 7.1 for a look at the influence that Kohlberg's theory in particular has had on moral education.

 Young children tend to state that people should not cheat because they'll be punished, whereas older children and adolescents are more likely to consider the reasons one might cheat as well as possible alternative actions. How would you classify each of these four children, according to the theories presented by Piaget and by Kohlberg?

Limitations of Classic Cognitive Theories

Despite the support that these cognitive approaches to explaining moral development have received, their usefulness is limited in several ways. First, young children have a greater capacity for moral reasoning than Piaget's theory indicates. For example, although young children judge people's actions by their physical consequences (such as how many cups are broken) more than older children do, still they are capable of focusing on the intentions behind behavior if those intentions are made salient (e.g., Nelson, 1980; Siegel & Peterson, 1998; Zelazo, Helwig, & Lau, 1996). In one study, even preschoolers could tell the difference between intentional lying and unintentional mistakes, and they judged real liars more harshly than bunglers (Siegel & Peterson, 1998).

Another important challenge to Piaget's theory is the finding that young children do not necessarily treat all rules and standards as equally important just because they are specified by parents or other authority figures. Moral philosophers point out that some standards, called **moral rules**, address fundamental moral issues of justice, welfare, and rights, such as rules about stealing, hurting others, or sharing. Other standards, called **conventional rules**, are more arbitrary and variable from one culture to another and are a function of social agreement, such as rules about appropriate dress, forms of address, and table manners. Finally, there are areas of functioning that individuals or families might have standards about—such as choices of friends or recreational activities or participation in family life—which are not governed by formal social rules in Western societies. We'll call these **personal rules** (see Turiel, 2006). Piaget assumed that young children treat all rules as "handed down from above," that is, as determined by authority figures. But researchers have found that even by age 3, children are more likely to judge violations of moral rules as more serious than violations of conventional rules (e.g., Smetana & Braeges, 1990). By ages 4 or 5 they believe that such moral rules should be obeyed despite what authority figures might say (e.g., Crane & Tisak, 1995; Smetana, Schlagman, & Adams, 1993; Tisak, 1993). For example, at 5, Jasmine believed it would be wrong to steal even if there were no laws against it and even if a friend's mother said it was okay. As children get older, they make clearer and clearer distinctions between moral and conventional rules, so that by age 9 or 10 children accurately categorize even unfamiliar rules (Davidson, Turiel, & Black, 1983). Turiel (1978) reexamined data from Hartshorne and May's (1928–1930) classic study of children's honesty and found that the participants were much more likely to cheat in academic tasks than they were to steal when given an easy opportunity. He argued that children probably saw the academic tasks as governed by conventional rules whereas stealing more clearly violates a moral rule.

By adolescence, children assume that their parents have a right to regulate and enforce moral behavior. They usually accept parents' regulation of conventional behavior as well, although there is more conflict with their parents in this domain than in the moral arena. Finally, with regard to personal issues such as appearance, spending, and friendship choices, adolescents balk at parental regulation, often arguing that parents have no legitimate authority in this domain (Smetana, 1988; Smetana & Asquith, 1994). Interestingly, Arnett (1999) argues that parents may push for their right to control personal behavior more as a function of how they judge that behavior (e.g., in some instances they may see it as crossing over into the moral domain) than because they are reluctant to grant their children personal freedom. So, in other words, parents and adolescents may differ in how they categorize rules and regulations. We address this issue again in Chapter 10.

Given what you have learned about cultural differences in self-concept development, you might wonder if children and adolescents make the same distinctions about personal, conventional, and moral domains of behavior in collectivist cultures as they do in the United States and other Western societies. The general answer to that question is "Yes." As Jensen (2008) notes, "children in many parts of the world recognize that not all issues are of the same hue" (p. 295). Even in the preschool years, children across cultures make a distinction between some foundational moral rules (e.g., it's wrong to hit or rob an innocent child) and more conventional or personal ones (e.g., it's wrong to eat soup with your fingers). But there is also substantial disagreement across cultures about the categorization of some behaviors. For example, in some parts of the world honoring a deathbed promise is a moral imperative, whereas Westerners are more likely to see it as a conventional rule.

Box 7.1: Morality as an Educational Goal

In 1917, W. J. Hutchins published the *Children's Code of Morals for Elementary Schools,* emphasizing "ten laws of right living": self-control, good health, kindness, sportsmanship, self-reliance, duty, reliability, truth, good workmanship, and teamwork. Hutchins's code was a widely used educational resource, supporting a character education movement that spanned the first three decades of the 1900s. This was a time of enormous change in the United States, marked by technological advances, population shifts that included immigration surges, and social and moral upheavals. Educators expressed concern about family breakups, increased political corruption and crime, media cynicism, and the decline of religion. Modern movie portrayals of speakeasies, crime syndicates, and loose morals in the "Roaring Twenties" probably capture some of the issues that Americans feared were having a detrimental influence on the youth of the day. Educators implemented character education by suffusing daily school activities with lessons in right living and by initiating student clubs in which moral behavior could be practiced (see Leming, 1997; McClellan, 1992).

As you saw in our discussion of moral development (this chapter), a massive study by Hartshorne and May published in the late 1920s led those researchers to conclude that moral training had little impact on children's moral behavior. These rather disconcerting results may have dampened educators' fervor for organized programs of character education. However, some features of these programs continue even today to be typical of most schools in the United States, such as student clubs and activity groups and "conduct" grades on report cards.

In the mid-1960s, there was a new surge of educational interest in what was now deemed "moral education," fueled by theory and research on moral reasoning and by renewed social interest. Several approaches to moral education became available to teachers, but the two most influential were Kohlberg's (1966) own prescription for translating his cognitive developmental model of moral reasoning into educational practice and a "values clarification approach" to moral education by Raths, Harmin, and Simon (1966). Although the latter approach provided a more detailed formula for teachers and students to follow and was probably more widely used, both approaches focused on encouraging students to examine their own thinking about morality and to come to their own conclusions. The teacher's role was to facilitate, not to impose any code or value system on students. Kohlberg's approach heavily emphasized peer discussions of moral dilemmas as a technique; "values clarification" provided a valuing process for students to follow as they critically examined the values they had learned thus far.

Many criticisms were leveled at these and other similar approaches to moral education. There is some limited evidence that peer discussions, skillfully facilitated by teachers, can help children and adolescents advance beyond their current level of moral reasoning (using Kohlbergian measures; see Althof & Berkowitz, 2006). But teachers found the facilitation of such discussions difficult, and they worried about some of their efforts ending in children rationalizing unacceptable behavior (Leming, 1986, 1997).

Support for the "moral education" movement had waned by the 1980s. But a new surge of interest in character education has emerged, fueled again by social concern with what appear to be declining morals. Parents and community leaders are looking to schools to develop systematic approaches to character development, hoping to counter rising crime and violence, increasing conduct problems in the schools, and apparently widespread malaise and disaffection even among our most affluent and privileged young people (see text, this chapter and Chapter 10). Like the character education programs of the early 1900s, newer programs focus on what their authors regard as widely accepted, even universal, standards of conduct. They often have two integrated goals: helping children understand why these standards are important and encouraging behavior consistent with these standards. Clearly, the current programs are more prescriptive than those developed in the 1960s and 1970s, but they are usually aimed at general standards that most people would agree are important (Althof & Berkowitz, 2006).

Schools often develop their own character education plans, but there are many packaged programs available to teachers. Some of the latter have been the subject of systematic outcome research; many have not. Let's consider briefly one program that incorporates some of the values targeted by most other programs and that uses a broad range of teaching strategies (from Leming, 1997).

Titled the "Child Development Project" (Developmental Studies Center, 1996), this program has the advantage of having been the focus of several evaluation studies. Designed for kindergarten through sixth grade, the program has as one goal to integrate ethical development with all aspects of social and intellectual development. To establish four core values (fairness, concern and respect for others, helpfulness, and responsibility), teachers use five techniques: focusing children's attention on prosocial examples of conduct; applying cooperative learning techniques; using examples from literature as well as real-life incidents to encourage a focus on others' needs and rights; involving children in helping activities; and encouraging self-control and moral reasoning by using an authoritative disciplinary style. There's more: The program is implemented schoolwide and includes a home program as well. A number of studies have compared children in the Child Development Project to a comparison group, using interview, questionnaire, and behavioral data. Leming (1997) summarizes the results as follows:

> [S]tatistically significant program effects have been detected for the following variables: a) self-esteem, b) sensitivity and consideration of others' needs, c) spontaneous prosocial behavior, d) interpersonal harmoniousness, e) preference for democratic values, and f) conflict resolution skills. (p. 18)

(See Leming, 1997, for a comparison of 10 programs, including this one, and Leming, 2008, for a discussion of the difficulties involved in systematically implementing such programs.)

In recent years, other major projects have been tested, incorporating many of the features of the Child Development Project (e.g., the Community Voices and Character Education Project—CVCE; see Lapsley & Narvaez, 2006). When implemented schoolwide, posttest effects on student behavior and reasoning, as well as on school climate, have been positive and significant.

(Box 7.1 continued)

Box 7.1 *Continued*

It appears that character education that has clear goals and specifies sound techniques for implementing those goals can be effective in encouraging some aspects of moral thinking, feeling, and behavior. Critics have raised concerns about at least some programs, worrying that children may be indoctrinated, drilled in specific behaviors rather than being encouraged to engage "in deep, critical reflection about certain ways of being" (Kohn, 1997). Indeed, if character education is based on drill and coercion, teachers can be expected to be no more effective in fostering the internalization of values than parents who use authoritarian techniques. But many character educators recognize such dangers. They encourage schools to include reasoning, emotions, and behavior in their notion of "character." They also foster the notion that character education must begin with the character of the school itself, which should be a caring community that shows respect toward all individuals and provides adult models of character (Character Education Partnership, 1995; see Lickona, 1998). Supporters also argue that many values are indeed shared across diverse religious, ethnic, geographic, and political communities and that if educators are careful to focus on these, character education makes sense (e.g., Berkowitz & Bier, 2004; Damon, 1995; Lapsley & Narvaez, 2006; Lickona, 1998).

Like Piaget's theory, Kohlberg's view may have some important limitations. When moral issues beyond the legalistic ones studied by Kohlberg are examined, both adults' and children's reasoning seems to include factors not described by Kohlberg. Gilligan (e.g., 1977, 1982) has argued that moral development follows different trajectories for males and females. She views Kohlberg's legalistic moral dilemmas and his approach to scoring people's reasoning as biased toward representing a more typically masculine approach to morality. Her concern is that Kohlberg's theory and the research it inspires tends to disregard the "different voice" women use in their approach to moral decision making. Males, she argues, are more likely to use a justice focus (sometimes called the **morality of justice**), whereas females are more likely to use a caring focus (**morality of caring**).

In her own research on moral reasoning, Gilligan (1977; Gilligan & Attanucci, 1988) included more practical dilemmas that are representative of the complex problems real people face, such as struggling with how to deal with an unplanned pregnancy. Although she found no significant differences in moral orientation (care vs. justice) between males and females, she did report some tendency in her data for men to focus on issues of justice and for women to focus on caring issues. However, her major finding has been that both women and men are concerned about both justice and caring and that together these concerns contribute to mature moral reasoning. A substantial body of research supports this conclusion (see Turiel, 2006). Perhaps the most valuable contribution of Gilligan's critique of Kohlberg's work is that she raised awareness of the need to study real-life moral problem solving and addressed the role that concerns about caring play in moral judgments. You will not be surprised to learn that concerns about care are universal, but that people in different cultures often focus on different aspects of care in their moral reasoning. For example, in many Eastern cultures, children and adults are more likely to emphasize the importance of role-based duties, whereas Westerners more often refer to interpersonal feelings when discussing care concerns (e.g., see Miller, 2006). (You will find more about Gilligan's ideas and related research in Chapters 8 and 11.)

Many researchers have studied children's thinking about real-life dilemmas in a child's world and have found that children consider matters of fairness even at ages when Kohlberg's scheme would assume they would not (e.g., Damon 1988; Gummerum, Keller, Takezawa, & Mata, 2008; McGillicuddy-DeLisi, Daly, & Neal, 2006; Sloane, Baillargeon, & Premack, 2012). For example, in studies of sharing and distributive justice, preschoolers and young school-aged children rarely justify acts of sharing on the basis of concern about punishment, as one might expect if they were at Kohlberg's preconventional stage. Rather, they talk about fairness, and if their actions do not quite measure up to what we might consider fair, they at least seem to feel a need to somehow explain why their selfish choices might actually be fair.

To illustrate, Damon (1988) describes a conversation between a 4-year-old and a researcher who asks the child if she would share some poker chips with an imaginary friend. The child initially decides to keep seven of nine chips, including all the blue ones and some of the white ones, and gives her friend "Jenny" two white ones. She explains that her "friend" is younger and that she herself has a blue dress, so clearly she should have the blue ones, and also that she is 4 and so should have four of the white ones. Even though the child's reasoning cannot disguise her blatant self-interest, she seems to feel an obligation to share (she gives away some white ones), and she wants to believe that she is being fair.

Even toddlers appear to have an incipient sense of fairness, showing surprise when rewards are not distributed evenly to equally deserving individuals (Sloane et al., 2012). Older elementary school children, still at a preconventional level of reasoning in Kohlberg's scheme, often try to balance a complex set of concerns in deciding what is fair, concerns not captured by Kohlberg's descriptions. As Damon (1988) indicates, children may now take into account hard work, poverty, talent, and issues of equality when trying to assess the best ways of distributing property or remuneration.

Another limitation of Kohlberg's work seems to be his assumption that moral reasoning is the prime determiner of children's moral behavior. As we have seen, moral reasoning is only imperfectly coordinated with action. Yet helpers who work with parents and teachers are often most concerned with encouraging children's moral behavior. In the next section, we will examine the many factors that influence children's prosocial or antisocial behavior.

Children's Prosocial Behavior

When a child voluntarily acts in ways that seem intended to benefit someone else, we credit her with **prosocial behavior** or **altruism**. Although prosocial behaviors are observed even in toddlers, they tend to increase with age, from preschool to grade school ages and continuing into adolescence (Eisenberg & Fabes, 1998). Altruistic tendencies are different from one child to another, and individual differences tend to be somewhat stable across age. In other words, a child who shows prosocial inclinations as a preschooler is somewhat more likely than other children to produce prosocial behavior in grade school.

Sharing, comforting a friend, helping a neighbor carry her groceries, collecting canned goods for victims of a flood—all are examples of simple prosocial behaviors that we might see from a child. You can probably see that whereas behaviors such as these benefit others, they can be motivated in many ways and could even provide some social reward to the benefactor. Sharing, for example, can help a child maintain a pleasant interaction.

When 15-month-old Michelle went trick-or-treating for the first time, as soon as an indulgent neighbor would put a treat in her bag, Michelle would reach into the bag and offer the neighbor a treat as well. She seemed to be sharing, literally, for the fun of the social exchange. When a child successfully comforts a crying friend she might be trying to regain her playmate's company. Or when she participates in an organized effort to provide relief to flood victims she may be hoping for positive attention from teachers or parents. For developmentalists, labeling an action altruistic or prosocial only specifies that it benefits someone other than the actor, not that unselfish motives are necessarily involved. Let's consider what factors have been found to influence the development of prosocial action in children, with an eye toward understanding how helpers might be able to promote children's prosocial tendencies.

Emotions as a Source of Helping Behavior

In many cases, our emotional reactions to others' distress can be an important source of helping behavior, and the emotion of empathy may be the linchpin (Hoffman, 1982; Kagan, 1984). **Empathy** can be thought of as "feeling with" another person—recognizing her emotional condition and experiencing what she is assumed to be feeling. Hoffman (1982) argued that children have a biological predisposition toward empathy, the earliest hint of which may be the contagious crying of some infants—that is, their tendency to cry when they hear other babies crying. In fact, offering comfort when others show distress is common in chimps as well as humans (Eisenberg, Fabes, et al., 2006). **Sympathy**, an emotion related to empathy, involves "feeling for" another: having concern for the other person, but not necessarily sharing the feelings of the other. Both empathy and sympathy seem to propel some prosocial acts from the time that toddlers begin to clearly differentiate self from other (e.g., Hepach, Vaish, & Tomasello, 2012; Miller, Eisenberg, Fabes, & Shell, 1996; Zahn-Waxler, Cole, Welsh, & Fox, 1995; see also Chapter 5). Children's empathic responses are also associated with their tendencies to inhibit antisocial behavior, as we will see in the next section. Toddlers' early helping behavior may be the result of their empathic feelings, but they still have little capacity to take another's point of view. Hoffman, for example, described the charmingly egocentric effort of a 13-month-old who sought out his own mother to comfort a crying toddler, even though the other child's mother was readily available.

Empathy and sympathy are evident in young children. However, their tendency to lead to effective prosocial action increases substantially with age, especially after the preschool years. Children's improving perspective-taking skills are an important ingredient. One reason appears to be that better role-taking ability can help a child understand how another is feeling and thereby increase the child's own empathic response (Roberts & Strayer, 1996). Also, increased understanding of another's emotions and thoughts should help a child assess what kind of prosocial action, if any, is likely to be beneficial.

In late childhood, the scope of empathy expands, probably influenced by increasing abilities to think about abstractions. Whereas younger children can empathize with particular people whom they observe, older children and adolescents can empathize with whole groups of people who are living in unfortunate circumstances, such as all those suffering from a famine, or from the abrogation of their rights, and so on (Hoffman, 1982).

Clearly, as important as prosocial emotions may be for altruistic behavior, other influences interact with those emotions in complex ways. These include not only advances in cognitive abilities such as perspective taking and abstract thinking but also individual temperamental and personality characteristics, parenting practices, and peer experiences. Also, prosocial behavior involves more than helping another in need. Behavior such as Michelle's spontaneous sharing of her Halloween treats often occurs in the absence of any apparent need on the part of the other and therefore seems not to rest on emotions like empathy or sympathy. Let's take a look at some of the other factors that can influence prosocial action.

Cognitive Contributions to Prosocial Behavior

Let's first consider how reasoning about other people's needs (called **needs-based reasoning**) changes with age, and then we will look at its relation to children's prosocial behavior. In needs-based reasoning, a person must weigh her own personal needs against those of others. For example, Eisenberg and her colleagues have posed moral dilemmas to children in which a child's needs are in competition with the needs of another. In one story, a child, on her way to a party, comes upon another child who has fallen and broken her leg. The first child must decide whether to continue on to the party, which is very important to her, or to find the parents of the injured child. (Compare this dilemma, focused on caring and concern, to Kohlberg's problems in social justice, like the story of Heinz and the druggist.) Eisenberg has found that preschoolers tend to be **hedonistic**—concerned for their own needs. By early elementary school, many children express recognition that another person's need is a good reason for helping—they are **needs oriented**—but they often do not express sympathy, nor do they talk about feeling guilty for not helping. By later elementary school, children begin to express recognition that helping is what is required or socially approved. At the next stage, in late elementary school or adolescence, expressions of sympathy for others, guilt about inaction, and to some minimal degree, reference to duty, become part of the reasoning process. Finally, some adolescents begin talking of the relationship of helping to one's self-respect and of being consistent with one's values. For these young people, it appears, moral values are becoming a core aspect of their self-concept (e.g., Eisenberg, Lennon, & Roth, 1983; Eisenberg, Spinrad, & Sadovsky, 2006).

We have seen in our discussion of the cognitive theories of moral development that moral reasoning is somewhat related to moral behavior. If the kind of moral reasoning that is assessed is similar to the kind of moral behavior, there is a stronger (but still moderate) relationship between reasoning and behavior. This is particularly true of needs-based reasoning and altruistic behavior. In middle childhood and adolescence, more advanced levels of needs-based reasoning tend to be associated with certain kinds of prosocial behavior. Specifically, if the behavior requires some real personal sacrifice, such as volunteering some free time after school, kids whose moral reasoning is more advanced are more likely to participate. Prosocial behaviors that incur little or no cost, such as helping a teacher to pick up the papers she has just dropped, are likely to occur regardless of a child's moral reasoning (e.g., Eisenberg et al., 1987).

Interestingly, moral reasoning, which is likely to benefit from interaction with peers (Tesson, Lewko, & Bigelow, 1987), tends to be more advanced in popular children with good social skills, at least for boys. Bear and Rys (1994) found that boys who tended to be aggressive and to have poor peer relations were also low in needs-oriented reasoning. One explanation may be that children with poor social skills have fewer opportunities for positive peer interactions, contributing to a lag in the development of their moral-reasoning skills. A number of intervention programs designed to promote children's moral functioning, including prosocial behavior and self-control, are focused on using peer discussions. For example, Gibbs (1987) describes a technique using small-group discussions aimed at encouraging empathic responding in delinquents. Actual problem incidents are re-created and discussed, and both peers and adults provide feedback to a participant about their own emotional reactions to the incident and to the participant's attitudes and emotions. Many violence prevention programs incorporate components designed to foster empathy development.

Another interesting observation is that for younger children whose moral reasoning may be needs oriented but at the most primitive level, their tendency to engage in prosocial behavior is especially dependent on their prosocial emotions—empathy and sympathy. With children and adolescents at more advanced levels of prosocial reasoning, reasoning is better matched to prosocial action regardless of how strong their prosocial emotions are (Eisenberg, Spinrad, et al., 2006; see also, Malti, Gummerum, Keller, & Buchmann, 2009). These findings demonstrate that different children can follow different paths to prosocial conduct, suggesting that counselors and other helpers should be able to gain inroads in moral development via more than one route (Hill & Roberts, 2010).

Temperament, Personality, and Prosocial Behavior

As we saw earlier, children who are prosocial in one situation are somewhat more likely than other children to be prosocial in other situations. Also, there is some consistency in the tendency to behave altruistically from early childhood through later childhood. These kinds of observations imply that temperamental or personality variables that are relatively stable across place and time might foster an "altruistic personality" (Eisenberg, Fabes, et al., 2006; Hill & Roberts, 2010). What might these characteristics be?

Personality factors, like sociability, are linked to prosocial behavior in children.

First, children's relative sociability or shyness might be an influence. Children who score low on social anxiety (behavioral inhibition or shyness) are a little more likely to help others than children who score high on this trait, especially when no one has requested their help, when assisting another requires initiating a social interaction, or when helping involves a stranger (e.g., Diener & Kim, 2004; Russell, Hart, Robinson, & Olson, 2003).

Second, as we saw in our discussion of moral reasoning, socially competent children who are popular with peers tend to show greater empathy and prosocial behavior (Eisenberg, Fabes, et al., 2006). It is difficult to sort out which is cause and which is effect in this relationship, but it seems likely that social competence and prosocial behavior are mutually causal, with several other intervening influences involved as well. Children who are empathic, for example, may do better at perspective taking, making them more appealing social partners, and may have closer friendships. The opportunities this creates for peer interaction help boost their perspective-taking skills, which in turn benefit their moral reasoning and empathy, and so on.

Another of these feedback loops may underlie a third link between personality and altruism: Older children and adolescents with a positive global self-concept generally tend to be more prosocial than other children (e.g., Larrieu & Mussen, 1986). Feeling competent and secure may help a child both focus her attention on others and believe that her help will be effective. But helping others also is likely to foster feelings of competency and self-worth (Damon, 1988, 1995; Yates & Youniss, 1996).

Assertiveness is a fourth personality variable tied to prosocial behavior. This characteristic helps illustrate that even though there is some tendency for individual children to be prosocial in many situations, there is also a great deal of situation-specific altruism. Assertive children, who will, for example, defend their possessions, are likely to be prosocial in situations in which no one has asked them to help, probably because offering assistance is, at least in part, an assertive act. Children who are unassertive are usually prosocial when it is requested of them, not when they must take the social initiative themselves. Their prosocial behavior seems to be based more on compliance than that of assertive children. It should be noted also that children whose behavior goes beyond assertiveness to being domineering are actually *less* likely than other children to behave altruistically, regardless of the situation (see Eisenberg & Fabes, 1998). Although assertiveness is positively linked to prosocial behavior, aggressiveness is not. Especially after the preschool years, aggressive children are less likely than others to behave prosocially (Eisenberg, Fabes, et al., 2006).

Finally, a child's capacity for self-regulation, which helps the child modulate her emotional reactions, may be important. You will recall that self-regulation, also known as **effortful control**, is defined as inhibiting a response that is "dominant" to perform a response that is less compelling (Rothbart & Bates, 1998). Eisenberg and Fabes (1992) hypothesized that empathic emotions, although they can motivate prosocial behavior, can also be counterproductive if they are experienced by a child as overwhelming. If the child cannot moderate such emotions, she might focus attention on her own discomfort, and doing so might reduce the chances of a sympathetic response to someone in need. Valiente and colleagues (2004) tested this hypothesis with 4- to 8-year-olds. Children watched a film about a girl who is burned in a fire and later endures cruel teasing by peers because of her scars. After the film, participants were asked about their "self-focused emotions"—feeling upset, scared, and so on—and about their sympathetic emotions—feeling concern, sadness for others, and so on. The children were also measured for effortful control. For example, they were asked to put together a puzzle "blind." The wooden shapes were covered by a cloth and children manipulated the pieces under the cloth (although it was possible to cheat by peeking at the pieces). How much time children persisted on puzzle solving without cheating or becoming distracted was the measure of effortful control. The higher children's scores were on effortful control, the better able they seemed to be at controlling their self-focused emotions during the film and the more sympathy they expressed.

Parents, Peers, and Prosocial Behavior

In Chapter 5 we began an examination of parenting behaviors and of the development of self-control, compliance, prosocial behavior, and conscience in infants and preschoolers. We observed that these aspects of moral development are, on the whole, most effectively launched when parents are authoritative in their style: on one hand, warm, responsive, and sensitive in their caregiving and, on the other hand, demanding, requiring that children live up to standards and values appropriate to their level of maturity (see Baumrind, 1989, 1993; Maccoby & Martin, 1983). The methods of control that seem to foster internalization of those standards and values in the long run involve mild power assertion, sufficient only to capture the child's attention but not to arouse a lot of anxiety, and induction (explaining why it is important to share, for example). It should be noted that parents who are demanding without warmth and sensitivity (the authoritarian style) may actually interfere with prosocial development. At least for toddlers, this parenting style has been associated with reductions in children's empathic responding (Robinson, Zahn-Waxler, & Emde, 1994; see Thompson, 2012). Extremes of negative parenting, resulting in child abuse, seem to suppress prosocial behavior. When abused toddlers and preschoolers see another child in distress, for example, they very rarely respond with sympathetic gestures. Rather, they are likely to respond with hostility and/or fear (e.g., Main & George, 1985; see also Harris, 2006).

In middle childhood and beyond, the same conclusions about what elements of parenting are most effective in promoting prosocial behavior (and inhibiting antisocial behavior) still apply (e.g., Padilla-Walker, Gustavo, Christensen, & Yorgason, 2012). There are also a number of other specific characteristics of parenting that seem to foster children's altruism. First, when parents have strong prosocial values, their elementary-school-aged children are more likely to be seen by peers as prosocial (Hoffman, 1975). Similarly, adults who show unusual prosocial tendencies, such as rescuers of Nazi victims in Europe during World War II, frequently report having had parents who strongly valued caring and helping behaviors (Oliner & Oliner, 1988).

Second, adult modeling of prosocial behavior seems to influence children's altruism. On the whole, models who are perceived by children as competent, models who have long-term, nurturant relationships with children, and models who express happiness after prosocial behavior (rather than receiving tangible rewards for their behavior) tend to foster children's prosocial behavior (see Eisenberg, Fabes, et al., 2006).

Finally, providing children with opportunities for prosocial action seems to help encourage a commitment to altruistic action. Eisenberg calls this "the foot in the door effect." For example, Eisenberg, Cialdini, McCreath, and Shell (1987) found that starting in middle childhood, children who are encouraged to donate in one context are more likely to engage in helping behavior later in another context. This was mostly true for children who valued being consistent. It may be that once children begin to form a stable self-concept, they are more likely to value consistency, and that practicing prosocial behavior then fosters further prosocial activities as children seek to maintain a coherent self-concept. But there are probably other benefits to practice in some contexts, such as gaining increased feelings of competence and obtaining social approval (Eisenberg, Fabes, et al., 2006).

Children's Antisocial Behavior

Antisocial behavior may look quite different as children grow and change, but it is generally distinguished by its intent to harm or injure another or by the perpetrator's disregard for the harm it might cause others (Dodge, Coie, & Lynam, 2006; Parke & Slaby, 1983). It might include physical, verbal, or social attacks (aggression) or it might involve acts like cheating, lying, and stealing. With regard to aggression, it is useful to distinguish **instrumental aggression** (using force or threat to obtain possession) from person-directed aggression.

 "You're my best friend, but you're not fair." This attempt at negotiation—a prosocial behavior—ends in relational aggression—an antisocial behavior.

Many aggressive, antisocial children have a hostile attributional bias. They assume negative intentions on the part of others and are often primed to want to "get even."

Aggression is characteristic of all mammalian species. It seems to be linked to the emotions of anger and frustration, and it clearly has some adaptive survival functions, such as facilitating self-protection in the face of threat (Dodge et al., 2006). Anger expression can serve a communicative function even in infancy. In one study, researchers restrained infants by grasping and holding their forearms about 6 inches in front of their bellies. As early as 7 months some babies' anger showed clearly on their faces, which they turned toward their mothers as if to say, "Hey, I don't like this!" (Stenberg & Campos, 1990).

Some displays of aggressive behavior are normative in early childhood. This behavior might be directed toward adults who serve as sources of frustration as children seek autonomy, or toward peers as children compete for attention or resources (e.g., toys). Temper tantrums with parents and power struggles with peers are not unusual. For example, observations of 12- to 18-month-olds indicate that nearly half of peer interactions involve some conflict (e.g., Caplan, Vespo, Pedersen, & Hay, 1991). Physical aggression usually declines substantially from ages 2 to 4. For example, in one large-scale American study "[t]he most frequent form of early aggression, hits others, occurred in about 70% of the sample at ages 2 and 3, but declined to 20% by ages 4 and 5" (National Institute of Child Health and Human Development [NICHD], 2004, p. 42). At the same time, verbal aggression tends to increase. As children grow in language facility, "using their words" becomes a more typical way of bullying others or expressing anger.

In elementary school, not only does overall aggressive behavior continue to decline for most children, but the nature of aggression changes. Instrumental aggression tends to give way to aggression that is person directed and more hostile than earlier forms (i.e., more strongly focused on hurting the other). This type of aggression can involve physical attacks but increasingly it involves "social aggression" or **relational aggression**, which is aimed at damaging peer relationships. Relational aggression might include social rejection, spreading rumors, teasing, demeaning and humiliating the other in front of peers, and so on. A great deal of research has been directed to relational aggression in recent years, partly because of the role it seems to have played in some school shootings, in which the shooter has been found to be a frequent victim of relational aggression (e.g., Harter, Low, & Whitesell, 2003). Some researchers have found that girls are more likely to use relational aggression than boys, but some studies find just the reverse pattern, or no difference in its use by gender (e.g., Spieker et al., 2012). What is clear is that girls are less likely than boys to use physical forms of aggression (Dodge et al., 2006).

Typically, aggression declines with increasing age, just as prosocial behavior tends to increase, although, as we will see in later chapters, some forms of aggression may increase somewhat in adolescence. Many of the same factors that facilitate prosocial development contribute to the decline of aggressive tendencies, such as feelings of empathy and sympathy, authoritative parenting, improvements in self-regulation, peer experiences that help children to increase their perspective-taking skills, and advances in cognitive skills in general (see Dodge et al., 2006). For example, empathy is linked to the inhibition, or control, of aggression (see Miller & Eisenberg, 1988). Presumably, when someone initiates an aggressive act, the ability to empathize with the distress of the target person can help inhibit continued aggression in that situation, and the anticipation of a target's distress may inhibit future episodes of aggressive behavior. A focus on the other, rather than the self, seems to be a key element of self-control in these situations.

The role of social cognition (especially perspective-taking skill) in the typical decline of aggression has been studied in some detail. Its importance is especially obvious when we look at more aggressive children, whose thinking styles fundamentally involve the misattribution of negative motives to others. In Figure 7.4 you will see an illustration of the **social information-processing** that Dodge and his

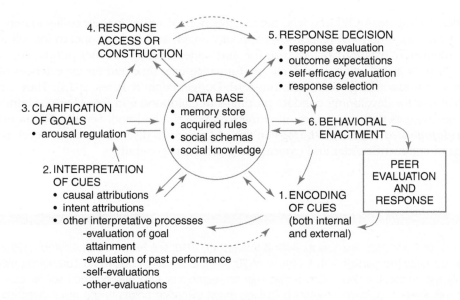

FIGURE 7.4   Social information-processing model.
SOURCE: Crick, N. R., & Dodge, K. A. (1994). A review and reformulation of social information-processing mechanisms in children's social adjustment. *Psychological Bulletin, 115,* 74–101. Reprinted with permission from the American Psychological Association.

colleagues have suggested is required to interpret others' behaviors and make decisions about how to respond in social situations (see Crick & Dodge, 1994, for a review). Let's imagine Brian waiting in line for a drink at the school water fountain. Two other youngsters, involved in a clandestine game of tag in the hallway, bump into him and knock his backpack to the floor. How might he respond?

Dodge's model suggests a typical sequence of mental activity for aggressive children. First, the child encodes cues selectively, focusing on situational cues that suggest threatening content. This tendency may develop as a response to harsh discipline, which enhances the hypervigilance needed to protect oneself from ever present threats to personal security (Dodge, Bates, & Pettit, 1990). Brian might attend more to the boy's body coming close and bumping him rather than to the smiles on the other boys' faces.

The child next interprets or attributes meaning to the cues. A biased interpretive style, called **hostile attributional bias** or hostile attribution of intent, characterizes aggressive individuals who tend to perceive threats even in neutral situations (de Castro, Veerman, Koops, Bosche, & Monshouwer, 2002). For example, Brian might conclude that the boys knocked the backpack off intentionally because they dislike him. The next step is to clarify goals. In Brian's emotionally aroused state, the primary goal might be to get even with the other boys for the perceived insult. For aggressive children, schemas or mental guides for social interaction may be organized around aggression. In other words, these individuals use aggressive schemas to make sense of or to figure out what has transpired socially. Because the situation is likely to be viewed through the lens of perceived hostility and because more socially acceptable responses have not been practiced, the likelihood of aggressive responding is high.

Brian next proceeds to access a behavioral response from his repertoire. Then he evaluates the response and enacts the behavior. Brian, still rather impulsive, is quick to respond in anger. He may start to punch the other boy for the perceived violation. For a child like Brian who is impulsive, who has experienced the benefits of aggression, or who has learned that aggression is a preferred means of problem solving, aggressive responding may become natural. Underdeveloped self-control and weaknesses in verbally expressive means of problem solving could add to the tendency to aggress. Children who fail to make normal strides in their ability to regulate their own emotional responses, especially anger, and whose concern for self is not adequately balanced by concern for, and understanding of other people are at risk for poor and declining academic performance over time and for experiences of peer victimization (e.g., Schwartz, Lansford, Dodge, Pettit, & Bates, 2013). They are also at risk for developing conduct problems in childhood and more serious criminal behavior as they move through adolescence and adulthood. See the **_Focus on Developmental Psychopathology_** in this chapter for a discussion of the development of conduct disorder and externalizing problems generally.

APPLICATIONS

A strong sense of self-worth and a sturdy moral compass are elements widely viewed as important for building and participating in a civil society. Some have recently argued that the two have parted ways and that, in Western cultures, the self has been emphasized over morality. Baumeister and Bowden (1994) put it this way: "[T]he modern growth of selfhood has included a love affair with it. Whereas, for centuries, morality and self-interest were regarded as mortal enemies, the modern individual has increasingly linked the self to positive values. Finding oneself, knowing oneself, cultivating oneself, and benefiting oneself are seen not only as moral rights, but even, increasingly, as moral duties" (p. 144). Nowhere is this trend more evident than in the pursuit of self-esteem. As we stated in Chapter 5, self-esteem has been touted as the holy grail of mental health particularly in the United States. Low self-esteem has been implicated as a key element in a wide variety of problems manifested by children, adolescents, and adults, including low academic motivation and diminished achievement (Carlson & Lewis, 1993), increasing abuse of drugs and alcohol (Kaplan, 1980), teenage pregnancy (Herold, Goodwin, & Lero, 1979), gang violence (Anderson, 1994), spousal abuse (Gondolf, 1985), hate crimes (Levin & McDevitt, 1993), and even murder (Kirschner, 1992).

Identifying low self-esteem as a correlate of mental health problems does not necessarily provide evidence of a causal relationship, as any student of statistics can point out. However, many preventive and remedial efforts are sometimes structured "as if" low self-esteem caused the problems directly. As a result, interventions are focused on changing affect. The premise is that if children feel better about themselves, they will then do better. Their general mental health will improve, and they will behave in prosocial ways.

Obviously, no one would argue that children should hold negative views of themselves! Abundant research has demonstrated that negative self-views are a feature of depression (Beck, 1963; Peterson, Maier, & Seligman, 1993) and that dwelling on one's negative attributes both prolongs and amplifies the depressive state (Nolen-Hoeksema, Morrow, & Fredrickson, 1993). But it is something different to assume that high self-esteem automatically causes positive outcomes. In fact, the goal of pursuing self-validation is viewed from many theoretical perspectives as maladaptive, whereas the goal of acquiring mastery in school and other pursuits is viewed as adaptive

(e.g., Rusk & Rothbaum, 2010; see Harter, 2012). Dryfoos (1990), in a review of 20 years of research, found no compelling evidence that high self-esteem is a necessary precursor for competence. In fact, much evidence points in the other direction, namely that competent performance results in feelings of high self-efficacy, and ultimately, self-esteem. In recent years the emphasis has clearly shifted toward a "skills-first" approach, that is, toward enhancing competencies that indirectly bolster self-esteem. From this perspective, feeling good becomes a "delicious by-product" of doing well (Seligman, 1995).

How great an effect can helpers have on the promotion of these outcomes in children? Morality and even self-esteem are broad constructs that are difficult to concretize in treatment plans. There is no clinical magic, which when applied, guarantees high self-esteem or morality, for advances in theory have outpaced practice applications in some areas. However, a few key points about the self-system and morality may help helping professionals make linkages to intervention.

Where Do We Start?

Nothing about the controversy over self-esteem promotion reviewed above should be interpreted as rejecting the importance of a supportive counseling relationship. Research on common factors in psychotherapies (Lambert & Bergin, 1994) points to the importance of empathy, encouragement, respect, and interest, among other things, for therapeutic change. Nonsupportive, nonaffirming counseling is an oxymoron. The point is that self-esteem enhancement may, in some cases, be a dicey primary objective. Crocker and Park (2004) argue convincingly that the pursuit of self-esteem has short-term emotional benefits but a big cost if one fails in the pursuit. Furthermore, autonomy, self-regulation, relatedness, and health can be compromised by the all-out striving to protect self-worth and avoid failure. Therefore, as Harter says, "It may be useful to make a distinction between the goal of our treatment (e.g., enhanced self-esteem or self-worth) and the target of our interventions" (Harter, 1988a, p. 152). As you have read, many (but not all) children who display oppositional behavior view themselves quite positively (Hughes, Cavell, & Grossman, 1997). For this group, their own estimates of their likeability and popularity do not jibe with teachers' and peers' appraisals. Despite the fact that others find them annoying, they view themselves as popular and likeable. More self-esteem enhancement may be a misguided treatment goal, regardless of whether the child's positive self-image is a true version of how she sees herself or a means of self-protection. This is particularly true for aggressive children who need to learn better ways to manage their feelings and behaviors. Thus, it might be preferable to target the skills and awareness that could lead to increased social self-efficacy.

However, many children, particularly nonaggressive, victimized ones, do suffer from feelings of low self-esteem that often coexist with more clearly defined clinical syndromes like anxiety or depression. The self-esteem of these children might be enhanced as a by-product of cognitive-behavioral interventions to improve coping skills and reduce anxiety as well as by peer group interventions to promote social development (see Chapter 8). Children are typically uninterested in and unable to comprehend abstract phenomenological insights about themselves, anyway. Helping them to focus on skills like coping with problem situations through greater awareness of their resources seems more effective.

What Do Schemas Have to Do with It?

Self-concept is complex, multidimensional, and strongly influenced by relationship history. So substantive changes in self-perceptions, like changes in other concepts (think of the round Earth), do not happen overnight. It takes time and a sufficient number of new experiences to eventually rewrite old cognitive and experiential scripts. Social information processing theories have demonstrated that schemas (including self- and relational schemas) are resistant to change and support consistency in perceptions. This is so, in part, because schemas are economical ways to predict and make sense of the world. They help us filter out a lot of unnecessary information, hone in on the data that have functional significance for us, disregard inconsistent information, and focus our attention on information that supports (or is consistent with) existing schemas. One can view the hostile attributional bias as a relational scheme that has functional significance for a child with a history of coercive interactions. This scheme is not a distortion of reality for someone whose safety once depended on assuming the imminent presence of threats. Obviously, this kind of social information processing bias may severely hurt a child's peer interaction in the present. Although our theoretical understanding of social information processing far outstrips our present understanding of successful interventions, it may be clinically useful to introduce new ways of interpreting social situations. A classic treatment sequence for many anger management programs includes helping clients to recognize provocative stimuli or events in the environment, to stop long enough to reduce levels of reactivity using deep breathing or backward counting, to change distorted thinking by using rational self-statements, and to practice more appropriate social behavior and emotion expression (Kendall, 1991).

The difficulty here is that those strategies that help children generate alternative interpretations, come up with alternative solutions to problems, or increase perspective-taking skills are typically carried out under nonthreatening, nonemotional, intellectualized conditions (called "cold cognitions"; Smith, Haynes, Lazarus, & Pope, 1993). In general, improvements in social-cognitive reasoning following these interventions have not been accompanied by improvements in actual social behavior (Beelman, Pfingsten, & Losel, 1994; Kendall, 1991). As we all know, those cognitive biases that provoke fights or lead to feeling depressed operate below the level of conscious awareness when personally significant and emotionally charged association networks become activated by some event. Bierman (2004) suggests using real conflict situations with real peers, as opposed to hypothetical ones, when working with children to increase the generalizabiliy of treatment effects. Videotaping children in social situations, reviewing the tape with the child, and stopping the action to process "online" those cues the child was attending to and how she was interpreting them may be a way to provide more access to "hot cognitions" (Putallaz, 1983).

Self-Concept, Perceived Competence, and the Looking Glass

The teachings of James and Cooley provide important implications for interventions in this area as well. It seems obvious, but still worth emphasizing, that words can and do hurt. Shaming, sarcasm, demeaning, and name calling by adults are incorporated by children and seep into the fabric of their self-concept. These internal voices can resonate in our psyches throughout adulthood, becoming the root of chronic self-reproach. Often they are coupled with the belief that we are not entitled to the painful feelings these negative messages elicited in the first place. Parents must be helped to understand the powerful looking glass their words create. By the same token, saying no to children should not be expected to hurt their self-esteem. Setting limits authoritatively by saying no when appropriate is necessary and needs to be disentangled from the idea that negative comments hurt children, an unfortunate conflation of ideas.

It is important for helpers to understand children's actual successes and their aspirations for success in the domains of self-concept that are personally important to them (see Chapter 5). Armed with this information, helpers may be able to help reduce the discrepancy between perceived and real competence. Very often, this may involve supporting skill development to enhance performance, such as in academic subjects or social interaction. Alternatively, children, as well as older individuals, can be helped to value components of their self-concepts in which they excel, such as academics, while reducing the importance of areas where they are less successful, such as athletics. Harter's suggestion is "to spend more psychological time in those life niches where favorable self-appraisals are more common" (Harter, 1999, p. 317). Remember, however, that working to reduce the importance of some components, such as behavioral conduct for an acting-out child, is not a good idea! In this case, the careful creation of a discrepancy may be what is called for.

Harter also recommends working toward a generally realistic appraisal of competencies. Bringing the self-perceptions of those who overrate their competencies more in line with external appraisers helps reduce the potential for highly inflated self-esteem. For underraters, the task is more difficult, particularly because higher order schemas, such as global self-esteem, are harder to change. Hattie (1992) believes that these kinds of self-views develop from early attachment experiences and provide durable working models of the self. One example of this might be the low global self-esteem and feelings of unworthiness of victims of severe early childhood abuse or neglect. Despite the relative intractability of such schemas, Harter argues that these self-representations may be more open to revision at critical developmental periods (e.g., transition to new school, adolescence, within intimate relationships) when the need for psychological reorganization occurs. Use of reframing strategies that encourage the person to revise beliefs about the possibility of changing her self-schema and that increase perceptions of personal control and self-efficacy may also be useful (Seligman, 1995). For older adolescents and adults, help in understanding the root causes of the negative self-schema (e.g., early abuse) may provide more cognitive control over these beliefs. Needless to say, change may be extraordinarily difficult in certain cases when the self-views are deeply negative and entrenched.

An "Inside" Job

Self-worth, particularly as linked to morality and a sense of character, is ultimately something that resides inside us. We have seen that it cannot be acquired in a social vacuum, dependent as we all are on the positive appraisals of significant others (Cooley, 1902). But just as true, it cannot be acquired by cosmetic or superficial means. Children have work to do in this area, and this "industry" is not always easy (Erikson, 1950/1963). It is unrealistic for parents and clinicians to assume that failure should be avoided at all costs, that children can be inoculated against self-doubt by unconditional love, or that being "the best" in some competitive arena (social, academic, athletic, or appearance) guarantees high self-esteem. Bednar and Petersen (1995) note that parents (and, by extension, therapists) make a critical mistake when emphasizing approval from others over approval from the self. Well-meaning adults, who are "oriented to avoiding rejection, train only for the development of the public self. The question of fostering the child's development of a private self may remain unasked and unanswered" (p. 353). Parents and teachers should be cautioned that very subtle messages can communicate the notion that pleasing others or winning others' regard is what constitutes self-worth in this world. Children should be helped to take personal responsibility for their actions and to choose internally motivated or learning goals (Pintrich, 2000) when possible. They can also be discouraged from excessive competition and overreliance on social comparison. These approaches can have positive effects on the internalization of personal standards and the fostering of a strong private self.

Moral Development: Putting Flesh on the Bone

Many programs in the past have tried to promote the development of moral reasoning using stage theories. These efforts typically included classroom presentations and discussions of moral dilemmas that students could resolve, requiring in the process some presentation of moral reasoning one level above that of the students (called "plus-one" programs). Other varieties of programs involved didactic instruction about specific character traits, one good quality at a time. Outcome research on these programs has been equivocal at best, even given their primary goal of stimulating students' level of moral reasoning (Enright, Lapsley, Harris, & Shawver, 1983). For one thing, the interventions in this category are directed toward children and adolescents as if they were homogeneous moral thinkers. Recall Piaget's notion of décalage and it becomes clear why we need to consider the variability in cognition among children. More important, these approaches focused on just one element: thinking. We are reminded again of Hartshorne and May's (1928–1930) conclusion that moral understanding does not guarantee moral behavior.

Contemporary writers have recognized the need to include affective aspects in the mix, what some are calling moral motives or moral personality, "the flesh vivifying the bare bones of cognition" (Walker & Hennig, 2004). It's difficult to conceive of morality without also considering its affective side. Developmentalists have long tied the concept of the moral self to concern for others. So perhaps, in a way that is similar to self-esteem, morality is the by-product of prosocial behavior. Schulman (2002) defines morality as composed of three interlocking systems: (1) empathy, (2) moral affiliations or identification with moral "others," and (3) principles or standards of right and wrong. Each can be fostered in specific ways. Empathy is primarily built through security of attachments and responsive caregiving. Affiliation with moral adults is a by-product of authoritativeness that provides a context for teaching about the reasons for rules and prohibitions. Children come to model the behavior and incorporate the reasoning of moral (just and caring) adults. Explicit teaching of principles, messages that encourage children to think about the effects of their behavior, and open discussion of moral dilemmas enhance the construction of a set of moral principles.

Damon (1995) reminds us that the development of morality is dependent on the contexts we inhabit. He notes that schooling provides an excellent opportunity to support the development of prosocial values and behavior. "Like a broad-spectrum vaccine that can block the growth of many dangerous viruses at once, a child's wholehearted engagement in schooling can stop destructive and wasteful activities before they begin to consume a child's life" (Damon, 1995, p. 195). The emphasis here, we stress, is on wholehearted engagement. Children need personal relationships with teachers who hold high intellectual, moral, and behavioral expectations in settings that are small enough to permit these relationships. They need rigorous and meaningful learning experiences that encourage diligence and depth of thinking, and they need high standards for behavior that actually hold them to account for their behavior. This is the crux of developmentally appropriate education at every level, given that most children excel when opportunities to develop competence and character are provided within a supportive environment (see Williams, Yanchar, Jenson, & Lewis, 2003, for an example of an exemplary high school program).

Finally, community organizations such as YMCA, sports leagues, and so on, composed of members who live and work in the communities they serve, have a critical part to play. The most successful ones provide a source of care and mentoring to children and require them to abide by strict rules and regulations. In this way, they provide a healthy dose of adjunct parenting by helping youth to internalize values and standards. Opportunities for children to provide meaningful service to others sharpen their sense of purpose and competence and reduce the demoralization that grows from excessive self-centeredness. Adults will provide a more powerful environment for moral development if we communicate some shared values to all our children through our words and deeds. Children learn the important messages best when homes, schools, and communities speak with one voice.

FOCUS ON DEVELOPMENTAL PSYCHOPATHOLOGY

Conduct Problems

Jason, at 3 years of age, is a high-energy youngster who never seems to sit still. He engages in daily bouts of toy grabbing, aggressive play, and fighting. His behavior definitely has an impulsive quality to it: strike now and think later! Two years later at age 5, Jason is still going strong. He communicates his strong-willed temperament in frequent temper tantrums over household rules. His developing language ability permits him to be more argumentative with adults and peers than he had been earlier. Problems with disobedience occur at home and at school. Jason frequently refuses to go to bed on time, pick up his toys, or take a bath. He rarely sustains attention to an activity for longer than 5 minutes. His mother resorts to spanking out of frustration, but she realizes that this is not effective in getting Jason to change his behavior. In squabbles with preschool classmates, Jason may throw something or hit another child. His teacher finds him a challenge to her patience and her classroom management skills.

Stop for a moment and reflect on 5-year-old Jason's behavior. How would you evaluate this youngster? Do you consider his behavior normal or problematic? Now consider him at age 8. He is in the third grade. His aggressive behaviors have persisted, primarily in the form of fighting and taunting other students. He is not well liked by classmates and has difficulty fitting into the social fabric of the class. His academic performance is marginal, and he finds schoolwork "boring." Jason has begun to steal toys and money from his classmates and has been caught vandalizing property belonging to one of his neighbors. How would you assess Jason's problems now?

If you view Jason's profile as problematic, your assessment is in line with current research on antisocial behavior. Antisocial behavior is a multidimensional term, which is usually characterized by the presence of aggression or the intent to harm another person. Recent formulations have recognized that antisocial behavior in adolescence and adults may also include such acts as risky sexual activity, substance abuse, defiance, cheating, lying, and vandalism (see Frick & Nigg, 2011). Antisocial behavior can be both overt, such as hitting, and covert, such as cheating. When these behaviors are serious enough to warrant a diagnosis in children and adolescents, **oppositional defiant disorder (ODD)** or **conduct disorder (CD)** are the most likely classifications depending on the nature, duration, and severity of symptoms. A diagnosis of **antisocial personality disorder (APD)** is typically reserved for adults (American Psychiatric Association [APA], DSM-V, 2013). In this section, we use the broad construct of conduct problems as a general descriptive term for externalizing problems that include disruptive, impulse control, and conduct disorders.

The scope of the problem. Conduct problems burden society with enormous economic and social costs. However one frames the problem—as aggression, behavior problems, conduct disorder, delinquency, or crime—its effects are borne by victims and their families, by perpetrators whose lives are restricted, and by taxpayers who fund the costs of incarceration, rehabilitation, treatment, and security (Krug, Mercy, Dahlberg, & Zwi, 2003). The exercise of criminal justice in the United States is a growth industry. The United States has the world's largest prison system and incarcerates more people than any other country (Currie, 1998; Walmsley, 2007). From 1982 to 2003, the number of individuals employed in the U.S. justice system increased by 86%. Total criminal justice expenditures increased 418% from 1982 ($36 billion) to 2003 ($185 billion). The number of incarcerated individuals has shown a steady increase since the 1980s, and, in 2005, more than 7 million people in the United States were either on probation, on parole, in prison, or in jail awaiting trial (U.S. Bureau of Justice Statistics, 2007: see Chapter 12).

Research clearly confirms that patterns of criminality can start early. A recent report of the Office of Juvenile Justice and Delinquency Prevention's Study Group on Very Young Offenders (Loeber & Farrington, 2000) states that child delinquents (ages 7 to 12) have "a 2- to 3-fold increased risk of becoming tomorrow's serious, violent and chronic offenders" (p. 738). Although rates of child delinquency are low compared to older offenders, they are nonetheless significant. One in 12 murders committed in 2002 (8%) involved a child offender, implicating them in an estimated 1,300 murders. More tellingly, approximately 48% of crimes committed by juveniles never get reported to the police (Snyder & Sickmund, 2006). Such evidence has led to the contemporary emphasis on prevention and early intervention to reduce the growth of chronic antisocial behaviors and, additionally, to reduce costs of supporting adolescent and adult offenders. Much more attention is now trained on early child delinquents

 Nicole and her mother describe a negative, defiant interaction pattern they have developed. Her mother reports, "Usually, she ends up winning" — suggesting that she gives up demands for compliance when the child becomes whiny and demanding.

and persistently disruptive children—those who have yet to commit crimes but whose behavior puts them on a pathway to later delinquency (Loeber & Farrington, 2000).

Pathways of antisocial behavior. Several developmental pathways can eventually lead to antisocial outcomes in adolescence and adulthood. One pathway has a life-course trajectory characterized by the presence of oppositional, noncompliant, and aggressive behavior that begins early, persists and diversifies over time, and becomes increasingly more serious. This **early-starter pathway** has been called life-course persistent (LCP; Moffit, 1993b). A second pathway for late starters, whose experience with delinquent activities begins at adolescence, is less likely to result in adult criminality. This **adolescent-onset or late-starter pathway** called adolescence-limited (AL) antisocial behavior, although serious, seems to be more reflective of a difficult or exaggerated reaction to the adolescent period (Moffit, 1993b). Both pathways are more complicated than they seem, and others have identified variations on these two pathways (see Loeber, Burke, & Pardini, 2009). However, early- and late-starter patterns remain among the best understood and have the most support from longitudinal studies (Farrington, 1995; Moffit, Caspi, Harrington, & Milne, 2002).

Most of the evidence for these models comes from studies on males, for males show higher rates of externalizing disorders compared to females across the life span (Moffit, Caspi, Rutter, & Silva, 2001). Some have questioned whether girls exhibit the LCP pattern at all. A recent report of the longitudinal Dunedin Multidisciplinary Health and Development Study (Odgers et al., 2008), which was initiated in 1972, provides evidence for the existence of this dual pathway in girls as well as boys. When girls show antisocial aggression in childhood and adolescence, they are also much more likely to have comorbid depression and anxiety. This phenomenon has been called "selective female affliction" (Eme, 1992). Rates of disorders are lower for girls in childhood but, when girls suffer from childhood disorders, the disorders are more serious.

In general, there is strong evidence for the continuity of antisocial behavior. People diagnosed as having antisocial personality disorder as adults almost always report histories of conduct problems in childhood and adolescence. Roughly two thirds of 3-year-olds who display extreme problems with impulsivity and defiance continue to show these behaviors at age 8, and these early problems are related to further difficulties in school (Campbell, 1987). Children diagnosed with conduct problems in adolescence have typically shown these problems since early childhood (Lahey, Loeber, Quay, Frick, & Grimm, 1992). Unfortunately, Odgers et al. (2008) report that violent, aggressive behaviors do not necessarily remit in time. Approximately one third of the LCP males in the Dunedin study were reconvicted of some new violence-related offence between the ages of 26 and 32. Three quarters of the LCP females in this group reported some form of physical violence directed toward themselves or others within the past year. Furthermore, there is some evidence that the incidence of conduct problems in childhood is increasing. When kindergarten teachers were surveyed by the National Center for Early Development and Learning, 46% indicated that more than half of their students did not have the

TABLE 7.4 When Should a Parent Seek Help?

- When child refuses to do what parent asks them to do 8 out of 10 times
- When a teacher or day care provider reports child has a problem with aggression toward peers and has difficulty making friends
- When parents feel they aren't successful in helping child reduce aggression
- When child has developmental problems making it difficult for him or her to learn social skills

SOURCE: Used with permission of Carolyn Webster-Stratton.

requisite emotion regulation skills and social competence to succeed in kindergarten (West, Denton, & Reaney, 2001).

On the other hand, some oppositional behaviors are relatively normal for young children of 4 and 5 years of age (Achenbach & Edelbrock, 1983). Sometimes caregivers fail to appreciate children's normal variations in activity level and willfulness. The important thing to remember is that, in the less extreme cases, these oppositional behaviors tend to recede around age 8. The developmental course that is problematic is one in which these behaviors are maintained into elementary school, then enlarged and expanded on in more delinquent ways. A number of risk factors, both internal and external, operate in synergistic fashion to set this LCP trajectory in motion. Like a storm that gathers strength as it moves along, early antisocial behaviors in certain cases are compounded by related problems in families, classrooms, and peer groups that often trap youngsters in a downward spiral. Table 7.4 provides some guidance about when a parent should seek outside help for a child exhibiting oppositional behaviors.

Physiological and Neuropsychological Influences

Certain physiological and neuropsychological characteristics have been identified as markers of risk. Children who had "difficult" temperaments as babies have been found to have significantly more behavior problems at age 3 than other children (Bates, Maslin, & Frankel, 1985). Efforts to understand the risks more specifically have included exploring genetic contributors, delayed neural maturation, sympathetic nervous system arousal, and circadian rhythm patterns. Molecular geneticists have discovered that the presence of the long allele version of the dopamine receptor D4 (DRD4) is implicated in higher levels of aggression, novelty-seeking, attention problems, and externalizing disorders (Benjamin, Ebstein, & Belmaker, 2002). When present in combination with the short allele version of the serotonin transporter gene (5-HTT), which is related to anxiety and depression, risks of comorbid internalizing and externalizing disorders accumulate substantially (Schmidt, Fox, & Hamer, 2007). Some research supports the relationship of hormones, specifically prenatal exposure to testosterone, to heightened aggressiveness and disinhibition in males (Baron-Cohen, 2002) which, in combination with slower brain maturation in certain areas, delays language and emotion regulation skills (McClure, 2000). Weaknesses in verbal skills and problem-solving abilities reduce children's ability to cope with problems verbally, to understand consequences, to take others' perspectives, and increase the odds of solving conflicts through physical force (Moffitt & Lynam, 1994). Deficits in emotion regulation that coexist with high activity levels appear to set the stage for conflictual behavior management situations at home and school (Barkley, 1997; Lahey, McBurnett, & Loeber, 2000).

The investigation of cardiac vagal tone as a biomarker of risk is another promising field of study. The two opposing components of the autonomic nervous system (ANS), the sympathetic and parasympathetic divisions, are mediated by the vagus nerve, which supplies fibers to the heart and other organs and feeds back input to the brain. The vagus nerve helps slow down the heart, acting, among other things, as an arm of the parasympathetic system to keep the ANS in balance (Porges, Doussard-Roosevelt, Portales, & Greenspan, 1996). Vagal tone refers to how effectively the vagus nerve mediates the parasympathetic system. An estimate of vagal tone can be derived from the ebb and flow of heart rate, a measure called respiratory sinus arrhythmia (RSA). Studies have shown that reduced vagal tone/low RSA is associated with aggression, hostility, and depression in children, adolescents, and adults (Beauchaine, 2001; Calkins, Graziano, & Keane, 2007).

Other biological markers related to problems with aggression are lower baseline levels of cortisol and lower morning-to-evening cortisol ratios compared to normal, nonaggressive samples. This abnormal cortisol pattern, observed in antisocial males and females, has also been associated with the tendency to sleep late and to stay up late, called "eveningness" as opposed to "morningness" (Carskadon, Viera, & Acebo, 1993). Recent evidence suggests that the tendency toward eveningness exists prior to the delayed phase preference changes ushered in at adolescence, and thus may represent a stable temperamental dimension of risk for externalizing problems. Susman and her colleagues (2007) report that eveningness was significantly associated with rule-breaking and conduct problems in boys and to relational aggression in girls, as has been observed in older groups.

Adverse Environmental Influences

Conditions such as poverty, substandard housing, low levels of parental education, teen parenting, parental substance abuse, membership of family or friends in gangs, large family size, inadequate educational opportunities, exposure to violence, and frequent residential moves exert great stress on family resources and are related to the development of antisocial behavior (e.g., Bolger & Patterson, 2001; Bradley & Corwyn, 2002; Rutter & Giller, 1983; Serbin & Karp, 2004). Such conditions increase the likelihood of hostile, harsh parenting; they heighten the risk of physical abuse, which is clearly related to later aggressive behavior (Cicchetti, 1989); and they are associated with chaotic home environments (noisy, lacking in routine, crowded) which also predict children's disruptive behavior (Jaffee, Hanscombe, Haworth, Davis, & Plomin, 2012).

More proximal influences include the characteristics of the parent–child relationship. Much of the current research on the early antecedents of antisocial behavior focuses on parent–child socialization practices. Patterson's influential model of **coercive family interaction** describes how children learn to act aggressively (see Figure 7.5). Based on the concept of negative reinforcement, Patterson and his associates have shown that young children learn to escape aversive consequences (such as turning

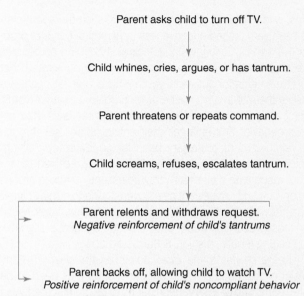

FIGURE 7.5 **Example of coercive parent–child interaction.**

off the TV) by whining, complaining, having tantrums, and so on, which cause parents to give up their demands for compliance (e.g., Snyder & Patterson, 1995). As soon as parents or caregivers cooperate with the child by backing off, the child reinforces the adults by stopping the unpleasant behavior (whining or crying). Sooner or later, these parents learn that the best way to escape or avoid the unpleasant situation their children create is by giving in to their children's demands. Thus, aggressive children reinforce parental cessation of demands by providing their parents with some short-lived peace and quiet. In such coercive interaction sequences, fairly typical in families of antisocial children, children are trained in the effectiveness of aggressive noncompliance and learn powerful parent-control strategies.

Both child and parent characteristics appear to contribute to these coercive cycles. Processes that foster and evolve from early insecure attachments (Fearon, Bakersman-Kranenburg, van IJzendoorn, Lapsley, & Roisman, 2010) are important, along with temperamental differences in children's proneness to anger (Kochanska, Barry, Stellern, & O'Bleness, 2009; Kochanska & Kim, 2012). Longitudinal studies have found that with insecure toddlers who are anger-prone, parents tend to use ever increasing power-assertive discipline strategies, and that by school age their children are rated both by themselves and by teachers as oppositional disruptive and callous. But securely attached toddlers who are anger-prone do not usually follow this negative pathway. For anger-prone toddlers, "early insecurity appeared to act as a catalyst for the parent-child dyad embarking on a mutually adversarial path toward antisocial outcomes, whereas security defused such a maladaptive dynamic" (Kochanska & Kim, 2012, p. 783).

Implications for Treatment

The best treatments for conduct problems are multidimensional, targeting individual, family, educational, and peer-related contexts. Despite this consensus, treatments are often based on "magic-bullet" approaches, as evidenced by court-mandated requirements for individual psychotherapy, group therapy, boot camps, wilderness programs, and the like. Such therapeutic efforts have very limited effectiveness in reversing conduct problems (Henggeler, Schoenwald, & Pickrel, 1995) and sometimes make problems worse. One famous study demonstrated that group treatments for antisocial youth pose a large iatrogenic increase in the rate and type of behavior problems. In other words, treating antisocial youth in group settings potentiates their antisocial behavior and enlarges their antisocial skill set through peer reinforcement of deviant behavior or "deviancy training" (Dishion, McCord, & Poulin, 1999). This finding received recent corroboration with a bit of a twist. Adolescents in mixed groups (with deviant and nondeviant peers) were found to display higher rates of deviant behavior and positive attitudes toward drug use than those receiving treatment in a homogeneous high-risk group setting (Poulin, Dishion, & Burraston, 2001).

Research has made three points crystal clear: (1) Early conduct problems in children are serious; (2) they need to be treated early; and (3) intervention needs to be multifaceted. Alan Kazdin (1995), a major figure in the study of child psychopathology, said that if antisocial behavior is not reversed by the end of the third grade, it will have progressed to a level comparable to chronic illness, like diabetes, and will need to be managed as such. Researchers have responded to the urgency of this message by creating theoretically sound and developmentally appropriate programs that have demonstrated efficacy.

Multisystemic therapy (MST; Henggeler, Mihalic, Rone, Thomas, & Timmons-Mitchell, 1998) is a treatment approach that provides family-based services for adolescent offenders who are at risk for out-of-home incarceration. Therapists who are part of a treatment team average 60 contact hours with families in their homes over 4 months. Treatment team members are available 24 hours a day and have small family caseloads. Therapists use techniques from behavioral, cognitive, and family-therapy traditions to support the family's cohesiveness, reduce problematic symptoms, and reinforce positive adjustment for the offending youth and family. One of the major program goals is the creation of a strong community support system for the family in order to promote treatment adherence. MST has been successful in reducing recidivism and need for placement. A recent meta-analysis of 11 studies (Curtis & Ronan, 2004) found 70% of families and youth who received MST showed improved functioning compared to those receiving other more conventional forms of treatment. Comprehensive school-based programs to reduce hostile attributional bias and promote effective conflict resolution have also shown promise. The Resolving Conflict Creatively Program (RCCP), which began in 1994 in the New York City public schools, has now been implemented in more than 400 urban, suburban, and rural schools in the United States (Brown, Roderick, Lantiere, & Aber, 2004). Aber and his colleagues (Aber, Jones, Brown, Chaudry, & Samples, 1998) showed that when students were taught a high number of lessons (an average of 23) by teachers with moderate levels of training in the program, the students demonstrated less dramatic increases in hostile attributions and fewer aggressive behaviors than comparison groups over time.

The Incredible Years (IY; Webster-Stratton et al., 2001) is a prevention program for at-risk children (ages 2 to 10) and their families that is intended to prevent conduct problems before they take root. Originally designed to treat clinic-referred children diagnosed with ODD, the program was adapted and expanded for use as a prevention program in preschools and elementary schools. The IY program incorporates programs for parents, children, and teachers. Parent training has three levels: basic (parenting skills, discipline), advanced (parent communication and anger management skills, conflict resolution), and school (home–school relationships, supporting educational achievement). Parents meet in small groups to discuss topics, watch videos of common problems, and role-play solutions. The curriculum for children, Dina Dinosaur Social Skills Curriculum, utilizes "child-size" dinosaur puppets and video vignettes to engage children in learning and practicing social and emotional skills. A third level of prevention includes a program for teachers that uses video, group discussion, and practice to help teachers learn effective management techniques for difficult behavior problems. All three curricula emphasize developing positive interpersonal relationships and effective emotion regulation skills. Program effectiveness studies show clear and sustained improvements in reducing conduct problems (Webster-Stratton & Hammond, 1997; Webster-Stratton & Reid, 2003), in improving school readiness and reducing classroom disruptive behavior in low-SES children (Webster-Stratton, Reid, & Stoolmiller, 2008), and reducing ADHD symptoms in preschool children (Jones, Daley, Hutchings, Bywater, & Eames, 2008). Encouraging research reports from programs like the ones mentioned here provide clinicians with excellent guidance in how to address conduct disorders effectively.

SUMMARY

Self-Concept

1. Although preschoolers can describe themselves, they have difficulty coordinating the different aspects of themselves. Also, they do not accommodate the opposition of some traits, such as "nice" and "mean," and they usually see themselves in an overly positive light. By middle childhood, the Me-self is becoming a more organized structure, although children still tend to emphasize the positive. Gradually, more traitlike concepts of self emerge, social comparison begins building on perspective-taking skills, and self-esteem tends to decline a bit.

2. During middle childhood and beyond, the self-concept can be divided into multiple domains, such as academic and nonacademic, and each of these can be further

differentiated. A global sense of self and self-esteem may coexist with these more differentiated assessments of self. Appearance is particularly associated with overall self-esteem, especially for girls.

3. Global self-esteem depends on competence in areas of importance to the individual, as William James suggested. In evaluating their own competencies, children may use concrete standards (e.g., making a team), but they are also influenced by social processes, as suggested by Cooley. They internalize the assessments of others, and they engage in social comparison, evaluating their own abilities and accomplishments against those of others who resemble them in some important way. They tend to be motivated by a self-enhancing bias, sometimes making downward social comparisons when their self-esteem is at stake. Children's self-appraisals come more and more into congruence with others' appraisals as they get older.

4. There is a small but stable gender difference in self-esteem favoring males in late childhood and early adolescence, but little evidence of a self-esteem slide for girls. Level of voice is one predictor of self-esteem, but girls' and boys' levels of voice do not appear to differ at adolescence.

5. Older views that marginalized groups would have lower self-esteem than mainstream groups due to the internalization of discriminatory appraisals are not supported by current research. African Americans, for example, have a slight self-esteem advantage over White Americans. In general, strong racial or ethnic identity correlates positively with level of global self-esteem, although findings vary from group to group and from individual to individual.

6. In different cultures, the judgments, beliefs, values, and expectations that influence self-concept are likely to differ. For example, individualistic cultures value independence more than collectivist cultures, which value interdependence more. As a result, both self-construals and the bases of self-worth evaluations tend to be different as well. For example, in individualist cultures, being proud of oneself, an element of self-esteem, is important and predicts positive outcomes if it is not overly inflated (narcissistic). But in collectivist cultures, having harmonious relationships is more important for self-respect. Pride in oneself is seen as arrogance, and self-criticism in the service of self-improvement is more valued.

The Moral Self

7. The meaning of morality varies across individuals, groups, and cultures, but generally includes fundamental principles necessary to successful functioning of society: concern for others, a sense of justice and fairness, trustworthiness or honesty, and self-control.

8. Emotions, cognitions, and behaviors are all part of morality, and are not always well coordinated.

9. In Freud's psychoanalytic theory, conscience emerges between ages 3 and 5, when children identify with the same-sex parent. In the process, children internalize the same-sex parent's values and rules, forming a superego. Much evidence is inconsistent with this view. For example, moral emotions and prosocial behavior begin as early as toddlerhood.

10. Piaget and Kohlberg propose cognitive theories, arguing that moral development is influenced by developmental changes in logical thinking and emerges in a series of stages. Although there is some clear support for these views, there are inconsistent findings. For example, Piaget assumed that preschoolers treat all rules as inviolable, determined by authorities. But even 3-year-olds judge violations of moral rules, such as rules about stealing, more seriously than violations of conventional rules, such as how one should dress.

11. Altruism may be motivated in many ways. Emotional reactions, such as empathy and sympathy, are important motivators. Even toddlers show signs that empathy can propel prosocial action such as sharing or comforting, but such emotions are much more effective motivators after the preschool years, as perspective-taking ability improves.

12. Needs-based reasoning can also affect prosocial behavior and shows predictable developments with age. It also tends to be more advanced in popular children with good social skills, especially boys. Also, younger children whose moral reasoning is needs oriented are not as likely as older children to engage in prosocial behavior unless they also experience prosocial emotions. For older children whose reasoning is needs oriented, the presence of such emotions is not so important.

13. Personality characteristics also affect tendencies toward prosocial behavior—characteristics such as sociability, social competence, positive self-concept, assertiveness, and effortful self-control.

14. Parents who use an authoritative parenting style with high levels of warmth and demandingness seem to promote prosocial behavior. Also, when parents have strong prosocial values their children are likely to follow suit. Providing children with opportunities to practice prosocial behavior increases further prosocial behavior, referred to as the "foot in the door effect."

15. Physical aggression, like hitting, is common in 2- and 3-year-olds but declines substantially by ages 4 and 5 and continues to decrease in middle childhood. Forms of aggression also change with age. Instrumental aggression gives way to person directed forms, such as relational aggression (e.g., spreading rumors, teasing).

16. Many factors contribute to declines in aggression with age, such as perspective-taking skills. For children who show high rates of aggression, social information processing often appears to involve a hostile attribution bias. That is, these children tend to misattribute negative motives to others. Hostile attributions lead these children to defend themselves or to extract revenge. Such children are using aggressive schemas to make sense of social interactions.

CASE STUDY

Kevin Miller, a White fifth-grade student at Greentree Elementary School, is in the principal's office with his parents. Mr. Dolan, the school principal, has just informed Mr. and Mrs. Miller that Kevin's fifth-grade trip privilege will be revoked because of an accumulation of disciplinary offenses. Kevin's behavior in fifth grade has become progressively more disruptive. This time, he has managed to create enough problems for his teachers to prevent his participation in the end-of-the-year event, which was planned as a reward for the students' effort and achievement.

Kevin is a very intelligent and physically attractive youngster with particular interests and abilities in sports and computer games. In second grade, he was identified as a candidate for the school's gifted student program, yet he invests little energy in schoolwork. He tells his teachers that he finds the assignments boring and can find no reason to involve himself in the learning process. He does little studying, but he manages to get by with a C+ average. In class, he talks to other students when he should be working, makes disrespectful comments to his teachers, and basically tries to get away with doing what he pleases most of the time.

Kevin relishes his position of power in the group. Many students in the class look up to Kevin because of his engaging bravado. They like him because he is often funny and provides a diversion from class work. Other students find him a nuisance who distracts the teachers from their instruction. Students know that if they work with Kevin on a group project, they may have a good time, but it will come with a price: getting in trouble with their teachers.

Kevin's parents have a long history of conferencing with the school principal and counselor. Over the years, problems have increased from some concerns about his attention span in the early grades to more serious issues. In fourth grade, Kevin was caught cheating on a test proctored by a substitute teacher. Kevin claimed that he was falsely accused because the teacher "didn't like him." At the beginning of fifth grade, Kevin responded to his English teacher, who was trying to get him to focus on a classroom writing assignment, with a profane comment. When confronted about his behavior, Kevin was convinced that he did not do anything seriously wrong. His explanation was that he was joking, and he suggested that the adults should "lighten up."

Kevin's parents believe it is their job to stand up for their only son and support him, even though they are unhappy about his frequent problems at school. The Millers describe their son as "lively and creative" and "smarter than they are" in some areas, such as computer literacy. Encouraged by the school counselor, they initiated private counseling for Kevin at the end of fourth grade. Kevin has seen his counselor sporadically for almost a year. Both parents believe that Kevin is a good boy whose irrepressible spirit and intellect get him into trouble with those who misunderstand him.

Faced with this new consequence, Kevin is quite upset. He was looking forward to the class trip and believes that the punishment is extreme. The Millers understand the principal's reasoning, but they also disagree with the punishment. They indicate that they will request a meeting with the superintendent to have the decision changed. They express the view that most kids behave like Kevin sometimes. From their perspective, Kevin should be allowed to express himself and to have the autonomy to make choices about what he does. They emphasize his persistence and interest in activities that engage his attention. They come close to faulting Kevin's teachers for failing to motivate him.

The district superintendent, after considering the case, decides that depriving Kevin of the trip would jeopardize any relationship teachers would be able to develop with him in the future. Kevin's consequence is changed to an in-school suspension; he is allowed to participate in the class trip.

Discussion Questions

1. What are the issues involved in Kevin's case? What assessment can you make of his moral development and his self-concept?
2. If you were his counselor, what would you recommend to promote healthy development?

PRACTICE USING WHAT YOU HAVE LEARNED

In the Pearson etext, apply these ideas to working with others.

Video Exercises

JOURNAL QUESTIONS

1. Give an example of a moral principle you learned as a child. How and when did you learn it? Provide an example from your own experience of an inconsistency between your level of moral reasoning and your behavior.

2. If you can remember struggling with some subject or concept in school, describe the impact of that experience on your sense of competence and industry. How have you resolved this struggle?

3. Rate your level of self-esteem on a scale of 1 (low) to 10 (high) in the following areas: academic, physical appearance, social (friendship relationships), athletic, and career success. Now rate each on a scale of 1 (not important) to 10 (very important) in terms of their significance to you. Where are the biggest discrepancies? How do these discrepancies affect your overall self-esteem?

4. How did your peers contribute to your understanding of yourself? Explain.

KEY CONCEPTS

academic self-concept (p. 247)
nonacademic self-concept (p. 247)
social comparison (p. 250)
self-enhancing bias (p. 250)
downward social comparisons (p. 250)
self-esteem slide (p. 253)
identification (p. 255)
premoral stage (p. 259)
heteronomous stage (p. 259)
immanent justice (p. 259)
autonomous stage (p. 259)
preconventional morality (p. 261)
conventional morality (p. 261)

postconventional morality (p. 261)
moral rules (p. 262)
conventional rules (p. 262)
personal rules (p. 262)
morality of justice (p. 264)
morality of caring (p. 264)
prosocial behavior or altruism (p. 265)
empathy (p. 266)
sympathy (p. 266)
needs-based reasoning (p. 266)
hedonistic (p. 267)
needs oriented (p. 267)
effortful control (p. 268)

antisocial behavior (p. 269)
instrumental aggression (p. 269)
relational aggression (p. 270)
social information-processing (p. 270)
hostile attributional bias (p. 271)
oppositional defiant disorder (ODD) (p. 275)
conduct disorder (CD) (p. 275)
antisocial personality disorder (APD) (p. 275)
early-starter pathway (p. 276)
adolescent-onset or late-starter
    pathway (p. 276)
coercive family interaction (p. 277)

CHAPTER 8

Gender and Peer Relationships: Middle Childhood Through Early Adolescence

It's recess time for the third graders at Columbus Elementary. Four girls take turns jumping rope, while other small clusters of girls are playing hopscotch or sitting and talking. One pair whispers conspiratorially, occasionally giggling and glancing up at the girls playing jump rope. One girl skips across the grass alone and then sits on a swing, watching three friends play a climbing game on the modern jungle gym. The game has something to do with the plot of a TV show they saw the night before. A crew of boys is playing a variant of tag, in which whoever is "it" must not only catch someone else (who will then become "it") but must also dodge the assaults of players who risk being caught to race past and punch the boy who is "it" in the back or arms. A boy watching on the sidelines suddenly jumps into the tag game, punching the player who is "it." The others gather round, shoving and yelling at the intruder. When he says, "I can play if I want to," one boy shouts more loudly than the rest, "Let him play, but he's gotta be it." In the remaining 10 minutes of recess, the intruder catches three different boys, but the captives are forcibly freed by their compatriots, and the intruder never escapes being "it" despite his bitter protests. Moments before the recess ends, he stomps off in a rage, shouting epithets at the others.

As the third graders move off the playground, recess begins for the higher grades. Soon a group of sixth graders, seven boys and one girl, are playing basketball on the paved court; another larger group, all boys, is playing soccer on a grassy field. Most of the sixth-grade girls are standing around in circles, talking.

We could watch a large assembly of elementary school children on any playground in the United States—the roof of a private Manhattan school; the small, fenced yard of a Chicago public school; or, as in this example, the ample playing fields, paved courts, and wood-chipped, well-equipped play area of a sprawling school in an affluent Seattle suburb. Despite the constraints of the setting, some key elements of the children's behavior would be strikingly similar. Most of the girls would be playing or talking in clusters of two or three, separately from the boys. The boys would be playing in larger groups, and often their play would consist of some mostly good-natured roughhousing. Some children would probably be alone. They might stand apart, or they might push their way into a group where they are not welcome and then find themselves in conflict with others. Occasionally, a child of one sex might play comfortably with a group of the opposite sex, but generally she or he will be a quiet, peripheral member of the group. More often than not, this child will be a girl. Sometimes, groups of boys will interfere with the play of a cluster of girls, most often to chase them or to upset their game. The girls might chase the boys back, always with their girlfriends along for support.

These patterns will be familiar to anyone who has ever participated in, or observed, a children's recess. In this chapter, we will examine two major features of child development that contribute to these patterns. The first is sex role development in childhood and early adolescence, including the formation of a gender identity and the acquisition of gender-related behaviors. (We will discuss the emergence of sexual orientation in Chapter 9.) The second is the formation and influence of peer relations in the lives of children and young adolescents, including both the degree to which children are able to establish satisfying relationships with their peers and the degree and kind of influence that peer groups wield. Sex role development and peer relations have traditionally been separate disciplines in the developmental sciences, and to some degree we will discuss them separately here. But, as you will see, it is becoming more and more clear not only that peer interactions differ as a function of gender but that peer processes may be very important in shaping gendered behavior.

For helpers, understanding the processes of sex role development can be a key element in providing valid supports to children and adults as they struggle with identity issues, self-acceptance, and self-esteem. Many coping difficulties, both externalizing and internalizing problems, are more typical of either one gender or the other in our society, or they have different features and implications depending on the sex of the client.

It has also become increasingly obvious that a major function of counselors, teachers and other helpers who work with children and adolescents is to identify and intervene with individuals whose peer relationships are distorted. Many developments—including perspective taking, as we have already seen, and sex role development, as we will see in this chapter—are now recognized to be at least partly a function of peer group interaction. Victims, bullies, and social isolates in the world of childhood are at risk for long-term social problems. Among the more spectacular examples are the child perpetrators of major community catastrophes, such as those at Columbine High School in 1998, whose actions appear to have been at least partly a function of peer relations gone awry (Greenfield & Juvonen, 1999; Harter Low, & Whitesell, 2003).

THE BIOLOGY OF SEX

You may recall from Chapter 2 that people have 23 pairs of chromosomes in the nuclei of their cells. In females, the 23rd pair, called the sex chromosomes, consists of two large X chromosomes. In males, the 23rd pair is mismatched: There is one X chromosome and one much smaller Y chromosome. (Go back to Figure 2.2 to see the difference.) When a woman produces an ovum (egg) with only half the typical number of chromosomes, one from each pair, the egg contains one of the woman's X chromosomes. Sperm also contain only one member of each pair of chromosomes, so half of the sperm a man produces will carry an X and half will carry a

Y chromosome. The role of heredity in sex determination begins at conception. If an X-carrying sperm fertilizes the egg, the zygote will have an XX pair and will develop into a female. Fertilization by a Y-carrying sperm will give the zygote an XY sex-chromosome pair, and a male will be the outcome. Unlike other chromosome pairs, the X and Y not only differ in size, they differ in function: Most of the genes on the X are not matched on the Y, and vice versa.

The chromosomal differences have some impact right from the start. For example, cells carrying the XY chromosome pair have a higher metabolic rate than XX carrying cells, so they divide more quickly and prenatal growth is faster (e.g., Pergament, Todydemir, & Fiddler, 2002). But the major differentiation of males and females begins at about 5 weeks after conception. By this point, the fetus has developed a pair of "indifferent" or unisex gonads that could become either ovaries or testes. We'll begin by following the process of differentiation into male structures. The key is a gene located only on the Y chromosome, called the **SRY gene** (sex-determining region of the Y chromosome). SRY codes for a transcription factor that binds to regulatory DNA, turning on genes that start the production of other proteins responsible for the development of gonads into testes. The cells of the testes begin to produce many masculinizing hormones, including **anti-Mullerian hormone (AMH)** and testosterone, one of several male hormones called **androgens**), which circulate throughout the body and influence the development of many different kinds of tissue.

All fetuses develop two sets of ducts, called the **Mullerian** and **Wolffian ducts**, which can differentiate into reproductive structures. Testosterone and other hormones stimulate the *Wolffian ducts* to develop into male structures, such as the seminal vesicles. *AMH* causes the deterioration of the *Mullerian ducts*, which could have developed into internal female parts: the fallopian tubes, uterus, and upper part of the vagina. By the third month, androgens are influencing the growth of male external genitalia from a whole set of "indifferent" structures. For example, the indifferent **genital tubercle** becomes a penis; in the absence of androgens it would have become a clitoris. Similarly, an area of genital swelling develops into a scrotal sac; without the androgens it would have become the labia majora (see Figure 8.1).

You can see that the SRY gene in the male begins a cascade of changes that result in a male reproductive system. Much of the process depends on high levels of circulating androgens, produced by the testes. Without the SRY gene and the male hormones, the default developmental path for all the indifferent structures is in the female direction (ovaries, clitoris, and so on). In females, the Mullerian tubes survive and evolve into female reproductive structures, and the Wolffian tubes deteriorate without androgens to stimulate their further development.

Females produce some androgens (both in the ovaries and the adrenal glands), just as males produce the female hormone, estrogen (from androgens as it happens; females produce estrogen more directly in their ovaries). The key to the determination of physical sexual characteristics is the amount and timing of androgen production. "If these hormones are not present in adequate amounts or over the correct temporal intervals, the natural tendency to retain female characteristics prevails" (Ward, 1992, p. 158), which is what happens in individuals with two X chromosomes. Males' androgen production begins surging at 5 weeks of gestation; the surge ends at about 28 weeks. There is another surge just after birth, peaking at 1 to 2 months, and then declining. Females' estrogen production surges a bit during this same post-natal period, which is sometimes called "mini-puberty" (see Eliot, 2012). After 5 months, both androgen and estrogen production is equally low for boys and girls until actual puberty. After puberty, males produce high levels of testosterone throughout adulthood, much higher than females, until a gradual decline begins at middle age (andropause). Females generally produce higher levels of estrogen than males until menopause.

You might think that males and females are conceived with equal frequency, given that X-carrying and Y-carrying sperm are produced in equal numbers. Yet male

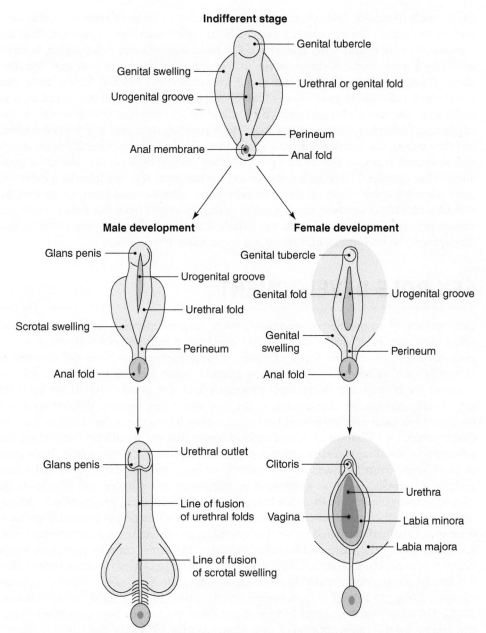

FIGURE 8.1   Prenatal differentiation of male and female external genitalia from the same structures.
SOURCE: From Blakemore, J. E.O., Berenbaum, S. A., & Liben, L. S. *Gender Development.* Copyright 2009. Psychology Press.

conceptions far outnumber female conceptions, with some estimates of the ratio (e.g., Pergament et al., 2002) being as high as 170 to 100! It is not clear why Y-carrying sperm have a better chance of winning the competition to fertilize an egg. But the male conception advantage turns out to be a good thing, because males are less likely to survive the prenatal period than females. More males are spontaneously aborted early in pregnancy, often before a woman knows that she is pregnant, and more are miscarried later in pregnancy. As a result, the actual birth ratio is about 105 males to 100 females.

The prenatal vulnerability of males is at least partly a function of their susceptibility to hereditary diseases, and that vulnerability continues into childhood. The problem for males is the mismatched sex chromosomes. The smaller Y chromosome does not carry most of the genes that the X chromosome does. There are a slew of **X-linked recessive disorders**, such as hemophilia, baldness, color blindness, night blindness,

Duchenne's muscular dystrophy, fragile X syndrome (a form of mental retardation), and so on, and males are much more likely to suffer from these disorders than are females. To understand why, consider color blindness. Normal color vision is influenced by a gene on the X chromosome that is ordinarily dominant over any defective allele. Thus, even if a girl (who has two X chromosomes) has a defective allele that could cause color blindness on one of her X chromosomes, she will not be color-blind as long as she has a normal color-vision allele on her other X chromosome. If she happens to inherit defective alleles from both parents, then she will be color-blind. In other words, for females only, color blindness, and all of the other X-linked recessive disorders, function like all inherited diseases caused by recessive, defective gene alleles (see Chapter 2). For males, the process is different. If a boy inherits a defective gene allele for color vision on the X chromosome, which comes from his mother, he will be color-blind because his Y chromosome, inherited from his father, bears no matching gene. This is true for all the X-linked recessive diseases. The result is that females tend to be carriers, and males are more likely to be victims.

SEX ROLE DEVELOPMENT

Descriptions of sex-related phenomena, such as gender-typed behavior or sexual orientation, can elicit strong feelings and can have significant political, religious, or personal implications. One focus of some of these feelings has been the denotation of words such as *sex* and *gender*. Some authors argue that the term *sex* should be reserved for biologically determined processes and that *gender* should be used for any socially influenced characteristics. Yet, we found this formula difficult to apply because biological and environmental causes play interactive roles in all of human development (see Chapter 2). Other authors argue that *sex* should be used when the reference is based on objective characteristics of males versus females (e.g., "members of both sexes were included in the study"), whereas *gender* should be used when making references based on judgments or inferences about males and females (e.g., "the feminine gender role includes being responsible for meal preparation"; Deaux, 1993). Yet, whether references are objectively based or a function of judgment or inference is not easily determined either. For example, in our culture we dichotomize sex, recognizing only the male and female categories, but some cultures recognize other categories as well (e.g., Nanda, 2008), and some people in our own culture believe that we should see gender as existing more on a continuum than as two clearly separate categories (e.g., Diamond & Butterworth, 2008; Fausto-Sterling, 2000; Savin-Williams, 2005). Therefore, inference and judgment influence even what are considered objective criteria for the categorization of individuals as male or female (or other).

The criteria that have been proposed for differentiating use of the terms *sex* and *gender* are difficult to apply consistently (see suggestions from Lee, Houk, Ahmed & Hughes, 2006). What we have done is to treat the terms as interchangeable, except where one word is used in a uniform, conventional way through much of the literature, as in the phrase *gender identity.*

Let's now take a look at the development of cognitive, social, and behavioral phenomena related to one's sex. The first part of our discussion of sex role development deals with the development of **gender identity**, a person's awareness of his or her own gender assignment and understanding of its meaning. The second part centers on *gender differences in behavior.* We will consider some of the processes that might account for these phenomena, and later we will examine how a helping professional could use this information to benefit his clients.

Gender Identity

Augustina was the youngest girl in a family of nine children. Her parents had emigrated from Italy to the United States before she was born in 1913. When she was an elderly woman, one of Augustina's memories of herself as a young child was that she had firmly believed she would be a man when she grew up. She remembered that sometime in her preschool years she was aware of being a girl, but she was excited about the prospect of becoming like her oldest brothers, whom she saw as confident, swaggering, well-dressed young men to whom her mother deferred and who could stand toe-to-toe with her imposing father. (In the cultural tradition of her family, men were more privileged and powerful than women.) She could also remember a feeling of bitter disappointment that hung with her for many months after she realized, sometime later, that she was destined to remain female and that she would inevitably become a woman.

Augustina's story illustrates some elements in the progress of *gender identity* for young children, although fortunately most kids do not associate negative feelings with the process but seem to wholeheartedly accept their status. The first step in the process is learning to categorize oneself as male or female. By late in their 1st year, babies seem to be able to make perceptual distinctions between the sexes. They can distinguish pictures of men from pictures of women (Poulin-Dubois & Serbin, 2006), and they can distinguish the voices of men from those of women (even when the voices are matched for pitch; Miller, 1983). Toddlers (about age 2) begin to show signs that they can discriminate some actions as more typical of one gender or the other. For example, they look longer (as if surprised) at a man putting on makeup than a woman doing so (Hill & Flom, 2007).

Children show some skill at labeling males and females and at understanding labels such as lady or man, girl or boy late in their second year (e.g., Zosuls, Ruble, Bornstein, & Greulich, 2009). Some children produce a gender label for themselves before age 2. The majority know a self-label by age 2½, and they can identify others who fit into the same category as they do (see Maccoby, 1998; Martin & Ruble, 2009).

As Augustina's experience illustrates, however, knowing your gender category today may not mean that you understand that it will stay that way forever. A second step in the process of identity formation is understanding **gender stability**, that over time, one's gender category usually stays the same: Boys grow into men, girls grow into women. A third step appears to be recognizing that gender category membership is permanent, that it could never change, even if one's behavior or appearance were changed to resemble the other gender. This is called **gender constancy** (see Slaby & Frey, 1975). Most children seem to have gender stability by 3 to 4 years old—a girl knows she was a girl yesterday and expects to be one again tomorrow. But even older preschoolers may not understand gender constancy. For this, children must realize that even if major surface changes were made—in hairstyle, dress, and behavior—the sex of the individual would not also change.

Controversy swirls around the question of when gender constancy develops. In some studies, preschoolers who are shown pictures of, say, a boy dressed up like a girl, with a long-haired wig and a dress, often express the belief that the boy has changed into a girl (e.g., DeLisi & Gallagher, 1991; Kohlberg, 1966). In other studies, even some 3-year-olds seem to have a pretty clear sense of gender constancy (e.g., Bem, 1989; Johnson & Ames, 1994). But it is safe to say that until about the time of school entry, a child's understanding of this concept can be fragile, and he can show uncertainty about the permanence of gender categories. By school age, children know their gender, and they understand that it is permanent (e.g., Ruble et al., 2007). But there are many other dimensions to gender identity that continue to evolve, like the child's comfort with his gender, as you will see in Box 8.1.

What influences affect the formation of a gender identity? How do children come to make gender a part of their self-concept? Like every other important behavioral development, many factors appear to contribute: social, cognitive, and biological.

The Role of Social Processes in Gender Identity

When babies are born, adults assign them to gender categories based on their genital characteristics. From the first, young children hear themselves described as male

Box 8.1: Beyond Gender Constancy: Gender Identity, Social Adjustment, and Ethnicity

Sebastian is a boy and he knows it. He understands that this gender category is essentially immutable. But at age 6, his gender identity is only beginning to develop. As he gets older, his self-knowledge will grow in many ways, as we saw in Chapter 7. This growth in self-awareness will come partly from his own active social comparisons and partly from the input and feedback about himself that he receives from others. In this process, Sebastian's sense of himself as a member of the "boy" category will differentiate. He will identify and evaluate his gender-typical behavior in many arenas, for example, "Do my interests match those of other boys?" or "Is my demeanor in the company of other boys typical?" Besides developing a more detailed and complex sense of himself as a boy, he will integrate much of this information into more general considerations of his gender typicality, such as, "Overall, am I a good fit with my gender category?" (Egan & Perry, 2001).

Do these more complex gender identities have any effects on children's psychosocial adjustment? Perry and colleagues (e.g., Egan & Perry, 2001) set out to find out. What they discovered was that in the United States, the impact of gender identity on adjustment can depend on whether children are members of the White majority or an ethnic/racial minority.

Let's begin by considering what the researchers learned about White children. In studies of hundreds of third to eighth graders, they measured various dimensions of gender (Carver, Yunger, & Perry, 2003; Egan & Perry, 2001; Yunger, Carver, & Perry, 2004). Three turned out to be especially important: felt gender typicality (compatibility), contentedness with gender assignment, and felt pressure for sex-typing. These dimensions were related to children's psychosocial adjustment, including peer acceptance, internalizing problems, and self-esteem.

To measure children's self-perceptions on dimensions of gender identity, researchers met with children individually and read them a set of statements, asking the children to rate how true the statements are of them. To assess Sebastian's felt gender compatibility, for example, one of the statements he would have rated is as follows:

"Some boys don't feel they are a good example of being a boy,	BUT	Other boys do feel they are a good example of being a boy."
Very true for me	Sort of true for me	Sort of true for me	Very true for me
☐	☐	☐	☐

To measure his contentedness with his gender assignment, Sebastian would rate statements like "Some boys wish it'd be okay for them to do some of the things that usually only girls do BUT other boys never wish it would be okay for them to do some of the things that only girls do." A statement about felt pressure for sex-typing would be "Some boys think their parents would be upset if they wanted to learn an activity that only girls usually do BUT other boys don't think their parents would be upset if they wanted to learn an activity that only girls usually do" (Egan & Perry, 2001).

Other measures focused on children's interest in stereotypical male (e.g., "using tools to make things") and female (e.g., "baking") activities and traits, their "intergroup bias" (whether and how strongly they valued their own gender over the other), their global self-esteem, and their perception of their own social competence. Peer perceptions of the participants were also sought. Classmates completed a sociometric assessment, indicating which children they liked the most and which they liked the least. In one study, peers indicated whether statements representing internalizing problems (e.g., "He says bad things about himself") or externalizing problems (e.g., "She hits and pushes others around") were true of participants.

Children varied widely on how they perceived their own gender typicality, how satisfied they were with their gender, and how much pressure they felt to conform to gender stereotypes. As you might expect, how typical children felt, and how content they were with their gender, were both correlated with their actual gender-typical activities and traits. But you might be surprised to learn that the correlations were only modest. Children do not all use the same criteria to judge what is typical for their gender and how closely they themselves match gender norms. They construct their own meanings for gender categories. These meanings are certainly affected by cultural stereotypes and norms, but they are also somewhat unique for each child. The characteristics one child weighs as important may not necessarily be as important to another child.

Longitudinally, there was some tendency for kids to increase in felt gender typicality over time; boys also showed a tendency to increase in gender contentedness, although girls did not. Girls at all ages felt less typical and less content with their gender than boys did, but they also reported less pressure to conform than boys. Yet for both boys and girls, the connections between gender identity and social adjustment were largely the same. Youngsters who reported feeling that they were not very typical of their gender had lower self-esteem than kids who felt more compatible with their gender. Perhaps children with low felt gender typicality fear rejection by peers or others, or they might just feel inadequate and out of step. Such feelings seem warranted: Children who felt less typical both considered themselves less socially competent and were less well liked by peers than youngsters who felt more typical.

We might expect that children who are dissatisfied with their gender assignment would be especially prone to social adjustment problems, such as depression or low self-esteem. Children at the extreme end of gender discontent—are often quite unhappy (e.g., Cohen-Kettenis, Owen, Kaijser, Bradley, & Zucker, 2003). But in the Perry studies of White children in the United States, whether dissatisfaction with gender assignment was problematic depended on whether children felt pressured by others (adults or children) to conform. In one study, children who scored low on gender contentment also tended to have internalizing problems, like self-deprecating behavior and social anxiety, but only if they felt that they were under pressure by others to conform to gender stereotypes (Yunger et al., 2004). In another study, such children were more likely to feel low self-esteem, but again, only if they felt social pressure to conform (Egan & Perry, 2001).

Some theorists have argued that when acceptance depends on fitting gender stereotypes, children are likely to limit the range of activities they explore and the talents that they choose to develop (e.g., Bem, 1981). As a result, children who feel strong pressure to conform have less opportunity to develop in ways that are maximally satisfying—that fit their preferences and inclinations—and they tend to be unhappy, anxious, and discontented with themselves. Although the research by Perry and colleagues supports this position to some extent, it also makes clear that felt pressure for gender conformity interacts with other aspects of gender identity in complex ways. High felt pressure is most problematic for children who sense that they do not fit in, either because they perceive their talents and interests to cross gender boundaries or because they are not as comfortable with their gender assignment as other children. Children who feel atypical are even likely to have problems with self-esteem when they do *not* feel much pressure from others to conform (see also Menon, 2011).

Egan and Perry (2001) argued that "children's adjustment is optimized when they (a) are secure in their conceptions of themselves as typical members of their sex yet (b) feel free to explore cross-sex options when they so desire" (p. 459). But do the same gender identity processes affect social adjustment for children in minority groups? Corby, Hodges, and Perry (2007) investigated, using the measures from Perry's earlier studies with White, Black, and Hispanic fifth graders from lower middle class neighborhoods.

In general, gender identity seemed to have less impact on social adjustment for the minority group children. For example, although gender *contentedness* was just as important for Black children's adjustment as it was for White children, it was not especially important for Hispanic children. Also, even though Black and Hispanic children felt *more* pressure for gender conformity than White children did, it did not seem to cause adjustment problems. In fact, Hispanic boys who felt a great deal of pressure to conform had fewer internalizing problems than other boys!

What can we make of these differences across U.S. subcultures? Corby et al. (2007) remind us that for children growing up with minority status, many features of experience, and many aspects of self-concept development, are different than for children with majority status (see Chapter 9). Even though gender seems important to all groups (e.g., minority children feel a lot of pressure to conform to gender expectations), in different developmental contexts it appears not to have the same meaning or power. For example, formulating a racial or ethnic identity, or coping with minority status, may have more influence on adjustment for some groups than gender identity dimensions (see Chapter 9). Clearly, we have much more to learn about the ways that culture moderates the effects of gender identity on children's social adjustment.

or female. They are told, "You're a big girl to help Daddy like that," "Mommy loves her sweet boy," or "You don't want to be a mean girl who makes her friend cry!" Children are literally surrounded by verbal reminders of their assigned gender. It's not surprising, then, that between 2 and 3, at the same time that they are learning other labels for themselves such as "naughty" or "nice" (see Chapter 5), nearly all children have learned their own gender label.

Research with **gender atypical** children suggests that social assignment to a gender category can influence gender identity. Gender-atypical children have either ambiguous genitalia or genitalia that are inconsistent with their sex chromosomes. In one example, biologically male children, with one X and one Y chromosome, have suffered surgical damage to their genitals during infancy, sometimes as a result of a botched circumcision. Faced with this difficult situation, some parents have raised these children as girls from infancy onward. One boy was reassigned by his family as a "girl" at age 7 months (Bradley, Oliver, Chernick, & Zucker, 1998). Physicians provided treatments with female hormones at puberty so that female secondary sexual characteristics would develop, such as enlarged breasts. At the most recent follow-up, in early adulthood, the young woman still accepted her female identity and was comfortable with her female role. (Note that the results in this case do not necessarily indicate that such a solution will be the right one in all cases. See the discussion below of another boy whose penis was ablated in infancy, and the very different outcome he experienced.)

Another gender-atypical problem is a condition called **congenital adrenal hyperplasia (CAH)**, in which biological females with two X chromosomes are exposed to high levels of androgens during prenatal and postnatal development. The overproduction of androgens by their own adrenal glands is caused by a defective gene. The upshot is that although CAH females usually have the internal organs of a girl, their external genitalia may be masculinized. They may, for example, have an enlarged clitoris that looks like a penis, and they have sometimes been misidentified at birth as boys. When these girls are properly diagnosed, a set of medical interventions can minimize the overproduction of androgens postnatally, and the genitalia can be surgically altered to resemble those of a girl. But John Money and his colleagues, who did extensive studies of children with CAH, concluded that if the diagnosis is not made before the age of 2½ to 3, a child's gender identity can be very difficult to alter (Erhardt & Baker, 1974; Money & Dalery, 1977; Money & Erhardt, 1972) and more recent studies seem to confirm this finding (Wolfle et al., 2002). Critics of Money's research program have questioned some of his evidence for the social construction of gender and caution against early gender assignment without the possibility of individual choice (Reis, 2007). Today, early misidentification of CAH girls is much less likely, and the American Academy of Pediatrics recommends that CAH girls identified as such in infancy should be raised as girls. It should be noted that sexual assignment or reassignment in infancy that involves surgery is becoming more and more controversial (see further discussion in the upcoming section "The Role of Biology in Gender Identity").

When CAH females are raised as boys, their gender identity is inconsistent with their biological sex, and yet most accept their gender assignment. Of course, their social assignment to the status of male may not be the only factor that supports their acceptance of a male identity. Their exposure to androgens appears to have a masculinizing effect on their behavior as well as on their genitalia, and this biologically generated difference in behavior may make a male identity a comfortable "fit" for some CAH females. Indeed, as you will see shortly, research with gender-atypical children demonstrates that nature and nurture operate in tandem with regard to the development of gender identity.

The Role of Cognition in Gender Identity

Forming a concept of oneself as either a boy or a girl is a cognitive task. Some theorists have argued that one's gender identity changes partly as a function of general developments in cognitive ability, especially logical thinking (e.g., Kohlberg, 1966). As we have seen, when children first categorize themselves as boys or girls, they may have done little more than learn a label. Their understanding of the implications of that label is limited. Gradually, they begin to recognize that there is stability to their category membership and, finally, that their category membership is constant, based on underlying properties that do not change when superficial perceptual characteristics alter. In a sense, gender is something that is conserved (at least under normal circumstances), much like number is conserved when candies in a pile are made to look different by spreading them out in a row. We have seen (Chapter 3) that a full understanding of number conservation typically is achieved between 5 and 7 years and seems to be based on the development of logical thinking. Gender constancy may also be dependent on the logical thinking skills that emerge as children reach middle childhood.

Although developments in logical thinking may be important, there are other cognitive factors that can influence the progress of gender identity, such as having accurate information about how gender is decided. As we pointed out earlier, adults assign babies to a gender category based on their genitalia. But unless young children are explicitly taught about the importance of genitals to gender assignment, they are likely to be unaware of the typical genital differences between the sexes. References to gender categorization are pervasive in our society, and they are a large part of children's daily experiences. Not only do children frequently hear themselves being categorized, but many references to other people contain gender labels, such as "This man will help us find the toy department." However, most of these references are not based on observation of people's genitals. They depend on people's other physical attributes, such as size and shape, and on more superficial characteristics, such as clothing and hairstyle. It's not really surprising, then, that young children are sometimes oblivious to the genital basis for gender assignment or that they might initially assume that gender categories are determined by superficial properties.

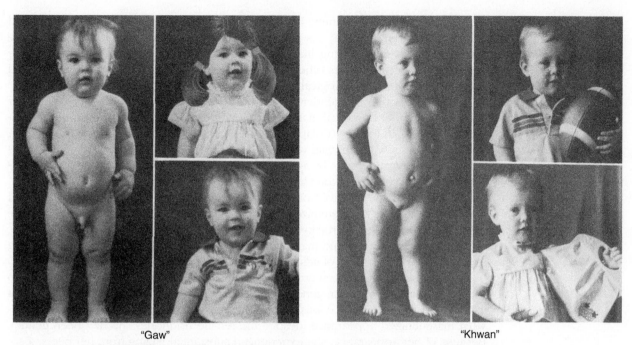

"Gaw"   "Khwan"

FIGURE 8.2 Photographs used to measure gender constancy in Bem's (1989) study.
SOURCE: Bern, S. L., (1989). Genital knowledge and gender constancy in school children. *Child Development, 60,* pp. 653, 654. Used by permission of John Wiley and Sons.

Researcher Sandra Bem (1989) tells the story of her son, Jeremy, who was informed about genital differences between boys and girls and about the importance of genitalia in gender assignment. One day, he chose to go off to nursery school wearing barrettes in his hair. When another little boy repeatedly insisted that Jeremy must be a girl because he was wearing barrettes, Jeremy just as vehemently insisted that he was a boy, because "wearing barrettes doesn't matter; being a boy means having a penis and testicles." Jeremy was even provoked enough at one point to pull down his pants to demonstrate. The other boy was not impressed. He said, "Everybody has a penis; only girls wear barrettes."

A study by Bem (1989) illustrates that when children do have knowledge of the genital basis of gender assignment, as Jeremy did, they are fortified with information that may help them to avoid some confusion about gender constancy. She presented 3- to 5-year-olds with two large photographs of nude toddlers. One was a boy (Gaw), and one a girl (Khwan; see Figure 8.2). Bem gave the pictured toddlers Thai names so that most North American youngsters would be unfamiliar with the names and would not associate them with gender. Children were asked to say whether a pictured toddler was a boy or a girl, and then were asked to explain how they knew. If no genital information was offered, the researcher probed by asking questions such as, "Can you point to anything about Gaw's body that makes Gaw a boy?" Nearly half of the children showed no awareness of the relevance of genitalia for specifying sex. The children who did know about genitals also seemed to have a better grasp of gender constancy. When they were shown pictures of Gaw or Khwan with cross-gendered clothes or hairstyles, they asserted that their genders had not changed.

It appears, then, that when adults provide appropriate scaffolding, giving children accurate information about how gender is assigned, children's understanding of their own gender identity is more advanced.

The Role of Biology in Gender Identity

If children are assigned to a gender based on their genitalia and if genitals are usually a product of underlying biological processes, then biology plays at least an indirect role in gender identity. But does biology have any other influence, beyond affecting the genitalia? That has proven a difficult question to answer, but there are some indicators that "feeling like a male" or "feeling like a female" may to some degree be related to factors other than social assignment to a gender category, and these factors could be biological.

Again, research on gender-atypical individuals provides some clues. Consider the case of another biological male, one of identical twins, who suffered surgical damage to his penis in infancy (Colapinto, 2001; Diamond & Sigmundson, 1997; Money & Tucker, 1975). As with the child we described earlier (Bradley et al., 1998), the parents raised this twin as a girl. Yet by age 10, unlike the child described by Bradley and colleagues, the girl twin was expressing dissatisfaction with her female gender assignment. At age 14, when she was told of her medical history, she took a stand: She refused hormone treatments that feminized her appearance. Male hormone treatments were begun, and surgical reconstruction of the penis was undertaken. By the time he was 25, the former girl was a married man. Tragically, he committed suicide at age 38, having experienced a long history of adjustment-related difficulties (Colapinto, 2000).

The case of the identical twin is no more than suggestive that biology can outdo social influences in affecting gender identity. First, this child's parents did not commit to a gender change until he was 17 months old. By puberty, this child had a somewhat masculinized appearance, despite the female hormones she had been getting. Because of her appearance, she experienced substantial hazing from her peers, a social factor that could have been important in creating her gender uncertainty and distress. Further, we cannot say how effective her own family had been in accepting her status as a girl and thus how unambiguous her socialization experiences had been. However, cases such as these raise the possibility that biology can exert an influence on how "male" or "female" one feels, or at least on how comfortable one is with a particular gender assignment. We should note that the results of this case appear to be quite different from the one reported earlier (Bradley et al., 1998).

Children sometimes undergo gender assignment or reassignment at birth because of conditions that cause malformations of genitalia. Large-scale studies of such children have produced conflicting results. In some, social reassignment of XY males to female identities, or of XX females to male identities, seems to work well (see Zucker, 1999, for a review). In more recent studies, although the majority accept reassignment comfortably, a sizeable minority of children have been reported to reject reassignment by the time they reach adolescence (Dessens, Slijper, & Drop, 2005; Meyer-Bahlberg, 2005; Reiner & Gearhart, 2004), suggesting that socialization may not be as powerful as it was once thought to be in the development of gender identity.

Because of the complexity of causal factors in gender identity development, as well as the increasing awareness of often subtle physical variations (nondimorphism) in internal and external reproductive organs, sex chromosomes, and hormones, many researchers and theorists have argued for recognition and cultural acceptance of **intersex** statuses (e.g., Diamond & Butterworth, 2008; Fausto-Sterling, 2000; Savin-Williams & Ream, 2007; see Byne et al., 2012). Blackless and colleagues (2000) report that some type of sexual nondimorphism is present in up to 2 out of every 100 live births. More recently, there has been consensus among some medical groups to replace the term "intersex" with "disorders of sex development" (DSD) in an effort to acknowledge the spectrum of human sexual biology. However, others have criticized this nomenclature for its divisive connotation and suggest replacing the term with "divergence of sex development" (Hughes, Houk, Ahmed, & Lee, 2006; Reis, 2007). As we noted earlier, it may be that for many people, "dichotomous models of gender fail to capture the complexity, diversity, and fluidity" of the gender experience (Diamond & Butterworth, 2008, p. 366).

Gender and Behavior

Many of us believe that males and females have at least some different behavioral tendencies, and some people believe that there are major differences in the distribution of personality traits between the sexes. Such beliefs about sex differences are called **gender stereotypes**. Researchers have found evidence for some of the differences that people believe in, but other stereotypes seem to arise from expectations that have no basis in fact. In this section, we will first take a look at some of the sex differences that have been found, especially in children. Then, we'll consider some of the theoretical explanations that have been proposed for sex differences. That is, when they actually exist, how do they develop?

Sex Differences in Behavior, Personality, and Preference

In 1974, Maccoby and Jacklin did a careful review of the scientific literature on sex differences. They surprised most observers by concluding that there were only four behaviors, skills, or tendencies that clearly differed for males and females: physical aggression, language skills, math skills, and spatial skills. Even in these domains, some behaviors differed across the life span (e.g., aggression) and others only during certain developmental periods, such as after puberty (e.g., certain math skills). Since 1974, researchers have acquired a valuable analytic tool for assessing the effects of variables such as sex. It's called **meta-analysis**, in which the results from a large number of studies on the same question—such as, "Are there sex differences in physical aggression?"—can be combined to produce an average estimate of the difference in a population (Glass, 1976).

The results of many meta-analyses are now available, and the list of "real" sex differences has lengthened (see Table 8.1). In addition, our knowledge of sex differences is now more fine-tuned. With regard to math, for example, among top-performing students, boys have an advantage over girls in complex problem solving. This is more likely to be true when problems can be solved using spatially based strategies. Yet, boys are also more numerous than girls among *underperformers* in math, and girls tend to outperform boys on computation (see Halpern et al., 2007, for a comprehensive review). We also have been collecting data for long enough, and in enough circumstances, that we know that these differences can change historically; that is, there are cohort effects. To add to the complexity, these effects can vary from one context to another. For example, historical change has affected math skills such that males and females in the United States today do not differ on most tests of math achievement before grade 12 (e.g., Hyde, Lindberg, Linn, Ellis, & Williams, 2008), even though they did differ two decades ago (e.g., Hyde, Fennema, & Lamon, 1990). The gender gaps that continue to exist seem to vary from one culture to another. The male advantage in complex problem solving (which continues to show up in the United States today as a gender difference on math SAT test performance) differs by country and culture. The more that cultural acceptance of male privilege characterizes a country, the more boys outnumber girls among top performers (Guiso, Monte, Sapienza, & Zingales, 2008). In countries where cultural attitudes strongly favor gender equality, such as Iceland, there are as many (or more) girls as boys among top math performers. One very large meta-analysis included the test data of nearly 500,000 14- to 16-year-olds in 69 nations. The analysis identified specific societal indicators of equality that are linked to disappearing math performance differences between boys and girls (Else-Quest, Hyde, & Lynn, 2010). These indicators are equal enrollment in school; larger shares of research jobs held by women; and larger numbers of women lawmakers (parliamentary representatives).

It is just as interesting to note the differences that have *not* been found as those that have. Among the common sex stereotypes, for example, are that females are more sociable, more dependent, and more prosocial than males and that males are more competent at analytical tasks. Although occasional studies have reported findings that are consistent with these expectations, in most studies such differences are not found. Similarly, arguments that males and females differ in moral reasoning have received a great deal of popular and scientific attention. As we mentioned in Chapter 7, Gilligan (e.g., 1977, 1982) proposed that males are more likely to focus

TABLE 8.1 A Sampling of Gender Differences

TRAIT OR QUALITY	MORE TYPICAL OF	TIME OF ONSET
Developmental vulnerability (learning disabilities, illness, accidents, etc.)	Boys	Prebirth
Activity level	Boys	Infant
Happy, excited mood	Boys	Infant/toddler
Risk taking	Boys	Infant/toddler
Physical aggression	Boys	Toddler
Faster reaction time	Boys	Preschool
Competitive play	Boys	Preschool
Discourse style	Boys	Preschool
Dominance seeking; clear group hierarchy	Boys	Preschool
Spatial skill: mental rotation	Boys	Middle childhood
Antisocial aggressive disorders	Boys	Middle childhood
Satisfaction with one's gender assignment	Boys	Middle childhood
Math problem solving	Boys	Middle childhood
Homosexuality, bisexuality	Boys	Adolescence
Preference for gender-typed toys	Both	Toddler
Preference for same-gender playmates	Both	Toddler
Quiet calm mood	Girls	Infant
Language onset (vocabulary)	Girls	Toddler
Collaborative discourse style	Girls	Preschool
Verbal achievement (reading, spelling, language tests)	Girls	Middle childhood
Emotional expressiveness	Girls	Middle childhood
Relational aggression (refusing friendship, exclusion from group)	Girls	Middle childhood
Depression	Girls	Adolescence
Social sensitivity	Girls	Adulthood

Key: Prebirth—Conception to birth; Infant—0 to 1 year; Toddler—1 to 3 years; Preschool—3 to 6 years; Middle childhood—6 years to puberty; Adolescence—Puberty to 18 years; Adulthood—18 years onward.

on issues of justice or fairness in their moral reasoning, but females are more concerned with issues of interpersonal responsibility and compassion. Yet the evidence indicates that boys and girls show no differences in their tendencies to focus on such issues and that both men and women raise both kinds of issues when they solve moral problems or judge moral maturity (e.g., Walker & Pitts, 1998). Occasionally, adolescent and adult females have been found to raise more concerns about people's needs than adolescent or adult males in addressing real-life dilemmas, but people of both genders raise such concerns quite frequently (see Jaffee & Hyde, 2000, for a meta-analysis; Turiel, 2006).

When sex differences are consistently found, they usually turn out to be small in size. Figure 8.3 illustrates the considerable overlap between males and females on those traits that show some sex difference. Some researchers have argued strongly

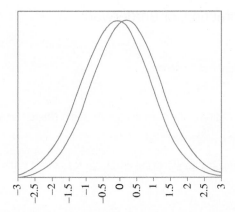

Depending on the characteristic, either boys or girls might have the higher average scores.

FIGURE 8.3 **Typical pattern of differences for characteristics that show a sex difference.**

that gender differences are too small to be important in development, especially considering that the average difference between genders is much smaller than the range of differences within each gender (Thorne, 1994).

However, average individual differences between the sexes may not be the important story in gender role development. More and more, developmentalists are recognizing that although boys and girls do not behave much differently in laboratory measures of personality or on individual abilities, they do spend their time differently. Specifically, girls spend their time interacting primarily with girls, and boys spend their time mostly with boys. In settings where there are both males and females of similar ages available, such as schools and playgrounds, and where there is freedom to choose one's companions, this sex segregation process begins by about 2½ for girls and by about 3 for boys, and it increases with age (see Martin, Fabes, Hanish, & Hollenstein, 2005). Sex segregation characterizes children around the world, in both industrialized and nonindustrialized societies (e.g., Omark, Omark, & Edelman, 1973; Whiting & Edwards, 1988). When children are about 4, the time they spend with same-sex peers is triple the time they spend with other-sex peers (Fabes, Martin, & Hanish, 2003). By the time children are 6, they spend 11 times more time with same-sex peers! During elementary school, sex segregation intensifies, and it begins to ease off only after puberty, when, drawn together by sexual interest, children begin to participate more readily in mixed-gender activities. During middle childhood, mixed-gender interactions, called **borderwork**, tend to be quite limited (Maccoby & Jacklin, 1987; Thorne, 1986, 1994). In fact, there seem to be unwritten "rules" that govern when it is acceptable for boys and girls to engage in mixed-gender interactions. Allen Sroufe and his colleagues (Sroufe, Bennett, Englund, Urban, & Shulman, 1993) observed 10- and 11-year-olds at a summer camp, for example, and identified a set of six rules that seemed to determine when children would cross the boundaries of their single-sex groups (see Table 8.2).

When children segregate by gender, other behaviors also tend to diverge. For example, suppose that Carissa and Duane, both 6 years old, are equally active when they play alone on the playground. They climb on the jungle gym with about average vigor for children their age, and they are more inclined to skip and

 In this typical example of borderwork on the playground, the grade-school boys watch and comment as the girls play jump rope, then begin their own, more rough-and-tumble activities with the jump rope once the girls have moved on.

As children mature, they spend increasingly greater amounts of time in sex-segregated peer groups.

TABLE 8.2 Rules Governing Mixed-Gender Interaction, or Borderwork

Rule:	The contact is accidental.
Example:	You're not looking where you are going and you bump into someone.
Rule:	The contact is incidental.
Example:	You go to get some lemonade and wait while two children of the other gender get some. (There should be no conversation.)
Rule:	The contact is in the guise of some clear and necessary purpose.
Example:	You may say, "Pass the lemonade," to persons of the other gender at the next table. No interest in them is expressed.
Rule:	An adult compels you to have contact.
Example:	"Go get that map from X and Y and bring it to me."
Rule:	You are accompanied by someone of your own gender.
Example:	Two girls may talk to two boys, though physical closeness with your own partner must be maintained and intimacy with the others is disallowed.
Rule:	The interaction or contact is accompanied by disavowal.
Example:	You say someone is ugly or hurl some other insult or (more commonly for boys) push or throw something at them as you pass by.

SOURCE: Sroufe, L. A., Bennett, C., Englund, M. and Shulman, S. (1993). The significance of gender. Child Development, 64, p. 456. Used with permission by John Wiley and Sons.

jog from place to place than either to walk or to run full tilt. When Carissa plays with her girlfriends, her activity level stays about the same. But when Duane plays with a group of boys, he is notably more active than when he plays alone: He moves more vigorously on the jungle gym or runs with greater intensity. "Boys are stimulated to high levels of activity by other boys" (Maccoby, 1998).

Children do somewhat different things in their same-sex groups. Perhaps most notable is that boys' play in groups is more physical and more aggressive than girls' play. This is true in all primate species, across cultures, and from the earliest ages that youngsters play together. (Ruble, Martin, & Berenbaum, 2006) When Carissa and her friends ride the wheeled vehicles in the play yard of their after-school child care center, they ride around carefully to avoid hitting each other. But when Duane and his friends are in the drivers' seats, their favorite thing to do is ram into each other—the harder the better (e.g., Dunn & Morgan, 1987; Fabes et al., 2003).

Good-natured physical roughness is called **rough-and-tumble play**, an almost exclusive property of boys' play with boys. Maccoby (2002) indicates that most boys are not consistently aggressive across situations. That is, physical aggressiveness is not so much a personality trait that you see when a child is in any situation—with adults, girls, or boys—although it can be for some children. More typically, it emerges when boys are with boys. Thus, it becomes an important defining feature of boys' social groups, which differ in specific ways from girls' social groups. Boys often use rough-and-tumble play to help establish dominance hierarchies within their groups, with more dominant boys less likely to back down and less often aggressed against. Generally, boys play in larger groups than do girls, who are more likely to play in twos and threes, and the boys' groups are more clearly structured hierarchically. Although girls' groups usually have their more and less dominant members, the rankings are not very stable, and leadership does not depend on toughness as much as on other leadership qualities, such as social skill (Maccoby, 1998; Martin & Fabes, 2001).

Girls' and boys' groups differ on other dimensions as well (Ruble et al., 2006). Boys compete with each other more than girls do. As preschoolers they compete for resources, such as attractive toys, and in middle childhood they compete in structured games. Girls' interactions tend to be more cooperative and to involve much more turn taking. These characteristics of gendered groups are integrally related to the kinds of activities that bring boys and girls together. In particular, boys seem to spend time with other boys who have shared interests, especially starting in middle childhood, and they are more likely than girls to be interested in sports and games and in adventure. For example, when boys pretend, their play tends to involve heroic or warlike themes (e.g., Flannery & Watson, 1993).

Girls often seem to get together just to be together, and their choice of companions is based more on personality (Erwin, 1985). On the whole, they tend to have broader interests than boys, and they are more interested in boys' activities than boys are in girls' activities. But they do have stronger tendencies than boys to like play that enacts family or school experiences, and increasingly from preschool onward, girls' pretend play themes have to do with adornment and beauty—being models or brides, doing glamorous or romantic things (Maccoby, 1998).

As you can see, girls' groups and boys' groups have different cultures to which the members, regardless of their individual characteristics, must adapt. A good example of this difference is the degree to which they use *collaborative* versus *domineering* discourse techniques (Leaper & Smith, 2004). In **collaborative or affiliative speech**, more often used in girls' groups, children's responses are keyed to what someone else has said, expressing agreement, making further suggestions, often in the form of a question rather than declarative or imperative sentences, which seems to soften the suggestion. For example, Carissa might say

Children construct internalized standards for appropriate gender-linked behavior partly based upon adult models and sanctions.

to a friend as they plan a game, "You want to be the mommy. Why don't we both be the mommy sometimes?" In **domineering or power-assertive speech**, more typical of boys' groups, commands and restrictions are common, as when Duane says, "Don't move that block; build the road there!" It is important to note that both boys and girls will use both kinds of discourse. It is the predominance of one type over the other that differs between their groups. On the whole, girls' discourse strategies are more "conflict mitigating" and boys strategies are more "egoistic"—threatening, demanding, interrupting, or ignoring of another's remarks (Maccoby, 1998).

Where do sex differences in behavior come from? There are theories that emphasize the importance of biology, of cognitive processes, and of socialization pressures. Clearly, all three, as always, are important. As you will see, some theorists emphasize the interaction of the three as children spend time in same-gender peer groups. It seems that gender segregation in childhood, perhaps the most pervasive sex difference, may be both an outcome of some sex differences and a source of others.

The Role of Biology in Generating Sex Differences

You learned earlier in this chapter that genetic differences between males and females normally influence the differential development of reproductive organs. You have seen that the prenatal release of masculinizing hormones (androgens) plays a major role in this process. Do masculinizing hormones also affect the developing nervous system, thus influencing postnatal behavior? In animals, there is evidence that prenatal hormones do affect neural structures (e.g., Wallen, 2005), and in both animals and humans, there appear to be effects on early behavior. For example, male rats whose exposure to prenatal androgens is delayed not only show a slight demasculinization of their genitalia but they also show more feminized play behaviors as pups (e.g., Ward, 1992; Ward & Stehm, 1991).

In humans, girls with CAH who are overexposed to prenatal (and sometimes postnatal) androgens have been found to exhibit more **tomboyism**—playing with boys and preferring boys' toys and activities—than non-CAH girls (for reviews see Berenbaum, 2004; Constantinescu & Hines, 2012). Findings such as these are open to several interpretations. For one, parents of girls with CAH may have doubts about their daughters' sexual identity that could affect their daughters' behavior, for another, these girls have many unusual experiences, such as genital surgeries and ongoing medical treatments, that could affect their behavioral development, and so on (see Collaer & Hines, 1995). However, the somewhat masculinized behaviors of CAH girls may also indicate a role for prenatal (or postnatal) hormones in some of the typical behavioral differences found between boys and girls. Two studies provide somewhat more convincing demonstrations of a role for prenatal androgens in the masculinizing of girls' behavior. The first is a large study of normally developing children. At 3 years old, girls were rated as more masculine in their activities if their mothers had had higher than average amounts of testosterone (an androgen) in their blood during pregnancy (Hines et al., 2002). The second is a study of 3- to 10-year-old CAH girls and their unaffected (non-CAH) siblings (Pasterski et al., 2005). The children were observed in toy play alone and also with each of their parents. The CAH girls made more spontaneous male-typical toy choices (e.g., trucks) than their unaffected sisters, even though their parents encouraged sex-typical toy play with their children and actually provided more positive feedback to CAH girls than to unaffected girls for play with female toys (e.g., dolls).

At puberty, hormonal changes and hormonal differences between boys and girls may cause some behavioral differences that emerge at about that time. For example, although depressive symptoms increase for both girls and boys after puberty, they increase more for girls; boys show more increases in aggressive, delinquent behaviors than girls (see Table 8.1 and Chapter 9). Could these differences in problem behavior be linked to hormones? It is a sensible question to ask, and some connections have been identified. For example, there is a link between boys' androgen levels and their aggressiveness (Buchanan, Eccles, & Becker, 1992). But androgens appear to more directly affect attempts to achieve social power (dominance seeking) which leads to aggression only in some people and some situations (Rowe, Maughan, Worthman, Costello, & Angold, 2004). Another complication in interpreting hormone–behavior connections is that whereas androgens may increase aggressiveness, one's experiences, such as family conflict, may change hormone levels (e.g., Steinberg, 1988). In particular, for males, aggression and dominance seeking can increase testosterone, an androgen (see Cacioppo & Berntson, 1992). So whether hormone levels cause or result from behavior and experience during and after puberty is not clear.

Research on brain structures has identified some sex differences (e.g., Sowell et al., 2007), supporting the idea that brain differences may underlie some gender differences, but many of the findings are controversial (see Ruble et al., 2006). Among the differences for which there is some evidence is greater lateralization in males than in females, that is, greater differentiation in the functioning of the two hemispheres of the brain, with language functions more clearly governed by the left hemisphere in males (e.g., Friederici et al., 2008). Even in children as young as 16 months, patterns of brain activation appear to be more lateralized for word comprehension in boys than in girls (as measured by functional magnetic resonance imaging, or fMRI; Molfese, 1990). But here again, findings are unclear. For example, one large fMRI study of older children found no sex difference in lateralization of language processing (Plante, Schmithorst, Holland, & Byars, 2006). If females *are* less lateralized, using more of both hemispheres for language functions, it could account for the female advantage in language. But this, and other brain differences, if they exist, could as easily be the result of different experiences. That is, when behavioral differences develop, they may cause differences in brain function rather than being the result of such differences. Given what we have learned about brain development (see Chapter 3), it seems likely that the causal links work both ways.

One other note of caution about relating brain differences to gender differences in behavior should be presented. Sometimes brain differences clearly are *not* related to behavioral differences. For example, in one study, intelligence as measured by standardized intelligence tests was correlated with more gray matter (thicker cortex) in the frontal and parietal lobes for men, but in women intelligence was correlated with more gray matter in different parts of the frontal lobes. There were no differences in these same men and women on intelligence. As the authors put it, "men and women apparently achieve similar IQ results with different brain regions, suggesting that . . . different types of brain designs may manifest equivalent intellectual performance" (Haier, Jung, Yeo, Head, & Alkire, 2005, p. 320).

The Role of Cognition in Generating Sex Differences

When Ben was 5 years old, he loved to sit with his mother early in the morning while she dressed for work. He especially enjoyed watching her comb her hair and tie it back with a ribbon. One day he asked if he could have a ribbon in his own hair. His mother, who tried to encourage nonsexist ideas in her children, tied a ribbon in Ben's hair, and he spent some happy moments admiring himself in the mirror. But soon he grew still, staring at his image, and he finally asked, "Do boys wear ribbons in their hair?" to which his mother responded, "Not usually." Ben grasped the ribbon and tore it off his head, pulling strands of hair along with it. Then, bursting into tears, he ran from the room. Despite his mother's neutrality, Ben was angry and humiliated that he had done a "girl" thing. Several cognitive theories of gender differences have been proposed to explain behaviors such as Ben's. We will examine them next.

Cognitive-Developmental Theories. Cognitive-developmental theorists such as Kohlberg (1966) have argued that when children acquire an understanding of the constancy of gender identity, partly as a function of advances in their logical thinking skills, they are intrinsically motivated to learn all they can about what it means to be male or female, and they are eager to behave in gender-appropriate ways. In other words, children actively seek to make their behavior consistent with their gender identity, whether or not they experience social pressure to do so. This process is often now referred to as **self-socialization**. The anecdote about Ben seems to illustrate the power of such a cognitively based motivational system. There is also research evidence to support a cognitive basis for at least some of children's gendered behaviors, although contrary to Kohlberg's notion, a full understanding of gender constancy does not seem to be required. Rather, establishing basic gender identity (i.e., learning one's own gender category) seems to be sufficient to foster a drive to learn about gendered behavior and a tendency to make gender-typical choices (e.g., Weinraub et al., 1984). Once gender stability is established, children are increasingly likely to make gender-based choices over what may be more attractive choices, as Ben did (see Martin, Ruble, & Szkrybalo, 2002; Ruble et al., 2006).

Cognitive-developmental theories also suggest that when children achieve gender constancy, their thinking about gender differences should become more "flexible" and less stereotyped. They now understand that superficial characteristics can change without changing one's underlying gender category. Therefore, children should be able to see that sex role stereotypes, such as girls wearing dresses and boys wearing pants, are social conventions, not moral imperatives or requirements for maintaining one's gender identity. Indeed, children's thinking about gender does become more flexible in middle childhood, as you will see in a later section (e.g., Conry-Murray & Turiel, 2012; Ruble et al., 2007). Some researchers theorize that young adolescents become somewhat more rigid in their thinking about what's permissible for people of different genders (Ruble et al., 2006). The **gender intensification hypothesis** suggests that one way young teens cope with the demands of establishing an adult identity is to fall back on stereotyped notions of masculinity or femininity (Hill & Lynch, 1983), but there is little evidence for this position, especially for U.S. adolescents today (Priess, Lindberg, & Hyde, 2009).

Gender Schema Theories. Cognitive theorists in the information processing tradition emphasize the role of **gender schemas** in influencing the behavior of children and adults (Bem, 1981; Markus, Crane, Bernstein, & Siladi, 1982). A gender schema is a network of expectations and beliefs about male and female characteristics. Schemas affect what we pay attention to, what we interpret, and what we remember about events. So, for example, if elementary school children hear stories or see pictures of men or women engaged in cross-sex behaviors—such as a woman doing carpentry work—they are likely to remember the pictures later in ways more consistent with their gender schemas. In this example, they might later remember that they heard about, or saw, a *man* working as a carpenter (e.g., Liben & Signorella, 1980, 1993; Welch-Ross & Schmidt, 1996).

Gender schemas seem to affect both how children evaluate behavior and the kinds of behaviors they choose for themselves. In one study, when preschoolers were told either that a boy or a girl had spilled some milk, they judged the behavior more negatively if they believed the child was a boy, apparently based on a "boys are bad" stereotype (Giles & Heyman, 2004). Many studies demonstrate the power of stereotypical beliefs on children's behavior. For example, when children are shown novel toys described as "girl" toys, girls play with the toys more and remember them better than if the same toys are described as "boy" toys; the reverse is true for boys (see Martin et al., 2002).

Gender schema theorists suggest that the schemas children have for their own sex affects what behaviors they choose to learn about and what behaviors they choose for themselves, but they do not account for the exact mechanisms by which schemas are constructed. Social experiences and available role models presumably affect sex differences by affecting what children know or believe about what is gender appropriate. But, according to these theorists, it is the schemas, not the social experiences directly, that motivate children to adopt sex-typed behavior. There is evidence that knowledge of stereotypes influences children's interests and judgments about what they are good at even when the sex difference is not real. For example, in a large U.S. sample of 6- to 10-year-olds, by second grade children endorsed the stereotype that boys are better than girls in math. Soon after, boys were more likely than girls to see themselves as good at math, even though typically the gender difference in math achievement emerges later in childhood (Cvencek, Meltzoff, & Greenwald, 2011). Research has not yet established clear links, however, between cognitive schemas and actual behavior.

Children's Knowledge of Gender Stereotypes. In general, cognitive theorists assume that the acquisition of knowledge about sex stereotypes influences the feminization and masculinization of children's behavior, regardless of whether others reward or otherwise pressure children to adopt gender-typed behavior. From this perspective, it is important to learn what children know about sex stereotypes and when they know it if we want to understand the development of sex differences.

Two-year-olds show little awareness of gender stereotypes. For example, Gelman, Taylor, and Nguyen (2004) recorded parent–child discussions of pictures depicting children and adults engaged in various activities. In the following exchange between a 2-year-old girl and her mother about a picture of a child playing with a toy truck, the little girl attributes ability not to gender categories but to individuals:

Mother:	Who can play with toy trucks?
Mother:	Hm?
Child:	Um, you.
	(Later . . .)
Mother:	Yeah, well who else?
Child:	Maybe Daddy.
Mother:	Daddy, yeah.
Child:	Maybe John.
Mother:	Yeah.

(*Source:* Gelman et al., 2004, pp. 103–104)

But by age 3, most children know something about gender-related preferences for toys and activities, and 4- to 6-year-olds have gendered expectations about people and their behaviors. In fact, 4-year-olds tend to be quite "sexist," regardless of whether their parents explicitly encourage such stereotyping. Contrast the above exchange with this dialogue from the same study between a 4-year-old boy and his mother about a picture of a male dancer:

Mother:	Who can be a ballet dancer?
Child:	I don't know.
Child:	Why is that a boy?
Mother:	Well, can a boy be a ballet dancer?
Child:	No.
Mother:	Why not?
Child:	(sighs)
Mother:	I've seen boy ballet dancers.
Child:	I don't think so.

(*Source:* Gelman et al., 2004, p. 106)

By school entry, about age 5 or 6, knowledge of gendered activities and occupations is very extensive (Liben, Bigler, & Krogh, 2002; Signorella, Bigler, & Liben, 1993). In middle childhood, children become more aware of psychological stereotypes, such as expecting boys to be more competent, and they begin to expect that a person with one gender-typical trait or behavior will have others as well. By age 10, children are aware of differences in the ways males and females are evaluated in their culture. In particular, they recognize that females and many female-typical behaviors are devalued (Intons-Peterson, 1988). Of course, such awareness may help explain why females show a greater susceptibility to depression beginning in early adolescence than males do.

Although knowledge of stereotypes increases dramatically in middle childhood, awareness that people vary in the degree to which they fit their gendered categories also grows. The following example of an exchange between a 6-year-old and her mother illustrates the child's incipient (if grudging) understanding that gender assignment does not necessarily dictate traits, abilities, or preferences:

Mother:	Does Cynthia ever play with trucks?
Child:	Sometimes.
Child:	Girl trucks.
Mother:	What are girl trucks?
Child:	Pink ones.
Mother:	Does Cynthia have pink trucks?
Child:	Yeah.
Mother:	Really?
Child:	(nods "yes")
Child:	Well she has pink cars but not pink trucks.
Mother:	So she drives the cars while you and Brian drive the trucks?
Child:	Yup.

(*Source:* Gelman, S.A., Taylor, M.G. & Nguyen, S.P. (2004). Mother-child conversations about gender. *Monographs of the Society for Research in Child Development, 69* (Serial No. 275). Republished with permission from Wiley-Blackwell.)

However, knowledge of stereotypes does not necessarily lead to conduct in keeping with those stereotypes (Liben & Bigler, 2002). Similarly, individuals may vary in their behavior (both consistent with and inconsistent with stereotypes) depending on context (Bandura, 1986). For example, female officers in the United States armed services may behave in stereotypically masculine ways while on duty but may act in more stereotypically feminine ways outside work. A young boy may play house with his sister at home but never do so with other boys at school.

Research also indicates that factors other than gender knowledge affect some sex differences. For example, cognitive theories explain children's preferences for same-sex playmates as a function of the human tendency to value members of one's own in-group over members of an out-group. Once children identify themselves as male or female, they should quickly begin the gender segregation process. But even though boys tend to learn their own gender category a bit earlier than girls do, girls show same-sex playmate preferences earlier than boys do. As Maccoby (1998) suggested, knowledge of one's own gender identity may be a necessary but not a sufficient condition for gender segregation. In the next section, we will examine some of the social influences that may directly affect the development of sex differences, including children's preferences for same-sex playmates.

The Role of Parenting in Generating Sex Differences

A number of theories, in many different traditions, have argued that parenting practices have a special role to play in the development of sex differences.

Freud's Psychoanalytic Theory. One of the oldest social influence theories of sex role development is Freud's psychoanalytic theory (e.g., Freud, 1935/1960; see also Chapter 1). Freud argued that at about age 3, children begin to have vague sexual needs. These needs create a family triangle that plays out somewhat differently for boys versus girls. Boys are buffeted by a tempest of motives and emotions called an **Oedipus complex**. First, they direct their sexual urges toward their mothers because they are most strongly attached to their mothers as primary caretakers. Then, this desire for the mother, to usurp her time, to be physically close to her, puts a boy in competition with his father for her affections. The boy fears that his more powerful father will retaliate with a physical punishment that fits the crime—castration. Finally, the boy is so terrified by the prospect of his father's retaliation that he redirects his energy into pleasing his father by identifying with him. This identification process involves both imitation and internalization. Identification explains why boys adopt sex-typed behaviors: They are acting like their fathers. It also explains how boys form a superego, a kind of conscience: They internalize their fathers' values (see Chapter 7).

In Freud's theory, girls go through a similar process called the **Electra complex**. They direct their initial sexual desires toward their fathers, even though they too are more strongly attached to their mothers. That is because they experience **penis envy**, a desire to have what they naively assume is the greater genital pleasure that must come with having the external genitalia of a male. Then they find themselves in competition with their mothers, although their fear of their mothers' displeasure is not so great as a boy's because they assume that somehow they have already been castrated. They do not understand that their genitalia are simply more internal than are a boy's. Eventually, they identify with their mothers to make peace, although because they do not fear castration, they do not identify as closely with their mothers as boys do with their fathers. Thus, girls too become gender typed in their behavior and form a superego. However, neither process is as intense for a girl as it is for a boy. This was Freud's way of explaining why women are "morally inferior" to men, a belief that was endemic to the time and place in which Freud himself was enculturated.

Although many aspects of Freud's tale of sexual desire, competition, and fear in young children have become deeply embedded in our culture, efforts to validate the theory have been unsuccessful. For example, one prediction we can make from Freud's theory is that traditional family structure—mother as primary caregiver, father as her sexual partner and a strong presence in the home—should be necessary for children to experience normal sex role development. Yet, sex role development is not impeded in children who come from single-parent homes, nor even in children who come from homes where both parents are of one sex (e.g., Bailey, Bobrow, Wolfe, & Mikach, 1995; Golombok & Tasker, 1996; Patterson, 2004).

There is also little evidence that children model themselves after a single identification figure. Rather, research indicates that children will model themselves after others whom they perceive to be like themselves (e.g., same gender; Bussey & Bandura, 1984), as the cognitive theorists predict, and whom they perceive as competent. It also helps if the model is not scary or punitive, but rather is perceived as nurturant (Bandura, 1977).

Social Learning Theories.   Social learning theorists argue that many parents and other adults influence children's sex-typed behaviors, both by modeling such behaviors and by differential treatment of boys and girls that teaches them to behave in sex-appropriate ways.

What evidence is there that adults actually do behave differently toward children based on gender? First, we should note that in many ways, boys and girls do not appear to be treated differently. Meta-analyses indicate no differences in how much parents interact with their sons and daughters, in how much parents encourage them to achieve, in how much parents encourage help seeking, in how much warmth or responsiveness parents show, or in how effectively parents communicate or reason with them (e.g., Lytton & Romney, 1991).

However, there are some important differences in parental behaviors. In what have been dubbed "Baby X" studies, adult participants interact with a baby they do not know (e.g., Seavey, Katz, & Zalk, 1975). When participants think they are interacting with a boy, they are more likely to handle the baby in active ways, such as bouncing; when they think the baby is a girl, they handle it more gently. Participants more often describe boys as big and strong, but they use terms like sweet and pretty more often with girls. As children get older, mothers talk more, use more supportive speech, and talk more about emotions with their daughters (e.g., Dunn, Bretherton, & Munn, 1987; Leaper, Anderson, & Sanders, 1998). Across cultures, girls are more often asked to help with infant sibling care, although across many cultures both boys and girls are recruited to care for young children (Best, 2010). Many parents place more pressure on preschool boys than girls not to cry or express feelings (Block, 1978). There are other parental differences as well, with fathers more likely than mothers to have different expectations of their sons than their daughters (Siegel, 1987). Fathers are more likely to be disapproving of cross-sex behavior in their sons than in their daughters, more likely to roughhouse with their sons, and more likely to be negative or confrontational with them (Maccoby, 1998). In the United States, this is true for Black, White and Latino fathers, who also engage in more literacy activities with their daughters than their sons by the time their children are 2 years old (Leavell, Tamis-LeMonda, Ruble, Zosuls, & Cabrera, 2012). Indeed, Katz and Walsh (1991) suggest that children come to see men as "the custodians of gender-role norms" (p. 349). Leavell et al. (2012) note that "fathers channel their children toward gender-typed activities well before their children have a clear understanding of gender roles" (p. 53). In some Western societies, boys typically experience stronger pressure to conform to gender-stereotypic behavior than do girls because the sanctions when boys deviate from such norms are more severe than they are for girls (Sandnabba & Ahlberg, 1999).

Other differences in adult socialization practices with boys versus girls may be particularly important in laying the groundwork for later sex differences in psycho-pathology. Keenan and Shaw (1997) reviewed a number of findings that are consistent with such a conclusion. They report that preschool girls, in contrast to boys, are more often reinforced by their parents for compliant behavior and more often ignored for attempts to direct interaction in free-play situations (Kerig, Cowan, & Cowan, 1993). Parents also socialize children to deal with conflict in different ways. Girls are more frequently encouraged to yield to peers in conflict situations, for example, by giving up a desired toy (Ross, Tesla, Kenyon, & Lollis, 1990). Girls are also taught, to a greater degree than boys, to take others' perspectives and feelings into account in situations involving conflict (Smetana, 1989). Preschool teachers have sometimes been found to react more negatively to girls than to boys for high levels of activity, including activity levels during play, and more positively to girls than to boys for dependency behaviors (Fagot, 1984). In sum, these authors conclude that

Although young children recognize gender differences and can articulate gender stereotypes, parental and other environmental influences have a big influence on gender-typical behaviors as children develop their own gender concepts.

there is evidence to suggest that early socialization experiences help channel the development of internalizing behaviors in girls and externalizing behaviors in boys.

Some research also suggests that parents' socialization behaviors can subtly vary depending on factors such as family composition and cultural background (see Leaper, 2002; Ruble et al., 2006). For example, in families with both male and female children, a mother's behaviors are more affected by the gender of the child she is relating to than in families with only girls or only boys (McHale, Crouter, & Whiteman, 2003). African American mothers convey less traditional gender-typed attitudes to their children than European American mothers, whereas Latina mothers convey more traditional attitudes (see Ruble et al., 2006).

When we evaluate typical differences in parents' socialization practices, we have to ask, to what extent are adults' behaviors causing sex differences in children, as social learning theorists would argue, and to what extent are they responses to already existing sex differences? As we have seen so many times, the causal processes here seem to be reciprocal. For example, parents make more attempts to "down-regulate" boys' emotional responses in the preschool years (Block, 1978), but boys may also be slower to develop self-regulatory skills than girls. It seems likely that parents are influenced in part by the fact that boys have more impulsive emotional outbursts and in part by their desire to teach boys not to display weakness (Maccoby, 1998). Another example is that parents talk more to their daughters than to their sons. This may influence girls' language development, but girls' vocabulary growth begins earlier than boys', and toddler girls are more talkative than toddler boys, which may help influence parents' behavior as well (Leaper & Smith, 2004).

The Role of Peer Interactions in Generating Sex Differences

We have already emphasized how intensive the sex segregation process is, beginning as early as 2½ years of age, and becoming by middle childhood the most extreme sex difference that there is: Girls spend much of their unstructured time with girls, boys with boys. As we have seen, gender segregation may be influenced by cognitive processes, such that when children become aware of their gender identity, they value members of the same in-group more than members of the out-group. Some preexisting sex differences, influenced by either biology or parenting or both, may also make same-gender companions more appealing. In particular, Maccoby (1990, 1998) has suggested that girls tend to be wary of boys' rough play and to turn away from it. If so, initial differences in children's play styles are then magnified in same-gender peer groups.

> Here is a plausible scenario: Individual boys, each prenatally sensitized (or primed by parents) to respond positively to overtures for rough, arousing play, will choose each other as playmates. . . . And girls, individually sensitized by their parents to others' feelings, or in a state of greater readiness to receive socialization inputs of this kind from their parents, will use (their) attributes to build a new and distinctively female type of interaction with their playmates . . . the whole is greater than the sum of its parts . . . merging individual children . . . into a group, will produce a new form of interaction that is different from what they have experienced with their parents. (Maccoby, 1998, pp. 296–297)

The important point is that within their gendered peer groups children develop interaction styles that are more differentiated than either biology or parenting would predict (see Martin et al., 2005). Martin and Fabes (2001) observed 3- to 5-year-olds' play-partner choices over a 6-month period. They found that "sex segregation was pervasive" among their 61 study participants. Over 80% of the children had clear same-sex play-partner preferences, even though teachers encouraged gender equity, and the stability of these preferences increased over the 6 months of the study. The results also demonstrated that same-sex peers seem to have a socializing influence on children, just as Maccoby suggests. Stereotyped sex differences, such as activity level differences, "developed or increased over time." Most interesting was that there was a **social dosage effect**: Children who spent more time in same-gender groups showed greater increases in gender-related behaviors even after only a few months. The social dosage effect also has been reported in studies of older children and adolescents (McHale, Kim, Dotterer, Crouter, & Booth, 2009).

In adolescence, when boys and girls begin to build cross-gender groups and relationships, their different interaction styles can create difficulties. For example, in studies of mixed-sex problem-solving groups, young women can be at a disadvantage. They tend to express agreement with others more often than young men do, consistent with their gendered discourse style, but unlike their experience in all-female peer groups, they may never get their chance to speak because males do less turn taking and are more domineering. Overall, they tend to have less influence on the outcome (Carli, 1990). Similarly, in heterosexual dyads, males do not offer as much support to their partners as females do for the expression of feelings. As you might expect, males seem less well prepared for the mutuality of intimate relationships, perhaps because of the discourse style they acquire in their larger, less intimate childhood groups (Leaper, 1994).

Gilligan (e.g., 1993) and Pipher (1994) describe females as "losing their voice" when they reach adolescence because they feel pressure to adapt themselves to what others want them to be. As we saw in Chapter 7, there is little evidence that girls' level of voice is compromised in this sense at adolescence (Harter et al., 1998; Steinberg & Monahan, 2007). Perhaps, instead, the more cooperative discourse style of females, in the face of the more egoistic male style, makes girls and women less powerful agents when interacting with males than when they are interacting with other females.

A Multidimensional Theory of Sex Differences in Behavior

As we have seen, several different explanations for gender differences in behavior have some empirical support, but all of them have some important limitations as well. Clearly what is needed is a multidimensional theory that takes into account multiple causal influences and that specifies how these influences transact to produce gender differences. A social-cognitive theory proposed by Bussey and Bandura (1999; see also Bandura & Bussey, 2004) takes a more complex approach to gender differences than the causal explanations we have considered so far. Bussey and Bandura specify three categories of variables that interact reciprocally to help shape the development of gender role, including gender differences in behavior. These factors include personal influences (cognitive conceptions of gender, affective, and biological features of the person), behavioral influences (learning of and execution of activities that are gender linked), and environmental influences (family, peer, and societal). All these influences interact reciprocally to mold the motivational and self-regulatory structures that determine behavior. For example, family and societal influences contribute to children's knowledge base about gender and gender-linked competencies by serving as models and by providing rewards or sanctions for gender-appropriate or inappropriate behavior. In addition, both proximal and distal social forces help shape children's patterns of expectations about how genders behave, their beliefs about how these behaviors will be evaluated by others, and their constructions about their own competence to enact the behaviors in gender-appropriate ways.

Although Bussey and Bandura (1999) specify that affective and biological features of the person are important, in their more detailed analyses of how various causes interact in gender role development they tend to emphasize social (especially parental) and cognitive factors. They suggest that at least initially adult sanctions and direct teaching contribute most to the production of behaviors that are considered gender appropriate. As you have seen, research attests to the important role that children's early socialization experiences play in the development of gender-linked behavior. Clearly, there are differences across cultures in the specifics of gender-appropriate behavior, but most cultures do place restrictions on what the genders should and should not do. Yet these behaviors are not shaped just by patterns of external contingencies. Children grow increasingly more adept at monitoring and evaluating themselves according to personal standards and according to the circumstances of the contexts in which they find themselves. Thus, cognitive factors play a larger role as children get older. Self-regulatory functions become progressively more internalized and direct children's behavior in ways that maximize self-satisfaction and minimize self-censure (Bandura, 1986). Children learn to anticipate the consequences of their actions and can thus predict the responses their behaviors will elicit from others. These emerging capacities for self-monitoring and prediction are linked to the development of internalized standards for performance, largely based upon how others in the social world have responded to the behavior, the models that have been observed, and what has been taught directly. Gender-linked behavior is thus maintained by ongoing social influences operating through psychological mechanisms such as motivation, expectancy for success, and self-efficacy. These internal mechanisms have been constructed in the process of interacting with a world in which gender is a highly salient social category.

Social-cognitive theory specifies that socialization by others and the self is embedded in cultural context. Not surprisingly, many gender differences described in this chapter are attenuated or even reversed in some cultures. For example, boys are typically more competitive than girls in the United States, Canada, and Mexico, but not in India. And in Israel, boys tend to be less competitive than girls (Strube, 1981). Among the cultural factors that seem to be important for some gender differences is how egalitarian a society's attitudes and institutions are. As you saw with math achievement, the more egalitarian the society, the fewer gender differences we tend to find.

Bussey and Bandura (1999) provide an attempt to take into account some of the complexity of interacting causal processes in gender role development, but much more work is needed to construct a theory that includes all the influences that we have seen to be important. Future theorists, for example, need to integrate the recent findings on peers' power to affect the development of gendered behavior. In the next section, we will take a broader look at the whole arena of peer relationships and the place of peers in the lives of children.

PEER RELATIONSHIPS

In 1958, the Primary Mental Health Project, a program for early identification of at-risk students, was initiated in the first grades of several schools in Monroe County, New York. Data from social work interviews with mothers, classroom observations, teacher reports, other school records, and psychological evaluations such as intelligence, personality, and achievement tests were compiled for each of the children in the hope of identifying variables that would predict later adjustment difficulties. Based on these multiple measures, children were given either a "red" or "non-red" tag. Red-tagged first graders were those whose behavior, educational achievement, and social-emotional functioning reflected moderate to severe maladaptation. Out of the total of three academic-year samples (1958–1959, 1959–1960, and 1960–1961), approximately one third of the youngsters received red tags (Cowen et al., 1963).

In a separate and fortunate development, the Medical Center of the University of Rochester initiated a county psychiatric registry concurrent with the school-based project. This registry provided an ongoing, longitudinal record of most persons in the county who were diagnosed with mental health problems and who had received treatment. These two unrelated sources of information made it possible to track the histories of the children in the Primary Mental Health Project 11 to 13 years later by means of registry entries (Cowen, Petersen, Babigian, Izzo, & Trost, 1973).

As they moved into early adulthood, individuals who had been red-tagged as children showed up in the registry in disproportionate numbers. They represented more than two out of every three individuals on the list of those needing psychiatric care. You already know from reading the previous chapters that there is evidence for continuity of behavioral and emotional problems over time, so this is not too surprising. What is intriguing about this story, however, is what predicted these later problems best. In other words, what kinds of measures separated youth who ended up in the registry from their age-mates who did not? If researchers had known the answer to this question, they might have been able to identify and treat children before more serious problems surfaced.

Remember that the researchers administered intelligence, personality, and achievement tests; obtained behavior rating scale data; amassed grade and attendance information; and interviewed parents. They also asked the children themselves to nominate their peers for various hypothetical roles, half positive (e.g., the lead character) and half negative (e.g., the villain) in a "Class Play" exercise (Bower, 1960). Researchers found through retrospective comparison that individuals on the county registry performed slightly less well than their age-mates on most assessment measures, but not significantly so. There was, however, one important exception: The extent to which children were nominated by their grade school peers for negative roles in the class play significantly predicted later membership in the registry. Children far and away outpredicted the adults in recognizing those children destined for later psychological problems. What did these children know?

As we have seen in our discussion of sex role development, peers are a significant force in the lives of children. The story of how effectively grade school children's feelings predicted their peers' later mental health outcomes introduces us to the fascinating world of the peer group, its dynamics in childhood and adolescence, and its relevance to later outcomes. In particular, it implies that peer relationships in childhood are significant predictors of later mental health and social adjustment.

The Peer Group, Social Competence, and Social Skills

What makes for good peer relationships? To answer this question, we need to understand something about the nature of peer groups and the distinctions researchers make between social competence and particular social skills. The study of the peer group may be distinguished from the study of simple social interactions or even the study of friendship relationships in ways that are familiar to helping professionals working in therapeutic settings. Group counseling, for example, differs from individual counseling not only because there are more people involved in the process but also because the interrelationships and dynamics become much more complex.

Around the world, children find friends among their peer groups, favoring others of the same gender and with similar interests.

> Groups are more than mere aggregates of relationships; through emergent properties such as norms or shared cultural conventions, groups help define the type and range of relationships and interactions that are likely or permissible. Further, groups have properties and processes, such as hierarchical organization and cohesiveness, that are not relevant to descriptions of children's experiences at lower levels of social complexity. (Rubin, Bukowski, & Parker, 1998, p. 623)

Social competence, a criterion for peer group acceptance, is a broad construct that is not restricted to one set of prescribed behaviors. Affective responses, such as empathy and valuing of relationships, and cognitive processes, such as perspective taking (see Chapter 5) and ability to make mature moral judgments (see Chapter 7), play a part in the repertoire of the socially adept individual. It is impossible to assess the social competence of a child without considering his skill in relating to others at every relationship level. Social but "nonfriend" interactions, as well as friendship relationships, are embedded within the larger peer group structure, each influencing and influenced by the other levels of social exchange. Remember, then, that a child's success or lack of success within his peer group is not independent of basic interaction skills or the kinds of friendship skills we discussed in Chapter 6.

Good **social skills** are important contributors to socially competent behavior at every level of interaction. They may be defined as discrete, observable behaviors such as making eye contact, using appropriate language, asking appropriate questions, and so forth that promote effective social interaction and that are part of the broader construct of social competence. Social skills training approaches grew out of the recognition that students who have peer group problems lack certain essential social skills or behave in ways that are counterproductive to smooth social exchange. Consequently, modeling, coaching, and reinforcement processes are used to teach students how to interact more adaptively in very basic ways.

Both correlational and experimental studies of social skills training programs lend modest support to their usefulness in improving peer acceptance (see Bierman, 2003; Ladd & Asher, 1985; Ladd & Mize, 1983; Michelson, Sugai, Wood, & Kazdin, 1983). One possible reason for their limited effects is the unidirectional approach typically employed in these interventions. In other words, treatment often assumes that the socially troubled individual owns the problem. There is evidence, however, that if children are disliked, peers also process information about them in biased ways. For example, children interpret negative acts as intentionally malicious when committed by disliked children but not when committed by popular children (Dodge, Pettit, McClaskey, & Brown, 1986; Veenstra, Lindenberg, Munniksma, & Dijkstra, 2010). Bierman (1986, 2003) found that greater success could be achieved by combining social skills training for individual children with attempts to enhance the cooperative nature of these children's peer groups. Thus, addressing the context within which the socially unskilled child functions, along with the transactional nature of his social interactions, allows for more lasting improvements. Social competence, including particular social skills, helps children experience success in friendship relationships. The same holds for children's success in the larger peer context.

Peer groups are complicated webs of social relationships, including friendship **dyads**, **cliques**, and **crowds**. These complex social networks emerge and take on great significance for children as early as middle childhood (Hallinan, 1979). In contrast, the social worlds of preschoolers and early elementary school children are less intricately constructed. By middle childhood, voluntary social or friendship groups of three to nine members, called cliques, become more common, although they are still rather informal. At this age the group's structure is flexible, and member turnover is common. The importance of cliques reaches a peak in early adolescence, followed by a general decline in importance over the course of high school (called **degrouping**; see Shrum & Cheek, 1987). Crowds are larger, reputation-based groups, composed of numerous cliques, that become more important in midadolescence (Dunphy, 1963). The significance of both cliques and crowds for adolescent development will be discussed in Chapter 10.

The peer group serves many important functions for children and adolescents. It provides opportunities for practice in communication, conflict resolution, joint goal setting, cooperative learning, and shared decision making. Important interpersonal goals—such as the development of empathy, tolerance for others, and a sense of belonging—are met within groups of peers. Skills acquired in activities such as team sports may provide training for certain competitive aspects of adult work roles (Lever, 1978). The peer group is like a real-world laboratory where the skills of living with and getting along with others are tried out and improved.

Zarbatany, Hartmann, and Rankin (1990) explored the function of competitive activities (sports, physical games) and noncompetitive activities (talking on telephone, watching TV) within peer groups of early adolescents. These authors found that the two kinds of activities were important for facilitating different aspects of socioemotional development and social competence. Whereas participation in competitive activities provided opportunities for self-understanding by defining personal strengths and weaknesses, participation in noncompetitive activities enhanced a sense of acceptance and belonging in relationship to others.

Analysis of the World of Peers

Sarah is a sixth grader who attends middle school in a midsized school district. The school is a mix of White, Black, and Asian youngsters whose families live and work in the surrounding communities. Some parents work in the new technology industry developing on the outskirts of the town center. Others are employed in the one manufacturing plant that still operates downtown.

Sarah is a talented member of her school's track team and sings in the concert choir. She is active in her school's student council as well. She has a few close friends whom she has known since early elementary school. Sarah is the one whom they depend on if they need some advice or help. She loves to spend time with her friends, texting, talking on the phone and going to movies.

Recently, Sarah's social life has become more important to her than ever. She spends a great deal of time in consultation with her friends, discussing what to wear and planning social activities. She pays a little less attention to her schoolwork now that she has so many other things to think about in her life. However, she still manages to maintain a B+ average. What can we say about Sarah and her place on the social map of middle school?

The attempt to answer this question presents us with an interesting challenge. We have noted the complexity of peer group structures, so you may have already guessed that there are several levels of analysis. In general, researchers have approached this question from two complementary yet distinct perspectives: analysis of the individual group member's characteristics within the peer group network and analysis of the different groups within the universe of peer groups. The first approach would help us understand Sarah's status within her peer group and would typically depend on sociometric assessment. The second approach would help us understand the number and nature of the peer groups in Sarah's school and would depend on more ethnographic means of analysis.

Measurement of Individuals Within the Peer Group

Sociometry

Before we can understand the kinds of categories that describe children's status within peer groups, we need to appreciate the means by which these differences were first identified. **Sociometry**, the classic way of assessing social competence, had its origins in the work of Moreno (1934), who used children's nomination of their peers to evaluate peer status. Moreno viewed group processes as a mixture of positive forces (attractions), negative forces (repulsions), and indifference (absence of attraction or repulsion). He proposed that the interpersonal relationships within a group could be mapped out on the basis of knowing these social forces. Since this introduction by Moreno, sociometric techniques have diversified and have been applied in a variety of ways. McConnell and Odom (1986) offer the general definition of sociometric measures as "tests in which children make preferential responses to statements about peers in their social group" (p. 217), resulting in a score that defines a child's social status.

Typically, children might be asked to select the classmate or classmates he would most like to play with, work with, or sit next to in class. Although many varieties of analysis have been used in sociometric studies, such as weighting the nominations, the most straightforward approach is to count the number of positive nominations or mentions a child receives. This number, then, reflects the child's **social preference** score. Sociometric techniques are most useful when they also include negative nominations, or children's mention of peers with whom they do not want to work or play. Researchers have found that children who are rejected by peers cannot be identified without the inclusion of negative nominations (Hartup, Glazer, & Charlesworth, 1967). Social preference scores may range from highly positive to highly negative.

A second score, called **social impact**, is computed by adding up the total number of nominations, both positive and negative. This measure indicates the degree to which the child gets noticed within his group (see Rubin, Bukowski, & Parker, 2006).

Sociometric Categories

Based on their scores on the dimensions of social impact and social preference, children can be classified into a variety of sociometric categories. Contemporary researchers most often use the methodology and categories identified by Coie and his associates (Coie, Dodge, & Coppotelli, 1982), which include five subgroups: **popular**, **average**, **neglected**, **rejected**, and **controversial**. Popular children receive many positive nominations and few negative nominations from their peers (high preference, high impact). Generally, they are well-liked members of the group and have relatively high visibility among their peers. Remember, however, that the term *popular* refers to a specific sociometric category and has a slightly more forgiving meaning than does the contemporary use of the term. In other words, a student does not have to be the captain of the football team to achieve popular status!

Average children are those who receive an average number of positive and negative nominations (near the mean for the group on preference and impact). *Neglected* children are those who receive few nominations, either positive or negative. This latter group is characterized by its low level of social impact. Students who fall into the *rejected* category receive many negative and few positive nominations. They are typically disliked (low preference) but have generally high visibility (high impact). The final category, called *controversial*, identifies a relatively small group of students who receive many positive and many negative nominations (high impact, average preference). They have been named controversial because they share many of the characteristics of both popular and rejected youngsters. They are seen by some peers as aggressive but as class leaders by others. These categories are presented graphically in Figure 8.4.

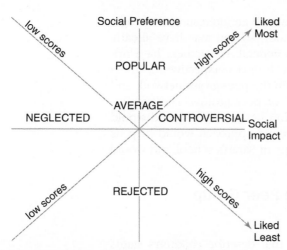

The relationships between positive and negative social choice measures, the dimensions of social preference and social impact, and five types of social status.

FIGURE 8.4 Dimensions and types of social statuses.

SOURCE: Coie, J. D., Dodge, K. A., & Coppotelli, H. (1982). Dimensions and types of social status: A cross-age perspective, *Developmental Psychology, 18,* 557–570. Adapted with permission from the American Psychological Association.

Individual Characteristics Related to Sociometric Status

What are the children in these categories like? Although it is tempting to think of each group as homogeneous in personality and behavior and thus clearly separable from the others, this kind of simplicity does not fit well with the facts. For example, all rejected children do not behave in aggressive ways. Nor do aggressive rejected children always behave aggressively. Popular children, despite their good qualities, are not perfect. They may also experience peer-related problems from time to time.

In this section, we will describe general identifying characteristics of the groups, with greatest emphasis on popular, rejected, and neglected categories, the three groups most frequently studied. The controversial category has been more difficult to examine because of its much smaller size and lack of measurement stability. Remember that the categories suggest general tendencies to behave or to process social information in certain ways much, but not all, of the time.

Popular

Popular children are notable for their use of perspective-taking skills. Upon entering a group, these children can adopt the group's frame of reference and join in without calling undue attention to themselves or to their own needs (Putallaz & Wasserman, 1990). They can be assertive, but they are not deliberately antagonistic or disruptive to others (Dodge, Schlundt, Schocken, & Delugach, 1983). In this, they demonstrate high levels of self-regulation and self-control. Popular children also manifest greater cognitive and social problem-solving ability than do children from other groups. Black and Hazan (1990) studied the language patterns of popular preschool children and found them to be particularly adept at communicating clearly with others and following others' conversations. Positive correlations have also been found between popular status and perceived social self-concept (Harter, 1981) and self-efficacy (Ladd & Price, 1987). For college students, high sociometric status (being liked and admired by peers) is a powerful predictor of feelings of well-being (Anderson, Kraus, Galinsky, & Keltner, 2012).

In general, popular students tend to be prosocial, cooperative, intelligent, and capable of working well with others. They are likely to enjoy close, dyadic relationships with friends, although the domains of popularity and friendship are not necessarily overlapping. In other words, popularity is not a prerequisite for friendship. Sociometrically average and neglected groups also develop friendships. Peer acceptance and friendship make separate contributions to children's overall adjustment. For example, loneliness in adolescence is more closely associated with lack of friendships than with low peer acceptance (see Ruben et al., 2006).

Certain other attributes, such as physical attractiveness (Langlois & Stephan, 1981) and scholastic competence (Coie & Krehbiehl, 1984), are also associated with popular status. If you think about Sarah, the sixth grader from our earlier example, you might conclude her sociometric status to be popular.

Rejected

The children who are rejected by their peers have received a great deal of research attention. Rejected children are the least socially skilled of all the groups and also the most heterogeneous category. Originally, researchers took the position that aggression was the primary attribute of children in this social group. In fact, being aggressive is still the most commonly cited behavior associated with being rejected by peers (e.g., Haselager, Cillessen, van Lieshout, Riksen-Walraven, & Hartup, 2002). However, it soon became clear that children can be rejected not only because they aggress against their peers (**rejected-aggressive** group) but also because they withdraw from them (**rejected-withdrawn** group).

The characteristics of rejected children contrast sharply with those of the popular group. Instead of modulating negativity, as is the case with popular children, rejected-aggressive youngsters demonstrate high levels

Both highly aggressive and highly withdrawn children can face rejection by peers. Efforts to enhance peer acceptance may be more effective when they address both rejected children and their peer groups as a whole.

of instrumental aggression, verbal negativity, and disruptiveness. You might wonder whether these children are rejected because they are aggressive or act aggressively because they have been rejected. Several longitudinal studies demonstrate a causal link between aggression and subsequent rejection. This evidence is different from most sociometric research findings because it helps to explain what causes a child to be rejected. Over a period of several days, Dodge (1983) observed the interactions of small groups of children who initially did not know each other. After each play session, children were asked to complete a sociometric measure for their group. As the experiment progressed, some children began to take on popular status, whereas others were rejected. As in other studies of this type (Coie & Kupersmidt, 1983; Kupersmidt, Burchinal, & Patterson, 1995), aggression was the characteristic that best predicted rejection by the other children when all other differences were controlled.

In addition to aggression, rejected youngsters are more likely to demonstrate lower levels of perspective taking, self-control, and positive social interaction skills. Particular deficits in information processing, marked by perceptions of hostile intent or hostile attributional bias (see Chapter 7), are significant features of their social cognition. Once rejected, these youngsters are prevented from engaging in the very kinds of social interactions that might help them develop more positive social skills. If you remember Jason, our example from Chapter 7, you might imagine him fitting into the rejected category. Controversial children also demonstrate high levels of aggressive behavior, but they possess correspondingly positive attributes, such as greater sociability and cognitive ability, that buffer their abrasive characteristics and may make them attractive to their peers.

As we indicated earlier, however, aggression is not characteristic of all rejected children. Even though estimates indicate that approximately 50% are aggressive (Bierman, 1986), another 10% to 20% are extremely withdrawn (Parkhurst & Asher, 1992). Interestingly, social withdrawal begins to elicit the disapproval of peers in middle to late childhood. Whereas isolation in early childhood is not nearly so stigmatizing (Younger, Gentile, & Burgess, 1993), presumably because it is not very important at this age, extreme social withdrawal in middle to late childhood is perceived as deviant and may provoke rejection by the group (Rubin, Coplan & Bowker, 2009).

Rejected-withdrawn children are more socially anxious than other groups and likely to behave in socially inappropriate ways. Poor perspective-taking skills and general social ineptness may lead these youngsters to behave in ways that are considered odd, infantile, unpredictable, or potentially embarrassing to peers. Consequently, popular peers may ostracize them, just as they ostracize their more aggressive counterparts, for failing to fit in. Children in the rejected category are at special risk for peer victimization (e.g., Hanish & Guerra, 2004). Both rejected-aggressive and rejected-withdrawn children do have social networks, but their social groups are smaller and are characterized by lower levels of intimacy and interaction (e.g., Ladd, Kochenderfer-Ladd, Eggum, Kochel, & McConnell, 2011). Overall, it is important for helping professionals to recognize that rejected children are a heterogeneous group.

Neglected

Neglected children can be distinguished from children in the average group primarily because they have somewhat lower levels of peer interaction. In their meta-analysis of peer relations studies, Newcomb, Bukowski, and Pattee (1993) reported some differences between neglected and average groups. Sociometrically neglected children are less aggressive than average children, are less likely to be highly visible within the peer group, and show less sociability, but they are perceived by their peers as relatively likeable. These authors conclude that neglected children are simply not choosing to participate very actively within their group of peers. Unlike rejected-withdrawn children, peers do not make them feel especially anxious (Ladd et al., 2011). Children in the neglected group are similar to those in the average group in their ability to have friendships and are as likely as other children to have a best friend (Ruben et al., 2009). Therefore, even though this group has certain sociometrically distinctive characteristics, neglected children are similar to average children in many respects. Being neglected, as distinct from being in the rejected-withdrawn subgroup, which also incurs high levels of peer neglect, does not seem to be associated with developmental problems (Rubin et al., 2006).

Average

Average children, as you might have guessed, receive an average number of nominations. They are at neither extreme on the impact or preference dimensions. They show lower levels of social competence than popular children and less aggression than rejected-aggressive youngsters. As with the neglected group, no problematic outcomes are associated with this sociometric category.

Gender and Cultural Differences

Differences between boys and girls across sociometric classifications have received relatively little research attention (Rubin et al., 2006; Ruble et al., 2006). Those studies that have addressed gender differences report that as children get older, particularly as they approach adolescence, greater intolerance of gender-inconsistent behavior is expressed for males than for females. Boys are more likely to be rejected for behaving in feminine ways, whereas girls who behave in masculine ways are more likely to be accepted by their peers (Berndt & Heller, 1986). Perhaps for this reason, socially withdrawn girls are less likely to be rejected than similar boys. It seems that shyness and social anxiety is perceived as more normative for girls (Gazelle, 2008).

Much of the data on peer relations and social status groups is drawn from research in the United States and Canada. Yet it seems very likely that peer relationships, including judgments of social behavior that affect acceptance or rejection of peers, would vary in different cultural contexts. Only limited information exists on cultural differences in peer group classifications, and some of it indicates that differences in values do have important effects. In China, for example, popular children are likely to be cautious, restrained, and shy (e.g., Chen, Ruben, & Li, 1995), whereas in North America such children are often rejected. Shy, socially anxious Chinese children are more likely to meet with approval and cooperation when they make social gestures, whereas North American children are likely to be ignored or victimized. Interestingly, some recent work indicates that things may be changing in China. Shyness and social withdrawal put children more at risk for social problems and feelings of depression than they once did (see Rubin, Coplan, Chen, Bowker, & McDonald, 2011). Chang et al. (2005) argue that over time, cultural change in China has weakened the link between shyness and popularity.

Generally, across Western and non-Western cultures, aggression is associated with peer rejection, and helpfulness is associated with popularity (e.g., Chang et al., 2005; see also Ruben et al., 2006). However, aggressive behavior is not necessarily associated with rejection in North America. When aggressive children are more socially competent in other ways (e.g., good at perspective taking) they may be considered part of the controversial category we have just discussed, and may even be perceived as popular, especially as children get older (e.g., Rodkin & Roisman, 2010; see Chapter 10). Research in China indicates that aggression is more severely sanctioned there, and that aggressive children are more likely to feel isolated, perhaps because of greater emphasis on maintaining harmony (see Rubin et al., 2011). And yet, a nationally representative study involving over 9,000 middle school children in China found bullying to be an important problem, with over 25% of both boys and girls affected (Cheng et al., 2010). Overall, it appears that despite some cross-cultural variation, aggressive behavior in children is a universal problem, with consequences for the perpetrators and the victims.

Even though all children, regardless of culture, are likely to experience some peer conflicts, societies differ in how adults intervene. In societies that value individualism, such as the U.S., children are often encouraged to verbally defend themselves, to negotiate, and to seek fairness for themselves, often with an adult acting as arbitrator. In more collectivist cultures, such as China and Japan, children at odds with peers are not likely to be singled out or to be encouraged to act on their own behalf. Rather, adults are likely to expect the peer group to manage the conflict and to establish harmony among themselves, bringing each child's behavior into line with group expectations (e.g., Tobin, Wu, & Davidson, 1989; see also Greenfield, Suzuki, & Rothstein-Fisch, 2006). There is an important lesson here for helping professionals:

> In a multi-cultural society such as the United States . . . there is a tendency for each interactant to see the other's behavior through the implicit lens of his or her own value system. It is therefore important for educators and clinicians to be aware of the potential differences between children to help each child to better understand that children may have different perspectives on proper peer interaction, and that these differences can be acknowledged, respected, and even appreciated. (Greenfield et al., 2006, p. 684)

Stability of Categories and Outcomes

Once classified, do children maintain their status in the peer group throughout childhood and adolescence? Many researchers have studied the long-term stability of these sociometric classifications (Asher & Dodge, 1986; Newcomb & Bukowski, 1984) and have found that the most extreme categories (popular and rejected) are also the most stable, at least over short periods (Rubin et al., 2006). Both neglected and controversial status categories show instability even in the short term. Those studies that have looked at the long-term stability of sociometric classifications have produced mixed results. In general, the impact of peer group classification is moderately stable, particularly for the broad dimensions of acceptance and rejection, with the category of peer rejection being the most stable of all. Denham and Holt (1993) propose that this stability stems from children's early experience with each other. Once a child's reputation has been formed on the basis of early social interaction, his reputation endures despite evidence to the contrary.

What are the long-term outcomes for children who belong to these different categories? Recently, a number of prospective or follow-up studies have used early peer group designations to predict later performance on various measures of adjustment, much like that of the Rochester Registry. The broad-based categories of early acceptance and rejection have been studied most frequently and provide the most consistent results.

Not surprisingly, peer acceptance has been associated with myriad positive outcomes, both psychologically and academically. The outcomes change dramatically, however, for rejected-aggressive children, who often have poorer academic records, are more likely to repeat grades, are absent more frequently, are at greater risk of dropping out, and report more criminal behavior and drug use (see Coie, Terry, Lenox, & Lochman, 1995; Ladd & Burgess, 1999; Parker & Asher, 1987; Wentzel & Asher, 1995). The strongest linkages, by far, have been found between early aggression and peer rejection on one hand, and later externalizing problems on the other hand—the early-starter model of antisocial development described in Chapter 7 (see Dodge et al., 2003).

Researchers have also investigated outcomes for rejected-withdrawn youngsters and have found evidence for later internalizing problems such as depression and loneliness (e.g., Gazelle & Rudolph, 2004). This is especially true for children who have no friendships (see Rubin et al., 2006). A prospective study by Ladd and Burgess (1999) followed three groups of children from kindergarten through second grade: aggressive, withdrawn, and those with a comorbid profile of aggression and withdrawal. Consistent with predictions from developmental psychopathology, the children with multiple risks were predisposed to the most severe and enduring outcomes. The children who exhibited aggression and withdrawal in kindergarten were the most likely of all the groups to have troubled relationships with teachers and peers in second grade, to report more loneliness and dissatisfaction, and to express greater feelings of victimization.

Measurement of the Peer Group: Another Level of Analysis

Let us turn our attention to peer groups, the cliques and crowds we referred to earlier. These are networks of like-minded individuals who become associated with a specific set of norms, dress, and behaviors, like "jocks" or "brains." When we examine peer processes from this angle, we do not focus on the accepted or rejected status of particular children. It is certainly possible to be a popular member of a group of jocks as well as a popular brain. These peer groups appear to develop more significance in late childhood to early adolescence for the reasons specified in previous sections of this chapter. Moreover, adolescents may be better able to recognize and describe their peer groups effectively because they become increasingly proficient in thinking abstractly about categories as a function of their cognitive development.

Brown (1990) noted that the term *peer group* has been used rather loosely in the past, often applied to the whole spectrum of peer relationships, from dyadic friendships to membership in large crowds. This lack of clarity compromises our understanding of the role that each type of relationship plays in development. We use the terms *peer group* and *clique* somewhat interchangeably here, consistent with the view that these units are small enough to allow for regular interaction among members and to serve as the center of most peer-related interaction. Crowds, as we noted earlier, are larger collectives, composed of multiple cliques, which serve as social categories for students rather than as actual friendship groups. You might think of crowds as actual peer "cultures" that represent approaches to behavior, attitudes, and values. In Chapter 10, we will take a closer look at crowds. As we noted already, crowds are a more potent force in the lives of middle and late adolescents than for elementary school and early adolescent children.

Peer group analysis at the level of cliques and crowds can be done in various ways. In general, identification of peer groups or cliques requires students to specify who "hangs around" with whom in their classroom. Based on this information, maps of the social structure of classrooms or schools can be drawn using sophisticated methodologies such as social network analysis (Cairns, Gariepy, & Kindermann, 1990) or composite social-cognitive mapping (Kindermann, 1993).

Why Do Cliques Form?

Perhaps you are wondering why cliques surface in middle childhood and take on such significance in the first place. Common terms such as *in-group, clique, pecking order,* and even more pedantic ones like *status hierarchy* make many adults uncomfortable, particularly when these terms are applied to children. This is so because these descriptors imply a set of winners and losers in the game of social relationships. Adults often prefer to believe that children are less critical and more tolerant of each other than these descriptors suggest. But like it or not, there is strong evidence for the existence of stable status groups among children and adolescents.

What motivates the development of distinct cliques? Two major forces are at work: first, the need to establish an identity, and second, the need for acceptance (approval) and belonging. As we shall see in Chapter 10, peers play a central role in the process of identity or self-development. The search for the self rests largely on comparing oneself to and distinguishing oneself from others by means of social comparison processes (see Chapter 6). One's own identity becomes more distinct to the degree that it can be contrasted to that of another. Children who tend to dress, act, or otherwise express themselves in similar ways gravitate to each other. Together, they form a type of social group that provides some identity to its own members and a basis of comparison to, and for, others. A group's identity is based on shared activities, values, clothes, and behaviors (see Fiske & Taylor, 1991, for a review). Recognizing and understanding group characteristics helps early adolescents construct a map of the social world and provides them with a knowledge base about human differences.

Individuals' needs for acceptance and belonging also help explain the significance of the peer group. Children as well as adults want to be liked by their associates and will typically engage in the kinds of behaviors that result in their friends' praise or approval (Hartup, 1983). In addition to this kind of external social reinforcement, youngsters are also motivated by more internal goals. Berndt and Keefe (1996) argue that children and adolescents are intrinsically motivated to identify with their friends in behavior, dress, and academic achievement, but because they get satisfaction from emulating their friends' characteristics and being part of a group, not because they fear retribution if they fail to conform.

Peer Groups' Influence on Behavior

Our understanding of peer group processes must accommodate the power of both their beneficial as well as their potentially harmful aspects. As a helper, you have undoubtedly read about peer pressure. If you are also the parent of a middle or high school–aged child, you may have lost some sleep over it. Adults frequently blame early to late adolescent behavior and misbehavior on peer pressure, a notion that almost always has a negative connotation. They may imagine that children and adolescents are forced to conform to peer group standards to avoid humiliation or punishment. No one disagrees that peers become increasingly more influential as children mature. However, studies also show that the influence of peers is primarily indirect rather than overtly coercive (Berndt, Miller, & Park, 1989). Furthermore, peers can motivate students to engage in beneficial as well as risky behaviors, such as avoidance of drugs (Steinberg, 1996; Steinberg & Monahan, 2007).

Of course, not all peer group effects are totally benign. The peer group delimits the range of opportunities by its very nature as a group with norms and roles. Within any peer culture, the range of acceptable activities is circumscribed. For example, the peer group determines who may be included as a member, how leisure time is spent, and how the members should dress and behave. In some cases, peer group members may use both indirect (e.g., teasing) and direct (e.g., confrontation) means to promote adherence to these group norms (Eder & Sanford, 1986). Unfortunately, the norms for certain groups may support deviant, antisocial behavior.

Many interventions that address typical developmental problems make the implicit assumption that peer pressure is a cause of most early to late adolescent difficulties. Many of these intervention models are built upon "resistance" training, which attempts to prepare children to do battle with dangerous peers. But is this the way it really works? And do these assumptions make sense?

It may be possible to shed some light on this issue, and to improve interventions as well, by reviewing a few principles of peer group dynamics. First, peer groups or cliques are generally homogeneous. There is a well-documented tendency for peer groups to exhibit **homophily**, or a degree of similarity among members on behavioral or attitudinal attributes of importance. This is why you can often identify the members of a group by the way they dress or on the basis of what they do after school. Second, groups are formed based on processes of **influence** and **selection** (Cohen, 1977; Kandel, 1978). Basically, *influence* refers to the fact that the peer group can cause an individual to conform to the norms of the group. For example, if a youngster is part of a peer group that disparages getting good grades, the child presumably reduces his investment in doing homework in order to be accepted by the group. Researchers have found that the influence of the group is not usually a result of coercive pressure, however. Instead, normative social processes, like positive reinforcement, observational learning, and in some cases discussion and information exchange seem to be important (e.g., Harakeh & Vollebergh, 2012). "The idea of a group of friends putting pressure on a single child to do whatever they want the child to do is a myth" (Berndt & Murphy, 2002, p. 283).

Less attention has been paid to the complementary process, called *selection*, in which individuals choose to affiliate with others who share similar behaviors or attributes. For example, youngsters who are highly motivated academically are drawn to peers who are similar in this respect. As children mature, they become more able to select the environments that suit them, perhaps influenced by their genetically based predispositions (Scarr & McCartney, 1983).

Contrary to conventional wisdom, which emphasizes the importance of peer influence, many recent studies have found that selection processes are at least as important in the formation of peer groups. For example, Kindermann (1993) investigated how fourth- and fifth-grade students' peer groups affected their academic motivation. He found evidence for an initial selection process, with students selecting a peer context early in the school year that reflected their unique level of motivation. Interestingly, membership in the high- or low-motivation peer groups predicted academic achievement at the end of the year, suggesting that some complementary peer influence processes were at work throughout the year to maintain the levels of motivation.

Ennett and Bauman (1994) looked at this issue as it relates to teenage cigarette smoking. Once again, they found support for both selection and influence processes. Adolescents were drawn to cliques where smoking was the norm if they smoked or viewed smoking as desirable (selection). But it was also the case that nonsmokers in smoking cliques were more likely to begin smoking than were nonsmokers in nonsmoking cliques (influence).

What is important to remember is that both processes contribute to peer group formation and maintenance. Overemphasis on peer influence processes may compromise our understanding of other dynamics, such as motivation to affiliate with similar individuals. Once established, peer groups constitute important social contexts for young people that reinforce certain ways of thinking and behaving. Obviously, peer groups differ in the degree to which they provide a healthy developmental context for children and adolescents, yet their impact can be profound regardless of their benefit or harm. Paxton and her associates (Paxton, Schutz, Weitheim, & Muir, 1999) studied female cliques that varied in their levels of concern about body image and eating. Those girls who showed higher levels of eating-related disorders also inhabited more negative social environments, which appeared to amplify their distorted ideas about body image.

Children's resilience is enhanced when they participate in beneficial activities along with other members of their peer group.

As children mature into adolescents, much more of their time is spent in the company of their peers. The body of research on peer relationships teaches us that we would do well to consider the peer network in our conceptualization of problems and in the structuring of our interventions. A recent study speaks clearly to this final point. Reasoning that some positive modification in environment could alter the course of development for at-risk students, Mahoney (2000) studied the trajectories of 695 boys and girls from elementary school to young adulthood. He specifically focused on the role that participation in extracurricular activities in school played in ameliorating the difficulties of those participants who were most at risk. Not too surprisingly, most of the students who participated in extracurricular activities (one or more years of involvement in 6th through 10th grades) graduated from high school and did not become involved in criminal activity as young adults. This result was most obvious for students in the highest risk category.

What was surprising, however, was that this benefit was limited to those high-risk students whose peer groups also participated in the activity. There was no appreciable gain from participation unless the youngster's peer group shared in the activity. Participation in positive, highly organized, and supervised activities enriched the adjustment of the whole group, reinforcing more socially adaptive behavior for everyone. It may be that raising the index of positive adaptation for the whole group attracts more adaptive members (selection) while providing a context that promotes healthier activity (influence).

APPLICATIONS

As children mature, they are exposed to influences from many contexts, and the relative power of these influences shifts with development. Friendships, peer groups, and other extrafamilial settings such as school play increasingly important roles.

Focusing on children's relationships with their peers has become a major clinical objective, given what we now understand about their importance. First of all, functioning well within a peer group is one of the most significant accomplishments in children's lives (Sullivan, 1965). Good peer relationships operate as a powerful protective factor, providing children and adolescents with experiences of friendship, opportunities for problem solving, and enhancement of perspective taking and empathy. The opportunity to feel validated by others in your age group, who share many of your ideas and feelings, contributes to a sense of self-worth, relatedness, and

security (Sullivan, 1953). Second, problematic peer relationships are risks because they elicit or maintain maladaptive behavior and deprive youngsters of the kinds of protective effects mentioned above. Peer group problems figure prominently in developmental models of antisocial behavior (the early-starter pattern). As you recall from Chapter 7, accumulated evidence supports links between early childhood characteristics, such as difficult temperament or poor emotion regulation, and family factors, such as poverty, poor parenting skills, or insecurity of attachment, and the development of coercive family interaction patterns. These, in turn, fuel social information-processing deficits that set the stage for aggression toward peers and problems with teachers once children enter school. Lack of academic success and chronic peer rejection reduce motivation for school work and promote positive identification with aggressive and deviant groups. Conduct disorder, possibly continuing as adult antisocial behavior, can be the final outcome of this developmental trajectory. Fortunately, not all children with these high-risk profiles demonstrate adult aggressive outcomes; approximately half show no disorders in adulthood (Cairns & Cairns, 2000). Yet we are well advised to take peer problems seriously because they figure so prominently in the histories of children with conduct disorders, which are the most frequent referral problems in outpatient clinics (McMahon, Greenberg, & CPPRG, 1995).

Assess Carefully

Helpers should keep in mind that there is more than one route to peer rejection. Understanding rejection profiles can help us tailor our interventions to be most effective. Although we tend to group rejected children together or divide them into aggressive and withdrawn types, Bierman (2004) emphasizes that we can differentiate the social behaviors that contribute to rejection into at least four constellations: aggressive/disruptive (fighting, stubbornness, threatening, lying, meanness); inattentive/immature (disruptive, irresponsible, dependent, poorly organized), low levels of prosocial behavior (uncooperative, temperamental, bossy, humorless); and socially anxious/avoidant (solitary, withdrawn, nervous, cries easily). As you have seen, it is possible for aggressive children to be rather well liked if, for example, their aggression (dominance and competitiveness) is balanced by strengths in areas like athletics and sense of humor. Rejection is more likely when aggression comes in the form of being a "sore loser" or a "hothead." Meanness without provocation, inability to regulate negative affect, deliberate disruption of peer group activity, and low rates of cooperative behavior are danger signals. Peer and teacher ratings of behaviors or direct observation in naturalistic settings are useful for assessment because aggressive children do not always report feelings of distress and may overestimate their own popularity.

Rejected-withdrawn children typically do not show aggression. These children annoy others by their strange or immature behavior, social awkwardness, and failure to "get" the rules governing social conventions. Because these are the children who are most likely to be victimized, self-reports of their own distress, loneliness, or social anxieties provide the most reliable estimate of problems. Some overlap in symptoms can exist in peer-problem profiles. Some victims can also be aggressive, for example, the "provocative" as opposed to "passive" victims described by Olweus (1993) (see also Cook, Williams, Guerra, Kim, & Sadek, 2010). These children retaliate aggressively to the taunts and teasing of their peers who are aggravated by their obnoxiousness. Careful observation and evaluation are required to understand the dynamics of each of these social categories for treatment purposes.

 This socially anxious girl responds well to play therapy in which she can project her feelings onto a toy.

Skills Are Not Enough

Rejected children have obvious deficits in what are popularly called social skills. Historically, the clinical approach to peer problems was based on a behavioral-psychoeducational model, focusing on manipulating the antecedent conditions and consequences of discrete behaviors, such as reinforcing children to make eye contact or approach a peer group. Evidence has demonstrated that these prescriptive teaching approaches fell far short of their mark. The focus on isolated skills does not generalize to naturalistic settings (Gresham, 1981) and does not appreciably alter the quality of peer relationships for rejected children (Asher, Markell, & Hymel, 1981). Given advances in developmental knowledge, emphasis has turned to promotion of social competence, a more broad-based concept that involves the "capacity to coordinate adaptive responses flexibly to various interpersonal demands, and to organize social behavior in different social contexts in a manner beneficial to oneself and consistent with social conventions and morals" (Bierman, 2004, p. 141). The key is that children need to learn to regulate their social behavior in contexts that are constantly changing. Thus, social interaction process skills might be construed as the overarching goal, even though one might also teach component skills when appropriate. Of note here is that many of the concepts we have been discussing such as social information processing, emotion regulation, perspective taking, empathy, and so forth play an enormous role in the pursuit of satisfying peer relationships. So, if teaching single skills is not advised and advancing social competence is preferred, what can we do to help?

Include the Peer Group

Interventions are most successful when they take into account the transactional nature of these problems, considering what elicits the difficulty and what sustains it. For example, one of the reasons behavioral skill-based approaches are not successful is because these interventions fail to change the target child's level of peer acceptance, even when the child's actual level of prosocial behavior has increased (Dodge, Coie, Pettit, & Price, 1990). Children acquire reputations in their social groups, generally pointing in either the "good" direction if the child is well liked and socially adept or in the "bad" direction if the child seems socially unskilled. Remember that children tend to see things concretely, in black-and-white terms, and that they will perceive new information selectively so that their schemas remain consistent. Interactions with the target child after a schema for that child has been constructed are marked by attention to evidence that confirms the disliked child's antisocial characteristics (called **confirmation bias**; Gurwitz & Dodge, 1977) and discounting of evidence that indicates a departure from his antisocial role. Children also interpret ambiguous or neutral behavior in ways that are consistent with their schema (Peets, Hodges, Kikas, & Salmivalli, 2007). Because these social forces operate to maintain homeostasis, they are quite resistant to change.

Efforts to enhance social competence should target not only the peer-rejected child but also the child's peer group (Mikami, Lerner, & Lun, 2010). Peers can be encouraged to initiate more positive interactions with a rejected child through cooperative activities. They may also be taught to clearly communicate that they will not tolerate aggression. The goal should be to create "niches of opportunity" (Bierman, 2004, p. 44) wherein the disliked child can behave more prosocially to modify the peer group's stereotypical schema.

Bierman and Furman (1984) found that combining cooperative activities with other social competence interventions had more lasting effects than cooperative activities alone. Olweus's

Bullying Prevention Program (Olweus & Limber, 2002) also takes a comprehensive approach. This program approaches bullying as a problem that resides in the whole system, not just within the bully or victim. Consequently, this universal intervention targets all individuals in a school through classroom meetings and activities that focus on effects of bullying, parent meetings, teacher training, and outcome assessment. It is very important for helpers to offer well-researched universal programs in schools, given that 70% to 80% of the children who need mental health treatment get their only services there (Burns et al., 1995).

Treat the System

Perhaps the most important clinical consideration that follows from recent research in the peer relations field is that interventions need to be directed simultaneously to multiple targets. One exemplary model based on the principles of prevention science is Fast Track, a 10-year, broad-based program that integrates both universal (school-based PATHS curriculum for all children) and targeted interventions (parent groups, social skills training for children, academic tutoring, and home visitations for high-risk children and their families). Interventions are theoretically driven by the developmental early-starter model of conduct disorder and designed to conform to the principles of prevention science. To assess the effectiveness of this program, participating schools have been randomly assigned to intervention and control conditions for purposes of outcome assessment. Early assessments (after the first 3 years) have indicated that treated children are significantly less aggressive, disruptive, and noncompliant than controls (CPPRG, 2002).

The backbone of the technique used with children in this program is described as social competence coaching (Bierman, Greenberg, & CPPRG, 1996). A few guidelines for effective coaching programs (from Bierman, 2004) can be useful for helpers:

1. The content of interventions should include important research-based domains of social competence that offer children a variety of behaviors, which can be flexibly applied to many different social situations. These domains include: social participation (how to join peers and feel comfortable in peer contexts, etc.), emotional understanding (how to identify and express feelings, etc.), prosocial behavior (how to interact cooperatively), self-control (how to cope effectively with frustration, etc.), communication skills (listening and speaking appropriately, etc.), fair-play skills (being a good sport, etc.), and social problem-solving skills (similar to the steps of the problem-solving models discussed in Chapter 6).

2. These skill domains should be taught by incorporating each of the following four steps: (a) presenting skills through modeling, discussion, giving examples and non-examples; (b) allowing children to practice skills using role-plays or other structured exercises; (c) providing feedback on children's performance by means of discussions, self-evaluations, and so on; and (d) fostering generalizations of skills to the real world of peer relationships. For this last goal, the more the actual peer group is involved in activities, the better one is able to create niches of opportunity for the child with social problems.

3. Create a positive environment so that changes can be practiced and sustained. The warmth and reinforcing qualities of the counselor or coach help reduce anxiety, motivate participation, and increase group cooperation.

Gender and Risk

What, if any, are the special needs and problems of children that attach to gender? Certain clinical syndromes are more frequently reported among boys, including ADHD and learning disorders. One's risk for internalizing disorders in adolescence is clearly increased by being female, as are risks for eating disorders and sexual abuse (American Psychiatric Association, 2000). Externalizing disorders are more often reported in boys, except for adolescent conduct disorder (Johnston & Ohan, 1999). However, some have suggested that we may have failed to recognize the distinct trajectory of girls' aggression that emerges by late childhood (Crick & Grotpeter, 1995). Girls tend to display a pattern of nonconfrontational, relational aggression (social ostracism, spreading rumors, alienation of others) along with direct confrontational approaches. In contrast, boys escalate their use of direct confrontational aggression at adolescence as the peer group's demands for masculine behavior increase. The fact that boys' aggression has been more visible should not diminish the importance of girls' antisocial behavior for treatment and prevention because of its links to later interpersonal problems with partners and children, anxiety, and depression (see Pepler et al., 2010).

The forms that problem trajectories take are also influenced by gender-role expectations. If girls' expression of emotions is tolerated, even encouraged, then boys' emotional expression is actively discouraged. You have learned that behaviors considered appropriate according to gender are more restrictive for boys than for girls and that parents often reinforce different behaviors for their sons and daughters.

Some authors, who provide clinical insights into the particular challenges faced by boys, argue that the "boy code" that is enforced in the masculine socialization process works like a gender straitjacket. Just as some girls' voices may be suppressed in certain contexts, they argue that some boys also go unheard (see Box 8.2). The boy code requires learning that feelings of fear, weakness, and vulnerability should be suppressed to appear brave and powerful. Although we may be primed to notice symptoms of depression in girls because they fit our conceptions of what depressed behavior looks like, we may miss the cues in boys. Adults need to avoid shaming boys for expressions of vulnerability and to provide them with the time and safety they need to open up. We should not take boys' stoicism as a given.

Evidence from many studies that have examined gender differences in behavior demonstrates that for most characteristics there is actually very little gender difference. Therefore, we need to remember that girls and boys have many similar qualities and needs. Feelings, either good or bad, should not be off-limits because one happens to be a boy or a girl. Counselors can help by examining their own schemas or constructions about what it means to be male and female. That way, we will not selectively attend to information that fits our schema while we discount other important information. For healthy development, both genders need safe spaces in which to exercise their power and to express their vulnerabilities.

Box 8.2: Meeting the Special Needs of Boys

Although boy babies are on average more active and intense in their reactions than girls, there is little consistent evidence of difference in emotion or emotional expression in the first two years (Blakemore, Barenboim, & Liben, 2009). By 3 to 4 years old, some differences in emotional expression are emerging, at least in U. S. samples, with boys beginning to hide feelings of sadness and fear more than girls (Kyratzis, 2001) and with girls beginning to hide feelings of pride more than boys (see Else-Quest, Higgins, Allison, & Morton, 2012). Way (2011) points out that learning to hide emotions linked with vulnerability, as boys seem more likely to do, can be an impediment to friendship and intimacy, even though friendship is as important to males as it is to females.

Pollack (1998) and Kindlon and Thompson (1990) make the case that boys need support if they are to preserve their emotional lives in a culture that undermines and constrains the expression of emotion among males. Too often, the only messages boys hear are those that advise them to be strong, competitive, and unemotional. These authors emphasize that this state of affairs is supported by multiple systems, from peer groups to adults, that do not take kindly to expressions of male vulnerability. In fact, boys are well schooled from their very early years in a "boy code" (Pollack, 1998) that prizes courage, activity, and strength, and devalues sensitivity and empathy. Sometimes the code prescribes that boys engage in bullying or be "silent witnesses to acts of cruelty to others" (Kindlon & Thompson, 1990, p. 82). In relation to adults, highly active and rambunctious boys are often more likely than girls to receive harsh punishment. As we have seen, harsh punishment is related to increases in aggression and reductions in empathy. The collective consequence of these gendered experiences can be the numbing of emotional awareness and its guarded expression.

These authors advocate that parents, teachers, and other helpers concerned about boys' development need to support the full range of boys' emotional expression by building upon their special strengths. One way is to capitalize on boys' task orientation by encouraging good problem solving. Another way is to respect their preference for activity by providing appropriate opportunities to exhibit strength and skill. Advocating a more oblique approach to the expression of emotion, Kindlon and Thompson (1990) suggest using indirect questions with boys that presuppose underlying emotional complexity, such as "I know you were disappointed about not getting a part in the play last year. Do you want to take the risk and try out again?" (p. 241) rather than "What do you want to do?" Above all, adults need to avoid harsh and shaming punishment, combat the culture of bullying, and model that it is acceptable for men to be both caring and strong. Thus, boys will be given permission to be strong and caring as well.

Boys may feel especially ill at ease in the culture of psychotherapy where emotional expression is often de rigueur. For counselors who work with young male clients, Kiselica (2003) offers some practical guidelines for making psychotherapy "male-friendly." Several of his suggestions are listed below.

- Be flexible about where to meet and how long to hold sessions.
- Display magazines or other reading material in your office that is of interest to boys, such as sports magazines.
- Avoid face-to-face seating arrangements in favor of a side-by-side setup; offer a snack to the boy before starting the counseling session.
- Become acquainted with contemporary teenage slang or be honest enough to ask what the boy's words mean if you are not familiar with the vocabulary.
- Pay attention to the boy's cues regarding pacing the session; be mindful of the boy's comfort level with respect to sensitive topics.
- Avoid asking too many questions; take the heat off from time to time by focusing on more practical problems like making a team or finding a job.
- Support autonomy strivings and motivation to continue therapy by scheduling appointments directly with the male client, if possible.
- Use appropriate humor and self-disclosure to facilitate engagement.

SUMMARY

The Biology of Sex

1. The sex chromosome pair consists of two XX chromosomes in females but an XY pair in males. Development in a male direction is initiated by expression of the SRY gene on the Y chromosome, which triggers the transformation of the indifferent gonads into testes. Testes produce masculinizing hormones, including androgens, which influence the development of internal and external reproductive organs and some brain structures. In the absence of the SRY gene and the masculinizing hormones, the natural course of development is in the female direction, beginning with the indifferent gonads becoming ovaries.

2. More males are conceived than females, but males are more vulnerable than females to a host of hereditary diseases because of their susceptibility to X-linked recessive disorders. One result is that many more males fail to survive the prenatal period, and males have higher mortality rates at all ages postnatally as well.

Sex Role Development

3. The first step is learning to label oneself as male or female by about age 2½. Next comes gender stability, by 3 or 4 years, which means realizing that gender doesn't fluctuate over time. Finally comes gender constancy, realizing

that gender cannot change. This may not emerge until age 6 or 7, although there is controversy on this issue.

4. Social processes, involving active teaching by others, influence learning one's gender identity. Gender-atypical children, whose genitalia are either ambiguous or inconsistent with their biological sex, often acquire the identity that is socially assigned even if it is inconsistent with their biological sex.

5. Cognitive development may also influence the acquisition of gender identity. For example, logical thinking may help a child understand gender constancy. Also, being given accurate information about what is and isn't important for gender assignment is helpful.

6. Biological sex may also influence children's gender identity, even when social input is inconsistent with biology. Some gender-atypical individuals have eventually rejected their assigned identity, apparently feeling more comfortable adopting an identity that is consistent with their biology.

7. Meta-analyses of many different behaviors, personality characteristics, and preferences have identified some that usually vary between males and females. Certain characteristics are found across the life span, whereas others typify specific developmental periods. Some have changed historically, such as differences in math problem solving. The average differences are usually quite small.

8. Perhaps more important than the small sex differences in laboratory measures of behavior, is that boys and girls spend their time differently: boys more often with boys, and girls with girls. Gender segregation begins as early as 2½ years old for girls and 3 years old for boys and increases with age. In their segregated groups, girls and boys behave differently. For example, boys are more active and engage in more aggressive play when they are with boys than with girls or adults. Girls' play and talk is more cooperative or collaborative, whereas boys' play and talk is more competitive and domineering.

9. Where do sex differences come from? Biology seems to play a role in some traits. For example, girls exposed prenatally to male hormones have stronger male play preferences in childhood than normal girls.

10. Cognitive developmental theories argue that children are motivated to acquire gender-appropriate behavior once they identify themselves as male or female. Gender schema theories also hypothesize that children choose to act in ways that are consistent with their gender schemas, that is, their networks of expectations and beliefs about male and female characteristics.

11. Parenting processes are also thought to contribute to gendered behavior. Freud's psychoanalytic theory posits that preschoolers identify with the same-sex parent in an effort to resolve the Oedipus complex (in boys) or the Electra complex (in girls). Identification involves imitation, so girls begin to act like their mothers, and boys begin to act like their fathers. There is little evidence to support this theory. Social learning theorists assume that parents play a more direct role, teaching children to adopt gendered behaviors through the use of rewards and punishments.

There are some differences in the ways parents treat girls and boys, and there are differences in the kinds of pressures they place. But there are many similarities as well.

12. Peers appear to play a role in engendering sex-typed behavior. Children spend a great deal of time in their sex-segregated peer groups, and in these groups some preexisting sex differences appear to be magnified. Recent research indicates that the more time preschoolers spend in gendered groups, the more sex-typed their behavior becomes (the social dosage effect).

13. Clearly what is needed to explain sex role development is a multidimensional theory that considers all the contributing elements: biology, cognitive processes, and parent and peer socialization pressures.

Peer Relationships

14. In a longitudinal study of children at risk for later mental health problems, one early risk factor stood out as highly predictive of later problems: peer rejection.

15. Evaluating social competence involves examining social skills at every level of social interaction, both within friendships and outside them. Interventions designed to improve specific children's social skills have moderate success, but they might have more success if both the disliked child and the children with whom the target child interacts were included.

16. Peer groups include dyads, cliques, and crowds. The clique and crowd structures begin to emerge in middle childhood and are crystallized in early adolescence. They play a role in the development of self-understanding, and they provide a sense of acceptance and belonging.

17. In sociometry, children's status among their peers is measured. Children in a class are asked to select which children they would most, or least, like to interact with in different contexts. Each child can be categorized on the basis of a social preference score (number of positive less negative nominations) and a social impact score (total nominations, positive and negative).

18. Popular children have high social preference and social impact scores. They have many social skills, tend to be attractive, and are cognitively competent as well.

19. Rejected children may be either aggressive or withdrawn, and neither group demonstrates the positive social skills of the popular children. They have low social preference scores but high social impact scores.

20. Neglected children have especially low social impact scores but are not perceived negatively by their peers. They may choose not to participate centrally in group activities.

21. Controversial children have some of the qualities of popular children and some of the qualities of rejected children. They are seen by some as leaders and by others as disruptive.

22. Average children score in the average range on both social preference and social impact. They have less social competence than popular children, more than rejected or neglected children.

23. Preferred qualities in peers seem to differ somewhat across genders and cultures. For example, boys, especially as they approach adolescence, are more likely to be rejected for cross-gendered behavior than girls. Shy, socially anxious behavior is valued more in some cultures, such as China, than in places like the United States. Aggressive behavior is generally sanctioned in all cultures, and bullying is found to be a problem cross-culturally, but there are differences as well. In the United States, children are expected to defend themselves in conflict situations, and adults serve as arbitrators. In more collectivist cultures, children who "fight back" are seen as behaving inappropriately, and peers are expected to help resolve conflicts.

24. Popular and rejected categories show the most stability over time and have fairly predictable long-term consequences: positive for popular children, negative for rejected children. The strongest links are found between rejected-aggressive status in childhood and later externalizing problems.

25. Cliques play a role in identity development. Kids with similar characteristics form groups that provide some identity and a basis for social comparison. Cliques also serve needs for acceptance and belonging.

26. Peer groups are formed and maintained both through influence and through selection processes. Influence is largely indirect (e.g., teasing) rather than directly coercive (e.g., confrontation) and can cause an individual to conform. Selection refers to the fact that individuals choose to affiliate with others like themselves.

CASE STUDY

Hyun-Ki's family emigrated from Korea 3 years ago and now lives in a large city on the West Coast. His parents moved to this location because they had relatives living in the same city, and they wanted the economic and educational opportunities that they believed the United States could afford their family. Both parents immediately found work in their relatives' small business.

The family lives in a modest home in a working-class neighborhood. The daughters, 16-year-old Sun and 17-year-old Cho, attend the local public high school, and they are diligent, academically advanced students. Hyun-Ki, a fifth grader, is the youngest child. He is quiet and socially reserved. He is also physically slight for his age, shorter than most of the boys and all the girls in his grade. His heavily accented English is somewhat difficult to understand, and he is sensitive about his speech. Consequently, he does not often volunteer to answer questions in class.

Although there are many ethnic groups represented among the students in his class, Hyun-Ki seems to get the brunt of the teasing, even from other Asian American students. When he enters the classroom, students snicker and deride him. "Look what he has on today!" they call out. They make fun of his speech and his reserved ways. When he walks down the hallway to his locker, he is aware of the disparaging looks he gets from some groups of students. Hyun-Ki has a Korean friend whom he sees every Sunday at church. The two boys enjoy spending time together after the service. Hyun-Ki and his friend share an interest in nature and biking. Hyun-Ki wishes he had a friend like this in his own classroom.

Mrs. Marshall, Hyun-Ki's teacher, has assigned a class project that is to be done by small groups of students. Peter, a boy in Hyun-Ki's group, is an outgoing and popular student who is considered one of the class leaders. He has called Hyun-Ki on the phone several times to discuss the project and is always friendly and pleasant toward him. In school, however, it is a different story. Peter is often part of the group of students who make fun of Hyun-Ki when they pass him in the hall. Hyun-Ki cannot understand why Peter is so nice to him on the phone and so mean to him at school.

Mrs. Marshall observes that Hyun-Ki is not participating very actively in the cooperative group assignment. From the teacher's perspective, Hyun-Ki is "too quiet" and has not contributed sufficiently to get a passing grade for the project. She also notes Hyun-Ki's reluctance to participate in the regular class discussions. She fears that Hyun-Ki's educational needs are not being met in her classroom. Hoping to intervene on the boy's behalf, Mrs. Marshall refers Hyun-Ki to the school's child-study team, whose role is to evaluate the special needs of students in the school.

Discussion Questions

1. How does your knowledge of the topics of sex role development culture and peer group processes contribute to your understanding of Hyun-Ki's situation?
2. How could you help Hyun-Ki's parents and teachers understand the situation? How would you suggest they help him?
3. What prevention efforts would you like to see initiated in this school?

PRACTICE USING WHAT YOU HAVE LEARNED

In the Pearson etext, apply these ideas to working with others.

Video Exercise

JOURNAL QUESTIONS

1. Gender-role training can be a straitjacket for both girls and boys. Reflect on the gender messages you received as a child and adolescent. Which ones were particularly restrictive? How did these messages affect the decisions you made in your life? Do you think gender-based messages have changed for more recent cohorts of children and adolescents?

2. Identify a gender-related issue that you are personally struggling with at the present time. How are you dealing with it? What resources would be helpful for you in dealing with it?

3. How would you assess your own peer status as an elementary school student? As a middle or junior high school student? As a high school student? What was the most difficult thing you experienced as a child or adolescent in relation to your peers? What could have made the situation better?

4. Give a personal example of an experience you had with peer pressure or peer influence. Has the nature of peer pressure changed?

KEY CONCEPTS

SRY gene (p. 284)
anti-Mullerian hormone (AMH) (p. 284)
androgens (p. 284)
Mullerian duct (p. 284)
Wolffian duct (p. 284)
genital tubercle (p. 284)
X-linked recessive disorders (p. 285)
gender identity (p. 286)
gender stability (p. 287)
gender constancy (p. 287)
gender atypical (p. 289)
congenital adrenal hyperplasia (CAH) (p. 289)
intersex (p. 292)
gender stereotypes (p. 293)
meta-analysis (p. 293)
borderwork (p. 295)

rough-and-tumble play (p. 296)
collaborative or affiliative speech (p. 297)
domineering or power assertive
     speech (p. 297)
tomboyism (p. 297)
self-socialization (p. 299)
gender intensification hypothesis (p. 299)
gender schema (p. 299)
Oedipus complex (p. 302)
Electra complex (p. 302)
penis envy (p. 302)
social dosage effect (p. 305)
social skills (p. 307)
dyads (p. 308)
cliques (p. 308)
crowds (p. 308)

degrouping (p. 308)
sociometry (p. 309)
social preference (p. 309)
social impact (p. 309)
popular (p. 310)
average (p. 310)
neglected (p. 310)
rejected (p. 310)
controversial (p. 310)
rejected-aggressive (p. 311)
rejected-withdrawn (p. 311)
homophily (p. 316)
influence (p. 316)
selection (p. 316)
confirmation bias (p. 318)

CHAPTER 9

Physical, Cognitive, and Identity Development in Adolescence

I could not prove the Years had feet—
Yet confident they run
Am I, from symptoms that are past
And Series that are done—
I find my feet have further goals—
I smile upon the Aims
That felt so ample—Yesterday—
Today's—have vaster claims—
I do not doubt the self I was—
Was competent to me—
But something awkward in the fit
Proves that—outgrown—I see—

EMILY DICKINSON (1862)

From Shakespeare's Romeo and Juliet to Salinger's Holden Caulfield to Margaret, the teenager in Judy Blume's novel who poignantly asked, "Are you there, God?" we have enjoyed many memorable literary examples of adolescents' coming of age. In many cultures and throughout many different historical periods, adolescence has evoked a certain fascination. We endow it with meaning and celebrate it as the time when innocent, dependent children are transformed into young adults. However, one reason this life stage is so interesting is that, in reality, it defies easy description. What are the tasks of adolescence, and are they completed by a certain chronological age? Are these tasks the same for all adolescents, or are there some that are culture or gender specific? Is adolescence a period of storm and stress or a relatively smooth transition? Should adolescents rebel against convention to define their uniqueness, or is rebellion a sign of maladjustment? Is legal adult status a real indicator of adulthood, or should we look to other indicators of cognitive and emotional maturity? And what is *really* happening within the adolescent brain? These are some of the topics we will discuss in the next two chapters.

Because of its child-to-adult metamorphosis, writers have long recognized the centrality of identity development to the adolescent period. Erik Erikson (1950/1963, 1968) is possibly best remembered for his writing on the topic of identity. Sometimes, however, his emphasis on the shaping of identity in adolescence, which has been the popular interpretation of Erikson's work, inadvertently suggests that there is no real sense of identity beforehand.

As we consider this important task of adolescence, we should note that Erikson himself was careful to emphasize the epigenetic nature of human development. The human being, like any other growing organism, has a "ground plan" (1968, p. 92) composed of parts that unfold or come into ascendancy at certain times, to eventually become a coherent whole. Success at each new developmental task requires qualities and skills acquired from the work of prior life stages and depends upon relative mastery of earlier tasks as a basis for moving ahead. Thus, far from being divorced from the child's earlier sense of self and self-in-relationship, adolescent identity is a synthesis of earlier elements with new, more cognitively and emotionally mature aspects of the self-system. Erikson makes this point succinctly in the following statement:

> A lasting ego identity, we have said, cannot begin to exist without the trust of the first oral stage; it cannot be completed without a promise of fulfillment which from the dominant image of adulthood reaches down into the baby's beginnings and which, by the tangible evidence of social health, creates at every step of childhood and adolescence, an accruing sense of ego strength. (1950/1963, p. 246)

Let us begin our look at the adolescent period with an exploration of the physical and cognitive changes that mark this time of life. Building on the growth and maturation of these systems, we will then consider how they support the process of adolescent identity development.

PHYSICAL DEVELOPMENT

When we think of physical development and the adolescent years, we are likely to think first of the sometimes startling changes associated with puberty. Recent discoveries about the adolescent brain have revealed changes that are less obvious externally but no less dramatic. In the first section of this chapter, we will examine the brain and body changes that characterize adolescence before moving on to a discussion of changes in cognition and identity.

Puberty: The Adolescent Metamorphosis

Rebecca recently had her 13th birthday. Her Aunt Cathy, who has just returned from a year abroad, hardly recognizes her. When she saw her last, Rebecca was a cute, pug-nosed pygmy with a sunny disposition and an easy laugh. Now she is 3 or 4 inches taller. But her rapid growth is not what surprises her aunt; it is the qualitative change in both her appearance and her manner. Her slim, child's body is softening and changing shape. Her breasts are emerging, her hips spreading. And her face is, well, a little weird. Suddenly she has a big nose and a pimply complexion. Although she seems genuinely happy to see her aunt, within the first hour of her reunion with the family Rebecca begins interjecting sarcastic remarks into the conversation, and she petulantly rolls her eyes at comments made by other members of her family. Little of what is said escapes her biting criticism. When her mildly exasperated mother gently suggests that she should spend some time studying for tomorrow's test, she suddenly seems near tears, whining, "I always have more to do than anyone else!"

Clearly, Rebecca has entered the land of puberty and has begun her trek across the divide from childhood to adulthood. Strictly speaking, **puberty** is a process of sexual maturation. When it is complete, boys and girls are fertile: Males can impregnate females, and females can conceive. But as most of us can recall from our own journey, puberty is related to a wide range of emotional, behavioral, and social changes as well.

A Glandular Awakening

The recent discovery of a chemical in the hypothalamus helps us understand what triggers the beginnings of puberty deep inside the brain. This signaling chemical was named **kisspeptin**, because it was discovered in Hershey, Pennsylvania, home of the famous Hershey Kiss (Oakley, Clifton, & Steiner, 2009). Kisspeptin triggers the activation of **gonadotropin releasing hormone (GnRH)**, which stimulates the pituitary and sets the reproductive axis into motion. The release of **follicle-stimulating hormone (FSH)** and **luteinizing hormone (LH)** from the pituitary stimulate other endocrine glands to increase their hormone production as well. These glands include the **gonads**—**testes** in males, **ovaries** in females—that now increase their production of both masculinizing hormones (**androgens**, such as **testosterone**) and feminizing hormones (**estrogen**). Interestingly, both kinds of hormones (as well as **progesterone**, which is involved in the reproductive cycle) are produced in males and in females, but they are produced in different ratios, so that increases in androgen production are much higher in boys than in girls, whereas estrogen production increases much more in girls. In combination with other hormones circulating in the blood, they cause a series of changes in children's bodies that promote the maturing of both **primary sexual characteristics** (those directly involved in reproduction, such as the genitalia) and **secondary sexual characteristics** (physical traits not directly involved in reproduction but indicative of sex, such as enlarged breasts in females and deeper voices in males). Early, outward signs of puberty are usually the appearance of pubic hair in both sexes (**pubarche**), the growth of the scrotum and testes in boys, and the budding of breasts in girls (**thelarche**). **Menarche** in girls (first menstruation) and **spermarche** in boys (first ejaculation) usually occur near the end of the process and are often treated as important social markers of sexual maturation. But fertility—ovulation in girls and adequate sperm production in boys—may not be achieved for a year or more after these outward manifestations of maturity (Chumlea, Schubert, Roche, Kulin, Lee, & Himes, 2003); Tanner, 1962, 1990; see Figure 9.1).

The timing of puberty appears to be affected by genetic factors: Identical twins usually begin and end the process within 2 to 3 months of each other, and mothers' and daughters' ages at menarche are correlated (Brooks-Gunn, 1991; Golub, 1992; Mustanski, Viken, Kaprio, Pulkkinen, & Rose, 2004). But environmental factors are clearly important as well. For example, a downward shift in the average age of menarche has been consistently reported (Steingraber, 2007). Today, the average age is just under 13 years, with slight variations across racial and ethnic groups, whereas in 1850 it was approximately 3 years later.

Because menarche and spermarche occur later in the maturational process, changes in breast development and pubic hair can be useful markers of pubertal onset. A recent study by Biro and colleagues (2010) of over 1,200 six to seven year old girls in Cincinnati, New York and San Francisco showed high rates of early breast development. The total sample included 31% African American, 30% Hispanic and 34% Caucasian females. At age 7, rates of stage 2 or higher breast development (on the 5-stage Tanner assessment, see Herman-Giddens & Bourdony, 1995) were found

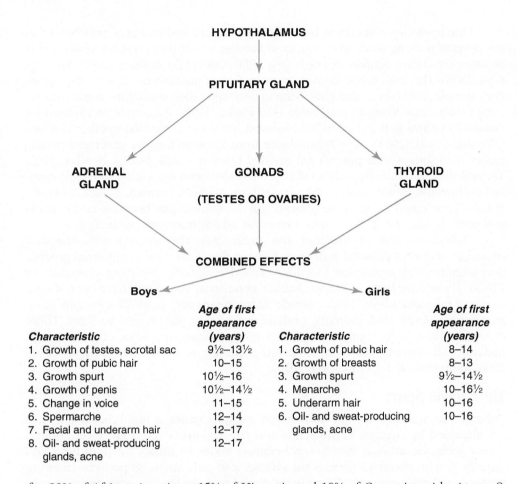

FIGURE 9.1 Typical sequences of pubertal change in males and females.
SOURCE: Arnett, J. J. (2013). *Adolescence and emerging adulthood* (5th Ed.). Upper Saddle River, NJ: Pearson Education, Inc. Used by permission of Pearson Education. permission of Pearson Education.

HYPOTHALAMUS

PITUITARY GLAND

ADRENAL GLAND | GONADS | THYROID GLAND

(TESTES OR OVARIES)

COMBINED EFFECTS

Boys | Girls

Characteristic	Age of first appearance (years)	Characteristic	Age of first appearance (years)
1. Growth of testes, scrotal sac	9½–13½	1. Growth of pubic hair	8–14
2. Growth of pubic hair	10–15	2. Growth of breasts	8–13
3. Growth spurt	10½–16	3. Growth spurt	9½–14½
4. Growth of penis	10½–14½	4. Menarche	10–16½
5. Change in voice	11–15	5. Underarm hair	10–16
6. Spermarche	12–14	6. Oil- and sweat-producing glands, acne	10–16
7. Facial and underarm hair	12–17		
8. Oil- and sweat-producing glands, acne	12–17		

for 23% of African American, 15% of Hispanic and 10% of Caucasian girls. At age 8, the rates of stage 2 or higher breast development had jumped to 42.9%, 30.9% and 18.3% respectively. The findings for Caucasian girls represented the greatest increase relative to studies conducted 10 years earlier, even though the absolute numbers were lowest for this group. Since early puberty in girls is a risk factor for later breast cancer, cardiovascular risk, elevated BMI, insulin resistance and a number of mental and behavioral health issues, this study prompts serious concern about the public health issues associated with the uptick in pubertal timing.

Signs of early puberty have been increasing in U.S. boys as well (Herman-Giddens et al., 2012). According to a comparable 5-stage assessment for male secondary sex characteristics, the approximate ages for stage 2 or higher genital development were 10.14 for non-Hispanic white, 9.14 for African American, and 10.04 for Hispanic boys. Pubarche occurred earliest for African American (10.25) boys compared to white (11.47) and Hispanic (11.43) samples. The results from this study showed pubertal onset occurring 6 months to 2 years earlier (depending upon groups) than data reported 20 years ago (Sun et al., 2002).

What might be causing this phenomenon? Body fat affects the timing of puberty in both girls and boys, such that higher ratios of fat are associated with earlier onsets, possibly through some association with leptin. **Leptin** is a hormone produced in fat tissue that may affect GnRH levels in the hypothalamus (Lassek & Gaulin, 2007). Children whose body fat is unusually low, such as those who are malnourished or who are heavily involved in athletics, are likely to begin puberty later than other children (Brooks-Gunn, 1991; Malina, 1983). Greater body mass in girls, while associated with earlier puberty, is also related to lower self-esteem. But a study from Norway illustrates the difficulty of untangling these variables. Lien and colleagues (Lien, Dalgard, Heyerdahl, Thoresen, & Bjertnessa, 2006) found that early maturing girls showed greater levels of mental stress, but the stress was largely due to dissatisfaction with body size rather than pubertal status.

One intriguing association between environment and timing of puberty is that the onset of puberty tends to be earlier in families where there is substantial conflict or other significant sources of stress (e.g., Ellis, 2004; Ellis & Essex, 2007; Tither & Ellis, 2008). This conclusion derives from studies of adolescents around the world. For example, Polish boys and girls living in crowded urban conditions begin puberty earlier than those living in rural areas (Hulanicka, 1999). Puberty is accelerated for Finnish boys and girls reared in father-absent homes as compared to other children (Mustanski et al., 2004). New Zealand girls from divorced families start menstruating earlier than girls whose parents are married (Moffitt, Caspi, Belsky, & Silva, 1992; Tither & Ellis, 2008). Early childhood abuse has also been associated with early menarche (Boynton-Jarrett, Wright, Putnam, Hibert, Michels, Forman, & Rich-Edwards, 2012). There could be multiple reasons for the correlations between family stress and puberty, but one is likely to be that stress affects hormone production.

Overall, aspects of nutrition and stress may also interact with chemical exposure to disrupt pubertal processes. Certain chemicals used in industrial production interfere with endocrine functions (called endocrine-disrupting chemicals or EDCs). These have been linked to changes in pubertal timing and have been shown to affect fat metabolism. EDCs include flame retardants, pesticides, certain pharmaceutical agents, lead, mercury, phthalates found in plastic, and so forth. These chemicals have been related to pubertal abnormalities in studies of animals and humans and warrant further investigation according to experts (Buck-Louis et al., 2008; Karapanou & Papadimitriou, 2010).

The Growth Spurt

Puberty corresponds with the **adolescent growth spurt**, a rapid increase in size accompanied by changes in the shape and proportions of the body. Over about a 4-year span, the average increase in height is about 10 inches for both boys and girls; boys gain about 42 pounds on average and girls about 38 pounds. Different parts of the body grow at different times. Facial features like the nose and ears usually grow before the skull does, accounting in part for Rebecca's strange appearance. It is likely that when her head growth catches up with her features, she will no longer seem to have a big nose. Hands, feet, and limbs usually grow before the torso, which can create awkwardness and adds to the odd look. There can even be asymmetries in growth between the two sides of the body, with one breast or one testicle growing before the other (Hofmann, 1997; Tanner, 1990).

Some aspects of the growth process play out differently for girls and boys. For girls, the growth spurt begins and ends about 2 years earlier than for boys. Besides other obvious differences, such as increased breast size and greater pelvic spread in girls and broader shoulders in boys, there are gender differences in internal growth. The size of the heart and lungs increases more in boys, for example, who also develop thicker bones and more muscle tissue than girls. Many of these changes contribute to average differences in physical strength and endurance between the sexes. Adolescent and adult males are typically stronger than females of the same general size. Thus, the adolescent growth spurt increases both internal and external **sexual dimorphism**, physical differences between the sexes (Chumlea, 1982; Malina, 1990).

The Changing Brain

Laurence Steinberg, a well-known researcher in the field of adolescent development, introduced a recent series of articles about the brain at adolescence in the following way: "Let me begin with what will surely strike many readers as obvious, but which needs to be said strenuously and incontrovertibly . . . the adolescent's brain is different from both the child's brain and the adult's brain. It is different with respect to both morphology and function, and at the levels of brain structures, regions, circuits, and systems. It is different with respect to grey matter, white matter, structural connectivity and neurotransmission. . . . Indeed, it appears that the brain changes characteristic of adolescence are among the most dramatic and important to occur during the human lifespan. Whether neurobiological differences between adolescents and adults should inform how society treats young people is open for debate, but whether such differences are real is not" (Steinberg, 2010, p. 160).

Whereas researchers once believed that brain development was largely complete by the onset of puberty (Siegler, 1998), the brain is far from finished at adolescence. It now appears that in many parts of the cortex, puberty is correlated with a "growth spurt" in synaptogenesis, followed by a long reprise of the pruning process that lasts, for some parts of the brain, into early adulthood. The pruning we described in the sections on infancy and early childhood took place primarily in the sensory and motor cortices of the brain. In adolescence, pruning occurs primarily in areas of the brain that are related to higher-order functions. Current evidence implicates the frontal lobes, which play a role in organization, planning, self-control, judgment, and the regulation of emotion; the parietal lobes, which are involved in integrating information; the temporal lobes, serving language functions and contributing to emotion regulation; and the corpus callosum, the network of fibers connecting the left and right sides of the cortex, aiding in information integration and other higher functions, such as consciousness (e.g., Casey, Giedd, & Thomas, 2000; for reviews, see Sowell, Thompson, & Toga, 2007; Toga, Thompson, & Sowell, 2006). Axon myelination continues, serving to connect the frontal cortex with other areas. At adolescence, the balance of grey to white matter shifts so that white matter comprises a higher proportion than at previous points of the life span (Spear, 2011). Ongoing myelination allows faster information processing during the teen years. Synaptogenesis, pruning, and myelination are thought to contribute to increased voluntary control of attention, more effective integration of information, and maturing of other executive functions (Gogtay et al., 2004; Luna et al., 2004; see Box 9.1). Some gender differences have also been noted, especially with regard to brain size. Males' brains tend to be larger than girls' brains overall. The amygdala tends to be larger and grows more rapidly in boys and the hippocampus tends to follow this pattern in girls (Lenroot & Giedd, 2010). As you will see in Chapter 10, brain changes in adolescence are also implicated in increased risk taking and greater involvement with peers (e.g., Reyna & Farley, 2006).

The Adolescent Brain and Stress

In the context of such rapid neurobiological changes, the adolescent period has been identified by some as a *sensitive period* for stress, even though the precise mechanisms for this phenomenon remain unclear (Blakemore & Frith, 2005; Romeo, 2010; Huttenlocher, 1979). Adolescents are particularly sensitive to social and emotional information, and this vulnerability shows up in studies of emotional information processing, emotion and behavior regulation, and stress reactivity. For example, adolescents process emotional information in ways that are different from pre-pubertal children and adults. Mid to late pubertal adolescents show greater pupil dilation to emotion-related words, rate themselves as higher in negative affect, and tend to remember more emotion-related words in delayed recall tasks than younger children, suggesting exaggerated limbic reactivity at puberty (Silk et al., 2009). While adults show increased amygdala responses only to images of fearful faces, adolescents show greater amygdala activation to both fearful and neutral faces (Thomas et al., 2001). Findings for adolescents of an exaggerated startle reflex (a measure of fear processing) (Quevedo, Benning, Gunnar, & Dahl, 2009), and stronger interference effects from emotional stimuli on task completion (Hare et al., 2008) lend further support to the proposition that the adolescent brain is particularly reactive to emotional information (Blakemore, 2008; Casey, Jones, & Hare, 2008).

Hormonal changes at puberty are considered important for triggering and moderating many of the brain changes we have described. Hormones can affect structural changes in the brain by influencing the onset or offset of genes. By doing

Box 9.1: The Limits of Guilt in Adolescence

Steven Drizin, a defense attorney who works with juvenile clients, provides the following case description:

> In November 1999, a Michigan jury convicted thirteen year old Nathaniel Abraham of second degree murder in the shooting death of Ronnie Greene, a crime committed when Abraham was only eleven years old. Under Michigan law, Judge Eugene Moore could have sentenced Nathaniel as a juvenile, as an adult, or given him a blended sentence that treated Nathaniel initially as a juvenile and then later as an adult if he failed to rehabilitate himself with services provided in the juvenile system. Judge Moore gave the boy the break of his life, sentencing Abraham as a juvenile and sparing him a sentence of between 8 and 25 years in prison. But the boy, who fidgeted and doodled during the judge's twenty-minute speech, didn't appreciate the judge's generosity. Reportedly, he turned to his attorney after the judge had concluded, and asked, 'What happened?' (Drizin, 2003, p. 8)

Drizin suggests that Nathaniel's response to his trial illustrates an important reason for treating juvenile offenders differently from adults: They are not necessarily fully capable of understanding the proceedings of a trial, participating in their own defense, or of making the many decisions that are required of an adult defendant.

The first juvenile justice system was established in Illinois in 1899. Within 25 years, in every part of the United States there were two systems of justice for individuals charged with crimes, one for adults and the other for juveniles (usually defined as those under the age of 18). The juvenile system emphasizes rehabilitation rather than punishment, and it reflects that focus even in the terminology that is used: "*petition* instead of *indictment, respondent* instead of *defendant*, and *disposition* instead of *sentencing*" (Trivits & Repucci, 2002, p. 694). The emphasis on rehabilitation is based on the belief that juvenile offenders are immature, not fully formed, and so can be reshaped or reformed. Further, the state's role is a parental one, to provide the right environment for future development.

But by the 1990s, "a legislative tsunami was washing over the United States" (Wilcox, 2003, p. 12). In one state after another, laws were altered to allow juveniles, especially adolescents, to be tried in adult criminal court, facing the same penalties that adults would face. A sense that predatory teens with well-established and irremediable character flaws were victimizing citizens and getting off too lightly in the juvenile justice system seemed to prevail. The United States is one of the only two UN member nations (the other is Somalia) that failed to ratify the Convention on the Rights of the Child, which prohibits execution and sentences of life without parole of children (Equal Justice Initiative, 2008). This "tough on crime" attitude has overwhelmed the reasoning that had inspired a different approach to juveniles a century before. Yet an appreciation for that reasoning is nonetheless reflected in some recent Supreme Court decisions. For example, in limiting the death penalty to individuals whose crimes were committed after their 16th birthday, the United States Supreme Court in 1998 acknowledged that teenagers, in comparison to adults, are likely to be less experienced, less intelligent, less educated, less

able to evaluate the consequences of their actions, and more motivated by the emotion of the moment or by peer pressure (Steinberg & Scott, 2003). Implied in this assessment is the belief that inspired the juvenile justice system: that at least until the age of 16, youngsters are not fully developed. Their misconduct is not necessarily a reflection of a well-established character but may be more affected by transient factors, and their future trajectory is malleable.

Based in part on research provided by developmental scientists, a 2005 U.S. Supreme Court decision prohibited the use of capital punishment for individuals who commit crimes when they are younger than age 18. Research findings on cognitive functioning, on brain development, on identity development, and on social interactive processes, like peer relations, has the potential to inform the way the justice system treats minors who commit less serious offenses as well. This research can be brought to bear on two critical questions. First, are teens as fully culpable as adults when committing the same crimes? And second, are adolescents competent to participate in the adult justice system?

Adolescent Culpability

Even when an individual is found guilty of a crime, her guilt can be mitigated under the law. "Mitigation places the culpability of a guilty actor somewhere on a continuum of criminal culpability and, by extension, a continuum of punishment" (Steinberg & Scott, 2003, p. 1010). Mitigation does not mean excusing the crime. The perpetrator is held responsible, but she is considered less than fully blameworthy. If by virtue of being an adolescent a guilty party's culpability were mitigated, then the punishments that would be appropriate would be altered as well. Indeed, interventions aimed at rehabilitation rather than punishment might be the wisest course.

Steinberg and Scott (2003) indicate that there are roughly three sources of mitigation in adult criminal law. The first is diminished capacity, which could be due to mental illness, emotional distress, intellectual impairment, or "susceptibility to influence or domination" (p. 1011). The second, compelling circumstances, occurs when an individual faces such pressure that even an ordinary, reasonable person could be expected to give in, such as acting in the face of extreme need or under threat of injury. The third source of mitigation is when the crime represents uncharacteristic behavior on the part of the perpetrator, as in the case of a first offense or when the crime is "aberrant in light of the defendant's established character traits and respect for the law's values" (p. 1011).

Are teens as fully culpable as adults? Steinberg and Scott (2003) argue that if we look at the developmental evidence, adolescents should be considered less culpable on the basis of all three sources of mitigation. First, their cognitive and psychosocial development is likely to affect their choices in ways not characteristic of adults. In essence, their decision making tends to be immature (or we could say impaired) in comparison to adults', suggesting *diminished capacity*. Reasoning ability improves throughout adolescence into adulthood. By midadolescence, many youngsters do well on tests of formal logic if they are given hypothetical problems that have logical solutions under conditions of low emotional arousal (like the scientific problem solving described in this chapter). But as you will see in Chapter 11, teens do not perform as well as young adults on the more ambiguous problems of real life, especially when they are emotionally invested in an issue (Blanchard-Fields, 1986). In addition, teens' decisions in real-life situations may be influenced by their psychosocial immaturity and lack of experience. As you will see in Chapter 10, adolescents are particularly susceptible to peer influence, they are high risk takers, and their self-control is not fully developed. Their capacity or tendency to think about future consequences is beginning to develop but is quite limited. Teens heavily weigh short-term gains in their decision making and tend to discount long-term considerations (e.g., Halpern-Felsher & Cauffman, 2001). When they are asked to imagine themselves or their circumstances in the future, teens use a much shorter time frame than adults do (e.g., Nurmi, 1991).

Adolescent characteristics that suggest diminished capacity from a legal standpoint appear to be linked to immature, and changing, neurological processes. The teenage brain shows gradual maturing of precisely those regions that affect long-term planning, judgment, decision making, regulation of emotion, impulse control, and the evaluation of risk and reward. Change in these areas continues throughout adolescence and into young adulthood.

Not only could adolescents be considered less culpable than adults on the basis of diminished capacity, but they are also more vulnerable to *compelling circumstances*. As Steinberg and Scott (2003) argue, "ordinary adolescents may respond adversely to external pressures that adults are able to resist" (p. 1014). For many of the reasons already indicated, they may be more easily provoked to aggressive responses by perceived threats. Their emotional lability and intensity seems to make many situations more stressful for adolescents than for adults. Also, their need for peer support and approval makes them especially susceptible to peer influence, whether in the form of direct pressure or as a result of the adolescent's own concern for fitting in.

Finally, adolescents' criminal actions may well qualify as *uncharacteristic behaviors* on the grounds that a teen's character and identity is relatively unformed. Identity formation is a major developmental task in adolescence and can involve assessment and reassessment of every aspect of the developing self, including the moral self. Teens who are immersed in this process often experiment with (or "try on") behaviors that are potentially dangerous, like drug use or antisocial acts, but for most adolescents this delinquent activity is relatively short-lived. It is referred to as "adolescence limited" behavior (see Chapter 10).

One arena in which this adolescence limited behavior has been observed is the perpetration of sex offenses. Trivits and Repucci (2002) examined recidivism rates across a wide range of studies of adolescents and adults convicted of sex crimes, such as rape, child molesting, and exhibitionism. On the whole, adolescents' recidivism rates over many years ranged from about 8% to 12% and were substantially lower than those of adult offenders, which ranged from about 20% to 40%. As Trivits and Repucci point out, sexual offenses may tend to have very different etiologies in adolescents as compared to adults, and patterns of sexual behaviors are likely to be less established among adolescents. Sexual misconduct in teens may often represent the kind of experimentation described earlier, associated with the fact that the adolescent's identity and character is very much a "work in progress."

Adolescent Competence to Stand Trial

The same characteristics that may mitigate adolescents' culpability raise questions about their competence to be processed in the system of justice designed for adults. In this system, a criminal defendant must be competent to stand trial, meaning that she must be able to assist her counsel in preparing her defense, understand the court proceedings well enough to participate, and be capable of making decisions about her rights, like whether or not to waive a jury trial or to accept a plea bargain. Fortunately, a research consortium, the MacArthur Research Network on Adolescent Development and Juvenile Justice, is undertaking studies that are designed to assess the degree to which teens have these capabilities. In one recent study (reported in Grisso et al., 2003, and in Steinberg et al., 2003), 1,000 juveniles (ages 11 to 17) and 500 young adults (ages 18 to 24) participated. Half of the participants were either in juvenile detention centers or adult jails, and the other half were drawn from the community (and matched for socioeconomic status, ethnicity, and so on). Each of them completed two measures. One was designed to assess competence to stand trial, including factors such as "understanding" (e.g., comprehension of courtroom procedures) and "reasoning" (e.g., recognition of information relevant to a legal defense). The other measure was designed to identify the kinds of choices that might be characteristic of the different age groups with regard to legal decisions. Participants heard stories about individuals charged with crimes and were asked to make decisions for them (e.g., about how to respond to police interrogation, whether to disclose information during consultation with an attorney, and how to respond to a plea agreement that would involve a guilty plea and testifying against other defendants).

The results support the conclusion that juveniles from 11 to 15 are significantly less competent than young adults to stand trial, whereas 16- to 17-year-olds are not significantly different from young adults. Substantially more young teens showed impairments in understanding or reasoning about court-related matters in comparison to young adults. Only age and intelligence were significant predictors of competence—neither gender, ethnicity, current status as an offender, nor socioeconomic status was important.

A similar pattern was obtained on the measures of decision making. Younger teens, ages 11 through 15, were significantly more likely to make decisions based on what authorities dictated. "Thus, compared with older adolescents and young adults, adolescents aged 15 and younger are more likely to recommend confessing to the police rather than remaining silent and accepting a plea bargain offered by a prosecutor rather than going to trial" (Steinberg et al., 2003, p. 10). The researchers looked at what considerations were involved in making these decisions and found that compared to older adolescents and adults, younger juveniles often failed to identify or to adequately evaluate risks or to take into account the long-range, as opposed to short-term, consequences of their choices.

In general, the results support Drizin's (2003) judgment that juvenile offenders, at least those under the age of 16, are substantially less likely than adults to have the ability to function adequately in the adult justice system.

so they alter protein synthesis, which is important for the growth and pruning of neurons, the production of neurotransmitters, and other neuromaturational processes. For example, among the changes that pubertal hormones initiate is a slow decrease in serotonin levels and increases in both dopamine levels and some enzymes that metabolize neurotransmitters. Basal cortisol levels in humans and animals have been found to rise over the transition to adolescence (Stroud et al., 2009). Animal studies confirm periods (infancy, childhood) of hyporesponsivity to stress hormones, presumably as protection for the developing brain, which are dramatically reversed at puberty when the brain becomes more sensitized to the effects of gonadal and stress-related hormones (McEwen, 2005; Lee, Brandy, & Koenig, 2003). Hormones are instrumental in laying down new neural pathways at adolescents, so overexpression of and increased sensitivity to cortisol during this period of rapid brain reorganization may signal a window of vulnerability for development of psychopathology (Spear, 2009). Recent longitudinal studies have found that levels of cortisol rise gradually through middle childhood and increase rapidly around age 13 (Walker & Bollini, 2002). Studies of adults have consistently linked increases in HPA reactivity, as measured by cortisol increases, with unipolar and bipolar disorders, schizophrenia, and PTSD (Muller, Holsboer, & Keck, 2002; Post, 2007; Walker & Diforio, 1997). Some evidence suggests a similar pattern for adolescent disorders, notably depression (Birmaher & Heydl, 2003; Goodyear, Park, Netherton, & Herbert, 2001; McEwen, 2005). Although all the mechanisms are not completely understood, some researchers believe that this normally heightened HPA reactivity sets the stage for increased vulnerability in adolescents who are at risk for psychiatric disorders. In other words, the surge in hormones may not just be a temporary blip during adolescence, leveling off and returning to some baseline at the end of puberty. Hormonal changes appear to have the capacity to organize the developing brain, by contributing to increases in stress-sensitivity and by activating genes involved in both normal and abnormal development (Romer & Walker, 2007).

Several recent human experimental studies have demonstrated that normally developing adolescents, compared to younger and older groups, display heightened stress reactivity on cortisol and other autonomic nervous system (ANS) measures during challenging situations. Stroud and colleagues (2009) assessed HPA axis and cardiac functions in a group of children (7–12) and adolescents (13–17) randomly exposed to two psychological stressors. Performance stress was assessed by requiring participants to make a 5-minute speech, answer mental arithmetic questions, and copy a picture from its mirror image in front of a small audience. Social stress was induced by means of a social rejection interaction involving confederates who gradually excluded the participant during conversation. While no significant differences were noted between age groups in self-reported distress, adolescents showed consistently more pronounced physiological responsiveness on all stress-related measures. Cortisol levels were highest in response to the performance stressors.

Several recent studies have considered the physiological effects that mental anticipation of a stressor and memories about past stressors have on stress reactivity in normal adolescents. Sumter, Bokhorsta, Miersa, Van Pelt, and Westenberg (2010) investigated this question in a large sample of 9- to 17-year-old boys and girls during the period prior to making a public presentation as well as during the actual task. Strongest cortisol rises were shown for adolescents during the anticipatory period, highlighting the potentially important role that perceptions of stress play in activating the stress response at adolescence (Folkman & Lazarus, 1988). A large prospective study of Dutch adolescents (Oldehinkel et al., 2010) also reported that level of perceived stress was positively associated with cardiac and cortisol measurements.

Adam (2006) investigated the normal fluctuations in emotional experience of adolescents' day-to-day lives using diary methods and cortisol sampling. Cortisol fluctuations covaried with momentary emotional states. When adolescents reported feeling angry or worried, their cortisol levels were significantly higher than what would normally be predicted for the individuals based on their typical daily patterns.

The physiological impact is also substantial when stressors involve peer rejection. Sebastian, Viding, Williams, and Blakemore (2010) asked young (11–13) and mid (14–15) adolescent female participants to play a 3-minute computer game called "cyberball" which manipulated inclusion and ostracism conditions as a function of being "thrown" the ball or ignored by two other players. Compared to adult studies using this manipulation, adolescents reported greater negative mood in both age groups, and younger adolescents also showed significant increases in distress. Even a short experience of social stress showed marked effects on affect. Considering the convergences of these factors, the "intersection of stress and the developing adolescent brain may represent a 'perfect storm' in the context of dysfunctional emotional development" (Romeo, 2010, p. 249).

Behavioral Changes with Puberty

Part of what surprised her aunt about Rebecca was how moody she had become. Parents whose children have gone through puberty often warn parents of younger children to "Enjoy them while they're young; you don't know what you're in for!" Parents of adolescents often assume that hormones are the underlying cause when their adolescents seem difficult, making comments such as "Her hormones are raging!" Adolescent moodiness—extreme and rapid swings in emotional tone—is indeed notorious. But how extreme is it, really? And how much of it can be attributed directly to the underlying hormonal changes of puberty?

Moodiness is part of a broader set of behavioral tendencies in teens that also includes conflict with parents, negative affect, and risky behavior, such as violating norms and recklessness (Arnett, 1999). G. Stanley Hall, an early developmental researcher, referred to the full complement of difficult behaviors as the "storm and stress" of adolescence (Hall, 1904). Although there is considerable variability in the degree to which adolescents experience storm and stress, with many teens showing few signs of it, a review of research on differences between adolescents and other age groups indicates that teens do indeed experience greater average storm and stress than other age groups (Arnett, 1999) Hollensteen & Lougheed, 2013. We will look more closely at some features of adolescent storm and stress in the next chapter. Let's consider here adolescent moodiness and negative affect.

Larson and Richards (1994) used a technique called the **experience sampling method** to gauge adolescents' moods. Participants in their study wore beepers throughout their waking hours. When they were beeped, they made notes about what they were doing, thinking, and feeling at that moment. In the course of a day, adolescents reported more mood disruptions, more feelings of self-consciousness and embarrassment, more extremes of emotion, and less happiness than younger children or adults. In addition, their emotional reactions to the very same events tended to be more intense than those of other age groups.

Petersen et al., 1993 reviewed studies of **depressed mood**, defined as a subclinical level of depression, and found

Adolescent moodiness and emotionality can be a trial for parents.

that about one third of teens experience depressed mood at any given time. Although clinical depression does not appear to be higher in samples of adolescents than in the general population, rates of clinical depression do increase at adolescence compared to childhood. As we have noted before, both depressed mood and clinical depression occur more often in females than in males, beginning in adolescence. Across recent studies, major depression rates for 12- to 19-year-olds range from 15% to 20%, with girls' rates about double that of boys' (Davila, 2008).

Moodiness does seem to be more characteristic of adolescents than of other age groups. Do hormones make it happen? As always, when we examine causes for behavior and for developmental changes in behavior, a multidimensional model seems to best fit the available data. Increases in hormone levels early in puberty are linked to increases in the sensitivity of sensory systems (Buchanan et al., 1992), perhaps contributing to correlated increases in negative mood (Brooks-Gunn & Warren, 1989) and in young adolescents' volatility (Buchanan et al., 1992). But hormonal changes are more likely to be predictive of mood if they are combined with negative life events, such as parental divorce or academic problems. In other words, risk factors potentiate each other.

Arnett (1999) provides an interesting example of the potential interaction of biological and social causes of mood disruption in teens. **Delayed phase preference** is a shift in sleep patterns that has been associated with hormonal changes at puberty. Adolescents are more comfortable staying up later in the evening and sleeping later in the morning than younger children (Carskadon, Vieria, & Acebo, 1993). Arnett asks whether requiring adolescents to start school earlier in the morning than younger children, a common practice in many school districts, might contribute to sleep deprivation in teens and by so doing, contribute to emotional volatility.

Moodiness seems to be strongly associated with changes in peer relationships, parent expectations, and self-concept that often accompany sexual maturation. In the next two sections, we will consider how some of these social and psychological repercussions of puberty function to affect mood. First, we'll examine how differently puberty seems to affect mood depending on whether its onset is early or late. Second, we will take a closer look at the gender difference in depressive symptoms that emerges in adolescence and consider how the different social experiences of girls and boys might contribute.

Early Versus Late Maturation. For girls, early sexual maturation is generally associated with greater storm and stress, including moodiness and depressive symptoms, than late sexual maturation (see Mendle, Turkheimer, & Emery, 2007). Thus, even though early and late maturers are subject to the same hormonal influences once puberty begins, early maturers seem to be more affected. The reasons must depend on factors other than hormones. Partly because most girls begin puberty before most boys, an especially early maturing girl is bigger than most of the other children her age. She is also heavier and so is more likely than other girls to be unhappy with her body in a culture that prizes slimness in females. Early sexual maturation (e.g., breast development) may make her a target for teasing or innuendo from peers. Also, being physically mature can be a source of outright rejection by less mature girls (Petersen, 1988). Parents of early-maturing girls tend to worry about their daughters being at risk for sexual experiences that they are not ready to handle, and they may limit their daughters' independence in ways that are grating. Parents' concerns may not be exaggerated: Early-maturing girls tend to have more behavior problems than other girls, especially if they become involved with older boys (e.g., Gowen, Feldman, & Diaz, 2004), and there is a slight tendency for early maturing girls to have their first sexual intercourse earlier than other girls (Zimmer-Gembeck & Helfand, 2008).

Early maturation in boys is a different story. Early-maturing boys seem to be less moody and less likely to exhibit depressed mood than later maturing boys. In fact, it is late-maturing boys who seem more affected by storm and stress. Being larger and stronger than other boys gives early-maturing boys an edge in socially approved male activities, such as athletics, whereas late-maturing boys are at a distinct disadvantage in the same activities. Generally, early-maturing boys are more confident than late-maturing boys, more popular, and more likely to be leaders among their peers. Late-maturing boys are more likely than other boys to be socially awkward, insecure, and variable in mood (Simmons & Blyth, 1987; Simmons et al., 1987). As with girls, early maturing boys tend to have first sexual intercourse somewhat earlier than other boys (Zimmer-Gembeck & Helfand, 2008).

Josh describes his experience as an early-maturing teenage boy. Notice how his social experiences are tied to his physical development. In what ways are his experiences typical of teens who reach puberty before their peers?

Clearly, the storm and stress that accompany the onset of puberty can vary dramatically depending on contextual factors. Overall, these findings suggest that the volatility and negativity of adolescents are largely related to the number of stressors with which they must cope.

Girls' Versus Boys' Susceptibility to Depression. Let's consider here why adolescent girls might be more susceptible to depression than boys. It is possible that sex differences in circulating hormones directly contribute. But most developmentalists argue that sex differences in social experience are likely to play a large role in the mix of causes. Remember that both boys and girls are more subject to depressive moods in adolescence than in the preadolescent period and that each gender experiences increased stress of various kinds (see Chapter 8). But on the whole, it may be that girls face more challenges to their self-esteem and more problems in living in early adolescence than boys do (Petersen, Sarigiani, & Kennedy, 1991). That is, girls must deal with more stressors simultaneously. As we have seen, self-esteem tends to decline more for girls than for boys at puberty (e.g., Robins & Trzesniewski, 2005). Also, in comparison to their male counterparts, females report experiencing more stressors from early adolescence onward (Compas, Howell, Phares, Williams, & Giunta, 1989; Wichstrom, 1999). Here are a few:

1. As we saw in the last chapter, by age 11 children are aware that the female gender role is less valued than the male role. They believe that there are greater restrictions on behavior for females and that there is gender-based discrimination (Brown & Bigler, 2005). They recognize that females are seen as less competent than males, and that traditional female occupations are less prestigious than male occupations (Ruble, Martin, & Berenbaum, 2006). As they integrate these beliefs into their self-concept, girls may begin to feel less worthwhile than boys, or at least less appreciated.

2. Although both boys and girls are concerned about **body image** (their concept of, and attitude toward, their physical appearance), girls worry more than boys about appearance and weight after puberty (e.g., Barker & Galambos, 2003; Jones, 2004; Smolak, Levine, & Thompson, 2001). As the discussion about gender differences in early and late maturation suggests, for boys, puberty is experienced as a move toward the male ideal: they grow taller, build muscle, and their voices deepen. But for girls, it often means a move away from the current thin, slim-hipped ideal (Harter, 2006). It should be noted that ethnicity moderates the role of body image in self-esteem. For example, some studies show that African American youth report more positive body images than White youth. Body ideals among African Americans are more consistent with actual body characteristics, which serves as a protective factor for adolescents (e.g., Paxton, Eisenberg, & Neumark-Sztainer, 2006). For other ethnic groups, especially for girls, thinness as a body ideal is well established by middle childhood and is directly associated with media exposure to this standard (e.g., how much adult programming children watch on television) (e.g., Dohnt & Tiggemann, 2006). As Harter (2006) points out, such " . . . images of female attractiveness are very punishing in that they are unattainable by the vast majority of girls and women in the culture" (p. 556).

3. Girls historically have more often had lower expectations of success than boys (Ruble, Gruelich, Pomerantz, & Gochberg, 1993).

4. Girls may be more stressed by the burgeoning of their sexuality and their sexual desirability. The traditional **double standard**, by which female sexual behavior is judged more harshly than male sexual behavior, has clearly diminished over the last half century, as the rates and acceptability of premarital sex have increased among teens of both sexes (Astin, Korn, Sax, & Mahoney, 1994). Yet, American college students still consider girls who have multiple sexual partners to be more immoral than boys who do (Crawford, 2003; Robinson, Ziss, Ganza, Katz, & Robinson, 1991), and among adolescents who

have intercourse, girls are more likely to judge themselves to be bad or unlovable than boys are to judge themselves negatively (Graber, Brooks-Gunn, & Galen, 1999). Thus, even though girls' acceptance of and experience with sexuality is increasing rapidly, they are still more subject to ambiguous messages about the acceptability of sex and seem to be more uncertain about what is appropriate for them in a world of shifting values (see Collins & Steinberg, 2006). In addition, the physical and social consequences of sexual activity are greater for girls. They are still the ones who get pregnant.

5. After puberty, girls and boys start interacting more in mixed-sex groups and in heterosexual dyads. In these contexts, the differences in their discourse styles may create more stress for girls. You'll recall from Chapter 8 that girls acquire a more cooperative discourse style and boys a more domineering style during childhood. One result is that when adolescent girls socialize with boys, they are less likely to influence the outcome of a discussion (see Maccoby, 1990). Also, in heterosexual pairs boys do not offer as much support to their partners as girls do (Leaper, 1994). As a consequence, these relationships may be less affirming and satisfying for girls than for boys (e.g., Pipher, 1994).

6. An emerging area of research finds strong links between adolescent romantic involvement and depression. Adolescents, who are steady or frequent daters, and those who engage in more sexual activity, are more prone to depression (e.g., Quatman, Sampson, Robinson, & Watson, 2001). In early adolescence, especially for girls, even typical romantic behaviors, such as flirting and kissing, are associated with increased depressive symptoms (e.g., Steinberg & Davila, 2008). Why this is so is not yet understood. However, issues such as those discussed in points 4 and 5 above may certainly be important (see Davila, 2008).

7. Because puberty comes earlier for girls, they are more likely than boys to simultaneously face both the changes of puberty and the difficult transition to secondary school (i.e., junior high or middle school; Petersen, Kennedy, & Sullivan, 1991; see Chapter 10 for a discussion of this transition).

Girls may be more subject to depression than boys not only because they face more challenges but because they often adopt a coping style, **rumination**, that increases the risk of depression (Nolen-Hoeksema & Girgus, 1994; Petersen et al., 1993). Rumination (Morrow & Nolen-Hoeksema, 1990) or self-focused attention (Ingram, Cruet, Johnson, & Wisnicki, 1988) may be defined as a stable, emotion-focused coping style that involves responding to problems by directing attention internally toward negative feelings and thoughts. Ruminating about problems includes both cognitive (self-focused cognitions) and affective (increased emotional reactivity) elements. Ruminative strategies may include isolating oneself to dwell on a problem, writing in a diary about how sad one feels, or talking repetitively about a negative experience with the purpose of gaining increased personal insight. In general, however, ruminative focusing on problems while in a depressed mood may actually make the depression worse.

Experimental studies have found that this type of heightened self-focus increases the duration and intensity of depressive episodes, particularly in adolescent and adult females (Greenberg & Pyszczynski, 1986; Ingram et al., 1988; Morrow & Nolen-Hoeksema, 1990), who are much more likely to exhibit this style of coping than are males (Butler & Nolen-Hoeksema, 1994). Adolescents and adults who ruminate are more likely to experience depression. To qualify as a gender-linked preexisting risk factor, gender differences in rumination and **distraction** must be shown to exist prior to adolescence, before the rise in levels of depression. A study of the coping styles of fourth- and fifth-grade children revealed that girls are more likely than boys to endorse ruminative coping choices when confronted with academic, family, and peer stressors, even though at these ages girls and boys show no differences in rates of depression (Broderick, 1998). Similar to Nolen-Hoeksema's (1987) finding that older males are more likely to dampen their stress-related negative affect, boys in this study were somewhat more likely to choose distracting or avoidant ways to handle problems than girls were. Girls, on the other hand, were prone to amplifying negative affect by providing responses to stressful situations that were both very negative ("I felt like I was going to die") and persistent ("I'd be in a bad mood all day"). Thus, it appears that when girls at puberty begin to face increased stress, they, more than boys, are more likely to bring to the task a coping style that puts them at greater risk of experiencing depression (Broderick & Korteland, 2004).

However, gender role also influences how children and early adolescents cope with problems. A ruminative coping style is most pronounced among girls and some boys whose gender roles are stereotypically feminine. These individuals identify themselves as relatively passive and nondominant and are less likely to cope by using active problem solving or distraction. Having a ruminative coping style, or being uncomfortable with or incapable of psychological distraction, may be a particularly heavy burden for feminine-identified boys, for whom such behavior is clearly contrary to the peer group's expectations for appropriate masculine behavior (Broderick & Korteland, 2004).

The Emergence of Sexuality and Sexual Preference

Sexual pleasure is a part of human functioning even in early childhood. Preschoolers and school-aged children may fondle their own genitals for the pleasure of it, and many engage in sex play with others. "Playing doctor," for example, has been known to involve disrobing or fondling the genitals of other children (see Shaffer, 1994). On average, children begin to show sexual attraction at **adrenarche**, when the adrenal glands increase their activity just before puberty, at about age 10 (Collins & Steinberg, 2006). However, the strength and urgency of the adult sex drive, emerging as a function of puberty, is a new experience to young adolescents. They are more sensitive to, and interested in, sexually relevant stimuli than younger children. Despite having spent most of childhood spontaneously segregating into single-gender groups, young adolescents begin to seek out opportunities to socialize in mixed-gender groups (Maccoby, 1998; Rubin et al., 2006).

Faced with their increased sexual interest, most adolescents begin to explore their sexuality. The earliest and most common activity throughout adolescence is sexual fantasizing, and the next step tends to be masturbation, especially for males (see Collins & Steinberg, 2006) which begins on average between 11 and 12 years. Table 9.1 indicates gender, ethnic, and grade differences of U.S. high school students reporting intercourse. It should be noted that as many as 50% of young adolescents also have sexual experiences with members of the same sex, primarily displaying

 Josh says there's no peer pressure to have a girlfriend, but he also says that some classmates brag or lie about having a sexual relationship. Might there be more implicit pressure than Josh realizes?

TABLE 9.1 Percentage of U.S. High School Students by Gender, Race, and Grade Endorsing "Ever Had Intercourse"

Race/Ethnicity	BOYS	GIRLS
White	44.0	44.5
Black	66.9	53.6
Hispanic	53.0	43.9
Grade		
9	37.8	27.8
10	44.5	43.0
11	54.5	51.9
12	62.6	63.6

[a]Data are from US YRBSS, 2011.

SOURCE: Eaton, D. K., Kann, L., Kinchen, S., Shanklin, S., Flint, K. H., Hawkins, J., et al. (2012). *Youth Risk Behavior Surveillance— United States, 2011 Surveillance Summaries. 61(SS04),* 1–162.

and touching genitals, and engaging in mutual masturbation. These activities seem to be partly a function of opportunity, because young adolescents still spend more of their time with same-sex than opposite-sex peers. For most youngsters, these sexual contacts are not indicators of a homosexual orientation (Masters, Johnson, & Kolodny, 1988; Savin-Williams & Ream, 2007).

Sexual maturation is a key determiner of sexual behavior, but many other factors come into play. Adolescents are often moved to engage in sexual behavior out of curiosity or because of pressure to have sex from partners or peer group (e.g., see Collins & Steinberg, 2006). Myriad other influences—from social class and ethnicity to religious background, geographic setting (urban versus rural), popular culture (as portrayed in movies, music, teen magazines, and Internet sites), and the quality of sex education in schools—play a part in when and whether adolescents become sexually active (e.g., Collins & Steinberg, 2006; Crump et al., 1999). Clearly, sexuality is a normative part of adolescent development, but early sexual debut is associated with more negative outcomes. Researchers are trying to better understand the normative processes that shape sexuality development in an effort to promote adolescent health. In the largest longitudinal study to date, the National Longitudinal Study of Adolescent Health (Add Study; Harris et al., 2009), researchers have been following over 6,000 adolescents in four waves since 1994. A recent examination of female participants in this sample (Reese, Haydon, Herring, & Halpern, 2012) examined the relationships between teen pregnancy and the timing and order of girls' sexual activity (see Table 9.2). The most common sequence, engaging in vaginal sex before oral-genital contact, was related to more teenage pregnancies compared to other types of sexual debuts.

Sexual Orientation

A central feature of sexual development in adolescence is the emergence of **sexual orientation**, referring to a preference for sexual partners of one's own sex (**homosexuality**) or the opposite sex (**heterosexuality**) or both (**bisexuality**). A large majority of adolescents eventually identify themselves as heterosexual. In a recent Youth Risk Behavior Surveillance (YRBS) survey of high school students across 9 states, approximately 93% identified themselves as heterosexual, 1.3% as gay or lesbian, 3.7% as bisexual and 2.5% as not sure of their sexual identity (CDC, 2011; Kann et al., 2011). The survey also inquired about type of sexual contact in which youth engaged. Most students across 12 states reported heterosexual contact (median = 53.5%). A smaller proportion (2.5%) reported sexual activity only with same-sex partners, 3.3% reported bisexual contact, and 40.5% reported no sexual contact.

Our understanding of how sexual orientation develops is increasingly better informed by research in neuroscience. Many theories that postulate environmental causes have no empirical support. The most famous of these is Freud's account of the Oedipal and Electra complexes (e.g., Freud, 1935/1960). As you will recall from Chapter 8, Freud proposed in his psychoanalytic theory that 3- to 5-year-olds compete with the same-sex parent for the attentions of the opposite-sex parent. To avoid the punitive consequences of such competition, boys eventually identify with their fathers and girls with mothers, imitating the behaviors and internalizing the values of that parent. According to Freud, this identification process explains why

TABLE 9.2 Sequence of Sexual Initiation and Relationship to Pregnancy

SEQUENCE OF SEXUAL INITIATION	PERCENTAGE REPORTING A PREGNANCY DURING TEEN YEARS
Vaginal sex first (54.7 % of the sample)	31.4%
Oral-genital sex first (9.9% of the sample)	7.9%
Both vaginal and oral-genital sex at the same time (35.5% of the sample)	20.5%

SOURCE: Reese, B. M., Haydon, A. A., Herring, A. H., & Halpern, C. T. (2012). The association between sequences of sexual initiation and the likelihood of teenage pregnancy. *Journal of Adolescent Health*. Available at www.sciencedirect.com.ezaccess.libraries.psu.edu/science/article/pii/S1054139X1200225X.

most children eventually adopt a heterosexual orientation. It is just one more way in which the child becomes like the same-sex parent. Homosexuality or bisexuality results when something goes wrong with the identification process: The Oedipal or Electra complex cannot unfold in the usual way because there is only one parent in the home, or the same-sex parent is too weak or shows little interest in the child, or the opposite-sex parent lacks the nurturing to be attractive or is too dominant.

Freud's theory of identification is not supported by the evidence. Adults who are homosexual or bisexual are not more likely than heterosexuals to come from one-parent homes or to have weak fathers or dominant mothers. Another environmental theory, the **seduction hypothesis**, is also unsupported. In this view, children or adolescents are seduced into homosexuality by homosexual pedophiles. Yet, survey research indicates that homosexuals often feel inklings of their sexual orientation long before their first sexual experience, and they are no more likely to have had early sexual experiences with predatory adults than are heterosexuals (See Bell, Weinberg, & Hammersmith, 1981). Even modeling by adults does not seem to affect children's sexual preference. Studies of children raised by homosexual partners indicate that they are no more likely to become homosexual themselves than children raised by heterosexuals. Children raised by homosexual parents are no more likely to be sexually abused than other children and their social-emotional adjustment, including relationships with peers, is comparable as well (Golombok et al., 2003; Herek, 2006, Patterson, 2004).

There is better evidence for biological influences on sexual orientation. Genes appear to play an important part. When one identical twin is homosexual, the other twin has about a 50% chance of also being homosexual, a much higher concordance rate than we find between less closely related family members (Bailey, Dunn, & Martin, 2000). But sexual orientation researchers have not yet agreed upon which genes are involved and how they are transmitted. Although some candidate genes have been identified (Hamer, Hu, Magnuson, Hu, & Pattatucci, 1993), results have been inconclusive because unraveling a complex behavior like sexuality is very difficult.

Prenatal hormones also play a role. Exposure to masculinizing hormones can affect the sexual orientation of human females. Girls who are exposed to high levels of prenatal androgens (congenital adrenal hyperplasia, or CAH; see Chapter 8) are often found to have a greater frequency of homosexual experiences and fantasies than their non-CAH female relatives (see Collaer & Hines, 1995). For males, delayed exposure to masculinizing hormones during prenatal development has been found to affect sexual behavior in several nonhuman mammalian species. For example, when a male rat fetus is prenatally stressed, effectively delaying its exposure to androgens, the rat in adulthood will show higher frequencies of female sexual posturing and lower frequencies of male sexual behaviors, such as mounting, than nonprenatally stressed males (see Chapter 8; Ward, 1992).

Other current theories about sexual orientation development have examined differences in handedness and finger-length ratios of the 2nd to 4th digits (see Rahman, 2005). The available evidence for consistent difference in left versus right handedness and finger length ratios support the androgen theory, since these observed effects serve as proxies for hormonal exposure. Recent work on the androgen hypothesis in humans more consistently supports this effect for homosexual women, but not necessarily for homosexual men. For males, homosexual orientation has been associated with both high and low levels of androgen exposure. Therefore, both level and timing of prenatal hormone exposure in concert with genetic influences need to be taken into account. Another theory, which has received considerable support, centers on fraternal birth order (FBO). Epidemiological evidence shows that homosexual males tend to have disproportionately higher numbers of older brothers compared to heterosexual males (Blanchard, 2004). The explanation for this robust finding suggests a possible role for immunology. The fraternal birth order theory posits that the maternal body begins to develop antibodies to male-linked (Y-chromosome) proteins during gestation. This antibody response accumulates with each successive male pregnancy and has an effect on prenatal brain development. Certain differences in areas of the brain, like the hypothalamic nuclei, have been related to sexual differentiation (Swaab, 2008). Bogaert (2006) found that this FBO effect held up across cultures and socioeconomic groups, and even when male siblings were raised in different households.

Savin-Williams (2005) argues that for up to 20% of teens, sexual orientation is a fluid concept (see also Diamond, 2007; Diamond & Butterworth, 2008; Thompson & Morgan, 2008). Regardless of how biology and environment transact in the determination of sexual preference, it should be noted that most homosexuals, like most heterosexuals, feel that their sexual orientation is not something they have chosen but that it is a part of what they are "naturally" (e.g., Money, 1988). Currently available evidence is strongest for prenatal influences on the development of gender identity and sexual orientation. There is no reliable evidence at this point that gender identity or sexual orientation is caused by environmental conditions after birth (see Swaab, 2008).

COGNITIVE DEVELOPMENT

When were you first introduced to the mysteries of algebra? When we asked a U.S. class of college sophomores that question, a few thought they might have been given a taste of algebra as early as sixth grade (at age 11 or 12). But the majority said it was between ninth to eighth grades (that is, between ages 15 to 14). The National Council on the Teaching of Mathematics (2000a, 2000b) recommends introducing the more concrete elements of algebra in Grades 5 through 8, as a generalization of arithmetic with some precursors to that as early as Grade 3. But the Council suggests that the more abstract concepts are better introduced in Grades 9 through 12.

Why do curriculum planners wait so long to introduce most aspects of algebra? Simple equations solving for x can be solved using basic mathematical operations such as adding, subtracting, multiplying, and dividing. In a culture known for its desire to do things faster and better, often pushing children along as quickly as possible, why do we wait until fifth or sixth grade to teach them to solve even simple equations? The answer seems to be, "because it does not work if we begin earlier." We make no faster progress if we introduce algebra in second grade than if we wait until later. The juggernaut seems to be that even the simplest algebraic equation involves the use of a symbol for the unknown, the x. You may recall your first algebra teacher defining those letters that appear in equations as "symbols for unknown numbers," representing "any possible number." When we ask children to use those letters to substitute for unknown numbers, we are asking them to reason logically about an abstraction, something that cannot be represented in concrete terms. The x can be defined or exemplified only in words or other symbols. There is no concrete example of "an unknown number."

In middle childhood, the period Jean Piaget referred to as the stage of concrete operational thought, children clearly can reason logically. They have the capacity to hold several pieces of information in mind at one time and to discover the relations among them. But, as we saw in Chapter 6, they seem to reason most effectively if the information they are working with can be represented readily in the concrete, real world, or at least if parallels can be found in the real world. In early adolescence, we begin to see this limitation of middle childhood recede. More and more, youngsters seem able to leave the ground of reality and to spin a logical tale with abstract contents, contents such as probabilities, hypothetical possibilities, and statements that are contrary to one's belief or even to fact.

Formal Operational Thought

Suppose you have two canisters of hard candy (see Figure 9.2). Your favorite flavor is lemon, the yellow candies. You know the first canister has one green

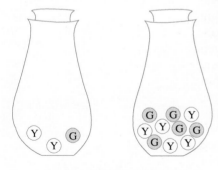

Y = Yellow Candies
G = Green Candies

FIGURE 9.2 From which canister are you more likely to get a yellow candy?

candy and two yellow ones. The second canister has five green and five yellow candies. To get a candy, you must shake one out of a canister, sight unseen. Which canister should you shake to be most certain of getting a yellow candy?

You are faced here with a probability problem. With the first canister, you would get a yellow candy 2 out of 3 times, or 67% of the time. With the second canister, you would get a yellow candy 5 out of 10 times, or 50% of the time. These odds make the first canister your best choice.

An 8-year-old would probably choose to take her chances with the second canister, arguing that it contains more yellow candies. But the absolute number of candies is not important in this case. Rather, the important features to compare are the relative proportions of yellow candies in each canister, which determine the probability of getting a yellow candy. The proportion of yellow candies is an abstraction, one that is difficult for an 8-year-old to reason about when faced with the concrete reality of a larger number of yellow candies in the second canister (see Piaget & Inhelder, 1951/1976).

Even as an adult, you may not have known which canister to choose. Perhaps you got confused about how to calculate the probabilities. Perhaps you were momentarily distracted by the concrete reality that is convincing to the 8-year-old—there are more yellow candies in the second canister. But now that you have run through this kind of problem and seen how it works, you are likely to see the importance of the more abstract concepts—the proportion of yellow candies in each canister—as opposed to the actual numbers of candies. Given another problem like this one, you have a good chance of figuring it out correctly. An 8-year-old, however, would not be likely to attack the next problem any differently, even with explanation and training. The 8-year-old's difficulty is not just inexperience with the probability concept; it is a failure to understand and reason effectively about an abstraction.

The problem of the yellow candy illustrates several characteristics of **formal operational thought**, the kind of thinking that Piaget and his colleague, Barbel Inhelder, identified as beginning at about 11 or 12 years (e.g., Inhelder & Piaget, 1955/1958). First, formal thought rises above particular contents and focuses on relationships that govern those contents—that is, on abstractions. In the candy example, the proportion of yellow to green candies, not the number of yellow candies, in each canister is what you had to reason about. Second, formal reasoning involves coordinating multiple relationships. In the candy example, the successful problem solver must discover the relationship between the two proportions, which are themselves relationships. Third, formal thought can be difficult even for adults. We all find logical thinking to be easier when the information we must contend with is more concrete. As a result, even adolescents and adults who are capable of formal thought do not always use it effectively (Gray, 1990). It helps if we have experience and training in solving a particular kind of problem (Overton, 1990) or if we have familiarity with the subject matter (the domain of knowledge; Schauble, 1996), just as we saw with younger children in Chapter 6. Across a number of studies using a variety of tests of formal operational thinking, researchers report that about 30% of young adolescents (about 13 years old) show a tendency to apply formal reasoning in some situations, and about 60% of older adolescents or young adults (college students) do so (see Cowan, 1978, for a summary of early work on this issue; see Kuhn, 1989, 2006, and Gray, 1990, for more recent findings).

As we have seen before, changes in cognitive ability usually occur gradually, not in startling stagelike shifts. The development of formal reasoning is no different, so that we see glimmerings of formal thought in middle childhood. The kinds of problem-solving strategies that children use at ages 9 or 10 are likely to be more elaborate than at ages 6 or 7, and they may even involve operating on relatively abstract contents (Kuhn, Garcia-Mila, Zohar, & Andersen, 1995; Kuhn & Franklin, 2006; Siegler, 2006; Zimmerman, 2007). But formal thinking is more likely to emerge in adolescence.

One way to think about the gradual improvement in formal or abstract reasoning skills is to view them as advances in information processing. Many of the information processing improvements that we described in middle childhood (see Chapter 6) continue through adolescence, linked in part to continuing brain development and in part to the child's growing knowledge base (Kuhn & Franklin, 2006). Processing speed increases, and, perhaps partly as a function of speed, the capacity of working memory continues to expand (Case, 1992). Another change is improvement in inhibitory ability, which primarily affects attentional control. We saw in Chapter 3 that advancing attentional control in the late preschool period is among the set of executive functions. Throughout middle childhood and early adolescence, children continue to get better at ignoring irrelevant stimuli (e.g., what is perceptually salient) during problem solving and focusing instead on what is important. This includes suppressing already learned information and responses in order to allow for new understandings and the practice of new responses. All of these processing changes probably contribute to what Piaget called formal thinking: the ability to identify, organize, and draw inferences about complex abstract content. However, while these processing changes may be necessary, they do not seem to be sufficient (Demetriou, Christou, Spanoudis, & Platsidou, 2002). More general cognitive control mechanisms, like meta-cognitive understanding of effective strategy use, emotion management and intentional efforts to acquire, compare and organize information are also important (see Halford & Andrews, 2006; Kuhn, 2000).

Educators have long recognized that more can be expected of adolescents, so that, as with algebra, more abstract subject matter is likely to be introduced to the curriculum after about age 12. In science classes, where younger students may be given laboratory assignments that consist of simple demonstrations, adolescents are often expected to generate and test hypotheses with thorough rigor (see below). In literature, teachers require students to begin to analyze works of fiction at multiple levels, going beyond the sequence of events that creates the story and looking for ironic, satiric, and metaphoric themes. These themes are abstractions, relationships among words on a different plane from the literal meaning. Some of us remember pining for the simpler, easier days when a story was just a story!

The capacity for formal thought can influence many aspects of adolescent life, from the approaches teens take to academic tasks to their views of religion and politics, their self-evaluation, and their relationships with parents and peers. In the following sections, we will look at some examples of these wide-ranging implications.

Scientific Problem Solving

This seventh-grade science class is attempting to solve the pendulum problem. Note in particular the student who tells Mr. Sowell, "The shorter and the heavier it is, the faster she goes." How does her response differ from those you'd expect of an older high-school student?

Suppose a high school physics teacher posed the following problem to her class: A pendulum is a swinging object at the end of a length of string. The important characteristics of a pendulum are the weight of the object, the length of the string, the force of the push that starts the swing, and the height of the dropping point. Some pendulums swing faster than others. *Your job is to figure out whether the length of the string makes any difference in the rate at which the pendulum swings.*

To solve this problem effectively, a student would need to understand the "control of variables strategy" (CVS). She would need to change the hypothesized cause of rate of swing—the length of the string—without letting any other important variable change simultaneously. Then, if a pendulum's rate of swing changed (which it would), the only possible explanation for that change would be the change in length, and she could conclude that length of the string changes the rate of swing. CVS is the essence of experimental procedure. A potential cause is changed, whereas all other potential causes (or variables) are controlled (held constant). Some elementary-school-aged children figure out CVS on their own when given problems like this one; most do not. But those who don't discover it themselves can be successfully trained to see its value and to use it consistently (Klahr & Nigam, 2004).

But if we change the problem, as follows, it becomes much more difficult, and most children do not do well on it until adolescence, either spontaneously or with training: A pendulum is a swinging object at the end of a length of string. The important characteristics of a pendulum are the weight of the object, the length of the string, the force of the push that starts the swing, and the height of the dropping point. Some pendulums swing faster than others. *Your job is to figure out why some pendulums swing faster than others* (problem adapted from Inhelder & Piaget, 1955/1958).

Consider how some high school students respond. One student makes a good start. She approaches the problem like this: "I think it could be any of the four characteristics that is important. First, I will try changing the weight of the object; then I'll change the length of the string; then I'll vary the force of the push; then I'll try changing the dropping point." The student makes a change in the weight with no effect on rate of swing. Then she changes the length of the string. Voila! The rate of swing changes. She stops her assessments and announces that she has found the solution: length of the string.

Another student approaches the task by changing more than one characteristic at a time. When she changes weight and length together, the rate of swing changes. She concludes that the rate of swing is a result of the combined effects of weight and length.

As teens acquire formal operational thinking skills, the science curriculum makes more demands for careful, abstract thought, such as requiring students to systematically generate and test hypotheses.

A third student tests each of the four characteristics and, of course, finds that changing the length affects rate of swing. But she continues her assessment, combining changes in pairs of characteristics: weight plus length, weight plus force of push, weight plus height of dropping point, and so on. Even though each pairing that includes a change of length affects the rate of swing, she continues her tests. She moves on to combine changes in weight plus length plus force of push, then weight plus length plus height of dropping point, and so on until she has tested every combination of three changes, and finally tests a combination of changes in all four characteristics at once. Only combinations in which length of string is changed affect rate of swing—no other combinations make a difference. Finally, she reports her conclusion: Length of string alone is the determining factor.

Only the third student has solved the problem using combinatorial logic, a type of formal operational thought. She has generated every possible hypothesis. Then, she has tested each hypothesis by holding constant all the factors that are not posited to contribute to the rate of swing by that hypothesis, so that by systematic examination of the results of all the tests she can eliminate all but the hypotheses that must be correct.

The first and second students provide two examples of concrete operational thinking. There is a degree of systematicity to their generation of hypotheses, but not a complete generation of all possibilities. Their conclusions are also too closely tied to concrete outcomes. When the "length of string hypothesis" works for the first student, she stops her testing, even though it remains possible that other characteristics could be involved or that some combination of characteristics could negate the effects of changing the string length. When the combination of weight and length works for the second student, she ends her investigation, drawing the false conclusion that the combination is important.

Adolescents who approach scientific problems by considering every possibility and then carefully testing each one are using formal operational reasoning. The pattern of results among all the tests is what drives the conclusions, not any particular concrete observation.

In effective scientific problem solving, we see another characteristic of people who use formal operational thought. They can generate and think about possibilities. What is real is just one of a full set of possibilities. These possibilities can be generated only in the realm of thought—they are abstractions, not dependent on observations.

As we noted in Chapter 6, even adults often fail to treat their own theories as just one in a set of possibilities. Even for individuals capable of formal thought, scientific reasoning often runs aground on the shoals of belief, so that evidence is distorted or ignored instead of carefully analyzed for overriding patterns. In other words, our motives and emotional commitments can sidetrack our logical reasoning (Kuhn, 1989, Kuhn & Frankin, 2006; Kuhn, Amsel, & O'Loughlin, 1988). It appears that those of us who overcome these common difficulties have learned to logically analyze our own thought processes (Kuhn, 1989, Moshman, 1998). When we have favorite theories (e.g., strong beliefs about the value of capital punishment or ideas about the best approach to bilingual education), we must take our own thinking about those theories as the subject of our formal reasoning, and we must monitor our own thought processes as we evaluate evidence, to ensure that we are maintaining logical consistency. As you will see, skill at such self-monitoring clearly advances in adolescence. However, the stronger our emotional commitment to an idea, the harder it is engage in such self-evaluation effectively and the less likely we are to do it (Kuhn, 1989, Kuhn & Franklin, 2006). Helpers often struggle to help clients see problematic situations in logical, objective ways to facilitate good decision making.

Constructing Ideals

Adolescents who are capable of generating possibilities, without regard for present reality, have acquired a powerful new cognitive tool that can be used to construct **ideals**: logically organized possible systems. As Cowan (1978) puts it, such individuals are "adept at generating ideas about the world as it could be" (p. 291). They might mentally construct an ideal political system, or religion, or school. They might also construct an ideal self, teacher, parent, or friend. Any of these ideal systems will make the real, imperfect forms seem shabby and inadequate by comparison. For some adolescents, this new capacity for constructing ideals leads to a zeal for reform. It may also contribute to a skeptical attitude toward childhood religious beliefs or toward parental politics and values (Cowan, 1978; Piaget, 1964/1968). A family belief system can become for the adolescent just one of many possibilities. Thus, the capacity to entertain possibilities and to construct ideals appears to contribute to a critical attitude, and to a skepticism about the justifications that others often give for the status quo. Rebecca's critical attitude in conversation with her family may be linked to her ability to construct ideals and her impatience with anything real that does not measure up.

The "cure" for a critical attitude is experience (Cowan, 1978; Piaget, 1964/1968). Ideals, by definition, are not real. They are perfect possibilities. But real systems and people are never perfect. Adolescent idealists are not familiar yet with the enormous complexity of putting ideas into action and with the actual limitations of the concrete world. Until they gain more experience of the difficulties, they are likely to be critical, even unforgiving. In essence, the adolescent's failure to understand the real limits of her ideas is a form of egocentrism. Interestingly, this seems to apply to her judgments not only of others but also of herself. The increase in depression in adolescence may in part be affected by a tendency to be discouraged by one's own imperfections: The real self never quite measures up to the ideal (e.g., Harter, 2006). An interesting feature of this new, self-critical attitude is that it is self-generated. Even when an adolescent's appearance or behavior does compare favorably to the standards that others hold, she may judge herself to be inadequate, based on her idealized version of the self. Such misplaced self-criticism can be very frustrating to adults who deal with adolescents, and it can play a role in some serious disorders, such as anorexia (Harter, 2006; Landa & Bybee, 2007; Vandereycken & Van Deth, 1994).

Advances in Metacognitive Skill: Thinking About Thought

In middle childhood, children gain some metacognitive skill, that is, some understanding of their own cognitive processes. They get better and better, for example, at assessing when they have studied a list of words enough to remember them on a test (e.g., Flavell, Friedrichs, & Hoyt, 1970). But planful, organized thinking about one's own thought processes involves logical thinking about an abstraction—thought. The capacity for formal operational thinking seems to give this process a strong boost. Adolescents are much more likely than children to "be introspective in an analytic mode, to think critically about themselves and about the way that they think and behave" (Cowan, 1978, p. 289).

On the positive side, improved metacognitive skill seems to benefit scientific thinking, making it possible for some teens to evaluate their theories or beliefs objectively, in the light of evidence,. Such skill also contributes to more careful planning and evaluation of one's activities. For example, once Rebecca sits down to study for her exam, she may test herself to determine what she has learned so far, evaluate the study strategies she has been using for their effectiveness, and allocate her study time planfully, spending the most time on the information she knows least well (e.g., Flavell & Miller, 1998).

On the more negative side, the self-evaluation and self-monitoring that come with improved metacognitive skill may also contribute to other forms of egocentrism that seem to emerge at adolescence. Elkind (1968), elaborating on some of Piaget's (1964/1968) ideas about adolescence, describes the young teen as intensely self-focused. In a sense, her new capacity for introspection, for evaluating her own mental processes, contributes to an inward focus that is distorting. Although she understands that others have minds of their own and that they have their own concerns, her own fascination with herself, enhanced by the compelling and unpredictable physical changes she is undergoing, leads her to mistakenly assume that others are as intrigued by and concerned about her as she is. Elkind calls this assumption the adolescent's **imaginary audience**. Because she is so sure that others are as interested in her as she is, she feels extremely self-conscious, acutely aware of her looks and her behavior in the presence of others (see also Harter, 2006).

Another feature of the adolescent's self-focus is a distorted view of her own importance. Elkind calls this assumption the **personal fable**. Adolescents often seem to feel that their experiences and concerns are unique. The personal fable may also include fantasies of having a special destiny, an important role to play in the lives of others or on the world stage. A feeling of being invulnerable, even immortal, called the **invincibility fable**, can be a part of this fantasy, perhaps contributing to increases in risk taking at adolescence. Adolescents may reason, for example, that others who drive drunk may get hurt in auto accidents or that others who have unprotected sex may get pregnant, but they don't believe that they themselves would suffer these consequences.

An adolescent's intense self-focus may contribute to a sense of uniqueness or invulnerability, called the invincibility fable.

The notions of imaginary audience and personal fable are useful, but researchers have raised a number of questions about where they originate and when they recede. Elkind (1968) characterized these egocentric developments as a product of formal operational skill, and he suggested that they diminish in later adolescence as a function of interpersonal experience. Sharing ideas and feelings with others, especially peers, helps an adolescent do a better job of perspective taking and helps her to recognize that others are focused on themselves and that her experiences are not unique.

Studies indicate that adolescents' self-focused thought is not as closely associated with the emergence of formal operational skills as Elkind suggested (Lapsley, FitzGerald, Rice, & Jackson, 1989). Lapsley (1993; Lapsley & Murphy, 1985) argues that the social realities of adolescence—the need to separate from parents, to form an adult identity—are at least as important in explaining the egocentrism of the adolescent. He contends that the imaginary audience may be an expression of intense anxiety associated with individuation and that the personal fable may be a useful fantasy for reducing some of that anxiety (see Blos, 1962, for a theoretical discussion of the separation-individuation process).

Whatever the cause or causes of adolescent egocentrism, recent research suggests that it is not a phenomenon that belongs exclusively to teens. Several studies have found that elements of the imaginary audience (extreme self-consciousness) and of the personal fable (a sense of invulnerability) continue at least into early adulthood, sometimes not showing much decline even then (e.g., Frankenberger, 2000; Quadrel, Fischhoff, & Davis, 1993). There is little disagreement that these egocentric tendencies begin in adolescence. It may be, however, that some of us are stuck with them far beyond our teen years.

The newer work on adolescent egocentrism reminds us that even if cognitive change contributes to these processes, the adolescent's cognitive abilities do not operate in a vacuum. They are among the many causal elements in a multidimensional mix. Adolescence brings a remarkable confluence of change into a child's life: change in thinking skills, biochemical and brain functioning, physical shape and size, peer and parental expectations, and educational structures and requirements. In addition, adult responsibility lurks just around the corner. In the next section, we return to the issue of how the child's self-concept evolves, in the midst of all this change, into an adult identity.

IDENTITY DEVELOPMENT

Some Basic Considerations

Identity, or **ego identity** as Erikson first called it, is a concept that is difficult to define. It incorporates and expands on all the dimensions of self-knowledge that have been discussed in previous chapters. Furthermore, it serves as the foundation for the behavioral, affective, and cognitive commitments to career, relationships, and political and religious belief systems that will be made in adulthood. Erikson himself seemed annoyed by others' attempts to reduce the concept of identity to a flat, mental picture of the self. He described himself as registering

> [A] certain impatience with the faddish equation, *never suggested by me*, of the term identity with the question "Who am I?". . . The pertinent question, if it can be put into the first person at all, would be "What do I want to make of myself, and what do I have to work with?" (Erikson, 1968, p. 314)

Note the dynamic, future-oriented quality implied in his statement, which integrates past accomplishments with new directions.

Erikson labeled the process of identity formation in adolescence a "crisis" of "identity versus identity confusion." But his view of the process is more accurately characterized as a specific challenge or task that asserts itself at a particular point in development (see Chapter 1). Erikson himself cautioned against thinking of life stages in terms of either-or propositions. In the case of identity, individuals make choices and have experiences that take them closer to or further away from a meaningful sense of self until one kind of resolution (e.g., identity achievement) predominates over the other (e.g., identity confusion, also called "diffusion"). Some authors suggest that using the term *identity exploration* instead of *identity crisis* for this stage is more appropriate (Marcia, Waterman, Matteson, Archer, & Orlofsky, 1993). Exploration reflects the prolonged effort involved in the discovery process, whereas crisis implies a short-term and possibly traumatic event.

Before we consider the way identity is conceptualized in most research studies, it is important to mention two aspects of Erikson's theory of identity that have generated some discussion: the stability of identity over time and its individualistic emphasis. First, the formation of an identity in adolescence, which is the subject of this section, is not the end of the story. Anyone who has counseled both adolescents and adults will recognize that growth and change of self-representations take place throughout the life span. What makes this particular period of the life cycle remarkable are the impressive strides young people make during the years of adolescence and young adulthood in developing the essential core of how they will be as adults.

All of our life stories are subject to revision by time, place, and circumstance. However, a core sense of self that "fits," to use the words of the poet at the beginning of this chapter, becomes clearer as the years unfold. Erikson (1968) captures the tension between continuity and change by writing that "ego identity could be said to be characterized by the actually attained but *forever to-be-revised* [italics added] sense of the reality of the Self within social reality" (p. 211).

Second, Erikson's identity theory has been criticized by some for being focused on the realization of the autonomous self at the expense of the collectivist self (Gilligan, 1982; Josselson, 1988). Erikson's theory has also been faulted for its "eurocentric" focus, which "assumes the necessity of individuation operationalized at its extreme" (Root, 1999, p. 69). It is true that classic developmental theories originally incorporated a masculine perspective, as we shall discuss in a later section on gender. However, the idea that identity formation requires valuing extreme individual autonomy may erroneously arise from the very nature of what constitutes identity, namely, the "I-ness" of the construct.

Consider these examples. You might be the type of person who tends to be competitive, who values personal ambition, and who single-mindedly pursues certain goals. Or you might be one who is more highly invested in membership in your social network, who works at being a good partner or friend, and whose values are based less on competition and more on meeting the goals of the whole group. Either way, you possess an identity! What has been overlooked in the individualistic–collectivist discussion is Erikson's primary contribution to theorizing about personality—namely, his emphasis on the power of social contexts to shape development. His writing clearly supports the importance of the cultural milieu as formative to personality development. His view is thus quite consistent with the contemporary notion that those values held in highest regard within one's cultural context strongly affect the nature of one's self-representations, worldviews, and commitments (e.g., Markus & Kitayama, 1991).

Adolescent Identity Development

So much has been written about adolescent identity development over the years that it is indeed a formidable task to summarize this wealth of theoretical and empirical knowledge. The most comprehensive empirical exploration of Erikson's theory is provided by James Marcia and his associates (Marcia, 1966, 1989, 1993), who developed a categorical system for labeling the dimensions or patterns that emerge in the identity development process. We will examine this body of work by focusing on the following questions: What are the categories of identity development? How are these categories assessed? Is there a universal sequence of change? Is the developmental trajectory always the same, or does it vary for different groups?

Identity Status

Individuals at adolescence and beyond may be characterized as belonging to one of four identity status categories: **diffusion**, **moratorium**, **foreclosure**, or **achievement**. These categories borrow from Erikson's conceptualization of identity development as a task involving exploration of various possible positions in the world and ultimately making mature commitments to certain ones, such as religion, career, political affiliation, and sexual orientation. Therefore, each status category can be defined by the presence or absence of exploration and commitment. Some of the names are similar to those used by Erikson in his writings. However, even though Erikson called the negative outcome associated with failure to achieve identity "identity diffusion," he did not develop the four identity status categories. Marcia and other researchers constructed these categories in their efforts to operationalize aspects of Erikson's ideas.

Let us consider each of the statuses and examine what they mean. *Diffusion* is the state that often characterizes young adolescents as they embark on the identity development process. In this state, they lack both exploration and commitment. Persons in the diffused category are not actively involved in exploring possible life choices, nor have they made any firm commitments to them. Although this state of affairs is fairly common in early adolescence, diffusion (or confusion) can be highly problematic later on in young adulthood. Persons whose identity is diffused may not trust their ability to find and commit to a meaningful path in life, or they might deny their need to do so. They may lack a sense of optimism about the future and, "many a sick or desperate late adolescent, if faced with continuing conflict, would rather be nobody or somebody totally bad, or, indeed, dead" (Erikson, 1968, p. 176). Alternatively, they may situate themselves within a highly controlling environment that dictates the conditions of their behavior and the nature of their views such as joining a gang.

Individuals in *moratorium* also display a lack of commitment, but they are distinguished from the identity diffused by virtue of their exploration. In other words, these adolescents and young adults are straining toward the future, looking for what they might make of themselves. They may demonstrate frequent shifts in goals and changes in behavior, along with the anxiety and exhilaration that accompany active experimentation. Consequently, these exploratory periods may look like "crises" to the observer. Erikson (1950/1963) defined *moratorium* as the essence of the adolescent mind and in so doing, helped make sense of the transitory, inconsistent, and often incomprehensible nature of many adolescent behaviors. The prize to be gained from this adolescent and early adult trial and error is an identity that has been personally constructed. **Constructed identity** is not based upon a predetermined set of expectations, but represents either a personal redefinition of childhood and early adolescent goals and values or perhaps something very different from them. In moratorium, the future may be perceived as difficult, exciting, or even anxiety producing, but it can be shaped by one's own decision making.

Foreclosure, the third status, describes a category of individuals who make commitments with little or no exploration of alternatives. This status, along with diffusion, may also characterize young people entering adolescence who incorporate the values and goals of significant others, such as their parents, without reflection. Their commitments are, by definition, premature, preordained by family obligation or constrained by circumstance. A very early marriage or settling very early on a career might be examples of this. These kinds of decisions are not always problematic, but they can be. The identity attained by those who are foreclosed is called a **conferred identity**, rather than a constructed one. Foreclosure's perspective on the future involves meeting the expectations of a "prearranged set of ideals, occupational plans, and interpersonal forms" (Marcia, 1993, p. 8). These individuals proceed into the future with the goals and values of early adolescence relatively intact and experience fewer difficulties along the way.

Identity achievement, the fourth of Marcia's categories, comprises individuals whose development has been marked by exploration and commitment to certain alternatives. They have decided on a game plan, so to speak, which may be revised as needed. Their identity has been constructed by their own efforts to shape and transform their earlier selves. In theory, at least, they have reached a valued end point. Studies have generally shown positive correlations between identity achievement and psychological well-being (Meeus, Iedema, Helsen, & Vollebergh, 1999). But is identity, once achieved, really the end of the story? We will discuss this issue in a later section.

Personal and Cognitive Characteristics of Each Identity Status

Much of the early research on identity focused on the behavioral and cognitive correlates of each identity status. Researchers found that those in the achieved category have a more internal locus of control as compared to diffused individuals, who are the most external (Dellas & Jernigan, 1987). Anxiety seems to be lowest for foreclosed groups, whereas it is relatively high among diffused groups and highest among those in moratorium (Marcia, 1967; Sterling & Van Horn, 1989). Foreclosed individuals report the highest levels of authoritarianism, conformity, and obedience to authority; those in moratorium report the lowest levels (Marcia et al., 1993; Podd, 1972). Autonomy is highest among achieved males and females and foreclosed women, but it is lowest in diffused males and females and foreclosed men (Schenkel & Marcia, 1972; Waterman, 1993).

In a study of the role of adolescent egocentrism in identity formation, O'Connor (1995) found that more egocentrism is associated with more exploration and, ultimately, with a greater likelihood of identity achievement, especially in males. Degree of exploration is also associated with more early childhood exposure to creative, technical, and cultural activities provided by parents, as demonstrated by Schmitt-Rodermund and Vondracek (1999). Providing children with early exploratory experiences was positively related to a broader range of interests in adolescence, more exploration in these areas, and later identity achievement.

More recent work links identity status to both risk-taking and prosocial behavior. Individuals in identity diffusion report more risk-taking and less prosocial behavior than individuals in other identity status groups. In addition, foreclosure is more strongly associated with religiosity (defined as strength of religious faith) than the other identity statuses (see Padilla-Walker, Barry, Carroll, Madsen, & Nelson, 2008).

Assessment of Identity Domains

To study identity development, it must be translated into something that can be measured. Erikson viewed occupation and ideology, both political and religious, as expressions of one's identity. Marcia (1964) constructed a standardized, semistructured **Ego Identity Interview** designed to assess these three domains of identity: vocational choice, religious beliefs, and political ideology, using samples of male college students. When his samples were expanded to include women, the domains of work–family conflict (Marcia & Friedman, 1970) and attitudes toward premarital intercourse (Schenkel & Marcia, 1972) were added to the interview schedule. Waterman (1993) distinguishes between the core dimensions that are covered in the majority of studies using the Ego Identity Interview and those that are only occasionally included. Core domains are vocational choice, religious beliefs, political ideology, gender-role attitudes, and beliefs about sexual expression. Supplemental domains include hobbies, friendships, dating relationships, role of spouse, role of parent, experiences at school, and issues of work–family balance. The interview format consists of general questions such as "Should one believe in God or not?" "What type of work would you like to do?" and "What do you see as the advantages and disadvantages of being single versus being married?" followed up by more specific probes. (See Marcia et al., 1993, for the complete interview.)

As you reflect on this approach, you may be reminded of the construct of self-concept, which was discussed in Chapters 5 and 7. The construction of ego identity in adolescence and beyond builds on or incorporates many of the components of self-concept developed earlier, such as social, academic, and physical self-concept. Identity may be construed as an overarching construct, with each domain representing a more specific aspect. Just as individuals vary in their level of self-esteem across domains, individuals will also show variation in the nature of their identity formation and in the timing of developmental progress. Thus, a person might be foreclosed in the area of religious identity but be in moratorium in the area of vocational choice.

Developmental Sequence in Identity Formation

Based upon the previous discussion, you may think the four statuses have the look of a linear, developmental stage model. Frequently, these statuses are interpreted to be synonymous with stages, and, in fact, Marcia (1967) originally proposed that each resided on a continuum, from diffusion to foreclosure to moratorium to achievement, with achievement representing the desirable end state. More recent research has prompted a rethinking of this perspective. Even though achieved and diffused statuses retain their ultimate significance as positive and negative outcomes, there are no compelling theoretical reasons to position foreclosure and moratorium adjacent to each other on the continuum. In addition, most of the studies done on the topic of identity development have used the categories to classify individuals rather than to follow their developmental progress (Meeus, 1996).

Those studies that have tried to find evidence for a universal, step-by-step sequence of identity development have largely come up short because there are many possible ways to move from category to category over time. The theoretical trajectory advanced in early work using Marcia's categories fails to describe other relatively common pathways. Think of a foreclosed individual who unexpectedly encounters a life event that forces her to rethink her commitments. Plunged back into moratorium, she can move into either achievement or diffusion. Another individual, who has become an identity achiever, may reenter moratorium if the goals she once chose no longer fit. Stephen, Fraser, and Marcia (1992) call the frequently observed cycles of movement from identity achievement to moratorium "MAMA" cycles (moratorium-achievement-moratorium-achievement). The pattern is not as neat as was originally anticipated.

So, are we to assume that the status categories merely provide a descriptive model for all possible states of identity development, or is there also evidence for some common developmental trajectory? In general, longitudinal studies of movement across statuses, or of "progressive developmental shifts" (Waterman, 1993), have been supportive of some developmental trends in identity formation.

Meeus and colleagues (1999), who worked with Dutch adolescents, developed a classificatory system based upon Marcia's, with two main distinctions. First, exploration and commitment are separately measured in Meeus's research to provide a more powerful way to demonstrate developmental trends. Second, his classification scheme is based on an individual's current identity development activity without reference to past behavior. For example, diffusion and moratorium categories are similar to Marcia's because the former reflects current disinterest in identity seeking and the latter reflects intense engagement in it. Foreclosure, on the other hand, has been renamed **closed commitment** because it signifies a high level of present commitment with low levels of coexisting exploration. **Achieving commitment** is used instead of achievement because it connotes a dynamic linkage between high levels of commitment and high levels of exploration. Meeus and colleagues explain the differences in approach this way:

> For Marcia, exploration is mainly important in the choice of a commitment, after which it is disregarded, whereas the new statuses are based on the idea that adolescents constantly reconsider their commitments. It is also hypothesized that not only do the commitments become stronger during the course of adolescence, but so too does the exploration of the commitments. A more solid identity structure arises, which is also more carefully considered. (Meeus et al., 1993, p. 433)

Based on their review of the identity development literature as well as the results of their own large-scale longitudinal studies, the conclusions provided by Meeus and his colleagues (1999) reinforce Waterman's (1993) finding of progressive developmental trends across categories. The number of achievements increases over time, whereas foreclosures decrease and diffusions decrease or remain the same. The number of moratoriums does not systematically increase or decrease over time. Thus, the categories defined by Marcia do have some directional, developmental significance. Generally, identity development proceeds toward achievement as a goal, with much of the movement accounted for by increases in achievement and decreases in foreclosure. These authors note, however, that a substantial percentage of adolescents remain in one of the other categories in some or all domains. Interestingly, these findings also indicate that individuals in both the achievement category and the foreclosed category experience high levels of psychological well-being.

Contrary to earlier theoretical perspectives, this suggests that foreclosure may be an adaptive end point for some individuals.

Identity Crisis: Truth or Fiction?

Research such as this indicates that moratorium should be considered a transitional state that has some elements of an identity crisis. Consider the following situation. If you are in diffusion or foreclosure, you might encounter situations, people, or new information that produce a state of disequilibrium. This exposure causes you to rethink old values and adopt new ideas, albeit after some anxiety and reflection. The physical, cognitive, and emotional changes that accompany adolescence, in addition to the more diversified experiences afforded by larger school settings, provide sufficient disruptions of old patterns to jump-start this process for most adolescents.

Consistent with the notion of constructed and conferred identities, Meeus and his associates (1999) found that individuals tended toward foreclosure in areas over which they had little control (e.g., school or work), which these authors called **closed identity domains**. They speculate that in these domains, adolescents "do not find it so useful to reflect intensively on their commitments because they can assert very little influence on them" (p. 456). Crises in more **open identity domains**, such as those involving personal relationships, were found to be shorter, under more personal control, and more likely to result in achieving commitments.

What influences the outcome of a crisis? Waterman (1993) lists a number of factors that support a positive resolution: successful accomplishment of earlier psychosocial tasks, availability of positive role models with achieved identities, and support for exploration of alternatives. Waterman (1993) and Marcia (1980) report that most of the work of identity development, as measured by transitions into and out of status categories, takes place during early adulthood. This is particularly true for students who attend colleges or universities, settings that facilitate exploratory processes. The results of Meeus's (1996) longitudinal study, however, indicate that the high school years are also a time of active identity formation. He found as many, or more, progressive developmental shifts during this period as in early adulthood.

Identity Development and Diverse Groups

Do individuals differ in their identity development processes because they are members of certain groups? In recent years, there has been intense clinical and research interest in the specific identity development patterns of groups differing in gender, race, ethnicity, and sexual orientation. This body of work developed as an offshoot of more classic identity research for a number of reasons. First, there has been general interest in understanding the differences that exist among groups of people. Demographic trends that project a growing multicultural citizenry and social movements that emphasize gay, lesbian, and women's rights, as well as pride in one's ethnic heritage, have sparked increased attention to these issues.

Second, there is a growing concern that traditional theories are insufficient to explain development because they are biased in favor of single-culture or single-gender models. Feminist writers (Archer, 1992; Enns, 1992; Miller, 1991), for example, point out the need to examine women's identity development separately from men's because of their belief that female and male developmental experiences are fundamentally different. Critical of traditional, monocultural approaches, counselors and other clinicians have also called for recognition and integration of diverse perspectives into practitioner training and therapeutic practice because of the relevance of gender, race, and sexual orientation to personal well-being and to client–counselor interaction (Sue, Arrendondo, & McDavis, 1992).

One of the first ways in which the message of diversity was originally promulgated was through an array of identity development theories based on group differences. Developmental schemes have been proposed for identity formation of Blacks (Cross, 1971), Hispanics (Bernal & Knight, 1993), Asian Americans (Sue, Mack, & Sue, 1998), Whites (Helms, 1990), womanists (Parks, Carter, & Gushue, 1996), and lesbians and gays (Cass, 1979). An example of the proliferation of theories can be observed in Eliason's (1996) summary review. She described 11 different theories of "coming out" or identity development for lesbian, bisexual, and gay individuals published in the social science literature. Similarly, Helms (1990) described 11 models of Black identity development.

Clearly, scholarly work in this area was long overdue. The effects of race, culture, class, and gender on development are highly significant. To their credit, these early identity theories broadened our perspective and continue to encourage a more inclusive look at developmental processes. In this section, we will try to examine some of the general issues that pertain to the literature on gendered and racial or ethnic identity development, search for some commonalities, and look at some newer empirical work.

Gender and Identity

Criticism of Erikson's developmental theory has centered on its emphasizing separateness or autonomy, a salient feature of masculine personality, as the desired goal of identity development (Marcia, 1980). Failure to give equal emphasis to the desirability of connectedness to healthy personality development has been viewed as a suppression of women's "voice" (Gilligan, 1982). Consequently, researchers have searched for gender differences in the identity formation process, investigating, for example, whether women's identity development proceeds via a different trajectory than the one traversed by men. Douvan and Adelson (1966) challenged Erikson's view by suggesting that women's successful identity formation depended upon prior resolution of intimacy issues, whereas men's successful resolution of intimacy issues depended first upon achieving identity. Note that in this formulation, the actual developmental progression is assumed to differ by gender, so that the sequence of stages and not simply the salient dimensions of identity are transposed.

How well has Erikson's theory fared when applied to women? Two main questions challenge researchers in this area. First, are certain identity domains differentially important to men versus women? Second, does Erikson's sequence of stages apply to males and females equally well? There is some support for the importance of interpersonal domains for women's identity development (Archer, 1992; Josselson, 1988; Kroger, 1983) and for the fact that relational issues may be more important for women's development than for men's (Meeus & Dekovic, 1995). Meeus and Dekovic, reporting on a cross-sectional study of 3,000 Dutch adolescents, found that girls were much more involved than boys in relationship-related activities (exploration) and experienced more personal satisfaction from them (commitment). Adolescent girls generally have been found to have closer friendships than boys and to be more vulnerable to distress when friendships end (see Collins & Steinberg, 2006), and both adolescent and adult females express more relationship-themed fears about their futures than do males (see Anthis, Dunkel, & Anderson, 2004).

Findings such as these, however, do not imply that other domains, such as vocation and religion, are unimportant for women. Nor should they suggest that relational issues are unimportant for men. In fact, Matteson (1993) summarized the large number of studies in this area and found inconsistent gender differences or no differences, depending upon the methodology employed. Similarly, Archer and Waterman (1988) found no differences between genders in levels of self-actualization, internal locus of control, social interdependence, or moral reasoning, suggesting more similarity than difference

Are relationship-related issues a more important part of the self-definition process for girls than for boys?

in identity development and individuation for males and females. It might be useful to interpret the results this way: When studies do identify differences in aspects of self-definition that are more important to one gender or another, it is more likely but not inevitable that women will assign interpersonal, communal aspects of themselves a higher priority.

The question of whether the actual pathways are different for males and females is also complicated. Erikson's proposal that a secure identity must be achieved before realizing intimacy has not been fully supported by research on either gender. Elkind (1967) suggested the reverse, that sharing perceptions and feelings with others helps all adolescents overcome egocentrism and develop a realistic view of themselves. Some studies indicate that more advanced identity achievement is linked to the formation of intimate relationships, but which is the cause and which the effect is not clear (see Brown, 2004, and Collins & Steinberg, 2006). As we have noted in earlier chapters, a secure sense of self and the ability to relate closely to others are very closely intertwined, such that the causal processes are probably bidirectional. At this point, growth in both autonomy and connection appear to be important to the development of males and females alike. Furthermore, whereas some girls may differ from some boys in their developmental routes, there is no evidence that different trajectories are characteristic of most or all girls versus boys.

Thus, it is likely that the achievement of identity and intimacy progress in tandem, with each gender's expression of the outcome looking somewhat different. Cramer (1999) observed that for males and females who have achieved identity, both genders have high levels of self-esteem, adequacy, and assertiveness. But males and females express these aspects of their personalities in different ways. Males are more likely to assert their adequacy in autonomous ways, whereas females more often do so within the context of social relationships. Overall, Waterman (1993) summarized available research by stating that the genders showed more similarities than differences in processes of identity formation but that the content of their identity choices might differ.

Racial and Ethnic Identity Theories

Distinct theoretical models have also been proposed to explain identity development in different racial and ethnic groups. Researchers have used multiple definitions of "ethnicity" in the studies done on this topic. For our purposes, we will use the term to signify one's sense of belonging to a group and one's beliefs or attitudes concerning group membership (Tajfel, 1981). Despite differences among particular groups, theories of racial or ethnic identity development have certain themes in common. Most describe an initial stage, not unlike diffusion, during which ethnic identity is either unrecognized or considered unimportant. Cross (1994) suggests that this stage may be accompanied by a preference for the dominant culture, although this is not the case for everyone. It may simply be that race or ethnicity is not yet a highly salient feature of one's self-concept. For example, having Mexican heritage may be less important to a young Mexican girl than the fact that she is smart in school, has lots of friends, and is the best soccer player on her team.

In most theories, this period is followed by a moratorium-like stage, typically triggered by some experience that thrusts the importance of one's race or ethnicity to the forefront. This stage is characterized by ambivalence or conflict, as the individual explores and comes to terms with her race or ethnicity. For many young adolescents, it is a time when the racism or cultural oppression that exists in society takes on personal significance. Experiences based on racial and ethnic stereotypes clearly can be salient and central to adolescent development. Here is how author Beverly Daniel Tatum (1997) explains the struggle that her 10-year-old son will likely have:

> When David meets new adults, they don't say, "Gee, you're Black for your age!" If you are saying to yourself, of course they don't, think again. Imagine David, at fifteen, six-foot-two, wearing the adolescent attire of the day, passing adults he doesn't

This teen recognizes that "there are certain things that people expect" from Asian children. How would you characterize this girl's ethnic identity at this point in her life?

know on the sidewalk. Do the women hold their purses a little tighter, maybe even cross the street to avoid him? Does he hear the sound of the automatic door locks on the cars as he passes by? Is he being followed around by the security guards at the local mall? As he stops in town with his new bicycle, does a police officer hassle him, asking where he got it, implying that it might be stolen? Do strangers assume he plays basketball? Each of these experiences conveys a racial message. At ten, race is not yet salient for David, because it is not yet salient for society. But it will be. (p. 54)

In a looking-glass society that sorts people on the basis of race, ethnicity, and appearance and then reflects back to them the measure of their worth, early adolescence is a time when many youngsters such as David, who are members of minority or marginalized groups, confront the negative stereotypes and discriminatory practices of others head on. In a startling real life example of such experiences, the first African American president of the United States, Barack Obama, tells the story of his own White grandmother, who admitted to him that she often had been fearful when she saw a Black man walking toward her, for no other reason than that he was Black. How do minority youth respond to such discriminatory views and behavior? Theories suggest that some adolescents may immerse themselves in their racial or cultural groups or even actively reject the dominant culture during this period.

In most theoretical formulations, the highest stage is achieved when the individual, having actively explored what her ethnicity means, affirms her identity as a member (commitment). Phinney (1989, 1990, 2003) argues that ethnic identity development can be seen as reflecting the same four statuses that characterize other aspects of identity, indicating the degree to which individuals have explored the meaning of their ethnicity/race in their lives. She asserts that the resolution—identity achievement—is twofold: (1) reconciling the differences that exist between the ethnic minority group and the dominant group, and (2) coming to terms with the lower status of one's group within the larger society. She also states, however, that this achievement does not necessarily need to coexist with a high level of involvement in one's own cultural group. The overall pattern of stages is similar to formulations of homosexual/bisexual identity development as well. Cross and Fhagen-Smith (2001), referring specifically to African American identity, suggest that adolescents can go through a process of exploration of what race means, and thereby achieve ethnic identity. Or if their families use positive racial socialization practices, they may have a foreclosed identity, which can be a positive result. But if they fail to commit to a racial identity during adolescence, they may be vulnerable to later discriminatory experiences that are likely to cause distress and instigate a rethinking of racial identity. In describing identity development of Latino adolescents, Supple and colleagues (Supple, Ghazarian, Frabutt, Plunkett, & Sands, 2006) identify a similar process. Their stages included exploration (engagement with cultural activities and roles), resolution (coming to understand the meaning of identifying with one's culture) and affirmation (accepting and identifying with oneself and one's group). This study found that exploration and resolution were primarily related to parental socialization efforts. However, affirmation of cultural identity depended as well on the interaction of parenting quality and environmental context, such as neighborhood safety. Highly supportive parenting, in the context of neighborhood security, was positively related to ethnic identity affirmation. Low quality, harsh parenting in the context of more dangerous surroundings showed the opposite effect. For Latino adolescents, strong ethnic identity operated as a protective factor and contributed to better academic performance. The authors conclude that ethnic identity is shaped by a number of interacting variables and is enhanced by the quality of the micro and exo-systems.

Other research seems consistent with this view. When minority group membership is central to high school and college students' identity, that ethnic identity appears to both increase sensitivity (awareness of) discrimination and protect psychological well-being in the face of discrimination (Neblett, Shelton, & Sellers, 2004; Greene, Way, & Pahl, 2006). Yip, Seaton, and Sellers (2006) found that for African American adolescents, college students, and adults, having an achieved ethnic identity status was associated with racial centrality (seeing race as an important aspect of self) and with private regard (seeing one's race as positive). For college students, achieved status also appeared to be a protective factor against depression.

Because having a strong ethnic identity confers many benefits on children, parents engage in **racial/ethnic socialization practices**. Racial/ethnic socialization includes several main elements (Boykin and Toms, 1985): (1) teaching about culture, cultural values, and participating in cultural activities, (2) preparing children for the possible experience of discrimination, and (3) providing them with opportunities for mainstream cultural experiences and egalitatrian relationships with others from different groups. In general, messages about racial and ethnic pride and participation in activities that reflect shared heritage lead to many positive increases in competence, identity, self-esteem, academic achievement, and less antisocial behavior (Wang & Huguley, 2012). Arming youth against the threat of racial discrimination has more mixed results. For example, preparing African American children for experiences of discrimination strengthened their connections with family members but lowered their academic performance and heightened depression and feelings of hopelessness in some studies (Davis & Stevenson, 2006; Evans et al., 2012). Some research showed that adolescents' expectations about discrimination fostered hostility and antisocial behavior (Hughes, Rodriguez, Smith, Johnson, Stevenson, & Spicer, 2006).). It is possible that teaching children about the realities of discrimination, which appears to be protective, needs to be decoupled from the promotion of mistrust. Providing opportunities for mainstream activities and fostering cross-racial friendships are related to better social skills and overall adjustment (Graham, Taylor, & Ho, 2009).

Issues in the Study of Racial or Ethnic and Sexuality Development

Remember the question posed about the true nature of Marcia's categories: Do they represent real stage transitions or do they simply classify groups of people? We can respond that evidence is sufficient to demonstrate a directional, developmental trend toward achievement and away from diffusion, despite the fact that individual trajectories may not follow the same course or sequence in detail. The research that supports this description has been longitudinal in design.

Until recently, much of the writing in the area of gender, racial or ethnic, and sexuality development has been theoretical rather than empirical. Much of the research was, and continues to be, cross-sectional, which cannot adequately elucidate the processes underlying development. Consequently, the unique stagewise progressions proposed in many identity theories have typically not been established as distinct developmental pathways. More longitudinal work is becoming available so that we can expect this situation to change in the near future (e.g., Diamond, 2008).

There are other methodological problems in the existing body of research as well. In the area of sexuality and gender development, for example, we have noted previously that there is considerable disagreement and uncertainty about what the categories of gender and sexual orientation are or should be, especially given that for many individuals a multiplicity of categorizations seem to apply (e.g., Diamond, 2007; Thompson & Morgan, 2008). Even terms such as *race, ethnicity*, and *culture* are often used by different authors to signify different things, adding to the confusion (e.g., Parke & Buriel, 2006). The term sexuality development has replaced sexual development over the past decade reflecting the fluidity and interconnectedness of physical and psychological development over the course of coming to understand one's sexuality.

Assuming that members of a race or ethnic group are homogeneous on variables such as ethnic identity is another problem. In a study of Latino/Latina adolescents living in the United States, Umana-Taylor and Fine (2001) found evidence for heterogeneity of ethnic identification among Colombian, Guatemalan, Honduran, Mexican, Nicaraguan, Puerto Rican, and Salvadoran participants. These authors concluded that grouping individuals from these Latino/Latina cultures into one collective ethnic group masked some real differences. The authors suggest the need to consider generational status, immigration history, and nationality to refine our understanding of ethnic identity.

Is whiteness a racial characteristic or a social-cultural one? Whatever stance you take on this issue, it is generally a good idea for people to consider the place of their own race, culture, and ethnicity in their self-definition. For members of the dominant White culture, race is often a nonissue in conceptualizations of identity, and many writers have pointed out that Whites are largely unaware of themselves in racial terms. In other words, White people fail to recognize how their being White

Box 9.2: Choosing an Identity: The Case of Multiracial Youth

Carlos was born in California. His mother is part Filipino and part Mexican. His father is White. In ninth grade, he filled out a questionnaire that asked him to "Select the major ethnic group that best describes you." Carlos picked "White." How did he make his choice?

That was the question that Melissa Herman (2004) addressed as she examined questionnaire data from nearly 9,000 adolescents surveyed in California and Wisconsin schools in the 1980s. Students were asked to "select the one major ethnic group that best describes you" with the choices being Black, Native American, White, Asian, Hispanic, and Pacific Islander. Students were also asked to select the ethnic background(s) of their parents, and in this case they were given the opportunity to select more than one answer. From the data they provided on their parents, Herman was able to identify nearly 1,500 kids with multiracial or multiethnic backgrounds.

Americans are frequently asked to identify race or ethnicity on questionnaires, from political surveys to SAT exams, and in many of these situations they are not given the choice of identifying themselves in more than one way. Herman looked for what factors seem to influence the choices that young people make when forced to choose. The questionnaire they completed also probed the teens' views of themselves and their ethnicity with questions on global self-esteem, on perceived importance of ethnic background for self-definition, on overall feelings about their ethnic background (from strongly negative to strongly positive), and on perceived ethnic discrimination (e.g., "How often are teachers unfair or negative to you because of your ethnic background?"). In addition, data were collected from other sources. The respondents' yearbook pictures were coded for apparent race by a group of independent observers. Demographic information like socioeconomic status was assessed by looking at parents' education level and at U.S. Census Bureau information on average income in a census tract.

Herman also looked at context variables. Did one or both parents reside with the adolescent? If just one, which one? What ethnic group characterized the adolescents' friends? What was the ethnic makeup of the student's neighborhood and school?

Herman categorized students as either monoracial or biracial, using a complex formula to determine biracial status if they reported more than two racial backgrounds for their parents. Biracial minority White adolescents, especially those whose minority category was "Black," were more likely to identify with their minority category than to identify as White, a finding reported by other researchers as well (e.g., Quintana, 1999). All groups felt positively about their ethnic background, and biracial adolescents' feelings were about the same as monoracials'. For example, monoracial Asians and biracial Asian Whites reported similar feelings about their ethnicity, although both were somewhat less positive than most other groups. Interestingly, although both monoracial non-Whites and biracial kids reported experiencing ethnic discrimination, they also had self-esteem scores that were comparable to those of Whites who reported experiencing little or no discrimination. In fact, monoracial Blacks had somewhat higher self-esteem scores than Whites, although monoracial Asians had somewhat lower scores.

How did students decide what racial identity to report? As we saw already, the majority of biracial adolescents identified with their minority category. Those biracial teens who identified as "White" were more likely than others to look White to observers or to live with a White parent. There were some effects of larger contexts as well, mostly for Hispanic White biracials. For these kids, living in a more affluent or White neighborhood predicted identifying as White. Ironically though, attending a largely White high school predicted identifying as Hispanic. Perhaps for some teens, under some conditions, being in the minority highlights their distinctiveness and makes a non-White category identification more likely. There were other findings that were specific to certain biracial groups. For example, Native American White biracials, even those who looked White to observers, almost never identified as being White.

Biracial adolescents' perceptions of the importance of ethnicity issues in their lives were among the strongest predictors of their identity choices. First, if a minority White biracial teen reported experiencing a good deal of ethnic discrimination, she was more likely to identify as non-White. Second, if she felt that ethnicity was an important aspect of her identity, she was also more likely to identify as non-White. Similarly, Quintana (1999) reported that for college students, sensitivity to ethnicity issues was a key factor in deciding their ethnic identity. Most of her respondents identified as non-White, they said, because they felt it was "the right thing to do." They cited reasons such as the history of oppression of non-White groups or their loyalty to a non-White parent (who was likely to be the parent with whom they had most contact). It is not clear from these data whether focus on ethnicity causes adolescents to adopt a minority identity or the reverse. More than likely, it is a bidirectional process, such that kids who are sensitive to ethnicity issues (e.g., who experience or have concern about racial discrimination) are prone to adopt a minority status, and kids who adopt a minority status are more likely to confront and be sensitized to issues like discrimination. In contrast, Whites do not usually perceive racial status to be an important aspect of their own identities, and they tend not to recognize the privilege it conveys. Herman found this to be true of both White monoracials and of biracials who identified as White in her study.

(i.e., the "in-group") in a society stratified on the basis of race influences their attitudes and behaviors toward themselves and toward members of other racial groups (i.e., the "out-groups"; see Helms, 1990). This myopic and possibly unintentional perspective comes at a price, these authors conclude, because it perpetuates one's point of view as the "real" one, serves as a filter for all information that is race related, and has the effect of maintaining White dominance or privilege. Essentially, it is a failure of perspective taking, with serious consequences for the broader society.

It seems reasonable to interpret the issues of race and ethnicity as content domains that figure prominently in the identities of group members, somewhat like vocation, ideology, and relationship domains. Fully understanding identity construction in adolescence requires uncovering the factors that influence how young people view themselves vis-a-vis these domains. (See Box 9.2.) Phinney (2000) noted that for members of ethnic minorities, identity development is more complex than it is for persons in the dominant culture because they have to confront and integrate more aspects of themselves. However, as with gender, the underlying developmental processes of identity formation, such as exploration and commitment, are the same.

APPLICATIONS

Adolescence is associated with major cognitive advances and gains in physical strength and vitality. However, this period is also notable for the onset of many physical and mental health problems that are *preventable* and that persist into adulthood, interfering with educational achievement and work productivity in long-lasting ways (Costello, Foley, & Angold, 2006; Spear, 2010). A recent Centers for Disease Control and Prevention (CDC) report (2010) confirms that behaviors which pose a physical and mental health risk across the lifespan often have their beginnings in childhood and adolescence and should be addressed by means of school health and other programmatic interventions to potentially reverse this trend.

Clearly, the dimensions of need are great, and evidence from large-scale epidemiological studies suggests the global scope of this problem (Patel, Flisher, Hetrick, & McGorry, 2007). Conduct problems have increased significantly over successive cohorts in the UK since 1958 (Collishaw, Maughan, Goodman, & Pickles, 2004). In Australia, affect-related disorders, including substance abuse disorders, contribute 60% to 70% of the disease burden in young people (Public Health Group, 2005). The U.S. Surgeon General's report (2001) concludes that 1 out of 5 children and adolescents in the United States suffers from significant social, emotional, and behavioral problems that place them at risk for school failure. A 1993 report by the American Academy of Pediatrics (AAP) that contained a list of threats to adolescent well-being was updated in 2001 to include the following items: school problems (including learning disabilities and attention difficulties), mood and anxiety disorders, adolescent suicide and homicide, firearms in the home, school violence, drug and alcohol abuse, HIV/AIDS, and the effects of media on violence, obesity, and sexual activity (AAP, 2001). These were called the "new morbidities." As Dahl (2004) observes, most of these threats derive from emotional and behavioral dysregulation. It is important for professionals to understand the scope of these competencies and these challenges in order to work effectively with youth. The topic of adolescent suicide, a major cause of mortality in adolescence, will be discussed in Chapter 10.

Growing Pains

Psychologically, all adolescents need room to grow and safe places to test their newly emerging selves. Using knowledge of the processes of exploration and commitment as a framework, counselors can start the assessment process by considering how the particular adolescent before them is going about meeting her needs for autonomy, relatedness, and competence. The ways in which adolescents try to meet each of these needs will look very different at age 14 than they did at age 8. Some teenage behaviors seem strange and annoying, but they might not be dangerous. Helping parents and others sort this out can be very helpful. In other cases when alternatives may be lacking, teenagers might try to meet their fundamental needs in ways that are potentially harmful. Helping adolescents find healthy and developmentally appropriate routes for expressing independence, for feeling part of a social group, and for experiencing satisfaction in accomplishment provides a sound basis for helping. Based upon the material presented in this chapter, counselors should also keep in mind that the teenage years are a time of active exploration. Striving to make early college decisions or committing to a career path while in high school may be developmentally inappropriate goals for many adolescents who lack the life experience necessary to make personally meaningful choices. Although teenagers who make these decisions may appear mature to observers and may establish themselves as role models for their peers, their behavior may actually reflect a pseudo-maturity that is more akin to premature foreclosure in certain domains, such as vocational identity.

A certain amount of egocentrism appears to go with the adolescent territory. It is often quite a bit easier for parents and other adults to respond authoritatively, with love and limits, to children when they are young. Something in the nature of their open dependence makes adults feel needed, valued, and important. The task often gets harder during the teenage years, at least in cultures and families that value independence and opportunities for personal expression. Being an adult authority figure in an adolescent's life may entail some hard times, when love and patience are put to the test. Sometimes adolescents' self-absorption seems impenetrable. In what may mirror adolescents' own sense of separateness, adults also can feel isolated.

Watching teenagers struggle with the problems of adolescence is painful, particularly when they behave egocentrically, when they are emotionally volatile, when they act as if they do not want or need our help, or when they actively rebel against the limits we have set. In some especially difficult situations, teenagers have managed to convince the adults around them that they are their equals and that they are entitled to wield much of the power. Some adults are inclined to avoid the grueling job of limit setter and enforcer because they may feel worn down, may have their own personal struggles to contend with, or may simply not know what to do. Sometimes parents take their cues, despite their better judgment, from other teenagers' more permissive families. Adults who are responsible for adolescents need to be committed to authoritative practices for the long haul. Despite their protestations, the last thing adolescents need is for parents, teachers, or counselors to disengage from them or abdicate their authoritative role (see Chapter 10). In particular, research has shown that involved and vigilant parenting has been critically important in protecting poor African American youth from potentially dangerous outcomes like delinquency (Brody et al., 2001).

Navigating Special Challenges

For adolescents from socially stigmatized or other disadvantaged groups, the process of resolving the challenge posed by Erikson (1968), "What do I want to make of myself, and what do I have to work with?" may be more complicated than for others. The constricted opportunity experienced by some adolescents because of societal discrimination, cultural intolerance, poverty, or lack of support can make the identity domains of relationships, school, and work "closed" domains, accommodating little positive exploration. Prevention and/or intervention in this situation might depend upon opening up opportunities for exploration as well as supporting commitments.

Given the salience of racial and ethnic group membership for minority individuals, the emergent identity development process in adolescence, and the benefits that attach to a healthy sense of self-worth in general, culturally sensitive efforts have been advanced that combine goals of fostering pride in one's group affiliation with meeting developmental challenges adaptively. Some of these efforts blend storytelling or narrative therapy with social-learning theory principles such as modeling and reinforcement. Costantino, Malgady, and Rogler (1994) developed narrative role-modeling therapy as a way to help Hispanic older children and early adolescents (ages 9 to 11) take pride in their heritage and learn to overcome obstacles using techniques of story construction and role-play. The group treatment consists of three phases: (1) group members create a story using a card from the picture set of the Tell-Me-a-Story (TEMAS) test (Costantino, Malgady, & Rogler, 1986) portraying multiracial Hispanic characters; (2) group members share their own personal experiences with problems depicted in the constructed

stories while the therapist reinforces adaptive responses; and (3) group members role-play the story which is videotaped and later discussed. In one study, results of this treatment showed reductions in conduct problems for the treatment group but these effects were strongest for the younger participants. Interventions intended for older participants (ages 12 to 14) aimed at enhancing pride in ethnic identity by highlighting stories of cultural heroes and heroines had mixed success (Malgady, Rogler, & Costantino, 1990). These researchers hypothesized that age and family context mediated outcomes for early adolescents. For example, even though female adolescents who lived with both parents felt "more Puerto Rican" after the intervention, their self-esteem decreased, possibly due to the idealized heroism of the role models compared to their own parents. As adolescents, they could construct ideals and were more able to use them to make social comparisons. In contrast, both males and females from single-parent homes reported higher self-esteem following the program. These results underscore the need for more context-specific and gender-specific research in culture-sensitive interventions as well as careful clinical judgment when selecting treatments.

An example of a culturally sensitive program that supports adolescent identity development more broadly is the Strong African American Families Program (SAAF; Brody et al., 2004). This prevention program, designed for rural African American mothers and their 11-year-old children, is based on strengthening parent and youth protective factors. Of primary interest here is that adaptive racial socialization is considered a protective factor based on evidence that minority children who receive explicit information about the nature of racial prejudice, adaptive ways of dealing with discrimination, and the clear message that they can be successful despite this reality have better academic success and more positive expectations about the future (Hughes & Chen, 1999).

Presumably, these active socialization practices assist adolescents in managing their personal encounters with racism and help reduce internalization of negative messages as their sense of personal identity matures. One trial of the 7-week program included seven separate meetings for mothers and adolescents (Brody et al., 2004). Parent sessions covered topics about involved parenting, racial socialization, and communication about sexuality and alcohol use. Youth sessions covered such topics as following family rules, setting goals for the future, adaptive ways of handling racism, and resistance strategies for alcohol and drugs. Joint parent–child sessions were also held once a week. Outcome assessment revealed increased goal-directed future orientation and more negative attitudes about drug and alcohol use for youth participants and improved communication skills for parent participants 7 months after program completion.

Programs such as this demonstrate a more layered approach to the developmental challenges facing adolescents in their search for identity, teaching them skills for meeting life's challenges and mobilizing important family support systems concurrently. Although not an explicit focus of these interventions, schools also have a part to play. Helms (2003) suggests that educators foster appreciation of students' cultures by infusing culture-specific information into academic work and group discussions. She advises professionals to model empathy for their students, to notice the ways that cultural differences play out in schools and affect student achievement, and to advocate for policies that promote healthy development for all.

Stages: Pros and Cons

Most identity development theories contain elements of exploration and commitment. But, as Savin-Williams and Diamond (1999) note in regard to "coming-out" models of gay, lesbian and bisexual identity, "with few exceptions, their empirical base is extraordinarily weak, in large part because they are top-down models and few researchers have been willing to investigate the methodological complexities of assessing these models" (p. 247). Helpers should be wary of rigid adherence to a single developmental pathway. Real life is rarely as orderly as the stage theories might suggest.

However, the goal of many of these theoretical frameworks is to promote sensitivity to the unique needs and particular challenges faced by members of specific groups. Even though external behaviors or outcomes may differ for different groups, underlying developmental processes are similar. For gay, lesbian, and bisexual adolescents, two central identity development processes, sexual questioning and disclosure to others, have been identified by Savin-Williams and Diamond (1999). These bear some resemblance to exploration and commitment. Individuals' paths through the processes of self-questioning and self-labeling, however, are extremely diverse, related to their gender, complicated by minority group membership, influenced by family acceptance or rejection, and without any one necessarily correct end point. These authors advise clinicians to be sensitive to the fact that lesbian, gay, and bisexual youth are struggling to come to terms with their own sexual orientation often *before* they understand what the issue really is. At first, conflicts might be expressed as feeling "different." This feeling can exist in the context of societal condemnation or actual threats and rejection, a state of affairs that exacerbates the sense of isolation. For some, the struggle can seriously undermine positive identity development and put them at risk for depression and even suicide (Garafolo, Wolf, Wissow, Woods, & Goodman, 1999).

As is the case with other identity domains, the timing and nature of sexual identity development is quite varied. Although more young people today begin to self-disclose shortly after puberty and to identify as gay, lesbian, or bisexual by the end of the adolescent period, others don't self-identify until late adolescence (Savin-Williams & Diamond, 1999). Contrary to what has been the conventional wisdom, the majority of gender-minority youth experience same-sex as well as other-sex attractions in the process of coming out (Garafolo et al., 1999). Consequently, clinicians should provide youth with support, information, and a safe place to explore their concerns without imposing any sexual identity on them prematurely. Putting youth in touch with agencies or support groups may be helpful in providing both a sense of belonging and the recognition that others have shared their struggles. Finally, counselors should not forget that

these youth are more than just the sum of their sexual identity. Positive development requires attention to the full range of adolescent experiences, including promoting positive peer and family relationships, successful academic performance, and vocational development (Diamond & Savin-Williams, 2003).

Sexuality in Adolescence

National surveys reflect what adults probably already know: Teenagers are engaging in sexual activity. Teens are also still at high risk for sexually transmitted diseases (STDs) because they are likely to have multiple sexual partners, to have older sexual partners, and to engage in unprotected sex. More than half of new HIV infections occur in young people under 25 years old, with males more likely than females to be newly infected (Harper, 2007). Female adolescents of color and male adolescents who have sex with other males " . . . are carrying the disproportionate burden of HIV infection and AIDS" (Harper, 2007, p. 806).

So despite some declines, these reports indicate that young people are engaging in sexual practices in greater numbers and at earlier ages than generations before them (Zimmer-Gembeck & Helfand, 2008). Yet most adolescents do not have accurate information about the risks associated with these practices. This may not be too surprising, given adolescents' egocentrism and their sense of invulnerability. A study published by the Washington, D.C. Urban Institute discovered that most teenagers did not believe that oral or anal sex was "real" sex. Thus, kids concluded, it was safe and had the added benefit of preserving girls' virginity (see Gaiter, 2001). Fewer than one quarter of teenagers ages 16 to 24 indicate that they have any knowledge at all about HIV/AIDS, according to an MTV survey of 4,140 U.S., Asian, European, and Latin American youth. Approximately one third of the group believed that only drug users who shared needles could get it; 16% believed that only homosexuals contracted the disease. This ignorance exists within a climate of adult reluctance to discuss sexuality and exaggerated and, some say, degrading sexual saturation in movies, music, TV, and Internet, all of which bombard media-savvy teenagers (Brown, Steele, & Walsh-Childers, 2002).

Caring adults need to address this situation with a combination of information, vigilance, empathy, awareness, and authority. Helpers can establish a trusting, nonpunitive relationship that fosters sharing of information and reduces the anxiety involved in disclosing personal information. With respect to younger adolescents who are particularly dependent upon the support of adults, counselors must work to include a family member or other guardian in treatment. Given the earlier onset of puberty today, experts recommend that efforts to educate about health and sexuality begin at earlier ages, before or at pubertal onset both for boys and for girls (Susman, Dorn, & Schiefelbein, 2003). Parents, by monitoring their children's behavior and by expressing their values, have more influence on the sexual behavior of early adolescents than of late adolescents (Zimmer-Gembeck & Helfand, 2008).

More research is needed to identify the most effective ways to reduce risky sexual behavior. In general, education about health promotion and disease prevention is an important component. Some research demonstrates that abstinence-only programs are ineffective in delaying sexual activity, pregnancy, and STDs compared to comprehensive sex education that incorporates discussion of the benefits of abstinence with information about contraception (Starkman & Rajani, 2002). Schools that offer on-site clinic services and health counseling to students have lower rates of pregnancy when compared with schools without these services (Zabin, Hirsch, Smith, Streett, & Hardy, 1986). A comprehensive look at U.S. sex-education programs suggests that offering abstinence as the *only* option for teenagers is not defensible from a scientific perspective and compromises the possibility of disseminating useful information about reproductive health (Santelli et al., 2006).

Education, important as it is, appears to be less effective than the combination of education and appropriate counseling. St. Lawrence and associates (1995) report that youth enrolled in a cognitive-behavioral treatment program that trained them in refusal skills, problem solving, knowledge of contraceptive choices, and coping had lower rates of risky sexual activity than youth given education alone. Based upon their work with HIV prevention in adults, Schreibmen and Freidland (2003) suggest that clinicians should incorporate prevention-focused information in each counseling session when dealing with clients at risk. Their advice might be useful to adapt to at-risk adolescents as well. Counselors' focus on prevention need not take the form of didactic messages but rather should be the basis for discussing practical steps toward risk reduction. Because topics of sexuality (or other risky behaviors, for that matter) may be difficult to broach, clinicians may use scripted phrases to introduce these issues sensitively. These are a series of questions that can draw clients into the conversation while minimizing discomfort. For example,

> "Now that we've finished discussing your medications, I'd like to ask you some questions about your sex and drug behaviors. What behaviors are you involved in now? Would you feel comfortable discussing them? Can you think of anything you might like to change about these behaviors? . . . How important is reducing risk behavior to you (on a scale of 1 to 10) and how confident are you that you can do this (on a scale of 1 to 10)?" (p. 1174)

Findings from the large Add study showed that parents played the key role in reducing their children's risky sexual behavior. The quality of the parent-adolescent relationship was related to lower levels of unprotected sex, later timing of first sexual experience, and reduced rates of sexually transmitted diseases (Deptula, Henry, & Schoeny, 2010). This association was especially strong in younger adolescents. These findings point to a role for strengthening family relationships as a means to address adolescent sexuality development.

Special Needs of Sexual Minority Youth

It is now quite clear that sexual minority youth (gay, lesbian, bisexual and transgender) suffer more than their heterosexual counterparts on a number of fronts. Results from a recent YRBSS study (Kann et al., 2011) of gay, lesbian and bisexual adolescents showed that these groups engage in much higher rates of health-compromising behavior than heterosexual peers

(e.g. not attending school because of safety issues, suicide-related behaviors, abuse of drugs and alcohol, unsafe sexual practices, poor diet, lack of exercise, smoking, etc.). They experience more family rejection, more bullying, more verbal abuse, and more overall stress than heterosexuals (Tolman & McClelland, 2011). The potentially negative social consequences of "coming out" make disclosure of sexual identity a particularly difficult developmental task.

Professionals who work with sexual minority youth can help them by attending to the special dimensions of their adolescent experience and by being alert to the risks associated with sexual minority status. The following clinical guidelines are offered by Telingator and Woyewodzic (2011).

1. As a helper, consider your own attitudes, anxieties, and judgments insofar as they influence the quality of the professional relationship.
2. Be aware that social stigma and fear of rejection can make a young person try to hide sexual identity and discount sexual feelings.
3. Allow for openness around the issues of sexuality, sexual attractions, and gender identity so that the young person experiences a place that is safe for honest self-exploration.
4. Consider that sexual identity development is a fluid process that may manifest in changing attractions and orientations over time.
5. Help the adolescent identify real and reliable sources of support among family, friends, and community members and assist the young person in accessing them.
6. Family support is the key protective factor. Work with the adolescent's family to strengthen attachments that will protect against risk. Clinical work with the family may involve supporting family members themselves and helping them understand fears and uncertainties about their child's sexual identity.

The Path Ahead

Some adolescents manage to make the transition to young adulthood in ways that evidence only mild or sporadic periods of upset, whereas others appear to be on a long roller-coaster ride. The temperament and capacities of the adolescent, the contributions of earlier experience, and the fit between the individual and the spheres that influence her will uniquely affect the adolescent experience. Despite the widely different ways that adolescents engage in the process of exploration, Erikson (1968) believed that the reward for the search was the achievement of "fidelity," or something to hold on to.

In other words, the adolescent who is in search of a way to be in the world, may appear confused, lost, and bewildering to others. Yet, this process is a necessary part of the moratorium that precedes the achievement of greater stability. As Josselson (1994) points out, this search is fundamentally a dialogue that the adolescent does not engage in alone. The success of adolescents' search for fidelity depends upon the community's fidelity to adolescents as they search.

FOCUS ON DEVELOPMENTAL PSYCHOLOGY

Eating Disorders

Food occupies a privileged place in human society. It supports life and social connectedness, offers pleasure, and communicates cultural and religious values. Maslow (1954), in his famous hierarchy of needs, puts food solidly at the foundation of the pyramid because of its importance to basic survival. Why, then, do some individuals refuse to eat or eat in such disordered ways as to create enormous emotional and physical suffering? These disturbances, called eating disorders (APA, 2000), are not a new phenomenon. Bulimic behaviors were seen in the ancient societies of Greece and Rome. Anorexia, or self starvation, was associated with fasting in the Middle Ages (Brumberg, 1988). But during the latter part of the 20th century, media images of shockingly emaciated anorexic figures and heartbreaking stories of bulimic binging and purging have raised public consciousness about eating disorders, to both fascinate and repel us.

Eating disorders are marked by dramatically aberrant patterns of eating which affect females far more often than males, with ratios between 10 or 20 to 1, although rates of eating pathology among males appear to be increasing (Carlatt, Camargo, & Herzog, 1997; Hoek, 1993). Homosexual males, in particular, are reported to suffer disproportionately from eating disorders compared to their heterosexual peers (Ricciardelli & McCabe, 2004). Eating disorders are frequently accompanied by other psychiatric conditions and have very high rates of inpatient hospitalization, suicide attempts, and, in the case of anorexia, the highest mortality rate of any mental illness (Birmingham, Su, Hlynsky, Goldner, & Gao, 2005). The DSM recognizes three conditions, anorexia nervosa (AN), bulimia nervosa (BN), and binge-eating disorder (BED).

Anorexia nervosa, a disorder characterized by refusal to maintain adequate body weight (below 85%) for age and height, has two subtypes. The restricting type maintains a malnourished state by not eating or by caloric restriction. The binge eating/purging type also shows marked weight loss but the course of disease is punctuated by bursts of binging and/or purging. Binges are typically followed by some type of compensatory action (self-induced vomiting, use of laxatives or diuretics, or extreme exercise routines). Those who suffer from AN have highly distorted cognitions about body shape and size.

The disease is deadly. Keel and colleagues (2003) report that those with anorexia are 57 times more likely to die from suicide than are their non-eating-disordered peers. They are also 12 times more likely than peers to die from causes unrelated to suicide. As an example of the variable course of the disorder in relative percentages, consider a hypothetical group of 10 people (100%) who suffer from AN. Roughly 5 will experience a reasonably successful recovery, 3 will continue to experience AN symptoms that manifest intermittently throughout adulthood, 1 will experience chronic AN symptoms, and 1 will die from the illness (Strober, Freeman, & Morrell, 1997). Rates of anorexia are reported to be increasing, despite the lack of extensive epidemiological studies (Johnson, Cohen, Kasen, & Brook, 2006). Although for years anorexia was regarded as a disease affecting mid to

high SES white females, incidence is also increasing within minority groups (Decaluwe, Braet, & Fairburn, 2003).

 Teens with anorexia often mention feeling pride in their ability to control themselves and their eating. This girl has been in treatment for 2 years with various therapists, a psychiatrist, and a nutritionist. Why might she, more so than others struggling with similar eating disorders, have a good chance of moving past this disorder?

Bulimia nervosa is characterized by repeated binge eating and compensatory behaviors at least once a week for 3 months. Those who suffer from BN may remain at normal weight but only do so by relying on purging, laxative use, or excessive exercise. Furthermore, like those who suffer from anorexia, they share cognitive distortions about body shape and size and the tendency to base their self-esteem on these dimensions. Bulimia manifests in two subtypes: purging, which includes regular self-induced vomiting or use of laxatives, enemas, and so on and non-purging, which includes excessive fasting or exercise. Binge eating disorder is characterized by periods of uncontrolled eating at least once a week for three months without any compensatory behavior.

Etiology of Eating Disorders

Many theories have been proposed to account for the puzzling phenomenon of disordered eating, including genetic, personality, family systems, cultural and developmental explanations. Clearly, eating disorders represent a good example of multiply determined disorders, for no one causal factor is sufficient to explain their emergence (Kaye, Klump, Frank, & Strober, 2000). Currently, the search is on for pathways that explain how these factors interact to result in eating pathology.

There is some evidence for the influence of genetically-transmitted risk insofar as AN and BN appear to cluster in families (Lilenfeld, Kaye, & Stroeber, 1997). For example, there is a 10-fold increased risk of suffering from anorexia among first-degree relatives of AN patients (Strober, Freeman, Lampert, Diamond, & Kaye, 2000) and a 2- to 4-fold increase in the probability of developing bulimia for first and second degree relatives of BN patients (Hsu, 1990). Research in molecular genetics is being carried out to identify the particular genetic variability associated with risk of AN, but understanding is still incomplete (Bulik, Sullivan, Tozzi, Furberg, Lichtenstein, & Pedersen, 2006). Researchers have also recognized that the hormonal and neurotransmitter abnormalities associated with AN and BN may result from malnutrition or even pre-morbid psychiatric conditions like depression, anxiety and substance abuse, so direction of effects needs to be carefully examined (Kaye et al., 2000).

The personality characteristics of eating disordered individuals have been the subject of great interest as well (Viousek & Manke, 1994). While both AN and BN types share preoccupations around food/eating, distortions in body image, and low self esteem, certain differences have been described which appear to predate diagnosis and persist even after recovery (Casper, 1990). Anorexics have been described as perfectionistic, conformist, obsessional, high in self-control, and rigid in their thinking. Restricting food intake fits into this constellation of personality traits and provides a source of control and security. Some bulimics, in comparison, may be impulsive, prone to self-mutilation and substance abuse, and dependent upon food to regulate dysphoric moods. Other bulimics have been described as self-effacing and guilt-prone. Their pattern of food restriction after binging is viewed as a means of alleviating guilt for over-indulgence. The line between AN and BN, however, is not completely clear; both disorders can share symptoms. For example, 25% to 39% of bulimics have a history of anorexia (Kaye et al., 2000).

The role of family dynamics in the development of eating disorders has been examined, largely through clinical case reports. In general, overcontrol or enmeshment is said to be prevalent in families of girls with anorexia whereas parental undercontrol and conflict is more prevalent in families of girls with bulimia (Minuchin, 1974). However, results from empirical studies have been more inconsistent (Archibald, Linver, Graber, & Brooks-Gunn, 2002). Some evidence for the role of culture, with its emphasis on narrowly defined standards of beauty, has also been demonstrated, influencing eating pathology in vulnerable individuals (Kaye et al., 2000).

Given that eating disorders typically emerge in adolescence, the developmental tasks of this period may constitute yet another set of risks that challenge the coping skills of vulnerable youth (Keel, Leon, & Fulkerson, 2001). Some of the age-related changes of this stage, such as normal accumulation of body fat and other physical changes, heightened self-consciousness, reliance on peer and societal standards for behavior and appearance, increased need for peer acceptance and approval, emergence of sexuality, greater demands for autonomy from parents, and so forth, increase the demands for effective coping. For some individuals, notably those with AN-related traits that constrain them, increase their harm-avoidance, and reduce their sensation-seeking, adolescence can be exceptionally difficult to navigate (Steiner et al., 2003). Stresses related to the adolescent transition can feel overwhelming, causing some individuals intense emotional distress. Unremitting pain can leave them feeling adrift and propel them toward methods of coping that can be ultimately destructive.

Risk Factors

Surprisingly, many of these risk factors associated with eating disorders have not been empirically tested. It is important for clinicians to understand what actually constitutes risk, so that interventions can target those factors that really make a difference to successful outcomes. Stice (2002) reviewed the research on risk factors and notes that some less well-reported risk factors are actually more influential in eating pathology than some that are part of conventional therapeutic wisdom. One of the strongest and most consistent risk factors for eating disorders was dissatisfaction with one's body, which could imply internalization of a thin-ideal for beauty. Body dissatisfaction

predicted negative affect, increases in dieting, bulimic symptoms, and compensatory behaviors to restrict weight. The actual size and shape of one's body (body mass) was not shown to predict disordered behavior directly. Instead it appears to amplify other risk factors, such as body dissatisfaction. Exposure to thin-ideal images in media can pose an indirect influence on body-dissatisfaction. However, such pressure to be thin exerts a significant impact only on those who are already dissatisfied with their bodies (Groesz, Levine, & Murnen, 2002).

A very important finding was the *causal* relationship between negative affect and body dissatisfaction creating, therefore, an indirect risk factor for eating pathology. When the capacity for emotion regulation is not up to the task of managing distress, one's perceptions of the world, oneself, and one's future can appear very bleak. Dissatisfaction spreads, and emotions become dysregulated. Pathological behaviors (e.g., binges) are more likely to occur in these circumstances. Perfectionism was also shown to be a risk factor for bulimia and an important element in maintaining eating disordered behaviors once they were established (Stice, 2002). This association, however, may be moderated by other variables including culture and race. For African American women who had strongly positive racial identity, body dissatisfaction did not significantly lower their self-esteem (Oney, Cole & Sellers, 2011).

The array of risk factors appear to operate similarly in predicting eating disorders in adolescent boys (Ricciardelli & McCabe, 2004), although variables implicated in the development of masculine body image, notably the influence of male peers and athletic participation, also need to be considered (Bardone-Cone, Cass, & Ford, 2008). A recent longitudinal study showed different trajectories for males and females suffering from bulimia. Although similar risk factors were operating for both groups (e.g., body dissatisfaction, alcohol use, anxiety, and depression), girls' risk of developing bulimia was greatest in mid-adolescence while risk peaked for males in the early 20's (Abebe, Lien, & von Soest, 2012).

The risks associated with dieting were somewhat more difficult to understand and may be related to type of eating pathology. Dieting has been demonstrated to promote binging through mechanisms of negative affect, which can arise from the physical and emotional stress of caloric deprivation. Other studies find that dieting curbed impulses to overeat and actually restrained binging. Despite suggestions that early puberty (menarche) and sexual abuse might be causally implicated in eating disorders, evidence does not support these as specific risks (Stice, 2002). Clearly, more research is needed to develop models that address the interaction of these important variables.

Prevention and Treatment Issues

Stice and Shaw (2004) offer some empirically based guidelines for prevention programs based on meta-analysis of evidence from 15 available programs. One major finding was that universal prevention programs were not as effective as selective interventions in producing beneficial results and reducing remission. The authors speculate that programs targeted to those at-risk or already experiencing some symptoms may be more effective because participants are more motivated to seek help. Also, universal prevention, typically provided before problems arise, may be directed toward an age group lacking the cognitive skills necessary to benefit. Consequently, programs offered to adolescents who were 15 years old or older were more successful than those offered to younger participants. Programs provided exclusively for females were more effective than combined programs. Brief programs were more effective than longer programs, provided that they offered more than a single session. Program content was less critical, but the strongest results were obtained from programs that targeted the risk factors mentioned above, for example, interventions to alter maladaptive attitudes toward thinness and negative affect.

Research on treatment of eating disordered populations suggest that manualized cognitive behavior therapy (CBT) is the preferred treatment protocol for BN and is effective in reducing distorted body-image cognitions as well as binging/purging for 30% to 50% of cases (Wilson, 2005). Existing evidence is equivocal about the added value of medication to an initial CBT treatment regimen. Recently, interest in mindfulness and acceptance-based treatments (see Chapter 14), such as Mindfulness-Based Stress Reduction (MBSR; Kabat-Zinn, 1994), Mindfulness-Based Cognitive Therapy (MBCT; Segal, Williams, & Teasdale, 2002), Dialectical Behavior Therapy (DBT; Linehan, 1993), and Acceptance and Commitment Therapy (ACT, Hayes, Strosahl, & Wilson, 1999), have been adapted for various problem areas, including eating disorders (see Telch, Agras, & Linehan, 2001). All these approaches share an emphasis on the cultivation of non-judgmental awareness of present experience in the service of developing emotion regulation skills or the "Wise Mind" (Linehan, 1993). All have demonstrated effectiveness in reducing negative affect and may thus target a central causal factor in eating pathology.

Mindfulness-based Eating Awareness Therapy (MB-EAT; Kristeller & Hallett, 1999) is a group treatment designed for binge-eating disorder that utilizes elements of MBSR and MBCT. Guided eating-related meditations and mindful eating exercises are an integral part of the program. The tools offered by the program help participants develop greater awareness of satiety mechanisms and eating behaviors without the critical judgments that often surround food. Mindful awareness, as is taught in the program, fosters self-acceptance and emotion regulation and helps reduce the need to use food for emotional nourishment. Smith and colleagues (2006) demonstrated the efficacy of this mindfulness-based approach in reducing binge-eating frequency as well as in reducing symptoms of anxiety and depression.

For anorexia nervosa, there are few treatment research studies available and existing treatment approaches have generally been less effective than those for BN (Wilson, 2005). Despite the fact that family therapy is widely used for AN, very little outcome evidence exists in the literature. For adolescents with AN, a specific type of structured family therapy does have some empirical support. This manualized method for family therapy, called the Maudsley Method (Dare & Eisler, 1997), has shown some benefits in promoting weight gain for the AN population. Initially, this structured approach focuses on weight gain and recruits the adolescent and the family as nonjudgmental partners who work together to accomplish this goal. Gradually, control over eating is returned to the adolescent. The benefits of this family-based treatment have been encouraging, showing gains that endure at five-year follow-up (Le Grange, 2005). Once satisfactory weight has been reestablished, CBT may be effective for preventing relapse (Berkman et al., 2006). Because not all affected individuals benefit from existing treatments, it is wise for clinicians to keep abreast of on-going research developments given the serious consequences of untreated illness.

SUMMARY

Physical Development

1. Puberty begins when the pituitary gland produces hormones that stimulate hormone production in the gonads. These and other circulating hormones promote the maturing of both primary and secondary sexual characteristics. The timing of puberty is affected both by genes and by environmental factors such as nutrition.

2. The adolescent growth spurt parallels puberty and includes large increases in height and weight. Different parts of the body grow at different times, such as the arms and legs before the torso. Gender differences in growth increase both internal and external sexual dimorphism.

3. The adolescent brain is under construction. Brain growth continues during adolescence, involving synaptogenesis, pruning, and continued myelination. Several areas of the cortex and the corpus callosum are involved in this development. Widespread reorganization makes adolescence a particularly vulnerable period for stress sensitivity and the development of psychopathology.

4. The storm and stress of adolescence includes characteristics such as increased conflict with parents, moodiness, negative affect, and risky behavior. Moodiness and negative affect, including depressed mood, are affected by increases in hormones, but only if they are combined with negative life events. In girls, early maturation usually means greater storm and stress; in boys, later maturation is more problematic. Generally, storm and stress seems to depend on the number of stressors children are experiencing.

5. At adolescence, girls are more susceptible to depressed mood than boys are, apparently because of differences in stress and methods of coping with stress. Among the stressors girls experience more than boys are the devaluing of the female role; worries about appearance and weight; fewer expectations of success; the double standard regarding sexuality; the use of a cooperative discourse that makes them less influential in mixed-sex groups; and earlier puberty, which means that girls are more likely to be making school transitions and coping

with the onset of puberty simultaneously. Girls are also more likely than boys to deal with stress using a ruminative coping style, which increases the risk of depression relative to the distracting style, which is more characteristic of boys.

6. Sexual activity and exploration, both with the opposite sex and with the same sex, increases at puberty. Sexual maturation is primarily responsible, but familial, social, and cultural factors are also important.

7. Sexual orientation becomes manifest in adolescence, with up to 97% of males and more than 98% of females becoming heterosexual. The development of sexual orientation is not well understood. Many traditional environmental theories, such as Freud's theory of identification and the seduction hypothesis, are not supported by evidence. Even modeling is not a viable explanation: Children parented by homosexuals are no more likely than other children to become homosexual. There is evidence for a strong biological contribution to sexual orientation, through prenatal hormones and heredity.

Cognitive Development

8. At Piaget's fourth stage in the development of logical thinking, 11- or 12-year-olds begin to be able to think logically about abstract contents, discovering relationships among relationships. Formal thought is difficult even for adults and is easier to apply in domains of knowledge with which we have some expertise.

9. When a formal operational thinker approaches scientific problems, she generates and considers every possible solution, then tests each one. The pattern of results among all the tests determines the conclusions. Generating and evaluating possibilities is a hallmark of formal operational thought.

10. With formal operations comes the ability to construct ideals, such as ideal political systems or ideal people. Young adolescents do not understand, however, that the real always falls short of the ideal. This failure to understand the limits of her ideas is a form of adolescent egocentrism, and it contributes to a critical attitude toward anything that is less than perfect, including the self.

11. Other aspects of adolescent egocentrism are derived from a distorting inward focus, which is partially a function of an improved capacity to think about one's own thinking. Self-focus may be a function of other factors as well, such as the need to form an adult identity. The imaginary audience and personal fable of adolescents are thought to be results.

Identity Development

12. Erikson's notion of an adolescent identity crisis is better characterized as an identity exploration, a search for answers to questions such as "What do I want to make of myself, and what do I have to work with?" Identity attainment does not imply that no further change occurs; identity is always to some degree in revision. Identity is also a product of the cultural contexts that shape development.

13. Marcia described four identity status categories. Diffusion characterizes adolescents who lack both exploration and commitment. Moratorium describes adolescents who are actively exploring but have made no commitments. Adolescents in foreclosure have not experienced exploration but have made commitments. Achievement comprises individuals whose development has involved exploration and has reached commitment. Each identity status is associated with certain personal and cognitive characteristics.

14. Assessment of identity status usually involves a semi-structured interview procedure in which status within several domains is assessed. For example, Marcia's original Ego Identity Interview assessed status in vocational choice, religious beliefs, and political ideology.

15. There is no fixed sequence of identity statuses, but longitudinal research has found some developmental trends. The number of achievements increases over time, foreclosures decrease, and diffusions decrease or remain the same. The number of moratoriums does not increase or decrease.

16. Both the high school and college years are times of active identity development. Successful accomplishment seems to rest partly on successful accomplishment of earlier psychosocial tasks, availability of positive role-models, and support for exploration.

17. There is a proliferation of theories to describe identity development in many diverse groups. Research on gender differences has produced inconsistent results: Some studies find gender differences, some do not. When differences are found, women, as a group, are more likely to assign interpersonal, communal aspects of themselves a higher priority. Suggestions that women achieve intimacy before identity are not supported by research. Growth in both autonomy and connection are important for both males and females, and for both, achievements in identity and intimacy issues seem to progress in tandem.

18. Achievement of ethnic identity has been described in different ways for many different groups, but most theories have some sequential aspects in common. Initially, race or ethnicity is not a salient feature of self-concept or one's search for identity. Then a moratorium-like period occurs, when the individual experiences some ambivalence or conflict that makes her ethnicity a personal matter, and she begins to explore its meaning (exploration). The highest stage is achieved when an individual affirms her identity as a group member (commitment). Identity development in homosexuals has been described in a similar way.

19. As yet, little longitudinal research is available to support these theories. At present, it seems reasonable to see race and ethnicity as content domains that figure prominently in the identities of group members, making identity development for minorities more complex than for majority group members. Evidence suggests that positive ethnic identity can serve as a protective factor during adolescence.

CASE STUDY

Dean is a White 16-year-old. He is a sophomore at George Washington Carver High School. He lives with his father and his stepmother in a semirural community in the South. His father and mother divorced when Dean was 8 years old, and both parents remarried shortly after the breakup. Dean's mother moved to another state, and, although she calls him from time to time, the two have little contact. Dean gets along well with his father and stepmother. He is also a good "older brother" to his 5-year-old stepbrother, Jesse.

Dean's father owns and operates an auto-repair shop in town. His wife works part time, managing the accounts for the business. She is also an active contributor to many community projects in her neighborhood. She regularly works as a parent volunteer in the elementary school library and is a member of her church's executive council. Both parents try hard to make a good life for their children.

Dean has always been a somewhat lackluster student. His grades fell precipitously during third grade, when his parents divorced. However, things stabilized for Dean over the next few years, and he has been able to maintain a C average. Neither Dean nor his father take his less-than-stellar grades too seriously. In middle school, his father encouraged him to try out for football. He played for a few seasons but dropped out in high school. Dean has a few close friends who like him for his easygoing nature and his sense of humor. Dean's father has told him many times that he can work in the family business after graduation. At his father's urging, Dean is pursuing a course of study in automobile repair at the regional vo-tech school.

Now in his sophomore year, Dean's circle of friends includes mostly other vo-tech students. He doesn't see many of his former friends, who are taking college preparatory courses. Kids in his class are beginning to drive, enabling them to go to places on weekends that had formerly been off-limits. He knows many kids who are having sex and drinking at parties. He has been friendly with several girls over the years, but these relationships have been casual and platonic. Dean wishes he would meet someone with whom he could talk about his feelings and share his thoughts.

Although he is already quite accustomed to the lewd conversations and sexual jokes that circulate around the locker room, he participates only halfheartedly in the banter. He has listened for years to friends who brag about their sexual exploits. He wonders with increasing frequency why he is not attracted to the same things that seem so important to his friends. The thought that he might be gay has crossed his mind, largely because of the scathing comments made by his peers about boys who show no interest in girls. This terrifies him, and he usually manages to distract himself by reasoning that he will develop sexual feeling "when the right girl comes along."

As time passes, however, he becomes more and more morose. His attention is diverted even more from his classwork. He finds it more difficult to be around the kids at school. Dean starts to drink heavily and is arrested for driving under the influence of alcohol. He is sentenced to a 6-week drug education program and is assigned community service. His parents are disappointed in him because of this incident, but they believe he has learned his lesson and will not repeat his mistake. Dean's father believes that his son will be fine as soon as he finds a girlfriend to "turn him around."

Discussion Questions

1. What are the issues facing Dean at this point in his development?
2. Enumerate the risks and the protective factors that are present in his life.
3. How would you, as his counselor, assess Dean's situation? What approaches could you take with this adolescent? What kinds of psycho-educational interventions might you consider within the school setting?

PRACTICE USING WHAT YOU HAVE LEARNED

In the Pearson etext, apply these ideas to working with others.

Video Exercise

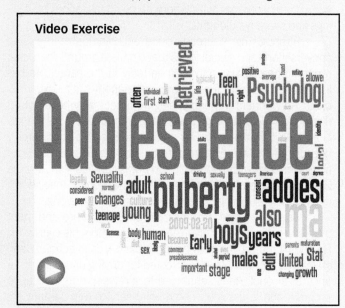

Video Exercise

JOURNAL QUESTIONS

1. Recount an example of the imaginary audience or the personal fable from your own adolescence. How can this knowledge help you in counseling young people?
2. Were you an early, an on-time, or a late-maturing adolescent? What impact did your physical development have on your adjustment and your peer group relationships?
3. Remember back to the time when you were 18 or 19. Using Marcia's identity categories, assess your own status in the following domains: relationships, career, religious or political ideology, ethnicity, and sexual orientation.
4. Reflect on the development of your cultural identity. How has this aspect of your self-system influenced your life?

KEY CONCEPTS

CHAPTER 10

The Social World
of Adolescence

The search for identity is considered the primary developmental task of the adolescent period. In this chapter, you will find that the outcome of an adolescent's search is very much affected by the social world. Peers play a critical role, and so do parents, schools, and neighborhoods. All are in turn influenced by the cultural and historical context in which the adolescent's identity is formed. Counselors, therapists, teachers, and other helping professionals who support adolescents through their explorations and struggles must consider the impact of these multiple, interdependent factors. As we have seen repeatedly, no single factor or influence fully explains any developmental outcome. In this chapter, we present a model of the mechanism for social identity development and explore research on the influence of peers, parents, schools, leisure, work, and culture on that process. We conclude with a discussion of implications for professionals who work with adolescents.

Let's begin with an example: As a balmy October turned into a frigid November, 12-year-old Tamara's mother repeatedly suggested to her daughter that they go shopping to replace Tamara's outgrown winter jacket. Tamara refused. She said she wasn't sure what sort of jacket she wanted, admitting that it depended on what the other girls in her class would be wearing. The popular girls had not yet worn jackets to school, despite the cold. They, too, were waiting and watching! Finally, in mid-December, one popular girl in the seventh-grade class capitulated to her mother's demands and made a jacket choice. Tamara and her classmates at last knew what to wear.

Parents and teachers are often perplexed, even dismayed, by the importance of peers to the adolescent. Why would an otherwise sensible young person become so dependent upon the actions and choices of others, and what role do parents and other concerned adults play in an adolescent's life when peers become so important?

Dependence upon peers is a normal and important developmental process for the young adolescent. As you will see, the search for identity (see Chapter 9) that characterizes the adolescent period takes place largely within the world of peers. The adolescent period roughly begins at puberty, although in today's world many of the processes discussed in this chapter are beginning to affect the lives of children even before the onset of puberty.

FRAMEWORKLESSNESS AND AUTONOMY: A MODEL OF ADOLESCENT SOCIAL IDENTITY

Theorists have long argued that one's identity develops within the context of interpersonal interactions (Cooley, 1902; Mead, 1934; see also Chapter 7). Erikson (1968) suggested that peers are particularly important in the construction of identity at adolescence, and Seltzer (1982) expanded upon Erikson's ideas, specifying how and why the peer group plays such a central role. To understand fully the function of peers, let's look again at what happens when a child enters adolescence. The body changes in appearance, adult sexual needs emerge, hormonal shifts may heighten irritability, the capacity to reflect on the future and on the self expands bringing its own brand of egocentrism, and demands for autonomy increase. All of these changes are supported by dramatic alterations in the adolescent brain. These profound shifts can produce a state of instability and anxiety unique to adolescence, which Seltzer calls **frameworklessness**.

Think about your own experiences as a young adolescent. Can you relate to the sense of frameworklessness?

> The adolescent is at sea. Previous boundaries and guideposts are no longer functional. In earlier developmental periods, expansion and growth exist within a context of familiar motion and exercise. The adolescent condition is different, however. The adolescent is possessed of new physical and intellectual capabilities that are both mystical and mystifying. . . . The allure of the adult world calls, and is strong, even as the safety of childhood is close and still beckons. Yet neither fits; the one is outgrown, the other not yet encompassable. (Seltzer, 1982, p. 59)

The adolescent's passage to adulthood is in some ways parallel to the infant's passage to childhood status. To exercise their developing skills and to explore the beckoning world, infants must give up the security of the caregiver's continual presence and care. Most attachment theorists believe that toddlers manage the stress of this separation by referring to their working model of the other, a kind of mental representation of the caregiver, which provides feelings of security and makes independent exploration possible. For adolescents, the task of establishing adult independence requires separating from caregivers on a new plane, a process traditionally called the "second" individuation (Blos, 1975). Adolescents rework their views of their parents, deidealize them, and loosen, somewhat, their emotional dependency (Steinberg & Belsky, 1991; Steinberg & Monahan, 2007). Figure 10.1 illustrates the typical decline between the ages of 11 and 17 years in adolescents' willingness to endorse the legitimacy of their parents' claims to authority or to endorse the notion that they (the children) are obligated to follow parental dictates. These data are from a large sample of Chilean youth, but young people in many countries, including the United States, show similar patterns of decline, with the steepest drop coming in early adolescence (Darling, Cumsille, & Martinez, 2008). Thus, it appears that in early adolescence the mental representation or concept of the parent becomes more peripheral to the child's self-system. However, a teenager's increasing individuation and sense of autonomy does not come without a price. As adolescents experience a loss in feelings of security, their sense of frameworklessness can increase.

But psychological separation from parents does not mean cutting ties in some dramatic fashion, even though stereotypes about adolescence might imply this. We know that emotional attachments persist in some form across the lifespan, and there is more than one pathway through the adolescent period. Cultural assumptions of interdependence and virtues such as filial piety can help shape alternative narratives

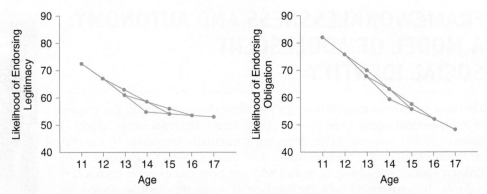

FIGURE 10.1 **Adolescents' likelihood of endorsing parental legitimacy and their own obligation to obey, by age.**
SOURCE: Darling, N., Cumsille, P., & Martinez, M. L. (2008). Individual differences in adolescents' beliefs about the legitimacy of parent authority and their own obligation to obey: A longitudinal investigation. *Child Development, 79,* 1103–1118. Reproduced with permission of Blackwell Publishing Ltd.

of adolescence with respect to parent–child relationships. While the movement toward separation and independence becomes stronger over the course of early adolescence in many countries, the same is not completely true for adolescents in China. For example, U.S. adolescents report more conflicts, less emotional closeness and a reduced sense of obligation to parents compared to their Chinese counterparts (Pomerantz, Qin, Wang, & Chen, 2009). Filial piety (see Chapter 5), which involves the sense of repaying and honoring parents for their role in raising them, appears to influence the developmental course of Chinese early adolescents substantially. Pomerantz and her colleagues (2011) found that Chinese adolescents' sense of obligation to parents increased over 7th and 8th grades compared to a declining pattern among U.S. youth (see Figure 10.2). The trend toward increasing levels of obligation to parents was associated with better grades, greater mastery of learning, and improved self-regulation. Adolescents in China and the United States who perceived greater obligation to please parents demonstrated higher achievement overall compared to those without a comparable sense of obligation.

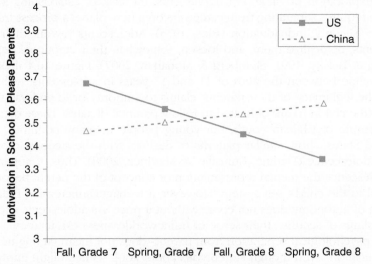

FIGURE 10.2 **Obligation to parents across two cultures.** U.S. and Chinese adolescents show differences in their academic motivation as a function of their intention to please parents.
SOURCE: Pomerantz, E. M., Qin, L., Wang, Q., & Chen, H. (2011). Changes in early adolescents' sense of responsibility to their parents in the United States and China: Implications for academic functioning. *Child Development, 82,* 1136–1151. Reproduced with permission of Blackwell Publishing Ltd.

In other words, even though decreasing connectedness to parents among early adolescents is culturally accepted in the United States, its normativeness does not prevent it from contributing to declines in academic performance. The authors of this study offer a possible explanation—"most likely because American children are in need of the motivation in the academic context that their sense of responsibility to their parents provides during the early adolescent years" (p. 1147).

The Peer Arena

Paradoxically, as children seek autonomy from their parents in early adolescence, they seem to become more dependent on their peers. In a classic study, Steinberg and Silverberg (1986) asked 10- to 16-year-olds in the United States questions about their relationships with parents and agemates. As most studies have found, children between fifth and eighth grades showed a marked increase in agreement on items assessing emotional autonomy from parents, such as "There are some things about me that my parents don't know" and "There are things that I would do differently from my mother and father when I become a parent." Yet, when the students in this study were asked "What would you really do?" if a friend suggested either some anti-social act such as cheating or some neutral act such as joining a club, they showed a marked decrease between the fifth and eighth grades in their ability to resist peer influence, as you can see in Figure 10.3. Newer studies indicate that increasing susceptibility to peer influence is greatest for anti-social or risky behaviors, and more likely for boys than for girls (e.g., Sim & Koh, 2003). Resistance to peer influence begins to rise in middle adolescence, increasing most between 14 and 18 years, with continuing, shallower gains in young adulthood (e.g., Steinberg & Monahan, 2007). Again, peer influence on risky behavior tends be greater and lasts longer, declining only after mid-adolescence (see Erickson, Crosnoe, & Dornbusch, 2000, and the discussion of risky behavior later in this chapter). Overall, it appears that between the ages of 11 and 14 children transfer at least some of their emotional dependency from their parents to their peers.

Why do peers become so important? Seltzer (1982) proposes that it is because adolescents share in common the unique state of frameworklessness. She describes nine basic characteristics that define this age group in contemporary society. Among them are similar chronological age and educational status and shared coping with feelings of aloneness and the loss of past certainties. Social psychologists established long ago that people under stress tend to affiliate with others perceived as having similar experiences (Schacter, 1959), so that adolescents' shared sense of instability makes the peer group a likely target of affiliation. The sometimes difficult movement toward identity can, at least in part, be shared.

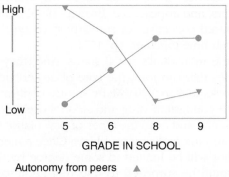

FIGURE 10.3   Parents, peers, and adolescent feelings of autonomy.
SOURCE: Based on Steinberg, L., & Silverberg, S. B. (1986). The vicissitudes of autonomy in early adolescence. *Child Development, 57,* 847. Reproduced with permission of Blackwell Publishing Ltd.

Peers are thus a source of support. But Seltzer (1982) argues also that the peer group becomes both the site and the raw material for constructing an identity. There are twin processes at work: The first is social comparison. As we saw in Chapter 7, younger school-aged children evaluate themselves in comparison to others. In later chapters we will find that adults continue to use social comparison as a means of self-assessment and self-refinement. But for adolescents, the lack of identity may make this process intense and more consuming.

Second is a process of **attribute substitution**, which involves both imitation and identification. Adolescents need to borrow and "try on" various behaviors and attributes that they observe in others because the state of frameworklessness leaves them without clearly defined ways of behaving and thinking. Peers become an important resource for such borrowing. A formerly quiet boy might imitate the wisecracking style of a friend, a girl may explore the mysteries of Buddhism espoused by a classmate, or a mediocre student might work for hours on a special project, mimicking the approach of a more successful peer. The borrowing goes beyond imitation to partial identification with friends, so that if a boy's friend has a special talent for hockey, the boy might appropriate a sense of accomplishment as a hockey player from his association with the friend. This appropriation of "stand-in elements" provides relief for the adolescent from the anxiety of being without a stable sense of self. The twin processes of social comparison and imitation appear to constitute a type of experimentation that is necessary for mature identity construction. At first, the trying-on process is rapid, intense, and undifferentiated, but toward later adolescence, some features actually become more stable elements that will form the foundation of the young adult's identity. Ideally, the goal of all this effort is the development or construction of a fundamental sense of what fits for the particular adolescent.

In summary, Seltzer (1982) argues that peers in large part provide the arena for identity formation. She also describes the Eriksonian ideal of unrestricted sampling of various "identities" as a normative process, but in reality what adolescents are able to do may be more circumscribed. As we will see in the next section, the structure of the peer culture may constrain the opportunity to try on some characteristics and behaviors.

THE STRUCTURE OF THE PEER NETWORK

As you saw in Chapter 8 by early adolescence a typical youngster is part of a nested set of peer relationships that seem to form concentric circles. He spends most of his time with one or two close friends, the innermost circle. A larger clique of about 6 to 10 members forms a less intimate second circle, composed of friends who eat lunch or go to class together. The clique's boundaries are somewhat permeable, and the membership may fluctuate. Finally, the much larger third circle is the adolescent's crowd. What crowd members share is not necessarily friendship, but similar interests, attitudes, behaviors, and appearance. Brown (1990) defined adolescent crowds as large "reputation-based collectives of similarly stereotyped individuals who may or may not spend much time together" (p. 177).

Crowds reflect the individual's social status. And, they ". . . demarcate different values and lifestyles that can form the core of an individual's identity" (Brown, Herman, Hamm, & Heck, 2008, p. 530). Many studies confirm that association with a crowd can be linked to youngsters' drug and alcohol use, sexual behavior, academic commitment, achievement, and even the types of psychiatric symptoms they display, such as externalizing and internalizing problems. Once a member, a teen's sampling of elements of behavior will be limited to some degree by the crowd to which the teen belongs. Few would be surprised to find that adolescents are strongly influenced by their closest friends. What is striking about the data on peer affiliation is how powerful crowd membership seems to be.

A classic example of the impact of crowds on adolescent behavior is provided by a large scale study by Steinberg and his associates (e.g., Lamborn, Mounts,

Steinberg, & Dornbusch, 1991; Mounts & Steinberg, 1995; Steinberg, 1996; Steinberg, Fegley, & Dornbusch, 1993; Steinberg, Lamborn, Darling, Mounts, & Dornbusch, 1994; Steinberg, Lamborn, Dornbusch, & Darling, 1992). More than 20,000 adolescents and their families from nine public high schools in Wisconsin and northern California were studied. Students came from ethnically and socioeconomically diverse communities (more than 40% were ethnic minorities) and from a variety of family structures (intact, divorced, and remarried). Student data were collected over a 3-year period from 9th through 12th grades. Teens answered questions about their emotional adjustment, academic achievement, and behavior, the parenting practices of their families, and their peer associations.

Steinberg (e.g., 1996) and his colleagues found a characteristic crowd structure that many other large-scale studies of U.S. teens have confirmed (e.g., Barber, Eccles, & Stone, 2001; Brown et al., 2008). Roughly 20% of students belong to popularity-conscious crowds ("populars" and "jocks"), who are moderately achievement oriented and may engage in some illicit behavior, such as drug use. About 20% belong to "alienated" crowds ("druggies" or "burnouts"), who are even less invested in academic success and who may be involved in heavy drug use and delinquent behavior. "Average" crowds, comprising about 30% of students, are not openly hostile to academics but, like the populars, are only moderately concerned about grades. In majority White high schools, some crowds are defined primarily by ethnicity (roughly 10% to 15% depending on the school), and academic achievement differences exist among these ethnically defined crowds. Less than 5% of high schoolers belong to crowds characterized by high academic achievement. These students are unlikely to use drugs and may form strong ties with teachers.

Distinct crowd structures also exist in other cultures. Researchers in Denmark, for example, found four major crowd categories: Alternative, Urban, Conventional, and Achievement-Oriented (Delsing, ter Bogt, Engels & Meeus, 2007). Alternative crowds ("punks," "metal heads," "goths") tended to display more nonconformist, rebellious behavior than more conventional crowds. The Urban crowd was characterized by an orientation to musical and cultural activities typically found in urban areas ("hip-hop," "rasta"). The Conventional crowd was made up of "normals," rural, and religious youth. The Achievement-oriented crowd ("posh," "brains") was oriented toward academic and financial success. Affiliation with the two nonconventional crowds (Alternative and Urban) was associated with higher rates of delinquency, aggression and depression.

In Singapore, where the cultural rules for dress and behavior are stricter and where a relatively strong norm for conformity exists, adolescents also identify with different crowds. Sim and Yeo (2012) identified seven primary crowd orientations from a large number of suggestions obtained from open-ended questions ("Nerd," "Gangster," "Athlete," "Computer Geek," "Joker," "Ordinary," and "Loner"). "Gangsters" were generally rebellious in the ways they dressed, were rude toward others and disinterested in academics. You may suspect some overlap between these and the crowds seen in U.S. schools, notably with jocks, brains, delinquents, and nerds. While groups in both cultures show a similar distinction between conventional and unconventional, there are also notable differences. Because of the cultural value placed on academic achievement and filial piety, "nerds" in Singapore were primarily identified with academic achievement rather than social awkwardness, and thus viewed much more positively. Although socializing and "partying" are common features of the "popular" crowd in the United States, a comparable "popular" group did not emerge in Singapore. The authors suggest that this is due to the relative absence of these types of activities among Singaporean youth. "Nerds" and "gangsters" were the largest and most commonly identifiable crowds. "Athletes" came in a distant third, a much less recognizable group compared to U.S. schools. Although the sample in this study did not represent the whole of Singapore, findings are interesting in light of how cultural values and practices shape adolescent behavior and identify formation.

 Teens and parents often use the word clique to describe all groups of friends. In these examples, are they talking about cliques, or are they talking about crowds?

How teens find a niche among the available crowds is not completely understood (Brown, 1990). Steinberg (1996) suggests three determining factors: children's personalities and interests as they enter adolescence; the types of crowds available; and the ways that parents attempt to manage their children's peer relationships. We'll take a close look at parents' role in children's crowd membership later in this chapter.

In Chapter 8 you learned that adults frequently attribute the behavior of adolescents to "peer pressure," what we have called the influence of peers, which implies that the individual teenager might conform to others' demands despite his or her better judgment. What research findings also show is that adolescents operate according to the principles of group dynamics that govern any social group—namely, they often choose to participate in shared norms, roles, and expectations, a process called **peer selection** (e.g., Cohen & Prinstein, 2006). They are influenced by peers, and sometimes that **peer influence** is related to negative control tactics by their peers, such as teasing and threats of rejection. Under the powerful influence of peers, teens may willingly engage in peer-sanctioned behavior. The willingness to be influenced by peers may be related to adolescents' identity processes. They are motivated to borrow styles, attitudes, behaviors and so forth from others, and they serve as models from whom others borrow. In the case of delinquent behavior, research has consistently shown that deviant peers mutually influence each other (Gifford-Smith, Dodge, Dishion, & McCord, 2005). Social processes are also amplified by the developmental changes in the teenage brain which affect risk taking.

Steinberg (1996) provides a specific example of the U.S. crowd's effects on academic achievement. Recall from the data on teens' distribution among their high school crowds that a relatively small percentage is committed to academic excellence (i.e., are A students). Membership in the largest, most appealing, and preferred crowds (populars, jocks, and average) prescribes more modest academic achievement. Most students in these crowds, representing about 50% of high schoolers, earn Bs on average.

Could it be that these data simply indicate that students who begin with only moderate academic commitments and abilities gravitate toward groups of similar individuals? Several longitudinal studies (e.g., Eccles & Barber, 1999; Steinberg, 1996; Kindermann, 2008) suggest otherwise. For example, after tracking students for 3 years who began with similar academic records and behavior profiles, Steinberg (1996) found that students' crowd affiliation was highly correlated with their later grades and delinquent activities. So, crowd membership made a unique contribution to these outcomes over and above early developmental characteristics.

What role do ethnicity and peer relationships play in academic achievement among U.S. adolescents, given that their peer networks are often based on shared ethnicity, even in heterogeneous school settings (Hamm, 2000)? Let's look at a study that examined this interplay. This study was based on a large representative sample of U.S. adolescents (Add Health study, see Chapter 9) over three waves from 1994 through 2002 (Goza & Ryabov, 2009). Peer networks, GPA, and odds of high school graduation were examined for approximately 14,000 students. Regardless of their racial/ethnic background, students generally had lower graduation rates in low SES schools compared to schools with higher school-wide SES. All students, especially non-Hispanic White students, had higher graduation rates when there was greater school-wide diversity in the student body.

When researchers took a closer look at the peer networks of African American, Latino, non-Hispanic White, and Asian students, certain unique effects on achievement and graduation rates were found. Remember that the amount of diversity in any school may be a substantial or a small percentage of overall school composition. Minority students may then have different experiences with regard to the availability of peer networks that are ethnically and racially similar. For African American students, membership in ethnically diverse peer networks contributed positively to their academic achievement, even though it was not related to their graduation rates. Findings were different for Asian, Latino and non-Hispanic White students. These three groups were more likely to graduate, and Asian and Latino students were more likely to have higher GPAs, when their peer networks were more homogeneous.

While research on crowd structure and social processes tell us much about adolescent peer behavior, we should remember that there are underlying brain changes that are also at work here. Areas of the brain involved in social information processing overlap in activation with areas that we refer to as the emotional brain system, which includes sub-cortical structures such as the amygdala, nucleus accumbens, and hippocampus. At puberty, there is both structural and functional change in these overlapping structures. We will provide more information about these brain changes in a later section of this chapter.

THE ROLE OF PARENTS

Given that peers become so important to young adolescents, what is the role of adults, especially parents, in adolescents' lives? A brief history of perspectives on adolescent development may be useful here. Early psychoanalytic writers described this period as one of conflict between parents and their teens that is sparked by the reemergence of latent sexual impulses as the child reaches puberty (Freud, 1958). The classic interpretation is that the young adolescent's emotional attachments become sexualized and need to be redirected to agemates. In this view, the child's press for autonomy creates conflict with the parents but is seen as normal and necessary. Neopsychoanalytic views have become more moderate over time (e.g., Blos, 1975), but still assume that the child's cognitive and affective detachment from parents is to be expected in the service of autonomy. Erikson's (1968) view of adolescence as a "normative crisis" supports this as a time of potential upheaval. The early psychoanalytic tradition framed the typical parent–adolescent relationship as a struggle, with teens trying to pull away from parents to the point of rebellion. Prescriptions for appropriate parental behavior often focused on the child's legitimate need to break away and the parents' responsibility to "let go" and allow their adolescents to "be themselves." Parents were advised to back off because teens must be free to explore with their peers to consolidate their identity.

In the 1970s and beyond, studies of adolescence contradicted earlier constructions based on psychoanalytic thought. They indicated that major transformations do occur in family relations as children pass through adolescence but that becoming more independent and personally responsible is not necessarily accompanied by emotional detachment from parents (Collins & Laursen, 2004). Offer (1969) reported that roughly two thirds of teens experienced adolescence as a tranquil period or at least experienced only minor conflicts with parents. Montemayor (1983) reported that in typical families, teens and their parents argued on average twice a week, hardly a matter of great concern. A more recent meta-analysis indicates that conflicts with parents occur most frequently in early adolescence. By middle adolescence, they begin to decline in frequency but tend to increase in intensity (Laursen, Coy, & Collins, 1998). Across cultures, both adolescents and parents view some aspects of parental control to be quite legitimate. Parents can exercise authority over *moral* issues (like stealing and justice) or even issues governed by *conventional* rules (such as table manners), especially when conventional

Parents who are invested in their adolescents' well-being balance acceptance with appropriate limit-setting and monitoring.

Camila, at age 16, states that friends say she and her mother seem like "best friends," but she then goes on to describe a variety of disagreements that she has with her parents. How does she try to exert her independence, and how do her parents respond?

rules have **prudential consequences** (having to do with an individual's health or safety; see Darling, Cumsille, & Martinez, 2007; Darling et al., 2008; Smetana, 1997). It's when parents impose rules on what their teens perceive as *personal* issues (like what you can say to a friend in an email, how you wear your hair, or what music you listen to) that conflicts are most likely to arise (Smetana & Daddis, 2002). For teens, gaining control over this personal domain is a way of establishing autonomy and therefore is an important identity issue (Smetana, Crean, & Campione-Barr, 2005). Observers began to argue that if disagreements with parents center on relatively mundane issues like music and hairstyles, perhaps the storminess of relations between parents and adolescents has been overstated (Rutter, 1995). Parenting prescriptions began to include the implicit advice, "Don't worry, things will work out fine." As you might guess, however, things may not be so simple.

Arnett (2000), for example, raises a word of caution. He suggests that conflicts over relatively minor matters are nonetheless stressful for both parents and children. He further warns that the "mundane" matters that adolescents argue with their parents about may not be as trivial as they seem. Rather, they

> . . . often concern issues such as when adolescents should begin dating and whom they should date, where they should be allowed to go, and how late they should stay out. All of these issues can serve as proxies for arguments over more serious issues such as substance use, automobile driving safety, and sex. (p. 320)

In other words, some of the behaviors that adolescents categorize as "personal," their parents probably see as "prudential/conventional" because the behaviors have potentially serious consequences for a teen's future (see Hasebe, Nucci, & Nucci, 2004; Smetana & Daddis, 2002).

Peer relationships, in particular, can be a flash point for parents and youth because what one group (adolescents) determines to be a matter of personal choice, the other (parents) may see as putting their child at some risk. What do parents of adolescents *really* know about their adolescent children's friendships and how much do teens tell them? Eighty-three percent of European-American high school and college students had lied to their parents in the past week according to a study by Arnett and colleagues (2004), and lies for the high school group most often involved peers and alcohol. Adolescents lied more to parents whom they perceived as controlling, cold, or rejecting (see also Tilton-Weaver et al., 2010). Consistent with their advances in cognition, adolescents make increasingly sophisticated decisions about what to disclose to parents. Information may be mangaged in various ways: full disclosure, partial story telling with details omitted, changing the subject or avoiding conversations, and outright lying (Darling, Cumsille, Caldwell, & Dowdy, 2006).

A small cross-cultural study investigated information management in African American and Hmong low-income samples (Bakken & Brown, 2010). Unlike the African American families in this study, the Hmong families were recent immigrants/ refugees to the United States who faced language and cultural barriers. The African American parents had a long history in the United States and were more knowledgeable about cultural norms. Hmong adolescents perceived their parents to be more restrictive and less able to help them with some of the challenges they faced. Understandably, Hmong parents wanted to protect and preserve the values of their culture, but frustrations and difficulties of life in a new country affected both parents' and adolescents' experience. Hmong adolescents justified withholding information from parents on pragmatic grounds (e.g., because they wouldn't understand) but also because they wanted to maintain good relationships with their parents. Hmong adolescents didn't want to worry parents by disclosing some aspects of teenage life in the United States. Younger African American adolescents believed that their parents had the resources to find out whether or not they were telling them the truth. Compared to older African American adolescents, younger adolescents engaged in more full disclosure. African American parents believed that they needed to balance their children's growing need for autonomy with their parental inclination to protect them from experiences of racial discrimination. Although African American youth could understand parental protectiveness, they were secretive about some things to preserve their own growing autonomy. Both universal aspects of adolescent autonomy-seeking and culturally specific rationales for information management were noted in this study. Even though the authors conclude that lying to parents is typically not a good idea, "more careful work is revealing that adolescents are both thoughtful and strategic in deciding what information about peers to share with parents. Often, they consider not only the quality of the parent-child relationship and the best interests of their parents but also their obligation to maintain confidence of peers" (Brown & Bakken, 2011, p. 155). It appears that the importance of peer relationships and the press for behavioral autonomy need to be appreciated by parents, serving to make their parenting strategies more flexible, though no less involved, at this age.

Research on the family as one supportive context for adolescent development has been growing rapidly. Its theoretical framework rests upon Baumrind's (e.g., 1971, 1978, 1991) studies of parenting styles, in which, you will recall from Chapter 5, she identified two important dimensions of parental behavior, each of which is predictive of a particular constellation of child characteristics. First is parental warmth or responsiveness. Responsive parents seem to encourage their children's self-acceptance, confidence, and assertiveness by being warm, involved, and accepting of their children's needs and feelings. They take their children's feelings and expressed needs seriously and are willing to explain their own actions, particularly when they impose limits on the child. The second dimension is parental control or demandingness. Demanding parents apparently foster self-discipline and achievement by making maturity demands on their children. They make and enforce rules, provide consistent supervision or **parental monitoring**, and confront their children when their behavior does not measure up. According to a large body of research by Baumrind and others, the most effective parenting style, authoritative parenting, combines high responsiveness and high demandingness.

Treating responsiveness and demandingness as two distinct dimensions, three other categories of parenting style can be derived. Besides authoritative, there are authoritarian, permissive (also called **indulgent**), and neglecting (also called uninvolved or **dismissive**) styles (Maccoby & Martin, 1983). Authoritarian parents are low on responsiveness but high on demandingness. Permissive parents are high on responsiveness but low on demandingness, and neglecting or dismissive parents are essentially disengaged, scoring low on both dimensions. Before you read Box 10.1 on how authoritative parenting of adolescents "looks in action," consider the evidence that it can positively influence teen behavior and well-being. Baumrind (e.g., 1991) assessed the behavior of parents and their young adolescents and found that "authoritative parents put out exceptional effort . . . and their adolescents were exceptionally competent (mature, prosocial, high internal locus of control, low internalizing and externalizing problem behavior, low substance use)" (Baumrind, 1993, p. 1308). In the large-scale study of 14- to 18-year-olds by Steinberg and his colleagues, parenting style was linked to four aspects of teens' adjustment: psychosocial development, school achievement, internalized distress, and problem behavior. The children of authoritative parents scored best on the majority of these indicators, and those of neglectful parents scored worst (Lamborn et al., 1991). After 1 year, the adolescents' adjustment status was reassessed. Parenting style was predictive of patterns of change over the year. For example, adolescents from authoritative homes showed increases in self-reliance, whereas other adolescents showed little change or, if they had neglectful parents, actually declined somewhat (Steinberg et al., 1994).

In general, research on parenting styles from as early as the 1940s (e.g., Baldwin, 1948) has produced results that are consistent with the large-scale studies of today, supporting the notion that both responsiveness and demandingness are beneficial. Overall, responsiveness seems more closely tied to adolescents' self-confidence and social competence, and demandingness is more closely associated with "good" behavior and self-control. Some work indicates that it can be useful to consider responsiveness as comprising separable factors: **acceptance** is being affectionate, praising the child, being involved in the child's life, and accepting the child's strengths and limitations, showing concern for the child's needs, and it is correlated with children's self-esteem and social adjustment. **Democracy** is the degree to which parents encourage children's psychological autonomy by soliciting their opinions or encouraging self-expression, and it is most closely linked to children's self-reliance, self-confidence, willingness to work hard, and general competence (Steinberg, 1996). *Democracy* is the opposite of "psychological control," which we described in Chapter 5: a parent's tendency to subvert an adolescent's autonomy by invalidating his feelings, constraining his verbal expressions, using love withdrawal, and so on. Psychological control predicts internalizing problems in adolescents, and to a lesser degree, externalizing problems (e.g., Barber et al., 2005).

Regardless of how we label the fundamental dimensions of parenting style, there is very strong empirical support for what constitutes "good parenting" for adolescents, and this support is surprisingly consistent across many cultures (Barber et al., 2005; Darling et al., 2008), from collectivist societies with more hierarchical family structures (such as China) to more individualistic cultures with more democratic family structures (such as the United States). It is also consistent across demographic and ethnic subgroups in the United States (e.g., Chung & Steinberg, 2006; Wang, Pomerantz, & Chen, 2008). One of the newer findings is that authoritative parenting's beneficial effects are partly determined by adolescents' willingness to accept their parents' authority on a variety of issues. When parents have established a warm family climate and are perceived by their children to monitor them closely, adolescents are more likely to endorse parental legitimacy and their own obligation to obey, even though they are more likely to argue with their parents (Darling et al., 2008). Ironically, effective parental monitoring depends partly on adolescents' willingness to disclose information about their behavior to their parents, which in turn depends on adolescents seeing their parents as warm and understanding (e.g., Smetana, 2008; Soenens, Vansteenkiste, Luyckx, & Goossens, 2006). Further, parents who are both high on acceptance/democracy *and* high on demandingness/monitoring are likely to make clearer distinctions between personal issues and other domains (moral and prudentially conventional) in their governance (Smetana, 1995, 2008), which may in turn help their children to feel more comfortable disclosing information.

But, relatively speaking, how powerful a role can such parental behaviors actually play in adolescence, when the influence of peers has been found to be so great? An important key to answering this question is to recall, again, that multiple determinants interact to affect outcomes at every developmental stage. Let's reconsider, for example, school achievement in the teen years. When authoritative parents involve themselves in their adolescents' schooling by attending school programs, helping with course selection, and monitoring student progress, their children are more likely to achieve (Gutman, Sameroff, & Eccles, 2002; Mounts & Steinberg, 1995; Steinberg, Lamborn, Dornbusch, et al., 1992). However, as we have seen, an adolescent's crowd affiliation also impacts school achievement. Steinberg (1996) found that teens who began with similar academic records showed change over time in school performance consistent with their crowd membership, indicating the importance of peer influence despite parental efforts.

Can parents affect crowd membership? Characteristic behaviors of the child are probably important in determining crowd membership, and a child's behaviors are associated with parenting style. Steinberg (1996) describes parenting as "launching" children on a trajectory through adolescence. But parental effects may be indirect. Research has shown for a long time that teenagers whose friends engage in delinquent behaviors are more likely to do so as well (see Brown & Bakken, 2011).

However, membership in delinquent crowds may be less the result of peer pressure and more the effect of intentional peer selection (Farrington, Loeber, Yin, & Anderson, 2002). Some parental behaviors, however, may have a moderating effect on peer selection processes. Monitoring and encouraging achievement, are correlated with children's choice of more academically oriented peers (e.g., Mounts & Steinberg, 1995). When urban parents in poor neighborhoods show high levels of monitoring and involvement their kids are more likely to steer clear of joining delinquent groups or gangs and less likely to become juvenile offenders (Chung & Steinberg, 2006; Walker-Barnes & Mason, 2001).

But the availability of crowds is also important. If, for example, all crowds value high academic achievement, or if none do, the child's trajectory with regard to school performance will be much less affected by authoritative parents who value academic excellence than if there is a diversity of crowds. Here is a clue to other ways in which parenting style may influence behavior. Steinberg proposes that authoritative parents, who are involved in their children's lives, may do things to help structure the child's

Box 10.1: Authoritative Parenting with Adolescents

Is authoritative parenting for real or some magician's trick? How can a parent, especially the parent of a savvy teenager, be warm, responsive, respectful, and democratic on one hand but firm, controlling, and watchful on the other?

Imagine that 14-year-old Risa bursts into the house on a Friday after school, literally jumping for joy at a party invitation she has just received. It's from Katy, one of the most popular girls in school, and being at the party will automatically define Risa as one of the popular elite. Risa prattles on about who will be there, and what to wear, and "Oh my god! I've got to start getting ready *now*!" Dad is working at home this afternoon, so he's the P.I.C.—parent in charge. First, he listens with interest and expresses understanding. It is not that difficult in this case. Risa is given to emotional extremes, but when the extreme is ecstasy, Dad has little trouble smiling, nodding, and reflecting ("This party is really something special!") compassionately. But before Risa bolts for the shower, Dad begins to ask questions about who, where, when, and under what circumstances. Risa's joyful prattle turns to impatient disdain: "It doesn't matter, and I don't have time to answer all these questions." Dad continues to try to reflect without being deflected. "I know you're busy, but the answers are very important to me. So let's just take a minute." Risa really does not know the answers, so Dad points out that he can find out more when he calls Katy's parents. "No! You can't! These kids don't even want to know I have parents. If you call I'll be completely humiliated!" Here is the challenge to the authoritative parent: balancing the child's feelings and concerns with the critical monitoring responsibility. Risa's dad stands firm: She is not permitted to attend parties where responsible adults are not present, and the only way to be sure is to speak directly to Katy's parents. Without belittling Risa's concerns, Dad insists on the phone call. He explains, as he has before, why unsupervised parties are not acceptable, and then invites Risa to help problem solve. "I know this is awkward, Risa. Let's try to think of ways to make this go smoothly for everyone. For example, I could call and thank Katy's parents for having the party at their house, and offer to bring over a case of soda." But Risa's idea of reasonable is not consistent with her

father's. She has an inkling that the party is not going to be supervised, and in any case she does not want to risk the popular crowd seeing her as a "baby." She attacks her father as "old-fashioned," "overprotective," and "stupid," alternately raging and whining.

At this point, it is difficult for parents to repeat explanations calmly and to hold firm. Sometimes they give up, or lose all patience. Personal assaults from the teenager complicate the parents' role: These attacks are hurtful and demeaning, and they too need to be addressed. In this case, Dad manages to respond, "I know you're upset, but your attacking me hurts my feelings, and it's not going to change my mind. Let's stick to the subject of the party." At another point, he takes a timeout for 5 minutes to cool down. Rarely do conflicts like these feel happily resolved in the immediate situation. In this case, Risa finally tells her father not to bother to call because she will not go to the party—she will call and make an excuse. She then sulks in her room all night. Both her mother and her father talk to her about it again, giving her an opportunity to vent, to discuss again the pros and cons of the rule about unsupervised parties, and to consider ways of promoting her relationships with her friends, such as having a party herself. Their restrictions on her social life never stop grating on Risa, but her parents hold firm.

These confrontations can be frightening for even the most confident parents. On a different occasion, Risa might just walk out rather than sulk in her room. Parents are dependent not only on the quality of the mutual caring that has been established with a child up to the teen years but also on the support that is available in the child's circle of friends. If her friends' parents routinely allow unsupervised parties, Risa's parents are soon going to feel besieged and may have limited success in helping Risa navigate her adolescence safely. On the other hand, if her friends' parents have similar values and are also authoritative, then the impact of her parents' authoritative style will be enhanced: Her psychosocial competence, including her self-esteem and self-reliance, will be benefited, and her chances of delinquency, drug abuse, and psychological distress will be reduced (Collins & Steinberg, 2006).

peer group options and thus indirectly affect achievement by affecting the accessibility of peers. Does the local high school have few, if any, academically oriented students? Parents may arrange for their children to go elsewhere; they might move, or put their children in private schools, or choose to home school. It is not uncommon for parents who live in dangerous environments to send their children to live for brief periods with relatives. Such behavior, of course, depends on income and on the availability of such options, but it also depends on parental involvement. Authoritative parents are invested parents, often making personal sacrifices to maintain their commitment to their view of good parenting (Greenberger & Goldberg, 1989).

Parenting Styles, Peers, and Ethnicity

The complex interplay of parenting style with peer influences stands out in bold relief when we look at teens in different ethnic groups in the United States. Several researchers have found that while the elements of effective parenting are generally applicable across subcultures (e.g., Chung & Steinberg, 2006), for minority youngsters authoritative parenting is not as strongly associated with positive outcomes as it is for White teens (e.g., Baumrind, 1972; Chao, 2001; Dornbusch, Ritter, Leiderman, Roberts, & Fraleigh, 1987; Walker-Barnes & Mason, 2001). Steinberg, Dornbusch, and Brown (1992) found ethnic differences in their large survey of adolescents, particularly in the likelihood of academic success: Authoritative parenting was not as good a predictor of academic success for teens from Asian American, African American, and Hispanic families as it was for White teens. However, Steinberg, Dornbusch, et al. (1992) found some fundamental similarities across all ethnic groups. First, not surprisingly, hard work is linked to academic success regardless of ethnicity; students who put in the most time on homework, for example, are the best school performers. Second, teens across all ethnic groups were equally likely to believe that getting a good education pays off. But the researchers also found some surprising differences in beliefs about the negative consequences of not getting a good education. Asian American students were most likely to believe that poor academic preparation could limit their job options later, whereas African American and Hispanic youngsters were the most optimistic, that is, the least likely to believe that poor academic preparation would hurt their job prospects.

These differences in belief systems were reflected in the degree to which various ethnic peer groups supported academic achievement: Asian crowds were usually highly supportive, whereas African American and Hispanic crowds were not. Unlike White students, minority students sometimes have little choice of which crowd to join, especially when they go to a school where White students are in the majority. They may see themselves as having access to one or a few crowds defined primarily by ethnicity. Steinberg, Dornbusch, et al. (1992) found that for all ethnic groups, the most successful students were those whose parents and peers supported academics. When peers were at odds with parents, the crowd's support, or lack of it, for homework and hard work was the better predictor of a student's day-to-day school behaviors. As Steinberg (1996) noted, even Asian students of disengaged parents are often "saved from academic failure" by their friends' support of academics (p. 157). Yet African American youngsters with authoritative parents often face giving up or hiding their academic aspirations to keep their friends because the crowds they join not only fail to support school effort but may even criticize it as an attempt to "act White" (Fordham & Ogbu, 1986). Indeed, at a very vulnerable age some Black adolescents may feel compelled to choose either to give up high academic standards, greatly limiting their future opportunities, or to be cut off from peer groups that help define their ethnic/racial identity (Ogbu, 2003).

The complex interactions between parenting and peer influences can also be seen in the arena of high-risk and deviant behavior. Again, an authoritative approach is the best protection a parent can provide. Lamborn, Dornbusch, and Steinberg (1996) found, for example, that children from permissive or disengaged families were most likely to experiment with alcohol and marijuana, and children from authoritative homes were least likely to do so. But they also found that the peer group had more influence than the parents on whether experimentation would lead to regular use. For example, even the most vulnerable youngsters, those who had experimented with drugs and whose parents were disengaged, were unlikely to become regular users if their peers were not.

As with school achievement, ethnicity and social class are among the predictors of drug use and deviant behavior in America, so that authoritative parenting is less effective for some teens than for others. But interestingly, several recent studies suggest that even among minority teens from poor neighborhoods, one component of authoritative parenting can be a strong force against deviant behavior and drug use: high levels of parental demandingness (behavioral control). Parents who closely monitor their children have teens who engage less often in delinquent behavior. These are parents who manage to keep track of their children and to place limits on where they spend their time after school and at night. These parents know with whom their children spend their time and what they spend their time doing. In one large, longitudinal study of rural preadolescent and adolescent children, one quarter of the sample was American Indian. About 4 years after the study began, a casino opened on the Indian reservation. Income supplements were paid to every Indian family thereafter, moving 14% of the Indian families out of poverty. Researchers found that for the children in these families (the "ex-poor"), there was a significant decline in conduct disorder and oppositional defiant disorders over 4 years. Statistical evaluation of a number of variables suggested that a key mediator of the children's behavioral change in the ex-poor families was that parents' time to supervise and monitor their children increased after the change in income (Costello, Compton, Keeler, & Angold, 2003).

Even when parents are not particularly warm or democratic, that is, when they are more authoritarian than authoritative, high levels of monitoring, especially for minority teens, can help protect youngsters from high-risk behavior (e.g., Fletcher, Steinberg, & Williams-Wheeler, 2004; Gorman-Smith, Tolan, Zelli, & Huesmann, 1996; Hoeve, Semon Dubas, Eichelsheim, van der Laan, Smeenk, & Gerris, 2009; Lamborn et al., 1996; Lansford, Deater-Deckard, Dodge, Bates, & Pettit, 2004; Walker-Barnes & Mason, 2001). Why are levels of parental monitoring and control so strongly associated with reduced levels of delinquent behavior among Black and other minority teens, even when parents appear to be authoritarian rather than authoritative in their style? As we indicated in Chapter 5, how children construe, or interpret, parenting behaviors may have an influence on how they respond to them. In some ethnic groups, under some environmental circumstances, parents who require absolute obedience to authority without question may be seen by children as operating out of love and affection. First, we have seen that in some cultures and ethnic minority groups, where control is perceived as normative, parents who use control tactics are nonetheless high on warmth (Collins & Steinberg, 2006). Second, if a family lives in a low-income neighborhood where the real dangers of risky behavior may be all too obvious to youngsters, an authoritarian style might be read by a child as an expression of concern. Interestingly, research on Black and White neighborhoods in the United States indicates that Black communities may be more dangerous places for children than White communities even when they are middle class. When Sampson, Morenoff, and Earls (1999) compared middle-class Black versus White communities, they found them to be quite similar internally. But the neighborhoods bordering Black and White communities could be quite different. For White middle-class families the surrounding neighborhoods were often affluent and reasonably safe; but Black middle-class enclaves were more likely to be surrounded by low-income and dangerous neighborhoods. Thus, Black parents, regardless of social class, may more often than White parents perceive a need to monitor and control their children closely to keep them safe. Their children, in turn, may perceive control as an indicator of affection. It should be noted, however, that regardless of ethnicity, when parents are low on warmth and high on harsh control, adolescents are less likely to be willing to reveal information to them, making the actual monitoring of adolescents' behavior more difficult (Smetana, 2008).

THE ROLE OF SCHOOL

As we have seen, the adolescent experience is strongly influenced by parents and peers. In addition, school plays a major part in the psychosocial, intellectual, and vocational development of adolescents. Teachers, curricula, school activities, and school culture all provide raw material contributing to the adolescent's growing sense of self and shaping experience-dependent learning.

Much has been written about the problems with American schools (National Center for Educational Statistics, 2002), and it is beyond the scope and purpose of this chapter to articulate all the aspects of the debate about American educational reform. It is important to note, however, that educational institutions have been increasingly challenged to make changes that support the developmental needs of adolescents (Carnegie Council on Adolescent Development, 1996). This movement derives both from the recognition that many contemporary adolescents face a host of social and academic problems that threaten their well-being (National Center for Educational Statistics, 2002) and from the increasing body of evidence that demonstrates a stage-environment mismatch between adolescents and their schools (Eccles et al., 1993; Eccles & Roeser, 2009).

Many researchers and theorists have noted a decline in academic orientation and motivation starting in the early adolescent years that for some individuals continues throughout high school or culminates in "dropping out" (e.g., Eccles & Roeser, 2011; Gutman, Sameroff, & Cole, 2003). Instructional practices such as whole-group lectures (Feldlaufer, Midgley, & Eccles, 1988), ability grouping (Oakes, Quartz, Gong, Guiton, & Lipton, 1993), and competitive rather than cooperative activities and assessment (Ward et al., 1982) all occur more frequently in middle and junior high schools than in the elementary grades. These practices have been linked to low levels of student motivation and heightened social comparison. For example, just as adolescents become exquisitely sensitive to their place in the peer scene, school-based evaluative policies such as "tracked" academic classes may make differences in ability more noticeable to the adolescent's peers and teachers, leading to decreased status for some (Eccles, Midgley, & Adler, 1984; Oakes 2005). Compared with elementary schools, middle or junior high schools place a heavier emphasis on discipline and teacher control and provide relatively fewer opportunities for student decision making (Brophy & Evertson, 1976; Midgley, Feldlaufer, & Eccles, 1988). In contrast to this traditional model, longitudinal research by Wentzel (1997) documents the benefits associated with a more personal system of middle and secondary schooling. She found that students who perceived their teachers as caring and supportive were more likely than were students of less nurturant teachers to show greater academic effort and to express more prosocial goals. Interestingly, when students described teachers "who cared," they named characteristics that were quite similar to those of authoritative parents.

The large size of most middle and secondary schools is another factor that detracts from personal, mentoring relationships between students and available adults. Ravitch (1983) writes that the trade-off for bigger, more "efficient" schools means "impersonality, bureaucratization, diminished contact between faculty and students, formalization of relationships among colleagues,

Large schools tend to be more impersonal and reduce adolescents' opportunities to be mentored by nurturing adults.

a weakening of the bonds of community" (p. 327). Large school size is correlated with lower scores on standardized test scores and higher drop out rates (see Benner, Graham, & Mistry, 2008), and smaller schools have been shown to promote prosocial behavior among teenagers (Barker & Gump, 1964) and more community activism among their adult graduates (Lindsay, 1984). Leithwood and Jantzi (2009) summarized the data on school size, concluding that elementary schools of 300 to 500 students or less and secondary schools of 600 to 1,000 had the highest levels of achievement.

Calls for smaller counselor-to-student ratios in secondary schools reflect the fact that critical goals such as curriculum choice and career planning are dependent upon personal knowledge of the student and a trusting relationship (Herr, 1989). Elkind (1984) asserts that the adolescent's identity formation is enhanced by being surrounded by a relatively small group of adults who know the student well and who, over time, are able to support the movement toward responsible autonomy. Indeed, adolescents who have more positive perceptions of relationships with teachers do better in school and perform better on achievement tests (e.g., Gregory & Weinstein, 2004; Woolley & Grogan-Kaylor, 2006).

The timing and types of transitions involved in the passage from primary to middle to secondary school are also important. These transitions represent turning points that involve a redefinition of social status (e.g., from middle school "top dog" to senior high "bottom dog," Entwisle, 1990) and the experience of several simultaneous stressors. Simmons and Blyth (1987) present evidence for "cumulative stress" theory in a study of the effects of different transition patterns on academic achievement and self-esteem. Investigating the school-related outcomes of students who followed a K–8, 9–12 transition model and those who followed a K–6, 7–9, 10–12 model, the researchers found more negative outcomes related to the latter plan. They interpreted these findings as resulting from an interaction between the stresses of puberty and the cumulative stresses inherent in multiple school changes. Of course, changing schools per se may not be the problem; it may be that moving from the more supportive elementary environment to the less supportive middle or junior high environment is the key stressor (e.g., Juvonen, 2007; Midgley, Feldlaufer, & Eccles, 1989). For students who might be already at risk, the cost of these educational practices could be extremely high. Feldlaufer et al. (1988) found that low levels of perceived teacher support were particularly harmful for low-achieving students who enter a less supportive classroom after a school transition.

But providing an emotionally supportive academic climate for young adolescents is not all that is needed to ensure their educational progress. Evidence from a study of 23 middle schools demonstrated that the combination of demanding teachers and rigorous curricula was strongly related to increased student achievement in mathematics, whereas warm teacher–student relations and communal classroom organization were not (Phillips, 1997). Perhaps we need to remember that both elements, responsiveness and demandingness, make important contributions to success in schools as well as in homes. In another study of middle school students, Wentzel (2002) found that teachers' high expectations for their students was most predictive of students' achievement and motivation to learn. But in addition, negative feedback or criticism from teachers, even in combination with high expectations, was found to be most clearly associated with diminished motivation and poor achievement. This finding applied to all students in her sample, regardless of gender, race, or ethnicity. She points out that "by creating a context free of harsh criticism *and* [italics added] one in which students are expected to do their best, teachers might be better able to convey information clearly and efficiently, encourage student engagement, and focus students' attention on academic tasks" (p. 298).

Finally, the level of involvement by parents in the schooling of adolescents also influences achievement outcomes. Despite scientific and government support of parental involvement as a critical ingredient in school success (e.g., U.S. Department of Education, 1990) particularly for poor and minority children (Comer, 1988), the idea of parents becoming involved in the academic life of the adolescent has

Leo, at age 16, has struggled with attention deficit disorder. Her comments show how important both adult support and peer collaboration are for a student's success in school.

been met with serious resistance. Consistent with the "hands-off" philosophy described earlier, many adults tend to leave the business of education to teachers or to the adolescents themselves. Involvement declines sharply at the middle and high school levels (Steinberg, 1996; Stevenson & Stigler, 1992). Steinberg has indicated that approximately one third of the students in his study said their parents were uninformed about their school performance, and another one sixth said that their parents did not care. More than 40% of participants said their parents did not attend any school function or activity. This parental unresponsiveness seems closely tied to the child's age and possibly to parental beliefs about an adolescent's right to autonomy. Parents and teachers tend to view various dimensions of involvement (e.g., monitoring homework and use of time, helping at school, attending meetings and conferences, plus serving as a partner with the school in decision making) as appropriately decreasing once the child has made the transition out of the elementary grades (see Stewart, 2008).

LEISURE AND WORK

Outside school, leisure activities occupy much of an adolescent's time. Leisure activities can promote skill mastery, such as sports participation, hobbies, and artistic pursuits, or they may be more purely recreational, such as playing video games, watching TV, daydreaming, or hanging out with friends (Fine, Mortimer, & Roberts, 1990). Young people who are involved in extracurricular activities sponsored by their schools and other community organizations—athletics, social service organizations, school newspaper staff, student government, band, and so on—are more likely to be academic achievers and to have other desirable qualities than students who are not involved in sponsored activities (see Mahoney, Larson, & Eccles, 2005; Mahoney, Harris, & Eccles, 2006) even though the gains are relatively modest. Longer and more intensive involvement is associated with better long-term effects, including greater educational, civic, and occupational success even in adulthood (e.g., Gardner, Roth, & Brooks-Gunn, 2008). Although there are general benefits to extracurricular participation, the kind of benefit varies somewhat by activity and not all the outcomes are positive. One longitudinal study followed over 1,000 Michigan young people for 14 years, beginning when they were in the 6th grade and keeping track of, among other things, their extracurricular involvements (Mahoney et al., 2005). High school participation in either prosocial activities or sports was associated with long-term educational achievements (e.g., going to college). But although kids who participated in prosocial activities were unlikely to use alcohol or other drugs in high school, those who participated in sports were more likely than most other teens to use alcohol in high school, perhaps because sports participation is also related to high stress (e.g., Larson, Hansen, & Moneta, 2006). Both personal qualities and peer influences appear to play a role in shaping these outcomes. For example, developing positive friendships through extracurricular activities seems to be one important pathway by which activity involvement influences later outcomes (e.g., Simpkins, Eccles, & Becnel, 2008).

Today's adolescents spend a lot of time doing work for pay. Mortimer (2005) reports that between 80% and 90% of teens are employed sometime during their high school years. Are there benefits to these early jobs for teens? It seems reasonable to propose some developmental advantages. Having adult responsibilities might help adolescents feel independent and grown up, enhancing self-esteem. Searching for work and being employed might provide training that is hard to come by in any other way, such as learning how to find a job, learning one's own job preferences, and clarifying one's work values. Parents often assume that working will help adolescents to learn to manage their money and their time. Mortimer et al. (1999) report that teens who work generally endorse many of these presumed benefits, seeing their jobs as helping them to be more responsible, to manage their time and their money, to establish a work ethic, and to learn social skills. Adolescents also list some

Leo's experiences with drama club and her job at Teen Empowerment both allow her to try out different roles and feel part of the larger community.

negative outcomes, primarily feeling fatigued and having less time for homework and leisure activities, but on balance they see their work in a positive light.

Do adolescents who work need to work—to save for college or even to help ease financial burdens at home? During the Great Depression, economic hardship did send adolescents into the workplace, and working was apparently linked to more responsible use of money and a more "adult" orientation (Elder, 1974). But the culture has changed dramatically since then. Whereas in 1940 only about 3% of 16-year-olds still in school were employed, by 1980 the government estimated that more than 40% were working. Of course, relatively more youngsters complete high school today than in 1940, so that today's students may be more representative of the general population, but there is evidence of a substantial shift in students' priorities as well. Middle-class teens are more likely to be employed than those from lower socioeconomic groups, and their money is unlikely to be saved or contributed to family expenses. Rather, working teens more frequently spend their money on materialistic pursuits: wardrobes, entertainment, drugs, and alcohol (e.g. Steinberg et al., 1993).

Cultural change has also affected the kinds of jobs adolescents acquire. In 1940, many teens worked on farms or in manufacturing, in jobs where they were supervised by adults (frequently adults who were family members or were known to their families), and they often received some training that was directly relevant to the jobs they would have after high school. Today, teens are much more likely to work in retail establishments, including restaurants, and to be under the direct supervision of other young people rather than adults. It appears that the work teens do today is often less educational than in 1940 and may have less long-term career value (Aronson, Mortimer, Zierman, & Hacker, 1996).

Although adolescents themselves seem enthusiastic about the value of their part-time work, researchers report that there can be some serious side effects. Note that negative consequences are substantially related to hours of employment—the more hours, the more problematic the effects in most cases. The most troublesome finding is that long hours of employment (especially 20 or more hours per week) are associated with increases in problem behaviors like theft (e.g., giving away store products to friends), school misconduct, alcohol and drug use, including cigarette smoking (e.g., Mihalic & Elliot, 1997; Mortimer et al., 1999). The effects of work on schooling and school involvement are mixed. Several large-scale studies have found no effects on students' grades but negative effects on total educational attainment. Years of schooling tend to be reduced for students who invest long hours in their jobs. Other studies have found negative correlations between working and grades even for relatively few hours of work (Largie, Field, Hernandez-Reif, Sanders, & Diego, 2001). Bachman, Safron, Sy, & Schulenberg, 2003 found that negative associations between schooling and work appear to be bidirectional—for example, teens with less school involvement are more likely to seek jobs, and once they are working substantial hours, teens become even less involved in school. A recent re-examination of data on part-time work (Monaghan, Lee, & Steinberg, 2011) helps strengthen earlier conclusions. Part-time work of moderate intensity (20 hours or less per week) was not associated with either positive or negative outcomes for adolescents. Contrary to the argument that adolescents acquired some psychological benefits from part-time work (Mortimer et al., 1999), this analysis showed negligible outcomes on academics, self-reliance, and self-esteem. Negative effects on academics and behavior were strongly related to high intensity work (more than 20 hours per week), especially when such work is begun during the course of the school year.

MEDIA AND THE CONSUMER CULTURE

No doubt about it, media plays a major role in the life of contemporary adolescents, and its use is increasing rapidly for both children and youth. A peek into ways young people consume electronic media shows some startling findings. The word

18-year-old Tim lives in a media-rich world, with both positive and negative influences. How does technology change adolescents' relationships with their friends and families?

"consume," often used in regard to media, is an interesting and apt choice because researchers have long been concerned about the effects of a steady diet of technology on the brains and behaviors of young people. A large-scale, nationally representative study by the Kaiser Family Foundation (2010) and its reanalysis by race (Northwestern University, 2011) shows that U.S. 3rd to 12th graders increased their total daily media consumption from 6 hours and 21 minutes in 2004 to 7 hours and 38 minutes by 2009, approximating the hours of a typical adult work day. Media usage takes up even more time than work, however, because it continues during the weekend. Rates of all media consumption (music, computers, video games, TV, and movies) except for print media increased over the three waves of the study (1999, 2004, 2009). What percentage of 3rd to 12th graders have a TV in their bedrooms? If you guessed slightly more that 7 out of 10 (71%,), you're correct. Cable TV and video game consoles are present in 50% of bedrooms. Computers, fast becoming a staple of the educational system, are also very common.

Consumption patterns differed between younger (8 to 10 years olds) and older groups as well as between racial/ethnic groups (see Figure 10.4). Media exposure was higher in Black, Hispanic, and Asian groups (by approximately 4 hours per day) compared to Whites and among boys (by approximately one hour per day) compared to girls (Center on Media and Human Development, 2011). Researchers concluded that a more realistic picture of media use should take into account exposure to multiple forms of media, because youth are often engaged in more than one form at the same time. When such multitasking is considered, the amount of time jumps to an average high of 10 hours and 45 minutes of media exposure per day.

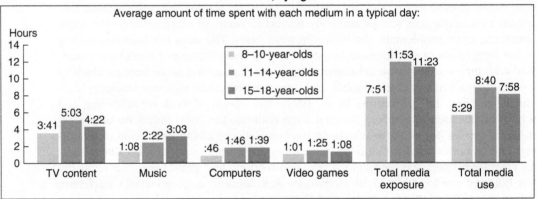

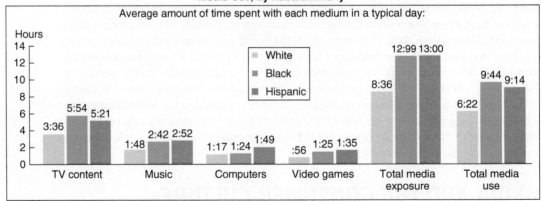

FIGURE 10.4 How much media do children and adolescents consume? Types and Extent of Media Use Among U.S. 3rd to 12th Graders.

SOURCE: The Henry J. Kaiser Family Foundation (2010, January 1). Generation M2: Media in the lives of 8- to 18-year-olds. From http://www.kff.org/other/poll-finding/report-generation-m2-media-in-the-lives/. Used by permission.

This study did *not* include time using cell or smart phones (talking, texting, tweeting, Internet, or movie viewing), which would have, most likely, increased the average amount of time spent on media use.

It is important for helping professionals to concern themselves with the effects of cultural forces on adolescent development if they are to take a position that promotes healthy growth and functioning. Jessor (1993) noted that the distal effects of the larger cultural context are rarely taken into consideration when studying development, although "understanding contextual change is as important as understanding individual change" (p. 120). Perhaps the major question to be addressed is: How adolescent-friendly is the society we live in? If family, peers, and teachers are fellow players in the unfolding drama of adolescent identity formation, the culture with its values and broader institutions provides the stage upon which that drama is acted out.

Many writers from diverse fields of study have noted a general loss of community and a focus on individualism and material success evident in American culture at this point in its history (Barber, 1992; Bellah, Madsen, Sullivan, Swidler, & Tipton, 1985; Hewlett & West, 1998; Lasch, 1991). In their discussion of a culture they call "poisonous," Hewlett and West describe punitive economic forces that undermine family stability and negative media forces that shape attitudes and beliefs. Few adults would deny that the exposure to the realities of the adult world that teens have today has been ratcheted up several levels compared to even recent generations. For example, media exposure to violent, sexualized, and commercial messages occurs at a more intense level and starts at earlier ages.

But how does this kind of media exposure affect children and adolescents and how much of a threat is it? The link between viewing televised violence and behaving aggressively for certain individuals has been well researched and is generally accepted (see Comstock & Scharrer, 1999). Modeling processes (see Chapter 1) are presumed to account for much of this relationship. Recent interest in the role of media as a socializer of values expands upon social learning principles to include constructivist conceptions of how individuals make sense of their environments. In other words, people use what they perceive as raw material from which to construct ideas, beliefs, and guiding principles. A recent longitudinal study offers strong support for this model with respect to violent video games (Willoughby, Adachi, & Good, 2012). Canadian adolescents were studied over the course of their high school years to investigate relationships between playing violent video games and later aggressive behavior. Even after controlling for other media use, quality of parenting, academic and school variables, sports involvement, depression, and deviant behaviors, the relationship between a steady diet of violent video game play and aggressive behavior was significant. Furthermore, the authors did not find support for the idea that more aggressive youth elected to play more violent video games (a selection effect). On the contrary, *playing the violent games themselves* was associated with increased levels of aggressive behavior for both boys and girls. There appears to be something unique about the violent video game effects insofar as the same increase in aggression was not seen in those youth who played nonviolent video games.

Violent video games are now played by adolescents around the world. Does violent video game play have the same causal relationship to aggressive behavior and cognitions across cultures? The answer appears to be yes. Results from a large meta-analysis of studies from Western countries and Japan showed that increased violent video game play was a causal factor in increasing aggressive behavior and cognitions and in reducing prosocial behavior and empathy (Anderson, Shibuya, Swing, Bushman, Sakamoto, et al., 2010) Neither gender nor age significantly moderated this relationship. This finding is important because it updates other analyses and strengthens the view that repeated practice shapes brain and behavior via processes of experience-dependent learning. This is a timely and practically important issue for parents, helpers, and public policy makers. The authors conclude that playing video games doesn't just involve moving a joystick. Players "are indeed interacting *with the game psychologically and emotionally*. It is not surprising that when the game involves rehearsing aggressive and violent thoughts and actions, such deep game involvement results in antisocial effects on the player. Of course, the same basic social–cognitive processes should also yield prosocial effects when game content is primarily prosocial . . . Video games are neither inherently good nor inherently bad. But people learn. And content matters" (Anderson et al., 2010, p. 171).

Another area of particular concern for adolescents is the learning of sexual messages and attitudes. Studies using correlational methods have found relationships between frequent viewing of televised portrayals of sexuality with more distorted cognitions, more liberal attitudes about sex, and more tolerance for sexual harassment (Strouse, Goodwin, & Roscoe, 1994). Frequent consumption of sexualized media has also been linked to increased sexual behavior—that is, more sexual partners and earlier sexual initiation than for individuals without such media exposure (Brown et al., 2002). This may have something to do with the perception that "everybody's doing it." Researchers have found that people's expectations or constructions about what is normative influence what they choose to do. Adolescents who believe that teens in general have frequent sexual experiences engage in riskier and more frequent sexual activity themselves (Whitaker & Miller, 2000).

A study by Ward (2002) employed both correlational and experimental methods to study whether television's messages influenced attitudes about sexuality in a multiethnic sample of older adolescents. This study confirmed that the three beliefs investigated in this study—that men are driven by sex, that women are sex objects, and that dating is a recreational sport—were very strongly related to heavy TV viewing and to personal involvement with TV. High personal involvement was measured by individuals' goals for TV (entertainment and a way to learn about the world), discussions about TV shows with others, and identification with TV characters, among other things. Outcomes of the experimental part of the study revealed that females more strongly endorsed the stereotypical beliefs after viewing sexual TV clips than did women who saw nonsexual episodes.

Interestingly, this pattern was not the same for males. Males' agreement with the three stereotypes was already much higher than women's, so it may not have been realistic to expect this experimental manipulation to generate higher rates of agreement. Another possibility is that males' attitudes might be differentially influenced by exposure to other types of media, such as music videos.

Certainly not all media use is associated with negative outcomes. Yet it is important to consider the impact of repeated exposure to the violent, sexual, and materialistic images in much of the media adolescents consume. Media messages can provide elements for the construction of identity via the processes we have described in this chapter. Moreover, media images serve as standards for social comparison, molding expectations for normative behavior and amplifying values that may be at odds with those of families and communities (Comstock & Scharrer, 2006). As the report from the Carnegie Council on Adolescent Development (1996) points out, adolescents are careening down the information superhighway, and electronic conduits (TV, videos, cable, computers, movies, and popular music) "have become strong competitors to the traditional societal institutions in shaping young people's attitudes and values" (p. 41). Also, newer interactive media applications (text messaging, e-mail, chat rooms, and so on) provide means for communicating with a broader segment of society, often anonymously. These venues offer youngsters new opportunities for risk taking and aggressive behavior. For example, "cyberbullying," using electronic forms of contact to carry out intentional, relational aggressive acts, is on the rise among adolescents (Raskauyskas & Stoltz, 2007; Smith et al., 2008). Unlike traditional bullying it tends to happen outside of school and can have a broad reach. Smith et al., for example, describe ". . . 'happy slapping,' where a victim is slapped or made to appear silly by one person, filmed by another, and the resulting pictures circulated on mobile phones . . ." (p. 376). Sexting, or the sending of sexually suggestive photos or messages, appears to be on the rise. A recent study showed that youth (aged 14–24) who were sexually active were more likely to engage in sexting. These adolescents and young adults were also more likely to share the suggestive pictures with friends (MTV, 2010). More research is needed to explore the effects of this trend most importantly on shaping attitudes and behaviors about sexuality.

How do contemporary cultural conditions interact with the adolescent's struggle for autonomy and self-definition? In the next section, we will explore some answers to this question.

RISKY BEHAVIOR AND SOCIAL DEVIANCE

Like it or not, teens assimilate views of acceptable behavior from many sources, including TV, movies, popular music, and the Internet.

Andy and Ben are talking about drinking and driving. They describe a typical "party"—one that involves lots of alcohol and not much parental supervision. They frequently drive home from these unsupervised events, believing that they are "responsible drivers" because they're so good at drinking and driving and have never had any accidents. It's not that Andy's and Ben's parents are intentionally neglectful. The teens just don't share this information with their parents. Andy and Ben simply believe they are very good at doing what they want to do without getting into trouble. They tend to think that other teenagers, those who aren't as smart or clever, might get into trouble, but not them. Are the behaviors Ben and Andy describe normal or deviant? Are they part of a passing phase or predictive of future problems? Should we crack down on these behaviors or look the other way? These questions pose real problems, not only for parents and helpers but also for social policy makers in fields such as education and criminal justice. These behaviors epitomize a paradox at this stage of development, for contravention of adult norms by experimentation with deviant behaviors has always been part of the adolescent experience and is, in fact, statistically normative (Barnes, Welte, & Dintcheff, 1992; Jessor et al., 1991; Reyna & Farley, 2006).

Risky behaviors are behaviors that constitute a departure from socially accepted norms or behaviors that pose a threat to the well-being of individuals or groups. Various writers have used different terms to refer to these behaviors, including *reckless, problem, deviant, antisocial,* and *delinquent.* Here we use the adjectives somewhat interchangeably, although risky and reckless connote slightly more benign behaviors than do deviant, antisocial, or delinquent. Even so, separating these activities into bad and not-so-bad is tricky because, as we shall see, they all pose potential dangers. They vary on a continuum of severity and, when severe, tend to appear in clusters in the lives of teenagers at risk. Some examples of these problem behaviors include drinking and other drug use, smoking, truancy, sexual behavior, high-speed driving, drunk driving, vandalism, and other kinds of delinquency. Society considers some of these behaviors to be not only reckless but illegal as well. Consequently, statistics show that fully four fifths of adolescent males have experienced some police contact for minor infractions during their teenage years (Farrington, 1989). Although most crime statistics indicate that males are disproportionately involved in these offenses, evidence points to increasing delinquency among girls, especially those who mature early (Henggeler, Schoenwald, Borduin, Rowland, & Cunningham, 1998; Odgers, Moffitt, Broadbent, Dickson, Hancox, Harrington, et al., 2008).

Risky behaviors escalate sharply during adolescence, peaking around age 17 and then dropping off in early adulthood for most individuals (Steinberg, 2008). Figure 10.5, for example, shows the drop in speeding while driving after the teen years. Not all adolescents experiment with reckless behavior, but a high percentage do. Thus, the proportion of adolescents who engage in some variety of reckless or deviant behavior is higher than for groups at any other stage of the life span.

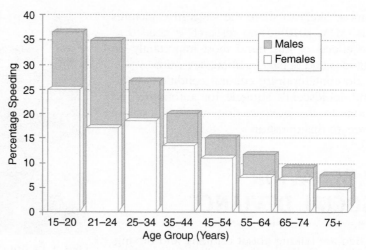

FIGURE 10.5 **Percentage of drivers who were speeding in fatal crashes in 1996, by age and sex.**
SOURCE: From U.S. Department of Transportation (1996, Fig. 4) as cited in Nell, V. (2002). Why young men drive dangerously: Implications for injury prevention. *Current Directions in Psychological Science, 11,* 75–79.

It is hard to get a handle on the actual amount of risky behavior enacted by adolescents. Juvenile crime rates have dropped overall since 1980. In 2010 the incidence was 55% lower that it was at its peak in 1994 (Puzzanchera & Adams, 2012; U.S. Bureau of Justice Statistics, 2000). Even though incidence rates of violent crime have fallen, the problems associated with risky behavior among teenagers have not disappeared. Consider that in the United States, approximately 3 million new cases of sexually transmitted diseases are diagnosed in adolescents each year, and two new young people are infected with HIV every hour (Centers for Disease Control, 2006). A decline in teenage pregnancy has continued since the 1990s into 2011. Reductions in sexual activity and increases in condom use may be the reason for this decline (Ventura & Hamilton, 2011). However, the number of babies born to teen mothers in the United States is still the highest of all developed countries. Great Britain, whose teenage birth rate is next highest, has only about half the teenage birth rate of the United States (e.g., United Nations Statistical Division, 2007).

In 1997, approximately 30% of children in 4th through 6th grades reported being offered drugs, representing an increase of 47% from 1993 to 1997 (Partnership for a Drug-Free America, 1998). When a national sample of adolescents was surveyed in the early 1990s about **binge drinking** (drinking at least five drinks in a row), 28% of high school seniors and 40% of 20- to 21-year-olds admitted they had binged on alcohol at least once during the previous 2-week period (Johnston, O'Malley, & Bachman, 1994). Results of the same survey in 2000 revealed that 30% of 12th graders, 26.2% of 10th graders, and 14.1% of 8th graders reported binge drinking in the 2 weeks prior to the survey. In addition, 12th graders' perceptions of the risks of drinking one or two alcoholic drinks decreased from 1990 to 2000 (Johnston, O'Malley, & Bachman, 2003). Data reported by the Partnership for a Drug-Free America (2006) indicate that alcohol use by teens has steadily declined since 1998. Still, in 2005, 28% of 7th to 12th graders reported binge drinking in the past 2 weeks. Furthermore, a significant increase in the use of painkillers (Vicodin and Oxycontin) was reported among 8th to 12th graders between 2002 and 2004 (Johnston, O'Malley, & Bachman, 2004). More recent statistics from 2009–2011 show some encouraging signs. Decreasing trends were reported for alcohol and tobacco use among teens. Marijuana use, however, increased over this period (see Substance Abuse and Mental Health Services Administration, 2011).

Sometimes, helpers choose to treat the reckless or deviant behaviors of adolescents as separable conditions. When this approach is used, interventions get targeted to specific problems, such as drug use or unsafe sexual practices or drunk driving. However, most problem behaviors come in packages. They frequently coexist on a spectrum of less harmful to dysfunctional. Consider Brianna, a high school sophomore who drinks alcohol at parties, but never to excess, and smokes cigarettes with her friends. She has tried pot now and again, but she thinks she does not want to try anything stronger until she gets older. She is an average student, has a sociable personality, and has stabilizing family and peer supports. Despite this, Brianna and her best friend recently were arrested for shoplifting in the local mall. The girls explained that they did this "on a dare."

Shauna is a 9th grader who has had academic and behavioral problems since elementary school. Her headstrong, impulsive, and aggressive characteristics have always put her at odds with people in authority. Her boyfriend is part of a gang that steals beer and cigarettes, later selling them to buy harder drugs. The lure of her boyfriend and his lifestyle is stronger than her single mother can overcome. Shauna is now pregnant and will soon drop out of high school. Although there are some similar features in both girls' risky behavior, namely, the easy availability of alcohol and drugs, freedom to spend time with peers who may influence risk taking, and the ubiquitous adolescent urge to experiment, there are also some important differences. Consequently, the level of intervention used to address Brianna's problem behaviors would probably be less effective with Shauna (see Box 1.2 in Chapter 1 on prevention issues).

Moffitt (1993a) makes a valuable contribution to understanding these differences by distinguishing between two major developmental trajectories of adolescent antisocial behavior: **life-course-persistent antisocial pattern** and **adolescence-limited antisocial patterns**. These developmental patterns are also called *early-starter* and *adolescent-onset trajectories*. (See Chapter 7 for descriptions.) The life-course-persistent pattern begins in early childhood and continues throughout life. In general, this pattern is associated with early conduct problems, aggressiveness, and academic difficulties, as typified by Shauna. For this particular package of problems, early intervention for children and families is most effective. In contrast, adolescence-limited antisocial behavior, such as Brianna's, develops in adolescence and usually ends shortly thereafter. The prognosis for the latter kind of pathway is generally more favorable.

Is adolescence-limited antisocial behavior the same as reckless behavior in adolescence? The answer may be a matter of degree. Certainly, some teenagers go to more extreme lengths, have more accumulated risk factors and fewer protective ones in their lives, and thus suffer more from the consequences of their behavior than others. But the paradox we introduced earlier seems to apply here. Behaviors traditionally considered deviant are increasingly becoming part of the experimental repertoire of teens who are considered well adjusted. Hersch (1998) closely followed the activities of adolescents in a suburban high school for several years. She got to know the students well, becoming an "insider" in the world of adolescents, and was able to document the escalation of dangerous pursuits as a normal part of contemporary adolescent life. "Behaviors once at the fringe of adolescent rebelliousness have not only permeated the mainstream culture of high school but are seeping into the fabric of middle school" (p. 156). As Jessica, an eighth-grade student interviewed by Hersch said, "This [smoking, using drugs, having sex] is *what you are supposed to do* [italics added]. . . . It's our teenage phase. You are only a kid once" (p. 156). Helpers who work on the front lines, in middle and high schools or in practices that include adolescents, deal with these problems and attitudes every day. Let us try to examine why reckless behavior is such a part of the adolescent phase in the first place, and then we will consider its benefits and costs to young people.

Setting the Stage for Risk Taking

Adolescent risk taking appears to be a result of complex interacting processes, from the brain changes that underlie emotional and cognitive developments from puberty onward to identity processes to parenting and community supports. Let's consider some of the important factors. First, adolescents tend to score higher than other age groups on a dimension called **sensation seeking**, which is defined as "the need for varied, novel, and complex sensation and experiences and the willingness to take physical and social risk for the sake of these experiences" (Zuckerman, 1979, p. 10).

Sensation seeking is related to the maturing of emotional brain systems and the relative imbalance that exists between appetitive functions (approach behaviors) and control (executive functions). At puberty, proliferation and then pruning of dopamine receptors creates a new pattern of receptor distribution throughout the brain (Steinberg, 2008). Dopamine is an important neurotransmitter in the processing of emotion, and puberty triggers ". . . a rapid and dramatic increase in dopaminergic activity . . . which is presumed to lead to increases in reward seeking" (Steinberg et al., 2008, p. 1764). The link between the reward system and the social processing system seems to play a role in adolescents' heightened interest in peers. Literally, peer acceptance appears to be more rewarding post-puberty than in childhood (Casey et al., 2008; Steinberg, 2008).

Human imaging studies show greater activation of parts of the emotional system relative to children or adults when adolescents are making risky choices (Casey et al., 2008). But why would having a mature emotional brain system make adolescents bigger risk takers than adults? As we have discussed in Chapter 9, the cognitive control system develops more slowly than the emotional system, and perhaps more importantly, connections between the cognitive control system and the emotional system develop slowly, continuing to grow through the mid-20s. Therefore, for adolescents "in emotionally salient situations, the limbic system will win over control systems given its maturity relative to the prefrontal control system" (Casey et al., 2008, p. 64). Figure 10.6 illustrates the relative rates of functional development for the emotional and cognitive control systems.

Ernst and her colleagues have expanded our understanding of adolescent risky behavior and cognitive control to include the increased sensitivity to stress present in adolescence. As we have described, cognitive control is primarily a function of the prefrontal cortex (PFC). Reward seeking is related to appetitive (approach) systems in the brain, and sensitivity to stress marked by emotional lability is related to the brain's threat-detection (avoidance) systems. The triarchic model (Ernst, Pine, &

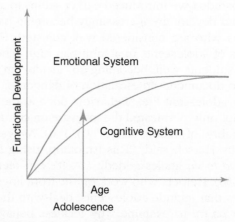

FIGURE 10.6 **A model of timing of functional maturation of the emotional and cognitive control systems of the brains.**
SOURCE: Based on Casey, B. J., Getz, S., & Galvan, A. (2008). The adolescent brain. *Developmental Review, 28*(1), 62–77. Used with permission from Elsevier.

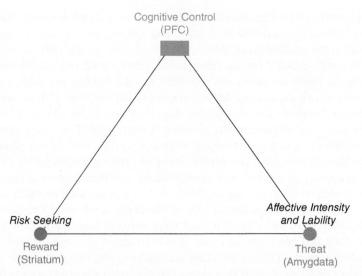

Cognitive Control
(PFC)

Risk Seeking

Affective Intensity
and Lability

Reward
(Striatum)

Threat
(Amygdata)

FIGURE 10.7 **Uneven brain development in adolescence.** Triadic Neural Systems Model (Ernst, Pine & Hardin, 2006). The reward and threat systems are more active during adolescence, tipping the balance needed for mature self-regulation, decision-making, and behavior.

SOURCE: Based on Richards, J. M., Plate, R. C., & Ernst. M. (2012). Neural systems underlying motivated behavior in adolescence: Implications for preventive medicine. *Preventive Medicine, 55*, S7–S16. Used with permission from Elsevier.

Hardin, 2006; Richards, Plate, & Ernst, 2012; see Figure 10.7) is a useful way of conceptualizing the mix of risky behavior, emotional dysregulation and reduced executive functioning characteristic of this period. The hyperactivity of both reward (mediated by the striatum) and avoidance (mediated by the amygdala) systems, in the context of an underdeveloped cognitive control system (mediated by the PFC), can help explain the sometimes inexplicable highs and lows of teenage behavior.

A second important factor may be that adolescent egocentrism supports the fiction that risky behavior is exciting but not potentially catastrophic. Arnett (1992) implicates adolescents' weaknesses in reasoning about probability, a kind of formal operational thinking, as particularly important here (See Chapter 9). Drawing upon Piaget's ideas, Arnett argues that

> . . . in every judgement of probability, there is a reference, implicit or explicit, to a system of distributions or frequencies. Adolescents' perceptions of these systems are skewed by their desire for sensation and by the personal fable that convinces them of their immunity from disaster. . . . But even if an adolescent were exceptionally proficient at estimating probabilities, on a given occasion, the likelihood of disaster resulting from drunk driving, or sex without contraception, or illegal drug use, or delinquency/crime is, in fact, statistically small—even when applied to others, and seen through the lens of sensation seeking and egocentrism, the perceived probability fades even further. (p. 350)

Recent empirical research supports some aspects of Arnett's analysis but not others. Adolescents who perceive the risks of certain behaviors seem to be somewhat less likely than others to ever engage in those risky behaviors; but adolescents who *do* engage in risky behavior actually seem to be well aware that they have put themselves at risk! There seem to be complicated processes at work here (see Reyna & Farley, 2006). It appears that some teens put themselves at risk because they are responding to triggers that cue big, short-term rewards; they do not do a cost/benefit analysis. This is what you would expect if the emotional system is activated without benefit of control from the cognitive system. However, even when adolescents feel vulnerable and *do* engage the cognitive control system, their approach to evaluating risk may keep them from being as risk averse as they should be. Reyna and Farley

(2006) suggest that when probability analyses are new to adolescents, they are likely to do cost/benefit assessments that favor risk taking, just as Arnett suggests. They often perceive the relative costs, which are usually low probability, as well worth the potential rewards. Adults, on the other hand, think about risk situations differently. They are more likely to assess risky behaviors, like having sex with a casual partner without a condom, as completely unacceptable, because *if* there were negative consequences, however low the probability, they would be catastrophic. As Reyna and Farley put it, adults eventually develop a more global or categorical approach to risk assessment, a sort of automatic response to the "gist" of the situation, rather than painstakingly weighing the probabilities of positive and negative outcomes. To illustrate, in a study of adolescents' versus adults' reaction time to questions such as, "Is it a good idea to set your hair on fire?" or "Is it a good idea to swim with sharks?" Baird and Fugelsang (2004) found that adolescents responded much more slowly than adults, as you would expect if they were actually taking a risk/benefit analysis approach. They did not respond more slowly to other, non-risk related questions.

Another important factor affecting adolescent risky behavior is the influence of peers. Arnett (1992) suggested that peers provide not only role models for deviancy but a kind of **collective egocentrism**. Shauna might reason, for example, that if her boyfriend and his friends aren't worried about getting caught in some illegal scheme, then neither should she worry. Each adolescent's judgment that "it probably won't happen to me" strengthens that of the other members of the peer group. Peers are definitely implicated in increased risk taking during adolescence, but there may be other reasons for their influence. We noted earlier that the presence of peers helps to activate reward-seeking behavior, because social information processing and reward are served by some of the same early maturing emotional brain areas. Steinberg (2008) argues that it is the same slowly developing connections between cognitive control systems (involving several cortical areas) and the subcortical emotional system that accounts for both the decline of risk taking and of peer influence in later adolescence and early adulthood. There is evidence to support these claims. For example, Paus and his colleagues (Paus, Leonard, Lerner, Lerner, Perron, Pike et al., 2011) report studies using imaging techniques to assess the degree of connectivity between regions of the cortex involved in self-control in a sample of 12- to 18-year-olds. Those participants who scored high on measures of resistance to peer influence showed more structural connectivity (controlling for age) than participants who scored low on such measures.

Are there any benefits for humans to having an adolescent period that involves increased sensation seeking and risk taking? Chronic, life-course-persistent antisocial behavior exacts an enormous cost from the individual involved, from his family, and from society in general. So it is hard to imagine any redeeming features to this condition. The impact of adolescent-limited antisocial behavior, however, is less clear-cut. In one view, recklessness in adolescents, especially in males, once had a strong fitness value (e.g., Nell, 2002; Steinberg & Belsky, 1996; Steinberg, 2008). Nell, for example, argues that in the evolutionary history of the human species, young males who were willing to risk their own safety to fight for territory and for dominance won the most desirable mates. The legacy of this evolutionary history is that, even today, adolescent boys are prepared, even more so than girls, to take risks and to engage in aggressive behavior. Research on the dopaminergic remodeling of the limbic and paralimbic systems that takes place at puberty indicates that ". . . it is more pronounced in males than in females" (Steinberg, 2008, p. 87), providing a neurological basis for greater risk taking in males during adolescence.

Another somewhat related view is that adolescent limited antisocial behavior is adaptive because it promotes individuation and self-determination. Goldstein (1990), for example, suggests that risky behavior is instrumental in relieving the **maturity gap** that afflicts adolescents who are caught in a time warp between physical and social maturity. To possess the symbolic trappings of adult status (sexual intimacy, material possessions, autonomy, and respect from parents), adolescents mimic the behavior of more advanced, and often more antisocial, peers, borrowing those elements that elicit respect from others and that affirm personal independence.

Maggs, Almeida, and Galambos (1995) found that increasing levels of engagement in risk-taking behavior across adolescence (disobeying parents, school misconduct, substance abuse, antisocial behavior) were associated with decreased levels of positive self-concept but with increased levels of peer acceptance. Wilson (1996) noted that some socially deviant behaviors of disadvantaged inner-city youth represent situationally adaptive means of coping with urban life. Engaging in risk-taking behavior thus represents a paradox that has both positive (status-provision) and negative (social-deviance) aspects. Arnett (1992) theorizes that reckless behavior is more a fact of life in cultures with **broad** as opposed to **narrow socialization** practices. Societies with broad socializing practices permit and encourage high levels of individual freedom of expression, have fewer social constraints, expect less community responsibility, and thus tolerate a wider variety of socially deviant behaviors. Cultures with narrow socialization practices, more characteristic of nonindustrialized cultures, exert more control over the expression of behaviors that violate social standards and expect more conformity from young members of the society.

So is reckless behavior among adolescents the price we must pay for living in a society that encourages freedom of expression? What kinds of trade-offs should we be willing to tolerate? Even though adolescent-limited antisocial patterns usually attenuate sometime in early adulthood, when more conventional roles of employee, spouse, or parent are assumed, we should not conclude that this pattern poses no risk at all. To be sure, Moffitt (1993a) notes that risky behavior, while enhancing peer involvement, may also ensnare adolescents in situations that can ultimately prove quite harmful, such as fostering drug dependence or depressing academic achievement. As Reyna and Farley (2006) argue, no matter how normative risk taking may be in adolescence, both its immediate and long term consequences can be so substantial that it is a matter of great social concern. Developing effective, empirically based interventions to eliminate the most consequential of the risks should be a high priority. Steinberg advocates a commonsense solution: making risky options less available to youth until they have greater maturity in making decisions. "Strategies such as raising the price of cigarettes, more vigilantly enforcing laws governing the sale of alcohol, expanding adolescents' access to mental-health and contraceptive services, and raising the driving age would likely be more effective in limiting adolescent smoking, substance abuse, pregnancy, and automobile fatalities than strategies aimed at making adolescents wiser, less impulsive, or less shortsighted. Some things just take time to develop, and, like it or not, mature judgment is probably one of them" (Steinberg, 2007, p. 58).

SOCIETY'S ROLE IN ADOLESCENT PROBLEM BEHAVIOR: THEN AND NOW

Let's reflect again about the continuum of narrow to broad socialization. At which point along the continuum would you place contemporary U.S. culture? Although there are certainly regional and ethnic variations, it is likely that you identify contemporary socializing practices as quite broad. Adolescents, and even younger children, seem to have a lot more freedom now than they have had in the past. However, we can also consider this question from a slightly different perspective, focusing not just on freedom but also on support. How much support does our contemporary culture provide for young people? How is level of support related to engagement in risky behavior? Has our collective level of responsibility changed in any way from that of the past decades, or is this idea just a nostalgic myth?

Siegel and Scovill (2000) provide a comprehensive look at the approach U.S. society has taken toward young people from the 1920s onward. In the 1920s, society viewed deviant adolescent behavior—as much a problem then as it is now—as an expression of youthful energies gone awry. In addition, social deviancy was considered an alternative pathway that some teenagers used to meet normal developmental goals, such as autonomy and relatedness, when more socially conventional means were unavailable to them. Consequently, it was generally believed that society as a whole was responsible for providing more productive outlets for adolescent energies. Many institutions and organizations were established to encourage teenagers to participate in socially constructive activities, to provide them with structured adult contact, and to facilitate prosocial interactions among youth themselves. Some examples of these organizations, most initiated before the 1920s, include Boy and Girl Scouts, Campfire Girls, Pioneer Youth of America, 4-H Clubs, Junior Achievement, Kiwanis, Order of the Rainbow for Girls, and Optimist International Boys' Work Council. Institutions dedicated to special interests, such as the National Recreation Association, the Girls' Service League of America, and the Sportmanship Brotherhood, as well as religiously affiliated groups such as the YMCA, the YWCA, the Knights of King Arthur, and the Ladies of Avalon, were also established. All were united in their purpose of providing guidance and character-building activities for youth.

Today, Siegel and Scovill (2000) point out, many of these age-appropriate community support systems have disappeared or have more limited scope. Consequently, the social envelope, which in the past strengthened families and schools and provided a safety net for youth who lacked family support or good educational opportunities, is weak or even absent. Many academic and recreational opportunities, often available free of charge to past generations of children and adolescents as part of their neighborhoods or communities, now come with a price tag. What has happened to cause this shift in attitudes and priorities?

Society's view of the cause of adolescent problem behaviors undoubtedly shapes its attitudes toward responsibility, prevention, and treatment. Contemporary society leans toward perceiving the source of deviancy as something within the individual adolescent rather than within society at large.

> While problem behavior was largely "socialized" through the 1960's, it has become "medicalized" in the 1990's. In an age in which we have been led to believe that there is a "magic scientific bullet" for nearly all physiological and social problems, we have "medicalized" problem behavior. An unspoken corollary of the "intrapsychic" view is that if the locus of the problem is in the adolescent, then parents and society are off the hook. The genetic or biological perspective provides that out: "There's nothing we could do; our child was born a delinquent." (Siegel & Scovill, 2000, p. 781)

No one should interpret these comments as suggesting that we return to either–or, nature–nurture thinking. As we have seen repeatedly, temperamental influences on behavior are strong, and they contribute significantly to developmental outcomes. What these authors recommend is a serious examination of the personal needs and rationalizations we adults use in interpreting adolescent problem behavior. If, as a society, we emphasize adolescent self-sufficiency and sophistication and deemphasize adolescent needs for adult time, guidance, and connection, then we do them, and us, a great disservice. Indeed, as we have seen, when adults closely monitor adolescents, they are less likely to engage in problem behaviors. The brain research that implicates increased sensation seeking along with immature self-regulatory processes as dual sources of risk taking makes it all the more obvious that adolescents need outside sources of support, structure, and control.

Parents, teachers, and other responsible adults who wish to limit adolescents' exposure to antisocial models or who wish to restrict their teens' experimentation are in a position of having to do battle with the culture. In many domains, the best judgment of responsible adults is at odds with information coming from the macrosystem. African American parents, for example, who recognize and support the value of academic achievement, report that music and movies that are made to appeal to their youngsters often explicitly disparage their values (Steinberg, 1996). Sometimes this battle can seem overwhelming. Steinberg estimates from his and other survey research that about 25% of American parents across all ethnic groups are disengaging from the struggle. He aptly describes them as follows:

> They have "checked out" of child-rearing. They have disengaged from responsibilities of parental discipline—they do not know how their child is doing in school, have no idea who their child's friends are, and are not aware of how their child spends his or her free time—but they have also disengaged from being accepting and supportive as well. They rarely spend time in activities with their child, and seldom just talk with their adolescent about the day's events. (p. 118)

As we have noted, adolescents whose parents are neglectful experience poorer social and academic outcomes than adolescents from authoritative families.

As Elkind (1994) has suggested, and as we noted earlier, the conceptualization of adolescents typical of the 1950s, 1960s and 1970s was that they should be "let go" to experiment and allowed to "be themselves." However, this idea developed within a culture that provided teenagers with a protective "adult envelope" that usually prevented their doing too much harm to themselves. In contemporary society, adolescence is not perceived as an adult apprenticeship but rather as an early pseudo-adulthood. Elkind believes that actively encouraging adolescent experimentation or, at least, looking the other way does not fit with postmodern realities.

With societal attitudes that place the burden of responsibility on the individual adolescent, with more mothers and fathers working longer hours, with larger classrooms and reductions in funding for recreational activities, and with fewer "old heads" around to listen and offer guidance, teens may come to depend more and more on their peers for support and information about life. In the colonized or segregated space Taffel (2001) dubs "Planet Youth," adolescent mimicry of risky behaviors may increasingly become the norm.

APPLICATIONS

Adolescence is the life stage characterized by the highest overall level of risk taking. Some risk taking is a healthy expression of autonomy in the service of identity development. Some risky pathways lead in less adaptive directions. Helping professionals who work with adolescents spend a good deal of their time attempting to encourage healthy behaviors and to discourage or reduce harmful ones. Clearly, there is no shortage of work in this area given the cultural possibilities for exploration in potentially dangerous areas like drugs, alcohol, sexuality, violence, and truancy that are open to younger and younger generations. What is the best way to make headway with adolescents given their natural proclivity to take risks? First, we need to recognize that adults can't prevent all risky behaviors. But assuming the attitude that "they'll grow out of it" can be ill-advised as well, given the convergence of research on the power of cumulative risk to affect later outcomes (Grant & Dawson, 1997; Robins & Pryzbeck, 1985). With regard to adolescent well-being, we introduce some ideas that draw upon developmental knowledge at the level of individual counseling, family and peer systems, and broad-based prevention. Approaches like these will not eliminate all risky behavior, but they can reduce it or help youth engage in it less impulsively.

The Personal Meaning of Risk

It would be easy if adolescents bought the argument that risky behaviors should be avoided. Some adolescents are inclined to do so, but many others seem impervious to adult logic. Those in the latter group might be more likely to show up in a counselor's office. Although we have discussed many of the theories about why adolescents take risks in general, it is important from a helping perspective to consider the personal motivation that drives a young person and, in so doing, to uncover the personal meaning of risky behavior for that individual. Counselors know how important empathy is for the success of therapeutic relationships. It is good to be mindful that, at its core, real empathy incorporates perspective taking. In work with adolescents, adults cannot assume that mature perspective-taking skills are on-line or that adolescent perspectives will necessarily resonate with their own adult points of view. Consequently, until we become aware of our own perspective and differentiate it from that of our adolescent clients, attempts to reason with youth across this "great divide" can be ineffective.

In individual counseling, a good place for the therapist to start might be with the questions "How does this young person perceive the risky behavior? What purpose does it serve?" Although not yet fully developed as an intervention strategy, Selman and Adalbjarnardottir (2000) describe a method for understanding adolescents' reasoning about risky behaviors that is based on social perspective taking. In their study, a developmental lens was applied to themes that emerged from extensive interviews with Icelandic adolescents about their alcohol use. The interview questions used in this study included two semistructured protocols, the Risky Business Interview (Levitt &Selman, 1993) and the Relationship Interview (Schultz, 1993), both comprised of open- and closed-ended prompts. The use of these instruments underscores the central connection between risky behavior and the world of peer relationships in adolescence.

In this research study, verbal responses of adolescent participants were coded to produce highly nuanced portraits of social perspective taking, meaning making, and relationships. Some have noted that this level of analysis may be too time consuming for clinicians to use on a regular basis (Nangle, Hecker, Grover & Smith, 2003). However, a few general implications can be adapted for clinical purposes to help us better understand adolescent thinking and behavior.

Recall that perspective taking develops in stagelike shifts from unilateral/noninclusive awareness of multiple perspectives to contextualized/highly inclusive awareness. The coordination of multiple perspectives gradually improves with time and experience. The theory posits that adolescents are likely to make more risky choices, especially in social contexts, when they lack the ability to coordinate their own perspectives with those of parents and other significant adults. Coordination of perspectives on risk actually involves the reciprocal interplay of three related competencies: (1) the adolescent's level of general knowledge about risks and their place in social interactions, (2) the variety of risk-management strategies that are available to the adolescent, and (3) the adolescent's level of awareness about the personal meaning of risky behavior. The last of these skills, personal meaning, is considered the "linchpin between understanding of factual knowledge and actual behavior—and between adolescents' perspectives on risk and relationship. Even individuals with sophisticated levels of understanding and a full repertoire of high-level social strategies are vulnerable to addictive influences of alcohol—especially if genetically disposed—if they do not have a mature perspective on what drinking means to them personally" (p. 62).

Consider the example of an adolescent who believes that adults prohibit alcohol because they don't want kids to drink, that kids should just go ahead and drink anyway to have fun with their friends, and that drinking makes kids "cool." Here we see a unilateral, undifferentiated perspective demonstrated in rule-based thinking (adults try to control people and drinking is

cool) and in one-way, nonmutual problem solving (just do what you want to do). Another adolescent with more highly developed perspective-taking skills might say that adults don't want kids to drink because kids might not be able to handle alcohol, that kids should go out with friends but stick to their own decision not to drink if they have to drive, and that drinking makes social situations easier so it might be hard to stop. Here the notion of intent to protect children, the costs as well as benefits of alcohol, and the possibility of more reciprocity in problem solving are apparent.

The authors hold that more mature functioning depends upon adolescents' ability to allow aspects of others' perspectives, even if these perspectives complicate the issue, into the thinking process. In other words, both the advantages and meaning of risk must be weighed simultaneously against the possibility of harm to oneself and to important relationships. This presents a difficult cognitive challenge for adolescents who, when confronted with such dilemmas, begin to wade into the muddy waters of ill-defined problems (see Chapter 11). Recall that formal operational skills, which are marked by increased capacity to reason about abstract ideas simultaneously and to engage in introspection, are still developing throughout the adolescent period. In general, the younger the adolescent, the less well-developed are these skills.

Interventions that provide factual information in isolation address only one part of the equation. Interventions that focus on changing behaviors may not work either if the adolescent does not "see" the point of changing behavior and thus become motivated to do so. Information and risk management skills need to be tied to personally meaningful real-world social contexts where costs and benefits of risk taking are acknowledged to coexist.

What are some specific ways to help adolescents become more reflective about their behaviors in the peer arena? Using the interviewing methods employed in this research as a springboard, helpers can start a dialogue with adolescent clients that focuses on coordinating their subjective points of view with the realities of alcohol (or other risks) and the wishes of adults who are important to them. The kinds of questions included in the interviews focus on perspective-taking deficits and are intended to move the adolescent toward more differentiated perspectives (see Table 10.1).

Professionals might apply these questions to the individual's actual risky behavior or employ videotaped or narrative vignettes as the basis for discussion. In addition to the questions in the table, other probes can help clinicians assess the maturity of adolescents' differentiation of feelings: "If you feel happy about drinking with your friends but you don't like it when your parents get angry about it, how do you feel overall? Can you have mixed feelings? How can feelings be mixed?" Others assess levels of self-reflection: "Can a person fool himself into thinking that he doesn't care about getting into trouble?" and "Is there a difference between fooling yourself and fooling another person? What is it?" (Questions are from Selman, 1979).

TABLE 10.1 The Risky Business Interview: Psychosocial Components, Issues, and Key Questions

PSYCHOSOCIAL COMPONENTS	ISSUES	KEY QUESTIONS
Understanding of the risk (here "drinking")	Initial (past) experiment	Why do you think someone your age starts to drink beer or other alcoholic drinks?
	Current purposes	Why do people your age like to drink these days?
	Further consequences	What can happen to people your age if they continue to drink? Is it more difficult for some people to stop drinking than others? Why?
Interpersonal strategies (from hypothetical dilemmas with parents[a] and peers)	Definition of the problem Alternative strategies	What is the problem in this dilemma? What are some ways they can solve these problems?
	Best strategy	What is the best way to solve this problem?
	Evaluation	How would they know the problem is solved?
Personal meaning of the risk	Past motivation for experimenting	When you first began drinking, why did you decide to give it a try?
	Present attitude	What are the reasons for your drinking *now*?
	Further orientation	Do you think at some time you might decide to change your drinking habit? If you decided to stop drinking, do you think you could stick to that decision if you wanted to? How do you know?

[a]Gunnar/Gudrun goes to a party one weekend evening and comes home late and drunk. His/her dad is waiting for him/her when he/she comes home and is very angry. He tells Gunnar/Gudrun that he/she is to be grounded for a month. Gunnar/Gudrun feels this is too severe a penalty and that he/she is old enough to decide for himself/herself whether he/she drinks or not. How can Gunnar/Gudrun deal with his/her father?

SOURCE: Selman, R. L. & Adalbjarnardottir, S. (2000). A developmental method to analyze the personal meaning adolescents make of risk and relationship: The case of "drinking." *Applied Developmental Science, 4*(1), 47–65. Reprinted by permission of Taylor & Francis Ltd.

The goal is to introduce some dissonance into the discussion to promote reflection and increase motivation to consider alternative ways of handling risks. The ultimate goal is more careful decision making. In practice, this approach blends developmental knowledge with an approach similar to motivational interviewing (Miller & Rollnick, 1991). Considering that many adolescents would be appropriately classified in the precontemplative stage (Prochaska & DiClemente, 1982) with regard to the risks they take, introducing some doubt in the context of a warm and supportive helping relationship might help them gain new perspective and assist them in managing the inevitable risks of adolescence.

Adolescent Health and Well-Being Matters

Prevention does work. The declining rate of infant mortality and infectious diseases across the globe provide two noteworthy examples. Countries around the world took this problem seriously and worked hard to reverse long-standing trends. Now, many of these same children face an adolescent period that does not support their health and well-being and amplifies their risk burden. Many non-communicable diseases related to self-jeopardizing behaviors, such as physical inactivity and obesity, tobacco and substance use, elevations in blood pressure, mental and emotional problems, have their start in adolescence. These risks can affect the quality of life these young people will experience as adults, and, by extension, future generations. These risks also contribute to approximately 70% of premature adult deaths (Resnick, Catalano, Sawyer, Viner, & Patton, 2012).

The world's youth population is now close to two billion, presenting us all with challenges for education and health care as well as opportunities to strengthen the future adult work force in productive ways. Many global institutions have recognized the need to pay attention to this growing demographic. For example, the United Nations Commission on Population and Development selected adolescents and youth as it 45th session theme in 2012. Advocates encourage a holistic, life-course approach to adolescent health and well-being, rather than an approach that focuses on single-problem issues, such as drug abuse. Arguably, advances in understanding adolescent brain development, developmental psychology and psychopathology, and the long-term consequences of harmful behaviors and contexts have added a sense of urgency to this agenda. Additionally, the gains in prevention science have made delivering on this growing knowledge base a more realistic possibility.

Increasingly, professional training in prevention science and evidence-based practice is being recommended for those who work with children and youth (Catalano, Fagan, Gavin, Greenberg, Irwin, Ross, & Shek, 2012). This requires understanding specific risks and protective factors faced by adolescents within their cultural context which informs and contributes to the effectiveness of interventions. Let's consider the context in light of the problem of youth suicide. Among our most important public health concerns, suicide is the third leading cause of mortality among young people. The whole range of suicide-related behaviors (ideation, attempts, self-harm and threats) is linked to mental health issues like depression and substance abuse. Suicide rates differ across cultural groups, suggesting some variation in the risks and preventions offered by the culture. Table 10.2 identifies key elements that are relevant to helping professional (Goldston et al., 2008).

The Power of Parents and Peers

In general, advocating for authoritative parenting and providing the information and support parents need to get the job done can have wonderfully beneficial effects on adolescents. Steinberg (1996) asserts that the high rates of parental disengagement in the United States amount to a public health problem that must be remedied by means of parent-education programs in communities and schools and through public-service programming. Encouragement and support should be given to adults who are trying to maintain connections with their adolescents, especially for teenagers at risk.

Steinberg (1994) found that parents of adolescents go through their own perilous transition and that 40% of them experience strong feelings of powerlessness, rejection, and personal regrets when their children become adolescents. Whereas sharing stories of problem behaviors is rather common among parents of younger children, parents of adolescents are often uncomfortable doing so (Sandmaier, 1996). Therefore, in addition to reconnecting adolescents to their families, mental health specialists need to reconnect adults to each other. Parent support or discussion groups, "safe-house" programs, and more informal "phone-tree" arrangements allow parents to communicate with each other. Taffel (1996) suggests that groups of parents develop common guidelines for their adolescents' social lives, related to concerns such as curfews, parties, and supervisory responsibility.

Ways to encourage parental involvement in education should also be strongly promoted. Many parents who have had unpleasant school experiences themselves resist dealing with school personnel despite their concern for their children. Sometimes schools present formidable obstacles, either real or perceived, to parents who wish to obtain help or information. Mental health practitioners can facilitate communication by advocating for parents, by explaining policy and procedures, and by working to develop good relationships with school personnel. Steinberg (1996) found that the most effective parental involvement strategy was to "work the system" on behalf of the student (for example, contacting the school when there is a problem, meeting with teachers or counselors, etc.). When school personnel encourage and facilitate this kind of participation instead of viewing it as an intrusion, it can be very helpful to the adolescents

they serve. For difficult teens who are failing in school, coordinating both systems (home and school) creates a powerfully watchful force that signals caring and demandingness. Some schools have created confidential hotlines to allow students to get their friends help if needed. Other implications drawn from the literature include supporting a wide variety of extracurricular activities that provide positive outlets for teens and limiting the number of hours spent in paid employment.

Efforts to change peer networks directly appear less realistic. Peer groups by their very nature represent adolescent attempts to establish independent social networks and to provide a supportive structure that is an alternative to parent and family (Eckert, 1989). Peer society is influenced by so many factors (individual personalities, availability of types, social context, ethnicity, media, and so forth) that single proximal interventions are likely to be difficult. Consequently, calls for changes in the broader societal context and in the more immediate family and school environment are thought to be the best way to exert influence on the chemistry of the peer groups formed. For example, in the matter of achievement, Steinberg (1996) strongly advocates refocusing the American discussion away from the problems of schools to the problem of changing adolescents' and parents' minds (or the collective culture's mind) about what is really important—schooling—and about what is less important: socializing, organized sports, paid employment, and so on.

This is not to suggest that counselors should necessarily leave peer groups alone. Indeed, the school counselor is in a unique position to provide information and a forum for discussion about important topics through developmental guidance programs. Other strategies, such as peer mediation and peer counseling, are useful approaches for teens because they capitalize on the adolescent's dependence upon peers.

Some research indicates that teens of all ethnic groups prefer not to seek help about personal problems from school professionals such as teachers and counselors but prefer to turn to their peers for advice about personal, educational and vocational concerns (Branwhite, 2000; Mau, 1995). As a way to engage adolescents, Taffel (1996) suggests including peers in the guidance process. In counseling sessions, constructing a genogram of the "second family," or the teen's peer group, can be a technique that allows the therapist to gain some entry into this system. Sometimes, he suggests, peers can be brought into the therapy process.

Pipher (1996), a family therapist who has written about the problems today's adolescents face, has taken therapists to task about the myopic focus of many traditional therapeutic practices. She notes that counseling theories, like the great therapists who developed them, are embedded in historical time and place. Ideas such as intrapsychic causes of distress and even the "dysfunctional family," if emphasized in counseling and diagnosis to the exclusion of culture, history, economics, and politics, ignore critical dimensions affecting adolescents and do a disservice to their already stressed families. She has argued that communities as well as families raise the nation's

TABLE 10.2   Adolescent Suicide Risk Across Cultures

CULTURAL GROUP	SPECIFIC RISKS	SPECIFIC PROTECTIVE FACTORS	HELP-SEEKING BEHAVIORS	PREVENTION AND TREATMENT
African American	Perceived discrimination; deindustrialization of inner cities leading to economic and social disadvantage; heightened sensitivity to inequities despite progress of civil rights movement; perceived pressure to adopt majority values; adoption of "cool pose" attitude of appearing invulnerable; disproportionate numbers of victim-precipitated suicide (e.g., shooting by gang or police) as a more culturally acceptable way to end one's life.	Religious orientation that supports meaning in life despite hardship; cultural capital and belonging to an interdependent social group.	Low rates of seeking help possibly due to distrust of professional mental health system; lack of adequate health coverage; culturally-inappropriate screening; an ethic that values personal expenditure of effort to cope with problems. Higher rates of help-seeking directed to members of clergy.	Gatekeeper model utilizing the Black church; training clergy and others to recognize risk and make referrals. Example: HAVEN program (Molock et al., 2008)
American Indian and Alaska Native Youth	Isolation of life on a reservation associated with poverty and social limitations; high rates of alcohol and substance use disorders; particular sensitivity to suicide contagion because of isolation; residual effects of ethnic cleansing trauma; high rates of complementary life-threatening/risky behaviors.	Spiritual orientation; traditional cultural values and identity provide grounding.	Distrust of the mental health system; Stigma associated with seeking professional mental health services; More adults and adolescents sought help from traditional community healers.	Tribes often strive to maintain their cultural integrity, so generic approaches may not be effective; Programs should integrate cultural values of the group. Example: Western Athabaskan Natural Helpers Program (May et al., 2005)
Asian American/Pacific Islander	Emphasis on interdependence and group harmony may serve to suppress conflict, leading to depression; loss of face and stresses of immigration for some may influence suicidal behavior.	Language fluency, ethnic pride and social support from families serve as protective factors for some groups.	Tendency not to disclose feelings may manifest in reporting more physical (rather than psychological) symptoms; long delays in accessing treatment may make problems more severe; loss of face may be a barrier to help-seeking.	No empirically-supported prevention programs at this point; Ethnically-matched therapists and centers and family involvement tends to result in longer treatment duration.
Latino/Latina	Familism may lead to stress that puts youth at odds with peers; traumatic immigration experiences and acculturation may be risks; culture-specific dissociative experiences (ataques de nervios) may precipitate suicide attempts.	Familismo also serves to bolster pride, family cohesion and sense of security.	Less likely to seek professional help due to language and structural barriers; Value of parental involvement in treatment may be difficult with limited numbers of bilingual helpers, especially for recent immigrant families.	No empirically supported prevention programs at this point; adaptations of CBT and interpersonal therapy for depression included parental involvement consistent with value of familismo; adaptations required for specific Latino groups rather than treating all the same.

SOURCE: Based on Goldston, D. B., Molock, S. D., Whitbeck, L. B., Murakami, J. L., Zayas, L. H., & Nagayama Hall, G. C. (2008). Cultural considerations in adolescent suicide prevention and psychosocial treatment. *American Psychologist, 63,* 14–31. Reprinted by permission of the American Psychological Association.

children and that therapists can do more harm than good by misdiagnosing problems and giving simplistic answers to complicated situations without according due consideration to the effects of the culture. She pointedly notes:

> In the past when therapists saw troubled teenagers, they could generally assume that the parents had problems. That's because most teenagers were fine. Troubled teens were an exception and required some explaining. Today most teenagers are not fine. At one time we helped kids differentiate from enmeshed families. Now we need to help families differentiate from the culture. (Pipher, 1996, p. 34)

Pipher (1996) advocates for "protecting" family time by deliberately limiting the encroachment of work and media entertainment and creating family rituals and celebrations to strengthen positive connections. Hewlett and West (1998) have called for a national initiative similar to the American Association of Retired Persons (AARP), called a Parents' Bill of Rights, which would guarantee family-friendly policies such as parenting leave, economic security, help with housing, responsible media, year-round educational programs, and quality schools, to name a few.

It Takes a Village

Because successful negotiation of the adolescent period depends upon the interaction of a number of variables—biology or genetics, social environment, perceptions, personality and behavior, individual counseling may only temporarily address problems unless the more systemic roots of the difficulties are also addressed (Cairns & Cairns, 1994). The fact that so many influential systems touch on adolescents' lives and that some systems, such as the peer network, can be resistant to adult intrusion makes it critical to use a wide-angle lens when evaluating and treating teenagers.

One way to put the pieces together comes from the work of prevention researchers who have stressed the need to view successful adolescent development as a function of interrelated risk and protective factors (Jessor, 1993). This two-pronged approach, building resilience while addressing risk, is central to the traditions of counseling (Van Hesteren & Ivey, 1990). In the past, many problem-reduction interventions (e.g., for drinking, drug use, smoking, etc.) were fear-based attempts to reduce these behaviors by providing information alone. Blum (2003) describes several characteristics of ineffective risk-reduction interventions. They include interventions that use scare tactics, are of short-term duration, that only provide factual information, that primarily target self-esteem, and that segregate at-risk students for special treatment. Some implications we can draw from these findings include the ineffectiveness of "talking at" adolescents, the futility of quick solutions, the importance of developmentally sensitive interventions, and the necessity of broad-based contextualized support.

Recently, we have witnessed an increased interest in supporting positive youth development. In general, these efforts recognize the importance of providing resources at all levels of the system. The Search Institute, for example, has identified useful lists of personal, family, and community assets that can serve as benchmarks for healthy adolescent development (Benson, 1997). Although positive youth development has been described in a variety of ways, some essential elements exist: the presence of caring adults and mentors on a regular basis, schools that build academic competence and offer vocational preparation, an atmosphere of hope, encouragement of positive values, and high but achievable expectations (Lerner, Fisher, & Weinberg, 2000). Clearly, professionals and nonprofessionals alike need to join forces to create the kinds of communities that offer these opportunities for everyone.

The Midwestern Prevention Project (Pentz, Mihalic, & Grotpeter, 2002) is a good example of a comprehensive, theoretically driven program that was developed to reduce or prevent adolescent use of gateway drugs. The program introduces 5 components in sequence every 6 months to 1 year over a 5-year period. The first component is the school-based program, begun during the transition to high school (either grades 6 or 7). School interventions include interactive classroom lessons that provide drug resistance training, initiation of peer counseling, and schoolwide efforts to make nonuse of drugs the social norm. During the 2nd year, parents are included in the program through parent education groups and opportunities for participation in leadership and mentoring activities. Community, religious, and political leaders are brought on board in years 3 through 5 to develop resources, plan, and implement initiatives that support adolescent health in the community as a whole. Mass media outlets (print, TV, and radio) are used throughout the entire 5-year period to introduce the program, promote the prevention message, and spotlight program successes. Overall, follow-up studies show significant reductions in use of cigarettes, marijuana, and, to a lesser extent, alcohol for those involved in the project (Pentz et al., 2002). Multisystemic Therapy (MST; Henggeler et al., 1998) is another effective prevention program that targets multiple levels of the system (family, peers, schools, and neighborhoods) to reduce antisocial behavior in at-risk populations.

Of course, limiting the possibility of exposure to harm, as Steinberg previously suggested, can go a long way to reducing threats to adolescent well-being. But restricting availability of alcohol or tobacco, monitoring adolescents' activities, providing interesting alternatives to harmful activities and other such changes depends upon the society's willingness to take adolescent health seriously. A list of developmentally healthy practices for adolescents is provided in Table 10.3.

To transform the social world of adolescents into a healthier place will take team effort. Neither families nor schools, two of our major socializing institutions, can do this alone. A few general guidelines from Siegel and Scovill (2000) summarize and reemphasize important points.

1. Take the social and cultural context seriously. Don't rely on intrapsychic interpretations alone when identifying or assessing problems. Don't blame everything on the adolescent brain. Adolescents do not engineer all their problems, despite how appealing that argument might appear.

TABLE 10.3 Risk Taking in Adolescence: Examples, Functions, Damaging and Healthy Practices

EXAMPLES OF ANTISOCIAL OR PROBLEM BEHAVIORS	POSSIBLE FUNCTIONS OF BEHAVIOR (I.E., OUTCOMES TEENS MAY BE SEEKING)	DEVELOPMENTAL TASK	DEVELOPMENTALLY DAMAGING PRACTICES	DEVELOPMENTALLY HEALTHY ALTERNATIVES
Skipping school, disobeying teachers	Expression of frustration with inability to succeed in school setting	Competence	Large schools, high student to teacher ratios in classrooms, ability grouping	Provide individualized programs where youth with a wide range of skills can be successful
Engaging in pseudoadult behaviors such as drinking, drug use, and early sexual activity	Means of coping with anxiety, frustration, and fear of inadequacy—seeking to be recognized as competent, capable, respected through mimicry of pseudoadult peers	Transition to adulthood	Lack of connectedness with adults created by lack of parental presence at home, few opportunities to develop relationships with adults at school or in the community, little one-on-one time with adults	Teach alternative methods for coping with stress, presence of adult role models, opportunities to learn career skills, involvement in mentoring or apprenticeship programs
"Teenage behaviors" (e.g., outrageous clothing, music, use of profanity), violation of minor rules such as curfew, status offenses	Means of making a personal statement (how I'm different, important, angry, etc.) seeking to be recognized as an individual of worth, capable of making a unique contribution	Identity, autonomy, individuation	Targeting of teens as consumer group by media, lack of opportunities for teens to make a positive contribution to family and society	Allow teens to participate in rule making; allow teens to participate in decision making; increase the types of contributions teens can make to society; increase variety of socially sanctioned clubs at school
Joining a gang, involvement with delinquent peers	Means of meeting the need to belong (I want to be part of something)	Intimacy, relationship building	Lack of opportunities to meet and interact with prosocial peers, coercive family interactions	Teach relationship enhancement skills, conversations skills, empathy skills; provide alternative niches or ecologies with prosocial peers and adults
"Acting out" (e.g., causing trouble at school, getting into fights, making threats, theft, running away)	To be heard or understood; to bring attention to perceived inequity of treatment	Identity, competence, industry	Failure to listen to teens, not allowing teens to participate in rule and decision making, doing things "to" teens rather than "with" them	Provide strong adult role models who listen to teens; teach youth to identify and express anger and other emotions (rational self-talk); teach negotiation skills; include teens in decision making
Smoking, having sex, drinking, status offenses	Way of asserting/affirming the transition from childhood to adulthood—seeking to be recognized as a person with an opinion that counts; attempting to establish a role for oneself	Transition to adulthood	Double standard of behavior for adults and teens	Create more formalized markers to acknowledge transitions; recognize the cost to children/adolescents when adults fail to "walk the way they talk"
Speeding, riding on the hoods of cars, "sensation seeking" (Zuckerman, 1979)	Way to avoid boredom and seek excitement—seeking a way to not feel put down, ignored or unimportant	Competence	Few community centers, clubs, or other environments where adult-monitored youth activities are provided	Develop exciting, adult-monitored activities for adolescents (e.g., midnight basketball)
Playing "chicken" with yourself and others, shoplifting, vandalism	Means of testing personal limits and status—seeking competence, finding something to be "in charge of"	Identity	Few opportunities for teens to succeed and to learn adult skills (e.g., career skills, communication skills) or to make a contribution to society	Create environments where adolescents can gain confidence and excel in something; broaden the scope of what defines success for adolescents beyond academics and sports
Violent behavior, law violations, conduct disorder	Expression of opposition to or outrage at adult authority—seeking control and power over disruptive/unsafe environment	Trust vs. mistrust, safety needs	Failure to protect children from poverty, child abuse, neglect, mistreatment, physiological disadvantages	Early childhood intervention has been most successful here; prognosis in adolescence is poor

SOURCE: Siegel, A.W., & Scoville, L.C. (2000). Problem behavior: The double symptom of adolescence. *Development and Psychopathology, 12*, 786–787. Used with permission by Cambridge University Press.

2. Consider adolescent problem behavior as a means to an end. Table 10.3 on the previous page provides some suggestions to help clinicians understand the functions that problem behaviors serve.

3. Construct healthy and attractive alternatives to help adolescents meet their developmental needs, including social as well as educational alternatives. Not all adolescents fit into the traditional academic mold for success, yet they want success and they are worthy of it.

SUMMARY

Frameworklessness and Autonomy: A of Adolescent Social Identity

1. The profound physical, cognitive, and social changes that accompany entry into adolescence create a state of instability and anxiety Seltzer called frameworklessness. Establishing adult independence requires separating from caregivers on a psychological level, with the concept of the parent becoming more peripheral to the adolescent's self-system, accompanied by a loss in feelings of security. Simultaneously, teens increase their affiliation with and dependency on peers, others who share their state of frameworklessness.

2. Peers are a source of support, of social comparison, and of attribute substitution or imitation and identification. Adolescents borrow from their peers' ways of behaving and thinking, providing some relief from the anxiety of being without a stable sense of self. Thus, peers provide an arena for identity formation.

The Structure of the Peer Network

3. Most adolescents have one or two best friends, who are part of a clique of individuals who tend to do things together. Larger groups composed of many cliques comprise crowds, whose members may not be friends but share interests, attitudes, behaviors, and appearance.

4. Most American high schools are characterized by fairly similar crowd structures, consisting of populars and jocks, some alienated groups such as druggies, an average crowd, and an academically high-achieving group. Crowd membership is likely to be determined by the child's personality and interests entering adolescence, the types of crowds available, and parents' attempts to manage peer relationships.

5. Crowds influence their members, but they are also freely selected by their members, who choose to participate in shared norms, roles, and expectations.

The Role of Parents

6. Parents have often been advised to let go—that conflicts with adolescents and adolescent rebellion is normal and not something to worry about. But more recent research has focused on whether certain kinds of parenting at adolescence may be more predictive of positive outcomes and have found that both warmth (responsiveness) and control (demandingness, close monitoring) are as important with adolescents as they are with younger children. This kind of authoritative parenting is associated with,

among other things, higher achievement, self-confidence, self-esteem, social adjustment, and self-control.

7. But crowd affiliations are also powerful in adolescence and can mitigate parent influences. The complex relationships among peers and parenting are evident across different ethnic groups and social classes. For example, Asian American teens tend to belong to ethnically defined crowds that usually value high achievement. Even if parents are not involved in their children's schooling, these teens are likely to be high achievers because of their crowd affiliation. Conversely, some Black teens are also members of ethnically defined crowds, and these crowds sometimes disparage school achievement as trying to act White. Even though parents are often quite supportive of school achievement, Black teens may sacrifice high grades, or hide them, to be true to their crowd.

The Role of School

8. Declines in academic orientation and motivation are noted in early adolescence and may be associated with shifting school structures and processes as children enter middle school or junior high school. Larger classes and schools, whole-group lecture, and heavy emphasis on competition are among these practices. Timing of the shift from elementary to secondary schools is also important: Later shifts are less stressful than earlier ones. Also, parental involvement declines sharply at secondary school levels, despite evidence that it remains just as important for teens' achievement as for younger children's.

Leisure and Work

9. When teens are involved in school- or community-sponsored out-of-school activities, they tend to be higher achievers and to have other desirable qualities. Many teens work for pay, but spending substantial hours working is associated with lower school achievement, less involvement in school activities, more drug and alcohol use, and more delinquency.

Media and the Consumer Culture

10. Adolescents, their peers, families, and schools are affected by the larger culture, and vice versa. Present culture may not be very "adolescent friendly" due to loss of community and a focus on individualism and material success. Negative media forces seem to shape attitudes and beliefs. Teens are increasingly exposed to violence,

sex, and commercial messages through the media, affecting what they view as normative and acceptable behavior. Thus, media messages often compete with other, more traditional messages from families and schools, and research demonstrates that media messages do influence teens' beliefs and behaviors.

Risky Behavior and Social Deviance

11. Risky behavior increases sharply during adolescence, peaking at about age 17, and rates of risky behavior have increased over the last one or two decades. Life-course-persistent antisocial behavior begins in childhood and continues throughout life, whereas adolescent-limited antisocial behavior develops in adolescence and usually ends shortly thereafter. Risky behavior, ranging from mild to severe, may be characteristic of adolescents for several reasons: the need for sensation seeking; egocentric beliefs about one's own invulnerability; modeling of deviant behavior by peers; and the exacerbation of illusions of invulnerability by the collective egocentrism of groups of peers.

12. Risky behavior may also provide some advantages in the teen years, making it, in some cases, adaptive. It can sometimes serve as an indicator of individuation and self-determination and as a source of peer acceptance. Thus, risk taking has both positive and negative aspects. It may be inevitable in cultures with "broad" socialization practices, which encourage high levels of individual freedom.

13. Although the United States provides high levels of freedom to adolescents, it may not provide adequate supports to ensure that risk taking is within reasonable limits. In the 1920s, concerns about adolescent risk taking fostered a sense of community responsibility to provide adequate supervision and healthy outlets for young people, and a number of youth-oriented institutions sprang up offering free services to teens. Today such community support systems are often in short supply, and costly when they are available. The current approach seems to be based on a reconceptualization of the issue. Risky behavior is seen as a problem of the individual rather than a problem of society as it was seen in the 1920s.

CASE STUDY

Mark Spencer is a White 16-year-old sophomore at a suburban public school. He lives with his mother, father, and older brother in a middle-class community. Mark has attended the local public schools since kindergarten, and until 8th grade he was an above-average student who frequently made honor roll. Mark's father Doug commutes to his job at an insurance company and in recent years has increased his hours at the office as his company has downsized and shifted responsibilities to remaining employees. His mother Joanne works as a secretary at a local real estate agency. Mark's brother Dave is a senior who is also an above-average student and who has been very active in intermural sports, especially soccer and baseball.

During middle school, Mark had a strong interest in scouting and was particularly involved in camping and developing survival skills. Several of Mark's friends in the scout troop left scouting in the 7th grade and began spending more time hanging out with girlfriends and playing sports. Mark continued scouting until 8th grade, but teasing from his friends became unbearable, and he finally gave up. Mark was shy with girls and not particularly interested in sports, so he was left with little in common with his middle school friends. At the same time, his grades began to slip.

When Mark's parents expressed concern about his poor grades, he told them that his teachers were jerks and his classes were boring. Although Doug and Joanne tried to encourage him to study more and to continue scouting or to try sports, Mark would generally react angrily, and his parents would back off to not upset him further. By 9th grade he was spending more and more time alone, playing video games and watching television in his room. When Mark turned 16, he begged for a car, and his parents agreed. Because they were so busy, Doug and Joanne

felt it would be helpful to give Mark more independence, and they hoped it would increase his social acceptance. Mark was one of the first students in the sophomore class to turn 16, and he found that his old friends' interest in him was piqued when he began driving his new car to school.

Mark began to hang out with his old friends, and began smoking, drinking, and experimenting with drugs. His grades slipped further, although with almost no effort he was able to maintain a C average. Once again his parents became concerned about his grades, particularly because college loomed. They even threatened to remove the television from his room, but, as usual, they backed down when confronted by his anger. Doug and Joanne were also loath to rock the boat when Mark finally seemed to be enjoying his social life. He was no longer moping around the house, watching TV, and worrying his parents.

When Mark asked to be allowed to drive his friends to a concert in a nearby city, with plans to spend the weekend at the home of a friend's uncle, his parents disagreed about how to handle his request. Joanne was afraid of giving him so much freedom and worried about the safety of the group. Doug, remembering how restrictive his own parents were, argued that "you're only young once" and that "you have to hope that what you've taught them up to now will stick, because that's all you can do. At 16, kids are really on their own."

The weekend trip was a disaster. After the concert, the group partied at the uncle's home, without adult supervision. Neighbors called the police about the noise. Parents were notified after the police found evidence of underage drinking. Mark persuaded his parents that he did not know the uncle would be away and that he had no control over his friends' drinking. Doug and Joanne gave Mark the benefit of the doubt, but a month later, Joanne found a bottle of vodka hidden in Mark's room. Both parents realized that they needed to seek help.

Discussion Questions

1. Consider the developmental path that Mark has followed. Describe the elements that have been influential in shaping this adolescent's experience.

2. Describe and comment on the parenting style used by Doug and Joanne. Evaluate the parents' approach to Mark throughout his early adolescence and suggest ways they might have responded differently.

3. What role could the school have played in modifying the course of Mark's development?

4. What specific suggestions for treatment might you make for Mark and his family?

PRACTICE USING WHAT YOU HAVE LEARNED

In the Pearson etext, apply these ideas to working with others.

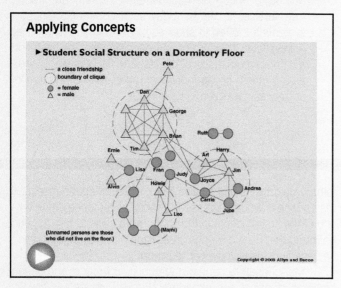

JOURNAL QUESTIONS

1. Compare and contrast the social world of adolescents today with that of your own adolescence. What similarities and differences do you find?

2. Think of a middle school, junior high school, or high school with which you are familiar. If you could change the school (academically, structurally, or otherwise), what changes would you make, and why?

3. Identify one action step that you could take to improve the lives of adolescents with whom you are in contact.

4. Consider your own level of media consumption. What portion of your day is spent consuming media? What are its benefits to you? What are its drawbacks? How does the prevalence of media in our culture affect our ability to sustain attention? What advice would you give parents who are concerned about their adolescent's media use?

KEY CONCEPTS

CHAPTER 11

Physical and Cognitive Development in Young Adulthood

Garrett, a 19-year-old, is a 2nd-year college student. He enjoys many privileges that could be construed as "adult." He drives a car, votes in elections, and owns a credit card. He shares an apartment near his college campus with two other undergraduates. He drinks alcohol with his friends at parties (albeit illegally) and has regular sexual relations with his girlfriend of 10 months. The couple split up once and subsequently reunited. During the separation, Garrett dated another young woman. At this point, Garrett and his girlfriend have no plans to marry. He wanted to get a job immediately after high school, but job opportunities in the trade he aspired to went to more experienced workers. He decided to give higher education a try. Garrett has little idea of what his ultimate career path will be. Garrett's father, who is divorced from Garrett's mother, pays for his tuition and housing costs. He has taken out loans to help finance his son's education. Garrett's mother provides him with an allowance for food. He works part-time for low wages at a clothing store in a local mall, which helps him pay for clothes and entertainment. Garrett is very responsible at work, but he is an unenthusiastic college student. His study habits lean toward procrastinating and then trying to make up for lost time by staying up all night to finish assignments by their deadlines. When Garrett broke his wrist playing sports, his mother had to take a few days off from her job to accompany him to doctor's visits. Her health insurance covered most of the bills. Yet, despite their financial support, Garrett's parents have no legal right to see Garrett's college grades.

Is Garrett an adult? Scholars are likely to disagree about the answer to this question. Most would agree that the onset of adolescence is marked by the changes of puberty. But there are no easily observed physical changes that signal entry into adulthood. Instead, adulthood is a social construction. One or more culturally determined criteria usually must be met before one's maturity is established (Hogan & Astone, 1986), and the criteria vary depending on the observer and the culture.

In the past, sociologists have emphasized the achievement and timing of **marker events** as criteria for adulthood. These have included completing formal education, entering the adult workforce, leaving the family home, getting married, and becoming a parent. Around the middle of the last century, a large proportion of the American population achieved these marker events between the ages of 18 and 24 (Rindfuss, 1991). However, if we evaluate our hypothetical student, Garrett, according to these traditional marker events, he would not be an adult despite being in the right age range.

From a sociological perspective, it seems to take longer to grow up today than it did at earlier points in history for many reasons. Some of these include the demand for a highly educated workforce and the increased cost of this education (Jacobs & Stoner-Eby, 1998), the difficulties inherent in earning enough to support children and in achieving stable employment (Halperin, 1998b), and the frequency of early, nonmarital sexual activity and the availability of contraception (Warner et al., 1998). All have had profound effects on the timing of life events. On one hand then, some markers of adulthood are considerably delayed. For example, the median age for marriage in 1976 was about 22 or 23. By 2006, the median age for marriage had risen to about 27, a difference of more than 4 years in only 30 years (Arnett, 2010). On the other hand, other indicators of adulthood, such as the onset of sexual activity, occur much earlier than they did in the past.

Such shifts in the timing of marker events appear to have delayed the onset of adulthood, especially in Western societies, where these shifts have most often occurred. However, even in more traditional, nonindustrialized cultures, the transition to adulthood can be a slow process. For example, after completing the puberty rites that induct boys into the adult ranks of some societies, young males in about 25% of cultures pass through a period of **youth** (Schlegel & Barry, 1991). In these societies, males are seen as needing a period of time to prepare for marriage. Serving as warriors during the transition period, for example, allows boys an opportunity to develop skills and to accumulate the material goods needed to afford a family. Girls enjoy a similar period of youth in 20% of cultures. Thus, even in many non-Western, traditional societies, the movement to full adult status takes time.

In cultures such as that of the United States, the pathways to adulthood are remarkable in their variability, so that specifying when adulthood has been achieved is difficult. Arnett (2000, 2004, 2007; Arnett & Taber, 1994) has explored a new way of conceptualizing adulthood. In addition to examining the timing of marker events, he considered individuals' own conceptions about what makes them adults. The reasoning goes like this: If one's own judgment of adult status were based on criteria other than marker events, we might find more consistency in criteria across cultures or even within the same culture over a certain period. Arnett (2000) asked young people in the United States to rate the importance of criteria in several areas (such as cognitive, behavioral, emotional, biological, and legal criteria, role transitions, and responsibilities) as definitions of adult status. He also asked participants whether they felt they had reached adulthood. A majority of respondents in their late teens and early twenties answered both "yes and no." Perhaps Garrett would say something similar. As you can see in Figure 11.1, the proportion of young people in Arnett's study who judged themselves to be adults gradually increased with age, with a clear majority of participants in their late 20s and early 30s doing so.

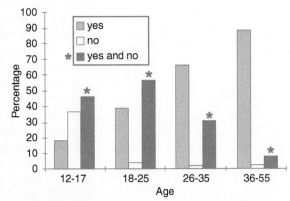

FIGURE 11.1 **"Do you feel that you have reached adulthood?"**

SOURCE: Arnett, J. (2000). Emerging adulthood: A theory of development from the late teens through the twenties. *American Psychologist, 55,* 472. Reprinted by permission of the American Psychological Association.

Can this delay in identifying oneself as an adult be attributed to the timing of role transitions? Apparently not. Chronological age and role transitions such as marriage and parenthood, on their own, were not considered significant markers. Arnett's respondents indicated that the two most important qualifications for adulthood are first, accepting responsibility for the consequences of one's actions and second, making independent decisions. Becoming financially independent, a traditional marker event, was third. Consequently, the subjective sense of being an adult may be more important than accomplishment and timing of discrete tasks. There is consensus among many researchers that a broad psychological shift toward increasing independence and autonomy characterizes the subjective experience of what it means to be an adult, at least for members of the American majority culture (Greene & Wheatley, 1992; Scheer, Unger, & Brown, 1994). Moreover, achieving a sense of autonomy is among the identity-related tasks described in Chapter 9. Because the shift to feeling autonomous is a lengthy process for many, Arnett (2000, 2004, 2007) advocates that the time period roughly between ages 18 and 25 be considered a distinct stage of life called **emerging adulthood**.

In past decades, adult status was conferred through the achievement of marker events, such as marriage and parenthood.

We should note that emerging adulthood is made possible by the kind of economic development that characterizes industrialized, Western cultures. If the labor of young people is not urgently needed for the economic well-being of their families, and if many occupations require extended years of education, then work is postponed, marriage and childbearing are likely to be delayed, and self-exploration can continue. Arnett (e.g., 2002) has argued that increasing **globalization** is spreading the experience of this new stage from Western societies to other parts of the world. *Globalization* is "a process by which cultures influence one another and become more alike through trade, immigration, and the exchange of information and ideas" (p. 774), a process that has shifted into high gear with advances in telecommunications and transportation. In developing countries, young people increasingly move from rural communities to urban centers as they pursue expanding economic opportunities. More occupational and lifestyle options are available, and self-development tends to continue well past the teen years. "For young people in developing countries, emerging adulthood exists only for the wealthier segment of society . . . however, as globalization proceeds . . . the emerging adulthood now normative in the middle class is likely to increase as the middle class expands" (p. 781).

Whereas Arnett (2000) found that American respondents to his questionnaire emphasized individualistic criteria in defining adulthood, we should note that they also acknowledged the importance of emotional support. As you will see in the next chapter, strong relationships with others are important in and of themselves and can provide a bulwark for the development of personal autonomy. Encouragement and tolerance for independent action and belief, however, may continue to be greater for young people in the American majority culture than for those in non-Western societies, such as China (e.g., Nelson & Chen, 2007), or in some diverse communities in the United States. Even so, several studies suggest that young people in minority samples can be characterized as defining adulthood much the way majority White samples do, and as experiencing the self-exploration or identity development that seems to be the hallmark of emerging adulthood. For example, Black males define manhood individualistically, characterized by personal responsibility and self-determination, much as Whites do (Hunter & Davis, 1992). Yip, Seaton, and Sellers (2006) investigated African American racial identity across the life span, and found that although more young adults had reached identity achievement status than adolescents, identity issues were still front and center for more than half of the college age group. Yip et al. argue that college experiences can "intensify the process of developing a racial and/or ethnic identity" (p. 1515). Deaux and Ethier (1998) make a similar argument, suggesting that college itself tends to serve as a catalyst for ethnic identity development, partly because of opportunities such as access to groups organized around race and college courses on racial or ethnic history. These kinds of experiences may make race and ethnicity more salient. Interestingly, Yip and her colleagues found that the only age group in which an identity status (diffusion) was linked to depression was the college age group, indicating that identity constructions in this age range have critical psychological consequences.

Whether or not emerging adults attend college, their social worlds are likely to expand beyond immediate family, friends, and neighbors (Arnett & Brody, 2008, p. 292). For African Americans, this often means moving into a much more ethnically diverse world than the schools and neighborhoods of their childhood. In college, fewer instructors or students are likely to be Black; in work environments, few employers and co-workers will be Black. **Minority stress**, the experience of prejudice and discrimination due to membership in a stigmatized group (Meyer, 2003) is very likely to increase. Arnett and Brody (2008) argue that dealing with identity issues with these added sources of stress may intensify the process. "We believe that identity issues are especially acute for African American emerging adults due to the injection of discrimination and prejudice, and that this may explain a range of puzzling findings" (p. 292). One is the **racial crossover effect**. African American adolescents engage in less substance use than White adolescents. But the reverse is true in adulthood, when African Americans use substances more than Whites. Another puzzling finding concerns male suicide rates. Males are much more prone to suicide than females. White males show a steady rise in suicide rates through much of adulthood, with the sharpest rise after age 65. But for Black males the peak suicide rate occurs much earlier, between 25 and 34. Arnett and Brody speculate that "there are uniquely formidable challenges to forming a Black male identity" in the United States and that for some the strain may become intolerable during early adulthood (p. 293).

Research on other ethnic minorities in the United States supports the idea that moving into a more ethnically diverse world after adolescence both extends the process of identity formation and increases its complexity. Fuligni (2007) looked at the children of Asian and Latin immigrant families and found, as you would expect, culture-specific concerns among young adults. The children of the immigrant families had a stronger sense of "family obligation" than European American offspring. They expected to support and assist their families in many ways (e.g., caring for siblings, providing financial support, living near or with the family) and believed that they should consider the family's wishes when making important decisions. Interestingly, the researchers found that these kinds of values, while strongest in the immigrant children, also increased in young adulthood for all ethnic groups, including the European Americans. Apparently, the importance of connection, as well as autonomy, becomes clearer after adolescence. Immigrant children were most likely, as young adults, to experience a much more expanded social world if they went to college than if they did not, and this happened most often for those of East Asian background. With these young people, Fuligni found a trend toward the kind of extended identity development that characterizes emerging adulthood. Their sense of obligation to family did not disappear, but it competed with new aspirations, "to be able to be doing something that I like" and "to be the person you're supposed to be" (p. 99).

Is a stage of emerging adulthood a good or a bad thing? Could it be viewed as a tendency for modern youth to simply avoid taking on adult roles and responsibilities, nurtured by overprotective, indulgent parents? Arnett (e.g., 2007) argues that in fact, there could be a grain of truth here; many young adults seem to "find it burdensome and onerous to pay their own bills and do all the other things their parents (have) always done for them" (p. 71). But he generally sees the ambivalence of young adults as a recognition of the value of an extended period of

 Gary grew up in a Vietnamese American family, who had certain expectations for his future. He describes clearly the stress that arises when need for autonomy and desire to meet family obligations come into conflict in young adulthood.

self-development to help them prepare more adequately for taking on adult roles in a complex society. He points out that few emerging adults fail to "grow up." By age 30 nearly all are stably employed, and three quarters are married and have a child. There is also evidence that as adolescents move into young adulthood today they are not substantially different from their counterparts in the 1970s. For example, high school seniors now and then report similar levels of loneliness, anti-social behavior, self-esteem, and life satisfaction (Trzesniewski & Donnellan, 2010).

But some theorists are not as sanguine about this new stage. Hendry and Kloep (2007), for example, express concern that young people are more often inadequately prepared for adulthood than they are benefiting from an extended transition into adulthood. Modern parents, they suggest, tend to both overindulge their children and to pressure them to excel, rather than assuring that their children are adequately educated in basic life skills. Although these competing views may both have "grains of truth"—only continuing research on this interesting new stage can resolve the issue.

In this and the next chapter we will examine some of the key characteristics of life after adolescence, primarily for young people in the United States. We will refer to the period from about 18 to 30 as **young adulthood**, although we acknowledge Arnett's (2000, 2010) argument that many 18- to 25-year-olds are better described as "emerging adults." The early years of young adulthood are often an extended period of transition involving exploration of potential adult identities.

In this chapter, we will begin by examining the physical characteristics of young adults and then move on to consider the cognitive changes that are likely in this period of life. In Chapter 12, we will explore the complexities of forming intimate, enduring adult attachments, maintaining or revamping family relationships, and making vocational commitments. That is, we will look at some of the myriad processes involved in taking one's place as a contributing member of an adult community.

PHYSICAL DEVELOPMENT IN YOUNG ADULTHOOD

Reaching Peak Physical Status

By age 18 to 20, most people have reached their full physical growth. Sometime between 18 and 30, all our biological systems reach peak potential. For example, we can see, hear, taste, and smell as well as we ever will; our skin is as firm and resilient as it can be; the potential strength of muscle and bone is as great as we will ever experience; and our immune systems provide us with the most effective protection we will ever have from diseases ranging from the common cold to cancer. Not all physical capacities reach their peak simultaneously. Visual acuity, for example, reaches a maximum level at about age 20, with little decline for most people until about age 40. But auditory acuity appears to peak before age 20 and may show some declines soon after (Saxon & Etten, 1987; Whitbourne, 1996).

There are certainly individual differences among us in the achievement of peak physical status—for example, some people reach their full height by age 15, whereas others may not finish growing until age 18 or 20. There are also substantial differences among different physical skills in the timing of peak performance, which is usually assessed by looking at the records of "super-athletes" (e.g., Tanaka & Seals, 2003; Schulz & Curnow, 1988). Schulz and Curnow examined athletic performance records for superathletes in a wide variety of sports. On one hand, they found that maximal performance for most sports is reached within the young adult period; on the other hand, they found that the average age of greatest skill (e.g., winning an Olympic gold medal in track or achieving a Number 1 world ranking in tennis) is different from one sport to another, and sometimes depends on which particular skill is examined within a given sport. For example, the average age at which Olympic swimmers win gold medals is 19; professional golfers typically do not achieve a Number 1 ranking until they have moved out of the young adult period, at age 34. For a professional baseball player, the average age for "most stolen bases" is 23, but the mean age for "peak batting average" is 28 and for "hitting the most doubles" is 32!

The differences in age of peak performance suggest that the relative importance of practice, training, knowledge, experience, and biological capacity varies from one skill to another. Skills that are based on muscle strength, flexibility, and speed of movement and response tend to peak early. Abilities that are heavily dependent on control, arm–hand steadiness, precision, and stamina tend to peak later. Overall, the greater the importance of cognitive factors in performance, factors such as strategy knowledge and use, the later a skill will top out (Schulz & Curnow, 1988).

An interesting finding from the research on superathletes is that physical development progresses at different rates for the two sexes. Men reach their peak of performance in many skills approximately 1 year later than women do. No simple explanation is available for the gender differences, but in some instances they appear to be based on earlier skeletal-muscular maturation in women. In other cases, they may depend on the fact that the smaller, more streamlined bodies of young adolescent females confer some speed advantages, as in long-distance swimming.

Superathletes are those whose performance of a skill seems to match their full potential. Most of the rest of us are not concerned about achieving maximal skill, but we usually are motivated to maintain our physical capacities at high levels—including not only performance skills, but also sensory abilities, good health, and youthful appearance—during and beyond the early adult period. Clearly, biology plays a role here. For example, regardless of activity level, muscular strength begins to decline somewhat by about age 30. But research supports the importance of lifestyle in this process. There are good habits that help maintain peak or near-peak functioning and appearance, and there are bad habits that can erode functioning (Whitbourne, 1996). For example, regular exercise can help both younger and older adults maintain muscle and bone strength and keeps the cardiovascular and respiratory systems functioning well. Smoking, poor diet, and a sedentary lifestyle accelerate loss of peak cardiovascular and respiratory functioning and loss of muscle and bone. Smoking or any excessive drug or alcohol use can diminish functioning in a variety of physiological systems. For example, smoking contributes to more rapid wrinkling of the skin, and alcohol causes damage to the nervous system, the liver, and the urinary tract.

"Eating right" is part of a healthy lifestyle. It means having regularly spaced meals (including breakfast) that are low in fat and that sample a range of food groups, allowing a proper balance of nutrients. Failure to eat right contributes to obesity, to depressed mood, and to many aspects of physical decline. Overweight and obesity are epidemic in the United States (65%) and Canada (59%), and weight gain is especially likely between the ages of 20 and 40 (Tjepkema, 2005; U.S. Department of Health and Human Services, 2005). Longitudinal studies that have followed participants for 40 to 50 years have made clear that people who fail to follow healthy lifestyles in their young adult years suffer from poorer health later and that they are less satisfied with their lives in late adulthood when compared to people who do adopt healthy habits in young adulthood (e.g., Belloc & Breslow, 1972; Mussen, Honzik, & Eichorn, 1982).

None of this information is likely to be new to you. Many Americans, including young adults, are aware of the benefits of a healthy lifestyle and of the liabilities that bad living habits pose. Do they heed what they know? We learned in Chapter 10 that adolescents often act in reckless ways that compromise their health and wellness. Often young adults are not much better. Consider their alcohol use. As we have seen, nearly half of college students report that they drink heavily, often binge drinking (i.e., having at least five drinks in a row), and many indicate that their drinking has caused them problems, such as having unplanned or unprotected sex, getting hurt, or causing property damage (e.g., Fromme, Corbin, & Kruse, 2008; Hingson, 2010). Studies of adolescents and young adults indicate that the ongoing development of memory and learning abilities may be inhibited in binge drinkers (Ballie, 2001). In a longitudinal study of 33,000 people, problem drinking and drug use shifted during the young adult period (Bachman, 1997; Johnston, O'Malley, Bachman, & Schulenberg, 2009). These problems began to decline as participants reached their mid-20s and as their reasons for drinking began to change. "To have a good time with my friends" was the most common reason given by younger participants, but it gradually declined after age 20 and was surpassed by the desire "to relax or relieve tension" as participants approached age 30 (see Figure 11.2; Patrick & Schulenberg, 2011). This study also indicated that being in college is a contributing factor to substance abuse in the United States, because college students drink more alcohol and smoke more marijuana than same-age peers who have never attended college.

Although the reasons for substance use in emerging adulthood do not seem to vary across demographic groups in the United States, the extent of substance use does. Alcohol consumption is greater for males than females, and it is greater for Caucasians than for other ethnic or racial groups, although Hispanics run a close second to Caucasians (e.g., Johnston et al., 2009; LaBrie, Atkins, Neighbors, Mirza, & Larimer, 2012; Smith et al., 2006). Sexual minority individuals appear to be at particular risk. Another large longitudinal study of adolescents and young adults found that even as teens, lesbian, gay and bisexual youth, especially girls, were at higher risk of alcohol abuse than heterosexuals (Dermody et al., 2013). And the risk disparity between sexual minorities and heterosexuals increased in young adulthood. It appears that the stresses of dealing with sexual identity issues, along with discrimination and victimization, may be important drivers of these differences in susceptibility to hazardous drinking (e.g., Hatzenbuehler, Corbin, & Fromm, 2011).

In addition to substance use problems, attending college appears to have negative health effects in general. In another survey, over 20,000 college students completed a questionnaire in the fall of their 1st year of college and again 1 year later (Keup & Stolzenberg, 2004). Over the course of that year, they reported substantial declines in their emotional well-being, in their physical health, and in their health habits (e.g., reduced levels of exercise). Fromme et al. (2008) also found substantial increases in alcohol and marijuana use, as well as sex with multiple partners, between high school and the end of freshman year of college in a sample of

FIGURE 11.2 Frequency of endorsement of five reasons for drinking in the young adult years.
SOURCE: Patrick, M. E., & Schulenberg, J. E. (2010). How trajectories of reasons for alcohol use relate to trajectories of binge drinking: National panel data spanning late adolescence to early adulthood. *Developmental Psychology, 47,* 314. Reprinted by permission of the American Psychological Association.

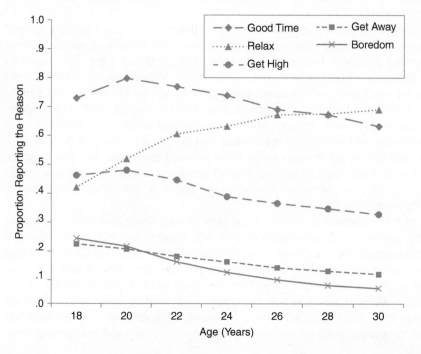

2,000 young people. There was some variability depending on whether students lived at home (less increase) or not, and whether they came from rural, urban (less increase), or suburban high schools, but in all cases there *was* an increase.

The unhealthy, underregulated lifestyles of many young adults are probably an outgrowth of multiple factors: poor application of problem-solving skills to practical problems (see the next section on cognitive development); perhaps a continuing sense of invulnerability that began in the adolescent years, which may be exacerbated by the fact that young adults can bounce back from physical stress far more readily than they will in later years; and the stresses of leaving home and facing the social and academic demands of college or the workplace—all steps that create new challenges to one's identity.

The Changing Brain

As we saw in Chapter 9, it is now clear that major brain developments continue in adolescence and into early adulthood, to the surprise of many researchers. Measures of brain growth (utilizing magnetic resonance imaging, or MRI, procedures) indicate that a resurgent growth of synapses (synaptogenesis) occurs around puberty in some parts of the brain, followed by a long period of pruning, which continues into the adult years (e.g., Petanjek, Judas, Simic, & Rasin, 2011). Such changes may mean an expanded capacity for cognitive advancement.

Hudspeth and Pribram (1992) measured brain activity in children and adults up to 21 years old (using electroencephalography, or EEG, technologies), and they were astonished to find accelerated maturing of electrical activity in the frontal cortex of the 17- to 21-year-olds. Pribram (1997) argues that such acceleration could mean that early adulthood is especially important for the advanced development of frontal lobe functions, such as the ability to organize and reorganize attention, to plan, and to exercise control over one's behavior and emotions. He suggests that the typical timing of a college education may be ideally suited to what he assumes is the heightened flexibility and plasticity of the frontal cortex in young adulthood. A great deal more research needs to be done to determine the degree to which accelerated brain growth is related to the acquisition of cognitive skills and to evaluate the direction of effects. To what extent are observed brain changes the cause, as opposed to the outcome, of learning and learning opportunities? Clearly, new technologies are making this an exciting time in the study of adult brain development.

COGNITIVE DEVELOPMENT IN YOUNG ADULTHOOD

Each year, millions of young people participate in a rite of passage that marks their entry into young adulthood, the transition to college. Although not all adolescents go on to higher education, statistics indicate the numbers continue to increase. A century ago, fewer than 5% of young adults attended college in the United States; today, more than 60% do (Arnett, 2000). So, at least for a sizable subset of American youth, the college experience represents a major influence on their cognitive and social development.

We can all picture the scenes: students piling out of cars driven by their anxious parents, descending on dorms at the beginning of the semester, bustling across campus as fall's first colors begin to tint the foliage, eagerly anticipating the educational challenges that await them in their classes, gathered late into the night, talking and laughing with their newfound community of peers, relishing the heady freedom of young adulthood.

If these images remind you of far too many movies you have seen, it may be because they have been overly romanticized, due in equal parts to advertising and to nostalgia. Below the attractive exterior these images suggest lays a core set of developmental challenges that await individuals at this time of life. For the most part, these tasks involve continuing the hard work of carving out an identity, now all the more pressing because of one's status as an "adult." Moreover, most of the work takes place outside the protected environments of home and high school, even though continuing attachments to family remain important, as we shall see in the next chapter.

In this section, we will examine the changes in cognitive functioning that appear to characterize many young adults. Most of the research on young adult development has been done on college students and focuses on the kinds of change that one can expect to find among people with the opportunity to continue their education beyond high school, delaying many other adult responsibilities. As we noted earlier, more than half of young Americans fall into this category. We know very little about cognitive change in those individuals who move directly from adolescence into the world of work. In the next chapter, we examine some of the special issues that may apply to this segment of our young people.

Unquestionably, early adulthood is a time of great learning. Whether in college or on the job, young people are faced with being the "novices," the "unknowledgeable," or the "inexperienced" when they enter the world of adults, and they spend a great deal of time building their knowledge base and becoming more expert in particular domains of knowledge, such as computer science or philosophy or mechanics. Not surprisingly, at the end of 4 years of college, students perform better on tests of general knowledge than they do as entering students, and the majority judge themselves to be "much stronger" than they were as 1st-year students in knowledge of a particular field (Astin, 1993). Comparable change measures are not available for young people who enter the workforce after high school, but it seems reasonable to assume that after 4 years on the job, some of which may be in job training programs, at least their knowledge of a particular field would have increased.

On the whole, longitudinal research on intellectual change across the life span indicates that many skills (such as spatial orientation abilities and inductive reasoning skills) improve throughout young adulthood, with measures of knowledge acquisition or breadth, such as understanding of verbal meanings, showing the most improvement in this time frame (e.g., Schaie, 1994). As long as opportunities to learn exist, the acquisition of knowledge seems to proceed rapidly during early adulthood. In later chapters, we will look in more detail at the typical progress of specific intellectual abilities throughout adulthood.

Logical Thinking: Is There Qualitative Change?

Is growth of knowledge and skill the only kind of cognitive change that we can expect to find in early adulthood? Or, as in childhood, does the nature of one's thinking and problem solving change as well? Piaget's analysis of structural shifts in children's logical thinking skills ends with the description of formal operational thought in the adolescent years (see Chapter 9). Formal operational thinking allows us to think logically about abstract contents. We can discover and understand the implications of relationships among pieces of information that may themselves be abstract relationships—such as proportions, for example. But many theorists have speculated that more advanced forms of rational thought are possible and emerge sometime in adulthood.

Several schemes, many borrowing heavily from Piaget's seminal work, attempt to describe the cognitive shifts that might occur in the adult years. Among these theories are those that propose a stage of adult cognitive thought that has variously been called **postformal** or **fifth-stage thinking**, implying an extension of Piaget's sequence of stages (e.g., Arlin, 1984; Basseches, 1984; Commons & Richards, 1984; Sinnott, 1984, 1998). Some of these theories actually elaborate a number of substages in the movement from formal operations to postformal thought. Two of these—Perry's (1970/1999) and Kitchener's (Kitchener & King, 1981; Kitchener, King, Wood, & Davison, 1989)—we describe in detail in later sections to illustrate the possible processes of change in young adulthood.

In all these theories, a fifth stage of logical thought is said to evolve as people begin to recognize that logical solutions to problems can come out differently depending on the perspective of the problem solver. In postformal thinking, the problem solver is said to coordinate contradictory formal operational approaches to the same problem. Each approach is logically consistent and leads to a necessary conclusion, and each can be valid. The postformal thinker can both understand the logic of each of the contradictory perspectives and integrate those perspectives into a larger whole. Although she will likely make a commitment to one of these for her purposes, she recognizes that more than one can be valid. Thus, postformal thought incorporates formal thinking and goes beyond it. The assumption is that one could not be a postformal thinker without going through Piaget's four stages of thought development.

As you can see, postformal stage theorists have incorporated some features of the Piagetian framework, including stage sequences, into their theories. They assume that there are qualitatively different structural organizations of thought and its contents at each stage. They also have a constructivist focus. That is, they assume that what one knows and understands about the world is partly a function of the way one's thought is, or can be structured. Yet gradual reorganizations of thought are possible as one confronts and accommodates her thinking to stimuli that cannot be fully assimilated into her current ways of thinking.

Some theorists disagree with the concept of a fifth stage of cognitive development. They often argue that the formal operational system of thinking is powerful enough to address any kind of logical problem. They are more inclined to see qualitative differences in adult problem solving and logical thinking not so much as an indication of a stage beyond formal operations but as a sign that the kinds of problems adults must solve are different from those that children are usually trained and tested on. As a result, adults must adapt their existing problem-solving skills to the new kinds of problems they face in adulthood (e.g., Chandler & Boutilier, 1992; Labouvie-Vief, 1984; Schaie, 1977–1978). Part of what people may learn as they confront adult problems and responsibilities is the limits of their own problem-solving abilities. That is, they may grow in metacognitive understanding, recognizing that in some circumstances logical thinking will lead to a clear solution but that in other circumstances they must make decisions based in part on values, needs, and goals (e.g., Chandler, Boyes, & Ball, 1990; Kuhn, Garcia-Mila, Zohar, & Andersen, 1995; Moshman, 1998).

In sum, theorists disagree about whether adult problem solving represents a fifth stage in the development of logical thinking or is a reflection of the fact that life presents adults with new problems. In the latter view, adults do not achieve a new rational system but learn to recognize the limits of their existing problem-solving systems and to evolve new strategies for applying them. Despite some disagreements, nearly all theorists agree that problem solving takes on a different look and feel in adulthood. In the following sections, we will summarize a few theoretical descriptions of adult logical thinking, and we will examine some of the research demonstrating that indeed, something changes as people face life's grown-up challenges.

Schaie's View of Adults Adjusting to Environmental Pressures

Schaie's (1977–1978; Schaie & Willis, 2000) theory emphasizes the importance of new roles, needs, and responsibilities in determining adult intellectual functioning. Schaie does not argue for postformal thought but for shifts in cognitive functioning, or in the use of knowledge and skills, that are straightforward adaptations to the new demands that adults face at different times of life. According to Schaie, we can think of the child and adolescent years as a time when the individual is sheltered from much of life's responsibilities. Schaie calls this the **acquisition stage** of cognitive development, when youngsters can learn a skill or a body of knowledge regardless of whether it has any practical goal or social implications. Practical problems and goal setting are monitored by parents and others who take on the responsibility for making decisions that will affect the child's life course. The child has the luxury of learning for learning's sake or problem solving just to sharpen her logical thinking skills. Many of the problems she confronts in this phase are those with preestablished answers.

In young adulthood the protections of childhood rapidly recede and the individual is faced with taking responsibility for her own decisions. The problems she must solve—such as how to maintain good health, what career path to choose, whom to vote for, or whether to marry—usually do not have preestablished answers. Many theorists have described these kinds of problems as **ill-defined** or **ill-structured**. Not only do they have no preestablished answers, but the "right" answer may be different depending on circumstances and on the perspective of the problem solver. Further, when we solve such problems we often do not have access to all the information that might be helpful.

Young adults are in the **achieving stage** of cognitive development, when an individual must apply her intellectual skills to the achievement of long-term goals, carefully attending to the consequences of the problem-solving process. Schaie assumes not that additional thinking skills are emerging beyond formal operational abilities but that previously acquired skills are being sharpened and honed on very different kinds of problems, such that the solution to one problem must be considered and adjusted relative to other life problems and goals. For example, an adult who is contemplating a divorce must contend with a number of issues: her future happiness, her economic status, and the well-being of her children, just to name a few.

According to Schaie, each new stage of adult life brings new kinds of problems, with different skills more likely to play an important role in one stage than in another. In middle adulthood, the **responsible stage**, ill-defined problems are still the norm, but problem solving must take into account not only one's own personal needs and goals but also those of others in one's life who have become one's responsibility: spouse, children, coworkers, members of the community. Schaie suggests that the greater impact of one's problem solutions leads adults to become more flexible in their thinking and to expand their knowledge and expertise and use those qualities more widely than before. For people who take on supervisory functions at work and in the community, the extended impact of one's problem solving is even greater than for others, and the responsible stage becomes the **executive stage**, requiring that one focus heavily on learning about complex relationships, multiple perspectives, commitment, and conflict resolution. Such individuals must sharpen skills in integrating and hierarchically organizing such relationships.

People's responsibilities usually narrow in early old age as their children grow up and retirement becomes an option. This is the **reorganizational stage**, when flexibility in problem solving is needed to create a satisfying, meaningful environment for the rest of life, but the focus tends to narrow again to a changed set of personal goals and needs. Practical concerns, such as planning and managing one's finances without an income from work, require applying one's knowledge in new ways.

As people move further into their elder years, called the **reintegrative stage**, they need less and less to acquire new domains of knowledge or to figure out new ways of applying what they know, and many are motivated to conserve physical and psychological energy. Schaie suggests that elderly people are often unwilling to waste time on tasks that are meaningless to them, and their cognitive efforts are aimed more and more at solving immediate, practical problems that seem critically important to their daily functioning.

A **legacy-leaving stage** may also characterize people whose minds are sound but whose frailty signals that their lives are ending. Such people often work on establishing a written or oral account of their lives or of the history of their families to pass on to others. Consider Jean, who used her considerable organizational ability to construct a detailed genealogy to pass along to her only son. The activity gave her a sense of satisfaction, purpose, and meaning. Clearly, these goals require substantial use of long-term memory and narrative skill, more than problem-solving skills, but as Schaie points out, such accounts do require decision making, or the use of judgment, about what is important and what is not.

Many of the problems that emerging adults face are ill-defined and have no right answers. The ability to deal with complexity is a characteristic of postformal thought.

This discussion of Schaie's theory has involved describing cognitive functions beyond early adulthood. We will return to the later stages in Chapters 13 and 14. For now, Schaie's depiction of cognitive functioning as heavily affected by the environmental pressures people face at different times of life should help set the stage for understanding other theories of young adult cognition. Most theories emphasize that advancements or changes in problem solving are embedded in the new experiences faced during adulthood.

Schaie's description of environmental pressures clearly is focused on typical middle-class experiences in Western cultures. He would probably be the first to acknowledge that adults in other cultures, or in some North American cultural groups, might show different shifts in the polishing or use of cognitive skills through life, depending on the unique demands that their environments impose. Arnett and Taber (1994) point out, for example, that in Amish communities within the United States, the importance of mutual responsibility and interdependence is emphasized from childhood through all phases of adulthood. A sense of duty and of the need to sacrifice on behalf of others is central to everyone's life within the culture. Thus, these obligations should be expected to affect cognitive functioning in important ways well before middle adulthood, which is when Schaie considers them to become influential. Keep in mind as you read the following accounts of postformal thought that they are almost entirely based on observations of members of the majority culture in Western societies and that it remains to be seen whether these conceptions adequately characterize adult cognitive development in other cultures.

 Amanda is still figuring out her adult roles and responsibilities. Which stage of Schaie's theory of development would you say best characterizes her?

Postformal Thought

Many theorists argue that the realities of adult experience actually lead to new forms of thought (e.g., Arlin, 1984; Basseches, 1984; Commons & Richards, 1984; Sinnott, 1984, 1998). The full flower of postformal thinking may not be realized until middle adulthood or even later, but the experiences of young adulthood contribute to the reconstruction of logical thinking. As we saw with formal operations, not all individuals will necessarily reach postformal operations. If they do, we can expect them to "skip in and out" of this type of thinking (Sinnott, 1998).

Sinnott (1984, 1998) captures many of the features of postformal thinking described by others. For Sinnott, the essence of postformal thought is that it is **relativistic**: "[S]everal truth systems exist describing the reality of the same event, and they appear to be logically equivalent" (1998, p. 25). The knower recognizes both the consistencies and the contradictions among the multiple systems of truth, or systems of formal operations, and depending on her goals and concerns, in many situations she will make a subjective commitment to one; in other situations, she may seek a compromise solution that integrates some of each perspective, but will not lose sight of the inherent contradictions.

For example, advanced study of a science often reveals that more than one theoretical system can account for much of the data, although perhaps not all of it. Let's use Sinnott's example from mathematics to begin our demonstration:

> The knower may be aware that both Euclidean and non-Euclidean geometries exist and that each has contradictory things to say about parallel lines. In Euclidean geometry parallel lines never come together; in non-Euclidean geometry, parallel lines eventually converge. These are two logically contradictory truth systems that are logically consistent within themselves and logically equivalent to one another. A mathematician bent on knowing reality must decide at a given point which system he or she intends to use, and must make a commitment to that system, working within it, knowing all along that the other system is equally valid, though perhaps not equally valid in this particular context. (Sinnott, 1998, p. 25)

In the behavioral sciences and the helping professions, we are quite familiar with the phenomenon of competing truth systems. For example, a counselor may be aware of multiple theories to account for snake phobias. One might be biologically based, another based on assumptions about the symbolic meaning of snakes in a person's life, and another a behavioral theory arguing that irrational fears are classically conditioned. Suppose she understands the logic of each theory and knows that each is supported by a set of evidence. Yet, in a therapeutic situation, she must make a commitment to one of these systems of "truth" for the purposes of developing a therapeutic plan that will achieve relief for her client as quickly as possible. As Sinnott argues, for her purposes that system then becomes her "true description of the world," but if she remains aware of the inherent contradictions among the different systems and realizes that each has some claim on being true, her thinking has postformal characteristics. Truth is relative, but one truth system may be more valid than another, depending on our goals. This example illustrates that descriptions of postformal thinking have parallels in the descriptions of "reflective practice" presented in Chapter 1.

Sinnott's characterization of postformal thought is consistent with what Chandler (1987; Chandler et al., 1990) calls **postskeptical rationalism**, in which we abandon

> the empty quest for absolute knowledge in favor of what amounts to a search for arguably good reasons for choosing one belief or course of action over another . . . an endorsement of the possibility and practicality of making rational commitments in the face of the clear knowledge that other defensible alternatives to one's views continue to exist. (Chandler et al., 1990, p. 380)

Interestingly, Chandler and his colleagues disagree that postskeptical rationalism actually represents thinking that is more advanced than formal operational thought. They are more inclined to see it as a result of self-reflection, a growing metacognitive awareness that is the product of "an ongoing effort to reflect on the status of the general knowing process" (p. 380) and to understand its strengths and its limits.

Whether relativistic thinking is truly postformal is perhaps less important than when and under what circumstances it emerges. Let's consider in greater detail two descriptions of cognitive change in the college years and the research in which they are grounded. In each of these theories, the final accomplishment is relativistic reasoning like that described by Sinnott. But each draws on data from studies of young adults to specify in detail how thinking might be restructured and why it is, especially for college students. They each describe a series of stages that we might consider substages in the progression from early formal operational thought to a postformal kind of thinking.

Perry's Theory of Intellectual and Ethical Development in the College Years

William Perry's (1970/1999) theory focuses on the cognitive and moral development of college students. Perry was a professor of education at Harvard and founder of the Harvard Bureau of Study Council, a counseling and tutoring center. Using many of Piaget's ideas, Perry proposed a stage-based theory that depicts the typical intellectual and ethical transitions experienced by students in higher education settings, from absolute adherence to authority to beliefs founded on personal commitment. Perry's theory examines the changes that occur over time in the structure of young adults' knowledge, or, put another way, the changes in their expectations and assumptions about the world.

Perry's original study involved hundreds of volunteer Harvard and Radcliffe students from 1954 through 1963. The theory was constructed from extensive interviews of students as they moved through their college years. In general, interview questions were open ended, such as "Why don't you start with whatever stands out for you about the year?" (Perry, 1970/1999, p. 21), allowing students maximum freedom to talk about their experiences. Initially, Perry considered the differences in students' thinking or worldviews to be a function of their personality differences. It was only after careful reflection on many transcriptions that Perry and his team of raters began to consider the possibility of a developmental sequence. He states, "We gradually came to feel that we could detect behind the individuality of the reports a common sequence of challenges to which each student addressed himself in his own particular way" (p. 8). Although Perry acknowledged that specific forms of knowing do vary across domains of knowledge (as we saw in our examinations of cognitive development in childhood), he believed it was possible to identify a dominant position or overarching form of thought for a given individual at a given time.

Perry constructed a sequence of nine "positions," or stages, ranging from extreme dualistic thinking to high levels of personally committed beliefs. What happens in between is the stuff of intellectual growth during the college years. Few students, if any, enter college at the first position, and few leave having achieved the ninth position. Like Piaget's theory, Perry's is a theory of continual movement and transition. Students "rest" for a time at each of the positions, but the dynamic clearly moves forward. From his perspective, the experience of a liberal arts college education accelerates the growth process, particularly in a society that values pluralism, because students are invariably confronted with diversity of thought, values, and beliefs.

Emerging adults may find the challenges of new academic and social responsibilities difficult to cope with, absent the familiar supports of home and family.

To understand Perry's ideas, let's consider each of the positions and the three alternatives to growth (see Table 11.1 for a summary).

TABLE 11.1 Moving Toward Postformal Thought: Descriptions by Perry and Kitchener

PERRY FROM DUALISM TO RELATIVISM	KITCHENER EMERGENCE OF REFLECTIVE JUDGMENT
Dualism	
Position 1: Strict Dualism There is right vs. wrong; authorities know the truth.	**Stage 1** Knowing is limited to single concrete instances.
	Stage 2 Two categories for knowing: right answers and wrong answers.
Position 2: Multiplicity (Prelegitimate) Multiple ideas exist; some authority knows what's right.	**Stage 3** Knowledge is uncertain in some areas and certain in others.
Position 3: Multiplicity (Subordinate) or Early Multiplicity Multiple perspectives are real and legitimate.	**Stage 4** Given that knowledge is unknown in some cases, knowledge is assumed to be uncertain in general.
Position 4: Late Multiplicity A. *Oppositional Solution:* Either "authority is right" or "no one is right." B. *Relative Subordinate Solution:* Some opinions are more legitimate (better supported); outside guidance may be needed to learn how to evaluate and to reach this conclusion.	**Stage 5** Knowledge is uncertain and must be understood within a context; can be justified by arguments within those contexts.
Relativism	
Position 5: Contextual Relativism Respectful of differing opinions, but belief that ideas can be evaluated based on evidence.	**Stage 6** Knowledge is uncertain; constructed by comparing and coordinating evidence and opinions.
Position 6: Commitment Foreseen Preference for a worldview begins to emerge despite awareness of legitimacy of other views.	**Stage 7** Knowledge develops probabilistically through inquiry that generalizes across domains.
Positions 7, 8, and 9: Commitment and Resolve "Flowering" of commitment; resolve to continue reflecting.	

SOURCES: Based on Kitchener, K. S., Lynch, C. L., Fischer, K. W., & Wood, P. K. (1993). Developmental range of reflective judgment: The effect of contextual support and practice on developmental stage. *Developmental Psychology, 29,* 893–906; and Perry, W. G. (1970/1999). *Forms of ethical and intellectual development in the college years: A scheme.* San Francisco, CA: Jossey-Bass.

Position 1: Strict Dualism. **Strict dualism** is really a downward extrapolation of higher stages, given that virtually no one enters college at this level. Strict dualistic thinking implies a rigid adherence to authoritarian views, a childlike division between in-group (the group that includes me, my family, and authorities who have the "right" idea) and out-group (the group that is "wrong" or has no legitimate authority). Individuals in this stage simply never think to question their belief that authority embodies rightness. Because most adolescents have struggled with parents over autonomy issues and have experienced peers and teachers who, at the very least, have exposed them to various viewpoints, it is unlikely that many students would enter college with this extremely simplistic view of the world.

Position 2: Multiplicity (Prelegitimate). **Multiplicity (prelegitimate)** is characterized by the student's first encounters with multiplicity, that is, multiple ideas, answers to life's questions, or points of view. Students now find themselves face-to-face with uncertainty when exposed to a mass of theories, social experiences, and information. Their confusion is exacerbated because they lack the structure to accommodate the sheer volume of ideas. Despite their confusion, however, individuals at this stage maintain the belief that some "authority" possesses the ultimate truth or right answers. It is just up to the individual to find it. It is not uncommon, according to Perry, for students to sort through and organize confusing or contradictory information by creating mental dichotomies. For example, they may distinguish between "factual" courses, such as those in the sciences, and "vague" courses, such as those in the humanities. Students who pursue fields that are relatively clear-cut, at least at the early stages of study, may experience confusion when they later have to confront the multiplicity inherent in advanced levels of study. (Remember our examples of multiple truth systems in advanced sciences.) As one student in Perry's study complained about an instructor:

> He takes all sort of stuff that, that isn't directly connected with what he's talking about . . . so you get just a sort of huge amorphous mass of junk thrown at you which doesn't really mean much until you actually have some sort of foundation in what the man is talking about. (1970/1999, p. 97)

Position 3: Multiplicity (Subordinate), or Early Multiplicity. In the stage of **multiplicity (subordinate)**, the individual grudgingly acknowledges the reality and legitimacy of multiple perspectives. For example, it becomes more difficult to deny that reasonable people can differ in their perspectives on life, and people who hold different views are not so easily dismissed as being wrong. Some of the students' beliefs in a **just world** (Lerner, 1980), beliefs that the world is fair and that people in it get what they deserve, are now reevaluated. Students realize that working hard on assignments or putting many hours into studying does not necessarily guarantee wished-for results. They may observe other students doing far less work than they do themselves and getting better grades. They may be distressed by their inability to understand "what the professors want." They are nudged toward the sometimes painful realization that even their professors and other authority figures around them don't have all the answers. They may also be distressed by the fact that their teachers continue to evaluate them, despite not having the "right" answers themselves.

Position 4: Late Multiplicity. **Late multiplicity** was the modal position of Harvard and Radcliffe students in the original study in the latter part of their first year. Perry's research identified two possible epistemologies or adaptations to the problem of multiplicity at this point in development. In effect, students at this stage now fully realize that even experts differ among themselves in regard to what is true. Students handle the realization in one of two ways. One response, identified as **oppositional**, is characterized by legitimizing multiplicity as one pole of a new kind of dualism. The right–wrong dualism of Position 1 moves to one end of a new continuum, with multiplicity on the other end. Individuals taking this view of the world succeed in maintaining a dualistic either-or structure in their thinking. In other words, either "authority is right" or "all opinions are equally right." One student in Perry's study captured the essence of this position when commenting to the interviewer about his English course: "I mean if you read them [critics], that's the great thing about a book like *Moby Dick*. Nobody understands it" (1970/1999, p. 108). The viewpoint that nobody possesses the truth, thus rendering all people's opinions equally valid, can provoke students to irritation when they believe their work or the content of their ideas has been evaluated unfairly.

The second alternative, called **relative subordinate**, is less oppositional. Students with this perspective begin to understand that some opinions are more legitimate than others, presaging the relativism of Position 5. The value of a perspective is now understood to be related to the supporting arguments and evidence for the position. However, the consideration of alternative points of view is still done primarily under the guidance of authority. A Perry interviewee reported that his first set of grades in a literature course was mediocre because he could not understand the kinds of thinking required:

> Finally I came to realize, about the middle of the second term, that they were trying to get you to look at something in a complex *way* and to try to weigh more factors than one, and talk about things in a concrete manner. That is, with words that have some meaning and some relevance to the material you were studying." (1970/1999, p. 112)

Often students receive explicit guidance in helping them weigh opinions or compare and contrast ideas. Instruction such as this fosters the kind of metacognition—awareness of how rational arguments are constructed and weighed—that is the foundation of later relativistic thinking.

Position 5: Contextual Relativism. The move to Position 5, **contextual relativism**, represents a major achievement in intellectual development. The first four positions are variants of a basic dualistic structure. The later positions represent a qualitatively different way of looking at the world. Kneflekamp (1999) reports on a common misunderstanding of Perry's theory, which confuses the "anything goes" quality of late multiplicity with the concept of relativism. He recalls what Perry himself used to say: "Relativism means *relative to what—to something—it implies comparison, criteria, and judgment!*" (pp. xix–xx). The individual can no longer accept the fiction that everyone's ideas are as good as everyone else's. Although she respects the rights of others to hold diverse views, the student at this stage possesses sufficient detachment to "stand back" on her own and consider ideas and values more objectively than before. In a very real way, the student develops the habit of thinking that relies on some standard of evidence that is appropriate to the domain in question. Students' new analytic abilities allow them to appreciate the merits of diverse perspectives and to find convincing elements in multiple points of view. Thinking relativistically, or thinking about knowledge in context, becomes more habitual.

Authority figures are seen more as colleagues than they were before, as people grappling with the same conflicts that beset students, only with more experience in dealing with those conflicts. They are figures no longer to be opposed but to be respected, as this 3rd-year college student from the study illustrates:

> I think when I was younger, when people in general are young, there's [*sic*] so many problems that they feel they don't have to face, and that's why they're indifferent to them. Either it's something that somebody else—the hierarchy, like the family—worries about, or it's something in the future that isn't any problem yet. And then you, when you mature you begin facing these problems for yourself, and looking at them, and then the family just becomes a help to people . . . with more, with a lot of experience. To help you, and not to take the brunt of the problem or something that's *your* worry. (Perry, 1970/1999, p. 138)

Position 5 also represents a watershed stage for religious belief, the point of demarcation between belief and the possibility of faith. No longer can an individual's religious belief rest on blind adherence to authority. Real faith, Perry purports, has been tested and affirmed in the context of a relativistic world. This implies that those who hold viewpoints other than one's own may be wrong, but no more wrong than oneself, given that the student now rejects the idea of absolute truth. With some effort, individuals come to respect and tolerate those who hold different viewpoints even while they struggle to clarify their own beliefs.

Position 6: Commitment Foreseen or Anticipation of Commitment. With **commitment foreseen**, we hear echoes of Erikson's discussion of identity development (see Chapter 9). Thinking at this stage incorporates a measure of moral courage, as the individual begins to affirm what it is she believes in, all the while knowing that reason will never provide absolute proof that her ideas or perspectives are right or better than others. Commitments to a set of beliefs, to a field of study or career, to relationships, and so forth, like the constructed commitments we discussed in Chapter 9, can take place "after detachment, doubt, and awareness of alternatives have made the experience of choice a possibility" (Perry, 1970/1999, p. 151). This way of thinking incorporates not only respect for diverse ideas and understanding of their rationales but also emerging, personally chosen, preferences for worldviews. One student captures this element of Position 6:

> It seems to me that so much of what I've been forced to do here, this taking of two sides at once, just suspends my judgment. There is a value in it, in seeing any perspective, or any one particular facet of, of a problem. But there's also a value in, in being able to articulate one side more than another. (p. 157)

One notices a general trend in thinking toward personal meaning making or reflective thinking.

Positions 7, 8, and 9: Commitment and Resolve. Perry discusses Positions 7 (**initial commitment**), 8 (**multiple commitments**), and 9 (**resolve**) together. Taken as a group, they suggest a flowering of the commitments anticipated in Positions 5 and 6. Changes in thinking are more qualitative than structural. According to Perry, 75% of students in the study had a level of commitment at Positions 7 or 8 at graduation. Despite its place at the end of the line, Position 9 does not imply a static resolution of existential conflict. On the contrary, it characterizes a state of courageous resolve to continue the work of reflecting on one's commitments throughout adulthood.

Perry also accounted for individuals who refrain from taking the intellectual challenge necessary for growth through these stages. Fallback positions include **temporizing**, **retreat**, and **escape**. Temporizing refers to delaying movement to the next stage. Escape characterizes a movement back to relativism when the demands of commitment prove too taxing. Retreat occurs when individuals revert to dualistic thinking in times of stress in order to seek the intellectual security of absolute right or wrong, a position that is unavailable at the level of committed relativism.

Although Perry's theory has been extremely popular, particularly among student personnel professionals, it has some limitations. The first five positions of the theory emphasize intellectual development; the last four pertain to moral and identity development. Thus, Perry's scheme incorporates several abstract constructs such as identity, ego development, and cognitive development simultaneously, making it difficult for researchers to agree on definitions and measurement. Some have noted that the lack of uniformity in assessment of stages prevents researchers from making valid comparisons of their findings across studies. Consequently, there is a paucity of recent empirical data on the linkages between Perry's theory and general cognitive processes in adulthood.

Some efforts have been made to address the issue of assessment. Several instruments and questionnaires have been developed to identify stages of reasoning that are less time consuming to administer than the interview method used in Perry's original work (see Baxter-Magolda & Porterfield, 1985; Moore, 1982; Taylor, M. B., 1983). Suggestions for informal assessment of cognitive development for use by residence life professionals have also been proposed (see Stonewater & Stonewater, 1983).

There is some research using Perry's framework to explore the connection between students' beliefs about knowledge and their approach to learning. For example, Ryan (1984) found that relativists were more successful in their college classes because they tended to use more constructivist approaches to studying course material. They paid attention to context, constructed meaningful interpretations of textual information, and summarized main ideas. Dualists, on the contrary, were more likely to focus on memorization of factual information. These differences were significant even when the effects of scholastic aptitude were eliminated statistically.

Using slightly different conceptual frameworks, other researchers have demonstrated that effective problem solving is related to relativistic thinking (Schommer, Crouse, & Rhodes, 1992) and that relativistic thinkers are more likely than dualistic thinkers to provide legitimate evidence to support their thinking and problem solving (Kuhn, 1992). Wilkinson and Maxwell (1991) found support for the relationship between college students' epistemological style (dualistic, multiplistic, or relativistic) and their approach to problem-solving tasks. Dualists took a rather narrow view of the tasks, breaking them down into unrelated, discrete parts and ignoring some important aspects. Relativists were more likely to consider the whole problem, processing and taking into cognitive account all of its components before attempting a solution.

Gilligan (1977) applied Perry's description of the development of relativistic thinking to an analysis of Kohlberg's scoring of young people's responses to moral dilemmas. She discussed a phenomenon called "late adolescent regression," wherein about one third of Kohlberg's samples actually regressed to lower levels on his scoring criteria. Gilligan argued that this "regression" actually indicates a more contextualized, relativistic stance in response to moral dilemmas, representing a more inclusive form of principled reasoning. As such, so-called regressions should more reasonably be considered advances. Kohlberg's original scoring system has since been revised.

Kitchener's Model of the Development of Reflective Judgment

As we noted earlier, and as helpers know all too well, many problems of adulthood are ill-defined. An ill-defined problem has neither one acceptable solution nor one agreed-on way to solve it (Kitchener, 1983). Should a talented athlete stay in college or accept an attractive job offer? Should a young woman pursue a high-powered career that will leave little room in her life for marriage and child rearing? How can a young adult deal with the pressures of academic and social life? Moreover, how do helpers deal with the messy issues that come to them on a daily basis?

Kitchener and her associates (Kitchener & King, 1981; Kitchener et al., 1989) have proposed a seven-stage theory outlining the development of **reflective judgment**, how people analyze elements of a problem and justify their problem solving (see Table 11.1). They presented individuals with a standard set of ill-structured problems from the social and physical sciences and questioned them about the reasoning they used in coming to conclusions about the problems. Like Perry, these researchers found a predictable, sequential progression that moved from a belief in the existence of absolute, fixed certainty to a kind of contextual relativism (see Kuhn, 2009; Moshman, 2008).

For Kitchener, different stages of thinking can be differentiated on the basis of three dimensions: certainty of knowledge, processes used to acquire knowledge, and the kind of evidence used to justify one's judgments. As you can see from Table 11.1, the early stages (1 through 3) are characterized by a belief in the existence of certainties and the use of personal justification ("This is just the way it is") or reliance on authorities for guidance. Individuals in the early stages also tend to use personal observation as evidence of the rightness of their judgments. Individuals in the middle stages (4 and 5), similar to Perry's multiplists, perceive knowledge as uncertain. They believe in the supremacy of personal opinion and tend to make judgments based on idiosyncratic kinds of reasoning. Those in the later stages (5 through 7) resemble Perry's contextual relativists in that they tend to make judgments based on a set of rules or logic in combination with personal reflection. For example, one reflective judgment problem concerned whether certain chemicals in foods, such as preservatives, are good or bad for us. The following is a prototypic example of a Stage 5 response to such a problem:

> I am on the side that chemicals in food cause cancer, but we can never know without a doubt. There is evidence on both sides of the issue. On the one hand there

is evidence relating certain chemicals to cancer, and on the other hand there is evidence that certain chemicals in foods prevent things like food poisoning. People look at the evidence differently because of their own perspective, so what they conclude is relative to their perspective." (Kitchener, Lynch, Fischer, & Wood, 1993, p. 896)

Some research demonstrates that reflective judgment is related to level of education (Dunkle, Schraw, & Bendixen, 1993; Kitchener & King, 1981) as well as to the kind of training one has received (Lehman, Lempert, & Nisbett, 1988). Graduate students, for example, reason at higher levels than do college undergraduates, and graduate students in psychology, a discipline that emphasizes statistical reasoning, show higher levels of proficiency on such tasks than do graduate students in chemistry, medicine, or law. Specific kinds of training or support appear to improve skills in reasoning and judgment. In one study, individuals from middle through graduate school were provided with prototypic statements like the one quoted above, with each statement modeling successively higher levels of reflective judgment, and then they were asked to explain the reasoning in the prototypic statement. The results indicated that after such modeling and practice, participants' own levels of reasoning on such problems had advanced.

One classic study illustrates that reflective judgment in social and personal issues tends to lag behind problem solving in domains that do not relate to one's own personal concerns (Blanchard-Fields, 1986). In this study, participants ranging in age from 14 to 46 were presented with two accounts of each of three events. One event that had little personal relevance for most people was an account of war (the Livia task) by two opposing parties (see Kuhn, Pennington, & Leadbeater, 1982, for a full description of the task). The remaining two events were characterized as "a visit to the grandparents" and "the pregnancy," and both events were rated by participants as emotionally involving. In the first of these, a teenage boy and his parent each present a story about a time when the boy was required to accompany his parents on a visit to his grandparents. The two stories are inconsistent in emotional tone and in many details (see Box 11.1 for the full text of the competing accounts). In the second emotionally involving event, a woman and a man each take a different stance on the woman's pregnancy, she favoring an abortion, he against an abortion. For each of the three events, study participants were asked to explain what the conflict was about and what happened. They also responded to probe questions such as "Who was at fault?" and "Could both accounts be right?" The participants' understanding and analysis of the events were scored based on six levels of reasoning, combining features of Perry's (1970/1999) and Kitchener and King's (1981) levels of cognitive maturity. Performance on the Livia task was better at earlier ages than performance on the more emotionally involving tasks. Performance continued to improve on all tasks from adolescence to young adulthood and from young adulthood to middle adulthood.

The following are examples of performance for these three age groups on the emotionally involving "visit to the grandparents" event (from Blanchard-Fields, 1986).

Level 2. This was the average level of response for adolescents on the two emotionally involving events. It is close to an absolutist conception of reality.

There's a lot more said by John of what they did and they had an argument and the parents did not say it like—how he talked, and that he wanted to be treated like an adult. It seems more right because I don't like the parents' talk." (p. 327)

Level 3. This level was about average for young adults in this sample. They recognized that different perspectives appear valid, but they tended to cling to the possibility that there may be an absolute truth, even in such ill-defined situations.

Yes [they could both be right]. I think you'd have to have a third person not involved emotionally with either party. They'd be able to write without feeling, the facts, just what happened. (p. 327)

Note that "just what happened" suggests one correct interpretation of events.

Level 4. This level was about average for middle-aged adults. They were not biased toward one side or the other, and the idea that more than one truth might exist was intimated, but there was still a strong sense that one can identify an essential similarity or truth despite the different perspectives.

> I think the accounts, as far as the actual events, are pretty much the same. The important differences are in the presentation . . . the important differences are in their perceptions of what was going on. The actual "this happened" are the same, but the interpretation of it is different. (p. 328)

Level 6. Perhaps you will recognize this relativistic view as one that helping professionals are trained to assume in highly personal matters. There is no hint here that one experience of the event was more valid than the other.

> They'd have to be able to really share [to resolve this conflict] . . . this way with each other, and even deeper, in terms of getting into some of their fears and some of their angers. They have to be able to accept it in each other, and maybe, they can resolve the conflict, only if they can accept feelings in each other. (Blanchard-Fields, 1986, p. 328)

Only a few participants, all of them middle-aged, responded at such an advanced relativistic level in this study. As Kuhn et al. (1995) point out, "topics in the social sphere both engage people and challenge them. They are easy to think about *but hard to think well about*" (p. 120, italics added). In Box 11.2 we consider some of the mistakes in problem solving that researchers have found to be quite common, even among adults. You will notice that these tend to occur in situations that can be very personally involving, so they have particular relevance to helping professionals.

Box 11.1: A Visit to the Grandparents

Blanchard-Fields (1986, p. 333) presented adolescents and adults with three tasks, each consisting of two discrepant accounts of the same event. Participants were interviewed to assess their reasoning about the events. The following are the two accounts for the task called "A Visit to the Grandparents."

Adolescent's Perspective

I'd been planning on spending the whole weekend with my friends. Friday, in school, we'd made plans to go to the video game arcade and the school carnival. We were all looking forward to a lot of fun. Saturday morning my parents surprised me by telling me that we were going to visit my grandparents that day. They reminded me that they'd planned this a long time ago. But how am I supposed to remember those things? So, we ended up in one of those big arguments with the typical results; I gave in and went with them. The worst part was when they lectured me on why it was my duty to go without ever once looking at my side of it. When we finally got to my grandparents, I had to do everything they wanted to do. I had to answer silly questions about school, play their games, and see their old slides and movies. It eventually blew up in an argument between me and my parents over the legal age for drinking.

Even though I was being as polite as I could, it was boring. I felt forced into everything. I just can't wait until I am free and out on my own. I was really angry with them. So, on the way home I told them that I wanted to be treated more like an adult; that I wanted more respect from them and I wanted them to take my plans seriously. They seemed to agree with this and decided that I was now old enough to make my own decisions.

Parents' Perspective

Two months had gone by since we had visited the grandparents. We try to visit them at least once a month, but everyone gets so busy that a month slips away very quickly. This time, we planned the visit far enough in advance so that everyone would come. When we tried to get John ready to go with us on Saturday morning, he put up a battle. After all, he hadn't seen his grandparents for a long time. They are getting old and won't be around much longer. We tried reasoning with John, stressing the importance of family unity and obligation as well as consideration of others. Certainly, in the future, he would regret not spending more time with his grandparents after they've gone. Although John was reluctant to go, he finally came with us and actually seemed to really enjoy himself. Since he seemed to be having a good time, we were surprised by how angry he became when we all got into a discussion about the legal age of drinking.

Even though he was reluctant to go with us at first, he seemed to have a good time, to enjoy the family closeness. He showed respect for his grandparents and seemed to understand how good it made them feel to see him. What this means to us is that he's old enough now to enjoy being with adults more and to learn from them. On the way home we agreed that John should take a more active part in discussions about family matters.

SOURCE: Blanchard-Fields, F. (1986). Reasoning on social dilemmas varying in emotional salience: An adult developmental perspective. *Psychology and Aging 1*, 325–333. Reprinted by permission of the American Psychological Association.

Box 11.2: Helper Beware: Decision-Making Pitfalls

Our ability to think our way logically through problems improves and expands throughout childhood and adolescence. As this chapter indicates, problem-solving skill continues to improve in adulthood as well, especially for ill-defined problems. We have also seen in this chapter that effectively using our logical abilities to make decisions can be especially difficult when we deal with social or emotional issues that have personal relevance. Among the many kinds of logical fallacies that commonly ensnare adults (see Stanovich, 1998) are some that may be especially problematic for helping professionals and their clients.

Suppose you want to encourage a client to consider beginning an exercise program. You are concerned that her sedentary lifestyle is contributing both to her depression and to other health problems. When you introduce the idea, however, she counters, "That won't help. I have a neighbor who has run 20 miles a week for all the years I've known her, but she had to be hospitalized last year because she was suicidal." The logical error that your client is making is sometimes called "the person who" fallacy. She is refuting a well-documented finding, like the correlation between regular exercise and well-being (both physical and emotional), by calling on knowledge of a person who is an exception. Especially when dealing with psychological and social issues, matters in which most of us have great personal interest, "people tend to forget the fundamental principle that knowledge does not have to be certain to be useful—that even though individual cases cannot be predicted, the ability to accurately forecast group trends is often very informative. The prediction of outcomes based on group characteristics is often called aggregate or actuarial prediction" (Stanovich, 1998, p. 149). So, for any individual, a prediction about the effectiveness of a treatment is more likely to be accurate if we base that prediction on general findings for people with that individual's characteristics than if we base it on one or a few other individuals whom we have known or observed.

Like many logical mistakes, "the person who" fallacy involves failing to step back and consider how well the evidence supports one's theory. Your hypothetical client has a theory that exercise will not relieve her depressive symptoms, perhaps motivated in part by her distaste for exercise. She is aware of one instance in which the prediction of her theory appears to have been correct. She fails to recognize that a single case is an inadequate test of a treatment's effectiveness. One outcome can be influenced by multiple factors, many of them unknown. Also, your client completely ignores the evidence *against* her theory: Proportionally, more people experience long-term emotional benefits from exercise than not. In other words, probabilistically, regular exercise has a good chance of helping.

Part of the reason that "the person who" fallacy occurs is because of the vividness effect. When we are trying to make decisions, some salient or vivid facts are likely to attract our attention regardless of their actual value as evidence. Even when other facts are available the *vividness* of personal experience or of the personal testimony of other individuals can be greater than that of any other information that we might access. Wilson and Brekke (1994) documented the strength of the vividness effect in a study of consumer behavior. Participants in the study were told they would be given

free condoms and that they could choose between two brands. They were also given access to two kinds of information about the condoms to help them choose a brand. One was an extensive analysis of survey data on the performance of condoms from a *Consumer Reports* magazine and the other was a pair of student testimonials. Objectively, the data from the *Consumer Reports* analysis were more useful in this case, but most participants asked for the testimonials as well, and when the testimonials were in conflict with the survey research, about one third of the participants were swayed by the testimonials. Thus, even in a situation in which *both* carefully collected group data *and* individual testimony were readily available, the vividness of the less appropriate individual testimony was hard for many participants to resist.

The insidiousness of vividness effects is especially problematic when testimonials are one's source of evidence for the effectiveness of a treatment. When your client's Cousin George swears that his son was relieved of his depression by "Dr. Olivino's oil immersion therapy," the appeal of Cousin George's testimonial may be irresistible to your client, especially when she observes for herself that George's son does indeed appear to be doing quite well. Unfortunately, people can be found to offer testimonials for any therapy or treatment that has ever been offered. One reason for the ready availability of testimonials is, of course, the placebo effect. People sometimes improve with attention or in the course of time, no matter what the medical or psychological intervention. The actual effectiveness of a treatment can only be determined in careful studies in which some participants are given the treatment and some are given a dummy, or placebo, version of the treatment. Typically in such studies, a substantial percentage of participants given the placebo control will improve, and typically they are convinced that their "treatment" is responsible. Clearly, the actual effectiveness of a treatment approach cannot be determined by testimonials. The only useful indicator of the effectiveness of a treatment is whether treatment participants are benefited more than placebo controls.

Counselors, too, often find the vividness effect hard to resist. For example, our own experience with individual cases often looms larger in our decision making about probable treatment outcomes than the actuarial evidence that is available to us from controlled studies of a treatment's effectiveness.

How can we protect ourselves and our clients from making poor decisions based on "the person who" fallacy and the vividness effect? Increased metacognitive awareness—that is, awareness of one's own thinking—seems to be the key. For example, educating clients to see that personal experience or the testimony of others can be limited in its generality, despite its vividness, can help them resist the appeal of such evidence. More generally, we can encourage clients to understand the decision-making process itself. When we try to decide whether a treatment should be pursued, we are actually evaluating the *theory* that a particular treatment alternative will cause improvement. Our task is to specify all the possible theories (treatment options) and to evaluate the evidence for each. When people have a favorite theory, they often do not realize that it is just a theory. As Kuhn (1991) points out, they think *with* their theory, not *about* their theory. In other words, the theory guides their thought and what they pay attention to instead of being an object of thought and evaluation. So, for example, if your client believes that Dr. Olivino's oil immersion therapy works, she will pay more attention to examples that support her theory and may either fail to look for, or will ignore, counterevidence.

Helping clients make better decisions, then, will include encouraging them to recognize that they are working with a theory,

not a fact. A theory must be justified by evidence, and *all* the available evidence, both pro and con, should be considered. In addition, alternative theories (treatment options) and the evidence for them should be considered. Testimonials or personal experiences are not likely to become less vivid in this process. But when our clients are armed with knowledge about the shortcomings of such data, they may become more cautious about using them as evidence.

APPLICATIONS

On the cusp of adulthood, individuals in their late teens and 20s confront a number of new developmental milestones. The serious tasks of consolidating an identity, solidifying a career path, and realizing the capacity for intimacy (Erikson, 1968; Keniston, 1971) are both challenging and time consuming. One competency required for each of these tasks is the ability to make decisions and choices given a wide array of possible alternatives. Helpers are frequently called on to help clients make decisions, and, to some, this is the quintessential role of the helper. Decision-making (Krumboltz, 1966; Stewart, Winborn, Johnson, Burks, & Engelkes, 1978) and problem-solving (D'Zurilla, 1986; Egan, 1975) models are widely used among clinicians to help people with personal and career-related issues.

Such models have in common a series of general steps, including (1) defining the problem, (2) setting realistic goals, (3) developing a variety of possible solutions, (4) assessing the costs and benefits of each alternative solution, (5) selecting and implementing one alternative, and (6) reviewing the effectiveness of the solution after implementation (Nezu, Nezu, & Lombardo, 2003). On its face, this strategy appears to incorporate some aspects of postformal thinking, specifically the relativistic, pro-and-con nature of solutions to fuzzy problems, for it is rare to find solutions to difficult problems that don't have potential disadvantages as well as advantages. But it can also suggest to more dualistic thinkers that problems are "well defined" and have correct solutions, if only someone can figure them out. Although most professonals understand that any solution or decision incorporates some good and some bad, their clients may not.

Given what we know about the importance of belief systems, the helper might be remiss if she did not consider the client's epistemology, or her beliefs about the nature of knowledge, when working on decision making—or other problems, for that matter. In other words, seeing a dilemma through the client's eyes requires an appreciation of the way she views truth, knowledge, and meaning in life.

If a client tends to see the world in absolute terms, she might be confused as to why alternatives are even being considered! Twenty-year-old Hannah recently moved into her boyfriend Mike's apartment near the college campus where both are students. She is upset that Mike wants to spend so much

time with his friends, playing basketball and going to bars. Hannah resents the fact that he doesn't spend his free time with her, and, to make matters worse, she believes drinking alcohol is morally wrong. Because the tension between the two is so great, Hannah consults a counselor for advice about how to change Mike's behavior. Hannah becomes indignant when the counselor asks her to consider the advantages of allowing Mike to socialize with his friends and to reflect on her role in the relationship problems. "Mike is the one with the problem," Hannah states emphatically. "I came here to find out how to get him to stop drinking and to spend time with me." Hannah will become frustrated if the counselor presses her to adopt a relativistic stance too quickly, and she may seek out another "authority." She will probably not return to this counselor.

Level of epistemological thinking also influences academic success. Research has demonstrated that students who believe that learning should be quick, that prolonged concentration is a waste of time, and that memorization of concrete facts is sufficient for learning demonstrate poor performance on mastery tests despite reporting high levels of confidence in their ability (Schommer, 1990). Students who perform better on mastery tests are more likely to disagree with the view that knowledge is certain and that single, simple answers are most reflective of reality (Schommer, 1993; see Muis, 2007). Skills in reflective thinking are also correlated with greater understanding of multicultural issues (King & Howard-Hamilton, 1999).

In general, relativistic thinking is considered to be more sophisticated because most problems in life involve uncertainty as well as some measure of uncontrollability. Expectations that complex problems should have clear-cut solutions can complicate the problem-solving process by increasing individuals' anxiety when simple answers prove inadequate (D'Zurilla, 1988). The ability to generate solutions, assess advantages and disadvantages of each, and then integrate aspects of several solutions into one presumes a level of epistemic knowledge that has come to terms with the ambiguity of real-world problems. Yet as Perry and others have demonstrated, this skill develops gradually; it does not necessarily come with a high school diploma. Professionals who are knowledgeable about cognitive development can help clients resolve specific problems and help them acquire more general skills in decision making, such as knowing when and where a strategy is effective.

Stonewater and Stonewater (1984) have proposed a problem-solving model based on Perry's theory that balances a bit of challenge (to introduce disequilibrium) with support and engagement by the counselor. They suggest that individuals who are closer to the dualistic end of the continuum need more carefully controlled exposure to diverse ways of thinking and can benefit from the provision of adequate structure as a framework for incorporating new ideas. For example, students who find the process of career selection overwhelming may be aided by a very specific set of activities that guides them through the exploration process. Students who are at the stages of dualism or early multiplicity may find that knowing what questions to ask or what criteria to investigate allows them to engage in the confusing career decision-making process with a supportive road map. In a process very consistent with Piaget's ideas, individuals will not be able to accommodate new ways of thinking if the complexity of the information is too great and the support is not sufficient. Likewise, individuals will not be motivated to accommodate at all if the challenge is minimal and support is overdone.

King and Kitchener (2002) offer specific suggestions for teachers and others who work with emerging adults. Several of these ideas can be useful in promoting reflective thinking about academic and psychoeducational content. First, demonstrate respect for young adults' thinking, keeping in mind that they are most likely to open up to new ways of reflection in a supportive atmosphere. Second, provide opportunities for young adults to gather information about an issue, evaluate the quality of that information, and draw conclusions based on that data. Third, teach young adults to explicitly examine the epistemological assumptions they use in making decisions about ill-defined problems.

The theories of cognitive development described in this chapter make another important contribution to the practicing clinician. They help us understand that certain kinds of thinking, sometimes labeled "irrational," may not be attributes of a dysfunctional personality style but rather the manifestation of a developmental stage. Construing clients' thinking and judgments from this perspective allows us to be more forgiving of their idiosyncrasies and more supportive about their potential for growth and change. Sometimes, clients with fairly rigid belief systems may not have been exposed to the kinds of contexts that encourage them to examine beliefs carefully or to consider alternative explanations. Or clients who hold less mature perspectives may be retreating from the confusion of too many ideas and too little support. Here the helper has a good opportunity to assess the person's thinking and provide a balance of support and challenge that facilitates progress from a dualistic, polarized belief system to one that is more cognitively complex (Sanford, 1962).

Putting Things Off

The road to adulthood is marked by a point when individuals are no longer bound by the externally controlled routines of home and school. This freedom can be exhilarating, but many are set adrift by the lack of structure. Feeling unsafe and frameworkless once again, many young people search for the certainty of "right" answers and struggle with the challenge of organizing large blocks of unstructured time to work on tasks that may have no clear-cut boundaries. In the past, they could rely on authoritative sources to provide guidelines and directions. Now, the need to become more self-reliant increases dramatically.

One problem that arises frequently at this point in the life span is procrastination. This problem has the power to derail, even if temporarily, emerging adults' potential success in academic and work environments. Procrastination is a multidimensional construct having motivational, behavioral, cognitive, and personality components, and may be the end product of diverse pathways. Those who investigate procrastination as a dispositional, traitlike characteristic (Paunonen & Ashton, 2001; Schouwenburg, 2004) report that procrastinators share low levels of trait conscientiousness (see the section on personality in Chapter 13), rendering this group more likely to be disorganized, poor at planning, and lacking the self-regulation needed to accomplish things in a timely way. Several subtypes have been identified within the general population of procrastinators. Those with low levels of conscientiousness and high levels of neuroticism tend to be fearful, anxiety-prone, and perfectionistic. These perfectionistic procrastinators abide by the "procrastinator's code" (Burka & Yuen, 1983), that specific cognitive tendency to equate failure in one area to a generalized sense of failure in all aspects of the self. An unrealistic set of perfectionistic standards and irrational beliefs, namely that failure is a fate worse than death, may fuel their avoidant behavior.

Those whose combination of personality traits includes low conscientiousness, low neuroticism, and high extraversion are more likely to procrastinate without the worry. These individuals also avoid tasks they consider unpleasant and prefer to engage in more satisfying pursuits but do not do so because they are averse to failure. Some have also identified a "rebellious" type of procrastinator who resists authority and asserts independence through procrastination. In counseling situations, care should be taken not to try to fit everyone who procrastinates into one of these "types" or to assume that patterns of dilatory behavior in certain contexts necessarily reveal the nature of that person's personality. Most of us have avoided aversive tasks at one time or another, and sometimes we may procrastinate in one setting (academic) but not in another (job). We suggest, as well, that there are developmental reasons for the ubiquity of procrastination at this stage of the life span. The landscape of emerging adulthood can be perceived by some as a frontier with open-ended possibilities and many high-stakes choices. The skills of decision making and self-management are honed in the identity development process, which proceeds concurrently with entry into college, military service, or the world of work. Procrastination may be the manifestation of confusion or lack of certainty about how to proceed. Although this is a growing area of research, we still need more evidence to sort out information about the nature of procrastination and ways to intervene to reduce it.

Behavioral approaches such as instruction in time management and organizational skills are very popular (Tuckman, Abry, & Smith, 2002). These techniques can be useful in helping students learn to segment tasks into manageable components, develop timelines and benchmarks for task completion, and provide themselves with regular feedback about performance. Other approaches blend behavioral elements with specific components that address underlying psychological needs. For example, van Essen, van den Heuvell, and Ossebaard (2004) developed a self-management course that facilitated self-reflection about personal reasons for procrastination as the basis for change. Rational Emotive Behavior Therapy (REBT) principles were incorporated to address the irrational beliefs that supported procrastination. These authors reported that the program was effective in enhancing self-efficacy and reducing procrastination. For perfectionistic procrastinators, helpers may find stress-management interventions such as guided relaxation training and systematic desensitization procedures helpful adjunctive therapies (Flett, Hewitt, Davis, & Sherry, 2004).

Growth and Change in Professionals' Epistemology

Don't be alarmed if you recognize that some aspects of your own thinking might seem dualistic or authority-oriented. Perry noted that new learning in any discipline can evolve in a similar stagelike way. Table 11.2 presents Stoltenberg and Delworth's (1987) model of stages in counselor development. As you can see, Level 1 counselors operate somewhat like dualists. They tend to be dependent on supervisors to tell them the "right" way to conceptualize cases. Level 1 counselors try to fit clients into categories and often rely on canned strategies. In general, they also tend to attribute too much pathology to their clients because of their own anxiety level. Level 2 counselors vacillate between dependence on supervisors and personal autonomy. Because they have more experience with difficult cases, they may be less optimistic about the possibilities for change in certain circumstances. As with multiplists, exposure to competing theories of human behavior and therapy undermines confidence in the validity of each. Counselors at this level are more skillful yet also more confused about their own efficacy. At Level 3, helping professionals are more independent and also more tolerant of divergent opinions. They come to accept the ambiguity that is inherent in the helping process. They are creative problem solvers and more objective in their assessment of their clients. In the fluid way they utilize the discipline's knowledge base to adjust to the needs of the client, these counselors truly embody the characteristics of reflective practice.

TABLE 11.2   Client Conceptualizations at Stages of Counselor Development

Level 1

Self- and Other-Awareness—Emotional and cognitive self-focus. *Indications:* Diagnoses/conceptualizations will be "canned" or stereotypical, trying to fit clients into categories. Incomplete treatment plans will focus on specific skills or interventions, often quite similar across clients. Treatment plans may not reflect diagnoses.

Motivation—High, with strong desire to learn to become effective diagnostician and therapist. *Indications:* Willing student, will seek out additional information from books, colleagues, and other sources.

Autonomy—Dependent. *Indications:* Relies on supervisor for diagnoses and treatment plans. Locus of evaluation rests with supervisor.

Level 2

Self- and Other-Awareness—Emotional and cognitive focus on the client. *Indications:* Realizes treatment plan is necessary and logical extension of diagnosis. May resist "labeling" client into diagnostic classifications. Treatment plans may prove difficult due to lack of objectivity. May reflect various orientations yet lacks integration.

Motivation—Fluctuates depending on clarity regarding various clients. *Indications:* May be pessimistic, overly optimistic or confident at times.

Autonomy—Dependency-autonomy conflict. *Indications:* May depend on supervisor for diagnoses and treatment plans for difficult clients, may avoid or resist supervisor suggestions concerning others. Confident with some less-confusing clients. More resistance to perceived unreasonable demands of supervisor, threats to tenuous independence and therapeutic self-esteem.

Level 3

Self- and Other-Awareness—Emotional and cognitive awareness of client and self. *Indications:* Able to "pull back" affectively and cognitively, monitor own reactions to client. The client's perspective and a more objective evaluation will be reflected in conceptualizations. Treatment plans will flow from diagnoses, taking into account client and environmental characteristics. Reflects therapist's own therapeutic orientation.

Motivation—Consistently high, based on greater understanding of personality-learning theory and self. *Indications:* Not as susceptible to permission or undue optimism. Diagnoses and treatment plans consistently thought through and integrated.

Autonomy—Independent functioning. *Indications:* Seeks consultation when necessary. Open to alternative conceptualizations and treatment approaches but retains responsibility for decisions. Makes appropriate referrals.

SOURCE: Stoltenberg, C. D. & Delworth, U. (1987). *Supervising counselors and therapists: A developmental approach.* San Francisco, CA: Jossey-Bass. Used with permission by John Wiley & Sons, Inc.

FOCUS ON DEVELOPMENTAL PSYCHOPATHOLOGY

Depression

Most people have some familiarity with the concept of depression, either from professional training and work with clients, from widespread coverage in popular media, or from all-too-common personal experience. Unfortunately, depression can be trivialized and misunderstood by those who have not lived through its torment. The novelist William Styron (1990), having suffered from clinical depression himself, takes issue with our limited understanding of this terrible ordeal. He described the experience as "a howling tempest in the brain," (p. 37), not at all consistent with the standard comments of people who have not experienced it, such as "We all have bad days" or "You'll pull out of it."

This misunderstanding might be clarified if depression were specified more clearly. Some advocate differentiating between a depressive symptom (e.g., sad mood), a depressive syndrome (e.g., sad mood plus anxiety), and a depressive disorder (Rutter, Tizard, & Whitmore, 1970). According to formal diagnostic criteria, depression is a serious mood disorder that has several presentations, including unipolar, bipolar, dysthymic, and cyclothymic forms. Some of the core features for major depressive disorder (MDD) include sad affect, anhedonia, fluctuations in weight and/or sleep, psychomotor changes, fatigue, cognitive impairments, feelings of guilt or worthlessness, and suicidal thoughts or acts. At least five symptoms must be present for at least 2 weeks, be clinically significant, and impair normal functioning in order to qualify for diagnosis (APA, 2013). Although this seems simple enough, diagnostic problems do result from the counting up of symptoms because normal mood fluctuations can be misconstrued as clinical depression. Evidence is building that it is the *number and intensity* of symptoms and not the presence of symptoms alone that should distinguish between depressed and nondepressed individuals (Angst & Merikangas, 2001; Slade and Andrews, 2005).

The various manifestations, symptom sets, risk factors, and courses of depression have led researchers to consider depression as a heterogeneous category of disorders (Chen, 2000; Chen, Eaton, Gallo, Nestadt, & Crum, 2000). Because all types of depression include alterations in mood, others argue that depression is best represented as a spectrum disorder, with unipolar depression on one end, atypical depression in the middle, and **bipolar disorder** at the other end (Akiskal & Benazzi, 2007). Although it is clear that children suffer from depression, the question of whether depression in childhood is qualitatively different from depression in adolescence and adulthood has not been resolved (Goodyear, 1996; Weiss & Garber, 2003). Nolen-Hoeksema (2008) sums up the issue, writing that "the notion that there is a coherent entity we call depression that will be identifiable in the body is just wrong, or at least, not very useful" (p. 178). Fundamentally, symptoms that collectively manifest as depression appear to arise from high levels of negative affect and stress.

Prevalence and Comorbidity

The World Health Organization predicts that depression will become the second most costly disease in the world by 2020

(WHO, 2004). The scope of the problem is staggering. Based on interviews used for the National Co-Morbidity Study (Kessler et al., 2003), the lifetime prevalence rate of MDD in the United States is 16.6%, or 32.6 to 35.1 million adults. Within the 12-month period prior to interview, 6.6% of U.S. adults (13.1 to 14.2 million) suffered from MDD. Among those in the 12-month MDD group, functional impairments were great. Approximately 97% reported significant problems in social relationships and work roles.

As we have noted, depression is not just a problem for adults. Rates of depression increase from approximately 4% in childhood (Angold & Rutter, 1992) to 5% to 15% in adolescence (Brooks-Gunn & Petersen, 1991). There is also good evidence that the incidence of MDD is increasing worldwide, and its age of onset is decreasing. This troubling finding means that depression has been appearing in successively younger generations since 1940 (Cross-National Collaborative Group, 1992; Kessler et al., 2003). Recently, a similar trend has been observed for bipolar illness (Chengappa et al., 2003). This phenomenon, called the "Birth Cohort Effect," cannot simply be explained by genetics, since genes presumably do not change so rapidly. Furthermore, earlier and earlier spikes in depression are supported by objective measures such as increases in hospitalizations and suicides.

 Feliziano, who has bipolar disorder, describes his experience with the depressive phases of his disorder. He recognizes that depression isn't a cognitive problem—he has no "reason" to be depressed. Rather, depression is a mood disorder.

Females are diagnosed with disproportionately higher rates of depressive syndromes and serious disorders than males from mid-adolescence through late adulthood (Compas et al., 1993). Before puberty, boys' rates of depressive symptoms and disorders are equal to or higher than those of pre-pubescent girls (Nolen-Hoeksema et al., 1992). Both genders suffer from bipolar disorder in equal numbers, an exception to the sex-based trends found in **unipolar disorders** (American Psychiatric Association, 2000). Females are also more likely than males to ruminate about their sad moods when depressed, to admit feeling sad, and to seek help (Nolen-Hoeksema, 2002). However, we can't assume from this evidence that males do not also suffer from depression in high numbers. Addis's (2008) Gendered Responding Framework of depression offers a way of understanding how male gender norms interact with the experience of negative affect. In this framework, males' experience of negative affect (grief, sadness, dysphoria) may be handled through distraction, anger, or avoidance because of prototypical masculine role expectations. Males, too, feel sad and upset, but they may learn, through social conditioning, to express their vulnerabilities in ways that don't neatly map onto available checklists of depressive symptoms.

Depression frequently coexists with other illnesses. In children, anxiety and impulse-control disorders have been found to manifest prior to depression and show high comorbidity with depression later on (Kessler et al., 2003). Angold and Costello (1993) reported that depressed children had rates of conduct problems 3 to 9 times higher and rates of anxiety disorders 2 to 25 times higher than nondepressed children. This pattern may point to a pathway from anxiety and/or behavioral problems to later depression in youth. As is the case in childhood, depression often coexists with other problems in adulthood, impacting physical health and mortality (Klerman & Weissman, 1989). Recently, Chatterji (2008) reported that people who suffered from depression in addition to a chronic illness such as diabetes, angina, arthritis, or asthma were in the poorest health category when compared to all other individuals.

The Perplexing Search for Causes

Despite enormous research efforts, the specific causes of depression remain unknown. The possible heterogeneity of the disease and the complexity of interacting influences make simple answers unlikely. However, some variables are clearly correlated with risk. Genetic/familial predispositions, early adverse life experiences, hormonal changes in puberty, cognitive and motivational processes such as attributional and coping style, number and intensity of stressors, and absence of protective factors like social support all have influential parts to play (Rutter, 1986). Much attention has focused on three main neurotransmitter systems: dopamine associated with loss of pleasure, norepinephrine associated with psychomotor retardation, and serotonin associated with depressive ideation (Sapolsky, 2004). There is no clear consensus about which system is most critical nor any clear understanding of whether there is too much or too little of some neurotransmitter in the brains of some depressed individuals. The question is complicated: Does a neurochemical imbalance cause depression or does depression (e.g., stress, trauma, distorted cognitions, etc.) cause a change in the chemistry of the brain? There is good evidence for the latter view, particularly in the case of early life stress.

In Chapter 2, we described the HPA axis as central to the body's stress response. Remember that the perception of a stressor causes the hypothalamus to trigger a cascade of neurochemical changes, via corticotrophin-releasing factor (CRF), that operate in a coordinated way to respond to threat. As it turns out, CRF is released from nerve terminals that also communicate directly with the serotonin, dopamine, and noradrenergic (epinephrine) systems, modulating the release of these neurotransmitters (Austin, Rhodes, & Lewis, 1997). Early exposure to adversity can alter the development of these systems and sensitize children so that it doesn't take much subsequent stress to activate the neurochemical pathways associated with depression (Graham, Heim, Goodman, Miller, & Nemeroff, 1999; Rudolph & Flynn, 2007). Even a genetically based biochemical imbalance can be an underlying diathesis that can be activated by adverse life experiences.

Sapolsky (2004) argues that the ability to recover from stress distinguishes who becomes depressed when stressed and who does not. The presence of a gene variant that limits the effectiveness of a neurotransmitter system to recover (like the 5-HTT gene mentioned in Chapter 7) may play a key role in determining who is most at risk. Certain medications, especially SSRIs (selective serotonin reuptake inhibitors), assist in the recovery of neurotransmitter systems and may explain their success in symptom reduction for some patients. It is important to emphasize, however, that reliable differences in neurotransmitter levels in the brains of depressed and nondepressed individuals have not been found, and medications are ineffective for a substantial percentage of depressed individuals (Leventhal & Martell, 2006).

Pathways of Risk

The recognition that serious adversities experienced in childhood are related to later depression is nothing new (Goodman, 2002). Early adverse experiences, such as parental loss, family disruption, and neglectful/abusive parenting, have long been considered serious contributors to psychopathology. To shed light on how these experiences might exert their impact, Duggal, Carlson, Sroufe, and Egeland (2001) followed a group of at-risk low-SES children from birth to age 17.5. During the group's first 3.5 years, the researchers conducted observations of mother–child interaction style so as to assess attachment-related constructs. A high percentage (19% of 168 children) demonstrated clinical depression in childhood and 18% did so in adolescence, rates higher than expected from epidemiological estimates. Two different pathways to depression were observed. Depression that presented first in childhood was best predicted by the accumulation of adverse family circumstances and characteristics. Think of these children as being born into very difficult or inadequate family circumstances. In this pathway, it was the *combination* of number and types of stressors on mothers, insensitive and emotionally unsupportive parenting, maternal depression, and abuse that was shown to "interfere with responsiveness to developmental needs, increasing the probability of depressive symptoms" (p. 159). Adolescent-onset depression, in contrast, was best predicted by maternal depression and lack of early supportive care, rather than the aggregate of factors that predicted prepubertal depression. Interestingly, gender differences emerged in pubertal depression pathways. Maternal depression, assessed when children were 7 or 8, predicted pubertal depression best for females, possibly because of sex-role identification processes. For males, unsupportive early care in infancy and early childhood was the strongest predictor of depression in adolescence. As the authors conclude, "for males, it seems to be what the caretaker did rather than who the caretaker was during childhood that is most relevant to depressive symptomatology in adolescence" (p. 160). All of these unfortunate circumstances could facilitate the particular cognitive vulnerabilities associated with depression: hopelessness, low self-worth, negative expectations, and cognitive distortions to name a few (Garber & Flynn, 2001). Findings such as these highlight the complex processes involved in the development of vulnerability to psychopathology.

Painful Passages

Stressors that occur after childhood and adolescence can also precipitate the emergence of depression in vulnerable individuals. The role transitions involved in moving out of the home into the larger world of adult responsibilities are one example. While not all emerging adults experience depression or even depressive symptoms, the challenges that are part of the developmental work of constructing an adult identity can take their toll on mental health. The separation and losses involved in the predictable life transitions and changes in interpersonal relationships that occur at this stage are stressful and can make already vulnerable individuals more vulnerable. Emerging adulthood typically involves a major separation from home—physically, psychologically, or both. For some, the combination of leaving family and friends, disruptions in romantic attachments, stresses of academic or work responsibilities, and the day-to-day challenges of caring for oneself may seem overwhelming. A stark reminder is the fact that the highest prevalence rate for depression across the entire life span occurs during the ages of 15 to 24 (Blazer, Kessler, McGonagle, & Schwartz, 1994).

The stress of the passage into adulthood can be especially intense for minority students in the United States, as you saw earlier in this chapter. Apparently as a result, minority college students can be more at risk of suffering from depression than majority students. The direct experience of racism and discrimination is not the only source of students' minority stress. Minority status often brings with it other problems, such as "interethnic difficulties (e.g., difficulty in making White friends), within-group conflicts (e.g., being viewed as "acting White"), and achievement stress (e.g., feeling less intelligent or less capable than others, or the pressure of high expectations for college success from one's family)" (Wei et al., 2010, pp. 411–412). An important factor that can reduce depression risk for minority students is **bicultural competence**, which involves having social skills for getting along in both the majority and minority culture "without compromising . . . one's sense of cultural identity" (LaFromboise, Coleman, & Gerton, 1993, p. 404). These skills include knowledge of beliefs and values in both cultures, a belief that one can function well in two cultural groups and maintain one's cultural identity, good communication skills, a repertoire of appropriate role behaviors in each culture, and so on. Minority students who perceive themselves as having such skills report fewer depressive symptoms and more feelings of psychological well-being (David, Okazaki, & Saw, 2009; Wei et al., 2010). Supporting bicultural competence may be an important added ingredient in any kind of treatment for minority students.

Fortunately, there are effective treatments for depression, including pharmacological, cognitive-behavioral (CBT), interpersonal (IPT), and mindfulness-based cognitive (MBCT) therapies. The foundations of interpersonal therapy may have particular relevance for development, insofar as the struggle involved in making normal life transitions is one of the primary factors assumed to cause the disorder. Interpersonal therapy (Klerman, Weissman, Rounsaville, & Chevron, 1984; Weissman, Makowitz, & Klerman, 2000) assumes that depression is affected by and affects interpersonal relationships, and aspects of the depressed person's social network are of primary importance in understanding and treating the disorder.

The theoretical foundations of the interpersonal approach derive from the work of Sullivan (1953) and Meyer (1957), among others, who emphasized the here and now social contexts of the depressed individual over causes of depression that were intrapsychic and rooted in the distant past. While IPT does not dismiss the cognitive processes that support depression, irrational, distorted thinking is not the primary focus of treatment. The causes of depression are presumed to be four broadly defined interpersonal situations: grief, role disputes (conflicts with significant others), life changes/role transitions, and significant interpersonal deficits. Using a time-limited approach (roughly up to 20 sessions) and functioning as a supportive ally, the therapist assesses symptoms, connects depression to one of the four major problematic areas, and assigns the client a "sick role" (Parsons, 1951). Assigning a sick role legitimizes the client's needs for support from others who may be included in the therapeutic process, temporarily frees the client from unmanageable responsibility, and allows the person to focus on recovery during the restricted period of therapy. During the intermediate stage of therapy, the therapist takes a moderately directive role and helps clients make real changes in relationships and renegotiate their roles in interpersonal contexts. In the case of difficult role transitions, such as the transition to adulthood, clients are helped to mourn the old "adolescent" role by reviewing what was good and bad about it, clarify feelings about the new role, and explore opportunities that the new role offers. When anxieties about one's ability to manage the new life stage successfully surface, expectations about what "being an adult" might be are discussed and readjusted if necessary. Sources of social support are identified and recruited and incentives for taking on new developmental challenges are created. The final stage of therapy acknowledges termination as a loss but also focuses on sustaining the gains made in therapy in the posttherapy social environment. Some techniques used in IPT include those common to supportive psychotherapies: questioning, clarification, support of emotional expression, behavior change strategies, and development of a strong therapeutic alliance. IPT has also been adapted for use with younger depressed adolescents (Mufson, Moreau, Weissman, & Klerman, 1993).

A key point in the interpersonal conceptualization of depression is its transactional emphasis. Unfortunately, it has been repeatedly demonstrated that depressed people suffer more frequent rejection from others than do nondepressed counterparts (Segrin & Abramson, 1994) and thus need to exert more effort and display more skill in order to overcome this social tendency. However, the life events that may have precipitated depression in vulnerable individuals in the first place, such as a move to a new school, reduction in contact with family and friends, and increased maturity demands, can produce symptoms (chronic fatigue, poor concentration, indecisiveness, sad mood, anhedonia, etc.) that make engaging in positive social interactions an enormous effort (Coyne, 1999). The vicious cycle is obvious. Regardless of theoretical bent, it is very important for helpers to pay serious attention to the environmental contexts that sustain depression. As Coyne warns, "depressed individuals' statements about themselves and their relationships get interpreted as enduring cognitive structures, a sociotropic trait, or working model of relationships, and these *reified entities* are then given causal priority over any interpersonal processes" (1999, p. 368). Even though IPT is an individual approach to counseling, the usefulness of including significant others in some manner in treatment should be emphasized. More research is needed to help us understand how to intervene in these interpersonal processes more directly.

SUMMARY

1. Specifying exactly when an individual reaches adulthood is surprisingly complex. Sociologists look to marker events, such as completing one's education, entering the workforce, leaving the family home, and so on. Young adults themselves tend to emphasize accepting responsibility for their own behavior and making independent decisions. In today's society, the period from about 18 to 25 may be described as a time of emerging adulthood.

Physical Development in Young Adulthood

2. Between 18 and 30, all biological systems reach peak potential. There are individual differences in when people reach peak potential, and there are differences among different systems and skills in the timing of peak status. For different skills, these differences reflect differences in the relative importance of practice, training, knowledge, experience, and biological capacity. Males and females also peak at different times.

3. Lifestyle affects the achievement and maintenance of peak or near-peak functioning. Healthy lifestyles include getting regular exercise, eating a healthy diet, and avoiding unhealthy behaviors such as smoking and drug use. Such behaviors in young adulthood are reflected in poorer health later in adulthood, yet many young adults have unhealthy, underregulated lifestyles, probably as a result of poor application of problem-solving skills, continued feelings of invulnerability, the fact that young adults "bounce back" quickly from physical stress, and the many stresses they face.

4. The pruning of synapses continues in young adulthood. The frontal lobes continue to mature, perhaps playing an important role in the young adult's advancing abilities in organization, attention, planning, and self-regulation.

Cognitive Development in Young Adulthood

5. Young adulthood is a time of great learning. We have clear data on the growth of knowledge in the college population (roughly 60% of young adults today), but it seems likely that rapid growth of knowledge characterizes all young adults as they gain training and experience in their vocations and avocations.

6. Logical thinking also appears to change beginning in young adulthood. Theorists and researchers disagree as to the nature of the change. Some propose that a more advanced kind of thinking, postformal or fifth-stage thinking, emerges. Others argue that the formal operational abilities of the adolescent period represent the most advanced form of thinking for humans but that adults learn to apply this kind of thinking to the more ill-defined or ill-structured problems that adults face. As part of this process, they may also gain better understanding of the limits of their own problem-solving abilities. That is, they may grow in metacognitive understanding.

7. Schaie argues against a new kind of adult thinking. Rather, he argues that at different times of adult life people face different kinds of problems, and different skills are brought to bear on those problems. He describes seven stages in adults' intellectual functioning, with each new stage a result of shifts in the challenges people face.

8. Theorists who argue that there is a stage of postformal thought suggest that it may not reach full development until middle adulthood, but its emergence begins in young adulthood. Most theorists, such as Sinnott, describe postformal thought as relativistic. The same reality can be described within several different truth systems, all of which are valid from one perspective or within some context. The postformal thinker recognizes the validity of different truth systems. She may make a subjective commitment to one in some situations or seek a compromise in other situations. Sinnott's description of postformal thought is similar to what Chandler called postrational skepticism, although Chandler disagrees that this kind of thinking is more advanced than formal operational thought.

9. Perry's stage theory of intellectual and ethical development in the college years describes a sequence of steps in the movement from more absolutist or dualistic thinking (there is one right answer, other answers are wrong) to relativistic thinking (there is more than one correct way to view the same issue). In addition to Perry's own longitudinal interview study, a number of researchers have provided some evidence for aspects of Perry's theory. For example, students' beliefs about knowledge have been found to relate to their approach to learning, as Perry's theory predicts.

10. Kitchener provides a seven-stage theory of the development of relativistic thinking, calling it reflective judgment. Research in which subjects are given ill-defined problems indicates that in the early stages of adult thinking, individuals believe in the existence of certainties. In the middle stages, people perceive knowledge as uncertain. In the later stages, they base their judgments on a set of rules or logic in combination with personal reflection. Essentially, they are relativistic.

11. Some research indicates that reflective judgment is related to level of education and to the specific kind of training people have received. Graduate students in psychology, for example, tend to show more proficiency than graduate students in other disciplines. Evidence also indicates that people are benefited by modeling of forms of thinking more advanced than their own.

CASE STUDY

Angela, a young Black woman, comes from a close-knit and very religious family that has always taken great pride in her accomplishments. Despite some minor rebelliousness during high school, Angela maintains close ties to her family and considers her parents and younger sister to be her best friends. A solid student all through school and a leader in her church's youth ministry, Angela knew for a long time that she wanted to go to college to be a teacher. Angela's father attended community college for 2 years, and her mother graduated from high school. Both parents were delighted when Angela became the first member of the family to pursue a baccalaureate degree.

Now in her first year at a state university in the South, she is getting used to college and to life in a dormitory. She enjoys the freedom and the challenge of college but is also experiencing some problems getting along with other students. Her roommate, a young White woman named Jen, poses a particular dilemma for her. It bothers Angela that Jen never goes to church, never prays, frequently spends the night at her boyfriend's apartment, and is an outspoken agnostic. Jen makes various comments about what she has learned in her religion and philosophy classes that trouble Angela, who firmly believes that Jen lacks a proper moral center. Angela has tried to convince Jen about the importance of belief in God and the consequences of her disbelief, but to no avail. Because it is important to Angela to maintain her beliefs, she starts to avoid being in the room when Jen is there and considers finding a new roommate.

During the spring semester, Angela develops a serious infection that confines her to bed and makes her unable to attend classes or to care for herself. She is both surprised and pleased when Jen comes to her assistance. Jen runs errands for her, brings her meals, and does her laundry. Even Jen's boyfriend pitches in to help Angela make up her missed assignments. She is touched by their generosity and confused about how this goodness can coexist with a nonreligious perspective on life. These are the kind of people she had thought were immoral. When the time comes to plan for next year's housing arrangement, Angela is uncertain. Her friends in the ministry counsel her to find a more appropriate roommate. Yet Angela cannot reconcile Jen's kindness toward her with what she believes to be an immoral lifestyle. This disjunction causes her great distress. She decides to seek out a counselor in the University Counseling Center to help her with her decision.

Discussion Questions

1. Discuss Angela's level of development according to the various theories presented in the chapter.
2. How would you respond to her problem as a counselor in a university setting? How would you take her cognitive development into account?

PRACTICE USING WHAT YOU HAVE LEARNED

In the Pearson etext, apply these ideas to working with others.

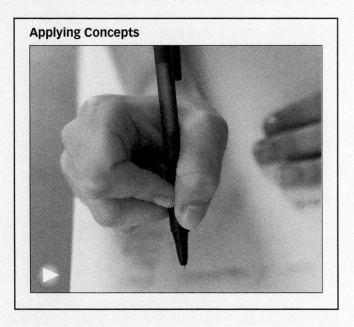

Applying Concepts

JOURNAL QUESTIONS

1. Give examples of your own thinking at one or more points in your life that reflected dualism, multiplicity, and relativism.
2. In what respect and in what areas have you achieved the stage of committed relativism? Discuss this process from your personal experience.
3. Describe your transition to college. What aspects of this adjustment were particularly difficult for you? If you were a helper working with similar problems, how would you approach them?

KEY CONCEPTS

marker events (p. 409)
youth (p. 409)
emerging adulthood (p. 410)
globalization (p. 410)
minority stress (p. 411)
racial crossover effect (p. 411)
young adulthood (p. 412)
postformal or fifth-stage thinking (p. 416)
acquisition stage (p. 417)
ill-defined or ill-structured problems (p. 418)
achieving stage (p. 418)
responsible stage (p. 418)
executive stage (p. 418)
reorganizational stage (p. 418)

reintegrative stage (p. 418)
legacy-leaving stage (p. 418)
relativistic thought (p. 419)
postskeptical rationalism (p. 420)
strict dualism (p. 422)
multiplicity (prelegitimate) (p. 422)
multiplicity (subordinate) (p. 422)
just world (p. 422)
late multiplicity (p. 422)
oppositional (p. 422)
relative subordinate (p. 423)
contextual relativism (p. 423)
commitment foreseen (p. 424)
initial commitment (p. 424)

multiple commitments (p. 424)
resolve (p. 424)
temporizing (p. 424)
retreat (p. 424)
escape (p. 424)
reflective judgment (p. 425)
"the person who" fallacy (p. 428)
actuarial prediction (p. 428)
vividness effect (p. 428)
placebo effect (p. 428)
bipolar disorder (p. 432)
unipolar disorder (p. 432)
bicultural competence (p. 434)

CHAPTER 12

Socioemotional and Vocational Development in Young Adulthood

What is required for a happy, well-adjusted adult life? For Sigmund Freud, both love and work are powerful methods by which we "strive to gain happiness and keep suffering away" (Freud, 1930/1989, p. 732). Love, he felt, may bring us closer to the goal of happiness than anything else we do. The disadvantage of love, of course, is that "we are never so defenseless . . . never so helplessly unhappy as when we have lost our loved object or its love" (p. 733). Work, from Freud's perspective, not only helps justify our existence in society, providing the worker with a "secure place . . . in the human community," but it also can be a source of special satisfaction if it is "freely chosen—if, that is . . . it makes possible the use of existing inclinations" (p. 732).

For Erikson (e.g., 1950/1963), both **intimacy** (love) and **generativity** (work) are arenas for expressing and developing the self, dominating the concerns of adults in their young and middle years. True intimacy and generativity require achieving an adult identity and are part of its further enrichment and evolution. "Intimacy is a quality of interpersonal relating through which partners share personal thoughts, feelings, and other important aspects of themselves with each other" (McAdams, 2000, p. 118). True intimacy is marked by openness, affection, and trust. Generativity is a motive or need that can be filled through one's vocation or avocations, through child rearing, or through community service. It includes productivity and creativity (Erikson, 1950/1963). Generativity is also a trait that people can be described as having when they are contributing members of society. "It is about generating: creating and producing things, people, and outcomes that are aimed at benefiting, in some sense, the next generation, and even the next" (McAdams, Hart, & Maruna, 1998). For most adults, achieving generativity is central to their belief in the meaningfulness of their lives. Erikson considered young adults to be especially driven by needs for intimacy, middle adults by needs for generativity. Modern research suggests that both are powerful influences on behavior throughout adulthood, although intimacy needs may predominate early and generativity needs later.

More recent conceptions of how adults achieve happiness or mental health or "wellness" are quite consistent with the importance that Freud and Erikson placed on love and work. Close relationships with lovers, friends, and family, as well as the opportunity to make productive use of one's time and talents, figure prominently in nearly all modern theorizing about what people need to be happy and well-adjusted (e.g., Ryan & Deci, 2000). From a developmental perspective, then, the period of young adulthood should be a time when identity issues are resolved sufficiently to allow a person to make significant progress on two major tasks: The first is establishing and strengthening bonds with people who will accompany him on his life journey, and the second is becoming a productive worker.

LOVE

Making connections with others in adulthood—establishing intimacy with a mate, making friends, reworking family ties—has been studied from many perspectives. One promising developmental approach examines the impact of attachment style, which is assumed to have its roots in infancy and childhood, on the formation of adult relationships.

Adult Attachment Theory

Attachment theory has enjoyed a prominent place in the child development literature since the groundbreaking work of John Bowlby and Mary Ainsworth (see Chapter 4). Following an explosion of studies on childhood attachment, researchers began to train their sights on attachment theorists' suggestion that early bonds with caregivers could have a bearing on relationship building throughout the life span (Ainsworth, 1989; Bowlby, 1980). Today, attachment theory provides a useful framework for conceptualizing adult intimacy. The abundance of research in this area makes it the most empirically grounded theory available for explaining the formation and nature of close interpersonal relationships throughout adulthood.

As we saw in Chapter 4, the process of attaching to a caregiver in infancy is considered species-typical. According to Bowlby (1969/1982, 1973, 1980), the attachment bonds of infancy serve survival needs. Infant behaviors, such as distress at separation, ensure proximity to the caregiver, who acts as a secure base for exploration, a safe haven in case of threat, and a preferred provider of emotional warmth and affect regulation.

How the attachment process unfolds is a function of the caregiving relationship. Depending on the caregiver's sensitivity and responsiveness, an infant becomes securely or insecurely attached to that caregiver. To the extent possible, he adapts his behavior to the caregiver's style to get his needs met, and he begins to internalize a working model of how relationships operate.

Despite diminishing demands for physical caretaking as individuals age, adults continue to need the emotional and practical support of significant others. As we have noted, Erikson (1950/1963) identified the achievement of intimacy as the central task of early adulthood. In his view, even though adults are much more independent than children, they still need to establish and maintain intimate connections to people who will provide them with love and care. Although you may never have thought of your adult relationships with significant others, including your bonds to your parents, as attachment relationships, many researchers believe that they are precisely that. Let us look more closely at the various manifestations of attachments in adulthood and consider a framework for organizing the existing research.

Research Traditions in Adult Attachment

Attachment theory has been used to understand relationships as divergent as those between parents and their adult children (Scharf, Mayseless, & Kivenson-Baron, 2004;

Vivona, 2000) and those between romantic partners (Simpson & Rholes, 2010). It provides a conceptual framework for individual differences in people's responses to bereavement and loss (Rando, 1993), to stress (Mikulincer & Florian, 1998), and to the processing of information about relationships (Dykas & Cassidy, 2011). And, as you will see below, attachment theory predicts intergenerational transmission of attachment classifications (van IJzendoorn, 1995). Among helping professionals, attachment theory has been used as a framework for explaining conflict resolution in interpersonal relationships (Creasey & Hesson-McInnis, 2001), family dysfunction (Byng-Hall, 1995), and psychopathology (Brennan & Shaver, 1998; Dozier, Stovall, & Albus, 1999), and it provides a basis for therapeutic interventions (Dozier & Tyrell, 1998).

One way to make sense of the multitude of studies on adult attachment is to identify which kind of attachment relationship is being explored. Simpson and Rholes (1998) offer a useful organizational framework that distinguishes between two major research traditions. First, there is a body of work that examines the outcomes of a person's attachment to his primary caregiver in infancy, once the person becomes an adult. This has been referred to as the **nuclear family tradition**. Research in this area seeks to understand the degree to which one's earliest attachments to primary caregivers may endure throughout life and how they might affect the quality of the caregiving provided to one's own children. A parallel line of research, called the **peer/romantic partner tradition**, focuses on the peer attachments of adults. Questions about how early attachments impact the quality of romantic and friendship relationships in adulthood form the core of inquiry from this angle. The two bodies of work share conceptual linkages, to be sure. However, they differ in their methodologies and even in their terminology, and they "tend to speak past each other" (Bartholomew & Shaver, 1998, p. 27).

It is sometimes assumed that findings from both traditions should converge into a coherent picture of an adult's attachment status. This has been a difficult goal to achieve, primarily because different domains are studied, different methodologies are used, and different typologies are employed. Despite these problems, there is some correlation between the different kinds of attachment findings in adulthood. As Bartholomew and Shaver (1998) note:

> When we step back from the details of specific measures and measure-specific findings, the results produced by attachment researchers are all compatible with the possibility that various forms of adult attachment arise from a continuous but branching tree of attachment experiences, beginning in infancy and developing throughout the life course. (p. 42)

We will continue our discussion of adult attachment by focusing on each approach in turn. First, we will consider how the nuclear family tradition contributes to our understanding of adult caregiving. Then we will present an overview of significant contributions from the peer/romantic partner tradition.

The Nuclear Family Tradition: The Past as Prologue

Does the nature of your attachment to your caregiver predict your behavior in adulthood, influencing the quality of attachment you will form with your own children? This is the intriguing question that is at the heart of the nuclear family line of research. We briefly examined this issue in Chapter 4. Now we'll take a closer look.

You may recall that the primary instrument used to measure the attachment representations of adults vis-à-vis their early caregivers is the Adult Attachment Interview (AAI) developed by Main and Goldwyn (1984). It is composed of a series of 18 open-ended questions with follow-up prompts that are transcribed verbatim by a trained interviewer. The questions concern memories of relationships with mother and father, recollections of stressful events such as separations, loss, harsh discipline, or abuse, interpretations of parental behaviors, and evaluation of the effects of these early events on the interviewee's later development.

Main and her colleagues (see Hesse, 2008) hypothesized that the primary task for the interviewee is to resurrect emotionally loaded memories of early childhood experiences while simultaneously presenting them in a coherent fashion to an interviewer. Because the questions deal with very complicated, personal, and often intense issues in a person's early history, they may never have been articulated by the individual prior to this interview experience. The rapidity of questioning, combined with the nature of the items and the interview setting, are thought to elicit material often heretofore unconscious, yet highly descriptive of the adult's state of mind regarding early attachments to primary caregivers. The assumption is that by adulthood, security has become a characteristic of the individual. Representations of different relationships—like relationships with mother versus father—tend to coalesce, and a single working model of attachment can be tapped (Furman & Simon, 2004).

Interviews are scored according to Grice's (1975) criteria for coherent discourse: truthfulness as supported by evidence, succinctness, relevance to the topic, clarity, and organization of responses. Additional scoring criteria include the coder's assessment of the interviewee's early attachment quality as well as an assessment of the language used in the interview (e.g., angry, passive, derogating). Four qualitatively different classifications, or attachment styles, are then assigned to adults based on their verbatim transcripts. These are secure or insecure (which includes three subcategories: dismissing, preoccupied, and unresolved) categories. Different classifications of insecurity are thought to reflect the different strategies and rules of information processing that the person has developed to manage the anxiety of early relationship failure, loss, or trauma. Let us examine each of these categories in turn (see Hesse, 2008, for more detail).

Autonomous (secure) adults provide a transcript that is coherent and collaborative. They answer questions with enough detail to provide sufficient evidence without giving excessive information. For example, incidents of caregiver insensitivity are described matter-of-factly, without embellishment or defensiveness. Secure adults also demonstrate the ability to integrate and monitor their thinking, summarize answers, and return the conversation to the interviewer. They seem to be less egocentric in their presentation than insecure individuals, and they demonstrate good perspective-taking skills. Secure individuals acknowledge the importance of attachment-related experiences in their development. Their memories of the parenting they received match up with the specific instances they present to the interviewer as illustrations. The emotions they express, both verbally and facially, are consistent with the content of their remarks (e.g., Roisman, Tsai, & Chiang, 2004).

Can adults be classified as secure if they have had less than favorable experiences as a child? Some individuals do come from circumstances of early adversity but describe their painful backgrounds truthfully and believably, while acknowledging the stressors their own parents faced. This ability to reflect on a difficult past realistically, yet with a certain level of generosity toward parents, results in a special classification called **earned secure**. Such adults appear to have come to terms with less than optimal early experiences, quite possibly with the help of a secure spouse or partner. Individuals in both secure categories typically have children who are securely attached to them (see Chapter 4 for a detailed discussion of children's attachment categories).

Dismissing (insecure) individuals provide transcripts that are characterized by markedly low levels of detail and coherence. They are likely to describe parents as very positive or idealized; however, they do not support their evaluations with any specific evidence. Whatever details these dismissive respondents offer may actually contradict their generally favorable presentation of parental behavior. They tend to minimize or avoid discussion of attachment-related issues and downplay the importance of close relationships. When discussing nonemotional topics, dismissing individuals generate coherent and comprehensive records and can talk at some length. Responses to attachment themes, in contrast, lack elaboration. Failure to remember is often cited as a reason for the impoverished answers. Adults classified as dismissive tend to have children who are in the avoidant attachment category.

The dismissive style has been linked to early experiences of rejection or other trauma and the development of repressive personality styles. Do these individuals simply hide their distress, or have they managed to actually suppress their attachment needs? Some evidence using an information-processing approach indicates that these individuals, over time, function with the goal of avoiding emotional thoughts and other reminders of unpleasant emotional experiences, such as parental unavailability (Fraley, Davis, & Shaver, 1998). This motivated avoidance may lead to less cognitive elaboration of attachment themes and reduction of behaviors that would encourage intimacy, such as sharing intimate conversation, mutual gazing, cuddling, and so on.

However, it is unlikely that the system has been deactivated completely. Dozier and Kobak (1992) provide interesting evidence that dismissive individuals do react strongly to emotional issues. These researchers interviewed college students using the AAI while measuring their rates of skin conductance. Dismissive subjects, although outwardly appearing unfazed during questioning, had significantly elevated levels of skin conductance, as compared to baseline levels, when asked questions about the emotional availability of their parents and the effects of early attachments on their self-development. Roisman et al. (2004) replicated these results cross-culturally, studying European Americans, Chinese Americans, and Chinese nationals who were students at a midwestern American university. This physiological phenomenon suggests that dismissive interviewees are effortfully engaged in diversionary tactics (either idealizing parents or restricting memory) to deal with the anxiety generated by the topics. This feature of the dismissive attachment style has been referred to as "deactivating" (see Roisman, 2007). Yet, the physiological data suggest that the emotional distress of the early attachment system may never be fully deactivated, but rather just kept at bay. The attachment system responds to emotionally provocative issues when they cannot be avoided.

Individuals in a third group, classified as **preoccupied** (insecure), typically violate the rule of collaboration on the AAI interview. These individuals provide very long, incoherent, egocentric responses that shift from topic to topic. They perform in ways that suggest they are overwhelmed by the emotional memories elicited by the interview questions and are sidetracked from the task of responding succinctly. Such speakers often sound angry, sad, or fearful, as if they have never resolved the painful problems of their childhood. Parents may be remembered as intrusive or egocentric. Their transcripts paint a picture of substantial enmeshment or preoccupation with parents, registered by angry, accusatory language or by conflicted descriptions that connote ambivalence and confusion about early relationships. This feature of the preoccupied attachment style has been referred to as "hyperactivating," and there is emerging evidence that individuals with hyperactivating responses to the AAI are more likely than others to show heart rate increases in situations that arouse the attachment system (Roisman, 2007). Both their facial expressions and self-reported emotions during the AAI are often inconsistent with the childhood memories they describe. For example, distressed facial expression might be combined with their description of a positive experience (e.g., Roisman et al., 2004). Linguistic features of their transcripts include run-on sentences, idiosyncratic uses of words, and juxtaposition of past and present tense, as though early problems continue to persist in the present. The children of preoccupied adults often have anxious-ambivalent attachments.

Individuals in the fourth category, called **unresolved** (insecure), produce transcripts characterized by marked lapses in logical thinking, particularly when these individuals discuss loss or other traumatic memories. One example of a lapse in reasoning might be an interviewee's mention of a deceased parent as still living. Hesse and Main (1999b) have suggested that these abrupt shifts may be related to temporary changes in consciousness, possibly due to the arousal of unintegrated fear. Individuals in this category may also receive a secondary classification of dismissive or preoccupied. The children of unresolved individuals show a higher frequency of disorganized attachment patterns than other children.

A fifth category, **cannot classify**, is used when protocols do not meet the criteria for other categories. Only a very small number of cases fall into this classification. Data on AAI classifications and psychopathology demonstrate that psychiatric disorders are clearly associated with insecure status and that, in particular, unresolved status is the clearest predictor of emotional disturbance (Dozier et al., 1999).

We have learned from longitudinal studies that an infant's attachment behavior, as measured by the strange situation test, reliably predicts the same individual's secure or insecure responses on the AAI in adolescence or adulthood (see Grossman, Grossman, & Waters, 2005; Simpson, Collins, Tran, & Haydon, 2007). As we saw in Chapter 4, however, a child's attachment status can become either more or less secure if he has either positive or negative experiences with close relationships after the infant–toddler period. Longitudinal studies in which participants have reached adolescence or young adulthood are finding that people can either "earn" security, as we have already noted, by experiencing later supportive relationships or can develop insecure representations of attachment if they experience negative life events after early childhood. Adults who were secure as children can later demonstrate insecure states of mind because of intervening, highly stressful events such as parental loss, divorce, abuse, illness, or psychiatric disorder. Such findings suggest that deviations from the predicted pathway are most likely explained by lawful rather than random discontinuity (Sroufe, Egeland, Carlson, & Collins, 2005; Weinfield, Sroufe, & Egeland, 2000).

In Search of the Working Model

Perhaps you are wondering if the attachment representation categories that are derived from adults' AAI performances could simply be measures of general linguistic style. If so, then interviews would have no particular relevance to attachment, and their predictive value for children's attachment characteristics might be coincidental. Crowell et al. (1996) investigated whether the different linguistic features used to make AAI classifications characterize individuals on other measures of discourse. Using the Employment Experience Interview, he examined a group of adults who had been assigned AAI classifications. The Employment Experience Interview had the same structure as the AAI and was coded using the same criteria. Note that the only difference between the two was in the nature of the questions: about job skills or early attachment relationships. Results showed differences among the transcripts (e.g., vague vs. clear discourse). However, the interesting finding was that respondents' classifications were different on each measure. In other words, an adult who might be judged "secure" on the employment interview could be "insecure" on the AAI. The researchers concluded that there is something unique about the attachment questions. They appear to provide a window into a person's state of mind concerning interpersonal representations.

The power of attachment theory rests on the concept of the inner working model. The AAI was designed to tap an adult's representation of attachments to primary caregivers. The assumption is that the individual's narrative reflects partly unconscious representations. Results are not considered to be a direct measure of an individual's attachment to any one person, but rather are an indicator of the individual's state of mind regarding attachment-related issues. Like an algorithm for our close interpersonal associations, the working model is thought to provide rules for processing information about relationships and for behaving in relationships.

Researchers agree that the working model of relationships that one has as an adult cannot simply be a carbon copy of the one that was formed with the primary caregiver in infancy. It is a cognitive structure or schema (often now described as a prototype) that must evolve with time and experience, becoming more elaborate, incorporating new elements into the original version in dynamic, qualitatively transformed ways. Like all cognitive schemas, our working models of relationships help us understand, predict, and act on information that is only fragmentary (Dykas & Cassidy, 2011). The obvious advantage is that they allow us to process information and to respond quickly. The downside is that we may fail to accommodate real differences in present relationships, and we may behave in these relationships in ways that are adapted to quite different circumstances.

For example, consider Sheila, whose mother was depressed and dependent. As a youngster, Sheila felt that her mother's needs always came before her own. Because even the simplest task was a chore for her mother, Sheila began taking on the care of the household and her younger siblings in order to spare her mother. Sheila grew increasingly competent as a caretaker, which, in turn, caused her mother to depend on her even more. As a young adult, Sheila has difficulty getting close to people. She bristles when any friend or romantic partner, in an attempt to get close to her emotionally, talks about a personal problem. She quickly changes the subject of conversation. Sheila's relationships in adulthood appear to be affected by the legacy of her earlier attachments. She exaggerates other people's reliance on her and fears she will be overcome by their needs, despite any real evidence for this.

Because this is a relatively new area of research, several important questions are yet unanswered. In particular, no one fully understands how the working model of infant–caregiver attachment gets transformed into a working model of attachments in adulthood. Main (1999) suggests that the multiple attachments formed in childhood coalesce into a "classifiable state of mind with respect to attachment in adulthood and that whatever this particular state of mind, it is predictive of a concordant and 'classifiable' form of caregiving" (p. 863). In this description, Main uses the phrase "state of mind with regard to attachment" instead of "working model" because she wants to avoid the oversimplified assumption that adult states of mind are always derivative of early experiences with parents in straightforward, linear ways. Main notes that insecure children often have multiple, contradictory models of attachment that are harder to integrate than those of secure children, who tend to have more unified models.

As we have seen, adults' attachment representations predict the quality of their attachments to their children (see Chapter 4). This link suggests that attachment representation is a determinant of parental caregiving behavior. Does attachment representation also affect the way that adults interact with other adults? If the working model, in fact, functions like an algorithm for close relationships, individual differences in attachment representations should also affect adults' ability to relate to others in romantic and friendship relationships. This is the subject of our next section.

The Peer/Romantic Relationship Tradition

Any reader of romance novels can testify that the topic of adult love relationships has considerable appeal. In the research community as well, quite a bit of time and energy has been devoted to understanding the formation and development of adult pair-bonds. Researchers have examined specific issues such as mate selection, relationship satisfaction, conflict resolution, relationship dissolution, and so on and have produced a wealth of findings in each of these areas. Studies have also been done that show consistent individual differences in adults' approaches to romantic relationships, sometimes called "love styles" (Lee, 1973). Similarly, there are theories about the elements of love, such as Sternberg's (1986) passion, intimacy, and commitment, and the ways they function in relationship formation. **Passion** refers to erotic attraction or feelings of being in love. *Intimacy* includes elements of love that promote connection and closeness, whereas **commitment** refers to making a decision to sustain a relationship with a loved one. We will discuss these elements further in the next chapter.

An early investigation by Shaver and Hazan (1988) contributed significantly to the growing body of knowledge on adult relationships by anchoring the fledgling field within the conceptual framework of attachment theory. These researchers tried to integrate the disparate threads of data into a comprehensive theory of

As she prepares to get married, this young woman struggles to sort out her feelings toward her fiancé and her family's—and her own—expectations of what marriage "should" be. What can you infer about her feelings toward passion, intimacy, and commitment with a husband?

relationships. Today, research conceptualizing adult pair-bonds as attachments represents the second influential offshoot of attachment theory.

Features of Adult Pair-Bonds

Do adult pair-bonds qualify as bona fide attachment relationships? Although there are some dissenting opinions (e.g., McAdams, 2000), many researchers answer yes (e.g., Haydon, Collins, Salvatore, Simpson, & Roisman, 2012). Consider Bowlby's definition of a behavioral system as a set of behaviors that serve the same function or goal. Human beings are equipped with multiple behavioral systems, meeting multiple goals, which interact in coordinated ways. In early childhood, attachment behavior—which includes proximity maintenance, separation distress, and treatment of the caregiver as both a safe haven and a secure base—is the most important behavioral system because it serves the ultimate goal of survival. When security is felt, other behavioral systems, such as exploration, can be activated. When security is threatened, the attachment system is triggered, and proximity-seeking behaviors increase.

In adulthood, as in childhood, particular behavioral systems are organized to meet specific needs. Attachment (based on the need for felt security) is just one of the adult behavioral systems serving psychosocial needs, which also include caregiving, sexual mating, and exploration. Because of their structure and function, pair-bonds in adults provide an effective way to integrate three of the basic systems: caregiving, attachment (felt security), and sexual mating (Simpson & Rholes, 2010). The support provided by the secure base of an attachment relationship also enhances exploration in adults, just as it does in children. Hazan and Zeifman (1999) conclude that adult attachments generally enhance reproductive success (or promotion of the species) as well as provide for the psychological and physical well-being of partners.

Infant–caregiver bonds and adult pair-bonds are notably similar in the kinds of physical contact they involve, such as mutual gazing, kissing, cuddling, and so on, and in the goals they serve (support, emotional closeness, etc.). Adult attachments, however, do differ from childhood attachments in the following three ways. First, the attachments adults have with adults are structured more symmetrically than are parent–child bonds. Both partners mutually provide and receive caregiving, whereas the parent is the unilateral source of caregiving for the child. Second, adults rely more than children do on "felt security" rather than on the actual physical presence of the attachment figure (Sroufe & Waters, 1977). Longer periods of separation can be tolerated by adolescents and adults because they understand that attachment figures will be dependable and available when they need contact. Third, adult attachments typically involve a sexual partner or peer rather than a parent figure.

The Process of Relationship Formation in Adulthood

How does the attachment system of early childhood become transformed into the attachments of adulthood? Hazan and Zeifman (1999) chart the progress of attachments by tracing the behaviors that serve the goals of the system. In infancy, as we have stated, all four functions of the attachment system (proximity maintenance, separation distress, secure base, safe haven) depend on the presence of an attachment figure, and infant behavior toward the caregiver clearly is adapted to meet these goals. As children get older, behaviors toward peers appear to serve some attachment functions as well. For example, children transfer some proximity-seeking behaviors to peers by early childhood. Children begin to spend more time with age-mates and seek them out as preferred playmates (Gottman, 1983). By

Adult pair-bonds meet multiple needs, such as attachment needs (especially the need for security), the need for caregiving or nurture, and sexual needs.

early adolescence, needs for intimacy and support are often met within the peer group (e.g., Steinberg & Monahan, 2007), suggesting that needs for a safe haven in times of distress are directed to peers as well as parents (see Chapter 10). By late adolescence and early adulthood, romantic partners may satisfy all the needs of the attachment system.

To provide support for this theory, Hazan and Zeifman (1999) asked children and adolescents from 6 to 17 years old a number of questions that tapped attachment needs. Researchers asked the participants whom they preferred to spend time with (proximity maintenance), whom they turned to if they were feeling bad (safe haven), whom they disliked being separated from (separation distress), and whom they could always count on when they needed help (secure base). Results of this study supported shifts away from parents to peers, apparently preparing the way for adult attachment behaviors. The great majority of respondents sought proximity to peers instead of parents at all ages. Between the ages of 8 and 14, participants' responses indicated a shift toward use of peers for safe haven as well. Most children and adolescents identified parents as their secure base and the source of their separation distress. However, among those older participants who had established romantic relationships, all four attachment needs were met in the context of their pair-bonds. See Figure 12.1 for a model of the attachment transfer process across age.

Individual Differences in Adult Attachments

The preceding discussion describes what might be considered normative processes involved in the development of adult attachments. Remember, however, that individuals differ in their states of mind regarding attachment experiences. Do these different "states of mind" predict different approaches to peer or romantic relationships in adulthood? To shed light on this question, we must recall that each tradition of attachment research has its own way of looking at these issues. Even though researchers start from the same premise, namely that adults' attachment styles will resemble Ainsworth's infant attachment typology, the typical measures used are different from those of the nuclear family tradition. Adult romantic relationship research began with self-report or questionnaire measures that were presumed to tap conscious, rather than unconscious, expectations about relationships. The sheer volume of work done in the area of measurement prevents a comprehensive discussion of this topic in this chapter. However, we will present an introduction to certain key issues and describe some important instruments. The interested reader is referred to Simpson and Rholes (1998) for a more thorough presentation.

DEVELOPMENTAL PHASE	TARGET OF ATTACHMENT BEHAVIORS	
	Parents	**Peers**
Infancy	proximity maintenance safe haven secure base	
Early Childhood	safe haven secure base	proximity maintenance
Late Childhood/ Early Adolescence	secure base	proximity maintenance safe haven
Adulthood		proximity maintenance safe haven secure base

FIGURE 12.1 Age changes in attachment and close relationships.
SOURCE: Hazan, C., and Shaver, R. (1994). Attachment as an organizational framework for research on close relationships. *Psychological Inquiry, 5,* 1–11. Reprinted by permission of Lawrence Erlbaum Associates.

TABLE 12.1 Three Attachment Prototypes in Peer/Romantic Tradition

Avoidant. I am somewhat uncomfortable being close to others; I find it difficult to trust them completely, difficult to allow myself to depend on them. I am nervous when anyone gets too close, and often, love partners want me to be more intimate than I feel comfortable being.

Anxious-ambivalent. I find that others are reluctant to get as close as I would like. I often worry that my partner doesn't really love me or won't want to stay with me. I want to get very close to my partner, and this sometimes scares people away.

Secure. I find it relatively easy to get close to others and am comfortable depending on them. I don't often worry about being abandoned or about someone getting too close to me.

SOURCE: Hazan, C., & Shaver, P. R. (1987). Romantic love conceptualized as an attachment process. *Journal of Personality and Social Psychology, 52,* 515. Reprinted by permission of the American Psychological Association.

The first influential measure of adult romantic attachment, developed by Hazan and Shaver (1987), asked adults to identify which of three statements (see Table 12.1) best captured their approach to and beliefs about romantic relationships. Descriptive statements represented avoidant, anxious-ambivalent, and secure classifications. As measurement was refined and attempts to integrate the fields of nuclear family and adult peer attachments increased, researchers recognized that the category called "avoidant" from Hazan and Shaver's instrument did not correspond to the "dismissing" category of the AAI. The avoidant person clearly acknowledged anxiety about getting too close to another, whereas the dismissive individual reported no subjective distress.

Faced with the needs to include both aspects of avoidance, Bartholomew and her colleagues (Bartholomew & Horowitz, 1991; Bartholomew & Shaver, 1998) proposed a new conceptual framework consisting of four categories across two dimensions. Figure 12.2 illustrates this typology which operationalized Bowlby's (1973) view that working models of the self and of others are interrelated. People are thought to develop expectations about how reliably their significant others will behave in close relationships, as well as expectations about how worthy or unworthy they are of care and support. Four categories of attachment orientation are defined by crossing the working model of self with the working model of others.

In Bartholomew's typology, **secure** individuals have internalized a positive sense of themselves along with positive models of others. In general, they expect

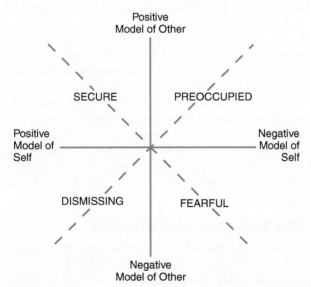

FIGURE 12.2 **Bartholomew's typology: A four-category model of adult attachment categories.**

SOURCE: Bartholomew, K., & Shaver, P. (1998). Methods of assessing adult attachment: Do they converge? in J. A. Simpson and W. S. Rholes (Eds.), *Attachment theory and close relationships* (pp. 25–45). New York, NY: Guilford Press. Used by permissions of Guilford Publications, Inc.

others to be available and supportive of their needs in close relationships. They are comfortable with emotional closeness but are also reasonably autonomous. Individuals classified as *preoccupied* hold positive models of others but negative models of themselves. Others are viewed as not valuing the preoccupied person as much as he values them. Preoccupied attachment is marked by emotional demandingness, anxiety about gaining acceptance from others, fear of and hypervigilance to cues of rejection, and excessive preoccupation with relationships.

The **avoidant** category is subdivided into two, based on reports of felt distress. *Dismissing* individuals are characterized by a positive model of the self but a negative model of the other. Denying the need for close relationships permits these adults to maintain a sense of superiority while devaluing the importance of others to their well-being. Self-sufficiency is preferred, and anxiety about attachment relationships is inhibited. A **fearful** attachment is the product of negative models of both self and others. For individuals with this style, attachments are desirable but seen as out of reach. Their desire for close relationships with others is thwarted by fear of rejection, and ultimately they withdraw. A high level of distress surrounds attachment themes.

The use of categories such as the ones we have just described is intuitively understandable and attractive but poses a number of problems. There is a danger of failing to recognize that individual differences often exist on a continuum, reflecting the degree to which a certain tendency is exhibited (e.g., high to low levels of anxiety), as opposed to differences in kind (highly anxious vs. not anxious). Therefore, measurements that place people in quadrants will undoubtedly mask the continuity that actually exists along the underlying dimensions. This kind of categorization may actually underestimate the real continuity of attachment patterns from childhood to adulthood and diminish the strength of associations between attachment research from the parental and romantic traditions (Fraley & Waller, 1998). It may be convenient to use a typology, but a number of studies suggest that attachment scales are really measuring two continuous dimensions: avoidance and anxiety (e.g., Brennan, Clark, & Shaver, 1998; Haydon, Roisman, & Burt, 2012; Roisman, Fraley, & Belsky, 2007; Roisman, 2009).

For helping professionals, a dimensional perspective may make it easier to think of individuals as operating within a range of possible behaviors. Specific attachment patterns should be viewed as tendencies to perceive and act in certain ways but not as guarantees that individuals will always operate according to type. So clinicians and other helpers should avoid "typecasting" clients on the basis of attachment categories that are fixed and orthogonal, a practice that can distort clinical judgment by acting as a cognitive bias or stereotype. It may be more helpful to keep in mind that the most basic issues involved in relationships concern a person's level of anxiety about social interaction and his level of approach or avoidance. The prototypical classifications may best represent individuals with very pronounced characteristics at the extremes of the anxiety-avoidance dimensions. It is probably more accurate to think of people having particular attachment styles rather than classifications, which is a less forgiving term. It may also be helpful to keep in mind that there is wide variability in behavioral expression of anxiety and of approach-avoidance in relationships.

Research on Young Adult Dyadic Relationships

Western research in the peer/romantic tradition has uncovered a number of interesting aspects of dyadic relationship patterns that are related to attachment style. The focus of most of this work has been the exploration of how individual differences in attachment orientations play out in areas of social interaction. Let us take a brief look at some of the results of these investigations in areas of concern to young adults: partner selection, satisfaction with and stability of relationships, and communication and conflict resolution styles. When appropriate, we will also consider how gender differences mediate these relationships.

Partner Selection. Attachment theory offers an intuitively reasonable framework for understanding why partners choose one another. First, secure individuals, who neither avoid intimacy nor are desperately in search of it, should be more likely to seek out balanced partners like themselves. Research indicates that secure individuals tend to be paired more often with other secure rather than insecure partners (Senchak & Leonard, 1992).

Insecure individuals, according to attachment theory, should also be likely to select partners who confirm their expectations or working models of close relationships. Avoidant partners, who are fearful or dismissing of intimacy, expect partners to cling and overwhelm them with their demandingness. Anxious partners, who crave closeness, may expect rejection and believe that their needs for intimacy will go unmet. Thus, a certain synergy might propel an avoidant individual to pair with an anxious one, fulfilling expectations of both partners.

Mate selection may be influenced by one's adult attachment status: Secure individuals are likely to be paired with other secure individuals.

Several studies have documented the fact that avoidant-avoidant and anxious-anxious pairings are rare. In Kirkpatrick and Davis's (1994) study of 354 heterosexual couples, not a single couple showed either of these patterns. From the perspective of attachment theory, such symmetrical matches would not make sense because they do not fit the expectations predicted from working models. What is far more likely is the complementary pairing of avoidant with anxious mates, and several studies have found a preponderance of anxious-ambivalent matches among insecure individuals (Collins & Read, 1990; Kirkpatrick & Davis, 1994; Pietromonaco & Carnelley, 1994; Simpson, 1990).

At this point, although the findings match the predictions of attachment theory, it is unclear whether romantic partners actually enter relationships with these complementary attachment styles or whether something in the nature of the relationship alters the attachment style. As you will see in Box 12.1, attachment styles can change with experience in a romantic relationship, but the probability of change is not large. Although distribution of attachment classification is independent of gender, gender-related stereotypes might be one possible contributor to changes in relationship quality over time. While traditional western stereotypes for masculinity might encourage greater emotional distance for males, recent cross-cultural research shows that dismissiveness in relationships is not characteristic of males in many non-western cultures (Schmitt, 2008).

Intimacy, Satisfaction, and Stability of Relationships. Consistent with attachment theory, the attachment styles of romantic partners help predict their emotional closeness and mutual acceptance—the intimacy of their relationships (e.g., Scharf et al., 2004). The quantity and quality of both caregiving and sexual experience are affected (see Simpson & Rholes, 2010). Highly avoidant partners tend to provide less physical comfort to their partners and their care tends to be less sensitive and nurturing. With primary romantic partners they engage in sex less frequently than secure people, even though they might be more inclined than others to have casual, uncommitted sex. Highly anxious partners are more controlling and intrusive in their caregiving than secure partners, and they are more likely to view sexual relations as a way of avoiding rejection and strengthening their attachment (see Mikulincer & Shaver, 2007).

Not surprisingly, feelings of commitment and relationship satisfaction are also tied to people's attachment styles. Some studies assess attachment status at one time and follow up later with assessments of partners' interactions and/or feelings about their relationships (e.g., Holland & Roisman, 2010; Kirkpatrick & Davis, 1994; Simpson, 1990). Secure individuals tend to experience more positive and less negative emotion,

Box 12.1: The Benefits of Love: Stability and Change in Adult Attachment Styles

A child's attachment status can change if the caregiving environment changes. We saw in Chapter 4, for example, that major disruptions of family life, such as parents' divorce or loss of employment, can impact the quality of care a child receives and alter the security of the child's attachment. Is an adult's attachment style open to revision? If so, it seems likely that such change would happen primarily in the context of major relationship shifts—after marriage, or with parenting, or because of the dissolution of an intimate partnership. Crowell, Treboux, and Waters (2002) studied stability and change in young adults' attachment representations after they were married, expecting that although stability might be the rule, the intimacy and intensity of marital relationships could be especially conducive to positive change for some individuals.

One hundred fifty-seven couples, averaging about 24 years old, were recruited for the study when they sought marriage licenses in one county of New York State. None was previously married and none had children. They had already been together for an average of 51 months, although most (about 67%) were still living separately, usually with their parents. These young men and women were tested 3 months before and 18 months after their weddings. At each assessment they were given an attachment classification based on an Adult Attachment Interview (AAI). In addition, participants completed a "Family Behavior Survey," answering questions about amount of happiness, discord, and aggression in their relationship. Finally, each partner participated in a "Current Relationship Interview." In these interviews, participants were required to use adjectives to characterize their own and their partners' behaviors, and they had to provide examples that supported those descriptions. They also talked about what factors were important aspects of, and influences on, their relationships, and about qualities of their interaction in different circumstances, such as when one partner was sick or upset. From these interviews, the researchers assigned each participant a relationship rating. A relationship, like an attachment status, could be classified as "secure," "dismissing," "preoccupied," or "unresolved." Individuals whose relationships were secure, for example, were likely to report examples of shared comfort and support, saw their partnership as an opportunity for both partners to grow, and spoke coherently about the importance of attachment elements, like emotional closeness. In dismissive relationships, individuals tended to express support for their partners only conditionally, that is, only for concerns that they regarded as important. They also talked more about the material or personal goals they had for their relationship (e.g., we'll be buying a house together) than they did about factors like their emotional bond. In preoccupied relationships, partners spoke of feeling anxious about their partners' expressed concerns and about the relationship, sometimes manifesting that anxiety as anger or confusion.

As expected, for the majority of participants (78%), attachment status remained stable through the marriage transition. This was especially true of those who began with a secure attachment. The relationships formed by secure partners were also more secure. As we would expect from other studies, the partnerships of secure individuals were more intimate from the beginning, and they had fewer difficulties, like arguments or verbal aggression, during the first 18 months of marriage. According to attachment theory, a working model of attachment *should* be fairly stable by adulthood, representing a characteristic state of mind in relationship contexts that affects the behavior of the individual and that in turn affects the responses of the relationship partner. As we have seen, these mental and behavioral patterns begin in infancy, evolve through childhood and adolescence, and become more entrenched with time. As a result, we should not only expect stability in the attachment status of the typical adult, but we should also find that his relationships tend to reflect his attachment style.

However, the idea of a "working model" is that it *can* be influenced by new input. If a new relationship provides truly different interactive experiences from those that have come before, then change is possible (Bowlby, 1988). Crowell et al. (2002) found that nearly all secure individuals remained secure at the end of the study, but over 20% of individuals who were insecure at the beginning of the study were secure by the second assessment. Those who changed were more likely to have been classified as preoccupied than dismissive at the beginning of the study. It may be that because dismissive individuals tend to avoid intimacy, they are less likely to experience the kinds of support that can transform one's expectations of relationships. The "became secure" participants were no more likely than the "stable insecure" participants to be paired with a secure partner, suggesting that "a committed, devoted, but insecure partner can be as effective as a secure partner in fostering growth and change, and may even be relatively tolerant and supportive of a partner's secure-base 'missteps'" (p. 476). The telling difference between the "became secure" and the "stable insecure" groups was that the "became secure" group had more positive relationships, even before the wedding. They were more intimate, happy, and passionate, and there was somewhat less discord than in the relationships of the "stable insecure" participants. The "became secure" group also tended to have more education and to have lived away from parents prior to marriage. "This suggests that experiences and opportunity in such settings (e.g., exposure to new ideas, new people, and new relationships), as well as physical and psychological distance from parents, facilitate the reconceptualization of childhood attachment relationships" (p. 476). If we think of the parent–child relationship as a child's "first love," it does indeed seem that love can be sweeter the second time around.

have more harmonious interactions with their partners, and report greater satisfaction in their relationships than those who are insecure. They also report more trust, commitment, and interdependence. Highly avoidant partners report weaker interdependence and less commitment; highly anxious people are more likely to say that their relationships lack trust. There are also some interesting gender differences. Avoidant males experience less distress when their relationships end than others, but that is not the case for avoidant females. Perhaps this is due to the commonly held perception that women are primarily responsible for maintenance of personal relationships and so they feel more accountable for the partnership's success.

The lowest levels of satisfaction are usually reported by couples composed of avoidant men and anxious women (e.g., Kirkpatrick & David, 1994). Yet these matches are typically about as stable as matches between more satisfied, secure partners. The couples who are most vulnerable to break up seem to be those made up of anxious men and avoidant women. Once again, this may have something to do with women being the stereotypical tenders of relationships. Avoidant women may be less skilled at accommodating, or less motivated to accommodate, the needs of the more dependent partner. Anxious women, overly concerned with possibilities of abandonment, might be more willing to do what it takes to maintain a relationship with an avoidant partner, perhaps explaining the high level of stability in these relationships.

Communication Style and Conflict Resolution. Consider for a moment a problem that you experienced at some time in one of your close relationships. Now reflect on how you dealt with that problem. Was your response typical of the way you usually deal with relationship problems? You undoubtedly know, by virtue of your training, that when faced with a relationship's inevitable glitches, it is a good idea to be open, nondefensive, reasonably assertive, and yet flexible enough to compromise. Keeping a clear head so that problem solving can be effective is another requirement. Easier said than done, you're probably thinking! Why is it often so hard to do this well?

One reason is that conflict and communication in close relationships frequently have one or more subtexts: love, loss, trust, and abandonment, to name a few. In short, conflicts are stressful, they elicit emotions, and, perhaps, they can trigger the patterns of emotion regulation learned in the earliest of attachment relationships. Many studies have documented the advantages of attachment security for interpersonal communication (e.g., Haydon, Collins, et al., 2012; Holland & Roisman, 2010; Keelan, Dion, & Dion, 1998; Mikulincer & Arad, 1999). Secure individuals display more reciprocity and flexibility in communication. Greater self-disclosure characterizes the communication of secure and anxious groups as compared to avoidant ones. Several studies also document the advantages of having a secure orientation when it comes to solving problems (Pistole, 1989). In general, secure individuals are more apt to compromise in ways that are mutually beneficial. Avoidant individuals tend to be more uncompromising, whereas anxious individuals tend to give in.

What actually happens when a couple has to deal with conflict in the relationship? According to attachment theory, the conflict produces stress, which activates the attachment system, makes the working models more accessible and influences how affect gets regulated. Simpson, Rholes, and Phillips (1996) asked 123 heterosexual couples, who had been dating from 6 months to 2 years, to discuss problems in their relationships. Participants were videotaped, and their interactions were rated by observers. Secure individuals were less defensive than insecure ones and held the most favorable views of their partners after discussing a major problem. Avoidant participants kept the greatest emotional distance in the discussion. Presumably uncomfortable with the expression of emotion, they appeared to minimize personal involvement. By the same token, they did not display evidence of anger, distress, or less positive views of their partners. Avoidant men provided less warmth and supportiveness to their partners, consistent with theoretical predictions. In contrast, avoidant women did not display this pattern in this study. The strength of society's mandate that women be relationship caretakers might, in certain circumstances, override avoidant dispositions. But this is not the case in every close relationship. In at least one other study, both men and women with avoidant styles were less likely to give emotional support to close friends (Phillips, Simpson, Lanigan, & Rholes, 1995).

Ambivalent partners in the study by Simpson and colleagues (1996) reacted with the most negative emotion to the discussion of problems, displaying high levels of stress and anxiety during the interaction. They also reported feeling more hostility and anger toward their partners after the session. Ambivalent couples report more disruptions and more shifts in satisfaction in general when compared to other types (Tidwell, Reis, & Shaver, 1996). Consistent with attachment theory, these individuals expect their partners to fail at meeting their needs in stressful situations. Rholes and his colleagues (Rholes, Simpson, & Stevens, 1998) explain the phenomenon in this way:

> Conflict elicits a cascade of unpleasant feelings in ambivalent persons, and it should raise doubts about the quality and viability of their current partner and relationship. Moreover, if fears of abandonment become salient, ambivalent partners ought to derogate the partner and relationship to minimize or "prepare for" potential loss. Persons who are not ambivalent, in contrast, may not experience conflict as aversive, but as an occasion in which open communication and the joint, constructive sharing of feelings can occur. (pp. 181–182)

Attachment style affects not only a couple's interactions in conflict situations. It also affects their physiological responses. We noted earlier that dismissive and preoccupied individuals appear to have distinctive physiological responses in situations that arouse the attachment system, such as participation in the AAI. Dismissive people tend to show increased electrodermal reactivity (i.e., increased skin conductance), which is associated with effortful emotional inhibition, whereas preoccupied people may show increased heart rate, associated with higher behavioral activation. Roisman (2007) observed both young engaged couples (ages 18 to 30) and older couples (older than 50, married for at least 15 years). After completing the AAI, the couples were asked to identify and discuss a problem area in their relationship and to try to resolve it. In these conflict discussions, dismissive individuals showed increased electrodermal reactivity and preoccupied individuals showed increased heart rate, regardless of age or length of relationship. In contrast, secure individuals showed little physiological change in these mildly stressful conversations. (Similar findings are reported by Holland & Roisman, 2010). The physiological data are consistent with the idea that dismissive adults are motivated to avoid their partners when asked to resolve problems in the relationship, whereas preoccupied adults tend to be emotionally overinvolved in their relationships.

In general, attachment theory serves as a useful template for conceptualizing the universal human needs served by close, interpersonal relationships as well as the systematic differences individuals display in their personal associations. Clinicians are already very familiar with the notion that certain qualities of family relationships experienced early in life tend to get repeated in later relationships. Although not derivative of attachment theory per se, psychoanalytic and some family therapy approaches, such as Bowen's (1978), advise clients to examine the nature of conflicted childhood relationships within one's family of origin in an effort to achieve insight and gain the freedom to make more adaptive relationship choices in the present.

WORK

For most young adults, the launching of a vocational life is as important a developmental task as the process of forming or reforming attachments. What are the key elements in a successful launch? A large body of theory and research has addressed this question. The theories share in common a general notion that career success and satisfaction depend heavily on matching the characteristics of an individual and the demands of a job. If this notion is correct, then self-knowledge is a critical element in career decision making. Thus, not only is establishing an occupational role an important part of identity or self-concept development, it is also an emergent property of that process. The stronger our sense of who we are as we become adults, the more likely we are to make good career choices. Two classic theories of career development will illustrate.

Some Theories of the Career Development Process

Holland's Theory of Personality–Environment Types

Holland (e.g., 1985, 1997) suggests that by early adulthood each individual has a **modal personal orientation**: a typical and preferred style or approach to dealing with social and environmental tasks. Holland proposed that most people can be categorized as having one of six modal orientations (described in Table 12.2), which can be seen as part of the individual's personality. According to Holland, a job or career typically makes demands on an individual that are compatible with one or more of these interactive types. That is, a job can be construed as creating an environment within which a certain personal orientation will lead to both success and happiness. For example, one of the personal orientation types is "social." A social type is likely to be sociable, friendly, cooperative, kind, tactful, and understanding and is often a good match to occupations that involve working with others to educate, to cure, or to enlighten them—such as counseling or social work. A contrasting type is the "enterprising" individual. He too is likely to be sociable, but more domineering, energetic, ambitious, talkative, and attention getting. He is also likely to be more effective in vocational tasks that involve maneuvering others to achieve goals, such as reaching a certain level of sales, or more efficiently delivering services as a salesperson, for instance, or an executive. Thus, each type of modal personal orientation, such as social or enterprising, is also a type of vocational environment. Usually, neither individuals nor environments fall neatly into only one "type." Holland and his colleagues have developed coding systems for rating both individuals and environments. In these systems, three-letter codes indicate the most characteristic style for the individual (e.g., Holland, Viernstein, Kuo, Karweit, & Blum, 1970) or the environment (e.g., Gottfredson, Holland, & Ogawa, 1982), as well as the second and third most characteristic styles. So, for example, a person (or environment) might be coded *RIS,* meaning primarily *realistic* (R), secondarily *investigative* (I), and finally *social* (S). (See Table 12.2 for some characteristics of these types for individuals.)

Studies spanning several decades have corroborated the notion that a good fit between modal orientation (also called personal style) and job characteristics is correlated with job satisfaction, performance, and stability, as well as feelings of personal well-being (for reviews see Kristof-Brown, Zimmerman, & Johnson, 2005; Nye, Su, Rounds, & Drasgow, 2012; Spokane & Cruza-Guet, 2005). For example, Gottfredson and Holland (1990) studied young adult bank tellers for 4 months after they were first hired. Congruence between an individual's personal style and job type was clearly correlated with job satisfaction. In two studies of school teachers, Meir (1989) examined several kinds of congruence or fit: between personal style and job type, between personal style and outside activities (avocations), and between the individual's particular skills and opportunities to use those skills on the job. All three kinds of congruence appeared to contribute to the participants' reported feelings of well-being. A person's happiness seems to be closely linked to the fit between his personality characteristics and both his work, as Holland predicted, and his leisure pursuits. It appears that creating a good match in one arena can help compensate for a lack of congruence in another.

One intriguing area of research on person-job fit explores how employees can actively improve fit by shaping their jobs to some extent. In this process, called **job crafting**, employees may initiate change in a number of different ways: by the kinds of tasks they choose or projects they launch, by negotiating with employers to modify job content, by proactively seeking feedback, by changing aspects of their jobs that

This career counselor, following John Holland's theory of personality-environment types, helps a college student think about and narrow down a diverse set of career interests and choose a major. What personality type does this young woman appear to have?

TABLE 12.2 Some Characteristics of Holland's Personality Types

REALISTIC	INVESTIGATIVE	ARTISTIC
Conforming	Analytical	Complicated
Dogmatic	Cautious	Disorderly
Genuine	Complex	Emotional
Hardheaded	Critical	Expressive
Inflexible	Curious	Idealistic
Materialistic	Independent	Imaginative
Natural	Intellectual	Impractical
Normal	Introverted	Impulsive
Persistent	Pessimistic	Independent
Practical	Precise	Introspective
Realistic	Radical	Intuitive
Reserved	Rational	Nonconforming
Robust	Reserved	Open
Self-effacing	Retiring	Original
Uninsightful	Unassuming	Sensitive

SOCIAL	ENTERPRISING	CONVENTIONAL
Agreeable	Acquisitive	Careful
Cooperative	Adventurous	Conforming
Empathic	Ambitious	Conscientious
Friendly	Assertive	Dogmatic
Generous	Domineering	Efficient
Helpful	Energetic	Inflexible
Idealistic	Enthusiastic	Inhibited
Kind	Excitement seeking	Methodical
Patient	Exhibitionistic	Obedient
Persuasive	Extroverted	Orderly
Responsible	Forceful	Persistent
Sociable	Optimistic	Practical
Tactful	Resourceful	Thorough
Understanding	Self-confident	Thrifty
Warm	Sociable	Unimaginative

involve relationships, and so on (Tims, Bakker, & Derks, 2012). You might think that job crafting opportunities would be limited to high level positions that allow employees a great deal of autonomy, but the data suggest that it happens at all levels of employment, especially among workers with good self-esteem, feelings of *self-efficacy* (see discussion later in this chapter), and self-regulation skills (Bakker, 2011). In one example, some nurses added the task of relating with and seeking information from patients' families to their specified tasks of patient care, improving the fit between their social needs and their job requirements (Wrzesniewski & Dutton, 2001). Lower ranking employees do seem to have different obstacles to face in job crafting than higher ranking employees. In particular, they are more likely to have to change others' expectations in order to modify their jobs to fit their own personal styles (Berg, Wrzesniewski, & Dutton, 2010).

Super's Developmental Approach

Super (e.g., 1972, 1984, 1990) agrees with Holland's notion that a satisfying work life is most likely when an individual's personal characteristics are well matched to the demands of a job. His theorizing about career development, however, focuses less on specifying personal style or job types and more on describing the developmental processes that determine both the emergence of one's **vocational self-concept** and the multiple factors that influence job choices throughout the life span. Vocational self-concept is part of one's total identity. It includes ideas about which qualities of the self would (or would not) provide a match to the requirements of an occupation (Super, 1984). Vocational self-concept is a function of two things: first, a person's view of his personal or psychological characteristics, and second, how he assesses his life circumstances, such as the limits or opportunities created by economic conditions; by his socioeconomic status; by his family, friendship network, and community; and so on.

Super described a series of typical life stages in the development of vocational self-concept and experience, beginning in childhood. In the **growth stage** (up to age 14 or so), children are developing many elements of identity that will have a bearing on vocational self-concept, including ideas about their interests, attitudes, skills, and needs. In the **exploratory stage**, which includes adolescence and young adulthood up to about age 24, vocational self-concept is tentatively narrowed down, but often career choices are not finalized. General vocational goals are formulated in the earlier part of this stage (**crystallization**), gradually leading to the identification of more specific vocational preferences (**specification**), and finally to the completion of education along with entry into full-time employment (**implementation**). In the **establishment stage**, from about 25 to 44, work experiences provide the laboratory within which the matching of vocational self-concept and job settings is tried out, sometimes reevaluated, sometimes confirmed, and eventually stabilized (**stabilization**). From about 45 to 64, in the **maintenance stage**, an individual makes ongoing adjustments to improve his work situation, often achieving more advanced status and seniority (**consolidation**). If not, this can also be a time of increasing frustration with work. Finally, in the **decline stage**, right before and after 65 for most people, the career winds down, with retirement planning and actual retirement taking precedence over career advancement and consolidation. Note that although these are typical life stages, at least partially verified by longitudinal research (e.g., Super & Overstreet, 1960), an individual can go through additional sequences of crystallization, specification, implementation, and stabilization when life circumstances change. These "mini-cycles" of reevaluation can be initiated by any number of events: disappointment with a career choice, job loss, changes in family life, and so on. Note the similarity to MAMA cycles in identity development described in Chapter 9.

Perhaps Super's most important insight is his recognition that career development is a continuing process. It serves as both a source of and an outgrowth of an individual's overall personal growth. For Super, a career is

> the life course of a person encountering a series of developmental tasks and attempting to handle them in such a way as to become the kind of person he or she wants to become. With a changing self and changing situations, the matching process is never really completed. (Super, 1990, pp. 225–226)

Classic career development theories emphasize the importance of fitting personal characteristics to the demands of the job. Self-knowledge is seen as critical to making the right career choices.

Research indicates that many aspects of a job beyond compatibility with one's interests and talents influence how rewarding it is. Quality of supervision, participation in decision making, interaction with others on the job, geographic location, personal health, pay, and a number of other factors are also correlated with job satisfaction and work engagement (e.g., Allen & Finkelstein, 2003; Bakker, 2011; Decker & Borgen, 1993; Perry-Jenkins, Repetti, & Crouter, 2000; Rhoades & Eisenberger, 2002). However, theories and research such as Holland's and Super's make the powerful suggestion that even when all these other factors are acceptable, a person's work responsibilities can be incompatible with his or her personality characteristics. Under these circumstances, although a hardworking individual could succeed in meeting his responsibilities, real satisfaction and the opportunity to truly excel are likely to elude him. We will have more to say about personality characteristics in Chapter 13.

The interdependence of career and self-development is an important focus of some career counseling approaches. McAuliffe (1993), for example, describes a developmentally oriented career counseling system that has an Eriksonian flavor. He argues that a central role of the counselor is to help clients address the following key question: "Who am I becoming and how shall I express this emerging self?" He points out that many clients may begin counseling with a different, but less helpful, way of conceptualizing their career issues. Some, for example, may be asking themselves, "What does my community, my family, my ethnic or religious group expect of me?" That is, they frame the issue such that their career, and their self-definition, is embedded in interpersonal relationships, not authored from within. Perhaps for this group, career identity represents a closed, rather than a constructed, facet of their identity (see Chapter 9). Other clients, especially those facing some career threat, such as downsizing, may begin with the question, "How do I maintain the current form I am in?" With this conceptual framework the self is embedded in what the person has always done, so that new career paths, expressing other needs or dimensions of the self, are not imaginable. The task for helpers may be to facilitate the development of a new, personally constructed sense of self as worker.

For many clients, then, career counseling may need to begin with help in reframing the way one construes the self. In McAuliffe's words,

> it is the counselor's challenge to assist clients in their transformations of meaning making. . . . For example, for the young adult college student whose seemingly simple dilemma is to choose between pursuing a parent-approved pre-medical track or to consider the internal voice that draws her to the social sciences, counseling would operate on two levels: one to weigh the pros and cons of various fields of study and the other to support and challenge the person so that the tacit assumptions about "who's in charge" become conscious, so that the dissonant voice that implicitly calls the person to author his or her own career can be considered. (1993, pp. 25–26)

The Realities of Career Development in Young Adulthood

For young adults launching a work life, many variables influence the speed and form of that process. Consider the prospects of two 18-year-olds, Akil and Jarod, who have just graduated from high school. Akil comes from a middle-class family. His parents take great pride in being the first ones in their own families to have graduated from college and to provide their children with a comfortable middle-class life. They expect their children to attend college and to select careers that will help them maintain or even improve on their socioeconomic status. They have several children to educate, but they are quite savvy about how to finance a college education, having put themselves through college, and they are convinced that college is a necessity for career success. Akil sees college as a necessary step on his way to a professional career, although his future plans are not specific. He expects his college experience to help him figure out what profession to enter.

The expectations that Jarod and his family have are quite different. Jarod's mother earns low wages working for a janitorial service, and she often puts in overtime to help make ends meet. Neither she nor Jarod's father (from whom she is estranged) completed high school, and both are quite proud that Jarod has. However, they have never even considered the possibility of college for Jarod. As they see it, he has completed his education and should now be able to earn a living. His mother expects him to find his own apartment to relieve the crowding in her small place. Jarod himself is quite unsure of what he can do in the world of work. He is simply hoping to find a job, any job, one that will give him a start, providing an opportunity to learn a skill and to find a niche.

Even if these two young men happen to have similar interests and personalities, their careers are likely to follow very different trajectories, largely because of the differences in their socioeconomic class, their families' views of education, and the opportunities that they perceive to be available to them. In the following sections, we will consider what the typical course of career development is for individuals like Akil and Jarod. We will specifically examine the characteristics of the process when young people move on to college from high school and when they do not. We will also consider the impact of other major factors on one's early career experiences, factors such as immediate environment, social class, race, and gender.

College Trajectories: Aspirations and Outcomes

In the United States, the percentage of high school students who say they plan to earn a bachelor's degree has skyrocketed in the past half century. By 2004, 89 percent of high school graduates aspired to do so (Rosenbaum, Stephan, & Rosenbaum, 2010). Young adults entering college have many hopes and expectations for the college years. Some of their concerns are incidental to the educational setting and are focused on either maintaining or establishing social networks or finding intimate relationships—the pursuit of *love*. But many of their hopes are relevant to *work*, their vocational lives. Some 1st-year students expect the college years to be a time of self-development, when they will "construct a philosophy of life" and become more clear about the course their adult lives might take. For most, very practical, work-related issues are among their highest priorities. The majority of students entering college indicate that "to get a better job" and "to make more money" are important reasons why they chose to go to college. Figure 12.3 illustrates that more recent cohorts of college students are even more likely to emphasize these kinds of practical career concerns than students did 20 or 30 years ago (Pryor et al., 2012).

The first vocationally relevant decision that students make is the choice of a major. Those students who are career oriented tend to decide on an occupation first and then select a major, whereas students more focused on self-development tend to select a major first and then consider possible occupational choices (Goodson, 1978). A majority of students change their majors at least once during college, although the changes they make are usually among related disciplines (Herr, Cramer, & Niles, 2003). There are substantial cohort differences regarding which majors and occupations are more popular with students. For example, Astin (1993) compared two large samples of college students who entered college 17 years apart, the first in 1968 and the second in 1985. Members of the 1985 cohort were more likely to want careers in business, law, or medicine and less likely to choose teaching or scientific research than members of the 1968 sample. Surveys of more recent cohorts indicate that the most popular majors in the 1990s were business, psychology, engineering, education, English literature, and accounting (Murray, 1996). By 2010 first-year college students were showing record-high interest in majors related to health careers, such as nursing, and the biological sciences. Although a smaller percentage chose

When Mak's early career expectations were not fulfilled, he searched for ways to make money to support himself. Focusing on his interests and his education, he has a job that he finds personally satisfying.

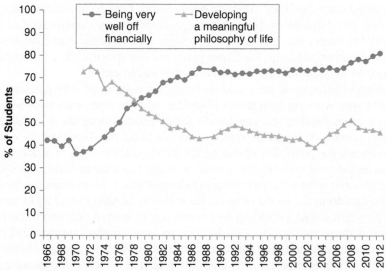

FIGURE 12.3 **What college students consider important reasons for attending college.**

SOURCE: © 2013 The Regents of the University of California. All Rights Reserved. Used by permission of John Pryor, Higher Education Research Institute.

Reflecting social and political change over recent decades, women often choose occupations traditionally occupied by men.

business than previously, it continued to be the most popular major (Higher Education Research Institute, 2004; Pryor et al., 2012).

We have seen that theorists such as Holland and Super argue that career choices often are, and should be, based on one's personal characteristics. What other factors, besides self-concept or personal style, might influence the choice of a major in college, and ultimately the choice of a career? First, cohort changes in choice of majors indicate that social and economic conditions influence choice of major. This includes economic upturns and downturns, change in the kinds of goods and services that are in demand, shifts in population size and composition, advances in technology, and developments in political and legal philosophy, such as in the area of civil rights law.

Some of the most interesting changes in majors and occupational choices across recent decades are gender specific and appear to reflect political and social trends in our beliefs about the role of women in society. The Higher Education Research Institute at UCLA reports that the proportion of women majoring in traditionally male-dominated fields, such as the biological sciences, the physical sciences, engineering, prelaw, premed, and business, increased dramatically in the last three decades of the twentieth century, as hiring patterns in related fields became less gender biased than they once were (Dey & Hurtado, 1999).

Social Class, Ethnicity, and Race

In addition to the influence of social, civil, and economic changes, other more stable factors appear to play a role. As the stories of Akil and Jarod indicate, socioeconomic status (SES) is important in shaping the expectations of young people, heavily influencing the educational choices that they make and the jobs to which they aspire. Research indicates that other family and environmental factors, such as race and ethnicity, also affect the choice of whether to go to college. Individuals from minority and low-SES groups are less likely than other groups to make the college choice. If an individual enrolls in college, are a student's career aspirations affected by such variables? Some indicators suggest that the answer is yes. To illustrate, the probability of **retention**, staying in college long enough to graduate, is related to SES (National Center for Education Statistics, 2012). The influence of

SES on retention is probably multifaceted. Often, low income high school students expect to go to college, and are encouraged to do so, but their high schools often do not provide adequate academic preparation (e.g., little or no access to AP courses or SAT preparation), and they may offer little access to counseling services designed to inform them of what will be required of them as they move on to college (Rosenbaum et al., 2010). Students who enroll in a 2- or 4-year institution often find that they must take remedial classes that are a financial drain, but which do not provide college credit. Lower SES students also have more problems paying for college, and they may receive less support from family and friends to remain in college than higher SES students do (e.g., Ryland, Riordan, & Brack, 1994).

Being of minority status is also linked to lower rates of retention (see Aud, KewalRamani, & Frohlich, 2011). Black and Native American students are at particular risk for dropping out, a problem that may be partially a result of the stress of dealing with minority status, such as feeling unwelcome or unsupported in predominantly White institutions (e.g., Newman & Newman, 1999; see Figure 12.4). How engaged and involved students feel in academic and social activities is clearly connected to retention rates (e.g., Pascarella & Terenzini, 2005). A student's "internal sense of validation"—a feeling that the institution and its representatives believe in and will support the student's ability to succeed—may be especially important here (Hurtado, Cuellar, & Guillermo-Wann, 2011). Institutions vary in how likely they are to create an inclusive educational environment where both faculty and staff engage in behaviors that support the success of individual students. What kinds of behaviors are important? A study of nearly 4,500 students from a wide range of 2- and 4-year institutions uncovered several key experiences that promoted students feelings of validation (Hurtado et al., 2011). First, students felt "academic validation in the classroom" when their instructors indicated that they were keyed into students' level of understanding, would provide students with adequate feedback, valued students' in-class contributions, were available to meet outside of class, encouraged questions and participation, and demonstrated concern for students. Students felt "general interpersonal validation" when faculty *and* staff showed interest in them, recognized students' achievements, believed in their potential, and encouraged students to get involved in campus activities. Unfortunately, minority students consistently reported experiencing substantially less validation, both academic and interpersonal, than White students.

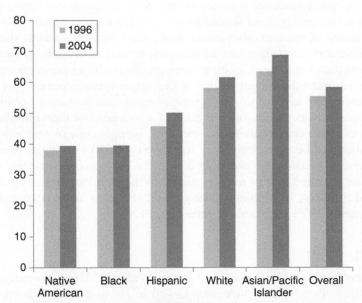

FIGURE 12.4 **Percentage of students graduating within six years of enrollment at 4-year colleges and universities (by first year of enrollment).**
SOURCE: National Center for Education Statistics (2012).

Do factors such as SES affect one's choice of a college major? There is indirect evidence that they can. For example, students attending private universities are more likely to choose premed majors than students attending public 4-year colleges, and students at public institutions are more likely to choose school teaching as a career than students at private universities (Astin, 1993). Given that SES has some influence on the choice of private versus public educational facilities, it appears that SES may contribute to these differences.

Other characteristics of the college environment also seem to influence choice of major or career (see Astin, 1993). For example, students are more likely to select college teaching as a career if they attend smaller colleges that provide high levels of student–faculty interaction, opportunities for independent research, and written evaluations of students' work. African American students are more likely to choose premed if they attend a traditionally Black college. Membership in a fraternity or sorority is linked to greater tendencies to select business or prelaw as a major. Of course, whether one attends a small college or a Black college, or joins a sorority or fraternity, is probably influenced by preexisting characteristics of the student. For example, extroverts appear to be more attracted to Greek life on campus than introverts (e.g., Sher, Bartholow, & Nanda, 2001). Therefore, it is difficult to say whether such features of college life have a causal influence on students' major or career choices or whether students who favor such environments also tend to prefer certain fields of study. It seems likely that the causal connections work both ways.

One role that the college experience seems to play in choosing a major and ultimately a career is that it provides opportunities to try out different choices with relatively little cost. Some students enter college aspiring to be lawyers or physicians or engineers, for example, only to find that the prelaw, premed, or engineering course work is not suitable to their interests or abilities. Such majors often lose enrollment as students move through their college years. Other majors tend to draw increasing numbers over the college years. Education and business majors are among these. Interestingly, some of the more academically challenging fields also increase their draw somewhat after students get a taste of college, fields like scientific research and college teaching (see Astin, 1993; Bright, Pryor, Wilkenfeld, & Earl, 2005).

Since one's choice of a college major is associated with college success as well as career choice, career counseling in college should begin with advisement on choice of a major. Unfortunately, leaving this task to relatively untrained faculty advisors seems to be insufficient for helping students to make good choices. Herr et al. (2003), in their text on career guidance throughout the life span, argue that career guidance professionals at the college level should provide students with assistance in selecting a major. In pursuit of this and other career goals, even 1st-year students should have help available in self-assessment and self-analysis, as well as in decision making.

It is clear that a college education plays a critical role in occupational opportunity. One's highest educational degree is the single most important predictor of level of job entry, and level of job entry weighs more heavily than IQ or job skill in predicting career advancement. But the value of a college education goes beyond its contribution to career development. For example, being a college graduate means a greater likelihood of being healthy or of having a successful marriage. Some of the effects of higher education are probably due to the income opportunities it creates and so are career linked; others may be related to the development of critical thinking skills and flexibility in problem solving that it seems to foster (Pascarella, Bohr, Nora, & Terenzini, 1995; Pascarella & Terenzini, 1991).

The Forgotten Half

The **forgotten half** was the name given by the William T. Grant Foundation Commission on Work, Family, and Citizenship (1988) to 18- to 24-year-olds who do not go to college. These were just under half of the total young adult population in the United States in 1988. They were described as the young people who build our homes, drive our buses, repair our automobiles, fix our televisions, maintain and serve our offices, schools and hospitals, and keep the production lines of our mills and factories moving. To a great extent, they determine how well the American family, economy and democracy function. They are also the thousands of young men and women who aspire to work productively but never quite "make it" to that kind of employment. For these members of the Forgotten Half, their lives as adults start in the economic limbo of unemployment, part-time jobs, and poverty wages. Many of them never break free. (1988, as cited in Halperin, 1998a, cover)

Ten years later, the American Youth Policy Forum sponsored a follow-up report on the forgotten half (Halperin, 1998a). The good news is that the high school dropout rate had declined since the original report, and the numbers of high school graduates entering 2- or 4-year colleges had increased, so that the proportion of young adults with no postsecondary training had dropped several percentage points, and that drop has continued (National Center for Education Statistics, 2012). The bad news, however, is that the real income of young adults in the United States had declined, and that downward trend has also continued. The most serious losses have been experienced by those with the least education. Further, poverty rates have increased for those at every educational level, but especially for those without a college degree (see Figure 12.5 for U.S. poverty rates by education in 2009). Graduation rates for those who begin college have improved over the last decade, but still only somewhat over half complete a degree (see Figure 12.4; National Center for Education Statistics, 2012).

Interestingly, the basic attitudes of young adults toward work and family do not differ regardless of whether they go to college. Young people usually rank good pay and opportunities for advancement as highly desirable features of a job. They also want their work to make a meaningful contribution to society. As for their social aspirations, young people of all backgrounds generally consider having a good marriage and having children to be important life goals for them (e.g., Hill & Yeung, 1999).

Despite the broad similarities in the goals of college and noncollege youth in the United States, the chances of achieving these goals are substantially reduced for the latter group. As we have already seen, education is a key predictor of employment success, career advancement, and general success in life, so that when a young person chooses to end education with high school, he limits his options and opportunities. "Until the last few decades, young people without an education beyond high school were often able to find family-sustaining work in service industries or manufacturing operations. Today, they face lives of grinding economic struggle virtually shut out from jobs that will allow them to build assets and support children of their own" (Pennington, 2003, p. 60). A number of other factors also affect the degree to which a young person's goals are likely to be achieved. These

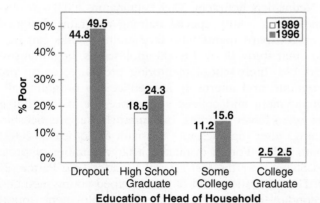

FIGURE 12.5 **Percentage of young adults (18- to 24-year-olds) living in poverty in the U.S. in 2009.**
SOURCE: Based on National Center for Education Statistics (2012). *Digest of Education Statistics: 2011.* Retrieved from http://nces.ed.gov/programs/digest/d11/.

factors include socioeconomic status, as was the case with Jarod. Even when young people fail to attend college, coming from a family of relatively high socioeconomic status provides opportunities and advantages that youth from lower SES families usually do not have. Another important factor is race, which can have a profound impact on the probability of employment across all education levels. Finally, a variety of "behavioral obstacles," including having a child early or out of wedlock and engaging in criminal behavior, are important determiners of whether young adults will make significant strides toward meeting their goals. Among noncollege youth, those most at risk of slipping into poverty, for example, are Blacks with criminal records who come from low-income families (e.g., Halperin, 1998b; Hill & Yeung, 1999). As we have discussed earlier, these outcomes may be the result of histories of accumulating and interlocking risks.

Although many factors can contribute to a slide into poverty, adequate educational preparation is clearly the most effective avenue to avoiding poverty and to achieving the typical goals that young people have for work and family. The problems faced by noncollege youth in America are partly a function of a disorganized and inadequate system for training adolescents and young adults for the kinds of skilled employment that are personally rewarding and that can provide an adequate income to support a family. As you have already seen, it is often difficult for high school students from lower income groups to get information that helps them prepare for the rigors of college (Rosenbaum et al., 2010). Young people face similar obstacles obtaining information on how to prepare themselves for particular jobs and occupations. Recommendations for improving the lot of noncollege youth begin with ideas for improving basic skill training in public schools, including the teaching of such traditional academic skills as reading, writing, math, and speaking abilities, as well as thinking skills, self-management, and social skills. The particular concern is to improve the quality of secondary education for students who go through general or vocational (noncollege preparatory) tracks in high school. These programs are often criticized for having watered-down, boring curricula (Bailey & Morest, 1998).

Next, reports on the forgotten half encourage providing high school students with better access to extensive vocational counseling; information and support for moving into post-secondary training designed to culminate with technical certificates or associates degrees; and with opportunities for work-based learning (e.g., Rosenbaum & Becker, 2011).

They also suggest increasing the participation of employers in providing training and apprenticeship programs, using the community college system to create expanded opportunities for technical training, and creating community-based resources to provide young adults with information about pathways into specific occupations (Bailey & Morest, 1998; Neumark & Rothstein, 2005; Pennington, 2003).

For some young adults, special training programs designed for economically disadvantaged participants who face multiple risks can be quite effective. In one longitudinal study of over 8,000 adolescents, beginning when they were 12 to 17 years old, high school mentoring programs, co-op programs, school enterprise programs, and internship/apprenticeship programs all had beneficial effects on employment and college attendance for males after graduation. For females, there were fewer benefits, but internship/apprenticeship programs led to better earnings after high school (Neumark & Rothstein, 2005). Similarly, the American Youth Policy Forum evaluated a large number of programs launched in the United States over the last several decades (see Partee, 2003; Hooker & Brand, 2009). The most successful of these helped young men and women move on to postsecondary education or to quality employment opportunities, simultaneously supporting the young adults they served and reaping economic and social benefits for their communities. For example, Job Corps, a public–private partnership administered by the U.S. Department of Labor, returned about $2.00 to society for every $1.00 invested. Private programs like Strive, operated in

New York City's Harlem, helped at-risk young adults sustain employment over multiple years. Like other effective interventions (see Box 1.2 in Chapter 1), these programs tend to have certain characteristics in common, such as implementation quality (e.g., sufficient and sustained resources, strong leadership, and professional staff development); caring and knowledgeable teachers, counselors, and mentors; high standards and expectations; and a holistic approach, meaning that they address multiple needs (e.g., providing child care and transportation, life skills and assertiveness training, individualized attention, and so on).

Many researchers note that there is a particularly sinister trend that affects the forgotten half. Arrest and imprisonment for minor crimes (e.g., drug possession) have increased dramatically since the early 1970s, especially for males, such that the United States now far outdistances every other country in the world in incarceration rates (numbers of prisoners per 100,000 people; see Figure 12.6). The number of young men incarcerated in U.S. prisons more than doubled between 1986 and 1995, continued to rise slowly until 2009, when the number leveled off and started to decline slightly (Carson & Sabol, 2012; Halperin, 1998b). Minority males have been especially affected. By 2008, for example, 1 in every 15 Black males, age 18 and older, was in prison, compared to 1 in every 106 White males (The Pew Center, 2008). The disparity in minority versus White incarceration rates for males has decreased somewhat in recent years, but it remains substantial. The rate of incarceration for both White and minority women is low in comparison, but it has shown a rise in recent years as well (Mauer, 2013).

> For some segments of society, crime control policy . . . has regressed to the point that imprisonment is the major governmental intervention in the transition to young adulthood. . . . This means that segments of the population are cut off from voting, employment, and community organizations. This disenfranchisement will further contribute to increased unemployment and undermine family life. (Laub, 1999)

Given that friendships, family ties, and a sense of belonging in a community play a significant role in a young adult's hope for the future and chances for upward mobility, school- and community-based vocational training and counseling seem like much better alternatives than jail for many adolescent and young adult delinquents. When we consider that young adult incarceration has cascading negative effects for the families of those who are jailed as well, the importance of implementing alternative interventions is strikingly clear (e.g., Green, Ensminger, Robertson, & Juon, 2006).

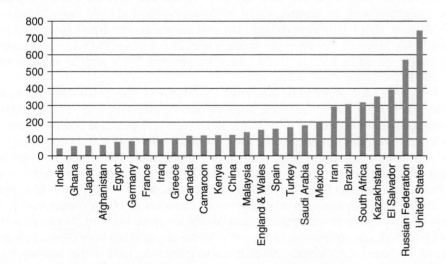

FIGURE 12.6 **Incarceration rates (per 100,000 people) in countries around the globe.**
SOURCE: Based on National Center for Education Statistics (2011). America's Youth: Transitions to Adulthood. Washington, DC: U.S. Department of Education. Retrieved from http://nces.ed.gov/pubs2012/1012026/chapter3_3.asp.

Women versus Men

Traditionally, gender has been a significant factor in career development. In 1957, Super found that a variety of career patterns characterized adults in the mid-20th century in the United States. For men, the "conventional career pattern" included a period or periods of "trial work," that is, trying out possible jobs and then launching into a stable career. The conventional career pattern for women, however, involved entry into work as a stopgap after high school or college. Once married, women tended to shift to full-time homemaking. Even in 1957, there were other patterns for both men and women that were common enough not to be considered atypical, but most of the alternative patterns also displayed gender differences. For example, women sometimes followed the "double-track career pattern," first establishing a career and then adding a second career as homemaker. Or they might show the "interrupted career pattern," first establishing a career, then marrying and becoming a full-time homemaker, and then shifting back to a career when home responsibilities were less pressing. Interestingly, none of the patterns Super characterized as typical of men included double-tracking or any kind of interruption based on family or homemaking concerns.

How important is gender in career development today? As we have already seen, there have certainly been substantial changes relevant to gender in our culture since 1950. These changes have grown out of the civil rights movement, the women's rights movement in particular, and are also linked to technological changes such as the availability of reliable contraceptives and an increase in the use of machines to do heavy labor. Many work-related gender differences have diminished, and some have even disappeared or reversed. For example, women now enter college in larger numbers than men do, whereas up until about 1980, men outnumbered women (U.S. Bureau of the Census, 2012). As we have already noted, women now often choose majors in college that traditionally were the preserve of men, such as premed and business. Women earn as many or more graduate degrees as men. Half of all MDs are now earned by women, as well as the majority of veterinary degrees. Women constitute nearly half of the employed labor force, and in 2006, women filled about 51% of executive, administrative, and managerial positions in the United States, more than doubling their representation in these kinds of jobs in 30 years (U.S. Bureau of Labor Statistics, 2010). Still, the representation of women in various jobs within these categories is often linked to gender traditions. Women are particularly under-represented in fields that are math intensive, such as engineering, math, physics, chemistry, economics, and computer science (Ceci & Williams, 2010). They are over-represented in fields that involve primarily caregiving, such as nursing, social work, education, and child care (Weisgram, Bigler, & Liben, 2010). Historical changes favoring greater gender equity have occurred in most fields, however. For example, women earn 29.6% of the PhDs in mathematics today (as compared to 5.9% in 1960); males are entering fields such as nursing and child care in increasing numbers as well.

Yet, gender continues to be a powerful predictor of vocational interests, more so than other individual differences, such as race or ethnicity (e.g., Fouad, 2004). Although men and women use most of the same criteria to evaluate potential careers (they try to match their interests, and they carefully consider professional advancement and income opportunities), women are more likely than men to consider relationships with people (opportunity for and kinds of) and altruistic concerns as important factors in selecting a career (e.g., Su, Rounds, & Armstrong, 2009; Weisgram et al., 2010). A greater focus on relational/social elements of career choice may help explain why women with exceptional math ability are more likely to choose paths to social and health science careers than careers in the physical sciences (Perez-Felkner, McDonald, Schneider, & Grogan, 2012). It is also interesting to note that women with outstanding math skills also tend to have outstanding verbal skills, whereas that is less likely to be true for men. As a result, such women may see themselves as having a wider range of good career options (Park, Lubinski, & Benbow, 2008).

Gender differences in career choice are also influenced at least in part by gender-role beliefs and life style preferences (Ceci & Williams, 2010). Both men and women anticipate that marriage and parenting will be important to their lives, for example, but men give greater priority to their role as breadwinner in the family, and women give greater priority to their role as caregiver (e.g., Vermeulen & Minor, 1998). Overall, women seem more concerned with work-life balance (Robertson, Smeets, Lubinski, & Benbow, 2010). For example, in surveys of young, high ability adults (e.g., graduate students), women say that they work fewer hours per week than men, and when asked about how many hours per week they are willing to work on their ideal job, they choose fewer hours than men.

Different role expectations are nowhere more evident than in the typical patterns of career development. There have been several noteworthy changes in career patterns for women, and to some extent for men, but these changes continue to reflect the tendency for women to focus more than men on family and child-rearing concerns at every stage of career planning. For example, despite the fact that both men and women have the right to take parental or family leaves in some companies in the United States (a right that is mandated by law in many European countries), it is quite rare for a man to exercise that right. The most dramatic change in women's career patterns since the 1950s has been the great increase in women's choice of a double-track pattern. To illustrate the enormity of the change, in 1950, most mothers of children under age 6 were full-time homemakers (88%). In 2009, more than 63% of U.S. mothers of preschoolers were employed, and the percentage of employed mothers continues to rise (U.S. Bureau of Labor Statistics, 2011).

Mothers who work are described as having two careers because they typically take more responsibility for child care and daily household tasks than fathers who work, although there is an increasing tendency for men to share somewhat more equitably in homemaking responsibilities and to make job-related decisions that take into account their parenting role (e.g., Bond, Thompson, Galinsky, & Prottas, 2002). Men have also become more likely to take their wives' careers into account in making other job-related decisions, such as whether to relocate (e.g., Gill & Haurin, 1998).

Despite some improvements, old habits do die hard. Women, for example, still make less money than men (U.S. Bureau of Labor Statistics, 2011). Unsurprisingly, researchers find that one contribution to earnings differences is the degree to which people endorse gendered separation of roles. In fact, women who endorse this view tend to earn less than other women, and men who endorse this view tend to earn more than other men (Judge & Livingston, 2008). "Overall, . . . although gender role attitudes are becoming less traditional for men and for women, traditional gender role orientation continues to exacerbate the gender wage gap" (Judge & Livingston, p. 994). Organizational structures, possibly constructed and maintained to build in certain privileges for select groups, are slow to change. Research has demonstrated that women in male-dominated occupations are not viewed as favorably as men, despite comparable skills. Their work is evaluated more negatively than men's, and they face more exclusion from the kinds of informal networks and social activities that often pave the way for advancement in the workplace (e.g., Eagly & Johannesen-Schmidt, 2001). Clearly, both traditional gender roles and the realities of secular change are influencing career patterns for both women and men. We will revisit the issue of dual careers and parenting in the next chapter.

Work and the Development of Self-Concept

As we have now seen, theorists in the arena of career development see an individual's vocational self-concept as critical for the evolution of a successful, satisfying career. Both Holland and Super specify the importance of self-knowledge in career development: accurate assessment of one's own style, interests, and characteristics. Super also emphasizes that one's vocational self both emerges from one's broader sense of identity and contributes to it. Thus, it seems that self-concept is a central force behind career development and is, in turn, a product of it. These ideas have formed the backbone of many career counseling approaches. In the following sections, we will consider how feelings and attitudes toward the self as a worker develop. What do these aspects of identity contribute to work and its role in the life of an adult and vice versa? We begin by recapping Erik Erikson's ideas about how work and self-concept are related in development.

Erikson's Theory of Identity Development

In Erikson's (1950/1963) view of the developing self-concept, children begin to formulate a sense of themselves as workers when they first confront serious work. In both nonindustrial and industrial societies around the world, children are expected to begin to work by the time they are 5 or 6 years old. In nonindustrial societies, they work alongside adults, caring for younger children, doing household tasks, helping with farm animals, working in the fields, or hunting. They are expected both to contribute to the productive efforts of the community and to learn the skills they will need as full-fledged adults. In most industrial societies today, children's work begins in school, where they are expected to achieve competence in basic skills, such as reading and arithmetic, that will serve them in nearly any adult work they might take on. Erikson argued that these early work experiences can provide a child with a feeling of **industry**, which is both a belief in his ability to master the skills and tools needed to be productive and a sense of "the pleasure of work completion by steady attention and persevering diligence" (p. 259). Feelings of industry help the child to be "an eager and absorbed unit of a productive situation" (p. 259). The child can, unfortunately, also slip into feeling inadequate and inferior if he cannot seem to master the skills that are required of him and begins to be discouraged about how effective he can be in contributing to productive work efforts. Feelings of inferiority can also begin at this point if social barriers, such as those experienced by the poor, limit a child's opportunities to try out challenging work, provide substandard educational opportunities, or lead him to question his abilities.

Thus, for Erikson, the elementary school years are a crucial time for establishing a strong sense of industry. In adolescence, teens work on fashioning an adult identity, which includes developing a sense of direction for their vocational lives. This process continues, as we have seen, well into young adulthood. Identity formation is influenced by the attitudes toward self that evolved in childhood. We can expect that young people who bring to this process a strong sense of industry will find the task of vocational self-development less cumbersome than those who are plagued by self-doubt.

As you know, Erikson theorized that in adulthood the process of self-concept development continues. Individuals with a sense of who they are and what they can do are motivated to use their lives and their skills to leave a legacy for the next generation. Erikson called this a need for generativity and hypothesized that generativity motives have a strong influence on one's work life as adults move into middle age. Concepts akin to what Erikson called "industry" and "generativity" have been the focus of intensive study in several different research traditions. In the following sections, we will take a closer look at some findings on the importance of these two aspects of self-concept for young adults.

The Importance of Industry. Erikson's ideas about one's sense of industry are similar to what Bandura and his colleagues have called **self-efficacy beliefs**, meaning beliefs about our ability to exercise control over events that affect our lives (see Bandura, 1989, for a summary). A positive, optimistic sense of personal efficacy, like a feeling of industry, motivates a person to work hard at a task and to persevere even in the face of obstacles. There is evidence that high levels of achievement usually depend on "an optimistic sense of personal efficacy" (Bandura, 1989, p. 1176; Cervone & Peake, 1986; Taylor & Brown, 1988).

Closely related to Bandura's work on self-efficacy is research by Dweck and her colleagues who have studied **mastery orientation** and the **helpless pattern** in school children and in college-aged adults (see Dweck & Allison, 2008). These are two different orientations to failure. Individuals with a mastery orientation move forward optimistically even when they fail. They assume that they *can* succeed with further effort. They construe failure as a challenge rather than as an obstacle. Individuals with a helpless pattern, however, often begin to denigrate their abilities when they encounter failure and typically stop applying themselves or trying to improve their performance. Dweck emphasizes the importance of our theories of intelligence or ability in influencing how we deal with failure. She has found that mastery-oriented people are likely to be **incremental theorists**, seeing intelligence as a dynamic and malleable quality that can be increased by hard work and instruction. People who show a helpless pattern are more often **entity theorists**, who see intelligence or ability as a fixed, concrete thing: "You can only have a certain amount of it, so you'd better show that it's enough and you'd better hide it if it isn't" (Dweck, 1999, p. 20).

When individuals with different orientations to failure move out of work environments where they have been successful into more challenging situations where they encounter more experiences of failure, they show different degrees of progress and different emotional reactions. Mastery-oriented people dig in and try harder and by that very effort make success more likely in the future. Helpless people tend to turn away from the new challenges. They seek tasks where they feel more certain they can succeed, settle for mediocre performance, or give up altogether. They also tend to feel more stress and shame when they find the new work they are faced with difficult. This pattern has been observed in children moving out of elementary school, where teachers often protect children from failure, into the more impersonal and competitive environment of a junior high school (e.g., Blackwell, Trzesniewski, & Dweck, 2007; Sorich & Dweck, 1996). It has also been found with young adults as they move through challenging college programs (Grant & Dweck, 2003; Robins & Pals, 1998). In both kinds of transitions, individuals with entity theories of ability performed less well than those with incremental theories, and they found their experiences in the new situations more emotionally distressing. This was true despite the fact that both groups entered the new environments with equally good credentials.

Findings like these might have particular significance for the patterns of career development observed among women and minorities. Gender differences in the choice of a career in male-dominated fields have been linked to lower self-efficacy in women, especially women who perceive themselves as highly feminine. Whereas women in general tend to have lower self-efficacy beliefs for "masculine" occupations requiring quantitative or leadership skills, males have about the same sense of efficacy for both masculine and "feminine" career options (Betz & Hackett, 1981; Betz & Schifano, 2000).

A closely related factor affecting self-efficacy for women and other minority group members is **stereotype threat**, the fear that a stereotype might be true or that one will be judged by that stereotype (see Schmader, 2010). When people are reminded of stereotypes that pertain to their own category (e.g., women, Blacks), they often show increased stress and reduced performance. For example, when researchers showed an engineering conference video to male and female math, science, and engineering students, females reacted differently depending on the gender stereotype cues in the video (Murphy, Steele, & Gross, 2007). Specifically, in a version of the video with no stereotype cue, equal proportions of men and women were depicted as attending the conference. In another version of the video, many more men were depicted than women, cuing the stereotype that engineering is a masculine profession. Men appeared to pay no attention to the cues, but women who watched the more stereotypical video were more physiologically reactive (e.g., their heart rates increased) and they reported both a lower sense of belonging and less willingness to attend the conference. In another study of gender stereotype threat, Krendl, Richeson, Kelley, and Heatherton (2008) used functional brain imaging techniques to demonstrate that creating a threat by calling attention to a gender stereotype literally changed how women's brains functioned as they solved math problems. College students were asked to solve math problems both before and after the researchers reminded them that "research has shown gender differences in math ability." Men's functioning was unaffected by the stereotype induction.

For women, performance on the math problems declined somewhat, and the parts of the cortex that they recruited to solve problems were different before and after the threat induction. Beforehand, they used neural networks that are typically associated with math learning, but afterward they showed more activation of neural regions associated with social and emotional processing. Such studies show us that when environmental cues trigger "entity" style thinking, people's performance tends to suffer (see Cimpian, Mu, & Erickson, 2012).

Why does stereotype threat impact performance? One important reason is that working memory space that should be available for learning or problem solving is partially taken up with concerns about being judged negatively. People under threat use up precious working memory space with worry about making mistakes, feeling too anxious, looking stupid to others, and so on. The following study illustrates that people are often paying close attention to their own anxiety when they are experiencing stereotype threat. In one condition, female participants were given a threat-cue: they were told that females' reaction times are slower than males' (Johns, Inzlicht, & Schmader, 2008). They then performed the task of identifying the position of a dot on a screen as quickly as possible. If the dot were preceded by an anxiety word in the location where the dot would appear, women who were given the threat-cue actually responded more quickly to the dot than they did if the dot were preceded by a neutral word in the same location. Women who were not given the threat-cue did not show this increased attention to anxiety-related stimuli: They responded with the same speed whether the dot was preceded by an anxiety word or a neutral word. In this particular study, being hypervigilant to anxiety was helpful to performance, but in most situations, it simply uses up memory space that is needed for the task at hand.

As we noted earlier, African American college students are more likely than White students to drop out of college. We also saw that when African American students attend Black colleges, they are more likely to pursue some particularly challenging majors, such as premed, than when they attend predominantly White colleges. Aronson and Fried (1998) posited that African American students are burdened by the stereotype that Blacks are less intelligent than Whites. Being in school with White students may have a tendency to evoke this stereotype and may make some Black students more susceptible to a helpless pattern, interfering with their achievement. In a now classic study, Aronson and Fried provided undergraduates with a training program that they hoped would reduce stereotype threat. The researchers hoped to foster a mastery orientation and thereby help improve achievement. Through film and lecture, citing scientific research, they instructed both Black and White undergraduates at Stanford University on the processes by which intelligence can actually be cultivated and changed. The training emphasized that when people take on new tasks and learn new skills there is neuronal growth so that they literally become smarter. To make sure that students had consolidated the information, participants were required to explain the incremental view of intelligence in letters to elementary school children. By the end of the school year, African American students who had been taught the incremental theory showed significant increases in achievement, reflected in their grade point averages. These students also were enjoying school more and felt more academically oriented than African American students in a control group, who had not been part of the incremental theory training.

There is evidence that many interacting variables in one's development affect the feelings of industry or positive self-efficacy or mastery orientation that people carry into adulthood. Such variables ultimately influence the likelihood of long-term achievement. These variables include parenting styles (e.g., Lamborn et al., 1991), teacher expectations (e.g., Rosenthal, 2003), stimulation and opportunities for personal challenge in one's home environment (e.g., van Doorninck, Caldwell, Wright, & Frankenberg, 1981), security of attachments (e.g., Jacobsen & Hofmann, 1997), and, as we have just seen, gender and cultural stereotypes. Dweck and her colleagues have also demonstrated that parents' and teachers' approaches to children's successes and failures play a role. For example, praising the whole person for success ("You're a smart girl" or "You're a good boy") tends to foster helplessness, apparently because it focuses attention on entity explanations rather than process or incremental explanations of performance. Praising process ("You found a good way to do it") fosters a mastery orientation (e.g., Cimpian, Arce, Markman, & Dweck, 2007; Kamins & Dweck, 1999; Ng, Pomerantz, & Lamb, 2007).

The Importance of Generativity.   How important are generativity needs in career development? As we have seen, Erikson described generativity as most influential in middle adulthood, but some recent work indicates that young adults are also influenced by generativity as they plan and launch their work lives.

Stewart and Vandewater (1998) examined two broad features of **generativity— desire** and **accomplishment**—and found that the desire for generativity is quite strong even in early adulthood and actually declines through middle and late adulthood. Desire was defined as expression of generativity goals, such as caring for future generations ("I'm concerned about the planet"), wanting to produce something of lasting value ("I want to write a major piece of nonfiction"), and being concerned about being needed ("It's nice to discover that my kids still come to me for advice and help"). In two cohorts of women who were studied longitudinally, such desires were strong through early adulthood, peaking in the early 30s and then declining. Generative accomplishment peaked later, in middle adulthood. The authors propose that "healthy early adulthood includes the formulation of generativity goals or desires, while healthy midlife includes the subjective experience of the capacity to be generative as well as the beginning of a sense of satisfaction in generative accomplishment" (p. 94). Stewart and Vandewater's results seem consistent with the finding, noted earlier, that even right after high school, young adults from all walks of life are likely to say that they would like their work to make a meaningful contribution (Hill & Yeung, 1999). We will look again at generativity issues in the next chapter, as we consider the development of adults in midlife.

APPLICATIONS

The search for intimacy in adulthood demonstrates the continuing human need for social connectedness. The deepest aspects of a person's emotional life as an adult are often expressed within the confines of pair-bonds. The importance of these associations is evidenced by the fact that the most common referral problems that counselors encounter are those involving interpersonal relationships (Veroff, Kulka, & Douvan, 1981). As we have seen, early attachment experiences can act as templates for the intimate relationships of adulthood. In particular, they may influence our willingness to rely on others to meet our needs for intimacy and to help us manage stress (approach). They can also affect how trusting we are that others will meet these needs (anxiety). These representations are intimately linked to how we view ourselves. Attachment theory provides a dynamic theoretical framework to explain the simultaneous pulls for intimacy and autonomy that can make interpersonal behaviors seem puzzling and contradictory. As the poet David Whyte puts it, "We are strange, difficult creatures who long for both freedom and belonging at the same time, and often run a mile when the real thing appears" (Whyte, 2001, p. 234).

Attachment in Counseling Contexts

The major theoretical tenets of attachment theory can be applied to individual, marital, and family therapies in some of the following ways.

1. For helpers who assume an attachment perspective, the therapeutic bond is the primary mechanism of change. The therapist functions as the secure base, provides the client with appropriate responsiveness and availability, and offers opportunities to explore models of self and others. Traditional views of therapy have long held that early attachment patterns carry over into therapeutic relationships (transference) and that therapy provides a chance for a corrective experience (Alexander & French, 1946). The way to revise insecure internal models, according to Bowlby (1988), is through the power of another, more secure and more responsive, base.

2. Therapeutic issues that are most applicable to an attachment-based approach include, but are not necessarily limited to, loss, separation, feelings of connectedness to others, and response to stress. Problems in close

interpersonal relationships—particularly pair-bonds—are viewed as recapitulations of early childhood problems. When clients are capable of insight, some connection between childhood patterns and adult attachment relationships might be appropriate. Clients can be helped to understand that their ideas of self and others might not conform to the reality of their present circumstances. In general, this involves helping clients articulate their feelings about current interpersonal encounters or conflicts, explore how they handle such situations, and draw connections between prior experiences in close relationships and present patterns of relating.

3. One central task for the therapist is to make attachment-based interpretations of how the client behaves in relationships. "The qualities Ainsworth called for—sensitivity in perceiving the patient's signals and the capacity to interpret them correctly and react to them appropriately and promptly—are just as necessary in the therapeutic situation and are just as helpful there as they are in the creation of attachment between mother and child" (Brisch, 1999, p. 79).

Remember that attachment is a flexible construct; many different behaviors can signal similar intent. Bowlby noted that when people feel threatened by loss of or separation from the secure base, the attachment system is activated and responds in protest (see Chapter 15). If protest behaviors prove ineffective in restoring connection, despair and detachment may follow. We have seen in earlier chapters what these behaviors look like in children. In adult partners whose attachment systems are activated due to conflict, protest can include crying, pleading, controlling, nagging, or seeking reassurance. Despair behaviors might include detachment, withdrawal from the partner, or anhedonia. These behaviors have been frequently reported in depressed individuals with respect to their partners (Anderson, Beach, & Kaslow, 1999; Coyne, 1976). Interpreting behaviors as expressions of attachment needs shifts the ownership for marital or family problems away from only one member of the system.

A principal task in therapy involves appraising what the verbal or nonverbal behaviors communicate about the felt security or insecurity of partners vis-à-vis each other. Emotionally distressed individuals or couples, viewed from this perspective, may be chronically "on alert," never quite sure that their bids for connection will be read accurately by intimate others, expecting rejection, and prepared to respond to threats of rejection by escalating demands or defensive withdrawal. Their real need for emotional closeness is hard to see when their bids for intimacy are accompanied by irritable, critical, or dismissive acts that are sometimes incorrectly interpreted by their counselors as resistance or regression.

4. Individuals can be helped to understand how their attachment needs are provoked and what their responses to provocation are. Although not an attachment-based therapy per se, Greenberg's (2002) emotion-focused therapy provides a framework for working with the deep emotions

at the heart of human relationships. In this model, the counselor acts as an "emotion coach" who guides clients to greater awareness and acceptance of their true feelings, helps them access their primary feelings, encourages them to listen to healthy feelings, and facilitates the transformation of less healthy ones. This approach can be useful for individuals as well as couples whose emotions are dysregulated or who are trapped in repetitive cycles of unresolved or unexpressed sadness or anger. In a manner that draws on many attachment-related concepts, the therapist provides a safe place in which clients can disclose "soft" attachment-related feelings of vulnerability, fear, loneliness, or grief through use of skills like reflective listening, use of "I" statements, nonblaming, and other structured activities (see Greenberg, 2002). The goal is to help clients use the wisdom of their emotions to achieve greater empathy for themselves and others, to improve emotion regulation skills, and, ultimately, to achieve greater intimacy with others.

5. The therapist has to be mindful of his own level of closeness and distance so as not to activate avoidance or dependency inadvertently (Brisch, 1999). With anxious clients, therapists need to monitor arrangements to avoid starting late, postponing sessions, taking frequent vacations, or other situations that trigger the client's needs for care. These events can be easily interpreted as rejection. For the avoidant client, too much emotional closeness may trigger anxiety as well and prompt premature termination.

6. Attachment behaviors are about exploration as well as connection. Healthy independence, assuming the presence of a secure base, should be a goal of therapy. It might be appropriate, therefore, for therapists to interpret their clients' need for a break in therapy or their desire for some choice in the counseling arrangements as a signal of healthy exploration rather than as indicating rejection of the therapy or therapist.

Attachment Applied to Couples and Families

One example of a therapy that applies attachment theory directly and that shares links with interpersonal therapy (see Chapter 11) is attachment-based family therapy (ABFT; Diamond, 1998; Diamond, Siqueland, & Diamond, 2003), a model typically used for families with adolescent children. According to ABFT, the major components of therapy are (1) alliance building, (2) reattribution, (3) teaching effective parenting, and (4) reattachment. Alliance building involves creating a relationship that provides a safe place for the therapeutic work and a source of ongoing support for family members. The target of alliance building, typically the relationship between therapist and client in individual counseling, is the relationship among family members. The therapist does, however, build personal alliances with parents and their adolescent to ensure a safe haven for expression of emotions and to provide the empathy needed for parents and children to feel heard and understood. "Alliance with the therapist is best understood as a transitional relationship that helps individual family members to uncover or learn about new parts of themselves" (Diamond & Diamond, 2002, p. 51). The task of reattribution involves helping family members conceptualize their conflicts in more positive ways. Questions take an attachment perspective by orienting clients' attention to a family member's need for connection. For example, asking parents "When your child feels so bad that she acts out, what is getting in the way of you being a resource for her?" (Diamond et al., 2003) makes the connection between negative emotion and problematic behavior explicit and evokes parents' motivation to help rather than blame. Effective parenting education may be part of the therapy if appropriate. Finally, the task of reattachment is accomplished by supporting communication and conflict resolution skills. The ultimate goals are to repair attachment relationships, strengthen emotional connections, and support family members' ability to recognize and acknowledge each other's needs for closeness and autonomy.

Caveats

Obviously, helpers should avoid overdiagnosing attachment-related problems because there is such wide individual and cultural variation within the range of normal functioning. Some people's relationships appear distant or enmeshed to observers, but they may be perfectly satisfactory to the couple involved. Clinicians should also resist viewing attachment style as a monolithic, traitlike characteristic that resides within a person. Working models of self and relationship are always shaped in context. Even though there has been a surge of interest in attachment-related issues in adulthood, many more questions remain to be answered by researchers (Colin, 1996). Caution is advised as well in regard to "attachment" therapies that try to rebuild attachments by resorting to high levels of confrontation and restraint to break down defenses. As we have noted in Chapter 4, these therapies, typically used with children, may involve coercive holding or "rebirthing" techniques that can be harmful.

The Counselor's Working Model

If counselors keep these reservations in mind, attachment theory can also help them understand the meaning in their own patterns of interaction, conflict resolution, and stress management. Dozier, Cue, and Barnett (1994) found that the therapists' level of attachment security was related to countertransference processes. In other words, secure therapists were more likely to respond empathically to the dependency needs of their dismissing or avoidant clients. They were able to see the needs hidden beneath a detached or a rejecting exterior, whereas insecure therapists were more likely to be driven away by the negativity. Secure therapists were also better able to manage clients with ambivalent attachment styles. They were less likely to get trapped into "taking care of" these clients by responding to their obvious needs rather than attending to the more important, underlying ones.

Are working models open to revision? Bowlby believed that working models can change in more positive directions, and recent research supports this (see Box 12.1). The question that needs much more empirical support concerns how this is accomplished. Bowlby (1988) viewed good therapy somewhat like good parenting. He theorized that in a relationship with an emotionally

available therapist, a person is able to reflect on the past, lower defenses, engage in perspective taking, know the experience of "felt security," and, together, co-construct a revision of the internal working model. Lopez and Brennan (2000) make a similar point by suggesting that counseling offers clients a context in which to learn ways of minimizing the negative consequences of insecure attachments (hyperactivation or deactivation) and to find ways of coping more effectively. Although more evidence is needed, some data indicate that attempts to improve social self-efficacy and perspective taking can mediate improvements in working model representations (Corcoran & Mallinckrodt, 2000).

If working models can be changed, it is probably a slow process. Revising representational models happens by engaging in a curative, therapeutic attachment that takes time, patience, and dedication. Slade (1999) draws our attention to the limitation of certain kinds of short-term, problem-centered therapies that are not well suited to reworking fundamental models of social and emotional relationships.

The Importance of Work

Finding a place in the world of work is another important challenge at this time of life. Historically, the helping professions has contributed significantly to the theory and practice of career development. A central tenet of this field is that finding a career is more than a simple choice. This task, like so many others, is a process that requires self-understanding and the ability to use self-knowledge to make informed decisions. Kegan (1982) believed that vocational development is a function of people's levels of self-awareness and the kinds of meaning they attribute to themselves as workers. His theoretical ideas have some things in common with Perry's scheme, which was described in Chapter 11.

According to Kegan, adolescent vocational aspirations are heavily influenced by family and peers. From their foreclosed position, adolescents often construe their early career aspirations as the "right" choice. When confronted with confusing or contradictory feedback about their skills or when given opportunities to pursue other career paths, they may cope by becoming even more rigidly entrenched in the pursuit of their original career goals. They mistake the form of the career (such as medical school) with the underlying functions it serves (such as prestige and service). In other words, vocational identity is construed as a position rather than as an aspect of one's self. Individuals at this stage may resist revising a career goal, even when personal experience or feedback from others challenges its suitability. With maturity, individuals can reflect on this dissonance, integrate the contradictions, and reach a new level of self-understanding and acceptance. They can also identify career goals that are a better fit with their underlying dispositions and goals. Counseling can be particularly helpful for those who need guidance in self-exploration and who may need to reconstruct new meanings about career (McAuliffe, 1993).

Building Self-Efficacy

One important component of success in life and work is the set of beliefs a person has about his ability to be successful. Self-efficacy is a construct that is meaningful in many different domains of development, as we have seen. It has rather recently been integrated into a model of career decision making (social cognitive career theory, SCCT; Lent, Brown, & Hackett, 1996) that is based on Bandura's (1977, 1997) self-efficacy theory. In this approach, client beliefs about how successful they will be in certain roles and work settings are given a prominent position in the career decision-making process. Our sense of self-efficacy shapes our best guess about whether some outcome is likely to be successful or not and, thus, influences the level of exploration we are willing to undertake in regard to pursuing that outcome. Self-efficacy level also influences our willingness to sustain effort in achieving desired outcomes and to learn the skills that might be needed for successful accomplishment of some goal. One's sense of self-efficacy is shaped by past experiences with success and failure as well as opportunities to try things out. These opportunities can be constrained by social class, gender, age, race, disability, the quality of educational experience, or family and peer influences.

Helpers can be both tutors and coaches in this process, scaffolding the development of a personal sense of efficacy in regard to many of life's important challenges. Because self-efficacy beliefs influence functioning in a whole host of ways, from making decisions (What major shall I select?) to behavioral performance (Shall I ask this person for a date? Or my boss for a raise?), it is a useful target for clinical intervention. Bussey and Bandura (1999) describe four major ways to instill a strong sense of self-efficacy.

1. Construct and try out graded mastery experiences that are tailored to the individual's level of ability and that maximize the chances of success. To do this effectively, helpers need to listen to clients explain why they try or don't try certain activities and what they think are their roadblocks to success. In relation to career counseling, Betz (2004) suggests asking clients what they would choose to do if they could do "anything," what skills they need to improve their career opportunities, and what they feel is standing in the way of improving their skills. These kinds of questions can reveal something about how clients view their own capabilities and limitations and thus provide a guide for selecting specific corrective experiences.

2. Discuss or provide models who demonstrate success in an area of difficulty for the client. Successful models encourage individuals to believe in their own capacity for success and provide skills and know-how to the motivated observer.

3. A third way to enhance self-efficacy is to apply social persuasion. This might be done by challenging erroneous beliefs about lack of ability, making attributions for failure to lack of effort (incremental) rather than lack of ability (fixed), and providing support as well as realistic, helpful suggestions for improvement.

4. Finally, attempt to reduce coexisting factors that lower self-efficacy, such as stress, depression, or features of the environment, like restricted opportunity structure, whenever possible. By means of these processes, clients revise versions of their expectancies, which can lead to changes in behavior.

"As they (clients) continue to accumulate more and more of such success experiences, processing this information within the therapy session helps them realign their anticipatory thoughts and feelings with an appropriate self-evaluation of the outcome of their response. Eventually, a new behavior pattern, together with a greater sense of self-efficacy, begins to emerge" (Goldfried, 1995, p. 113).

Adjusting to the World of Work

Finding productive work enhances our lives, but choosing a career is only one step in the career development process. People also need to adjust to the demands of the workplace. Hershenson's (1996) contextual model proposes that work adjustment is most likely to occur if the ongoing characteristics of the individual (work values, skills, goals, habits, etc.) mesh with the day-to-day demands of the job (behavioral expectations, skill requirements, available rewards, and opportunities). For example, an organizational position that is highly structured and requires adherence to routine may be unsatisfying to an individual with high needs for autonomy and little motivation to work in a corporate culture. Helping clients consider the person–environment dimensions of a career can promote more successful adjustment.

Of course, not all problems in the workplace are amenable to change. Finding the ideal fit, although a desirable goal, is not always realistic. The workplace is harsh and unsatisfying for many people due to job-related threats to health, lack of job security, lack of control over tasks performed, and pressure to increase productivity with limited time and resources (Tomasik & Silbereisen, 2012). In his description of the state of work in the United States at the beginning of this century, Reich (2000) pointed to several significant changes that have had profound effects on workers: the end of steady, dependable work, the obsolescence of loyalty between employers and employees, the ever-widening inequality of wages, and the shrinking time factor. "In 1999, the average middle-income married couple with children worked a combined 3,918 hours—about seven weeks more *than a decade before*" (pp. 111–112; italics added). Since 2007, the worst global financial crisis since the Great Depression has put many people out of work around the world. Young adults have been the most affected, but people in every age bracket find themselves either unemployed or threatened by the possibility, often needing to reexamine and/or restructure their career goals in order to improve their chances of re-employment (Tomasik & Silbereisen, 2012).

Work stresses, especially periods of unemployment, can have adverse effects on workers and their families, especially on their dependent children (see Paul & Moser, 2009; Wanberg, 2012). In 1996, Jones was already suggesting that helpers help clients consider workplace safety and stability issues when contemplating career choices. In a departure from more traditional ways of viewing career development, he suggested that helpers avoid portraying job success as the primary means of achieving self-esteem. For many people, work may never be particularly meaningful or personally satisfying. The stresses of the contemporary working world should also be factored in when clients come to counseling for other problems, such as problems in relationships or difficulties with children. He also suggested that helpers take an advocacy position on issues related to work, such as government or company policies that support high-quality child care. Given the importance of love and work in adults' lives, understanding and supporting successful adjustment in these two areas is a worthy task for clinicians.

In times of high unemployment, career counselors often find themselves focused on re-employment strategies with their clients. Specific training to boost job search skills (such as locating opportunities and improving interviewing techniques) and helping clients to cultivate resilience and persistence in the face of rejection (an aspect of self-efficacy) are often key features of interventions for the unemployed (Wanberg, 2012).

SUMMARY

1. Freud characterized love and work as the means by which adults strive for happiness. Erikson described intimacy—closeness to another that is marked by trust, openness, and affection—as the goal of young adulthood, and generativity—creating, producing, and contributing to the human community—as the goal of middle adulthood. Recent conceptions of mental health or "wellness" also emphasize both having close relationships and feeling competent and productive as essential ingredients for happiness.

Love

2. Attachment theory provides one framework for conceptualizing adult intimacy. It suggests that early bonds with caregivers could have a bearing on relationship building in adulthood and that intimate adult relationships provide some of the same benefits as infant–adult relationships: a secure base, safe haven, and emotional warmth.

3. Two traditions or lines of inquiry characterize adult attachment research: the nuclear family tradition, exploring how early attachments might affect the quality of caregiving that an adult gives his own children, and the peer/romantic partner tradition, which focuses on the peer attachments of adults.

4. The Adult Attachment Interview (AAI) consists of questions about early memories of relationships with parents. Autonomous (secure) adults provide a coherent, collaborative narrative, acknowledging the importance of attachment-related experiences in their development. Individuals described as earned secure appear to have come to terms with painful backgrounds. They reflect on their past realistically, acknowledging their parents' perspective. Autonomous adults tend to have securely attached children.

5. Dismissing (insecure) adults describe parents positively but provide either no evidence or contradictory evidence. Generally, they downplay the importance of early relationships. Their children tend to form avoidant attachments.

6. Preoccupied (insecure) individuals provide long, incoherent, egocentric monologues. They seem overwhelmed by the interview questions and are often angry, sad, or fearful. They seem preoccupied with parents, who are remembered as intrusive or egocentric. Their children often have anxious-ambivalent attachments.

7. Unresolved individuals produce narratives with notable lapses in logical thinking. Their children have a tendency to show disorganized attachment patterns. Insecure adults are the most likely to be emotionally disturbed.

8. Longitudinal studies find that an individual's infant attachment status (as measured by the strange situation test) predicts his adult AAI attachment status, although intervening events can shift that status from secure to insecure or vice versa.

9. AAI narratives are different from other interview narratives with the same interviewees, suggesting that the AAI specifically reflects a person's state of mind regarding interpersonal representations. This working model of attachments is assumed to be a schema that has evolved with time and experience and that serves as a guide for understanding, predicting, and acting.

10. Adult pair-bonds integrate three basic behavioral systems: caregiving, attachment, and sexual mating. The attachment system involves proximity seeking and separation distress and serves safe haven and secure base functions. Attachment functions gradually transfer from parents to peers and, eventually, to romantic partners. Proximity seeking begins to shift as early as the preschool years. Between 8 and 14 years, peers also provide safe haven. Eventually attachments to romantic partners involve proximity seeking and separation distress, and they also serve safe haven and secure base functions.

11. The measurement procedures and typologies in the peer/romantic relationship tradition have been different from those in the nuclear family tradition. Several typologies have been proposed, and in the most recent work it is suggested that people may be better characterized as differing along two continuous dimensions, one having to do with their degree of anxiety about close relationships and the other with their approach-avoidance tendencies.

12. Partner selection can be predicted to some degree by the attachment characteristics of the partners. Secure individuals tend to pair with secure partners; anxious and avoidant individuals tend to pair up; but anxious-anxious pairs or avoidant-avoidant pairs are uncommon. Whether individuals actually enter relationships with these characteristics or tend to evolve these styles within their relationships has not been determined.

13. Partnerships between secure individuals seem to involve more positive and less negative emotions than other pairings. Male avoidant individuals show less distress during

breakups than other males, but females of all attachment types show similar levels of distress. Ambivalent partners are most stressed by conflict within a relationship.

Work

14. In Holland's theory of career development, people are categorized as having one of six modal personal orientations, part of their personality. Jobs or careers make demands that are compatible with one or more of these orientations. A good fit between modal orientation and job characteristics benefits job satisfaction and feelings of well-being.

15. In Super's theory, the focus is on the development of a vocational self-concept, part of one's total identity. He describes five stages in its development, from the growth stage in early childhood through the decline stage in people of retirement age. Super emphasizes that career development is a continuing, lifelong process. Many career counseling approaches emphasize the important relationship between career and self-development, with self-discovery an important ingredient in career satisfaction.

16. College students' first vocationally relevant decision is choice of a major. Whereas personal characteristics and interests influence the choice, so do cultural changes (e.g., economic shifts) and cohort characteristics. Ethnic and socioeconomic differences appear to influence not only who attends college but also the likelihood of college retention and career choices. Career counseling in college should begin with advisement on choice of a major.

17. For the forgotten half, those who do not attend college, the chances of achieving career goals shared by all young adults (e.g., good pay, opportunities for advancement, opportunities to make a meaningful contribution to society) are substantially reduced. As with college students, factors such as socioeconomic status and ethnicity affect these chances as well.

18. Career opportunities for noncollege young people could be improved if there were more systematic and effective resources for them, such as basic skill training in public schools, extensive vocational counseling, and opportunities for work-based learning. Some well-designed training interventions for high-risk groups have been successful, such as the Job Corps program.

19. Traditionally, women with careers have followed different career paths from men. Substantial changes have occurred, such as women outnumbering men in college. But there are still gender differences: Some careers are still highly gendered, and women are still more likely to consider the impact of career choices on their relationship opportunities, although men are increasingly attending to such concerns as well.

20. Self-concept and self-understanding are central features of many theories of career development. How do basic feelings and attitudes toward the self as a worker develop? Erikson describes a sense of industry, belief in one's ability to work productively and expectation of satisfaction from work, as beginning in middle childhood, when children have their first work experiences. Generativity becomes important in adulthood, as people become motivated to leave a legacy for the next generation.

21. Bandura has studied self-efficacy beliefs, beliefs in one's own ability to affect events, as motivating people to work hard and persevere even in the face of failure. Such beliefs are correlated with high levels of achievement.

22. Mastery orientation is similar to self-efficacy and to a sense of industry. Mastery-oriented individuals move forward even when they fail, apparently because they are incremental theorists, believing that hard work and instruction can affect ability. Conversely, people who show a helplessness pattern, who give up when they fail, tend to be entity theorists, seeing ability as fixed.

23. Differences in self-efficacy beliefs, or mastery orientation, may have significant effects on minority groups and women. Stereotype threat, the fear that an inferiority stereotype might be true, can influence achievement. In some research, stereotype threat has been reduced and achievement improved when individuals have received intensive training on the scientific evidence for the malleability of intelligence and ability.

CASE STUDY

Tayib, who is 29 years old, works as a paralegal in a public defender's office. His parents came to the United States from India before he was born. Tayib's extended family in India are highly educated people, and his parents encouraged him to get a good education as well. Although he considered going to law school, Tayib never felt confident enough to pursue this goal. In his current place of employment, many coworkers rely on his conscientiousness. He feels that others, including his superiors, often take advantage of him by giving him the most difficult cases to sort out and the shortest deadlines for getting them done. He was recently passed over for a promotion by his boss, who decided to fill the higher level post by hiring someone from outside the department. He feels unsatisfied in his position, but he thinks that his chances for advancement may be best if he remains in civil service. His parents encourage him to find a position with more prestige and a better income.

Tayib has been dating Rachael, a 27-year-old White woman with a young son, for the past 6 months. Rachael works as a public relations executive in one of the corporate offices in the city. Rachael and her son, Luke, share an apartment with one of Rachael's girlfriends. This has been her living arrangement since the breakup of her relationship with Luke's father,

Kevin, 3 years ago. The couple were never married, a factor that led to strained relationships with her own mother and father.

Tayib and Rachael are both interested in finding someone with whom they can have a serious relationship. Lately, however, their relationship has not been going as smoothly as it did in the beginning. As Luke's 4th birthday approached, Rachael wanted to plan a celebration for him. Tayib had already taken Luke and Rachael to an amusement park as a birthday present for the youngster. Rachael decided to have a special birthday dinner for Luke and invited her parents and Tayib. Tayib, in the midst of an important project at work, declined the invitation.

Rachael feels totally rejected by his refusal to attend the dinner. She cannot understand why she and Luke mean so little to Tayib. She believes that she does everything she possibly can in order to keep Tayib interested in her. She prepares meals for him, works on her appearance, listens to him talk about problems at work, calls him to let him know she cares about

him, and tries to accommodate her schedule to his. She wonders now if she will ever find someone who wants to make a commitment to her. Tayib can't understand why Rachael is so upset about the dinner. Since she is a working woman with a child to support, he feels that she should understand how important it is to have and keep a job. Tayib begins to wonder if she really understands what is important to him. Although the two do not discuss this incident directly, they both feel tension growing in the relationship.

Discussion Questions

1. What are the issues involved in this case?
2. From an attachment perspective, what inferences can you draw about the relationship styles of Tayib and Rachael?
3. What are the challenges each person faces at this point in his or her development? How would you help them cope with these challenges?

PRACTICE USING WHAT YOU HAVE LEARNED

In the Pearson etext, apply these ideas to working with others.

Case Study

Latisha: HIV Positive and Looking for Work

Latisha is a 35-year-old black female who has been HIV positive for five years. She comes into the career center at the local community college looking for some advice on careers. Latisha is referred to you, a career counselor at the center. Latisha states she contracted HIV from a boyfriend who was shooting drugs with a needle. Initially, Latisha was very ill with HIV, and she thought her life was all but over. She lost interest in doing things for herself. She moved into her mother's house and waited to die; however, with the encouragement of her mother and doctors, and with antiretroviral drug therapy, she has stabilized and is feeling well enough to pursue something for herself. Currently, Latisha states that she is not symptomatic. Therefore, she has enrolled in a local community college, but she is unsure which major to choose because she is not sure what her long-term limitations might be. You arrange a time to meet with Latisha and discuss her concerns, interests, and options.

Applying Concepts

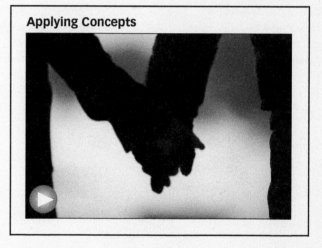

JOURNAL QUESTIONS

1. Write a brief relationship autobiography describing how you behaved, thought, and felt about one significant relationship. How would you describe your own attachment style?
2. Describe how you solve conflicts in your closest relationship. How do you deal with stress in this relationship? Explain how these patterns relate to what you experienced in your family of origin.
3. How has your own career history changed since you held your first job? What were the influences (both internal and external) on your career trajectory? How would you evaluate your sense of self-efficacy regarding your career?

KEY CONCEPTS

intimacy (p. 438)
generativity (p. 438)
nuclear family tradition (p. 440)
peer/romantic partner tradition (p. 440)
autonomous (p. 441)
earned secure (p. 441)
dismissing (p. 441)
preoccupied (p. 442)
unresolved (p. 442)
cannot classify (p. 443)
passion (p. 444)
commitment (p. 444)
secure (p. 447)

avoidant (p. 448)
fearful (p. 448)
modal personal orientation (p. 453)
job crafting (p. 453)
vocational self-concept (p. 455)
growth stage (p. 455)
exploratory stage (p. 455)
crystallization (p. 455)
specification (p. 455)
implementation (p. 455)
establishment stage (p. 455)
stabilization (p. 455)
maintenance stage (p. 455)

consolidation (p. 455)
decline stage (p. 455)
retention (p. 458)
forgotten half (p. 460)
industry (p. 466)
self-efficacy beliefs (p. 466)
mastery orientation (p. 466)
helpless pattern (p. 466)
incremental theorists (p. 467)
entity theorists (p. 467)
stereotype threat (p. 467)
generativity desire (p. 469)
generativity accomplishment (p. 469)

13

Middle Adulthood: Cognitive, Personality, and Social Development

What is the nature of development at midlife? This is a perplexing question because adult lives are complex and multifaceted. Adults seek out jobs, select them, and sometimes ascend to positions of responsibility in their fields of work. Adults also change employment voluntarily to work in other settings or in other careers. Some adults lose their jobs and may experience unemployment or underemployment. Some work at multiple jobs. Adults take on leadership, executive, or mentoring roles in their communities. Adults move from one location to another, historically now more than ever before. They marry, cohabitate, divorce, date, and often go on to marry again. Some adults have children and grandchildren; others are childless. Adults may have responsibilities for the care of their own aging parents. Those who are parents or stepparents have to deal with the ever-changing developmental needs of their children. Adults are also affected by the close relationships they share with partners or friends. They may experience financial difficulties. They may sustain illness themselves or experience the illness or loss of loved ones. Some adults experience catastrophic events, such as wars, accidents, or natural disasters. Many more deal with chronic adversities such as discrimination of one sort or another, mental problems such as depression, or simply the gradual physical changes involved in the aging process. Moreover, many of these events occur simultaneously.

The complexity of people's experience and functioning is what is most striking about middle adulthood. How are we to make sense of all the variables operating in adult lives? Is there some coherent scheme that helpers can use to understand development in the adult years? In Chapter 1, we examined some of the many theoretical approaches that explain developmental processes, including stage models, such as Erikson's or Piaget's, and incremental models, such as learning and information processing accounts. As we have seen throughout this book, these approaches to development can be quite helpful in understanding some aspects of psychological functioning, but modern theorists typically turn to multidimensional models, which are focused on the complexity of interrelated causal processes in development. Recall in Bronfenbrenner's multidimensional model, for example, the description of proximal processes in development—reciprocal interactions between an "active, evolving biopsychological human organism and the persons, objects, and symbols in its immediate environment" (Bronfenbrenner & Morris, 1998, p. 996). These proximal processes are modified by more distal processes, some within the organism, such as genes, and some outside the organism, such as the family, the workplace, the community, the broader economic and political context, and other aspects of the culture.

As we saw in Chapter 1, multidimensional theories of adult development, called **life span developmental theories or models**, address all the fundamental questions of development, including the role of heredity and environment in adulthood and the extent to which adult characteristics are continuous with previous traits and propensities versus how much genuine change there is in adult behavior. Life span developmental models (e.g., Baltes, Lindenberger, & Staudinger, 2006) make one fundamental assumption in addressing such questions—that from birth to death, adaptation continues. The development of psychological functioning does not end or become fixed when adulthood is reached but goes on until death. The reciprocal interaction of many biological and environmental factors forms an ever-changing "architecture" or scaffolding that supports the development of behavioral and mental functioning (e.g., Baltes et al., 2006). Thus, middle adulthood is not some kind of holding pattern before the slide into death. An adult's cognitive and socioemotional functioning continues to evolve through her 30s, 40s, 50s, and beyond.

LIFE SPAN DEVELOPMENTAL THEORY

Historically, developmental study in North America focused on children and adolescents. With some rare exceptions, such as Erikson's stage theory, adulthood was given short shrift in most theory and research. Yet in some parts of Europe, such as Germany and Belgium, interest in development over the whole life span was the scientific norm. Baltes et al. (2006) speculate that when developmental psychology became a specialty in the United States around 1900, the strong influence of Darwinian theories, which describe growth as a process of maturation, may have helped establish childhood as the primary focus of attention. In contrast, in German-speaking countries, important essays on development began to emerge in the 18th and 19th centuries, before there was much biological science. Early developmental writings were rooted more in philosophy and the humanities, with a special emphasis on concerns about how to optimize human functioning. Thus, there was no special impetus to limit the discussion of development to descriptions of the childhood period.

Around the middle of the 20th century, some American developmentalists began to shift their attention from the growth that characterizes childhood to the declines of aging, and developmental psychology was soon represented by two somewhat independent groups, the child developmentalists and the gerontologists. Even today, textbooks often reflect this disjunction. Chapters on middle adulthood discuss career motivation, stress, marriage, family roles, sexuality, and leisure time, which are all important issues for adults. But there is often a notable absence of an overarching framework for understanding how middle adult life is linked to the childhood years, on one hand, and to old age, on the other.

Life span developmental theory provides such an organizational framework. It can be construed as a kind of macrotheory under whose umbrella all the processes of **ontogeny**, or the development of organisms, fall into place. This orientation offers a clear benefit to those in the helping professions. First, it provides a way of organizing developmental processes across the life cycle. Think of the multiplicity of challenges and possibilities in adult life, some of which we mentioned at the beginning of this chapter. Rather than viewing them as disconnected parts of a life story, helpers can interpret the choices people make and the ways they adapt as reflecting some degree of lawful continuity. Second, life span developmental theory emphasizes the importance of learning about successful or effective development. Thus, this perspective fits well with therapeutic or psychoeducational goals. Let's now consider some of the elements of life span developmental theory.

Gains and Losses in Development: The Changing Architecture of Biology and Culture

Natural selection through many generations has created a biological trajectory that tends to optimize development in most typical environments, allowing most individuals to grow up and become fully functioning adults who can contribute to the success of the species by reproducing. Of course, basic cultural supports—adequate parenting, nutrition, education, protection from environmental hazards, and so on—are fundamental for the success of this process as well. As individuals move through adulthood, the biological supports for life weaken because the reproductive process is complete, and the selection pressure that the need for reproductive success creates for a species is no longer operative. Thus, biological dysfunctions are more likely. "Evolution and biology are not good friends of old age" (Baltes, 1997, p. 368). During middle adulthood (defined here as ages 30 to 55), people begin to depend more and more on cultural supports for adequate functioning. Indeed, "old age" exists primarily because of modern culture. Advances in economics, nutrition, general knowledge, technology, and medicine have compensated for the weakening of the biological supports for life. As a result, from 1900 to 1995, the average life span increased in Western societies from about 45 years to around 75 years! For the U.S. population, life expectancy at birth increased to 76 (males) and 78 (females) by 2008. Some racial disparities continue to exist, for example between Whites and African-Americans, but the gap has narrowed for the first time in many years (Harper, Rushani, & Kaufman, 2012). Hispanic males (78) and females (83) showed the longest life expectancies compared to other groups (National Center for Health Statistics, 2012).

Viewing development as a life span process makes clear that development or change in functioning with age involves both gains and losses for the individual. Gains are most obvious early in life, losses are more obvious later. But once we are sensitized to the fact that development involves both, we begin to notice that gains and losses characterize change throughout life. Thus, children, not just adults, experience some losses in the normal course of development. One familiar illustration is characteristic of language development. As an infant, you were capable of hearing and producing all of the kinds of sound distinctions that are used across all human languages. But as you learned your native language, you became less adept at discriminating and producing sounds that were not part of that language. If you were introduced to a second language after the preschool years, you probably had trouble producing sounds that were not part of your native tongue, and so you probably speak the second language with a "foreign accent." Another example, suggested by Baltes (1997), is that as adolescents strive for personal autonomy, their relationships with their parents are often strained, as we have seen. The intimacy of the parent–child relationship is diminished for both partners as the adolescent struggles to achieve an adult identity.

Of course, loss is more obvious to us in adulthood as biological declines occur. We saw in Chapter 11, for example, that our biological systems, like our sensory

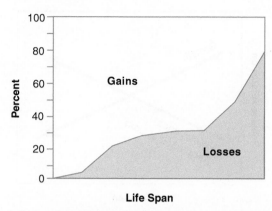

FIGURE 13.1 **The shifting relationship between gains and losses across the life span.**
SOURCE: Baltes, P. B. (1997). On the incomplete architecture of human ontology: Selection, optimization, and compensation as foundation of developmental theory. *American Psychologist, 52,* 366–380. Reprinted with permission from the American Psychological Association.

abilities and our immune functions, all reach peak potential between ages 18 and 30. Many of these systems begin to decline soon after (see below). But the increase in losses through adulthood should not mask the fact that the gains also continue. For example, in Chapter 11 we discussed the gains in postformal thinking that seem to characterize some people as they move into middle adulthood. Other examples of gains will become clear throughout this chapter. However, the relative balance of gains and losses clearly shifts across the life span, until eventually losses outstrip gains for most people in old age (see Figure 13.1).

Development as Growth, Maintenance, and Regulation of Loss

Life span developmental theory defines development as a process of adapting to the constant flux of influences in our lives (see Baltes, 1997; Baltes et al., 2006). One kind of adaptation is **growth**. We grow when we add new characteristics, understandings, skills, and so on to our behavioral repertoire. So, for example, an adult might grow by becoming more expert at some task at work, or she might acquire a more balanced and thus empathic perspective on her relationship with her parents. Another kind of adaptive functioning is **maintenance** or **resilience**, finding ways to continue functioning at the same level in the face of challenges or restoring our functioning after suffering some loss. For example, an adult might maintain the concept of herself as a poet despite repeated rejections of her work by persistently revising and resubmitting her work until eventually a piece is published. Or despite the death of a partner, she might eventually reestablish intimacy in her life by returning to social circulation and finding a new partner. A third kind of adaptation is **regulation of loss**. Like maintenance, this form of adaptation involves reorganizing the way we behave. But unlike maintenance, regulation of loss involves adjusting our expectations and accepting a lower level of functioning. Suppose that a woman who prides herself on her ability to remember names, faces, and telephone numbers suffers a reduction in learning ability as she ages. She adapts by using strategies that include writing down essential information that she previously would have recalled. She accepts that she will never have the breadth of information available to her that she had before, but by using her new strategies she ensures that she will remember what is really necessary.

According to life span developmental theory, all three adaptive processes—growth, maintenance, and regulation of loss—are part of development from infancy through old age. What changes is the relative probability of each. Growth is much more characteristic of children than it is of the elderly, and regulation of loss is much

 This 50-year-old man describes his transition into middle age. As you watch, think about how his experience shows the three adaptive processes—growth, maintenance, and regulation of loss.

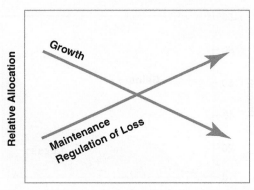

FIGURE 13.2 **The relative increase in maintenance and regulation of loss and the relative decrease in growth as adaptive processes across the life span.**
SOURCE: Baltes, P. B. (1997). On the incomplete architecture of human ontology: Selection, optimization, and compensation as foundation of developmental theory. *American Psychologist, 52,* 366–380. Reprinted with permission from the American Psychological Association.

more characteristic of the elderly (see Figure 13.2). The middle adult years appear to be a time when the balance is shifting among the three adaptive processes. All three processes occur across the life span. Children experience the need to compensate for loss through maintenance or regulation, and adults of all ages experience growth. However, knowing the relative proportions of each, given a client's stage of life, may provide professionals with a frame for understanding presenting problems. We will have more to say about how these processes affect coping with stress in Chapter 14.

Defining Successful Development at Any Age

As adulthood proceeds, the more physical and psychological resources an individual has will affect the likelihood that individual will be able to adapt well. Consider the nature of developmental success at different times in the life of Emma, now a 91-year-old woman. Emma never married or had children, which she experienced as a loss. In her young adulthood, she compensated for her childlessness by dedicating her considerable talents to teaching poor urban children in public schools. In middle adulthood, she became an administrator, developing innovative programs for young children and mentoring teachers in the public school system. In her early old age, the physical demands of a daily work schedule became too great, so she retired. This change diminished her power to influence the lives of young children in the public schools. But she managed the loss, maintaining her view of herself as a child advocate, by serving on the governing boards of nonprofit organizations that provide services for children. Now, Emma suffers from a number of biological losses—near blindness, breathing problems, and general frailty—and she has confined her living space to her small apartment. A good deal of her functioning involves regulating her biological losses by living a quiet, sedentary life in her small space and depending on some outside help, which she has the means to pay for as a result of careful financial planning. But she also continues to grow: She has learned to use a computer, and she has begun to write for her own enjoyment. She also maintains her contacts with friends through e-mail, phone calls, and visits.

Growth, maintenance, and regulation of loss are part of human adaptation, but their relative proportions change at different points of the life cycle.

At each stage of her life, Emma found ways to manage losses through maintenance or regulation and to continue to grow. The balance of losses and gains in her life has now clearly shifted so that much of her adaptive energy is dedicated to managing losses. With the help of technological supports, such as the computer, Emma has minimized the overwhelming losses of her late life and has continued to maximize her gains, to the extent possible. She provides an example of successful development even in old age.

Our description of successful development will sound familiar to most helpers because it is clearly continuous with what we think of as healthy coping. The life span developmental view helps us see that healthy coping evolves and changes throughout life. What is adaptive coping at one stage of life may be less adaptive at another. In the following sections, we will consider some relatively stable influences on adult life as well as the sources of change. As we look at these influences, we will begin to identify what resources the mature individual brings to the task of development and which of these resources might most effectively contribute to success. In Chapters 14 and 15, we examine additional aspects of the adaptive developmental process that characterizes adult life.

INFLUENCES ON ADULT DEVELOPMENT: SOURCES OF STABILITY

A popular series of films produced by the British Broadcasting Company (BBC) documented the lives of several men and women at 7-year intervals, from the time they were 7 years old to age 56. The series set out to investigate the truth of the proverb: *Give me a child until he is 7, and I'll show you the man.* The eight documentaries clearly depict many changes that occur over the intervening 49 years. Yet they also illuminate the thread of stability that runs through these individual lives. For example, Nick, who at age 7 expressed the desire "to find out all about the moon," became a professor of science in adulthood. Sue, who was a vibrant, independent youngster, is now a fun-loving, independent woman. What kind of continuity is typical of people in general? What are the sources of relative stability in development from childhood through adulthood?

Longitudinal studies have found substantial stability in personality characteristics across the life span (e.g., Allemand, Zimprich, & Masten, 2008; Terraciano, Costa, & McCrae, 2006; Terraciano, McCrae, & Costa, 2006; Shiner, Masten, & Roberts, 2003; see Roberts, Walton, & Viechtbauer, 2006, for a meta-analysis; see McAdams & Olson, 2010, for a review). In much of this research, personality is construed as a set of traits that may be likened to the temperament characteristics of infants (see Chapter 4). Perhaps the most influential—and well supported—trait theory of personality has been developed by McCrae and Costa (e.g., 2008) who specifically assume that traits are biologically based, inherent tendencies that persistently influence thoughts, feelings, and behavior throughout life.

What are these traits that appear to be so stable? In the 1980s, researchers recognized that the thousand of words used to describe aspects of human personality (called trait adjectives) could be reliably boiled down to five, yielding the "Five Factor Model" of personality (see McCrae & Costa, 2008). The **Five Factor Model (Big 5)**, as they are called, represent the most basic dimensions of personality: **neuroticism** (N), **extraversion** (E), **openness** (O), **agreeableness** (A), and **conscientiousness** (C). Table 13.1 provides additional detail on these dimensions, describing some of the qualities of individuals at the "high" end of each dimension. Cross-sectional studies of personality traits as measured by questionnaires find evidence of striking similarity across adult cohorts in the degree to which they are characterized by each of these traits, even when different instruments are used. There are some shifts in these traits with age that characterize people in general, and these may be linked to maturation

TABLE 13.1 The Big 5 Personality Traits

TRAIT	CHARACTERISTICS
Neuroticism	Tense, touchy, self-pitying, unstable mood, anxious, self-conscious
Extraversion	Outgoing, active, assertive, energetic, talkative, enthusiastic
Agreeableness	Warm, sympathetic, generous, forgiving, kind, affectionate, compliant
Conscientiousness	Organized, planful, reliable, responsible, careful, efficient, self-controlled
Openness to experience	Creative, artistic, curious, insightful, original, wide-ranging interests, positive orientation to learning

SOURCE: Based on McCrae, R. R., & John, O. T. (1992). An introduction to the five-factor model and its applications. *Journal of Personality, 60,* 175–215. Reprinted with permission from the American Psychological Association.

or to age-typical experiences. Conscientiousness and agreeableness tend to increase somewhat throughout early and middle adulthood, whereas neuroticism, openness, and extraversion tend to decline somewhat (see Allemand, Zimprich, & Hendriks, 2008). And, there is some change in these traits within individuals over time—for example, some individuals may become more or less extroverted as they grow older (e.g., Roberts & Mroczek, 2008). Relatively speaking, however, despite the potential for change, longitudinal evidence supports the notion that personality traits are largely stable after age 30 (see McAdams & Olson, 2010; McCrae & Costa, 2008).

Personality traits in adults and the typical age changes in these traits are quite similar across many cultures (see McCrae & Costa, 2008). In an impressive cross-sectional study of adults in five different cultures, McCrae et al. (1999) found highly consistent trends among German, Italian, Portuguese, Croatian, and Korean groups. Despite their differing historical experiences and cultural contexts, older individuals across cultures were slightly higher in agreeableness and conscientiousness and somewhat lower in extraversion and openness to experience than younger adults. The authors suggest that these trends are universal and maturity-dependent. In other words, "persons grow and change, but they do so on the foundation of enduring dispositions" (Costa & McCrae, 1994, p. 36).

The Link to Temperament

Where do these adult traits come from? Some researchers have looked for links between childhood temperament characteristics and adult personality dispositions because both are construed to have some basis in biology. Rothbart and her colleagues (Rothbart, Ahadi, & Evans, 2000) call adult personality an outcome of temperament because it arises from constitutionally based differences in systems such as reactivity (excitability, responsivity) and self-regulation (modulation of activity). A growing literature in the field of developmental psychobiology provides evidence for brain-mediated systems of positive approach, fear, irritability or anger, effortful control, and reactive orienting (Rothbart, Derryberry, & Posner, 1994; Stifter, Dollar, & Cipriano, 2010). As children develop and experience age-related changes, their temperamental characteristics become increasingly more differentiated and integrated into more mature self-systems. So, for example, early manifestations of positive approach, such as smiling and laughing, may be translated into more mature forms, such as social extraversion. When Rothbart and her associates (2000) correlated young adults' temperaments with their Big 5 personality traits, they found evidence for relationships between extraversion and positive approach, between effortful attention and conscientiousness, between irritability or anger and neuroticism, and between orienting sensitivity and openness to experience. Additional cross-cultural support is provided by McCrae and his colleagues (2000) who found modest correlations between the temperamental characteristics of German, British, Turkish, Czech, and Spanish samples with their adult personality traits.

But what if we looked at individual development over time? Would early temperamental patterns reliably predict adult personality? Caspi (2000; Slutske, Moffitt, Poulton, & Caspi, 2012) investigated the continuity of temperament in a cohort of New Zealanders from age 3 to age 32. The sample for this study consisted of all children born in Dunedin, New Zealand, between April 1972 and March 1973. Temperamental characteristics were assessed at various points by means of parent report, clinical examiner ratings, and self-report. Data on home environment, school, employment, and social history were also gathered. The assessment measures reflected the typologies, developed by Chess and Thomas, that were available in 1972 (see Chess & Thomas, 1987): undercontrolled or difficult (impulsive, restless, negative), inhibited or slow-to-warm-up (introverted, fearful), and well-adjusted or easy (see Chapter 4).

Results paint a picture of moderate personality stability over time. At age 21 and again at age 32, the 10% of children identified at age 3 as undercontrolled were more likely than other groups to be aggressive, sensation-seeking, impulsive, prone to gambling and troubles with the law. They also tended to experience higher levels of interpersonal conflict in family and romantic relationships. Even if the surface features of behavior changed over time, these undercontrolled children were more likely to grow up to be adults whose behavior reflected a similar lack of control and problematic adjustment. The inhibited children (8% of the sample) at 21 were more likely than the other participants to have suffered from depression. As adults, they were more shy, fearful, and nonassertive and less connected to sources of social support.

Several possible explanations might account for trait stability over time. First, genes probably play a role in stability of personality. McCue, Bacon, and Lykken (1993) found that of the roughly 50% consistency in twins' personality traits measured over 10 years, about 80% of that similarity could be attributed to genetics. Remember, however, that we do not inherit trait patterns per se. As multidimensional models of development predict, personality features are also shaped by both biological and socio-contextual circumstances. The transactional interplay between individual and context is what sculpts personality.

Viewed from this perspective, personality or trait consistency will be highest if other variables, in addition to biology, provide support or scaffolding for that consistency. For example, the individual's environment should remain consistent. A classic study by Helson and Roberts's (1994) is illustrative here. Eighty-one women from Mills College were followed from ages 21 to 52. Those women whose level of ego development showed no change or whose level of ego development even slightly decreased over the years of the study were the least likely to have experienced disruptive experiences or high levels of responsibility. They seemed to have found comfortable niches for themselves that required little accommodation or change. Personality could remain fairly consistent over time, because these women appeared to have selected environments that suited their personalities in the first place. Or they may have behaved in ways that communicated their reluctance to change, thus eliciting compliance from others.

Yet another possible explanation for continuity is that certain kinds of personality styles show more consistency than others. Clausen (1993), for example, suggested that planful competence, a trait found in people who are highly dependable and self-reliant, tends to be consistent across adulthood. Similarly, Hampson (2008) reports that high levels of conscientiousness in childhood tend to predict well-being in adulthood, and she speculates that conscientious individuals may ". . . gravitate to niches that are compatible with their attributes, including relatively safe environments for work and leisure. . . and are likely to evoke positive reactions in other people, which will serve over time to sustain these traits and related behaviors" (p. 265). These conclusions have been supported in more current research as well (Burt & Paysnick, 2012). Generally, people who possess resilient characteristics tend to be more stable and consistent throughout life. Perhaps any strong, "achieved" identity operates as a cognitive schema or organizer that interprets information and situations in ways that promote consistency with one's personality or reputation (Vandewater, Ostrove, & Stewart, 1997; see McAdam & Olson, 2010).

INFLUENCES ON ADULT DEVELOPMENT: SOURCES OF CHANGE

Although personality characteristics can be a relatively stable set of influences on the adult's development, there are many changes to which an adult must adapt. Some changes may be strongly age determined or *age graded*, such as physical changes that come more or less inevitably with time. Some changes are more a function of historical circumstance and are called *history-graded changes*. These include events that we share with our whole cohort, like living through the Great Depression or the Iraq War. Some circumstances that affect people's lives can be unique to cultural groups. Finally, there are changes that apply specifically to our own lives. These are *nonnormative changes*, often accidents of fate, like being in a train wreck or winning the lottery.

Age-Graded Changes

We will consider three kinds of age-graded changes. The first two are the physical and cognitive changes that have been documented as a function of aging in adulthood. The last concerns shifts in the relative importance of various life tasks that seem to occur with age. These shifts in life tasks, described by theorists such as Erik Erikson and Daniel Levinson, are generally thought to be a product of one's psychological response to reaching adulthood and facing the typical burdens and challenges that life presents to all of us. All three kinds of change represent challenges to our adaptive functioning as we get older.

Physical Changes in Adulthood

Bodily changes may be the most obvious ones in adult life. By about age 30, as people enter middle adulthood, there begins a shift from **adolescing**, or growing up, to **senescing**, or "growing down" (Levinson, 1986). Although there are physical declines that most people are aware of fairly early in this process, such as some skin wrinkling or hair loss, most declines are much more subtle, such as a decrease in the effectiveness of immune processes or in cardiovascular functioning. For the most part, people continue to feel that they are at peak or near peak levels of physical functioning until they are 40 or older. In their 40s and 50s, most people become more aware of physical losses. In the United States, the majority of middle adults enjoy good health, but this period is one in which many individuals, especially those in lower socioeconomic groups, begin to deal with chronic illnesses and other health problems that can limit their activities. In the 40s, 7% of adults have some kind of disability; by the early 60s, 30% do (Lachman, 2004).

Most sensory systems decline in sensitivity or acuity, although there is considerable variation among the systems and among individuals. The aging of the visual and auditory systems is probably best understood (e.g., Li-Korotky, 2012; Owsley, 2011). Visual acuity declines with age but is maintained at near peak levels until about age 40 and then noticeably wanes. Individuals who never before wore glasses or contact lenses are likely to need them now, and those who required some visual correction in the past begin to experience more frequent prescription changes, or they now need bifocals or trifocals. Middle adults also begin to notice that they need more light to see well than their younger friends, and they may begin to notice that it takes longer to adapt to lighting changes than it used to. They are most likely to be bothered when there is a sudden change in lighting: coming out of a dark movie theater into daylight or encountering the headlights of an oncoming car on a dark road. Changes in the neurons of the retina, as well as changes in the cornea and lens of the eye, all contribute to these growing problems.

Similar declines in hearing or auditory sensitivity begin in the 30s. Sensitivity to high-frequency (high-pitched) sounds declines earlier and more rapidly, and the losses are usually greater in men than in women. Note that women's voices are therefore more difficult to hear in the later years than are men's, so that men are more likely to have difficulty hearing women than vice versa. There is much individual variation in the degree and kind of hearing loss, but most individuals find their lives somewhat affected by the end of middle age (Frisina, 2009; Murphy, Daneman, & Schneider, 2006).

Among the functional systems that show developmental changes sometime in middle adulthood is the reproductive system. As with the sensory systems, noticeable changes tend to begin in the 40s and 50s. The menstrual cycle usually begins to shorten and becomes somewhat more erratic by the time a woman is in her late 30s. The female **climacteric**, the gradual reduction of reproductive ability, ending in **menopause**, the cessation of menstruation, usually begins in the 40s and continues for at least 10 years (Berecki-Gisolf, Begum, & Dobson, 2009; Foxcroft, 2009). The climacteric is largely a function of a reduction in circulating **estradiol**, a form of the primary female hormone, and **estrogen**, produced by the ovaries. Having less estradiol eventually influences many other changes: the thinning and coarsening of pubic hair, the thinning and wrinkling of the labia, and changes in vaginal chemistry that can cause dryness and a greater likelihood of vaginal infections. Women commonly experience other physical symptoms as well, such as fatigue, headaches, insomnia, nightsweats, and hot flashes—sudden sensations of intense heat along with sweating that can last for as long as a half an hour. One reason for such symptoms is that lowered estrogen triggers the release of other hormones and these have widespread effects on the body, such as altering its temperature control mechanisms. Despite these changes, and despite a general slowing of sexual response times, sexual functioning and sexual pleasure seem to be affected very little for most women (Avis, Stellato, Crawford, Johannes, & Longcope, 2000). Many researchers have found only small declines, if any, in the frequency of female sexual activity in middle age (see Table 13.2). Women report less sexual activity than men at every age. A key ingredient for maintaining an active sex life is having a sexual partner, and women are more likely than men to be without a partner (Karraker, DeLamater, & Schwartz, 2011). They are more likely to be widowed than men, and they are less likely to re-partner after either the death of a spouse or a divorce. In one large scale U.S. study, 89% of 57- to 64-year-old men reported having a sexual partner, compared to 74% of women. Although 78% of men ages 75 to 85 still had partners, only 40% of women did (Waite, Laumann, Das, & Schumm, 2009).

For men in the middle years, changes in the production of *testosterone*, the primary male hormone, are not as dramatic. Some controversy has existed over whether testosterone production declines at all in healthy men, but longitudinal studies in recent years confirm that small average declines do occur, starting as early as the 20s, a process referred to as **andropause** (Feldman et al., 2002; Meletis & Wood, 2009). Men with health problems, such as cardiovascular disease and overweight, are likely to show a larger drop in testosterone. Lower testosterone levels are thought to contribute to some aspects of physical aging in men, such as loss of muscle mass and bone density. Some erectile dysfunction is also experienced by

TABLE 13.2 Frequency of Sexual Activity by Age and Gender

	M	F	M	F	M	F	M	F	M	F
AGE	**18–26**		**27–38**		**39–50**		**51–64**		**65+**	
N	254	268	353	380	282	295	227	230	212	221
>1/wk	53%	46%	60%	49%	54%	39%	63%	32%	53%	41%
"rarely"	13%	17%	9%	12%	8%	21%	8%	21%	11%	22%

SOURCE: Kellett, J. M. (2000). Older adult sexuality. In L.T. Szuchman, & F. Muscarella (Eds.), *Psychological perspectives on human sexuality* (p. 357). Used by permission of of John Wiley & Sons, Inc.

about 50% of men between 40 and 70 years old, but this seems to be more related to changes in the circulatory system than to hormones. Healthy men remain fertile through old age, even though reproductive structures like the testes, seminal vesicles, and prostate gland do undergo some changes (e.g., Plas, Berger, Hermann, & Pfluger, 2000). These changes have little effect on sperm production, but they result in reduced amounts of seminal fluid by the 40s and 50s and a steady decline in the volume and force of ejaculations. Yet, as with women, whereas sexual response times begin to increase in middle age, sexual functioning and sexual pleasure can be maintained (see Table 13.2). For a man with an available sexual partner, how sexually active he will be in his older years is closely correlated with how strong his sex drive was in his younger years (see Kellett, 2000) and with his general physical health (Karraker et al., 2011). For both men and women, understanding that sexual activity need not be derailed by the normal changes in sexual function that come with age (e.g., slower responses, erectile changes, vaginal dryness, and so on; Lindau et al., 2007) can be key to maintaining a satisfying sex life.

In today's popular culture, personal worth is linked to physical beauty, defined in part as a youthful, fit appearance. In such a climate, the most problematic physical changes of middle adulthood for some people can be the wrinkling and sagging of the skin and an increase in body fat (e.g., Bessenoff & Del Priore, 2007). Weight gain is not inevitable in middle adulthood, but rather is directly linked to overeating, poor nutrition, or inadequate exercise. Chronic stress and inadequate sleep have also been related to weight gain (Beccuti & Pannain, 2011; Dallman, Pecoraro, Akana, laFleur, Gomez, Houshyar, et al., 2003). Unfortunately, the typical habits of many Americans do result in their gaining weight throughout middle adulthood, mostly around the waist and hips. Among the factors contributing to the wrinkling and sagging process are changes in the layers of the skin. For example, **elastin**, a substance in the cells of the dermis, or middle layer of skin, allows the skin to stretch and contract as we move. After age 30, elastin gradually becomes more brittle, reducing skin elasticity. Areas of the body containing fat, such as the arms, legs, torso, and breasts, usually begin to sag by the 40s and 50s.

Developmental changes in some systems, such as **nocioception** or pain sensitivity, may increase in sensitivity as people age. Although many questions about this developmental process are still unanswered, studies of age-related pain sensitivity point to some overlap with stress and systemic inflammatory processes, another age-related phenomenon. Researchers describe a cascade of events. At the outset, psychological stress amplifies limbic and sympathetic nervous system reactivity, as we have described in earlier chapters. This contributes to stress-induced pain sensitivity, chronic SNS activation, and constriction of peripheral muscle tissue. Pain-sensitive neurons (nociceptors) deep inside muscle tissue pick up the signals and amplify sensitivity. Ultimately, a cycle may begin that leads to heightened pain experience, supported by chemicals related to a chronic inflammatory response (Vierck, 2006).

Cognitive Changes in Adulthood

Age-graded changes in cognitive functioning are experienced throughout adulthood. An enormous research literature exists on adult cognitive change. We humans, including developmental researchers, seem to worry a great deal about what kinds of intellectual declines we can expect as we get older and how we might avoid them. Early findings, from cross-sectional studies (Schaie, 1994) showed that most intellectual skills declined fairly steadily after age 25. But in such cross-sectional studies, different ages are represented by people from different cohorts. Many factors contribute to what appear to be age decrements. This is so because different cohorts are often different in breadth of educational, economic, and cultural opportunities (Flynn, 2012; Gerstorf, Ram, Hoppmann, Willis, & Schaie, 2011). Prospective or longitudinal research, which follows people over time, suggests a different and more complex picture of intellectual change in adulthood. Although some abilities begin to decline early, many cognitive capacities seem to show improvements with age and show only small average declines after ages 55 to 60.

One way to make sense of the mixed pattern of improvement and decline through adulthood is to categorize cognitive skills with regard to how heavily they depend on two kinds of underlying intellectual resources: *fluid* and *crystallized* intelligence (Horn & Cattell, 1966). **Fluid intelligence** is also called the **mechanics** of intelligence (e.g., Baltes et al., 2006), and refers to basic operational characteristics that seem to directly reflect how well the "hardware" of the nervous system is working, affecting the efficiency of processes like reasoning. Fluid, or mechanical, functions include such things as processing speed and inhibitory mechanisms. They are the most likely kinds of intellectual processes to show declines sometime in middle adulthood. For example, information processing speed may begin to slow down as early as age 30 and declines fairly rapidly after age 40, so that we are slower to take in information as we get older and slower to respond to it (e.g., Kail & Salthouse, 1994; Tucker-Drob, 2011). Inhibitory mechanisms show decrements by about age 40, so that in some tasks, older adults are more easily distracted by irrelevant stimulation than younger adults (e.g., Zacks & Hasher, 1994; Gopie, Craik, & Hasher, 2011).

The cognitive processes called *executive functions (EFs)* are closely linked to fluid intelligence. EFs—working memory, self-regulation (inhibitory control), and cognitive flexibility—are recruited when we effortfully pursue goals, rather than functioning more automatically or intuitively. You have seen the importance of EFs for the development of skills that support children's success in school (see Chapters 3 and 6). They are important for adult functioning as well, including job success, good quality of life, and even marital harmony (see Diamond, 2013). EFs involve activation of the prefrontal cortex, and they affect strategic planning and problem solving, creative thinking, maintaining attention on what is important in a situation, adapting to changing circumstances, avoiding impulsive actions, and so on. EFs show some declines in middle adulthood. These declines are related to changes in fluid intelligence, especially changes in processing speed and ability to gate out irrelevant stimuli.

Working memory provides a good example here. You know that *working memory* stores information that we are thinking about or working with at the present moment. It has a limited capacity, so that only a restricted number of information units can be retained there at one time, and usually only for 15 to 30 seconds, unless we actually keep working with them, that is, unless we make an effort to pay attention to the information. To put it a different way, working memory is the active, attentive part of the mind, where we consciously think and learn. In late middle adulthood, working memory capacity seems to decline. Fewer pieces of information can be attended to at one time, and either problem solving or learning or both can be somewhat affected as a result. Imagine a situation in which you look up and dial a 10-digit phone number, and then you immediately attempt to redial the number. Suppose that at age 30, you could remember about 6 of the digits when you redialed. At age 50, given the same kind of memory task, you would probably remember only 5 of the digits. Clearly, what we are describing here are not catastrophic losses. The modest change is more a nuisance factor than anything else. Most people, by about age 50, notice that they have a little more difficulty than they used to recalling the name of a new acquaintance or solving a complex problem that requires attending to several pieces of information at once. Declines in fluid intelligence seem to make the difference. Slower processing speed may make it harder to keep as many pieces of information in mind simultaneously as we once could or make it difficult to work our way through to the end of a problem before some of the information that we need has disappeared from short-term storage (Verhaeghen, 2012). Reduced inhibitory control is also important. For example, we might experience at times "a kind of 'mental clutter' in which extraneous thoughts and plans can interfere with, and possibly crowd out, goal-relevant thoughts and plans" (Zacks, Hasher, & Li, 2000, p. 297).

Another intellectual resource is called **crystallized intelligence** or the **pragmatics** of intelligence (e.g., Baltes et al., 2006). It is the compilation of skills

This woman has noticed declines in her fluid intelligence and her executive functions throughout middle adulthood.

and information we have acquired in the course of our lives. Crystallized intelligence, or pragmatics, is a little like the pile of software programs that most of us accumulate for our computers. Our knowledge of language, of how to do a job or to play an instrument, the strategies we have learned for memorizing information or solving problems—all forms of declarative and procedural knowledge (see Chapter 6)—are included. Crystallized intelligence is less likely than fluid intelligence to show declines with age and, for some individuals, can increase even into old age. For most people in middle adulthood, and for most abilities, declining fluid resources are usually balanced or outweighed by continuing steady increases in crystallized resources (Baltes et al., 2006). It is only after about age 60 that losses in fluid intelligence may be great enough to contribute to overall declines in intellectual functioning.

Problem solving in middle adulthood provides a good illustration of the interactive influences of mechanics and pragmatics in overall functioning. As you have just seen, working memory *is* disrupted by mechanical declines with age. Working memory is where we solve problems, but age-related declines in working memory affect problem solving most when either the information that is relevant to the solution or the problem-solving situation is new. When middle adults are solving familiar, everyday problems or problems in areas of their own expertise, the crystallized resources at their disposal often help them to be more effective than younger adults (e.g., Salthouse, 2012).

Learning and long-term storage of information also reveal the complex interrelations of mechanics and pragmatics with age. Although the limitations of working memory make it more difficult to get new information into long-term memory, we nonetheless do continue to learn in middle and late adulthood, storing new information from our experiences despite our reduced efficiency. Thus, both younger and older adults add new information to episodic memory—memory for personal experiences—but younger subjects typically learn more with greater ease (e.g., Addis, Wong, & Schacter, 2008). To put it differently, we are somewhat less likely, as we get older, to remember specific daily experiences, such as where we parked the car at the shopping mall. However, information already learned appears to be maintained as well as in our younger years. In fact, an older person's semantic memory, her store of factual information, seems to have a richer network of interrelationships as a result of her greater experience, allowing her to retrieve information through many more routes than a younger person can (e.g., MacKay & Abrams, 1996; Salthouse, 2012). As Pak and Stronge (2008) point out, younger adults may have the edge in games that require speedy responding (e.g., a video game), but older adults often outperform younger ones on memory games (e.g., Trivial Pursuit and Jeopardy).

Charness and Bosman (1990) provide an interesting example of the differential effects of age changes in fluid and crystallized intelligence on performance in adulthood. They describe two kinds of chess competitions. In tournament chess, participants make their moves quickly, after deliberating for about 3 minutes. In correspondence chess, the participants can have 3 days to make a move. Clearly, tournament chess makes greater demands on processing speed, whereas correspondence chess seems to draw much more completely on one's knowledge and experience. Not surprisingly, then, top performers win their first world championship in tournament chess at much younger ages, about age 30 on average, than they do in correspondence chess, where the average first-time champion is 46! It is not unusual for middle-aged chess devotees to adapt to declines in fluid intelligence by shifting their focus from tournament chess to correspondence chess as they get older.

In Chapter 15 we will look more closely at cognitive changes in late adulthood, focusing especially on how older adults compensate for losses in fluid intelligence and on the debate over the growth of wisdom.

Life-Task or Life-Course Changes in Adulthood

People experience another kind of age-graded change as they move through adulthood. Life-course changes, brought on by shifts in the life tasks that seem most important to us at different times of our lives, have been described by many different theorists. Although each of these theorists tends to emphasize somewhat different aspects of the life experience, you will see commonalities in their observations as we briefly summarize a sampling of these descriptions.

You may recall that Schaie (1977–1978; Schaie & Willis, 2000; see also Chapter 11) proposed a series of stages in adult life, each of which requires the development of new ways to apply and use one's intellectual resources. These changes are directly related to shifts in family roles and in the life tasks that we face as we grow older. In the *achieving stage* of young adulthood, the individual must learn to use logical thinking skills to plan the achievement of long-term goals. In the *responsible stage* of middle adulthood, one must learn to use her problem-solving skills not only to achieve her own goals but also to help coordinate her needs with those of others for whom she is responsible at home, at work, and in the community. In the *reorganizational stage* of one's elder years, one's focus narrows again to reaching personal, practical, day-to-day goals as an adult devotes her thinking skills to managing her losses. Finally, in late adulthood, people move into the *reintegrative stage*, when their goals are primarily to conserve energy, and perhaps into a *legacy-leaving stage*, when they use their cognitive resources to help them leave behind a written or oral account of their experience or wisdom.

Schaie emphasizes the shifting allocation of intellectual skills across adulthood, as people confront different kinds of problems related to their age and stage of life. Most other theorists emphasize changes in personality. They do not focus on personality traits, which, as we have seen, are relatively stable in middle adulthood and beyond, but rather they describe structural changes in self-concept and in self-expression.

Perhaps the best-known theory of life-course changes in self-concept is Erik Erikson's, by now quite familiar to you. Erikson (e.g., 1950/1963) describes three stages in self-development in adulthood, based on the kinds of life tasks that become most important to people as they find themselves fully matured and facing the fact that this is the one life that they have to live. Very briefly, in young adulthood, intimacy (vs. isolation) is one's quest: finding a way to validate and expand her own sense of self by committing to a shared life with others. In middle adulthood, generativity (vs. stagnation) becomes most important, giving one's own life purpose by producing and building for the next generation, through work, community service, or child rearing. By old age, establishing **ego integrity (vs. despair)** becomes life's task. Ideally, a process of life review helps the elderly adult to develop a sense that her own life is "something that had to be," that she has lived a life that has order, meaning, and dignity (see Chapter 1, especially Table 1.1).

Erikson argued that different concerns reach ascendancy in different age periods. Vaillant (1977; Vaillant & Koury, 1994) suggested that two more adult life stages should be added to Erikson's scheme, reflecting that forming deep bonds, becoming productive, and finding meaning in one's life are recurring themes throughout adulthood. In one's mid-20s, **career consolidation (vs. self-absorption)** is a key focus of self-development. In this phase of life, in addition to ongoing intimacy concerns, making a commitment to work that brings personal satisfaction, regardless of its other rewards, rather than just having a job, becomes important. The most positive development for this period is that such a commitment emerges as an important part of one's identity.

Vaillant also described a stage that comes near the end of Erikson's generativity stage, in late middle adulthood. This he called the **keeper of meaning (vs. rigidity)** stage, when the adult expands her generative concerns beyond just making a productive contribution, in order to actually preserve something that is part of the culture. In this sense, adults seek ways to establish the meaningfulness of the work or contributions they have made. For example, Tien, a woman who worked as an aid at her children's day care center, might move on after her own children are grown to join a child care advocacy group in her community, hoping to ensure that future generations of children in her region will have access to the high-quality child care she was able to provide her own children.

TABLE 13.3 Adult Life Stages: Some Theories of Self-Development

APPROXIMATE AGE PERIOD	ERIKSON	VAILLANT	LOEVINGER	GOULD
Adolescence	Identity (vs. Identity Diffusion)	(like Erikson)	Conscientious—Conformist	Separating from parents: becoming independent
Young Adulthood	Intimacy (vs. Isolation)	(like Erikson)	Individualistic	"Nobody's baby": becoming a competent, self-maintaining adult
Middle Adulthood (Early)	Generativity (vs. Stagnation)	Generativity—Career consolidation (vs. Self-Absorption); producing	Autonomous	Opening up: exploring inner consciousness; coming to deeper understanding of self and needs
Middle Adulthood (Late)		Generativity—Keeper of Meaning (vs. Rigidity); giving, mentoring		Midlife: finding the courage and resourcefulness to act on deeper feelings; awareness of pressure of time
Late Adulthood	Ego Integration (vs. Despair)		Integrated	Beyond midlife: establishing true autonomy; becoming inner-directed rather than governed by roles; "I own myself"

As we saw in Chapter 12, research indicates that both intimacy and generativity are central to the lives of young adults. Later in this chapter we will discuss research on how these concerns tend to play out in the arenas of marriage, family life, parenting, and work during the middle years of adulthood.

Several other theorists have proposed stages in adult personality development that repeat many of the themes that we see in Erikson's work. They all emphasize that people have fundamental concerns or needs that shift in importance from one adult stage to another. We will briefly describe Levinson's theory here; some additional theories (e.g., Gould, 1978; Loevinger, 1976) are included in schematic comparison in Table 13.3.

In Levinson's account (e.g., Levinson, 1986; Levinson & Levinson, 1996; Levinson, Darrow, Klein, Levinson, & McKee, 1978), a person's life has structure at any given time. One's **life structure** is a pattern of relationships between the self and the external world, such as relationships to one's "spouse, lover, family, occupation, religion, leisure, and so on" (Levinson, 1986). There may be many components to the life structure, but Levinson found that at any one time there are usually only one or two really significant, defining components for the self, usually marriage-family and/or occupational components. Levinson identified three major adult stages, or eras: early, middle, and late adulthood. Each of these eras begins with a 5-year transitional period and is marked by a smaller mid-era transition, when the life structure's effectiveness for serving the person's goals is reexamined and may be altered.

Whereas Erikson and Vaillant suggest that certain life tasks occur in relatively predictable sequence (e.g., first intimacy needs are greater, then generativity needs), Levinson (1986) argues that life events unfold in many ways depending on a particular individual's life circumstances, gender, and culture and that specific concerns are not necessarily more important in one era than in another. What is predictable, he argues, is the sequence of age periods for building and changing first one life structure and then another. The experience of life changes from one era to the next. Put a different way, what is inevitable in adulthood is that a person will establish and then revise her life structure at particular times as she ages.

In sum, many theorists have identified life-course changes affecting self-concept or self-expression during adulthood. There is by no means complete agreement among these theorists on the character of these changes. For example, following Jung (1963), Levinson (e.g., 1986) and Gould (1978) describe the midlife transition as an often tumultuous time, a period of major upheaval and self-evaluation, not unlike adolescence. You may have heard it referred to as a "midlife crisis." Their research, consisting of longitudinal interview studies of relatively small and somewhat selective samples of adults, tends to support these claims (e.g., Gould, 1978; Levinson et al., 1978; Levinson & Levinson, 1996). But in much larger interview and questionnaire studies, many researchers have found little evidence of widespread midlife distress, although they have found indications of shifting concerns at midlife (e.g., Almeida & Horn, 2004; McCrae & Costa, 2003; Vaillant, 1977). Crisis-level distress seems most likely to occur as a function of major life events, like financial problems or job loss, which can happen at any time. Individuals who score high on the personality trait of neuroticism are particularly likely to suffer acute distress (see Lachman, 2004).

Regardless of such disagreements, there is some similarity among the theoretical descriptions of adult life-course changes. The available empirical work supports the general idea of such change. Some longitudinal research also indicates that major aspects of self, such as intimacy, may be reworked with every major life change, rather than being fully resolved at specific times in the life course (e.g., Whitbourne, Sneed, & Sayer, 2009). Despite the enormous variation in the immediate details of adult lives—from culture to culture, from cohort to cohort, from family to family, and from individual to individual—there appear to be some life changes that are widely experienced. These changes lead each of us to reformulate, or at least reevaluate, ourselves and our lives periodically. Much more research is needed to establish the specifics of these changes and whom they do and do not affect.

For professionals, awareness of potential stage changes can help enrich our understanding of clients. For example, suppose a woman at 45 comes to a counselor looking for help with marital problems she has tolerated for 20 years. We might be inclined to wonder, why now, and, how likely is it that change can be effected after so many years of entrenched behavior patterns? The answers to both questions may be partly a function of life stage. Many theorists see the 40s as a time when reassessment of one's life structure is very likely and when willingness to act on the basis of one's individual propensities, rather than strictly in adherence with social expectations, increases (see Table 13.3). Vaillant (1977) suggests that generativity needs are likely to reorganize, so that direct caregiving to one's spouse or children is less likely to meet one's needs than opportunities to seek broader meaning in one's life by finding ways to preserve the culture. Thus, not only is it a likely time for this woman to reassess her life, but it may also be a time when she will be open to trying new ways of meeting her needs.

History-Graded Changes

The historical events that affect our whole cohort are another source of change in adult lives. People are partly a product of the historical context in which they develop. Imagine that you were a young adult parent trying to support your children during the years of the Great Depression. You would take a job wherever you found one, no matter how difficult the work, and you would probably be grateful for it. What effect might years of deprivation and struggle have on your tendency toward conscientiousness? Or think about moving through early adulthood during the social upheavals and sexual revolution of the 1960s. Do you think this experience might have some effect on your openness to experience? History-graded events, also called **cohort effects**, provide a context for development and also influence it directly (e.g., Rogler, 2002).

The year of your birth marks your entry into a cohort of peers who accompany you through age-graded developmental changes (toddlerhood, puberty, and so on) within the context of a specific set of historical events (wars, technological shifts, etc.). The effect of history is particularly linked to a person's age and stage of life (such as coming of age in a time of war, when you could be drafted into military service). In addition to age-graded and history-graded changes, we also progress through stages of the family life cycle as child, parent, grandparent, and so on. Researchers who take a **life-course perspective** remind us that development is influenced by the intersection of chronological age (life time), family-related roles (family time), and membership in a birth cohort (historical time; Elder & Shanahan, 2006). If society experiences an economic recession that results in a lengthy period of corporate downsizing, a young father who has just completed a training program in computer repair might see his chances of getting a well-paying job shrink. He may have to wait to buy a first house, ultimately limiting the lifetime equity he can accrue. Because his family must continue to reside in a low-cost apartment, his preschool son might also be affected because of missed educational opportunities that would have been available with a move to a more advantaged school district. Note that despite the important implications of the economic downturn for this young parent's life, his own grandparents, who are retired and receiving a fixed pension, would not be much affected.

Twenge (2000) provides an example of how sociocultural and historical context influences the personality development of cohorts of individuals. She reviewed published reports of child and adolescent anxiety from 1952 to 1993 to see if levels had changed over these years. Her distressing finding showed that the average child in America during the 1980s scored higher on anxiety than child psychiatric patients from the 1950s. Further analysis allowed her to demonstrate that these increases were associated with the breakdown of social connections and with increases in physical and psychological threats. Economic recessions were not related to the increase in anxiety. Twenge's results imply that recent cohorts are living in a world that is less favorable to their positive development than the world in which their own parents grew up. A context that provides for fewer or weaker social bonds at the same time that threats are expanding heightens the sense of vulnerability for these young people, who are truly growing up in an "age of anxiety."

The Social Gradient and Life-Course Development

What has been absent from some formulations of history-graded effects is the role of culture. Sociocultural effects on development are not restricted to time-limited incidents nor do they necessarily exert the same influence on all members of a generation. Developmental change also results from structural features of society. For individuals and families, one's place on the rungs of society's status and economic ladders has long-term consequences. Lower status contributes to poorer life outcomes on a number of measures, especially to disturbingly higher rates of illness as people age (see Figure 13.3). Socioeconomic status (SES) is a complex concept that has typically been assessed using indicators like education, income, and zip code. Historically, researchers often considered it a nuisance variable that needed to be statistically controlled so that the "real" differences could emerge. Nuisance variables are hypothesized to be extraneous to the effects researchers intend to investigate. More contemporary views recognize that SES effects are real, direct and powerful (Adler et al., 1994). Increasingly, researchers are adopting the term **socioeconomic position (SEP)**, instead of SES, because it reflects a more systems-centered approach and recognizes the contributions of societal stratification on development. Because the most common impulse within society is to organize itself in a hierarchical fashion, those at the bottom usually end up with restricted access to resources and opportunities. This step-wise top-to-bottom phenomenon is called the **social gradient**. Marmot and Wilkinson (2009) explain how SEP impacts life chances:

> Social organization also structures advantage and disadvantage longitudinally. Advantage or disadvantage in one phase of the life course is likely to have been preceded by, and to be succeeded by, similar advantage or disadvantage in the other phases of life. A child raised in an affluent home is likely to succeed educationally, which will favour entry to the more privileged sectors of the labour market, where an occupational pension scheme will provide financial security in old age. At the other extreme, a child from a disadvantaged home is likely to achieve few

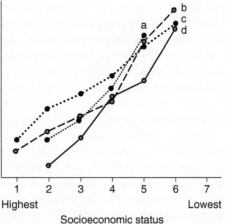

(a) Osteo- arthritis	(b) Chronic Disease	(c) Hyper- tension	(d) Cervical Cancer
25	150	16	30
20	125	14	25
15	100	12	20
10	75	10	15
5	50	8	10

FIGURE 13.3   The social gradient in health. Rates of selected illnesses (osteoarthritis, chronic diseases, hypertension, and cervical cancer) per 100,000 as a function of socioeconomic status.

SOURCE: Matthews, K. & Gallo, K. (2011). Psychological perspectives on pathways linking socioeconomic status and physical health, *Annual Review of Psychology, 62,* 501–530. Republished with permission of Annual Reviews, Inc.

> educational qualifications and, leaving school at the minimum age, to enter the unskilled labour market where low pay and hazardous work combine with no occupational pension, which ensures reliance on welfare payments in old age. (p. 41)

Life at the bottom of the social ladder is not easy. Across the world, the poor suffer most in terms of morbidity and mortality compared to their more advantaged peers. Figure 13.3 depicts the linear increase in incidence rates for disease by SES level.

The study of SEP represents an example of a multidimensional, life-course approach to development that incorporates societal/cultural considerations. The impact of socially embedded influences can be studied at the individual or group level, at sensitive periods of development, and longitudinally across the life span. Neuroscientific research is also targeting the processes through which SEP becomes embodied via brain pathways that mediate its effects (Gianaros & Manuck, 2010). Figure 13.4 presents potential ways to measure SEP at different stages of the life span.

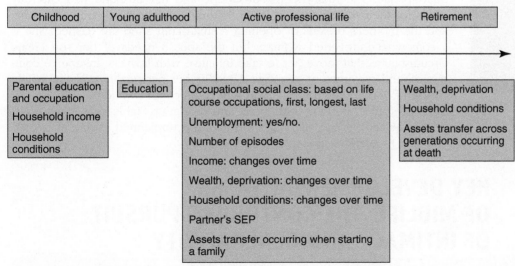

FIGURE 13.4   Measuring the socioeconomic trajectory over the life span. Examples of life-course measures for socioeconomic position.

SOURCE: Galobardes, B., Lynch, J., & Smith, G. D. (2007). Measuring socioeconomic position in health research. *British Medical Bulletin, 81–82,* 21–37. Used by permission of Oxford University Press.

For the most part, life circumstances associated with low SEP include economic hardship (not having necessary resources like food and shelter), loss of job, income, housing or material possessions, debt, evictions, and insecurity. Now, consider the effects of sytematic discrimination. What might membership in a socially devalued group add to the list of hardships? Would it matter if the individuals felt they had adequate resources to cope with discrimination? Life course researchers are also beginning to examine the long-term impact of racial discrimination on life span development, especially in health-related areas. Just as the sociocultural influences of one's era may create an "age of anxiety," so too might they affect disease processes. The disparities in health among different racial and ethnic groups have been well-documented (CDC, 2011). Effects of race frequently co-vary with socioeconomic status, but the particular contribution of racial discrimination appears to increase the damaging effects. Reliable data has shown that for certain historically disadvantaged groups, especially African Americans, the health disparities are stark. Heart disease, diabetes, strokes, hypertension, and obesity occur at much higher rates for African Americans than for all other major racial/ethnic groups (Mays, Cochran, & Barnes, 2007). The search is on for a comprehensive understanding of how poverty and racism "gets under the skin" by altering physiological reactivity to result, ultimately, in these dramatic health disparities (McEwen, 2012). A clearer understanding of the mechanisms will increase our repertoire of effective prevention strategies (Brondolo, Gallo, & Myers, 2009).

Nonnormative Changes

Just as history-graded changes can significantly affect the development of a whole cohort, individual lives are also changed by unexpected events. These events are called nonnormative events, "bolt from the blue" experiences that we don't anticipate, yet that can have powerful developmental effects. Crises such as traumatic illnesses, accidents, imprisonment, the untimely death of a loved one, or even positive events such as winning a lottery can be considered nonnormative. They create new sets of circumstances for people, and these have the potential to alter developmental trajectories (Datan & Ginsburg, 1975).

Imagine a woman at age 45 who has worked hard as a parent and homemaker and looks forward to seeing each of her children move into adult independence. A car accident suddenly leaves her 19-year-old son a quadriplegic. The financial resources she and her husband had carefully saved for their retirement and their children's college years are soon gone, and the mother's dreams of opening a small craft shop are dashed. She is a somewhat introverted woman, but the special needs of her son create circumstances that move her to take initiative with lawyers, insurance companies, and government agencies. Literally, her personality and the whole course of her life begin to move in a new direction. So middle age, like the "ages" before it, is both continuous and changing. Stable personality traits are influenced by age, life stage, history, and unplanned events as people continue to adapt to life.

What do you think might be the nonnormative and cohort effects of the events of September 11, 2001, on your life?

KEY DEVELOPMENTAL TASKS OF MIDLIFE: THE CONTINUING PURSUIT OF INTIMACY AND GENERATIVITY

In middle adulthood, as in young adulthood, loving relationships and productive, meaningful work continue to be critical elements in the construction of a satisfying life. As you know, Erikson saw intimacy, broadly defined as sharing oneself with another, as a more prominent concern in young adulthood and generativity, defined as the need to create and produce, as a more central focus of middle adulthood. However, it is clear from available research that although the relative balance between these two concerns may shift (see Chapter 12), both remain important in middle adulthood and beyond. In the following sections we will further explore intimacy issues by examining how marital relationships form, develop, and sometimes fail during adulthood. We will continue our discussion of generativity by considering the parental role from the adult's perspective, and we will touch on other generativity issues in the middle years, having to do with work and community.

Intimacy: Marriage and Other Primary Relationships

One of the most valuable adaptations we humans can make is to establish and maintain close interpersonal relationships. In adulthood, close ties take on a variety of forms, and the number and diversity of forms is increasing. Marriage has provided the traditional structure within which such relationships exist. Approximately 58% of the U.S. population were married in 2010, a figure down from 62% in 1990 (U.S. Bureau of Census, 2012; see Figure 13.5). One quarter of all households in the United States were single-person households. Cohabitation was also on the rise. Although there has been a steep rise in the number of people living alone or as unmarried partners, this condition might be temporary for some. Estimates of the marriage rate for people over their lifetimes predict that approximately 90% of the population will have been married at least one time (e.g., Whitehead & Poponoe, 2003).

The definition of "family" has indeed become more inclusive in the 21st century and refers to more than the traditional nuclear family with its own biological children. Particularly since the social changes initiated in the 1960s, people have felt freer to meet their needs for intimacy and connection in a variety of ways. Extended, multigenerational families, adoptive and foster families, same-sex unions, remarried or blended families, single-parent families, and "families" composed of several people living together without legal ties are all examples of new trends in family formation. To illustrate, one-third of the children adopted in the United States in 2001 went to single women (Coontz, 2005). Some individuals will be part of several different kinds of families as they progress through their lives.

Clearly, psychological wellness does not depend upon any one specific relationship configuration. Kaslow (2001) encourages clinicians to expand their definition of family and to work toward ways of promoting optimal functioning for each of these forms. It is important to recognize, as Coontz (2005) has argued, "moving in

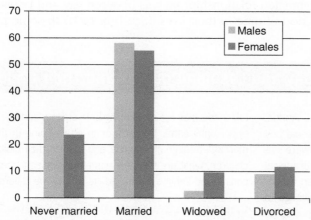

FIGURE 13.5 **Percentage of U.S. population over age 15 in different marital status categories in 2010.**
SOURCE: U.S. Bureau of the Census (2012). America's families and living arrangements: 2010, Table 57. Retrieved from http://www.census.gov/compendia/statab/2012/tables/12s0057.pdf.

lockstep through a series of predictable transitions is no longer a route to personal security. Each man and woman must put together a highly individualized sequence of transitions . . . a 'do-it-yourself' biography" (p. 277). Whether or not people are married, helpers must offer resources that promote healthy relationships and, where children are involved, to improve parenting. Despite greater social acceptance of alternative family styles, researchers have discovered that good marriages or primary relationships confer a number of physical and psychological benefits that other states may not provide (e.g., Diener, Tamir, & Scollon, 2006; Lucas, 2007). For example, married people report generally higher levels of happiness than unmarried people (Hoppmann, Gerstorf, Willis, & Schaie, 2011). They have lower rates of mental illness, drug and alcohol abuse, and physical illness than their unmarried counterparts. They report higher levels of sexual and emotional satisfaction (Waite & Joyner, 2001). Research has even documented that married partners tend to live longer (Friedman et al., 1995). Perhaps the day-to-day economic and social support that accrues to married couples over the years helps to account for some of these effects. Married couples may also receive more social approval and less social rejection than individuals in other situations, although tolerance for alternative family arrangements is growing. The economic benefits that come with marital status in U.S. culture, including those that provide retirement income for surviving spouses, probably make a major contribution to the increased happiness and even health of married people over time. In one study, single mothers who were the sole support for their children for a period of 10 years or more during their lifetimes were 55% more likely to live in poverty at ages 65 to 75, regardless of their current marital status (Johnson & Favreault, 2004). Marriage appears to serve as an economic protective factor, given the structure of the current laws and benefit systems in the United States. More research is needed to understand whether the same benefits are conferred by alternative relationship forms as well. One thing that is clear at this point is that many factors mediate and moderate the benefits of marriage (and other intimate partnerships). One factor is gender. For example, women overall are likely to be less satisfied with their marriages over time than men. Two thirds of divorces filed after age 40 are initiated by women (Hacker, 2003). Another factor is socioeconomic status. For example, women without high school degrees are more likely to divorce (60 % rate) than women with college degrees (33% rate) (see Coontz, 2005).

Although we use marriage as the prototypical vehicle to illustrate the development of intimacy over the adult life span, we acknowledge that this is not the only road, nor even the best one, for many people. We do not underestimate the importance of friendships nor devalue single status in adulthood. However, as you have seen, demographics show that the majority of people will marry or participate in some kind of committed relationship, such as between gay and lesbian couples, for at least some period of time in their lives. (See Box 13.1.) In some Latin American

Box 13.1: Changing Families: Gay and Lesbian Couples and Their Children

In 2002, Steve Lofton and Roger Croteau, residents of Florida, achieved media fame when they tried to adopt a 10-year-old boy who had been their foster child since infancy. These men were surrogate parents to five foster children at the time, several with special needs, but state law prohibited adoption of minor children by gay adults. Lofton and Croteau eventually lost their court challenge to Florida's adoption laws, and the child they had raised was put up for adoption by strangers, despite the child's wish to stay with his foster parents (Patterson, 2004).

Lofton and Croteau are among a growing cohort of gay and lesbian adults who head households, form families, and raise children. In many instances, they are challenging both custom and law by asking for the opportunity either to marry or to attain some of the legal rights of marriage through civil unions, and to raise their biological or adopted children. What are the developmental consequences of these newly constituted families, for the adults and for the children they raise?

Characteristics of Committed Relationships Between Gay and Lesbian Adults

Although media images of gay and lesbian relationships often suggest they are unstable and dysfunctional, ". . . research has documented that many contemporary lesbians and gay men establish enduring intimate relationships" (Peplau & Fingerhut, 2007, p. 418). In a review of existing literature, Herek (2006) found that across many studies 40% to 70% of gay men and 45% to 80% of lesbian women were in committed relationships, many of which had lasted for at least a decade (see also Herek, Norto, Allen, & Sims, 2010). The 2010 U.S. Census reported over 600,000 same-sex, cohabiting couples (O'Connell & Feliz, 2011). Such couples appear to be similar to heterosexual couples in many ways. The stability of their relationships depends on the same factors as the stability of heterosexual relationships: "positive attraction forces, such as love and satisfaction, the availability of alternatives, and barriers to leaving a relationship, such as psychological, emotional and financial costs" (Peplau & Fingerhut, 2007, p. 412). Many researchers have found the quality of same-sex relationships to be similar to, or better than, male–female relationships, and the processes that determine quality are the same, such as the use of positive communication styles (e.g., Balsam, Beauchaine, Rothblum, & Solomon, 2008; Gottman et al., 2003; Roisman, Clausell, Holland, Fortuna, & Elieff, 2008). In a five-year study that controlled for factors such as age and education, relationship satisfaction was the same for married heterosexual and co-habiting homosexual couples at the start of the study, and for both types of couple, satisfaction declined somewhat over time, at similar rates (Kurdek, 1998).

Some differences have been identified between homosexual and heterosexual couples. One difference is that same-sex couples generally get less support from relatives than heterosexual couples, and they are more likely to rely on friendship networks (Kurdek, 2004). When the partners' commitment has some legal status, via civil unions or marriage, relationships with extended family seem to be more supportive, although it is difficult to say whether couples with supportive families are more likely to legalize their relationships or whether families become more supportive when couples legalize their relationships (e.g., Balsam et al., 2008).

Another difference is that same-sex couples, especially lesbian couples, are more likely to endorse equal power in their relationships, and they tend to be more egalitarian in the way they divide household chores, decision making, and child rearing duties (see Herek, 2006; Patterson, Sutfin, & Fulcher, 2004). There are some differences in exclusivity and frequency of sexual relations as well (see Peplau & Fingerhut, 2007, for a summary). Gay men are less likely to restrict sex to their primary partner than lesbian or heterosexual women or heterosexual men, and male couples are more likely to openly agree to be non-exclusive than female couples or male-female couples. For all types of couple, the frequency of sexual relations is quite variable, usually declining over time. However, on the average, gay couples have more frequent sex than heterosexual couples, who have more frequent sex than lesbian couples (see Peplau & Fingerhut, 2007). In a longitudinal study, Balsam et al. (2008) found that for lesbian couples, having more sex was an important predictor of relationship quality, more so than for gay or heterosexual couples. The authors suggest that it may be especially important for lesbian couples to overcome whatever problems they face in maintaining a good sexual relationship.

There is considerable controversy in the United States about whether committed gay and lesbian couples should be awarded some legal recognition, either through marriage or through civil unions. Legalizing such relationships would redress some problems that same-sex couples face. For example, without legal recognition of a relationship, even when couples have longstanding stable relationships, if one partner is ill or dies the other partner can be barred from making health care decisions or funeral arrangements for that partner, or may be faced with no right or access to the other partner's financial resources. Research on the psychological and behavioral effects of legal unions on same-sex partners is in its infancy. After Vermont passed a law allowing civil unions, Balsam et al. (2008) compared same-sex couples who obtained civil unions there to married heterosexuals from the same families and to same-sex couples from the same friendship networks who were not in civil unions. The same-sex couples who were not in civil unions were more likely to terminate their relationships during the three years of the study than either same-sex couples in civil unions or married heterosexual couples, whose relationships were equally stable. Much more research is needed, and with many states now legalizing same-sex marriages additional studies should soon be available. However, it appears from this study that being in a legalized relationship may confer somewhat greater stability on same-sex relationships, perhaps partly because it creates a barrier to dissolution of the relationship and partly because of the public nature of the commitment. Consider the assessment of one lesbian study participant:

> Having a civil union has been good for us. Relationships can be hard at times and having at least one formal barrier helps make you think about splitting up . . . In the past few years (since the civil union) it's seemed as if it was O.K. to have some separate interests . . . it proved to my partner that she didn't have to worry if I was gone playing tennis, golf or whatever with someone else. So that's been really good. (p. 112)

The Children of Gay and Lesbian Parents

Many gay and lesbian adults have biological children from prior heterosexual relationships. Others use artificial insemination, surrogacy, or some combination of modern technologies in order to have biological children. And many others adopt. Few states are like Florida, forbidding adoption on the basis of sexual orientation, although courts in many states have been more likely to grant adoptions to gay or lesbian parents if the children are difficult to place for some reason, such as disability or illness. Recent estimates indicate that nearly 14% of gay couples and 27% of lesbian couples are raising children (Krivickas & Lofquist, 2011). State laws differ greatly, affecting the kinds of family arrangements that gay and lesbian parents can construct. In some states, a gay or lesbian adult can raise a biological child or adopt a child, but his or her partner cannot become a legal co-parent, so the partner's relationship to the child does not have legal status (meaning, for example, that the partner cannot sign a school permission form or be sure that he or she would be granted custody if the legal parent were to die). In other states, co-parenting by same-sex adults is permitted. Different legal and informal arrangements probably affect the kinds of stress and stability that are likely to characterize a family, but little is known yet about these differences.

(Box 13.1 continued)

Box 13.1 *Continued*

Are there any special risks or protective factors that affect children raised by same-sex couples? A growing body of research, some of it longitudinal, some of it using large representative samples, compares outcomes for children reared by homosexual and heterosexual couples. Many more studies include lesbian than gay couples, but both groups are represented in the literature. In general, the findings are quite consistent: The risk of problematic outcomes is no greater for children of homosexual parents than for children reared by heterosexual couples (see reviews by Herek, 2006; Meezan & Rauch, 2005; Patterson, 2004). Meezan and Rauch summarize four key findings to date:

- The parenting styles of homosexual parents are like those of heterosexual parents, although gay and lesbian parents are somewhat more likely to report using strategies consistent with an authoritative parenting style (high levels of warmth and control). Despite the stereotypic concern that gay fathers might be more likely to sexually abuse their children, gay men are no more likely than heterosexual men to sexually abuse children (see Patterson, 2004).

- Children of lesbian and gay parents do not seem more confused about their gender identities than children of heterosexual parents (e.g., Bos & Sandfort, 2010). They tend to engage in less gender stereotypic toy play than children reared by heterosexual parents, perhaps because their parents are likely to be more liberal in their attitudes toward gender nonconformity (e.g., Goldberg, Kashy, & Smith, 2012). The vast majority of children grow up to be heterosexual, regardless of their parents' sexual orientation, and it appears that base rates of homosexuality are about the same for children of homosexual and heterosexual parents. Daughters in lesbian-headed households are more willing to accept others' alternative sexual identities, more likely to have homosexual friends, and more willing to say that they

would consider same-sex relationships. Both boys and girls in lesbian-headed households are also more likely as children to express concern that they might become homosexual, a concern that disappears in adolescence.

- No differences have been found in the cognitive abilities, self-esteem, and social or emotional development of children reared by homosexual parents.

- The majority of studies find no difficulties with peers related to the social stigma of having homosexual parents, although parents worry that their children will be ridiculed, and children sometimes engage in behaviors that keep their families' characteristics hidden. Rivers, Poteat, and Noret (2008) also found that children of same-sex couples report using fewer school-based supports than children of heterosexual couples. Apparently, school staff are unlikely to acknowledge alternative family structures and children often feel that school-based supports are not really intended for them.

Overall, gay and lesbian parents appear to be as successful at child rearing as heterosexual parents. Consider a study that included lesbian and heterosexual couples and their children. The children were all conceived through artificial insemination arranged through the same sperm bank, so that one parent was biologically related to the child and one was not. When children averaged 7 years old, both parents and children were assessed using a variety of scales. The results did not depend on the parents' sexual orientation but on the same risk and protective factors that appear to affect all parents and their children. ". . . Family process variables such as parental adjustment and couple adjustment were more strongly related to children's outcomes than were family structural variables such as parental sexual orientation or relationship status" (Fulcher, Sutfin, Chan, Scheib, & Patterson, 2005, p. 294).

---

cultures, there is a historical acceptance of long-term consensual unions (Landale & Fennelly, 1992) even though couples are not formally wed. Even after divorce, in the United States over half of individuals are likely to remarry within 5 years (Kreider, 2006). Although the traditional marital and family life cycle may not be the best descriptive fit for everyone, there are aspects of its stages that can help us understand many kinds of close adult relationships. The nature of intimate relationships, inside or outside marriage, is defined by mutual sharing of joys and sorrows, reaching compromises and working out problems, and developing a sense of "we-ness."

The Family Life Cycle

Marriages (and other primary relationships) change as partners age and the demands of family life ebb and flow. The **family life cycle**, a normative, stagelike sequence of traditional family development in intact marriages, has been described in several ways. Figure 13.6 shows a well-known early example proposed by Duvall (1971) that depicts a historically traditional breakdown of time. Duvall emphasized the time spent in each of the stages of family life as partners become parents, rear and launch their children, become "empty-nesters," and subsequently face old age. Carter and McGoldrick (1999) developed a similar model that incorporates the tasks

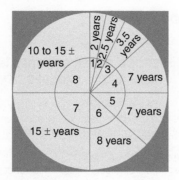

1. Married Couples (without children).
2. Childbearing Families (Oldest child, birth–30 months).
3. Families with Preschool Children (Oldest child 30 months–6 years).
4. Families with Schoolchildren (Oldest child 6–13 years).
5. Families with Teenagers (Oldest child 13–20 years).
6. Families as Launching Centers (First child gone to last child leaving home).
7. Middle-aged Parents (Empty nest to retirement).
8. Aging Family Members (Retirement to death of both spouses).

FIGURE 13.6 The family life cycle: Approximate number of years spent in each stage for families with children.
SOURCE: Duvall, E. M. (1971). *Family development* (4th ed.). Boston, MA: Allyn and Bacon. Used with permission from Pearson Education, Inc.

that accompany each stage (see Table 13.4). In the next section, we borrow from this latter model to highlight some important transitions and challenges facing families. Then we take a closer look at marriage itself and address theories of marital satisfaction and dysfunction.

Stages of the Family Life Cycle

Finding a mate is a task that typically involves a relatively lengthy period of experimentation, given that people in the United States marry at later ages than they did in previous generations. Mate selection has been compared to a "filtering process" by which people go through the step-by-step elimination of ineligible candidates until they settle on a partner (Janda & Klenke-Hamel, 1980). According to this theory, people initially select potential dates on the basis of physical attractiveness and personality characteristics from a pool of available, eligible candidates. Further sorting or filtering out follows on the basis of **homogamy**, or similarity to oneself in religion, SES, race, education, and so on, as well as on personality **compatibility** (Diamond, 1986). A trial period, such as an engagement or a period of cohabitation, represents the final step in the decision-making or filtering process.

If homogamy and compatibility are the actual standards for mate selection, what about love? In the United States, most people believe that love is the most important consideration when choosing a mate. You might be surprised to learn that this belief is not universal. People from other cultures considered other factors to be more important. Males in South Africa, for example, considered a mate's maturity and ability to keep house as more significant than love in choosing a partner. Chinese women valued emotional stability and the desire for a family as important criteria for mate selection (see Buss, 1989).

Sternberg's (1986, 2006) view of love, composed of the three elements of passion, intimacy, and commitment, which were introduced in Chapter 12, may help us understand these differences. The romantic ideal of love portrayed in many movies and songs embodies the element of passion. This is the aspect of love most closely associated with sexuality and romance. Love that includes passion without intimacy or commitment is called infatuation. Intimacy refers to feelings of attachment or emotional closeness. It characterizes one's willingness to trust another, to value her

TABLE 13.4 Family Life Cycle Stages, Transitions, and Tasks

FAMILY LIFE CYCLE STAGE	EMOTIONAL PROCESS OF TRANSITION: KEY PRINCIPLES	SECOND-ORDER CHANGES IN FAMILY STATUS REQUIRED TO PROCEED DEVELOPMENTALLY
Leaving home: single young adults	Accepting emotional and financial responsibility for self	a. Differentiation of self in relation to family of origin b. Development of intimate peer relationships c. Establishment of self in respect to work and financial independence
The joining of families through marriage: the new couple	Commitment to new system	a. Formation of marital system b. Realignment of relationships with extended families and friends to include spouse
Families with young children	Accepting new members into the system	a. Adjusting marital system to make space for children b. Joining in child rearing, financial and household tasks c. Realignment of relationships with extended family to include parenting and grandparenting roles
Families with adolescents	Increasing flexibility of family boundaries to permit children's independence and grandparents' frailties	a. Shifting of parent–child relationships to permit adolescent to move into and out of system b. Refocus on midlife marital and career issues c. Beginning shift toward caring for older generation
Launching children and moving on	Accepting a multitude of exits from and entries into the family system	a. Renegotiation of marital system as a dyad b. Development of adult-to-adult relationships between grown children and their parents c. Realignment of relationships to include in-laws and grandchildren d. Dealing with disabilities and death of parents (grandparents)
Families in later life	Accepting the shifting generational roles	a. Maintaining own and/or couple functioning and interests in face of physiological decline: exploration of new familial and social role options b. Support for more central role of middle generation c. Making room in the system for the wisdom and experience of the elderly, supporting the older generation without overfunctioning for them d. Dealing with loss of spouse, siblings, and other peers and preparation for death

SOURCE: Carter, B. & McGoldrick, M. (2005). *The expanded family life circle: Indvidual, family and social perspectives* (3rd ed.). Upper Saddle River, NJ: Pearson Education, Inc. Used by permission of Pearson Education, Inc.

support, and to care about her well-being. (Note that Sternberg defines "intimacy" differently from Erikson, who defines it more broadly.) According to Sternberg, when intimacy is present in a relationship without the other elements, a state of liking exists, which is similar to friendship.

The third element, commitment, is present when partners agree to love each other or make a commitment to sustain that love. Maintaining a commitment without intimacy or passion results in the state of "empty love." Sternberg proposed that any of the three elements can be either present or absent in a relationship, accounting for eight different kinds of love (see Table 13.5). He has expanded on these ideas by suggesting that people hold implicit narratives for love or "love stories," which direct their choice of a mate and the course of their relationships (see Sternberg, 2006). Sternberg posits that those who have matching scripts, or similar implicit narratives, stand the best chance of having a compatible relationship. Each script emphasizes certain elements, such as emotional maturity or the commitment factor, as more important than others, and "love scripts" are heavily influenced by cultural values. In contemporary U.S. culture, elements of romance and sexual passion are typically central to the definition of love and are considered very important for relationship satisfaction and mate selection. These authors conclude that love is a social construction and that we are strongly influenced by the conceptions of love that are taught by our culture.

Once the members of a couple make a commitment to each other, they begin to develop a new marital or relationship system that is a creative synthesis of the

TABLE 13.5   Sternberg's Eight Kinds of Love

KINDS OF LOVE	ELEMENTS*		
	INTIMACY	PASSION	DECISION/COMMITMENT
Nonlove	−	−	−
Liking	+	−	−
Infatuation	−	+	−
Empty Love	−	−	+
Romantic Love	+	+	−
Companionate Love	+	−	+
Fatuous Love	−	+	+
Consummate Love	+	+	+

*Element present (+) or absent (−)

SOURCE: Sternberg, R. J. (1986). A triangular theory of love. *Psychological Review, 93,* 123. Reprinted with permission from the American Psychological Association.

couple's original family systems. Marriages, then, are more than the joining of two individuals. The couple must develop a sense of "we-ness" that is not so rigid that it isolates them from their original family systems nor so weak that it dissolves under pressure from them.

With time, the couple may become parents, creating a new rung on the generational ladder and reaching a new stage in the family life cycle. Caretaking responsibilities then must be integrated into the marital relationship, and each partner needs to adjust to the new parental role. As children move through the adolescent period, the family needs to adapt to children's increasing demands for independence. They must learn how to provide the stability and flexibility that characterize authoritative parenting for adolescents.

Next, a couple must deal with the transition of launching their children and renegotiating the marital relationship. Adult children need to balance the attachments they have with parents with those they form outside the family. Parents need to strive for acceptance of their adult children's extrafamilial attachments as well as of their careers and other personal choices. Overall, all generations need to work toward two goals: tolerance of independence and maintenance of connections. Among families in later life, the transitions involved in grandparenthood, loss of spouse, and physical decline produce further challenges that must be dealt with flexibly.

Marriage and Its Discontents

Recall that the great majority of individuals marry at least once during their lifetimes. Clearly, many of these unions do not last "till death do us part." People still divorce in record numbers despite a modest decline in the divorce rate since 1979. It is surprisingly difficult to determine accurately the likelihood that a marriage will end in divorce, but common estimates based census data in the United States are that 40 to 50% of first marriages and up to 60% of remarriages end in divorce. These rates do not account for the number of unions that break up without benefit of legal divorce.

Women typically experience a 45% drop in standard of living following a divorce. Each year approximately one million children witness the dissolution of their parents' marriages and subsequently often share in their mothers' reduced circumstances. Yet divorce wreaks more than financial hardship for children. Researchers have documented increased emotional and behavioral problems, such as

Pam describes some of the challenges raising her children following her divorce. How can Pam—and other mothers and fathers in similar situations—help to alleviate the risks that children like Laurel face?

underachievement, antisocial behavior, and depression in children and adolescents after divorce (e.g., Lansford, 2009; see Box 13.2). Given that divorce is sometimes the best or the only alternative to a troubled marriage and that not every child of divorce suffers dire consequences, we should nonetheless consider how to help prevent what is so often a powerfully negative event in people's lives.

Box 13.2: When Parents Divorce

Georgia and Jim, an affluent white couple, were married for 12 years. Georgia had an impairment that made it impossible for her to drive, although she competently handled most aspects of child rearing and homemaking. She felt isolated in a suburban neighborhood without public transportation, living far from her extended family. Jim brushed aside Georgia's frustrations. He felt that suburban environments were best for children. He believed that he was more than generous with his time as the family "chauffer;" and that Georgia was dismissive of the benefits of his successful career. Jim made lots of time for his family, somewhat enjoying his power as transportation guru, and he was jealous of his relationship with the beautiful and gregarious Georgia. He feared what "too much freedom" might bring. Georgia defied Jim's controlling strategies in a variety of ways. Vitriolic battles ensued, with mutual accusations of disloyalty, brutality, and unfaithfulness.

The couple's children, ages 3, 5, and 9, were caught in the headlights as their parents' fears and frustrations drove a once vital marital relationship into a brick wall. Divorce proceedings were marked by repeated custody and financial court battles. Eventually Georgia moved the children to an urban condominium; Jim found a house with some acreage 2 hours away. The oldest child, Emily, was continually torn by conflicting loyalties, as she was treated by both parents as confidant and ally in their battles. At the worst of times, Emily, still a preadolescent, was often in charge of her younger siblings overnight, while their mother explored her new-found freedom. Emily was strictly enjoined not to reveal this arrangement to anyone, especially her father. Her father was not much more responsible, at times insisting on extensive visits from his children, during which he pumped them for information about their mother, and at other times "punishing" their mother by refusing to see the children or to send support payments.

Although this family's story has unique features, it also has many characteristics that are relatively common to the divorce experiences of children: long standing parental conflict, to which the children are witnesses and unwitting pawns; parents so stressed and absorbed by their problems that their parenting breaks down in critical ways; dramatic changes in the living arrangements of the children. Although not true in this case, many custodial mothers experience a substantial decline in their standard of living; it is not unusual for mothers and children to slip into poverty. It is not surprising that "children often report their parents' marital transitions to be their most painful life experience" (Hetherington, Bridges, & Insabella, 1998, p.170).

Are There Any Consistent Developmental Consequences for Children of Divorce?

Overall, children whose parents divorce (or divorce and remarry) have higher rates of behavioral, emotional and cognitive problems than children whose parents maintain a stable marriage (the "continuously married"). As we review some of these outcomes, however, keep in mind that the impact of divorce on children in specific cases depends on multiple characteristics of the children, the parents, the family, and the community, which all interact in complex ways. Understanding the impact of divorce requires a multidimensional or systems perspective. Individual studies of the consequences of divorce sometimes yield inconsistent results, some finding serious, long-term consequences for children, and others suggesting only temporary problems. Fortunately, meta-analyses and reviews of large numbers of studies have begun to clarify not only what problems tend to occur, but also how the complex blending of risk and protective factors contributes either to sustaining these problems or to mitigating them. The following summary is largely based on meta-analyses and reviews by Amato and colleagues (Amato, 2001, 2005; Amato & Keith, 1991), by Lansford (2009) and by Hetherington et al., (1998).

What Are the Most Likely Problems for Children of Divorce?

Compared to children of continuously married parents, the children of divorce tend to have lower grades and achievement test scores. They are more likely to display externalizing problems (e.g., conduct problems) and/or internalizing problems (e.g., depression). They are likely to have fewer friends and less peer support, and their self-esteem is likely to suffer. As children get older, new problems may emerge. Adolescents and young adults can have more difficulty establishing and maintaining intimate relationships. They are more likely to be sexually active at earlier ages and to have out-of-wedlock children. Dropping out of school, trouble finding and maintaining employment, illicit drug use, and other forms of delinquency are all more common for youth from divorced families, regardless of ethnicity. In adulthood, children of divorce have more trouble staying married, partly because of other outcomes of divorce (like early child bearing) and partly, it appears, because their marital interactions are more likely to involve negative exchanges, such as criticism and contempt. Divorce rates tend to be higher for adults who experienced their parents' divorce during childhood. Intergenerational transmission of marital strife and divorce even extends to the third generation, with the children of the children of divorce more likely to divorce (Amato & Cheadle, 2005).

How Common Are These Problems and Why Do They Occur?

It appears that 20% to 25% of children whose parents divorce have one or more of these problematic outcomes, while about 10% of children of continuously married parents do (Hetherington et al., 1998). The increased risk for children of divorce is clear, but it is also clear that the majority of children of divorce are able to overcome the difficulties that their parents' marital changes create for them. Children who have adjustment problems in the first year or two after a divorce often show improvements thereafter, although new developmental challenges, such as becoming an adolescent, can precipitate new problems. Among the risk and protective factors that contribute to differential outcomes are individual factors, like parents' personalities and children's temperaments, and family factors, like how much conflict children witness and the post-divorce financial arrangements and re-marriages of their parents.

For example, children's characteristics matter. An intelligent child with an easy temperament and good social relationships is likely to weather the storm of divorce, even in very difficult circumstances, more effectively than a child with a difficult temperament or one with a history of cognitive or social problems. Both boys and girls are negatively affected by divorce, but some girls show remarkable resilience, rising to the challenge of increased responsibility, especially in a mother-headed household. Boys are less likely to do so. Yet boys adjust better to a mother's remarriage, apparently benefiting from a stepfather in the home, whereas girls tend not to adjust well to living in stepfamilies (see Hetherington et al., 1998).

Another important factor is children's exposure to parental conflict, during the marriage, and after a divorce. Children whose married parents are chronically in conflict, creating a hostile household environment, often do *better* if their parents divorce, especially if they are less exposed to conflict after the divorce *and* their parents' distress is reduced (Amato, 2005). Conflict, whether before or after divorce, in which children are "caught in the middle" because their parents fight about them, communicate through them, or denigrate each other to the children is especially harmful (Hetherington et al., 1998). Parental conflict appears to have *direct* consequences. It increases children's anger, sadness, fear, and insecurity (e.g., Davies & Woitach, 2008), and these negative emotions are related to later behavior problems (e.g., Crockenberg & Langrock, 2001). But perhaps more important are the *indirect* consequences. Parents in conflict tend to interact with their children less effectively, apparently due to their own stress. They behave more negatively and less sensitively toward their children than other parents (e.g., Cox, Paley, & Harter, 2001). Even infants suffer the effects: Their attachments are less secure and their emotion regulation is less adequate when their parents frequently argue (e.g., Crockenberg, Leerkes, & Lekka, 2007). In a 30-year study of personality development, Block and Block (2006) found that boys who were going to experience their parents' divorce in their future tended to be undercontrolled (e.g., aggressive) before the divorce, suggesting that for some children, family dysfunction begins to take its toll well before divorce.

Many risk factors seem to have effects by influencing the quality of the parenting children receive. Divorced or divorcing parents tend to be less sensitive and responsive to their children's needs and less likely to control and monitor their children than continuously married parents (e.g., Hetherington et al., 1998). Responding to children's increased distress and insecurity can be a challenge that parents are ill-equipped to handle when they themselves are highly stressed. We have seen that one risk factor, parent conflict, affects children partly by reducing parenting quality. Parents' emotional distress also puts children at risk (e.g., chronic anger, anxiety, depression, loneliness, and so on) at least in part by affecting the quality of parent–child interactions. Another risk factor for children is parental re-marriage. Children's adjustment problems tend to increase, and some of this increase is due to declines in parenting quality associated with remarriage. Even though parents may experience emotional and material benefits from re-partnering, their own stress often increases as they face new challenges, such as managing new financial arrangements, new relationships and new family roles (e.g., step-parenting). It is not unusual for step-parents to assume disciplinary authority too quickly, before children have had a sufficient opportunity to build the kinds of ties that make discipline effective (e.g., warm, affectional, trusting bonds) (Browning & Bray, 2007). Another risk factor, separation from the noncustodial parent (usually the father), seems to be a problem more because of changes in the quality of the parent–child relationship than because parent and child spend less time together. The noncustodial parent is likely to find his or her new role quite difficult to navigate, often failing to appropriately enforce controls in order to avoid alienation from the child. Yet, if noncustodial parents maintain an authoritative style with their children, despite having less time with them, children are protected (see DeGarmo, 2010). "Competent, supportive, authoritative noncustodial parents can have beneficial effects for children, and these effects are most marked for . . . parents and children of the same sex" (Hetherington et al., 1998, p. 173).

Clearly, parenting quality and consistency is not all that is important for long-term child outcomes after divorce. Some factors—such as the temperament of the child and the problems of moving into poverty—have direct or moderating influences on outcomes. But parenting quality turns out to be a critical mediator of many of the effects of parents' marital transitions on children's outcomes. Fortunately, it is a factor that is amenable to intervention. Many family courts now offer or require mediation and/or education for parents that is aimed at highlighting the importance of understanding the needs of their children and making those needs a priority in their divorce agreements. At least one comprehensive court related intervention, "The Collaborative Divorce Project" (Pruett, Insabella, & Gustafson, 2005), has demonstrated significant benefits. Compared to controls, intervention parents were more accepting of each others' importance in parenting their children, parents' conflict and distress were reduced, fathers' involvement was increased, fathers were more reliable in making child support payments, and teacher ratings of children's cognitive functioning was improved. If Georgia and Jim had been required to participate in such a program, perhaps Emily and her siblings would have been protected from some of the negative consequences of their parents' divorce.

What Makes a Marriage Fail?

Consider two final statistics from the 1997 census data: Only 4.2% of all divorces were attributed to financial problems, whereas 80% were attributed to irreconcilable differences (U.S. Bureau of the Census, 1998). What makes a difference irreconcilable? How do some people manage to reconcile their conflicts whereas others do not? Are the differences due to the nature of the conflicts or to something about the individuals themselves? These are some of the questions that marital and family researchers have attempted to answer. Increasingly, researchers have relied upon longitudinal studies to describe the course of marriage and to help them identify predictors of distress and divorce as they develop over time. On a more fine-grained level, they have also explored the nature of distressed and nondistressed couples' interaction so that therapeutic recommendations can be made. We will focus on some important research findings in both of these areas to give helpers a framework for understanding the life of a marriage, the behaviors that lead to successful outcomes, and the behaviors that may foreshadow divorce.

Research done in the 1970s indicated consistent U-shaped patterns for quality of marriage. Couples' satisfaction declined shortly after the marriage, reached a low point when children were adolescents, and recovered initial levels of satisfaction when children were launched (Burr, 1970; Rollins & Feldman, 1970). The problem with this portrayal is that these early studies were cross-sectional rather than longitudinal. The high level of satisfaction reported by long-married couples could have been due to the fact that these marriages were happy enough to have survived, long after less satisfied unions had dissolved. Vaillant and Vaillant (1993) collected assessments of marital satisfaction both prospectively (in a longitudinal study) and retrospectively (in which couples reported what they could remember of their marriages over the past 40 years). Results were different depending on how the data were collected. Although retrospective accounts resembled the U-shaped curve found in previous research, prospective ratings showed gradual declines in satisfaction over the entire course of the marriage for both partners, with somewhat greater declines in women's ratings. It appears that fluctuations in the family life cycle did not predict changes in marital satisfaction but were an artifact of the cross-sectional design.

If life cycle changes do not influence satisfaction, then what does? And why, at least for some, does marital satisfaction persistently decline? Let us consider three contemporary hypotheses about marital success and breakdown for some possible answers. Imagine three hypothetical newlywed couples, the Grays, the Whites, and the Greens. Mr. and Mrs. Gray are very much in love. Even when they are in the presence of other people, they behave as if they see only each other. They are highly affectionate and romantic, and their courtship was a whirlwind of exciting events. The Grays believe that they are one another's soul mates, possessing few, if any, negative characteristics. They have no doubts about the happiness that awaits them in marriage.

The Whites are also an affectionate couple. Their view of each other, however, is not quite as rosy as that of the Grays. Their engagement period was a long one because both husband and wife worked to save up enough money to buy a house. Shortly after the wedding, Mrs. White noticed that her husband was becoming less willing to part with any of his income for furniture or other items for the house that she considered important. This has already become a source of tension in the marriage.

The Greens met each other through an online dating website because each was having difficulty meeting eligible romantic partners. Mrs. Green was very insecure in social situations and worried constantly that she would never find a husband. Mr. Green did not want to get married so soon, but he consented because he was afraid that he might lose his chance. Their courtship was a rocky one from the start.

As you read about each of these couples, did you think one or more of them would be more likely to divorce than another? If so, why? Your answers might illustrate popular hypotheses about why marriages succeed or fail. Those who espouse the **disillusionment model** might choose the hypothetical Grays as the couple most likely to experience marital breakdown. This view posits that overly romantic idealizations of marriage and blissfully optimistic views of one's partner set people up for eventual disappointment. Such fantasies cannot coexist for long with the reality of married life (Miller, 1997; Waller, 1938). The rise in divorce rates and incidence of cohabitation might be partially attributable to the fact that young adults today have high expectations for marriage. Barich and Bielby (1996) reported that contemporary young adults had higher expectations than their 1960s counterparts that marriage would satisfy their needs for emotional security, personality development, and companionship. Disappointment in these areas might be seen as a reason to abandon the relationship.

However, another possibility is that the Grays are not especially likely candidates for divorce because they will work hard to maintain their favorable beliefs about each other, despite the inevitable challenges of marriage. Their positive illusions are supportive of the relationship; thus they may be reluctant to abandon them to face reality. This perspective is called the **maintenance hypothesis** (Karney & Bradbury, 1997; Murray, Holmes, & Griffin, 1996).

Perhaps you thought that the Whites were the most likely couple to divorce because of the growing tension in the marriage. Another perspective on marital breakdown, built on **social exchange and behavioral theories**, proposes that increasing problems and mounting conflicts gradually escalate to overwhelm the originally positive perceptions spouses held for each other. Over time, couples who experience chronic conflict and who fail to negotiate it adequately may "fall out of love" with each other once they perceive that the costs of the relationship outweigh its benefits. In truth, no marriage escapes conflict. Approximately half of all divorces occur within the first 7 years of marriage (Cherlin, 1981), suggesting that satisfaction makes its steepest slide during the early period. At this point in development, couples must adjust to each other, work out routines for household tasks, pool resources, and if they have children, take care of them. Several studies have implicated the transition to parenthood as the culprit in the loss of marital satisfaction. For example, Belsky and his colleagues found that many new parents experience a sharp drop in positive interactions and a dramatic increase in conflict following the birth of the first child (Belsky & Kelly, 1994; Belsky, Spanier, & Rovine, 1983). But even couples who remain childless report similar declines in satisfaction. Several prospective studies of young couples' marriages have found much higher rates of divorce among childless couples than among those with children (Cowan & Cowan, 1992; Shapiro, Gottman, & Carrere, 2000). Thus, the existence of conflict in a marriage is simply not a good predictor of its prognosis, but the way couples handle it may be, as we will see later on.

Finally, let's consider the Greens. You may have predicted this couple's marital demise because they seem to bring more personal problems into the marriage in the first place. **Intrapersonal models**, which draw on theories of attachment or personality, emphasize the contribution of one's personal history or temperament to the success or failure of relationships. In some studies, intrapersonal variables like a person's tendency to make positive or negative attributions about her partner and her expectations about the future of the relationship have been found to affect relationship quality over time (e.g., McNulty & Karney, 2004). Another important factor is how quickly an individual recovers from conflict (Salvatore, Kuo, Steele, Simpson, & Collins, 2011). Individual traits are also important. One particularly robust finding from many investigations of marriages is that neuroticism is moderately related to lower levels of marital satisfaction and higher levels of relationship dissolution (Karney & Bradbury, 1995; Kelly & Conley, 1987; Kurdek, 1993). Also, people who have higher levels of negative affect tend to view life as more stressful (Marco & Suls, 1993). These individuals may be more easily overwhelmed by the conflicts that are inherent in family life and, therefore, more prone to marital distress.

In an empirical test of this hypothesis, Karney and Bradbury (1997) measured the level of marital satisfaction of 60 newlywed couples at 6-month intervals over a period of 4 years. A measure of neuroticism was obtained for each participant at each of the first two data collections. Questions examined things such as tendency to worry and moodiness. Measures of initial satisfaction and observations of problem-solving interactions were also collected.

The researchers found that marital satisfaction declined, on average, for all participants over the 4 years, replicating many earlier findings. However, the drop in satisfaction was several times greater for couples who divorced than for those who remained together. Spouses' levels of neuroticism, a presumably stable variable, were related primarily to how satisfied they were at the beginning of the marriage and less so to rates of change in satisfaction. The way couples solved problems was also strongly related to the rates of decline in satisfaction. In this case, both intrapersonal and interpersonal variables made independent contributions to the health of the relationship but in different ways and at different points in time.

Keeping Love Alive

Although the models we have described all may contribute something to our understanding of marriage, each by itself is inadequate to explain its complexity. The marital trajectory seems to be affected by intrapersonal (traits, expectations), interpersonal (problem-solving skills), situational (life stresses, environmental conditions), and developmental (transitions, role change) factors. A comprehensive, multidimensional theory of marriage or other committed relationships has yet to be developed. Nevertheless, we can learn a great deal from the research that has been done, particularly during the last decade, to help us improve the relationships of our clients.

Some of the most helper-friendly information comes from the "love-lab" of John Gottman, who has a unique approach to the study of marital dynamics. Gottman and his colleagues have spent years observing and videotaping couples interacting with each other to understand, from the inside out, what makes marriages work or fail. Gottman (1993, 1999) has used this descriptive approach as a step toward building a theory of marital stability and dissolution that can be closely tied to clinical application.

Research on marital communication styles has helped clinicians understand more about the elements of successful relationships.

Three fundamental ideas are important in understanding Gottman's research. First, he conceptualizes marriage or any primary relationship as a new system that represents a synthesis of the pre-existing elements of each partner's personal history and temperament. Second, he draws upon systems theory to describe marriage as a relational system that seeks a stable or **homeostatic steady state** (von Bertalanffy, 1968). This steady state is maintained over time by the couple's unique balance of positive and negative elements in areas of interactive behavior, perception, and physiology. Behavior refers here to a couple's interactions and accompanying affect; perception refers to self-perceptions and attributions directed to partners; and physiology refers to the autonomic, endocrine, and immune system functioning of the partners. Third, he premises his approach on research done in the last few decades, which consistently documents a ratio of high negative to low positive behaviors in distressed/divorcing couples as opposed to nondistressed/stable couples.

Thinking about a marital relationship as a ratio of positive and negative factors is somewhat like considering the relationship to have a typical kind of "weather," for example, sunny, calm, cloudy, stormy, and so forth. The marital climate or stable steady state is made up of uninfluenced (intrapersonal elements like neuroticism) and influenced (couple's interaction) elements. From a systems perspective, a marital union tends toward stability in its positivity to negativity ratio over time. Obviously, contextual features and crises also play a part in the nature of relationships, but these factors are not emphasized because they are less predictable.

Gottman and his colleagues developed ways to measure levels of positivity and negativity in couples' behavioral interactions, in their perceptions of each other, and in their physiological states, such as arousal or calmness, using observational coding systems, measures of physiological responding, and questionnaire and interview data. Over several extensive longitudinal studies, they set out to predict which couples would divorce and which would remain together. Moreover, they sought to determine whether particular elements were associated with marital breakup or success (see Gottman, 1994a; Gottman & Levenson, 2000).

In general, making this kind of marital "weather report" has surprising predictive ability. Assessments done at the beginning of a marriage, including those made from videotapes of the first 3 minutes of a newlywed marital conflict discussion, predicted later outcomes with a high degree of accuracy (Carrere & Gottman, 1999; Carrere, Buehlman, Gottman, Coan, & Ruckstuhl, 2000; Gottman & Levenson, 2000). What turns out to predict marital dissolution best? A high level of **negative affect reciprocity** is a distinguishing feature. This construct refers to the likelihood that negative emotions in one partner will follow from the other partner's negativity. You may think of it as the likelihood that partners will bring out the worst in each other. This is accomplished through the combined influences of information processing biases (e.g., seeing the other's qualities as negative), heightened physiological arousal (e.g., interpreting arousal as anger), negative behavioral interactions (e.g., being critical and defensive), and failing to respond to a partner's bids for attention.

But a number of fine points bear mentioning. As it turns out, conflict and angry feelings are part of all intimate relationships, so simply trying to avoid conflict won't help. Furthermore, not all negative affect is equally deleterious to relationships. Anger can play a constructive function when it is a justifiable reaction to a partner's behavior or reflects airing of grievances (Gottman, 1994b). The trick is to distinguish between functional and dysfunctional types of negativity. Other researchers have drawn similar distinctions (e.g., Markman, Stanley, & Blumberg, 1994), but, for the sake of simplicity, we will present Gottman's definitions here.

The four kinds of negativity that do the most damage to relationships and that are highly predictive of divorce are criticism, defensiveness, contempt, and stonewalling (see Table 13.6). The presence of these **"four horsemen of the apocalypse"** (Gottman, 1999), particularly contempt, can be very destructive. But suppose you recognize some of these elements in your own close relationship? Does this forecast an inevitable breakup? You may be somewhat relieved to know that Gottman found criticism, defensiveness, and stonewalling even in happy marriages. In couples headed toward divorce, however, these three behaviors were more frequent, contempt was also present, and there was much less positive affect in the relationship overall. Most important, the distressed couples he observed were not skilled in repairing the relationship after conflict occurred. Instead, prolonged periods of unrelieved distress, accompanied by heightened physiological arousal, fueled negative perceptions of the partner, overwhelmed spouses' positive feelings for each other, and led to a state of isolation and loneliness. Over time, if negativity surpassed positivity, it contributed to the derailment of the relationship.

TABLE 13.6   Gottman's Four Horsemen of the Apocalypse

1. *Criticism:* Implying that one's partner has some global deficiency that is part of his/her personality: "You always . . .; You never. . . ."
2. *Defensiveness:* Failure to take responsibility and defending oneself against criticism: "Who me? . . . I do not!"
3. *Contempt:* A statement or nonverbal behavior that puts down the partner while elevating the speaker to a superior position (such as insulting, using hostile humor, or mocking the partner).
4. *Stonewalling:* Verbal or nonverbal behaviors that communicate impassiveness (looking away, looking bored).

SOURCE: Based on Gottman, J. M. (1999). *The marriage clinic: A scientifically based marital therapy.* New York, NY: Norton.

With the accumulation of stresses and losses that we all experience in adulthood, it makes sense that good coping skills would be an essential component of personal and interpersonal wellness. Therefore, a critical part of marriage maintenance (and probably that of any close relationship) is the capacity to repair the frayed relationship after conflict. Gottman observed that the particular type of conflict style that couples demonstrated did not matter as much as the amount of overall positivity in the relationship (humor, interest, affection, and validation) and the couples' ability to soothe hurt or angry feelings. Some couples tended to avoid conflict, others embraced it with gusto, whereas some discussed their differences with the validating ("I hear what you are saying. . .") style of counselors. Surprisingly, all three types could be very happily married if the steady state ratios of positivity to negativity in their relationships were 5 to 1. In other words, if a marital climate has substantially more periods of sun than rain, the chances of long-term success are pretty good.

Generativity: Making a Mark at Midlife

Establishing generativity is the primary developmental task of middle adulthood according to Erikson (1950/1963). Generativity has been described as having several components (e.g., McAdams, 2006; Stewart & Vandewater, 1998). As we saw in Chapter 12, two primary components are desire and accomplishment (Stewart & Vandewater). Desire refers to wanting to be creative, productive, or giving, and accomplishment means actually feeling that you are creative, productive, or giving. Generative desire is more characteristic of young adults, but generative accomplishment is more typical of middle adults.

The Experience of Child Rearing

For many people, raising children is a significant part of adult life. Parents experience more stress than nonparents, but they usually view their parenting role as a generative process (Marks, Bumpass, & Jun, 2003). The nature and quality of the parenting experience, including the parent's feelings of generativity, change substantially as both children and parents grow older.

Each major period or stage of a child's life creates new challenges for a parent, challenges that the parent is more or less prepared to face depending on her age and stage of life, her personality and coping skills, her socioeconomic status, and the available support systems. For example, the gratifications of parenthood and marriage are usually greater for older rather than younger first-time parents. Older parents tend to have a more fully developed self-concept and greater self-esteem, are more advanced in their careers, have more money, and are more likely to find balancing work and family responsibilities easier to negotiate. Older fathers spend more time caring for their children than younger fathers, a factor that not only increases satisfaction with parenting but also improves satisfaction for both partners. Older dads also tend to be less physical with their young children (e.g., less tickling and chasing), and to engage their children in more cognitively stimulating activities than younger dads (see Parke, 2002). Research on mothers indicates that age is not a factor in how likely mothers are to meet their infants' health, safety and survival needs; younger mothers are as effective as older mothers in feeding, holding and establishing positive emotional bonds. Yet older mothers tend to have more basic knowledge about children and parenting than younger mothers (Bornstein, Cote, Haynes, Hahn, & Park, 2010). This may help explain why, even with social class controlled, older moms provide more cognitive stimulation to their infants. They talk to them more and use more diverse vocabulary, and they provide more exploratory opportunities (e.g., Moore & Brooks-Gunn, 2002; Bornstein, Putnick, & Suwalsky, & Gini, 2006).

Not surprisingly, very young first-time parents (under 20) are at greater risk than other groups to find that the stress of parenting outweighs its satisfactions. They typically complete fewer years of education than older parents and have lower incomes. They are more likely to divorce than other groups, and their children are more likely to experience developmental problems (e.g., Boden, Fergusson, & Horwood, 2007; Furstenberg, Brooks-Gunn, & Chase-Lansdale, 1987). The satisfactions of parenting, like all other developmental outcomes, are a function of many interacting risk and protective factors.

The normative experience of parents as they move through each stage of parenting is that the challenges bring both intense new stresses and delightful new pleasures (Delmore-Ko, Panser, Huntsberger, & Pratt, 2000). For example, in the newborn period, first-time parents often feel distressed and overwhelmed (Harwood, McLean, & Durkin, 2007; Meijer & van den Wittenboer, 2007; Nomaguchi & Milkie, 2003) and are likely to experience a decline in marital satisfaction (Twenge, Campbell, & Foster, 2003). Caring for an infant is far more demanding than most people expect it to be. Distress is linked to insufficient sleep, money worries, anxieties about the baby's dependency and vulnerability, feelings of uncertainty about one's caretaking skill, difficulty balancing the needs of self, partner, and baby, and disillusionment with the "yucky" side of infant care (such as mounds of laundry, endless spit-up, and baffling crying fits just when it's time for the parents to eat dinner). Simultaneously, however, most parents of newborns report feeling like they have now truly grown up, that their lives have new purpose and meaning, and that they have a strong sense of shared joy. The transition to parenting involves tasks and demands that are transformative for many first time parents. For example, gender role attitudes tend to become somewhat less egalitarian and more traditional as mothers and fathers attempt to adapt to their new roles (e.g., Katz-Wise, Priess, & Hyde, 2010). For both mothers and fathers, personal identity becomes somewhat less focused on work and more on family, although the shift in work salience tends to be greater for mothers.

A core feature of generativity is taking care of or showing concern for the next generation.

The parent of the toddler or preschooler must begin to discipline a child who is still very dependent but who is skilled enough to need continuous supervision. Because a toddler is a proficient climber, for example, a parent can no longer put her in a crib to keep her safe while the parent takes a quick shower or talks on the phone. Parents begin to have conflicts with their children as disciplinary efforts are resisted by a child who has little capacity to take the parent's perspective. Also, partners often find themselves in conflict about their children as they negotiate disciplinary styles, time commitments, and divisions of labor. And parents feel physically exhausted as they try to keep up with energetic, active youngsters who have little self-control. Although many parents experience this period as especially stressful, there are new pleasures as well (Crnic & Booth, 1991; Edwards & Liu, 2002). Children begin to talk, to participate in organized activities, and to do things on their own, such as feeding themselves. Their temperaments are blossoming into personalities, and a new little self becomes part of the family system. Most parents experience these developments as intriguing and as a source of pride, despite the heavy dose of frustration that these advances can bring.

As children move into middle childhood, the family waters are often somewhat becalmed. If there is a honeymoon period between parents and children, this is it. The child's thinking is more logical, she has a growing capacity to take another's perspective, and she can in many situations keep herself safe, so that supervision can be reduced. At the same time, the child does not yet feel much ambivalence about her dependence on her parents, and parents still enjoy the role of preferred companion. There are plenty of challenges in this period, of course. Outside factors—such as peers, teachers, and the media—are increasingly influential. Helping children learn to interpret and negotiate the outside world and to deal with the stress it creates can be difficult (e.g., Collins, Madsen, & Susman-Stillman, 2002).

 While raising three boys, Julie finds that her discipline style has changed over time and also that it is quite different than her husband's style. What sorts of new challenges might she expect as the boys grow into adolescence?

Parenting usually becomes more demanding and difficult when children reach adolescence. The child's push for independence, parental worries about the child's risk taking and sexual maturity, and the child's often critical and rejecting attitudes are tough to bear, even when parents are well versed in the needs of adolescents. Many parents reach their 40s and 50s when their children are adolescents, so that they are beginning to confront their own physical aging and perhaps engage in a "midlife review" at the same time. Steinberg and Silk (2002) report that adolescent development and parental distress about midlife are interacting factors. For example, parents whose teens are actively dating and involved in mixed-sex activities are more likely to express midlife concerns and to feel less satisfaction with their lives than parents whose teens are not yet dating. Parent and adolescent bickering over mundane matters and adolescents' de-idealization of parents can also take a toll on parents' well-being. Many studies find this period to be when parents' marital and life satisfaction reaches its lowest point.

The **launching period**, when emerging adults begin to move away and become more self-sufficient, brings some new challenges. On the whole, by the time adult children are in their twenties parents begin to feel the benefits of fewer parental responsibilities, and their relationships with their children improve (e.g., Fingerman, 2003). We often hear about how sad parents are, especially mothers, when their young adult children depart, leaving an "empty nest." Lewis and Lin (1996) report that although parents often anticipate that the transition will be difficult for them, only about 25% feel very unhappy. The loneliness of the empty nest may be more profound for people in more interdependent cultures, especially when adult children leave to pursue lifestyles different from those of their parents (Liu & Guo, 2007). Western research shows that fathers with traditional gender expectations and roles may experience more distress than mothers. They may struggle more with the concept of their adult children becoming autonomous, which modifies their role as decision maker and changes the structure of the family (e.g., Lewis & Lin, 1996). Mothers, who typically do more of the day-to-day child rearing, are more struck by the relief they experience from those duties. Their greater involvement may also lead them to prepare more and to do more planning for the next phase of their lives. There is, however, a strong link between both mothers' and fathers' feelings of well-being and generativity, on one hand, and their children's functioning, on the other. If adult children are seen as personally and socially well-adjusted, parents are likely to experience greater self-acceptance, purpose in life, and feelings of mastery (e.g., Ryff, Lee, Essex, & Schmutte, 1994).

The typical parent is exiting middle age when her children are entering it. Parents whose children are over 30 years old may find the quality of their relationships changing further, such that they now tend to relate to their children more as equals. Adult children often begin to identify with their parents, appreciating more profoundly what an adult's life is like than they ever could before. Exchange of support seems to become more and more complementary. However, the relationship is still not likely to be completely egalitarian. Assistance and support, such as financial help, are still more likely to be provided by the older generation to the younger one (Birditt, Fingerman, & Zarit, 2010; Byers Levy, Allore, Bruce, & Kasl, 2008).

As adults move through middle age, they sometimes find themselves in the role of **kinkeeper**, the person in an extended family who helps the generations maintain contact with one another (e.g., Sinardet & Mortelmans, 2009). They may also take on new family responsibilities involving care of an ailing parent or another elderly relative. Most adults in the United States enter midlife with one or both parents living, but by the end of midlife, 77% have lost both parents and many have participated in some way in their parents' terminal care (Lachman, 2004). Women are much more likely to play these roles than men in most cultures, although many men take on some kinkeeping or caregiving responsibilities. These tasks can be particularly challenging if they coincide with the adolescence of one's children. People who carry these double responsibilities are described as being in the **sandwich generation** (e.g., Hamill & Goldberg, 1997; Zal, 1992). Many factors affect how stressful this position is, such as the coping style of the sandwiched individual, educational, financial, and cultural factors, and the availability of other family help, especially the support of the partner. As with the challenges of parenting, kinkeeping and elder care can put caregivers at risk for physical and mental health problems (Hsing-Yi & Chiou, 2010). Yet it can also bring emotional rewards, such as feelings of mastery and meaningfulness (e.g., Martire, Stephens, & Townsend, 1998). See Box 15.1 in 15.1.

Work and Community Involvement

Our careers begin in young adulthood, but it is in the middle adult years that people usually feel they are becoming expert in their work. The full fruits of a career are likely to be experienced in this stage of life, and for many, identity is heavily affected by work (Sterns & Huyck, 2001). Incomes for both men and women tend to reach their peak, and top levels of management and professional advancement are most likely to characterize people in this age period as well. Work intensity and time invested in work usually increase in the first half of middle adulthood and then begin to taper off, as many people begin to strike a balance between time spent working and time spent with family and friends and in community service. This shift seems to be motivated for some people by increased confidence in their productivity and their value in the workplace, allowing them to invest more energy and effort into other aspects of their lives. For others, the shift may be motivated by a sense that their work will not bring them the satisfactions they may have once expected or dreamed about (e.g., Levinson, 1986).

This temporal pattern, of course, varies considerably across individuals and life circumstances, such as social class and marital status. It is also linked somewhat to gender. In married couples, women who continue to work after having children generally give more priority to child rearing over career responsibilities (e.g., McElwain, Korabik, & Rosin, 2005). Men are less likely to do so, although fathers are more likely to modify the intensity of their work effort in dual-earner couples, which now represent the most typical arrangement in the American middle class. With this change has come a shift in role structures, with men becoming more active, involved parents and taking on more household responsibilities, although women still shoulder more of these burdens (Bond et al., 2002). There is some evidence that for more recent cohorts of U.S. parents, self-esteem goes up for fathers who adjust their work schedules to accommodate family needs, even though they are likely to worry about negative effects on their careers. And, just like mothers who choose to give up careers to care for children, "stay at home" dads, whose numbers are growing (e.g., an increase of 60% from 2004 to 2006) tend to miss the daily adult interactions they had in the workplace (Cynkar, 2007). For mothers in recent cohorts, self-esteem tends to decline if they cut back on employment to take care of family responsibilities; older cohorts of men show a similar tendency (Carr, 2002). Note the impact of historical context on the interplay of social roles and psychological functioning.

The picture is a little different in non-Western countries. In a recent analysis (Chandra, 2012), work-life balance was more likely to be considered the responsibility of employers in Western countries. Employee assistance programs, flexible work schedules, and so on have become more common in the United States and Europe, and both genders share in the benefits. In Asian countries, the problem of balancing home and work was perceived to be an issue for women who retained primary responsibility for household duties. Individuals were expected to take responsibility for balancing jobs and family. In many cases, women were expected to limit their career options in the service of motherhood, which was considered their preeminent role.

Western researchers have found that participating in multiple roles (active parent, spouse, worker, caregiver to aging parents, and so on) makes middle adulthood hectic. Professionals frequently work with middle adults who are struggling to find effective ways of resolving what is called "work-life conflict" (e.g., Schultheiss, 2006; Somech, 2007). Yet, despite the challenge, multiple roles can contribute to life satisfaction, to mental health, and to better relationships (see Brummelhuis & Bakker, 2012).

In dual career households, the degree to which both parents modify their work time and share child care and household duties is a significant factor in determining marital satisfaction and feelings of spousal commitment, especially for women (e.g., Feeney, Peterson, & Noller, 1994; Hyde, DeLamater, & Durik, 2001; Schafer & Keith, 1980).

One of the benefits of participating in multiple roles is **role buffering**: If one role is a source of psychological stress or failure experiences, success and satisfaction in another role may compensate. For example, when women interrupt their careers to take on full-time parenting, they may in midlife restart their careers or start new ones, especially after their children reach adolescence. For them, the intensity of work involvement may be greater than it would otherwise be at this stage of their lives, and it can be out of phase with their husbands' work involvement, because they are at an earlier point in career development. Yet, the opportunity to be productive in another setting seems to provide a buffer against some of the stresses involved in parenting an adolescent (e.g., Larson & Richards, 1994).

Money and promotion are the external markers of achievement for middle adults, but a sense of generative accomplishment appears to be more dependent on how creative and productive we feel. The latter experiences are in turn related to how challenging the work is and to the level of interest and expertise that we bring to the work (see Csikszentmihalyi, 1999; Myers, 1993; Ryan & Deci, 2000). McAdams (2006; Mansfield & McAdams, 1996) explains generativity as constituting both **agency** and **communion**. Agency "involves generating, creating, and producing things, ideas, people, events, and so on as powerful extensions or expressions of the self [italics added]" (Mansfield & McAdams, 1996, p. 721). Agentic generativity, then, depends on self-knowledge, a sense of identity, and the opportunity to work on tasks that match our interests, values, and skills, all key features of successful career planning, as we saw in Chapter 12. Generativity also involves communion, expressed "in the adult's desire to care for the next generation, even to the point of sacrificing his or her own well-being for the good of those who will follow" (pp. 721–722). Behaviors involving giving, offering, and contributing are aspects of communion. Research indicates that adults who are identified by others as "generative" do tend to combine both agency and communion in the concerns that they express and in their occupational and community behaviors (Mansfield & McAdams, 1996). See Box 13.3.

McAdams and his colleagues have developed a variety of measures of generativity. For example, on a 20-item questionnaire respondents rate the degree to which statements are true of them, such as, "I have a responsibility to improve the neighborhood in which I live" (McAdams & de St. Aubin, 1992). In a measure of generative goals, respondents are asked to describe 10 "personal strivings," and the responses are coded for "generative imagery" (McAdams, de St. Aubin, & Logan, 1993). Using these techniques, people who rate high on generativity are found to be more likely to use authoritative, child-centered parenting styles; are more actively involved in political, religious, and social reform activities; and report higher levels of self-esteem and happiness than people who score low on generativity (see McAdams & Bowman, 2001, for a review).

One of the more interesting differences between midlife adults who score high versus low on generativity measures is in the kind of narrative they produce when asked to tell their life stories. McAdams (e.g., 2006; McAdams & Olson, 2010) argues that the narratives we construct about our lives are reconstructions that are based on the real events in our lives but that they also indicate our characteristic ways of making sense of things. They contribute to and reflect our identities and our sense of well-being. Generative adults, for example, tend to tell life stories with "redemption" themes (McAdams & Bowman, 2001). That is, even though the individual may describe many serious difficulties, her story often progresses from describing an emotionally negative event or bad scene to an emotionally positive or good outcome. Conversely, adults low on generativity tend to include more "contamination" sequences in their life stories. These are descriptions that go from good or positive experiences to negative outcomes.

Box 13.3: Men, Women, and Leadership

In high school, Regina loved math and science, and as a 1st-year college student she signed up to be a chemistry major. Regina liked her courses, but she also loved to party, and hours in the lab, along with grinding competition with premed students in organic chemistry, were not much fun. She began to feel that she was floundering—how could she combine her sociability with her sharp, analytic intellectual style to carve out a future? To satisfy distribution requirements she signed up for an economics course her second semester, and the rest is history. Regina became a very successful economics major, and by the time she was a senior was being wooed by several major banking institutions for their management training programs. It was the early 1970s in corporate America, and recruitment of at least some women for executive management tracks was beginning to be "politically correct." But a foot in the door is only that. What did it take for Regina to become one of the top ranking banking executives in the United States by the time she was 50?

Early research on gender and leadership seemed to indicate that women and men have different "leadership styles." This research often involved bringing together strangers to accomplish some goal and assigning one participant as leader. Under these conditions, gender seems to make a big difference: Men are more "task oriented," focusing on doing whatever will get the job done, whereas women tend to be more "interpersonal," putting more time and effort into the quality of the social interaction. But in a meta-analysis of leadership style research, Eagly and Johnson (1990) found that when actual managers who occupy the same organizational positions are compared, both women and men are characterized by task-oriented, not interpersonal, styles. They did find one sex difference in leadership style, however. Women were more likely to be democratic, whereas men were more likely to be autocratic.

Social role theory, like that of Eagly and her colleagues, paints a complex picture of what contributes to leadership development and success for women and men in today's world (e.g., Eagly, 2007). When an individual fills a role, like a leadership role, the role itself influences their behavior. But their occupational role is only one of many social roles they are fulfilling. Another important one is their gender role, which is comprised of a set of expectancies, or "shared beliefs that apply to individuals on the basis of their socially identified sex" (Eagly & Johannesen-Schmidt, 2001, p. 783). Understanding leadership behavior and its effectiveness, for men or women, requires understanding how the demands of these various roles are met within the particular organizational context.

As we saw in Chapter 8, expectancies or stereotypes about gender differences may or may not actually be real, and even when they are substantiated by empirical measures (e.g., males on average are more physically aggressive than females), average sex differences in behavior or traits tend to be small. The range of differences among individuals of the same sex is much greater than the average differences between sexes. But social role theorists argue that the importance of sex differences is not just a function of their real size but of the impact they have on people's expectations of their own and others' behavior, as well as on how people interpret behavior. An example of how people's interpretations are affected by sex stereotypes comes from research on anger expressed in the workplace. Brescoll and Uhlmann (2008) report that in simulated job interviews, when women professionals expressed anger their reactions were attributed to internal characteristics (e.g., "She's an angry person" or "She is out of control"), but when males expressed anger their reactions were attributed to external circumstances.

Two aspects of gender roles that are important in the discussion of leadership are *agency*, which is more strongly ascribed to men, and *communion*, which is seen as more characteristic of women. As you have seen in the discussion of generativity, *agency* is a kind of powerful "get things done" expression of self. It can be captured by descriptors like *assertive, ambitious, dominant, controlling, forceful, independent*, and *confident. Communion* involves expression of concern for others. Descriptors like *affectionate, helpful, sensitive to others, sympathetic*, and *nurturing* apply.

Social role theory predicts that how a woman or a man will behave in a managerial or other leadership position is largely constrained by the nature of the position. They do not discount the influence of individual characteristics, like personality traits, but they emphasize that regardless of the individual filling the role, certain task requirements must be met, such as supervising the work of others, planning, gathering information, and disseminating it. These responsibilities require agentic behavior, and managers tend to behave agentically regardless of gender, as the meta-analysis by Eagly and Johnson illustrates. People also adjust their agentic behavior depending on whether they are interacting with subordinates or with a boss. Moskowitz, Suh, and Desaulniers (1994) used an experience sampling method to monitor managers' interpersonal behavior at work for 20 days. The same individuals were highly agentic with their subordinates, but less agentic with their superiors. It seems clear that managerial status predicts agentic behavior. But in the Moskowitz et al. study, the same participants' communal behavior was affected by their gender role, not by their managerial status: Women behaved more communally than men, especially with other women.

It appears, then, that women and men may tend to display different leadership styles, not with regard to whether they are task oriented or agentic, but with regard to how they treat people in the process. In other words, although their agentic behavior is constrained by their managerial role, their communal behavior is constrained by their own or others' expectations with regard to gender. Eagly and her colleagues propose that an important reason for this gender difference is that when women are leaders, there is an incongruity in role expectations that does not hold for men. *Agency* is important for leadership and is also expected of men. Therefore, people are likely to accept a domineering, even autocratic, management approach from men. Women must be agentic as leaders because the role requires it, but agency is incongruent with the female gender role and may tend to be perceived negatively by others as a result. In other words, many people may feel ambivalent about yielding power to women. Therefore, for many leadership positions, women will be more successful if they exercise their authority with

(Box 13.3 continued)

Box 13.3 *Continued*

special attention to at least some communal aspects of the process. They may have to be more democratic, inviting others to participate more in decision making, whereas men may have more freedom to be authoritarian if they choose. Fortunately, women are more likely than men to have developed skill using a collaborative, negotiating style as we saw in Chapter 8.

Western scientific research supports this analysis. Eagly, Makhijani, and Klonsky (1992) did a meta-analysis of studies in which participants rated others' leadership skill. In all of these studies, the behaviors of men and women leaders had been equated by the researchers. Participants gave significantly lower ratings to women who behaved autocratically than to men. Eagly and Johannesen-Schmidt (2001) report on an international study of managerial style in primarily Western countries. They assessed the behaviors and effectiveness of 2,874 female and 6,126 male managers, looking at ratings by subordinates, peers, superiors, and by the managers themselves. The most effective managers of either gender were characterized by the same leadership behaviors: acknowledging good performance by followers (giving performance-based rewards), developing and mentoring their followers, attending to followers' individual needs, and inspiring their followers' optimism and excitement about the future as well as their respect and pride in their leader. Women managers outscored men on all of these behaviors, especially the most communal of them (e.g., attending to the individual needs of their followers). The least effective managers were those who focused on their followers' mistakes, procrastinated in solving problems, and were absent or uninvolved at critical times. These were not common behaviors for any of these managers, but they were more common for men than for women.

Why were women leaders more effective than men? Eagly and Johannesen-Schmidt (2001) offer two explanations. First, women probably have to meet a higher standard to be successful managers.

"Men may have greater leeway to remain in leadership roles, despite poor performance" (p. 793). Second, the behaviors that are especially effective for leaders—for example, individualized consideration, rewarding positive performance—"may involve being attentive, considerate, and nurturing" (p. 793), communal behaviors that women may be more likely to engage in because of gender role expectations. A more recent meta-analysis suggests that women are more likely than men to be transformational leaders. Such leaders more typically gain the trust of employees, show the capacity to innovate, and are able to empower others (Eagly, Johannesen-Schmidt, & vanEngen, 2003)

The studies we have reviewed thus far suggest that men are less likely than women to be penalized for autocratic, domineering behavior in leadership positions. But this situation may not hold for all racial and ethnic groups, at least in the United States. In one study, researchers asked participants to rate the performance of a leader who was confronting a subordinate employee (Livingston, Rosette, & Washington, 2012). The leader was presented in one of two ways: either as demanding and assertive (dominant) or as encouraging and compassionate (communal). A photograph portrayed the leader either as a Black man or woman or as a White man or woman. Participants tended to rate communal leaders more positively than dominant leaders, regardless of race or gender, consistent with the research we have just reviewed. But dominant leaders were rated differently depending on race and gender. If the leader were White, a dominant man was seen as a better leader than a dominant woman, as you might expect. But the reverse was true when the leader was portrayed as Black. A dominant woman was given much higher scores than a dominant man. Although research examining the intersection of race and gender roles in the workplace is in its infancy, this study suggests that minority group members may face very different sets of gender role expectations than Whites.

Generative adults also are more likely to describe themselves as "sensitized to others' suffering at an early age" and as "guided by a clear and compelling ideology that remains relatively stable over time" (McAdams & Bowman, 2001, p. 14). Overall, there is a progressive structure to the generative adult's life story that suggests a reasonably coherent sense of a self who is moving in a positive direction and who feels able and willing to make a difference. In particular, such individuals seem to be able to move on despite sometimes serious setbacks. People low in generativity by midlife, however, seem to be stuck, "unable to grow." McAdams and Bowman (2001) describe one woman who, at 41, is still setting goals that are markedly like those she set as a young woman—"to graduate from high school" and to be "better able to take care of myself." She tells the interviewer that she is "desperately seeking" herself. Unfortunately, her persistent expectation that what appears to be good will turn out bad—reflected in the many contamination sequences she includes in her life story narrative—seems to make her quest overwhelming.

Generativity seems to be foreshadowed in the personality characteristics that emerge in adolescence and young adulthood. Petersen and Steward (1996) found that individuals who as adolescents already had strong power and achievement needs, combined with strong needs for affiliation, were most likely to demonstrate generativity when they reached middle adulthood. The Big 5 personality traits can play a role as well. Aspects of extraversion (which is somewhat agentic) and agreeableness (especially altruism, which is strongly communal) are correlated with generativity (see Cox, Wilt, Olson, & McAdams, 2012). Finally, as we pointed out above, identity development contributes to generativity. For example, self-knowledge can help a person make choices, such as choices of career and community activities that provide a good match to her skills and interests, so that she can maintain her intrinsic motivation to produce and create.

APPLICATIONS

The middle years are a challenging period of life. Adults have to contend with jobs, children, partners, and themselves, as well as the unexpected crises that occur. They bring very different experiences and dreams into adulthood. It is impossible to establish a life-stage trajectory that could take into account all this diversity with any level of precision. However, there do seem to be powerful themes, such as the quest for intimacy and generativity that characterize most adult lives.

We have seen that many theorists (e.g., Erikson, 1950/1963; Levinson, 1986; Vaillant, 1977) have attempted to specify these themes and their typical progress, though they all seem to recognize that we cannot expect every life story to unfold in some inevitable sequence of events or experiences. These same theorists have also described psychological requirements for healthy functioning as people move through adulthood. One consistent message that these authors communicate in various ways is this: Adults have to grow up. Growing up is not always easy and often not much fun, particularly in an age and in a society that heavily invests in the notion of personal satisfaction, youth, and freedom of choice. However, the very nature of the life cycle makes certain changes inevitable, and once those changes are accepted, they can be the source of great personal satisfaction and pride.

Adult Commitments

For most married people and other intimate partners, both joyous and painful experiences make up the fabric of close relationships and both wax and wane over the course of the life span. Some of these changes are predictable: when a new baby arrives, when children become adolescents, when adult children marry, when parents age and die, when partners experience age-related declines or the onset of illness. Some changes are due to unpredictable events: the loss of a job or the demands of a new one, an unexpected illness, a relocation, a war or economic recession.

Professionals who work with couples can find it helpful to identify the sources of stress as coming from nonnormative or normative causes. Couples in crisis, for example, may be reeling from an unexpected and rather obvious stressor that has taken its toll on the relationship. On the other hand, changes involved in predictable life events, such as steadily accumulating time demands or eroding incomes of working families with children, can affect the quality of relationships just as significantly and may not be quite as obvious to the people involved.

Furthermore, changes that come with daily give and take, such as increased realization of a partner's flaws and idiosyncracies combined with greater awareness of personal needs and preferences, can set the stage for relationship conflict.

Clinicians often report that couples come to counseling after their relationships have reached a state of meltdown. Partners can become trapped in destructive patterns of relating that create persistent distress (Weiss & Hayman, 1990). In the demand–withdraw pattern, for example, one partner withdraws to escape the demands of the other and, as a result, demands escalate and withdrawal is reinforced. Various methodologies have been employed to address couple difficulties, including behavioral approaches to improving communication and problem-solving skills, cognitive techniques for changing negative thoughts, affective or emotion-focused methods for teaching partners to own and express feelings more effectively, and intrapsychic models that relate present problems to early attachment histories. At this point, both behavioral marital therapy (BMT; Jacobson & Addis, 1993) and emotionally focused couples therapy (EFT; Johnson, Hunsley, Greenberg, & Schindler, 1999) have demonstrated empirical support. Insight-oriented couples therapy (IOCT; Snyder & Wills, 1989), which fosters awareness of the nature of relationship problems and promotes positive interaction, has also demonstrated long-term effectiveness in helping distressed couples (Snyder, Wills, & Grady-Fletcher, 1991).

A few common themes have emerged from this growing body of research to guide professionals who work in this area. Simply stated, relationships tend to flourish when the psychological atmosphere is positive, and they tend to deteriorate when it becomes negative. Because stress and disagreements are an inevitable part of all long-term relationships, successful therapies appear to blend skills of conflict management with those of positive relationship enhancement. This is the theme of Gottman's approach to marital therapy. He has made the interesting observation, based upon his studies of marital interaction, that the content of couples' problem discussions remains remarkably stable over time. Fully 69% of the time, couples' arguments are about a problem that has existed in the relationship for a long time (Gottman, 1999). These "perpetual problems," which have to do with partners' personalities, may be expressed in the partners' different behavioral styles or ways of approaching issues such as money, sex, or in-laws. As we have learned, there is evidence for continuity in many temperamental characteristics, and they constitute relatively stable features of individuals' behavior and cognition throughout their life span. Based on his work, Gottman (1999) suggests that therapists "encourage couples to think of these relationship problems as inevitable, much the way we learn to deal with chronic physical ailments as we get older. The chronic back pain, the trick knee and tennis elbow or irritable bowel do not go away, but we learn to have a dialogue with these problems. We keep trying to make things a little better all the time, but we learn to live with these problems and manage our world so as to minimize them. . . . So it is in all relationships" (p. 57).

The target of therapist intervention will undoubtedly depend upon the nature of the problem as well as therapist orientation. However, most couple therapists, regardless of orientation, know to set clear limits on hostile and aggressive displays in therapy sessions to guard against further erosion of the partnership. Gottman (1999) translates findings from a large set of research studies into several core strategies that clinicians can teach clients in order to foster relational well-being.

1. *Calm down.*   Emotions such as anger are highly arousing and can escalate into a cascade of negative feelings that shut down real communication. Gottman (1994) describes in precise detail how these escalating emotions affect interaction:

   "From the data gathered in our lab, we've seen how quickly discussions fall apart as soon as one spouse's heart rate begins to soar. Because physical responses are such an accurate barometer of your ability to communicate at a particular moment, tracking your arousal level during intense conversation will help keep your discussions on track as well. (p. 176)"

   This requires that each person be aware of his or her own physiological and emotional reactions. We will have more to say about this in Chapter 14. However, we see this as a two-step process in actual practice: becoming aware of one's reactivity and taking steps toward regulating it effectively. Awareness can be fostered by helping clients learn to take their pulse rate as a measure of physiological arousal, to learn to ask for and take time-outs, and to engage in relaxation activities in order to return to baseline levels of arousal, a process that takes an average of 20 minutes after becoming aroused. Gottman notes that this is a particularly important step for males who typically get physiologically "flooded" with emotion more quickly than women and who take longer to return to baseline (Levenson & Gottman, 1985).

2. *Speak nondefensively.*   The emphasis on improving communication has a long-established history in marital therapy and in relationship education (Halford, Markman, Kline, & Stanley, 2003). The goal of such interventions is generally to help couples express their feelings and disagreements in ways the other can understand. What is critical here appears to be reducing the tendency to come out swinging when conflicts arise. Called "harsh startups" by Gottman and Silver (1999), a conversation about a problem that starts with criticism, contempt, or sarcasm is likely to become an argument that deteriorates quickly. This speedy

buildup of emotional negativity results in feelings of being flooded and can lead one or both partners to protect themselves by stonewalling. Taking a "softer" approach when addressing potentially difficult issues can reduce defensive responding and maintain a more positive state.

3. *Validate.*   Among the Zulu, a person is traditionally greeted with a word that is roughly translated to mean "I see you." The response to this greeting is "I am here." Notice the direction of this interchange: Until you see me, I am not here. We are psychologically "here" because we are seen and known by intimate others, much in the way Cooley describes the looking-glass phenomenon. In the intimate world of close relationships, individuals do not need so much for their partners to solve their problems as for their partners to see and validate what they're going through.

   Counselors are often called upon to help couples work on empathy-building, particularly when their attachment relationship is weakened due to neglect, injury, or prolonged conflict. Sometimes old wounds reemerge in the present and need to be readdressed. Success in relationships often depends upon "the wounded partner being able to express deep hurts and losses and the other partner staying emotionally engaged and actively responding to these emotions with compassion and comfort" (Johnson, 2003, p. 373). Browning's (1998) empathy-expansion procedure helps partners address a long-standing relationship hurt through a specific process facilitated by the therapist. Through a sequence of steps, the counselor coaches one partner to recognize and apologize for the injury that has been causing the impasse. The goal is to enhance empathic responding and to give the aggrieved partner real validation for his or her pain. Clearly, this is most appropriate for couples who are motivated to put past hurts behind them and who are willing to "do whatever it takes" to mend the relationship.

4. *Overlearning.*   In the spirit of the graded mastery experiences described in Chapter 12, small successes in important areas can reap rewards in increased motivation. Applied to relationships, practicing behaviors of self-soothing, nondefensive listening and validating fosters good emotion regulation, increases the level of positivity in the relationship and, over time, becomes more automatic. These overlearned responses can be especially useful when conflicts arise.

5. *Pay attention to the little things.* A final recommendation reflects the importance of cultivating positive affect in daily interactions. In one study, the use of humor, affection, and playfulness in addition to noticing and responding to partners' bids for attention in the course of daily life were strongly associated with better conflict resolution and greater marital satisfaction overall (Driver & Gottman, 2004). In particular, a husband's playfulness and enthusiasm were related to his wife's willingness to be more affectionate when the couple did experience a conflict. It appears that relationship satisfaction is not only related to how conflicts are resolved but also to the quality of the emotional connection constructed bit by bit though the mundane interchanges that fill couples'

lives. These authors suggest that this aspect of a relationship might be amenable to therapeutic intervention. "Building positive affect during everyday life may be easier to influence than directly changing positive affect during conflict. For example, it may be easier to teach a couple to use enthusiastic responses in daily moments than to ask them to use affection during an argument" (p. 312).

 How does the counselor guide this couple to come to a better understanding of their own emotions and communication styles?

Out of Work

The experience of nonnormative events can affect well-being and, in some cases, permanently alter one's life course. Job loss represents a particular challenge to the normative expectations that most adults hold about their lives: to provide for themselves and their loved ones consistently and independently. When workers lose their jobs, a singular expression of their generative capacity is compromised (see Fouad & Bynner, 2008). A recent longitudinal study of more than 24,000 German respondents over 15 years found that for people who experienced episodes of unemployment, their lives were never quite the same (Lucas, Clark, Georgellis, & Diener, 2004). Workers experienced a decline in overall life satisfaction following job loss and a trending upward toward pre-unemployment levels of satisfaction after reemployment. Nevertheless, their sense of life satisfaction did not return to baseline, even many years after being reemployed.

The connection between job loss and mental and physical health problems is quite strong (Kessler, Turner, & House, 1989). Although financial strain is the most significant reason for depression following job loss, Price, Choi, and Vinokur (2002) have shown that the effects on physical and mental health are mediated by the erosion of a sense of personal control that accompanies the reduction of financial resources. Furthermore, these elements operate transactionally. As the authors indicate, "while job loss and financial strain may influence depression, depression, in turn, may reduce access to opportunities to reduce financial strain through reemployment. Thus, chains of adversity are clearly complex and may contain spirals of disadvantage that reduce the life chances of vulnerable individuals still further" (2002, p. 310). The ripples extend to children, as well, who suffer from more behavioral and academic problems when their parents are under financial strain (Conger, Ge, Elder, Lorenz, & Simons, 1994).

Helpers who work with people experiencing job loss need to take into account such psychological consequences, namely increased stress, anxiety, feelings of hopelessness, as well as physical problems that may arise, as they help clients deal with this stressful event. Sometimes, individuals might try to cope through behaviors like excessive use of drugs or alcohol. Although the ultimate goal of counseling may be to find new employment, it is important to remember that the clients' confidence may be badly bruised and in need of shoring up. This might help explain why some clients do not pursue reemployment in active ways like sending out resumes or going on job interviews. It may be their way of avoiding further damage to self-esteem (Price, 1992).

Prevention programs offer some demonstrated success in curtailing the downward spiral of disadvantage following job loss. Participants in the JOBS project, developed by researchers at the Michigan Prevention Research Center, showed more success in finding reemployment, demonstrated fewer symptoms of depression, and reflected better overall adjustment than nonparticipants at a 2-year follow up (Vinokur, Price, & Schul, 1995; Vinokur, Schul, Vuori, & Price, 2000). This program is delivered to small groups of 12 to 18 participants who meet for five 4-hour counseling sessions. There are three main elements to the program: (1) building skills for the job search, such as improving resume writing, learning to "think like" the employer, networking and contacting potential employers; (2) increasing participants' sense of self-efficacy through graded exposure exercises, role-modeling, and reinforcement of effective behavior; and (3) inoculating participants against setbacks that they might encounter in the job search process by identifying possible barriers while practicing the skills needed to overcome the obstacles (Price & Vinokur, 1995).

Off-Time

Adulthood is a time when individuals may have to contend with the realization that events or accomplishments that they once wished for have not been achieved. Individuals of all ages may feel distressed by a sense that they did not meet their developmental goals or expectations "on-time." Feeling "off-time," as it relates to such things as getting married, having children, reaching career goals, or other normative achievements, reflects the fact that we all have a set of age-related expectations for the appropriate timing of major life events. This phenomenon is called the **social clock**. Clinicians should be sensitive to this particular source of distress in the lives of their clients to help them cope more effectively. Certainly helpers can support client strivings to find outlets for generative needs that might be met in flexible ways. Even the strains of caring for children or older relatives can be reframed as valuable contributions. For clients without such responsibilities, other outlets might be explored.

Becoming generative can be viewed as a way of growing up, by taking and accepting responsibility for oneself and for dependents, by forgiving past generations for what they may have done, and by working to leave a legacy. As we have learned, flexibility and adaptability in the face of life's demands support this process. One developmental task involves the shift in expectations that may occur gradually over this time from adolescent idealism to mature acceptance of reality (Gould, 1978).

Adulthood means getting far enough outside oneself to do as Margaret Mead urged:

> "to cherish the life of the world," that is, to connect with life itself rather than just with oneself, to overcome the narcissism of our youth and make give-and-take connections from which we can feel the pain and pleasure of others rather than crouching selfishly and alone in our own protective skins. . . . The maturing function of psychotherapy is to get people past a narcissistic state where they notice only what other people do and how it makes them feel, and move them into a mature state where they notice what they do and how it makes other people feel. (p. 257)

FOCUS ON DEVELOPMENTAL PSYCHOPATHOLOGY

Post-Traumatic Stress Disorder

Human beings are born with the capacity to experience fear, one of our primary emotions. Fearfulness has evolutionary significance and is necessary for survival. Imagine how long our ancestors would have survived had they not become attuned to the signs of predators and other threats. But is there a difference between fear and anxiety? And when does anxiety become an anxiety disorder? Fear may be considered a hard-wired response to an immediate threatening stimulus, the kind that makes your palms sweat, your heart race, and your stomach tie itself into a knot. Fear triggers the "fight or flight" changes of the body-mind first proposed by Walter Cannon (Bracha, Ralston, Matsukawa, Williams, & Bracha, 2004; Cannon, 1929). Anxiety has been viewed as that uneasy sense of imminent danger. In other words, we get anxious about the possibility of something fearful happening.

In learning theory terms, both classical and operant conditioning processes are in play. Stimuli that actually cause fear or pain, such as loud noises or electric shock, can become associated with other neutral stimuli. In the end, these classically conditioned stimuli elicit the same physiological fear response as the original stimuli because of powerful learned associations. Termination of aversive stimuli results in escape learning, and escape behaviors are reinforced by virtue of their power to provide relief. Ultimately, avoidance conditioning patterns develop whereby individuals tend to avoid settings or situations that *may cause* distress because they have learned a set of anticipatory cues. Avoidance is strengthened through the process of negative reinforcement. Consider a woman who, as a result of early experiences of punishment or love withdrawal for expressing anger toward parents or others, has learned to suppress these threatening feelings. Such early aversive consequences can result in long-term patterns of conflict avoidance as well as avoidance of her own subjective angry feelings. The process is a maladaptive turn of events. What was once adaptive, avoiding pain and discomfort, becomes a generalized operating principle in circumstances that may not be particularly threatening. The maladaptive result, called "experiential avoidance" or anxious apprehension and avoidance of one's own real experience can be quite problematic (Hayes, 2004). Opportunities to become more assertive and less anxious in social situations are effectively shut down through avoidance patterns.

When fear and anxiety become overwhelming, individuals can develop anxiety disorders, which cause significant restriction in their lives and persistent intrusion into their states of mind. Unfortunately, anxiety disorders are very common. One in four adults suffers from some clinically significant form of anxiety (Keltner, Folks, Palmer, & Powers, 1998). Anxiety also accompanies many other mental illnesses, including depression, schizophrenia, and substance abuse. Previously, anxiety disorders were defined as the class of disorders that shared the characteristic feature of anxiety. DSM-V has revised its diagnostic criteria for anxiety disorders due to better understanding of their causes. Those that remain in the anxiety disorder category include panic, phobia, and generalized anxiety disorders. Post-traumatic stress disorder (PTSD) is now in a class of disorders called Stressor and Trauma-Related Disorders, given its clear association with traumatic events (APA, 2013).

PTSD, together with dementia and substance-induced disorders, is one of the very few diagnostic categories in the DSM whose onset has a clearly identifiable cause, namely the experience of a traumatic event. However, as we shall see, not everyone who is exposed to trauma develops PTSD. From a developmental perspective, it is a good example of the interaction of genetic and environmental influences on psychopathology.

The scientific study of trauma and its effects is a relatively recent phenomenon. Perhaps the incidence of horrific events around the globe, from wars, abuse and terrorist attacks to natural disasters, has sharpened our awareness of the psychological sequelae of such traumas. Kessler and colleagues (Kessler, Sonnega, Bromet, Hughes, & Nelson, 1995) used epidemiological data to conclude that 50% to 60% of individuals will experience a serious trauma sometime during their lives, even though many will not suffer from PTSD. Still, when PTSD was introduced into the DSM-III in 1980, it was criticized as a conglomeration of symptoms that were patched together to constitute a mental illness in order to procure needed treatment and benefits for Vietnam veterans (Kirk & Kutchins, 1997). Critics of the diagnosis claimed that it was one more example of the psychiatric establishment creating a mental illness out of a normal human response to unusually terrifying events. Researchers have sought to test the charge that PTSD is a Western social construction and have found that the symptoms of PTSD are expressed by individuals throughout the world who have been exposed to traumatic incidents (Keane, Marshall, & Taft, 2006). Perhaps early scientific attention to extreme trauma exposure, despite the ongoing controversy, has paved the way for a more nuanced understanding of the mechanisms that operate in all humans when under serious or sustained stress.

Diagnostic Features

For diagnosis of PTSD, a person must have experienced, witnessed, or been confronted with an event so traumatizing that it results in symptoms of *re-experiencing*, *hyperarousal*, cognitive alterations and *avoidance*. Such events could include the experience of war, torture, rape, or physical/sexual abuse, to name a few. Some suggest that witnessing such events or being a relative or helper of trauma victims is also sufficient for traumatization, a phenomenon called secondary or vicarious traumatization (McCann & Pearlman, 1990). Symptoms of *re-experiencing* might be manifested by the presence of flashbacks, recurrent dreams, or heightened fear and anxiety when exposed to internal or external trauma-related cues. Symptoms of *hyperarousal* might include irritability, lack of concentration, hypervigilance, sleep problems or heightened startle response. Symptoms of *avoidance* include behaviors that serve to allow victims to avoid people, places, or things that could trigger an association with the trauma. Avoidance tactics may also extend to avoiding thoughts and feelings that elicit memories of trauma, possibly in an attempt to down-regulate the intensity of re-experiencing. Symptoms also include *altered cognition and mood* related to the traumatic event.

PTSD affects individuals of all races and ethnicities, although rates tend to be slightly higher for females and low income groups (Brewin, Andrews, & Valentine, 2000; Tolin & Foa, 2006). PTSD appears to be more common among members of minority groups according to some studies. In their review, Pole, Gone and Kulkarni (2008) present evidence of higher PTSD rates and/or symptom severity for Latino American groups and some evidence for higher rates and severity for other U.S. minority groups (African American, Pacific Islander American, and American Indian). Cultural differences in symptom expression, coping style, and stressor profiles (e.g. discrimination) may present unique risks for PTSD development in racial and ethnic minority subgroups. Unfortunately, the suffering of PTSD tends to endure. Schnurr and colleagues (2000) found that complete PTSD symptomology continued to plague 32% of soldiers exposed to mustard gas a full 50 years after their exposure in World War II.

Who Develops PTSD?

Let's consider the interesting question of who develops PTSD. Researchers suggest that the development of this disorder rests upon a combination of factors: biological vulnerability, psychological vulnerability, and the experience of trauma. Some of us, because we possess certain genes, are particularly sensitive to stressful experiences (Stephenson, 2003). Recent research has focused on specific variants of a gene called FKBP5 (Ising et al., 2008), which is involved in the body's stress response as it mediates the action of cortisol, a major player in the HPA axis (see Chapter 2). A recent study of 900 individuals (primarily Black, low income individuals seeking general medical, non-psychiatric, hospital services) was carried out to assess relationships among genes, early history and PTSD (Binder et al., 2008). Participants' early history of childhood trauma/abuse was determined in order to explore the impact of early experience on later PTSD symptomotology. All participants reported experiencing significant adult (non-child abuse) traumatic events. Interestingly, the presence of a particular variant of the FKBP5 gene did not independently predict PTSD symptomotology, despite the occurrence of significant adult life stress. However, those participants who possessed a gene variant *and* reported early child abuse were significantly more likely to demonstrate PTSD symptoms after traumatization in adulthood. Early social trauma (as occurs in child physical or sexual abuse) for individuals with a particular genetic pattern thus appears to heighten vulnerability for PTSD in later life, should they be exposed to precipitating incidents. As we have discussed and as the authors propose, patterns of cortisol receptors are shaped in the developing brain by early experience, and the experience of abuse may make individuals' neurophysiology more sensitive to the effects of stress over time. This understanding appears to be supported by evidence from combat veterans who served in Afghanistan. Berntsen and colleagues (2012) found that the experience of adversity in childhood was a better predictor of which soldiers developed PTSD than the trauma experienced in deployment.

Difficulties in executive functions prior to a traumatic incident also increases the probability of developing PTSD. You have seen that executive functions involve the capacity to inhibit distractions and voluntarily direct attention to certain objects of attention. Some research suggests that compromised ability to disengage attention from stimuli that are highly salient can make it difficult to disengage from later traumatic memories, exacerbating symptoms of PTSD (Aupperle, Melrose, Stein, & Paulus, 2012). Early assessment of relevant executive functions might help professionals identify those who are most susceptible to developing this disorder.

Five Features of Treatment

Just as we are discovering what causes PTSD to develop in certain individuals, we are learning what works and what does not work in treatment. Hobfoll and colleagues (2007) have sifted through the evidence on PTSD treatments and concluded that five essential elements should be present in public health and clinical interventions for PTSD. The first element is to address safety. This means providing a safe place for victims, promulgating media messages of safety and resilience rather than those of continuing threat, limiting exposure to media that evokes threatening cues, restricting the amount of talk about traumatic events to reduce hyperarousal, and using techniques to ground individuals in their immediate, safer reality, once they are out of imminent danger.

The second element is calming. Victims should receive prompt, practical assistance for their most pressing needs (e.g., food, shelter, etc.) and accurate information about the well-being of their loved ones. Subsequently, anxiety-management techniques, such as therapeutic grounding, relaxation training with imagery, stress inoculation training, mindfulness practices, yoga, and coping skills training might be employed. These interventions are useful in interrupting the development of avoidance behaviors, which, as we have already noted, can seriously impair functioning. In some cases, anti-anxiety medication may be useful, but benzodiazepine tranquilizers are contraindicated because they can exacerbate PTSD symptoms. Another recent approach, psychological debriefing, is not recommended by these authors because of equivocal empirical findings and the possibility of enhancing hyperarousal for some victims (van Emmerik, Kamphuis, Hulsbosch, & Emmelkamp, 2002).

Efforts to support self and collective efficacy is the third element. Specifically, promoting individuals' sense of efficacy in relation to coping with trauma is important. Interventions should draw on local community supports to provide a caring network for victims. Emphasis on setting reasonable goals for rebuilding lives after trauma promotes a sense of personal control, healthy adaptation, and resilience. Cognitive-behavioral therapy approaches may be useful in this regard. A closely linked principle is connectedness, the fourth element. Interventions and community reorganization efforts (in the case of mass trauma) should be structured to bolster connections among survivors and their social networks. Victims should be educated in how to access what they need, materially and interpersonally, through partnerships with families, social agencies, churches, and so on. Supports should be clear and reliable so as to assure trauma survivors of predictable assistance.

Finally, efforts should include the element of instilling hope. Hope counteracts the tendency of victims to perceive their future as foreshortened, to question their ability to survive, and to succumb to resignation and even despair. Approaches that

help individuals deal with irrational fears and unrealistic expectations, de-catastrophize, and identify existing strengths permit hope to take hold in the midst of great suffering. However, the authors caution helpers not to encourage victims to see benefits and meaning in a traumatic event before they are ready to do so. Hobfoll, Canetti–Nisim, and Johnson (2006) found that benefit-finding as a therapeutic technique was related to increases in PTSD symptoms, greater defensiveness, and potential for retaliation, possibly because benefit-finding may be perceived as an attempt to minimize the real struggles and hardships associated with traumatic events.

SUMMARY

Life Span Developmental Theory

1. The complexity of adult development makes it clear that multidimensional models are needed to adequately understand the processes of change. Life span developmental models focus on both hereditary and environmental influences and on the continuities and changes that characterize adults. They emphasize that adaptation continues from birth to death.

2. Baltes describes the architecture of biology and culture, a web of interacting organismic and environmental influences on development. During childhood, he argues, optimal development is strongly supported by the processes of natural selection, such that most people reach adulthood and can contribute to the success of the species by reproducing. But biological supports weaken by middle adulthood, as selection pressures decline. Thus, from middle adulthood on, more cultural supports are required to ensure optimal development.

3. Throughout the life span, change involves both gains and losses, but the relative balance of gains and losses shifts as people move toward old age. Adaptation throughout life involves growth, maintenance or resilience, and the regulation of loss, but growth is more common in childhood, whereas regulation of loss is more common in old age. Successful development, or healthy coping, at any age is the relative maximization of gains and the minimization of losses, but coping changes as people age.

Influences on Adult Development: Sources of Stability

4. The Big 5 personality traits—neuroticism, extraversion, openness, agreeableness, and conscientiousness—are relatively stable after approximately age 30, according to cross-sectional, longitudinal, and cross-cultural research.

5. Adult personality traits are somewhat correlated with temperament in childhood. Although heredity is implicated in

the development and stability of traits, a relatively stable environment is probably equally important.

Influences on Adult Development: Sources of Change

6. Age-graded change refers to change that comes as a function of time. Some predictable physical changes in adulthood include declines in sensory ability and in reproductive ability (much more for women than for men). Appearance changes as skin wrinkles and sags, and weight gain is common though not inevitable.

7. Cognitive changes with age are best studied with longitudinal methods. A mixed pattern of improvement and decline occurs, related to differences in fluid intelligence (mechanics) versus crystallized intelligence (pragmatics). Fluid or mechanical processes, such as processing speed and inhibitory mechanisms, begin to show declines in middle adulthood. Crystallized resources, including all forms of declarative and procedural knowledge, are not as likely to decline, and for many people they increase throughout middle and even old age. Only after about age 60 do losses in fluid intelligence somewhat outweigh crystallized gains for the average individual.

8. The relative losses and gains are illustrated by memory effects. The capacity of working memory declines with age, which can affect problem solving negatively, as fewer pieces of information can be held in mind simultaneously. Semantic memory, however, continues to expand with age, as we learn more and more information, and often older adults solve problems better than younger ones because they are more likely to have expertise they can bring to the task.

9. Life-task or life-course changes are age-graded changes in the tasks and responsibilities that confront us or seem important as we age. Theorists such as Schaie, Erikson, Vaillant, Levinson, Jung, Gould, and so on have all described stages or phases in life-task change. Despite the significant differences in the lives of individuals, there do

seem to be relatively predictable sequences of change in our concerns as we move through adulthood.

10. History-graded changes affect the development of a whole cohort. A life-course perspective emphasizes that development is influenced by chronological age, family-related roles, and membership in a birth cohort. Thus, the same historical events can have different effects on members of different cohorts. Recent cohorts of children are experiencing a time of increased breakdown in social connections. Apparently as a result, they experience more anxiety than older cohorts did as children.

11. Nonnormative changes refer to unexpected events, such as an accident or untimely death of a loved one that can alter developmental trajectories.

Key Developmental Tasks of Midlife: The Continuing Pursuit of Intimacy and Generativity

12. Adults involved in a primary relationship such as marriage are generally happier than single adults. Other relationships, such as friendships, are also important sources of life satisfaction. Critical features of such relationships involve sharing, working out problems, and developing a sense of "we-ness."

13. The family life cycle begins with mate selection, a kind of filtering process based largely on homogomy and compatibility. Love is also seen as important in our culture. Sternberg described three elements: passion, intimacy, and decision/commitment. Once a commitment is established, a blending of family systems is involved, not just a joining of individuals. Other stages in the more typical family life cycle include becoming parents and then the transition of launching and renegotiating the marital relationship.

14. A high percentage of marriages end in divorce in the United States, often creating financial hardship for the wife and emotional and behavioral difficulties for children. For many people, marital satisfaction persistently declines over the life of a marriage. Theories about the causes of marital harmony and discord include the disillusionment model (when romantic notions are dashed, marriages fail), the maintenance hypothesis (romantic couples work to maintain their illusions and therefore their marriage), and the social exchange and behavioral theories (marriages fail when problems and conflict escalate to become overwhelming because of inadequate strategies for coping with conflict). Intrapersonal models draw on attachment theory and notions about temperament to explain marital success or failure.

15. Studies of marital dynamics suggest that marriages are successful or satisfying to the extent that positive factors outweigh negative factors, including interactive behaviors, perceptions, and physiology (e.g., endocrine functioning). High levels of negative affect reciprocity (likelihood that negativity in one partner will be followed by negativity from the other) is especially predictive of marital dissolution. What are termed the *four horsemen of the apocalypse* are especially problematic: criticism, defensiveness, contempt, and stonewalling.

Generativity: Making a Mark at Midlife

16. Each period of a child's life presents new challenges to parents. A parent's age, SES, personality and coping skills, and support systems all contribute to how satisfying parenting is (e.g., older parents generally find parenting more rewarding than younger parents).

17. Most parents find their task both stressful and rewarding. Infants are far more difficult to care for than most people expect, but they also bring joy to most parents. Toddlers, combining new skills with poor self-control or understanding, need very close supervision, so they are time and energy consuming. As their unique "selfhood" begins to blossom, they also become more interesting. In middle childhood, parenting is usually much easier as children become logical thinkers but are still relatively unambivalent about their dependence on their parents. Adolescent children are usually experienced as more demanding and difficult as they push for independence, take more risks, and de-idealize their parents. The launching period usually is experienced as positive, as parents have fewer responsibilities and their children become more self-sufficient. Parents of middle adults relate to their children more as equals, although assistance and support still tends to flow more from parent to child.

18. Sometimes middle-aged adults find themselves with dual caregiving responsibilities—parents to their children and caretaker for their aging parents. This sandwiched position can be very stressful, depending on factors such as the availability of other sources of support.

19. In middle age, people generally feel they have reached the peak of their career in terms of expertise, income, and advancement. Work intensity and time invested increase in the first half of middle adulthood and taper off thereafter, with most people increasing time spent with friends and family. This pattern can vary dramatically across individuals and is linked to gender. A rise in dual-career couples in recent decades is linked to increases in men's involvement in family roles. Middle adults usually function in many roles, which can increase stress but also allows for role buffering.

20. A sense of generative accomplishment depends on how creative and productive adults feel. Two kinds of generativity have been described: agency (creating, producing) and communion (wishing to care for the next generation). People who score high on measures of generativity report higher levels of self-esteem and happiness than others. A coherent sense of a self moving in a positive direction seems to characterize people who score high on generativity.

CASE STUDY

Lupe is a 45-year-old Mexican American woman. She has two adult children, a son and a daughter, as well as one granddaughter. She lives in a small apartment near her mother, now in her late 60s. Lupe visits her mother several times a week to check on her health and her emotional state. Although she is relatively self-sufficient, Lupe's mother expects this kind of attention from her daughter. Lupe has always been very responsible and concerned about the well-being of her family members. Even though this takes a lot of her time, she faithfully attends to her mother's needs without complaint.

When Lupe's children were young, she and her children's father lived together. He left the family after a few years, however, because he found the stress of family life to be overwhelming. In particular, he felt that he could not make enough money to support two children. Although he and Lupe were never legally married, she considered them to be a "married" couple. Single now for 16 years, she feels that she would like to meet someone with whom she could share her life. This is a new feeling for Lupe. Until recently, she was too distracted with the problems of raising her children to think about herself. Now she feels that she only has a limited amount of time left to pursue some of her own wishes. She can envision herself, like her mother, old and alone, and that prospect disturbs her. She has started to attend social functions at her church and has accepted some social invitations from members of the congregation. Lupe feels comfortable with this approach, because she is very close to the members of her parish community.

Lupe's life has recently become more complicated. Her daughter, Lucia, and her 2-year-old granddaughter, Eva, have moved in with her. Lucia and her boyfriend, Tomas, were living together and were planning to marry. Their relationship deteriorated after the baby's birth, and the couple fought frequently. Lucia accused Tomas of spending too much of his paycheck on frivolous things. Tomas, in response, withdrew even further, spent more time with his friends, and continued to spend money as he pleased. Lucia finally took the baby and threatened not to come back.

In addition to this, Lupe was injured on her job as a practical nurse in a large hospital. She was trying to prevent a patient from falling and hurt her back in the process. She will need to receive physical therapy, which means she will be out of work for a few months. Her physician, noticing her depressed mood, referred her to a counselor at the local mental health clinic.

Discussion Questions

1. What are the developmental stresses (age-related) and contextual stresses (nonnormative) in Lupe's life at the present time? Consider her age, family role, and cultural context.
2. What are Lupe's sources of strength? What aspects of her cognitive functioning and her personality might support her resilience in the face of difficulties?
3. What is the potential impact of Lucia's return on her mother? On Eva? On Tomas?
4. What advice might you give to Lupe? To Lucia and Tomas?

PRACTICE USING WHAT YOU HAVE LEARNED

In the Pearson etext, apply these ideas to working with others.

Video Exercise

Video Exercise

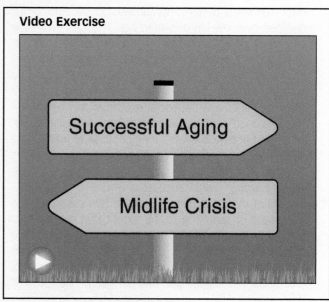

JOURNAL QUESTIONS

1. If you can, ask your parent or a member of your family to describe you using the Big 5 personality traits. Which of your personality traits have remained stable over time? Which have changed?

2. Do you think people normally go through a midlife crisis? Why or why not?

3. Consider a major event that has occurred in your lifetime (like a war, recession, revolution, major shift in technology, etc.). What effect has this had on your life? Now think of someone from an older or younger generation. Do you think the effects will be similar or different from your own? What is the impact of developmental timing on history-graded change?

4. Think of a married (or otherwise committed) couple you know well. What are the major challenges of their marriage? What are the benefits? What style of relating best characterizes the couple?

5. What are the normative and nonnormative challenges you are facing now? How are you coping with each? What other coping strategies could you try?

KEY CONCEPTS

life span developmental theories or models (p. 479)
ontogeny (p. 480)
growth (p. 481)
maintenance or resilience (p. 481)
regulation of loss (p. 481)
Five Factor Model (Big 5) (p. 483)
neuroticism (p. 483)
extraversion (p. 483)
openness (p. 483)
agreeableness (p. 483)
conscientiousness (p. 483)
adolescing (p. 486)
senescing (p. 486)
climacteric (p. 487)
menopause (p. 487)
estradiol (p. 487)

estrogen (p. 487)
andropause (p. 487)
elastin (p. 488)
nocioception (p. 488)
fluid intelligence (mechanics) (p. 489)
crystallized intelligence (pragmatics) (p. 489)
ego integrity (vs. despair) (p. 491)
career consolidation (vs. self-absorption) (p. 491)
keeper of meaning (vs. rigidity) (p. 491)
life structure (p. 492)
cohort effects (p. 493)
life-course perspective (p. 494)
socioeconomic position (SEP) (p. 494)
social gradient (p. 494)
family life cycle (p. 500)
homogomy (p. 501)
compatibility (p. 501)

disillusionment model (p. 506)
maintenance hypothesis (p. 507)
social exchange and behavior theories (p. 507)
intrapersonal models (p. 507)
homeostatic steady state (p. 508)
negative affect reciprocity (p. 509)
"four horsemen of the apocalypse" (p. 509)
launching period (p. 512)
kinkeeper (p. 512)
sandwich generation (p. 512)
role buffering (p. 514)
agency (p. 514)
communion (p. 514)
social role theory (p. 515)
social clock (p. 519)
post-traumatic stress disorder (PTSD) (p. 520)

CHAPTER 14

Living Well: Stress, Coping, and Life Satisfaction in Adulthood

Although young adults often feel as though life is still "about to happen," during middle adulthood people see themselves as having "grown up." Their lives have all the trappings of adults in their culture. For North Americans this is likely to mean they are married or have a life partner, have children, are owners or leasers of major possessions like a car or a house, and have substantial commitments to their work, place of worship, or other community organizations.

So how does it feel to be all grown up? Are most people satisfied with their lives? What does it take to be happy as an adult? Western philosophers have debated the ingredients of "the good life" since the days of the ancient Hebrews and Greeks. Religious traditions throughout the world champion virtues that constitute "right living," and that lead to true happiness, either in this life or the next. For helping professionals, the question of what constitutes well-being is at the heart of their work. Although ameliorating psychopathology is an important clinical focus, it is subsumed by the broader goal of promoting well-being, happiness, and the fulfillment of human potential.

Happiness is currently a focus of intense research interest, both at the individual and societal levels of analysis (Diener, 2000; Myers, 1993; Veenhoven, 1984). **Subjective well-being (SWB)** is frequently used synonymously with happiness, possibly because its dimensions have been well-studied. The most commonly used measurements of SWB incorporate three separable factors: overall life satisfaction, frequency of positive and of negative moods (Diener, Emmons, Larsen, & Griffin, 1985; Diener et al., 2009). Measuring life satisfaction usually involves asking people to rate their level of agreement with statements like "So far I have gotten the important things I want in life" or ranking one's place on a ladder where the top rung is the very best life possible and the bottom is the worst (Cantril, 1965). Frequencies of positive and of negative affective experiences are measured by asking people to rate how many times they felt a variety of emotions (e.g., joyful, angry, good, or bad) over a certain period of time. The life satisfaction estimate of SWB represents the cognitive aspect of happiness whereas reports of positive-negative experience represent its more emotional elements. Retrospective self-reports are not the only methods used in this kind of work. See Box 14.1 for a description of another promising way to assess emotional experience.

A rapidly growing body of studies from the social science literature has led to some surprising revelations about what is really important for people to sustain a sense of well-being as they negotiate the complex and frequently stressful realities of adulthood.

Midlife is often the time when adults take stock of their lives.

Box 14.1: Measuring What Makes People Happy

In most cases, the constructs of life satisfaction and subjective well-being are studied by asking respondents to complete questionnaires. Participants might be asked to respond on a scale of 1 to 10 to questions like "I believe that I make enough money" or "I am getting what I want out of my life." Such survey results can be very enlightening, but they cannot answer some of the most interesting questions about people's lived experience in a real-time context. For that data, researchers can utilize the technique called the **experience-sampling method (ESM)**. Typically, those who use this methodology give participants beepers that are programmed to beep at various points during the day. The beep alerts participants to record what they are doing and how they are feeling at that moment. This strategy is a good way to observe lives as they unfold. However, it can be expensive and intrusive to participants. Furthermore, events are recorded as discrete snapshots instead of a reflection of the ebb and flow of well-being across situations.

Recently, Kahneman and his associates (Kahneman, Krueger, Schkade, Schwartz, & Stone, 2004) developed an alternative approach called the **day reconstruction method (DRM)**, which combines elements of experience sampling with elicitation of memories of affective experience. One major difference is that DRM does not require beepers or present-moment reporting of experience. Instead, participants are asked to recall the previous day and to construct a running account or diary that describes the day's events. The instructions direct participants to "think of your day as a continuous series of scenes or episodes in a film. Give each episode a brief name that will help you remember it (for example 'commuting to work', or 'at lunch with B?')" (p. 1778). After the day's "scenes" are remembered and described, participants respond to more structured questions about each one, including how they felt while each was happening. Indices of positive affect (happy, friendly, enjoying myself) and negative affect (frustrated, depressed, hassled, angry, worried, criticized) are gathered. The result is a chronology of daily events linked to subjective ratings of positive or negative feeling.

This method was used to gather information about the life satisfaction of a sample of 909 racially diverse, middle-class women.

The average age of participants was 38 years. Results demonstrate that this method can access information that other methods generally cannot. For example, most surveys of life satisfaction report that people believe their children to be a source of great happiness. In this study, the activity of *taking care of children* ranked close to the bottom of enjoyable activities. Only working, housework, and commuting had lower positive ratings. The authors suggest that this finding may be due to the fact that DRM taps experience instead of the kind of global beliefs that are assessed in traditional life satisfaction surveys. Respondents may feel less constrained by socially appropriate or "belief-based generic judgments" (Kahneman et al., p. 1777) such as the valuing of children. With this method, they report on the reality of their lived experience. Activities that were associated with the most positive affect were intimate relations, socializing, and relaxing. This methodology reveals how enjoyable people's lives are on a day-to-day basis instead of global estimates of life satisfaction.

Similar to other research reported in this chapter, the life circumstances of these women, such as income, religion, and education, made only modest contributions to the affective quality of their daily lives. What did matter? Things that made for a happy day were related to their personality and mental health (like absence of depression) and, notably, the quality of their sleep! The authors found very large differences in women's enjoyment of home-related activities as a function of good or poor sleep, which had a surprisingly powerful impact on the quality of their satisfaction and enjoyment of life overall. In the work arena, job pressure exerted a similarly large effect. Although factors like job security and the presence of adequate benefits were important predictors of job satisfaction, they did not influence women's daily enjoyment at work. What made for a happier workday was less pressure to work quickly and more opportunities to talk with coworkers. Overall, life satisfaction, based upon results of this study, was determined by the difference in net negative and net positive affect. This study suggests that it may be the little things in our day-to-day lives that can make us happy.

LIFE SATISFACTION: WHAT IS A WELL-LIVED LIFE?

Worldly Goods and Well-Being

First, let's consider the importance of money. Although we would probably all concede some truth to the saying "money can't buy happiness," research indicates that most of us *believe* that even a little more income would improve our lives and make us happier (Myers, 2000). On the whole, happiness and income are correlated, but the relationships are complicated.

The relationship between material goods and life satisfaction is a complicated one.

It is true that the poor are not as happy as the rich. But people with adequate though modest incomes report nearly the same levels of life satisfaction as the wealthiest individuals, both within and between cultures and subcultures (see Table 14.1). Even people who have a sudden economic windfall, like those who win a lottery, "typically only gain a temporary jolt of joy from their winnings" (Myers, 2000, p. 61).

But a recent cross-national study of 158 nations shows the complexity involved in studying this subject. Diener, Tay, and Oishi (2013) showed that actual household income level (not national GDP) was related to all dimensions of SWB. Over the course of this 7-year study, individuals' satisfaction with rising incomes was more than a transitory blip, suggesting these increases had a long-lasting cumulative effect. The rise in family income appeared to affect SWB if it offered increased purchasing power and was accompanied by optimism about the future. Previously, work had indicated that those whose incomes increased over time did not experience more happiness than people whose incomes failed to increase (see Diener, Lucas, & Scollon, 2006; Diener & Seligman, 2004). This 2013 study may represent an advance over earlier work because of the size and representativeness of the sample as well

TABLE 14.1 Life Satisfaction for Various Groups

GROUP	RATING
Forbes magazine's "richest Americans"	5.8
Pennsylvania Amish	5.8
Inughuit (Inuit people in northern Greenland)	5.8
African Maasai	5.7
Swedish probability sample	5.6
International college-student sample (47 nations in 2000)	4.9
Illinois Amish	4.9
Calcutta slum dwellers	4.6
Fresno, California, homeless	2.9
Calcutta pavement dwellers (homeless)	2.9

NOTE: Respondents indicated their agreement with the statement "You are satisfied with your life" using a scale from 1 (complete disagreement) to 7 (complete agreement); 4 is a neutral rating.

SOURCE: Diener, E., & Seligman, M. E. P. (2004). Beyond money: Toward an economy of well-being. *Psychological Science in the Public Interest, 5,* 1–31. Reprinted by permission of Blackwell Publishing.

as the use of consistent measurements. It's important to note that the observed relationship did not obtain unless the *average* person in the country, not just its wealthy citizens, experienced the income gains.

So rising incomes appear to make people happy if a number of other conditions are met. For North Americans, per capita income and standard of living rose steadily from the mid 1950s through the late 1990s, yet the percentage of people who claimed to be very happy remained level or declined slightly (see Figure 14.1). At the same time, rates of depression and other pathologies soared. Myers (2000) calls this inverse ratio of affluence to pathology "the American paradox." The materialistic goals that motivate many Americans (and Europeans and Japanese, to name a few other national groups for whom we have data) do not appear to bring happiness, and they seem to have some toxic side effects.

This paradox may have many sources; we will mention a few. First, it may be linked to what is described as the "hedonic treadmill" (Brickman & Campbell, 1971). When people are driven to strive for material gain, they are often quickly habituated to each new level of wealth and thus can't be satisfied (Kasser & Ryan, 1996). Pittman (1985) argued "Wealth is addictive. It enticingly offers happiness, but it cannot provide satisfaction, so those who attain some of it keep thinking more of it will provide satisfaction" (p. 470). Ironically, the more an individual strives for further material gain, the less attention he is likely to give to other pursuits that are more strongly linked to satisfaction, like having supportive social relationships.

Second, the lifestyle that affluence makes possible may reduce some of the forces that ordinarily help create supportive relationships (Luthar, 2003). For example, people who can buy services from the marketplace, such as child care and elder care, are less likely to turn to family, friends, and neighbors for those kinds of support (Putnam, 2000). Further, people living in affluent societies rarely need to rely on others for physical support in "tough times," such as help with food, clothing, and shelter, and so opportunities for friends and neighbors to demonstrate "genuine friendship" by making sacrifices for one another are minimal. Absent such opportunities, it may be more difficult for people to feel that others in their lives can be relied upon (Tooby & Cosmides, 1996).

Third, having material resources allows people to make choices and to control much of their lives. But the more control people have, the more likely they are to expect to be able to create a "perfect" life (Schwartz, 2000). Of course, perfection is impossible to achieve. However, when people fail to do so, they blame themselves, creating fertile ground for depression. Because materialistic cultures foster the belief that material gain brings happiness, affluent people who do become depressed often feel confused and guilty, making it difficult to reach out to friends and share their distress (Wolfe & Fodor, 1996).

These analyses suggest that whereas material gain is a source of well-being, supportive relationships might also be. In what follows we will explore several

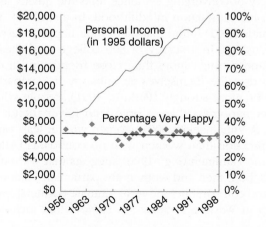

FIGURE 14.1 Economic growth and happiness in the U.S.

SOURCE: Myers, D. G. (2000). The funds, friends, and faith of happy people. *American Psychologist, 55,* 56–67. Reprinted with permission from the American Psychological Association.

factors that are positively correlated with well-being, including social relationships. We'll begin with the characteristics of the individual himself.

Personality and Well-Being

Could personality be more important than external conditions for explaining life satisfaction? Personality traits like extroversion and neuroticism *are* strongly correlated with subjective well-being measures, much more so than external factors like wealth (see Diener, Oishi, & Lucas, 2003; Weiss, Bates, & Luciano, 2008). Extroverts, who tend to focus interest on things outside the self, are happier than introverts, who focus more attention on their own interior experience. Not surprisingly, neuroticism, which includes tendencies to be self-conscious, anxious, hostile and impulsive, is negatively correlated with happiness. To a lesser extent, conscientiousness, which includes planfulness and self-control, is positively correlated with well-being. Personality probably influences well-being for many reasons. One is that personality traits affect what information people pay attention to and remember. Information that is congruent with an individual's personality is more likely to be fully processed. For example, extroverts process rewarding stimuli for longer periods than introverts (Derryberry & Reed, 1994). In addition, people who approach situations differently may construe the same life events in different ways (Lyubomirsky, 2001).

Could personality moderate the impact of money on happiness? It appears that it does. Let's consider a person high in neuroticism. By definition, he feels the slings and arrows of daily life more intensely. When income level does not match expectations, this perceived lack might have a more powerful impact on his overall well-being than it would for a less anxious person. High neuroticism is linked to more active social-comparison processes (Olson & Evans, 1999) that can also exaggerate perceived deficiencies. Studies of adults from large representative samples in Germany, Australia, and the UK bear this out. Soto and Luhmann (2013) found that income had a more powerful influence on SWB for individuals high in neuroticism than it did for their more extroverted and less anxious peers.

Relationships and Well-Being

 Forty-five-year-old Jeff points out that his happiness in middle adulthood is directly related to his relationship with his wife. Do you think his later age for marriage affects his outlook toward relationships and his own happiness?

As we saw in Chapter 12, many theorists, like Freud and Erikson, have emphasized the importance of "love" for happiness. Evidence strongly supports this view. Regardless of personality characteristics, social relationships appear to be essential ingredients of well-being. Both extroverts and introverts report more pleasant emotions in social situations (Pavot, Diener, & Fujita, 1990). *Receiving* social support is clearly linked to better coping with life's stresses, as you will see later in this chapter, but having opportunities to *give* social support is also a key ingredient in happiness. Life is more stressful for people who have limited opportunities to be a source of support to others or who experience limited success in their efforts to do so (Brown, Nesse, Vinokur, & Smith, 2003; Herzberg et al., 1998).

A wide variety of converging evidence links the quality and quantity of social relationships with life satisfaction in adulthood. In a study of "very happy people," Diener and Seligman (2002) found that *all* of their happiest respondents had "excellent" social relationships. In a survey of 800 college graduates, those who valued material success and prestige more than close friends and a close marriage were twice as likely to describe themselves as unhappy in comparison to people who valued relationships more strongly (Perkins, 1991). People with more friends also experience greater happiness than people with fewer friends (Hintikka, Koskela, Kontula, Koskela, & Viinamaeki, 2000). Women with at least one confidant are less susceptible to depression than women with no confidants (Antonucci, Lansford, & Akiyama, 2001), and Hammen (e.g., 1996) suggests that without strong, positive interpersonal bonds, both men and women are particularly vulnerable to depression.

Marriages (and comparable long-term intimate partnerships) are a major source of companionship in Western societies. In surveys that include tens of thousands of people from the United States and many other countries, married women and men report more happiness than unmarried people (e.g., Mastekaasa, 1994). Being married is also associated with a lower risk of depression (Myers, 2000).

Do social relationships cause happiness, or are happy people more likely to be involved in social relationships? There is evidence that it works both ways. People who are more secure, who have more positive attitudes and better social skills are more likely to successfully make friends, develop confidants, and create long-term partnerships, as we have seen in our earlier discussions of friendship (e.g., Chapter 6) and marriage (e.g., Chapters 12 and 13). But when we study life satisfaction within individuals over time, we find that social relationships do affect people's happiness as well. The same people are happier when they are with others than

Life satisfaction in adulthood is strongly correlated with good social relationships.

when they are by themselves. For example, Kahneman and colleagues tracked women's affective states during 15 daily activities—like exercising, resting, commuting, and so on—and found that emotions were more positive when people were with others than when they were alone (Kahneman et al., 2004; see Box 14.1). People whose closest relationships end, as with divorce or death of a partner, may show precipitous declines in well-being. Their life satisfaction recovers only slowly and not usually to the same level as before the loss (e.g., Diener & Seligman, 2004; see also Figure 14.2).

The importance of social relationships for well-being is consistent across cultures. When people feel supported by family and friends they weather life's difficulties more effectively. But fine-grained analyses demonstrate that how people derive support from their interpersonal connections differs across cultural groups. For example, Kim, Sherman, and Taylor (2008) found in a series of studies that European Americans generally seek *explicit* support in times of trouble. They share their troubles with others, soliciting solace and advice and even material help. Asians and Asian Americans, however, prefer not to bring their personal problems to the attention of others. Rather, they are likely to seek *implicit* support. They obtain comfort from reminding themselves of close others or by spending time in their company, but without discussing their problems. In experiments in which participants were

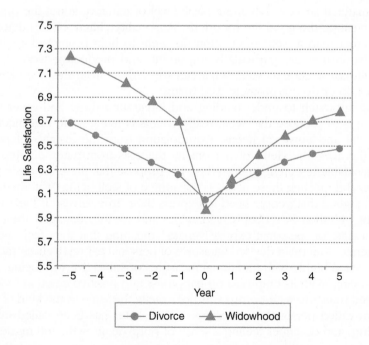

FIGURE 14.2 Life satisfaction before and after divorce or death of a spouse.
SOURCE: Diener, E., & Seligman, M. E. P. (2004). Beyond money: Toward an economy of well-being. *Psychological Science in the Public Interest, 5,* 1–31. Reprinted by permission of Blackwell Publishing.

required to seek either explicit or implicit support under stressful circumstances, European Americans reported reduced distress and showed lower levels of cortisol only if they explicitly sought help, whereas Asian Americans showed these benefits only with implicit support. Kim et al. (2008) argue that the interpersonal processes that most benefit us depend on our cultural assumptions:

> "People in more individualistic cultures share the cultural assumption that individuals should proactively pursue their well-being and that others have the freedom to choose to help according to their own volition. In contrast, people in the more collectivistic cultures may be relatively more cautious about bringing personal problems to the attention of others for the purpose of enlisting their help because they share the cultural assumption that individuals should not burden their social networks and that others share the same sense of social obligation." (p. 519)

Work, Achievement, Generativity, and Well-Being

As theorists like Freud and Erikson proposed, work experience and the general sense of oneself as a competent worker are also important predictors of happiness. Feeling that one is making progress toward challenging goals, both in work and in nonwork settings, is thus correlated with well-being (see Ryan & Deci, 2003). Similarly, scores on measures of generativity are predictors of well-being (e.g., Ackerman, Zuroff, & Moskowitz, 2000). As we have seen, generativity is a sense that one's skills and efforts are creatively or productively contributing to the world—to family, coworkers, community, or future generations.

Work experiences in general are often associated with subjective well-being. In the study by Kahneman et al. (2004) comparing affective states during daily tasks, people generally reported positive emotions at work, although not as positive as during sex or socializing after work. *Congruence* between personality characteristics and the skills and qualities required for a job is part of what makes work satisfying. But there are also many characteristics of the workplace itself that contribute to happiness. Opportunities for personal control, the variety of tasks, the support of the supervisor, interpersonal contact and coworker relationships, good pay and fringe benefits, respect and status can all influence the degree of satisfaction people derive from work (e.g., Chiaburu & Harrison, 2008; Warr, 1999).

Universal Needs and Values and Well-Being

In sum, material success, beyond a basic level of comfort, is not the primary ingredient in creating the good life for adults. Personality characteristics that support an "other" rather than a "self" orientation do seem to help promote happiness. Good social relationships are particularly important, and productive work opportunities support life satisfaction as well. What can we deduce from this overview of factors that either do or do not promote well-being?

One approach to understanding and integrating these and other findings on well-being is to propose that what really counts is living a life that meets our most fundamental and universal needs. Extrapolating from the insights of philosophers through the ages, the views of personality theorists from many different traditions, and the available research, modern theorists propose that there are basic psychological needs, and meeting these needs is the source of well-being. Waterman (1993), for example, argued that people need to express their "true selves." If their activities are congruent with their own deeply held values and are fully engaged, then people can achieve a state of "personal expressiveness," meaning that they feel intensely alive and authentic. Waterman devised measures of personal expressiveness and found that they correlated highly with traditional measures of subjective well-being. But subjective well-being, with its emphasis on happiness and positive emotion (what has also been called **hedonic well-being**) was not exactly the same as the kind of feeling that Waterman called personal expressiveness. The latter has been called **eudaemonic well-being**, and describes feeling a sense of purpose, growth, and mastery.

In a similar vein, Ryff and her colleagues (e.g., Ryff & Keyes, 1995; Ryff & Singer, 2008) differentiated **psychological well-being** from subjective well-being, defining it as "the striving for the realization of one's true potential" (Ryff, 1995, p. 100). They list six fundamental elements of psychological well-being: autonomy, personal growth, self-acceptance, life purpose, mastery, and positive relatedness. Questionnaire measures of these six aspects of experience are highly correlated with measures of positive affect in which individuals are asked to describe how intensely they usually experience 20 different positive feeling states (e.g., interest, excitement, strength, etc.; Urry, et al., 2004).

In what is called **self-determination theory**, Ryan and Deci (2000; see also Deci & Ryan, 2008; Ryan, Huta, & Deci, 2008) have also argued that self-realization is at the core of eudaemonic well-being. They suggest that life satisfaction is derived from the fulfillment of fundamental psychological needs for **autonomy** (feeling that one's behaviors are self-endorsed), **competence** (expressing one's talents and skills), and **relatedness** (opportunities to feel cared for and valued by others). These psychological needs, like hunger and other basic physiological needs, are energizing. Their relative salience and the ways in which they are satisfied can be different across the life span and in different cultures. But there is cross-cultural evidence that satisfaction of these needs supports feelings of well-being in general (e.g., Deci et al., 2001; Ryan et al., 1999). A recent meta-analysis of studies from health care settings showed that promotion of autonomy, competence, and relatedness by providers had positive effects on patient physical and mental health (Ng et al., 2012). It is not difficult to see how research on subjective well-being can be interpreted as consistent with this view. For example, a wide range of studies indicate that focusing on, investing in, and acting within social relationships predicts well-being, findings that support the existence of a universal need for relatedness. Also, the fact that feelings of well-being are linked to opportunities to express one's skills and personality traits in one's work could be support for the importance of both autonomy (involvement in intrinsically motivated activity) and competence needs.

The Importance of Meaning, Religion, and Spirituality

Many observers of human nature have proposed that the well-lived life is one that is grounded in the conviction that life has meaning. Park and Folkman (1997) define *meaning* as simply the perception of significance, and they propose that the need to find meaning may be intrinsic to human beings. They differentiate between "global meaning," a sense of what the universe and human existence is about, or what is universally true, and a sense of "situational meaning," finding a purpose for one's own life. Generally, they see the second as heavily dependent on the first.

Baumeister (1991) argues that we humans have a need to understand our lives, to see them as making sense, and he proposes four reasons why people seek meaning. First, they feel a need for their lives to have a purpose, which basically is synonymous with having goals. Such goals help people place their current actions in context, providing a connection between past, present, and future. In other words, they help us see our lives as coherent and making sense. Second, when people have a sense of meaning in their lives, they feel like they have control, that what they do is consistent with a purpose they endorse, helping them meet what self-determination theory describes as the need for autonomy (see Ryan, Huta, & Deci, 2008). Third, a sense of meaning helps people define what actions are legitimate and what actions are not. In this way, people can justify their actions and construct or identify values, morals, and ethics to help guide their behavior. Fourth, a sense of meaning helps people value themselves, fostering self-worth. Baumeister also suggests that becoming part of a social group helps people feel valued and valuable and enhances their sense of meaning.

As we have seen, despite the growth of wealth in the United States and other affluent nations in the last several decades, depression and other mental health problems have been on the rise (Diener & Seligman, 2004). Perhaps one of the reasons that increased wealth is not substantially correlated with well-being is that it is often linked to the valuing of materialistic goals, the pursuit of material goods, status, and financial advancement over other life goals. When materialism substitutes for a philosophy of life that provides a deeper sense of meaning and purpose, it may block the development of true life satisfaction.

Some of the reasons for seeking meaning that Baumeister proposes are associated with the basic self-actualization needs or values that Ryan and Deci and others have specified, such as needs for autonomy and relatedness. In fact, one way to construe self-realization is that it means to find your true meaning or value—where and how you fit into a larger whole. Because religious traditions are in large part institutionalized meaning systems, they can help people establish global meaning, which in turn can support the creation of situational meaning. In Box 14.2, we review some scientific work on the role of spiritual and religious experience in adult life.

Culture and Well-Being

So far, we've identified multiple influences on well-being: money, personality, relationships, achievement, values, meaning, and religion. Cross-cultural research offers us the opportunity to examine the relative influence of such factors on happiness among people all across the globe. Even though cultural comparisons of any sort should be done carefully, this research can help us understand different socialization practices related to life satisfaction and identify possible cultural universals in development (Tov & Diener, 2007). For example, self-esteem figures more prominently in the overall satisfaction of people from cultures that privilege individualism (Diener & Diener, 1995). In comparison, people from collectivist cultures have higher levels of life satisfaction when their social relationships were satisfying (Kang, Shaver, Sue, Min, & Jing, 2003; Oishi, Diener, Lucas, & Suh, 1999). Some have even suggested that there may be different definitions of what constitutes happiness across cultures. Chinese, for example, prize peace of mind (peaceful, calm) over the kinds of positive experience (elated, excited) valued in Western cultures (Lee, Lin, Huang, & Fredrickson, 2012). Such cultural differences have important implications for assessment of SWB and for analyses of research results.

As you have seen, money is related to happiness, but groups that differ widely in income ("Richest Americans" and African Maasai) report similar levels of SWB (see Table 14.1). Researchers noted that the Maasai take great pride and satisfaction in their culture and its long history, possibly overriding the importance of excessive material goods in their prescription for happiness (Biswas-Diener, Vitterso, & Diener, 2005). A recent study using 2005–2006 Gallup poll data explored effects of material and nonmaterial resources on well-being across 132 countries in the world (Diener, Ng, Harter, & Arora, 2010). The three dimensions of subjective well-being (life satisfaction, positive and negative experiences during the previous day) were assessed along with family income. The presence of a TV, computer, and/or Internet access in the home yielded a measure of material fulfillment beyond basic needs. Scores were also calculated for number of times in the past year respondents lacked basic food and shelter. Researchers added items that assessed social psychological variables. For example, individuals were asked whether they had friends or family to count on in times of need. Relative to the previous day, participants were asked to report the level of respect they felt from others, the opportunities they had to learn something new, and the amount of control they had over their own time.

Across the world, money and well-being were correlated. However, income (assessed by GDP) was most strongly related to the cognitive, life satisfaction aspect of well-being and less to experience of positive affect. Participants who lived in economically advantaged countries reported higher levels of overall life satisfaction even if their personal income levels were low. The affective components of well-being were most strongly associated with social-psychological variables. For example, countries that ranked lower on the income scale often had higher levels of positive affect based on their social capital. The conclusion reached by the authors

Box 14.2: Spirituality, Religion, and Well-Being

Personality theorists have sometimes argued that spirituality is built into the human psyche. Carl G. Jung in particular felt that religion and spirituality are expressions of an innate need "to find meaning in life, to create a sense of wholeness or completeness, and to connect with something larger than the individual self" (Compton, 2005, p. 210). Modern researchers make a distinction between spirituality and religion (or religiosity). A person can have a spiritual side or spiritual strivings without practicing a particular religion, although the two are closely allied for many people (Hill et al., 2000). Both are concerned with "a search for the sacred" (Zinnbauer, Pargament, & Scott, 1999), which means attempting to identify, articulate, or move toward an understanding or association with a divine being, or divine object, or some kind of ultimate reality or truth (Hill et al., 2000). Religion also involves affiliation with "a covenant faith community" that has prescriptive and revelatory teachings and may include rituals, all of which are intended to support the search for the sacred and to encourage morality (Dollahite, 1998). Religion also may serve nonsacred goals, like creating a social identity (Hill et al., 2000). The empirical study of spirituality and religion is beginning to paint a picture of the role that both play in adults' everyday psychological functioning.

Religiosity and Well-Being

A majority of the world's population report that religion is an important part of their lives (Diener, Tay, & Myers, 2011). In fact, large representative studies do show that religion adds a small but significant boost to SWB for people in the United States, even after their life circumstances are taken into account. Across the world's four major religions, Hinduism, Christianity, Buddhism, and Islam, adherents tended to report higher SWB in each of its three dimensions compared to nonreligious counterparts. But what are the life circumstances that moderate this relationship? Diener and colleagues (2011) confirmed that economic development and security contribute to religiosity both at individual and societal levels. In countries where life circumstances are more difficult, levels of religiosity tend to be high and being religious adds to SWB. Nonreligious individuals in religious societies tend to report the least SWB, especially in terms of social support and positive affect. An inverse relationship was found for relatively advantaged countries where, in general, level of need is low and security is high. In these societies, organized religion is rated as less important to overall happiness. Nonreligious individuals in economically developed, nonreligious societies also report high levels of SWB. It is possible that the positive relationship between religiosity and SWB observed in the United States is due to this country's economical advantage and moderate religiosity (Diener et al., 2011).

Why might religion contribute to happiness? Both Eastern and Western religions and philosophies prescribe regulation of negative or destructive emotions, like anger and envy. Some religious movements (e.g., charismatic movements) also emphasize cultivating strong positive emotions, but others foster moderation of all emotional reactions (Emmons & Paloutzian, 2003). In traditional Buddhist teachings, the presence of compassion and serenity and the absence of destructive emotions, like envy and anger, are cultivated

through meditative practices (Compton, 2005). As reported in the text, Davidson and his colleagues (2003) have found that areas of the brain associated with positive mood show increased activity during meditation. They have also found that the most experienced practitioners, such as Tibetan monks, show the most extreme shifts toward patterns associated with positive emotions.

Many less striking studies have demonstrated that adherence to religious practices by people of many different faiths is moderately correlated with measures of subjective well-being in the U.S. For example, widowed women who worship regularly report more joy in their lives than those who do not (e.g., Siegel & Kuykendall, 1990). Indeed, after many kinds of negative life experiences—divorce, unemployment, death of a child, and so on—religious people seem to recover more happiness more quickly than the nonreligious (e.g., Ellison, 1991). These benefits are more likely to accrue to people who are active religious participants (attending services, praying, meditating) than to those who describe themselves as pro-religious but are not active practitioners (e.g., George, Larson, Koenig, & McCullough, 2000). In survey assessments of spiritual commitment (e.g., asking whether people agree with statements like "My religious faith is the most important influence in my life," or "I feel very close to God"), those who score highest are also more likely than those who score lowest to rate themselves as "very happy" (Myers, 2000).

When researchers assess psychological well-being, focusing on people's feelings of mastery, growth, and purpose rather than on subjective well-being (that is, measures of happiness or positive mood), there is a strong relationship between religiosity and well-being (Poloma & Pendleton, 1990). This connection is thought to be mediated by the fact that spirituality and religion support people's efforts to find meaning in life and may help them construct a sense of how their own lives fit into a larger plan or system. Professionals need to be aware of the importance of religious and spiritual issues in their clients' lives and work respectfully with these beliefs (see Zinnbauer & Pargament, 2000).

Sorting Out the Benefits of Religiosity

Another important reason why religious belief benefits people may be that religious communities provide their members with social support, a critical ingredient in well-being (Myers, 2000). The role of religion in fostering hope and optimism may also be important. Seligman (2002) describes a survey of religious congregations in which level of hope was the best predictor of feelings of well-being. Diener and colleagues (2011) suggested that religion may increase happiness through the mechanisms of social support, feelings of respect, purpose, and meaning.

It should be noted that religions, like all human institutions, have their darker side. For example, although some religious doctrines and practices foster positive feelings, such as hope and compassion, others foster emotions and attitudes, such as guilt and fear of retribution, that can be harmful in excess. Another example is that some religious doctrines and beliefs encourage a distrust or intolerance of others, especially outgroup members, or promote retribution or revenge against those who are construed as evil or guilty

(Box 14.2 continued)

Box 14.2 *Continued*

(Chatters, 2000). Freud, having seen the dark side, assumed that religion must be "corrosive to happiness" (Myers, 2000, p. 63). Indeed, current evidence suggests that only positive elements of religious doctrine are correlated with well-being (Pargament, Smith, Koenig, & Perez, 1998). U.S. Muslims who used positive religious coping after the attacks of September 11th showed more post-traumatic growth compared to peers who engaged in negative religious coping. Those who coped positively called on a basic sense of trust in the divine and perceived the tragic events as out of their control. Those who used negative coping were more likely to view the challenges they faced after the attacks as a punishment for their lack of devotion (Abu-Raiya, Pargament, & Mahoney, 2011).

Spirituality, Religion, and Personality

One question that researchers have asked is whether there is a link between spirituality or religiosity and personality. Do personality characteristics, like the Big 5 (see Chapter 13), affect the degree to which people are drawn to spiritual exploration or religious involvement? One meta-analysis found that across a large number of studies, high agreeableness and conscientiousness were associated with religiousness (Saraglou, 2002). One interesting set of studies by Piedmont and colleagues suggests that there may even be a sixth personality trait that specifically relates to spirituality or "spiritual transcendence," which can be defined as the ability to view life from a perspective that transcends space and time and to achieve a sense of fundamental unity with nature. These investigators consulted theological experts from many different Eastern and Western faith traditions to develop an assessment of spiritual transcendence that seemed to be common to all faiths. They then developed the "spiritual transcendence scale," which required individuals to rate how true spiritually based statements are of them, statements such as "I find inner strength and/or peace from my prayers or meditations" and "I feel that on a higher level all of us share a common bond." Piedmont has found that adults' scores on spiritual transcendence improve prediction of important characteristics like interpersonal style above and beyond their scores on the Big 5 personality traits (e.g., Piedmont, 1999; Piedmont & Leach, 2002).

Developmental Shifts in Spirituality and Faith

In what ways does the understanding and experience of spirituality change across the life span? Fowler (1981) interviewed over 350 individuals, ranging in age from 3 to 84 years, exploring their past and "life-shaping experiences," their values and commitments, and their religious thoughts and feelings. From these interviews, he derived a description of six stages in the development of faith. His definition of *faith* is "our way of finding coherence in and giving meaning to the multiple forces and relations that make up our lives" (p. 4). Faith and religion are not synonymous in his view. People with no religious commitments still develop faith, construed as "an orientation of the total person, giving purpose and goal to one's hopes and strivings, thoughts and actions" (p. 14). He acknowledged that because his interviewees were all reared in Judeo-Christian traditions, it remained

to be seen what elements of his descriptions represented universal features of faith development and which were specific to Western culture. As always with stage theories, the ages are approximate and there is substantial variability, with some individuals moving more slowly than others, and many not progressing past the first few stages. Fowler found only one person who had achieved Stage 6. Note that the most advanced middle-aged adults in this model can be expected to move through Stages 4 and 5, as they come to understand the inherent inconsistencies in any spiritual perspective and how profoundly unknowable ultimate truth is. As you will see in Chapter 15, Fowler's description of these stages is consistent with features of a definition of *wisdom*.

Stage 1 (0 to 6 years): Intuitive-projective

At these ages children are intuitive, egocentric, and not logical. Their understandings of sex, death, and taboo begin, and they may be overwhelmed by a sense of danger with regard to doing what's wrong versus right.

Stage 2 (7 to 12 years): Mythic-literal

At these ages children can narrate a life story of sorts. They tend to repeat what they have been taught by parents and other close adults about truths and beliefs, which then serve as their morals and rules. They still literally see God as a father, and they see distinct categories of right and wrong.

Stage 3 (13 to 20 years): Synthetic-conventional

By adolescence, the individual is constructing a life story. A "they" beyond the family is ascribed the authority to dictate values and beliefs, so faith remains conformist at this stage. Beliefs are not yet understood to be abstractions, and when others have different beliefs, they are judged to be wrong.

Stage 4 (21 to 30 years): Individuative-reflective

Authority is shifting from the "they" to the self. People can recognize inconsistencies and conflicts in the beliefs and morals they have been taught, and they can think critically about them. People take responsibility for making commitments to a worldview, lifestyle, beliefs, and attitudes. They see those commitments as individual, belonging to self.

Stage 5 (31 to 60 years): Conjunctive

In early midlife, some individuals begin to see both sides of a problem at once and are able to resolve the conflicts in their beliefs using dialectical (postformal) thinking. The individual begins to appreciate the unknowable—what must be the unfathomable complexity of ultimate truth.

Stage 6 (over 60): Universalizing

Transcending specific belief systems, perceiving a universal community, this individual actively makes "real and tangible . . . the imperatives of absolute love and justice," unfettered by concerns about self. People at this stage live with "felt participation in a power that unifies and transforms the world."

TABLE 14.2 Dimensions of Well-Being Across the Globe

COUNTRY	INCOME/GDP- GROSS DOMESTIC PRODUCT	SOCIAL- PSYCHOLOGICAL VARIABLES	WELL-BEING	POSITIVE FEELINGS	*LOW* NEGATIVE FEELINGS
United States	1	19	16	26	49
Denmark	5	13	1	7	1
Israel	20	56	11	61	64
New Zealand	22	12	9	1	22
South Korea	24	83	38	58	77
Costa Rica	41	6	18	4	38
Sierra Leone	87	80	87	87	86

(1 = highest reported well-being; 89 = lowest reported well-being in ranking for 89 countries sampled)

Selected Rankings of Countries (Out of 89) on Income, Well-Being, Social-Psychological Variables and Affect.

SOURCE: Diener, E., Ng, W., Harter, J., & Arora, R. (2010). Wealth and happiness around the world: Material prosperity predicts life evaluation, whereas psychological prosperity predicts positive feelings. *Journal of Personality and Social Psychology, 99,* 52–61. Reprinted with permission from the American Psychological Association.

was that happiness is a product of many things beside money; paying attention to social-psychological sources of well-being contributes to happiness and productivity. Table 14.2 offers findings from a small group of countries.

If you look closely at the findings from this study, you'll notice that no country takes first place across all rankings. Generally, most people in the world report being relatively happy except for those who live in extreme circumstances. But take a closer look at Denmark. Denmark is a high-income country that has consistently ranked near the top on cognitive and affective measures of SWB and has been called "chronically happy" (Biswas-Diener, Vitt erso, & Diener, 2010; Gallup, Inc, 2007). What might account for the rising tide of happiness in Scandinavia? Using multiple measures of life satisfaction, income, affect, and social resources, researchers discovered that high levels of past, present, and predicted future happiness were best explained by relatively greater income equality in Denmark compared to the United States. In other words, Denmark's poorest citizens were much more satisfied than their low-income peers in the United States, a phenomenon the researchers called "The Danish Effect." Citizens of the United States were higher in emotionality (both positive and negative) than the Danes. However, while positive emotionality was higher for advantaged U.S. citizens, negative affect was also higher among the more disadvantaged. The Danes were less emotional by comparison and tended to show less extreme highs and lows in overall satisfaction.

STRESS, COPING, AND WELL-BEING IN MIDLIFE

In Chapter 13 you saw that nonnormative events are often the source of traumatic loss regardless of when they occur during the life span. The normative changes associated with growing older produce more predictable losses. Even when adults are healthy and self-sufficient, the physical changes of midlife and late life "raise concerns and lamentations about the woes of getting older" (Whitbourne, 2001, as cited in Lachman, 2004).

Clearly, the capacity to adapt to stress and challenge is critical to survival at every stage of the life span. In many ways throughout this text, we have emphasized the important goal of fostering resilience in children, adolescents, and adults and the promotion of effective coping regardless of one's age or stage in life. Resilience refers to the presence of healthy coping and adaptation *in spite of* challenges and

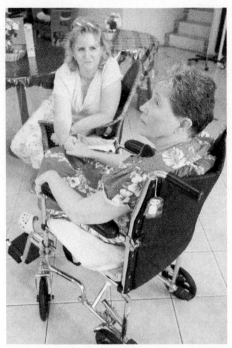

Resilience involves the ability to flourish despite the challenges that life presents.

risks, or in the words of Ryff and Singer, "the capacity to flourish under fire" (Ryff & Singer, 2003, p. 15). Resilience can also be described as "bouncing back" after the inevitable struggles and setbacks of life. To understand and foster resilience, we must consider the nature of the risks and protective factors that mark each individual's life and attend to the ways that these might change as a function of age. We will also consider some important contributions to fostering resilience from research in positive psychology.

Midlife brings its own set of challenges, not the least of which is the recognition of "time left to live," slowly accumulating losses related to getting older, and often great demands in the areas of the family and workplace. Some research suggests that stress is higher among young and middle-aged adults than it is for older adults (Chiriboga, 1997). Older adults are often more skilled at managing their emotions and sustaining joy. But it may also be that the life space midlife adults occupy is filled with more conflicting pulls on time and attention than it is for older individuals. In the middle years, adults are frequently in positions of increased responsibility and authority at work; they may have obligations to children and grandchildren; they may also take on the physical, emotional, or financial care of aging parents. All these situations can increase risk load. These circumstances are a defining characteristic of the sandwich generation, namely that group of individuals described in Chapter 13 who have caregiving responsibilities for generations both younger and older than themselves.

Who, then, are the resilient people? Questions about who thrives and why they do so defy easy answers. True to the principles of multifinality and equifinality (see Chapter 1), eventual life outcomes are dependent upon a whole array of variables that interact in complicated ways. What we are learning, however, is that pathways to adult disorder and well-being are not random but have their roots in the experiences of childhood and each succeeding stage. And, as with earlier parts of the lifespan, there are multiple pathways to well-being as well as to disorder.

The Wisconsin Longitudinal Study (Singer & Ryff, 1999), one early, comprehensive study of adult development, offers a look at the lives of adults who graduated from Wisconsin High Schools in 1957. This study of 10,317 men and women provides extensive information about participants' education, IQ, employment, marriage/family status, experience of stressful life events, accomplishments, goals, social support, and history of depression gathered over three data collections in 1957, 1975, and 1992/1993. Such a rich body of information offers many windows into adult development.

One subgroup that was studied intensively was the group of resilient women. *Resilient women* were defined as those who had experienced depression sometime during their lives but who had subsequently regained a high level of well-being (Singer, Ryff, Carr, & Magee, 1998). Aggregating the life stories of this group, the authors identified four pathways to wellness following the experience of adversity. Their life stories reflected a diversity of experiences in the following major areas: educational level of parents; alcoholism in the home as a child; marriage or cohabitation with an alcoholic as an adult; being a single parent; upward or downward mobility at work; and comparisons with parents and siblings with regard to education, finances, and occupation.

One group of resilient women had more cumulative advantages than the other groups, namely, educated parents, family financial stability, stable marriages, and so on. These women, however, did experience stressful life events, like the death of a parent or the onset of chronic illness, that presumably were related to their depression. A second group experienced more childhood adversity, including growing up in a family where there were problems with alcoholism. Women in this group also experienced similar losses and illness in adulthood. A third group was advantaged in childhood but experienced important setbacks in adulthood, like involuntary unemployment or divorce. The fourth group had lives that incorporated mixtures of advantages and disadvantages throughout early childhood and adulthood. What this work most clearly illustrates is the presence of multiple pathways to resilience. All four groups of women had at least one experience with depression, yet found their way out of it to reclaim a sense of well-being. Although not directly assessed in this sample, the ways in which these women perceived their difficulties and dealt with them most likely played a role in their resilient outcomes.

Certain elements were identified as protective factors that seemed to buffer the adversity that occurred in other domains. Some of these were childhood advantages, like educated parents, no problems with alcohol either in the family of origin or within marriage, and not having to raise children alone. Other advantages included social attachments (like close confidants, friends, spouses, church, or civic groups), relatively stable or upward mobility in employment with only one involuntary job loss, and positive social comparisons with parents and siblings with regard to economic and educational achievement. Clearly, all of these women faced stressful circumstances and suffered because of them. But their ability to flourish despite adversity raises intriguing questions about the nature of stress and coping over the life span.

The stressful circumstances of middle age are frequently a taxing set of demands related to managing family and work in the context of diminishing resources, such as time and energy. When circumstances exist that buffer the effects of competing role demands, such as good social support and adequate income, these demands may be perceived as less stressful. However, when the demands are too great given available resources, **role strain** (Goode, 1960) can occur, taking a toll on health and well-being. Perrone and Worthington (2001) found that having more resources, including income and social support, was associated with greater marital satisfaction among their sample of dual-income couples and presumably compensated for some of their work strains. Some others have demonstrated that multiple roles can be beneficial when they buffer the negative effects of one role with the protective function of a more satisfying one. Rozario, Morrow-Howell, and Hinterlong (2004) found that older caregivers with multiple productive roles reported more positive health outcomes compared to those without such roles.

Social support, as found in marriage or other close relationships, can be a potent protective factor in managing stress and promoting health. In a sample of middle-aged rural adults, Wickrama and associates found that unsupportive or distressed marital relationships were linked to early onset of hypertension for both husbands and wives. Problematic relationships with children contributed independently to the early onset of hypertension for mothers, but not for fathers. Husbands' satisfaction with employment, particularly the opportunity for advancement in the workplace, was negatively related to early onset of hypertension (Wickrama et al., 2001). These results suggest that chronic exposure to stressors in relationships can have direct negative effects on health and that these effects may be further exacerbated by gender-salient roles and expectations.

Work, children, spouses, friends, money, health, family . . . It's obvious that there are many challenges in adulthood, and some of these are certainly outside of our control. But what part can our attitudes play in supporting resilience? Let's review some features of stress and coping and then explore what research is learning about the role of a healthy mind in living well.

Stress: A Review

The nature and effect of stress on individuals is important to review because of its clear impact on emotional and physical health. Some have argued that the term *stress* is vague and open to many interpretations (Kemeny, 2003); consequently we adopt the recommended term *stressors*. Stressors have been divided into two varieties: **life events** (Holmes & Rahe, 1967) which are discrete, often traumatic, events that have a clear onset (like a death or accident) and **daily hassles** (Lazarus &

Folkman, 1984), which are chronic, problematic situations (like day-to-day care of a sick relative or chronic illness). Research has suggested that chronic daily stress is very important in the development of psychological (Compas, Davis, Forsythe, & Wagner, 1987) as well as physical symptoms (Selye, 1980). For example, the stress of keeping a job while caring for a sick child or older relative may cause a person to go without sleep for a prolonged period of time. As a result the caregiver might succumb to illness herself due, in large part, to physical exhaustion. In some cases, stressors aggregate in people's lives, often subsequent to a traumatic event, and with this accumulation, their power amplifies the allostatic load (Garmezy, 1993). Caregivers like the one just described can lose a job, thus causing them to forfeit access to health care coverage and enough income to maintain a house or an automobile. Such cycles of disadvantage can exert a powerful impact on the lives of children as well as adults and have been consistently linked to the onset of physical and mental health problems (Turner & Lloyd, 1995).

A phenomenon that has been useful in explaining the effects of cumulative stressors on vulnerability is called **kindling-behavioral sensitization** (Post, 1985; 2007). This psychological model has been useful in conceptualizing mechanisms involved in drug tolerance, epilepsy, and affective disorders (Goddard, McIntyre, & Leech, 1969). Kindling-sensitization describes a process of progressive illness severity or illness incidence that results from gradual increases in sensitivity to stressful triggers. Consider how this model is applied to affective disorders. An initial episode of depression is triggered by stressful life events (Dohrenwend & Dohrenwend, 1974), which leaves residual neurological changes in the individual's brain (neurotransmitters, receptors, etc.) rendering him more reactive to stressors. Following this experience of "sensitization," subsequent episodes of depression can occur spontaneously or with very little external provocation (Kendler, Thornton, & Gardner, 2001). How the stress system develops in infancy and early childhood provides a foundation for later stress sensitivity (see Chapters 2 and 4).

Hlastala and her colleagues (2000) investigated whether this model explained the progression of episodes of bipolar disorder over the life span. The number of previous bipolar episodes per se did not predict later episodes of disorder. However, increasing age was related to increasing incidents of bipolar illness. As people got older, their episodes were preceded by relatively less external stress. This suggests that some specific aspects of the aging process, possibly medical or biological factors, may interact with stressors in a way that heightens vulnerability. Mroczek and Almeida (2004) report a similar finding showing that older adults reported heightened stress reactivity, consistent with kindling, when compared to younger groups. "A lifetime of frequent activation of the neural pathways associated with negative affect may bring about such sensitization" (p. 371). Even if people report more life satisfaction as they age, they may still be more affected by stressors.

Diatheses and Stress

Many contemporary models that address the development of problems posit a **diathesis-stress** transaction. **Diatheses** are premorbid conditions or predispositions that render individuals vulnerable to some disorder under certain circumstances. Individual vulnerability or diatheses may be genetically based (e.g., inherited traits) or acquired through learning (as in the case of self-defeating cognitions or early attachments). These underlying vulnerabilities may come to light only if individuals experience a sufficient number, type, or intensity of stressful experience to trigger the manifestation of disorder. According to this model, people of all ages with multiple or severe underlying vulnerabilities require less situational stress to trigger a maladaptive outcome. This is one way to explain why only a portion of individuals, such as those who experienced early abuse, go on to develop post-traumatic stress disorder after trauma (see Chapter 13). Presumably, those individuals who possess sufficient levels of preexisting biological and environmental vulnerabilities reach a tipping point when traumatic stress is experienced, whereas others do not (McKeever & Huff, 2003).

Those who flourish despite challenging circumstances might enjoy the protections of biology or environment, but explanations are far from crystal clear at this point. Nonetheless, these questions are attracting the attention of many contemporary researchers who are interested in understanding what contributes to positive development. One approach has been provided by Tedeschi and Calhoun (2004) who offer evidence for a phenomenon they call **post-traumatic growth**. This is defined as "positive psychological change experienced as a result of the struggle with highly challenging life circumstances" (p. 1). People who evidence post-traumatic growth, following experiences like bereavement, accident, illness, and so on, are marked by demonstrable improvements in psychological functioning that exceed pretraumatic event levels. Some of these gains include an altered set of priorities about life, a greater appreciation for one's life, closer and more positive relationships with others, improved sense of life's possibilities, and heightened spirituality (Tedeschi & Calhoun, 1996). These authors provide evidence that post-traumatic growth is related to certain personality traits, notably extroversion and openness to experience, and to a lesser extent, dispositional optimism. Growth following trauma is believed to occur via the mechanism of cognitive processing, which refers to qualitative shifts in schemata about the self and the world that need to occur to accommodate the enormously traumatic event. "This process is likely to involve a powerful combination of demand for emotional relief and cognitive clarity, that is achieved through construction of higher order schemata that allow for appreciation of paradox" (Tedeschi & Calhoun, 2004, p. 15). Others have pointed out that part of this process also includes the construction of positive illusions, like the belief that trauma makes one a better person (Taylor, 1983). These cognitive distortions may protect traumatized individuals by reinforcing their sense of mastery and self-worth along with soothing the acute stress (Maercker & Zoellner, 2004). Monumental positive experiences, like the birth of a child, can also enhance growth in comparable ways and should not be discounted as a vehicle for positive development (Aldwin & Levenson, 2004).

Stressors and the Body-Mind

It is worthwhile to revisit the body's way of reacting to stressors and examine how they affect a variety of physiological systems to appreciate these processes more fully. As you may recall from Chapter 2, stressors engage the body's autonomic nervous system, activating the HPA axis, causing the release of hormones into the bloodstream, and preparing the body to respond to the perceived attack. Although this process serves us well in emergency situations or in relatively short hormonal bursts, there are costs associated with chronic activation of the system (Sapolsky, 1992). For example, during the acute phase of the body's stress response, immune system functioning is depressed.

Remember that stressors mobilize the body's energy resources to enhance certain functions (such as motor and sensory abilities, all the better to see and run away from the big, bad threat). The immune system, intended to surround and destroy attacking foreign bodies such as viruses or bacteria, requires mobilization of the body's energy to do its work as well. Our immune system operates through a process of inflammation to limit the spread of such harmful pathogens and to repair their damage.

Each of these important processes requires that the body's energy be directed to different ends (Maier, Watkins, & Fleshner, 1994). During a stressful event, energy reserves need to be devoted to the immediate fight-flight-freeze response and any alternative expenditure of energy, such as that required for reproductive system functions, is suppressed in service of the more immediate need. If homeostasis does not resume following the acute stress-response phase, the ill effects of chronic stress result. Chronically increased levels of cortisol, the body's primary stress hormone, are linked to cardiovascular decline in middle-aged and older adults (e.g., Hawkley & Caccioppi, 2007). High levels of cortisol can also dysregulate immune functions and reduce the body's capacity to protect itself against disease. You may have noticed, for example, that when you are dealing with some ongoing stressor, you might be more likely to catch a cold or flu, an example of the process of **immunosuppression**. This occurs because cortisol inhibits the proliferation or blunts the responses of certain types of cytokines (e.g., Kemeny, 2003; Robles, Glaser, & Kiecolt-Glaser, 2005).

Another immune system process, inflammation, is also affected when the body confronts chronic stressors. Chronic stress exposure increases cortisol production, but also desensitizes the immune cells' ability to respond to cortisol's instructions to inhibit inflammatory processes. Consequently, high concentrations of proinflammatory cytokines, which are related to maladaptive inflammation, go unchecked. Many disease conditions, such as cardiovascular disease, allergies, rheumatoid arthritis, and other autoimmune disorders, have been associated with unregulated inflammatory processes (Kemeny, 2003; Steptoe, Willemsen, Owen, Flower, & Mohamed-Ali, 2001). These immune-related effects have been demonstrated in a study of adult parents of children with pediatric cancer. This group, presumably under chronic stress, showed impairment in the capacity of their immune system to downregulate inflammatory processes in comparison to parents of healthy children (Miller, Cohen, & Ritchey, 2002).

Maier and Watkins (1998) conclude from their review of research that psychological stressors, such as traumatic environmental events, operate on the body in much the same way as infectious agents. The effects on the body can include some combination of fever, increased sleep, reduction in eating and drinking, reduced exploration and activity, reduced aggression, reduction in social interaction, cognitive alterations, increased pain sensitivity, increased HPA activity, and depressed mood. Viewed from this perspective, these authors argue that certain types of depression are associated with hyperactivation of the immune response, even though the precise direction of these effects is still unclear. The important point in this discussion is the establishment of the connection between emotional experiences and the dysregulation of body mechanisms (like immune system functioning).

> The argument is not that depression is caused by immune activation. The argument is that whatever does cause depression (e.g., negative cognitions about the self or loss of a loved one) may have access to the same neural circuitry that evolved to mediate sickness and activate that circuitry. Some of the symptoms of depression, particularly the vegetative symptoms, may then be the result of this process and represent essentially *sickness* responses. In addition, as noted earlier, the circuit is bi-directional, and the products of these activated immune cells in turn provide signals to the brain. It is conceivable that this positive feedback circuit could help to maintain depression. (Maier & Watkins, 1998, p. 98)

Recent evidence has clearly supported the existence of bidirectional communication processes between the brain and the immune systems in relation to stressors, be they psychological or physical (Pert, 1997; Sternberg, 2001). Pert, for example, discovered that opiate receptors for the body's natural opiates, called **endorphins**, are present on the surface of cells in the immune system (spleen and thymus). This discovery uncovered the connections between the brain, the immune system and emotions, linking the mind and body in new and exciting ways. As we are learning, the brain and the immune system operate together in a highly orchestrated dance that maintains homeostasis or balance within systems of the body-mind. Originally, it was thought that the brain "talked" and the immune system responded. Now researchers increasingly recognize that the brain also "listens" to the communication of the immune system, which sends its chemical messengers to various parts of the nervous system, including the brain. Findings such as these have helped usher in a new field, **psychoneuroimmunology**, the study of the interactions between the central nervous system, the immune system and behavior (Cohen & Williamson, 1991).

Coping with Stress

Given that everyone deals with stressors in their lives, that they critically influence our health, and that many of them derive from the aging process itself, the question becomes how best to manage inevitable stressful circumstances. Do people learn to restrict their exposure to stressful experiences as they age? Or do they learn better ways of managing stress? What separates resilient individuals from those who adapt less effectively? Why is it that not all people who experience similarly stressful events suffer similar adverse consequences?

We suggest that management of stress is essentially the same thing as coping. Many typologies have been developed to explain the nature of coping and a voluminous body of research has been devoted to the question of whether coping in certain ways makes a difference in outcomes. The highly influential model proposed by Lazarus and Folkman (1984) makes a basic distinction between efforts aimed at changing the situation (problem-focused, problem-solving) and those directed toward emotion management (emotion-focused, tension-reduction). The two-dimensional model of primary and secondary control (Rothbaum, Weisz, & Snyder, 1982; see also Chapter 15) emphasizes the role of controllability of stressors as a determinant of coping responses. The repression-sensitization model (Byrne, 1964; Krohne & Rogner, 1982) describes coping behavior as a trait-like characteristic or style of coping that has two primary manifestations. The first (sensitizing) is marked by typically heightened perception of threat and increased attention to stressful information; the second (repression) is characterized by appraisal of stressors as less threatening and/ or avoidance. This conceptualization bears some resemblance to other models such as approach-avoidance (Roth & Cohen, 1986), monitoring-blunting (Miller & Green, 1984), and rumination-distraction (Nolen-Hoeksema, 1987).

At present, researchers have recognized that some of these dichotomous distinctions fail to capture the real nature of coping, which does not manifest in mutually exclusive categories. Virtually all coping needs to accommodate cognitive (decision making) as well as emotional (anxiety management) aspects. Therefore, attempts to compartmentalize coping into sets of behaviors that address problem fixing or feeling better do not acknowledge that some coping falls outside these boundaries (such as seeking social support) and that categories are not mutually exclusive (such as taking a "mental health" day that allows you to avoid an unpleasant meeting and makes you feel more relaxed at the same time). Lazarus himself (Lazarus, 1996) stated that treating problem- and emotion-focused coping as two highly distinctive types leads to oversimplification of the nature of coping itself. These distinctions are also problematic because they do not consider the function or intention of the coping behavior. In a recent review, Skinner and her colleagues state:

> If the ways that an individual copes are assembled based on the specific stressor(s) and situational constraints, then any way of coping can be locally adaptive. For example, if a set of stressors is actually uncontrollable, it may be adaptive to give up (to conserve resources). Or if an important goal is arbitrarily blocked, it may be adaptive to attack the obstacle (to defend the goal). In this sense, given the right circumstances, every possible way of coping can be appropriate, normative or right. (Skinner, Edge, Altman, & Sherwood, 2003, p. 231)

Hobfoll (1989, 2001) presents a theory of coping with stressors that is relevant to midlife and aging because it emphasizes the centrality of loss experiences. His theory, called conservation of resources (COR) theory, posits that the primary stress trigger is loss, either through a primary loss event (bereavement, injury), transitions that involve loss (children leaving home, retirement), threats to aspects of the self (demotion, lack of acknowledgment for accomplishments), or challenges that incorporate some aspects of loss (job promotion that involves a move to a new location). Even though some of these events might have positive elements, the experience of stress, according to this theory, is the consequence of the loss component.

Researchers have demonstrated that people tend to weigh resource loss as more important in their lives than resource gain (Kahneman & Tversky, 1984; Tversky & Kahneman, 1974). In other words, negative events in people's lives appear to produce more powerful physiological, emotional, and cognitive consequences than do positive events. Resource loss is a critical predictor of distress following traumatic events, such as those due to natural disasters (Freedy, Saladin, Kilpatrick, Resnick, & Saunders, 1994), as well as in more chronic, day-to-day stressful events (Siegrist, 1996). That is, "losses make us hurt more than gains make us feel good" (Schwartz, 2004).

To deal with loss in its multiplicity of forms, individuals tend to act in ways that conserve their resources. Resources may be understood as things that people value in and of themselves or things that enable people to achieve or obtain that which is important to them (Baltes, 1987; Hobfoll, 1989). Resources can include objects (material possessions like a home or car), conditions (marriage, job status), personal characteristics (self-esteem, hope), or energies (time). When stressed, people seek to minimize the cost to their net resource capacity. Individuals also seek to increase their resources during nonstressful times, to accumulate a reserve. These ideas bear some resemblance, from a behavioral perspective, to the "sickness" response of the body under attack that was previously described.

Do the conceptual frameworks proposed to explain coping apply equally well to all cultural groups? It's true that the physiological mechanisms of the stress response are universal. But what about the ways individuals appraise and respond to the threats they perceive in their worlds? Even within groups, there is room for differences in assessment of what is stressful and how best to deal with it. The existence of relatively systematic preferences in coping behaviors within cultural groups, however, might indicate emic (culture-specific) dimensions of coping (see Kuo, 2011). Some researchers have identified the individualistic-collectivistic dimension of culture as a likely candidate to explain observed differences (Chun, Moos, & Cronkite, 2006). In cultures that are more individualistic, the reasoning goes, an autonomous, direct approach to problem-solving best fits the context. In more collectivistic cultures, managing one's own response to difficulties might be preferred over attempts to change the situation. Such a response could be seen as striving to maintain harmony within the group. As with most all behaviors, selecting a coping response has a great deal to do with the values, beliefs, and attitudes of one's cultural framework. It also has to do with the nature of the stressors that individuals face. Research has begun to identify unique cross-cultural variations. Table 14.3 contains examples of differences in coping responses to a national tragedy, the World Trade Center attacks of September 11, 2001. This field is emerging as one of particular interest to professionals engaged in helping clients manage stress by capitalizing on cultural strengths.

Wellness

Mary, at age 42, describes how serious health complications altered her outlook about aging, stress, and life satisfaction. Why does Mary show such resilience?

With increasing attention to the negative effects of chronic stressors, there is a complementary, growing interest in the interrelationships among health, coping, and stress management. The emphasis these days is not on any rigid "right" or "wrong" strategy for coping, but on adaptive flexibility (Bonanno, Papa, Lalande, Westphal, & Coifman, 2004). Certain resources have been construed as particularly important to the process of healthy coping. A general sense of self-efficacy (Bandura, 1989), optimism (Schier & Carver, 1985), self-esteem (Rosenberg, 1979), personal control over important goals (Seligman, 1975), and social support (Sarason & Sarason, 1985) are among the characteristics that are associated with greater physical and emotional health and well-being.

But how does one demonstrate these qualities in the midst of stress? What if the stressor is uncontrollable, such as the onset of chronic ailments as people age? Is it just a fortunate few, blessed by temperament, who tend toward resilience? In line with COR theory, it makes sense to support the development of attributes like self-efficacy and optimistic cognitions because these qualities serve as protective factors in the face of hardship. But there is currently a strong interest in the pivotal role positive emotions play in the experience of well-being and their role in the stress management process. The encouraging news is that these qualities can be cultivated as well. See Table 14.4 for a list of such qualities.

TABLE 14.3 Examples of Cultural Influences on Coping in the United States After World Trade Center Attacks

SAMPLE STUDIED AND METHOD	STYLE OF COPING	COPING STRENGTHS RELATED TO CULTURE	COPING CHALLENGES RELATED TO CULTURE	SOURCE
Interviews from first generation immigrants from **South Asia** who lost a relative. (Group of 11 included participants from India, Bangladesh, and Guyana.)	Use of relational coping; use of distraction; reliving memories of the deceased; emotional coping (getting angry); cognitive coping (making sense of it); religious/spiritual coping; avoidance; use of indigenous healers	Use of fatalistic beliefs that "suffering is part of destiny" to cope; reliance on community (including indigenous healers and kinship members); increased reliance on religious ritual	Inability to perform cultural rituals (e.g., burial practices) impeded the grieving process; loss of a potential income earner shifted the collective balance vis a vis roles in family; being targeted as the "enemy" affected well-being	Inman, Yeh, Madan-Bahel, & Nath, 2007
Interviews from first generation **East Asian** immigrants who lost a relative. (Group of 11 included participants from China, Philippines, and Korea.)	Primary use of collectivistic ways of coping and support-seeking within the family; some use of distraction (focus on work, cooking, and going out)	Reliance on family and indigenous sources of support; use of spiritual and religious practices	Did not utilize mental health system due to shame and norms about emotional expression; sense of forbearance (bearing up) impeded self-disclosure	Yeh, Inman, Kim, & Okubo, 2006
Interviews from Indian-American **Sikh** males (N = 5) living in NYC.	Primary use of social support; religious coping; increased communication with Sikh community and family members, especially wives	Use of service as a way to cope (*seva* = selfless acts for others' benefit); emphasized nonviolence (not responding to hate with hate); educated others about their religious beliefs	Misidentification by others (due to uncut hair/turban/beard) as anti-American; physical and verbal threats and abuse	Ahluwalia & Pellettiere, 2010
Self-report assessments from 138 **Muslims** living in the United States.	Primary use of social support and religious and spiritual coping; some utilized avoidant coping (social isolation) which was related to depression	Increased religious practices (fasting, prayer, reading Qura'n); reached out to communities of faith for support; provided education about Muslim faith	Physical attacks, anti-Muslim comments; endured special security measures; experienced bullying, discrimination, and violence directed to personal property (setting fire to home)	Abu-Raiya, Pargament, & Mahoney, 2011

As we have emphasized, not everyone who is exposed to the same stressor will have the same response. This is due, in part, to the way people appraise threats relative to the way they appraise their capacities to deal with them. The appraisal part of coping is the target for many cognitive and behavioral interventions that are geared toward self-efficacy and that enhance a sense of mastery and personal control. But affective elements are also in play in stress management, coping, and more generally, well-being.

The Affectivity Connection

Human emotional experience can be broadly construed as positive and negative and recent conceptualizations link positive and negative emotions to separate neurobiological systems (Watson, Wiese, Vaidya, & Tellegen, 1999). **Negative affectivity**, or the extent to which a person experiences nervousness, fear, anger, sadness, contempt, and guilt, is a part of the **behavioral-inhibition system**. This circuit is related to withdrawal and avoidance behaviors shaped through evolution to help people keep out of harm's way. **Positive affectivity**, or the extent to which a person experiences enthusiasm, alertness, joy, confidence, and determination, is part

TABLE 14.4 Psychological Resilience Factors: Attitudes and Behaviors That Can Help Maintain Well-Being During Stress

1. Positive attitude: optimism and sense of humor
   Optimism is strongly related to resilience
   Optimism is partly inherited but can be learned through cognitive behavioral therapy
   Putative neurobiological mechanisms: strengthens reward circuits, decreases autonomic activity

2. Active coping: seeking solutions, managing emotions
   Resilient individuals use active rather than passive coping skills (dealing with problem and with emotions versus withdrawal, resignation, numbing)
   Can be learned: work on minimizing appraisal of threat, creating positive statements about oneself, focusing on aspects that can be changed
   Putative neurobiological mechanisms: prevents fear conditioning and learned helplessness, promotes fear extinction
   Facing fears: learning to move through fear
   Fear is normal and can be used as a guide for action
   Facing and overcoming fears can increase self-esteem and sense of self-efficacy
   Practice undertaking and completing challenging or anxiety-inducing tasks
   Putative neurobiological mechanisms: promotes fear extinction, stress inoculation

3. Cognitive flexibility/cognitive reappraisal: finding meaning or value in adversity
   Traumatic experiences can be reevaluated through a more positive lens
   Trauma can lead to growth: learn to reappraise or reframe adversity, finding its benefits; assimilate the event into personal history; accept its occurrence; and recover
   Recognize that failure is an essential ingredient for growth
   Putative neurobiological mechanisms: alters memory reconsolidation, strengthens cognitive control over emotions

4. Moral compass: embrace a set of core beliefs that few things can shatter
   Live by a set of guiding principles
   For many, moral compass means religious or spiritual faith
   Altruism strongly associated with resilience: selfless acts increase our own well-being
   Putative neurobiological mechanisms: spirituality/religiosity associated with strong serotonergic systems; morality has neural basis, likely evolved because adaptive

5. Physical exercise: engage in regular physical activity
   Physical exercise has positive effects on physical and psychological hardiness
   Effective at increasing mood and self-esteem
   Putative neurobiological mechanisms: promotes neurogenesis, improves cognition, attenuates HPA activity, aids in regulation of emotion, boost immune system

6. Social support and role models or mentors
   Establish and nurture a supportive social network
   Very few can "go it alone," resilient individuals derive strength from close relationships
   Social support is safety net during stress
   Role models and mentors can help teach resilience: imitation is powerful mode of learning
   Putative neurobiological mechanisms: oxytocin mediates initial bonding/attachment
   "Mirror"/Von Economo neurons involved in neuronal imprinting of human values

NOTE: HPA, hypothalamic-pituitary-adrenal axis.

SOURCE: Haglund, M. E. M., Nestadt, P. S., Copper, N. S., Southwick, S. M., & Charney, D. S. (2007). Psychobiological mechanisms of resilience: Relevance to prevention and treatment of stress-related psychopathology. *Development and Psychopathology, 19*, 889–920. Reprinted with the permission of Cambridge University Press.

of the **behavioral facilitation system**, that system intended to allow people to respond to reinforcement and to approach and engage with the environment. Both positive and negative affectivity have trait-like as well as state-like qualities. This means that individuals' emotions may change from happy to sad based on certain events. But it also means that people tend to vary in their baseline levels of positive and negative affectivity or emotional style overall.

Studies of the brain indicate that the left prefrontal cortex (LPC) is activated during the experience of positive emotions, whereas the right prefrontal cortex (RPC) is activated during periods of negative emotion (Davidson, 2000). This prefrontal asymmetry can be measured in individuals in resting states and points to what might be thought of as temperamentally related emotional style. When researchers asked participants to watch film clips designed to elicit positive (animals at a zoo) and negative (a burn victim) emotional responses, having recorded their baseline brain activity prior to exposure to the films, they found reliable individual differences in responses that were predicted by prefrontal activity. Those with higher left frontal activity reported more positive affect in response to the positive stimuli; those with the reverse prefrontal pattern reported more fear and disgust in response to the negative stimuli. These results suggest that people are different in their tendencies to respond to emotional stimuli (Tomarken, Davidson, & Henriques, 1990).

So what does this have to do with stress and coping? As you might imagine, negative affectivity has been associated with greater reactivity to stress (Watson & Pennebaker, 1989). Research also demonstrates that the immune systems of individuals with greater left PFC activation were less compromised following a traumatic stressor (Davidson, Coe, Dolski, & Donzella, 1999). In other research, participants viewed an emotionally distressing film while hemispheric activity and hormone levels were measured. Researchers employed a procedure that allowed participants to see the film using only their right or left hemisphere. Results demonstrated that viewing the film using the right hemisphere was associated with a significantly higher release of cortisol than was left-hemisphere viewing. The authors concluded that cortisol regulation may be related to RH activation (Wittling & Pflüger, 1990). Cohen and his colleagues found that people who tended to have a positive emotional style were significantly more likely, compared to those with a negative emotional style, to be resistant to the common cold (Cohen, Doyle, Turner, Alper, & Skoner, 2003).

Does this mean that those of us with higher levels of RPC activation are doomed to a life of greater unhappiness? Keep in mind that the impact of negative things is stronger than the impact of good ones in general, so to some degree we are all in the same boat (Baumeister, Bratslavsky, Finkenauer, & Vohs, 2001). The good news is that emotional affectivity is not a zero sum game; in other words, positive and negative affectivity circuits are independent of each other rather than opposite ends of a continuum (Cacioppo & Gardner, 1999; Diener & Emmons, 1985). People do not express only one type of emotionality or the other but can have access to the full range of emotions. So even if we view the pattern of trait-like negative affectivity as a risk factor, emerging research suggests that we can encourage the development of positive emotions through certain practices. As Ingram and Price (2001) conclude, "Even though vulnerability is conceptualized as a trait according to some conceptualizations, vulnerability is not necessarily permanent or unalterable. Corrective experiences can occur that may attenuate the vulnerability, or, alternately, certain experiences may increase vulnerability factors" (p. 12).

What are the protections against encroaching stress sensitivity due to temperament, stressful life events, or age? In general, cultivating mindfulness and positive emotions are increasingly viewed as antidotes to stress and health-compromising emotions like anger and hostility (e.g., Goleman, 2003; Lyubomirsky, King, & Diener, 2005; Hölzel et al., 2011; Srivastava, McGonigal, Richards, Butler, & Gross, 2006). Mindfulness (or mindfulness meditation) involves cultivating attention in a way that can benefit health and well-being. (See the applications section for more description.) **Meditation**, as used in this context, refers to a "family of complex emotional and attentional regulatory training regimes developed for various ends, including the cultivation of well-being and emotional balance" (Lutz, Slagter, Dunne, & Davidson, 2008, p. 163). Two general families of meditation practice include focus (practice in stabilizing attention, noticing distractions, shifting attention, etc.) and open-monitoring (nonreactive meta-awareness of experience) to which compassion or kindness practices are sometimes added (Kok, Coffey, Cohn, Catalino, Vacharkulksemsuk, Algoe et al., 2013; Lutz et al., 2008). If you remember that the brain is our gatekeeper for stress, it makes sense that improving its ability to respond to events in a more regulated, less reactive way could reduce the harmful impact of a stress-system on overdrive. It is also reasonable to conclude that practicing a positive emotional style may serve as an antidote, buffering the effects of stress. You might have thought of emotional style as a hard-wired tendency. Recent research is revolutionizing our way of thinking about emotion and providing support for the view that the brain is somewhat plastic with regard to affective style, more similar to an incremental viewpoint. Although much more work needs to be done in this area, current research offers some tantalizing possibilities.

Much has been written about the nature and consequences of negative emotions. Fear prepares us to escape; anger helps us protect ourselves; sadness allows us to grieve a loss. But what is the evolutionary role of positive emotion? Positive emotions serve to undo or reverse the potentially harmful impact of negative emotions (Fredrickson, 2001). This makes sense if we consider the destructive effects of chronically activating the body's stress response.

Stress revs up the system for a reason, but when the stressor has been avoided or conquered, the stress response system needs to revert to baseline in order to prevent damage. However, as you have read, chronic activation of brain-based stress responses can make the system super-sensitive. Attention becomes hyperfocused on threatening details and individuals feel as if they are living under siege. Figure 14.3 depicts the cognitive, emotional and physical outcomes associated with chronic stress.

Mindfulness and positive emotions, states of mind that can be practiced, promote recovery from stress. They allow individuals to let go of distress and replace the narrowed focus on threat with a more expansive attention (*broaden*). "Because positive emotions arise in response to diffuse opportunities, rather than narrowly focused threats, positive emotions momentarily broaden people's attention and thinking, enabling them to draw on higher-level connections and a wider-than-usual range of percepts or ideas. In turn, these broadened outlooks often help people to discover and build consequential personal resources" (Fredrickson, Cohn, Coffey, Pek, & Finkel, 2008, p. 1045). Accumulating resources may be gained in physical (fewer illnesses), social (more friendships), psychological (increased optimism) or intellectual (mindfulness or creativity) domains. Figure 14.4 illustrates the resiliency process.

Fredrickson and her colleagues (2008) tested the "build" portion of the theory by exploring whether a daily practice of lovingkindness meditation (LKM; see Applications) would increase participants' experience of positive emotions and add to their repertoire of positive resources to impact long-term well-being. At the end of the 9-week study, the positive emotions experienced by participants in the daily LKM group (such as love, joy, gratitude, contentment, hope, pride, interest, amusement, and

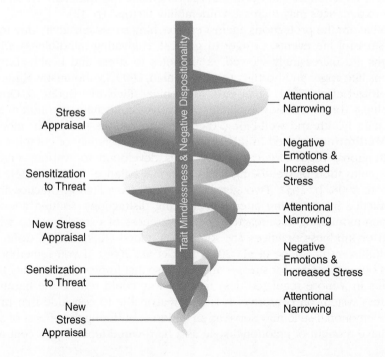

FIGURE 14.3 The downward spiral of stress reactivity. Chronic activation of the stress response can lead to a downward spiral of negative physical and emotional consequences.
SOURCE: Garland, E. L., Fredrickson, B. L., Kring, A. M., Johnson, D. P., Meyer, P. S., & Penn, D. L. (2010). Upward spirals of positive emotions counter downward spirals of negativity: Insights from the broaden-and-build theory and affective neuroscience on the treatment of emotion dysfunctions and deficits in psychopathology. *Clinical Psychology Review, 30 (7)*, 849–864. Used with permission from Elsevier.

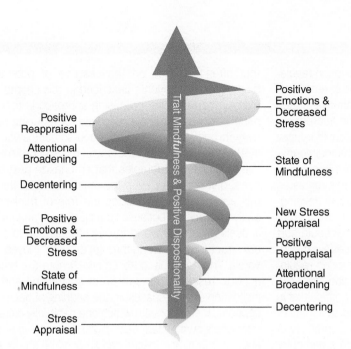

FIGURE 14.4 The upward spiral of positive emotions and resilience. The experience of positive emotions broadens attention and contributes to building a reserve of personal resources.

SOURCE: Garland, E. L., Fredrickson, B. L., Kring, A. M., Johnson, D. P., Meyer, P. S., & Penn, D. L. (2010). Upward spirals of positive emotions counter downward spirals of negativity: Insights from the broaden-and-build theory and affective neuroscience on the treatment of emotion dysfunctions and deficits in psychopathology. *Clinical Psychology Review, 30 (7)*, 849–864. Used with permission from Elsevier.

awe) were three times as great as they were at week 1. Furthermore, these changes were associated with increased resources like self-acceptance, mindfulness, better health, and improved social relationships. The authors conclude that the path to improved life satisfaction was heavily impacted by positive emotions. "Positive emotions emerged as the mechanism through which people build the resources that make their lives more fulfilling and help keep their depressive symptoms at bay" (p. 1057).

In a study that investigated the effectiveness of meditation for reducing anxiety and enhancing positive mood, Davidson and his colleagues (Davidson et al., 2003) explored the effects of a meditation course on brain and immune system functioning. A group of healthy male and female employees at a biotechnology corporation were recruited to participate in an 8-week meditation-based stress reduction program at their workplace, forming a treatment group and a wait-list control. Before beginning the program, participants' brain electrical activity was measured while they were asked to write about a series of positive and negative events in their lives. At the end of the 8 weeks, the same assessments of brain activity were performed. Participants also rated their experience of positive and negative emotions following each group session. Finally, all participants (including the wait-list group) were vaccinated with flu influenza vaccine at the end of the 8 weeks. Blood samples were obtained 3 to 5 weeks and again at 8 to 9 weeks postvaccination to assess the immune response.

Results demonstrated that meditators showed a significant increase in left prefrontal brain activity, related to the experience of positive affectivity, compared to the control group. Self-report measures reflected a significant decrease in anxiety for those in the program compared to those who did not participate. Interestingly, program participants reported significant decreases in their own experiences of negative affectivity over time, whereas control group members did not. When blood draws were examined, participants in the meditation group had significantly increased concentrations of antibodies in their blood compared to nonmeditators. This finding suggests a greater and more rapid immune system response compared to controls. These findings are promising because they reflect that even a relatively short intervention carried out in a work setting can reduce negative affectivity and anxiety and promote health and well-being.

APPLICATIONS

Threaded throughout this book is the theme of emotion regulation, that capacity that allows us to regulate levels of emotional arousal. The behaviors and capacities that constitute emotion regulation also include recognition of feelings and appropriate expression and modulation of emotional expression. In infancy and toddlerhood, attachments with caregivers channel youngsters' developing capacity to self-soothe, to tolerate frustration, and to stay for longer and longer periods of time in a regulated emotional state. In childhood and adolescence, social development is promoted by the young person's ability to delay gratification in service of peers, to control impulses that could hurt or antagonize others, and to benefit from capacities for friendship. In emerging and young adulthood, good emotion regulation is associated with better overall adjustment and satisfying communication in close relationships. Conversely, difficulties in emotion regulation have been associated with a wide variety of problems. Recall that temperamental differences in intensity of perceived emotions can make emotion regulation a particular challenge for some children.

What we have been calling "emotion regulation" typically refers to the experience of negative emotions—that is, what we do when we feel bad or when we don't get our own way. Helpers might be heartened by the growing literature indicating that emotional affectivity, both positive and negative, is not immutable and can be shaped by certain practices. All the efforts to support resiliency affirm this conclusion. As Davidson reflects about his own work, "It was the possibility of altered *traits* of consciousness that was particularly appealing to me. Altered traits implied the transformation of consciousness and personality in an enduring fashion to foster increased well-being" (Davidson, 2002, p. 107).

Helping professionals should be proud of their history of fostering wellness in various ways (see Keyes & Haidt, 2003; Walsh, 2003). The paths to well-being include the development of mastery and optimism, teaching of effective problem solving and decision making, encouragement of social competence, support for health-promoting behaviors related to diet and exercise, and advocacy for improved environmental circumstances. In this press toward well-being, however, it is important to take note of the real suffering that serious negative life events produce in the lives of those who sustain them. There are no easy therapeutic interventions that can guarantee rapid recovery or put an end to serious distress, such as simply reframing the problem or learning to perceive stressful events in different ways. Often the coping process, as in the case of recovery from addictions or traumatic assault, happens one step at a time on a day-to-day basis. Helpers clearly have much to offer their clients in this regard. But we should not forget that clients' struggles to cope with stressors and to make their own lives meaningful have a great deal to teach us as well.

Mindfulness

Within the body of techniques that address stress reduction, interventions that target stress-reactivity—the quick response that often switches on the cascade of potentially harmful biopsychological events described in this chapter—are particularly important. One promising approach is to work with the mind's own plasticity and capacity for reducing negative reactivity through present-moment and somatic awareness (Cioffe, 1991; Kabat-Zinn, 2003). Therapy of this sort provides an alternative to traditional therapies that emphasize past history, future goals, distraction, or even the restructuring of thinking. In fact, this approach deemphasizes the role of thinking and verbal analysis precisely because "the illusion of language is that one is dealing with the world through thought. In fact, one is actually structuring the world through thought" (Hayes, 2002, p. 104). Varela, Thompson, and Rosch (1991) note the tendency of the mind to reside in the domain of abstraction and refer to this inclination as "the spacesuit, the padding of habits and preconceptions, the armor with which one habitually distances oneself from one's own experience" (p. 25). As we have noted, worrying about something stressful can amplify the stress. Even without the presence of stressors, our minds are constantly engaged in inner conversations that remove us from the direct experience of what is actually happening in the present moment.

The direct experience of the present, as opposed to mental reruns of past events, discursive ruminations about abstract ideas, or fantasy scenarios about future possibilities, is a very different type of mental event. Being present in the moment involves stepping out of the automatic pilot mode that characterizes much of our mental life. With practice in noticing and taking account of the present moment, it becomes possible to disengage from dominating ruminative patterns of thinking. Moreover, it becomes possible to extricate oneself from the attitude of abstraction to reconnect the mind and body. Approaches that foster somatic present-moment awareness help develop the skill of being in the "here and now" without attaching any evaluative valence to the experience. Attention available for discursive thought is deliberately reduced, whereas nonjudgmental acceptance of one's experience and also oneself is increased. Greater awareness of present-moment experience improves the capacity to respond to stressors in a more skillful and less reactive way.

Recently researchers have proposed that one of the key features of cognitive therapy—that is, metacognitively standing back from one's negative thoughts to notice their accuracy—promotes the type of psychological decentering or distancing that helps interrupt the ruminative cycle. This phenomenon, often called **mindfulness**, has been defined as "paying attention in particular way: on purpose, in the present moment, and nonjudgmentally" (Kabat-Zinn, 1994). Teasdale and colleagues (Teasdale et al., 2000; Teasdale et al., 2002) view mindfulness as the main ingredient in therapeutic change in cognitive behavioral therapy because of its capacity to short circuit negative thought cycling, to liberate us from the tyranny of the mental rules we establish for ourselves and others, and to allow for dispassionate observation of thinking.

Meditation-based mindfulness approaches are beginning to be subject to enthusiastic inquiry by those who translate

Eastern traditions for modern Western readers (Goleman, 2003; Kabat-Zinn, 2005). Mindfulness-based stress reduction (MBSR), developed by Kabat-Zinn and colleagues at the University of Massachusetts Stress Reduction Clinic, is a generic program based on a psychoeducational rather than a clinical treatment model. Originally developed as a hospital-based program for stress reduction, MBSR programs have proliferated in recent years to include training for groups as diverse as students, educators, corporate employees, health care professionals, attorneys, inmates, clergy, and athletes. The course has a structured curriculum that is taught in a group format over 8 weeks and involves daily homework practice. In comparison to therapies that emphasize discussion or analysis, MBSR emphasizes practice in working with attention. A core feature of mindfulness is learning to transform stressful situations by going through them in a skillful way, not trying to avoid or eradicate them. Essentially, to be mindful is to develop skills in attention and moment-to-moment awareness. Therefore, developing the ability to take note of thoughts, feelings, and sensations increases the capacity to work skillfully with negative ones and replace automatic, habitual, and often judgmental reactions with relaxed observing and awareness.

Some of the session themes include noticing the automaticity of thinking and behavior, becoming more aware of bodily sensations, learning how to get "unstuck" from reactive patterns, enhancing stress hardiness, and so forth. The program employs various activities such as walking, sitting, and eating meditation, yoga/mindful movement, and discussion. One of the primary foundations of the program is daily home practice.

MBSR principles have been incorporated into cognitive-behavioral therapy resulting in a new treatment modality called mindfulness-based cognitive therapy (MBCT; Segal, Williams, & Teasdale, 2002). This approach was designed to reduce the risk of depressive relapse. Mindfulness approaches are also a prominent part of Linehan's (1993) Dialectical Behavior Therapy, originally designed for individuals diagnosed with borderline personality disorder, as well as in Acceptance and Commitment Therapy (Hayes, 2004).

MBSR outcome studies show improvements in physical and psychological functioning for individuals suffering from chronic pain (Kabat-Zinn, Lipworth, Burney, & Sellers, 1986; Randolph et al., 1999), in overall quality of life, stress reduction, and sleep quality for cancer patients (Carlson, Speca, Patel, & Goodey, 2004; Shapiro, Bootzin, Figueredo, Lopez, & Schwartz, 2003), in healing of psoriasis (Kabat-Zinn et al., 1998), in immune system functioning among HIV-positive patients (Robinson, Mathews, & Witek-Janusek, 2003), in reduction of pain, fatigue, and sleep disturbances associated with fibromyalgia (Weissbecker, et al., 2002), in symptom reduction among women with binge-eating disorder (Kristeller, Hallett, & Brendan, 1999), as well as decreases in anxiety and depression (Kabat-Zinn et al., 1992) and reduction in depressive relapse (Ma & Teasdale, 2004). In general, meditative practices improve functioning on a number of important health indices related to longevity: increased immune and cardiovascular system functioning and reduced pain sensitivity (Alonso-Fernandez & De la Fuente, 2011; Kok, Waugh, & Fredrickson, 2013). Meta-analyses (Grossman, Niemann, Schmidt, & Walach, 2004; Hofmann, Sawyer, Witt, & Oh,

2010) reported that MBSR was an effective intervention for enhancing both physical and mental wellness and for improving coping with both day-to-day and more serious stressors.

Forgiveness

Part of the acceptance process must involve forgiveness of past hurts. Increasingly, forgiveness is being accorded more importance in therapeutic contexts as it is shown to contribute to physical and psychological features of well-being (McCullough & Witvliet, 2002). For example, consider this empirical study of the effects of forgiveness or lack of forgiveness on physiology. Witvliet, Ludwig and Vander Laan (2001) asked participants in this study to imagine a person who had harmed or mistreated them. Participants were then instructed to rehearse unforgiving feelings (like holding the grudge) for a brief period of time while physiological measurements were made. They were next instructed to practice forgiving responses (like empathizing with the offender by trying to take an alternative perspective on the offense) while the same assessments were taken. Blood pressure, facial tension, cardiovascular reactivity, arterial pressure and sympathetic nervous system arousal as measured by skin conductivity were all significantly higher in the unforgiving condition. Participants reported more negative mood (angry, sad, aroused, etc.) while being unforgiving. Furthermore, negative physiological effects of the period of "holding a grudge" as measured by cardiovascular and sympathetic nervous system indicators persisted into the subsequent stage of the experiment. This finding suggests that the physiological systems activated in the unforgiving state may resist healing, contribute to overall stress, and have implications for overall health.

Forgiveness does not involve excusing hurtful behavior, necessarily reconciling with the offender, suppressing one's pain or forgetting the offense. Rather, it involves a shift in thoughts, feelings and behaviors in relation to offenders in a more positive direction (McCollough, Pargament, & Thoresen, 2000). It generally involves a long and gradual process of transforming the tendency to seek revenge and to let go of enmity. As Kornfield puts it, "Forgiveness means giving up all hope of a better past" (Kornfield, 2002, p. 25).

Forgiveness therapy (Enright & Fitzgibbons, 2000) proposes a series of stages that map the process of forgiveness in a therapeutic setting. The first phase, uncovering, is spent in a thorough examination of the traumatic injury or event. Recognizing and confronting anger or shame, readjusting an old view of a "just world," and coming to terms with the injury are parts of this process. In phase two, the decision phase, injured clients face up to the realization that carrying the burden of rage or seeking revenge may be an unskillful resolution. Here the therapist attempts to motivate clients to see the benefits of forgiveness to physical and emotional well-being. Perhaps for the first time, forgiveness is seen as a possibility. In the work phase, clients might be asked to write about whom it is they wish to forgive. Reframing questions posed by the therapist, such as "What was it like for the offender when he or she was growing up?" encourage perspective taking and empathy, which may plant the seeds of compassion. The authors caution that compassion aids in the healing process but must unfold in its own time, so therapists should not rush this process. Clients may also be asked to write about the impact that acceptance and forgiveness might have on their lives. In the last phase, called deepening, clients continue to construct a narrative to account for the painful experience, which allows the episode to become integrated into a meaningful life story. Sometimes, sharing one's story with others or working to help others who have been similarly hurt provides a therapeutic resolution.

Self-Compassion: Spirals of Positivity

Looking ahead toward the last of Erikson's psychosocial tasks, we see that everyone needs to come to terms with his or her own life story, regardless of the paths their lives have taken. "Coming to terms" may include forgiving ourselves for real or imagined offenses as well as forgiving those who might have hurt us. The fact that people are developmentally more inclined to take stock in midlife (Erikson, 1968) does not mean that reflection is nonexistent at other points in the life span. However, the salience of this theme in the "second half of life" (Jung, 1963) suggests that self-acceptance is truly a life's work. The world's great religions have all adopted some version of the "golden rule," to love both one's neighbor and oneself. The great philosophical traditions have also championed the values of love for all humanity. But what does it really mean to love oneself? Clearly, this advice has merit not only on theological or philosophical grounds. Self-acceptance and self-compassion offer many advantages for personal happiness, adjustment, and physical health. Empathy for others also makes relationships less confrontational and more satisfying. Perhaps those in the helping professions need to be particularly mindful of their own needs for self-care because they so often share in the emotional experiences of others. Compassion is an exceptionally important quality for helpers that can support their work with clients and improve their own psychological wellbeing (see Germer & Siegel, 2012).

A meditation practice, akin to those described earlier, can be useful to enhance positive affectivity by cultivating lovingkindness. *Lovingkindness* may be defined as an attitude that extends care and empathy toward self and others (Goleman, 2003). This should not be mistaken for some transient sentimental state. Rather it is the basis for a broad-based altruism and a strong positive regard for others. The lovingkindness exercise is essentially a way to practice benevolence directed first toward oneself and then toward friends, neutral acquaintances, and finally enemies. Often people find it easier to be compassionate toward others than toward themselves; indeed, practicing self-acceptance at an affective level may seem strange to many of us in the West.

Disrespect for ourselves and disregard for our basic physical, social, and emotional needs underlies many self-destructive behaviors that take their toll on health and happiness. To cultivate this attitude of compassion in this way, the person first concentrates his attention, repeats inwardly a set of phrases "May I be happy; May I be peaceful; May I be healthy and strong" and so forth, as he generates the emotions of compassion. Recent research using neuroimaging techniques has shown that such practice produces long-lasting alterations in brain function in areas related to development of positive affective states (Lutz, Greischan, Rawlings, Ricard, & Davidson, 2004). Savoring the positive moments of life mindfully, expressing gratitude, cultivating optimism, and acceptance by not trying to avoid the less pleasant realities of life are all resilience-building strategies. Kok et al. (2013) summarize these points well.

> "Most advice dispensed about how people might improve their physical health calls for increased physical activity, improved nutritional intake, and reductions in tobacco and alcohol use. Alongside this good advice, we now have evidence to recommend efforts to self-generate positive emotions as well. Recurrent momentary experiences of positive emotions appear to serve as nutrients for the human body, increasing feelings of social belonging and giving a needed boost to parasympathetic health, which in turn opens people up to more and more rewarding positive emotional and social experiences. Over time, this self-sustaining upward spiral of growth appears to improve physical health."

Positive practices that help us manage stress and regulate mood are beneficial for clients and helpers alike. One broad implication we can draw from work in this area is that well-being is not just the "absence" of disorder, experienced only some of the time by a fortunate few. Instead, it involves the deliberate cultivation of those elements that make life worthwhile.

SUMMARY

Life Satisfaction: What Is a Well-Lived Life?

1. Subjective well-being, an individual's overall satisfaction with life and general happiness, is usually measured using questionnaires or interviews asking people to rate their lives or their feelings about their lives on a continuum, say from "very happy" to "very unhappy." SWB includes cognitive (satisfaction) as well as affective (positive and negative experience) elements. New ways of measuring daily experience are contributing to this body of research.

2. The well-being of individuals and of national populations is correlated with wealth but its strength depends upon measures used. People who are poor report less well-being than those who are not, but after a certain basic level of income is attained, greater wealth is not strongly associated with greater happiness. Actual increases in disposable income are related to life satisfaction especially when optimism about the future and low income disparity are present.

3. The American paradox, which characterizes many wealthy nations, is that as income and standard of living have increased steadily in recent decades, so have emotional problems such as depression. There may be several

reasons, among which are that pursuit of material gain may put many people on a hedonic treadmill. Because they expect more money to make them happier, when it doesn't they feel compelled to further pursue material gain. Also, the lifestyles made possible by affluence tend to reduce the need for support from others, limiting opportunities for others to demonstrate genuine friendship. Income inequality may play a role because disadvantaged individuals report more negative experiences. Finally, having wealth means having control. When that control can't create a "perfect" life, people may blame themselves, fostering depression.

4. Some personality characteristics, like extroversion and neuroticism, are strongly correlated with subjective well-being measures.

5. Social relationships appear to be essential to well-being. Giving and receiving social support are both important. People who are happy have better social relationships, but social relationships also play a causal role in creating happiness. Having friends, confidants, and marriage partners are all linked to well-being. Some cultural groups with strong social connections report high levels of happiness even though income is relatively low.

6. Work also is linked to happiness. People who feel generative report more well-being. Well-being is also associated with making progress toward goals and having opportunities to exercise skills.

7. People may have universal psychological needs that must be met to feel satisfied with life. Among those that have been suggested are needs for autonomy, competence, and relatedness. When such needs are met, people are thought to experience psychological well-being (also called eudaemonic well-being), which is distinguished from subjective well-being (also called hedonic well-being). Although the two kinds of well-being are closely correlated, psychological well-being specifically involves feeling a sense of purpose, growth, and mastery.

8. Many theorists propose that having a sense that one's life has meaning (situational meaning) that is linked to the meaning or purpose of the universe and of human kind (universal meaning) is an important ingredient in well-being. Religion and spirituality is an important source of happiness for a majority of people in the world. Levels of religiosity vary in terms of a country's economic status and level of strife.

Stress, Coping, and Well-Being in Midlife

9. Many stressors affect people at midlife including awareness of limited time left to live, accumulated losses related to aging, and increased responsibilities and obligations in the family and at work that can cause role strain. What determines resilience in this stage of life? Among the protective factors identified in one large-scale study of adults were childhood factors (e.g., educated parents), social attachments (e.g., confidants and spouses), stable employment, and positive social comparisons with parents and siblings.

10. Two kinds of stressors are life events, which are discrete events, and daily hassles, which are more chronic. The cumulative effects of chronic stressors on the body is called allostatic load. People can experience gradually increasing sensitivity to stressful triggers, called kindling-behavioral sensitization.

11. Diathesis-stress models suggest that some individuals have specific vulnerabilities (diatheses) to a disorder under the right stress conditions. This would explain, for example, why only some people develop post-traumatic stress disorder after experiencing traumatic events.

12. Some people experience post-traumatic growth, positive psychological change after struggling with difficult circumstances. Personality traits like extroversion and openness are linked to this kind of change.

13. In response to stress, the body mobilizes energy to enhance functions that would support fight or flight, such as motor and sensory abilities. In response to disease, the immune system also mobilizes energy to fight pathogens. The two systems direct energy to different ends; when under stress, the body inhibits functions that support the immune system, causing immunosuppression.

14. The new field of psychoneuroimmunology, the study of interactions between the central nervous system, the immune system and behavior, indicates that the brain influences the immune system, and the immune system also influences the brain, playing a role, for example, in depression.

15. Management of stress, or coping, has often been conceptualized as constituting binary approaches, such as problem-focused versus emotion-focused coping. But instead of mutually exclusive categories of coping behavior, there may be many ways of coping that work differently depending on the situation. At midlife, stress may be largely a function of loss. To deal with loss, people act in ways to conserve or rebuild their resources.

16. Cultural groups appear to cope in different ways using strategies that reflect core values such as individualism or collectivism.

17. Among the ways of conserving or rebuilding resources is to cultivate a sense of self-efficacy, mastery, and control. Cultivation of positive affectivity, and reduction of negative affectivity, is also beneficial. The left prefrontal cortex is activated during the experience of positive emotions, and the right prefrontal cortex is activated during periods of negative emotion. More negative affectivity is associated with greater reactivity to stress. Immune responses are less compromised during stress when positive emotions are increased.

18. The brain is the gatekeeper to stress, so cultivating healthy mental habits can serve as one antidote to health-compromising reactivity. The practice of mindfulness meditation and positive emotions has been shown to promote good health, especially by improving immune and cardiovascular functioning and reducing pain perception.

CASE STUDY

David is a 52-year-old White male who has spent the last 24 years in the human resource field. Most recently, he held the position of supervisor in the billing department of a midsized hospital in a rural state. He worked hard to obtain a master's degree while on the job at the hospital and always had high aspirations for himself professionally. David has three children from his first marriage, which ended in divorce. His first wife Anne, who is 50, works as a preschool teacher in another part of the state. Their children's ages are 16, 20, and 22. Both older children started to attend college but may have to drop out temporarily due to financial difficulties. David feels that it is his responsibility to support his children's education, and he has been paying as much of their tuition as he can afford. David and his second wife live in a new, but modest home in a community on the outskirts of the state capital close to David's job. David's second wife, Sandy, has twin 14-year-old boys. One of the twins has a serious learning disability and needs extra tutoring and a great deal of parent support to keep up academically. Sandy works part time in a department store to be home to help her sons. David and Sandy have a good relationship. Sandy's widowed mother lives nearby and helps with the twins on a regular basis.

Recently, the hospital system that employs David merged with a large network of medical providers to cut costs and use resources more efficiently. David's job at the hospital is becoming more complicated, requiring more and more processing of information that involves advanced computer technology. At a recent professional meeting, David learned from others in his network that many jobs were being cut and many tasks redistributed to the employees that remained. David feels that this has already happened in his workplace. He has noted a dramatic increase in the amount of paperwork required and a distinct decrease in the time allotted to meet deadlines. His supervisory responsibilities have expanded to include workers from another unit that merged with his own in a major departmental

realignment. David's direct supervisor will be retiring soon, and David will be a candidate for that position. He knows that this promotion would mean more income, but it would also mean even more work responsibility. David now spends his weekends going to the office to catch up on tasks. He is not as available as he once was to spend time with his children, and this has caused some problems in his relationship with his wife. He is starting to feel that all the paperwork his job requires is not meaningful in ways that are important to him.

David has recently begun to suffer from significant pain in his lower back that he believes might be related to a traffic accident that happened when he was younger. The pain keeps him from sleeping well and has contributed to his feeling more "on edge" during the day. David's physician prescribes two medications to help him sleep better and to reduce anxiety. David has started to drink a few beers when he comes home at night to "calm himself down" as well. The sleep medication he has been taking helps him fall asleep, but now he wakes up at 3:00 am with his mind racing. He's recently learned that his 16-year-old son has been cutting classes and failing tests. His ex-wife, who has custody of their teenage son, has been pressuring him to help her with this problem situation.

Discussion Questions

1. Identify the risks and protective factors that are present in David's life story. What information, not presented here, would be helpful to know if you were to make a more comprehensive list of risks and protections?
2. How do you conceptualize David's situation? What aspects are relate to his midlife stage?
3. What treatment approach would you take if he were to come to you for help? What other behavioral changes might you suggest?

PRACTICE USING WHAT YOU HAVE LEARNED

In the Pearson etext, apply these ideas to working with others.

Video Exercise

JOURNAL QUESTIONS

1. What is your stereotypic view of midlife? Does it or does it not conform to what you have read in this chapter? Explain how your thinking about midlife might have changed.
2. What is your view of a well-lived life? Consider each of the aspects in this chapter (money, social relationships, values, meaning, religion/spirituality, and work) and describe their importance to you. What are your priorities? How do you plan to realize your goals?
3. What does spirituality mean to you? What does "faith" mean to you? Are they the same?
4. What do you imagine will be the way you will deal with the expected and unplanned stressors of your own midlife period?
5. How do you deal with stress in your life now? What part do your mental habits play in generating your stress?

KEY CONCEPTS

subjective well-being (SWB) (p. 526)
experience-sampling method (ESM) (p. 527)
day reconstruction method (DRM) (p. 527)
hedonic well-being (p. 532)
eudaemonic well-being (p. 532)
psychological well-being (p. 533)
self-determination theory (p. 533)
autonomy (p. 533)
competence (p. 533)

relatedness (p. 533)
role strain (p. 539)
life events (p. 539)
daily hassles (p. 539)
kindling-behavioral sensitization (p. 540)
diathesis-stress (p. 540)
diatheses (p. 540)
post-traumatic growth (p. 541)
immunosuppression (p. 542)

endorphins (p. 542)
psychoneuroimmunology (p. 542)
negative affectivity (p. 545)
behavioral-inhibition system (p. 545)
positive affectivity (p. 545)
behavioral facilitation system (p. 546)
meditation (p. 547)
mindfulness (p. 550)

CHAPTER 15

Gains and Losses in Late Adulthood

As people move into old age, in their 60s and 70s, or into old-old age, in their 80s and 90s, both gains and losses continue. However, losses may considerably outweigh gains. "Even in young people's lives, not everything goes well. Old age is a genuinely difficult situation with lots of sadness and frustration. Many things do not go well" (Pipher, 1999, p. 26). How can the elderly effectively manage the ever-increasing losses they experience? For example, can their developmental trajectory be a positive one when they experience multiple health problems or find themselves in chronic pain? An important focus of this chapter will be to identify the means by which elderly adults manage their lives and the extent to which they can grow, maintain themselves, and regulate their losses.

Clearly, different people manage their late-life losses with varying degrees of success. But you may be surprised to learn that for a majority of us, successful development is what we can expect for much of our old age. At age 81, Helen still maintains her job in a bookstore. As one of the oldest siblings in a large working-class family, she learned early to value hard work and has always been active and productive. Her job provides her with opportunities to maintain her skills as well as the chance to learn new ones, such as the new computerized system her company uses to inventory material. Helen is fortunate in that her health is good, aside from some problems with arthritis that slow down her movement. She recognizes that she must regulate her activity now more than before, reducing extraneous activities so she can be well rested and prepared for work, thus optimizing her performance there. She is an avid crossword puzzle fan, her recipe for staying mentally active. When she noticed herself becoming more forgetful, she compensated by writing notes to herself and establishing and following set routines. She travels and volunteers less these days, compared to what she did years ago when her husband was alive. Now she chooses to spend more time with her family and has eliminated activities she considers unnecessary. She knows what she can do and what gives her a sense of satisfaction. Helen's adaptation is a good example of how a person can cope successfully with the challenges of aging.

In what follows, we will first review the nature of the losses and challenges that typically confront people in old age. Then we will look at the ways in which the elderly cope with these challenges, paying special attention to the processes that seem most important for the lifelong experience of psychological well-being. The fact that the world's aging population is rapidly increasing adds a level of urgency to these issues if we are to support healthy development at all points in the lifespan (see Figure 15.1).

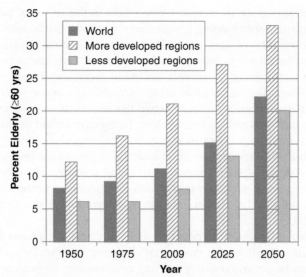

FIGURE 15.1 **The growing aging population across the world.** The numbers of aged are predicted to rise sharply across the world in coming years.

SOURCE: United Nations World Population Aging 2009; http://www.un.org/esa/population/publications/WPA2009/WPA2009-report.pdf.

PHYSICAL, COGNITIVE, AND SOCIOEMOTIONAL CHANGE IN LATE LIFE

Challenge and Loss in Late Adulthood

Physical Change

A gradual decline from peak functioning is characteristic of most physiological systems beginning as early as age 30. By late adulthood, the losses are usually noticeable and have required some adjustment in expectations or lifestyle. A lifelong runner who still entered marathons at age 62 remarked, "At 30, my goal was to win. At 50, I celebrated every race that I finished. Today, I'm delighted to be at the starting line."

Maintaining good physical and mental health becomes more challenging with age, as the immune system becomes progressively less effective in staving off cancer and infections and as the cardiovascular, respiratory, and organ systems function less adequately. Chronic illness and the need for more vigilant health maintenance increase dramatically with age. Age shifts in the leading causes of death illustrate these changing health concerns. In the United States, accidents are the leading cause of death in adults up to age 45. But at 45, heart disease and cancer take over as the leading causes of death, followed by cerebrovascular diseases and chronic respiratory illness (U.S. National Center for Health Statistics, Health, United States, 2010). People of any age can suffer from acute or chronic illnesses, such as cancer, heart problems, diabetes, and so on. But the risk of these illnesses climbs dramatically and steadily in our later years.

Among the continuing declines of old age are two that are common and often especially debilitating. First are increasing sensory deficits (see Chapter 13). Changes in the visual system can be particularly important for one daily activity: driving. A number of aging changes make driving more difficult, including loss of visual acuity, loss of sensitivity to movement in the periphery, increased recovery time after exposure to glare, and reduced night vision. These changes do not contribute significantly to accident rates until people reach their mid-70s (Whitbourne, 2002; U.S. Bureau of the Census, 2012).

A second important decline in older adults is the onset of pain, stiffness, and swelling of joints and surrounding tissues that we call **arthritis**. After 65, about half of women and about 40% of men experience the most common form, **osteoarthritis**, which involves the thinning, fraying, and cracking of cartilage at the ends of bones. Ordinarily, this cartilage helps protect our joints from the friction of bone to bone contact. As cartilage degenerates and other joint changes occur, such as the growth of bony spurs and modifications in connective tissues, joints may stiffen and swell. The upshot is often pain and reduced movement. Being overweight or overusing a particular joint (for example, the knees in sports like running and tennis) can contribute to susceptibility, but ordinary degeneration with age is part of the problem. Osteoarthritis can range from being a painful nuisance to being a source of major disability. It can affect the performance of simple tasks, such as opening a jar or walking, as well as more complex skills such as playing the piano or swinging a golf club (Whitbourne & Whitbourne, 2011).

How older individuals respond to daily physical symptoms has a substantial impact on their overall health over time. Being proactive in seeking help when health problems begin and making a strong commitment to treatment, such as sticking to medical treatment plans or exercise regimens is important. In a longitudinal study of people above age 60, Wrosch and Schultz (2008) found that the use of such health management control strategies was directly related to health maintenance versus decline. We have repeatedly examined the role of stress in inflammatory and disease-related processes throughout the lifespan. In old age, stress-related allostatic load contributes to disease burden and lowered quality of life (see Prasad, Sung, & Aggarwal, 2012 for a review of inflammation's role in chronic diseases of aging). Of particular significance are studies that implicate stress in telomere shortening. **Telomeres** are the protective ends of chromosomes that are shortened by physiological and psychological stress as well as age. When stress is chronic, accelerated cell aging has been observed both in children and adults. Shortness of telomeres is associated with earlier mortality (Lin, Epel, & Blackburn, 2011) but some shortening may be reversed with effective stress management strategies such as mindfulness meditation (Epel, Daubenmier, Moskowitz, Folkman, & Blackburn, 2009). Not all stress is bad, however. Exercise is a beneficial form of physical stress that provides abundant benefits for all age groups. Physical activity includes things like walking a pet or gardening. Remaining as active as possible in later life, both through structured exercise and physical activities, helps reduce stress and promotes health. Other mild stress, such as the stress of caloric restriction and exposure to cognitive stimulation, also appears to reduce deterioration in aging individuals (Mattson, Chan, & Duan, 2002).

Attention to health maintenance is an important aspect of successful coping in late adulthood.

Brain and Cognitive Change

Cognition depends on a healthy and well-functioning brain. This means, among other things, that synaptic connections operate smoothly and the integrity of white matter is preserved. You have seen that healthy brain development proceeds in an organized fashion with the frontal lobes last to mature. As people age, those portions of the brain that matured last tend to be most vulnerable. Vascular problems and atrophy affect the frontal lobes first in late life, although this phenomenon does not account for all the cognitive changes of aging (Raz, 2000). Thus, executive functions, largely controlled via frontal lobe funtioning, are areas that generally show earliest age-related declines. Continuous decrements on many neurological measures related to cognition like brain volume, cortical thickness, neurotransmitter efficiency, and so forth extend from the decade of the twenties onward (see Salthouse, 2009). In this section we'll take a look at these changes and provide a brief review of related material from Chapter 13.

You probably recall that reserachers make a distinction between fluid and crystallized intelligence as a way of describing two types of intellectual resources. In previous chapters we call these categories mechanics (fluid) and pragmatics (crystallized). Another way to think about this distinction is to consider fluid intelligence as the processing efficiency of the cognitive system and crystallized intelligence as the product of that processing (Salthouse, 2006). For many years, correlational studies of cognitive aging in adults have reported declines in both fluid and crystallized intelligence (Jones &Conrad, 1933; see Figure 15.2a).

Longitudinal studies paint a different picture. They suggest that crystallized intelligence, as represented by measures of verbal ability and factual knowledge, does not decline until the mid-70s, and the declines are modest thereafter (Schaie, 1996). Many old individuals show no declines in some areas, and some who have maintained good health actually continue to improve on crystallized intelligence measures. For example, in one longitudinal study of 70- to 100-year-olds, vocabulary knowledge increased until age 90 and showed only slow declines thereafter (Singer, Verhaeghen, Ghisletta, Lindenberger, & Baltes, 2003). In contrast, gradual decrements in fluid intelligence, marked by slower processing speed and reduced inhibitory functions occur with age. Such declines may limit the efficiency of working memory operations, such as learning and problem solving, but these effects may be balanced by the maintenance or advancement of crystallized intelligence or pragmatics (see Figure 15.2b).

Interestingly, even for people who perform well on cognitive tasks well into old age, there appear to be changes in the areas of the brain that are being activated. In brain imaging studies, older adults frequently show *underactivation* of some brain sites and *overactivation* of other sites, especially the prefrontal lobes, relative to younger adults. Also, older adults are more likely to involve both sides of the brain in performing a task when younger adults may only use one side. There could be many reasons for these differences in brain utilization, but some evidence indicates that compensation for loss is often involved, helping the older individual to maintain levels of performance. This is a little like using a back-up reserve and can be successful at moderate levels of task difficulty. When the demands exceed capacity, a resource ceiling is reached, which might explain age-related cognitive declines (see Reuter-Lorenz & Cappell, 2008).

Despite the fact that longitudinal results have been the dominant paradigm for interpreting age changes in cognition, some researchers have questioned the accuracy of these results. Salthouse (2009) showed that reanalyzing the longitudinal data while extracting the effects of prior testing or "practice effects" changes the picture. After statistically removing the practice effects, results from longitudinal findings more closely mirror the declines observed in cross-sectional analyses. These findings, however, should not diminish the importance of longitudinal work. They do suggest, however, the need to more clearly identify true maturational change, devoid of practice effects, and to factor in the developmental stage at which the learning occurs relative to when it is lost.

Craik and Bialystok (2006) offer a framework (see Figure 15.2c) for understanding age changes in cognition that integrates cross-sectional and longitudinal results. These authors use a different way of characterizing cognitive functions: **representations** and **control**. Representations are the kinds of schemas or sytems of schemas one develops over time to interact with the world. In previous chapters we described Piaget's famous stage theory, a narrative of how representations develop from reflexes to abstract thought across the years of childhood and adolescence. Representational systems can involve declarative (language or world history) or procedural (playing chess or driving a car) knowledge. Representations are the foundation of crystallized intelligence. Control involves the ways one works with knowledge and includes attention, learning efficiency, flexibility of working memory, inhibitory

 Alvin and his partner/ caregiver describe the challenges of living with dementia.

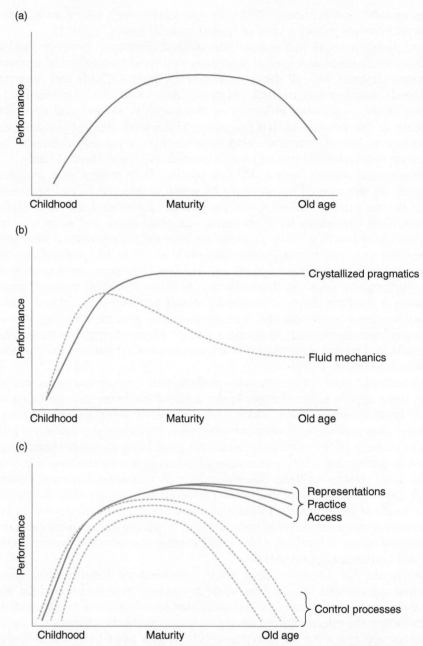

FIGURE 15.2 Three models of cognitive change throughout the lifespan. Part a reflects an inverted u-shaped curve of cognitive development. Performance increases in childhood, is maintained in adulthood, and decreases thereafter. Part b illustrates differing trajectories for fluid and crystallized intelligence. Part c incorporates executive processes informed by neuroscientific findings that show more subtle patterns of maintenance and decline.

SOURCE: Craik, F. J. M. & Bialystok, E. (2006). Cognition through the lifespan: Mechanisms of change. *Trends in Cognitive Sciences, 10,* 131–138. Used with permission from Elsevier.

control and processing speed. Both representations and control features interact. Consider how your attention is drawn to certain kinds of information which, in turn, results in the construction of new schemas or representations of the world. As your understanding grows in a particular domain, so does your expertise.

At older ages, the process of forming new representations is more challenging despite the retention of previously learned representational systems. It appears that using these systems contributes to their maintenance, supporting the proverbial "use it or lose it" advice. But even previously learned representations depend upon control funtions in order to be accessed and used. For example, the name of that elementary school classmate you're trying to recall does you no good buried in your memory unless you can access it. Peak levels of cognitive control functions occur in young adulthood, and gradually decrease thereafter.

Craik and Bialystok posit that research on cognition in childhood and late life are separated by differences in language and emphases. "In development, the primary emphasis is on the changes in representations as the child constructs a coherent interpretive basis for understanding the world; in cognitive aging, the primary emphasis is on decline in control processes as they produce impairments of access to existing knowledge, integration of new and existing information, and translation of knowledge into timely and adaptive action" (Craik & Bialystok, 2006, p. 136). But a more holistic approach to cognition and, in particular, to executive functions across the lifespan can help us map existing knowledge onto new findings in neuroscience. This approach also offers a potential paradigm for studying remediation efforts to increase cognitive reserve (Reuter-Lorenz & Mikels, 2006).

Dementia.   **Dementia** is a syndrome that affects multiple functional domains due to chronic and progressive disease processes in the brain. Cognitive and emotional skills like memory, judgement, language, self-regulation, and motivation are progressively diminished. **Alzheimer's disease (AD)** is the most common type, accounting for 60% of all cases. Frontotemporal dementia (deterioration primarily in frontal and temporal lobes), vascular dementia (related to problems with blood flow to the brain), and dementia with Lewy bodies (or protein build-up) have also been identified. Among these four main types of dementia, there is a great deal of overlap and combined types are frequent (World Alzheimer Report, 2009). The World Health Organization estimates that 35.6 million people around the world were living with dementia in 2010 and rates are predicted to double every 20 years (Alzheimer's Association, 2012).

AD is diagnosed primarily by its clinical characteristics and by excluding other possible causes of dementia. Diagnostic procedures continue to be improved, and skilled clinicians can be quite accurate once a comprehensive evaluation is performed. At this point, however, only autopsy can definitively conclude the presence of AD. Typically dementia progresses in stages. There is a prodromal period, lasting for a year or two, when symptoms (e.g., memory loss) do not reach a clinical threshold but are more impaired than what would be normal for that age. In its early stages, it looks like absentmindedness: forgetting where you recently put something or forgetting something that happened in the last few days or the last few hours. Difficulties with decision making, word-finding, regulating moods, or completing complex tasks might be present. Some pharmaceutical treatments are currently being tested for symptom reduction at this stage, but, thus far, daily exercise and cognitive stimulation have shown the greatest benefit (see Morley, 2011; Cheng, Chow, Song, Yu, Chan, et al., 2012).

More general confusion may follow in the middle stage (second to fourth or fifth year). Individuals might have difficulty remembering even very recent events, wander away from home and get lost, and become unable to prepare meals or perform other self-care tasks. People at this stage may be quite distressed by their memory loss, perhaps even paranoid if they frequently cannot remember what they have done or where they have put things. They may also conclude that others are responsible for these lapses. A relative of one of the authors, for example, would insist that people had entered her apartment and had turned on her TV when she wasn't looking. Others may become hostile in their frustration and confusion. One elderly man, believing that an intruder had entered his home, assaulted his own son each time the latter visited. In later stages, memory and language problems get worse, disorientation is extreme, and physical coordination is affected. Eventually, in the last stage (fifth year and after), Alzheimer's patients, often mute and bedridden, need full-time care and supervision, and death is the outcome (see Alzheimer's Association, 2012).

This is not the only course of the disease. Early-onset AD strikes 40- to 50-year-olds, ends in death after about 5 years, and clearly has a genetic contribution. In all forms of AD, extensive brain changes include the formation of **plaques**, clumps of insoluble protein that are damaging to neurons, and **tangles**, twisted filaments of another protein, which may interfere with communication between neurons and even cause cell death (Braak & Braak, 1991). **Amyloid precursor protein (APP)** and several enzymes that operate on it appear to play an initial role in development of plaque formation (Ballard, Gauthier, Corbett, Brayne, Aarsland, & Jones, 2011). Related inflammatory processes also appear to be important precursors of dementia. These inflammatory processes can start up to 10 to 20 years before actual symptoms appear (Friedrich, 2013). Early stage studies have also found noticeable brain changes in AD including thinning in several areas of the brain (Dickerson et al., 2008). The inability to remember things after an intervening distraction or period of time (either several minutes or longer), called delayed recall, is considered one of the best preclinical signs of approaching AD (Salmon & Bondi, 2009).

Many of us have seen the ravages of dementia in a relative or friend, and we worry that extreme memory loss and disorientation are the inevitable consequences of aging. But they are not. Normal aging does not lead to dementia, although the frequency of illnesses and conditions that cause dementia does increase with age. Among these are cardiovascular problems that limit the oxygen supply to the brain for some period of time. These include **cerebrovascular accidents**, or **strokes**, in which an artery serving the brain is either clogged or bursts. A single stroke can lead to acute onset of dementia. More typically, many minor strokes (**multi-infarct dementia**) can gradually do sufficient damage to cause dementia. Hypertension (high blood pressure), or hypertension combined with diabetes, increases the risk of this type of dementia (Whitbourne & Whitbourne, 2011).

Although AD and other forms of dementia are not characteristic of the majority of elderly, there is some suspicion that the formation of plaques and tangles may occur to some extent in all of us. Some environments seem to enhance or reduce AD rates. For example, lifelong education and intellectual stimulation seem to decrease the risk (Snowdon, 1997; Wilson et al, 2010).

Terminal Drop and Terminal Decline. **Terminal drop** and **terminal decline** describe the phenomena of deteriorating cognitive ability as adults approach the end of their lives. In the months and years prior to death, individuals may show a substantial decline in intellectual functioning as indicated by scores on intelligence tests (e.g., Berg, 1987; Wilson, Beck, Bienias, & Bennet, 2007). Figure 15.3 illustrates this finding from one set of longitudinal data. Once used synonymously, researchers are now distinguishing between the terms _drop_ and _decline_. The former change is more precipitous while the latter suggests a gradual process. Researchers using a large-scale Canadian sample (MacDonald, Hultsch, & Dixon, 2011) found little support for the terminal drop trajectory for aggregated cognitive measures used in this study. Instead, the evidence showed greater support for the model of terminal decline. Abrupt declines in cognition may be observed in certain circumstances, and more research is needed to determine why they occur, given the clinical importance of such meaningful changes. Either way, patterns of cognitive deterioration appear to reflect the individual's declining health status, although there also appear to be some individual differences in deterioration processes linked to genetic susceptibility (Wilson et al., 2007). Interestingly, people often seem to be able to detect in themselves whatever changes in health status are predictive of death. A number of studies have found that when older adults self-rate their health as "poor," they are much more likely to die within the next few years than when they rate their health as "excellent" (e.g., Wolinsky & Johnson, 1992). Apparently, people often realize

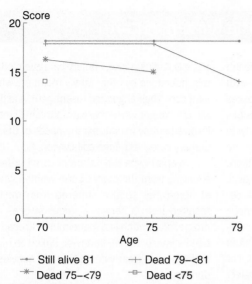

FIGURE 15.3 The relationship between survival scores on an IQ test of verbal meaning in a longitudinal study.
SOURCE: Berg, S. (1996). Aging, behavior, and terminal decline. In James E. Birrens, et al. (Eds.), *Handbook of the psychology of aging (4th ed.).* Burlington, MA: Elsevier Science (USA). Used with permission from Elsevier.

when they are going into decline. In Box 15.1, we examine the effect on caregivers when the elderly reach the end stage of their lives.

Autobiographical Memory. One cognitive function that has particular significance for one's sense of self as well as for social interactions throughout the life span is called **autobiographical memory**. This is the remembered self, "representations of who we have been at various points in the past" (Fitzgerald, 1999, p. 143). It draws from several long-term memory systems (see Chapter 6 for an introduction to these systems). When we recall specific experiences in our lives we are calling on episodic memory; when we remember that we know some fact we're using our semantic memory; and when we remember how to do something we depend on our procedural memory. Autobiographical memory has often been treated as synonymous with episodic memory, which is a very important part of it, but our self-recollections are not episodic alone.

Autobiographical memory is important in many ways. It provides us with a "sense of identity in narrative form" (Fitzgerald, 1999, p. 143). It also is a source of information about social interactions that have worked and that have not worked for us in the past. When we draw on autobiographical memory to tell stories about ourselves to others, it helps us reveal and share ourselves, get closer to others, create impressions, even teach lessons (Fitzgerald, 1999; Hyman & Faries, 1992).

One stereotype that people often have about the aged is that they remember more about their early lives than about what has happened to them recently. Studies of autobiographical memory indicate that this belief is only partially true. Elderly people actually do remember their more recent experiences better than earlier experiences, although the stories that they tell about themselves are often well-rehearsed experiences from the distant past.

There are two very salient characteristics of self-memories for adults of all ages. One is **recency**: The strength of a memory declines the more time has passed since the memory was formed. That is, we are more likely to remember something that has happened to us recently than something that happened in the more distant past. One way to study autobiographical memory is to say a word, like "dog," and ask a person to report a specific experience in his life that the word calls to mind.

Box 15.1: The Burden of Care

In the United States, most elderly people are in good enough health to take full responsibility for their own lives and well-being. But with advancing age the chance of chronic illness or disability increases and for many, there comes a time when full self-care is impossible. For approximately 80% of the frail elderly, family members provide the care that is needed, and often one person bears most of the responsibility (Martin, 2000). For these primary caregivers, there may be rewards, but there often are costs as well—psychological, physical, occupational, social and financial—that together are described as the *care burden*. This burden can bring with it serious consequences for caregivers and sometimes, for patients. For caregivers of patients with dementia, for example, quality of life often declines, and their physical and mental health is jeopardized. For patients, care burden sometimes contributes to the abuse or neglect of the patient or to generally poor standards of care (Papastavrou, Kalokerinou, Papacostas, Tsangari, & Sourtzi, 2007).

Benefits and Burden

A caregiver may reap emotional benefits from her role if her self worth is tied in part to "an ethic of responsibility and care" (Martin, 2000, p. 988). In Asian cultures, filial piety (*xaio*) provides an explicit cultural norm that guides caregiving behavior. Children are taught to care for aging parents as a form of gratitude and respect (Wang, 2004). But even in cultures without such explicit norms, children usually care for their parents in old age (Montgomery, Borgatta, & Borgatta, 2000). Good quality caregiving can promote feelings of competency and self-esteem. For some caregivers there may be financial benefits associated with caregiving as well, as when the primary caregiver anticipates having some priority in the patient's will. In some circumstances, caregiving can be a satisfying aspect of a reciprocal relationship in which the patient continues to serve as a source of emotional and social support to the caregiver. Interestingly, the burden of care is not necessarily reduced by the positive elements of caregiving. For example, caregivers who report strong feelings of general mastery (vis a vis their caregiving) have often been found to experience more care burden than other caregivers, perhaps because those who are more effective tend to work harder (e.g., Greenberger & Litwin, 2003; Halm, Treat-Jacobson, Lindquist, & Savick, 2006).

There are many sources of care burden, such as fatigue, uncertainty about the future, uncertainty about care procedures, discomfort with the tasks required, and so on. The role strain that caregivers experience, trying to balance the needs of the patient with other responsibilities such as work, parenting, and self-care is an important part of the problem. The time and energy consumed both by the physical needs of patients and by their psychological and behavioral difficulties contribute heavily. In one study of over 800 caregivers, researchers found that burden was largely predicted by the degree of physical and/or psychological disability of the patient (Martin, 2000). For caregivers, the psychological and physical consequences of care burden can be profound. The risk of depression and suicide is substantial. Health decline and increased risk of death are common. Emotional turmoil, including feelings of anger, helplessness, guilt, and loss, are typical (see

Mace & Rabins, 1999). Primary caregivers often feel unfairly treated or misunderstood by other family members who are less involved in patient care. Their anger and resentment, and the chances of a long-term rift, are greater when more distant family members justify their lesser involvement by minimizing the needs of the patient or the sacrifice of primary caregivers (Ingersoll-Dayton, Neal, Ha, & Hammer, 2003).

To appreciate the nature of care burden, consider the following excerpts from the diary of one woman who cared for her husband at home. Her spouse suffered from multi-infarct disease, which resulted from a series of minor strokes. Damage to the brain is progressive, much like Alzheimer's disease. The changes in her husband's interpersonal behavior, linked to his growing confusion and memory loss, clearly constitute the heaviest part of this caregiver's burden.

August 28th:

(Charlie said) . . . "We don't even have any water in the house." Oh no, I thought, not again, but he went on. "And since we don't have water in the house they're going to condemn it for sure."

"They're not going to condemn it," I said. "I told you that before."

"That's all you know about it. You're just dumb and stupid, that's all." He was ranting like a maniac. "I never saw anybody so ignorant." He kept going on and on, but . . . I managed to change the subject.

It's so hard to contend with something like this, to keep loving someone who calls you names and treats you like an enemy. I remember how nice it used to be to sit here in the evening and enjoy the TV together. And how Charlie used to laugh and joke around. I also remember how thoughtful he used to be. How warm, generous and loving, and how close we were. Now, he's so wrapped up in his own mixed up world and in his own thoughts, he hardly pays any attention to what's going on around him, or what I'm doing. He doesn't seem to have a grasp on reality, and yet, his family thinks he's just fine, that he's just a little forgetful.

September 15th:

. . . It's 8:30 P.M. He's sitting on the sun porch and he's been crying for over an hour and I don't know what to do. I've tried everything I can think of to quiet him down, but he still just keeps right on crying. When I ask him why he's crying he says, "I don't know." It hurts to see him like this.

March 18th:

. . . I heard loud weird noises coming from the kitchen . . . I hurried into the dinette area just in time to see Charlie raise his arm and throw a handful of ice cubes into one of my cooking pans . . . Water and ice cubes were everywhere.

"What are you doing?" I yelled.

"I have to," he shouted. "We're running out of water."

"We aren't running out of water," I yelled back. "Now, put everything down and leave it alone."

"Get away!" he threatened and he took a swing at me . . .

. . . Every time I tried to stop him, he'd come at me with fury in his eyes, clenched fists, arms swinging, yelling that we were running out of water.

(Shiplett, 1996)

Primary Caregivers

Most primary caregivers are either adult children or spouses of the patient. Among all racial and ethnic groups, women, especially daughters, are more likely to be primary caregivers. Aronson and Weiner (2007) claim that women today actually spend more total time caring for older parents than they do caring for children. When multiple family members contribute, there appear to be some differences in the tasks that female and male caregivers perform. Women are more likely to provide routine hands-on care, whereas men are more likely to provide help in specific situations. Men are more likely to use formal services than women, and they are less likely to feel a conflict with their employment responsibilities, perhaps because less is typically expected of men as caregivers. Many studies indicate that care burden tends to be greater for women than for men, although this gender difference can be moderated by ethnicity. Specifically, African American women report less care burden than White women, whereas African American men report more care burden than White men. Given that African American households are more likely to include extended family members than White households, it may be that African American women expect to care for frail, elderly relatives, whereas African American men may have less expectation of such responsibilities. African American families may also provide more support to women caregivers than White families.

The aforementioned virtue of filial piety may affect the nature and quality of caregiving among Asian families. A study of Caucasian-Canadian, Chinese-Canadian, and Hong-Kong Chinese caregivers explored the strength of traditional cultural attitudes and caregiving quality (Chappell & Funk, 2012). Contrary to expectations, filial piety did not predict behaviors related to care of basic daily needs because children cared for parents across all cultures examined. However, both Chinese groups were more likely to provide greater emotional support to aging parents, possibly demonstrating one distinctive effect of cultural socialization. Further research into cultural differences seems especially important if it can help illuminate environmental factors that explain caregiving patterns and mitigate the burden of care (see Martin, 2000, for a review).

Helping Caregivers

Delehanty and Ginzler (2005), in their guide for caregivers, remind us of the lesson that airline safety instructions impart: "In the event the oxygen masks deploy due to loss of cabin pressure, put on your own mask first, then assist others." The point is, of course, that a caregiver whose mental or physical resources are depleted can actually endanger herself *and* those who are dependent on her.

Consider these quotes from Mace and Rabins (1999), one from a patient's daughter and another from a patient's husband, both primary caregivers:

My mother would scratch at herself in one spot until it bled. The doctor said we had to stop it. I tried everything until one day I guess I snapped: I grabbed her and shook her and I screamed at her. She just looked at me and began to cry. (p. 218)

Sometimes I couldn't stand it. My wife would get to me so, always on about something, and the same thing over and over. Then I would tie her into her chair and go for a walk. I felt terrible about it, but I couldn't stand it. (p. 217)

Most guidelines for caregivers emphasize the critical importance of "timeouts," regular daily or weekly respites from the constancy of caregiving tasks (e.g., Delehanty and Ginzler, 2005; Mace and Rabins, 1999). To make timeouts possible, caregivers need access to resources, such as adult day care programs, professional in-home aids, or regular substitutes among family and friends. Avoiding isolation and reserving time for socializing is critical. Many communities, especially through their medical facilities, offer either individual or group interventions to educate and support caregivers. These services teach caregivers what to expect, how to cope, and how to access resources, and help them to understand their own emotions and the behaviors of difficult patients. A meta-analysis of studies of treatment interventions for primary caregivers found significant benefits of both individual and group approaches (Yin, Zhou, & Bashford, 2002). Interestingly, although women caregivers reported more care burden than men before intervention, women tended to benefit more. Also, there were cultural moderators: Group interventions were more effective than individual interventions for non-White caregivers, but for White caregivers both forms were equally effective.

The impact of the caregiver's role, and the need for support, is poignantly expressed in the words of one husband caregiver as he tried to write a journal about his wife's illness: "I realized that I was telling the story of my own deterioration. I gave up my job to take care of her, then I had no time for my hobbies, and gradually we stopped seeing our friends" (Mace & Rabins, 1999, p. 214). Clearly, helpers can play a role in reducing the costs of care burden, both by advocating for community resources for caregivers and by providing a range of interventions to meet caregivers' needs.

Regardless of the age of the respondent, half of all such cue-prompted memories will be from the most recent 12 months of his life. Eighty percent are from the most recent decade. "The remembered self is largely a now-self, not a distant-self," even for old people (Fitzgerald, 1999, p. 159).

This may sound a bit confusing, given that adults learn new information less efficiently with age. As we saw in Chapter 13, information in working memory is

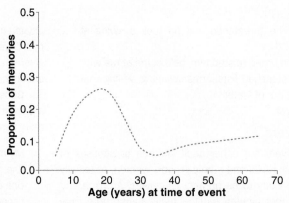

FIGURE 15.4 **Proportion of reported flashbulb memories by age and time of event for older adults.**
SOURCE: Based on Fitzgerald, J. M. (1999). Autobiographical memory and social cognition. Development of the remembered self-adulthood. In Thomas M. Hess (Ed.). *Social cognition and aging.* Elsevier Science. Burlington, MA: Elsevier Science (USA).

not as easily transferred to long-term memory at later ages. However, older people nonetheless do continue to learn, and newer memories are more readily retrieved than older memories.

However, a second salient feature of self-memories is a phenomenon that is ignominiously called **"the bump"** or the "reminiscence bump." Regardless of age, adults' cue-prompted memories of the self from the young adult period (from about ages 18 to 22) are slightly but reliably overproduced (see Berntsen & Rubin, 2002). That is, more memories are produced from this era than we would predict on the basis of recency (see Figure 15.4). If we explore autobiographical memory in a different way, by asking adults to tell us about their **flashbulb memories**, nearly all of what they tell us comes from the bump era (e.g., Fitzgerald, 1988). Flashbulb memories in these studies are defined as recollections that are especially vivid and personally relevant. It appears that when people talk about memories that are intense and important to them, they draw very heavily on experiences from young adulthood, even in their old age. If we ask people to tell stories that they would include in a book about themselves, again, a disproportionate number of the narratives come from the bump era (Fitzgerald, 1992). Similar results come from studies in which people are asked to name the most memorable books they have read (Larsen, 2000), the songs they find most desirable to listen to (Holbrook & Schindler, 1989), or the films that help describe their era (Schulster, 1996). That is, the elderly refer more often to items from their young adulthood than from any other time of their lives. Fitzgerald (1999) argues that the strength of the bump phenomenon for people's most important memories and preferences reveals the significance of late adolescence and young adulthood as a period of intense self-development. This phenomenon might also be explained by the fact that these events tend to be positive in tone and reflect a bias toward remembering pleasant things (Thomsen, Pillemer, & Ivcevic, 2011). It's also been proposed that these reminiscence events were encoded more strongly in memory in the first place, given their highly emotional charge (Dolcos, Labar, & Cabeza, 2005).

However, the recency effect in cue-prompted memory research makes it very clear that people continue to add to their self-stories throughout their adulthood and that healthy older people have their recent past available to them despite some declines in learning efficiency.

Stereotypes and Age Discrimination

Among the challenges that elderly people face are stereotyped attitudes and responses from others based on age category rather than on actual characteristics.

TABLE 15.1 Traits Associated with Stereotypes of Older Adults

STEREOTYPE	TRAITS
Negative	
Severely impaired	Slow-thinking, incompetent, feeble, inarticulate, incoherent, senile
Despondent	Depressed, sad, hopeless, afraid, neglected, lonely
Shrew/curmudgeon	Complaining, ill-tempered, demanding, stubborn, bitter, prejudiced
Recluse	Quiet, timid, naïve
Positive	
Golden ager	Active, capable, sociable, independent, happy, interesting
Perfect grandparent	Loving, supportive, understanding, wise, generous, kind
John Wayne conservative	Patriotic, conservative, determined, proud, religious, nostalgic

SOURCE: Hummert, M. L. (1999). A social cognitive perspective on age stereotypes. In Thomas M. Hess (Ed.), *Social cognition and aging*. Burlington, MA: Elsevier Science (USA). Used with permission from Elsevier.

An *age stereotype* can be defined as a set of widely held beliefs about the characteristics of older people. These knowledge structures or schemas can lead to relatively uniform treatment of older people regardless of their own individual characteristics. They are thought to account for certain discriminatory or demeaning practices, such as mandatory retirement and patronizing talk (Hummert, 1999).

Research on the content of old-age schemas in Western cultures has identified seven common stereotypes. Four of these are negative, such as "severely impaired" or "shrew/curmudgeon," but three are more positive, such as "perfect grandparent" (Hummert, Garstka, Shaner, & Strahm, 1994). A description of each is provided in Table 15.1. A recent study involving participants from 26 countries asked individuals to assess "typical" adolescents, adults and old people from their own country on Big 5 personality characteristics (Chan et al., 2012). Stereotypic views of older people tended to be very similar across all cultures included in this study. Old people were viewed as less active, extraverted, and impulsive compared to other age groups. They were also perceived as more agreeable and more apt to prefer to follow a routine in their daily lives.

Facial features associated with aging play a significant role in activating these stereotypes. The older people look, the more likely they are to be described in ways that fit a negative stereotype. In one study, participants were asked to match the photographs of people perceived to be in their 60s, 70s, or 80s with trait sets describing either positive or negative stereotypes (Hummert, Garstka, & Shaner, 1997). The older the appearance of the person in the picture, the more likely participants were to match the picture with a negative stereotype. Gender of the pictured person played a role as well. For example, pictures of unsmiling women were more likely to be matched with a negative stereotype than pictures of unsmiling men. Many studies find that people are more likely to see men than women as losing more general competence or agentic ability with age, yet they are more likely to judge women as needing more help with age (Kite, Stockdale, Whitley, & Johnson, 2005).

Because of age stereotypes, the very same behavior in younger versus older individuals is perceived differently. For example, the seriousness and the causes of a memory failure, such as forgetting the name of a new acquaintance, tend to be perceived quite differently depending on whether the failure is ascribed to a 30-year-old or to a 70-year-old. When younger adults forget, the cause is more likely to be seen as transient and external, such as "that's a hard thing to remember." When older people forget, the cause is more likely to be seen as something stable and internal, such as having a poor memory (see Erber & Prager, 1999; and Kite et al., 2005, for reviews).

When age stereotypes are triggered, the quality of social interactions can be affected. For example, people, including clinicians, often use "patronizing talk" when speaking with an elderly person. This kind of conversation has many characteristics: simplified vocabulary and sentence structure, slower pace, careful articulation, an overly familiar or overbearing tone, and disapproving, controlling, or superficial content (e.g., Hummert & Ryan, 1996; Hummert, Shaner, Garstka, & Henry, 1998). Hummert (1999) has argued that such talk is probably grounded in stereotypic ideas about declining memory and hearing abilities in the aged.

It appears, then, that aging brings with it stereotypic reactions and expectations from others, which seem likely to interfere with satisfying social interactions. Researchers have found that when older individuals perceive themselves as the target of age discrimination, their sense of well-being is negatively affected (Gartska, Schmitt, Branscombe, & Hummert, 2004). Also, the experience of stereotype threat may actually impair performance. For example, O'Brien and Hummert (2006) gave people in late middle age (48–62 years) a memory task, and either implied that they were in the "older" group by saying that their performance would be compared to younger adults, or implied that they were "younger" by saying they would be compared to older adults (over age 70). Participants performed significantly better when they saw themselves as the "younger" group than if they were characterized as the "older" group! Thus, even older people appear to have negative stereotypes about the elderly, having internalized these beliefs when they were younger. Harmful aging self-stereotypes, often operating below the level of awareness, can impact health and well-being, as Levy (2003) has shown in a series of experiments. When primed by negative stereotypes of aging, elderly participants showed reductions in cognitive performance, will-to-live, and cardiovascular functioning.

Some research also indicates that the conversational styles of older people often include features that may cue stereotypes. For example, older people are sometimes prone to making "painful self-disclosures" to relative strangers about illnesses, loss of a loved one, and other personal problems (e.g., Coupland, Coupland, Giles, Henwood, & Wiemann, 1988). For the elderly, self-disclosures may serve self-presentational goals, such as indicating resilience, but for younger listeners they tend to strengthen stereotypes of the elderly as weak or lonely. Thus, misinterpretations of some characteristic behaviors of older adults probably contribute to stereotypic responses from others (Hummert, 1999).

The Shrinking Social Convoy

Aging brings with it the more and more frequent experience of social loss. Friends, partners, and relatives may die or suffer from debilitating disorders such as Alzheimer's disease. In one study of 85-year-olds, 59% of the men and 42% of the women had lost a friend to death in the past year (Johnson & Troll, 1994). But illness and death are not the only sources of social loss. When people retire they lose daily contact with their colleagues at work. If the elderly person is constrained by limited finances or health problems, opportunities to visit others or to be part of club or other social activities may be reduced. Adult children may move to geographically distant locations. The elderly may leave behind neighbors and shopkeepers of long acquaintance if they move from a larger home to an apartment, an adult community, or an assisted-living facility. The shrinking of the social network and the pain of bereavement are problems that increase in late adulthood (Rook, 2000).

In Chapter 10, we noted that adolescents are largely segregated into age-bound communities that share language, interests, and a dress code, among other things. Mary Pipher (1999) proposes that the physical, cognitive, and social changes of late life segregate older people as well, in ways that are important for helpers to understand. As we have noted, older people often live in circumstances that separate them from their families and their communities, often because poor health makes independent living impossible. Although these arrangements may provide the benefit of day-to-day care and companionship, they may also prevent older people from interacting with members of younger generations and deprive them of opportunities for service to others. Thus, some of their own developmental needs may be going unmet. "The old look for their existential place. They ask, 'How did my life matter? Was my time well spent? What did I mean to others?'" (Pipher, 1999, p. 15). Social segregation creates islands of culture that discourage intergenerational bonding and may make older people feel less valued and useful to others.

The elderly are restricted in other, less obvious ways. Older individuals may sometimes use language in ways that position them within a cultural group or cohort that is separate from younger generations (e.g., using "depression" primarily to mean a period of economic downturn rather than a mental health problem). Many elderly people also feel segregated from society because it simply moves too fast. Pipher (1999) recalls the adjustments she needed to make when interviewing her older clients:

> I learned to let the phone ring fifteen times. I learned to wait at doors five minutes after I rang the bell. I had to slow down to work with the old. Their conversation is less linear, and there are pauses and repetitions. Points are made via stories; memories lead to more memories. . . . When I walked the old, I walked slowly and held hands at intersections or when sidewalks were slick. . . . Because their bones break more easily, the old are afraid of falling . . . a broken hip can mean the end of independent living. (p. 27)

In the next section, we will consider how older adults face these and many of the other losses and challenges that we have described. Later in this chapter, we will take a special look at bereavement across the life span, with particular attention to how the elderly cope with the deaths of those close to them and with their own dying process.

Maintaining Well-Being in the Face of Loss: Successful Aging

How do aging adults adapt to, or cope with, the increasing losses they face? Baltes and colleagues (e.g., Baltes & Baltes, 1990; Baltes, Lindenberger, & Staudinger, 2006) suggest that three processes are key to successful development at any age, and especially in the later years. The first is **selection**. This is a process of narrowing our goals and limiting the domains in which we expend effort. It is not difficult to see that selection is important at any time in the life cycle. For example, at 20, Len selected a career, limiting the possible directions his life could take but also enabling him to achieve high levels of expertise and productivity by focusing his training and practice on career-related skills. At 62, Len selected family life instead of career. Because he felt his stamina waning somewhat, and despite the many satisfactions he still gained from his work, he decided to retire earlier than originally planned so that he could give more energy to developing relationships with his young grandchildren.

The second process is **optimization**, finding ways to enhance the achievement of remaining goals or finding environments that are enhancing. Len, for example, traded in his sporty two-door coupe for a larger sedan so that he could take the grandchildren on excursions to movies or museums. He also moved from a small apartment in the city to a place in the suburbs, closer to his children with amenities such as a yard where he could entertain his family.

The final process that contributes to successful development is **compensation**. When a loss of some kind prevents the use of one means to an end, we can compensate by finding another means. For example, by age 76, as Len's eyesight began to fail, chauffeuring his grandchildren was no longer possible. He now entertains the youngest ones at his home most of the time, planning special events such as "video marathons" and backyard camping "trips."

Baltes provides the following example of successful development in old age:

> When the concert pianist Arthur Rubinstein, as an 80-year-old, was asked in a television interview how he managed to maintain such a high level of expert piano playing, he hinted at the coordination of three strategies. First, Rubinstein said that he played

 Thelma, at age 81, engages in all three processes that are key to successful development at this age. Can you identify examples of selection, optimization, and compensation?

fewer pieces (selection); second, he indicated that he now practiced these pieces more often (optimization); and third, he said that to counteract his loss in mechanical speed he now used a kind of impression management such as introducing slower play before fast segments, so to make the latter appear faster (compensation). (Baltes, Lindenberger, & Staudinger, 1998, p. 1055)

The three combined processes of successful development are called **selective optimization with compensation** (e.g., Baltes et al., 2006). Table 15.2 summarizes some everyday sayings that seem to promote the three processes of selection, optimization, and compensation, and it provides examples of questionnaire items that have been used to assess these processes.

As previously discussed, meeting basic needs for autonomy, competence, and relatedness substantially determines a person's sense of well-being and life satisfaction, according to self-determination theory (see Chapter 14). Several theorists argue that whatever challenges we face in meeting our needs, there are two broad types of strategies that people use to control their destinies. Heckhausen (e.g., Heckhausen, 1999; Wrosch, Heckhausen, & Lachman, 2006) refers to primary and secondary control strategies. When our control efforts are attempts to affect the immediate environment beyond ourselves, we are exerting **primary control**. The growth of competencies of all kinds serves primary control functions and contributes to feelings of mastery and self-esteem. When we choose to develop some competencies and not others (that is, when we engage in selection, such as choosing a career) we are using a primary control strategy. When new retirees freely choose and plan their retirements, they are using primary control strategies (see Box 15.2).

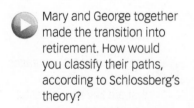

Mary and George together made the transition into retirement. How would you classify their paths, according to Schlossberg's theory?

From the perspective of self-determination theory, exercising primary control could serve autonomy, competence, and/or relatedness needs. **Secondary control** generally refers to our attempts to modify our expectations in the face of things we can't change. We are using secondary control strategies when, for example, we change our aspirations and goals because we cannot do everything we used to do or when we minimize the importance of specific needs after failing to achieve some end.

TABLE 15.2 Selection, Optimization, and Compensation: Brief Definitional Frames and Examples from Proverbs and Questionnaire Items

STRATEGY	ROLE IN DEVELOPMENT	SAMPLE PROVERB	SAMPLE QUESTIONNAIRE ITEM
Selection	Concerns directionality and focus of developmental outcomes such as goals.	Jack-of-all-trades, master of none. Those who follow every path, never reach any destination. Between two stools you fall to the ground.	I always focus on the most important goal at a given time. When I think about what I want in life, I commit myself to one or two important goals. To achieve a particular goal, I am willing to abandon other goals.
Optimization	Concerns the acquisition and refinement of means and their coordination to achieve goals/outcomes.	Practice makes perfect. If at first you don't succeed, try, try, and try again. Strike the iron when it's hot.	I keep working on what I have planned until I succeed. I keep trying until I succeed at a goal. When I want to achieve something, I can wait for the right moment.
Compensation	Concerns maintenance of functioning by substitution of means in situation of losses of means.	There are many hands; what one cannot do, the other will. When there's no wind, grab the oars. Those without a horse walk.	When things don't work the way they used to, I look for other ways to achieve them. When things aren't going so well, I accept help from others. When things don't go as well as they used to, I keep trying other ways until I can achieve the same result I used to.

SOURCE: Baltes, P. B., Lindenberger, U., & Staudinger, U. (2006). Life span theory in developmental psychology. In W. Damon & R. M. Lerner (Eds.), *Handbook of child psychology Vol. 1. Theoretical models of human development* (6th ed., pp. 569–664). Hoboken NJ: Wiley. Reproduced with permission of John Wiley & Sons Inc.

Box 15.2: Navigating the Transition to Retirement

Beverly, a counseling psychologist and community activist, began to think about her retirement in earnest when she was 57 years old, after a bout with cancer. She recuperated well and her prognosis was good, but the sudden confrontation with ill health helped her to see that she might not always be able to work. Until then, she had vaguely assumed she would work until she dropped. Indeed, at first, she couldn't imagine her life without the challenge of a full schedule of diverse clients and community speaking engagements. But her illness led her to examine her goals for the future more carefully. She decided that in time she would like to reduce her work commitments to have time for other interests. She had always wanted to explore her artistic talent, and when her long-time partner retired, they both hoped to have more time and energy to pursue the activities they enjoyed together, especially international travel. By the age of 65, Beverly felt she was ready to make the change. She stopped taking new clients and reduced her speaking engagements to one or fewer a month. She began thinking of herself as a retiree.

Most modern adults, both men and women, have been part of the workforce for 30 or more years by the time they retire. How do they navigate the sometimes dramatic transition from being a worker to being a retiree?

Not everyone who can retire chooses to do so. And when people retire (defined by *Webster's* dictionary as "withdrawal from one's position or occupation") the strategies people devise for making the shift are quite diverse. Nancy Schlossberg, a retired counselor herself, identified multiple paths from an interview study of 100 retirees. Some were "continuers" who continued to use their work skills part time or in different settings. Beverly is a continuer; she maintains a small client roster and continues her community activities at a reduced level. "Involved spectators" keep a hand in their previous work but adopt some new role. Schlossberg herself is an example of this category. A former counseling professor, she became an author and consultant who applied her counseling knowledge to developing guidelines for retirees. "Adventurers" leave behind their old work skills and develop new talents or skills, sometimes taking on a new job. "Easy gliders" try to keep their time unscheduled. They seem especially comfortable with the flexibility they have without work or other regular commitments. "Searchers" in Schlossberg's study have not yet found a path that works for them, but see themselves in a trial-and-error phase. "Retreaters" seem to give up on finding a satisfactory lifestyle and become depressed (Dittman, 2004; Schlossberg, 2004).

Some of the diversity in Schlossberg's findings may reflect not only different pathways of retirement but also different stages of retirement. Atchley (1976) argued that adjustment to retirement follows a typical progression for many people. Stage 1, honeymoon, is a time when people focus on the pleasures of being free from the constraints of old schedules, dress codes, and other work demands. In Stage 2, disenchantment occurs when people begin to experience an emotional "letdown" as they face the day-to-day realities of retirement, such as separation from work colleagues, uncertainties about how to feel competent and in control, a sense of diminished generativity and meaningfulness, new tensions that may arise with one's partner, financial concerns, and perhaps, boredom.

Stage 3, reorientation, can be a time of active trial and error. The retiree seeks solutions for the problems that retirement presents and tries strategies for building a satisfactory life. In Stage 4, stability is achieved. The retiree finds a functional path that seems to work. Life span theorists would say that *selective optimization with compensation* is achieved. Finally, Stage 5 is termination, the end-of-life transition, when the individual's health declines and she becomes dependent on others for her care.

There are certainly substantial individual differences in the retirement experience that depend on many factors, such as health, financial security, and marital status. For example, although research on the effects of marital status is limited, it suggests some complex processes at work. In one study, married and remarried women rated themselves as healthier and more satisfied with retirement than unmarried (divorced, widowed, never married) women; yet the two groups scored about the same on overall feelings of well-being (Price & Joo, 2005). Another study examined the retirement status of married partners, and found in general, that satisfaction was greater when both partners were retired. Also, if one partner were still working, satisfaction of the retired partners tended to be lower if they felt that their decision-making power in the relationship had diminished (Szinovacz & Davey, 2005). This was true for both genders.

Despite the importance of individual circumstances, research suggests that Atchley's stage descriptions do capture some predictable phases of retirement for many people. In addition, there may be several cycles of reorientation and stability, with the same individual renegotiating her retirement strategy several times as her life continues to change with the death of a partner, shifting health status, financial changes, and so on. The longer we live, the more cycles we are likely to experience.

Reitzes and Mutran (2004) found general support for the idea that retirement is a dynamic, and to some degree, stagelike process. Satisfaction was high after 6 months (honeymoon), but had declined after a year (disenchantment) and had increased again after 2 years (reorientation and stability). They also identified a number of individual difference factors that impact how well people adjust to the retirement transition both in the honeymoon stage and thereafter. They assessed 800 men and women who were between the ages of 58 and 64 and who were employed full time (at least 35 hours per week) as the study began. The participants represented a random sample of people in this age range living in the Raleigh–Durham–Chapel Hill, North Carolina metropolitan area, so the sample was diverse with respect to race and socioeconomic status. The participants completed an initial screening, and they were tracked with follow-up phone calls until they retired. About 600 of the original sample had retired within 5 years. Those who were willing to continue the study were reassessed at 6 months, 1 year, and 2 years postretirement.

In addition to providing information on income, pension eligibility, health status, marital status, and so on, at every assessment period the participants completed a questionnaire designed to measure their attitudes toward retirement. At the preretirement assessment, they also completed measures of their self-esteem, the social roles they filled in their current lives (e.g., parent,

(continued)

Box 15.2 *Continued*

spouse, widow/widower, divorcee, etc.), and their "friend identity," which captured how they viewed themselves in the friend role. The participant rated herself as a friend on a five-point scale, from (1) passive to (5) active, from (1) anxious to (5) confident, and from (1) unsuccessful to (5) successful. The researchers also collected information on the participants' retirement experience, like how much retirement planning the participants had done preretirement, what reasons they had for retirement, whether they continued working in any capacity during retirement, and so on.

Reitzes and Mutran found little difference between men and women or among different socioeconomic groups with regard to the basic ingredients of a successful retirement. Several factors at preretirement were strong predictors of positive attitudes toward retirement both early in retirement and later: pension eligibility, high self-esteem, and a positive friend identity. Not surprisingly, pension eligibility allows a degree of financial security that reduces some of the stress of the shift to retirement. As Reitzes and Mutran suggest, individuals with a strong sense of self-worth and who feel confident about their relationships with friends probably are better able to organize and structure new opportunities with confidence. High self-esteem helps people be optimistic that they will be successful in new activities and pursuits. A positive friend identity would seem to be especially valuable when release from work constraints provides more time for interactions with friends.

Some other factors were very helpful for ensuring a happy honeymoon phase: being in control of the decision to retire (that is, doing so voluntarily), and approaching retirement with a plan of action. People who felt that they had no choice but to retire, because of the conditions of their employment or because of ill health, were not as happy as others in the 1st year of retirement. The same was true for people who had not carefully considered what they would do in retirement. These individuals were less satisfied at the start, but with time their situations tended to improve, and they were often doing as well as other retirees after 2 years.

One retiree provides a good example of some of these factors at work, and of the typical stages that many retirees experience. Jack just plunged into retirement optimistically with no plan but his usual belief that he could "handle it." For a while he enjoyed finishing some carpentry projects he had never had time for and some travel. But he was deep into disillusionment within a few months. He missed the opportunity to interact with colleagues and he missed the status he had achieved in his work life. With some help from a counselor, he identified the problems and mapped out some alternative solutions. He chose to begin consulting on a part-time basis (often voluntarily for nonprofit organizations), which brought him in touch with a wider range of people and helped him feel generative. At 72, Jack still enjoys good health, and after 4 years of retirement he believes that this is the best time of his life.

Both primary and secondary control may involve cognition and action, although primary control is almost always characterized in terms of behavior engaging the external world, whereas secondary control is predominantly characterized in terms of cognitive processes localized within the individual. (Schultz & Heckhausen, 1996, p. 708)

When primary control efforts fail or we suffer losses that we cannot overcome, secondary controls are likely to become important. Schultz and Heckhausen indicate that our repertoire of both primary and secondary control strategies will increase with age until late midlife but that the sheer weight of late-life declines will make primary control decline as well, so that people are likely to use more secondary control strategies in old age. Heckhausen (1997) found, for example, that adults in their 60s demonstrated more flexibility in adjusting their goals than adults in their 20s. When young, middle-aged, and elderly adults were asked to state their five most important goals and plans for the next 5 years, there was a clear shift in aspirations across age (Heckhausen, 1997). Elderly people had fewer aspirations regarding work, finances, and family and more aspirations related to health, community, and leisure pursuits than young adults. Heckhausen argues that these shifts reflect the fact that older people generally have less primary control potential over work, finances, and family. They therefore shift their goals in a compensatory way to those over which they may be able to take some primary control.

On the whole, how well do people in old age adapt to the challenges of late life? There is a tendency for a terminal decline in well-being that is driven by changes associated with impending death such as health decline, cognitive and physical disability (Gerstorf et al., 2008). Yet, as we suggested earlier in this chapter, generally older people report high levels of well-being. Ryff and Keyes (1995) analyzed measures of six dimensions of well-being from interviews with 1,108 adults. The responses of young (25 to 29), middle-aged (30 to 64), and old (65 or over) adults were compared, and several measures were found to increase over age. Old adults scored higher on a measure of positive relationships than both younger groups. They scored as well as the middle-aged and higher than the young adults on measures of environmental mastery and autonomy, and they scored as well as both younger groups on self-acceptance. Older adults did score lower than the younger groups on two dimensions of well-being: purpose in life and personal growth. Perhaps as a person leaves behind the arenas in which generativity is most directly expressed—work, parenting, and community service—opportunities to feel useful or to grow seem diminished. This conclusion is consistent with findings that elderly women who continue to care for a disabled adult child report a much greater sense of purpose in life than elderly women who do not have such responsibilities (Kling, Seltzer, & Ryff, 1997). Generativity issues aside, results of these studies suggested that aging and a sense of well-being were often quite compatible and that some aspects of well-being actually improved in old age. More recent population-based longitudinal studies using Ryff's dimensions, however, failed to find the expected increases in well-being into old age (Springer, Pudrovska, & Hauser, 2011). Some of these differences may be due to methodological problems; thus, more research is needed to clarify maturational trends across specific dimensions of well-being.

Wisdom, Aging and Culture

Wisdom is often perceived as going hand in hand with advanced age. If that is true, then the well-being elders do manifest may be related to the wisdom they accrue over the years. But what exactly is wisdom anyway? And does everyone achieve it in late life? The search for wisdom has been at the heart of religious and philosophical systems since ancient times. Its study as a Western scientific topic, however, began in earnest only in the 1970s. This may be due, in no small part, to the breadth of the topic and the difficulties posed in defining and measuring it.

Wisdom has been called "expertise in the fundamental pragmatics of life" (Baltes et al., 1998, p. 1970). We have seen that the practical problems adults must face do not necessarily have one right answer. As young adults gain experience with the complexities of such ill-defined problems, the adolescent expectation that logical, absolute right answers always exist may give way to a more relativistic perspective. This perpective acknowledges that there are multiple, contextually embedded truth systems (e.g., Perry, 1970/1999). But wisdom encompasses more than cognitive skills. A wise person is an expert in the "psychological art of life" (Staudinger 1999, p. 343) that includes aspects of motivation, emotion regulation, other-directed versus self-involved orientation, tolerance for ambiguity, and insight. Wise people recognize and deal with the dialectics inherent in human existence (e.g., good and bad, strength and weakness, self-interest and altruism) in a balanced way. They often help guide others to do the same. "Mastery of such dialectics in the sense of wisdom does not mean that a decision for either one or the other side is taken but rather that both sides are essential for grasping human existence. Wisdom embraces these contradictions of life and draws insights from them. It further develops heuristics about when and under which circumstances to focus on which side of each of these opposites (Staudinger & Gluck, 2011, p. 217)."

Messages about wise ways of navigating life's challenges are embedded in culture. In fact, researchers often use folk theories of wisdom as a starting point for their work. Transmitted across generations in folk tales and proverbs, these insights have, according to Csikszentmihalyi and Rathunde (1990), universal evolutionary value. Table 15.3 contains proverbs from different cultures, each offering advice about anger and conflict. Do you notice any similar themes? Can you come up with proverbs that present an opposing message? If so, they may be examples of the dialectic we've described.

For some elderly people, wisdom may be a special asset in managing the problems of life.

TABLE 15.3 Wisdom Across Cultures: Wise Counsel About Anger

PROVERB	ORIGIN
He who is slow to anger is better than the mighty; and he who rules his spirit, than he who captures a city.	Old Testament, Book of Proverbs 16:32
Life is short, but troubles make it longer.	Roman proverb
If you fear something, you give it power over you.	African Proverb
When anger and revenge get married, their daughter is called cruelty.	Russian Proverb
Force, no matter how concealed, begets resistance.	Lakota (Sioux) Proverb
The man who strikes first admits that his ideas have given out.	Chinese Proverb
A knife wound heals, but a tongue wound festers.	Persian Proverb
Holding on to anger is like grasping a hot coal with the intent of throwing it at someone else; you are the one who gets burned.	Indian Proverb (Buddhaghosa)
For what cannot be cured, patience is best.	Irish Proverb
Don't notice the tiny flea in the other person's hair and overlook the lumbering yak on your own nose.	Tibetan Proverb
Two wrongs don't make a right.	English Proverb
He who starts up in anger, sits down with a loss.	Turkish Proverb
Never do anything out of anger; would you hoist your sails during a storm?	Arabic Proverb

SOURCE: Mieder, W. (1993). *The Prentice Hall encyclopedia of world proverbs.* Upper Saddle River, NJ: Pearson Education, Inc. Used with permission from Pearson Education.

So, is wisdom universal or culture-specific? Perhaps there are some distinctions in the way wisdom is defined that differentiate East and West (Takahashi & Overton, 2005). Western cultural views tend to emphasize the cognitive aspects of wisdom, such as breadth of knowledge and ability to analyze. Eastern cultures take a more expansive view, incorporating both cognition and affect into their understanding of wisdom. However, similarities across cultures are greater than these distinctions. Staudinger and Gluck (2011) make clear that the consensus across cultures is that wisdom represents the "perfect integration of mind and character for the greater good" (p. 221).

Is wisdom more likely in old age in all cultures? In a program of research on wisdom by Staudinger, Baltes, and their colleagues, Western participants were told about people experiencing difficult real-life problems and were asked to describe and explain what the fictional people should do. One example of such a real-life problem, along with a response that received a low score for wisdom and one that received a high score, is presented in Table 15.4. Scores for wisdom were based on raters' judgments of how rich the respondent's factual and procedural knowledge seemed to be, whether the response took into account the developmental context, the degree to which the response reflected a relativistic view and a recognition of uncertainty, as well as attempts to manage uncertainty (e.g., Staudinger & Baltes, 1996).

Findings from studies using this technique indicate that wisdom, as defined by Staudinger and Baltes (1996), does seem to require experience and thus is somewhat enhanced by age. The years from 15 to 25 appear to be very important for wisdom acquisition (Pasupathi, Staudinger, & Baltes, 1999, 2001), but after 25, the proportion of people whose wisdom scores are above average does not change substantially. After 75, fewer people continue to function at above-average levels on

TABLE 15.4 Wisdom Problem and Abbreviated Responses

Wisdom Problem

A 15-year-old girl wants to get married right away. What should one/she consider and do?

Low Wisdom-Related Score

A 15-year-old girl wants to get married? No, no way, marrying at age 15 would be utterly wrong. One has to tell the girl that marriage is not possible. (After further probing) It would be irresponsible to support such an idea. No, this is just a crazy idea.

High Wisdom-Related Score

Well, on the surface, this seems like an easy problem. On average, marriage for 15-year-old girls is not a good thing. But there are situations where the average case does not fit. Perhaps in this instance, special life circumstances are involved, such that the girl has a terminal illness. Or the girl has just lost her parents. And also, this girl may live in another culture or historical period. Perhaps she was raised with a value system different from ours. In addition, one has to think about adequate ways of talking with the girl and to consider her emotional state.

SOURCE: Baltes, P. B., & Staudinger, O. M. (2000). Wisdom: A metaheuristic (pragmatic) to orchestrate mind and virtue toward excellence. *American Psychologist, 55,* 122–136. Used with permission from the American Psychological Association.

measures of wisdom (Baltes & Staudinger, 2000). Studies using somewhat different methods have found a tendency for wisdom to increase well into middle adulthood (e.g., Blanchard-Fields, 1986, 2007) but also to decline thereafter (e.g., Labouvie-Vief, Chiodo, Goguen, Diehl, & Orwoll, 1995). Grossman and colleagues (2010) reported that older Americans displayed wiser reasoning in relation to solving interpersonal conflicts than did younger or middle aged Americans.

The developmental trajectory of wisdom aquisition, however, may not be the same for all cultural groups. Let's consider the ways that people deal with conflict. Kunzmann and Baltes (2003) found that individuals scoring high on wisdom tend to prefer cooperative conflict management, as opposed to dominance strategies. They also score high on involvement with others, yet at the same time tend to moderate their emotional reactivity more than other people. They also seem more committed than others to pursuits that have the goal of enhancing the growth and potential of both themselves and other people. Consistent with themes presented in prior chapters, Some Eastern cultures tend to privilege harmony and cohesion in social relationships. Their conflict management strategies tend to be indirect and considerate of multiple points of view. Behaviors that assert autonomy and independence, leading to more direct conflict management strategies, are more characteristic of people in the United States. Grossman and his colleagues (2010) reasoned that the sensitivity to social cues young children learn in interdependent cultures may foster an earlier development of wise reasoning skills for solving conflict. Consistent with previous findings, older North Americans in this cross-cultural study gave wiser responses to questions about inter-group conflict than did younger and middle aged Americans. However, younger and middle-aged Japanese participants gave wiser answers when compared to younger U.S. groups, suggesting cultural differences in wisdom development. Elderly Americans reasoned more wisely about inter-group conflict whereas Japanese elderly were wiser with regard to interpersonal conflict.

Let's take a closer look at some ways of operationalizing wisdom. Theorists from the neo-Piagetian perspective argue that relativistic thinking represents a new, qualitatively more advanced form of logical thinking, called postformal thought. Others regard more relativistic thinking as a function of reflection and experience, perhaps benefited by advancing metacognitive understanding of the limits of one's own thought processes. In the latter view, relativistic thought does not represent a qualitatively different level of functioning, but the outcome of accumulating knowledge. From either perspective, the result for some, though not all, adults is the achievement of wisdom.

Researchers from the Max Plank Institute in Germany (The Berlin Wisdom Project; Baltes & Smith, 2008) have been at the forefront of this research agenda.

This group posits five criteria for a wise person. The first is a deep fund of factual knowledge about life, human nature, and relationships with others. The second involves well-developed procedural knowledge about how to deal with life and its conflicts. The ability to consider life's challenges from multiple perspectives and to work toward decisions that balance one's own and others' interests are the third and fourth criteria. Finally, understanding that true certainty is impossible for life's ill-defined problems and coming to peaceful terms with uncertainty is the fifth criterion in this typology of wisdom. Identifying criteria makes it a little easier to assess the components of wisdom.

One interesting research finding is that, in addition to age and culture, training and experience in occupations that involve managing and reviewing life's problems seem to promote wisdom. Clinical psychologists, for example, receive higher wisdom scores than people with similar levels of education who are in fields that do not focus on "the fundamental pragmatics of life" (e.g., Smith, Staudinger, & Baltes, 1994). Clinical training itself seems to be important, because even when analyses controlled for the contribution of intelligence and personality differences across professions, clinicians had a wisdom advantage (e.g., Staudinger, Maciel, Smith, & Baltes, 1998).

Social-Emotional Experience in Late Life

Perhaps you are wondering how late-life increases in wisdom might co-exist with cognitive declines? Contemporary research paints a nuanced picture of gains and losses that appear in old age. Evidence supports growth in some areas of socioemotional functioning as long as certain conditions (such as relatively good health and social support) are present. The socioemotional domain seems to be enhanced and better regulated with age. One reason is that older adults become more selective about the social relationships in which they invest their time. They tend to selectively invest in fewer social relationships, keeping or replacing close, deeply satisfying relationships and eliminating more peripheral ties (Carstensen, 1998). Figure 15.5 demonstrates that in one study the number of very close social partners stayed about the same for people ranging in age from 69 to 104, but the numbers of less close social partners dropped dramatically (Lang & Carstensen, 1994). Laura Carstensen and her colleagues explain this socioemotional selectivity as a function of people's expectations that the time remaining in their lives is limited (e.g., Carstensen & Mikels, 2005; Charles & Carstensen, 2008). In both Western and Eastern cultures, they have found that people of any age will become more selective about whom they spend time with if they perceive their remaining time in life to be constrained (e.g., Fredrickson & Carstensen, 1990; Fung, Carstensen, & Lutz, 1999). Because older people (and others who expect their lives to end soon) pay more attention to their feelings, their emotional

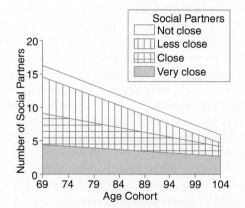

FIGURE 15.5 **Numbers of very close social partners are maintained in old age.**
SOURCE: Lang, F. R., & Carstensen, L. L. (1994). Close emotional relationships in late life: Further support for proactive aging in the social domain. *Psychology and Aging, 9,* 315–324. Used with permission from the American Psychological Association.

experiences are more enhanced and complex (Carstensen, 1998). For older adults, emotional characteristics play a greater role than for younger adults in how they categorize potential social partners (Frederickson & Carstensen, 1990). Older adults also remember relatively more emotional information from descriptions of people than younger adults do (Carstensen & Turk-Charles, 1994).

While this selectivity may benefit socioemotional satisfaction, what about cognition? A U.S. study of White and African American elderly living in the community points in a different direction. This study found that the number of social networks an older person had was related to less cognitive decline even after controlling for baseline differences in education, SES, health, depression, and intellectual ability (Barnes, de Leon, Wilson, Bienias, & Evans, 2004). The authors concluded that it may be important for older individuals to retain as many social connections and engage in as much social interaction as possible presumably to enhance cognitive reserve. Social relationships serve a strong protective function. Other studies suggest that they play a causal role in preventing onset of dementia (Fratiglioni, Wang, Ericsson, Maytan, & Winblad, 2000) and in promoting recovery after illness, such as stroke (Glymour, Weuve, Fay, Glass, & Berkman, 2008).

Self-reported emotional well-being seems to increase over the years of adulthood, although some decrements after age 60 have been reported (Charles & Carstensen, 2008). Compared to younger adult cohorts, older individuals report more satisfying friendships, marriages, and family relationships. They also report less conflict with others, possibly because of improved emotion regulation over the years (Charles & Piazza, 2007). Older adults are more likely to remember positive experiences than negative ones when compared to younger adults (Charles, Mather, & Carstensen, 2003). Older adults' neural processing of emotional information involves greater activation of the amygdala when viewing positive images as compared to negative images, whereas no such difference occurs for younger adults (Mather, 2004; see also, Kisley, Wood, & Burrows, 2007). When older adults think about emotion arousing experiences in their lives, they show less heart rate reactivity than younger adults, especially for negative emotions like anger and fear (Labouvie-Vief, Lumky, Jain, and Heinze, 2003).

In one experience-sampling study (Carstensen, Pasupathi, Mayr, & Nesselroade, 2000), negative emotional states ended more quickly for older participants, but positive states lasted just as long as they did for the younger participants. In a variety of cultures, older adults describe themselves as having greater control over their emotions than younger adults do (Gross et al., 1997). When older and younger adults listened to taped conversations containing negative remarks, presumably about them, older adults tended to "emotionally disengage" more than younger adults, reporting less anger and less interest in the speakers (Charles & Carstensen, 2008). In direct observations of conflict management between spouses, older couples were more skillful than long-married middle-aged couples at interspersing positive, affectionate statements with negative ones and keeping negative expressions to a minimum (e.g., Levenson, Carstensen, & Gottman, 1993, 1994). It appears that older people may be wise in the ways they deal with emotions: Don't dwell on sorrow, and make happiness last.

Besides focusing on the positive, older people may be more accepting of things they cannot change. Shallcross and her colleagues (2013) explored connections between emotional well-being and acceptance, "the process of deliberately and non-judgmentally engaging with negative emotions" (p. 734) in an effort to reconcile the inevitable declines of late life with increases in positive affect. Indeed, age-related trends were found for increased acceptance and decreased anger and anxiety among participants ranging from 21 to 73. Interestingly, and consistent with other research, sadness did not decrease with age despite the observed growth in positive affect.

While well-being increases up to a point, depressive symptoms also increase in old age. Overall rates of major depressive disorder (MDD) are lower among older groups but minor depression and subclinical symptoms of depression increase from middle adulthood into very old age (Blazer, 2003; Buchteman, Luppa, & Heller, 2012). It is difficult to establish accurate prevalence estimates because different methodologies and assessments, developed on younger age cohorts, may not reliably capture the nature of late life depression (Edelstein, Drozdick, & Ciliberti, 2010). Co-occuring cognitive declines and physical illnesses also complicate diagnostic efforts. Rates of MDD among community-dwelling adults aged 65 and above range from 1% to 5% (Fiske et al,. 2009) and increase (12.4% to 14.4%) among long-term care residents (Teresi, Abrams, Holmes, Ramirez, & Eimicke, 2001). Rates of depressive symtpoms that are clinically relevant are much higher. Depressive symptoms have been reported by over a third of aged 65 and older adults living in the community (Sirey, Bruce, Carpenter, Booker, Reid, et al., 2008), although other estimates are lower. Those above 85 show very high rates (43.9%; see Luppa, Sikorski, Luck, Weyerer, Villringer et al., 2011). African Americans showed more severe symptoms than other groups in a recent study (Shellman, Granara, & Rosengarten, 2011) although more research is needed to clarify cultural differences. Symptom recognition is important because of the relationship of depressive symptoms to more serious physical and mental health problems.

Depressive symptoms in late life are different from those that younger people are likely to report. The elderly are more likely to report loss of interest, hopelessness, and helplessness as well as somatic symptoms. Pain, insomnia, and loss of appetite are common. Older individuals are less likely than younger adults to report guilt, self-deprecation, dysphoric mood, or suicidal ideation (see Edelstein et al., 2010). Fortunately, despite the intractability of many health problems in old age, research on the effectiveness of treatment for depressive symptoms has been encouraging. As with younger clients, elderly people, including nursing home residents, respond positively to a variety of psychotherapeutic interventions, including cognitive behavioral, brief psychodynamic, interpersonal, life-review, and problem-solving therapies (Antognini & Liptzin, 2008; Pot et al., 2010).

EXPERIENCING LOSS

Death and Dying

In the expectable rhythm of life, most people begin to take the prospect of their own mortality more seriously during middle adulthood. Illness, the deaths of parents, spouses, siblings, or friends, the experience of watching adult children struggle with problems, and many other bumps in the road grow more frequent, and they signal what has already been lost. At some point, we begin to think of time not as unlimited "time to live" but as "time left to live." In old age, the reality of death and loss are inescapable. Even though advances in medicine have extended life and greatly improved its quality for many people, all of us face the certainty of death. And though death can occur at any point in the life cycle, the proportion of individuals who die in late adulthood is much greater than at any other time. Currently, close to 80% of the U.S. population live beyond age 65. Of this group, more than 75% will struggle with heart disease, cancer, stroke, lung disease, or dementia during their last 12 months of life (Lynn, 2000). Despite these statistics, elderly individuals report less anxiety about death and are more realistic about its inevitability than are middle-aged adults (Gesser, Wong, & Reker, 1988).

Professional helpers will undoubtedly come face to face with the emotionally challenging issues of death and dying in their work. They may be called on to support children who experience a parent's death, relatives or friends of a suicide victim, families struggling to cope with the aftermath of a fatal accident, or individuals facing their own deaths from illnesses such as cancer or HIV/AIDS. Or they may work with the elderly, for whom the prospect of death ever more insistently intrudes into daily life. Death in later life is generally expected. The experience of death for younger persons can be particularly traumatic. Although the older person and his family may have time to prepare themselves for the separation, death at earlier ages defies the natural order. Even though we present the issues of death and dying in the context of later life, many of the issues involved in dying and bereavement are similar across the life span. First we will consider the issues involved in dying. Then we will look at the psychological work of bereavement.

Facing Death

Dame Cicely Saunders, founder of the modern hospice movement, recounted a dying patient's words to her: "I thought it so strange. Nobody wants to look at me" (Ewens & Herrington, 1983, p. 5). This remark captures many elements that describe the experience of dying: general reluctance to address the topic of death openly, anxiety about death that informs this reluctance, guilt that emanates from the lack of openness, and the loneliness and isolation of the dying person. If death is a part of every human life, why do many of us avoid discussing it? Death clearly represents unknown territory, and it is difficult to comprehend a more painful or stressful life event than the prospect of dying or of losing a loved one. According to some existential therapists, fear of death is the ultimate source of anxiety and the foundation of most depression and alienation (May, 1979). Some people have also pointed out that the advances of modern medicine, despite their obvious benefits, have encouraged us to think of dying in some of the same ways we conceptualize treatable illnesses (Kane, 1996).

Fortunately, much progress has been made in understanding death and dying relatively recently. Modern U.S. culture is very gradually moving away from one that denies or sanitizes death to one that supports death with dignity. Courageous pioneers such as Elisabeth Kubler-Ross (1969) have directed our collective attention to the issues facing the dying and the bereaved and, in doing so, have shed much-needed light on their needs and concerns. Faced with a growing population of elderly and prompted by advances in research, the field of medicine has taken steps toward more compassionate care of the dying. An emerging consensus among medical specialties regarding **end-of-life care** is reflected in the development of a set of core principles for providers (see Table 15.5). These 11 principles list the responsibilities of end-of-life caregivers to patients and their patients' families or support systems. Societies such as the American Medical Association and the Joint Commission on the Accreditation of Healthcare Organizations, to name a few, have adopted these principles (Cassel & Foley, 1999). In general, the principles support more humanistic approaches to end-of-life care, including better pain management, continuity of care, and attention to the psychological dimensions of death and dying. These principles are reflected at the practical level in state initiatives such as Oregon's policies to improve end-of-life care (Wyden, 2000).

What Is a Good Death?

Most people hope for a good death, but what does that really mean? As the poet Robert Frost observed, "Hope does not lie in a way out, but in a way through." You

---

TABLE 15.5 Core Principles for End-of-Life Care

1. Respecting the dignity of both patients and caregivers;
2. Being sensitive and respectful of the patient's and family's wishes;
3. Using the most appropriate measures that are consistent with patient choices;
4. Encompassing alleviation of pain and other physical symptoms;
5. Assessing and managing psychological, social, and spiritual/religious problems;
6. Offering continuity (the patient should be able to continue to be cared for, if so desired, by his/her primary care and specialist providers);
7. Providing access to any therapy that may realistically be expected to improve the patient's quality of life, including alternative and nontraditional treatments;
8. Providing access to palliative care and hospice care;
9. Respecting the right to refuse treatment;
10. Respecting the physician's professional right to discontinue some treatments when appropriate, with consideration for both patient and family preferences;
11. Promoting clinical evidence–based research on providing care at end-of-life.

SOURCE: Cassel, C. K., & Foley, K. M. (1999). *Principles for care of patients at the end of life: An emerging consensus among the specialities of medicine.* Used with permission from the Millbank Memorial Fund. Available at www.milbank.org.

might imagine that dying quickly without unnecessary suffering or dying at home surrounded by loved ones would provide good ways through this final passage. But preferences may be different for different people. Steinhauser and her colleagues (Steinhauser et al., 2000) investigated the relative importance of factors that signify a good death in a survey of 2,000 seriously ill patients, physicians, recently bereaved family members, and other care providers. There was general agreement among all respondents that certain attributes were highly important. These included elements of symptom management and care (freedom from pain and anxiety, freedom from shortness of breath, being touched, and kept clean), certain practical details (having financial affairs in order, knowing what to expect about one's condition), and patient–professional relationship quality (having caring, trustworthy providers who listen). In addition, specific psychological attributes (maintaining dignity, not dying alone, having the opportunity to resolve unfinished business and saying good-bye) were also rated highly by all respondents. The entire patient group expressed concern about being burdensome to their families. Somewhat surprisingly, they also viewed being able to help others as an important contribution to their end-of-life quality, suggesting the significance of generativity across the life span.

But some differences among respondents were noted as well. Though many people assume that patients prefer to die at home, this was not the overwhelming preference of this sample. In contrast to the value placed on autonomous decision making by many professionals, members of certain cultures prefer to share decision making with relatives because this is perceived as supportive (Searight & Gafford, 2005). Members of Chinese, Pakistani, and Hispanic communities may actively strive to protect their loved ones from knowledge of the full extent of their illness because it is deemed impolite, cruel, or deleterious to health (Talamantes, Lawler, & Espino, 1995). In some Asian communities, a family's desire for extraordinary measures to preserve the life of a relative may reflect the deep reverence they have for their elders. African American patients were more likely than their White counterparts to want all available life-sustaining treatments. They were also less likely to utilize hospice services or to have prepared advanced directives (see below). Wicher and Meeker (2012) suggest that some of these preferences may be shaped by African American cultural and religious perspectives on death. It is important to recognize that there are many ways to define a good death. It is incumbent on caregivers not to make assumptions about their clients, but to ask for and listen to individuals' needs.

Despite the importance of these individual differences, many studies have demonstrated that **palliative care** (Hanson, Danis, & Garrett, 1997; Singer, Martin, & Merrijoy, 1999) and the ability to prepare for death (Christakis, 2000; Emanuel & Emanuel, 1998) are two of the most consistently wished-for aspects of end-of-life care reported by patients and families. *Palliative care*, or comfort care, involves services provided by caregivers from several disciplines. It embodies a comprehensive approach to care that addresses pain management, emotional and spiritual care, and psychological support for caregivers and survivors (Billings, 1998).

The philosophy of care embodied in the modern **hospice movement**, which serves people suffering from terminal illness, is a good example of a palliative, patient-centered approach. Considered a hospitable respite for weary travelers in medieval times, hospice is now a place where people on another kind of journey, from life to death, can find peace and comfort. The hospice philosophy of end-of-life care says much about its philosophy of death, primarily about what the dying person needs in order to have a good death (Callanan & Kelley, 1992). Hospice emphasizes the importance of giving patients as much knowledge about their condition as possible so that they maintain some control over their care. The focus is not on curing disease but on managing symptoms and pain by means of palliative (pain-reducing) medicine. Perhaps more difficult to manage are other aspects of dying: the emotional, social, and spiritual sequelae of illness. In this approach to treatment, patients and their families are assisted in coping with the feelings of depression, anxiety, rejection, abandonment, and spiritual discomfort that may arise from the process of dying and losing a loved one.

Some studies have found that hospice patients are more satisfied with their care than conventional hospital patients (Kane, Wales, Bernstein, Leibowitz, & Kaplan, 1984) and that provision of hospice care in nursing homes improves quality of care there (Baer & Hanson, 2000; Wilson, Kovach, & Stearns, 1996). As noted earlier, there are clear worldwide trends toward improving end-of-life care by incorporating palliative care for all patients, regardless of setting (Lynn, 2000). In some areas, coalitions of hospitals, hospices, medical practices, nursing associations, long-term care facilities, social workers, and pastoral and mental health counselors have been formed to provide high-quality, comprehensive services to seriously ill individuals and their families (Mitka, 2000).

Having a good death appears to be related to the person's ability to make informed decisions about treatment, a notion congruent with what has been said about the psychological benefits of control. However, even though the importance of this kind of control has generally been acknowledged by practitioners of palliative care, studies suggest that a significant number of patients, even the most highly educated ones, still misunderstand the treatment options available to them. Silveira and her associates (Silveira, DiPiero, Gerrity, & Feudtner, 2000) examined whether knowledge about end-of-life options such as **refusal of treatment, physician-assisted suicide, active euthanasia**, and **double effect** was improved among patients who had signed **advance directives or living wills**, who had experienced previous illness, or who had previously cared for a dying loved one. *Refusal of treatment* refers to patients' refusal of any food, water, or medical treatment that prolongs life. *Physician-assisted suicide* involves prescribing medicine that enables patients to take their own lives. *Active euthanasia* refers to injection of a medication by someone else that causes immediate death. The *double effect* means giving medication intended to relieve pain even though there is a chance that death can result. *Advance directives* or *living wills* are statements, typically in writing, that describe a person's wishes regarding medical treatment in the event of incurable illness.

The results of the study showed that knowledge about end-of-life treatment options was generally poor. It was not improved for those who had signed advance directives or who were ill themselves. Knowledge was somewhat more accurate for those who had cared for dying loved ones. In general, caregivers often wait too long to discuss end-of-life preferences. Decisions may be made in haste, when the dying person is too ill or caregivers too distressed to make reflective choices (Gleeson & Wise, 1993). It is important, therefore, to initiate conversations about end-of-life decisions well in advance of the stresses of illness.

The Process of Dying

In the late 1950s, Elisabeth Kubler-Ross (Kubler-Ross, 1969), a Swiss-born psychiatrist, began to study the ways that people who were dying faced death. At that time, the dying were largely invisible among hospital patients, and she encountered a high degree of professional resistance to her work. When she asked her fellow physicians to recommend to her their dying patients so that she could talk to them, she was told that there were no dying patients in her 600-bed hospital (Ewens & Herrington, 1983). But after meeting people who realized that they were dying and after listening carefully to their stories, she described responses to death that appeared to characterize the process: denial, anger, bargaining, depression, and acceptance. Each of these responses represents a type of coping or defense mechanism for dealing with death. Perhaps it was unfortunate that she referred to these processes as "stages" and linked them together in sequence. Although Kubler-Ross herself (Kubler-Ross, 1974) emphasized that the stages do not always occur in order and that they can and often do occur simultaneously, the use of a stair-step approach is fraught with the kinds of problems we discussed in Chapter 1. Foremost, perhaps, is that a stage sequence can be irresistible to helpers who are looking for fixed, clear guidelines for understanding grief.

Criticism of the model has centered on the overall lack of empirical evidence for the existence of stages (Kastenbaum, 1986; Klass, 1982) and the problems that arise when professionals and caregivers use the stages as a road map by which to evaluate functional versus dysfunctional adjustment to death and dying (Corr, 1993). The belief among some helping professionals that these five responses are the only appropriate ones for the dying represents another limitation of the model as it is applied to practice. Studies of individuals who have received terminal diagnoses do provide some support for the initial manifestation of shock or disbelief as well as for the presence of greater acceptance before death (Kalish, 1985). In general, however, helpers should remember that there is much greater variation in the process than is allowed for by a strict interpretation of these stages. Perhaps the reactions can be viewed as some important ways that people cope with impending loss, but by no means is the sequence fixed nor the range of coping mechanisms exhaustive.

With these caveats in mind, let us consider each of these coping mechanisms in more detail. **Denial** may follow the initial shock that is associated with news of a terminal illness. At best, it temporarily protects the person from the reality of a terrifying situation. Denial is associated with feelings of numbness or disbelief and buffers the person from the full weight of the threat. Considered in this way, some measure of denial can be adaptive. It allows a person to temper the emotional impact, thus rendering it more manageable (Janoff-Bulman, 1993).

Anger is a normal reaction to separation and loss. Anger may be directed toward God ("Why me?"), toward others ("Why didn't you do something to help me?"), or toward the disease itself, which is viewed as an enemy to be battled. Often this is a very difficult response for family members to tolerate from loved ones who are dying. Resentment or hostility toward family members or caregivers who are healthy may reflect the depth of the dying person's pain and cries out for caregivers' compassion. Anger can ebb and flow throughout the course of illness, depending upon the individual and the specific circumstances (Rosenblatt, Walsh, & Jackson, 1972).

The essence of **bargaining** is to try to postpone the inevitable by making promises, usually to a higher power. Sometimes individuals will try to delay death until some memorable event, such as an anniversary or a child's marriage, takes place. The individual may offer some prize, such as "a life dedicated to God," if the chance to live longer is granted.

Depression as a reaction to impending death is characterized by sadness and feelings of hopelessness. Kubler-Ross distinguished between reactive depression, or depression that results from loss of functioning or other problems associated with the disease process, and preparatory depression, which is related to prospective loss and separation. **Acceptance** is characterized by a sense of peace and relative tranquility, which suggests that the person has come to terms with his impending death. We stress, however, that this peace is relative. No one should be evaluated on how quickly or completely she accepts death. Remember, too, that these reactions, although important, do not reflect all possible ways of managing the dying process.

It is helpful for professionals to understand that the dying process may also be distinguished by the nature of illness. Figure 15.6 illustrates some trajectories of dying for patients suffering from three common diseases: cancer, heart disease, and dementia (Eti, 2011). Awareness of these patterns can enhance provision of palliative care. Professionals can better help families understand prognoses and make more informed decisions about treatment.

Bereavement

Life is death

kept at an arm's length.

Love is grief

dressed in its Sunday best.

And sadness is the tax

assessed on any happiness.

—From *St. James' Park Epistle* by Thomas Lynch

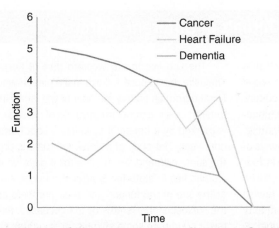

FIGURE 15.6 **Trajectories of illness in common diseases of aging.** The trajectories of cancer, organ failure (heart failure) and dementia, show different pathways.
SOURCE: Eti, S. (2011). Palliative care: An evolving field in medicine. *Clinics in Office Practice, 38,* 159–171. Used with permission from Elsevier.

Sadness is not the sole province of the dying person. Those who suffer the loss of loved ones are themselves deeply grieved. Grief is a universal reaction to loss or separation, and, as you recall from the discussion of attachment theory, it takes a number of behavioral forms, such as active distress, protest, and searching for the lost attachment figure. Grief has been described with great poignancy from the earliest times by philosophers, poets, and religious leaders. It has been memorialized in song and codified in ritual. Grief is often so unsettling to observe that it elicits from others a desire to give comfort and solace. Many religious and secular customs have grown up around the grieving process in an attempt to help people survive the rigors of suffering and to give meaning to death. Culture also plays a role in determining how grief is expressed, for example, as an emotional versus a physical set of symptoms (Kleinman & Kleinman, 1985). Box 15.3 describes various rituals from different cultures that demonstrate some of the diversity in people's beliefs about, and experiences with, death.

Helping professionals are often called upon to offer support to people who have experienced the loss of loved ones. An extensive clinical folklore has developed, primarily about the ways that grief should be expressed and the best ways to help people express it. In the 1980s, a vibrant debate commenced when researchers began to question the lack of empirical support for many of these traditionally accepted assumptions about grief. A number of inconsistencies or "myths" about grieving were uncovered in the process (Wortman & Silver, 1989, 2001), and researchers and clinicians have since continued this important dialogue. What follows is a discussion of some classic approaches to grief, an examination of some of the major tenets of bereavement counseling, and a brief summary of evidence from recent studies.

Classic Approaches to Bereavement

Freud's (1917/1957) theorizing about grief and mourning was very influential in shaping the legacy that came to be known as **grief work**. In simple terms, Freud believed that individuals who lose a loved one (or object) must withdraw their emotional attachments or energy (or libido) and detach (or decathect) from the lost object. Loss causes great pain, and bereaved people, Freud believed, inevitably need to struggle with the process of letting go. As manifestations of their mourning, they may lose interest in the world, prefer to isolate themselves from others, dwell on thoughts of the deceased, and suffer from depression. Gradually, the reality of loss is accepted. From Freud's perspective, successful resolution involves **decathecting**, or detaching emotionally, from the former relationship and reinvesting psychic energy into the formation of new attachments.

 Bob, age 81, and his family describe their experience learning about and living with the deaths of family members. How do Bob and his children differ in their bereavement processes?

Box 15.3: Funeral Rituals in Different Cultures

In virtually every culture, distinct funeral rituals have evolved that are fascinating reflections of people's beliefs about death. Social anthropologists suggest that these rituals serve to bind a culture together by expressing its "collective representations" about fundamental issues such as life, death, and spirituality (Metcalf & Huntington, 1991). To illustrate the diversity of beliefs and the many ways of demonstrating grief, we present a look at funeral practices in four cultures: the Chinese of San Francisco's Chinatown (Crowder, 1999; Hill, 1992), the Luo of Kenya (Nyamongo, 1999), traditional Jewish families (Schindler, 1996), and the San Francisco gay community during the last decades of the 20th century (Richards, Wrubel, & Folkman, 1999–2000).

For the Chinese, a funeral signifies the important transition from family member to ancestor, that beneficent spirit who will look out for the family's well-being from the spirit world. The connection between living family members and their ancestors is so important that, prior to the mid-20th century, Chinese immigrants living in the United States routinely returned their dead to China to be buried next to other family members. The Chinese community in San Francisco practiced elaborate traditional rituals, complete with funeral processions and brass bands. Funerals drew large groups of family members and friends, and they provided an occasion to tell the world about the accomplishments of the deceased. So fundamentally important was this practice that funerals in the Chinese province of Gansu were held *before* the person dies, so that he could be present to hear about the good things he had accomplished in his lifetime (2001, N. Zhang, personal communication).

Chinese funerals in San Francisco may incorporate Christian or Buddhist elements into a ceremony that traditionally consists of five parts: the visit, the service, the procession, the burial, and the dinner. The visit, or wake, allows visitors to view the body of the deceased. Near the body are placed a portrait of the dead person, usually framed with flowers, and items of food, such as chicken, vegetables, rice, and tea, intended to sustain the soul of the person through the journey to the afterlife. Various items such as jewelry, money, and clothing are placed in the coffin for his use as well. The funeral service, usually held the day after the visit, includes prayers and a eulogy. The funeral procession consists of a hearse, the funeral cortege, and a band, which plays hymns and other traditional music. On its way to the cemetery, the procession typically stops at the deceased's home or place of business. The portrait of the dead person is then taken from the hearse and set up facing the building. The mourners bow to pay their respects and may toss "spirit money," pieces of white paper in the shape of bills that are intended to placate malevolent spirits, into the air. Some relatives and friends await the procession at the house and greet the spirit of the ancestor with offerings of food, incense, and candles. At the gravesite, members of the funeral party, males first, followed by females, toss dirt, flowers, coins, or rice into the grave. The ritual is concluded with a formal seven-course meal, because seven is the number for death. At the center of each table is a cup of white rice liquor in honor of the departed.

The Luo live in the western part of Kenya near Lake Victoria. They, like the Chinese, believe that a person who dies becomes transformed from an earthly member of the family into a spiritual one. The funeral ritual is a transformative rite of passage. Death among the Luo is marked by a funeral fire, which is kept burning for approximately one week. The body of a deceased male is prepared by the men of the same clan and lies in state for 4 days, while that of a deceased woman lies in state for 3. After the burial, animals are slaughtered at the site of the funeral fire. Their numbers and kind depend upon the socioeconomic status of the deceased. Relatives and neighbors might contribute some animals for slaughter, knowing that the same will be done for them in their time of bereavement.

During the period of mourning, the sons of the deceased keep company around the fire. Their wives stay together in the house of the deceased, avoiding any sexual contact because of their belief that sexual relations will cause the death of their own sons. The widow of a deceased man is inherited by the dead man's brother, thus transferring her care to another relative and giving him the benefit of an additional laborer.

Traditional Jewish funeral practices emphasize honoring the deceased as well as giving the bereaved time and freedom to grieve. Jewish law is very sensitive to the emotional pain experienced by grieving persons and structures rituals to provide explicit comfort for them. During the funeral service, an emotional eulogy encourages mourners to vent their feelings by crying. A similarly cathartic release is elicited during the recitation of the *Kaddish*, or ritual prayer. Flowers are not customarily given in this cultural tradition because they signify happiness, an emotion that is discordant with the painfulness of death.

Throughout the period of mourning, called *Aninut*, great care is taken to support the bereaved. Jewish law indicates that those who have experienced a loss should be exempt from normal religious obligations, such as studying the scriptures. Customs such as *Kreiah*, or the ritual tearing of garments and the breaking of a shard on the lintel of the deceased's house, provide religious sanctions for outward displays of anger and sadness during the time of mourning. The period of *Shiva*, a 7-day mourning period, is dedicated to visiting and consoling the bereaved. Providing emotional comfort and social support for the survivors is viewed as an important religious obligation that helps to move people beyond the pain of their loss to a state of acceptance. Once the official 12-month grieving period is over, the *Kaddish* prayer is recited again, and excessive outward displays of mourning are expected to cease.

A relatively new culture, that of the gay community in San Francisco, developed its own ways of dealing with bereavement due to the unfortunate increase in HIV/AIDS related deaths in that community. Because many members of this community died in hospice or home settings, their dying often took the form of a vigil. Family and friends attended the dying person, keeping him as comfortable as possible while saying their good-byes. After death, rituals such as bathing and dressing the body honored the wishes of the deceased and allowed the bereaved to feel connected to the loved one. Photos could be placed around the bedside, and valued objects, such as letters or items of religious significance, were placed near the body. Funeral services could combine elements of formal religious rites with those that signified some personal meaning. For example, planting trees in the loved one's memory, burning incense, playing music, and so forth might be incorporated into the service.

These examples, although certainly not exhaustive, emphasize the healing function of rituals, either traditional ones or those that are newly created. Whatever their type or origin, regardless of their religious or cultural underpinnings, rituals appear to draw people together in their encounter with death. They give voice to fears and to sadness, and they signify love and respect for the persons who have died.

Freud presented these theoretical ideas on mourning well in advance of some important deaths that were to occur in his own personal life. The loss of his daughter at age 25 and of his grandson at age 4 affected him greatly. He wrote that his life was permanently altered by these enormous losses and that, although acute grief may subside, people "remain unconsolable and will never find a substitute" (Freud, 1929/1961, p. 239). These words suggest that Freud, in his later years, recognized that one does not necessarily recover from grief nor cut the cords of old attachments. However, his earlier notion that active grieving leads to recovery is one idea that he never formally revised and one that has permeated the canon of grief counseling. Other assumptions, that successful resolution of grief necessitates detachment from lost loved ones and reinvestment in other relationships and that abnormal mourning may follow from conflicted relationships, have also influenced clinical practice.

Bowlby's (1969/1982, 1980) highly influential construction of the bereavement process, based on attachment theory, depicts his view of typical human reactions to the experience of separation from or loss of attachment figures. The theory was initially developed to describe the responses of children temporarily separated from their caregivers (see Chapter 4, Box 4.2) and was later adapted to describe permanent separation, or bereavement, in adults. Bowlby's description of various reactions to separation gave rise to popular stage conceptions of dying, such as those of Kubler-Ross (Archer, 1999).

Bowlby's description of the grieving process includes four phases. At first, the loss is met by disbelief, a phase Bowlby called **shock**. The grieving person may experience numbness or feelings of unreality. Emotions may be blunted, and some individuals may even appear unaffected by the loss. Others may display emotional outbursts or may experience dizziness or other physical symptoms. The sense of disbelief eventually subsides when the reality of loss sets in. A second phase, **protest**, follows. Bereaved individuals may experience periods of obsessive yearning or searching for the lost loved one as well as bouts of restlessness or irritability.

The subsequent period, called **despair**, may be characterized by great sadness; social withdrawal; sleeping, eating, or somatic disturbances; and other symptoms of depression or emotional upset. People may experience flashbacks or intrusive memories of the deceased. They may actively seek support from others by telling and retelling the story of their loss. Yet, as with a child whose attachment figure has left him, the comfort of others cannot replace the presence of the lost loved one. Gradually, the bereaved person begins to adjust to the loss. Bowlby used the term **reorganization** to describe the last phase of grieving a permanent separation. Taking a position in opposition to Freud's, Bowlby believed that bereaved individuals do not decathect, or detach, from their lost loved ones. Instead, they discover

Funeral traditions vary dramatically across cultures, reflecting fundamental beliefs about life, death, and spirituality.

ways to hold on to the memory of the deceased and integrate that memory into their current life and new attachments. They heal, in part, by drawing comfort from the sense of the deceased person's presence (see Fraley & Shaver, 1999).

Assumptions About Grief Work and Empirical Support

As we have noted, a number of assumptions about bereavement, many derived from classic theories such as these, have been reexamined in the light of new evidence and cross-cultural information. One of the most prevalent myths is that people need to deal with their loss, by confronting the pain in an active way, for healing to occur. Avoiding the sadness, it is assumed, leads to later emotional problems. The tenets of *grief work* explicitly encourage bereaved individuals to confront and "work through" their feelings about loss for recovery to take place (Parkes & Weiss, 1983; Stroebe, 1992). This process, often facilitated by therapeutic intervention, might involve reflecting upon one's relationship to the deceased, expressing anger and other negative emotions related to the death, questioning and trying to construct meaning from the death, and ultimately resigning oneself to the loss. Unexpressed grief and unexamined loss, which have not been integrated into one's revised view of the world and the self, are thought to place the bereaved person's long-term physical and psychological well-being at risk. Another assumption is that the normal grieving process evolves in a sequence of stages that take a usually brief but arbitrarily determined period of time, such as 6 months to a year, to complete.

Those studies that have investigated the existence of stages in bereavement find little evidence to support the belief that people grieve in a linear, predictable fashion (van der Waal, 1989–1990; Wortman & Silver, 1987). Although many people do report initial shock and, later, some measure of reorganization, the intervening process does not necessarily follow in a clear sequence of compartmentalized, independent reactions. There is also a great deal of confusion over how long the manifestations of grief should persist before the grief is judged "abnormal." Previous diagnostic criteria (American Psychiatric Association, *DSM IV-TR*, 2000, p. 740) indicated that a clinician may consider a diagnosis of major depression if the depressive symptoms attendant to bereavement persist beyond two months. However, it is common for people to show grief symptoms much longer than 2 months. Several studies report gradual declines in depressive symptoms within the first 2 years after loss (Middleton, Raphael, Burnett, & Martinek, 1997; Stroebe & Stroebe, 1993), but depression may persist even longer (Martinson, Davies, & McClowry, 1991), particularly if the circumstances surrounding the death have been especially traumatic. Such findings have led to criteria for use in the diagnosis of **complicated or abnormal grief** that allow for longer periods of normal grieving (see Horowitz et al., 1997).

Controversy surrounds the recent decision to allow a diagnosis of depression two weeks after bereavement (DSM-V, 2013). At issue is the distinction between normal and complicated (also called chronic, unresolved, pathological) grieving and the decision to treat it as depression needing medication (see Francis, 2010). Abnormal grief was viewed by Bowlby (1980) as grief that is either excessive and protracted or absent. At one end of the continuum is chronic grief, which, like a preoccupied attachment, is marked by persistent yearning, anxiety, and unremitting distress. This type of mourning immobilizes bereaved individuals and prevents their return to normal functioning. Absence of grieving, on the other end of the continuum, was viewed by Bowlby and others (Deutch, 1937; Parkes, 1965) as a maladaptive defense against the trauma of loss. In this response, characteristic of a highly avoidant attachment pattern, bereaved individuals suppress grief and try to exclude frightening and painful feelings from consciousness. Despite the lack of consistency in empirical support, the concept of abnormal grief has been accepted in clinical practice (Rando, 1993). It is widely assumed that people should demonstrate great distress after a loss and that failure to do so is abnormal, a condition often called the "requirement of mourning" (Wright, 1983).

In general, some recent research has failed to find support for the assumption that all people need to work through loss in the highly cathartic fashion advised by advocates of grief work to adjust successfully. Contrary to what helping professionals might expect, a certain amount of detachment during the grieving process predicts healthy recovery for some bereaved individuals. Bonanno and Keltner (1997; see also Bonanno & Kaltman, 1999 for a review) provide data demonstrating that minimizing expression of negative emotions can offer some benefit to the bereaved. In this study of individuals whose spouses had died, the remaining partners who manifested a high degree of emotional distress (fear, anger, disgust, and the like) at 6 months after their loss continued to report poorer outcomes after 2 years. Those individuals who had lower initial levels of distress had better health and lower levels of grief after 2 years. Similarly, in a study designed to explore the coping styles of bereaved individuals, Bonanno and his colleagues (Bonanno, Znoj, Siddique, & Horowitz, 1999) reported that some detachment or emotional dissociation was not related to the development of later adjustment problems but was, in fact, predictive of positive outcomes. Neimeyer (2000) concludes from an examination of research that the use of grief-focused interventions with individuals who are not highly distressed risks doing them harm.

Other studies of bereaved individuals (Lund et al., 1985–1986; Vachon et al., 1982), of parents whose babies died from SIDS (Wortman & Silver, 1987), and of individuals who experienced spinal cord injuries (Dinardo, 1971) showed similar results. Those individuals who demonstrated the highest levels of distress initially were also most distressed and less effective in coping with the loss up to several years later. Individuals who showed lower levels of initial distress were generally better adjusted later and were not more likely to experience delayed grief reactions. One conceptual explanation for these findings draws on the framework of individual differences in attachment representations. Specifically, adjustment to loss may be less difficult for individuals whose emotional systems can be deactivated more easily (avoidant) than for those who have difficulty suppressing emotions (ambivalent) (see Fraley & Shaver, 1999). Another hypothesis is linked to gender. For example, one study demonstrated that females gave priority to sharing feelings after a loss, while males viewed problem-solving approaches as more important (Hopmeyer & Werk, 1994). Also, extreme levels of distress might indicate longstanding difficulties in emotion regulation or stress sytem activation. Certainly, much more research is needed to understand fully the significance of individual differences in grieving.

Overall, the evidence presented above should not be interpreted to suggest that outward signs of distress are necessarily unhealthy. Either side of an either-or argument is problematic. Just as a prescription to demonstrate intense grief is not right for everyone, neither is the advice to remain stoic. What we need to understand are the mechanisms that might explain individual differences in grief reactions, in hopes of constructing a more comprehensive theory of grieving. For those who take the stoic approach, perhaps it is not simply detachment, or the temporary psychic space it provides, but also the restricted focus on loss that makes for better overall adjustment. The traditional advice of grief work, which is to confront pain head-on, may be problematic for some people because of the risk of chronically activating systems related to yearning or "pining" for the lost loved one. Rumination, an emotion-focused style of coping, is correlated with poor adjustment. Excessive preoccupation with the deceased or obsessive dwelling on thoughts of pain and sadness may qualify as rumination.

In a longitudinal study of hundreds of bereaved individuals conducted over 18 months, Nolen-Hoeksema and Larson (1999) found that the use of rumination as a way to cope with loss was highly related to depression at each interview point. In addition, people who ruminated tended to have great difficulty finding meaning in the loss, despite the significant amount of time they spent trying to do so. These findings are consistent with the strong association between ruminative coping and depression in general (Nolen-Hoeksema, 1991).

You might wonder how a bereaved person can make sense of his loss, another assumed measure of successful grieving, if he does not engage in some rumination. Yet, is it really necessary for people to make sense of the loss to adapt successfully? Davis, Lehman, and Wortman (1997) report that not all people who struggle to make sense of deaths, accidents, illnesses, and other tragedies are able to explain these events in satisfactory ways. Many people do not try to do so, preferring to move ahead with their lives without searching for existential or philosophical meaning.

Davis and his associates (Davis, Wortman, Lehman, & Silver, 2000) reported very consistent findings from several studies that investigated the benefits of meaning-making for later adjustment. In general, individuals who were able to derive meaning from the event relatively early on were least distressed at follow-up interviews. Interestingly, those who were able to find something positive in the experience or who were able to reappraise the loss to extract some benefit from it were the best adjusted. Religious or spiritual beliefs often helped people find meaning in the loss. However, others found that loss precipitated a cascade of doubts about faith because it shattered their views of a just world. Those who did not initiate a search for meaning were also found to have relatively good adjustments. It was the group that struggled for meaning without finding it that suffered most in this study.

Nolen-Hoeksema and Larson (1999) reported significant associations in their bereavement study between the tendency to ruminate and the inability to find meaning in the experience of loss. The highest level of distress at follow-up interviews was demonstrated by the group who struggled continually to make sense of the inexplicable. Certain contextual circumstances may make it more difficult for people to find meaning or benefits from the deaths of loved ones. Among these kinds of deaths are those that occur suddenly (Parkes & Weiss, 1983); deaths of children (Nolen-Hoeksema & Larson, 1999); deaths due to intentional, malicious causes such as homicide (Murphy, 1997); and deaths due to the negligence of others, such as those involving motor vehicle accidents (Wortman, Battle, & Lemkau, 1997). Some measure of restitution made by the perpetrators of these acts can be beneficial in reducing the bereaved families' distress and promoting resolution of grief (Davis et al., 2000).

An Integrated Perspective on Grief

As research in this area increases, more sophisticated models of grieving have been developed (Cook & Oltjenbruns, 1998; Rubin, 1981). One such model that weaves together some of the theoretical and empirical threads described above is the **dual-process model** proposed by Stroebe and Schut (1999). This conceptualization depicts an interplay of stressors and coping strategies within a flexible, oscillating framework. Specifically, the authors propose that bereaved individuals simultaneously engage in two kinds of coping mechanisms, approach and avoidance, that wax and wane over the course of grieving.

Approach tendencies are reflected in activities synonymous with grief work: confronting the painful reality of death, expressing sadness, and gradually desensitizing oneself to the reminders of loss. Approach tendencies can be tolerated for only so long. They are **loss focused** and can lead to rumination or excessive preoccupation and, often, great distress. According to the dual-process model, the loss-focused work of grieving is balanced by parallel activities that are **restoration focused**. This type of coping strategy is directed toward handling the practical tasks that need to be done to carry on with daily life. For example, a widow might experience intense periods of grief during which she focuses on memories of her life with her deceased spouse; however, she might also have dependent children who need care. Attending to their needs serves as a distraction, mitigating the periods of loss-related distress. Both loss and restoration coping strategies are part of the grieving process, and Stroebe and Schut view their dynamic oscillation as a healthy regulatory mechanism. Bereaved individuals go back and forth between emotion-focused (loss-oriented) and problem-focused (restoration-oriented) modes of coping. This approach-avoidance interplay protects bereaved individuals from the exacting extremes of unrelieved distress or rigid mental suppression. In general, there is more loss-oriented coping early in the grieving process and more restoration-oriented coping at later points. Traditional conceptions of abnormal grief can be viewed as "disturbances of oscillation" (Stroebe & Schut, 1999, p. 217), either overly loss oriented or excessively avoidant. Figure 15.7 presents a diagram of the dual-process model of coping.

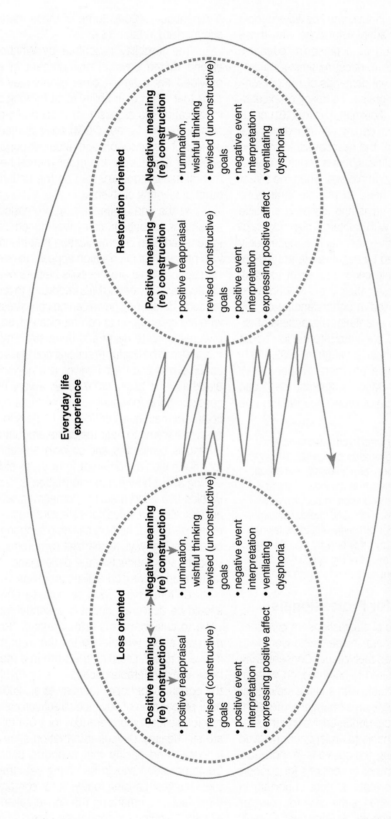

FIGURE 15.7 A dual-process model of coping with loss: pathways.

SOURCE: Stroebe, M. S., & Schut, H. (2001). Model of coping with bereavement: A review. In M. S. Stroebe, R. O Hansson, W. Stroebe & H. Schut (Eds.), *Handbook of bereavement research: Consequences, coping, and care* (p. 397). Used by permission of the authors.

APPLICATIONS

This chapter presents information about some key ways people change in later life and how they adapt to or cope with those changes. Coping has been defined as a person's "cognitive and behavioral efforts to manage (reduce, minimize, master, or tolerate) the internal and external demands of the person–environment transaction that is appraised as taxing or exceeding the resources of the person" (Folkman, Lazarus, Gruen, & DeLongis, 1986, p. 572). Adaptive coping, or managing the demands of life relatively well, is at the heart of achieving and maintaining optimal health and wellness. This is certainly true at any age, but perhaps even more so in old age, when the threat of overtaxed resources and the need to tolerate limitations becomes inevitable. Life involves gains and losses. It is naïve to assume that everyone can and will maintain a high quality of life right up to their death. But on the other hand, unnecessarily pessimistic views of old age, fueled by negative stereotypes of the elderly, restrict the ways people choose to adapt to aging and limit their sense of control over their lives. Helpers who are knowledgeable about and skilled in understanding coping mechanisms can promote healthy adaptation, regardless of client age (Ponzo, 1992). Sources of concrete information about how to cope with getting old (Skinner & Vaughan, 1983/1997), how to understand the perspective of elders (Pipher, 1999), and how to deal with dementia (Mace & Rabins, 1999) can help clinicians build their foundation of knowledge. Whitbourne (1989) summarizes the task:

> The main point that a clinician must keep foremost in mind when working with an aging client is the need to be flexible. The aging process involves multiple physical, psychological, and social demands that can all potentially impact on the individual's ability to function. Clinicians may be called upon to perform advocacy services, environmental interventions, and interdisciplinary consultations, which they would not ordinarily regard as falling within the domain of "psychotherapy." It is only by maintaining an open approach to the multiple needs of the aged client that the clinician can hope to bring about successful change. (p. 168)

A Good Fit: Adaptations for Professionals

Myers and Harper (2004) offer useful suggestions for clinicians who work with older clients. In general, helpers who work with this population may be younger than their clients. Consequently, more time and sensitivity are required to build rapport with individuals who may be less comfortable with sharing feelings or with asking questions of "authority" figures. Younger professionals also need to be prepared to deal nondefensively with older clients who might view them as unable to understand the lived experience of old age. Lengthening the sessions in individual counseling and increasing the number of sessions for support groups or other group therapy formats is more important in reducing relapse for older clients than is the case for younger ones. Psychological treatments should be modified as well. Many typical counseling approaches can be accommodated to meet the needs of older clients (Gellis & Kenaley, 2008; Kennedy,

& Tanenbaum, 2000). Some of these modifications have been summarized in Table 15.6.

The flexibility described by Whitbourne above should extend to the physical environment in which counseling is provided. For example, older clients may have physical limitations that affect their ability to sit for long periods or may need modifications to assessment procedures due to hearing or vision problems. Lyness (2004) advises medical and counseling professionals who work with an older population to screen routinely for depression and other mental health issues because mental health concerns can be the underlying cause of many other presenting problems.

At the end of life, helping professionals can bring a real advantage to patient care: well-honed communication skills. Patient-centered communication that blends empathic listening with provision of information appears to offer patients the greatest support. What are the skills helpers need for delivering bad news when it is needed? It's important to remember that delivering such life-altering news can be very stressful for professionals who are called upon to communicate it. So, awareness of one's own response to dying and understanding of best practices in this area can be useful. Practicing compassion for oneself as well as for clients and their families is a powerful resource. Barclay, Blackhall, and Tulsky (2007) offer a very helpful review of key considerations for culturally appropriate communication of difficult information. It's critical for helpers to understand that not everyone wants to hear the same amount of information about prognosis, symptoms, and so forth. Sometimes patients' wishes for information are different from those of families. Carefully inquiring about how much information is desired as the dialogue unfolds is a good practice. Sometimes separate conversations are indicated, provided consistent information is delivered. When prognosis is poor, helpers can help support realistic expectations by discussing ways to manage symptoms, providing emotional support, and connecting the patient and family with resources rather than offering unrealistic promises.

Cultures differ with respect to how directly bad news should be delivered, and it is essential for helpers to be sensitive to cultural norms in this regard. "Here the difference is *not only* about whether to tell the truth, but also about *what it means to tell*. Learning the truth in a more indirect way may be seen as preferable because the ambiguity allows the patient the possibility of hope" (Barclay et al., 2007, p. 963). In general, prior preparation of advance directives can provide an opportunity for discussing preferences for truth-telling while individuals are still healthy. Difficult information should be conveyed with language and pacing that supports patients' understanding. Communication should be caring yet straightforward. The authors suggest pausing to check for comprehension after every three facts. Summarizing the conversation aids understanding as well. Planning for continuing care that includes that patient and/or family can help convey the reality of continuing support through the process.

TABLE 15.6 Therapeutic Adaptations for Older Clients

TYPE OF THERAPY	EXAMPLES OF TARGET THERAPEUTIC OUTCOMES	SOME ADAPTATIONS FOR OLDER CLIENTS
Brief Psychodynamic	Resolving survivor guilt; reducing negative attitudes toward self related to aging.	Recognition and skillful handling of age-specific transference issues, (e.g., client's view that younger therapist is inexperienced and unable to help).
Cognitive Behavioral	Changing dysfunctional thoughts; active problem solving.	Understanding of older clients' learning styles; recognition of cognitive and sensory impairments that might interfere with learning; use of concrete written material and practice.
Behavioral Therapy for Depression	Improving mood through increasing positive reinforcement.	Provision of methodical and concrete approaches to identify and engage in positive, mood-enhancing experiences and systematically avoid unpleasant experiences.
Interpersonal Therapy for Depression	Improving interpersonal relationships through time-limited approach to problem-solving using therapist as supportive resource.	Active therapeutic stance that focuses on solving real problems within the context of old age; provision of ample social support.
Life Review or Reminiscence Therapy	Finding meaning in life at present by reflecting on and integrating past conflicts.	Empathic listening that provides a context for a review of the past; review of memorabilia like photographs, journals, and writing exercises.
Problem-Solving Therapy	Finding ways to view problems more realistically and solve them more effectively.	Careful listening to client's problems, empathy, encouragement and support for trying new solution in a personal context.
Group Therapy	Addressing multiple needs of older clients, particularly clients in institutionalized settings.	Screening of participants to ensure a relatively high degree of homogeneity in cognitive and sensory functioning; provision of structured format; ample positive reinforcement of group members; timing of meeting in midmorning to early afternoon.

SOURCE: Based on Kennedy, G. J., & Tanenbaum, S. (2000). Psychotherapy with older adults. *American Journal of Psychotherapy, 54*, 386–407.

Healthy Aging and Prevention

The amount of research on aging continues to grow, due, at least in part, to the aging of the world's population. One wave of research is focused on "successful aging," a perspective that assumes that healthy functioning and even the achievement of certain gains is possible in late life. One such initiative is actually a series of studies called the MacArthur study because of the financial support provided by the John D. and Catherine T. MacArthur Foundation (Rowe & Kahn, 1998). The fruits of 10 years of intensive investigations involving thousands of participants, millions of dollars, and the combined expertise of biologists, neuropsychologists, sociologists, epidemiologists, geneticists, and gerontologists, among others, tell us a great deal about successful aging.

To summarize briefly, enjoying a healthy and productive old age is possible. The more physically and mentally fit older individuals are, the more likely they will age successfully. Clearly, one's lifestyle prior to old age can have a tremendous influence on the quality of later life. A healthy diet and regular exercise, including aerobics and weight training, confers a real physical advantage. Although maintaining healthy habits provides protection from disease and should, ideally, be maintained consistently, the MacArthur study revealed that positive changes in eating and exercise habits, even in old age, can help people live longer and healthier

Older people often meet their needs to feel competent and productive by engaging in part-time or volunteer work.

lives. Equally important to successful aging are social relationships. It turns out that older people benefit more from emotional than instrumental support in many cases. So while it can be very helpful to offer help with housecleaning, providing a patient listening ear may go a longer way toward promoting well-being.

A sense of being productive also appears to be a benchmark of healthy aging as well. Healthy men and women are three times more likely than those with physical or mental health problems to be engaged in paid work or volunteer activities. However, as we have seen, even people with physical limitations often manage, with some creativity, to engage in activities that keep them in touch with the world. Productive engagement with others, in whatever form it takes, is linked to a sense of mastery or personal self-efficacy. A "can-do" attitude contributes enormously to well-being. Professionals can facilitate the development of self-efficacy by fashioning opportunities for older individuals that reflect their self-endorsed goals and that challenge their capacities without overwhelming them. Helpers also need to provide encouragement to older people to engage in these challenges, give confirming feedback for mastery, and help dispel negative stereotypes that lead to passivity and hopelessness.

 Through her volunteer work in the community, Marie, at age 92, feels productive and remains socially engaged.

When Losses Occur

What should we do to help when the losses of later life occur? Based on recent longitudinal studies, several principles appear to be important. Helping professionals should be aware that grief has many affective, behavioral, and physical manifestations and that there is wide variation in expressions of mourning at the level of the individual and culture. The oversimplified use of stage theories may suggest that there is one correct way to grieve and one circumscribed time frame in which to do so. One can only imagine how discouraging it must be for a bereaved person to be told that she is not grieving correctly. In our fast-paced world, it is often difficult to let people take the time they need to heal. Helpers should not hold prescriptive rules for how long grief should last, because many people continue to grieve well beyond the limits of several months or even years.

Remember as well that the absence of overt, intense grief is not necessarily problematic. Not everyone who fails to demonstrate great distress or who does not search for meaning in a loss will suffer eventual emotional problems. Furthermore, we often expect people to "recover" from a loss by returning to an earlier level of functioning, despite evidence that this is often impossible.

Difficulties in the grief process may be considered to be an imbalance between too much expression and too little, but even this is mediated by personality, gender, culture, and beliefs. Some interventions that have traditionally been favored by helping professionals, such as active grief work interventions, may not be useful and may actually be more distressing for individuals given to ruminative tendencies. Even support seeking, a style of coping that involves seeking help from other people, may be

a source of stress unless those sought after for help are themselves compassionate and willing to listen (Nolen-Hoeksema & Larson, 1999). Efforts to personalize interventions depending upon needs and characteristics of clients are important.

Several sets of tasks have been developed that describe the responsibilities of helpers or other caregivers in times of bereavement (Rando, 1993; Worden, 1982). The following is a brief description of Worden's tasks with evidence-based recommendations derived from the bereavement coping project of Nolen-Hoeksema and Larson (1999). Keep in mind that bereaved individuals differ in their needs, so these recommendations should be considered general guidelines.

1. Bereaved individuals may need support in order to accept the reality of loss. Providing assistance with funeral arrangements and helping to prepare meals or clean up are all useful ways to be of help. It is important not to "push" the person to accept the loss but to be respectful of the individual's style of coping.

2. Helpers and other loved ones should allow bereaved persons to identify and express feelings if they want to do so. Judicious use of open-ended questions and provisional language ("Sometimes people say that they occasionally feel anxious or impatient. I wonder if you ever feel that way?" Nolen-Hoeksema & Larson, 1999, p. 182) can promote feelings of safety and acceptance.

3. Bereaved persons need to learn how to live without their lost loved ones. For example, they may need to learn restoration-focused tasks previously handled by the deceased, such as managing finances or cooking for children. The helper can scaffold the development of these skills by anticipating possible needs, helping to break them down into manageable tasks, and providing concrete assistance or information.

4. Survivors may need help in finding a place in their lives for the deceased. This may take many forms, depending upon the individual, but generally entails finding a way to maintain some emotional connection. For some people, talking about the deceased is easier and more beneficial than talking about themselves. Silverman (2000) noticed in her work with bereaved children that they were much more articulate when asked to talk about the person who died than they were when asked to talk about their own feelings about the death. She called this process "constructing a relationship to the deceased."

5. The next task for helpers requires them to be patient and allow time and a nurturing context for grieving. It's worth considering very carefully the risks and benefits of treating grief as an illness that needs medication. While this may surely be advisable in certain cases, it's also possible to turn what is an expectable reaction to loss into a disorder. "Medicalizing normal grief stigmatizes and reduces the normalcy and dignity of the pain, short-circuits the expected existential processing of the loss, reduces reliance on the many well-established cultural rituals for consoling grief, and would subject many people to unnecessary and potentially harmful medication treatment" (Francis, 2010, p. 46).

6. Helpers may need to help normalize grief for the bereaved. Grieving people often report fears about "going crazy" because of symptoms such as visual or sensory hallucinations, panic attacks, and other signs of intense distress. Learning that these are common occurrences in bereavement that will go away in time is very reassuring.

7. Helpers should provide continuing support, as needed, to help survivors weather the trials of grieving and to assist them in examining the effectiveness or ineffectiveness of their coping strategies. Taking notice of strategies that are effective is an empowering exercise because it allows people to recognize that they have some choice. Strategies that are less helpful can be identified, and more useful possibilities can be suggested.

8. Finally, helpers need to identify and find other sources of support if they, for whatever reason, cannot provide for the range of needs described above.

Integrity: The Life Cycle Completed

From Erikson's (1950/1963) perspective, people struggle continuously throughout the life cycle with the "hazards of existence" (p. 274) and should not expect to reach a level of achievement in any of the stages that is completely impervious to conflict. The negative pole of each developmental task represents its counterpoint, a reminder of each stage's dynamic quality (see Chapter 1, Table 1.2). The period of old age is no exception. Facing old age and death are awesome challenges. Yet over a lifetime, the struggles of earlier stages ideally bear fruit. The resulting integrity, that sense of coherence or wholeness that comes from "acceptance of *one's own and only life cycle* [italics added]" (p. 268) is the product of strengths accumulated from each earlier period: hope, self-control, direction, love, devotion, affiliation, and care. Renunciation, the outcome of the final stage according to Erikson, is consummate generativity. It embodies acceptance of the natural order, namely that wisdom which allows us to view death as a stage of life. "Healthy children will not fear life," Erikson wrote, "if their elders have integrity enough not to fear death" (p. 269).

Erikson's view of the life span, then, is less of a straight line and more of a circle, with its final stage a gift of courage and caring for the generations that follow. In his psychosocial view of development, the quality of life from beginning to end is touched by its social intersections. As we are learning, positive relationships keep people well (Ryff & Singer, 2000); they offer long-term protective factors. Nurturing others, so necessary for survival of our species, returns on the investment at the end of life when we receive others' care. As we age, some have suggested the need to reminisce or review life events as a way of integrating the features of one's identity and achieving integrity (Butler, 1963). Part of the benefit of this process, undoubtedly, involves sharing the story with others.

We have provided throughout this book descriptions of various aspects of human functioning: attachments, social networks, cognition, brain development, identity, marriage, adaptation, family ties and aging, among many others. There is much left to learn about these topics and about how that knowledge can be used to benefit individuals and societies. Research agendas continuing into the 21st century promise to improve even further our working knowledge of the life span and offer potential avenues for best practice. With this knowledge, helping professionals will be in a unique position to foster resilience, to cultivate compassion for themselves and others, and to create conditions that support well being for all members of the human family in the face of life's challenges.

SUMMARY

Physical, Cognitive, and Socioemotional Change in Late Life

1. Despite the increasing number of losses older people experience as they move into old age (60s and 70s) or into old-old age (80s and 90s), most older individuals manage to adapt to old age successfully.

2. As people age, they experience declines in many physical systems, including the immune and sensory systems. Arthritis, particularly osteoarthritis, is especially common.

3. Cognitive change across the lifespan shows a nuanced pattern of change. Perspectives from longitudinal, cross-sectional and integrated models describe maintenance or even gains in some crystallized knowledge (representation) but declines in fluid processes (control) mediated by executive functions. Executive functions are typically the first to show decrements in the aging process. Cognitive functioning in old age is related to overall health, and substantial declines in cognitive functioning, known as dementia, are usually due to cardiovascular accidents or disease processes such as Alzheimer's disease. Brain changes associated with dementia can start many years before symptoms become evident. Current thinking implicates both genetic and physiological influences (e.g., inflammation) on disease progression. Terminal drop or decline refers to a rapid decline in intellectual functioning shortly before death.

4. Studies of autobiographical memory indicate that, contrary to stereotypic notions, older people remember their more recent experiences better than earlier experiences (recency), even though older adults learn new information less efficiently than younger adults. However, if adults are asked about flashbulb memories, especially vivid and personally relevant recollections, their reports are largely about events in their early adulthood, referred to as the bump period. That is probably why elderly people often tell stories about their early years.

5. As people age, their network of friends and family members shrinks. Social loss is exacerbated by negative stereotypes about aging that assume all elderly people share

certain negative characteristics. These stereotypes can lead to discriminatory or demeaning practices that interfere with positive social interactions. Stereotypes of aging are similar across cultures. Negative self-stereotypes of aging also affect performance and mood of older individuals.

6. Three processes appear to be important for successful development in old age. Selection involves limiting activities to a few that are particularly rewarding. Optimization involves finding ways of enhancing achievement of remaining goals. Compensation involves finding new means to achieve our ends. Together these processes are called selective optimization with compensation.

7. There are other, similar ways of describing adaptation processes. In self-determination theory, three needs are said to motivate adaptation at any age: autonomy, competence, and relatedness.

8. Another description of techniques for facing challenges emphasizes two broad strategies. Primary-control strategies are attempts to affect the immediate environment and often increase feelings of mastery and self-esteem. Secondary-control strategies are attempts to change ourselves, such as changing goals. If the latter approach allows a person to then take primary control over some stressor, feelings of happiness and well-being are likely to be enhanced.

9. On the whole, older people seem to cope well with the challenges of late life according to their self-reports. They compare positively with younger adults on some aspects of well-being, such as positive relationships and self-acceptance. Reported well-being does declines in later life.

10. Does increased wisdom help the elderly to cope? Wisdom involves superior knowledge, judgment, emotion regulation, and advice-giving with regard to important questions about life. Research indicates that it is somewhat more likely to characterize older rather than younger adults, although wisdom seems to be as much a quality of the individual person as it is of age. Cross-cultural similarities and differences have been observed in wisdom acquisition and expression.

11. As people age, they pay more attention to their feelings, and their emotions are more enhanced and complex. Positive emotions are as common among the old as the young. Negative emotions, except for sadness, occur less often. Emotion regulation seems to improve. Yet, rates of clinically important depressive symptoms and incidence of minor depression increase into old age.

Experiencing Loss

12. Elderly people report less anxiety about death than younger people. Dying adults often must deal with others' reluctance to deal with death and may feel lonely and isolated.

13. A good death for most people includes symptom management and care (such as freedom from pain, being clean), practical details (such as knowing what to expect), a good patient–professional relationship, and certain psychological attributes (such as maintaining dignity, not dying alone). But many people have very individual needs and desires as well. For example, some people prefer to die at home, but many do not. Palliative care, such as that promoted by the hospice movement, is important to most people.

14. People who sign living wills or advance directives do not necessarily know more about their end-of-life options, although those who have recently cared for a dying patient are more aware.

15. Kubler-Ross described several reactions to dying that are called stages but that do not necessarily occur for all dying adults and do not occur in any fixed sequence: These are denial, anger, bargaining, depression, and acceptance. The dying process is also influenced by the nature of the terminal illness. Knowledge of typical trajectories can improve effectiveness of palliative care.

16. Both Freud and Bowlby proposed influential theories of the grief process. Freud originally believed that bereaved individuals needed to withdraw from the lost loved one and reinvest emotional energy into forming new attachments. Bowlby used attachment theory concepts to describe stages of the grief process: shock, protest, despair, and reorganization. Assumptions derived from these theories have been disputed by contemporary researchers. In particular, the existence of a stage sequence of grief reactions has not been validated. The concept of abnormal grief and the need for cathartic grief work have been called into question as well.

17. Contemporary models of grieving include diverse ways of coping with loss. The dual-process model of Stroebe and Schut incorporates both loss-focused elements and restoration-focused elements within a flexible framework. Current controversies exist regarding whether to treat grief as a form of depression needing medication.

CASE STUDY

Isabelle and her husband Victor lived together for 53 years in a small, close-knit Italian American section of a big city. Victor made a living for the family working as a forklift operator. Isabelle, a stay-at-home mother when her children were young, returned to work as a sales clerk once the youngest two children entered high school. Isabelle enjoyed her years of full-time mothering, but she also loved the social interaction and camaraderie she found in her job. The family has four grown children, Paul, 51, Sophia, 49, and twins Lenore and Joseph, 45. Paul and his wife own and operate a small restaurant in a nearby suburb. They have two young adult children. Sophia, also married with two children, teaches in a middle school about an hour away from her parents' home. Lenore has recently remarried after a divorce. She lives with her second husband and her three children in the city. Joseph is a salesperson who has never married but who lives in another state with his longtime partner, Joanne.

At this time, the family is struggling to come to grips with Victor's recent death. After years of robust health, Victor was diagnosed with pancreatic cancer. During the last 4 months of his life, he was in and out of the hospital as his health demanded. Isabelle tried to care for him as best she could, but it was very difficult. The side effects of Victor's treatment protocol left him feeling ill and in need of constant care. The family members tried to help, but the greatest burden fell to Paul because in this family the oldest child is perceived to have the most responsibility.

As time went on and it became clear that Victor was dying, Isabelle mentioned to her children that their father had not wanted any extraordinary measures to be used to keep him alive in his final illness. Victor had never put this in writing, but Isabelle was sure of his wishes. Victor's family physician, a deeply religious man, Victor's older brother, and Joseph all strongly disagreed with this plan. They believed that every effort should be made to save Victor's life. One night, Victor lapsed into a coma and was having trouble breathing. Joseph prevailed upon his mother to allow the physician to insert a ventilator. Joseph's siblings were very upset about this turn of events, for they believed it caused their father unnecessary suffering. Victor died several days later.

Now 4 months after the death of her husband, Isabelle is grieving the loss of her spouse. She lives alone but is seriously contemplating asking her son Paul to let her move in with his family. She quit her job at the department store because she felt she was unable to concentrate well enough to perform in a satisfactory manner. She has been unable to sleep through the night, and her mind keeps returning to memories of Victor during his illness.

Relationships are strained among the children. Neither daughter speaks to Joseph or Joanne because of their disagreement about Victor's care. Joanne believes that Joseph should "move on" and concentrate on her and their life together. Lenore avoids calling her mother because she does not want to hear her repeat the same troubles over and over again. She uses her hectic schedule as a full-time mother as an excuse. Sophia is somewhat more attentive, but she is also uncomfortable listening to her mother's reminiscences. She wants to believe that her mother is still the same vibrant person she has always known, so she discounts the sadness she hears in Isabelle's voice. Paul is overwhelmed by the responsibility he feels for his family, his business, and his mother. He knows his mother is grieving, but he cannot find a way to make her feel better. For her part, Isabelle feels that she has come to the end of her life as well. She believes that she will end up like many of the other lonely widows she knows in her neighborhood.

Discussion Questions

1. What are the emotional and behavioral responses of each person to Victor's death?
2. Identify the stressors that are operating on this family. Distinguish between those that can be controlled and those that cannot be changed. Develop a list of coping strategies that might be useful in dealing with these problems.
3. As a helper, how would you begin to work with this family? With Isabelle?

PRACTICE USING WHAT YOU HAVE LEARNED

In the Pearson etext, apply these ideas to working with others.

Applying Concepts

Case Study

An Elderly Couple Living with Mild Dementia in Unsanitary Conditions

Lydia and John were a couple in their nineties who lived in their own home and had been married over 60 years. Both were confused and forgetful. They had two sons who were in their seventies and lived in nearby towns. One son was estranged from them. The other was somewhat involved in their lives, but he had a mentally ill wife, as well as health problems of his own to deal with.

JOURNAL QUESTIONS

1. Identify someone you know whom you believe to be aging successfully. Write a letter to this person (to be given or not) describing how you think the person is dealing with growing old and why you admire the person.
2. What would you do if you had only 6 months to live?
3. What kind of ceremony or funeral ritual would you like to have when you die? Why would you choose this particular type of ritual?
4. Interview someone from a culture that is different from your own. Explore attitudes about the elderly, perspectives on aging and death, and end-of-life rituals or practices that are characteristic of this culture. How are they different from your own?

KEY CONCEPTS

arthritis (p. 558)
osteoarthritis (p. 558)
telomeres (p. 558)
representations (p. 559)
control (p. 559)
dementia (p. 561)
Alzheimer's disease (AD) (p. 561)
plaques (p. 562)
tangles (p. 562)
amyloid precursor protein (APP) (p. 562)
cerebrovascular accidents (strokes) (p. 562)
multi-infarct dementia (p. 562)
terminal drop (terminal decline) (p. 562)
autobiographical memory (p. 563)
recency (p. 563)
"the bump" (p. 566)
flashbulb memories (p. 566)
selection (p. 569)

optimization (p. 569)
compensation (p. 569)
selective optimization with compensation (p. 570)
primary control (p. 570)
secondary control (p. 570)
stages of retirement (p. 571)
honeymoon (p. 571)
disenchantment (p. 571)
reorientation (p. 571)
stability (p. 571)
termination (p. 571)
wisdom (p. 573)
end-of-life care (p. 579)
palliative care (p. 580)
hospice movement (p. 580)
refusal of treatment (p. 581)
physician-assisted suicide (p. 581)

active euthanasia (p. 581)
double effect (p. 581)
advance directives (living wills) (p. 581)
denial (p. 582)
anger (p. 582)
bargaining (p. 582)
depression (p. 582)
acceptance (p. 582)
grief work (p. 583)
decathecting (p. 583)
shock (p. 585)
protest (p. 585)
despair (p. 585)
reorganization (p. 585)
complicated or abnormal grief (p. 586)
dual-process model (p. 588)
loss-focused grief (p. 588)
restoration-focused grief (p. 588)

A Practitioner's Guide to Psychological Science

Understanding the Scientific Process

We have argued that information gained from scientific research on development is important for helping professionals to know. Yet, practitioners often do not find research results helpful or relevant to the problems they face with their clients. What is going on here? Is scientific work of practical value? It can be, but only if the practitioner understands the scientific process.

Most of us are enculturated to believe that the sciences provide answers to life's conundrums, and sometimes they do. For example, at one time the causes of diseases such as tuberculosis or polio were a mystery, but biological research has now established that microorganisms are the culprits. The path that biologists followed to achieve this insight was a laborious and time-consuming one, with many wrong turns or apparent missteps. Adequate scientific answers almost always are found at the end of similarly circuitous routes. As a result, practitioners closely allied to any scientific field sometimes find that the best scientific information of today can change tomorrow. In addition, scientists may offer competing answers to the same question until enough work has been done on a phenomenon to validate one answer, or some amalgam of previous answers. It is not unusual for practitioners faced with competing scientific "answers" to begin to wonder, "What good is science?"

Let's address this question by first looking at the nature of the scientific process. Then we will examine how practitioners can effectively use science to achieve their goals.

Psychology as the Study of Human Behavior

The study of human behavior and its associated mental processes—motivations, cognitions, emotions, and so on—is a topic of great interest to most of us, and it is the subject of many disciplines besides the social sciences. Most of the humanities, such as literature, history, and philosophy, are focused primarily on human behavior. What differentiates these disciplines are the *methods* that they use to gain understanding. For example, the study of *literature* is in part the study of human behavior as seen through the eyes of great writers of fiction. Through their literary work, writers share with us their observations and beliefs about human motivation, morality, social functioning, and so on. *History* examines the unfolding of human behavior in past events, lining up the facts that can be uncovered about the actions of real people in earlier times and speculating about the connections between these actions and their underlying causes. *Philosophers* usually focus their attention on human behavior as well, but their preferred method is rational analysis. For example, a particular philosopher may take human language as her subject matter and attempt to analyze its sources and its implications for the operation of the human mind. The social sciences are like these other disciplines in their subject matter, human behavior, but they use different methods—the methods of science.

The Three Steps in Scientific Investigation

Across different scientific disciplines—psychology, biology, physics, or any other science—the subject matter changes, but the general methods are the same. Some specific techniques may vary, adapted to the particulars of the topics under scrutiny, but three broad steps are alike for all sciences: description, explanation, and verification.

Description

Description is a research step aimed at answering factual questions about a phenomenon, questions such as who, what, when, where, and with whom. Suppose we were interested in understanding the phenomenon of juvenile delinquency. We would begin our scientific exploration by seeking answers to questions such as the following: *Who* engages in juvenile delinquency? (What are the usual ages, gender, socioeconomic status, family characteristics, intellectual characteristics, academic performance, social skills, personality characteristics, and so on, of children identified as delinquent?) *What* kinds of behaviors usually characterize delinquency? (Are most delinquents truants, or nonviolent thieves, or violent murderers, or other kinds of perpetrators?) *Where* and *when* are delinquent acts most likely to occur? *With whom* are delinquents likely to associate and to commit their evil deeds?

Explanation

With an arsenal of facts gained from descriptive research, we are ready to take the next step, **explanation**. At this point, we frame a *theory* or set of *hypotheses* about *how* the facts are related to each other and *why* they occur. Our other theoretical commitments are likely to influence us here. For example, we may tend to make stage assumptions, or we may be more apt to formulate incremental theories. Our theories may be broad in scope, attempting to integrate all the data we've collected, or they may be simple hypotheses, focused on particular aspects of the facts. In formulating a theory, we should meet certain criteria. First, the theory must be *comprehensive*, that is, either it must take into account all of the known facts (for a broad theory) or at least it should not be inconsistent with any of the known facts (for a more simple, focused hypothesis). Second, it must be presented with sufficient clarity that we can make *verifiable predictions* from it.

A note of caution here: It is important to recognize that by definition, a theory or hypothesis is an *inference* rather than an observed fact. Statements about causes are always inferences, because causal relationships cannot be directly observed. We can obtain evidence for them—as you will see in the next step—but we cannot actually *prove* them without a doubt.

Verification

The gathering of evidence for our theories, or **verification**, is the third step in scientific method. Verification processes provide means of judging theories *objectively,* on the basis of factual support, rather than *subjectively,* on the basis of how appealing they might be or how well they might fit our biases. At this point again, the scientist turns to research. It is not good enough for a theory to be effective at post hoc explanation, that is, comprehensively explaining the facts we already have. To be really convincing, a theory must generate predictions about events or behaviors that have not yet been observed. Research is designed to test those predictions. If they come true, there is evidence to support the theory. If the predictions fail to come true, there is evidence against the theory. Albert Einstein's theory of relativity revolutionized physics, posing relationships among known facts and suggesting causal processes not previously proposed. It was appealing because it helped explain some findings that had not fit with previous theories. But, like any scientific theory, Einstein's view had to pass the litmus test; could it predict events not previously observed? Despite the abstractness of his principles, the theory did succeed in generating a few predictions about concrete events that had not yet been observed, and these predictions did come true. Thus, Einstein's idea now has the status of being not just a creative explanation of known data, but a theory with supporting evidence.

Suppose, however, that we formulate a theory that sounds good, but its predictions do not come true. Or, as more often happens, some of its predictions come true, and some do not. Or, even more disconcerting, the predictions of our theory come true, but so do the predictions of a very different theory to explain the same phenomenon! This is a situation that drives many students of a science, and allied practitioners, to distraction: scientists providing more than one answer to the same question!

There is a scientific approach to resolving such dilemmas. The next step is to go back to the explanation process, taking the new data we have gained from our verification efforts to craft a new, or at least a modified theory. Then we move forward again to the verification process. Science advances in this fashion, taking the evidence (both pro and con) gathered from testing one theory to help develop a better one, then subjecting the new theory to the same rigorous tests, until eventually we have a theory that encompasses all the known facts and can generate valid predictions.

In our everyday lives, all of us sometimes operate a little like scientists. Suppose there is a phenomenon that concerns us. Perhaps a close friend begins to behave erratically, laughing or grunting inappropriately during conversations, having animated discussions with no one at all, acting irritable or becoming strangely silent. Our first step in confronting this problem is somewhat comparable to the scientist's *description* process. We try to

gather more facts about our friend's behavior from coworkers, family, and friends, and we make more observations of our own. Our second step is similar to the scientist's *explanation* process: We try to develop a coherent theory that will explain how these facts fit together and why they are happening at all. Perhaps we hypothesize a schizophrenic breakdown or the onset of a degenerative brain disorder. At this point, however, our approach to our friend's behavior will probably lose its resemblance to the scientific process. Scientists would put all action on hold, make predictions from their theories, and proceed to test the predictions in carefully designed studies (see *Testing Theories Scientifically*). In our everyday lives, however, we are more likely to jump into practical application, such as urging the family to seek medical help. We rarely have the time or the resources to actually verify our theories in systematic ways. We simply act on them and hope that we've made the right guesses. Scientists advance more slowly to action, avoiding practical application until theories are strongly supported by evidence.

Helping professionals, too, use a process closely akin to scientific method if they follow the tenets of reflective practice. First, as in the scientist's description process, they gather all the information they can about a client and the client's problem. This part of reflective practice includes examining theories and information available from scientific work that might be relevant, as well as considering both standard practices for dealing with similar problems and the practitioner's own experiences. From all of this information, the practitioner formulates hypotheses about the client and about the most appropriate clinical strategy (as in the scientist's explanation process) and then "tests" these hypotheses (as in the scientist's verification process). However, for the practitioner, testing hypotheses occurs in the practice itself, so that, unlike the scientist, helping professionals apply and adjust their hypotheses in the context of practice. In sum, scientifically generated knowledge informs clinical practice not by providing *answers* but by providing *options* for the development of hypotheses that can be tested in application and by suggesting strategies for handling problems.

Testing Theories Scientifically

To understand how scientific research is done, let's consider examples of studies aimed at testing one hypothesis drawn from behaviorist theories in the middle of the last century. The hypothesis was an effort to explain why babies become both more positively responsive to their mothers over time (e.g., smiling more to them than to other people) and why babies seem to become more unwilling to be cared for by others, especially strangers. The argument was that if babies get most of their nurture from their mothers, mothers are rewarding babies' positive social behaviors (smiling and vocalizing) along with babies' more negative help-seeking behaviors (crying). The result, in this view, is that babies *both* learn to behave more socially around their mothers *and* they begin to rely more and more on their mothers to take care of their needs. We will refer to the combination of positive social behaviors and help-seeking as infants' "dependency."

The proposal that "nurturance causes infant dependency" is a simple theory or hypothesis. "Nurturance" is the single postulated cause, or **causal variable**, and "infant dependency" is what is said to be affected by the cause, or the **outcome variable**. Some theories are much more complex, posing more than one cause, suggesting interactions among causes, or speculating about effects on more than one outcome variable. But regardless of how complex a theory becomes, it can be verified only by testing its predictions. There are two general techniques for testing the predictions of any theory—**experiments** and **correlational studies**. These techniques can be as complex as the theories that inspire them, but no matter how complex they become, they are only extensions of the basic experimental or correlational procedures that we will now describe.

Experiments

An experiment is a study in which the researcher purposely changes (or manipulates) the causal variable in order to observe or measure the effects of the manipulation on the outcome variable. In a good experiment, the researcher also takes care that nothing else systematically changes at the same time as the causal variable. This ensures that if the outcome variable does seem to be affected, only the postulated causal variable could be responsible. When a scientist succeeds in eliminating alternative explanations for the changes in the outcome variable, we say that the researcher has exercised *control* over other, possible causes.

When proposed causes of human behavior are put to experimental test, psychologists use standard procedures adapted to the study of people. Rheingold (1956) conducted an experiment to test the hypothesis we have framed as "nurturance causes infant dependency." She studied babies in an orphanage, whose many caregivers usually had time only to meet basic physical needs. Rheingold increased babies' nurturance from a single caregiver (the causal variable), and she measured babies' dependency with that caregiver (the outcome variable). However, she needed to be sure that no other changes in the babies' lives could account for any observed change in the babies' dependency over time. If Rheingold were studying inanimate objects, she might have been able to make certain that nothing else changed at the same time that she changed the causal variable. But with human infants, it was not possible to simply keep everything else from changing. In most studies with humans, researchers simply do not have that much power. For example, the babies' nurturance was increased for a 8-week period. But during this period the babies changed in age as well, a process that could not be stopped. There may also have been other, less obvious changes in the babies' experiences. For example, the orphanage could have contracted to buy baby formula from a different vendor, so that the taste and quality of the babies' food could have changed. Rheingold exercised control over all of these alternative explanations of the outcome not by preventing them from changing, but by using a **control group**.

The control group was a second group of babies from the same orphanage nursery who experienced all of the "unstoppable" changes that the first group of babies (the experimental group) experienced: They got older in the 8 weeks of the study, and if anything else in the nursery changed, such as the baby formula, it changed for them, too. However, Rheingold did not make any changes to nurturance for these babies. Over time, the experimental group babies showed more positive social behaviors to the primary caregiver as expected, although their negative help-seeking behaviors did not increase. The control group babies showed no change in dependency behaviors, even though they experienced everything that the experimental group babies did except for increased single-caregiver

nurturance. Only the change in nurturance could have been the cause of greater dependency in the experimental group babies.

Experiments with humans usually "control" causes other than the postulated causal variable by incorporating control groups to which the experimental group can be compared. The experimental group is defined as the group for which the causal variable is purposely changed. The control group is a group like the experimental group in every way except that the causal variable is not purposely changed. Chemists and other scientists who study the inanimate, physical world need not use control group procedures, but psychologists need this technique because, either for practical or ethical reasons, they cannot necessarily prevent other possible causes from changing during the course of an experiment.

Correlational Studies

Sometimes, both in psychology and in other sciences, predictions cannot be tested using experiments. Remember, in an experiment, the researcher purposely changes the causal variable. But what if the researcher does not have the power to change the causal variable? In some sciences, such as astronomy, this is usually the case. Suppose an astronomer hypothesizes that "meteor showers cause temperature increases in the outer atmosphere of planet X" (a hypothesis invented by a textbook author who knows little about astronomy). To do an experiment, the astronomer would have to manipulate the occurrence of meteor showers (the causal variable) and then observe or measure atmospheric temperature (the outcome variable) to see whether it also changes. But astronomers cannot (at least at the present time) manipulate the occurrence of meteor showers, so such an experiment could not be done. The alternative, in such a case, is to do a *correlational study,* a technique in which both the causal variable and the outcome variable are measured or observed, and nothing is actually manipulated by the researcher. The research question is, do the two variables change together in the ways predicted by the hypothesis? In this astronomical example, the prediction is that the more intense a naturally occurring meteor shower is, the greater the temperature increase in planet X's atmosphere will be.

A correlational study can determine whether changes in the causal variable are matched by predicted changes in the outcome variable. What a correlational study *cannot* do is tell us whether the changes in the causal variable actually determined the matching changes in the outcome variable. For example, an astronomer would not know if some other variable might also have changed when the meteor shower occurred. If it did, the other variable might actually have caused the increased temperature of planet X's atmosphere. Only experiments, with proper controls, can tell us whether the postulated causal variable is the real cause. But when the predictions of a theory come true in a correlational study, it is still evidence *for* the theory that made the prediction, because the results are consistent with the theory. And, when the predictions do not come true, it is still evidence *against* the theory, because the results are inconsistent with the theory.

Correlational studies are usually done in the social sciences when experiments are either impractical or unethical. Consider again the hypothesis that "nurturance causes infant dependency." Rheingold was able to purposely change the amount of nurturance orphanage babies received from a single caregiver because she was able to supply the personnel, and no one considered the changes unethical. But if Rheingold had wanted to change the nurturance of babies being cared for by their own parents, it is unlikely that the parents would have considered that reasonable. Parents have their own ideas about the nurturance their babies should get. For this reason, when Ainsworth and her colleagues (e.g., Ainsworth, Bell, & Stayton, 1972; Ainsworth, Blehar, Waters, & Wall, 1978) wanted to look at the relationship between maternal nurturance and infant dependency, they did a correlational study. They asked parents only to allow them to watch the nurturing process. Over a period of many months, they observed and measured mothers' nurturance of their infants (the causal variable in this hypothesis) and also measured infants' dependency (the outcome variable in this hypothesis). The hypothesis predicts that the more nurturance that mothers give their babies, the more dependent the babies become. This would be a **positive correlation**: The two variables would change in the same direction, either both increasing or both decreasing. Just as with Rheingold's study, the prediction came true only in part. By late infancy, babies whose mothers had provided the most nurturance were more positively responsive to their mothers, but they were *less dependent* than other babies with regard to help-seeking behaviors. For example, they cried less frequently. So there was a negative correlation between mothers' nurturance and these dependency behaviors. That is, the variables of nurturance and infant help-seeking changed in opposite directions, so that as one increased, the other decreased.

When theories are tested, mixed findings like Rheingold's and Ainsworth's are typical. No single study, either an experimental or correlational study, is ever a sufficient test of a theory. Theories become more convincing as the stockpile of supporting evidence grows. If the evidence is mixed, it's time to go back to the drawing board and consider how to change or replace this theory in order to explain all of the findings. As we saw in Chapter 4, the studies of nurturance and dependency just described have led most researchers to prefer a more complex explanation of their relationship, now referred to as "attachment theory."

A Special Case: Studying Age Effects

Suppose we have a theory that some behavior or skill changes with age, for example, "In adulthood, aging causes declines in intelligence." We can use only correlational studies to test hypotheses where age is the causal variable, because age is not something that a researcher can directly change or manipulate. So age is observed, and the outcome variable (such as intelligence in this hypothesis) is observed or measured. However, age can be observed in three different ways, and each method has its own advantages and disadvantages.

Cross-Sectional Studies

In **cross-sectional studies**, different ages are represented by different groups of people. For example, a group of 20-year-olds might represent young adults, a group of 40-year-olds might represent middle-aged adults, and a group of 70-year-olds might represent older adults. Then all the subjects would be measured for the outcome variable (such as intelligence). When age and intelligence have been examined in this way, typically intelligence scores have declined with age as our sample hypothesis predicts.

But in cross-sectional studies, what look like the effects of age could be the result of *cohort* differences. Participants in each age group belong to a cohort: They were born in the same historical period, and they grew up at about the same time. People in different age groups belong to different cohorts. When it appears that age is causing some change, such as a decline in intelligence, the change could be the result of other differences among the cohorts. For example, educational approaches and opportunities may have changed dramatically from the time that today's 70-year-olds were kids to the time that today's 40-year-olds were kids, and these changes in education may be the cause of their differences in measured intelligence. Age may have nothing to do with it!

Longitudinal Studies

Some researchers study age and its effects by doing **longitudinal** research. Only one group of subjects, all the same age, participates. They are measured several times as they get older. For example, in place of the cross-sectional study we just described, we could do a longitudinal study testing the intelligence of one group of participants several times throughout their lives, starting when they were all 20 years old.

This kind of design eliminates cohort differences because only one cohort is included. In longitudinal studies of overall intelligence, no declines are usually found until after age 50 or 60, and many individuals show increasing scores through much of adulthood, indicating that the steady declines in intelligence often observed in cross-sectional studies are due to cohort effects (see Chapter 13 and 15).

But longitudinal studies have their own disadvantages. First, they can take so long that the original researchers are retired or dead before the studies are completed! Second, age is not the only thing that could be causing the observed changes. Cultural changes could also be a cause of what look like age changes. For example, medical care and nutrition improved dramatically after World War II. If subjects in our imaginary longitudinal study have benefitted from such improvements, they may actually enjoy greater mental alertness as older adults than they did when they were young, helping them to perform better in a testing situation even though other elements of intelligence have not actually improved and may even have declined as a function of age.

Take heart, however, because there is a way to combine the advantages of both cross-sectional and longitudinal studies that helps to isolate the effects of age.

Sequential Studies

A **sequential** study is like a cross-sectional study in that more than one cohort is included, and it is like a longitudinal study in that each cohort is measured at more than one age. Suppose again that we want to know if intelligence changes with age. We might include three cohorts in our study. Let's say one cohort, born in 1930, is measured at age 60 and again at 70; the second cohort, born in 1940, is measured at ages 50 and 60; and the last cohort, born in 1950, is measured at ages 40 and 50. All subjects are measured in the years 1990 and 2000. Our study will be 10 years long, but we will have information on whether intelligence increases or decreases over each 10-year age period from age 40 to age 70. The subjects who were born first may not have intelligence scores as high as those born later, but we are examining increases or decreases with age, not absolute scores. And cultural changes will be uniform for all cohorts because they are all being measured at the same times. Cultural changes could still explain results if all groups change the same way from the first to the second testing, but if there are improvements in some cohorts and declines in others, these differences cannot be explained by cultural change and are more likely the result of age.

Qualitative Research Methods

Qualitative research methods afford the developmentalist another, less traditional way of doing research. **Qualitative research** has been defined as "any kind of research that produces findings not arrived at by means of statistical procedures or other means of quantification" (Strauss & Corbin, 1990, p. 17). This definition appears to allow for many types of methodologies and techniques and may seem somewhat ambiguous. One way to clarify the concept is to view qualitative research as a way of answering questions not readily answerable by quantitative methods. For example, qualitative studies can be aimed at providing rich descriptive information about some concept or experience that is not well understood. Rather than using tests or other assessment instruments, the qualitative researcher may choose to interview the participants, make observations, or gather life histories. Although one of the purposes of this kind of research is to build theory, the actual data are not analyzed and tested as in more traditional methods. Instead, the data are the "voices" of the participants, who are allowed to speak for themselves. The data are not categorized according to any predetermined scheme but are allowed to evolve in novel ways. Consider, for example, the question of how middle-aged men cope over time with the death of a spouse when adolescent children are still in the home. A researcher may legitimately choose to study this topic using standardized questionnaires or interviews in an effort to categorize the fathers according to various established typologies of coping behavior. In contrast, a qualitative analysis would probably involve extensive, ongoing interviews without a predetermined typology or way of categorizing the fathers and would allow a "theory" of fathers' coping styles to build over the course of the project.

Daniel Levinson's study of the stages of a woman's life represents a good example of a qualitative research project (Levinson & Levinson, 1996). Using methods he called biographical interviewing and biographical reconstruction, he studied 45 women in order to learn about "the nature of women's development and about specific life issues relating to friendship, work, love, marriage, motherhood, good times and bad times, the stuff life is made of" (pp. 7–8). Levinson's intensive work with these participants resulted in complex, descriptive narratives that provided a framework for a theoretical construction about women's life trajectories.

Qualitative research approaches differ from more traditional methodologies in a number of ways. First, the data, as we have indicated, consist primarily of the words and actions of participants instead of numerical scores or frequencies. Second, the design of a study may change as the study progresses and the "data" are collected and considered. Third, a qualitative researcher may appear to be less objective than the more traditional researcher and may write about the study in a narrative style. Sometimes the data are reported in the first person. Fourth, no hypothesis is used to guide the study. However, a research question identifies the topic of the project, as in "How do middle-aged men, with adolescent children, cope with the death of a spouse?" Other differences exist as well, but these are some of the primary ones. Despite these differences, qualitative and traditional (quantitative) research methods share some similar features. Both approaches can be descriptive and have theory building as their goal (see *Understanding the Scientific Process*). Most importantly, perhaps, both maintain their own rigorous standards for reliability and validity (Lincoln & Guba, 1985).

Qualitative and quantitative methods can enhance each other by approaching a problem from more than one direction. A number of years ago a consortium of editors of developmental psychology journals endorsed the importance of qualitative methods and encouraged researchers to use them in their research projects. They argued that quantitative tools alone "cannot reveal the complex processes that likely give rise to normal and abnormal behavior among different children and adolescents" (Azar, 1999, pp. 20–21).

Caveat Emptor

Helping professionals rely on research to inform their practice with children, adults, and families, and they may be faced with choices about which interventions would be most effective and in which circumstances. Contemporary practice guidelines encourage the use of empirically supported treatments and interventions (Chambless & Ollendick, 2001). Although many programs and practices are advertised as "research based," this term may sometimes be applied loosely and inaccurately, especially when those making the claim do not show any supporting documentation. Helping professionals should be aware that empirically-supported treatments need to be shown more effective than a placebo in at least two well-designed and well-controlled studies (or in a large number of single-subject studies). The studies must be carried out using a treatment manual that provides a framework for intervention and allows for replication by others. Reputable research support for interventions can usually be found in published studies that have been subjected to rigorous peer review. The process of review by peers within the research community assures that the reported findings are legitimate and that they have passed the test of scientific research. Such care provides a means of quality control for helping professionals and others who are consumers of scientific research.

Glossary

academic self-concept: One of two divisions of children's general self-concept, referring to sense of self as an achiever in school subjects. Can be further divided into specific school subject areas such as math, science, English, and social studies.

acceptance: A reaction to impending death that is characterized by a sense of peace and relative tranquility, suggesting that one has come to terms with the inevitable.

acceptance factor: An aspect of parental responsiveness that includes being affectionate, praising the child, being involved in the child's life, and showing concern for the child's needs; correlated with children's self-esteem and social adjustment.

accommodation: In Piaget's theory of cognitive development, the adaptation process by which existing knowledge structures are modified somewhat when an individual is exposed to new information.

achievement: One of Marcia's four identity status categories characterizing individuals whose development has been marked by exploration and then commitment to certain alternatives. Persons in this category have constructed their identity by their own efforts to shape and transform their earlier selves.

achieving commitment: An alternative name for Marcia's "achievement" that is used by Meeus and colleagues, because it emphasizes the dynamic linkage between high levels of commitment and high levels of exploration.

achieving stage: In Schaie's theory, the stage of cognitive development when a young adult must apply her intellectual skills to the achievement of long-term goals, carefully attending to the consequences of the problem-solving process.

acquisition stage: In Schaie's theory, the time in cognitive development (during childhood and adolescence) when an individual is sheltered from the majority of life's responsibilities and can learn a skill or a body of knowledge regardless of whether it has any practical goal or social implications.

active euthanasia: Injection of a medication by someone else that causes immediate death.

activity level: The intensity and quantity of movement an individual displays; one aspect of infant temperament.

actuarial prediction: Predicting an individual's outcome based on group characteristics, such as predicting how likely an individual is to suffer a heart attack based on the frequency of heart attacks in large samples of people with similar characteristics (same age, gender, socioeconomic status, etc.).

adaptation: In Piaget's theory of cognitive development, the process by which the human mind constructs its knowledge, both assimilating new information to existing knowledge structures or understandings, and accommodating those structures to create a better fit to what is new.

adolescence-limited antisocial pattern: A developmental pattern of adolescent antisocial behavior that develops in adolescence and usually ends shortly thereafter.

adolescent growth spurt: Corresponding with puberty, a rapid increase in size accompanied by changes in the shape and proportions of the body.

adolescent-onset or late-starter model: A developmental pathway of antisocial behavior that begins in adolescence and is not likely to result in adult criminality. Although serious, it seems to be reflective of a difficult or exaggerated reaction to the adolescent period.

adolescing: The process of advancing with age, improving or growing.

adrenal glands: Situated at the top of the kidneys, these glands are important in the stress system. They respond to ACTH (released by the pituitary when threats are perceived) by producing cortisol. They also produce epinephrine and norepinephrine as part of the stress reaction. Adrenal glands are also involved in androgen production.

adrenarche: The point just before puberty when the adrenal gland increases its activity and children begin to show sexual attraction.

adrenocorticotropic hormone (ACTH): A hormone, released into the bloodstream during the body's response to stress, which prompts the adrenal glands to release "stress hormones."

Adult Attachment Inventory (AAI): A structured interview in which adults describe their memories of the parenting they received and their evaluation of whether and how that parenting influenced their own development. Based on coding of the verbatim transcripts, adults are categorized as having one of four attachment styles: autonomous (secure), dismissing (insecure), preoccupied (insecure), and unresolved (insecure). The security of an adult's attachment style tends to be correlated with the attachment security of his or her own infants.

advance directives (living wills): Statements, typically in writing that describe a person's wishes regarding treatment in the event of incurable illness.

age-graded changes: Changes to which a person must adapt that are strongly age determined, such as physical changes.

agency: In cognitive functioning, the ability to act without an external trigger or to engage in self-motivated behavior. In social-emotional functioning, a constituent of generativity that involves generating, creating, and producing things, ideas, people, events, and so on as powerful extensions of the self.

agreeableness (A): One of the Big 5 personality traits that is described using synonyms including *warm, sympathetic, generous, forgiving, kind,* and *affectionate.*

alleles: Different forms of the same gene, such as the many forms of the eye color gene.

allostatic accommodation: The dynamic stress process that allows for adjustments to be made within a range of possibilities across a variety of systems to suit the circumstances. The process finds the best balance possible, rather than returning to a fixed set point.

allostatic load: The physiological wear and tear on the body that results from ongoing adaptive efforts to maintain stability (homeostasis) in response to stressors.

allostasis: "Balance through adaption." In this model of stress processes, the central nervous system (CNS) controls multiple interacting regulatory processes so that the best balance for each specific challenge is found, rather than returning to a fixed set point.

Alzheimer's disease (AD): A brain disease that leads to dementia. Becomes more prevalent with age. Extensive brain changes including the development of plaques and tangles lead to the common symptom characteristics of the disease including absentmindedness, confusion, language and memory problems, disorientation, and problems with physical coordination. The eventual outcome is death.

amygdala: A brain structure that influences motivation, emotional control, fear responses, and interpretation of nonverbal, emotional expressions.

amyloid precursor protein (APP): Protein produced by a gene that is found in the brain, spinal cord, and other organs. Mutations in the gene alter APP and are implicated in early-onset Alzheimer's disease (AD) and plaque formation.

anal stage: In Freud's theory, the second of psychosexual stage, beginning in the 2nd year of life, when the anal area of the body becomes the focus of greatest pleasure. During this stage, parenting practices associated with toilet training that are either overcontrolling or overindulgent could have long-lasting effects on personality development.

androgens: Male hormones, produced in the testes that contribute to the development of male reproductive organs and may affect some aspects of brain development.

andropause: A decline in testosterone production in men as a function of age.

anger: A type of coping mechanism experienced by one nearing death that is a normal reaction to separation and loss. May be directed toward God, toward others, or toward the disease itself.

antisocial behavior: Behavior characterized by the presence of aggression or the intent to harm another person. More broadly may include such acts as risky sexual activity, substance abuse, defiance, cheating, lying, and vandalism.

antisocial personality disorder: A personality disorder used for adult diagnosis that is characterized by antisocial behavior of long duration. APD is often preceded by serious conduct problems in childhood and adolescence.

Anti-Mullerian hormone (AMH): A hormone produced in the testes during prenatal development which causes the deterioration of the Mullerian ducts, which otherwise would develop into fallopian tubes, uterus and part of the vagina.

anxious ambivalent: An attachment category describing babies who show a great deal of distress on separation from their mothers, and who may act angry when reunited with the mother, alternately approaching and resisting her, or who may respond listlessly to her efforts to comfort. They seem preoccupied with their mothers and rarely return to exploration after a separation.

anxious arousal: A state that children are thought to experience when parents discipline them. Hoffman proposed that mild forms help a child pay attention to the parent's socialization message, but more intense arousal attracts the child's attention to other concerns, like their own fear.

arthritis: A debilitating disease common in the elderly that is characterized by the onset of pain, stiffness, and swelling of joints and surrounding tissues.

assimilation: In Piaget's theory of cognitive development, the process of interpreting new stimulation or information as fitting with what one already knows, sometimes distorting the new information as a result.

association area: A part of the cortex that is not a "primary" area involved in vision, hearing, sensory, or motor functions. Integrates information coming from the various primary cortical areas and appears to be important for complex cognitive functioning.

attachment theory: According to Bowlby, the infant and his primary caregiver(s) participate in an interactive system that has evolved to keep the infant safe and ensure survival. As the infant changes cognitively and emotionally, an affectional bond with the caregiver emerges in stages, with a full-fledged attachment likely by about 7 or 8 months.

attention deficit hyperactivity disorder (ADHD): A disorder that is characterized by one or more of a cluster of symptoms that are especially problematic for school performance: poor attentional control, restlessness or hyperactivity, and impulsivity.

attention-persistence: Length of uninterrupted orienting or attention to a single activity and tendency to return to a task after interruption; an aspect of infant temperament.

attribute substitution: A process involving imitation and identification in which adolescents need to borrow and "try on" various behaviors and attributes that they observe in others, because the state of frameworklessness leaves them without clearly defined ways of behaving and thinking.

atypical depression: Atypical depression has many of the typical characteristics of depression, but individuals with atypical depression are likely to show improvements in mood with positive experiences. Also characterized by weight gain and sensitivity to interpersonal rejection.

authoritarian style: An interactive parenting style that combines low levels of warmth (cold emotional climate) with high levels of control or demandingness. Associated with negative emotional tone, poor social skills, and other negative outcomes in children.

authoritative style: An interactive parenting style that combines high levels of warmth (affection, sensitivity and responsivity) with moderate to high levels of control or demandingness. Associated with many positive child outcomes.

autism spectrum disorder (ASD): Developmental disorder that is diagnosed early (typically around age 3). Children on this spectrum are characterized by difficulties in social development, showing impairments in the basic skills necessary for building a theory of mind: joint attention, imitation, and the turn-taking routines needed to cement solid interpersonal relationships. A variety of other symptoms, including impaired language development, mental retardation, special cognitive skills, physical awkwardness, and so on, characterize some children on this spectrum. Generally, even children with good language facility have problems with the pragmatics of language and with communicating effectively with others.

autobiographical memory: What we remember of our own history of experiences, including representations of who we have been at various points in the past. Largely synonymous with episodic memory.

autonomic functions: A set of bodily functions, such as those involving the organ systems, that is outside an individual's conscious control.

autonomous (secure): An attachment category characterizing adults who provide an Adult Attachment Inventory transcript that is coherent and collaborative. They integrate and monitor their thinking, summarize answers, return the conversation to the interviewer, demonstrate good perspective-taking skills, acknowledge the importance of attachment-related experiences in their development, and tend to have children who are securely attached.

autonomous stage: Stage of moral development described by Piaget that begins in middle childhood. Children now understand that rules are based on social agreements and can be changed.

autonomy: In Ryan and Deci's self-determination theory, one of three basic or universal needs. Being in control of oneself, or feeling that one's behavior is congruent with one's "true self," meaning that it is intrinsically motivated.

autonomy versus shame and doubt: The crisis faced in the second of Erikson's "Eight Stages of Man," in which the 1- to 3-year-old child may develop feelings of autonomy ("I can do things myself") or of shame and self-doubt, depending on whether his caregiver strikes the right balance between exercising control and being sensitive to the child's new need for independence.

autosomes: The 22 of 23 pairs of chromosomes in humans that are matched (they look and function alike).

average: A sociometric category that includes those children who receive an average number of positive and negative nominations from their peers (near the mean for the group on social preference and social impact).

avoidant: An attachment category describing babies who typically fail to cry when separated from their mothers in a strange situation test. They actively avoid or ignore her when she returns, sometimes combining proximity seeking and moving away, but mostly turning away and often appearing unemotional. In Bartholomew's typology of adult attachments, a category that is subdivided into two types (dismissing and fearful) based on the individual's reports of felt distress.

axon: A long extension, projecting from the cell body of a neuron, which is like a cable attached to a piece of electronic equipment. Electrical impulses travel from the cell body through the axon toward synapses with other neurons.

axon terminals: Structures found at the ends of axons, which contain tiny sacs of neurotransmitters.

babbling: Infant vocal sounds, usually beginning around 6 months of age, consisting of repeated consonant-vowel-consonant sequences such as "bababa" or "doodoo-doo." By 9 months of age, they tend to be limited to the sounds permissible in the baby's native language.

bargaining: A reaction to impending death that serves as an attempt to postpone an inevitable death by making promises, usually to a divine other, or trying to delay death until some memorable event has taken place.

basic emotions: Those core affects that have old neurobiological underpinnings. According to Izard, they include joy/happiness, interest, sadness, anger, disgust and fear.

basic trust: In Erikson's theory of personality development, an infant's ability to see others as dependable and trustworthy as a result of caregiving that is timely, sensitive to the infant's needs, and consistently available.

behavioral facilitation system: Neural system that regulates approach behaviors, response to incentives, positive affect, and psychomotor activity.

behavioral inhibition: In late infancy and childhood, a tendency toward shyness, manifested as avoidance or distress in new situations. This trait is linked to high reactivity (including irritability in response to new sensory stimulation) in early infancy.

behavioral inhibition system: Neural system that regulates withdrawal and avoidance behaviors.

behaviorist tradition: Approaches to explaining learning in which behavioral change is seen as a function of chains of specific environmental events, such as those that occur in classical and operant conditioning.

Big 5: See *five factor model of personality.*

binge drinking: Drinking many drinks in a row.

bidirectional processes: Reciprocal relationships between causal mechanisms. Factors that result in developmental change often moderate each others' influence. For example, genetic influences are moderated by environmental processes and vice versa.

bipolar disorder: An affective disorder that is generally characterized by episodes of mania or hypomania, sometimes alternating with episodes of depression.

bisexuality: A characteristic of individuals who have interest in sexual relations with partners of both sexes.

body image: The concept of, and attitude toward one's physical appearance.

borderwork: Interactions between boys and girls during middle childhood when there appear to be unwritten rules governing when and how the two genders will interact.

brainstem: A set of lower brain structures that include the medulla, pons, and midbrain.

broad socialization: Socialization that permits and encourages high levels of individual freedom of expression, has few social constraints, expects less community responsibility, and thus tolerates a wide variety of socially deviant behaviors.

Bronfenbrenner's bioecological theory: A comprehensive developmental model proposed by Bronfenbrenner that takes into account the many levels of influence the environment can have on an individual. The interacting systems in this model are the microsystem, the mesosystem, the exosystem, and the macrosystem.

"the bump": A salient feature of self-memories, also called the "reminiscence bump." Regardless of age, adults' cue-prompted memories of the self from the young adult period (ages 18–22) are slightly but reliably overproduced.

cannot classify: An attachment category characterizing adults who may have psychiatric disorders and who do not fit in any of the other four attachment style categories.

career consolidation (vs. self-absorption): A life stage that Vaillant added to Erikson's sequence of stages, characterizing the mid-20s, when in addition to ongoing intimacy concerns, one becomes concerned with making a commitment to work that brings personal satisfaction, regardless of its other rewards, rather than just having a job.

carrier: Someone with a gene that is unexpressed in his phenotype but can be passed on to offspring.

causal variable: The postulated cause of a given phenomenon.

central sulcus: A fissure in the cerebrum that is used to locate the parietal lobe, which sits behind this fissure.

centration: A characteristic of preoperational thought in which the child tends to focus on one salient feature of an experience or event at a time.

cerebellum: A brain structure located in the hindbrain that is involved in the planning, coordination, and smooth operation of complex motor activities.

cerebral cortex: The outer layer of the gray matter of the cerebrum, which is the highest and most recently evolved portion of the brain.

cerebrovascular accident (stroke): A cardiovascular problem in which an artery serving the brain is either clogged or bursts.

cerebrum: The highest brain structure, comprising two thirds of the forebrain, and coordinating most other brain activity. Involved in higher brain processes like thinking, language, decision-making, and so on.

child centered: Describes caregivers who set aside their own needs (for time and convenience) to meet a child's developmental needs.

chromosomes: Forty-six tiny strands of DNA, found in the nucleus of each cell of the body, which are the source of biological inheritance.

chunking: The cognitive process of linking several pieces of information together into a single meaningful unit, such as remembering the digits 1, 7, 7, and 6 by thinking of the year 1776.

circuits: Series of neurons that are joined via their synaptic connections into groups and are part of larger organizations of neurons.

classical conditioning: A process by which a change in behavior takes place when a neutral event or stimulus is associated with a stimulus that causes an automatic response. As a result the neutral stimulus causes the person to make the same automatic response in the future.

climacteric: The gradual reduction of reproductive ability in women usually beginning in their late 30s when the menstrual cycle begins to shorten and become somewhat more erratic as a result of a reduction in the amount of circulating estradiol.

cliques: Voluntary social or friendship groups of three to nine members characterizing children in early to middle adolescence.

closed commitment: Meeus and colleagues' alternative name for Marcia's "foreclosure." It signifies an identity with a high level of present commitment and low levels of coexisting exploration.

closed identity domains: Areas of identity in which individuals tend toward foreclosure because they have little control over them.

coaction: The intricate pattern by which genes and environment mutually influence one another. The activity of the genes is affected by the environment of the cell that is affected by other levels of the environment including the outside world. One result is that the same complement of genes produces different outcomes in different environments. Also, the same environment can have different effects on outcomes when interacting with different genes.

code switching: Shifting from one form or style of speech to another depending on context, such as shifting from using slang with friends to using more polite forms with authority figures.

codominance: A type of relationship between two alleles of the same gene (located at matching sites on a pair of chromosomes) in which neither allele is suppressed, producing a blended outcome.

coercive family interaction: Patterson's description of how children learn to act aggressively. Aggressive children respond to parental demands by behaving aversively (whining, etc.), parents retreat, rewarding the child's noncompliance, and parents are reinforced with short-lived peace and quiet. Children are trained in the effectiveness of aggressive noncompliance and learn powerful parent-control strategies.

cognitive flexibility: The ability to readily shift one's way of thinking about a problem, categorizing material, or responding

to a situation when the more practiced or typical way of dealing with the situation is not effective or appropriate.

cohort: A group of people who were born in the same historical period and grew up at about the same time.

cohort effects: Also called history-graded events, they are events that provide a context for development and also influence it directly. The year of your birth marks your entry into a cohort of peers who accompany you through age-graded developmental changes within the context of a specific set of historical events.

collaborative or affiliative speech: A type of speech, more often used among girls, in which children's responses are keyed to what someone else has said, expressing agreement or making further suggestions, often in the form of a question rather than declarative or imperative sentences.

collective egocentrism: Peer influences on maintaining risky behavior; each adolescent's illusion of invincibility strengthens that of the other members of the peer group.

commitment: An element of love that refers to making a decision to sustain a relationship with a loved one.

commitment foreseen: Position 6 in Perry's model in which thinking incorporates not only respect for diverse ideas and understanding of their rationale, but also the individual's affirmation of what it is she believes in, all the while knowing that reason will never provide absolute proof that her ideas or perspectives are right or better than others.

committed compliance: Describes toddlers' eager and enthusiastic willingness to go along with parental requests. Predicts measures of internalization and conscience in the later preschool period.

communion: A constituent of generativity that is expressed in the adult's desire to care for the next generation, even to the point of sacrificing her own well-being for the good of those who will follow.

compatibility: A standard for mate selection in which one chooses a potential mate based on how his or her personality meshes with one's own personality.

compelling circumstances: Conditions that mitigate the guilt of a criminal defendant because he or she faced such pressure when the crime was committed that even an ordinary, reasonable person could be expected to have acted in the same way, such as acting in the face of extreme need or under threat of injury.

compensation: A process that contributes to successful development. When a loss of some kind prevents the use of one means to an end, the individual finds another means.

competence: In self-determination theory, feeling effective in one's interactions with the social environment and experiencing opportunities to exercise and express one's capacities.

complicated or abnormal grief: A response to bereavement that is generally accompanied by other disorders such as major depression, substance abuse, or post-traumatic stress disorder that is intense and lasts for an extended period of time, greatly interfering with functioning. Abnormal grief may also be marked by a complete absence of grief and the total inability to experience grief reactions.

compulsive caregiving: Describes a behavioral pattern in which children (usually insecurely attached, avoidant children) take emotional care of their parents.

compulsive self-sufficiency: Describes a behavioral pattern in which children (usually insecurely attached, avoidant children) appear very self-possessed, perhaps related to experiences of shaming for expressions of dependency or needs for closeness.

concordance: Similarity in some trait or behavior between members of a twin pair.

concrete operational stage: In Piaget's theory of cognitive development, the period from about age 6 to 12 when children begin to think logically but have difficulty applying logical thought to abstract contents.

conditioned response: In classical conditioning, when a neutral stimulus has been conditioned to produce an automatic response. For example, if an animal hears a tone (neutral stimulus) every time it eats, it may begin to salivate (conditioned response) automatically when it hears the tone.

conditioned stimulus: A formerly neutral stimulus that has become associated with a stimulus that causes an automatic response, thus causing the same automatic response in the future.

conduct disorder (CD): A pattern of serious behavior problems that violate the basic rights of others, such as stealing, aggression, or property destruction. Presently, this diagnosis requires a persistent pattern of aggression in youth.

conferred identity: The identity attained by those who are foreclosed (individuals who make commitments with little or no exploration of alternatives).

confirmation bias: When a child's peers have already developed schemas or constructions for him that are built on his social reputation, the interactions with the target child that follow are marked by attention to evidence that confirms the target child's characteristics.

congenital adrenal hyperplasia (CAH): A gender-atypical condition in which biological females with two X chromosomes are exposed to high levels of androgens (male hormones) during prenatal and postnatal development.

conscience: An internalized slate of standards and principles that constitutes a person's primary guide to action. May cause feelings of discomfort or distress when the violation of a rule is contemplated or carried out.

conscientiousness (C): One of the Big 5 personality traits that is described using synonyms including *organized, planful, reliable, responsible, careful,* and *efficient.*

consolidation: In Super's theory, achievement of advanced status and seniority in the workplace that often accompanies the maintenance stage.

constructed identity: The identity not based upon a predetermined set of expectations, but rather representative either of a personal redefinition of childhood and early adolescent goals and values or perhaps something very different from them.

constructivist: An approach to explaining the acquisition of knowledge (e.g., in Piaget's theory). Constructivist theories assume that individuals actively create their own knowledge by interpreting new information in light of prior learning and by restructuring prior knowledge, or by co-constructing knowledge in interactions with others. Individuals are not seen as passive receptors of information who acquire knowledge via external manipulations.

contextual relativism: Position 5 in Perry's model that represents a major achievement in intellectual development because the student now possesses analytic abilities that allow her to appreciate the merits of diverse perspectives and to find convincing elements in multiple points of view. Thinking relativistically, or thinking about knowledge in context, becomes more habitual.

contingency management system: Presenting and withdrawing reinforcers and punishments in a systematic and consistent way to effect behavioral change.

control dimension (parental demandingness): One of two major features of parenting style. The degree to which parents impose discipline, requiring their children to curb some of their behaviors and to perform other behaviors that are suitable to their level of maturity.

control: According to Craik and Bialystock (2006), similar to fluid intelligence, this refers to the way the brain works with information.

control group: In experimental design, a group like the experimental group in every way except that the causal variable is not purposely changed.

controversial: A sociometric category that identifies a relatively small group of children who receive many positive and many negative nominations from peers (high social impact, average social preference).

conventional morality: Kohlberg's second stage of moral reasoning in which what is right depends on others' approval or on the need to maintain social order.

conventional rules: Social rules of conduct that vary from one culture to another and are a function of social agreement, such as rules about appropriate dress, forms of address, and table manners.

corpus callosum: A network of fibers that connects the right and left cerebral hemispheres of the brain. Its maturation from early childhood through adolescence contributes to coordination and integration of information and aids in the development of consciousness.

correlational studies: Often utilized when experiments are impractical or unethical, a technique in which both the causal variable and outcome variable are measured or observed, and nothing is actually manipulated by the researcher. Such studies can determine whether changes in the causal variable are matched by predicted changes in the outcome variable, but they cannot determine whether changes in the causal variable *caused* the changes in the outcome variable.

corticotrophin releasing hormone (CRF): A hormone produced by the hypothalamus

that stimulates the pituitary gland to release adrenocorticotrophic hormone (ACTH)

cortisol: A hormone, released during the body's response to stress, that increases blood glucose levels and affects the immune response.

counting all strategy: Rudimentary addition strategy of young children. For example, given the problem of adding 2 plus 3, holding up two fingers on one hand, three fingers on the other hand and counting all of them.

counting on strategy: Addition strategy of young children. For example, given the problem of adding 2 plus 3, starting at 2 and counting three more digits on from there.

critical period: A certain time frame in which some developments, such as first language learning, must take place or the opportunity is missed.

cross-fostering study: Research that involves separating animal offspring from their biological mothers to be reared by mothers with different genetic or behavioral characteristics in order to assess the effects of biology and environmental factors separately.

cross-sectional studies: A study design in which different ages are represented by different groups of people as opposed to one group of people over time.

crowds: Large, reputation-based groups, composed of numerous cliques that form in early to midadolescence.

crystallization: In Super's theory, the formulation of general vocational goals in the early part of the exploratory stage.

crystallized intelligence (pragmatics): The compilation of skills and information we have acquired in the course of our lives that can be viewed as the software programs of our nervous system.

culture: Shared traditions, attitudes, values, and beliefs handed down from one generation to the next.

cytokines: These chemical messengers are produced by the body as part of its immune response. These proteins can either promote inflammation or reduce it.

cytoplasm: The jellylike substance that fills a cell between its outer membrane and its nucleus. Cytoplasm comprises an array of organic structures (organelles) and chemicals.

daily hassles: Category of stressor that is chronic and cumulative in its effect.

day reconstruction method (DRM): Method of research in which participants revive memories of a previous day, describe the days' experiences, and rate affective valence of experiences.

deacetylation: An epigenetic change that makes the expression of a gene less likely. It involves the removal of an acetyl group (an organic molecule) from the histones that bind with DNA and results in tightening the binding, typically decreasing transcription of a gene.

décalages: Within-stage variations in Piaget's cognitive stage theory. Children sometimes show more advanced or less advanced functioning in one or another cognitive domain than is typical of their overall stage of development.

decathecting: Detaching emotionally from the relationship one had experienced with a loved one prior to their death and reinvesting psychic energy into the formation of new attachments.

decentration: A characteristic of concrete and formal operational thought in Piaget's cognitive theory. Attending to multiple pieces of information (or multiple aspects of a situation) at one time; a necessary ingredient in logical thinking.

declarative knowledge: Knowledge about facts (semantic information) and events (episodic information).

decline stage: In Super's theory, just before and after age 65, when one's career winds down, retirement is planned and takes precedence over career advancement and consolidation.

deferred imitation: Imitation in which children observe the actions of another on one occasion, and then imitate those actions sometime later. In order to do so, the child must be able to recall the observed actions.

degrouping: A general decline in the importance of cliques over the course of the high school years.

delayed phase preference: A shift in sleep patterns characterized by staying up later in the evening and sleeping later in the morning than younger children that has been associated with hormonal changes at puberty.

demand characteristics: Behavioral tendencies that often either encourage or discourage certain kinds of reactions from others.

dementia: Cognitive functioning that is so severely impaired that it negatively affects ability to relate to others and to manage one's own daily activities.

demethylation: An epigenetic change that makes the expression of a gene more likely. It involves the removal of a methyl group (an organic molecule) from either a coded gene or from regulatory DNA. Or, it can involve the removal of a methyl group from histones that bind with DNA.

democracy factor: An aspect of parental responsiveness. The degree to which parents encourage children's psychological autonomy by soliciting their opinions or encouraging self-expression. Related to children's self-reliance, self-confidence, willingness to work hard, and general competence.

dendrites: Small projections that grow out from a neuron's cell body; they receive transmissions from other neurons.

denial: A type of defense mechanism for dealing with stressful events, such as approaching death, associated with feelings of numbness or disbelief that buffers the person from the full weight of the threat.

deoxyribonucleic acid (DNA): A complex organic substance that comprises chromosomes and genes.

depressed mood: A subclinical level of depression.

depression: A pattern of symptoms that include depressed mood, sadness, feelings of hopelessness, and loss of pleasure or interest in formerly pleasurable activities (also called *clinical depression* or *major depressive disorder*). In clinical usage,

various subtypes of depression have been identified and all cause significant impairment in functioning.

description: The first step in the scientific method, aimed at answering factual questions about a phenomenon, such as who, what, when, where, and with whom.

despair: The third phase in the grieving process characterized by great sadness; social withdrawal; sleeping, eating, or somatic disturbances; and other symptoms of depression or emotional upset.

developmental psychopathology: A relatively new and influential field that has applied a developmental focus to the study of abnormal behavior and dysfunction.

diathesis: Underlying predispositions to some disease or abnormal condition.

diathesis-stress: Model for the development of psychopathology that assumes a genetic predisposition (diathesis) that confers particular sensitivity to environmental risk (stress). See also, *genetic vulnerability*.

differential emotions theory: Izard's view that facial expressions in infants are the direct manifestation of underlying neural processes related to the emotion expressed. For example, a sad expression implies the operation of the neural circuitry associated with sadness, so that if a baby looks sad, he is sad.

differential susceptibility: Some physiological makeups can make an individual more likely to be affected by environmental influences than other people. For example, a child with a highly reactive temperament might be benefited more than other children by positive parenting but harmed more than others by negative parenting.

differentiation: The process by which a global skill or activity divides into multiple skills or begins to serve multiple functions.

difficult babies: A temperament type described by Thomas and Chess. These babies are fearful, irritable, active, display low levels of positive affect, are irregular in biological rhythms, and so on, making them more challenging to care for than other babies.

diffusion: One of Marcia's four identity status categories that often describes young adolescents as they embark on the identity development process. The individual is not actively involved in exploring possible life choices, nor has she made any firm commitments to them.

digit span tests: A test of working memory in which a series of digits are presented and the participant must repeat them in the correct order.

diminished capacity: One source of mitigation in adult criminal law. A guilty actor is considered less than fully blameworthy because of some deficiency at the time of the offense. Perhaps he was mentally ill, emotionally distressed, or intellectually impaired.

discipline: The tendency of parents to limit or demand behavior by exerting or requiring control.

discordance: Dissimilarity in some trait or behavior between members of a twin pair.

disenchantment: The second stage of retirement, when people begin to experience an

emotional "letdown" as they face the day-to-day realities of the change, such as separation from work colleagues, uncertainties about how to feel competent and in control, a sense of diminished generativity and meaningfulness, new tensions that may arise with one's partner, financial concerns, and perhaps, boredom.

dishabituation: After habituating to one stimulus, an infant may show reinstatement of the orienting response if the stimulus is changed. This response is dishabituation and indicates that the baby has noticed the difference between the original stimulus and the new stimulus.

disillusionment model: The view that posits that overly romantic idealizations of marriage and blissfully optimistic views of one's partner set people up for eventual disappointment.

dismissing (insecure): An attachment style characterizing adults whose Adult Attachment Inventory transcripts provide little detail and coherence. They may describe their parents positively but provide either no evidence or contradictory evidence. They downplay close relationships and tend to have children who are in the avoidant attachment category. In Bartholomew's typology, these individuals prefer self-sufficiency and maintain a sense of superiority while devaluing the importance of others to their well-being.

dismissive parenting: Also called neglecting, a parenting style that describes parents who are essentially disengaged, scoring low on both responsiveness and demandingness.

disorganized-disoriented: An attachment category describing babies who produce contradictory and even bizarre behaviors in the strange situation test, showing both an inclination to approach the mother when stressed and a tendency to avoid her when she approaches.

distal processes: Factors outside the immediate external environment, including internal forces (genes) and external forces (features of the educational system or of the broader culture), which modify the proximal processes in Bronfenbrenner's bioecological model and other multidimensional theories.

distraction: A coping style that involves deliberate focusing on neutral or pleasant thoughts or engaging activities that divert attention in more positive directions. Distraction can attenuate depressive episodes.

dizygotic (fraternal) twins: Twins who develop from two separate zygotes. Their genotypes are as similar (or different) as any two siblings.

domain of knowledge: A specific subject matter, such as mathematics or chess or history.

domain specific: Describing a level of knowledge or skill that has been achieved in one subject area but not in others, such as being able to think logically about math but not about baseball or biology.

dominant-recessive: A type of relationship between two alleles of the same gene, in which one allele is expressed whereas the other is suppressed.

domineering or power-assertive speech: Discourse containing many commands and restrictions. Tends to be "egotistic," ignoring others' remarks, and often includes threats and interruptions, more typical of males than females.

dopamine: A neurotransmitter and a hormone that serves many functions in the body. As a neurotransmitter, it is involved in several brain processes, including reward systems. Low levels of dopamine production are associated with Parkinson's disease.

dose–response relationship: With regard to problem behaviors in children, mothers who experience fewer stressors during pregnancy tend to have children with fewer internalizing or externalizing problems later, whereas mothers with higher levels are more likely to have children with more problems later.

double effect: Giving medication intended to relieve pain even though there is a chance that death can result.

double standard: The idea that female sexual behavior is judged more harshly than male sexual behavior.

Down syndrome (Trisomy 21): A disorder caused by an extra copy of chromosome number 21 and often characterized by mental retardation, flattened facial features, poor muscle tone, and heart problems.

downward social comparisons: Comparing oneself to less competent or less successful peers when one's own self-esteem is at stake. Such comparisons protect the individual from negative self-evaluations.

dual-process model: The model that proposes that bereaved individuals simultaneously engage in two kinds of coping mechanisms, approach and avoidance, that wax and wane over the course of grieving.

dyads: A social unit or "group" that consists of two people.

early-starter model: One developmental pathway to antisocial behavior. Oppositional behavior begins in early childhood, persists and diversifies over time, and becomes increasingly more serious.

earned secure: An attachment style characterizing adults who in Adult Attachment Inventory transcripts reveal experiences of early adversity, describe their painful backgrounds truthfully, acknowledge the stressors their own parents faced, and come to terms with their early experiences. Their children are usually securely attached.

easy babies: A temperament type described by Thomas and Chess. These babies are placid, not very active, show positive affect, and are regular in their rhythms, making them easier to care for than other babies.

ecobiodevelopmental (EBD): Describes the view that psychosocial problems affect the functioning of both mind and body, and thus should not be seen as substantially different from other biological impairments.

effortful control: The inhibition of a compelling response that is "dominant" or preferred (e.g., eating dessert) to perform a response that is less compelling (e.g., complying with a diet). Plays a role in regulating or modulating emotional reactions.

ego: In Freud's personality theory, the second of three aspects of personality, which represents the rational, realistic self that seeks to meet bodily needs in sensible

ways that take into account all aspects of a situation.

egocentric speech: Speech for self, a use of language typical of preschoolers that has no apparent communicative function. Piaget suggested that it serves no useful purpose, but Vygotsky argued that it is the precursor of inner speech and important for problem solving, planning, and self-control.

egocentrism: A failure to recognize one's own subjectivity. One fails to see things realistically because one is, in a sense, trapped in one's own perspective, and cannot imagine that others may have a different perspective on the same situation.

ego identity: Includes all the dimensions of self-knowledge and serves as the foundation for the behavioral, affective, and cognitive commitments to career, relationships, and political and religious belief systems that will be made in adulthood.

Ego Identity Interview: A standardized, semistructured interview designed by Marcia to assess these core domains of identity: vocational choice, religious beliefs, and political ideology, gender-role attitudes, and beliefs about sexual expression through first asking general questions and then following up with more specific probes. Supplemental domains may include hobbies, friendships, dating relationships, role of spouse, role of parent, experiences at school, and issues of work–family balance.

ego integrity (vs. despair): In Erikson's theory, the result of life review in the elderly. Integrity is a sense that one's own life is "something that had to be," and had order, meaning, and dignity. Despair is a sense of hopelessness, that one's life has no coherence or meaning.

elaboration strategy: A memory strategy that requires finding or creating some kind of meaningful link between to-be-remembered items, such as creating a story that includes all the items.

elaborative style: A style that characterizes some adults' conversations with children about past experiences. Adults using this style engage in lengthy discussions providing lots of details, asking questions and encouraging children to provide details as well.

elastin: A substance in the cells of the dermis, or middle layer of skin, that allows the skin to stretch and contract as we move.

Electra complex: In Freud's theory, the belief that young girls direct their sexual urges toward their fathers, even though they are more strongly attached to their mothers, because they experience penis envy. Young girls find themselves in competition with their mothers, although their fear of their mothers' displeasure is not as great as a young boy's because they assume that somehow they have already been castrated. The girl will identify with her mother to make peace and, therefore, become gender typed in her behavior and form a superego.

embryo: After conception, the fertilized egg travels down the fallopian tube to the uterus, increasing in size. Once the growing organism attaches to the uterine wall (implantation) it is called an embryo.

emerging adulthood: The time period from about 18 to 25, which is characterized by the shift toward increasing independence and autonomy.

emotion schemas: Mental experience that includes feelings, memories, thoughts, images, and noncognitive elements like hormonal shifts that interact with and may amplify a basic emotional experience.

emotional intelligence: The ability to perceive emotions, to identify and understand their meaning, to integrate them with other kinds of cognition, and to manage them.

empathy: "Feeling with" another person, recognizing her emotional condition and experiencing what she is assumed to be feeling.

end-of-life care: Principles that support more humanistic approaches to aiding individuals nearing death including better pain management, continuity of care, and attention to the psychological dimensions of death and dying.

endocrine system: A system of ductless glands that secrete their hormones directly into the bloodstream; responds to messages from the hypothalamus.

endophenotypes: Biobehavioral processes that are intermediary between the actual genes that contribute to disorders and their expressed behavioral manifestations.

endorphins: Biochemical substances produced by the body under conditions of stress or vigorous exercise that serve to alleviate pain.

English language learner (ELL): A term used to describe school children in the United States from immigrant families for whom English is a second language. Many have little or no exposure to English prior to entering school.

entity theorists: A theory of intelligence usually held by individuals who show a helpless pattern and who see intelligence or ability as a fixed, concrete thing.

epigenesis: The control of genetic expression by both regulatory DNA and environmental factors.

epigenetic model: A type of multidimensional or systems theory, which assumes that development is the result of complex interactions between genetic and environmental factors. Developmental change is bidirectional with the environment influencing biology and biology influencing the environment.

epigenetics: See *epigenesis.*

epigenome: The full set of factors, from DNA to outside world that controls the expression of coded genes.

epinephrine: Also called adrenaline, it is a substance that is both a hormone and a neurotransmitter. One place it is produced is in the adrenal glands as part of the body's response to stress. Among its effects is increased heart rate.

episodic: Description of knowledge of the events that one has experienced. This knowledge is organized around time and space.

Erikson's psychosocial stages: Erik Erikson's eight-stage model of personality that focuses on explaining attitudes and feelings toward the self and others. The first five correspond to the age periods in Freud's psychosexual stages, whereas three adult life stages suggest that personality development continues until death.

escape: Perry's characterization of the behavior of individuals who revert to relativism when the demands of commitment are too stressful.

establishment stage: In Super's theory, the final stage in the development of vocational self-concept (about 25 to 44), when work experiences provide the laboratory within which the matching of vocational self-concept and job settings is tried out, sometimes reevaluated, sometimes confirmed, and eventually stabilized.

estradiol: A form of the primary female hormone, estrogen, produced by the ovaries.

estrogen: A feminizing hormone that is produced by the ovaries in females and to a lesser extent by the testes in males.

ethnic group: People who share cultural traditions, attitudes, values, and beliefs that have been handed down through generations.

ethologists: Biologists who do careful observations of animal behavior in natural environments.

ethnicity: People are considered to share ethnicity when they have a common ancestry, language, and place of origin, as well as a sense of belonging to the same group.

eudaemonic well-being: A term synonymous with psychological well-being.

executive stage: In Schaie's theory, a stage that some middle adults experience who take on executive functions at work and in the community that extends beyond the responsible stage. This stage requires one to focus heavily on learning about complex relationships, multiple perspectives, commitment, and conflict resolution.

exosystem: In Bronfenbrenner's bioecological model, the level of the environment that children may not directly interact with but that influences them nonetheless.

experience-dependent: Describes neural growth that is stimulated by environmental experiences and may vary from one individual to another.

experience-expectant: Describes neural growth that requires a certain kind of environmental stimulation that is almost certain to occur in the experience of most members of a species. An example is development of the visual system that requires exposure to light in order to occur.

experience sampling method (ESM): A research technique in which participants are interrupted at random times during the day and asked to report on what they are doing, thinking, and feeling.

experiments: A technique for testing the predictions of a theory in which the researcher purposely manipulates the causal variable to observe the effects of the manipulation on the outcome variable.

explanation: The second step in the scientific method, when the researcher frames a theory or set of hypotheses about how the facts gained from descriptive research are related to each other and why they occur.

exploratory play: Play that involves manipulating objects, checking out their properties, sorting and/or organizing them. Through exploratory play, children can learn about object properties, spatial relations, numerical relations, categorical relations, and so on. Begins in infancy.

exploratory stage: In Super's theory, the second life stage in the development of vocational self-concept from about 14 to 24, in which vocational self-concept is tentatively narrowed down, but often career choices are not finalized.

externalizing problems: Problem behavior that involves engaging in inappropriate conduct, especially aggressive acts.

extraversion (E): One of the Big 5 personality traits that is described using synonyms including *outgoing, active, assertive, energetic, talkative,* and *enthusiastic.*

false belief tasks: Tasks in which one person has correct knowledge of a situation, but another person (or the same person at another time) has incorrect knowledge, or a "false belief." Used to test children's theory of mind, specifically their understanding of others' mental states.

family life cycle: A normative, stage-like sequence of traditional family developments in intact marriages as partners become parents, rear and launch their children, become "empty nesters," and subsequently face old age.

fast mapping: The rapidity with which young children add new words to functional vocabulary after only one or two exposures.

fearful: In Bartholomew's typology of adult attachment categories, a subcategory of avoidant attachment. Describes individuals who have negative models of both self and others and who see relationships as desirable but out of reach. Their desire for close relationships with others is thwarted by fear of rejection, and ultimately they withdraw. A high level of distress surrounds attachment themes.

fearfulness or reactivity: In infants, proneness to crying or pulling away from new sensory stimuli.

fetal alcohol effects (FAE): Symptoms, usually in the form of cognitive impairments, affecting babies who do not have the physical or structural problems of fetal alcohol syndrome (FAS) but who were exposed to small amounts of alcohol prenatally.

fetal alcohol syndrome (FAS): A condition found in babies who are exposed to alcohol prenatally. It is characterized by a unique facial configuration (small head, widely spaced eyes, flattened nose) as well as possible mental retardation and behavioral problems.

five factor model of personality (Big 5): The five most basic dimensions of personality including neuroticism (N), extraversion (E), openness (O), agreeableness (A), and conscientiousness (C).

flashbulb memories: Recollections that are especially vivid and personally relevant because of the emotions associated with them.

fluid intelligence (mechanics): Basic operational characteristics that seem to directly reflect how well the "hardware" of the nervous system is working. Its functions include such things as processing speed and inhibitory mechanisms.

follicle-stimulating hormone (FSH): Hormone that stimulates the gonads.

forebrain: The largest and most recently evolved portion of a mammalian brain; includes the cerebrum.

foreclosure: One of Marcia's four identity status categories that describes individuals who make commitments with little or no exploration of alternatives. They incorporate the values and goals of significant others without reflection.

forgotten half: The name given to 18- to 24-year-olds who do not go to college.

formal operational stage: In Piaget's theory of cognitive development, a stage that begins at about 11 or 12 years, when children are able to engage in thinking that (1) rises above particular contents and focuses on relationships that govern those contents (abstractions), (2) involves coordinating multiple relationships, and (3) can be difficult even for adults.

"four horsemen of the apocalypse": The four kinds of negativity that do the most damage to relationships and that are highly predictive of divorce. They are criticism, defensiveness, contempt, and stonewalling.

frameworklessness: A state of instability and anxiety unique to adolescents. This state is a result of the body changing in appearance, the emergence of adult sexual needs, hormonal shifts, the expanding capacity to reflect on the future and the self, and increased maturity demands.

Freud's psychosexual stages: The five developmental stages that Freud believed were initiated by changes in the id and its energy levels.

friendship skills: Behavioral skills, such as appropriate assertiveness, good communication, and conflict resolution that maintain and enhance friendships.

friendship understanding: A child's changing knowledge of what friendship implies.

friendship valuing: Emotional attachment or investment that a child makes in a friendship.

frontal lobe: The part of the cerebrum that is situated at the top front part of each hemisphere and controls voluntary muscle movements and higher-level cognitive functions such as planning, goal setting, and decision-making.

gender atypical: Individuals who have either ambiguous genitalia or genitalia that is inconsistent with their sex chromosomes.

gender constancy: Recognizing the permanency of one's gender category membership and understanding that it could never change.

gender identity: The awareness of one's own gender assignment and understanding of its meaning.

gender intensification hypothesis: A hypothesis that suggests that one way young teens cope with the demands of establishing an adult identity is to fall back on stereotyped notions of masculinity or femininity.

gender schema: A network of ideas and expectations of male and female beliefs about male and female characteristics that affect what we pay attention to, what we interpret, and what we remember about events.

gender stability: The understanding that over time, one's gender category stays the same: Boys grow into men, girls grow into women.

gender stereotypes: The beliefs and expectations that individuals have concerning the different behavioral tendencies and distribution of personality traits between the sexes.

gene expression: The process by which DNA information is transmitted and translated to cells.

gene regulation: The promotion or inhibition of gene transcription. Intergenic DNA and an array of factors in the cellular environment and beyond are involved in gene regulation.

general adaptation syndrome: The way that organisms respond to threats to their well-being. The response has three phases: alarm, resistance, and exhaustion.

generalization: The process by which learned behaviors may be extended to new events that are very similar to events in the original learning context.

generativity: A motive or need that can be filled through one's vocation or avocations, through child rearing, or through community service. It includes productivity and creativity. Generativity also describes people who are contributing members of society.

generativity accomplishment: A sense of satisfaction in making a meaningful contribution.

generativity desire: Expression of generativity goals, such as caring for future generations, wanting to produce something of lasting value, and being concerned about being needed.

genes: Functional units or sections of DNA that provide a blueprint or code to the cell for how to produce proteins and enzymes. Found on chromosomes, they come in matching pairs, one from each parent.

genetic counselors: People who help screen candidates for testing that would help determine the risk of genetic disorders for their offspring. Genetic counselors provide information and support to prospective parents regarding their choices about testing, childbearing, and parenting.

genetic vulnerability (diathesis-stress): A physiological makeup (diathesis) that makes an individual more prone to the negative effects of unsupportive parenting or other negative environmental influences (stress) than other people.

genital stage: The fifth and last of Freud's psychosexual stages, when the changes of puberty mean that id energy is especially invested in adult sexual impulses.

Genital tubercle: A prenatal structure in both male and female fetuses. In males, it becomes the penis as a result of effects of circulating androgens. In females, it becomes a clitoris.

genomic imprinting: A process in which some gene alleles in the sperm or the ovum are deactivated. Imprinted gene alleles do not influence the phenotype of the offspring.

genotype: An individual's genetic endowment, including both expressed and unexpressed genes.

germinal period: The first two weeks of pregnancy, beginning at fertilization and ending at implantation in the uterine lining.

glia: Supporting cells in the central nervous system that provide a type of scaffolding for the neurons.

globalization: The process by which, as a result of international communication, transportation, and trade, countries around the world influence one another's lifestyle, economics, and culture, so that similarities among nations increase along with interaction.

glucocorticoid: A set of hormones referred to as "stress hormones," such as cortisol, that play a role the body's reaction to stress.

gonads: Testes in males and ovaries in females. Produce eggs (ova) in females and sperm in males. Increase their hormone production at puberty after being stimulated by hormones released from the pituitary gland in response to the maturing hypothalamus.

gonadotropin releasing hormone (GnRH): Substance released in the brain that triggers a hormonal cascade related to activity of the reproductive system.

goodness of fit model: Thomas and Chess's view that when adults provide care that is adjusted to the temperament of an infant or child, even difficult early temperaments are unlikely to lead to later adjustment problems.

grief work: A process that explicitly encourages bereaved individuals to confront and "work through" their feelings about loss for recovery to take place.

growth: Developmental change or adaptation to the constant flux of influences on our lives that involves adding new characteristics, understandings, skills, and so on to our behavioral repertoire.

growth stage: In Super's theory, the first stage in the development of vocational self-concept lasting until about age 14. Many elements of identity develop in this stage including ideas about their interests, attitudes, skills, and needs.

guided imagery: A technique used to aid memory of an event or person. For example, a child might be asked to pretend that an event occurred, then create a mental picture of the event and its details.

habituation: A decrease in an infant's responses to a stimulus over time, including decreased looking, decreased sucking, a return to a resting heart rate, and so on.

habituation paradigm: A research technique that takes advantage of a baby's tendency to orient to new stimulation and to habituate to repeated or old stimulation. Once an infant habituates to one stimulus a new stimulus can be presented. The baby's reorienting to the new stimulus (or failure to do so) reveals whether or not she perceives or notices the differences between the stimuli.

heart rate regulation (HRR): Also called heart rate variability. Heart rate accelerates on the in-breath and decreases on the out-breath. Higher rates of heart rate variability between in and out breaths during respiration is a mark of health and efficient operation of the vagus nerve. Lower rates of heart-rate variability, referred to as low vagal tone, suggest that an individual is chronically mobilized to respond to perceived threat.

hedonic well-being: A term synonymous with subjective well-being.

hedonistic: Preschool-aged children's tendency to be more concerned about their own needs than those of someone else in need.

helpless pattern: An orientation to failure in which individuals begin to denigrate their abilities when they encounter failure and typically stop applying themselves or trying to improve their performance.

hemispheric specialization: The two symmetrical halves of the cerebrum process information from and control opposite sides of the body. They also control some different higher cognitive functions, with the left hemisphere largely responsible for language and the right hemisphere largely responsible for visual-spatial skills.

heteronomous stage: Stage of moral development described by Piaget characterizes children from about ages 5 through 8, when they regard rules as immutable, existing outside the self, and requiring strict adherence.

heterosexuality: A sexual preference for partners of the opposite sex.

hidden object test: A research technique invented by Piaget to assess object permanence in infants from 6 months old. An interesting object, like a small toy, is placed in front of a baby within her reach. As the baby watches, the experimenter covers the object so that it is out of sight. If the baby searches for the object under the cloth she demonstrates that she has a sense of the continued existence of absent objects.

hierarchical integration: The organization and integration of activities and skills from one stage of development into broader, more complex patterns at the next stage.

hindbrain: The part of the mammalian brain that evolved first. Includes the medulla, pons, cerebellum, and reticular formation.

hippocampus: The region of the forebrain that plays a role in emotions, the ability to remember, and the ability to compare sensory information to expectations.

histones: Proteins that wrap around DNA to help form chromosomes.

history-graded changes: Changes in our life experience that are a function of historical circumstance, including events that we share with our whole cohort.

homeostatic steady state: A stable state maintained over time by a couple's unique balance of positive and negative elements in areas of interactive behavior, perception, and physiology.

homeostasis: A stable state maintained by reflexive, physiological feedback loops, primarily controlled by lower-level brain areas that balance internal systems around a fixed set-point, something like a thermostat. Sometimes used to describe the body's response to stressors.

homogamy: A standard for mate selection in which one chooses a potential mate based on her or his similarity to oneself in religion, SES, race, education, and so on.

homophily: A degree of similarity among members of a peer group on behavior or attitudinal attributes of importance.

homosexuality: A sexual preference for partners of one's own sex.

honeymoon: The earliest stage of retirement, when people focus on the pleasures of being free from the constraints of old schedules, dress codes, and other work demands.

hospice movement: A patient-centered approach for people suffering from terminal illness that emphasizes the importance of giving patients as much knowledge about their condition as possible so that they maintain some control over their care, and focuses not on curing disease but on managing symptoms and pain by means of palliative medicine.

hostile attributional bias: A tendency to interpret or perceive what is neutral behavior as threatening. Often characterizes aggressive individuals.

Huntington's chorea: A lethal genetic disorder, usually beginning between 30 and 40 years of age, that causes the nervous system to deteriorate, leading to uncontrolled movements, increasingly disordered psychological functioning, and eventually death. Because the dominant, defective alleles causing this disorder do not have their effects until after the childbearing years, it continues to be passed from one generation to another.

hypothalamic-pituitary-adrenal (HPA) axis: The system involved in the body's physical response to stress. When a person experiences or anticipates stress, the amygdala detects the danger and informs the hypothalamus, which communicates the danger to the pituitary gland, which responds by releasing adrenocorticotropic hormone (ACTH) into the bloodstream. ACTH causes the adrenal glands to release the hormones epinephrine, norepinephrine, and cortisol, which travel back to the brain and prepare the body to resist the stressor.

hypothalamus: The brain structure that plays a role in emotions, ability to remember, and ability to compare sensory information to expectations.

"I" or self-as-subject: The part of the self that is an active agent or is the knower. The part of the self that experiences a sense of subjective self-awareness.

id: In Freud's personality theory, one of three aspects of personality. Represents the biological self and its function are to keep the individual alive. It is irrational, blindly pursuing the fulfillment of physical needs or "instincts," such as the hunger drive and the sex drive.

ideals: Imagined, logically organized, perfect systems (such as political systems or persons) that do not match reality.

identification: Trying to become like another person by both imitating the model's behaviors and internalizing her attitudes, standards, and values.

ill-defined or ill-structured problems: Problems faced in adulthood that lack pre-established answers. The "right" answer to an ill-defined problem may be different depending on circumstances and on the perspective of the problem solver.

imaginary audience: An individual's mistaken assumption that others are as

intrigued by and concerned about him as he is. A characteristic feature of adolescents' self-focuses.

immanent justice: The expectation that misbehavior will eventually be punished, even if no one knows about it, as though some higher authority is always watching.

immigrant family: A family in which at least one parent was born outside of the country of residence.

immigrant paradox model: A view that expects children from immigrant families to be more successful than other children of similar SES because immigrant families have strengths or protective factors (such as cultural values) that moderate the risks they face.

immigrant risk model: A view that expects children from immigrant families to be especially vulnerable to academic or social problems because of an accumulation of risk factors, such as low SES, lack of skill with the language of the country of residence, ethnic stereotypes, and so on.

immunosuppression: Suppressed or weakened state of the immune system.

implantation: The process by which a zygote, which has migrated down the mother's fallopian tube into the uterus, becomes attached to the uterine lining.

implementation: In Super's theory, completion of education along with entry into full-time employment that is the final step in the exploratory stage.

incremental models: Theoretical models in which change is considered steady and specific to particular behaviors or mental activities, rather than being marked by major, sweeping reorganizations that affect many behaviors at once, as in stage theories.

incremental theorists: Usually mastery-oriented people who see intelligence as a dynamic and malleable quality that can be increased by hard work and instruction.

indicated prevention: A category of prevention efforts that address individuals who show subclinical symptoms of disorders.

induction: One method parents use to enforce control of children's behavior. Involves use of explanation, giving reasons for rules and appealing to children's desires to be grown-up. The most effective way to promote the internalization of rules.

indulgent parenting: Also called permissive parenting, it is a parenting style that describes parents who are high on responsiveness but low on demandingness.

industry: In Erikson's theory, an aspect of self-concept that develops as a function of the first work experiences in childhood. A belief in one's ability to master the skills and tools needed to be productive and an expectation of pleasure in completion of challenging work.

infantile amnesia: The difficulty people experience remembering events in their lives before they were 3 or 4 years old.

inferior colliculi: Small structures in the midbrain involved in receiving sensory input from the ears.

influence: The process by which a peer group can cause an individual to conform to the norms of the group.

information processing theories: Theories that tend to liken human cognitive functioning to computer processing of information.

initial commitment: Position 7 in Perry's model that, taken together with multiple commitments (Position 8) and resolve (Position 9), suggests a flowering of the commitments anticipated in Positions 5 and 6. Changes in thinking are more qualitative than structural.

inner speech: Internal, subvocal dialogue that in Vygotsky's theory facilitates thinking.

instrumental aggression: Using force or threat to obtain possession of a desired object or goal.

intention: A mental state, such as a plan or a desire that is the source of voluntary action.

intergenerational transmission: When parents repeat with their children the patterns of trauma, rejection, and maltreatment that they experienced as children from their own parents.

internalization: The process by which children adopt adults' standards and rules as their own.

internalizing problems: Problem behavior that involves negative feelings about self and other symptoms of depression.

interneuron: One of two main types of neurons in systems of neurons. These have short projections (e.g., short axons) and affect other cells relatively close to the circuit of which they are a part.

interpersonal orientation: The way an individual characteristically interacts on a social level.

intersensory integration (or intermodal perception): The notion that the senses are already somewhat related very early in infancy, perhaps at birth, and that when babies perceive an object in one way, they can construct some notion of the object's other perceptual characteristics.

intersex: One or more categories of gender identity along a continuum from "male" to "female," based on subtle physical variations (nondimorphism) in internal and external reproductive organs, sex chromosomes, and hormones.

intimacy: A quality of interpersonal relating through which partners share personal thoughts, feelings, and other important aspects of themselves with each other. True intimacy is marked by openness, affection, and trust.

intrapersonal models: Drawing on theories of attachment or personality, this model emphasizes the contribution of one's personal history or temperament to the success or failure of relationships.

invincibility fable: A feeling of being invulnerable, or even immortal that can be part of an adolescent's personal fable.

irritability or negative emotionality: The infant's tendency to cry, squirm, and otherwise react with fussiness to negative or frustrating events. An aspect of infant temperament.

just world: Beliefs that the world is fair and that people in it get what they deserve.

karyotype: A display of the actual chromosomes from human body cells, photographed under a microscope and laid out in matching pairs.

keeper of meaning (vs. rigidity): A stage of life that Vaillant added to Erikson's sequence of stages, characterizing late middle adulthood when the adult expands his generative concerns beyond just making a productive contribution, to actually preserve something that is part of the culture and, in doing so, establish the meaningfulness of the work or contributions he has made.

kindling-behavioral sensitization: Phenomenon characterized by progressive illness severity or illness incidence following an initial illness episode due to increased sensitivity to stressful triggers.

kinkeeper: The person in an extended family who helps the generations maintains contact with one another.

knowledge base: An individual's mentally stored information. Adults generally have a larger base for most domains of knowledge than children do.

kwashiorkor: A condition occurring in children who suffer severe protein and calorie shortages, which is characterized by stunted growth, a protuberant belly, and extreme apathy. Although therapeutic diets can reverse some effects, cognitive impairments are likely to persist.

late multiplicity: Position 4 in Perry's model in which students fully realize that even experts differ among themselves in regard to what is true. Students handle this realization by embracing either the oppositional or relative subordinate response to late multiplicity.

latency stage: The fourth of Freud's psychosexual stages, beginning around age 5, during which the id's energy is not especially linked to any particular pleasure or body part, and the potential conflicts among the three aspects of personality are largely latent and unexpressed.

launching period: The time when emerging adults begin to move away from home and become more self-sufficient.

legacy-leaving stage: In Schaie's theory, a late life stage when the mind is sound but frailty signals that life is ending. Individuals often work on establishing a written or oral account of their lives or of the history of their families to pass on to others.

leptin: Hormone found in fat tissue that plays a role in appetite and eating behavior.

life-course-persistent antisocial pattern: A developmental pattern of adolescent antisocial behavior that begins in early childhood and continues throughout life. This pattern is generally associated with early conduct problems, aggressiveness, and academic difficulties.

life-course perspective: The view that development is influenced by the intersection of chronological age (life time), family-related (family time), and membership in a birth cohort (historical time).

life events: Category of stressor that is discrete, often traumatic, and with a clear onset.

life span development or life span developmental psychology: The study of human development from conception to death.

life span developmental theories or models: A type of multidimensional theory that emphasizes the continuity of developmental processes from birth through death. Developmental change, seen as adaptation, involves proximal interactions between the organism and the immediate context modified by more distal processes both within the individual and in the environment.

life structure: A pattern of relationships between the self and the external world, such as relationships to one's spouse, lover, family, occupation, religion, leisure, and so on.

limbic system: A collection of structures in the brain that includes the hippocampus, amygdala, septum, thalamus, and hypothalamus. These structures produce feelings such as pleasure, pain, anger, sexuality, fear, and affection. Referred to as the "emotional brain" and works in concert with other parts of the brain, such as the frontal lobes.

longitudinal: A study design in which one group of subjects is measured several times as they grow older, eliminating cohort differences.

long-term memory: An almost unlimited mental store of knowledge.

looking-glass self: According to Cooley, a self-concept that develops from the reflected appraisals of others, primarily attachment figures.

loss-focused grief: Confronting the painful reality of death, expressing sadness, and gradually desensitizing oneself to the reminders of loss that can lead to rumination or excessive preoccupation and, often, great distress.

love withdrawal: One method parents use to enforce control of children's behavior. Involves parents withdrawing attention or affection, expressing disappointment or disillusionment with a child, turning away from a child, cutting off verbal or emotional contact, or enforcing separations. Generates high anxiety and elicits immediate compliance.

lowest observable adverse effect level: A level of prenatal alcohol exposure at which a fetus will experience some functional impairment but is not likely to sustain structural malformations.

luteinizing hormone (LH): Hormone that stimulates the gonads.

macrosystem: In Bronfenbrenner's bioecological model, the customs and character of the larger culture that help shape the microsystems.

maintenance hypothesis: The view that couples typically work hard to maintain their favorable beliefs about each other, despite the inevitable challenges of marriage. Positive illusions support the relationship, and people are often reluctant to abandon them to face reality.

maintenance or resilience: In life span developmental theory, a kind of adaptation that involves finding ways to continue functioning at the same level in the face of challenges or to restore one's functioning after suffering some loss.

maintenance stage: In Super's theory, a stage from about age 45 to 64, when an individual makes ongoing adjustments to improve her work situation, often achieving more advanced status and seniority.

making interesting sights last: Occurs when an infant's behavior accidentally produces an interesting event, the child notices the effect, and repeats the action. A precursor to intentional behavior in Piaget's view.

marker events: Events that are used as criteria for adulthood, including completing formal education, entering the adult workforce, leaving the family home, getting married, and becoming a parent.

mastery orientation: An orientation to failure in which individuals move forward optimistically, assuming that they can succeed with further effort. They seem to construe failure as a challenge rather than as an obstacle.

maturity demands: Parents' requirements that children perform behaviors that are suitable to their level of maturity.

maturity gap: A time in adolescence when physical maturity is achieved but social maturity is not. Adolescents may mimic the behavior of more advanced peers to possess the symbolic trappings of adult status (sexual intimacy, material possessions, autonomy, and respect from parents).

means–end behavior: A type of intentional behavior that characterizes infants by 8 to 12 months. Babies divert their attention from a goal, such as grasping a toy, in order to produce another action that will help achieve the goal.

mediated learning: A central concept in Vygotsky's theory. The child's acquisition of knowledge is "mediated" in the sense that it is highly influenced by the surrounding environment and culture.

mediating variables: Intermediate links in a causal chain. For example, if early poverty causes reading problems in school, and reading problems cause later depression, then reading problems serve as a mediating variable.

mediation: In Vygotsky's theory, the intermediary role of other people in determining the meaning of signs and symbols, like words, which in turn affect the child's thinking.

meditation: Family of techniques intended to train attention and improve regulatory functions.

medulla: A brain structure found in the hindbrain that helps to regulate functions that are basic for survival, such as heart rate, blood pressure, and respiration.

melancholic depression: A classification used for a severe form of depression in which the depressive symptoms do not abate when positive experiences occur. Other features include psychomotor and cognitive disturbances, loss of appetite, lack of motivation and excessive feelings of guilt.

"Me" self-concept: The known part of the self that is the object of one's own or others' observations.

memory strategies: Potentially conscious activities a person may voluntarily carry out to remember something.

menarche: A girl's first menstruation.

menopause: The cessation of menstruation that usually begins in the 40s and continues for at least 10 years.

mesosystem: In Bronfenbrenner's bioecological model, the network of microsystems that relate with and modify one another.

messenger ribonucleic acid (mRNA): The organic compound that cells synthesize by copying strands of DNA. The sequence of bases in a gene is replicated in the mRNA, and then the RNA serves as a "messenger" to the cell from the gene, guiding the cell's construction of a protein.

meta-analysis: An analytic tool for assessing the effects of variables in which data from a large number of studies on the same topic are analyzed together to determine which effects are consistent across studies and what the strength of those effects are.

metacognition: The ability to think about and understand one's own cognitive processes and their effects.

method of control: A technique that parents use to enforce control of their children's behavior. The three primary methods are power assertion, love withdrawal, and induction.

methylation: An epigenetic change that makes the expression of a gene less likely. It involves the addition of a methyl group (an organic molecule) to DNA, either to the coded gene or to regulatory DNA. Or, it can involve the addition of a methyl group to histones that bind with DNA.

microsystem: In Bronfenbrenner's bioecological model, the immediate environment where proximal processes are played out.

midbrain: A set of brain structures that are between hindbrain and forebrain and include the superior colliculi, inferior colliculi, and the substantia nigra.

mindfulness: Paying attention on purpose in the present moment with attitudes of curiosity, patience, nonjudgement and openness.

minimum sufficiency principle: Long-term internalization of rules in children is best facilitated by mild power assertion, rather than harsh power assertion.

minority stress: The experience of prejudice and discrimination based on membership in a stigmatized group.

mirror neurons: These neurons are activated both when a person performs a particular action and also when that person observes someone else performing that action. They appear to help with the understanding of others' actions.

mitigation: When the perpetrator of a crime is guilty and is held responsible for the crime but is considered less than fully blameworthy. Mitigation applies not only to degree of culpability but also to degree of punishment.

mitochondria: Small organelles within cells that produce energy for the cell's metabolism and overall function.

mitosis: A kind of cell division that produces two new cells identical to the original cell.

modal personal orientation: In Holland's theory, an aspect of personality that is a typical and preferred style or approach to dealing with social and environmental tasks. Most jobs or careers will be compatible with one of the six orientations: realistic, investigative, artistic, social, enterprising, and conventional.

modeling: See *observational learning.*

moderating variables: Causal factors that interact with other causal variables, altering and sometimes even eliminating the effects of other variables altogether.

monozygotic (identical) twins: Twins who develop from a single zygote and have exactly the same genotype.

morality of caring: A focus on concern for others (as opposed to establishing justice) when making moral evaluations decisions and when evaluating decisions of others.

morality of justice: A focus on establishing justice (as opposed to concern for others) when making moral decisions and when evaluating decisions made by others.

moral rules: The standards used to address fundamental issues of justice, welfare, and rights, such as rules about stealing, hurting others, or sharing. Rules of behavior that are relatively universal as opposed to being culturally based.

moratorium: One of Marcia's four identity status categories in which individuals are actively involved in exploring possible life choices, but not having made any firm commitments to them.

Mullerian ducts: Prenatal structures in both male and female fetuses that can develop into fallopian tubes, uterus and part of the vagina. These are destroyed by anti-Mullerian hormone in male fetuses.

multidimensional theories: A class of theoretical models in which theorists consider development to be the result of the relationships among many causal components. They generally apply to all domains of development from the cognitive to the social and suggest that there are layers, or levels, of interacting causes for behavioral change: physical/molecular, biological, psychological, social, and cultural. These models may also be called transactional, relational, systems, or bioecological models.

multi-infarct dementia: A number of minor strokes that gradually do sufficient damage to cause dementia.

multiple commitments: Position 8 in Perry's model that, taken together with initial commitment (Position 7) and resolve (Position 9), suggests a flowering of the commitments anticipated in Positions 5 and 6. Changes in thinking are more qualitative than structural.

multiplicity (prelegitimate): Position 2 in Perry's model that is characterized by the student's first encounters with multiplicity, that is, multiple ideas, multiple answers to life's questions, or multiple points of view. Individuals in this stage face confusion, yet maintain the belief that some "authority" possesses the ultimate truth or right answers.

multiplicity (subordinate): Position 3 in Perry's model in which the individual grudgingly acknowledges the reality and legitimacy of multiple perspectives. Individuals in this stage find it more difficult to deny that reasonable people can differ in their perspectives on life, and people who hold different views are not so easily dismissed as being wrong.

mutation: A change in the chemical structure of an existing gene, sometimes occurring spontaneously and sometimes occurring due to environmental influences, such as exposure to radiation or toxic chemicals.

myelination: The phenomenon in which glial cells wrap themselves around the axons of neurons, providing an insulating sheath that facilitates the conduction of electrical impulses.

narrative: A story or event description that conveys the full sense of an experience or gets at the point of an event while taking into account what the listener needs to hear to understand.

narrative skill: The ability to tell a coherent story.

narrow socialization: Socialization more characteristic of nonindustrialized cultures that exert extensive control over the expression of behaviors that violate social standards and expect substantial conformity from young members of the society.

needs-based reasoning: Reasoning about other people's needs in which one must weigh one's own personal needs against those of others.

needs oriented: Describes the understanding that another person's need is a good reason for helping, usually characteristic of children sometime in the elementary school years.

negative affectivity: The state or trait tendency to experience nervousness, fear, anger, sadness, contempt, or guilt.

negative affect reciprocity: A tendency for negative emotions in one partner to follow from the other partner's negativity.

negative correlation: A relationship between variables in which they change together but in opposite directions, so that as one increases, the other decreases.

negative reinforcement: Withdrawal of an aversive experience, which serves as a rewarding consequence of a behavior. For example, rewarding your dog for sitting on command by removing a restraining muzzle.

neglected: A sociometric category that includes those children who receive few nominations, either positive or negative, from their peers. Neglected children are characterized by their low level of social impact.

neglecting–uninvolved style: An interactive parenting style that combines low levels of warmth (emotional distance) and low levels of control or demandingness, so that parents invest very little time or attention in a child. Associated with many negative child outcomes.

neoPiagetians: Theorists who explain Piaget's stages or revise the stages using many information processing concepts. These theorists attempt to combine the best components of both Piagetian and information processing approaches.

nerve growth factor: A substance found within the brain that is absorbed by neurons and aids in the process of synapse production.

neural pruning: A gradual process in brain development that continues through adolescence into young adulthood in which neurons die off and many synaptic connections are selectively discarded.

neural tube: A structure that represents the first step in the development of an embryo's central nervous system. It is formed when a sheet of cells from the embryo's upper surface turns inward and curls into a tube.

neurons: The building blocks of the brain, these nerve cells are specialized for the transmission of electrical impulses.

neuroplasticity: The malleability of the human brain, its capacity to change and grow especially in response to new environmental input. Includes the capacity of neurons to shift functions to compensate for damage to other cells or because they have been transplanted to a different part of the brain.

neuroticism (N): One of the Big 5 personality traits that is described using synonyms including *tense, touchy, self-pitying, unstable, anxious,* and *worrying.*

neurotransmitters: Chemical substances found in the nervous system that communicate messages between neurons when released. The chemical message, once picked up by the dendrites, the cell body or the axon of a neighboring neuron, is read by that cell as a message to "fire" or "stop firing."

neurulation: The prenatal formation of a neural tube that begins the development of the central nervous system.

nociception: Processes that allow individuals to experience pain or other noxious stimuli.

no observable effect level: The threshold of alcohol ingestion by a pregnant mother above which the fetus will experience some functional impairment.

nonacademic self-concept: One of two major divisions of a child's general self-concept that includes his view of self in the social, emotional, and physical domains.

noncoded genes: Sections of intergenic DNA that do not code for protein production. They function to either initiate or prevent a gene's transcription.

nondeclarative knowledge: Knowledge that one cannot adequately put into words and might not enter awareness, including procedural knowledge, knowing how to do things.

nonnormative changes: Changes that are expected, such as the death of a family member.

norepinephrine: Also called noradrenaline, it is one of the stress hormones released by the adrenal glands and has no effects on heart rate and other "fight or flight" responses in the body. Also functions as a neurotransmitter.

normative: What is typical or usual in development.

nuclear family tradition: A body of work that examines the outcomes of a person's attachment to his primary caregiver in infancy, once the person becomes an adult.

nucleus: In the brain, a cluster of cells creating a functional structure.

number conservation task: A procedure designed by Piaget to test children's understanding of number. Children must be able to recognize that the number of items in a set does not change when the appearance of the set changes; for example, when a row of buttons is spread out or bunched together.

object concept: Understanding of what an object is, including recognition that an object has properties that can stimulate all of our senses and that an object has "permanence"—it continues to exist even when we do not perceive it.

object permanence: The fact that objects has a separate existence from the perceiver; that is, they continue to exist even when no one perceives them.

observational learning (or modeling): Learning by imitation. Occurs when an individual repeats an act or sequence of actions that she has observed another individual (the model) performing.

occipital lobe: The part of the cerebrum, located at the back of each hemisphere that processes visual information.

Oedipus complex: In Freud's theory, the belief that young boys direct their sexual urges toward their mothers because they are most strongly attached to their mothers as primary caretakers. This desire for the mother, to usurp her time, to be physically close to her, puts a boy in competition with his father for her affections. The boy fears that his more powerful father will retaliate with a physical punishment that fits the crime—castration. The boy is so terrified by the prospect of his father's retaliation that he redirects his energy into pleasing his father by identifying with him.

ontogeny: The development of organisms.

open identity domains: Areas, such as those involving personal relationships, in which individuals assert much control and can be successful in achieving commitment.

openness (O): One of the Big 5 personality traits that is described using synonyms including *creative, artistic, curious, insightful, original,* and *wide-ranging interests.*

operant: An accidental or random action.

operant conditioning: The process by which a person learns to produce a formerly random behavior (or operant) in response to a cue because the behavior was previously reinforced in that situation.

oppositional: In Perry's theory, a response to late multiplicity characterized by legitimizing multiplicity as one pole of a new kind of dualism and the right–wrong dualism of Position 1 (strict dualism) at the other end of the new continuum. Allows individuals to maintain a dualistic either-or structure in their thinking.

oppositional defiant disorder (ODD): A pattern of hostile, negative, or defiant behaviors, such as arguing with adults, spitefulness, or throwing tantrums. One type of conduct problem typically seen in children and youth.

optimization: A process of finding ways to enhance the achievement of remaining goals or finding environments that are enhancing that is key to successful development.

oral fixation: In Freud's personality theory, an excessive need for oral pleasures (such as eating or talking) that results from extreme denial or excessive indulgence of them during the oral stage.

oral stage: The first of Freud's psychosexual stages, corresponding to the 1st year of life, when Freud believed that a disproportionate amount of id energy is invested in drives satisfied through the mouth.

organization strategy: A memory strategy that involves sorting items to be learned on some meaningful basis, such as grouping the names by region.

orienting response: In infants, a set of behaviors that suggest that the baby is attending to a stimulus. May include head turn toward the stimulus, looking, decreased heart rate, and increased sucking.

orthogenetic principle: The notion that as behavior becomes differentiated or elaborated, the multiple behaviors that develop also are hierarchically organized or controlled by higher levels of functioning. For example, with age the generalized distress of newborns differentiates into several different negative emotions, such as anger and sadness, the expression of which is controlled by higher brain processes.

osteoarthritis: The most common form of arthritis, which involves the thinning, fraying, and cracking of cartilage at the ends of bones.

other-directed coping behaviors: Efforts to deal with stress that appear to be aimed at changing the behaviors of others, such as when infants use facial expressions, movements, and verbalizations that seem designed to get a caregiver to respond positively in an interaction.

other-transforming: An immature interpersonal style in which an individual tries to dominate or coerce a friend into meeting his needs. Acting to change or transform the other; can involve bullying, aggression, or manipulation.

outcome variable: The variable that is said to be affected by the cause of a given phenomenon.

ovaries: Female gonads that primarily produce estrogen and progesterone, but also produce lesser amounts of androgens (such as testosterone). Site of egg (ovum) production in females.

ovum: Reproductive egg cell, containing only 23 chromosomes, produced in and released by the ovaries of females.

oxytocin: A neuropeptide hormone that facilitates social bonding.

pair therapy: Selman's approach to treating children and adolescents with social interactive difficulties. Two individuals with equally ineffective social styles, such as a controlling child and a fearful one, meet regularly with a helper who encourages them to be effectively assertive and empathic.

palliative care: Comfort care that involves services provided by caregivers from several disciplines embodying a comprehensive approach to care that addresses pain management, emotional and spiritual care, and psychological support for caregivers and survivors.

parasympathetic nervous system: Whereas the sympathetic nervous system arouses the body in response to threat, once the threat is reduced this system counteracts the arousal, down regulating the heart and lung activity for example and restoring energy to maintenance systems such as digestion, growth and reproduction once the threat has passed.

parent centered: Describes parents whose interactions with their children are driven by parental needs rather than focusing on children's needs. Parents with this approach may make hostile attributions when children's needs are out of line with their own.

parental monitoring: Consistent parental supervision.

parenting styles: Approaches that characterize parents' typical interactions with and attitudes toward their children. Four styles have been identified, combining and crossing the positive and negative poles of two parenting dimensions—warmth and control. These styles are often predictive of child characteristics.

parietal lobe: A part of the cerebrum located between the frontal lobe (at the front of the cerebrum) and the occipital lobe (at the back of the cerebrum) and above the temporal lobe (on the side of the cerebrum) of each hemisphere. It processes somatosensory information such as touch, temperature, and pain.

passion: An element of love that refers to erotic attraction or feelings.

peer influence: The individual adolescent's behavior, values, and attitudes are affected and/or determined by peer group norms.

peer selection: Choosing peers based on behaviors, preferences, attitudes, and so on that are similar to one's own.

peer/romantic partner tradition: A body of work that focuses on the peer attachments of adults by questioning how early attachments impact the quality of romantic and friendship relationships in adulthood.

penis envy: According to Freud's theory, a girl's desire to have what she naively assumes is the greater genital pleasure that must come with having the external genitalia of a man.

period of the embryo: Lasting from the 4th through the 8th week of gestation, the time that most of the body's organ systems and structures are forming.

period of the fetus: Lasting from the 9th week of gestation until birth, the time of rapid growth and further differentiation when the reproductive system forms, gains in body weight occur, and the brain and nervous system continue to develop.

period of the zygote: Approximately a 2-week period from the time of fertilization of a human ovum by a sperm to the time of implantation in the uterine wall.

permissive style: An interactive parenting style that combines moderate to high levels of warmth (positive emotional climate, sensitivity and responsivity) with low levels of control or demandingness. Associated with impulsive behavior and low levels of self-reliance in children.

personal fable: A distorted view of one's uniqueness that is a feature of adolescents' egocentrism.

personal rules: Rules about areas of functioning that individuals or families might have standards about, such as

choices of friends or recreational activities or participation in family life, that are not governed by formal social rules in Western societies.

"the person who" fallacy: Refuting a well-documented finding by calling on knowledge of a person who is an exception.

perspective taking: Consideration of the viewpoints of others; putting oneself, metaphorically, in the shoes of another and seeing self and others from that alternative stance.

phallic stage: The third of Freud's psychosexual stages, lasting from age 3 to about 5, in which id energy is focused primarily in the genital region. This stage draws the greatest parental discipline, leads to feelings of guilt and the development of the superego, and can have long-lasting effects on how a child copes with postpubertal sexual needs.

phenotype: The aspect of a genetic blueprint that is actually expressed in the physical and behavioral characteristics of an individual.

Phineas Gage matrix: Syndrome related to injury of the frontal cortex. Consists of cognitive dysfunctions (such as poor planning, inadequate decision-making, inability to take another's perspective, and problems in sustaining employment) and emotional problems (such as shallow affect, lack of an enriched emotional life, lack of passion and initiative, and a diminished sense of pleasure and pain).

phonology: The sound system of a language; includes rules for arranging the basic sounds or "phonemes" of the language.

physician-assisted suicide: The prescribing of medicine that enables patients to take their own lives.

Piaget's cognitive development: Jean Piaget's theory of the development of cognition, which outlines four childhood stages in which the capacity to think logically about both concrete and abstract concepts evolves.

placebo effect: Occurs when individuals receiving a placebo (a "dummy" version of a treatment) experience improvement in their symptoms and attribute the improvement to the placebo.

placenta: A nourishing barrier that surrounds the developing fetus, allowing nutrients from the mother's blood to pass to the fetus's blood while allowing waste to be removed by the mother's blood. Otherwise, it keeps the two circulatory systems separate.

plaques: In the brain, clumps of insoluble protein that are damaging to neurons and associated with Alzheimer's disease.

pleasure principle: The pursuit of gratification, which motivates the id in Freud's personality theory.

polygenic: Describes traits that are affected by the products of multiple gene pairs, often located on different chromosomes, so that any one pair of gene alleles has only a limited affect on a given trait.

pons: A brain structure located in the hindbrain that is involved in the regulation of the sleep–wake cycle.

popular: A sociometric category that includes those children who receive many

positive nominations and few negative nominations from their peers (have high social preference and high social impact). Popular children are generally well-liked members of the group and have relatively high visibility among their peers.

positive affect: Tendency to express happy mood states by smiling and laughing especially to social stimuli. An aspect of infant temperament.

positive affectivity: The state or trait tendency to experience enthusiasm, alertness, joy, confidence, and determination.

positive correlation: A relationship between variables in which they change in the same direction, either both increasing or both decreasing.

positive reinforcement: A rewarding consequence of a behavior in the presence of a cue. Rewarding consequences increase the likelihood of that behavior in the future when the proper cue is provided. For example, if you give a food treat to your dog when she sits on command, the food treat is a positive reinforcement, and she is likely to repeat the sit in the future when she hears the command.

postconventional morality: Kohlberg's third stage of moral reasoning achieved by some adults in whom what is considered right is defined not by specific rules or laws but by general processes such as democratic principles or individual rights.

postformal or fifth-stage thinking: Characteristic of a stage beyond Piaget's sequence of stages that describes the changes in logical thinking that might occur in the adult years. Characterized by the ability of the problem solver to coordinate contradictory formal operational approaches to the same problem. The postformal thinker can understand the logic of each of the contradictory perspectives and integrate the perspectives into a larger whole.

postrational skepticism: A characterization of postformal thought that suggests that the search for absolute truth gives way to a search for arguably good reasons for choosing one belief or course of action over another; an endorsement of the possibility and practicality of making rational commitments in the face of the clear knowledge that other defensible alternatives to one's views continue to exist.

post-traumatic growth: Positive psychological change experienced as a result of the struggle with highly stressful or traumatic events.

post-traumatic stress disorder (PTSD): A trauma or stress-related disorder that follows a traumatic event. PTSD is characterized by clinically significant symptoms such as re-experience of the traumatic event, general numbing of responsiveness to others, heightened arousal, disturbed sleep, and so forth

power assertion: One method parents use to enforce control of children's behavior. Can involve physical punishment or the threat of physical punishment, or it can involve withdrawal of privileges. Effective for the immediate control of behavior, but over the long term, children show higher levels of anger, aggressiveness and anxiety.

pragmatics: One of the aspects of language that children must learn that goes beyond learning semantics and syntax and involves using the language effectively to communicate. Includes skills such as crafting a narrative and "code switching," using different language styles in different contexts.

preconventional morality: Kohlberg's first stage of moral reasoning characterizing middle childhood in which what is right is what avoids punishment, what conforms to the dictates of authority, or what serves one's personal interests.

preferential response paradigms: Approaches to studying infant behavior and mental functioning. Multiple stimuli are presented to an infant (e.g., two visual stimuli) and researchers record (e.g., by measuring looking time) which stimulus the baby responds to more (prefers).

premoral stage: In Piaget's theory of moral development, characterizes preschoolers who are unconcerned about established rules or standards.

preoccupied (insecure): An attachment style classifying adults who provide transcripts in the Adult Attachment Inventory that are not collaborative and that are characterized by very long, incoherent, egocentric responses that shift from topic to topic. They indicate substantial enmeshment or preoccupation with parents, registered by angry, accusatory language or by conflicted descriptions that connote ambivalence and confusion about early relationships. Their children tend to have anxious-ambivalent attachments. In Bartholomew's typology, these individuals are emotionally demanding, anxious about gaining acceptance, fearful of rejection, and preoccupied with relationships.

preoperational egocentrism: The tendency of preschoolers to be aware only of their own perspective. Demonstrated in their expectations that others will know what they know, believe what they believe, and so on.

preoperational stage: In Piaget's theory of cognitive development, the time period from approximately age 2 to 7 when children are capable of representational thought but appear to be prelogical in their thinking.

pre-self: An infant's early inklings of the permanence of her body, its separateness from others, and the rhythms of interpersonal connections.

pretend play: Play in which children (beginning at about age 2) behave "as if" objects or people were something or someone else, that is, treating them as symbols. In social pretend play, children enact roles "as if" they themselves were other people, simulating the actions or characteristics of others and interacting with other children playing other roles.

prevention science: A new and evolving multidisciplinary mix of human development, psychopathology, epidemiology, education, and criminology that offers us useful guidelines for understanding what constitutes effective prevention.

primary control: Control efforts that are attempts to affect the immediate environment beyond ourselves.

primary prevention: An attempt to forestall the development of problems by promoting health and wellness in the general population through group-oriented interventions.

primary sexual characteristics: The physical traits directly involved in reproduction, such as the genitalia.

principle of equifinality: Many early developmental pathways can produce similar outcomes.

principle of multifinality: The same developmental pathways may result in a wide range of possible outcomes.

procedural knowledge: Describes the often unconscious, nondeclarative knowledge of how to do things that underlies many physical skills.

production deficiency: Failure to use a memory strategy one has knowledge of even in a situation where it is ordinarily helpful.

progeria: A fatal genetic disorder that causes rapid aging, so that by late childhood its victims are dying of "old age." Because progeria sufferers do not survive long enough to reproduce, the disease must be caused by a genetic mutation.

progesterone: A hormone involved in the reproductive cycle, especially in females.

projection neuron: One of two main types of neurons in systems of neurons. These have long projections, especially axons that extend far away from the cell body.

prosocial behavior or altruism: Voluntarily acting in ways that seem intended to benefit someone else.

protective factors: Aspects of the organism or the environment that moderate the negative effects of risk.

proteins: The chemical building blocks of the body that are constructed when cells follow the codes provided by genes.

protest: The second phase in the grieving process where bereaved individuals may experience periods of obsessive yearning or searching for the lost loved one as well as bouts of restlessness or irritability.

proximal processes: Reciprocal interactions between a person and her immediate external environment, including other people, the physical environment, or informational sources such as books or movies. In Bronfenbrenner's biological model, all developments are a function of these processes.

proximity maintenance: One of three purposes of the attachment system. Bonds between infant and caregiver encourage and sustain physical closeness.

prudential consequences: Negative effects on an individual's health, safety, or future as a result of an action that violates some social expectation or rule. Getting arrested or having an accident would be a prudential consequence of driving too fast.

psychological well-being: Feeling a sense of purpose, growth, and mastery, or that one is striving for realization of one's true potential.

psychoneuroimmunology: The study of the interactions between the central nervous system, the immune system, and behavior.

psychosocial development: Change with age in the psychological processes of interpersonal understanding, skills, and values that affect an individual's capacity for interpersonal relationships, including friendships.

puberty: A process of sexual maturing in late childhood related to a wide range of emotional, behavioral, and social changes.

qualitative research: Any kind of research that does not use statistical procedures or quantitative methods to arrive at conclusions.

racial crossover effect: African American adolescents are less likely to use illicit substances than White adolescents, but the reverse is true for adults.

racial group: Groups of people, like Blacks, Whites, and Asians, who have historically been assumed to be genetically different, identifiable by variations in hair, skin color, bone structure, or other physiological markers. Genetic indicators of race have not been found, so that racial groups appear to be a social construction.

reactive attachment disorder (RAD): A lack of ability to form affectional bonds with other people and a pattern of markedly disturbed social relationships. RAD can result when a child receives grossly neglectful or pathological care in the early years.

reality monitoring: The ability to distinguish what is imagined from what is real.

reality principle: A focus on understanding the world and behavioral consequences that leads to sensible and self-protective behavior. In Freud's personality theory, the ego operates on this principle.

recall: Remembering information or events that are not currently available to the senses. Requires the ability to mentally represent the absent information.

recency: A salient characteristic of self-memories. The tendency to remember something that has happened to us recently better than something that happened in the more distant past.

receptor: A chemical located either on the surface of a cell or inside a cell that binds to a transcription factor (coming either from outside or inside the cell) and allowing the transcription factor to then bind with a regulatory portion of DNA to begin the transcription of a gene.

recognition: Remembering in the sense of knowing that information currently available to the senses has been previously experienced.

reflective judgment: In Kitchener's theory of the development of problem solving, the analysis of the elements of a problem and justification of problem solutions.

reflective practice: A method used by counselors that emphasizes careful consideration of theoretical and empirical sources of knowledge, as well as one's own beliefs and assumptions, as a precursor to practice.

refusal of treatment: Patients' refusal of any food, water, or medical treatment that prolongs life.

regulation of loss: In life span developmental theory, a kind of adaptive functioning that involves reorganizing the way we behave by adjusting our expectations and accepting a lower level of functioning.

rehearsal: A strategy for remembering that usually involves continuing to actively process to-be-remembered material, like repeating it to oneself.

reinforcement: An event that an individual experiences as pleasurable or rewarding, which increases the frequency of a behavior that occurred immediately before the pleasurable event.

reintegrative stage: In Schaie's theory, the elder years when individuals do not often need to acquire new domains of knowledge or to figure out new ways of applying what they know. Many are motivated to conserve energy (physical and psychological). Cognitive efforts are aimed at solving immediate, practical problems that seem critically important to daily functioning.

rejected: A sociometric category that includes those children who receive many negative nominations and few positive nominations from their peers. Rejected children are typically disliked (low social preference) but have generally high visibility (high social impact).

rejected-aggressive: Describes children who are rejected because they aggress against their peers.

rejected-withdrawn: Describes children who are rejected because they withdraw from their peers.

relatedness: In self-determination theory, one of three basic needs. Feeling that one is important to others and valued enough to be sensitively and responsively cared for, from infancy onward.

relational aggression: A type of aggression in which relationships are manipulated and/or damaged in order to hurt an individual.

relative subordinate: In Perry's theory, a response to late multiplicity in which students (primarily under the guidance of authority) begin to understand that some opinions are more legitimate than others. The value of a perspective is now understood to be related to the supporting arguments and evidence for the position.

relativistic thought: The essence of postformal thought in which several truth systems exist describing the reality of the same event, and they appear to be logically equivalent.

reorganization: The last phase in the grieving process in which the grieving individual discovers ways to hold on to the memory of the deceased and integrate that memory into their current life and new attachments.

reorganizational stage: In Schaie's theory, a stage of early old age, when responsibilities narrow as children grow up and retirement becomes an option. Flexibility in problem solving is needed to create a satisfying, meaningful environment for the rest of life, but the focus tends to narrow to a changed set of personal goals and needs.

reorientation: The third stage of retirement, which is a time of active trial and error. The retiree seeks solutions to the problems that retirement presents and tries strategies for building a satisfactory life.

representational thought: The capacity to think about things or events that are not currently stimulating one's senses. Utilizes mental images or symbols to "re-present" the absent experience.

representations: According to Craik and Bialystock (2006), the kinds of schemas or systems of schemas one develops over time to interact with the world; the foundation of crystallized intelligence.

representations of interactions (or RIGs): A kind of sensorimotor or procedural memory or expectation that infants form of how interactions with others are likely to proceed. These representations are based on repeated experiences and are preverbal and unconscious.

resilience (resilient): The quality that permits developmental success for some individuals despite grave setbacks, early adversity, or other risk factors. (Describes a person who has this quality.)

resolve: Position 9 in Perry's model that, taken together with initial commitment (Position 7) and multiple commitments (Position 8), suggests a flowering of the commitments anticipated in Positions 5 and 6. Position 9, although placed at the end of the line, does not imply a static resolution of existential conflict; rather, it characterizes a state of courageous resolve to continue the work of reflecting on one's commitments throughout adulthood.

respondent: An automatic response to a stimulus. For example, a rapidly approaching visual stimulus can automatically elicit an eye blink, which is a respondent.

responsible stage: In Schaie's theory, the stage of cognitive development faced during middle adulthood in which ill-defined problems remain the norm, but problem solving must now take into account not only one's own personal needs and goals but also those of others in one's life that have become one's responsibility (spouse, children, coworkers, member of the community).

restoration-focused grief: A type of coping strategy directed toward handling the practical tasks that need to be done to carry on with daily life.

retention: Staying in college long enough to graduate.

reticular activating system: A set of brain structures including the reticular formation located in the brain stem that filters out some of the stimuli we perceive and alerts higher structures to "pay attention" to other stimuli.

reticular formation: A bundle of neural tissue in the brainstem that acts together with other nuclei to form the reticular activating system, which affects attention to incoming stimuli.

retreat: Perry's characterization of the behavior of individuals who move back to dualistic thinking in times of stress to seek the intellectual security of absolute right and wrong.

retrieval: What we usually mean by remembering, that is, getting information out of mental storage so we can use it.

retrieval strategy: An approach to finding and recovering information stored in memory. In math, this refers to solving arithmetic problems by recovering a memorized answer (e.g., remembering that 3 plus 2 equals 5 rather than solving the problem).

reversible relationship: A kind of logical relationship in which one change reverses the effects of another change (and also implies the existence of its reverse). For example, in math, subtraction is the reverse of addition.

rhythmicity: The predictability of an individual's sleep, feeding, elimination, and other biological cycles. An aspect of infant temperament.

risk factors: Aspects of the organism or the environment that compromise healthy development.

risky behaviors: Behaviors that constitute a departure from socially accepted norms or behaviors that pose a threat to the well-being of individuals or groups.

role buffering: For individuals who participate in multiple roles, such as "mother," "wife," "caregiver to ailing parent," and "employee," if one role is a source of psychological stress or failure experiences, success and satisfaction in another role may compensate.

role strain: The stress or strain of meeting obligations that are associated with certain roles (e.g., caregiver).

rough-and-tumble play: Good-natured physical roughness that is an almost exclusive property of boys' play with boys.

rumination: Repeated focusing of attention on negative mood and cognitions. Rumination is sometimes viewed as an ineffective emotion regulation strategy that is related to avoidance of emotional experience.

safe haven: One of the three purposes of the attachment system. Bonds between infant and caregiver make the caregiver a source of comfort when distressed.

sandwich generation: Those who carry the double responsibilities of taking care of both an elderly relative and their own children.

scaffolding: The process whereby more advanced thinkers or more capable members of a culture provide novice learners with a supportive temporary prop that enables the novice to learn and to reach higher levels of thinking.

scientific concepts: In Vygotsky's theory, culturally defined concepts that can provide children with a basis for organizing their thinking in line with the knowledge and skills of the culture.

script: A schematic representation of the typical features of an event and the order in which they happen.

secondary control: Control efforts that involve attempts to change ourselves.

secondary prevention: An attempt to reduce the incidence of disorders among those who are at high risk or to provide treatment to forestall the development of more serious psychopathology in cases that are already established.

secondary sexual characteristics: Physical traits not directly involved in reproduction but indicative of sex, such as enlarged breasts in females and deeper voices in males.

secure base: One of the three purposes of the attachment system. The bond between infant and caregiver provides the infant a protective resource as she develops and learns.

securely attached: An attachment category describing babies who typically show distress on separation from the mother in the strange situation test, but who greet her happily on her return, usually seeking comfort by reaching to be picked up. Once reassured they tend to return to exploring. In Bartholomew's description of adult attachment categories, describes individuals who expect others to be available and supportive of their needs in close relationships, who are comfortable with emotional closeness, but are also reasonably autonomous.

seduction hypothesis: Freud's early view that some psychopathology stems from infantile sexual molestation.

selection (as an adaptive strategy): A process of narrowing our goals and limiting the domains in which we expend effort that is important for successful development.

selection (as a peer group process): The process by which individuals choose to affiliate with others who share similar behaviors or attributes.

selective attention: Deployment of attention to only a chosen subset of the information available for processing in a situation. Selective attention to information that must be remembered later can be used as a memorization strategy.

selective optimization with compensation: The three combined processes of successful development according to life span development theory (selection, optimization, and compensation).

selective prevention: A category of prevention efforts that target individuals at some epidemiological risk.

self-conscious emotions: Emotions that require self awareness (self-recognition), and are directly relevant to the self, such as pride, shame, embarrassment and guilt. These emotions require more cognitive capacity than basic emotions such as fear, and they do not emerge until the second year of life.

self-control or behavior regulation: Ability to stop the self from performing a proscribed act or to make the self perform an act that is not appealing or attractive in itself.

self-determination theory: The theory that three basic psychological needs including autonomy, competence, and relatedness motivate our adaptation efforts at any age.

self-directed coping behaviors: Efforts to deal with stress that appear to be aimed at self comfort. In infants these behaviors include looking away from the source of distress or self-stimulating behavior, such as rocking and sucking.

self-efficacy beliefs: Beliefs about our ability to exercise control over events that affect our lives.

self-enhancing bias: The motivation to maintain moderately positive beliefs about oneself, which is reflected in a tendency to make comparisons of oneself to people who are similar.

self-esteem: A person's evaluation of his or her attributes or the positive or negative valence associated with those attributes. In William James's opinion, self-esteem depends on the number of successes we enjoy relative to our aspirations.

self-esteem slide: A drop in self-esteem presumably experienced by girls at adolescence.

self-instruction (or self-monitoring): The clinical and educational practices in which the general goal is to affect some behavior change (such as control of impulsivity or improvement in test-taking skills) by attending to, regulating, and sometimes changing cognitions.

self-organizing: Filtering incoming information through one's own existing mental constructs and influencing the environment's inputs with one's actions and reactions.

self-recognition: Awareness of self, usually manifested by the individual's display of self-directed behavior on viewing her own reflection. For example, a child capable of self-recognition will touch a spot of rouge on her nose when she looks in a mirror rather than touching the mirror.

self-regulation: An individual's ability to prevent himself or herself from making a dominant, preferred or automatic response in order to perform a nondominant response, such as when a hungry person is served food at a restaurant but waits to eat until everyone at the table has been served.

self-socialization: Actively seeking to make one's behavior consistent with his or her gender identity without needing social pressure to do so. An intrinsically motivated process that fosters gender role development. Once children have learned their gender label, they attempt to learn what it means to be male or female and then choose to behave in gender consistent ways.

self-system: A term currently used in place of the "self" because "self" seems too unidimensional. Includes multiple aspects of the self, such as self-concept, self-regulation, and self-esteem.

self-transforming: An immature interpersonal style in which an individual gives in so as to reduce the level of tension. He changes his own behaviors or feelings in order to conform to the needs or demands of another.

semantic: Describing knowledge about factual information, rules, and concepts.

semantics (semantic system): An aspect of a language that children must learn, including the words and word parts that express meanings in that language, also called the meaning system of a language.

senescing: The process of declining with age or "growing down."

sensation seeking: The need for varied, novel, and complex sensation and experiences and the willingness to take physical and social risk for the sake of these experiences.

sensorimotor stage: In Piaget's theory of cognitive development, the period from birth to about age 2 when infants are not yet capable of representational thought, so they are unable to form mental images or to plan their behavior. Babies have sensory experiences, organize them on the basis of inborn reflexes or patterns of motor responses, and make motor responses to them.

sensory integration dysfunction: A disorder marked by difficulties such as extreme hypersensitivity or hyposensitivity to sensations such as bright lights, loud sounds, pain, certain textures, or human touch. Usually includes motor clumsiness, balance problems, fidgeting, and poor eye–hand coordination.

sensory memory: Very brief retention of sensory experiences.

separation anxiety: Distress of an infant or young child when a primary caregiver leaves the child in someone else's care. Usually begins in the second half of the

1st year, demonstrating the infant's capacity to recall the absent caregiver, and is viewed as a sign of attachment to that caregiver.

septum: A brain structure located in the forebrain that is part of the limbic system or "emotional brain," which produces feelings such as pleasure, pain, anger, sexuality, fear, and affection.

sequential: Describes a kind of study that is like a cross-sectional study in that more than one cohort is included, but is like a longitudinal study in that each cohort is measured at more than one age.

sex chromosomes: The 23rd pair of chromosomes, which play a major role in sex determination. In females these are two relatively large X chromosomes, whereas in males this pair consists of one X chromosome and one much smaller Y chromosome.

sexual dimorphism: Both internal and external physical differences between the sexes, which increase during the adolescent growth spurt.

sexual orientation: A preference for partners of one's own sex (homosexuality), the opposite sex (heterosexuality), or both (bisexuality).

shock: The first phase in the grieving process when the loss is met by disbelief and the grieving person may experience blunted emotions, or emotional outbursts.

sickle-cell anemia: A hereditary disease caused by a recessive, defective gene allele affecting the red blood cells. These are abnormally (half-moon) shaped and not as efficient as normal, round red blood cells in carrying oxygen to the tissues. Symptoms can include breathing problems, a variety of organ dysfunctions, and sometimes early death. Most common in individuals of African descent.

slow mapping: After a word has been added to a child's vocabulary, it may take multiple exposures to the word in different situations for a child to work out the word's full meaning, including what features are defining versus characteristic, and the other words to which it is related.

slow-to-warm-up babies: A temperament type described by Thomas and Chess. These babies are like easy babies in most ways, but they are like difficult babies in their fearfulness, showing more wariness in new situations than most other babies.

social clock: The set of age-related expectations that we all have for the appropriate timing of major life events.

social cognition: A person's mental processing (thoughts, beliefs, and so on) of information about other people and their reasoning about social relationships.

social comparison: The process whereby people observe the performance of others and use it as a basis for evaluating their own abilities and accomplishments.

social competence vs. performance: Social competence is a set of abilities that are important for peer group acceptance; not one set of prescribed behaviors, but rather a range of effective responses, cognitive processes, and abilities to make mature judgments. Performance refers to the child's actual use of skills for getting along with others. Adequate competence (e.g., perspective taking) is necessary but not sufficient for good performance (social functioning).

social dosage effect: The more time children spend in same-gender groups the more gender-typical behaviors they exhibit.

social exchange and behavior theories: Related to marriage, views that assume satisfaction results from negotiated exchange between partners. Problems arise when costs of relationship exceed benefits.

social gradient: Stepwise fashion in which outcomes improve as a function of improvement in social position.

social impact: A sociometric measure that is computed by adding the total number of nominations a child receives from her peers, both positive and negative, which indicates the degree to which a child gets noticed within her group.

social information-processing: Model used to explain idiosyncratic ways of processing social information, such as use of a hostile attributional bias to interpret neutral social cues.

social learning theories: Theories that focus specifically on how children acquire personality characteristics and social skills.

social preference: A sociometric measure that is computed by adding the total number of positive nominations a child receives from his peers, which indicates the degree to which a child is positively viewed by his social group.

social referencing: A baby's adjustment of its reactions to objects or events based on feedback provided by a caregiver. For example, a baby may look at a caregiver's facial expression before approaching a new toy.

social role theory: The view that the social roles an individual fills, such as parent, spouse, manager, and so on, are important influences on her behavior, and that different individuals will typically behave in similar ways when filling the same role.

social skills: Discrete, observable behaviors such as making eye contact, using appropriate language, asking appropriate questions, and so forth, which promote effective social interaction and which are part of the broader construct of social competence.

socialize: To limit some behaviors of the child while demanding others, so that the child will be safe and she will learn the standards of her culture and behave in ways that are conventionally acceptable.

sociocultural theories: Theories in the tradition of Vygotsky, arguing that important aspects of cognitive development may be qualitatively different in different cultures.

socioeconomic position (SEP): The measure of an individual's or group's position within hierarchically organized society, which determines access to resources and opportunities within the society.

socioeconomic status (SES) group: Social standing or power characterizing adults in a household. Characteristics defining SES include educational background, income, and occupational type.

sociometry: The classic way of assessing social competence and determining the kinds of categories that describe children's status within peer groups. Usually involves asking members of a social group (e.g., children in a classroom) to indicate which members of the group they prefer to spend time with (sit with, play with, etc.) and which they do not.

specification: In Super's theory, the identification of specific vocational preferences during the middle of the exploratory stage.

spermarche: A boy's first ejaculation.

SRY gene: Located on the Y chromosome in males, this gene codes for a transcription factor that binds to regulatory DNA. At about 5 weeks gestation, it turns on genes that start the production of other proteins responsible for the development of gonads into testes.

stability: The fourth stage of retirement, when the retiree settles into a lifestyle that is satisfactory to her.

stabilization: In Super's theory, an individual's settling on a vocational self-concept and job that completes the establishment stage.

stage: A period of time, perhaps several years, during which a person's activities (at least in one broad domain) have certain characteristics in common.

stages of retirement: For many people, adjustment to retirement follows a typical stagelike progression, from honeymoon to disenchantment to reorientation to stability to termination.

stereotype induction: An interview strategy that involves slanting the interviewee's view of an individual, such as implying that an alleged perpetrator is a bad person to encourage children to reveal information.

stereotype threat: The fear that a stereotype might be true of oneself or that one will be judged by that stereotype.

still-face paradigm: A research technique for assessing infant coping strategies. The infant is seated facing the mother who is instructed to interact in normally pleasant and playful ways at first and then is asked to change her behavior and to be completely unresponsive or withdrawn.

storage: The acquisition knowledge or learning; maintaining information in memory.

stranger anxiety: The tendency of an infant or young child to be wary of strangers and to seek the comfort and protection of the primary caregiver when a stranger is present. May begin early in infancy but is likely to intensify at about 8 months when separation anxiety begins.

strange situation test: A measurement technique designed by Ainsworth to assess the quality of an infant's attachment to a caregiver. Infants (12 months or older) and their caregivers are brought to a room (the strange situation) where the child experiences a series of eight 3-minute episodes, each one introducing changes in the social situation, some of which are likely to be stressful, such as an episode when the mother leaves the baby with a stranger. The infant's willingness to explore the toys and his reactions to his mother and the strangers are observed.

stress: A response to an environmental condition or stimulus that requires adaptation from an organism.

strict dualism: Position 1 in Perry's model that implies a rigid adherence to authoritarian views and a childlike division between in-group and out-group. Individuals in this stage never think to question their belief that authority embodies rightness.

subgranular zone: An area of the brain, part of the hippocampus, where new neural stem cells can be generated in adults, apparently supporting learning and memory.

subjective well-being: An individual's experience of overall life satisfaction, including satisfaction with particular domains of life, frequency of positive mood, and relative infrequency of negative mood.

substantia nigra: One structure in the midbrain. It is involved in vision, hearing, and consciousness.

subventricular zone: An area of the brain near the ventricles where new neural stem cells can be generated in adults. These cells migrate to the olfactory bulb and appear to play a role in maintaining its functioning.

superego: In Freud's personality theory, the last of three aspects of personality, which serves as an "internalized parent" that causes one to feel guilty if his behavior deviates from parental and societal restrictions.

superior colliculi: Structures in the midbrain that play a role in vision, hearing, and consciousness.

symbolic artifacts: Analogical symbols, such as pictures or maps or scale models that are both concrete objects themselves and symbols for other things. To understand a symbolic artifact, a child must mentally represent the same thing in two ways at once.

symbols: Representational indicators or stand-ins for other things, such as words serving as symbols for concepts or drawings serving as symbols of objects.

sympathetic nervous system: When a threat is perceived, this system releases important chemicals such as epinephrine (adrenaline) and norepinephrine (noradrenalin) that send a burst of energy to those organs necessary for fight or flight (e.g., heart, lungs) while diverting energy from less necessary systems (e.g., growth, reproduction).

sympathy: An emotion related to empathy that involves "feeling for" another; that is, having concern for the other person, but not necessarily sharing the feelings of the other.

synapses: Connections among neurons, usually between the dendrite of one neuron and the axon of another neuron, or between the dendrites of one neuron and the cell body of a second neuron. At the synapse there is a gap between neurons, which can be bridged by chemicals called neurotransmitters.

synaptic gap: The space between neurons where they "connect." In transmission of an electrical impulse from one neuron to the next, the gap is bridged by the release of chemicals called neurotransmitters from the first neuron, which then stimulate or inhibit an electrical impulse in the second neuron.

synaptic overproduction: The generation of more synapses than are needed in the process of brain growth. Those synapses that are not used are later eliminated or "pruned."

synaptogenesis: The generation of synapses or connections between neurons, usually as a result of the growth of axons and dendrites.

synchrony: Infant–adult interactions are often characterized by this repetitive-rhythmic organization. Nonverbal behaviors occur in a patterned, temporally coordinated sequence.

syntax (grammar): The aspect of language that specifies how to link words into meaningful sentences. A system of rules for generating and decoding sentences.

systems theories: Another term for multi-dimensional models.

tangles: Twisted filaments of protein, which may interfere with communication between neurons and even cause cell death; they are associated with Alzheimer's disease.

telomere: The ends of the chromosome that are progressively shortened by cell division; telomeres are related to cellular aging and cell death.

temperament: Describes the usual emotional and behavioral characteristics of a given individual. For infants, includes activity level, degree of fearfulness and irritability, attention persistence, typical mood, and so on.

temporal lobe: The part of the cerebrum that is situated on the sides of each hemisphere and is responsible for auditory processing. The left temporal lobe is especially important in language processing.

temporizing: Perry's description of what individuals are doing when they delay movement to the next stage of thought development.

teratogens: Substances or agents that can cross the placental barrier and produce fetal deformities when taken or absorbed by the mother during pregnancy.

terminal drop (terminal decline): A substantial decline in intellectual functioning that adults may show as they approach the end of their lives, between 6 months and 5 years prior to death.

termination: The fifth and final stage of retirement, which is the end-of-life transition when the individual's health declines and he becomes dependent on others for care.

tertiary prevention: An attempt to rehabilitate persons with established disorders; similar to treatment.

testes: Male gonads that primarily produce androgens (such as testosterone), but also produce lesser amounts of estrogen and progesterone. Site of sperm production in males.

thalamus: A part of the forebrain that relays information from sensory organs and other brain structures to appropriate sites on the cerebral cortex.

theory of mind: Degree of knowledge of the existence of mental (psychological) processes in self and other people. Includes understanding that people have thoughts, beliefs, intentions, desires, feelings, and so on, that these mental experiences may or may not reflect reality accurately, and that they may be different in other people than they are in the self. Makes possible the capacity to take the perspective of another person.

time-out: A disciplinary technique in which for a short span of time a child is required to discontinue his involvement in ongoing activities to quietly sit somewhere apart. This technique involves mild power assertion and is suitable for use with toddlers and preschoolers.

tomboyism: A trait girls exhibit when they prefer to play with boys and prefer boys' toys and activities.

tools or signs: In Vygotsky's theory, anything that people use to help them think and learn, such as numbering or writing systems.

transcription: The complex chain of cellular processes that involves translating the code specified by a gene into the production of a protein. This series of biochemical events ultimately accounts for genetic expression or influence.

transcription factor: Chemicals in cells that bind with the regulatory portions of the DNA, initiating the uncoiling of strands of DNA at a gene location and allowing mRNA production to begin. Transcription factors cannot bind to the regulatory DNA unless they first bind to another chemical called a receptor.

trust versus mistrust: The crisis faced in the first of Erikson's "Eight Stages of Man," in which the responsiveness of an infant's caregiver will determine whether the baby establishes basic trust and a sense of being valuable.

uncharacteristic behavior: A condition that mitigates a criminal defendant's guilt because the crime is not typical of her, such as when it is a first offense or is not consistent with the individual's values.

unipolar disorder: A term used to indicate a clinical course marked by episodes of depression but not of mania.

universal prevention: A category of prevention efforts that are directed to the general population.

unresolved (insecure): An attachment style characterizing adults whose Adult Attachment Inventory transcripts show marked lapses in logical thinking, particularly during discussions of loss or other traumatic memories. These individuals may receive a secondary classification of dismissive or preoccupied, and often have children who show more disorganized attachment patterns than other children.

utilization deficiency: A situation in which using a memory strategy does not seem to boost memory.

vagal tone: Refers to degree of healthy functioning of the vagus nerve as it regulates heart rate. Heart rate variability on the in-breath versus the out-breath is healthy. Low levels of variability in ordinary circumstances suggest low vagal tone and indicate that the individual may be chronically mobilized to respond to threat.

vagus nerve: The vagus nerve connects brainstem areas that control ancient fight, flight, or freeze responses with various organs such as larynx, heart, and intestines. It plays a key role in heart rate regulation.

verification: The third step in the scientific method, when the researcher judges a theory objectively by testing predictions about events and theories to see if they come true.

visual acuity: The level of detail that one can see. Young infants have substantially less visual acuity than adults.

vividness effect: Occurs during decision-making when some salient or vivid facts attract our attention regardless of their actual value as evidence.

vocabulary spurt: Describes the rapid growth of productive vocabulary from 50 to about 500 words in just a few months. Tends to occur between 18 and 24 months in most children.

vocational self-concept: Part of one's total identity that includes ideas about which qualities of the self would or would not provide a match to the requirements of an occupation. Includes person's view of his own characteristics and of his life circumstances, such as the limits or opportunities created by economic conditions and so on.

voicing: In phonology, vibration of the vocal cords in the production of a sound. Some consonant sounds in English are voiced (e.g., the d and v sounds) and some, which are identical to the voiced consonants in other ways, are not voiced (e.g., t and f).

warmth dimension (parental responsiveness): One of two major features of parenting style. The degree to which parents create a positive emotional climate for their children by listening to them, being involved and interested in their activities, accepting them, making positive attributions about their behavior, and being sensitive and supportive.

wisdom: Expertise in the fundamental pragmatics of life. Superior knowledge and judgment in solving problems or addressing issues that arise in the course of living and that affect the meaning and quality of life.

Wolffian-ducts: Prenatal structures in both male and female fetuses. In males, high levels of androgens stimulate these ducts to develop into male reproductive structures, such as seminal vesicles. In females, these ducts deteriorate.

working memory: The part of the cognitive machinery that holds information one is actively thinking about at the moment; also referred to as short-term memory.

working model: In Bowlby's attachment theory, an individual's mental representation of self, other, and relationships, which serves as a prototype of social functioning and affects the individual's expectations and behaviors in future relationships? A cognitive schema that begins in infancy and is refined and elaborated over time; a state of mind about attachment-related issues.

X chromosomes: The female sex chromosomes, a matched pair of elongated chromosomes that determine that one will be a female.

X-linked recessive disorders: A class of genetic disorders that are carried on the X chromosome and are recessive, meaning that they are more likely to affect males, who do not have a matching X chromosome that might have the corresponding (and dominant) normal gene. Examples include hemophilia, baldness, color blindness, night blindness, and Duchenne's muscular dystrophy.

Y chromosome: The male sex chromosome, which pairs with an X chromosome and determines that one will be a male.

young adulthood: The time period from about 18 to 30 years that is often an extended period of transition involving exploration of potential adult identities.

youth: A period of time after completing puberty that serves as a transition into adulthood.

zone of proximal development: In Vygotsky's theory, the range of concepts and skills that a learner is to understand or perform only with support or scaffolding from someone else.

zygote: An ovum that has been fertilized by a sperm and thus contains a full complement of 46 chromosomes, half from the mother and half from the father.

References

Abbott, L. C., & Winzer-Serhan, U .H. (2012). Smoking during pregnancy: Lessons learned from epidemiological studies and experimental studies using animal models. *Critical Review of Toxicology, 42*, 279–303.

Abebe, D., Lien, L., & von Soest, T. (2012). The development of bulimic symptoms from adolescence to young adulthood in females and males: A population-based longitudinal cohort study. *International Journal of Eating Disorders, 45*, 737–745.

Aber, J. L., Jones, S., Brown, J. L., Chaudry, N., & Samples, F. (1998). Resolving Conflict Creatively: Evaluating the developmental effects of a school-based violence prevention program in the neighborhood and classroom context. *Development and Psychopathology, 10*, 187–213.

Aboud, F. (1977). Interest in ethnic information: A cross-cultural developmental study. *Canadian Journal of Behavioral Science, 9*, 134–146.

Abrams, K. Y., Rifkin, A., & Hesse, E. (2006). Examining the role of parental frightened/frightening subtypes in predicting disorganized attachment within a brief observational procedure. *Development and Psychopathology, 18*, 345–361.

Abu-Raiya, H., Pargament, K. I., & Mahoney, A. (2011). Examining coping methods with stressful interpersonal events experienced by Muslims living in the United States following the 9/11 attacks. *Psychology of Religion and Spirituality, 3*, 1–14.

Achenbach, T., & Edelbrock, C. S. (1983). *Manual for the Child Behavior Checklist and Revised Child Behavior Profile*. Burlington: University of Vermont, Department of Psychiatry.

Ackerman, S., Zuroff, D. C., & Moskowitz, D. S. (2000). Generativity in midlife and young adults: Links to agency, communion, and subjective well-being. *International Journal of Aging and Human Development, 50*, 17–41.

Ackil, J. K., & Zaragoza, M. S. (1995). Developmental differences in eyewitness suggestibility and memory for source. *Journal of Experimental Child Psychology, 60*, 57–83.

Acolet, D., Modi, N., Giannakoulopoulos, X., Bond, C., Clow, A., & Glover, V. (1993). Changes in plasma cortisol and catecholamine concentrations in response to massage in preterm infants. *Archives of Disease in Childhood, 70* (1, Spec. No.), F80.

Adam, E. K. (2006). Transactions among adolescent trait and state emotion and diurnal and momentary cortisol activity in naturalistic settings. *Psychoneuroendocrinology, 31*, 664–679.

Addis, D. R., Wong, A. T., & Schacter, D. L. (2008). Age-related changes in the episodic simulation of future events. *Psychological Science, 19*, 33–41.

Addis, M. E. (2008). Gender and depression in men. *Clinical Psychology Science and Practice, 15*, 153–168.

Adler, N. E., Boyce, T., Chesney, M. A., Cohen, S., Folkman, S., Kahn, R. L., et al. (1994). Socioeconomic status and health: The challenge of the gradient. *American Psychologist, 49*, 15–24.

Afifi, T. O., Mota, N. P., Dasiewicz, P., MacMillan, H. L., & Sareen, J. (2012). Physical punishment and mental disorders: Results from a nationally representative US Sample. *Pediatrics, 130*, 184–192.

Afshari, R., Bhopal, R. S., & Afshari, R. (2002). Changing pattern of use of 'ethnicity' and 'race' in scientific literature. *International Journal of Epidemiology, 31*, 5, 1074.

Aguiar, A., & Baillargeon, R. (1999). 2.5-month-old infants' reasoning about when object should and should not be occluded. *Cognitive Psychology, 39*, 116–157.

Aguiar, A., & Baillargeon, R. (2002). Developments in young infants' reasoning about occluded objects. *Cognitive Psychology, 45*, 267–336.

Ahnert, L., Pinquart, M., & Lamb, M. (2006). Security of children's relationships with nonparental care providers: A meta-analysis. *Child Development, 77*, 664–679.

Ainsworth, M. D. S. (1967). *Infancy in Uganda: Infant care and the growth of love*. Baltimore: The Johns Hopkins University Press.

Ainsworth, M. D. S. (1989). Attachments beyond infancy. *American Psychologist, 44*, 709–716.

Ainsworth, M. D. S., Bell, S. M., & Stayton, D. J. (1972). Individual differences in the development of some attachment behaviors. *Merrill-Palmer Quarterly, 18*, 123–143.

Ainsworth, M. D. S., Blehar, M. C., Waters, E., & Wall, S. (1978). *Patterns of attachment*. Hillsdale, NJ: Erlbaum.

Akiskal, H. S., & Benazzi, F. (2007). Continuous distribution of atypical depressive symptoms between major depressive and bipolar II disorders: Dose-response relationship with bipolar family history. *Psychopathology, 41*, 39–42.

Aksan, N., Kochanska, G., & Ortmann, M. R. (2006). Mutually responsive orientation between parents and their young children: Toward methodological advances in the science of relationships. *Developmental Psychology, 42*, 833–848.

Akshoomoff, N., Pierce, K., & Courchesne, E. (2002). The neurobiological basis of autism from a developmental perspective. *Development and Psychopathology, 14*, 613–634.

Al-Namlah, A. S., Fernyhough, C., & Meins, E. (2006). Sociocultural influences on the development of verbal mediation: Private speech and phonological recoding in Saudi Arabian and British samples. *Developmental Psychology, 42*, 117–131.

Aldwin, C. M., & Levenson, M. R. (2004). Posttraumatic growth: A developmental perspective. *Psychological Inquiry, 15*, 19–22.

Alexander, F., & French, T. M. (1946). *Psychoanalytic therapy*. New York: Rolande.

Allemand, M., Zimprich, D., & Hendriks, A. A. J. (2008). Age differences in five personality domains across the life span. *Developmental Psychology, 44*, 758–770.

Allemand, M., Zimprich, D., & Martin, M. (2008). Long-term correlated change in personality traits in old age. *Psychology of Aging, 23*, 545–557.

Allen, T. D., & Finkelstein, L. M. (2003). Beyond mentoring: Alternative sources and functions of developmental support. *Career Development Quarterly, 51*, 346–355.

Alliance for Childhood. (2000). *Fool's gold: A critical look at children and computers*. College Park, MD: Alliance for Childhood.

Almeida, D. M., & Horn, M. C. (2004). Is daily life more stressful during middle adulthood? In O. G. Brim, C. D. Ryff, & R. C. Kessler (Eds.), *How healthy are we? A national study of well-being at midlife* (pp. 425–451). Chicago: University of Chicago Press.

Alonso-Fernandez, P., & De la Fuente, M. (2011). Role of the immune system in aging and longevity. *Current Aging Science, 4*, 78–100.

Als, H. (1986). A syntactive model of neonatal behavioral organization: Framework for the assessment of neurobehavioral development in the premature infant and for support of infants and parents in the neonatal intensive care environment. *Physical and Occupational Therapy in Pediatrics, 6*, 3–53.

Althof, W., & Berkowitz, M. W. (2006). Moral education and character education: Their relationship and roles in citizenship education. *Journal of Moral Education, 35*, 495–518.

Alzheimer's Association, (2012). Alzheimer's disease facts and figures. *Alzheimer's & Dementia, 8*. Retrieved October 13, 2013 from https://www.alz.org/downloads/facts_figures_2012.pdfh15

Amato, P. R. (2001). Children of divorce in the 1990s: An update of the Amato and Keith (1991) meta-analysis. *Journal of Family Psychology, 15*, 355–370.

Amato, P. R. (2005). The impact of family formation change on the cognitive, social, and emotional well-being of the next generation. *The Future of Children, 15*, 75–96.

Amato, P. R., & Cheadle, J. (2005). The long reach of divorce: Divorce and child well-being across three generations. *Journal of Marriage and Family, 67*, 191–206.

Amato, P. R., & Keith, B. (1991). Consequences of parental divorce for children's well-being: A meta-analysis. *Psychological Bulletin 10*, 26–46.

American Academy of Pediatrics, Committee on Psychosocial Aspects of Child and Family Health (1998). Guidance for effective discipline. *Pediatrics, 101*, 723–728.

American Academy of Pediatrics [AAP]. (2001). Policy statement: Children, adolescents and television. *Pediatrics, 107*, 423–426.

American Academy of Pediatrics., American Public Health Association, and National Resource Center for Health and Safety in Child Care. (2002). *Caring for our children: National health and safety performance standards: Guidelines for out-of-home child care* (2nd ed.). Elk Grove Village, IL: American Academy of Pediatrics.

American Academy of Pediatrics. (2011). Media use by children younger than 2 years. *Pediatrics, 128*, 1040–1045.

American Academy of Pediatrics. (2012). Policy statement: Breastfeeding and the use of human milk. *Pediatrics, 129*, e827–e841.

American Psychiatric Association [APA]. (2013). *Diagnostic and statistical manual of mental disorders* (5th ed.). Arlington, VA: American Psychiatric Publishing.

American Psychiatric Association [APA]. (2000). *Diagnostic and statistical manual of mental disorders* (4th ed.). Washington, DC: Author.

American Psychological Association's Board of Educational Affairs. (1995). *Learner-centered psychological principles: A framework for school redesign and reform*. Washington, DC: American Psychological Association.

American Psychological Association. (2003). Guidelines on multicultural education, training, research, practice, and organizational change for psychologists. *American Psychologist, 58*, 377–402.

American Speech-Language-Hearing Association. (1997–2004). *How does your child hear and talk?* Rockville, MD: Author. Retrieved October 30, 2004, from http://www.asha.org/public/speech/development/child_hear_talk.html

Anand, B. K., & Brobeck, J. R. (1951). Hypothalamic control of food intake in rats and cats. *Yale Journal of Biology and Medicine, 24*, 123–140.

Anda, R. F., Brown, D. W., Felitti, V.J., Bremner, J. D., Dube, S. R., & Giles, W. H. (2007) Adverse childhood experiences and prescribed psychotropic medications in adults. *American Journal of Preventive Medicine, 32,* 389–394.

Anda, R. F., Felitti, V. J., Bremner, J. D., Walker, J. D., Whitfield, C., Perry, B. D., et al. (2006). The enduring effects of abuse and related adverse experiences in childhood: A convergence of evidence from neurobiology and epidemiology. *European Archives of Psychiatry and Clinical Neuroscience, 256,* 174–186.

Andersen, S. L., & Teicher M. H. (2008). Stress, sensitive periods and maturational events in adolescent depression. *Trends in Neurosciences, 31,* 183–191.

Anderson, C., Kraus, M. W., Galinsky, A. D., Keltner, D. (2012). The local ladder effect: Social status and subjective well being. *Psychological Science, 23,* 764–771.

Anderson, C. A., Shibuya, A., Ihori, N., Swing, E. L., Bushman, B. J., Sakamoto, et al. (2010). Violent video game effects on aggression, empathy, and prosocial behavior in Eastern and Western countries: A meta-analytic review. *Psychological Bulletin, 136,* 151–173.

Anderson, D. R., Huston, A. C., Schmitt, K. L., Linebarger, D. L., & Wright, J. C. (2001). Early childhood television viewing and adolescent behavior. *Monographs of the Society for Research in Child Development, 66* (Serial No. 264).

Anderson, E. (1994, May). The code of the streets. *Atlantic Monthly, 273*(5), 81–94.

Anderson, P., Beach, S. R. H., & Kaslow, N. J. (1999). Marital discord and depression: The potential of attachment theory to guide integrative clinical intervention. In T. Joiner & J. C. Coyne (Eds.), *The interactional nature of depression* (pp. 271–297). Washington, DC: American Psychological Association.

Anderson, R. N., & Smith, B. L. (2003). Deaths: Leading causes for 2001. *CDC National Vital Statistics Report, 54*(9).

Andrews, G., & Halford, G. S. (2002). A cognitive complexity metric applied to cognitive development. *Cognitive Psychology, 45,* 153–219.

Angold, A., & Costello, E. J. (1993). Depressive comorbidity in children and adolescents: Empirical, theoretical and methodological issues. *American Journal of Psychiatry, 150,* 1779–1791.

Angold, A., & Rutter, M. (1992). Effects of age and pubertal status on depression in a large clinical sample. *Development and Psychopathology, 4,* 5–28.

Angst, J., & Merikangas, K. R. (2001). Multi-dimensional criteria for the diagnosis of depression. *Journal of Affective Disorders, 62,* 7–15.

Antell, S. E., & Keating, D. P. (1983). Perception of numerical invariance in neonates. *Child Development, 54,* 695–701.

Anthis, K. S., Dunkel, C. S., & Anderson, B. (2004). Gender and identity status differences in late adolescents' possible selves. *Journal of Adolescence, 27,* 147–152.

Antognini, F. C., & Liptzin, B. (2008). Psychotherapy for late-life mood disorders. In J. M. Ellison, H. Kyomen, & S. Verma (Eds.), *Mood disorders in later life* (2nd ed; pp. 315–337). New York: Informa Healthcare.

Antonucci, T. C., Lansford, J. E., & Akiyama, H. (2001). Impact of positive and negative aspects of marital relationships and friendships on well-being of older adults. *Applied Developmental Science, 5,* 68–75.

Archer, J. (1999). *The nature of grief: The evolution and psychology of reactions to loss.* London: Routledge.

Archer, S. L. (1992). A feminist's approach to identity research. In G. R. Adams, R. Montemayor, & T. P. Gullotta (Eds.), *Advances in adolescent development: Vol. 4.*

Adolescent identity formation (pp. 25–49). Newbury Park, CA: Sage.

Archer, S. L., & Waterman, A. S. (1988). Psychological individualism: Gender differences or gender neutrality? *Human Development, 31,* 65–81.

Archibald, A. B., Linver, M. R., Graber, J. A., & Brooks-Gunn, J. (2002) Parent-adolescent relationships and girls' unhealthy eating: Testing reciprocal effects. *Journal of Research on Adolescence, 12,* 451–461.

Aries, P. (1960). *Centuries of childhood: A social history of family life* (R. Baldick, Trans.). New York: Knopf.

Arlin, P. K. (1984). Adolescent and adult thought: A structural interpretation. In M. L. Commons, F. A. Richards, & C. Armon (Eds.), *Beyond formal operations* (pp. 258–271). New York: Praeger.

Arnett, J. J. (1992). Reckless behavior in adolescence: A developmental perspective. *Developmental Review, 12,* 339–373.

Arnett, J. J. (1999). Adolescent storm and stress, reconsidered. *American Psychologist, 54,* 317–326.

Arnett, J. J. (2000). Emerging adulthood: A theory of development from the late teens through the twenties. *American Psychologist, 55,* 469–480.

Arnett, J. J. (2002). The psychology of globalization. *American Psychologist, 57,* 774–783.

Arnett, J. J. (2004). *Emerging adulthood: The winding road from the late teens through the twenties.* New York: Oxford University Press.

Arnett, J. J. (2007). Emerging adulthood: What is it, and what is it good for? *Child Development Perspectives, 1,* 68–73.

Arnett, J. J. (2010). Oh, grow up! Generational grumbling and the new life stage of emerging adulthood-Commentary on Trzesniewski & Donnellan (2010). *Perspectives on Psychological Science, 5,* 89–92.

Arnett, J. J., (2013). Adolescence and emerging adulthood (5th Ed.). Upper Saddle River, NJ: Pearson Education, Inc. Reprinted and Electronically reproduced by permission of Pearson Education.

Arnett, J. J., & Brody, G. H. (2008). A fraught passage: The identity challenges of African American emerging adults. *Human Development, 51,* 291–193.

Arnett, J. J., & Taber, S. (1994). Adolescence terminable and interminable: When does adolescence end? *Journal of Youth and Adolescence, 23,* 517–523.

Arnold, L. E., Chuang, S., Davies, M., Abikoff, H. B., Conners, C. K., Elliott, G. R. (2004). Nine months of multicomponent behavioral treatment for ADHD and effectiveness of MTS fading procedures. *Journal of Abnormal Child Psychology, 32,* 39–51.

Aronson, J., & Fried, C. (1998). *Reducing stereotype threat and boosting academic achievement of African Americans: The role of conceptions of intelligence.* Unpublished manuscript.

Aronson, K., & Weiner, M. B. (2007). *Aging parents, aging children.* Lanham, MD: Rowman & Littlefield.

Aronson, P. J., Mortimer, J. T., Zierman, C., & Hacker, M. (1996). Generational differences in early work experiences and evaluations. In J. T. Mortimer & M. D. Finch (Eds.), *Adolescents, work, and family: An intergenerational developmental analysis* (pp. 25–62). Newbury Park, CA: Sage.

Arredondo, P., & Perez, P. (2006). Historical perspectives on the multicultural guidelines and contemporary application. *Professional Psychology : Research and Practice, 37,* 1–5.

Asher, S. R., & Dodge, K. A. (1986). Identifying children who are rejected by their peers. *Developmental Psychology, 22,* 444–449.

Asher, S. R., Markell, R. A., & Hymel, S. (1981). Identifying children at risk in peer relations: A critique of the rate-of-interaction approach to assessment. *Child Development, 52,* 1239–1245.

Ashwood, P., Krakowiak, P., Hertz-Picciotto, I., Hansen, R., Pessah, I., & Van de Water, J. (2011). Elevated plasma cytokines in autism spectrum disorders provide evidence of immune dysfunction and are associated with impaired behavioral outcome. *Brain, Behavior and Immunity, 25,* 40–45.

Asperger, H. (1991). "Autistic psychopathy" in childhood. In U. Frith (Ed. & Trans.), *Autism and Asperger syndrome* (pp. 37–92). Cambridge, England: Cambridge University Press. (Original work published 1944)

Astin, A. W. (1993). *What matters in college? Four critical years revisited.* San Francisco: Jossey-Bass.

Astin, A. W., Korn, W. S., Sax, L. J., & Mahoney, K. M. (1994). *The American freshman: National norms for fall 1994.* Los Angeles: Higher Education Research Institute, UCLA.

Atchley, R. C. (1976). *The sociology of retirement.* New York: Wiley.

Atzil, S., Hendler, T., & Feldman, R. (2011). Specifying the neurobiological basis of human attachment: Brain, hormones, and behavior in synchronous and intrusive mothers. *Neuropsychopharmacology, 36,* 2603–2615.

Aucoin, K. J., Frick, P. J., & Bodin, S. D. (2006). Corporal punishment and child adjustment. *Journal of Applied Developmental Psychology, 27,* 527–541.

Aud, S., KewalRamani, A., and Frohlich, L. (2011). *America's Youth: Transitions to Adulthood* (NCES 2012–026). U.S. Department of Education, National Center for Education Statistics. Washington, DC: U.S. Government Printing Office.

Aupperle, R. L., Melrose, A. J., Stein, M. B., & Paulus, M. P. (2012). Executive function and PTSD: Disengaging from trauma. *Neuropharmacology, 62,* 686–694.

Austin, M. P., Hadzi-Pavlovic, D., Saint, K., & Parker, G. (2005). Antenatal screening for the prediction of postnatal depression: Validation of a psychosocial Pregnancy Risk Questionnaire. *Acta Psychiatrica Scandinavica, 112,* 310–317.

Austin, M., Rhodes, J., & Lewis, D. (1997). Differential distribution of corticotrophin-releasing hormone immunoreactive axons in monoaminergis nuclei of the human brainstem, *Neuropsychopharmacology, 17,* 326–341.

Averhart, C. A., & Bigler, R. S. (1997). Shades of meaning: Skin tone, racial attitudes, and constructive memory in African American children. *Journal of Experimental Child Psychology, 67,* 363–388.

Avis, N. E., Stellato, R., Crawford, S., Johannes, C., & Longcope, C. (2000). Is there an association between menopause status and sexual functioning? *Menopause, 7,* 297–309.

Axline, V. (1947). *Play therapy: The inner dynamics of childhood.* New York: Houghton Mifflin.

Azar, B. (1999, February). Consortium of editors pushes for shift in child research methods. *APA Monitor, 30,* 20–21.

Bachman, J. (1997). *Smoking, drinking, and drug use in young adulthood: The impact of new freedoms and responsibilities.* Mahwah, NJ: Erlbaum.

Bachman, J. G., Safron, D. J., Sy, S. R., & Schulenberg, J. E. (2003). Wishing to work: New perspectives on how adolescents' part-time work intensity is linked to educational disengagement, substance use, and other problem behaviors. *International Journal of Behavioral Development, 27,* 301–315.

Baer, W. M., & Hanson, L. C. (2000). Families' perceptions of the added value of hospice in the nursing home. *Journal of the American Geriatric Society, 48,* 879–882.

Badanas, L. S., Dmitrieva, J., & Watamura, S. E. (2012). Understanding cortisol reactivity across the day at child care: The potential buffering role of secure attachments to caregivers. *Early Childhood Research Quarterly, 27,* 156–165.

Bahrick, L. E., & Pickens, J. N. (1995). Infant memory for object motion across a period of three months: Implications for a four-phase attention function. *Journal of Experimental Child Psychology, 59,* 343–371.

Bailey, B. A., McCook, J. G., Hodge, A., & McGrady, L. (2012). Infant birth outcomes among substance using women: Why quitting smoking during pregnancy is just as important as quitting illicit drug use. *Maternal and Child Health, 16,* 414–422.

Bailey, J. M., Bobrow, D., Wolfe, M., & Mikach, S. (1995). Sexual orientation of adult sons of gay fathers. *Developmental Psychology, 31,* 124–129.

Bailey, J. M., Dunne, M. P., & Martin, N. G. (2000). Genetic and environmental influences on sexual orientation and its correlates in an Australian twin sample. *Journal of Personality and Social Psychology, 78,* 524–536.

Bailey, T., & Morest, V. S. (1998). Preparing youth for employment. In S. Halperin (Ed.), *The forgotten half revisited: American youth and young families, 1988–2008* (pp. 115–136). Washington, DC: American Youth Policy Forum.

Baillargeon, R. (2000). Reply to Bogartz, Shinskey, and Schilling; Schilling; and Cashon and Cohen. *Infancy, 1,* 447–462.

Baird, A. A., & Fugelsang, J. A. (2004). The emergence of consequential thought: Evidence from neuroscience. *Philosophical Transactions of the Royal Society of London, Series B: Biological Sciences, 359,* 1797–1804.

Bakermans-Kranenburg, M. J., & van IJzendoorn, M. H. (2004). No association with the dopamine D4 receptor (D4DR) and -521 C/T promoter polymorphisms with infant disorganization. *Attachment and Human Development, 6,* 211–218.

Bakermans-Kranenburg, M. J., van IJzendoorn, M. H., & Juffer, F. (2003). Less is more: Meta-analyses of sensitivity and attachment interventions in early childhood. *Psychological Bulletin, 129,* 195–215.

Baker-Ward, L., Ornstein, P. A., & Holden, D. J. (1984). The expression of memorization in early childhood. *Journal of Experimental Child Psychology, 37,* 555–575.

Bakker, A. B. (2011). An evidence-based model of work engagement. *Current Directions in Psychological Science, 20,* 265–269.

Baldwin, A. L. (1948). Socialization and the parent–child relationship. *Child Development, 19,* 127–136.

Ballard, C., Gauthier, S., Corbett, A., Brayne, C., Aarsland, D., & Jones, E. (2011). Alzheimer's disease. *The Lancet, 377,* 1019–1031.

Ballie, R. (2001). Teen drinking more dangerous than previously thought. *Monitor on Psychology, 32,* 12.

Balsam, K. F., Beauchaine, T. P., Rothblum, E. D., & Solomon, S. E. (2008). Three-year follow-up of same-sex couples who had civil unions in Vermont, same-sex couples not in civil unions, and heterosexual married couples. *Developmental Psychology, 44,* 102–116.

Baltes, M. M., & Baltes, P. B. (1990). *The psychology of control and aging.* Hillsdale, NJ: Erlbaum.

Baltes, P. B. (1997). On the incomplete architecture of human ontogeny: Selection, optimization, and compensation as foundation of developmental theory. *American Psychologist, 52,* 366–380.

Baltes, P. B., Lindenberger, U., & Staudinger, U. M. (1998). Life-span theory in developmental psychology. In W. Damon (Series Ed.) & R. M. Lerner (Vol. Ed.), *Handbook of child psychology: Vol. 1. Theoretical models of human development* (5th ed., pp. 1029–1143). New York: Wiley.

Baltes, P. B., Lindenberger, U., & Staudinger, U. (2006). Life span theory in developmental psychology. In W. Damon & R. M. Lerner (Series Eds.) & R. M. Lerner (Vol. Ed.), *Handbook of child psychology: Vol. 1. Theoretical models of human development* (6th ed., pp. 569–664). Hoboken, NJ: Wiley.

Baltes, P. B., & Smith, J. (2008). The fascination of wisdom: Its nature, ontogeny, and function. *Perspectives on Psychological Science, 3,* 56–64.

Baltes, P. B., & Staudinger, U. M. (2000). Wisdom: A metaheuristic (pragmatic) to orchestrate mind and virtue toward excellence. *American Psychologist, 55,* 122–136.

Bamshad, M. J., & Olson, S. E. (2003). Does race exist? *Scientific American, 289,* 78–85.

Bandura, A. (1974). Behavior theory and the models of man. *American Psychologist, 29,* 859–869.

Bandura, A. (1977). *Social learning theory.* Upper Saddle River, NJ: Prentice Hall.

Bandura, A. (1986). *Social foundations of thought and action: A social cognitive theory.* Upper Saddle River, NJ: Prentice Hall.

Bandura, A. (1989). Human agency in social cognitive theory. *American Psychologist, 44,* 1175–1184.

Bandura, A. (1990). Conclusion: Reflections on nonability determinants of competence. In R. J. Sternberg & J. Kolligian, Jr. (Eds.), *Competence considered* (pp. 316–352). New Haven, CT: Yale University Press.

Bandura, A. (1997). *Self-efficacy: The exercise of control.* New York: Freeman.

Bandura, A. (1999). Social cognitive theory of personality. In L. Pervin & O. John (Eds.), *Handbook of personality* (2nd ed., pp. 154–196). New York: Guilford Press.

Bandura, A., & Bussey, K. (2004). On broadening the cognitive, motivational, and sociocultural scope of theorizing about gender development and functioning: Comment on Martin, Ruble, and Szkerybalo (2002). *Psychological Bulletin, 130,* 691–701.

Banich, M. T. (2009). Executive function: The search for an integrated account. *Current Directions in Psychological Science, 18,* 89.

Banks, W. C. (1976). White preference in blacks: A paradigm in search of a phenomenon. *Psychological Bulletin, 83,* 1179–1186.

Barber, B. K., Stolz, H. E., & Olsen, J. A. (2005). Parental support, psychological control, and behavioral control: Assessing relevance across time, culture, and method. *Monographs of the Society for Research in Child Development, 70* (Serial No. 282), vii–151.

Barber, B. L., Eccles, J. S., & Stone, M. R. (2001). Whatever happened to the jock, the brain, and the princess? Young adult pathways linked to adolescent activity involvement and social identity. *Journal of Adolescent Research, 16,* 429–455.

Barber, B. R. (1992). *An aristocracy of everyone: The politics of education and the future of America.* New York: Oxford University Press.

Barclay, J. S., Blackhall, L. J., & Tulsky, J. A. (2007). Communication strategies and cultural issues in the delivery of bad news. *Journal of Palliative Medicine, 10,* 958–977.

Bardone-Cone, A. M., Cass, K. M., & Ford, J. A. (2008). Examining body dissatisfaction in young men within a biopsychosocial framework. *Body Image, 5,* 183–194.

Barich, R. R., & Bielby, D. D. (1996). Rethinking marriage: Change and stability in expectations. *Journal of Family Issues, 17,* 505–525.

Barker, E. T., & Galambos, N. L. (2003). Body dissatisfaction of adolescent girls and boys: Risk and resource factors. *Journal of Early Adolescence, 23,* 141–165.

Barker, R. G., & Gump, P. V. (1964). *Big school, small school: High school size and student behavior.* Stanford, CA: Stanford University Press.

Barkley, R. A. (1997). Behavioral inhibition, sustained attention, and executive function: Constructing a unified theory of ADHD. *Psychological Bulletin, 121,* 65–94.

Barnes, G. M., Welte, J. W., & Dintcheff, B. (1992). Alcohol misuse among college students and other young adults: Findings from a general population study in New York State. *International Journal of the Addictions, 27,* 917–934.

Barnes, L. L., de Leon, C. F. Mendes, Wilson, R. S., Bienias, J. L., & Evans, D. A. (2004). Social resources and cognitive decline in a population of older African Americans and whites. *Neurology, 63,* 2322–2326.

Barnett, D., Ganiban, J., & Cicchetti, D. (1997). Maltreatment, emotional reactivity, and the development of type D attachments from 12 to 24 months of age. Unpublished manuscript.

Barnett, W., Jung, K., Yarosz, D., Thomas, J., Hornbeck, A., Stechuk, R., & Burns, S. (2008). Educational effects of the Tools of the Mind Curriculum: A randomized trial. *Early Childhood Research Quarterly, 23,* 299–313.

Barnett, W. S., & Masse, L. N. (2007). Comparative benefit-cost analysis of the Abecedarian program and its policy implications. *Economics of Education Review, 26,* 113–125.

Baron, R. M., & Kenny, D. A. (1986). The moderator-mediator variable distinction in social psychological research: Conceptual, strategic, and statistical considerations. *Journal of Personality and Social Psychology, 51,* 1173–1182.

Baron-Cohen, S. (2000). Is Asperger syndrome/high-functioning autism necessarily a disability? *Development and Psychopathology, 12,* 489–500.

Baron-Cohen, S. (2002). The extreme male brain theory of autism. *Trends in Cognitive Science, 6,* 248–254.

Barr, D. (1997). Friendship and belonging. In R. L. Selman, C. L. Watts, & L. H. Schultz (Eds.), *Fostering friendship: Pair therapy for treatment and prevention* (pp. 19–30). New York: Aldine de Gruyter.

Barrera, M., Jr., & Sandler, I. N. (2006). Prevention: A report of progress and momentum into the future. *Clinical Psychology: Science and Practice, 13,* 221–226.

Barrera, M., Jr., Castro, F. G., & Holleran-Steiker, L. K. (2011). A critical analysis of approaches to the development of preventive interventions for subcultural groups. *American Journal of Community Psychology, 48,* 439–454.

Bartholomew, K., & Horowitz, L. (1991). Attachment styles among young adults: A test of the four category model. *Journal of Personality and Social Psychology, 61,* 226–244.

Bartholomew, K., & Shaver, P. R. (1998). Methods of assessing adult attachment: Do they converge? In J. A. Simpson & W. S. Rholes (Eds.), *Attachment theory and close relationships* (pp. 25–45). New York: Guilford Press.

Basseches, M. (1984). *Dialectical thinking and adult development*. Norwood, NJ: Ablex.

Bateman, D., Ng, S., Hansen, C., & Heagarty, M. (1993). The effects of intrauterine cocaine exposure in newborns. *American Journal of Public Health, 83*, 190–194.

Bates, J. E., Maslin, C. A., & Frankel, K. A. (1995). Attachment security, mother-child interaction, and temperament as predictors of behavior-problem ratings at age three years. *Monographs of the Society for Research in Child Development, 50*, 167–193.

Bauer, P. J. (2006). Event memory. In W. Damon & R. M. Lerner (Series Eds.), D. Kuhn & R. S. Siegler (Vol. Ed.), *Handbook of child psychology: Vol. 2. Cognition, perception and language* (6th ed., pp. 373–425). Hoboken, NJ: Wiley.

Baumeister, R. F. (1991). *Meanings of life.* New York: Guilford Press.

Baumeister, R. F., & Bowden, J. M. (1994). Shrinking the self. In T. M. Brinthaupt & R. P. Lipka (Eds.), *Changing the self: Philosophies, techniques, and experiences.* Albany: State University of New York Press.

Baumeister, R. F., Bratslavsky, E., Finkenauer, C., & Vohs, K. D. (2001). Bad is stronger than good. *Review of General Psychology, 5*, 323–370.

Baumrind, D. (1971). Current patterns of parental authority. *Development Psychology Monographs, 4*(1, Pt. 2), 1–103.

Baumrind, D. (1972). An exploratory study of socialization effects on Black children: Some Black/White comparisons. *Child Development, 43*, 261–267.

Baumrind, D. (1978). Parental disciplinary patterns and social competence in children. *Youth and Society, 9*, 239–276.

Baumrind, D. (1989). Rearing competent children. In W. Damon (Ed.), *Child development today and tomorrow* (pp. 349–378). San Francisco: Jossey-Bass.

Baumrind, D. (1991). Parenting styles and adolescent development. In J. Brooks, R. Lerner, & A. C. Petersen (Eds.), *The encyclopedia of adolescence* (pp. 758–772). New York: Garland.

Baumrind, D. (1993). The average expectable environment is not good enough: A response to Scarr. *Child Development, 64*, 1299–1317.

Baumrind, D. (2001). *Does causally relevant research support a blanket injunction against the use of spanking?* Paper presented at the annual meeting of the American Psychological Association, San Francisco.

Bavelier, D., Green, C. S., & Dye, M. W. G. (2010). Children, wired: For better and for worse. *Neuron, 67*, 692–701.

Baxter-Magolda, M., & Porterfield, W. D. (1985). A new approach to assessing intellectual development on the Perry Scheme. *Journal of College Student Personnel, 21*, 46–58.

Bean, R. A., Bush, K. R., McKenny, P. C., & Wilson, S. M. (2003). The impact of parental support, behavioral control, and psychological control on the academic achievement and self-esteem of African American and European American adolescents. *Journal of Adolescent Research, 18*, 523–541.

Bear, G. G., & Rys, G. S. (1994). Moral reasoning, classroom behavior, and sociometric status among elementary school children. *Developmental Psychology, 30*, 633–638.

Beauchaine, T. (2001). Vagal tone, development, and Gray's motivational theory: Toward an integrated model of autonomic nervous system functioning in psychopathology *Development and Psychopathology, 13*, 183–214.

Beauchaine, T. P., Neuhaus, E., Brenner, S. L., & Gatzke-Kopp, L. (2008). Ten good reasons to consider biological processes in prevention and intervention research. *Development and Psychopathology, 20*, 745–774.

Beccuti, G., & Pannain, S. (2011). Sleep and obesity. *Current Opinion in Clinical Nutrition and Metabolic Care, 14*, 402–412.

Beck, A. T. (1963). *Depression: Causes and treatment*. Philadelphia: University of Pennsylvania Press.

Bednar, R. L., & Petersen, S. R. (1995). *Self-esteem: Paradoxes and innovations in clinical theory and practice* (2nd ed.). Washington, DC: American Psychological Association.

Beeghly, M., & Cicchetti, D. (1994). Child maltreatment, attachment, and the self-system: Emergence of an internal state lexicon in toddlers at high social risk. *Development and Psychopathology, 6*, 5–30.

Beelman, A., Pfingsten, U., & Losel, F. (1994). Effects of training social competence in children: A meta-analysis of recent evaluation studies. *Journal of Clinical Child Psychology, 23*, 260–271.

Beilin, H. (1999). Understanding the photographic image. *Journal of Applied Developmental Psychology, 20*, 1–30.

Bell, M. A., & Fox, N. A. (1992). The relations between frontal brain electrical activity and cognitive development during infancy. *Child Development, 63*, 1142–1163.

Bell, A., Weinberg, M., & Hammersmith, S. (1981). *Sexual preference: Its development in men and women*. Bloomington: Indiana University Press.

Bell, R. Q., & Chapman, M. (1986). Child effects in studies using experimental or brief longitudinal approaches to socialization. *Developmental Psychology, 22*, 595–603.

Bell, R. Q., & Harper, L. V. (Eds.). (1977). *Child effects on adults*. Hillsdale, NJ: Erlbaum.

Bellah, R. N., Madsen, R., Sullivan, W. M., Swidler, A., & Tipton, S. M. (1985). *Habits of the heart: Individualism and commitment in American life*. New York: Harper & Row.

Bellamy, C. (2005). *The state of the world's children: 2005*. New York: UNICEF.

Belloc, N. B., & Breslow, L. (1972). Relationships of physical health status and health practices. *Preventive Medicine, 1*, 409–421.

Belsky, J. (2005). Differential susceptibility to rearing influence: An evolutionary hypothesis and some evidence. In B. J. Ellis & D. F. Bjorklund (Eds.), *Origins of the social mind: Evolutionary psychology and child development* (pp. 139–163). New York: Guilford Press.

Belsky, J. (2006). Determinants and consequences of infant-parent attachment. In L. Balter & C. S. Tamis-LeMonda (Eds.), *Child psychology: A handbook of contemporary issues* (2nd ed., pp. 53–77). New York: Psychology Press.

Belsky, J., Garduque, L., & Hrncir, E. (1984). Assessing performance, competence, and executive capacity in infant play: Relations to home environment and security of attachment. *Developmental Psychology, 20*, 406–417.

Belsky, J., & Kelly, J. (1994). *The transition to parenthood: How a first child changes a marriage. Why some couples grow closer and some grow apart*. New York: Dell.

Belsky, J., & Pluess, M. (2009). Beyond diathesis-stress: Differential susceptibility to environmental influences. *Psychological Bulletin, 135*, 885–908.

Belsky, J., Spanier, G., & Rovine, M. (1983). Stability and change in a marriage across the transition to parenthood. *Journal of Marriage and the Family, 45*, 567–577.

Belsky, J., Vandell, D. E., Burchinal, M., Clarke-Stewart, K. A., McCartney, K., Owen, M. T., et al. (2007). Are there long-term effects of early child care? *Child Development, 78*, 681–701.

Belsky, J., & Volling, B. L. (1987). Mothering, fathering, and marital interaction in the family triad during infancy: Exploring family systems' processes. In P. W. Berman & F. A. Pedersen (Eds.), *Men's transitions to parenthood: Longitudinal studies of early family experience* (pp. 37–63). Hillsdale, NJ: Erlbaum.

Bem, S. L. (1981). Gender schema theory: A cognitive account of sex typing. *Psychological Review, 88*, 354–364.

Bem, S. L. (1989). Genital knowledge and gender constancy in preschool children. *Child Development, 60*, 649–662.

Bendersky, M., & Lewis, M. (1998). Arousal modulation in cocaine-exposed infants. *Developmental Psychology, 43*, 555–564.

Benjamin, J., Ebstein, R. P., & Belmaker, R. H. (Eds.). (2002). *Molecular genetics and the human personality*. Washington, DC: American Psychiatric Association Press.

Benner, A. D., Graham, S., & Mistry, R. S. (2008). Discerning direct and mediated effects of ecological structures and processes on adolescents' educational outcomes. *Developmental Psychology, 44*, 840–854.

Benson, P. (1997). *All kids are our kids*. San Francisco: Jossey-Bass.

Berecki-Gisolf, J., Begum, N., & Dobson, A. J. (2009). Symptoms reported by women in midlife: Menopausal transition or aging? *Menopause-The Journal of the North American Menopause Society, 16*, 1021–1029.

Berenbaum, S. A. (2004). Androgen and behavior: Implications for the treatment of children with disorders of sexual differentiation. In O. H. Pescovitz & E. A. Eugster (Eds.), *Pediatric endocrinology: Mechanisms, manifestations, and management* (pp. 275–284). Philadelphia: Lippincott, Williams, & Wilkins.

Berg, J. M., Wrzesniewski, A. M., & Dutton, J. E. (2010). Perceiving and responding to challenges in job crafting at different ranks: When proactivity requires adaptivity. *Journal of Organizational Behavior, 31*, 158–186.

Berg, S. (1987). Intelligence and terminal decline. In G. L. Maddox & E. W. Busse (Eds.), *Aging: The universal experience* (pp. 414–415). New York: Springer.

Berkman, N. D., Bulik, C. M., Brownley, K. A., Lohr, K. N., Sedway, J. A., Rooks, A., et al. (February 2006). *Management of Eating Disorders Evidence Report*. Evidence Report/Technology Assessment Number 135. AHRQ Publication No. 06-E010. Prepared by RTI International–University of North Carolina Evidence-Based Practice Center under Contract No. 290-02-0016. Rockville, MD: Agency for Healthcare Research and Quality.

Berkowitz, M. W., & Bier, M. C. (2004). Research based character education. *Annals of the American Academy of Political and Social Science, 591*, 72–85.

Berlin, L. J., Appleyard, K., & Dodge, K. A. (2011). Intergenerational continuity in child maltreatment: Mediating mechanisms and implications for prevention. *Child Development, 82*, 162–176.

Bernal, M. E., & Knight, G. P. (1993). *Ethnic identity: Formation and transmission among Hispanics and other minorities*. Albany: State University of New York Press.

Bernard, K., Dozier, M., Bick, J., Lewis-Morrarty, E., Lindhiem, O., & Carlson, E. (2012). Enhancing attachment organization among maltreated children: Results of a randomized clinical trial. *Child Development, 83*, 623–636.

Berndt, T. J. (1982). The features and effects of friendship in early adolescence. *Child Development, 53*, 1447–1460.

Berndt, T. J., & Heller, K. A. (1986). Gender stereotypes and social inferences: A developmental study. *Journal of Personality and Social Psychology, 50,* 889–898.

Berndt, T. J., & Keefe, K. (1996). Friends' influence on school adjustment: A motivational analysis. In J. Juvonen & K. R. Wentzel (Eds.), *Social motivation: Understanding children's school adjustment.* New York: Cambridge University Press.

Berndt, T. J., Miller, K. A., & Park, K. (1989). Adolescents' perceptions of friends' and parents' influence on aspects of school adjustment. *Journal of Early Adolescence, 9,* 419–435.

Berndt, T. J., & Murphy, L. M. (2002). Influences of friends and friendships: Myths, truths, and research recommendations. *Advances in Child Development and Behavior, 30,* 275–310.

Berninger, V. W., & Hart, T. M. (1992). A developmental neuropsychological perspective for reading and writing acquisition. *Educational Psychologist, 27,* 415–434.

Bernstein, A. C., & Cowan, P. A. (1975). Children's concepts of how people get babies. *Child Development, 46,* 77–91.

Berntsen, D., Johannessen, K. B., Thomsen, Y. D., Bertelsen, M., Hoyle, R. H., & Rubin, D. C. (2012). Peace and war: Trajectories of posttraumatic stress disorder symptoms before, during, and after military deployment in Afghanistan. *Psychological Science, 23,* 1557–1565.

Berntsen, D., & Rubin, D. C. (2002). Emotionally charged autobiography memories across the life span: The recall of happy, sad, traumatic and involuntary memories. *Psychology and Aging, 17,* 636–652.

Berntson, G. G., & Cacioppo, J. T. (2007). Integrative physiology: Homeostasis, allostasis and the orchestration of systemic physiology. In J. T. Cacioppo, L. G. Tassinary, & G. G. Berntson (Eds.), *Handbook of Psychophysiology* (3rd ed., pp. 433–452). Cambridge, UK: Cambridge University Press.

Bessenoff, G. R., & Del Priore, R. E. (2007). Women, weight, and age: Social comparison to magazine images across the lifespan. *Sex Roles, 56,* 215–222.

Best, J. R., & Miller, P. H. (2010). A developmental perspective on executive function. *Child Development, 81,* 1641–1660.

Best, D. L. (2010). Gender. In Bornstein, M. H. (Ed.), *Handbook of cultural developmental science* (pp. 209–222). New York: Psychology Press.

Bettleheim, B. (1967). *The empty fortress: Infantile autism and the birth of the self.* New York: Free Press.

Betz, N. E. (2004). Contributions of self-efficacy to career counseling: A personal perspective. *Career Development Quarterly, 52,* 340–353.

Betz, N. E., & Hackett, G. (1981). The relationship of career-related self-efficacy expectations to perceived career options in college women and men. *Journal of Counseling Psychology, 28,* 399–410.

Betz, N. E., & Schifano, R. S. (2000). Evaluation of an intervention to increase realistic self-efficacy and interests in college women. *Journal of Vocational Behavior, 56,* 35–52.

Beuf, A. H. (1977). *Red children in White America.* University Park: Pennsylvania State University Press.

Bialystok, E., Craik, F. I., M., Green, D. W., & Gollan, T. H. (2009). Bilingual minds. *Psychological Science in the Public Interest, 20,* 89–129.

Bialystok, E., & Viswanathan, M. (2009). Components of executive control with advantages for bilingual children in two cultures. *Cognition, 112,* 494–500.

Bidell, T. R., & Fischer, K. W. (1997). Between nature and nurture: The role of human agency in the epigenesis of intelligence. In R. J. Sternberg & E. L. Grigorenko (Eds.), *Intelligence, heredity, and environment* (pp. 193–242). New York: Cambridge University Press.

Bierman, K. (1986). Process of change during social skills training with preadolescents and its relation to treatment outcomes. *Child Development, 55,* 151–162.

Bierman, K. L. (2003). *Peer rejection: Developmental processes and intervention.* New York: Guilford Press.

Bierman, K. L. (2004). *Peer rejection: Developmental processes and intervention strategies.* New York: Guilford Press.

Bierman, K. L., & Furman, W. (1984). The effects of social skills training and peer involvement on the social adjustment of preadolescents. *Child Development, 55,* 151–162.

Bierman, K. L., Greenberg, M. T., & the Conduct Problems Prevention Research Group. (1996). Social skills training in the Fast Track Program. In R. D. Peters & J. McMahon (Eds.), *Preventing childhood disorders, substance abuse, and delinquency* (pp. 65–89). Thousand Oaks, CA: Sage.

Bigler, R. S., & Liben, L. S. (1992). Cognitive mechanisms in children's gender stereotyping: Theoretical and educational implications of a cognitive-based intervention. *Child Development, 63,* 1351–1363.

Billings, J. A. (1998). What is palliative care? *Journal of Palliative Medicine, 1,* 73–81.

Binder, E. B., Bradley, R. G., Liu, W., Epstein, M. P., Deveau, T. C., Mercer, K. B., et al. (2008). Association of *FKBP5* polymorphisms and childhood abuse with risk of posttraumatic stress disorder symptoms in adults. *Journal of the American Medical Association, 299,* 1291–1305.

Binet, A., & Simon, T. (1916). *The development of intelligence in children.* Baltimore, MD: Williams and Wilkins.

Bird, A. P. (2002). DNA methylation patterns and epigenetic memory. *Nature, 447,* 396–398.

Birditt, K. S., Fingerman, K. L., & Zarit, S. H. (2010). Adult children's problems and successes: Implications for intergenerational ambivalence. *The Journals of Gerontology Series B: Psychological Sciences an Social Sciences, 65B,* 145–153.

Birkeland, M. S., Melkevik, O., Holsen, I., & Wold, B. (2012). Trajectories of global self-esteem development during adolescence. *Journal of Adolescence, 35,* 43–54.

Birmaher, B., & Heydl, P. (2003). Biological studies in depressed children and adolescents. *International Journal of Neuropsychopharmacology, 4,* 149–157.

Birmingham, C., Su, J., Hlynsky, J., Goldner, E., & Gao, M. (2005). The mortality rate from anorexia nervosa. *International Journal of Eating Disorders, 38,* 143–146.

Biro, F. M., Galvez, M. P., Greenspan, L. C., Succop, P., Vangeepuram, N., Pinney, et al. (2010). Pubertal assessment method and baseline characteristics in a mixed longitudinal study of girls. *Pediatrics.* doi:10.1542/peds.2009-3079

Bishop, J. B., Witt, K. L., & Sloane, R. A. (1997). Genetic toxicities of human teratogens. *Mutation Research, 396,* 9–43.

Biswas-Diener, R., Vitterso, J., & Diener, E. (2005). Most people are pretty happy, but there is cultural variation: The Inughuit, the Amish, and the Maasai. *Journal of Happiness Studies, 6,* 205–226.

Biswas-Diener, R., Vitterso, J., & Diener, E. (2010). The Danish effect: Beginning to explore high well-being in Denmark. *Social Indicators Research, 97,* 229–246.

Blackless, M., Charuvastra, A., Derryck, A., Fausto-Sterling, A., Lauzanne, K., & Lee, E. (2000). How sexually dimorphic are we? Review and synthesis. *American Journal of Human Biology, 12,* 151–166.

Blackman, J. A. (2002). Early intervention: A global perspective. *Infants and Young Children, 15,* 11–19.

Blackwell, L. S., Trzesniewski, K. H., & Dweck, C. S. (2007). Implicit theories of intelligence predict achievement across an adolescent transition: A longitudinal study and an intervention. *Child Development, 78,* 246–263.

Blakemore, J. E. O., Berenbaum, S. A., & Liben, L. S. (2009). *Gender development.* New York: Taylor & Francis Group.

Blakemore, S. J. (2008). Development of the social brain during adolescence. *The Quarterly Journal of Experimental Psychology, 61,* 40–49.

Blakemore, S. J. (2012). Imaging brain development: The adolescent brain. *NeuroImage, 61,* 397–406.

Blakemore, S. J., & Frith, U. (2005). *The learning brain: Lessons for education.* Oxford, UK: Blackwell.

Blair, C. (2002). School readiness: Integrating cognition and emotion in a neurobiological conceptualization of children's functioning at school entry. *American Psychologist, 57,* 111–127.

Blair, C., Granger, D., Willoughby, M., Mills-Konce, R., Cox, M., Greenberg, M. T., et al. (2011). Salivary cortisol mediates effects of poverty and parenting on executive functions in early childhood. *Child Development, 82,* 1970–1984.

Blanchard, R. (2004). Quantitative and theoretical analyses of the relation between older brothers and homosexuality in men. *Journal of Theoretical Biology, 230,* 173–187.

Blanchard-Fields, F. (1986). Reasoning on social dilemmas varying in emotional salience: An adult developmental perspective. *Psychology and Aging, 1,* 325–333.

Blanchard-Fields, F. (2007). Everyday problem solving and emotion: An adult developmental perspective. *Current Directions in Psychological Science, 16,* 26–31.

Blaser, E., & Kaldy, Z. (2010). Infants get five stars on iconic memory tests: A partial-report test of 6-month-old infants' iconic memory capacity. *Psychological Science, 21,* 1643–1645.

Blasi, A., Mercure, E., Lloyd-Fox, S., Thomson, A., Brammer, M., Sauter, D., et al. (2011). Early specialization for voice and emotion processing in the infant brain. *Current Biology, 21,* 1220–1224.

Blazer, D. G. (2003). Depression in late life: Review and commentary. *Journal of Gerontology, 58,* 249–265.

Blazer, D. G., Kessler, R. C., McGonagle, K. A., & Schwartz, M. S. (1994). The prevalence and distribution of major depression in a national community sample: The national comorbidity survey. *American Journal of Psychiatry, 151,* 979–986.

Blewitt, P. (1989). Category hierarchies: Levels of knowledge and skill. *Genetic Epistemologist, 17,* 21–30.

Blewitt, P. (1994). Understanding categorical hierarchies: The earliest levels of skill. *Child Development, 65,* 1279–1298.

Blewitt, P., Rump, K. M., Shealy, S. E., & Cook, S. A. (2009). Shared book reading: When and how questions affect young children's word learning. *Journal of Educational Psychology, 101,* 294–304.

Block, J. H. (1978). Another look at sex differentiation in the socialization behaviors of mothers and fathers. In J. Sherman &

F. L. Denmark (Eds.), *The psychology of women: Future directions of research* (pp. 29–87). New York: Psychological Dimensions.

Block, J., & Block, J. H. (2006). Venturing a 30-year longitudinal study. *American Psychologist, 61,* 315–327.

Block, M. L., & Calderón-Garcidueñas L. (2009). Air pollution: mechanisms of neuroinflammation and CNS disease. *Trends in Neuroscience, 32,* 506–516.

Bloom, L. (1998). Language acquisition in its developmental context. In W. Damon (Series Ed.), D. Kuhn & R. S. Siegler (Vol. Eds.), *Handbook of child psychology: Vol. 2. Cognition, perception, and language* (5th ed., pp. 309–370). New York: Wiley.

Blos, P. (1962). *On adolescence: A psychoanalytic interpretation.* New York: Free Press.

Blos, P. (1975). The second individuation process of adolescence. In A. Esman (Ed.), *The psychology of adolescence* (pp. 156–176). New York: International Universities Press.

Blum, R. W. (2003). Positive youth development: A strategy for improving adolescent health. In I. B. Weiner (Series Ed.), F. Jacobs, D. Wertlieb, & R. M. Lerner (Vol. Eds.), *Handbook of applied developmental science: Vol. 2. Enhancing the life chances of youth and families* (pp. 237–252). Thousand Oaks, CA: Sage.

Boden, J. M., Fergusson, D. M., & Horwood, L. J. (2007). Early motherhood and subsequent life outcomes. *The Journal of Child Psychology and Psychiatry, 49,* 151–160.

Bodhi, B. (Ed.). (1999). *A comprehensive manual of Abhidhamma: The philosophical psychology of Buddhism.* Seattle, WA: BPS Pariyatti Editions.

Bodrova, E., & D. J. Leong. (2007). *Tools of the Mind: The Vygotskian Approach to Early Childhood Education* (2nd ed.). Upper Saddle River, NJ: Pearson Education/Merrill.

Boduroglu, A., Shah, P., & Nisbett, R. E. (2009). Cultural differences in allocation of attention in visual information processing. *Journal of Cross-Cultural Psychology, 40,* 349–360.

Bogard, K., & Takanishi, R. (2005). PK-3: An aligned and coordinated approach to education for children 3 to 8 years old. *Social Policy Report, 19,* 3–23.

Bogaert, A. F. (2006). Biological versus nonbiological older brothers and men's sexual orientation. *Proceedings of the National Academy of Sciences. USA, 103,* 10771–10774.

Bogels, S. M., Lehtonen, A., & Restifo, K. (2010). Mindful parenting in mental health care. *Mindfulness, 1,* 107–120.

Bokhorst, C. L., Bakermans-Kranenburg, M. J., van IJzendoorn, M. H., Fonagy, P., & Schengel, C. (2003). The importance of shared environment in mother-infant attachment security: A behavioral genetic study. *Child Development, 74,* 1769–1782.

Boland, A. M., Haden, C. A., & Ornstein, P. A. (2003). Boosting children's memory by training mothers in the use of an elaborative conversational style as events unfold. *Journal of Cognition and Development, 4,* 39–64.

Bolger, K. E., & Patterson, C. J. (2001, April). Developmental pathways from child maltreatment to peer rejection. *Child Development, 72,* 549–568.

Bolger, K. E., & Patterson, C. J. (2003). Sequelae of child maltreatment: Vulnerability and resilience. In S. S. Luthar (Ed.), *Resilience and vulnerability: Adaptation in the context of childhood adversities* (pp. 156–181). Cambridge, England: Cambridge University Press.

Bolotin, S. (1999, February 14). The disciples of discipline. *The New York Times Magazine,* pp. 32–77.

Bonanno, G. A., & Kaltman, S. (1999). Toward an integrative perspective on bereavement. *Psychological Bulletin, 125,* 760–776.

Bonanno, G. A., & Keltner, D. (1997). Facial expression of emotion and the course of conjugal bereavement. *Journal of Abnormal Psychology, 106,* 126–137.

Bonanno, G. A., Papa, A., Lalande, K., Westphal, M., & Coifman, K. (2004). The importance of being flexible: The ability to both enhance and suppress emotional expression predicts long-term adjustment. *Psychological Science, 15,* 482–487.

Bonanno, G. A., Znoj, H., Siddique, H. I., & Horowitz, M. J. (1999). Verbal-autonomic dissociation and adaptation to midlife conjugal loss: A follow-up at 25 months. *Cognitive Therapy and Research, 23,* 605–624.

Bond, J. T., Thompson, C., Galinsky, E., & Prottas, D. (2002). *Highlights of the national study of the changing workforce.* New York: Families and Work Institute.

Booth, C. L., Clarke-Stewart, K. A., Vandell, D. L., McCartney, K., & Owen, M. T. (2002). Childcare usage and mother-infant "quality time." *Journal of Marriage and Family, 64,* 16–26.

Booth, C. L., Kelly, J. F., Spieker, S. J., & Zuckerman, T. G. (2003). Toddlers' attachment security to child-care providers: The Safe and Secure Scale. *Early Education and Development, 14,* 83–100.

Bornstein, M. H., Putnick, D. L., Suwalsky, J. T. D., & Gini, M. (2006). Maternal chronological age, prenatal and perinatal history, social support, and parenting of infants. *Child Development, 77,* 875–892.

Bornstein, M. H., & Colombo, J. (2010). Infant cognitive functioning and child mental development. In S. Pauen & M. H. Bornstein (Eds.), *Early childhood development and later achievement.* New York: Cambridge University Press.

Bornstein, M. H., Cote, L. R., Haynes, O. M., Hahn, C-S., & Park, Y. (2010). Parenting knowledge: Experiential and sociodemographic factors in European American mothers of young children. *Developmental Psychology, 46,* 1677–1693.

Borod, J. C., Koff, E., & Buck, R. (1986). The neuropsychology of facial expression: Data from normal and brain-damaged adults. In P. Blanck, R. Buck, & R. Rosenthal (Eds.), *Nonverbal communication in the clinical context.* University Park: Pennsylvania State University Press.

Bos, H. M. W., & Sandfort, T. (2010). Childen's gender identity in lesbian and heterosexual two-parent families. *Sex Roles, 62,* 114–126

Botvin, G. J., & Griffin, K. W. (2005). Prevention science, drug abuse prevention, and Life Skills Training: Comments on the state of the science. *Journal of Experimental Criminology, 1,* 63–78.

Bouchard, T. J., Lykken, D. T., McGue, M., Segal, N. L., & Tellegen, A. (1990). Sources of human psychological differences: The Minnesota study of twins reared apart. *Science, 250,* 223–228.

Bouwmeester, S., & Verkoeijen, P. P. J. L. (2011). Why do some children benefit more from testing than others? Gist trace processing to explain the testing effect. *Journal of Memory and Language, 65,* 32–41.

Bowen, M. (1978). *Family therapy in clinical practice.* New York: Jason Aronson.

Bower, E. M. (1960). *Early identification of emotionally handicapped children in school.* Springfield, IL: Charles C. Thomas.

Bowlby, J. (1969/1982). *Attachment and loss: Vol. 1. Attachment.* New York: Basic Books.

Bowlby, J. (1973). *Attachment and loss: Vol. 2. Separation.* New York: Basic Books.

Bowlby, J. (1980). *Attachment and loss: Vol. 3. Loss: Sadness and depression.* New York: Basic Books.

Bowlby, J. (1988). *A secure base: Parent-child attachment and healthy human development.* New York: Basic Books.

Boyer, T. W., Levine, S. C., & Huttenlocher, J. (2008). Development of proportional reasoning: Where young children go wrong. *Developmental Psychology, 44,* 1478–1490.

Boykin, A. W., & Toms, F. D. (1985). Black child socialization: A conceptual framework. In H. P. McAdoo & J. L. McAdoo (Eds.), *Black children: Social, educational, and parental environments* (pp. 33–52). Newbury Park, CA: Sage.

Boynton-Jarrett, R., Wright, R., Putnam, F., Hibert, E., Michels, K., Forman, M., & Rich-Edwards, J. (2012). Childhood abuse and age at menarche, *Journal of Adolescent Health.* http://dx.doi.org.ezaccess.libraries .psu.edu/10.1016/j.jadohealth.2012.06.006

Braak, H., & Braak, E. (1991). Neuropathological staging of Alzheimer-related changes. *Acta Neuropathologica, 82,* 239–259.

Bracha, H. S., Ralston, T. C., Matsukawa, J. M., Williams, A. E., & Bracha, A. S. (2004). Does "Fight or Flight" need updating? *Psychosomatics, 45,* 448–449.

Bradley, R. H., & Corwyn, R. F. (2002). Socioeconomic status and child development. *Annual Review of Psychology, 53,* 371–399.

Bradley, R. H., & Corwyn, R. F. (2008). Infant temperament, parenting, and externalizing behavior in 1st grade: A test of the differential susceptibility hypothesis. *Journal of Child Psychology and Psychiatry, 49,* 124–131.

Bradley, S. J., Oliver, G. D., Chernick, A. B., & Zucker, K. J. (1998). Experiment of nurture: Ablatio penis at 2 months, sex reassignment at 7 months, and psychosexual follow-up in young adulthood. *Pediatrics, 102,* 132–133.

Brainerd, C. J. (1996). Piaget: A centennial celebration. *Psychological Science, 7,* 191–195.

Brand, R. J., & Dixon, W. E. (2013). Difficulty calming predicts infant TV use and mediates the relationship between TV and later attention problems. Poster presented at the biennial meetings of the Society for Research in Child Development, Seattle, Washington.

Brand, R. J., Hardesty, S., & Dixon, W. E. (2011). Toddler's difficult temperament predicts television use. Poster presented at the biennial meetings of the Society for Research in Child Development, Montreal, Canada.

Branwhite, T. (2000). *Helping adolescents in school.* Westport, CT: Praeger.

Brauner, J., Gordic, B., & Zigler, E. (2004). Putting the child back into child care: Combining care and education for children ages 3–5. *Social Policy Report, 18,* 3–15.

Brazelton, T. B. (1986). Issues for working parents. *American Journal of Orthopsychiatry, 56,* 14–25.

Brazelton, T. B., & Greenspan, S. I. (2000). *The irreducible needs of children: What every child must have to grow, learn, and flourish.* Cambridge, MA: Perseus.

Brennan, K. A., Clark, C. L., & Shaver, P. R. (1998). Self-report measurement of adult attachment: An integrative interview. In J. A. Simpson & W. S. Rholes (Eds.), *Attachment theory and close relationships* (pp. 46–76). New York: Guilford Press.

Brennan, K. A., & Shaver, P. R. (1998). Attachment styles and personality disorders: Their connections to each other and to parental divorce, parental death, and perceptions of parental caregiving. *Journal of Personality, 66,* 835–878.

Brescoll, V. L., & Uhlmann, E. L. (2008). Can an angry woman get ahead? Status conferral, gender, and expression of emotion in the workplace. *Psychological Science, 19,* 268–275.

Brestan, E. V., & Eyberg, S. M. (1998). Effective psychosocial treatment of conduct-disordered children and adolescents: 29 years, 82 studies, and 5275 kids. *Journal of Clinical Child Psychology, 27,* 180–189.

Brewin, C. R., Andrews, B., & Valentine, J. D. (2000). Meta-analysis of risk factors for posttraumatic stress disorder in trauma-exposed adults. *Journal of Consulting and Clinical Psychology, 68,* 748–766.

Brickman, P. D., & Campbell, D. T. (1971). Hedonic relativism and planning the good society. In M. H. Appley (Ed.). *Adaptation level theory: A symposium* (pp. 287–304). New York. Academic Press.

Bridgett, D. J., Gartstein, M. A., Putnam, S. P., McKay, T., Iddins, E., Robertson, C., et al. (2009). Maternal and contextual influences and the effect of temperament development during infancy on parenting in toddlerhood. *Infant Behavior and Development, 32,* 103–116.

Bright, J. E. H., Pryor, R. G. L., Wilkenfeld, S., & Earl, J. (2005). The role of social context and serendipitous events in career decision making. *International Journal for Educational and Vocational Guidance, 5,* 19–36.

Brisch, K. H. (1999). *Treating attachment disorders: From theory to therapy.* New York: Guilford Press.

Britton, J. R., Britton, H. L., & Gronwaldt, V. (2006). Breastfeeding, sensitivity, and attachment. *Pediatrics, 118,* e1436–e1443.

Broderick, P. C. (1998). Early adolescent differences in the use of ruminative and distracting coping styles. *Journal of Early Adolescence, 18,* 173–191.

Broderick, P. C., & Korteland, C. (2002). Coping style and depression in early adolescence: Relationships to gender, gender role, and implicit beliefs. *Sex Roles: A Journal of Research, 46,* 201–213.

Broderick, P. C., & Korteland, C. (2004). A prospective study of rumination and depression in early adolescence. *Clinical Child Psychology and Psychiatry, 9,* 383–394.

Broderick, P. C., & Mastrilli, T. (1997). Attitudes concerning parental involvement: Parent and teacher perspectives. *Pennsylvania Educational Leadership, 16,* 30–36.

Brody, G. H., Ge, X., Conger, R., Gibbons, F. X., Murry, V. M., Gerrard, M., et al. (2001). The influence of neighborhood disadvantage, collective socialization, and parenting on African American children's affiliation with deviant peers. *Child Development, 72,* 1231–1246.

Brody, G. H., Murry, V. M., Gerrard, M., Gibbons, F. X., Molgaard, V., McNair, L., et al. (2004). The Strong African American Families Program: Translating research into prevention programming. *Child Development, 75,* 900–917.

Bronfenbrenner, U. (1979). *The ecology of human development: Experiments by nature and by design.* Cambridge, MA: Harvard University Press.

Bronfenbrenner, U., & Ceci, S. J. (1994). Nature-nurture reconceptualized in developmental perspective: A bioecological model. *Psychological Review, 101,* 568–586.

Bronfenbrenner, U., & Morris, P. A. (1998). The ecology of developmental processes. In W. Damon (Series Ed.) & R. M. Lerner (Vol. Ed.), *Handbook of child psychology: Vol. 1. Theoretical models of human development* (5th ed., pp. 993–1028). New York: Wiley.

Bronfenbrenner, U., & Morris, P. A. (2006). The bioecological model of human development. In W. Damon & R. M. Lerner (Series Eds.),

R. M. Lerner (Vol. Ed.), *Handbook of child psychology: Vol. 1. Theoretical models of human development* (6th ed., pp. 793–828). Hoboken, NJ: Wiley.

Brooks-Gunn, J. (1991). Maturational timing variations in adolescent girls, antecedents of. In R. M. Lerner, A. C. Petersen, & J. Brooks-Gunn (Eds.), *Encyclopedia of adolescence* (Vol. 2). New York: Garland.

Brooks-Gunn, J. (2003). Do you believe in magic? What we can expect from early childhood intervention programs. *Social Policy Report, 17,* 3–14.

Brooks-Gunn, J., Han, W., & Waldfogel, J. (2002). Maternal employment and child cognitive outcomes in the first three years of life: The NICHD study of early child care. *Child Development, 73,* 1052–1072.

Brooks-Gunn, J., & Petersen, A. C. (1991). Studying the emergence of depression and depressive symptoms during adolescence. *Journal of Youth and Adolescence, 20,* 115–119.

Brooks-Gunn, J., & Warren, M. P. (1989). Biological and social contributions to negative affect in young adolescent girls. *Child Development, 60,* 40–55.

Brooten, D., Youngblut, J. M., Brown, L., Finkler, S. A., Neff, D. F., & Madigan, E. (2001). A randomized trial of nurse specialist home care for women with high-risk pregnancies: Outcome and costs. *American Journal of Managed Care, 7,* 793–803.

Brophy, J. E., & Evertson, C. M. (1976). *Learning from teaching: A developmental perspective.* Boston: Allyn & Bacon.

Brown, B. B. (1990). Peer groups and peer cultures. In S. S. Feldman & G. R. Elliott (Eds.), *At the threshold: The developing adolescent* (pp. 171–196). Cambridge, MA: Harvard University Press.

Brown, B. (2004). Adolescents' relationships with peers. In R. Lerner & L. Steinberg (Eds.), *Handbook of adolescent psychology* (2nd ed., pp. 363–394). Hoboken, NJ: Wiley.

Brown, B. B., Herman M., Hamm, J. V., & Heck, D. J. (2008). Ethnicity and image: Correlates of crowd affiliation among ethnic minority youth. *Child Development, 79,* 529–546.

Brown, C., & Chu, H. (2012). Discrimination, ethnic identity, and academic outcomes of Mexican immigrant children: The importance of school context. *Child Development, 83,* 1477–1485.

Brown, C. S., & Bigler, R. S. (2005). Children's perceptions of discrimination: A developmental model. *Child Development, 76,* 533–553.

Brown, J., Steele, J., & Walsh-Childers, K. (2002). *Sexual teens, sexual media: Investigating media's influence on adolescent sexuality.* Hillsdale, NJ: Erlbaum.

Brown, J. L., Roderick, T., Lantiere, L., & Aber, J. L. (2004). The Resolving Conflicts Creatively Program: A school-based social and emotional learning program. In J. E. Zins, R. P. Weissberg, M. C. Wang, & H. J. Walberg (Eds.), *Building academic success on social and emotional learning: What does the research say?* (pp. 151–169). New York: Teachers College Press.

Brown, L., & Gilligan, C. (1992). *Meeting at the crossroads: Women's psychology and girls' development.* Cambridge, MA: Harvard University Press.

Brown, R. (1973). *A first language: The early stages.* Cambridge, MA: Harvard University Press.

Brown, R., & Hanlon, C. (1970). Derivational complexity and order of acquisition. In J. R. Hayes (Ed.), *Cognition and the development of language* (pp. 11–53). New York: Wiley.

Brown, S. L., Nesse, N. M., Vinokur, A., & Smith, D. M. (2003). Providing social support may be more beneficial than receiving it: Results from a prospective study of mortality. *Psychological Science, 14,* 320–327.

Browning, S. W. (1998). The empathy expansion procedure: A method of assisting couples in healing from traumatic incidents. In L. L. Hecker & S. A. Deacon (Eds.), *The therapist's notebook: Homework, handouts, and activities for use in psychotherapy.* New York: Haworth Press.

Browning, S., & Artelt, E. (2012). *Stepfamily therapy: A 10-step clinical approach.* Washington, D.C.: American Psychological Association.

Browning, S., & Bray, J. H. (2009). Treating stepfamilies: A subsystems-based approach. In M. Stanton & J. Bray (Eds.), *Blackwell handbook of family psychology.* London: Blackwell Publishing.

Brubaker, R. (2009). Ethnicity, race, and nationalism. *Annual Review of Sociology, 35,* 21–42.

Bruck, M., & Ceci, S. J. (2012). Forensic developmental psychology in the courtroom. In M. Bruck & S. J. Ceci (Eds.), *Coping with psychiatric and psychological testimony: Based on the original work by Jay Ziskin* (6th ed., pp. 723–736). New York: Oxford University Press.

Bruck, M., Ceci, S. J., & Principe, G. F. (2006). The child and the law. In W. Damon & R. M. Lerner (Series Eds.), K. A. Renninger & I. E. Sigel (Vol. Ed.), *Handbook of child psychology: Vol. 4. Child psychology in practice* (6th ed., pp. 776–816). Hoboken, NJ: Wiley.

Bruer, J. T. (December, 1999). Neural connections: Some you use, some you lose.? *Phi Delta Kappan,* 264–277.

Brumberg, J. J. (1988). *Fasting girls: The emergence of anorexia nervosa as a modern disease.* Cambridge, MA: Harvard University Press.

Brynner, J. M., O'Malley, P. M., & Bachman, J. C. (1981). Self-esteem and delinquency revisited. *Journal of Youth and Adolescence, 10,* 407–441.

Buchanan, C. M., Eccles, J. S., & Becker, J. B. (1992). Are adolescents the victims of raging hormones? Evidence for activational effects of hormones on moods and behavior at adolescence. *Psychological Bulletin, 111,* 62–107.

Buchtemann, D., Luppa, M., Bramesfeld, A., & Riedel-Heller, S. (2012). Incidence of late-life depression: A systematic review. *Journal of Affective Disorders, 142,* 172–179.

Buck Louis, G. M. L., Gray, E., Marcus, M., Ojeda, S. R., Pescovitz, O. H., et al. (2008). Environmental factors and puberty timing: Expert panel research needs. *Pediatrics, 12* (Supplement 3), 192–207.

Buckingham, D., & Willett, R. (2006). *Digital generations: Children, young people, and new media.* Mahwah, NJ: Erlbaum.

Buckner, J. D., Lopez, C., Dunkel, S., & Joiner, T. E. (2008). Behavior management training for the treatment of Reactive Attachment Disorder. *Child Maltreatment, 13,* 289–297.

Bugental, D. B., & Grusec, J. E. (2006). Socialization processes. In W. Damon & R. M. Lerner (Series Eds.), N. Eisenberg (Vol. Ed.), *Handbook of child psychology: Vol. 3. Social, emotional, and personality development* (6th ed., pp. 366–428). Hoboken, NJ: Wiley.

Bulik, C. M., Sullivan, P. F., Tozzi, F., Furberg, H., Lichtenstein, P., & Pedersen, N. L. (2006). Prevalence, heritability and prospective risk factors for anorexia nervosa. *Archives of General Psychiatry, 63,* 305–312.

Burka, J. B., & Yuen, L. M. (1983). *Procrastination: Why you do it, what to do about it.* Reading, MA: Addison-Wesley.

Burns, B. J., Costello, E. J., Angold, A., Erkanli, A., Stangl, D., & Tweed, D. L. (1995). Children's mental health service use across service sectors. *Health Affairs, 14,* 147–159.

Burns, B. J., Hoagwood, K., & Mrazek, P. J. (1999). Effective treatments for mental disorders in children and adolescents. *Clinical Child and Family Psychology Review, 2,* 199–254.

Burr, W. R. (1970). Satisfaction with various aspects of marriage over the life cycle: A random middle class sample. *Journal of Marriage and the Family, 32,* 29–37.

Burt, K. B., & Paysnick, A. A. (2012). Resilience in the transition to adulthood. *Development and Psychopathology 24,* 493–505.

Buss, D. M. (1989). Sex differences in human mate preferences: Evolutionary hypotheses tested in 37 cultures. *Behavioral and Brain Sciences, 12,* 1–49.

Bussey, K., & Bandura, A. (1984). Influence of gender constancy and social power on sex-linked modeling. *Journal of Personality and Social Psychology, 47,* 1292–1302.

Bussey, K., & Bandura, A. (1999). A social cognitive theory of gender development and differentiation. *Psychological Bulletin, 106,* 676–713.

Butler, L. D., & Nolen-Hoeksema, S. (1994). Gender differences in response to depressed mood in a college sample. *Sex Roles, 30,* 331–346.

Butler, R. N. (1963). The life review: An interpretation of reminiscence in the aged. *Psychiatry, 26,* 65–76.

Byers, A. L., Levy, B. R., Allore, H. G., Bruce, M. L., & Kasl, S. V. (2008). When parents matter to their adult children: Filial reliance associated with parents' depressive symptoms. *The Journals of Gerontology Series B: Psychological Sciences and Social Sciences, 63,* P33–P40.

Byne, W., Bradley, S. J., Coleman, E., Eyler, A. E., Green R., Menvielle, E., et al. (2012). Treatment of gender identity disorder. *American Journal of Psychiatry 169,* 875–876.

Byng-Hall, J. (1995). *Rewriting family scripts: Improvisation and systems change.* New York: Guilford Press.

Byrne, B. M., & Shavelson, R. J. (1996). On the structure of social self-concept for pre-, early- and late adolescents: A test of the Shavelson, Hubner, and Stanton (1976) model. *Journal of Personality and Social Psychology, 70,* 599–613.

Byrne, D. (1964). Repression-sensitization as a dimension of personality. In B. A. Maher (Ed.), *Progress in experimental personality research* (pp. 169–220). New York: Academic Press.

Cacioppo, J. T., & Berntson, G. G. (1992). Social psychological contributions to the decade of the brain: Doctrine of multilevel analysis. *American Psychologist, 47,* 1019–1028.

Cacioppo, J. T., & Gardner, W. L. (1999). Emotion. *Annual Review of Psychology, 50,* 191–214.

Cairns, R. B., & Cairns, B. D. (1994). *Lifelines and risks: Pathways of youth in our time.* New York: Cambridge University Press.

Cairns, R. B., & Cairns, B. D. (2000). The natural history and developmental functions of aggression. In A. J. Sameroff, M. Lewis, & S. M. Miller (Eds.), *Handbook of developmental psychopathology* (2nd ed., pp. 403–429). New York: Kluwer Academic/Plenum Press.

Cairns, R. B., Gariepy, J. L., & Kindermann, T. A. (1990). *Identifying social clusters in natural settings.* Unpublished manuscript, University of North Carolina at Chapel Hill, Social Development Laboratory.

Calkins, S. D., Graziano, P. A., & Keane, S. P. (2007). Cardiac vagal regulation differentiates among children at risk for behavior problems. *Biological Psychology, 74,* 113–308.

Callanan, M., & Kelley, P. (1992). *Final gifts: Understanding the special awareness, needs and communications of the dying.* New York: Bantam Books.

Cameron, C. A., & Wang, M. (1999). Frog, where are you? Children's narrative expression over the telephone. *Discourse Processes, 28,* 217–236.

Cameron Ponitz, C. E., McClelland, M. M., Jewkes, A. M., Connor, C. M., Farris, C. L., & Morrison, F. J. (2008). Touch your toes! Developing a direct measure of behavioral regulation in early childhood. *Early Childhood Research Quarterly, 23,* 141–158.

Campbell, J. D. (1990). Self-esteem and clarity of the self-concept. *Journal of Personality and Social Psychology, 59,* 538–549.

Campbell, J. D., & Lavallee, L. F. (1993). Who am I? The role of self-concept confusion in understanding the behavior of people with low self-esteem. In R. F. Baumeister (Ed.), *Self-esteem: The puzzle of low self-regard* (pp. 3–20). New York: Plenum Press.

Campbell, S. B. (1987). Parent-referred problem 3-year-olds: Developmental changes in symptoms. *Journal of Child Psychology and Psychiatry, 28,* 835–845.

Campos, J., Barrett, K., Lamb, M., Goldsmith, H., & Sternberg, C. (1983). Socioemotional development. In P. H. Mussen (Ed.), *Handbook of child psychology: Vol. 2. Infancy and developmental psychology* (pp. 783–915). New York: Wiley.

Campos, J. J., Campos, R. G., & Barrett, K. C. (1989). Emergent themes in the study of emotional development and emotion regulation. *Developmental Psychology, 25,* 394–402.

Cannon, W. B. (1929). *Bodily changes in pain, hunger, fear and rage: An account of recent research into the function of emotional excitement* (2nd ed.) New York: Appleton-Century-Crofts.

Cannon, T. D., & Keller, M. C. (2006). Endophenotypes in the genetic analysis of mental disorders. *Annual Review of Clinical Psychology, 2,* 267–290.

Canobi, K. H., Reeve, R. A., & Pattison, P. E. (1998). The role of conceptual understanding in children's addition problem solving. *Developmental Psychology, 34,* 882–891.

Cantor, J., & Wilson, B. J. (1998). Helping children cope with frightening media presentations. *Current Psychology: Research & Reviews, 7,* 58–75.

Cantril, H. (1965). *The pattern of human concerns.* New Brunswick, NJ: Rutgers University Press.

Caplan, M., Vespo, J. E., Pedersen, J., & Hay, D. F. (1991). Conflict over resources in small groups of 1- and 2-year-olds. *Child Development, 62,* 1513–1524.

Carlatt, D. J., Camargo, C. A., & Herzog, D. B. (1997). Eating disorders in males: A report on 135 patients. *American Journal of Psychiatry, 154,* 1127–1132.

Carlson, E. A. (1998). A prospective longitudinal study of disorganized/disoriented attachment. *Child Development, 9,* 1970–1979.

Carlson, J., & Lewis, J. (1993). Motivation: Building students' feelings of confidence and self-worth. In J. Carlson & J. Lewis (Eds.), *Counseling the adolescent: Individual, family and school interventions* (2nd ed., pp. 249–270). Denver, CO: Love.

Carlson, L. E., Speca, M., Patel, K. D., Goodey, E. (2004). Mindfulness-based stress reduction in relation to quality of life, mood, symptoms of stress and levels of cortisol, dehydroepiandrosterone sulfate (DHEAS) and melatonin in breast and prostate cancer outpatients. *Psychoneuroendocrinology, 29,* 448–474.

Carlson, S. M., Moses, L. J., & Claxton, L. J. (2004). Individual differences in executive functioning and theory of mind: An investigation of inhibitory control and planning ability. *Journal of Experimental Child Psychology, 87,* 299–319.

Carnegie Council on Adolescent Development. (1996). *Great transitions: Preparing adolescents for a new century.* New York: Carnegie Corporation of New York.

Carr, D. (2002). The psychological consequences of work-family trade-offs for three cohorts of men and women. *Social Psychology Quarterly, 65,* 103–124.

Carrere, S., Buehlman, K. T., Gottman, J. M., Coan, J. A., & Ruckstuhl, L. (2000). Predicting marital stability in divorced and newlywed couples. *Journal of Family Psychology, 14,* 42–58.

Carrere, S., & Gottman, J. M. (1999). Predicting divorce among newlyweds from the first three minutes of a marital conflict discussion. *Family Process, 38,* 293–301.

Carskadon, M., Vieria, C., & Acebo, C. (1993). Association between puberty and delayed phase preference. *Sleep, 16,* 258–262.

Carson, E. A., & Sabol, W. J. (2012). *Prisoners in 2011.* Washington, D. C.: U.S. Department of Justice, Bureau of Justice Statistics. Retrieved from http://bjs.gov/content/pub/pdf/p11.pdf

Carstensen, L. L. (1998). A life-span approach to social motivation. In J. Heckhausen & C. S. Dweck (Eds.), *Motivation and self-regulation across the life span* (pp. 341–364). Cambridge, England: Cambridge University Press.

Carstensen, L. L., & Mikels, J. A. (2005). At the intersection of emotion and cognition: Aging and the positivity effect. *Current Directions in Psychological Science, 14,* 117–121.

Carstensen, L. L., Pasupathi, M., Mayr, U., & Nesselroade, J. R. (2000). Emotional experience in everyday life across the adult life span. *Journal of Personality and Social Psychology, 79,* 644–655.

Carstensen, L. L., & Turk-Charles, S. (1994). The salience of emotion across the adult life span. *Psychology and Aging, 9,* 259–264.

Carter, B., & McGoldrick, M. (Eds.). (1999). *The expanded family life cycle: Individual, family and social perspectives* (3rd ed.). Boston: Allyn & Bacon.

Carter, C. S. (2003). Developmental consequences of oxytocin. *Physiology & Behavior, 79,* 383–397.

Cartwright, D. (1950). Emotional dimensions of group life. In M. L. Reymert (Ed.), *Feelings and emotions* (pp. 437–447). New York: McGraw-Hill.

Carver, L. J., & Vaccaro, B. G. (2007). 12-month-old infants allocate increased neural resources to stimuli associated with negative adult emotion. *Developmental Psychology, 43,* 54–69.

Carver, P. R., Yunger, J. L., & Perry, D. G. (2003). Gender identity and adjustment in middle childhood. *Sex Roles, 49,* 95–109.

Case, R. (1985). *Intellectual development: Birth to adulthood.* New York: Academic Press.

Case, R. (1991). Stages in the development of the young child's first sense of self. *Developmental Review, 11,* 210–230.

Case, R. (1992). *The mind's staircase: Exploring the conceptual underpinnings of children's thought and knowledge.* Hillsdale, NJ: Erlbaum.

Casey, B. J., Giedd, J. N., & Thomas, K. M. (2000). Structural and functional brain development and its relation to cognitive development. *Biological Psychology, 54,* 241–257.

Casey, B. J., Jones, R. M., & Hare, T. A. (2008). The adolescent brain. *Annals of the New York Academy of Sciences, 1124,* 111–126.

Casper, R. C. (1990). Personality features of women with good outcome from restricting anorexia nervosa. *Psychosomatic Medicine, 52,* 156–170.

Caspi, A. (2000). The child is father of the man: Personality continuities from childhood to adulthood. *Journal of Personality and Social Psychology, 78,* 158–172.

Caspi, A., McClay, J., Moffitt, T. E., Mill, J., Martin, J., Craig, I. W., et al. (2002). Role of genotype in the cycle of violence in maltreated children. *Science, 297,* 851–855.

Cass, V. (1979). Homosexual identity formation: A theoretical model. *Journal of Homosexuality, 4,* 143–167.

Cassel, C. K., & Foley, K. M. (1999). *Principles for care of patients at the end of life: An emerging consensus among the specialties of medicine.* New York: Millbank Memorial Fund.

Cassidy, J., & Berlin, L. J. (1994). The insecure/ambivalent pattern of attachment: Theory and research. *Child Development, 65,* 971–991.

Cassidy, J., Woodhouse, S. S., Sherman, L. J., Stupica, B., & Lejuez, C. W. (2011). Enhancing infant attachment security: An examination of treatment efficacy and differential susceptibility. *Development and Psychopathology, 23,* 131–143.

Ceci, S. J., & Bruck, M. (1998). Children's testimony: Applied and basic issues. In W. Damon (Series Ed.), I. E. Sigel, & K. A. Renninger (Vol. Eds.), *Handbook of child psychology: Vol. 4. Child psychology in practice* (5th ed., pp. 713–774). New York: Wiley.

Ceci, S. J., Bruck, M., & Battin, D. B. (2000). The suggestibility of children's testimony. In D. F. Bjorklund (Ed.), *False-memory creation in children and adults: Theory, research, and implications* (pp. 169–201). Mahwah, NJ: Erlbaum.

Ceci, S. J., & Liker, J. (1986). A day at the races: A study of IQ, expertise, and cognitive complexity. *Journal of Experimental Psychology: General, 115,* 255–266.

Ceci, S. J., & Williams, W. M. (2010). Sex differences in math-intensive fields. *Current Directions in Psychological Science, 19,* 275–279.

Ceci, S. J., Loftus, E. W., Leichtman, M., & Bruck, M. (1994). The role of source misattributions in the creation of false beliefs among preschoolers. *International Journal of Clinical and Experimental Hypnosis, 62,* 304–320.

Ceci, S. J., Papierno, P. B., & Kulkofsky, S. (2007). Representational constraints on children's suggestibility. *Psychological Science, 18,* 503–509.

Ceci, S. J., Rosenblum, T., de Bruyn, E., & Lee, D. Y. (1997). A bio-ecological model of intellectual development: Moving beyond h-sup-2. In R. J. Sternberg & E. L. Grigorenko (Eds.), *Intelligence, heredity, and environment* (pp. 303–322). New York: Cambridge University Press.

Centers for Disease Control and Prevention Youth Risk Behavior Survey. (2011). *Sexual identity, sex of sexual contacts, and health-risk behaviors among students in grades 9–12.* Retrieved April 18, 2013 from www.cdc.gov/yrbs

Centers for Disease Control and Prevention [CDC]. (2011). Health disparities and inequalities report: United States, 2011.

MMWR Surveillance Summaries 2011,60: US Department of Human Services.

Centers for Disease Control and Prevention [CDC]. (2012). Retrieved from http://www.cdc.gov/chronicdisease/overview/index.htm

Center for the Developing Child at Harvard University. (2007). *A science-based framework for early childhood policy: Using evidence to improve outcomes in learning, behavior, and health for vulnerable children.* Retrieved from http://www.developingchild.harvard.edu

Center on Media and Human Development. (2011). Children, Media, and Race: Media Use Among White, Black, Hispanic, and Asian American Children. Retrieved November 16, 2012 from http://web5.soc.northwestern.edu/cmhd/wp-content/uploads/2011/06/SOCconfReportSingleFinal-1.pdf

Cervone, D., & Peake, P. K. (1986). Anchoring, efficacy, and action: The influence of judgmental heuristics on self-efficacy judgments and behavior. *Journal of Personality and Social Psychology, 50,* 492–501.

Chaffin, M., Hanson, R., Saunders, B. E., Nichols, T., Barnett, D., Zeanah, C., et al. (2006). Report of the APSAC Task Force on attachment therapy, reactive attachment disorder, and attachment problems. *Child Maltreatment, 11,* 76–89.

Chan, C. C. Y., Tardif, T., Chen, J., Pulverman, R. B., Zhu, L., & Meng, X. (2011). English- and Chinese-learning infants map novel labels to object and actions differently. *Developmental Psychology, 47,* 1459–1471.

Chan, W., McCrae, R. R., de Fruyt, F., Jussim, L., Löckenhoff, C. E., deBolle, M., et al. (2012). Stereotypes of age differences in personality traits: Universal and accurate? *Journal of Personality and Social Psychology,* doi: 10.1037/a0029712

Chandler, M. J. (1987). The Othello effect: Essay on the emergence and eclipse of skeptical doubt. *Human Development, 30,* 137–139.

Chandler, M. J., & Boutilier, R. G. (1992). The development of dynamic system reasoning. *Human Development, 35,* 129–137.

Chandler, M. J., Boyes, M., & Ball, L. (1990). Relativism and stations of epistemic doubt. *Journal of Experimental Child Psychology, 50,* 370–395.

Chandra, V. (2012). Work–life balance: eastern and western perspectives. *The International Journal of Human Resource Management, 23,* 1040–1056.

Chang, L., Lei, L., Li, K., Liu, H., Guo, B., Wang, Y., et al. (2005). Peer acceptance and self-perceptions of verbal and behavioral aggression and social withdrawal. *International Journal of Behavioral Development, 29,* 48–57.

Chao, R. K. (1994). Beyond parental control and authoritarian parenting style: Understanding Chinese parenting through the cultural notion of training. *Child Development, 65,* 1111–1119.

Chappell, N. L., & Funk, L. (2012). Filial responsibility: Does it matter for care-giving behaviours? *Ageing and Society, 32,* 1128–1146.

Character Education Partnership. (1995). *Eleven principles of effective character education.* Washington, DC: Author.

Charles, S. T., & Carstensen, L. L. (2008). Unpleasant situations elicit different emotional responses in younger and older adults. *Psychology and Aging, 23,* 495–504.

Charles, S. T., Mather, M., & Carstensen, L. L. (2003). Aging and emotional memory: The forgettable nature of negative images for older adults. *Journal of Experimental Psychology: General, 132,* 310–234.

Charles, S. T., & Piazza, J. R. (2007). Memories of social interactions: Age differences in emotional intensity. *Psychology and Aging, 22,* 300–309.

Charness, N., & Bosman, E. A. (1990). Expertise and aging: Life in the lab. In T. H. Hess (Ed.), *Aging and cognition: Knowledge organization and utilization* (pp. 343–385). Amsterdam: Elsevier.

Charney, D. S., & Nestler, E. J. (2009). *Neurobiology of mental illness* (3rd ed.). Oxford: Oxford University Press.

Chase, W. G., & Simon, H. A. (1973). Perception in chess. *Cognitive Psychology, 4,* 55–81.

Chase-Lansdale, P. L., & Brooks-Gunn, J. (1994). Correlates of adolescent pregnancy and parenthood. In C. B. Fisher & R. M. Lerner (Eds.), *Applied developmental psychology* (pp. 207–236). New York: McGraw-Hill.

Chatterji, S. (2008). Depression: Greater effect on overall health than angina, arthritis, asthma or diabetes. *Evidence-Based Mental Health, 11,* 57.

Chatters, L. M. (2000). Religion and health: Public health research and practice. *Annual Review of Public Health, 21,* 335–367.

Chen, C., & Stevenson, H. W. (1988). Cross-linguistic differences in digit span of preschool children. *Journal of Experimental Child Psychology, 46,* 150–158.

Chen, E. (2004). Why socioeconomic status affects the health of children: A psychosocial perspective. *Current Directions in Psychological Science, 13,* 112–115.

Chen, E., Miller, G. E., Kobor, M. S., & Cole, S. W. (2011). Maternal warmth buffers the effects of low early-life socioeconomic status on pro-inflammatory signaling in adulthood. *Molecular Psychiatry, 16,* 729–737.

Chen, L. (2000). Understanding the heterogeneity of depression through the triad of symptoms, course and risk factors: a longitudinal, population-based study. *Journal of Affective Disorders, 59,* 1–11.

Chen, L., Eaton, W. W., Gallo, J. J., Nestadt, G., & Crum, R. M. (2000). Empirical examination of current depression categories in a population-based study: Symptoms, course, and risk factors. *American Journal of Psychiatry, 157,* 573–580.

Chen, X., & French, D. C. (2008). Children's social competence in cultural context. *Annual Review of Psychology, 59,* 591–616.

Chen, X., Rubin, K. H., & Li, B. (1995). Social and school adjustment of shy and aggressive children in China. *Development and Psychopathology, 31,* 531–539.

Cheng, S., Chow, P. K. M., Song, Y. Q., Yu, E. C., Chan, A. C., Lee, T., et al. (2012). Mental and physical activities delay cognitive decline in older persons with dementia. *American Journal of Geriatric Psychiatry.* doi:10.1097/JGP.0b013e31826d6af1

Cheng, Y., Lee, S., Chen, H., Wang, P., & Decety, J. (2012). Voice and emotion processing in the human neonatal brain. *Journal of Cognitive Neuroscience, 24,* 1411–1419.

Cheng, Y., Newman, I. M., Qu, M., Mbulo, L., Chai, Y., Chen, Y., et al. (2010). Being bullied and psychosocial adjustment among middle school students in China. *Journal of School Health, 80,* 193–199

Chengappa, K., Kupfer, D. J., Frank, E., Houck, P. R., Grochocinski, V. J., Cluss, P. A., et al. (2003). Relationship of birth cohort and early age at onset of illness in a bipolar disorder case registry. *American Journal of Psychiatry, 160,* 1636–1642.

Cherlin, A. (1981). *Marriage, divorce, remarriage.* Cambridge, MA: Harvard University Press.

Chess, S., & Hassibi, M. (1978). *Principles and practice of child psychiatry.* New York: Plenum Press.

Chess, S., & Thomas, A. (1987). *Origins and evolution of behavior: From infancy to early adult life.* Cambridge, MA: Harvard University Press.

Chi, M. T. H. (1978). Knowledge structures and memory development. In R. S. Siegler (Ed.), *Children's thinking: What develops?* Hillsdale, NJ: Erlbaum.

Chi, M. T. H., Hutchinson, J. E., & Robin, A. F. (1989). How inferences about novel domain-related concepts can be constrained by structured knowledge. *Merrill-Palmer Quarterly, 35,* 27–62.

Chi, M. T. H., & Koeske, R. D. (1983). Network representation of a child's dinosaur knowledge. *Developmental Psychology, 19,* 29–39.

Chiaburu, D. S., & Harrison, D. A. (2008). Do peers make the place? Conceptual synthesis and meta-analysis of coworker effects on perceptions, attitudes, OCBs, and performance. *Journal of Applied Psychology, 93,* 1082–1103.

Chiriboga, D. A. (1997). Crisis, challenge, and stability in the middle years. In M. E. Lachman & J. B. James (Eds.), *Multiple paths of midlife development* (pp. 293–322). Chicago: University of Chicago Press.

Chiu, L. H. (1972). A cross-cultural comparison of cognitive styles in Chinese and American children. *International Journal of Psychology, 7,* 235–242.

Choi, I., Nisbett, R. E., & Norenzayan, A. (1999). Causal attribution across cultures: Variation and universality. *Psychological Bulletin, 125,* 47–63.

Chow, S-M., Haltigan, J. D., & Messinger, D. S. (2010). Dynamic infant-parent affect coupling during the face-to-face/still-face. *Emotion, 10,* 101–114.

Chomsky, N. (1968). *Language and mind.* New York: Harcourt Brace World.

Christakis, D. A., Zimmerman, F. J., DiGiuseppe, D. L., & McCarty, C. A. (2004). Early television exposure and subsequent attention problems in children. *Pediatrics, 113,* 708–714.

Christakis, N. (2000). *Death foretold: Prophecy and prognosis in medical care.* Chicago: University of Chicago Press.

Chumlea, W. C., Schubert, C. M., Roche, A. F., Kulin, H. E., Lee, P. A., Himes, J. H., et al. (2003). Age at menarche and racial comparisons in US girls. *Pediatrics, 111,* 110–113.

Chun, C.-A., Moos, R. H., & Cronkite, R. C. (2006). Culture: A fundamental context for the stress and coping paradigm. In P. T. P. Wong & L. C. J. Wong (Eds.), *Handbook of multicultural perspectives on stress and coping* (pp. 29–53). New York: Springer.

Chung, H. L., & Steinberg, L. (2006). Relations between neighborhood factors, parenting behaviors, peer deviance, and delinquency among serious juvenile offenders. *Developmental Psychology, 42,* 319–331.

Cicchetti, D. (Ed.). (1984). *Developmental psychopathology.* Chicago: University of Chicago Press.

Cicchetti, D. (1989). How research on child maltreatment has informed the study of child maltreatment: Perspectives from developmental psychopathology. In D. Cicchetti & V. Carlson (Eds.), *Child maltreatment: Theory and research on the causes and consequences of child abuse and neglect* (pp. 377–431). New York: Cambridge University Press.

Cicchetti, D., & Rogosch, F. A. (1996). Equifinality and multifinality in developmental psychopathology. *Development and Psychopathology, 8,* 597–600.

Cicchetti, D., & Rogosch, F. A. (2001). The impact of child maltreatment and psychopathology upon neuroendocrine functioning. *Development and Psychopathology, 13,* 783–804.

Cicchetti, D., Rogosch, F. A., Gunnar, M. R., & Toth, S. L. (2010). The differential impacts of early abuse on internalizing problems and daytime cortisol rhythm in school-aged children. *Child Development, 81,* 252–269.

Cicchetti, D., Rogosch, R. A., & Toth, S. L. (2011). The effects of child maltreatment and polymorphisms of the serotonin transporter and dopamine D4 receptor genes on infant attachment and intervention efficacy. *Development and Psychopathology, 23,* 357–372.

Cicchetti, D., & Sroufe, L. A. (2000). The past as prologue to the future: The times, they've been a-changin'. *Development and Psychopathology, 12,* 255–264.

Cicchetti, D., & Toth, S. L. (Eds.). (1994). *Rochester Symposium on Developmental Psychopathology: Vol. 5. Disorders and dysfunctions of the self* (pp. 79–148). Rochester, NY: University of Rochester Press.

Cicchetti, D., & Toth, S. L. (2006). Developmental psychopathology and preventive intervention. In W. Damon & R. M. Lerner (Series Eds.), K. A. Renninger & I. E. Sigel (Vol. Eds.), *Handbook of child psychology: Vol. 4. Child psychology in practice* (6th ed., pp. 497–547). Hoboken, NJ: Wiley.

Cimpian, A., Arce, H.-M. C., Markman, E. M., & Dweck, C. S. (2007). Subtle linguistic cues affect children's motivation. *Psychological Science, 18,* 314–316.

Cimpian, A., Mu, Y., & Erickson, L. C. (2012). Who is good at this game? Linking an activity to a social category undermines children's achievement. *Psychological Science, 23,* 533–541.

Cioffe, D. (1991). Beyond attentional strategies: A cognitive-perceptual model of somatic interpretations. *Psychological Bulletin, 109,* 25–39.

Clark, K. B., & Clark, M. P. (1939). The development of consciousness of self and the emergence of racial identification in Negro preschool children. *Journal of Social Psychology, 10,* 591–599.

Clark, M. L. (1982). Racial group concept and self-esteem in black children. *Journal of Black Psychology, 8,* 75–88.

Clark, R., Hyde, J. S., Essex, J. J., & Klein, M. H. (1997). Length of maternity leave and quality of mother-infant interactions. *Child Development, 68,* 364–383.

Clausen, J. A. (1993). *American lives: Looking back at the children of the Great Depression.* New York: Free Press.

Cline, F. (1991). *Hope for rage and rage-filled children: Attachment theory and therapy.* Golden, CO: Love and Logic Press.

Cohen, G. L., & Prinstein, M. J. (2006). Peer contagion of aggression and health risk behavior among adolescent males: An experimental investigation of effects on public conduct and private attitudes. *Child Development, 77,* 967–983.

Cohen, J. M. (1977). Sources of peer group homogeneity. *Sociology of Education, 50,* 227–241.

Cohen, L. B., & Cashon, C. H. (2006). Infant cognition. In W. Damon & R. M. Lerner (Series Eds.), D. Kuhn & R. S. Siegler (Vol. Eds.), *Handbook of child psychology: Vol. 2. Cognition, perception and language* (6th ed., pp. 214–254). Hoboken, NJ: Wiley.

Cohen, S., Doyle, W. J., Turner, R. B., Alper, C. M., & Skoner, D. P. (2003). Emotional style and susceptibility to the common cold. *Psychosomatic Medicine, 65,* 652–657.

Cohen, S., & Williamson, G. M. (1991). Stress and infectious diseases in humans. *Psychological Bulletin, 109,* 5–24.

Cohen-Kettenis, P. T., Owen, A., Kaijser, V. G., Bradley, S. J., & Zucker, K. J. (2003). Demographic characteristics, social competence, and behavior problems in children with gender identity disorder: A cross-national, cross-clinic comparative analysis. *Journal of Abnormal Child Psychology, 32,* 41–53.

Coie, J., Terry, R., Lenox, K., & Lochman, J. (1995). Childhood peer rejection and aggression as predictors of stable patterns of adolescent disorder. *Development & Psychopathology, 7,* 697–713.

Coie, J. D., Dodge, K. A., & Coppotelli, H. (1982). Dimensions and types of social status: A cross-age perspective. *Developmental Psychology, 18,* 557–570.

Coie, J. D., & Krehbiehl, G. (1984). Effects of academic tutoring on the social status of low-achieving, socially rejected children. *Child Development, 55,* 1465–1478.

Coie, J. D., & Kupersmidt, J. (1983). A behavioral analysis of emerging social status in boys' groups. *Child Development, 54,* 1400–1416.

Coie, J. D., Watt, N. F., West, S. G., Hawkins, J. D., Asamow, J. R., Markman, H. J., et al. (1993). The science of prevention: A conceptual framework and some directions for a national research program. *American Psychologist, 48,* 1013–1022.

Colapinto, J. (2000). *As nature made him: The boy who was raised as a girl.* New York: Harper Perennial.

Colby, A., & Damon, W. (1992). *Some do care: Contemporary lives of moral commitment.* New York: Free Press.

Colcombe S. J., Erickson K. I., Raz N., Webb, A. G., Cohen N. J., McAuley, E., et al. (2003). Aerobic fitness reduces brain tissue loss in aging humans. *Journals of Gerontology Series A: Biological Sciences and Medical Sciences. 58,* 176–180.

Cole, M. (1996). *Culture in mind.* Cambridge, MA: Harvard University Press.

Cole, D. A., Maxwell, S. E., & Martin, J. M. (1997). Reflected self-appraisals: Strength and structure of the relation of teacher, peer, and parent ratings to children's self-perceived competencies. *Journal of Educational Psychology, 89,* 55–70.

Cole, M. (1998). *Cultural psychology: A once and future discipline.* Cambridge, MA: Belknap.

Cole, M. (2006). Culture and cognitive development in phylogenetic, historical, and ontogenetic perspective. In W. Damon & R. M. Lerner (Series Eds.), D. Kuhn & R. S. Siegler (Vol. Eds.), *Handbook of child psychology: Vol. 2. Cognition, perception and language* (6th ed., pp. 636–683). Hoboken, NJ: Wiley.

Cole, M., & Packer, M. (2011). Culture in development. In M. H. Bornstein & M.E. Lamb (Eds.) *Developmental science: An advanced textbook* (pp. 51–107). New York: Psychology Press.

Cole, M., & Wertsch, J. V. (1996). Beyond the individual-social antinomy in discussions of Piaget and Vygotsky. *Human Development, 39,* 250–256.

Coles, R. (1970). *Erik H. Erikson: The growth of his work.* Boston: Little, Brown.

Colin, V. L. (1996). *Human attachment.* New York: McGraw-Hill.

Collaer, M. L., & Hines, M. (1995). Human behavioral sex differences: A role for gonadal hormones during early development? *Psychological Bulletin, 118,* 55–107.

Collier, V. P., & Thomas, W. P. (2004). The astounding effectiveness of dual language education for all. *NABE Journal of Research and Practice, 2,* 1–20.

Collins, N. L., & Read, S. J. (1990). Adult attachment, working models, and relationship quality in dating couples. *Journal of Personality and Social Psychology, 58,* 644–663.

Collins, W. A., & Laursen, B. (2004). Parent-adolescent relationships and influences. In R. Lerner & L. Steinberg (Eds.), *Handbook of adolescent psychology* (2nd ed., pp. 331–361). New York: Wiley.

Collins, W. A., Maccoby, E. E., Steinberg, L., Hetherington, E. M., & Bornstein, M. H. (2000). Contemporary research on parenting: The case for nature and nature. *American Psychologist, 55,* 218–232.

Collins, W. A., Madsen, S. D., & Susman-Stillman, A. (2002). Parenting during middle childhood. In M. H. Bornstein (Ed.), *Handbook of parenting: Vol. 1. Children and parenting* (2nd ed., pp. 73–101). Mahwah, NJ: Erlbaum.

Collins, W. A., & Steinberg, L. (2006). Adolescent development in interpersonal context. In W. Damon & R. M. Lerner (Series Eds.), N. Eisenberg (Vol. Ed.), *Handbook of child psychology: Vol. 3. Social, emotional, and personality development* (6th ed., pp. 1003–1067). Hoboken, NJ: Wiley.

Comer, J. P. (1988). Educating poor minority children. *Scientific American, 5,* 42–48.

Committee for Economic Development. (2006). *The economic promise of investing in high quality pre-school: Using early education to improve economic growth and the fiscal sustainability of states and the nation.* Washington DC: Committee for Economic Development.

Committee on Psychosocial Aspects of Child and Family Health, Committee on Early Childhood, Adoption, and Dependent Care, and Section on Developmental and Behavioral Pediatrics, Shonkoff, J. P., Siegel, B. S., Dobbins, M. I., Earls, M. F., Garner, A. S., et al. (2012). Early childhood adversity, toxic stress, and the role of the pediatrician: Translating developmental science into lifelong health. *Pediatrics, 129,* 224–231.

Commons, M. L., & Richards, F. A. (1984). A general model of stage theory. In M. L. Commons, F. A. Richards, & C. Armon (Eds.), *Beyond formal operations: Late adolescent and adult cognitive development* (pp. 120–140). New York: Praeger.

Compas, B. E., Davis, G. E., Forsythe, C. J., & Wagner, B. M. (1987). Assessment of major and daily stressful events during adolescence: The Adolescent Perceived Events Scale. *Journal of Consulting and Clinical Psychology, 55,* 534–541.

Compas, B. E., Howell, D. C., Phares, V., Williams, R. A., & Giunta, C. (1989). Risk factors for emotional/behavioral problems in young adolescents: A prospective analysis of adolescent and parental stress and symptoms. *Journal of Consulting and Clinical Psychology, 57,* 732–740.

Compton, W. C. (2005). *Introduction to positive psychology.* Belmont, CA: Thomson/Wadsworth.

Comstock, G., & Scharrer, E. (1999). *Television: What's on, who's watching, and what it means.* San Diego, CA: Academic Press.

Comstock, G., & Scharrer, E. (2006). Media and popular culture. In W. Damon & R. M. Lerner (Series Eds.), K. A. Renninger & I. E. Sigel (Vol. Eds.), *Handbook of child psychology: Vol. 4. Child psychology in practice* (6th ed., pp. 817–863). Hoboken, NJ: Wiley.

Conduct Problems Prevention Research Group [CPPRG]. (1999). Initial impact of the Fast Track Prevention Trial for conduct problems: II. Classroom effects. *Journal of Consulting and Clinical Psychology, 67,* 648–657.

Conduct Problems Prevention Research Group [CPPRG]. (2002). Evaluation of the first 3 years of the Fast Track Prevention Trial with children at high risk for adolescent conduct problems. *Journal of Abnormal Child Psychology, 30,* 19–35.

Conger, R. D., & Elder, G. H., Jr. (in collaboration with Lorenz, F. O., Simons, R. L., & Whitbeck, L. B.). (1994). *Families in troubled times: Adapting to change in rural America.* Hillsdale, NJ: Aldine.

Conger, R. D., Ge, X., Elder, G., Lorenz, F., & Simons, R. (1994). Economic stress, coercive family process, and developmental problems in adolescents. *Child Development, 65,* 541–561.

Conley, D., & Bennett, N. (2002). Comment: Outcomes in young adulthood for very low birth-weight infants. *New England Journal of Medicine, 347,* 141–143.

Constantinescu, M., & Hines, M. (2012). Relating prenatal testosterone exposure to postnatal behavior in typically developing children: Methods and findings. *Child Development Perspectives, 6,* 407–413.

Conry-Murray, C., & Turiel, E. (2012). Jimmy's baby doll and Jenny's truck: Young children's reasoning about gender norms. *Child Development, 83,* 146–158.

Cook, A. S., & Oltjenbruns, K. A. (1998). The bereaved family. In A. S. Cook & K. A. Oltjenbruns (Eds.), *Dying and grieving: Life span and family perspectives* (pp. 91–115). Fort Worth, TX: Harcourt, Brace.

Cook, C. R., Williams, K. R., Guerra, N. G., Kim, T. E., & Sadek, S. (2010). Predictors of bullying and victimization in childhood and adolescence: A meta-analytic investigation. *School Psychology Quarterly, 25,* 65–83.

Cooley, C. H. (1902). *Human nature and the social order.* New York: Scribner's.

Coontz, S. (2005). *Marriage, a history: From obedience to intimacy or how love conquered marriage.* New York: Viking.

Corbie-Smith, G., Henderson, G., Blumenthal, C., Dorrance, J., & Estroff, S. (2008).Conceptualizing race in research. *Journal of the National Medical Association, 100,* 1235–1243.

Corby, B. C., Hodges, E. V. E., & Perry, D. G. (2007). Gender identity and adjustment in Black, Hispanic, and White preadolescents. *Developmental Psychology, 43,* 261–266.

Corcoran, K. O., & Mallinckrodt, B. (2000). Adult attachment, self-efficacy, perspective-taking, and conflict resolution. *Journal of Counseling and Development, 78,* 473–483.

Corr, C. A. (1993). Coping with dying: Lessons that we should and should not learn from the work of Elisabeth Kubler-Ross. *Death Studies, 17,* 69–83.

Costa, P. T., & McCrae, R. R. (1994). Set like plaster? Evidence for the stability of adult personality. In T. F. Heatherton & J. L. Weinberger (Eds.), *Can personality change?* (pp. 21–40). Washington, DC: American Psychological Association.

Costantino, G., Malgady, R. G., & Rogler, L. H. (1986). *The TEMAS thematic perception test: Technical manual.* Los Angeles: Western Psychological Association.

Costantino, G., Malgady, R. G., & Rogler, L. H. (1994). Storytelling-through-pictures: Culturally sensitive psychotherapy for Hispanic children and adolescents. *Journal of Clinical Child Psychology, 23,* 13–20.

Costello, E. J., Compton, S. N., Keeler, G., & Angold, A. (2003). Relationships between poverty and psychopathology: A natural experiment. *Journal of the American Medical Association, 290,* 2023–2063.

Costello, E. J., Erkanli, A., Copeland, W., & Angold, A. (2010). Association of family income supplements in adolescence with development of psychiatric and substance abuse disorders in adulthood among an American Indian population. *Journal of the American Medical Association, 303,* 1954–1960.

Côté, S. M., Borge, A. I., Geoffroy, M-C., Rutter, M., & Tremblay, R. E. (2008). Nonmaternal care in infancy and emotional/behavioral difficulties at 4 years old: Moderation by family risk characteristics. *Developmental Psychology, 44,* 155–168.

Coughlin, C. R. (2009). Prenatal choices: Genetic counseling for variable genetic diseases. In V. Ravitsky, A. Fiester, & A. L. Caplan (Eds.), *The Penn Center guide to bioethics* (pp. 415–424). New York: Springer.

Coupland, N., Coupland, J., Giles, H., Henwood, K., & Wiemann, J. (1988). Elderly self-disclosure: Interactional and intergroup issues. *Language and Communication, 8,* 109–133.

Courage, M. L., Edison, S. C., & Howe, M. L. (2004). Variability in the early development of visual self-recognition. *Infant Behavior and Development, 27,* 509–532.

Courage, M. L., & Setliff, A. E. (2009). Debating the impact of television and video material on very young children: Attention, learning, and the developing brain. *Child Development Perspectives, 3,* 72–78.

Cowan, C. P., & Cowan, P. A. (1992). *When partners become parents.* New York: Basic Books.

Cowan, N. (2001). The magical number 4 in short-term memory: A reconsideration of mental storage capacity. *Behavioral & Brain Sciences, 24,* 87–185.

Cowan, P. A. (1978). *Piaget with feeling: Cognitive, social and emotional dimensions.* New York: Holt, Rinehart & Winston.

Cowan, W. M. (1979). The development of the brain. In R. R. Llinas (Ed.), *The workings of the brain: Development, memory, and perception.* New York: Freeman.

Cowen, E. L., Hightower, A. D., Pedro-Carroll, J. L., Work, W. C., Wyman, P. A., & Haffey, W. G. (1996). *School-based prevention for children at risk: The Primary Mental Health Project.* Washington, DC: American Psychological Association.

Cowen, E. L., Izzo, L. D., Miles, H., Telschow, E. F., Trost, M. A., & Zax, M. A. (1963). A mental health program in the school setting: Description and evaluation. *Journal of Psychology, 56,* 307–356.

Cowen, E. L., Petersen, A., Babigian, H., Izzo, L. D., & Trost, M. A. (1973). Long-term follow-up of early detected vulnerable children. *Journal of Consulting and Clinical Psychology, 41,* 438–446.

Cox, M. J., Paley, B., & Harter, K. (2001). Interparental conflict and parent-child relationships. In J. H. Grych & F. D. Fincham (Eds.), *Interparental conflict and child development: Theory, research and application* (pp. 249–272). New York: Cambridge University Press.

Cox, K. S., Wilt, J., Olson, B., & McAdams, D. P. (2012). Generativity, the Big Five, and psychosocial adaptation in midlife adults. *Journal of Personality, 78,* 1185–1208.

Coyne, J. C. (1976). Depression and the response of others. *Journal of Abnormal Psychology, 85,* 186–193.

Coyne, J. C. (1999). Thinking interactionally about depression: A radical restatement. In T. Joiner & J. C. Coyne (Eds.), *The interactional nature of depression* (pp. 365–392). Washington, DC: American Psychological Association.

Craik, F. J. M., & Bialystok, E. (2006). Cognition through the lifespan: Mechanisms of change. *Trends in Cognitive Sciences, 10,* 131–138.

Crain, W. (1992). *Theories of development: Concepts and applications* (3rd ed.). London: Prentice-Hall.

Crain, W. (2005). *Theories of development: Concepts and applications* (5th ed.). Upper Saddle River, NJ: Pearson/Prentice Hall.

Cramer, P. (1999). Development of identity: Gender makes a difference. *Journal of Research in Personality, 34,* 42–72.

Crane, D. A., & Tisak, M. (1995). Mixed-domain events: The influence of moral and conventional components on the development of social reasoning. *Early Education and Development, 6,* 169–180.

Crawford, M. (2003). Sexual double standards: A review and methodological critique of two decades of research. *Journal of Sex Research, 40,* 13–26.

Creasey, G., & Hesson-McInnis, M. (2001). Affective responses, cognitive appraisals, and conflict tactics in late adolescent romantic relationships: Associations with attachment orientations. *Journal of Counseling Psychology, 48,* 85–96.

Crick, N. R., & Dodge, K. A. (1994). A review and reformation of social information processing mechanisms in children's social adjustment. *Psychological Bulletin, 115,* 74–101.

Crittendon, P. M. (1994). Peering into the black box: An exploratory treatise on the development of self in young children. In D. Cicchetti & S. L. Toth (Eds.), *Rochester Symposium on Developmental Psychopathology: Vol. 5. Disorders and dysfunctions of the self* (pp. 79–148). Rochester, NY: University of Rochester Press.

Crittendon, P. M. (1997). Patterns of attachment and sexual behavior: Risk of dysfunction versus opportunity for creative integration. In L. Atkinson & K. J. Zucker (Eds.), *Attachment and psychopathology* (pp. 47–93). New York: Guilford Press.

Crittendon, P. M., & DiLalla, D. L. (1988). Compulsive compliance: The development of an inhibitory coping strategy in infancy. *Journal of Abnormal Child Psychology, 16,* 585–599.

Crnic, K. A., & Booth, C. L. (1991). Mothers' and fathers' perceptions of daily hassles of parenting across early childhood. *Journal of Marriage and the Family, 53,* 1042–1050.

Crockenberg, S. C. (2003). Rescuing the baby from the bathwater: How gender and temperament (may) influence how child care affects child development. *Child Development, 74,* 1034–1038.

Crockenberg, S., & Langrock, A. M. (2001). The role of emotion and emotional regulation in children's response to interparental conflict. In J. H. Grych & F. D. Fincham (Eds.), *Child development and interparental conflict: Theory, research and application* (pp. 129–156). New York: Cambridge University Press.

Crockenberg, S. C., Leerkes, E. M., & Bárrig Jó, P. S. (2008). Predicting aggressive behavior in the third year from infant reactivity and regulation as moderated by maternal behavior. *Developmental and Psychopathology, 20,* 37–54.

Crockenberg, S., Leerkes, E. M., & Lekka, S. K. (2007). Pathways from marital aggression to infant emotion regulation: The development of withdrawal in infancy. *Infant Behavior & Development, 30,* 97–113.

Crockenberg, S., & Litman, C. (1991). Effects of maternal employment on maternal and two-year-old child behavior. *Child Development, 62,* 930–953.

Crocker, J., & Knight, K. M. (2005). Contingencies of self-worth. *Current Directions in Psychological Science, 14,* 200–203.

Crocker, J., & Major, B. (1989). Social stigma and self-esteem: The self-protective properties of stigma. *Psychological Review, 96,* 608–630.

Crocker, J., & Park, L. E. (2004). The costly pursuit of self-esteem. *Psychological Bulletin, 130*(3), 392–414.

Crosnoe, R. (2006). *Mexican roots, American schools: Helping Mexican immigrant children succeed.* Stanford, CA: Stanford University Press.

Crosnoe, R., & Fuligni, A. J. (2012). Children from immigrant families: Introduction to the special section. *Child Development, 83,* 1471–1476.

Cross, C. P., Copping, L. T, & Campbell, A. (2011). Sex differences in impulsivity: A meta-analysis. *Psychological Bulletin, 137,* 97–130.

Cross, W. E. (1971). The Negro to Black conversion experience. *Black World, 20,* 13–17.

Cross, W. E. (1994). Nigrescence theory: Historical and explanatory notes. *Journal of Vocational Behavior, 44,* 119–123.

Cross, W. E. Jr., & Fhagen-Smith, P. (2001). Patterns of African American identity development: A life span perspective. In B. Jackson & C. Wijeyesinghe (Eds.), *New perspectives on racial identity development: A theoretical and practical anthology* (pp. 243–270). New York: NYU Press.

Cross-National Collaborative Group. (1992). The changing rate of major depression: Cross-national comparisons. *Journal of the American Medical Association, 268,* 3098–3105.

Crowder, L. S. (1999). Mortuary practices in San Francisco Chinatown. *Chinese America, History & Perspectives,* pp. 33–47.

Crowell, J. A., Treboux, D., & Waters, E. (2002). Stability of attachment representations: The transition to marriage. *Developmental Psychology, 38,* 467–479.

Crowell, J. A., Waters, E., Treboux, D., O'Connor, E., Colon-Downs, C., Feider, O., et al. (1996). Discriminant validity of the Adult Attachment Interview. *Child Development, 67,* 2584–2599.

Crump, A. D., Haynie, D. L., Aarons, S. J., Adair, E., Woodward, K., & Simons-Morton, B. G. (1999). Pregnancy among urban African-American teens: Ambivalence about prevention. *American Journal of Health Behavior, 23,* 32–42.

Csikszentmihalyi, M. (1999). If we are so rich, why aren't we happy? *American Psychologist, 54,* 821–827.

Csikszentmihalyi, M., & Rathunde, K. (1990). The psychology of wisdom: An evolutionary interpretation. In R. J. Sternberg (Ed.). *Wisdom: Its nature, origins and development.* (pp. 25–51). Cambridge, UK: Cambridge University Press.

Csoka, A. B., & Szyf, M. (2009). Epigenetic side-effects of common pharmaceuticals: A potential new field in medicine and pharmacology. *Medical Hypotheses, 73,* 770–780.

Cultice, J. C., Somerville, S. C., & Wellman, H. M. (1983). Preschooler's memory monitoring: Feeling-of-knowing judgments. *Child Development, 54,* 1480–1486.

Currie, E. (1998). *Crime and punishment in America.* New York: Metropolitan Books, Henry Holt.

Curtis, M.A., Kam, M., Faull, R. L. M. (2011). Neurogenesis in humans. *European Journal of Neuroscience: Special Issue: Adult Neurogenesis, 33,* 1170–1174.

Curtis, N. M., & Ronan, K. R. (2004). Multisystemic treatment: A meta-analysis of outcome studies. *Journal of Family Psychology, 18,* 411–419.

Cvencek, D., Meltzoff, A. N., & Greenwald, A. G. (2011). Math-gender stereotypes in elementary school children. *Child Development, 82,* 766–779.

Cynkar, A. (2007). Stay-at-home dads report high job satisfaction. *Monitor on Psychology, 38,* 57.

Cyr, C., Euser, E. M., Bakermans-Kranenburg, M. J., & van IJzendoorn, M. H. (2010). Attachment security and disorganization in maltreating and high-risk families: A series of meta-analyses. *Development and Psychopathology, 22,* 87–108.

Dahl, R. E. (2004). Adolescent brain development: A period of vulnerabilities and opportunities. *Annals of the New York Academy of Sciences, 1021,* 1–22.

Daley, S. (1991, January 9). Little girls lose their self-esteem on way to adolescence, study finds. *The New York Times,* p. B6.

Dallman, M. F., Pecoraro, N., Akana, S. F., la Fleur, S. E., Gomez, F., Houshyar, H., et al. (2003). Chronic stress and obesity: A new view of "comfort food." *Proceedings of the National Academy of Sciences of the United States of America, 100,* 11696–11701.

Damasio, A. R. (1994). *Descartes' error: Emotion, reason, and the human brain.* New York: Grosset/Putnam.

Damasio, A. (2003). The person within. *Nature, 423,* 227.

Damon, W. (1988). *The moral child: Nurturing children's natural moral growth.* New York: Free Press.

Damon, W. (1995). *Greater expectations: Overcoming the culture of indulgence in America's homes and schools.* New York: Free Press.

Damon, W., & Hart, D. (1988). *Self-understanding in childhood and adolescence.* New York: Cambridge University Press.

Damon, W., & Hart, D. (1992). Self-understanding and its role in social and moral development. In M. H. Bornstein & M. E. Lamb (Eds.), *Developmental psychology: An advanced textbook* (3rd ed., pp. 421–464). Hillsdale, NJ: Erlbaum.

Danese, A., & McEwen, B. (2012). Adverse childhood experiences, allostasis, allostatic load, and age-related disease. *Physiology and Behavior, 106,* 29–39.

Dare, C., & Eisler, I. (1997). Family therapy for anorexia nervosa. In D. M. Garner & P. E. Garfinkel (Eds.). *Handbook of Treatment for Eating Disorders* (2nd ed.). New York: Guilford Press.

Darling, N., Cumsille, P., Caldwell, L. L., & Dowdy, B. (2006). Predictors of adolescents' disclosure to parents and perceived parental knowledge: Between- and within-person differences. *Journal of Youth and Adolescence, 35,* 667–678.

Darling, N., Cumsille, P., & Martinez, M. L. (2007). Adolescents as active agents in the socialization process: Legitimacy of parental authority and obligation to obey as predictors of obedience: *Journal of Adolescence, 30,* 297–311.

Darling, N., Cumsille, P., & Martinez, M. L. (2008). Individual differences in adolescents' beliefs about the legitimacy of parental authority and their own obligation to obey: A longitudinal investigation. *Child Development, 79,* 1103–1118.

Darling, N., & Steinberg, L. (1993). Parenting style as context: An integrative model. *Psychological Bulletin, 113,* 487–496.

Darwin, C. (1872/1965). *The expression of emotions in man and animals.* Chicago: U of Chicago Press.

Datan, N., & Ginsberg, L. H. (Eds.). (1975). *Life-span developmental psychology: Normative life crises.* New York: Academic Press.

David, E. J. R., Okazaki, S., & Saw, A. (2009). Bicultural self-efficacy among college students: Initial scale development and mental health correlates. *Journal of Counseling Psychology, 56,* 211–226.

Davidson, P., Turiel, E., & Black, A. (1983). The effect of stimulus familiarity on the use of criteria and justifications in children's social reasoning. *British Journal of Developmental Psychology, 1,* 49–65.

Davidson, R. J. (1992). Anterior cerebral asymmetry and the nature of emotion. *Brain and Cognition, 20,* 125–151.

Davidson, R. J. (2000). Affective style, psychopathology, and resilience: Brain mechanisms and plasticity. *American Psychologist, 55,* 1193–1214.

Davidson, R. J. (2002). Toward a biology of positive affect and compassion. In R. J. Davidson & A. Harrington (Eds.), *Visions of compassion: Western scientists and Tibetan Buddhists examine human nature* (pp. 107–130). New York: Oxford University Press.

Davidson, R. J., (2012). *The emotional life of your brain.* New York: Hudson Street Press.

Davidson, R. J., Coe, C. C., Dolski, I., & Donzella, B. (1999). Individual differences in prefrontal activation asymmetry predicts natural killer cell activity at rest and in response to challenge. *Brain, Behavior, and Immunity, 13,* 93–108.

Davidson, R. J., & Fox, N. A. (1989). Frontal brain asymmetry predicts infants' response to maternal separation. *Journal of Abnormal Psychology, 98,* 127–131.

Davidson, R. J., & Irwin, W. (1999). The functional neuroanatomy of emotion and affective style. *Trends in Cognitive Science, 3,* 11–21.

Davidson, R. J., Kabat-Zinn, J., Schumacher, J., Rosenkranz, M., Muller, D., Santorelli, S. F., et al. (2003). Alterations in brain and immune function produced by mindfulness meditation. *Psychosomatic Medicine, 65,* 564–570.

Davies, P. T., & Woitach, M. J. (2008). Children's emotional security in the interparental relationship. *Current Directions in Psychological Science, 17,* 269–274.

Davila, J. (2008). Depressive symptoms and adolescent romance: Theory, research, and implications. *Child Development Perspectives, 2,* 26–31.

Davis, C. (1852). *Lecture on the duties and relations of parents, teachers, and pupils as connected with education.* Delivered at the First Session of the Teachers' Institute at the Normal School at Ypsilanti, MI. Free Press Book and Job Office.

Davis, C. G., Lehman, D. R., & Wortman, C. B. (1997). *Finding meaning in loss and trauma: Making sense of the literature.* Unpublished manuscript, University of Michigan.

Davis, C. G., Wortman, C. B., Lehman, D. R., & Silver, R. C. (2000). Searching for meaning in loss: Are clinical assumptions correct? *Death Studies, 24,* 497–540.

Davis, G., & Stevenson, H. (2006). Racial socialization experiences and symptoms of depression among black youth. *Journal of Child and Family Studies, 15,* 293–307.

Davis, J. (1997). *Mapping the mind: The secrets of the human brain and how it works.* Secaucus, NJ: Birch Lane Press.

Davis-Kean, P. E., Jager, J., & Collins, W. A. (2009). The self in action: An emerging link between self-beliefs and behaviors in middle childhood. *Child Development Perspectives, 8,* 184–188.

Dawson, G. (2008). Early behavioral intervention, brain plasticity, and the prevention of autism spectrum disorder. *Development and Psychopathology, 20,* 775–803.

Dawson, G., Carver, L., Meltzoff, A., Panagiotides, H., McPartland, J., & Webb, S. (2002). Neural correlates of face recognition in young children with autism spectrum disorder, developmental delay, and typical development. *Child Development, 73,* 700–717.

Dawson, G., Frey, K., Panagiotides, H., Yamada, E., Hessl, D., & Osterling, J. (1999). Infants of depressed mothers exhibit atypical frontal electrical brain activity during interactions with mother and with a familiar, non-depressed adult. *Child Development, 70,* 1058–1066.

Dawson, G., Klinger, L. G., Panagiotides, H., Lewy, A., & Castelloe, P. (1995). Subgroups of autistic children based on social behavior display distinct patterns of brain activity. *Journal of Abnormal Child Psychology, 23,* 569–583.

Dawson, G., Rogers, S., Munson, J., Smith, M., Winter, J., Greenson, J., et al. (2010). Randomized controlled trial of the Early Start Denver Model: A developmental behavioral intervention for toddlers with autism: Effects on IQ, adaptive behavior, and autism diagnosis. *Pediatrics, 125,* 17–23.

Deater-Deckard, K., Dodge, K. A., Bates, J. E., & Pettit, G. S. (1996). Physical discipline among African American and European American mothers: Links to children's externalizing behaviors. *Developmental Psychology, 32,* 1065–1072.

Deaux, K. (1993). Commentary: Sorry, wrong number: A reply to Gentile's call. Sex or gender? [Special section]. *Psychological Science, 4,* 125–126.

Deaux, K., & Ethier, K. A. (1998). Negotiating social identity. In J. K. Swim (Ed.), *Prejudice: The target's perspective* (pp. 301–323). San Diego, CA: Academic Press.

De Bellis, M. D., Baum, A. S., Birmaher, B., Keshavan, M. S., Eccard, C. H., Boring, A. M., et al. (1999). Bennett Research Award. Developmental traumatology. Part I: Biological stress systems. *Biological Psychiatry, 45,* 1259–1270

Decaluwe, V., Braet, C., & Fairburn, C. G. (2003). Binge eating in obese children and adolescents. *International Journal of Eating Disorders, 33,* 78–84.

DeCasper, A. J., & Fifer, W. P. (1980). Of human bonding: Newborns prefer their mothers' voices. *Science, 208,* 1174–1176.

DeCasper, A. J., Lecaneut, J., Busnel, M., Granier-Deferre, C., & Maugeais, R. (1994). Fetal reactions to recurrent maternal speech. *Infant Behavior and Development, 17,* 159–164.

DeCasper, A. J., & Prescott, P. A. (1984). Human newborns' perception of male voices: Preference, discrimination, and reinforcing value. *Developmental Psychobiology, 17,* 481–491.

DeCasper, A. J., & Spence, M. J. (1986). Newborns prefer a familiar story over an unfamiliar one. *Infant Behavior and Development, 9,* 133–150.

de Castro, B. O., Veerman, J. W., Koops, W., Bosche, J. D., & Monshouwer, H. J. (2002). Hostile attribution, intent, and aggressive behavior: A meta-analysis. *Child Development, 73,* 916–934.

DeCatanzaro, D. A. (1999). *Motivation and emotion: Evolutionary, physiological, developmental, and social perspectives.* Upper Saddle River, NJ: Prentice Hall.

Deci, E. L., & Ryan, R. M. (2008). Self-determination theory: A macrotheory of human motivation, development, and health. *Canadian Psychology, 49,* 182–185.

Deci, E. L., Ryan, R. M., Gagne, M., Leone, D. R., Usunov, J., & Kornazheva, B. P. (2001). Need satisfaction, motivation, and well-being in work organizations of a former Eastern Bloc country: A cross-cultural study of self-determination. *Personality and Social Psychology Bulletin, 27,* 930–942.

Decker, P. J., & Borgen, F. H. (1993). Dimensions of work appraisal: Stress, strain, coping, job satisfaction, and negative affectivity. *Journal of Counseling Psychology, 40,* 470–478.

DeGarmo, D. S. (2010). Coercive and prosocial fathering, antisocial personality, and growth in children's postdivorce noncompliance. *Child Development, 81,* 503–516.

de Jong, M. T., & Bus, A. G. (2002). Quality of book-reading matters for emergent readers: An experiment with the same book in a regular or electronic format. *Journal of Educational Psychology, 94,* 145–155.

Delehanty, H., & Ginzler, E. (2005). *Caring for your parents: The complete AARP guide.* New York: Sterling.

DeLisi, R., & Gallagher, A. M. (1991). Understanding of gender stability and constancy in Argentinean children. *Merrill-Palmer Quarterly, 37,* 483–502.

Dellas, M., & Jernigan, L. P. (1987). Affective personality characteristics associated with undergraduate ego identity formation. *Journal of Adolescent Research, 3,* 306–324.

Delmore-Ko, P., Pancer, S. M., Hunsberger, B., & Pratt, M. (2000). Becoming a parent: The relation between prenatal expectations and postnatal experience. *Journal of Family Psychology, 14,* 625–640.

DeLoache, J. S. (1987). Rapid change in the symbolic functioning of very young children. *Science, 238,* 1556–1557.

DeLoache, J. S. (1999, April). *Becoming symbol minded.* Paper presented at the biennial meetings of the Society for Research in Child Development, Albuquerque, NM.

DeLoache, J. S., Chiong, C, Sherman, K., Islam, N., Vanderborght, M., Troseth, G. L., et al. (2010). Do babies learn from baby media? *Psychological Science, 21,* 1570–1574.

DeLoache, J. S., Miller, K. F., & Pierroutsakos, S. L. (1998). Reasoning and problem solving. In W. Damon (Series Ed.), D. Kuhn & R. S. Siegler (Vol. Eds.), *Handbook of child psychology: Vol. 2. Cognition, perception, and language* (5th ed., pp. 801–850). New York: Wiley.

DeLoache, J. S., Miller, K. F., & Rosengren, K. (1997). The credible shrinking room: Very young children's performance in symbolic and non-symbolic tasks. *Psychological Science, 8,* 308–313.

DeLoache, J. S., Simcock, G., & Macari, S. (2007). Planes, trains, automobiles—and tea sets: Extremely intense interests in very young children. *Developmental Psychology, 43,* 1579–1586.

Demetriou, A., Christou, C., Spanoudis, G., & Platsidou, M. (2002). The development of mental processing: Efficiency, working memory, and thinking. *Monographs of the Society for Research in Child Development, 67* (Serial No. 268), vii–154.

Dempster, F. N. (1981). Memory span: Sources of individual and developmental differences. *Psychological Bulletin, 89,* 63–100.

Denham, S. A., & Holt, R. W. (1993). Preschoolers' likability as cause or consequence of their social behavior. *Developmental Psychology, 29,* 271–275.

Deptula, D. P., Henry, D. B., & Schoeny, M. E. (2010). How can parents make a difference? Longitudinal associations with adolescent sexual behavior. *Journal of Family Psychology, 24,* 731–739.

Dermody, S. S., Marshal, M. P., Cheong, J-W., Burton, C., Hughes, T., Aranda, F., et al. (2013). Longitudinal disparities of hazardous drinking between sexual minority and heterosexual individuals from adolescence to young adulthood. *Journal of Youth and Adolescence.* doi: 10.1007/s10964-013-9905-9

Derryberry, D., & Reed, M. A. (1994). Temperament and attention: Orienting toward and away from positive and negative signals. *Journal of Personality and Social Psychology, 66,* 1128–1139.

Dessens, A. B., Slijper, F. M. E., & Drop, S. L. S. (2005). Gender dysphoria and gender change in chromosomal females with congenital adrenal hyperplasia. *Archives of Sexual Behavior, 34,* 389–397.

Dettling, A. C., Gunnar, M. R., & Donzella, B. (1999). Cortisol levels of young children in full-day child care centers: Relations with age and temperament. *Psychoneuroendocrinology, 24,* 519–536.

Dettling, A. C., Parker, S., Lane, S. K., Sebanc, A. M., & Gunnar, M. R. (2000). Quality of care and temperament determine whether cortisol levels rise over the day for children in full-day childcare. *Psychoneuroendocrinology, 25,* 819–836.

Deutch, H. (1937). Absence of grief. *Psychoanalytic Quarterly, 6,* 12–22.

Developmental Studies Center. (1996). *Child development project.* Oakland, CA: Author.

Dewey, J. (1911). *Development. The middle works of John Dewey* (Vol. 6). Carbondale, IL: Southern Illinois University Press.

Dewey, J. (1933/1998). *How we think: A restatement of the relation of reflective thinking to the educative process.* Boston: Houghton Mifflin.

Dey, E. L., & Hurtado, S. (1999). Students, colleges, and society: Considering the interconnections. In P. G. Altbach, R. O. Berndahl, & P. J. Gumport (Eds.), *American higher education in the twenty-first century: Social, political, and economic challenges* (pp. 298–322). Baltimore: Johns Hopkins University Press.

Diamond, A. (2005). Attention-deficit disorder (attention-deficit/ hyperactivity disorder without hyperactivity): A neurobiologically and behaviorally distinct disorder from attention-deficit/hyperactivity disorder (with hyperactivity). *Development and Psychopathology, 17,* 807–825.

Diamond, A. (2013). Executive functions. *Annual Review of Psychology, 64,* 135–168.

Diamond, A., Barnett, W. S., Thomas, J., & Munro, S. (2007). Preschool program improves cognitive control. *Science, 318,* 1387.

Diamond, G. S. (1998, August). *Anatomy of a family-based model for treating adolescent depression.* Paper presented at the American Psychological Association Convention, San Francisco.

Diamond, G. S., & Diamond, G. M. (2002). Studying a matrix of change mechanisms: An agenda for family-based process research. In H. A. Liddle, D. A. Santisteban, R. F. Levant, & J. H. Bray (Eds.), *Family psychology: Science-based interventions* (pp. 41–66). Washington, DC: American Psychological Association.

Diamond, G., Siqueland, L., & Diamond, G. M. (2003). Attachment-based family therapy for depressed adolescents: Programmatic treatment development. *Clinical Child and Family Psychology Review, 6,* 107–127.

Diamond, J. (1986). I want a girl, just like the girl? *Discover, 7,* 65–68.

Diamond, L. M. (1998). Development of sexual orientation among adolescent and young adult women. *Developmental Psychology, 34,* 1085–1095.

Diamond, L. M. (2007). A dynamical systems approach to female same-sex sexuality. *Perspectives on Psychological Science, 2,* 142–161.

Diamond, L. M. (2008). Female bisexuality from adolescence to adulthood: Results from a 10-year longitudinal study. *Developmental Psychology, 44,* 5–14.

Diamond, L. M., & Butterworth, M. (2008). Questioning gender and sexual identity: Dynamic links over time. *Sex Roles, 59,* 365–376.

Diamond, L. M., & Savin-Williams, R. C. (2003). Gender and sexual identity. In I. B. Weiner (Series Ed.), R. M. Lerner, F. Jacobs, & D. Wertlieb (Vol. Eds.), *Handbook of applied developmental science: Vol. 1. Applying developmental science for youth and families: Historical and theoretical foundations* (pp. 101–121). Thousand Oaks, CA: Sage.

Diamond, M., & Sigmundson, K. (1997). Sex reassignment at birth: Long-term review and clinical implications. *Archives of Pediatric Adolescent Medicine, 151,* 298–304.

Dick, D. M., & Rose, R. J. (2002). Behavior genetics: What's new? What's next? *Current Directions in Psychological Science, 11,* 70–74.

Dickerson, B. C., Bakkour, A., Salat, D. H., Feczko, E., Pacheco, J., Greve, D. N., et al. (2008). The cortical signature of Alzheimer's disease: Regionally specific cortical thinning relates to symptom severity in very mild to mild AD dementia and is detectable in asymptomatic amyloid-positive individuals. *Cerebral Cortex Advanced Access.* doi:10.1093/cercor/bhn113

Dickinson, D. K., McCabe, A., Anastasopoulos, L., Peisner-Feinberg, E. S., & Poe, M. D. (2003). The comprehensive language approach to early literacy: The interrelationships among vocabulary, phonological sensitivity, and print knowledge among preschool-aged children. *Journal of Educational Psychology, 95,* 465–481.

Diener, E. (2000). Subjective well-being: The science of happiness, and a proposal for a national index. *American Psychologist, 55,* 34–43.

Diener, E., & Diener, M. (1995). Cross-cultural correlates of life satisfaction and self-esteem. *Journal of Personality and Social Psychology, 68,* 653–663.

Diener, E., & Diener, M. (2009). Cross-cultural correlates of life satisfaction and self-esteem. In E. Diener (Ed.), *The collective works of Ed Diener* (pp. 71–91). New York: Springer Science and Business Media.

Diener, E., & Emmons, R. A. (1985). The independence of positive and negative affect. *Journal of Personality and Social Psychology, 47,* 71–75.

Diener, E., Emmons, R. A., Larsen, R. J., & Griffin, S. (1985). The Satisfaction with Life Scale. *Journal of Personality Assessment, 49,* 71–75.

Diener, E., Lucas, R. E., & Scollon, C. N. (2006). Beyond the hedonic treadmill: Revising the adaptation theory of well-being. *American Psychologist, 61,* 305–314.

Diener, E., Ng, W., Harter, J., & Arora, R. (2010). Wealth and happiness around the world: Material prosperity predicts life evaluation, whereas psychological prosperity predicts positive feelings. *Journal of Personality and Social Psychology, 99,* 52–61.

Diener, E., Oishi, S., & Lucas, R. E. (2003). Personality, culture, and subjective well-being: Emotional and cognitive evaluations of life. *Annual Review of Psychology, 54,* 403–425.

Diener, E., & Seligman, M. E. P. (2002). Very happy people. *Psychological Science, 13,* 80–83.

Diener, E., & Seligman, M. E. P. (2004). Beyond money: Toward an economy of well-being. *Psychological Science in the Public Interest, 5,* 1–31.

Diener, E., Tamir, M., & Scollon, C. N. (2006). Happiness, life satisfaction, and fulfillment: The social psychology of subjective well-being. In P. A. M. Van Lange (Ed.), *Bridging social psychology: Benefits of transdisciplinary approaches* (pp. 319–324). Mahwah, NJ: Erlbaum.

Diener, E., Tay, L., & Myers, D. (2011). The Religion Paradox: If religion makes people happy, why are so many dropping out? *Journal of Personality and Social Psychology 101,* 1278–1290.

Diener, E., Tay, L., & Oishi, S. (2013). Rising income and the subjective well-being of nations. *Journal of Personality and Social Psychology, 104,* 267–276.

Diener, E., Wirtz, D., Tov, W., Kim-Prieto, C., Choi, D., Oishi, S., et al. (2009). New measures of well-being: Flourishing and positive and negative feelings. *Social Indicators Research, 39,* 247–266.

Diener, M. L., & Kim, D. Y. (2004). Maternal and child predictors of preschool children's social competence. *Applied Developmental Psychology, 25,* 3–24.

Dinardo, Q. (1971). *Psychological adjustment to spinal cord injury.* Unpublished doctoral dissertation, University of Houston, TX.

Dion, K. K., Berscheid, E., & Walster, E. (1972). What is beautiful is good. *Journal of Personality and Social Psychology, 24,* 285–290.

DiPietro, J. A. (2004). The role of prenatal maternal stress in child development. *Current Directions in Psychological Science, 13,* 71–74.

Dishion, T. J., McCord, J., & Poulin, F. (1999). When interventions harm: Peer groups and problem behavior. *American Psychologist. 54,* 755–764.

Dittman, M. (2004). A new face to retirement. *Monitor on Psychology, 35,* 78–79.

Dix, T., Gershoff, E. T., Maunier, L. N., & Miller, P. C. (2004). The affective structure of supportive parenting: Depressive symptoms, immediate emotions, and child-oriented motivation. *Developmental Psychology, 40,* 1212–1227.

Dix, T., Stewart, A. D., Gershoff, E. T., & Day, W. H. (2007). Autonomy and children's reactions to being controlled: Evidence that both compliance and defiance may be positive markers in early development. *Child Development, 78,* 1204–1221.

Dixon, J. A., & Moore, C. F. (1990). The development of perspective taking: Understanding differences in information and weighting. *Child Development, 61,* 1502–1513.

Dodge, K. A. (1983). Behavioral antecedents of peer social status. *Child Development, 54,* 1386–1399.

Dodge, K. A., Bates, J. E., & Pettit, G. S. (1990). Mechanisms in the cycle of violence. *Science, 250,* 1678–1683.

Dodge, K. A., Coie, J. D., & Lynam, D. (2006). In W. Damon & R. M. Lerner (Series Eds.), N. Eisenberg (Vol. Ed.), *Handbook of child psychology: Vol. 3. Social, emotional, and personality development* (6th ed., pp. 719–788). Hoboken, NJ: Wiley.

Dodge, K. A., Coie, J. D., Pettit, G. S., & Price, J. M. (1990). Peer status and aggression in boys' groups: Developmental and contextual analyses. *Child Development, 61,* 1289–1309.

Dodge, K. A., Lansford, J. E., Burks, V. S., Bates, J. E., Pettit, G. S., Fontaine, R., et al. (2003). Peer rejection and social information-processing factors in the development of aggressive behavior problems in children. *Child Development, 74,* 374–393.

Dodge, K. A., Pettit, J. M., McClaskey, C. L., & Brown, M. M. (1986). Social competence in children. *Monographs of the Society for Research in Child Development, 51,* 1–80.

Dodge, K. A., Schlundt, D. G., Schocken, I., & Delugach, J. D. (1983). Social competence and children's social status: The role of peer group entry strategies. *Merrill-Palmer Quarterly, 29,* 309–336.

Dohnt, H., & Tiggemann, M. (2006). The contribution of peer and media influences to the development of body satisfaction and self-esteem in young girls: A prospective study. *Developmental Psychology, 42,* 929–936.

Dohrenwend, B. S., & Dohrenwend, B. P. (1974). Overview and prospects for research on stressful life events. In B. S. Dohrenwend & B. P. Dohrenwend (Eds.), *Stressful life events: Their nature and effects* (pp. 313–331). New York: Wiley.

Dolcos, F., Labar, K. S., & Cabeza, R. (2005). Remembering one year later: Role of the amygdala and the medial temporal lobe memory system in retrieving emotional memories. *Proceedings of the National Academy of Sciences, 102,* 2626–2631.

Dollahite, D. C. (1998). Fathering, faith, and spirituality. *Journal of Men's Studies, 7,* 3–15.

Donovan, W. L., Leavitt, L. A., & Walsh, R. (1990). Maternal self-efficacy: Illusory control and its effect on susceptibility to learned helplessness. *Child Development, 61,* 1638–1647.

Dornbusch, S. M., Ritter, P. L., Leiderman, P. H., Roberts, D. F., & Fraleigh, M. J. (1987). The relation of parenting style to adolescent school performance. *Child Development, 58,* 1244–1257.

Douglas, M. K., Pierce, J. U., Rosenkoetter, M., Pacquiao, D., Callister, L. C., Hattar-Pollara, et al. (2011). Standards of practice for culturally competent nursing care: 2011 update. *Journal of Transcultural Nursing, 22,* 317–333.

Douvan, E., & Adelson, J. (1966). *The adolescent experience.* New York: Wiley.

Dozier, M., Cue, K., & Barnett, L. (1994). Clinicians as caregivers: Role of attachment organization in treatment. *Journal of Consulting and Clinical Psychology, 62,* 793–800.

Dozier, M., & Kobak, R. R. (1992). Psychophysiology in attachment interviews: Converging evidence for deactivating strategies. *Child Development, 63,* 1473–1480.

Dozier, M., Stovall, K. C., & Albus, K. E. (1999). Attachment and psychopathology in adulthood. In J. Cassidy & P. R. Shaver (Eds.), *Handbook of attachment: Theory, research, and clinical applications* (pp. 497–519). New York: Guilford Press.

Dozier, M., & Tyrell, C. (1998). The role of attachment in therapeutic relationships. In J. A. Simpson & W. S. Rholes (Eds.), *Attachment theory and close relationships* (pp. 221–248). New York: Guilford Press.

Driver, J. L., & Gottman, J. M. (2004). Daily marital interactions and positive affect during marital conflict among newlywed couples. *Family Process, 43,* 301–304.

Drizin, S. A. (2003). Research on juvenile competency: A defender's perspective. *Social Policy Report, 17*(4), 8–9.

Dryfoos, J. G. (1990). *Adolescents at risk: Prevalence and prevention.* New York: Oxford University Press.

Dryfoos, J. G. (1997). The prevalence of problem behaviors: Implications for programs. In R. P. Weissberg, T. P. Gullotta, R. L. Hampton, B. A. Ryan, & G. R. Adams (Eds.), *Enhancing children's wellness* (Vol. 8, pp. 17–46). Thousand Oaks, CA: Sage.

Dube, S., Felitti, V. J., Dong, M., Giles, W. H., & Anda, R. F. (2003). The impact of adverse childhood experiences on health problems: Evidence from four birth cohorts dating back to 1900. *Preventive Medicine, 37,* 268–277.

Duckworth, A. L., & Seligman, M. E. P. (2006). Self-discipline outdoes IQ in predicting academic performance of adolescents. *Psychological Science, 16,* 939–944.

Dubowitz, H., Papas, M. A., Black, M. M., & Starr, R. H. (2002). Child neglect: Outcomes in high risk urban preschoolers. *Pediatrics, 109,* 1100–1107.

Duggal, S., Carlson, E. A., Sroufe, L. A., & Egeland, B. (2001). Depressive symptomatology in childhood and adolescence. *Development and Psychopathology, 13,* 143–164.

Duncan, G. J., & Brooks-Gunn, J. (Eds.), (1997). *Consequences of growing up poor.* New York: Sage.

Duncan, R., & Cheyne, J. A. (2002). Private speech in young adults: Task difficulty, self-regulation, and psychological predication. *Cognitive Development, 16,* 889–906.

Duncan, L. G., Coatsworth, J. D., & Greenberg, M. T. (2009). A model of mindful parenting: Implications for parent-child relationships and prevention research. *Clinical Child and Family Psychology Review, 12,* 255–270.

Dunkle, M. F., Schraw, G., & Bendixen, L. (1993, April). *The relationship between epistemological beliefs, causal attributions, and reflective judgment.* Paper presented at the Annual Meeting of the American Educational Research Association, Atlanta, GA.

Dunn, J. (2004). *Children's friendships: The beginnings of intimacy.* Oxford, England: Blackwell.

Dunn, J., Bretherton, I., & Munn, P. (1987). Conversations about feeling states between mothers and their young children. *Developmental Psychology, 23,* 132–139.

Dunn, S., & Morgan, V. (1987). Nursery and infant school play patterns: Sex-related differences. *British Educational Research Journal, 13,* 271–281.

Dunphy, D. C. (1963). The social structure of urban adolescent peer groups. *Sociometry, 26,* 230–246.

Durrant, J., Ensom, R., & the Coalition on Physical Punishment of Children and Youth (2004). *Joint statement on physical punishment of children and youth.* Ottawa (ON): The Coalition; 2004. Available: www.cheo.on.ca/en/physicalpunishment

Durrant, J., & Ensom, R. (2012). Physical punishment of children: lessons from 20 years of research. *Canadian Medical Association Journal, 184,* 1373–1377.

Duvall, E. M. (1971). *Family Development* (4th ed.). Philadelphia: J. B. Lippincott.

Dweck, C. S. (1999). *Self-theories: Their role in motivation, personality, and development.* Philadelphia: Taylor & Francis.

Dweck, C. S., & Allison, M. (2008). Self-theories motivate self-regulated learning. In D. H. Schunk & B. J. Zimmerman (Eds.), *Motivation and self-regulated learning: Theory, research, and applications* (pp. 31–51). Mahwah, NJ: Erlbaum.

Dweck, C. S., & Elliott-Moskwa, E. S. (2010). Self theories: The roots of defensiveness. In J. E. Maddux & J. Price (Eds.), *Social psychological foundations of clinical psychology* (pp. 136–153). New York: Guilford Press.

Dye-White, E. (1986). Environmental hazards in the work setting. Their effect on women of child-bearing age. *American Association of Occupational Health and Nursing Journal, 43,* 76–78.

Dykas, M. J., & Cassidy, J. (2011). Attachment and the processing of social information across the life span: Theory and evidence. *Psychological Bulletin, 137,* 19–46.

Dykiert, D., Der, G., Starr, J. M., & Deary, I. J. (2012). Sex differences in reaction time mean and intraindividual variability across the life span. *Developmental Psychology, 48,* 1262–1276. doi: 10.1037/a0027550

D'Zurilla, T. J. (1986). *Problem-solving therapy: A social competence approach to clinical intervention.* New York: Springer.

D'Zurilla, T. J. (1988). Problem-solving therapies. In K. S. Dobson (Ed.), *Handbook of cognitive-behavioral therapies* (pp. 85–135). New York: Guilford Press.

Eagly, A. H. (2007). Female leadership advantage and disadvantage: Resolving the contradictions. *Psychology of Women Quarterly, 31,* 1–12.

Eagly, A. H., & Johannesen-Schmidt, M. C. (2001). The leadership styles of women and men. *Journal of Social Issues, 57,* 781–797.

Eagly, A. H., Johannesen-Schmidt, M. C., & van Engen, M. L. (2003) Transformational, transactional, and laissez-faire leadership styles: A meta-analysis comparing women and men. *Psychological Bulletin, 129,* 569–591.

Eagly, A. H., & Johnson, B. T. (1990). Gender and leadership style: A meta-analysis. *Psychological Bulletin, 108,* 233–256.

Eagly, A. H., Makhijani, M. G., & Klonsky, B. G. (1992). Gender and the evaluation of leaders: A meta-analysis. *Psychological Bulletin, 117,* 125–145.

Easterbrooks, M. A., & Goldberg, W. A. (1990). Security of toddler-parent attachment: Relation to children's sociopersonality functioning during kindergarten. In M. T. Greenberg, D. Cicchetti, & E. M. Cumings (Eds.), *Attachment in the preschool years* (pp. 221–244). Chicago: University of Chicago Press.

Eaton, W. O., & Enns, L. R. (1986). Sex differences in human motor activity level. *Psychological Bulletin, 100,* 19–28.

Eccles, J., Midgley, C., & Adler, T. (1984). Grade-related changes in the school environment: Effects on achievement motivation. In J. J. Nicholls (Ed.), *Advances in motivation and achievement* (Vol. 3, pp. 283–331). Greenwich, CT: JAI Press.

Eccles, J. S., & Barber, B. L. (1999). Student council, volunteering, basketball, or marching band: What kind of extracurricular involvement matters? *Journal of Adolescent Research, 14,* 10–43.

Eccles, J. S., Midgley, C., Wigfield, A., Buchanan, C. M., Reuman, D., Flanagan, C., et al. (1993). Development during adolescence: The impact of stage-environment fit on young adolescents' experiences in schools and in families. *American Psychologist, 48,* 90–101.

Eccles, J. S., & Roeser, R. W. (2009). Schools, academic motivation, and stage-environment fit. *Handbook of Adolescent Psychology.* New York: Wiley.

Eccles, J. S., & Roeser, R. W. (2011). Schools as developmental contexts during adolescence. *Journal of Research in Adolescence, 21,* 225–241.

Eckert, P. (1989). *Jocks and burnouts: Social categories and identity in the high school.* New York: Teachers College Press.

Edwards, A. C., Dodge, K. A., Latendresse, S. J., Lansford, J. E., Bates, J. E., Pettit, G. S., et al. (2010). MAOA-uVNTR and early physical discipline interact to influence delinquent behavior. *Journal of Child Psychology and Psychiatry, 51,* 679–687.

Edelstein, B. A., Drozdick, L. W., & Ciliberti, C. M. (2010). Assessment of depression and bereavement in older adults, In P. Lichtenberg (Ed.), *Handbook of assessment in clinical gerontology* (2nd ed., pp. 3–43). San Diego, CA: Elsevier Academic Press.

Eder, D., & Sanford, S. (1986). The development and maintenance of interactional norms among early adolescents. *Sociological Studies of Child Development, 1,* 283–300.

Edwards, C. P., & Liu, W.-L. (2002). Parenting toddlers. In M. H. Bornstein (Ed.), *Handbook of parenting: Vol. 1. Children and parenting* (2nd ed., pp. 45–71). Mahwah, NJ: Erlbaum.

Egan, G. (1975). *The skilled helper: A model for systemic helping and interpersonal relating.* Monterey, CA: Brooks/Cole.

Egan, S. K., & Perry, D. G. (2001). Gender identity: A multidimensional analysis with implications for psychosocial adjustment. *Developmental Psychology, 37,* 451–463.

Egeland, B., Bosquet, M., & Chung, A. L. (2002). Continuities and discontinuities in the intergenerational transmission of child maltreatment: Implications for breaking the cycle of abuse. In K. D. Browne, H. Hanks, P. Stratton, & C., Hamilton (Eds.), *Early prediction and prevention of child abuse: A handbook* (pp. 217–232). New York: Wiley.

Eisen, M. L., Goodman, G. S., Qin, J., Davis, S., & Crayton, J. (2007). Maltreated children's memory: Accuracy, suggestibility, and psychopathology. *Developmental Psychology, 43,* 1275–1294.

Eisenberg, N., Cialdini, R., McCreath, H., & Shell, R. (1987). Consistency-based compliance: When and why do children become vulnerable? *Journal of Personality and Social Psychology, 52,* 1174–1181.

Eisenberg, N., & Fabes, R. A. (1992). Emotion, regulation, and the development of social competence. In M. S. Clark (Ed.), *Review of personality and social psychology* (Vol. 12, pp. 34–61). Newbury Park, CA: Sage.

Eisenberg, N., & Fabes, R. A. (1998). Prosocial development. In W. Damon (Ed.) & N. Eisenberg (Vol. Ed.), *Handbook of child psychology: Vol. 3. Social, emotional, and personality development* (5th ed., pp. 701–778). New York: Wiley.

Eisenberg, N., Fabes, R. A., & Spinrad, T. L. (2006). Prosocial development. In W. Damon & R. M. Lerner (Series Eds.), N. Eisenberg (Vol. Ed.), *Handbook of child psychology: Vol. 3. Social, emotional, and personality development* (6th ed., pp. 646–718). Hoboken, NJ: Wiley.

Eisenberg, N., Lennon, R., & Roth, K. (1983). Prosocial development: A longitudinal study. *Developmental Psychology, 19,* 846–855.

Eisenberg, N., Shell, R., Pasternack, J., Lennon, R., Beller, R., & Mathy, R. M. (1987). Prosocial development in middle childhood: A longitudinal study. *Developmental Psychology, 24,* 712–718.

Eisenberg, N., Spinrad, T. L., & Sadovsky, A. (2006). Empathy-related responding in children. In N. Eisenberg, T. L. Spinrad, & A. Sadovsky (Eds.), *Handbook of moral development* (pp. 517–549). Mahwah, NJ.: Erlbaum.

Ekman, P. (1992). Are there basic emotions? *Psychological Review, 99,* 550–553.

Ekman, P. (1994). Strong evidence for universals in facial expression: A reply to Russell's mistaken critique. *Psychological Bulletin, 115,* 268–276.

Ekman, P. (1999). Basic emotions. In T. Dalgleish & T. Power (Eds.), *Handbook of cognition and emotion* (pp. 45–60). New York: Wiley.

Ekman, P., & Friesen, W. V. (1969). The repertoire of nonverbal behavior: Categories, origins, uses, and coding. *Semiotica, 1,* 49–98.

Ekman, P., & Friesen, W. V. (1971). Constants across cultures in the face and emotion. *Journal of Personality and Social Psychology, 17,* 124–129.

Ekman, P., & Oster, H. (1979). Facial expression of emotion. *Annual Review of Psychology, 30,* 527–554.

Elder, G. (1974). *Children of the Great Depression.* Chicago: University of Chicago Press.

Elder, G. H., Jr., & Shanahan, M. J. (2006). The life course and human development. In W. Damon & R. M. Lerner (Series Eds.), R. M. Lerner (Vol. Ed.), *Handbook of child psychology: Vol. 1. Theoretical models of human development* (6th ed., pp. 665–715). Hoboken, NJ: Wiley.

Eliason, M. J. (1996). Identity formation for lesbian, bisexual and gay persons: Beyond a "minoritizing" view. *Journal of Homosexuality, 30,* 31–58.

Eliot, L. (2009). *Pink brain, blue brain.* Boston: Harcourt.

Elkind, D. (1967). Egocentrism in adolescence. *Child Development, 38,* 1025–1031.

Elkind, D. (1968, May 26). Giant in the nursery—Jean Piaget. *The New York Times Magazine,* 25–80.

Elkind, D. (1981). *Children and adolescents.* New York: Oxford University Press.

Elkind, D. (1984). *All grown up and no place to go: Teenagers in crisis.* Reading, MA: Addison-Wesley.

Elkind, D. (1994). *Ties that stress: The new family imbalance.* Cambridge, MA: Harvard University Press.

Elkonin, D. B. (2005). Chapter 1: The subject of our research: The developed form of play. *Journal of Russian and East European Psychology, 45,* 22–48.

Ellis, B. J. (2004). Timing of pubertal maturation in girls: An integrated life history approach. *Psychological Bulletin, 130,* 920–958.

Ellis, B. J., & Essex, M. J. (2007). Family environments, adrenarche, and sexual maturation: A longitudinal test of a life history model. *Child Development, 74,* 1799–1817.

Ellis, N. C., & Hennelly, R. A. (1980). A bilingual word-length effect: Implications for intelligence testing and the relative ease of mental calculation in Welsh and English. *British Journal of Psychology, 71,* 43–51.

Ellison, C. G., (1991). Religious involvement and subjective well-being. *Journal of Health and Social Behavior, 32,* 80–99.

Else-Quest, N. M., Higgins, A., Allison, C., & Morton, L. C. (2012). Gender differences in self-conscious emotional experience: A meta-analysis. *Psychological Bulletin, 138,* 947–981.

Else-Quest, N. M., Hyde, J. S., & Linn, M. C. (2010). Cross-national patterns of gender differences in mathematics: A meta-analysis. *Psychological Bulletin, 136,* 103–127.

Emanuel, E., & Emanuel, L. (1998). The promise of a good death. *The Lancet, 251,* 21–29.

Emde, R. N., Biringen, Z., Clyman, R. B., & Oppenheim, D. (1991). The moral self of infancy: Affective core and procedural knowledge. *Developmental Review, 11,* 251–270.

Emde, R. N., & Buchsbaum, H. (1990). "Didn't you hear my mommy?" Autonomy with connectedness in moral self-emergence. In D. Cicchetti & M. Beeghly (Eds.), *The self in transition: Infancy to adulthood* (pp. 35–60). Chicago: University of Chicago Press.

Emde, R. N., Johnson, W., & Easterbrooks, M. (1987). The dos and don'ts of early moral development: Psychoanalytic tradition and current research. In J. Kagan & S. Lamb (Eds.), *The emergence of morality in young children* (pp. 245–276). Chicago: University of Chicago Press.

Eme, R. F. (1992). Selective female affliction in the development of disorders of childhood: A literature review. *Journal of Clinical Child Psychology, 21,* 354–364.

Emmons, R. A., & Paloutzian, R. F. (2003). The psychology of religion. *Annual Review of Psychology, 54,* 377–402.

Ennett, S. T., & Bauman, K. E. (1994). The contribution of influence and selection to adolescent peer group homogeneity: The case of adolescent cigarette smoking. *Journal of Personality and Social Psychology, 67,* 653–663.

Enns, C. Z. (1992). Toward integrating feminist psychotherapy and feminist philosophy. *Professional Psychology: Research and Practice, 23,* 453–466.

Enright, D. R., Lapsley, D. K., Harris, D. J., & Shawver, D. J. (1983). Moral development interventions in early adolescence. *Theory into Practice, 22,* 134–145.

Enright, R. D., & Fitzgibbons, R. P. (2002). *Helping clients forgive: An empirical guide for resolving anger and restoring hope.* Washington, DC: American Psychological Association.

Ensor, R., & Hughes, C. (2008). Content or connectedness? Mother-child talk and early social understanding. *Child Development, 79,* 201–216.

Enticott, P. G., Kennedy, H. A., Rinehart, N. J., Tonge, B. J., Bradshaw, J. L., Taffe, J. R., et al., (2012). Motor neuron activity associated with social impairments but not age in autism spectrum disorder. *Biological Psychiatry, 71,* 427–433.

Entwisle, D. R. (1990). Schools and the adolescent. In S. S. Feldman & G. R. Elliott (Eds.), *At the threshold: The developing adolescent* (pp. 197–224). Cambridge, MA: Harvard University Press.

Epel, E., Daubenmier, J., Moskowitz, J. T., Folkman, S., & Blackburn, E. (2009). Can meditation slow rate of cellular aging? Cognitive stress, mindfulness, and telomeres. *Annals of the NY Academy of Science, 1172,* 34–53.

Equal Justice Initiative. (2008). *Cruel and unusual: Sentencing 13- and 14-year-old children to die in prison.* Montgomery, AL: Equal Justice Initiative.

Erber, J. T., & Prager, I. G. (1999). Age and memory: Perceptions of forgetful young and older adults. In T. M. Hess & F. Blanchard-Fields (Eds.), *Social cognition and aging* (pp. 197–217). San Diego, CA: Academic Press.

Erel, O., Oberman, Y., & Yirmiya, N. (2000). Maternal versus nonmaternal care and seven domains of children's development. *Psychological Bulletin, 126,* 727–747.

Erhardt, A. A., & Baker, S. W. (1974). Fetal androgens, human central nervous system, differentiation, and behavior sex differences. In R. C. Friedman, R. M. Richart, & R. L. Van de Wiele (Eds.), *Sex differences in behavior* (pp. 33–51). New York: Wiley.

Erickson, K., Crosnoe, R., & Dornbusch, S. M. (2000). A social process model of adolescent deviance: Combining social control and differential association perspectives. *Journal of Youth and Adolescence, 29,* 395–425.

Erickson, M. F., Sroufe, L. A., & Egeland, B. (1985). The relationship between quality of attachment and behavior problems in preschool in a high-risk sample. In I. Bretherton & E. Waters (Eds.), Growing points of attachment theory and research. *Monographs of the Society for Research in Child Development, 50* (Serial No. 209), 147–166.

Erikson, E. H. (1950/1963). *Childhood and society* (2nd ed.). New York: Norton.

Erikson, E. H. (1968). *Identity, youth, and crisis.* New York: Norton.

Eriksson, P. S., Perfilieva, E., Bjork-Eriksson, T., Alborn, A. M., Nordborg, C., Peterson, D. A., et al. (1998). Neurogenesis in the adult human hippocampus. *Nature Medicine, 4,* 1313–1317.

Ernst, M., Pine, D. S., & Hardin, M. (2006). Triadic model of the neurobiology of motivated behavior in adolescence. *Psychological Medicine, 36,* 299–312.

Eti, S. (2011). Palliative care: An evolving field in medicine. *Primary Care: Clinics in Office Practice, 38,* 159–171.

Erwin, P. (1985). Similarity of attitudes and constructs in children's friendships. *Journal of Experimental Child Psychology, 40,* 470–485.

Ewens, J., & Herrington, P. (1983). *Hospice.* Santa Fe, NM: Bear & Co.

Eysenck, H. J., & Schoenthaler, S. J. (1997). Raising IQ level by vitamin and mineral supplementation. In R. J. Steinberg & E. Grigorenko (Eds.), *Intelligence, heredity, and environment* (pp. 362–393). Cambridge, England: Cambridge University Press.

Ezzo, G., & Bucknam, R. (1995). *On becoming babywise: Vol. 2: Parenting your pretoddler.* Sisters, OR: Multnomah Books.

Ezzo, G., & Bucknam, R. (1999). *On becoming childwise: Parenting your child from three to seven years*. Sisters, OR: Multnomah Books.

Fabes, R. A., Martin, C. L., & Hanish, L. D. (2003). Young children's play qualities in same-, other-, and mixed-sex peer groups. *Child Development, 74,* 921–932.

Fagot, B. I. (1984). The consequences of problem behavior in toddler children. *Journal of Abnormal Child Psychology, 12,* 385–397.

Farah, M. J., Rabinowitz, C., & Quinn, G. E. (2000). Early commitment of neural substrates for face recognition. *Cognitive Neuropsychology, 17,* 117–124.

Farrington, D. P. (1989). Self-reported and official offending from adolescence to adulthood. In M. W. Klein (Ed.), *Cross-national research in self-reported crime and delinquency*. Boston: Kluwer Academic.

Farrington, D. P. (1995). The development of offending and antisocial behavior from childhood: Key findings from the Cambridge Study in Delinquent Development. *Journal of Child Psychology and Psychiatry, 36,* 929–964.

Fausto-Sterling, A. (2000). *Sexing the body: Gender politics and the construction of sexuality*. New York: Basic Books.

Feagans, L., & Farran, D. C. (1981). How demonstrated comprehension can get muddled in production. *Developmental Psychology, 17,* 718–727.

Fearon, R. P., Bakersman-Kranenburg, M. J., van IJzendoorn, M., H., Lapsley, A-M, & Roisman, G. I. (2010). The significance of insecure attachment and disorganization in the development of children's externalizing behavior: A meta-analytic study. *Child Development, 81,* 435–456.

Feeney, J., Peterson, C., & Noller, P. (1994). Equity and marital satisfaction over the family life cycle. *Personality Relationships, 1,* 83–99.

Fein, G. (1981). Pretend play in childhood: An integrative review. *Child Development, 52,* 1095–2018.

Feinman, S., & Entwisle, D. R. (1976). Children's ability to recognize other children's faces. *Child Development, 47,* 506–510.

Feldlaufer, H., Midgley, C., & Eccles, J. S. (1988). Student, teacher, and observer perceptions of the classroom environment before and after the transition to junior high school. *Journal of Early Adolescence, 8,* 133–156.

Feldman, H. A., Longcope, C., Derby, C. A., Johannes, C. B., Araujo, A. B., Coviello, A. D., et al. (2002). Age trends in the level of serum testosterone and other hormones in middle-aged men: Longitudinal results from the Massachusetts male aging study. *Journal of Clinical Endocrinology and Metabolism, 87,* 589–598.

Feldman, J., & Kazdin, A. E. (1995). Parent management training for oppositional and conduct problem children. *The Clinical Psychologist, 48,* 3–5.

Feldman, R. (2007). Parent-infant synchrony: Biological foundations and developmental outcomes. *Current Directions in Psychological Science, 16,* 340–345.

Feldman, R., & Eidelman, A. I. (2007). Maternal postpartum behavior and the emergence of infant-mother and infant-father synchrony in preterm and full-term infants: The role of neonatal vagal tone. *Developmental Psychobiology, 49,* 290–302.

Felitti, V. J., Anda, R. F., Nordenberg, D., Williamson, D. F., Spitz, A. M., Edwards, V., et al. (1998). Relationship of childhood abuse and household dysfunction to many of the leading causes of death in adults: The Adverse Childhood Experiences (ACE) Study. *American Journal of Preventive Medicine, 14,* 245–258.

Fenson, L., Dale, P. S., Reznick, J. S., Bates, E., Thal, D. J., & Pethick, S. J. (1994). Variability in early communicative development. *Monographs of the Society for Research in Child Development, 59*(5, Serial No. 242).

Ferguson, C. J., & Donnellan, M. B. (2013). Is the association between children's baby video viewing and poor language development robust? A reanalysis of Zimmerman, Christakis, and Meltzoff (2007). *Developmental Psychology*. Advance online publication. doi:10.1037/a0033628

Fernald, A. (2010). Getting beyond the "convenience sample" in research on early cognitive development. *Behavior & Brain Sciences, 33,* 91–92.

Fernald, A., Perfors, A., & Marchman, V. A. (2006). Picking up speed in understanding: Speech processing efficiency and vocabulary growth across the second year. *Developmental Psychology, 42,* 98–116.

Fernyhough, C., & Fradley, E. (2005). Private speech on an executive task: Relations with task difficulty and task performance. *Cognitive Development, 20,* 103–120.

Ferrari, P. F., & Fogassi, L. (2012). *The primate mind: Built to connect with other minds*. Cambridge, MA: Harvard University Press.

Festinger, L. (1954). A theory of social comparison. *Human Relations, 7,* 117–140.

Field, T., & Diego, M. (2008). Vagal activity, early growth and emotional development. *Infant Behavior and Development, 31,* 361–373.

Field, T., Fox, N., Pickens, J., & Nawrocki, T. (1995). Relative right frontal activation in 3- to 6-month-old infants of depressed mothers. *Developmental Psychology, 31,* 358–363.

Field, T., Grizzle, N., Scafidi, F., & Schanberg, S. (1996). Massage and relaxation therapies' effects on depressed adolescent mothers. *Adolescence, 31,* 903–1002.

Field, T., Hernandez-Reif, M., & Diego, M. (2006). Intrusive and withdrawn depressed mothers and their infants. *Developmental Review, 26,* 15–30.

Field, T., Hernandez-Reif, M., Diego, M., Feijo, L., Vera, Y., Gil, K., & Sanders, C. (2007a). Responses to animate and inanimate faces by infants of depressed mothers. *Early Child Development and Care, 177,* 533–539.

Field, T., Hernandez-Reif, M., Diego, M., Feijo, L., Vera, Y., Gil, K., & Sanders, C. (2007b). Still-face and separation effects on depressed mother-infant interactions. *Infant Mental Health Journal, 28,* 314–323.

Field, T., Hernandez-Reif, M., & Freedman, J. (2004). Stimulation programs for preterm infants. *SRCD Social Policy Report, 18,* 1–19.

Field, T., Scafidi, F., & Schanberg, S. (1987). Massage of preterm infants to improve growth and development. *Pediatric Nursing, 13,* 385–387.

Field, T., Schanberg, S. M., Scafidi, F., Bauer, C. R., Vega-Lahr, N., Garcia, R., et al. (1986). Tactile/kinesthetic stimulation effects on preterm neonates. *Pediatrics, 77,* 654–658.

Fine, G. A., Mortimer, J. T., & Roberts, D. F. (1990). Leisure, work, and the mass media. In S. S. Feldman & G. R. Elliott (Eds.), *At the threshold: The developing adolescent* (pp. 225–253). Cambridge, MA: Harvard University Press.

Fingerman, K. L. (2003). *Mothers and their adult daughters: Mixed emotions, enduring bonds*. Amherst, NY: Prometheus Books.

Fink, G. (Ed.) (2009). *Stress Science: Neuroendocrinary*. San Diego, CA:Academic Press.

Fischer, K. W., & Bidell, T. R. (2006). Dynamic development of action and thought. In W. Damon & R. M. Lerner (Series Eds.), R. M. Lerner (Vol. Ed.), *Handbook of child psychology: Vol. 1. Theoretical models of human development* (6th ed., pp. 313–399). Hoboken, NJ: Wiley.

Fischer, R., & Schwartz, S. (2011). Whence differences in value priorities?: Individual, cultural, or artifactual sources. *Journal of Cross-Cultural Psychology, 42,* 1127–1144.

Fisher, C. B., & Lerner, R. M. (1994). *Applied developmental psychology*. New York: McGraw-Hill.

Fiske, A. P., Kitayama, S., Markus, H. R., & Nisbett, R. E. (1998). The cultural matrix of social psychology. In D. T. Gilbert & S. T. Fiske (Eds.), *The handbook of social psychology, Vol. 2* (4th ed., pp. 915–981). New York: McGraw-Hill.

Fiske, S. T. (2009). Cultural processes. In G. G. Berntson & J. T. Cacioppo (Eds.), *Handbook of Neuroscience for the Behavioral Sciences* (pp. 985–1004). New York: Wiley.

Fiske, S. T., & Taylor, S. E. (1991). *Social cognition* (2nd ed.). New York: McGraw-Hill.

Fitzgerald, J. M. (1988). Vivid memories and the reminiscence phenomenon: The role of a self narrative. *Human Development, 31,* 261–273.

Fitzgerald, J. M. (1992). Autobiographical memory and conceptualizations of the self. In M. A. Conway, D. C. Rubin, H. Spinnler, & W. A. Wagenaar (Eds.), *Theoretical perspectives on autobiographical memory* (pp. 99–114). Boston: Kluwer Academic Press.

Fitzgerald, J. M. (1999). Autobiographical memory and social cognition: Development of the remembered self in adulthood. In T. M. Hess & F. Blanchard-Fields (Eds.), *Social cognition and aging* (pp. 145–171). San Diego, CA: Academic Press.

Flannery, K. A., & Watson, M. W. (1993). Are individual differences in fantasy play related to peer acceptance levels? *Journal of Genetic Psychology, 154,* 407–416.

Flavell, J. H. (1963). *The developmental psychology of Jean Piaget*. New York: Van Nostrand.

Flavell, J. H., Botkin, P., Fry, C. L., Wright, J., & Jarvis, P. (1968). *The development of role-taking and communication skills in children*. New York: Wiley.

Flavell, J. H., Friedrichs, A. G., & Hoyt, J. D. (1970). Developmental changes in memorization processes. *Cognitive Psychology, 1,* 324–340.

Flavell, J. H., & Miller, P. H. (1998). Social cognition. In W. Damon (Series Ed.), D. Kuhn & R. S. Siegler (Vol. Eds.), *Handbook of child psychology: Vol. 2. Cognition, perception, and language* (5th ed., pp. 851–898). New York: Wiley.

Flavell, J. H., Miller, P. H., & Miller, S. A. (1993). *Cognitive development* (3rd ed.). Upper Saddle River, NJ: Prentice Hall.

Flavell, J. H., Mumme, D. L., Green, F. L., & Flavell, E. R. (1992). Young children's understanding of different types of beliefs. *Child Development, 63,* 960–977.

Flavell, J. II., Flavell, E. R., & Green, F. L. (1987). Young children's knowledge about the apparent-real and pretend-real distinctions. *Developmental Psychology, 23,* 816–822.

Fletcher, A. C., Steinberg, L., & Williams-Wheeler, M. (2004). Parental influences on adolescent problem behavior: Revisiting Stattin and Kerr. *Child Development 75,* 781–796.

Flett, G. L., Hewitt, P. L., Davis, R. A., & Sherry, S. B. (2004). Description and counseling of the perfectionistic procrastinator. In H. C. Schouwenburg, C. H. Lay, T. A. Pychyl, & J. R. Ferrari (Eds.), *Counseling the procrastinator in academic settings* (pp. 181–194). Washington, DC: American Psychological Association.

Flynn, J. R. (2012). *Are we getting smarter? Rising IQ in the twenty-first century*. New York: Cambridge University Press.

Foley, M. A., Harris, J., & Hermann, S. (1994). Developmental comparison of the ability to discriminate between memories for symbolic play enactment. *Developmental Psychology, 30*, 206–217.

Folkman, S., & Lazarus, R. S. (1988). The relationship between coping and emotion: Implications for theory and research. *Social Science Medicine, 26*, 309–1003.

Folkman, S., Lazarus, R. S., Gruen, R. J., & DeLongis, A. (1986). Appraisal, coping, health status, and psychological symptoms. *Journal of Personality and Social Psychology, 50*, 571–579.

Folstein, S., & Rutter, M. (1977). Infantile autism: A study of 21 twin pairs. *Journal of Child Psychology and Psychiatry, 18*, 297–321.

Fordham, S., & Ogbu, J. U. (1986). Black students' school success: Coping with the burden of "acting white." *Urban Review, 18*, 176–206.

Fouad, N. A. (2004). Cross-cultural differences in vocational interests: Between-groups differences on the strong interest inventory. *Journal of Counseling Psychology, 49*, 283–289.

Fouad, N. A., & Bynner, J. (2008). Work transitions. *American Psychologist, 63*, 241–251.

Fowler, J. W. (1981). *Stages of faith: The psychology of human development and the quest for meaning.* San Francisco: Harper & Row.

Fox, N. A., Hane, A. A., & Pine, S. S. (2007). Plasticity for affective neurocircuitry: How the environment affects gene expression. *Current Directions in Psychological Science, 16*, 1–5.

Fox, N. A., Kimmerly, N. L., & Schafer, W. D. (1991). Attachment to mother/attachment to father: A meta-analysis. *Child Development, 62*, 210–225.

Foxcroft, L. (2009). *Hot flushes, cold science: A history of the modern menopause.* London: Granta Publishers.

Fraley, R. C., Davis, K. E., & Shaver, P. R. (1998). Dismissing-avoidance and the defensive organization of emotion, cognition, and behavior. In J. A. Simpson & W. S. Rholes (Eds.), *Attachment theory and close relationships* (pp. 249–279). New York: Guilford Press.

Fraley, R. C., & Shaver, P. R. (1999). Loss and bereavement: Attachment theory and recent controversies concerning "grief work" and the nature of detachment. In J. Cassidy & P. R. Shaver (Eds.), *Handbook of attachment: Theory, research and clinical applications* (pp. 735–759). New York: Guilford Press.

Fraley, R. C., & Waller, N. G. (1998). Adult attachment patterns: A test of the typological model. In J. A. Simpson & W. S. Rholes (Eds.), *Attachment theory and close relationships* (pp. 77–114). New York: Guilford Press.

Francis, A. (2010). The medicalization of grief. *Psychiatric Times*, March 16, 2010.

Francis, R. C. (2011). *Epigenetics: The ultimate mystery of inheritance.* New York: W.W. Norton.

Frankenberger, K. D. (2000). Adolescent egocentrism: A comparison among adolescents and adults. *Journal of Adolescence, 23*, 343–347.

Fratiglioni, L., Wang, H. X., Ericsson, K., Maytan, M., & Winblad, B. (2000). Influence of social network on occurrence of dementia: A community-based longitudinal study. *The Lancet, 355*, 1315–1319.

Frede, E. (2008). Top 10 pre-K questions: What parents need to know about high quality preschool. Retrieved August 20, 2008, from http://nieer.org/docs/index.php?DocID=189

Fredrickson, B. L. (2001). The role of positive emotions in positive psychology: The broaden-and-build theory of positive emotions. *American Psychologist, 56*, 218–226.

Fredrickson, B. L. (2013). Positive emotions broaden and build. In E. Ashby Plant & P. G. Devine (Eds.), *Advances on Experimental Social Psychology, 47*, 1–53.

Fredrickson, B. L., & Carstensen, L. L. (1990). Choosing social partners: How old age and anticipated endings make us more selective. *Psychology and Aging, 5*, 335–347.

Fredrickson, B. L., Cohn, M. A., Coffey, K. A., Pek, J., & Finkel, S. M. (2008). Open hearts build lives: Positive emotions, induced through loving-kindness meditation, build consequential personal resources. *Journal of Personality and Social Psychology, 95*, 1045–1062.

Freedy, J. R., Saladin, M. E., Kilpatrick, D. G., Resnick, H. S., & Saunders, B. E. (1994). Understanding acute psychological distress following natural disaster. *Journal of Traumatic Stress, 7*, 257–273.

Freidrich, L. K., & Stein, A. H. (1973). Aggressive and prosocial television programs and the natural behavior of preschool children. *Monographs of Society for Research in Child Development, 38* (Serial No. 3).

Freud, A. (1958). Child observation and prediction of development. *The Psychoanalytic Study of the Child, 13*, 92–116.

Freud, S. (1905/1989). Three essays on the theory of sexuality. In P. Gay (Ed.), *The Freud reader.* New York: Norton.

Freud, S. (1917/1957). Mourning and melancholia. In J. Strachey (Ed.), *Standard edition of the complete works of Sigmund Freud.* London: Hogarth Press.

Freud, S. (1920/1955). Beyond the pleasure principle: In J. Strachey (Ed. and Trans.), *The standard edition of the complete psychological works of Sigmund Freud* (Vol. 18, pp. 7–64). London: Hogarth Press.

Freud, S. (1929/1961). To Ludwig Binswanger [Letter]. In E. L. Freud (Ed.), *Letters of Sigmund Freud 1873–1939* (T. & J. Stern, Trans.). London: Hogarth Press.

Freud, S. (1930/1989). Civilization and its discontents. In P. Gay (Ed.), *The Freud reader* (pp. 722–772). New York: Norton.

Freud, S. (1935/1960). *A general introduction to psychoanalysis.* New York: Washington Square Press.

Freud, S. (1949/1969). *An outline of psychoanalysis.* New York: Norton.

Freud, S. (1956). *Delusion and dream: An interpretation in the light of psychoanalysis of Gravida, a novel, by Wilhelm Jensen.* Boston: Beacon Press.

Frick, P. J., & Nigg, J. T. (2011). Current issues in the diagnosis of attention deficit hyperactivity disorder, oppositional defiant disorder, and conduct disorder. *Annual Review of Clinical Psychology, 8*, 77–107.

Friederici, A. D. A., Pannekamp, A., Partsch, C-J., Ulmen, U., Oehler, K., et al. (2008). Sex hormone testosterone affects language organization in the infant brain. *NeuroReport, 19*, 283–286.

Friedman, H. S., Tucker, J. S., Schwartz, J. E., Tomlinson-Keasey, C., Martin, L. R., Wingard, D. L., et al. (1995). Psychosocial and behavioral predictors of longevity: The aging and death of the "Termites." *American Psychologist, 50*, 69–78.

Friedman, S. L., & Boyle, D. E. (2008). Attachment in US children experiencing nonmaternal care in the early 1990s. *Attachment & Human Development, 10*, 225–261.

Friedrich, M. J. (2013). Studies suggest potential approaches for early detection of Alzheimer Disease. *JAMA, 309*, 18–19. doi:10.1001/jama.2012.105106

Frisina, R. D. (2009). Age-related hearing loss: Ear and brain mechanisms. *Annals of the New York Academy of Sciences, 1170*, 708–717.

Fromme, K., Corbin, W. R., & Kruse, M. I. (2008). Behavioral risks during the transition from high school to college. *Developmental Psychology, 44*, 1497–1504.

Fruzzetti, A. E., Shenk, C., & Hoffman, P. D. (2005). Family interaction and the development of borderline personality disorder: A transactional model. *Development and Psychopathology, 17*, 1007–1030.

Fuhs, M. W., & Day, J. D. (2011). Verbal ability and executive functioning development in preschoolers at Head Start. *Developmental Psychology, 47*, 404–416.

Fulcher, M., Sutfin, E. L., Chan, R. W., Scheib, J. E., & Patterson, C. J. (2005). Lesbian mothers and their children: Findings from the contemporary families study. In A. M. Omoto & H. S. Kurtzman (Eds.), *Sexual orientation and mental health* (pp. 281–299). Washington DC: American Psychological Association.

Fuligni, A. J. (2007). Family obligation, college enrollment, and emerging adulthood in Asian and Latin American families. *Child Development Perspectives, 1*, 96–100.

Fung, H., Carstensen, L. L., & Lutz, A. (1999). The role of time perspective in age differences in social preferences. *Psychology and Aging, 14*, 595–604.

Furman, W., & Simon, V. A. (2004). Concordance in attachment states of mind and styles with respect to fathers and mothers. *Developmental Psychology, 40*, 1239–1247.

Furstenberg, F. F., Brooks-Gunn, J., & Chase-Lansdale, L. (1987). *Adolescent mothers in later life.* New York: Cambridge University Press.

Furstenberg, F. F., Brooks-Gunn, J., & Chase-Lansdale, L. (1989). Teenaged pregnancy and childbearing. *American Psychologist, 44*, 313–320.

Gage, F. H. (2000). Mammalian Neural Stem Cells. *Science, 287*, 1433.

Gaiter, J. M. (2001). Let's talk about sex and health. *Essence, 32*, 214.

Galindo, C., & Fuller, B. (2010). The social competence of Latino kindergartners and growth in mathematical understanding. *Developmental Psychology, 40*, 579–592.

Gallup, Inc. (2007). *The state of global well-being 2007.* New York: Gallup Press.

Galvan, A., Hare T. A., Parra C. E., Penn J., Voss H., Glover G., et al. (2006). Earlier development of the accumbens relative to orbitofrontal cortex might underlie risk-taking behavior in adolescents. *Journal of Neuroscience, 26*, 6885–6892.

Ganzel, B., & Morris, P. (2011). Allostasis and the developing human brain: Explicit consideration of implicit models. *Development & Psychopathology, 2nd Special Issue on Allostasis, 23*, 953–974.

Ganzel, B., Morris, P., & Wethington, E. (2010). Allostasis and the healthy human brain: Integrating models of stress from the social and life sciences. *Psychological Review, 117*, 134–174.

Garafolo, R., Wolf, R. C., Wissow, L. S., Woods, E. R., & Goodman, E. (1999). Sexual orientation and risk of suicide attempts among a representative sample of youth. *Archives of Pediatrics and Adolescent Medicine, 153*, 487–493.

Garbarino, J. (1999). *Lost boys: Why our sons turn violent and how we can save them.* New York: Free Press.

Garber, J., & Flynn, C. A. (2001). Predictors of depressive cognitions in young adolescents. *Cognitive Therapy and Research, 25*, 353–376.

Garcia Coll, C. T. (1990). Developmental outcome of minority infants: A process oriented look into our beginnings. *Child Development 61*, 270–289.

Garcia Coll, C., & Marks, A. K. (2009). *Immigrant stories: Ethnicity and academics in middle childhood*. New York: Oxford University Press.

Gardner, H. (1983). *Frames of mind: The theory of multiple intelligences*. New York: Basic Books.

Gardner, H. (1991). *The unschooled mind: How children think, how schools should teach*. New York: Basic Books.

Gardner, M., Roth, J., & Brooks-Gunn, J. (2008). Adolescents' participation in organized activities and developmental success 2 and 8 years after high school: Do sponsorship, duration, and intensity matter? *Developmental Psychology, 44*, 814–830.

Garmezy, N. U. (1993). Vulnerability and resilience. In D. C. Funder, R. D. Parke, & C. Tomlinson-Keasey (Eds.), *Studying lives through time: Personality and development* (pp. 377–398). Washington, DC: American Psychological Association.

Gartska, T. A., Schmitt, M. T., Branscombe, N. R., & Hummert, M. L. (2004). How young and older adults differ in their responses to perceived age discrimination. *Psychology and Aging, 19*, 326–335.

Gathercole, S. E. (1998). The development of memory. *Journal of Child Psychology & Psychiatry & Allied Disciplines, 39*, 3–27.

Gauvain, M. (2001). *The social context of cognitive development*. New York: Guilford Press.

Gauvain, M., & Munroe, R. L. (2009). Contributions of societal modernity to cognitive development: A comparison of four cultures. *Child Development, 80*, 1628–1642.

Gazelle, H. (2008). Behavioral profiles of anxious solitary children and heterogeneity in peer relations. *Developmental Psychology, 44*, 1604–1624.

Gazelle, H., & Rudolph, K. D. (2004). Moving toward and moving away from the world: Social approach and avoidance trajectories in anxious youth. *Child Development, 75*, 829–849.

Geary, D. C. (2006). Development of mathematical understanding. In W. Damon & R. M. Lerner (Series Eds.), D. Kuhn & R. S. Siegler (Vol. Ed.), *Handbook of child psychology: Vol. 2. Cognition, perception and language* (6th ed., pp. 777–810). Hoboken, NJ: Wiley.

Gee, J. P. (2003). *What video games have to teach us about learning and literacy*. New York: Palgrave Macmillan.

Geist, E. A., & Gibson, M. (2000). The effect of network and public television programs on four- and five-year-olds' ability to attend to educational tasks. *Journal of Instructional Psychology, 27*, 250–261.

Gellis, Z & Kenaley, B. (2008). Problem-solving therapy for depression in adults: A systematic review. *Social Work Practice, 18*, 117–131.

Gelman, R. (1982). Basic numerical abilities. In R. J. Sternberg (Ed.), *Advances in the psychology of human intelligence* (Vol. 1). Hillsdale, NJ: Erlbaum.

Gelman, R., & Gallistel, C. R. (1978). *The child's understanding of numbers*. Cambridge, MA: Harvard University Press.

Gelman, R., & Williams, E. M. (1998). Enabling constraints for cognitive development and learning: Domain specificity and epigenesis. In W. Damon (Series Ed.), D. Kuhn & R. S. Siegler (Vol. Eds.), *Handbook of child psychology: Vol. 2. Cognition, perception, and language* (5th ed., pp. 575–630). New York: Wiley.

Gelman, S. A., Taylor, M. G., & Nguyen, S. P. (2004). Mother-child conversations about gender. *Monographs of the Society for Research in Child Development, 69* (Serial No. 275), vii–127.

Germer, C. K., & Siegel, R. D. (Eds.) (2012). *Wisdom and compassion in psychotherapy*. New York: Guilford Press.

George, L. K., Larson, D. B., Koenig, H. G., & McCullough, M. E. (2000). Spirituality and health: What we know, what we need to know. *Journal of Social and Clinical Psychology, 19*, 102–119.

Gergen, K. J. (1971). *The concept of self*. New York: Holt, Rinehart and Winston.

Gershoff, E. T. (2002). Corporal punishment by parents and associated child behavior and experiences: A meta-analytic and theoretical review. *Psychological Bulletin, 128*, 539–579.

Gershoff, E. T. (2008). *Report on physical punishment in the United States: What research tells us about its effects on children*. Columbus, OH: Center for Effective Discipline.

Gershoff, E. T., Grogan-Kaylor, A., Lansford, J. E., Chang, L., Zelli, A., Deater-Deckard, K., et al. (2010). Parent discipline practices in an international sample: Associations with child behaviors and moderation by perceived normativeness. *Child Development, 81*, 480–495.

Gershoff, E. T., Lansford, J. E., Sexton, H. R., Davis-Kean, P., & Sameroff, A. J. (2012). Longitudinal links between spanking and children's externalizing behaviors in a national sample of White, Black, Hispanic, and Asian American families. *Child Development, 83*, 838–884.

Gerstorf, D., Ram, N., Estabrook, R., Schupp, J., Wagner, G. G., & Lindenberger, U. (2008). Life satisfaction shows terminal decline in old age: Longitudinal evidence from the German socio-economic panel study (SOEP). *Developmental Psychology, 44*, 1148–1159.

Gerstorf, D., Ram, N., Hoppman, C., Willis, S. L., & Schaie, K. W. (2011). Cohort differences in cognitive aging and terminal decline in the Seattle Longitudinal Study. *Developmental Psychology, 47*, 1026–1041.

Gerth, H., & Mills, C. W. (1953). *Character and social structure: The psychology of social institutions*. New York: Harcourt, Brace.

Geschwind, N. (1990). Specializations of the human brain. In R. R. Llinas (Ed.), *The workings of the brain: Development, memory, and perception* (pp. 105–120). New York: Freeman.

Gesser, G., Wong, P. T., & Reker, G. T. (1988). Death attitudes across the life span: The development and validation of the Death Attitude Profile (DAP). *Omega: Journal of Death and Dying, 18*, 113–128.

Gianaros, P. J., & Manuck, S. B. (2010). Neurobiological pathways linking socioeconomic position and health. *Psychosomatic Medicine 72*, 450–461.

Gibbons, J. L. (1998). Introduction to adolescents in a changing world: Intracultural diversity in developmental contexts. *Cross Cultural Research, 32*, 211–216.

Gibbs, J. (1987). Social processes in delinquency: The need to facilitate empathy as well as sociomoral reasoning. In W. Kurtines & J. Gewirtz (Eds.), *Moral development through social interaction*. New York: Wiley.

Gibbs, J. C., Basinger, K. S., Grime, R. L., & Snarey, J. R. (2007). Moral judgment development across cultures: Revisiting Kohlberg's universality claims. *Developmental Review, 27*, 443–500.

Giedd, J. N., Clasen, L. S., Lenroot R., Greenstein, D., Wallace, G. L., Ordaz, S., et al. (2006). Puberty-related influences on brain development. *Molecular and Cellular Endocrinology, 254–255*, 154–162.

Giedd, J. N., & Rapoport, J. L. (2010). Structural MRI of pediatric brain development: What have we learned and where are we going? *Neuron, 67*, 728–734.

Gifford-Smith, M., Dodge, K. A., Dishion, T. J., & McCord, J. (2005). Peer influence in children and adolescents: Crossing the bridge from developmental to intervention science. *Journal of Abnormal Child Psychology, 33*, 255–265.

Giles, J. W., & Heyman, G. D. (2004). When to cry over spilled milk: Young children's use of category information to guide inferences about ambiguous behavior. *Journal of Cognition and Development, 5*, 359–386.

Gill, H. L., & Haurin, D. R. (1998). Wherever he may go: How wives affect their husband's career decisions. *Social Science Research, 29*, 264–279.

Gillespie, C. F., & Nemeroff, C. B. (2007). Corticotropin-releasing factor and the psychobiology of early-life stress. *Current Directions in Psychological Science, 16*, 85–89.

Gilligan, C. (1977). In a different voice: Women's conceptions of self and of morality. *Harvard Educational Review, 47*, 481–517.

Gilligan, C. (1982). *In a different voice*. Cambridge, MA: Harvard University Press.

Gilligan, C. (1993). Adolescent development reconsidered. In A. Garrod (Ed.), *Approaches to moral development: New research and emerging themes*. New York: Teachers College Press.

Gilligan, C., & Attanucci, J. (1988). Two moral orientations: Gender differences and similarities. *Merrill-Palmer Quarterly, 23*, 77–104.

Gilstrap, L. L. (2004). A missing link in suggestibility research: What is known about the behavior of field interviewers in unstructured interviews with young children? *Journal of Experimental Psychology: Applied, 10*, 13–24.

Ginsburg, H. P. (1989). *Children's arithmetic: How they learn it and how you teach it* (2nd ed.). Austin, TX: Pro-Ed.

Glass, G. (1976). Primary, secondary and meta-analysis of research. *Educational Research, 5*, 3–8.

Gleason, M. M., Fox, N. A., Drury, S., Smyke, A., Egger, H. L., Nelson, C.A., et al. (2011). Validity of evidence-derived criteria for reactive attachment disorder: Indiscriminately social/disinhibited and emotionally withdrawn/inhibited types. *Journal of the American Academy of Child and Adolescent Psychiatry, 50*, 216–234.

Gleeson, K., & Wise, S. (1993). The do-not-resuscitate order. Still too late. *Archives of Internal Medicine, 153*, 1999–2003.

Glenberg, A. M. (2011). Introduction to the mirror neuron forum. *Perspectives on Psychological Science, 6*, 363–368.

Glymour, M. M., Weuve, J., Fay, M. E., Glass, T., & Berkman, L. F. (2008). Social ties and cognitive recovery after stroke: Does social integration promote cognitive resilience? *Neuroepidemiology, 31*, 10–20.

Goddard, L. S., McIntyre, D. C., & Leech, C. K. (1969). A permanent change in brain function resulting from daily electrical stimulation. *Experimental Neurology, 25*, 295–330.

Gogtay, N., Giedd, J. N., Lusk, L., Hayashi, K. M., Greenstein, D., Vaituzis, A. C., et al. (2004). Dynamic mapping of human cortical development during childhood through early adulthood. *Proceedings of the National Academy of Science, 101*, 8174–8179.

Goh, J. O., Chee, M. W., Tan, C., Venkatraman, V., Hebrank, A., Leshikar, E. D. et al. (2007). Age and culture modulate object processing and object-scene binding in the ventral visual area. *Cognitive, Affective, & Behavioral Neuroscience, 7*, 44–52.

Goh, J. O., & Park, D. C. (2009). Culture sculpts the perceptual brain. J. Y. Chiao (Ed.), *Progress in Brain Research, 178*, 95–111.

Gold, P. W., & Chrousos, G. P. (2002). Organization of the stress system and its dysregulation in melancholic and atypical depression: High vs low CRH/NE states. *Molecular Psychiatry, 7*, 254–275.

Goldberg, A. E., Kashy, D. A., & Smith, J. Z. (2012). Gender-typed play behavior in early childhood: Adopted children with lesbian, gay and heterosexual parents. *Sex Roles, 67,* 503–515.

Goldfried, M. R. (1995). *From cognitive-behavior therapy to psychotherapy integration.* New York: Springer.

Goldhaber, D., & Hannaway, J. (2009). Overview. In D. Goldhaber & J. Hannaway (Eds.), *Creating a new teaching profession* (pp. 3–14). Washington, DC: Urban Institute Press.

Goldstein, A. P. (1990). *Delinquents on delinquency.* Champaign, IL: Research Press.

Goldstein, M. H., King, A. P., & West, M. J. (2003). Social interaction shapes babbling: Testing parallels between birdsong and speech. *Proceedings of the National Academy of Sciences, 100,* 8030–8035.

Goldston, D. B., Molock, S. D., Whitbeck, L. B., Murakami, J. L., Zayas, L. H., & Nagayama Hall, G. C. (2008). Cultural considerations in adolescent suicide prevention and psychosocial treatment. *American Psychologist, 63,* 14–31.

Goleman, D. (1995). *Emotional intelligence.* New York: Bantam Books.

Goleman, D. (1998). *Working with emotional intelligence.* New York: Bantam Books.

Goleman, D. (2003). *Destructive emotions: How can we overcome them?* New York: Bantam Books.

Golinkoff, R. M. (1983). The preverbal negotiation of failed messages: Insights into the transition period. In R. M. Golinkoff (Ed.), *The transition from prelinguistic to linguistic communication.* Hillsdale, NJ: Erlbaum.

Golombok, S., Perry, B., Burston, A., Murray, C., Mooney-Somers, J., Stevens, M., et al. (2003). Children with lesbian parents: A community study. *Developmental Psychology, 29,* 20–33.

Golombok, S., & Tasker, F. (1996). Do parents influence the sexual orientation of their children? Findings from a longitudinal study of lesbian families. *Developmental Psychology, 32,* 3–11.

Golub, S. (1992). *Periods: From menarche to menopause.* Newbury Park, CA: Sage.

Gondolf, E. W. (1985). *Men who batter.* Holmes Beach, FL: Learning Publications.

Goode, W. J. (1960). A theory of role strain. *American Sociological Review, 25,* 483–496.

Goodman, G. S., & Clarke-Stewart, A. (1991). Suggestibility in children's testimony: Implications for child sexual abuse investigations. In J. L. Doris (Ed.), *The suggestibility of children's recollections* (pp. 92–105). Washington, DC: American Psychological Association.

Goodman, S. H. (2002). Early experiences and depression. In I. H. Gotlib and C. L. Hammen (Eds.), *Handbook of Depression and Its Treatment* (pp. 245–267). New York: Guilford Press.

Goodson, W. D. (1978). Which do college students choose first—their major or their occupation? *Vocational Guidance Quarterly, 30,* 230–235.

Goodyear, I. M. (1996). Physical symptoms and depressive disorders in childhood and adolescents. *Journal of Psychosomatic Research, 41,* 405–408.

Goodyear, I. M., Park, R., Netherton, C. M., & Herbert, J. (2001). Possible role of cortisol and dehydroepiandrosterone in human development and psychopathology. *British Journal of Psychiatry, 179,* 243–249.

Goossens, F. A., & Van IJzendoorn, M. H. (1990). Quality of infants' attachments to professional caregivers: Relation to infant-parent attachment and day-care characteristics. *Child Development, 61,* 832–837.

Gopie, N., Craik, F. I. M., & Hasher, L. (2011). A double dissociation of implicit and explicit memory in younger and older adults. *Psychological Science, 22,* 634–640.

Gopnik, A., & Astington, J. W. (1988). Children's understanding of representational change and its relation to the understanding of false belief and the appearance-reality distinction. *Child Development, 59,* 26–37.

Gordon, B., Ornstein, P. A., Clubb, P. A., Nida, R. E., & Baker-Ward, L. E. (1991). *Visiting the pediatrician: Long-term retention and forgetting.* Paper presented at the annual meeting of the Psychonomic Society, San Francisco.

Gorman-Smith, D., Tolan, P. H., Zelli, A., & Huesmann, L. R. (1996). The relation of family functioning to violence among inner city youths. *Journal of Family Psychology, 10,* 115–129.

Goswami, U. (2008). *Cognitive development: The learning brain.* New York: Psychology Press.

Gottesman, I. I., & Gould, T. D. (2003). The endophenotype concept in psychiatry: etymology and strategic intentions. *American Journal of Psychiatry, 160,* 636–645.

Gottfredson, D. C., Fink, C. M., Skroban, S., Gottfredson, G. D., & Weissberg, R. P. (1997). Making prevention work. In R. P. Weissberg, T. P. Gullotta, R. L. Hampton, B. A. Ryan, & G. R. Adams (Eds.), *Healthy children 2010: Establishing preventive services* (pp. 219–252). Thousand Oaks, CA: Sage.

Gottfredson, G. D., & Holland, J. L. (1990). A longitudinal test of the influence of congruence: Job satisfaction, competency utilization, and counterproductive behavior. *Journal of Counseling Psychology, 37,* 389–398.

Gottfredson, G. D., Holland, J. L., & Ogawa, D. K. (1982). *Dictionary of Holland occupational codes.* Palo Alto, CA: Consulting Psychologists Press.

Gottlieb, G. (1992). *Individual development and evolution: The genesis of novel behavior.* New York: Oxford University Press.

Gottlieb, G. (2003). Probabilistic epigenesis of development. In J. Valsiner & K. J. Connolly (Eds.), *Handbook of developmental psychology* (pp. 3–17). London: Sage.

Gottman, J. M. (1983). How children become friends. *Monographs of the Society for Research in Child Development, 48* (3, Serial No. 201).

Gottman, J. M. (1993). A theory of marital dissolution and stability. *Journal of Family psychology, 7,* 57–75.

Gottman, J. M. (1994a). *What predicts divorce? The relationship between marital processes and marital outcomes.* Hillsdale, NJ: Erlbaum.

Gottman, J. M. (1994b). *Why marriages succeed or fail: And how you can make yours last.* New York: Simon & Schuster.

Gottman, J. M. (1999). *The marriage clinic: A scientifically-based marital therapy.* New York: Norton.

Gottman, J. M., & Levenson, R. W. (2000). The timing of divorce: Predicting when a couple will divorce over a 14-year period. *Journal of Marriage and the Family, 62,* 737–745.

Gottman, J. M., Levenson, R. W., Gross, J., Frederickson, B. L., McCoy, K., Rosenthal, L., et al. (2003). Correlates of gay and lesbian couples' relationship satisfaction and relationship dissolution. *Journal of Homosexuality, 45,* 23–43.

Gottman, J., & Silver, N. (1999). *The seven principles for making marriages work.* New York: Three Rivers Press.

Gould, R. L. (1978). *Transformations: Growth and change in adult life.* New York: Simon & Schuster.

Gowen, L. K., Feldman, S. S., & Diaz, R. (2004). A comparison of the sexual behaviors and attitudes of adolescent girls with older versus similar-aged boyfriends. *Journal of Youth and Adolescence, 33,* 167–175.

Goza, F., & Ryabov, I. (2009). Adolescents' educational outcomes: Racial and ethnic variations in peer network importance. *Journal of Youth and Adolescence, 38,* 1264–1279.

Graber, J. A., Brooks-Gunn, J., & Galen, B. R. (1999). Betwixt and between: Sexuality in the context of adolescent transitions. In R. Jessor (Ed.), *New perspectives on adolescent risk behavior* (pp. 270–318). New York: Cambridge University Press.

Graham, Y. P., Hein, C., Goodman, S. H., Miller, A., & Nemeroff, C. B. (1999). The effects of stress on brain development; Implications for psychopathology. *Development and Psychopathology, 11,* 545–565.

Grant, B. F., & Dawson, D. (1997). Age of onset of alcohol use and its association with DSM-IV alcohol use and dependence: Results from the National Longitudinal Alcohol Epidemiological Survey. *Journal of Substance Abuse, 9,* 103–111.

Grant, H., & Dweck, C. S. (2003). Clarifying achievement goals and their impact. *Journal of Personality and Social Psychology, 85,* 541–553.

Gray, J. A. (1990). Brain systems that mediate both emotion and cognition. *Cognition and Emotion, 4,* 270–288.

Gray, J. A., & McNaughton, N. (2000). *The neuropsychology of anxiety.* Oxford: Oxford University Press.

Gray, W. M. (1990). Formal operational thought. In W. F. Overton (Ed.), *Reasoning, necessity, and logic: Developmental perspectives* (pp. 227–254). Hillsdale, NJ: Erlbaum.

Gray-Little, B., & Hafdahl, A. R. (2000). Factors influencing racial comparisons of self-esteem: A quantitative review. *Psychological Bulletin, 126,* 26–54.

Green, K. M., Ensminger, M. E., Robertson, J. A., & Juon, H-S. (2006). Impact of adults sons' incarceration on African American mothers' psychological distress. *Journal of Marriage and Family, 68,* 430–441.

Greenberg, J., & Pyszczynski, T. (1986). Persistent high self-focus after a failure and low self-focus after success: The depressive self-focusing style. *Journal of Personality and Social Psychology, 55,* 1039–1044.

Greenberg, L. S. (2002). *Emotion-focused therapy: Coaching clients to work through their feelings.* Washington, DC: American Psychological Association.

Greenberg, L. S., & Safran, J. D. (1989). Emotion in psychotherapy. *American Psychologist, 44,* 19–29.

Greenberg, M. T., & Kusche, C. (1998). Preventive intervention for school-age deaf children. *Journal of Deaf Studies and Deaf Education, 3,* 49–63.

Greenberg, M. T., & Kusche, C. (2002). Promoting alternative thinking strategies (PATHS). In D. S. Elliot (Series Ed.) & S. F. Mihalic (Contributing Ed.), *Blueprints for violence prevention: Book Ten.* Boulder: University of Colorado, Center for the Study and Prevention of Violence.

Greenberg, M. T., & Speltz, M. L. (1988). Attachment and the ontogeny of conduct problems. In J. Belsky & T. Nezworski (Eds.), *Clinical implications of attachment* (pp. 177–218). Hillsdale, NJ: Erlbaum.

Greenberger, E., & Goldberg, W. (1989). Work, parenting, and the socialization of children. *Developmental Psychology, 25,* 22–35.

Greenberger, H., & Litwin, H. (2003). Can burdened caregivers be effective facilitators of elder care-recipient health care? *Journal of Advanced Nursing, 41,* 332–341.

Greene, A. L., & Wheatley, S. M. (1992). "I've got a lot to do and I don't think I'll have the time": Gender differences in late adolescents' narratives of the future. *Journal of Youth and Adolescence, 21,* 667–685.

Greene, M. L., Way, N., & Pahl, K. (2006). Trajectories of perceived adult and peer discrimination among Black, Latino, and Asian American adolescents: Patterns and psychological correlates. *Developmental Psychology, 42,* 218–238.

Greenfield, P. M. (1994). Independence and interdependence as developmental scripts: Implications for theory, research, and practice. In P. M. Greenfield & R. R. Cocking (Eds.), *Cross-cultural roots of minority child development* (pp. 1–40). Hillsdale, NJ: Erlbaum.

Greenfield, P. M., & Juvonen, J. (1999, July/August). A developmental look at Columbine. *APA Monitor.*

Greenfield, P. M., & Suzuki, L. K. (1998). Culture and human development: Implications for parenting, education, pediatrics, and mental health. In W. Damon (Series Ed.), I. E. Sigel & K. A. Renninger (Vol. Eds.), *Handbook of child psychology: Vol.4. Child psychology in practice* (5th ed., pp. 1059–1109). New York: Wiley.

Greenfield, P. M., Suzuki, L. K., & Rothstein-Fisch, C. (2006). In W. Damon & R. M. Lerner (Series Eds.), K. A. Renninger & I. E. Sigel (Vol. Eds.), *Handbook of child psychology: Vol. 4. Child psychology in practice* (6th ed., pp. 655–699). Hoboken, NJ: Wiley.

Greenough, W. T., & Black, J. E. (1992). Induction of brain structure by experience: Substrates for cognitive development. In M. R. Gunnar & C. A. Nelson (Eds.), *Minnesota Symposium on Child Psychology: Vol. 24. Developmental behavioral neuroscience* (pp. 155–200). Hillsdale, NJ: Erlbaum.

Greenspan, S., & Weider, S. (1999). A functional developmental approach to autism spectrum disorders. *Journal of Association for Persons with Severe Handicaps, 24,* 147–161.

Greenspan, S. I. (2003). Child care research: A clinical perspective. *Child Development, 74,* 1064–1068.

Greenspan, S. I., & Weider, S. (1997). An integrated developmental approach to interventions for young children with severe difficulties in relating and communicating. *Zero to Three, 17*(5), 279–306.

Greenspan, S. L. (1981). *The clinical interview of the child.* New York: McGraw-Hill.

Gregory, A., & Weinstein, R. S. (2004). Connection and regulation at home and in school: Predicting growth in achievement for adolescents. *Journal of Adolescent Research, 19,* 405–427.

Gresham, F. M. (1981). Social skills training with handicapped children: A review. *Review of Educational Research, 51,* 139–176.

Grice, P. (1975). Logic and conversation. In P. Cole & J. L. Moran (Eds.), *Syntax and semantics: Vol. 3. Speech acts* (pp. 41–58). New York: Academic Press.

Grisso, T., Steinberg, L., Woolard, J., Cauffman, E., Scott, E., Graham, S., et al. (2003). Juveniles' competence to stand trial: A comparison of adolescents' and adults' capacities as trial defendants. *Law and Human Behavior, 27,* 333–363.

Groesz, L. M., Levine, M. P., & Murnen, S. K. (2002). The effects of experimental presentation of thin media images on body dissatisfaction: A meta-analytic review. *International Journal of Eating Disorders, 31,* 1–16.

Gross, J. J., Carstensen, L. L., Pasupathi, M., Tsai, J. L., Gottestam, K., & Hsu, A. Y. C. (1997). Emotion and aging: Changes in experience, expression, and control. *Psychology and Aging, 12,* 590–599.

Grossman, K. E., Grossman, K., & Waters, E. (Eds.) (2005). *Attachment from infancy to adulthood: The major longitudinal studies.* New York: Guilford Press.

Grossman, P., Niemann, L., Schmidt, S., & Walach, H. (2004). Mindfulness-based stress reduction and health benefits. *Journal of Psychosomatic Research, 57,* 35–43.

Grossmann, I., Na, J., Varnum, M. E., Park, D. C., Kitayama, S., & Nisbett, R. E. (2010). Reasoning about social conflicts improves into old age. *Proceedings of the National Academy of Sciences, 107,* 7246–7250.

Grossmann, K. E., Grossmann, K., Huber, F., & Wartner, U. (1981). German children's behavior towards their mothers at 12 months and their fathers at 18 months in Ainsworth's strange situation. *International Journal of Behavioral Development, 4,* 157–181.

Grusec, J. E., & Goodnow, J. J. (1994). Impact of parental discipline methods on the child's internalization of values: A reconceptualization of current points of view. *Developmental Psychology, 30,* 4–19.

Grusec, J. E. (2011). Socialization processes in the family: Social and emotional development. *Annual Review of Psychology, 62,* 243–269.

Grunstein, M. (1997). Histone acetylation in chromatin structure and transcription. *Nature, 389,* 349–352.

Guiso, L., Monte, F., Sapienza, P., & Zingales, L. (2008). Culture, gender, and math. *Science, 320,* 1164–1165.

Gummerum, M., Keller, M., Takezawa, M., & Mata, J. (2008). To give or not to give: Child's and adolescents' sharing and moral negotiations in economic decision situations. *Child Development, 79,* 562–576.

Gunnar, M. R., Kryzer, E., Van Ryzin, M. J., & Phillips, D. A. (2010). The rise in cortisol in family day care: Associations with aspects of care quality, child behavior, and child sex. *Child Development, 81,* 851–869.

Gunnar, M. R., Kryzer, E., Van Ryzin, M. J., & Phillips, D. A. (2011). The import of the cortisol rise in child care differs as a function of behavioral inhibition. *Developmental Psychology, 47,* 792–803.

Gurwitz, S. B., & Dodge, K. A. (1977). Effects of confirmations and disconfirmations on stereotype-based attributions. *Journal of Personality and Social Psychology, 35,* 495–500.

Gutman, L. M., Sameroff, A. J., & Cole, R. (2003). Academic growth curve trajectories from 1st grade to 12th grade: Effects of multiple social risk factors and preschool child factors. *Developmental Psychology, 39,* 777–790.

Gutman, L. M., Sameroff, A. J., & Eccles, J. S. (2002). The academic achievement of African-American students during early adolescence: An examination of multiple risk, promotive, and protective factors. *American Journal of Community Psychology, 30,* 367–399.

Haas, R. H. (2010). Autism and mitochondrial disease. *Developmental Disabilities Research Reviews, 16,* 144–153.

Hacker, A. (2003). *Mismatch: The growing gulf between women and men.* New York: Scribner.

Haden, C. A., Ornstein, P. A., Eckerman, C. O., & Didow, S. M. (2001). Mother-child conversational interactions as events unfold: Linkages to subsequent remembering. *Child Development, 72,* 1016–1031.

Haier, R. J., Jung, R. E., Yeo, R. A., Head, K., & Alkire, M. T. (2005). The neuroanatomy of general intelligence: Sex matters. *Neuorimage, 25,* 320–327.

Haith, M. M., & Benson, J. B. (1998). Infant cognition. In W. Damon (Series Ed.), D. Kuhn & R. S. Siegler (Vol. Eds.), *Handbook of child psychology: Vol. 2. Cognition, perception, and language* (5th ed., pp. 199–254). New York: Wiley.

Halford, G. S., & Andrews, G. (2006). Reasoning and problem solving. In W. Damon & R. M. Lerner (Series Eds.), D. Kuhn & R. S. Siegler (Vol. Eds.), *Handbook of child psychology: Vol. 2. Cognition, perception and language* (6th ed., pp. 557–608). Hoboken, NJ: Wiley.

Halford, W. K., Markman, H. J., Kline, G. H., & Stanley, S. M. (2003). Best practice in couple relationship education. *Journal of Marital and Family Therapy, 29,* 385–406.

Hall, G. S. (1904). *Adolescence: Its psychology and its relation to physiology, anthropology, sociology, sex, crime, religion, and education* (Vols. 1 & 2). New York: Appleton-Century-Crofts.

Hall, T. M., Kaduson, H. G., & Schaefer, C. E. (2002). Fifteen effective play therapy techniques. *Professional Psychology: Research and Practice, 33,* 515–522.

Hallinan, M. T. (1979). Structural effects on children's friendships and cliques. *Social Psychology Quarterly, 42,* 43–54.

Halm, M. A., Treat-Jacobson, D., Lindquist, R., & Savik, K. (2006). Correlates of caregiver burden after coronary artery bypass surgery. *Nursing Research, 55,* 426–436.

Halperin, S. (Ed.). (1998a). *The forgotten half revisited: American youth and young families, 1988–2008.* Washington, DC: American Youth Policy Forum.

Halperin, S. (1998b). Today's forgotten half: Still losing ground. In S. Halperin (Ed.), *The forgotten half revisited: American youth and young families, 1988–2008* (pp. 1–26). Washington, DC: American Youth Policy Forum.

Halpern, D. F., Benbow, C. P., Gearty, D. C., Gur, R. C., Hyde, J. S., & Gernsbacher, M. A. (2007). The science of sex differences in science and mathematics. *Psychological Science in the Public Interest, 8,* 1–51.

Halpern-Felsher, B., & Cauffman, E. (2001). Costs and benefits of a decision: Decision-making competence in adolescents and adults. *Journal of Applied Developmental Psychology, 22,* 257–273.

Hambrick, D. Z., & Meinz, E. J. (2011). Limits on the predictive power of domain-specific experience and knowledge in skilled performance. *Current Directions in Psychological Science, 20,* 275–279.

Hamer, D., & Copeland, P. (1998). *Living with our genes: Why they matter more than you think.* New York: Doubleday.

Hamer, D. H., Hu, S., Magnuson, V. L., Hu, N., Pattatucci, A. M. (1993). A linkage between DNA markers on the X chromosome and male sexual orientation, *Science, 261,* 321–327.

Hamill, S. B., & Goldberg, W. A. (1997). Between adolescents and aging grandparents: Midlife concerns of adults in the sandwich generation. *Journal of Adult Development, 4,* 135–147.

Hamilton, J. E. (1993, June). Smart ways to use time-out. *Parents Magazine,* 110–112.

Hamm, J. V. (2000). Do birds of a feather flock together? Individual, contextual, and relationship bases for African American, Asian American, and European American adolescents' selection of similar friends. *Developmental Psychology, 36,* 209–219.

Hammen, C. (1996). Stress, families, and the risk for depression. In C. Mundt, M. J. Goldstein, K. Hahlweg, & P. Fiedler (Eds.), *Interpersonal factors in the origin and course of affective disorders* (pp. 101–112). London: Gaskell-Royal College of Psychiatrists.

Hampson, S. E. (2008). Mechanisms by which childhood personality traits influence adult well-being. *Current Directions in Psychological Science, 17,* 264–268.

Hamre, B. K., & Pianta, R. C. (2005). Can instructional and emotional support in the first-grade classroom make a difference for children at risk of school failure? *Child Development, 76,* 949–967.

Hamre, B. K., & Pianta, R. C. (2007). Learning opportunities in preschool and early elementary classrooms. In R. C. Pianta, M. J. Cox, & K. L. Snow (Eds.), *School readiness and the transition to kindergarten in the era of accountability* (pp. 40–83). Baltimore: Brookes.

Han, W-J. (2012). Bilingualism and academic achievement. *Child Development, 83,* 300–321.

Hane, A. A., & Fox, N. A. (2006). Ordinary variations in maternal caregiving influence human infants' stress reactivity. *Psychological Science, 17,* 550–556.

Hane, A. A., & Philbrook, L. E. (2012). Beyond licking and grooming: Maternal regulation of infant stress in the context of routine care. *Parenting: Science and Practice, 12,* 144–153.

Hanish, L. D., & Guerra, N. G. (2004). Aggressive victims, passive victims, and bullies: Developmental continuity or developmental change. *Merrill-Palmer Quarterly, 50,* 17–38.

Hansen, R., Ozonoff, S., Krakowiak, P., Angkustsiri, K., Jones, C., Deprey, L., et al. (2008). Regression in Autism: Prevalence and associated factors in the CHARGE study. *Academic Pediatrics, 8,* 25–31.

Hanson, L., Danis, M., & Garrett, J. (1997). What is wrong with end-of-life care? Opinions of bereaved family members. *Journal of the American Geriatric Society, 45,* 1339–1344.

Hanson, R. F., & Spratt, E. G. (2000). Reactive Attachment Disorder; What we know about the disorder and implications for treatment. *Child Maltreatment, 5,* 137–145.

Harakeh, Z., & Vollebergh, W. A. M. (2012). The impact of active and passive peer influence on young adult smoking: An experimental study. *Drug and Alcohol Dependence, 121,* 220–223.

Hare T. A., Tottenham, N., Galvan, A., Voss, H.U., Glover, G.H., & Casey, B. J. (2008). Biological substrates of emotional reactivity and regulation in adolescence during an emotional go-nogo task. *Biological Psychiatry, 63,* 927–934.

Harper, G. W. (2007). Sex isn't that simple: Culture and context in HIV prevention interventions for gay and bisexual male adolescents. *American psychologist, 62,* 806–819.

Harper, S., Rushani, A., & Kaufman, J.S. (2012). Trends in the Black-White life expectancy gap, 2003–2008. *Journal of the American Medical Association, 307,* 2257–2258.

Harris, J. R. (1998). *The nurture assumption: Why children turn out the way they do.* New York: Touchstone.

Harris, K. M., Halpern, C. T., Whitsel, E., J., Hussey, Tabor, J., Entzel, P., et al. (2009). The National Longitudinal Study of Adolescent Health: Research Design [WWW document]. URL: http://www.cpc.unc.edu/ projects/addhealth/design

Harris, P. L. (2006). Social cognition. In W. Damon & R. M. Lerner (Series Eds.), D. Kuhn & R. S. Siegler (Vol. Eds.), *Handbook of child psychology: Vol. 2. Cognition, perception and language* (6th ed., pp. 811–858). Hoboken, NJ: Wiley.

Harris-Britt, A., Valrie, C., Kurtz-Costes, B., & Rowley, S. (2007). Perceived racial discrimination and self-esteem in African American youth: Racial socialization as a protective factor. *Journal of Research on Adolescence, 17,* 669–682.

Harrison, L. J., & Ungerer, J. A. (2002). Maternal employment and infant–mother attachment security at 12 months postpartum. *Developmental Psychology, 38,* 758–773.

Hart, B., & Risley, T. R. (1992). American parenting of language-learning children: Persisting difference in family-child interactions observed in natural home environment. *Developmental Psychology, 28,* 1096–1105.

Hart, B., & Risley, T. R. (1995). *Meaningful differences in the everyday experience of young American children.* Baltimore: Brookes.

Harter, S. (1981). A new self-report scale of intrinsic versus extrinsic orientation in the classroom: Motivational and informational components. *Developmental Psychology, 17,* 300–312.

Harter, S. (1985). *The self-perception profile for children.* Unpublished manual, University of Denver, CO.

Harter, S. (1988a). Developmental and dynamic changes in the nature of the self concept: Implications for child psychotherapy. In S. R. Shirk (Ed.), *Cognitive development and child psychotherapy* (pp. 119–160). New York: Plenum Press.

Harter, S. (1988b). *The self-perception profile for adolescents.* Unpublished manual, University of Denver, CO.

Harter, S. (1990). Causes, correlates, and the functional role of global self-worth: A life-span perspective. In R. Sternberg & J. Kolligian, Jr. (Eds.), *Competence considered* (pp. 67–98). New Haven, CT: Yale University Press.

Harter, S. (1993). Causes and consequences of low self-esteem in children and adolescents. In R. F. Baumeister (Ed.), *Self-esteem: The puzzle of low self-regard* (pp. 3–20). New York: Plenum Press.

Harter, S. (1999). *The construction of the self: A developmental perspective.* New York: Guilford Press.

Harter, S. (2006). The self. In W. Damon & R. M. Lerner (Series Eds.), N. Eisenberg (Vol. Ed.), *Handbook of child psychology: Vol. 3. Social, emotional, and personality development* (6th ed., pp. 505–570). Hoboken, NJ: Wiley.

Harter, S. (2012). *The construction of the self: Developmental and sociocultural foundations* (2nd ed.). New York: Guilford Press.

Harter, S., Low, S., & Whitesell, N. R. (2003). What have we learned from Columbine: The impact of the self-system on suicidal and violent ideation among adolescents. *Journal of Youth Violence, 2,* 3–26.

Harter, S., & Pike, R. (1984). The pictorial scale of perceived competence and social acceptance for young children. *Child Development, 55,* 1969–1982.

Harter, S., Waters, P. L., Whitesell, N. R., & Kastelic, D. (1998). Level of voice among female and male high school students: Relational context, support, and gender orientation. *Developmental Psychology, 34,* 892–901.

Hartshorne, H., & May, M. A. (1928–1930). *Studies in the nature of character* (Vols. 1–3). New York: Macmillan.

Hartup, W. W. (1983). Peer relations. In P. H. Mussen (Series Ed.) & E. M. Hetherington (Vol. Ed.), *Handbook of child psychology: Vol. 4. Socialization, personality and social development* (pp. 103–196). New York: Wiley.

Hartup, W. W., Glazer, J., & Charlesworth, R. (1967). Peer reinforcement and sociometric status. *Child Development, 38,* 1017–1024.

Harwood, R. L., Schoelmerich, A., Schulze, P. A., & Gonzalez, Z. (1999). Cultural differences in maternal beliefs and behaviors: A study of middle-class Anglo and Puerto Rican mother-infant pairs in four everyday situations. *Child Development, 70,* 1005–1016.

Harwood, K., McLean, N., & Durkin, K. (2007). First-time mothers' expectations of parenthood: What happens when optimistic expectations are not matched by later experiences? *Developmental Psychology, 43,* 1–12.

Hasebe, Y., Nucci, L., & Nucci, M. S. (2004). Parental control of the personal domain and adolescent symptoms of psychopathology: A cross-national study in the United States and Japan. *Child Development, 75,* 815–828.

Haselager, G. J. T., Cillissen, H. N., van Lieshout, C. F. M., Riksen-Walraven, J. M. A., & Hartup, W. W. (2002). Heterogeneity among peer-rejected boys across middle childhood: Developmental pathways of social behavior. *Child Development, 73,* 446–456.

Hastings, P. D., & Grusec, J. E. (1998). Parenting goals as organizers of responses to parent-child disagreement. *Developmental Psychology, 34,* 465–479.

Hatfield, E., & Sprecher, S. (1986). Measuring passionate love in intimate relationships. *Journal of Adolescence, 9,* 383–410.

Hattie, J. (1992). *Self-concept.* New York: Erlbaum.

Hatzenbuehler, M. L., Corbin, W. R., & Fromme, K. (2011). Discrimination and alcohol-related problems among college students: A prospective examination of mediating effects. *Drug and Alcohol Dependence, 115.* doi:10.1016/ j.drugalcdep.2010.11.002

Hauser, S. T. (1999). Understanding resilient outcomes: Adolescent lives across time and generations. *Journal of Research on Adolescence, 9,* 1–24.

Hawkley, L. C., & Cacioppo, J. T. (2007). Aging and loneliness: Downhill quickly? *Current Directions in Psychological Science, 16,* 187–191.

Hayatbakhsh, M. R., Flenady, V. J., Gibbons, K. S., Kingsbury A. M., Hurrion, E., Mamun A., et al. (2012). Birth outcomes associated with cannabis use before and during pregnancy. *Pediatric Research, 71,* 215–219.

Haydon, K. C., Collins, W. A., Salvatore, J. E., Simpson, J. A., & Roisman, G. I. (2012). Shared and distinctive origins and correlates of adult attachment representations: The developmental organization of romantic functioning. *Child Development, 83,* 1689–1702.

Haydon, K. C., Roisman, G. I., & Burt, K. B. (2012). In search of security: The latent structure of the Adult Attachment Interview revisited. *Development and Psychopathology, 24,* 589–606.

Hayes, B. K., Goodhew, A., Heit, E., & Gillan, J. (2003). The role of diverse instruction in conceptual change. *Journal of Experimental Child Psychology, 86,* 253–276.

Hayes, C. D. (Ed.). (1987). *Risking the future: Adolescent sexuality, pregnancy, and childbearing* (Vol. 1). Washington, DC: National Academy Press.

Hayes, D. S., & Birnbaum, D. W. (1980). Preschoolers' retention of televised events: Is a picture worth a thousand words? *Developmental Psychology, 16,* 410–416.

Hayes, S. C. (2002). Acceptance, mindfulness and science. *Clinical Psychology: Science and Practice, 9,* 101–106.

Hayes, S. C. (2004a). Acceptance and commitment therapy and the new behavior therapies: Mindfulness, acceptance and relationship. In S. C. Hayes, V. M. Follette, & M. M. Linehan (Eds.), *Mindfulness and acceptance: Expanding the cognitive-behavioral tradition* (pp. 1–29). New York: Guilford Press.

Hayes, S. C., Strosahl, K., & Wilson, K. (1999). *Acceptance and commitment therapy: Understanding and treating human suffering.* New York: Guilford Press.

Hayne, H., Herbert, J., & Simcock, G. (2003). Imitation from television by 24- and 30-month-olds. *Developmental Science, 6,* 254–261.

Hazan, C., & Shaver, P. (1987). Romantic love conceptualized as an attachment process. *Journal of Personality and Social Psychology, 52,* 511–524.

Hazan, C., & Shaver, P. R. (1994). Attachment as an organizational framework for research on close relationships. *Psychological Inquiry, 5,* 1–22.

Hazan, C., & Zeifman, D. (1999). Pair bonds as attachments. In J. Cassidy & P. R. Shaver (Eds.), *Handbook of attachment: Theory, research, and clinical applications* (pp. 336–377). New York: Guilford Press.

Healy, J. M. (1998). *Failure to connect: How computers affect our children's minds for better or worse.* New York: Simon & Schuster.

Heckhausen, J. (1997). Developmental regulation across adulthood: Primary and secondary control of age-related challenges. *American Psychologist, 33,* 176–187.

Heckhausen, J. (1999). *Developmental regulation in adulthood: Age-normative and sociostructural constraints as adaptive challenges.* New York: Cambridge University Press.

Heckman, J. J. (2006). Skill formation and the economics of investing in disadvantaged children. *Science, 312,* 1900–1902.

Heijmans, B. T., & Mill, J. (2012). Commentary: The seven plagues of epigenetic epidemiology. *International Journal of Epidemiology, 41,* 74–78. doi: 10.1093/ije/dyr225

Heijmans, B. T., Tobi, E. W., Stein, A. D., Putter, H., Blauw, G. J., Susser, E. S., et al. (2008). Persistent epigenetic differences associated with prenatal exposure to famine in humans. *Proceedings of the National Academy of Sciences, 105,* 17046–17049.

Heim, C., Young, L. J., Newport, D. J., Mietzko, T., Miller, A. H., & Nemeroff, C. B. (2009). Lower CSF oxytocin concentrations in women with a history of childhood abuse. *Molecular Psychiatry, 14*(10), 954–958.

Heine, S. J., & Hamamura, T. (2007). In search of East Asian self-enhancement. *Personality and Social Psychology Review, 11,* 4–27.

Heine, S. J., Kitayama, S., Lehman, D. R., Takata, T., Ide, E., Leung, C., et al. (2001). Divergent consequences of success and failure in North America and Japan: An investigation of self-improving motivations and malleable selves. *Journal of Personality and social Psychology, 81,* 599–615.

Helms, J. E. (1990). An overview of Black racial identity theory. In J. E. Helms (Ed.), *Black and White racial identity: Theory, research and practice* (pp. 9–32). New York: Greenwood Press.

Helms, J. E. (2003). Racial identity in the social environment. In P. B. Pedersen & J. Carey (Eds.), *Multicultural counseling in schools: A practical handbook* (2nd ed., pp. 44–58). Boston: Allyn & Bacon.

Helson, R., & Roberts, B. W. (1994). Ego development and personality change in adulthood. *Journal of Personality and Social Psychology, 66,* 911–920.

Hendry, L. B., & Kloep, M. (2007). Conceptualizing emerging adulthood: Inspecting the emperor's new clothes? *Child Development Perspectives, 1,* 74–79.

Henggeler, S. W., Mihalic, S. F., Rone, L., Thomas, C. R., & Timmons-Mitchell, J. (1998). *Blueprints For Violence Prevention, Book 6: Multisystemic Therapy.* Boulder, CO: Center for the Study and Prevention of Violence.

Henggeler, S. W., Schoenwald, S. K., Borduin, C. M., Rowland, M. D., & Cunningham, P. B. (1998). *Multisystemic treatment of antisocial behavior in children and adolescents.* New York: Guilford Press.

Henggeler, S. W., Schoenwald, S. K., & Pickrel, S. G. (1995). Multisystemic therapy: Bridging the gap between university- and community-based treatments. *Journal of Consulting and Clinical Psychology, 63,* 709–717.

Henrich, J., Heine, S. J., & Norenzayan, A. (2010). The weirdest people in the world? *Behavior & Brain Sciences, 33,* 61–135.

Herek, G. M. (2006). Legal recognition of same-sex relationships in the United States. *American Psychologist, 61,* 607–621.

Hepach, R., Vaish, A., & Tomasello, M. (2012). Young children are intrinsically motivated to see others helped. *Psychological Science, 23,* 967–972.

Herman, M. (2004). Forced to choose: Some determinants of racial identification in multiracial adolescents. *Child Development, 75,* 730–748.

Herman-Giddens, M. E., & Bourdony, C. J. (1995). *Assessment of sexual maturity stages in girls. Report MA0089.* Elk Grove Village (IL): American Academy of Pediatrics.

Herman-Giddens, M. E., Steffes, J., Harris, D., Slora, E., Hussey, M., Dowshen, S.A., et al. (2012). Secondary sexual characteristics in boys: Data from the pediatric research in office settings network. *Pediatrics,* July 2012 Pediatrics peds.2011–3291; published ahead of print October 20, 2012, doi:10.1542/peds.2011–329

Herold, E., Goodwin, M., & Lero, D. (1979). Self-esteem, locus of control, and adolescent contraception. *Journal of Psychology, 101,* 83–88.

Herr, E. L. (1989). *Counseling in a dynamic society: Opportunities and challenges.* Alexandria, VA: American Counseling Association.

Herr, E. L., Cramer, S. H., & Niles, S. G. (2003). *Career guidance and counseling through the life span: Systematic approaches* (6th ed.). New York: HarperCollins.

Hersch, P. (1998). *A tribe apart: A journey into the heart of American adolescence.* New York: Fawcett Columbine.

Hershenson, D. B. (1996). Work adjustment: A neglected area in career counseling. *Journal of Counseling and Development, 74,* 442–446.

Hertenstein, M. J. (2002). Touch: Its communicative functions in infancy. *Human Development, 45,* 70–94.

Hertz-Picciotto, I., Croen, L., Hansen, R., Jones, C., van de Water, J., & Pessah, I. (2006). The CHARGE study: An epidemiologic investigation of genetic and environmental factors contributing to autism. *Environmental Health Perspectives, 1141,* 1119–1125.

Herzberg, D. S., Hammen, C., Burge, D., Daley, S. E., Davila, J., & Lindberg, N. (1998). Social competence as a predictor of chronic interpersonal stress. *Personal Relationships, 5,* 207–218.

Hesse, E. (2008). The Adult Attachment Interview: Protocol, method, of analysis, and empirical studies. In J. Cassidy & P. R. Shaver (Eds.), *Handbook of attachment: Theory, research and clinical applications* (2nd ed., pp. 552–598). New York: Guilford Press.

Hesse, E., & Main, M. (1999a). Frightened behavior in traumatizing but non-maltreating parents: Previously unexamined risk factor for offspring. In D. Diamond & S. J. Blatt (Eds.), *Psychoanalytic theory and attachment research I: Theoretical considerations. Psychoanalytic Inquiry, 19,* 481–540.

Hesse, E., & Main, M. (1999b). Second generation effects of unresolved trauma in non-maltreating parents: Dissociative, frightened and threatening parental behavior. *Psychoanalytic Inquiry, 19,* 481–540.

Hetherington, E. M. (1998). Relevant issues in developmental science. *American Psychologist, 53,* 93–94.

Hetherington, E. M., Bridges, M., & Insabella, G. M. (1998). What matters? What does not? Five perspectives on the association between marital transitions and children's adjustment. *American Psychologist, 53,* 167–184.

Hewage, C., Bohlin, G., Wijewardena, K., & Lindmark, G. (2011). Executive functions and child problem behaviors are sensitive to family disruption: A study of children of mothers working overseas. *Developmental Science, 14,* 18–25.

Hewlett, S. A., & West, C. (1998). *The war against parents: What we can do for America's beleaguered moms and dads.* Boston: Houghton Mifflin.

Hibel, L. C., Granger, D. A., Blair, C., Cox, M. J., and The Family Life Project Key Investigators. (2011). Maternal sensitivity buffers the adrenocortical implications of intimate partner violence exposure during early childhood. *Development and Psychopathology, 23,* 689–701.

Higgins, E. T. (1991). Development of self-regulatory and self-evaluative processes: Costs, benefits, and tradeoffs. In M. R. Gunnar & L. A. Sroufe (Eds.), *Minnesota Symposium on Child Development: Vol. 23. Self processes and development* (pp. 125–166). Hillsdale, NJ: Erlbaum.

Higher Education Research Institute (HERI). (2004). *The American Freshman: National Norms for Fall 2004.* www.gseis.uda.edu/heri/findings.html

Hill, A. M. (1992). Chinese funerals and Chinese ethnicity in Chiang Mai, Thailand. *Ethnology, 31,* 315–330.

Hill, J. P., & Lynch, M. E. (1983). The intensification of gender-related role expectations during early adolescence. In J. Brooks-Gunn & A. C. Petersen (Eds.), *Girls at puberty: Biological and psychosocial perspectives* (pp. 201–228). New York: Plenum Press.

Hill, M. S., & Yeung, W. J. (1999). How has the changing structure of opportunities affected transitions to adulthood? In A. Booth, A. C. Crouter, & M. J. Shanahan (Eds.), *Transitions to adulthood in a changing economy: No work, no family, no future?* (pp. 3–39). Westport, CT: Praeger.

Hill, P. C., Pargament, K. I., Wood, R. W., Jr., McCullough, M. E., Swyers, J. P., Larson, D., et al. (2000). Conceptualizing religion and spirituality: Points of commonality, points of departure. *Journal of Theory in Social Behavior, 30,* 51–77.

Hill, P. L., & Roberts, B. W. (2010). Propositions for the study of moral personality development. *Current Directions in Psychological Science, 19,* 380–383.

Hill, S. E., & Flom, R. (2007). 18- and 24-month-olds' discrimination of gender-consistent and inconsistent activities. *Infant Behavior & Development, 30,* 168–173.

Hines, K. A., McCarthy Veach, P., & LeRoy, B. S. (2010). Genetic counselors' perceived responsibilities regarding reproductive issues for patients at risk for Huntington disease *Journal of Genetic Counseling, 19,* 131–147.

Hines, M., Golombok, S., Rust, J., Johnston, K. J., Golding, J., & Avon Longitudinal Study of Parents and Children Study Team. (2002). Testosterone during pregnancy and gender role behavior of preschool children: A longitudinal, population study. *Child Development, 73,* 1678–1687.

Hingson, R. W. (2010). Magnitude and prevention of college drinking and related problems. *Alcohol Research & Health, 33*, 45–54.

Hintikka, J., Koskela, T., Kontula, O., Koskela, K., & Viinamaeki, H. (2000). Men, women and friends: Are there differences in relation to mental well-being? *Quality of Life Research, 9*, 841–845.

Hirsh-Pasek, K., Golinkoff, R. M., Berk, L. E., & Singer, D. G. (2009). *A mandate for playful learning in preschool: Presenting the evidence*. New York: Oxford University Press.

Hlastala, S. A., Frank, E., Kowalski, J., Sherrill, J. T., Tu, X. M., Anderson, B., et al. (2000). Stressful life events, bipolar disorder, and the "Kindling Model." *Journal of Abnormal Psychology, 109*, 777–786.

Hobfoll, S. E. (1989). Conservation of resources: A new attempt at conceptualizing stress. *American Psychologist, 44*(3), 513–524.

Hobfoll, S. E. (2001). The influence of culture, community, and the nested-self in the stress process: Advancing conservation of resources theory. *Applied Psychology: An International Review, 50*, 337–421.

Hobfoll, S. E., Canetti-Nisim, D., & Johnson, R. J. (2006). Exposure to terrorism, stress-related mental health symptoms, and defensive coping among Jews and Arabs in Israel. *Journal of Consulting and Clinical Psychology, 74*, 207–218.

Hobfoll, S. E., Watson, P., Bell, C. C., Bryant, R. A., Brymer, M. J., Friedman, et al. (2007). Five essential elements of immediate and midterm mass trauma intervention: empirical evidence. *Psychiatry 70*, 283–315.

Hobson, P., Ouston, J., & Lee, A. (1988). What's in a face? The case of autism. *British Journal of Psychology, 79*, 441–453.

Hoek, H. W. (1993). Review of epidemiological studies of eating disorders. *International Review of Psychiatry, 5*, 61–74.

Hoeve, M., Semon Dubas, J., Eichelsheim, V. I., van der Laan, P. H., Smeenk, W., & Gerris, J. R. M. (2009). The relationship between parenting and delinquency: A meta-analysis. *Journal of Abnormal Child Psychology, 37*, 749–775.

Hofer, M. A. (1994). Hidden regulators in attachment, separation, and loss. *Monographs of the Society for Research in Child Development, 59*, 1–207.

Hoffman, M. L. (1975). Altruistic behavior and the parent–child relationship. *Journal of Personality and Social Psychology, 31*, 937–943.

Hoffman, M. L. (1982). Development of prosocial motivation: Empathy and guilt. In N. Eisenberg (Ed.), *The development of prosocial behavior* (pp. 281–313). New York: Academic Press.

Hoffman, M. L. (1983). Affective and cognitive processes in moral internalization. In E. T. Higgins, D. Ruble, & W. Hartup (Eds.), *Social cognition and social development: A sociocultural perspective* (pp. 236–274). New York: Cambridge University Press.

Hofmann, A. D. (1997). Adolescent growth and development. In A. D. Hofmann & D. E. Greydanus (Eds.), *Adolescent medicine* (3rd ed.). Stamford, CT: Appleton and Lange.

Hofmann, S. G., Sawyer, A. T., Witt, A. A., & Oh, D. (2010). The effect of mindfulness-based therapy on anxiety and depression: A meta-analytic review. *Journal of Consulting and Clinical Psychology, 78*, 169–183.

Hogan, D. P., & Astone, N. M. (1986). The transition to adulthood. *American Sociological Review, 12*, 109–130.

Holbrook, M., & Schindler, R. M. (1989). Some exploratory findings on the development of musical taste. *Journal of Consumer Research, 16*, 119–124.

Holland, A. S., & Roisman, G. I. (2010). Adult attachment security and young

adults' dating relationships over time: Self-reported, observational, and physiological evidence. *Developmental Psychology, 46*, 552–557.

Holland, J. L. (1985). *Making vocational choices: A theory of vocational personalities and work environments* (2nd ed.). Upper Saddle River, NJ: Prentice Hall.

Holland, J. L. (1997). *Making vocational choices: A theory of vocational personalities and work environments* (3rd ed.). Odessa, FL: Psychological Assessment Resources.

Holland, J. L., Viernstein, M. C., Kuo, H. M., Karweit, N. L., & Blum, S. D. (1970). *A psychological classification of occupations* (Report No. 90). Baltimore: Johns Hopkins University, Center for the Study of Social Organization of Schools.

Holmes, T. H., & Rahe, R. H. (1967). The Social Readjustment Rating Scale. *Journal of Psychosomatic Research, 11*, 213–218.

Holleran Steiker, L. K. (2008). Making drug and alcohol prevention relevant: Adapting evidence-based curricula to unique adolescent cultures. *Family & Community Health, 31*, 52–60.

Hollenstein, T., & Loughheed, J. P. (2013). Beyond storm and stress: Typicality, transactions, timing, and temperament to account for adolescent change. *American Psychologist, 68*, 444–454.

Hölzel, B. K., Lazar, S. W., Gard, T., Schuman-Olivier, Z., Vago, D. R., & Ott, U. (2011). How does mindfulness meditation work? Proposing mechanisms of action from a conceptual and neural perspective. *Perspectives on Psychological Science 6*, 537–559.

Homer, B. D., Brockmeier, J., Kamawar, D., & Olson, D. R. (2001). Between realism and nominalism: Learning to think about names and words. *Genetic, Social, and General Psychology Monographs, 127*, 5–25.

Hooker, S., & Brand, B. (2009). *Success at every step: How 23 programs support youth on the path to college and beyond*. Washington, DC: American Youth Policy Forum.

Hopmeyer, E., & Werk, A. (1994). A comparative study of family bereavement groups. *Death Studies, 18*, 243–256.

Hoppmann, C. A., Gerstorf, D., Willis, S. L., & K. W. Schaie (2011). Spousal interrelations in happiness in the Seattle Longitudinal Study: Considerable similarities in levels and change over time. *Developmental Psychology, 47*, 1–8.

Horn, J. L., & Cattell, R. B. (1966). Refinement and test of the theory of fluid and crystallized intelligence. *Journal of Educational Psychology, 57*, 253–270.

Horney, K. (1950). *Neurosis and human growth*. New York: Norton.

Hornig, M., Briese, T., Buie, T., Bauman, M. L., Lauwers, G., et al. (2008). Lack of association between measles virus vaccine and autism with enteropathy: A case-control study. PLoS ONE, 3: e3140.doi:10.1371/journal.pone.0003140

Horowitz, M. J., Siegel, B., Holen, A., Bonanno, G. A., Milbrath, C., & Stinson, C. H. (1997). Diagnostic criteria for complicated grief disorder. *American Journal of Psychiatry, 154*, 904–910.

Hoshman, L. T., & Polkinghorne, D. E. (1992). Redefining the science-practice relationship and professional training. *American Psychologist, 47*, 55–66.

Howes, C., & Olenick, M. (1986). Family and child care influences on toddler's compliance. *Child Development, 57*, 202–216.

Hsing-Yi C., H., Chiou, C., & Chen, N. (2010). Impact of mental health and caregiver burden on family caregivers' physical health. *Archives of Gerontology and Geriatrics 50*, 267–271.

Hsu, L. K. G. (1990). *Eating disorders*. New York: Guilford Press.

Hu, V. W. (2012). From genes to environment: Using integrative genomics to build a Systems-Level understanding of Autism Spectrum Disorders. *Child Development, 84*, 1–15.

Hudspeth, W. J., & Pribram, K. H. (1992). Psychophysiological indices of cognitive maturation. *International Journal of Psychophysiology, 12*, 19–29.

Hughes, C., & Dunn, J. (1998). Understanding mind and emotion: Longitudinal associations with mental-state talk between young friends. *Developmental Psychology, 34*, 1026–1037.

Hughes, D., & Chen, L. A. (1999). The nature of parents' race-related communications to children: A developmental perspective. In L. Bolter & C. S. Tamis-LeMonda (Eds.), *Child psychology: A handbook of contemporary issues* (pp. 467–490). Philadelphia: Psychology Press.

Hughes, D., Rodriguez, J., Smith, E. P., Johnson, D. J., Stevenson, H. C., & Spicer, P. (2006). Parents' ethnic-racial socialization practices: A review of research and directions for future study. *Developmental Psychology, 42*, 747–770.

Hughes, J. N., Cavell, T. A., & Grossman, P. B. (1997). A positive view of self: Risk or protection for aggressive children? *Development and Psychopathology, 9*, 75–94.

Hughes I. A., Houk, C., Ahmed, S. F., & Lee, P. A. (2006). Consensus statement on management of intersex disorders. *Archives of Diseases in Childhood, 91*, 554–563.

Hulanicka, B. (1999). Acceleration of menarcheal age of girls from dysfunctional families. *Journal of Reproductive and Infant Psychology, 17*, 119–132.

Hummert, M. L. (1999). A social cognitive perspective on age stereotypes. In T. M. Hess & F. Blanchard-Fields (Eds.), *Social cognition and aging* (pp. 176–196). San Diego, CA: Academic Press.

Hummert, M. L., Garstka, T. A., & Shaner, J. L. (1997). Stereotyping of older adults: The role of target facial cues and perceiver characteristics. *Psychology and Aging, 12*, 107–114.

Hummert, M. L., Garstka, T. A., Shaner, J. L., & Strahm, S. (1994). Stereotypes of the elderly held by young, middle-aged, and elderly adults. *Journal of Gerontology: Psychological Sciences, 49*, P240–P249.

Hummert, M. L., & Ryan, E. B. (1996). Toward understanding variations in patronizing talk addressed to older adults: Psycholinguistic features of care and control. *International Journal of Psycholinguistics, 12*, 149–169.

Hummert, M. L., Shaner, J. L., Garstka, T. A., & Henry, C. (1998). Communication with older adults: The influence of age stereotypes, context, and communicator age. *Human Communication Research, 25*, 124–151.

Hunter, A., & Davis, J. E. (1992). Constructing gender: An exploration of Afro-American men's conceptualization of manhood. *American Sociological Review, 12*, 109–130.

Hurtado, S., Cuellar, M., & Guillermo-Wann, C. (2011). Quantitative measures of students' sense of validation: Advancing the study of diverse learning environments. *Enrollment Management Journal, 5*, 53–71.

Hurtado, N., Marchman, V. A., & Fernald, A. (2008). Does input influence uptake? Links between maternal talk, processing speed and vocabulary size in Spanish-learning children. *Developmental Science, 11*, F31–F39.

Huttenlocher, P.R. (1979). Synaptic density in human frontal cortex: Developmental changes and effects of aging. *Brain Research, 163*, 195–205.

Huttenlocher, J., & Smiley, P. (1990). Emerging notions of persons. In N. L. Stein,

B. Leventhal, & T. Trabasso (Eds.), *Psychological and biological approaches to emotion* (pp. 283–295). Chicago: University of Chicago.

Huttenlocher, P. (1994). Synaptogenesis, synapse elimination, and neural plasticity in human cerebral cortex. In C. A. Nelson (Ed.), *Minnesota Symposium on Child Psychology: Vol. 27. Threats to optimal development: Integrating biological, psychological, and social risk factors* (pp. 35–54). Hillsdale, NJ: Erlbaum.

Hyde, J. S. (1984). How large are gender differences in aggression? A developmental meta-analysis. *Developmental Psychology, 20,* 722–736.

Hyde, J. S., DeLamater, J. D., & Durik, A. M. (2001). Sexuality and the dual-earner couple: Part II. Beyond the baby years. *Journal of Sex Research, 38,* 10–23.

Hyde, J. S., Fennema, E., & Lamon, S. J. (1990). Gender differences in mathematics performance: A meta-analysis. *Psychological Bulletin, 107,* 139–155.

Hyde, J. S., Lindberg, S. M., Linn, M. C., Ellis, A. B., & Williams, C. C. (2008). Gender similarities characterize math performance. *Science, 321,* 494–495.

Hyman, I. E., & Faries, J. M. (1992). The function of autobiographical memory. In M. A. Conway, D. C. Rubin, H. Spinnler, & W. A. Wagenaar (Eds.), *Theoretical perspectives on autobiographical memory* (pp. 207–221). Boston: Kluwer Academic Press.

Hyson, M., Copple, C., & Jones, J. (2006). Early childhood development and education. In W. Damon & R. M. Lerner (Series Eds.), K. A. Renninger & I. E. Sigel (Vol. Eds.), *Handbook of child psychology: Vol. 4. Child psychology in practice* (6th ed., pp. 3–47). Hoboken, NJ: Wiley.

Ingersoll-Dayton, B., Neal, M. B., Ha, J., & Hammer, L. B. (2003). Redressing inequity in parent care among siblings. *Journal of Marriage and Family, 65,* 201–212.

Ingram, R. E., Cruet, D., Johnson, B., & Wisnicki, K. (1988). Self-focused attention, gender, gender-role, and vulnerability to negative affect. *Journal of Personality and Social Psychology, 55,* 1039–1044.

Ingram, R. E., & Price, J. M. (2001). *Vulnerability to psychopathology: Risk across the lifespan.* New York: Guilford Press.

Inhelder, B., & Piaget, J. (1955/1958). *The growth of logical thinking from childhood to adolescence.* New York: Basic Books.

Inhelder, B., & Piaget, P. (1964). *The early growth of logic in the child.* New York: Harper & Row.

Inman, A. G, Yeh, C. J., Madan-Bahel, A., & Nath, S. (2007). Bereavement and coping of South Asian Families post 9/11. *Journal of Multicultural Counseling and Development, 35,* 101–115.

Institute of Medicine. (1994). *Reducing risks for mental disorders: Frontiers for preventive intervention research.* Washington, DC: National Academy Press.

Ising, M., Depping, A. M., Siebertz, A., Lucae, S., Unschuld, P. G., Kloiber, S., et al. (2008). Polymorphisms in the FKBP5 gene region modulate recovery from psychosocial stress in healthy controls. *The European Journal of Neuroscience, 28,* 389–398.

Izard, C. E. (1971). *The face of emotion.* New York: Appleton-Century-Crofts.

Izard, C. E. (1979). *The maximally discriminative facial movement coding system (Max).* Newark, DE: University of Delaware, Information Technologies and University Media Services.

Izard, C. E. (1991). *The psychology of emotions.* New York: Plenum Press.

Izard, C. E. (1992). Basic emotions, relations among emotions, and emotion-cognition relations. *Psychological Review, 99,* 561–565.

Izard, C. E. (1993). Four systems for emotion activation: Cognitive and noncognitive processes. *Psychological Review, 100,* 68–90.

Izard, C. E. (2004). The generality-specificity issue in infants' emotion responses: A comment on Bennett, Bendersky, and Lewis, 2002. *Infancy, 6,* 417–423.

Izard, C. E. (2006). Experts' definitions of emotion and their ratings of its components and characteristics. Unpublished manuscript, Newark, DE, University of Delaware.

Izard, C. E. (2007). Basic emotions, natural kinds, emotion schemas, and a new paradigm. *Perspectives on Psychological Science, 2,* 260–277.

Izard, C. E. (2009). Emotion theory and research: Highlights, unanswered questions, and emerging issues. *Annual Review of Psychology, 60,* 1–25.

Izard, C. E., Dougherty, L. M., & Hembree, E. A. (1983). *A system for identifying affect expression by holistic judgments (Affex).* Newark, DE: University of Delaware, Computer Network Services and University Media Services.

Izard, C. E., & Malatesta, C. Z. (1987). Perspectives on emotional development I: Differential emotions theory of early emotional development. In J. D. Osofsky (Ed.), *Handbook of infant development* (2nd ed., pp. 494–554). New York: Wiley.

Jackson, L. A., von Eye, A., Biocca, F. A., Barbatsis, G., Zhao, Y., & Fitzgerald, H. E. (2006). Does home Internet use influence the academic performance of low-income children? *Developmental Psychology, 42,* 429–435.

Jackson, M. I., Kiernan, K., & McLanahan, S. (2012). Immigrant-native differences in child health: Does maternal education narrow or widen the gap? *Child Development, 8,* 1501–1509.

Jacobs, J. A., & Stoner-Eby, S. (1998). Adult enrollment in higher education and cumulative educational attainment, 1970–1990. *The Annals of the Academy of Political and Social Science, 559,* 91–108.

Jacobs, J. E., Lanza, S., Osgood, D. W., Eccles, J. A., & Wigfield, A. (2002). Changes in children's self-competence and values: Gender and domain differences across grades one through twelve. *Child Development, 73,* 509–527.

Jacobsen, T., & Hofmann, V. (1997). Children's attachment representations: Longitudinal relations to school behavior and academic competency in middle childhood and adolescence. *Developmental Psychology, 33,* 703–710.

Jacobson, N. S., & Addis, M. E. (1993). Research on couples and couple therapy: What do we know? Where are we going? *Journal of Consulting and Clinical Psychology, 61,* 547–557.

Jacobvits, D., Leon, K., & Hazen, N. (2006). Does expectant mothers' unresolved trauma predict frightened/frightening maternal behavior? Risk and protective factors. *Development and Psychopathology, 18,* 363–379.

Jaenisch, R. (1997). DNA methylation and imprinting: why bother? *Trends in Genetics, 13,* 323–329.

Jaffee, S., & Hyde, J. S. (2000). Gender differences in moral orientation: A meta-analysis. *Psychological Bulletin, 126,* 703–726.

Jahromi, L. B., Putnam, S. P., & Stifter, C. A. (2004). Maternal regulation of infant reactivity from 2 to 6 months. *Developmental Psychology, 40,* 477–487.

Jahromi, L. B., & Stifter, C. A. (2007). Individual differences in the contribution of maternal soothing to infant distress reduction. *Infancy, 11,* 255–269.

James, W. (1890). *Principles of psychology.* Chicago: Encyclopedia Britannica.

Janda, L. H., & Klenke-Hamel, K. E. (1980). *Human sexuality.* New York: Van Nostrand.

Janoff-Bulman, R. (1993). *Shattered assumptions: Toward a new psychology of trauma.* New York: Free Press.

Jansen, J., de Weerth, C., & Riksen-Walraven, J. M. (2011). Breastfeeding and the mother-infant relationship: A review. *Developmental Review, 28,* 503–521.

Jensen, L. A. (2008). Through two lenses: A cultural-developmental approach to moral psychology. *Developmental Review, 28,* 289–315.

Jensen, P. S., & Hoagwood, K. (1997). The book of names: DSM-IV in context. *Development and Psychopathology, 9,* 231–249.

Jessor, R. (1993). Successful adolescent development among youth in high-risk settings. *American Psychologist, 48,* 117–126.

Ji, L. J., Zhang, Z., & Nisbett, R. E. (2004). Is it culture or is it language? Examination of language effects in cross-cultural research on categorization. *Journal of Personality and Social Psychology, 87,* 57–65.

Jin, M. K., Jacobvitz, D., Hazen, N., & Jung, S. H. (2012). Maternal sensitivity and infant attachment security in Korea: Cross-cultural validation of the strange situation. *Attachment & Human Development, 14,* 33–44.

Johns, M., Inzlicht, M., & Schmader, T. (2008). Stereotype threat and executive resource depletion: Examining the influence of emotion regulation. *Journal of Experimental Psychology: General, 137,* 691–705.

Johnson, A., & Ames, E. (1994). The influence of gender labeling on preschoolers' gender constancy judgments. *British Journal of Developmental Psychology, 12,* 241–249.

Johnson, C. A., Pentz, M. A., Weber, M. D., Dwyer, J. H., Baer, N., MacKinnon, D. R., et al. (1990). Relative effectiveness of comprehensive community programming for drug abuse prevention with high-risk and low-risk adolescents. *Journal of Consulting and Clinical Psychology, 58,* 447–456.

Johnson, C. L., & Troll, L. (1994). Constraints and facilitators to friendships in late, late life. *The Gerontologist, 34,* 79–87.

Johnson, C. P., & Myers, S. M. (2007). American Academy of Pediatrics, Council on Children with Disabilities. Identification and evaluation of children with autism spectrum disorders. *Pediatrics, 120,* 1183–1215.

Johnson, J. G., Cohen, P., Kasen, S., & Brook, J. S. (2006). Eating disorders during adolescence and the risk for physical and mental disorders during early childhood. *Archives of General Psychiatry, 59,* 545–552.

Johnson, K. E., Alexander, J. M., Spencer, S., Leibham, M. E., & Neitzel, C. (2004). Factors associated with the early emergence of intense interests within conceptual domains. *Cognitive Development, 19,* 325–343.

Johnston, L. D., O'Malley, P. M., Bachman, J. G., & Schulenberg, J. E. (2009). *Monitoring the Future national survey results on drug use, 1975–2008.: Vol. 1. Secondary school students* (NIH Publication No 09-7402). Bethesda, MD: National Institute on Drug Abuse.

Johnson, R. W., & Favreault, M. M. (2004). Economic status in later life among women who raised children outside of marriage. *Journals of Gerontology: Series B: Psychological Sciences & Social Sciences, 59,* 315–323.

Johnson, S. M. (2003). The revolution in couple therapy: A practitioner-scientist perspective. *Journal of Marital and Family Therapy, 29,* 365–384.

Johnson, S. M., Hunsley, J., Greenberg, L., & Schindler, D. (1999). Emotionally-focused couples therapy: Status and challenges.

Clinical Psychology: Science and Practice, 6, 67–79.

Johnson, S. P. (2003). The nature of cognitive development. *Trends in Cognitive Science, 7,* 102–104.

Johnson, T. H. (1960). *The complete poems of Emily Dickinson.* Boston: Little, Brown.

Johnston, C., & Ohan, J. L. (1999). Externalizing disorders. In W. K. Silverman & T. H. Ollendick (Eds.), *Developmental issues in the clinical treatment of children* (pp. 279–294). Needham Heights, MA: Allyn & Bacon.

Johnston, L. D., O'Malley, P. M., & Bachman, J. G. (1994). *National survey results on drug use from the Monitoring the Future Study: 1975–1993.* Rockville, MD: National Institute on Drug Abuse.

Johnston, L. D., O'Malley, P. M., & Bachman, J. G. (2004). *The monitoring the future national survey results on adolescent drug use. Overview of key findings, 2003.* Bethesda, MD: National Institute on Drug Abuse.

Johnston, L. D., O'Malley, P. M., Bachman, J. G., & Schulenberg, J. E. (2009). *Monitoring the Future national survey results on drug use, 1975–2008.: Vol. 1. Secondary school students* (NIH Publication No 09-7402). Bethesda, MD: National Institute on Drug Abuse.

Jones, D. C. (2004). Body image among adolescent girls and boys: A longitudinal study. *Developmental Psychology, 40,* 823–835.

Jones, H. E., & Conrad, H. (1933). The growth and decline of intelligence: a study of a homogeneous group between the ages of ten and sixty. *Genetic Psychological Monographs 13,* 223–298.

Jones, K., Daley, D., Hutchings, J., Bywater, T., & Eames, C. (2008). Efficacy of the Incredible Years Programme as an early intervention for children with conduct problems and ADHD: long-term follow-up. *Child: Care, Health and Development 33,* 749–756.

Jones, L. K. (1996). A harsh and challenging world of work: Implications for counselors. *Journal of Counseling and Development, 74,* 453–459.

Jordan, P., & Hernandez-Reif M. (2009). Reexamination of young children's racial attitudes and skin tone preferences. *Journal of Black Psychology, 35,* 388–403.

Josselson, R. L. (1988). *Finding herself: Pathways of identity development in women.* New York: Jossey-Bass.

Josselson, R. L. (1994). The theory of identity development and the question of intervention: An introduction. In S. Archer (Ed.), *Interventions for adolescent identity development* (pp. 12–25). Thousand Oaks, CA: Sage.

Judd, C. M., Park, B., Ryan, C. S., Bauer, M., & Kraus, S. (1995). Stereotypes and ethnocentrism: Diverging interethnic perceptions of African American and White American youth. *Journal of Personality and Social Psychology, 69,* 460–481.

Judge, T. A., & Livingston, B. A. (2008). Is the gap more than gender? A longitudinal analysis of gender, gender role orientation, and earnings. *Journal of Applied Psychology, 93,* 994–1012.

Juffer, F., Bakermans-Kranenburg, M. J., & van IJzendoorn, M. H. (2007). *Promoting positive parenting: An attachment-based intervention.* Mahwah, NJ: Lawrence Erlbaum.

Jung, C. G. (1928). *Two essays on analytical psychology.* New York: Dodd, Mead.

Jung, C. G. (1963). *Memories, dreams, reflections.* New York: Random House.

Jung, S., Fuller, B., & Galindo, C. (2012). Family functioning and early learning practices in immigrant homes. *Child Development, 83,* 1510–1526.

Juvonen, J. (2007). Reforming middle schools. *Educational Psychologist, 42,* 197–208.

Kabat-Zinn, J. (1994). *Wherever you go, there you are.* New York: Hyperion.

Kabat-Zinn, J. (2003). Mindfulness-based interventions in context: Past, present and future. *Clinical Psychology: Science and Practice, 10,* 144–156.

Kabat-Zinn, J. (2005). *Coming to our senses: Healing ourselves and the world through mindfulness.* New York: Hyperion.

Kabat-Zinn, J., Lipworth, L., Burney, R., & Sellers, W. (1986). Four-year follow-up of a meditation-based stress reduction program for the self-regulation of chronic pain: Treatment outcomes and compliance. *Clinical Journal of Pain, 2,* 159–173.

Kabat-Zinn, J., Massion, A. O., Kristeller, J., Peterson, L. G., Fletcher, K., Pbert, L., Linderking, W., & Santorelli, S. F. (1992). Effectiveness of a meditation-based stress reduction program in the treatment of anxiety disorders. *American Journal of Psychiatry, 149,* 936–943.

Kabat-Zinn, J., Wheeler, E., Light, T., Skillings, A., Scharf, M., Cropley, T. G., et al. (1998). Influence of a mindfulness-based stress reduction intervention on rates of skin clearing in patients with moderate to severe psoriasis undergoing phototherapy (UVB) and photochemotherapy (PUVA). *Psychosomatic Medicine, 60,* 625–632.

Kaffman, A., & Meaney, M. J. (2007). Neurodevelopmental sequelae of postnatal maternal care in rodents: Clinical and research implications of molecular insights. *Journal of Child Psychology and Psychiatry, 48,* 224–244.

Kagan, J. (1981). *The second year: The emergence of self-awareness.* Cambridge, MA: Harvard University Press.

Kagan, J. (1984). *The nature of the child.* New York: Basic Books.

Kagan, J. (1994). Yesterday's premises: Tomorrow's promises. In R. D. Parke, R. A. Ornstein, J. J. Rieser, & C. Sahn-Waxler (Eds.), *A century of developmental psychology* (pp. 551–568). Washington, DC: American Psychological Association.

Kagan, J. (2002). *Surprise, uncertainty, and mental structures.* Cambridge, MA: Harvard University Press.

Kagan, J., & Fox, N. A. (2006). Biology, culture, and temperamental biases. In W. Damon & R. M. Lerner (Series Eds.), N. Eisenberg (Vol. Ed.), *Handbook of child psychology: Vol. 3. Social, emotional, and personality development* (6th ed., pp. 167–225). Hoboken, NJ: Wiley.

Kagan, J., Kearsley, R., & Zelazo, P. (1978). *Infancy: Its place in human development.* Cambridge, MA: Harvard University Press.

Kagan, J., Snidman, N., Kahn, V., & Towsley, S. (2007). The preservation of two infant temperaments into adolescence. *Monographs of the Society for Research in Child Development, 72,* 1–75.

Kagan, S. L., & Kauerz, K. (2007). Reaching for the whole: Integration and alignment in early education policy. In R. C. Pianta, M. J. Cox, & K. L. Snow (Eds.), *School readiness and the transition to kindergarten in the era of accountability* (pp. 11–30). Baltimore: Brookes.

Kahneman, D., Krueger, A. B., Schkade, D., Schwarz, N., & Stone, A. (2004). A survey method for characterizing daily life experience: The day reconstruction method. *Science, 306,* 1776–1781.

Kahneman, D., & Tversky, A. (1984). Choices, values and frames. *American Psychologist, 39,* 341–350.

Kail, R. (1993). Processing time decreases globally at an exponential rate during childhood and adolescence. *Journal of Experimental Child Psychology, 56,* 254–265.

Kail, R., & Salthouse, T. (1994). Processing speed as a mental capacity. *Acta Psychologica, 86,* 199–225.

Kaiser Family Foundation (2010). *Generation M2: Media in the lives of 8- to 18-year-olds.* Retrieved November 16, 2012 from http://www.kff.org/entmedia/upload/8010.pdf

Kalish, R. A. (1985). The social context of death and dying. In R. H. Binstock & E. Shanas (Eds.), *Handbook of aging and the social sciences* (2nd ed., pp. 147–170). New York: Van Nostrand Reinhold.

Kamii, C. (1986). Place value: An explanation of its difficulty and educational implications for the primary grades. *Journal of Research in Childhood Education, 1,* 75–86.

Kamii, M. (1990). Why Big Bird can't teach calculus: The case of place value and cognitive development in the middle years. In N. Lauter-Klatell (Ed.), *Readings in child development* (pp. 101–104, 170). Mountain View, CA: Mayfield.

Kamins, M. L., & Dweck, C. S. (1999). Person versus process praise and criticism: Implications for contingent self-worth and coping. *Developmental Psychology, 35,* 835–847.

Kandel, D. B. (1978). Homophily, selection, and socialization in adolescent friendships. *American Journal of Sociology, 84,* 427–436.

Kane, R. S. (1996). The defeat of aging versus the importance of death. *Journal of the American Geriatric Society, 44,* 321–325.

Kane, R., Wales, J., Bernstein, L., Leibowitz, A., & Kaplan, S. (1984). A randomized controlled trial of hospice care. *The Lancet, 302,* 890–894.

Kang, S., Shaver, P. R., Sue, S., Min, K., & Jing, H. (2003). Culture-specific patterns in the prediction of life satisfaction: Roles of emotion, relationship quality, and self-esteem. *Personality and Social Psychology Bulletin, 29,* 1596–1608.

Kann, L., Olsen, E. O., McManus, T., Kinchen, S., Chyen, D., Harris, W. A., et al.; Centers for Disease Control and Prevention [CDC]. (June 2011). *MMWR Surveillance Summaries 2011, 60*(7), 1–133.

Kanner, L. (1943). Autistic disturbances of affective contact. *The Nervous Child, 2,* 217–250.

Kaplan, H. B. (1980). *Deviant behavior in defense of self.* New York: Academic Press.

Kaplow, J. B., & Widom, C. S. (2007). Age of onset of child maltreatment predicts long-term mental health outcomes. *Journal of Abnormal Psychology, 116,* 176–187.

Karraker, A., DeLamater, J., & Schwartz, C. R. (2011). Sexual frequency decline from midlife to later life. *The Journals of Gerontology, Series B: Psychological Sciences and Social Sciences, 66,* 502–512.

Karapanou, O., & Papadimitriou, A. (2010). Determinants of menarche. *Reproductive Biology and Endocrinology, 8,* 115: http://www.rbej.com/content/8/1/115

Karen, R. (1998). *Becoming attached: First relationships and how they shape our capacity to love.* New York: Oxford University Press.

Karmiloff-Smith, A. (1992). *Beyond modularity: A developmental perspective on cognitive science.* Cambridge, MA: MIT Press.

Karmiloff-Smith, A. (2000). Why babies' brains are not Swiss army knives. In H. Rose & S. Rose (Eds.), *Alas, poor Darwin* (pp. 173–187). New York: Harmony Books.

Karney, B. R., & Bradbury, T. N. (1995). The longitudinal course of marital quality and stability: A review of theory, method, and research. *Psychological Bulletin, 118,* 3–34.

Karney, B. R., & Bradbury, T. N. (1997). Neuroticism, marital interaction, and the trajectory of marital satisfaction. *Journal of Personality and Social Psychology, 72,* 1075–1092.

Kartner, J., Keller, H., Chaudhary, N., & Yovsi, R. D. (2012). The development of mirror self-recognition in different sociocultural contexts. *Monographs of the Society for Research in Child Development, 77,* 1–101.

Kaslow, F. W. (2001). Families and family psychology at the millennium. *American Psychologist, 56,* 37–46.

Kasser, T., & Ryan, R. M. (1996). Further examining the American dream: Differential correlates of intrinsic and extrinsic goals. *Personality and Social Psychology Bulletin, 22,* 280–287.

Kastenbaum, R. (1986). *Death, society, and human experience* (3rd ed.). Columbus, OH: Merrill.

Katz, L. C., & Shatz, C. J. (1996). Synaptic activity and the construction of cortical circuits. *Science, 274,* 1133–1138.

Katz, P. A., & Walsh, V. (1991). Developmental aspects of gender role flexibility and traditionality in middle childhood and adolescence. *Child Development, 30,* 272–282.

Katz, P., & Zalk, S. (1974). Doll preferences: An index of racial attitudes? *Journal of Educational Psychology, 66,* 663–668.

Katz-Wise, S. L., Priess, H. A., & Hyde, J. S. (2010). Gender-role attitudes and behavior across the transition to parenthood. *Developmental Psychology, 46,* 18–28.

Kawabata, Y., & Crick, N. R. (2008). The role of cross-racial/ethnic friendships in social adjustment. *Developmental Psychology, 44,* 1177–1183.

Kaye, W. H., Klump, K. L., Frank, G. K. W., & Strober, M. (2000). Anorexia and Bulimia Nervosa. *Annual Review of Medicine, 51,* 299–313.

Kazdin, A. E. (1991). Effectiveness of psychotherapy with children and adolescents. *Journal of Consulting and Clinical Psychology, 59*(6), 785–798.

Kazdin, A. E. (1995). *Conduct disorders in childhood and adolescence* (2nd ed.). Thousand Oaks, CA: Sage.

Kazdin, A. E. (2003). Psychotherapy for children and adolescents. *Annual Review of Psychology, 54,* 273–276.

Keane, T. M., Marshall, A. D., & Taft, C. T. (2006). Posttraumatic stress disorder: Etiology, epidemiology, and treatment outcome. *Annual review of clinical psychology, 2,* 161–197.

Keel, P. K., Dorer, D. J., Eddy, K. T., Franko, D., Charatan, D. L., & Herzog, D. B. (2003). Predictors of mortality in eating disorders. *Archives of General Psychiatry, 60,* 179–183.

Keel, P. K., Leon, G., & Fulkerson, J. A. (2001). Vulnerability to eating disorders in childhood and adolescence. In Ingram, R. E. & Price, J. M. (Eds.), *Vulnerability to psychopathology: Risks across the lifespan* (pp. 389–411). New York: Guilford Press.

Keelan, J. P. R., Dion, K. K., & Dion, K. L. (1998). Attachment style and relationship satisfaction: Test of a self-disclosure explanation. *Canadian Journal of Behavioural Science, 30,* 24–35.

Keenan, K., & Shaw, D. (1997). Developmental and social influences on young girls' early problem behavior. *Psychological Bulletin, 121,* 95–113.

Kegan, R. (1982). *The evolving self.* Cambridge, MA: Harvard University Press.

Kellett, J. M. (2000). Older adult sexuality. In L. T. Szuchman & F. Muscarella (Eds.), *Psychological perspectives on human sexuality* (pp. 355–379). New York: Wiley.

Kelley, P., & Camilli, G. (2007). The impact of teacher education on outcomes in center-based early childhood education programs: A meta-analysis. A National Institute for Early Education Research Working Paper. Retrieved May 3, 2008, from http://nieer.org/resources/research/Teacher_Ed.pdf

Kellman, P. J., & Arterberry, M. E. (2006). Infant visual perception. In W. Damon & R. Lerner (Series Eds.), D. Kuhn & R. Siegler (Vol. Eds.), *Handbook of child psychology: Vol. 2. Cognition, perception, and language* (6th ed., pp. 109–160). New York: Wiley.

Kelly, E. L., & Conley, J. J. (1987). Personality and compatibility: An analysis of marital stability and marital satisfaction. *Journal of Personality and Social Psychology, 52,* 27–40.

Keltner, N. L., Folks, D. G., Palmer, C. A., & Powers, R. E. (1998). *Psychobiological foundations of psychiatric care.* Elsevier Health Sciences.

Kemeny, M. E. (2003). The psychobiology of stress. *Current Directions in Psychological Science, 12,* 124–129.

Kempermann G., Kuhn H. G., & Gage F. H. (1998). Experience-induced neurogenesis in the senescent dentate gyrus. *Journal of Neuroscience 18,* 3206–3212.

Kendall, P. C. (1991). *Child and adolescent therapy.* New York: Guilford Press.

Kendall, P. C. (1993). Cognitive-behavioral therapies with youth: Guiding theory, current status, and emerging developments. *Journal of Consulting and Clinical Psychology, 61,* 235–247.

Kendler, K. S., Thornton, L. M., & Gardner, C. O. (2001). Genetic risk, number of previous depressive episodes, and stressful life events in predicting onset of major depression. *American Journal of Psychiatry, 158,* 582–586.

Keniston, K. (1971). *Youth in dissent: The rise of a new opposition.* New York: Harcourt Brace Jovanovich.

Kennedy, G. J., & Tanenbaum, S. (2000). Psychotherapy with older adults. *American Journal of Psychotherapy, 54,* 386–407.

Kerig, P. K., Cowan, P. A., & Cowan, C. P. (1993). Marital quality and gender differences in parent–child interaction. *Developmental Psychology, 29,* 931–939.

Kernberg, O. (1976). *Object relations theory and clinical psychoanalysis.* New York: Aronson.

Kersten-Alvarez, L. E., Hosman, C., Riksen-Walraven, J. M., & Van Doesum, K. (2011). Which preventive interventions effectively enhance depressed mothers' sensitivity? A meta-analysis. *Infant Mental Health, 32,* 362–376.

Kessler, R. C., Berglund, P., Demler, O., Jin, R., Merikangas, K. R., & Walters, E. E. (2005). Lifetime prevalence and age-of-onset distributions of DSM-IV disorders in the National Comorbidity Survey Replication. *Archives of General Psychiatry, 62,* 593–602.

Kessler, R. C., Berglund, P., Demler, O., Jin, R., Koretz, D., Merikangas, K. R., et al. (2003). The epidemiology of major depressive disorder: Results from the National Comorbidity Survey Replication (NCS-R). *JAMA, 289,* 3095–3105.

Kessler, R. C., Sonnega, A., Bromet, E., Hughes, M., & Nelson, C. B. (1995). Posttraumatic stress disorder in the national comorbidity survey. *Archives of General Psychiatry, 52,* 1048–1060.

Kessler, R. C., Turner, J. B., & House, J. S. (1989). Unemployment, reemployment, and emotional functioning in a community sample. *American Sociological Review, 54,* 648–657.

Keup, J. R., & Stolzenberg, E. B. (2004). *The 2003 Your First College Year (YFCY) survey: Exploring the academic and personal experiences of first-year students.* Los Angeles: National Resource Center for The First-Year Experience & Students in Transition & Higher Education Research Institute at UCLA.

Keyes, C. L. M., & Haidt, J. (2003). *Flourishing: Positive psychology and the well-lived life.*

Washington, DC: American Psychological Association.

Kiang, L., Harter, S., & Whitesell, N. R. (2007). Relational expression of ethnic identity in Chinese Americans. *Journal of Social and Personal Relationships, 24,* 277–296.

Kibbe, M. M., & Leslie, A. M. (2011). What do infants remember when they forget? Location and identity in 6-month-olds' memory for objects. *Psychological Science, 22,* 1500–1505.

Killen, M., & Smetana, J. (2008). Moral judgment and moral neuroscience: Intersections, definitions, and issues. *Child Development Perspectives, 2,* 1–6.

Kilmartin, C. T. (1994). *The masculine self.* New York: Macmillan.

Kim, H. S., Sherman, D. K., & Taylor, S. E. (2008). Culture and social support. *American Psychologist, 63,* 518–526.

Kimbro, R. T., Lynch, S. M., & McLanahan, S. (2008). The influence of acculturation on breastfeeding initiation and duration for Mexican-Americans. *Population Research and Policy Review, 27,* 183.

Kindermann, T. A. (1993). Natural peer groups as contexts for individual development: The case of children's motivation in school. *Developmental Psychology, 29,* 970–977.

Kindermann, T. A. (2008). Effects of naturally existing peer groups on changes in academic engagement in a cohort of sixth graders. *Child Development, 78,* 1186–1203.

Kindlon, D., & Thompson, M. (1990). *Raising Cain: Protecting the emotional life of boys.* New York: Ballantine Books.

King, P. M., & Howard-Hamilton, M. F. (1999). *Becoming a multiculturally competent student affairs professional.* Final report submitted to the National Association of Student Personal Association, 1999. Retrieved from http://www.naspa.org

King, P. M., & Kitchener, K. S. (2002). The reflective judgment model: Twenty years of research on epistemic cognition. In B. K. Hofer & P. R. Pintrich (Eds.), *Personal Epistemology* (pp. 37–62). Mahwah, NJ: Erlbaum.

Kirk, S. A., & Kutchins, H. (1997). *Making us crazy. DSM: The psychiatric bible and the creation of mental disorders.* Hawthorne, NY: Aldine de Gruyter.

Kirkpatrick, L. A., & Davis, K. E. (1994). Attachment style, gender, and relationship stability: A longitudinal analysis. *Journal of Personality and Social Psychology, 66,* 502–512.

Kirschner, D. (1992). Understanding adoptees who kill: Dissociation, patricide, and the psychodynamics of adoption. *International Journal of Offender Therapy and Comparative Criminology, 36,* 323–333.

Kitayama, S., Duffy, S., Kawamura, T., & Larsen, J. T. (2003). Perceiving an object and its context in different cultures: A cultural look at new look. *Psychological Science, 14,* 201–206.

Kitayama, S., & Park, J. (2010). Cultural neuroscience of the self: Understanding the social grounding of the brain. *Social Cognitive and Affective Neuroscience, 5,* 111–129.

Kitayama, S., & Uskul, A. (2011). Culture, mind, and the brain: Current evidence and future directions. *Annual Review in Psychology, 62,* 419–449.

Kiselica, M. S. (2003). Transforming psychotherapy in order to succeed with adolescent boys: Male-friendly practices. *Journal of Clinical Psychology, 59,* 1225–1236.

Kisley, M. A., Wood, S., & Burrows, C. L. (2007). Looking at the sunny side of life. *Psychological Science, 18,* 838–843.

Kitchener, K. S. (1983). Cognition, metacognition, and epistemic cognition: A three-level model of cognitive processing. *Human Development, 4,* 222–232.

Kitchener, K. S., & King, P. M. (1981). Reflective judgment: Concepts of justification and their relationship to age and education. *Journal of Applied Developmental Psychology, 2,* 89–116.

Kitchener, K. S., King, P. M., Wood, P. K., & Davison, M. L. (1989). Sequentiality and consistency in the development of reflective judgment: A six-year longitudinal study. *Journal of Applied Developmental Psychology, 10,* 73–95.

Kitchener, K. S., Lynch, C. L., Fischer, K. W., & Wood, P. K. (1993). Developmental range of reflective judgment: The effect of contextual support and practice on developmental stage. *Developmental Psychology, 29,* 893–906.

Kite, M. E., Stockdale, G. D., Whitley, B. E., Jr., & Johnson, B. T. (2005). Attitudes toward younger and older adults: An updated meta-analytic review. *Journal of Social Issues, 61,* 241–266.

Klahr, D., & Nigam, M. (2004). The equivalence of learning paths in early science instruction: Effects of direct instruction and discovery learning. *Psychological Science, 15,* 661–667.

Klass, D. (1982). Elisabeth Kubler-Ross and the tradition of the private sphere: An analysis of symbols. *Omega, 16,* 241–261.

Klein, M. (1921/1945). *Contributions to psychoanalysis.* London: Hogarth.

Kleinman, A., & Kleinman, J. (1985). Somatization: The interconnections in Chinese society among culture, depressive experiences, and the meanings of pain. In A. Kleinman & B. Good (Eds.), *Culture and depression: Studies in the anthropology and cross-cultural psychiatry of affect and disorder* (pp. 429–490). Berkeley: University of California Press.

Klerman, G. L., & Weissman, M. M. (1989). Increasing rates of depression. *JAMA, 261,* 2229–2235.

Klerman, G. L., Weissman, M. M., Rounsaville, B. J., & Chevron, E. S. (1984). *Interpersonal psychotherapy for depression.* New York: Basic Books.

Kling, K. C., Hyde, J. S., Showers, C. J., & Buswell, B. N. (1999). Gender differences in self-esteem: A meta-analysis. *Psychological Bulletin, 125,* 470–500.

Kling, K. C., Seltzer, M. M., & Ryff, C. D. (1997). Distinctive late-life challenges: Implications for coping and well-being. *Psychology and Aging, 12,* 288–295.

Klinnert, M. (1984). The regulation of infant behavior by maternal facial expression. *Infant Behavior and Development, 7,* 447–465.

Kneflekamp, L. L. (1999). Introduction. In W. G. Perry, *Forms of ethical development in the college years: A scheme* (p. xix). San Francisco: Jossey-Bass.

Kochanska, G. (1995). Children's temperament, mothers' discipline, and security of attachment: Multiple pathways to emerging internalization. *Child Development, 66,* 597–615.

Kochanska, G. (1998). Mother-child relationship, child fearfulness, and emerging attachment: A short-term longitudinal study. *Developmental Psychology, 34,* 480–490.

Kochanska, G., Aksan, N., & Joy, M. E. (2007). Children's fearfulness as a moderator of parenting in early socialization: Two longitudinal studies. *Developmental Psychology, 43,* 222–237.

Kochanska, G., Aksan, N., & Koenig, A. L. (1995). A longitudinal study of the roots of preschoolers' conscience: Committed compliance and emerging internalization. *Child Development, 66,* 1752–1769.

Kochanska, G., Barry, R. A., Stellern, S. A., & O'Bleness, J. J. (2009). Early attachment organization moderates the parent-child mutually coercive pathway to children's antisocial conduct. *Child Development, 80,* 1288–1300.

Kochanska, G., Gross, J. N., Lin, M-H., & Nichols, K. E. (2002). Guilt in young children: Development, determinants, and relations with a broader system of standards. *Child Development, 73,* 461–482.

Kochanska, G., & Kim, S. (2012). Toward a new understanding of legacy of early attachments for future antisocial trajectories: Evidence from two longitudinal studies. *Development and Psychopathology, 24,* 783–806.

Kochanska, G., Koenig, J. L., Barry, R. A., Kim, S., & Yoon, J. E. (2010). Children's conscience during toddler and preschool years, moral self, and a competent, adaptive developmental trajectory. *Developmental Psychology, 46,* 1320–1332.

Kochanska, G., Tjebkes, T. L., & Forman, D. R. (1998). Children's emerging regulation of conduct: Restraint, compliance, and internalization from infancy to the second year. *Child Development, 69,* 1378–1389.

Kohlberg, L. (1966). Moral education in the school. *School Review, 74,* 1–30.

Kohlberg, L. (1976). Moral stages and moralization: The cognitive developmental approach. In T. Lickona (Ed.), *Moral development and behavior: Theory, research and social issues* (pp. 31–53). New York: Holt, Rinehart and Winston.

Kohlberg, L. (1984). *Essays on moral development: The psychology of moral development.* San Francisco: Harper & Row.

Kohlberg, L. A. (1966). A cognitive-developmental analysis of children's sex role concepts and attitudes. In E. E. Maccoby (Ed.), *The development of sex differences* (pp. 82–173). Stanford, CA: Stanford University Press.

Kohn, A. (1997, February). How not to teach values: A critical look at character education. *Phi Delta Kappan,* 428–439.

Kok, B. E., Coffey, K. A., Cohn, M. A., Catalino, L. I., Vacharkulksemsuk, T., Algoe, S. et al. (2013). How positive emotions build physical health: Perceived positive social connections account for the upward spiral between positive emotions and vagal tone. *Psychological Science, 24,* 1123–1132.

Kok, B. E., Waugh, C. E., & Fredrickson, B. L. (2013). Meditation and health: The search for mechanisms of action. *Social and Personality Psychology Compass, 7,* 27–39.

Kolb, B., Gibb, R., & Robinson, T. E. (2003). Brain plasticity and behavior. *Current Directions in Psychological Science, 12,* 1–5.

Kolb, B., & Wishaw, I. Q. (2006). *An introduction to brain and behavior* (2nd ed.). New York: Worth.

Kondo-Ikemura, K. (2001). Insufficient evidence. *American Psychologist, 56,* 825–826.

Konner, M. J., & Worthman, C. (1980). Nursing frequency, gonadal function and birth-spacing among !Kung hunters and gatherers. *Science, 207,* 788–791.

Kopp, C. B. (1982). Antecedents of self-regulation: A developmental perspective. *Developmental Psychology, 18,* 199–214.

Kopp, C. B., & Wyer, N. (1994). Self-regulation in normal and atypical development. In D. Cicchetti & S. L. Toth (Eds.), *Rochester Symposium on Developmental Psychopathology: Vol. 5. Disorders and dysfunctions of the self* (pp. 31–56). Rochester, NY: University of Rochester Press.

Kornfield, J. (2002). *The art of forgiveness, loving-kindness, and peace.* New York: Bantam Books.

Kotch, J. B., Blakely, C. H., Brown, S. S., & Wong, F. Y. (Eds.). (1992). *A pound of prevention: The case for universal maternity care in the United States.* Washington, DC: American Public Health Association.

Krain, A. L., & Castellanos, F. X. (2006). Brain development and ADHD. *Clinical Psychology Review, 26,* 433–444.

Krendl, A. C., Richeson, J. A., Kelley, W. M., & Heatherton, T. F. (2008). The negative consequences of threat. *Psychological Science, 19,* 168–175.

Kreutzer, M. A., Leonard, C., & Flavell, J. H. (1975). An interview study of children's knowledge about memory. *Monographs of the Society for Research in Child Development, 40* (Serial No. 159).

Kreider, R. M. (2006). *Remarriage in the United States.* Poster presented at the annual meeting of the American Sociological Association, Montreal, Canada. Retrieved from http://www.census.gov/hhes/socdemo/marriage/data/sipp/us-remarriage-poster.pdf

Kristeller, J. L., & Hallett, C. B. (1999). An exploratory study of meditation-based intervention for binge eating disorder. *Journal of Health Psychology, 4,* 357–363.

Kristeller, J., Hallett, L., & Brendan, C. (1999). An exploratory study of a meditation-based intervention for binge eating disorder. *Journal of Health Psychology, 4,* 357–363.

Kristof-Brown, A. L., Zimmerman, R. D., & Johnson, E. C. (2005). Consequences of individuals' fit at work: A meta-analysis of person-job, person-organization, person-group, and person-supervisor fit. *Personnel Psychology, 58,* 281–342.

Krivickas, K. M., & Lofquist D. (2011). Demographics of same-sex couple households. Washington DC: U.S. Bureau of the Census. Retrieved from http://www.census.gov/hhes/samesex/data/acs.html

Kroger, J. (1983). A developmental study of identity formation among late adolescent and adult women. *Psychological Documents, 13* (Ms. No. 2537).

Krohne, H. W., & Rogner, J. (1982). Repression-sensitization as a central construct in coping research. In J. G. Schulterbrandt & A. Raskin (Eds.), *Depression in childhood: Diagnosis, treatment, and conceptual models* (pp. 1–25). New York: Raven.

Krug, J., Mercy, L., Dahlberg, A., & Zwi, A. B. (2003). The world report on violence and health. *The Lancet, 360,* 1083–1088.

Krueger, A. B. (1999). Experimental estimates of education production functions. *Quarterly Journal of Economics, 114,* 497–532.

Kruger, A. C. (1992). The effect of peer and adult-child transductive discussions on moral reasoning. *Merrill-Palmer Quarterly, 38,* 191–211.

Kruger, A. C., & Tomasello, M. (1986). Transactive discussions with peers and adults. *Developmental Psychology, 22,* 681–685.

Krumboltz, J. D. (1966). Behavioral goals for counseling. *Journal of Counseling Psychology, 13,* 153–159.

Kubler-Ross, E. (1969). *On death and dying.* New York: Macmillan.

Kubler-Ross, E. (1974). *Questions and answers on death and dying.* New York: Macmillan.

Kuczynski, L. (1984). Socialization goals and mother–child interaction: Strategies for long-term and short-term compliance. *Developmental Psychology, 20,* 1061–1073.

Kuhl, P. K., Stevens, E., Hayashi, A., Deguchi, T., Kiritani, S., & Iverson, P. (2006). Infants show a facilitation effect for native language phonetic perception between 6 and 12 months. *Developmental Science, 9,* F13–F21.

Kuhn, D. (1989). Children and adults as intuitive scientists. *Psychological Review, 96,* 674–689.

Kuhn, D. (1991). *The skills of argument.* Cambridge, England: Cambridge University Press.

Kuhn, D. (1992). Thinking as argument. *Harvard Educational Review, 62,* 155–178.

Kuhn, D. (2000a). Does memory development belong on an endangered topic list? *Child Development, 71,* 21–25.

Kuhn, D. (2000b). Metacognitive development. *Current Directions in Psychological Science, 9,* 178–181.

Kuhn, D. (2005). *Education for thinking.* Boston, MA: First Harvard University Press.

Kuhn, D. (2009). The importance of learning about knowing: Creating a foundation for development of intellectual values. *Child Development Perspectives, 3,* 112–117.

Kuhn, D. (2011). What is scientific thinking and how does it develop? In D. Kuhn (Ed.), *The Wiley-Blackwell handbook of childhood cognitive development* (2nd ed., pp. 497–523). Malden, MA: Wiley-Blackwell.

Kuhn, D., Amsel, E., & O'Loughlin, M. (1988). *The development of scientific reasoning skills.* New York: Academic Press.

Kuhn, D., & Franklin, S. (2006). The second decade: What develops (and how). In W. Damon & R. M. Lerner (Series Eds.), D. Kuhn & R. S. Siegler (Vol. Eds.), *Handbook of child psychology: Vol. 2. Cognition, perception and language* (6th ed., pp. 953–993). Hoboken, NJ: Wiley.

Kuhn, D., Garcia-Mila, M., Zohar, A., & Andersen, C. (1995). Strategies of knowledge acquisition. *Monographs of the Society for Research in Child Development, 60* (Serial No. 245).

Kuhn, D., Pennington, N., & Leadbeater, B. (1982). Adult thinking in developmental perspective. In P. B. Baltes & O. Brim (Eds.), *Life span development and behavior* (pp. 157–195). New York: Academic Press.

Kulis, S., Marsiglia, F. F., Elek, E., Dustman, P., Wagstaff, D. A., & Hecht, M. L. (2005). Mexican/Mexican American adolescents and keepin' it REAL: An evidence-based substance use prevention program. *Children and Schools, 27,* 133–145.

Kunzmann, U., & Baltes, P. B. (2003). Wisdom-related knowledge: Affective, motivational, and interpersonal correlates. *Personality and Social Psychology Bulletin, 29,* 1104–1119.

Kupersmidt, J. B., Burchinal, M., & Patterson, C. J. (1995). Developmental patterns of childhood peer relations as predictors of externalizing problems in adolescence. *Child Development, 61,* 1350–1362.

Kuo, B. C. H. (2011). Culture's consequences on coping: Theories, evidences, and dimensionalities. *Journal of Cross-Cultural Psychology, 42,* 1084–1100.

Kupfer, D. J., Regier, D. A., & Kuhl, E. A. (2008). On the road to DSM-V and ICD-II. *European Archives of Psychiatry and Clinical Neuroscience, 258,* 2–6.

Kurdek, L. A. (1993). Predicting marital dissolution: A 5-year prospective longitudinal study of newlywed couples. *Journal of Personality and Social Psychology, 64,* 221–242.

Kurdek, L. A. (1998). Relationship outcomes and their predictors: Longitudinal evidence from heterosexual married, gay cohabiting, and lesbian cohabiting couples. *Journal of Marriage and the Family, 60,* 553–568.

Kurdek, L. A. (2004). Are gay and lesbian cohabiting couples really different from heterosexual married couples? *Journal of Marriage and Family, 66,* 880–900.

Kurtz, B. E., Carr, M., Borkowski, J. G., Schneider, W., & Rellinger, E. (1990). Strategy instruction and attributional beliefs in West Germany and the United States: Do teachers foster metacognitive development? *Contemporary Educational Psychology, 15,* 268–283.

Kuwabara, M., Son, J. Y., & Smith, L. B. (2011). Attention to context: U.S. and Japanese children's emotional judgments. *Journal of Cognition and Development, 12,* 502–517.

LaBrie, J. W., Atkins, D. C., Neighbors, C., Mirza, T., & Larimer, M. E. (2012). Ethnicity specific norms and alcohol consumption among Hispanic/Latino/a and Caucasian students. *Addictive Behaviors, 37,* 573–576.

Labouvie-Vief, G. (1984). Logic and self regulation from youth to maturity: A model. In M. L. Commons, F. A. Richards, & C. Armon (Eds.), *Beyond formal operations: Late adolescent and adult cognitive development* (pp. 158–179). New York: Praeger.

Labouvie-Vief, G., Chiodo, L. M., Goguen, L. A., Diehl, M., & Orwoll, L. (1995). Representations of self across the life span. *Psychology and Aging, 10,* 404–415.

Labouvie-Vief, G., Lumley, M. A., Jain, E., & Heinze, H. (2003). Age and gender differences in cardiac reactivity and subjective emotion responses to emotional autobiographical memories. *Emotion, 3,* 115–126.

Lachman, M. E. (2004). Development in midlife. *Annual Review of Psychology, 55,* 305–331.

Ladd, G. W., & Asher, S. R. (1985). Social skills training and children's peer relations. In L. L'Abate & M. Milan (Eds.), *Handbook of social skills training and research* (pp. 219–244). New York: Wiley.

Ladd, G. W., & Burgess, K. B. (1999). Charting the relationship trajectories of aggressive, withdrawn, and aggressive/withdrawn children during early grade school. *Child Development, 70,* 910–929.

Ladd, G. W., Kochenderfer-Ladd, B., Eggum, N. D., Kochel, K. P., & McConnell, E. M. (2011). Characterizing and comparing the friendships of anxious-solitary and unsociable preadolescents. *Child Development, 82,* 1434–1453.

Ladd, G. W., & Ladd, B. K. (1998). Parenting behaviors and parent-child relationships: Correlates of peer victimization in kindergarten? *Developmental Psychology, 34,* 1450–1458.

Ladd, G. W., & Mize, J. (1983). A cognitive-social learning model of social skills training. *Psychological Review, 90,* 127–157.

Ladd, J. M., & Price, J. M. (1987). Predicting children's social and school adjustment following the transition from preschool to kindergarten *Child Development, 58,* 1168–1189.

LaFromboise, T., Coleman, H. L. K., & Gerton, J. (1993). Psychological impact of biculturalism: Evidence and theory. *Psychological Bulletin, 114,* 395–412.

Lahey, B. B., McBurnett, K., & Loeber, R. (2000). Are attention-deficit/hyperactivity disorder and oppositional defiant disorder developmental precursors to conduct disorder? In A. J. Sameroff, M. Lewis, & S. M. Miller (Eds.), *Handbook of developmental psychopathology* (2nd ed., pp. 431–446). New York: Kluwer Academic/Plenum Press.

Lahey, B., Loeber, R., Quay, H. C., Frick, P. J., & Grimm, J. (1992). Oppositional defiant and conduct disorders: Issues to be resolved for DSM-IV. *Journal of the American Academy of Child and Adolescent Psychiatry, 31,* 539–546.

Laible, D. J., & Thompson, R. A. (2002). Mother-child lessons in emotion, morality, and relationships. *Child Development, 73,* 1187–1203.

Lamb, M. E., & Ahnert, L. (2006). Nonparental child care: Context, concepts, correlates, and consequences. In W. Damon and R. M. Lerner (Series Eds.), K. A. Renninger & I. E. Sigel (Vol. Eds.), *Handbook of child psychology: Vol. 4. Child psychology in practice* (6th ed., pp. 950–1016). Hoboken, NJ: Wiley.

Lamb, M. E., & Lewis, C. (2004). The development and significance of father-child relationships in two-parent families. In M. E. Lamb (Eds.), *The role of the father in child development* (4th ed., pp. 272–306). Hoboken, NJ: Wiley.

Lamb, M. E., & Lewis, C. (2011). The role of parent-child relationships in child development. In M. H. Bornstein & M. E. Lamb (Eds.). *Developmental science: An advanced textbook* (pp. 469–517). New York: Psychology Press.

Lambert, M. J., & Bergin, A. E. (1994), The effectiveness of psychotherapy. In A. E. Bergin & S. L. Garfield (Eds.), *Handbook of psychotherapy and behavior change* (4th ed., pp. 143–189). New York: Wiley.

Lamborn, S. D., Dornbusch, S. M., & Steinberg, L. (1996). Ethnicity and community context as moderators of the relations between family decision making and adolescent adjustment. *Child Development, 67,* 283–301.

Lamborn, S. D., Mounts, N. S., Steinberg, L., & Dornbusch, S. M. (1991). Patterns of competence and adjustment among adolescents from authoritative, authoritarian, indulgent, and neglectful families. *Child Development, 62,* 1049–1065.

The Editors of The Lancet. (2010). Retraction—ileal-lymphoid-nodular hyperplasia, non-specific colitis, and pervasive developmental disorder in children. *The Lancet, 375,* 445.

Landa, D. E., & Bybee, J. A. (2007). Adaptive elements of aging: Self-image discrepancy, perfectionism, and eating problems. *Developmental Psychology, 43,* 83–93.

Landale, N. S., & Fennelly, K. (1992). Informal unions among mainland Puerto Ricans: Cohabitation or an alternative to legal marriage? *Journal of Marriage and the Family, 54,* 269–280.

Landreth, G. L. (2002a). *Play therapy: The art of the relationship* (2nd ed.). New York: Brunner-Routledge.

Landreth, G. L. (2002b). Therapeutic limits in the play therapy relationship. *Professional Psychology: Research and Practice, 33,* 529–522.

Landry, S. H., Smith, K. E., Swank, P. R., Assel, M. A., & Vellet, S. (2001). Does early responsive parenting have a special importance for children's development or is consistency across childhood necessary? *Developmental Psychology, 37,* 387–403.

Lang, F. R., & Carstensen, L. L. (1994). Close emotional relationships in late life: Further support for proactive aging in the social domain. *Psychology and Aging, 9,* 315–324.

Langlois, J. H., Ritter, J. M., Casey, R. J., & Savin, D. B. (1995). Infant attractiveness predicts maternal behaviors and attitudes. *Developmental Psychology, 31,* 164–172.

Langlois, J. H., & Stephan, C. W. (1981). Beauty and the beast: The role of physical attraction in peer relationships and social behavior. In S. S. Brehm, S. M. Kassin, & S. X. Gibbans (Eds.), *Developmental social psychology: Theory and research* (pp. 152–168). New York: Oxford University Press.

Lansford, J. E. (2009). Parental divorce and children's adjustment. *Perspectives on Psychological Science, 4,* 140–152.

Lansford, J. E., Chang, L., Dodge, K. A., Malone, P. S., Oburu, P., Palmerus, K., et al. (2005). Physical discipline and children's adjustment: Cultural normativeness as a moderator. *Child Development, 76,* 1234–1246.

Lansford, J. E., Deater-Deckard, K., Dodge, K. A., Bates, J. E., & Pettit, G. S. (2004). Ethnic differences in the link between physical discipline and later adolescent externalizing behaviors. *Journal of Child Psychology and Psychiatry, 45,* 801–812.

Lansford, J. E., Wager, L. B., Bates, J. E., Pettit, G. S., & Dodge, K. A. (2012). Forms of spanking and children's externalizing behaviors. *Family Relations, 61,* 224–236.

Lapsley, D. K. (1993). Toward an integrated theory of adolescent ego development: The "new look" at adolescent egocentrism. *American Journal of Orthopsychiatry, 63,* 562–571.

Lapsley, D. K., FitzGerald, D. P., Rice, K. G., & Jackson, S. (1989). Separation-individuation and the "new look" at the imaginary audience and personal fable: A test of an integrative model. *Journal of Adolescent Research, 4,* 483–505.

Lapsley, D. K., & Murphy, M. N. (1985). Another look at the theoretical assumptions of adolescent egocentrism. *Developmental Review, 5,* 201–217.

Lapsley, D. K., & Narvaez, D. (2006). Character education. In W. Damon & R. M. Lerner (Series Eds.), K. A. Renninger & I. E. Sigel (Vol. Eds.), *Handbook of child psychology: Vol. 4. Child psychology in practice* (6th ed., pp. 248–296). Hoboken, NJ: Wiley.

Largie, S., Field, T., Hernandez-Reif, M., Sanders, C. E., & Diego, M. (2001). Employment during adolescence is associated with depression, inferior relationships, lower grades, and smoking. *Adolescence, 36,* 395–401.

Larrieu, J. A., & Mussen, P. (1986). Some personality and motivational correlates of children's prosocial behavior. *Journal of Genetic Psychology, 147,* 529–542.

Larsen, S. F. (2000). Memorable books: Recall of reading in its personal context. In M. S. MacNealey & R. Kreuz (Eds.), *Empirical approaches to literature and aesthetics: Advances in discourse processes* (Vol. 52, pp. 583–599). Norwood, NJ: Ablex.

Larson, R. W., Hansen, D. M., & Moneta, G. (2006). Differing profiles of developmental experiences across types of organized youth activities. *Developmental Psychology, 42,* 849–863.

Larson, R., & Richards, M. H. (1994). *Divergent realities: The emotional lives of mothers, fathers, and adolescents.* New York: Basic Books.

Lasch, C. (1991). *The true and only heaven: Progress and its critics.* New York: Norton.

Lassek, W. D., & Gaulin, S. J. (2007). Menarche is related to fat distribution. *American Journal of Physical Anthropology, 133,* 1147–1151.

Laub, J. H. (1999). Alterations in the opportunity structure: A criminological perspective. In A. Booth, A. C. Crouter, & M. J. Shanahan (Eds.), *Transitions to adulthood in a changing economy: No work, no family, no future?* (pp. 48–55). Westport, CT: Praeger.

Laursen, B. M., Coy, K. C., & Collins, W. A. (1998). Reconsidering changes in parent-child conflict across adolescence: A meta-analysis. *Child Development, 69,* 817–832.

Lazarus, R. S. (1996). The role of coping in the emotions and how coping changes over the life course. In C. Malatesta-Magni & S. H. McFadden (Eds.), *Handbook of emotion, adult development, and aging* (pp. 289–306). New York: Academic Press.

Lazarus, R. S., & Folkman, S. (1984). *Stress, appraisal, and coping.* New York: Springer.

Leaper, C. (1994). Exploring the correlates and consequences of gender segregation: Social relationships in childhood, adolescence, and adulthood. In B. Damon (Series Ed.) & C. Leaper (Vol. Ed.), *New directions for child development: The development of gender relationships.* San Francisco: Jossey-Bass.

Leaper, C. (2002). Parenting girls and boys. In M. H. Bornstein (Ed.), *Handbook of parenting: Children and parenting* (pp. 189–225). Mahwah, NJ: Erlbaum.

Leaper, C., Anderson, K. J., & Sanders, P. (1998). Moderators of gender effects on parents' talk to their children. *Developmental Psychology, 34,* 3–27.

Leaper, C., & Smith, T. E. (2004). A meta-analytic review of gender variations in children's language use: Talkativeness, affiliative speech, and assertive speech. *Developmental Psychology, 40,* 993–1027.

Leavell, A. S., Tamis-LeMonda, C. S., Ruble, D. N., Zosuls, K. M., & Cabrera, N. J. (2012). African American, White and Latino fathers' activities with their sons and daughters in early childhood. *Sex Roles, 66,* 53–65.

Lebel, C., Roussotte, F., & Sowell, E. R. (2011). Imaging the impact of prenatal alcohol exposure on the structure of the developing human brain. *Neuropsychological Review, 21,* 102–118.

L'Ecuyer, R. (1992). An experimental-developmental framework and methodology to study the transformations of the self-concept from infancy to old age. In T. M. Brinthaupt & R. P. Lipka (Eds.), *The self: Definitional and methodological issues* (pp. 96–136). Albany: State University of New York Press.

LeDoux, J. (1996). *The emotional brain: The mysterious underpinnings of emotional life.* New York: Simon & Schuster.

LeDoux, J. (2012). Rethinking the emotional brain. *Neuron, 73,* 653–668.

LeDoux, J. E. (2000). Emotion circuits in the brain. *Annual Review of Neuroscience, 23,* 155–184.

Lee, J. A. (1973). *The colors of love: An exploration of the ways of loving.* Don Mills, Ontario, Canada: New Press.

Lee, P.A., Houk, C.P., Ahmed, S.F., & Hughes I.A. (2006). International consensus conference on intersex organized by the Lawson Wilkins pediatric endocrine society and the European society for paediatric endocrinology: Consensus statement on management of intersex disorders. *Pediatrics, 118,* 488–500.

Lee, P. R., Brandy, D., & Koenig, J. I. (2003). Corticosterone alters N-methyl-D-aspartate receptor subunit mRNA expression before puberty. *Molecular Brain Research, 115,* 55–62.

Lee, Y.-C., Lin, Y.-C., Huang, C.-L., & Fredrickson, B. L. (2013). The construct and measurement of peace of mind. *Journal of Happiness Studies, 14,* 571–590.

Le Grange, D. (2005). The Maudsley family-based treatment for adolescent anorexia nervosa. *World Psychiatry, 4,* 142–146.

Lehman, D. R., Lempert, R. O., & Nisbett, R. E. (1988). The effects of graduate training on reasoning. *American Psychologist, 43,* 431–442.

Leibowitz, S. F., Hammer, N. J., & Chang, K. (1981). Hypothalamic paraventricular nucleus lesions produce overeating and obesity in the rat. *Physiology and Behavior, 27,* 1031–1040.

Leichtman, M. D., Wang, Q., & Pillemer, D. B. (2003). Cultural variations in interdependence and autobiographical memory: Lessons from Korea, China, India, and the United States. In R. Fivush & C. A. Haden (Eds.), *Autobiographical memory and the construction of a narrative self* (pp. 73–97). Mahwah, NJ: Erlbaum.

Leithwood, K., & Jantzi, D. (2009). A review of empirical evidence about school size effects. *Review of Educational Research, 79,* 464–490.

Leming, J. S. (1986). Kohlbergian programs in moral education: A practical review and assessment. In S. Modgil & C. Modgil (Eds.), *Lawrence Kohlberg: Consensus and controversy* (pp. 245–262, 275–276). Philadelphia: Falmer Press.

Leming, J. S. (1997). Whither goes character education? Objectives, pedagogy, and research in education programs. *Journal of Education, 179,* 11–34.

Leming, J. S. (2008). Theory, research, and practice in the early twentieth century character education movement. *Journal of Research in Character Education, 6,* 17–36.

Lenroot, R. K., & Giedd, J. N. (2010) Sex differences in the adolescent brain. *Brain and Cognition, 72,* 46–55.

Lenroot, R. K., & Giedd, J. N. (2011). Annual research review: Developmental consideration of gene by environment interactions. *Journal of Child Psychology and Psychiatry, 52,* 429–441.

Lenroot, R. K., Gogtay, N., Greenstein, D. K., Wells, E. M., Wallace, G. L., Clasen, L., et al. (2007). Sexual dimorphism of brain developmental trajectories during childhood and adolescence. *NeuroImage, 36,* 1065–1073.

Lengua, L. J., Honorado, E., & Bush, N. R. (2007). Contextual risk and parenting as predictors of effortful control and social competence in preschool children. *Journal of Applied Developmental Psychology, 28,* 40–55.

Lent, R. W., Brown, S. D., & Hackett, G. (1996). Career development from a social cognitive perspective. In D. Brown, L. Brooks, & Associates (Eds.), *Career choice and development* (3rd ed., pp. 373–421). San Francisco: Jossey-Bass.

Leong, D. J., & Bodrova, E. (2012). Assessing and scaffolding make-believe play. *Young Children, January,* 28–43.

Lerner, M. J. (1980). *The belief in a just world: A fundamental delusion.* New York: Plenum Press.

Lerner, R. M. (1996). Relative plasticity, integration, temporality, and diversity in human development: A developmental contextual perspective about theory, process, and method. *Developmental Psychology, 32,* 781–786.

Lerner, R. M. (1998). Theories of human development: Contemporary perspectives. In W. Damon (Series Ed.) & R. M. Lerner (Vol. Ed.), *Handbook of child psychology: Vol. 1. Theoretical models of human development* (5th ed., pp. 1–24). New York: Wiley.

Lerner, R. M., Fisher, C. B., & Weinberg, R. A. (2000). Toward a science for and of the people: Promoting civil society through the application of developmental science. *Child Development, 71,* 11–20.

Lerner, R. M., Rothbaum, F., Boulos, S., & Castellino, D. R. (2002). Developmental systems perspective on parenting. In M. H. Bornstein (Ed.), *Handbook of parenting, Vol. 2: Biology and ecology of parenting* (2nd ed., pp. 315–344). Mahwah, NJ: Erlbaum.

Lester, B. M., Freier, K., & LaGasse, L. (1995). Prenatal cocaine exposure and child outcome: What do we really know? In M. Lewis & M. Bendersky (Eds.), *Mothers, babies, and cocaine: The role of toxins in development* (pp. 19–39). Hillsdale, NJ: Erlbaum.

Levenson, R. W., Carstensen, L. L., & Gottman, J. M. (1993). Long-term marriage: Age, gender, and satisfaction. *Psychology and Aging, 8,* 301–313.

Levenson, R. W., Carstensen, L. L., & Gottman, J. M. (1994). Marital interaction in old and middle-age long-term marriages: Physiology, affect, and their interrelations. *Journal of Personality and Social Psychology, 67,* 56–68.

Levenson, R. W., & Gottman, J. M. (1985). Physiological and affective predictors of change in relationship satisfaction. *Journal of Personality and Social Psychology, 49,* 85–94.

Leventhal, A. M., & Martell, C. R. (2006). *The myth of depression as disease: Limitations and alternatives to drug treatment.* Westport, CT: Praeger.

Lever, J. (1978). Sex differences in the complexity of children's play and games. *American Sociological Review, 43,* 471–483.

Levin, J., & McDevitt, J. (1993). *Hate crimes: The rising tide of bigotry.* New York: Plenum Press.

Levine, S., (2000). Influence of psychological variables on the activity of the hypothalamic–pituitary–adrenal axis. *European Journal of Pharmacology. 405,* 149–160.

Levinson, D. J. (1986). A conception of adult development. *American Psychologist, 41,* 3–13.

Levinson, D. J., Darrow, C. N., Klein, E. B., Levinson, M. H., & McKee, B. (1978). *The seasons of a man's life.* New York: Knopf.

Levinson, D. J., & Levinson, J. D. (1996). *The seasons of a woman's life.* New York: Knopf.

Levitt, M. Z., & Selman, R. L. (1993). *A manual for the assessment and coding of personal meaning.* Unpublished manuscript, Harvard University, Cambridge, MA.

Levy, B. (2003). Mind matters: Cognitive and physical effects of aging self-stereotypes. *Journal of Gerontology, 58,* 203–211.

Levy, S. E., Mandell, D. S., & Schultz, R. T. (2009). Autism. *The Lancet, 374,* 1627–1638.

Lewandowsky, S., & Thomas, J. L. (2009). Expertise: Acquisition, limitations, and control. *Reviews of Human Factors and Ergonomics, 5,* 140–165.

Lewis, M. (1993). The emergence of human emotions. In M. Lewis & J. Haviland (Eds.), *Handbook of emotions* (pp. 563–573). New York: Guilford Press.

Lewis, M. (1994). Myself and me. In S. T. Parker, R. W. Mitchell, & M. L. Boccia (Eds.), *Self-awareness in animals and humans: Developmental perspectives* (pp. 20–34). New York: Cambridge University Press.

Lewis, M. (2008). Self-conscious emotions: Embarrassment, pride, shame, and guilt. In M. Lewis, J. Haviland-Jones, & L. Feldman Barrett (Eds.), *Handbook of emotions* (3rd ed., pp. 742–756). New York: Guilford Press.

Lewis, M., & Brooks-Gunn, J. (1979). *Social cognition and the acquisition of the self.* New York: Plenum Press.

Lewis, M., & Michalson, L. (1983). *Children's emotions and moods: Developmental theory and measurement.* New York: Plenum Press.

Lewis, M. D. (2000). Self-conscious emotions: Embarrassment, pride, shame, and guilt. In M. Lewis & J. Haviland (Eds.), *Handbook of emotions* (2nd ed., pp. 623–636). New York: Guilford Press.

Lewis, M. D., & Carmody, D. P. (2008). Self-representation and brain development. *Developmental Psychology, 44,* 1329–1333.

Lewis, M. D., & Ramsay, D. (2004). Development of self-recognition, personal pronoun use, and pretend play during the second year. *Child Development, 75,* 1821–1831.

Lewis, R. A., & Lin, L. W. (1996). Adults and their midlife parents. In N. Vanzetti & S. Duck (Eds.), *A lifetime of relationships* (pp. 364–382). Pacific Grove, CA: Brooks/Cole.

Lewit, E. M., & Baker, L. S. (1995). School readiness. *Critical issues for children and youths, 5,* 128–139.

Lewkowicz, D. J., & Turkewitz, G. (1980). Cross-modal equivalence in early infancy: Auditory-visual intensity matching. *Developmental Psychology, 16,* 597–607.

Lewkowicz, D. J., & Turkewitz, G. (1981). Intersensory interaction in newborns: Modification of visual preferences following exposure to sound. *Child Development, 52,* 827–832.

Li, J., Holloway, S. D., Bempechat, J., & Loh, E. (2008). Building and using a social network: Nurture for low-income Chinese American adolescents' learning. *New Directions for Child and Adolescent Development, 121,* 9–25.

Li-Korotky, H-S. (2012). Age related hearing loss: Quality of care for quality of life. *The Gerontologist, 52,* 265–271.

Liben, L. S., & Bigler, R. S. (2002). The developmental course of gender differentiation. *Monographs of the Society for Research in Child Development, 67,* 1–147.

Liben, L. S., Bigler, R. S., & Krogh, H. R. (2002). Language at work: Children's gendered interpretations of occupational titles. *Child Development, 73,* 810–828.

Liben, L. S., & Signorella, M. L. (1980). Gender-related schemata and constructive memory in children. *Child Development, 57,* 11–18.

Liben, L. S., & Signorella, M. L. (1993). Gender-schematic processing in children: The role of initial interpretations of stimuli. *Developmental Psychology, 29,* 141–149.

Lickona, T. (1998, February). A more complex analysis is needed. *Phi Delta Kappan, 79,* 449–454.

Lieberman, A. F., Chu, A., Van Horn, P., & Harris, W. W. (2011). Trauma in early childhood: Empirical evidence and clinical implications. *Development and Psychopathology, 23,* 397–410.

Lieberman, A.F., & Van Horn, P. (2005). *Don't hit my mommy: A manual for Child-parent Psychotherapy with young witnesses of family violence.* Washington, DC: Zero to Three Press.

Lien, L., Dalgard, F., Heyerdahl, S., Thoresen, M., & Bjertnessa, E. (2006). The relationship between age of menarche and mental distress in Norwegian adolescent girls and girls from different immigrant groups in Norway: Results from an urban city cross-sectional survey. *Social Science & Medicine, 62,* 285–295.

Lilenfeld, L. R., Kaye, W. H., & Strober, M. (1997). Genetics and family studies of anorexia nervosa and bulimia nervosa. *Bailliere's Clinical Psychiatry: International Practice and Research, 3,* 177–197.

Lin, J., Epel, E., & Blackburn, E. (2011). Telomeres and lifestyle factors: Roles in cellular aging. *Mutation Research, 730,* 85–89.

Linares, L. O., Heeren, T., Bronfman, E., Zuckerman, B., Augustyn, M., & Tronick, E. (2001). A mediational model for the impact of exposure to community violence on early child behavior problems. *Child Development, 72,* 639–652.

Lincoln, Y. S., & Guba, E. G. (1985). *Naturalistic inquiry.* Beverly Hills, CA: Sage.

Lindau, S. T., Schumm, L. P., Laumann, E. O., Levinson, W., O'Muircheartaigh, C. A., & Waite, L. J. (2007). A study of sexuality and health among older adults in the United States. *The New England Journal of Medicine, 357,* 762–774.

Lindquist, K. A., Wager, T. D., Kober, H., Bliss-Moreau, E., & Barrett, L. F. (2012). The brain basis of emotion: A meta-analytic review. *Behavioral and Brain Sciences, 35,* 121–143.

Lindsay, P. (1984). High school size, participation in activities, and young adult social participation: Some enduring effects of schooling. *Educational Evaluation and Policy Analysis, 6,* 73–83.

Linehan, M. (1993). *Skills training manual for treating borderline personality disorder.* New York: Guilford Press.

Liotti, G. (1992). Disorganized/disoriented attachment in the etiology of the dissociative disorders. *Dissociation, 5,* 196–204.

Liston, C., McEwen, B. S., & Casey, B. J. (2009). Psychosocial stress reversibly disrupts prefrontal processing and attentional control.

Proceedings of the National Academy of Science, 106, 912–917.

Liu, L. J., & Guo, Q. (2007). Loneliness and health-related quality of life for the empty nest elderly in the rural area of a mountainous county in China. *Quality of Life and Research, 16,* 1275–1280.

Livingston, R. W., Rosette, A. S., & Washington, E. F. (2012). Can an agentic black woman get ahead? The impact of race and interpersonal dominance on perceptions of female leaders. *Psychological Science, 23,* 354–358.

Locke, J. L. (1993). *The child's path to spoken language.* Cambridge, MA: Harvard University Press.

Lodge, J., Tripp, G., & Harte, D. K. (2000). Think-aloud, thought-listing, and video-mediated recall procedures in the assessment of children's self-talk. *Cognitive Therapy and Research, 24*(4), 399–418.

Loeber, R., Burke, J. D., & Pardini, D. A. (2009). Development and etiology of disruptive and delinquent behavior. *Annual Review of Clinical Psychology, 5,* 291–310.

Loeber, R., & Farrington, D. P. (2000). Young children who commit crime: Epidemiology, developmental origins, risk factors, early interventions, and policy implications. *Development and Psychopathology, 12,* 737–762.

Loevinger, J. (1976). *Ego development: Conception and theory.* San Francisco: Jossey-Bass.

Loftus, E. F. (1979). *Eyewitness testimony.* Cambridge, MA: Harvard University Press.

Lomax, E. M. R., Kagan, J., & Rosenkrantz, B. G. (1978). *Science and patterns of child care.* San Francisco: Freeman.

Looft, W. R. (1972). Egocentrism and social interaction across the lifespan. *Psychological Bulletin, 78,* 73–92.

Lopez, F. G., & Brennan, K. A. (2000). Dynamic processes underlying adult attachment organization: Toward an attachment theoretical perspective on the healthy and effective self. *Journal of Counseling Psychology, 47,* 283–300.

Love, J. M., Harrison, L., Sagi-Schwartz, A., van Ijzendoorn, M. H., Ross, C., Ungerer, J. A., et al. (2003). Child care quality matters: How conclusions may vary with context. *Child Development, 74,* 1021–1033.

Lovaas, O. I. (1987). Behavioral treatment and normal educational and intellectual functioning in young autistic children. *Journal of Consulting and Clinical Psychology, 55,* 3–9.

Lucas, R. E. (2007). Personality and the pursuit of happiness. *Social and Personality Psychology Compass, 1,* 168–182.

Lucas, R. E., Clark, A. E., Georgellis, Y., & Diener, E. (2004). Unemployment alters the set point for life satisfaction. *Psychological Science: Research, Theory, and Application in Psychology and Related Sciences, 15,* 8–13.

Lugo-Gil, J., & Tamis-LeMonda, C. S. (2008). Family resources and parenting quality: Links to children's cognitive development across the first 3 years. *Child Development, 79,* 1065–1085.

Lui, T., Howard, R. M., Mancini, A. J., Weston, W. L., Paller, A. S., Drolet, B. A. et al. (2001). Kwashiorkor in the United States: Fad diets, perceived and true milk allergy, and nutritional ignorance. *Archives of Dermatology, 137,* 630–636.

Lumey, L. H., Stein, A. D., Kahn, H. S., Van Der Pal-De Bruin, K. M., Blauw, G. J., Zybert, P. A. et al. (2007). Cohort profile: The Dutch Hunger Winter families study. *International Journal of Epidemiology, 36,* 1196–1204.

Luna, B., Garver, K. E., Urban, T. A., Lazar, N. A., & Sweeney, J. A. (2004). Maturation of cognitive processes from late childhood to adulthood. *Child Development, 75,* 1357–1372.

Lund, D. A., Dimond, M. F., Caserta, M. S., Johnson, R. J., Poulton, J. L., & Connelly, J. R. (1985–1986). Identifying elderly with coping difficulties after two years of bereavement. *Omega, 16,* 213–224.

Luppa, M., Sikorski, C., Luck, T., Weyerer, S., Villringer, A., König, H., et al. (2012). Prevalence and risk factors of depressive symptoms in latest life—results of the Leipzig Longitudinal Study of the Aged (LEILA 75+). *International Journal of Geriatric Psychiatry, 27,* 286–295.

Luthar, S. (2003). The culture of affluence: Psychological costs of material wealth. *Child Development, 74,* 1581–1983.

Lutz, A., Greischar, L. L., Rawlings, N. B., Ricard, M., & Davidson, R. J. (2004). Long-term meditators self-induce high-amplitude gamma synchrony during mental practice. *Proceedings of the National Academy of Sciences, 101,* 16369–16373.

Lutz, A., Slagter, H. A., Dunne, J. D., & Davidson, R. J. (2008). Attention regulation and monitoring in meditation. *Trends in Cognitive Sciences, 12,* 163–169.

Lyness, J. M. (2004). Treatment of depressive conditions in later life: Real-world light for dark (or dim) tunnels. *Journal of the American Medical Association, 291,* 1626–1628.

Lynn, J. (2000). Learning to care for people with chronic illness facing the end of life. *Journal of the American Medical Association, 284,* 2508–2513.

Lyons-Ruth, K. (1996). Attachment relationships among children with aggressive behavior problems: The role of disorganized early attachment patterns. *Journal of Consulting and Clinical Psychology, 64,* 64–73.

Lytton, H., & Romney, D. M. (1991). Parents' differential socialization of boys and girls: A meta-analysis. *Psychological Bulletin, 109,* 267–296.

Lyubomirsky, S. (2001). Why are some people happier than others? The role of cognitive and motivational processes in well-being. *American Psychologist, 56,* 239–249.

Lyubomirsky, S., King, L. A., & Diener, E. (2005). The benefits of frequent positive affect: Does happiness lead to success? *Psychological Bulletin, 131,* 803–855.

Ma, H., & Teasdale, J. (2004). Mindfulness-based cognitive therapy for depression: Replication and exploration of differential relapse prevention effects. *Journal of Consulting and Clinical Psychology, 72,* 31–40.

Maccoby, E. E. (1990). Gender and relationships: A developmental account. *American Psychologist, 45,* 513–520.

Maccoby, E. E. (1998). *The two sexes: Growing up apart, coming together.* Cambridge, MA: Harvard University Press.

Maccoby, E. E. (2002). Gender and group process: A developmental perspective. *Current Directions in Psychological Sciences, 11,* 54–58.

Maccoby, E. E., & Jacklin, C. N. (1974). *The psychology of sex differences.* Stanford, CA: Stanford University Press.

Maccoby, E. E., & Martin, J. A. (1983). Socialization in the context of the family: Parent-child interaction. In P. H. Mussen (Series Ed.) & E. M. Hetherington (Vol. Ed.), *Handbook of child psychology: Vol. 4. Socialization, personality and social development* (4th ed., pp. 1–101). New York: Wiley.

MacDonald, K. B., & Parke, R. D. (1986). Parent-child physical play: The effects of sex and age of children and parents. *Sex Roles, 15,* 367–379.

MacDonald, S. W. S., Hultsch, D. F., & Dixon, R. A. (2011). Aging and the shape of cognitive change before death: Terminal decline or terminal drop? *The Journals of Gerontology, Series B: Psychological Sciences and Social Sciences, 66,* 292–301.

Mace, N. L., & Rabins, P. V. (1999). *The 36-hour-day: A family guide to caring for persons with Alzheimer's disease, related dementing illnesses, and memory of later in life* (3rd ed.). Baltimore: Johns Hopkins University Press.

Macfie, J., Cicchetti, D., & Toth, S. L. (2001). Dissociation in maltreated versus nonmaltreated preschool-aged children. *Child Abuse & Neglect, 25,* 1253–1267.

MacKay, D. G., & Abrams, L. (1996). Language, memory, and aging: Distributed deficits and the structure of new-versus-old connections. In J. E. Birren & K. W. Schaie (Series Eds.), R. P. Abeles, M. Gatz, & T. A. Salthouse (Vol. Eds.), *Handbook of the psychology of aging* (4th ed., pp. 287–307). San Diego, CA: Academic Press.

Mackie, S., Shaw, P., Lenroot, R., Pierson, R., Greenstein, D. K., Nugent, T .F., 3rd, et al. (2007). Cerebellar development and clinical outcome in attention deficit hyperactivity disorder. *American Journal of Psychiatry, 164,* 647–655.

MacLean, P. D. (1952). Some psychiatric implications of the physiological studies on the frontotemporal portion of the limbic system. *Electroencephalography and Clinical Neurophysiology, 4,* 407–418.

MacLean, P. D. (1970). The triune brain, emotion, and scientific basis. In F. O. Schmidt (Ed.), *The neurosciences: Second study program* (pp. 336–349). New York: Rockefeller University Press.

Maercker, A., & Zoellner, T. (2004). The Janus-face of self-perceived growth: Toward a two-component model of posttraumatic growth. *Psychological Inquiry, 15,* 41–48.

Maggs, J. L., Almeida, D. M., & Galambos, N. L. (1995). Risky business: The paradoxical meaning of problem behavior for young adolescents. *Journal of Early Adolescence, 15,* 344–362.

Magnuson, K. A., & Duncan, G. J. (2006). The role of family socioeconomic resources in the black-white test score gap among young children. *Developmental Review, 26,* 365–399.

Mahler, M. S., Pine, F., & Bergman, A. (1975). *The psychological birth of the human infant: Symbiosis and individuation.* New York: Basic Books.

Mahoney, J. L. (2000). School extracurricular activity participation as a moderator in the development of antisocial patterns. *Child Development, 71,* 502–516.

Mahoney, J. L., Harris, A. L., & Eccles, J. S. (2006). Organized activity participation, positive youth development, and the over-scheduling hypothesis. *Society for Research in Child Development Social Policy Report, 20,* 1–30.

Mahoney, J. L., Larson, R. W., & Eccles, J. S. (2005). *Organized activities as contexts of development: Extracurricular activities, after-school and community programs.* Mahwah, NJ: Erlbaum.

Maier, S. F., & Watkins, L. R. (1998). Cytokines for psychologists: Implications of bi-directional immune-to-brain communication for understanding behavior, mood, and cognition. *Psychological Review, 105,* 83–107.

Maier, S. F., Watkins, L. R., & Fleshner, M. (1994). Psychoneuroimmunology: The interface between behavior, brain and immunity. *American Psychologist, 49,* 1004–1017.

Main, M. (1996). Overview of the field of attachment. *Journal of Consulting and Clinical Psychology, 64,* 237–243.

Main, M. (1999). Epilogue: Attachment theory: Eighteen points with suggestions for future studies. In J. Cassidy & P. R. Shaver (Eds.), *Handbook of attachment: Theory, research, and clinical applications* (pp. 845–887). New York: Guilford Press.

Main, M., & George, C. (1985). Responses of abused and disadvantaged toddlers to distress in agemates: A study in the day care setting. *Developmental Psychology, 21,* 407–412.

Main, M., & Goldwyn, R. (1984). Predicting rejection of her infant from mother's representation of her own experience: Implications for the abused-abusing intergenerational cycle. *International Journal of Child Abuse and Neglect, 8,* 203–217.

Main, M., & Goldwyn, R. (1985–1994). *Adult attachment classification system.* Unpublished manuscript, University of California at Berkeley.

Main, M., & Hesse, E. (1992). *Frightening, frightened, timid/deferential, dissociated, or disorganized behavior on the part of the parent: Coding system.* Unpublished manuscript, University of California at Berkeley.

Main, M., Kaplan, N., & Cassidy, J. (1985). Security in infancy, childhood, and adulthood: A move to the level of representation. In I. Bretherton & E. Waters (Eds.), Growing points of attachment theory and research. *Monographs of the Society for Research in Child Development, 50* (Serial No. 209), 55–104.

Main, M., & Solomon, J. (1986) Discovery of a new, insecure-disorganized/disoriented attachment pattern. In T. B. Brazelton & M. Yogman (Eds.), *Affective Development in Infancy* (pp. 95–124). Norwood, NJ: Ablex.

Main, M., & Solomon, J. (1990). Procedures for identifying infants as disorganized/disoriented during the Ainsworth strange situation. In M. Greenberg, D. Cicchetti, & E. M. Cummings (Eds.), *Attachment in the preschool years: Theory, research, and intervention* (pp. 121–160). Chicago: University of Chicago Press.

Majidi, N. E., Bouchard, M. H., Gosselin, N., & Carrier, G. (2012). Relationship between prenatal exposure to polychlorinated biphenyls and birth weight: A systematic analysis of published epidemiological studies through a standardization of biomonitoring data. *Regulatory Toxicology and Pharmacology, 64,* 161–176.

Malgady, R. G., Rogler, L. H., & Costantino, G. (1990). Hero/heroine modeling for Puerto Rican adolescents: A preventive mental health intervention. *Journal of Consulting and Clinical Psychology, 58,* 469–474.

Malina, R. M. (1983). Menarche in athletes: A synthesis and hypothesis. *Annals of Human Biology, 10,* 1–24.

Malina, R. M. (1990). Physical growth and performance during the transitional years (9–16). In R. Montemayor, G. R. Adams, & T. P. Gullotta (Eds.), *From childhood to adolescence: A transitional period?* (pp. 41–62). Newbury Park, CA: Sage.

Malti, T., Gummerum, M., Keller, M., & Buchmann, M. (2009). Children's moral motivation, sympathy, and prosocial behavior. *Child Development, 80,* 442–460.

Mandler, J. M. (2004). *The foundations of mind: Origins of conceptual thought.* New York: Oxford University Press.

Mangelsdorf, S., Gunnar, M., Kestenbaum, R., Lang, S., & Andreas, D. (1990). Infant proneness-to-distress temperament, maternal personality, and mother-infant attachment: Associations and goodness of fit. *Child Development, 61,* 820–831.

Mansfield, E. D., & McAdams, D. P. (1996). Generativity and themes of agency and communion in adult autobiography. *Personality and Social Psychology Bulletin, 22,* 721–731.

Marcia, J. E. (1964). *Determination and construct validity of ego identity status*. Unpublished doctoral dissertation, University of California at Davis.

Marcia, J. E. (1966). Development and validation of ego identity status. *Journal of Personality and Social Psychology, 3*, 551–558.

Marcia, J. E. (1967). Ego identity status: Relationship to change in self-esteem, "general maladjustment," and authoritarianism. *Journal of Personality, 35*, 118–133.

Marcia, J. E. (1980). Identity in adolescence. In J. Adelson (Ed.), *Handbook of adolescent psychology* (pp. 159–187). New York: Wiley.

Marcia, J. E. (1989). Identity and intervention. *Journal of Intervention, 12*, 401–410.

Marcia, J. E. (1993). The status of the statuses: Research review. In J. E. Marcia, A. S. Waterman, D. R. Matteson, S. L. Archer, & J. L. Orlofsky (Eds.), *Ego identity: A handbook for psychosocial research* (pp. 22–41). New York: Springer-Verlag.

Marcia, J. E., & Friedman, M. L. (1970). Ego identity status in college women. *Journal of Personality, 38*, 249–263.

Marcia, J. E., Waterman, A. S., Matteson, D. R., Archer, S. L., & Orlofsky, J. L. (1993). *Ego identity: A handbook for psychosocial research*. New York: Springer-Verlag.

Marco, C. A., & Suls, J. (1993). Daily stress and the trajectory of mood: Spillover, response assimilation contrast, and negative affectivity. *Journal of Personality and Social Psychology, 64*, 1053–1063.

Marcus, R. F. (1975). The child as elicitor of parental sanctions for independent and dependent behavior: A simulation of parent-child interaction. *Developmental Psychology, 11*, 443–452.

Marcus, R. F. (1976). The effects of children's emotional and instrumental dependent behavior on parental response. *Journal of Psychology, 92*, 57–63.

Markides, K. S., & Coreil, J. (1986). The health of Hispanics in the southwestern United States: An epidemiologic paradox. *Public Health Reports, 101*, 253–265.

Markman, H. J., Stanley, S., & Blumberg, S. L. (1994). *Fighting for your marriage: Positive steps for preventing divorce and preserving a lasting love*. San Francisco: Jossey-Bass.

Marks, N. F., Bumpass, L. L., & Jun, H. (2003). Family roles and well-being during the middle life course. In O. G. Brim, C. D. Ryff, & R. Kessler, (Eds.), *How healthy are we: A national study of well-being in midlife* (pp. 514–549). Chicago: University of Chicago Press.

Markus, H. (1977). Self-schemata and processing information about the self. *Journal of Personality and Social Psychology, 35*, 63–78.

Markus, H., Crane, M., Bernstein, S., & Siladi, M. (1982). Self-schemas and gender. *Journal of Personality and Social Psychology, 42*, 38–50.

Markus, H., & Kitayama, S. (1991). Culture and the self: Implications for cognition, emotion, and motivation. *Psychological Review, 98*, 224–253.

Markus, H. R., & Kitayama, S. (2010). Cultures and selves: A cycle of mutual constitution. *Perspectives on Psychological Science, 5*, 420–430.

Markus, H., & Nurius, P. (1986). Possible selves. *American Psychologist, 41*, 954–969.

Marmot, M., & Wilkinson, R. (2009). Social determinants of health. The life course, the social gradient, and health. Published to Oxford Scholarship Online: September 2009, doi: 10.1093/acprof:oso/9780198565895.001.0001

Marsh, H. W. (1990). The structure of academic self-concept: The Marsh/Shavelson model. *Journal of Educational Psychology, 82*, 623–636.

Marsh, H. W. (1994). Using the National Longitudinal Study of 1988 to evaluate theoretical models of self-concept: The Self-Description Questionnaire. *Journal of Educational Psychology, 86*, 107–116.

Marsh, H. W., & Hattie, J. (1996). Theoretical perspectives on the structure of the self-concept. In B. A. Bracken (Ed.), *Handbook of self-concept* (pp. 38–90). New York: Wiley.

Marsh, H. W., & Roche, L. A. (1996). Structure of artistic self-concepts for performing arts and non-performing arts students in a performing arts high school: "Setting the stage" with multigroup confirmatory factor analysis. *Journal of Educational Psychology, 88*, 461–477.

Marsh, H. W., & Shavelson, R. (1985). Self-concept: Its multifaceted, hierarchical structure. *Educational Psychologist, 20*, 107–123.

Martel, J. G. (1974). *Smashed potatoes: A kid's-eye view of the kitchen*. Boston: Houghton Mifflin.

Martin, C. D. (2000). More than the work: Race and gender differences in caregiving burden. *Journal of Family Issues, 21*, 986–1005.

Martin, C. L., & Fabes, R. A. (2001). The stability and consequences of young children's same-sex peer interactions. *Developmental Psychology, 37*, 431–446.

Martin, C. L., Fabes, R. A., Hanish, L. D., & Hollenstein, T. (2005). Social dynamics in the preschool. *Developmental Review, 25*, 299–327.

Martin, C. L., & Ruble, D. N. (2009). Patterns of gender development. *Annual Review of Psychology, 61*, 353–381.

Martin, C. L., Ruble, D. N., & Szkrybalo, J. (2002). Cognitive theories of early gender development. *Psychological Bulletin, 128*, 903–933.

Martinson, I. M., Davies, B., & McClowry, S. (1991). Parental depression following death of a child. *Death Studies, 15*, 259–267.

Martire, L. M., Stephens, M. A. P., & Townsend, A. L. (1998). Emotional support and well-being of midlife women: Role-specific mastery as a mediational mechanism. *Psychology and Aging, 13*, 196–404.

Marvin, R. S., Cooper, G., Hoffman, K., & Powell, B. (2002). The Circle of Security project: Attachment-based intervention with caregiver-preschool child dyads. *Attachment and Human Development, 4*, 107–124.

Marx, K., & Engels, F. (1972). The German ideology. In R. C. Tucker (Ed.), *The Marx-Engels reader*. New York: Norton. (Original work published 1846)

Masangkay, Z. S., McCluskey, K. A., McIntyre, C. W., Sims-Knight, J., Vaughn, B. E., & Flavell, J. H. (1974). The early development of inferences about the visual percepts of others. *Child Development, 45*, 237–246.

Mashburn, A. J., Pianta, R. C., Barbarin, O. A., Bryant, D., Hamre, B. K., Downer, J. T., et al. (2008). Measures of classroom quality in prekindergarten and children's development of academic, language, and social skills. *Child Development, 79*, 732–749.

Maslow, A. H. (1954). *Motivation and personality*. New York: Harper & Row.

Mastekaasa, A. (1994). Marital status, distress, and well-being: An international comparison. *Journal of Comparative Family Studies, 25*, 183–206.

Masters, W. H., Johnson, V. E., & Kolodny, R. C. (1988). *Human sexuality* (3rd ed.). Boston: Little, Brown.

Masuda, T., & Nisbett, R. E. (2001). Attending holistically versus analytically: Comparing the context sensitivity of Japanese and Americans. *Journal of Personality and Social Psychology, 81*, 922–934.

Masuda, T., & Nisbett, R. E. (2006). Culture and change blindness. *Cognitive Sciences, 30*, 381–399.

Mather, M., Canli, T., English, T., Whitfield, S., Wais, P., Ochsner, K., et al. (2004). Amygdala responses to emotionally valenced stimuli in older and younger adults. *Psychological Science, 15*, 259–263.

Matsuzawa, J., Matsui, M., Konishi, T., Noguchi, K., Gur, R. C., Bilker, W., et al. (2001). Age-related changes of brain gray and white matter in healthy infants and children. *Cerebral Cortex, 11*, 335–342.

Matteson, D. R. (1993). Differences within and between genders: A challenge to the theory. In J. E. Marcia, A. S. Waterman, D. R. Matteson, S. L. Archer, & J. L. Orlofsky (Eds.), *Ego identity: A handbook for psychosocial research* (pp. 69–110). New York: Springer-Verlag.

Mattson, M. P., Chan, S. L., & Duan, W. (2002). Modification of brain aging and neurodegenerative disorders by genes, diet, and behavior. *Physiological Review, 82*, 637–672.

Mau, W. (1995). Educational planning and academic achievement of middle school students: A racial and cultural comparison. *Journal of Counseling and Development, 73*, 518–526.

Mauer, M. (2013). The changing racial dynamics of women's incarceration. Washington, DC: The Sentencing Project. Retrieved from http://sentencingproject.org/doc/publications/rd_Changing%20Racial%20Dynamics%202013.pdf

May, P. A., Serna, P., Hurt, B. L., & DeBruyn, L. M. (2005). Outcome Evaluation of a Public Health Approach to Suicide Prevention in an American Indian Tribal Nation. *American Journal of Public Health, 95*(7), 1238–1244.

May, R. (1979). *Psychology and the human dilemma*. New York: Norton.

Mayer, J. D., & Cobb, C. D. (2000). Educational policy on emotional intelligence. Does it make sense? *Educational Psychology Review, 12*, 163–183.

Mays, V. M., Cochran, S. D., & Barnes, N. W. (2007). Race, race-based discrimination and health outcomes among African-Americans. *Annual Review of Psychology, 58*, 201–225.

Maxwell, J. S., Shackman, A. J., & Davidson, R. J. (2005). Unattended facial expressions asymmetrically bias the concurrent processing of nonemotional information. *Journal of Cognitive Neuroscience 17*(9), 1386–1395.

McAdams, D. P. (2000). Attachment, intimacy, and generativity. *Psychological Inquiry, 11*, 117–120.

McAdams, D. P. (2006). The redemptive self: Generativity and the stories Americans live by. *Research in Human Development, 3*, 81–100.

McAdams, D. P., & Bowman, P. J. (2001). Narrating life's turning points: Redemption and contamination. In D. P. McAdams, R. Josselson, & A. Lieblich (Eds.), *Turns in the road: Narrative studies of lives in transition* (pp. 3–34). Washington, DC: American Psychological Association.

McAdams, D. P., & de St. Aubin, E. (1992). A theory of generativity and its assessment through self-report, behavioral acts, and narrative themes in autobiography. *Journal of Personality and Social Psychology, 62*, 1003–1015.

McAdams, D. P., de St. Aubin, E., & Logan, R. L. (1993). Generativity among young, midlife, and older adults. *Psychology and Aging, 8*, 221–230.

McAdams, D. P., Hart, H. M., & Maruna, S. (1998). The anatomy of generativity. In D. P. McAdams & E. de St. Aubin (Eds.), *Generativity and adult development: How and why we care for the next generation* (pp. 7–44). Washington, DC: American Psychological Association.

McAdams, D. P., & Olson, B. D. (2010). Personality development: Continuity and change over the life course. *Annual Review of Psychology, 61,* 517–542.

McAlister, A., & Peterson, C. C. (2006). Mental playmates: Siblings, executive functioning and theory of mine. *British Journal of Developmental Psychology, 24,* 733–751.

McAuliffe, G. J. (1993). Constructive development and career transition: Implications for counseling. *Journal of Counseling and Development, 72,* 23–28.

McBride, S. L., & DiCero, K. (1990). Separation: Maternal and child perspectives. In N. Lauter-Klatell (Ed.), *Readings in child development.* Mountain View, CA: Mayfield.

McCann, I. L., & Pearlman, L. A. (1990),. Vicarious traumatization: A framework for understanding the psychological effects of working with victims. *Journal of Traumatic Stress, 3,* 131–149.

McCartney, K., Burchinal, M., Clarke-Stewart, A., Bub, K. L., Owen, M. T., Belsky, J., et al. (2010). Testing a series of causal propositions relating time in child care to children's externalizing behavior. *Developmental Psychology, 46,* 1–17.

McCartney, K., Dearing, E., Taylor, B. A., & Bub, K. L. (2007). Quality child care supports the achievement of low-income children: Direct and indirect pathways through caregiving and the home environment. *Journal of Applied Developmental Psychology, 28,* 411–426.

McCauley, T., & White, D. A. (2011). A latent variables examination of processing speed, response inhibition, and working memory during typical development. *Journal of Experimental Child Psychology, 108,* 453–468.

McClellan, B. E. (1992). *Schools and the shaping of character: Moral education in America, 1607–present.* Bloomington, IN: ERIC Clearinghouse for Social Studies/Social Science Education and the Social Studies Development Center.

McClelland, M. M., & Cameron, C. E. (2012). Self-regulation in early childhood: Improving conceptual clarity and developing ecologically valid measures. *Child Development Perspectives, 6,* 136–142.

McClure, E. B. (2000). A meta-analytic review of sex differences in facial expression processing and their development in infants, children, and adolescents. *Psychological Bulletin, 126,* 424–453.

McConnell, S. R., & Odom, S. L. (1986). Sociometrics: Peer-referenced measures and the assessment of social competence. In P. S. Strain, M. J. Guralnick, & H. M. Walker (Eds.), *Children's social behavior: Development, assessment, and modification* (pp. 215–284). New York: Academic Press.

McCrae, R., & Costa, P. T. (Eds.). (2003). *Personality in adulthood: A five-factor theory perspective* (2nd ed.). New York: Guilford Press.

McCrae, R. R., & Costa, P. T. (2008). The five-factor theory of personality. In O. P. John, R. W. Robins, & L. A. Pervin (Eds.), *Handbook of personality: Theory and research* (3rd ed., pp. 159–181). New York: Guilford Press.

McCrae, R. R., Costa, P. T., Ostendorf, F., Angleitner, A., Hrebickova, M., Avia, J., et al. (2000). Nature over nurture: Temperament, personality and life span development. *Journal of Personality and Social Psychology, 78,* 173–186.

McCrae, R. R., Costa, P. T., Pedroso de Lima, M., Simoes, A., Ostendorf, F., Angleitner, A., et al. (1999). Age differences in personality across the adult life span: Parallels in five cultures. *Developmental Psychology, 35,* 466–477.

McCrae, R. R., & John, O. T. (1992). An introduction to the five-factor model and its applications. *Journal of Personality, 60,* 175–215.

McCue, M., Bacon, S., & Lykken, D. T. (1993). Personality stability and change in early adulthood: A behavioral genetic analysis. *Developmental Psychology, 29,* 96–109.

McCullough, M. E., Pargament, K. I., & Thoresen, C. T. (Eds.). (2002). *Forgiveness: Theory, research and practice.* New York: Guilford Press.

McCullough, M. E., & Witvliet, C. V. (2002). The psychology of forgiveness. In C. R. Snyder & S. J. Lopez (Eds.), *Handbook of positive psychology* (pp. 446–458). New York: Oxford University Press.

McEachin, J. J., Smith, T., & Lovaas, O. I. (1993). Long-term outcome for children with autism who received early intensive behavioral treatment. *American Journal of Mental Retardation, 97,* 359–391.

McElwain, A. K., Korabik, K., & Rosin, H. M. (2005). An examination of gender differences in work-family conflict. *Canadian Journal of Behavioral Science, 37,* 283–298.

McEwen, B. (1998) Protective and damaging effects of stress mediators. *New England Journal of Medicine, 338,* 171–179.

McEwen, B. S. (2005). Glucocorticoids, depression, and mood disorders: Structural remodeling in the brain. *Metabolism: Clinical and Experimental, 54,* 20–23.

McEwen, B. S. (2012). Brain on stress: How the social environment gets under the skin. *Proceedings of the National Academy of Sciences of the United States of America, 109,* 171–180.

McEwen, B. S., & Gianaros, P. J. (2010). Central role of the brain in stress and adaptation: Links to socioeconomic status, health, and disease. *Annals of the New York Academy of Sciences, 1186,* 190–222.

McEwen, B. S., & Sapolsky, R. M. (1995). Stress and cognitive function. *Current Opinion in Neurobiology, 5,* 205–216.

McEwen, B. S., & Seeman, T. (1999). Protective and damaging effects of stress mediators: Elaborating and testing the concepts of allostasis and allostatic load. In N. E. Adler, M. Marmot, B. S. McEwen, & J. Stewart. (Eds.). Annals of the New York Academy of Sciences: Vol. 896. *Socioeconomic status and health in industrialized nations- Social, psychological, and biological pathways* (pp. 30–47). New York: NY Academy of Sciences.

McEwen, B. S., & Stellar, E. (1993). Stress and the individual: Mechanisms leading to disease. *Archives of Internal Medicine, 153,* 2093–2101.

McGillicuddy-DeLisi, A. V., Daly, M., & Neal, A. (2006). Children's distributive justice judgments: Aversive racism in Euro-American children? *Child Development, 77,* 1063–1080.

McGuigan, F., & Salmon, K. (2004). The time to talk: The influence of the timing of adult-child talk on children's event memory. *Child Development, 75,* 669–686.

McHale, S. M., Crouter, A. C., & Whiteman, S. D. (2003). The family contexts of gender development in childhood in adolescence. *Social Development, 12,* 125–148.

McHale, S. M., Kim, J-Y., Dotterer, A. M., Crouter, A. C., & Booth, A. (2009). The development of gendered interests and personality qualities from middle childhood through adolescence: A biosocial analysis. *Child Development, 80,* 482–495.

McKeever, V. M., & Huff, M. E. (2003). A diathesis-stress model of posttraumatic stress disorder: Ecological, biological, and residual stress pathways. *Review of General Psychology, 7,* 237–250.

McLoyd, V. C., & Smith, J. (2002). Physical discipline and behavior problems in African American, European American, and Hispanic children: Emotional support as a moderator. *Journal of Marriage and the Family, 64,* 40–54.

McMahon, J. R., Greenberg, M. T., & the Conduct Problems Prevention Research Group [CPPRG]. (1995). The Fast Track Program: A developmentally focused intervention for children with conduct problems. *Clinician's Research Digest* (Suppl. Bulletin 13), 1–2.

McNeil, N. M., Fyfe, E. R., Petersen, L. A., Dunwiddie, A. E., & Brletic-Shipley, H. (2011). Benefits of practicing $4 = 2 + 2$: Nontraditional problem formats facilitate children's understanding of mathematical equivalence. *Child Development, 82,* 1620–1633.

McNulty, J. K., & Karney, B. R. (2004). Positive expectations in the early years of marriage: Should couples expect the best or brace for the worst? *Journal of Personality and Social Psychology, 86,* 729–743.

Mead, M. (1928). *Coming of age in Samoa: A psychological study of primitive youth for western civilization.* New York: William Morrow.

Mead, G. H. (1934). *Mind, self, and society.* Chicago: University of Chicago Press.

Meaney M. (2001). Maternal care, gene expression, and the transmission of individual differences in stress reactivity across generations. *Annual Review of Neuroscience, 24,* 1161–1192.

Meaney, M. J. (2010). Epigenetics and the biological definition of gene × environment interactions. *Child Development, 81,* 41–79.

Meaney, M. J., Diorio, J., Donaldson, L., Yau, J., Chapman, K., & Seckl, J. R. (2000). Handling alters the expression of messenger RNAs for AP-2, NGFI-A and NGFI-B in the hippocampus of neonatal rats. *Journal of Neuroscience, 20,* 3936–3945.

Meeus, W. (1996). Studies on identity development in adolescence: An overview of research and some new data. *Journal of Youth and Adolescence, 25,* 569–597.

Meeus, W., & Dekovic, M. (1995). Identity development, parental and peer support in adolescence: Results of a national Dutch study. *Adolescence, 30,* 931–944.

Meeus, W., Iedema, J., Helsen, M., & Vollebergh, W. (1999). Patterns of adolescent identity development: Review of literature and longitudinal analysis. *Developmental Review, 19,* 419–461.

Meezan, W., & Rauch, J. (2005). Gay marriage, same-sex parenting, and America's children. *The Future of Children, 15,* 97–115.

Meichenbaum, D. (1986). Cognitive behavior modification. In F. Kanfer & A. Goldstein (Eds.), *Helping people change: A textbook of methods* (3rd ed., pp. 346–380). New York: Pergamon Press.

Meichenbaum, D. H., & Goodman, J. (1971). Training impulsive children to talk to themselves: A means for self-control. *Journal of Abnormal Psychology, 77,* 115–126.

Meijer, A. M., & van den Wittenboer, G. L. H. (2007). Contribution of infants' sleep and crying to marital relationship of first-time parent couples in the 1st year after childbirth. *Journal of Family Psychology, 21,* 49–57.

Meir, E. I. (1989). Integrative elaboration of the congruence theory. *Journal of Vocational Behavior, 35,* 219–230.

Meletis, C. D., & Wood, S. G. (2009). *His change of life: Male menopause and healthy aging with testosterone.* Westport CT: Praeger.

Melinder, A., Forbes, D., Tronick, E., Fikke, L. M., & Gredeback, G. (2010). The development of the still-face effect: Mothers do matter. *Infant Behavior and Development, 33,* 472–481.

Meltzoff, A. N. (1988). Infant imitation and memory: Nine-month-old infants in immediate and deferred tests. *Child Development, 59,* 217–225.

Meltzoff, A. N. (1990). Foundations for developing a concept of self: The role of imitation in relating self to other and the value of social mirroring, social modeling, and self practice in infancy. In D. Cicchetti & M. Beeghly (Eds.), *The self in transition: Infancy to childhood* (pp. 139–164). Chicago: University of Chicago Press.

Meltzoff, A. N., & Borton, R. W. (1979). Intermodal matching by human neonates. *Nature, 282,* 403–404.

Meltzoff, A. N., & Moore, M. K. (1977). Imitation of facial and manual gestures by human neonates. *Science, 198,* 75–78.

Mendle, J., Turkheimer, E., & Emery, R. E. (2007). Detrimental psychological outcomes associated with early pubertal timing in adolescent girls. *Developmental Review, 27,* 151–171.

Menon, M. (2011). Does felt gender compatibility mediate influences of self-perceived gender nonconformity on early adolescents' psychosocial adjustment? *Child Development, 82,* 1152–1162.

Mercer, J., Sarner, L., & Rosa, L. (2003). *Attachment therapy on trial: The torture and death of Candace Newmaker.* Westport, CT: Praeger.

Merewood, A. (1991, April). Sperm under siege. *Health,* 53–57, 76–77.

Mesman, J., van IJzendoorn, M. H., Bakermans-Kranenburg, M. J. (2009). The many faces of the still-face paradigm: A review and meta-analysis. *Developmental Review, 29,* 120–162.

Metcalf, P., & Huntington, R. (1991). *Celebrations of death: The anthology of mortuary ritual* (2nd ed.). New York: Cambridge University Press.

Meyer, A. (1957). *Psychobiology: A science of man.* Springfield, IL: Charles C. Thomas.

Meyer, I. H. (2003). Prejudice, social stress, and mental health in lesbian, gay, and bisexual populations: Conceptual issues and research evidence. *Psychological Bulletin, 129,* 674–697.

Meyer-Bahlberg, H. F. (2005). Gender identity outcome in female-raised 46, XY persons with penile agenesis, cloacal exstrophy of the bladder, or penile ablation. *Archives of Sexual Behavior, 34,* 423–438.

Michelson, L., Sugai, D., Wood, R., & Kazdin, A. E. (1983). *Social skills assessment and training with children: An empirical handbook.* New York: Plenum Press.

Middleton, W., Raphael, B., Burnett, P., & Martinek, N. (1997). Psychological distress and bereavement. *Journal of Nervous and Mental Diseases, 185,* 447–453.

Midgley, C., Fedlaufer, H., & Eccles, J. S. (1988). The transition to junior high school: Beliefs of pre- and post-transition teachers. *Journal of Youth and Adolescence, 17,* 543–562.

Midgley, C., Feldlaufer, H., & Eccles, J. S. (1989). Student/teacher relations and attitudes toward mathematics before and after the transition to junior high school. *Child Development, 60,* 981–992.

Mihalic, S. W., & Elliot, D. (1997). Short- and long-term consequences of adolescent work. *Youth and Society, 28,* 464–498.

Mikulincer, M., & Arad, D. (1999). Attachment working models and cognitive openness in close relationships: A test of chronic and temporary accessibility effects. *Journal of Personality and Social Psychology, 77,* 710–725.

Mikulincer, M., & Florian, V. (1998). The relationship between adult attachment styles and emotional and cognitive reactions to stressful events. In J. A. Simpson & W. S. Rholes (Eds.), *Attachment theory and close relationships* (pp. 143–165). New York: Guilford Press.

Mikulincer, M., & Shaver, P. R. (2007). *Attachment in adulthood: Structure, dynamics, and change.* New York: Guilford Press.

Miller, A. (1981). *The drama of the gifted child.* New York: Basic Books.

Miller, D. L. (1983). Developmental changes in male/female voice classification by infants. *Infant Behavior and Development, 6,* 313–330.

Miller, G. E., Cohen, S., & Ritchey, A. K. (2002). Chronic psychological stress and the regulation of pro-inflammatory cytokines: A glucocorticoid-resistance model. *Health Psychology, 21,* 531–541.

Miller, J. B. (1991). The development of women's sense of self. In J. V. Jordan, A. G. Kaplan, J. B. Miller, I. P. Stiver, & J. L. Surrey (Eds.), *Women's growth in connection* (pp. 11–26). New York: Guilford Press.

Miller, J. G. (1999). Cultural psychology: Implications for basic psychological theory. *Psychological Science, 10,* 85–91.

Miller, J. G. (2006). Insights into moral development from cultural psychology. In M. Killen & J. Smetana (Eds.), *Handbook of moral development.* New York: Erlbaum.

Miller, P. A., & Eisenberg, N. (1988). The relation of empathy to aggression and externalizing/ antisocial behavior. *Psychological Bulletin, 103,* 324–344.

Miller, P. A., Eisenberg, N., Fabes, R. A., & Shell, R. (1996). Relations of moral reasoning and vicarious emotion to young children's prosocial behavior toward peers and adults. *Developmental Psychology, 32,* 210–219.

Miller, P. H. (1994). Individual differences in children's strategic behavior: Utilization deficiencies. *Learning and Individual Differences, 6,* 285–307.

Miller, P. J., Fung, H., Lin, S., Chen, E. C-H., & Boldt, B. R. (2012). How socialization happens on the ground: Narrative practices as alternate socializing pathways in Taiwanese and European-American families. *Monographs of the Society for Research in Child Development, 77* (1, Serial No. 302).

Miller, R. S. (1997). We always hurt the ones we love: Aversive interactions in close relationships. In R. M. Kowalski (Ed.), *Aversive interpersonal behaviors* (pp. 11–29). New York: Plenum Press.

Miller, S. A. (2012). *Theory of mind: Beyond the preschool years.* New York: Psychology Press.

Miller, S. M., & Green, M. L. (1984). Coping with stress and frustration: Origins, nature, and development. In M. Lewis & C. Saarni (Eds.), *The socialization of emotions* (pp. 263–314). New York: Plenum Press.

Miller, W. R., & Rollnick, S. (1991). *Motivational interviewing: Preparing people to change addictive behavior.* New York: Guilford Press.

Minuchin, S. (1974). *Families and family therapy.* Cambridge, MA: Harvard University Press.

Mitka, M. (2000). Suggestions for help when the end is near. *Journal of the American Medical Association, 284,* 2441–2444.

Mix, K. S., Moore, J. A., & Holcomb E. (2011). One-to-one play promotes numerical equivalence concepts. *Journal of Cognition and Development, 12,* 463–480.

Moffitt, T. E. (1993a). Adolescence-limited and life-course persistent antisocial behavior: A developmental taxonomy. *Psychological Bulletin, 100,* 674–701.

Moffitt, T. E. (1993b). The neuropsychology of conduct disorder. *Development and Psychopathology, 5,* 135–151.

Moffitt, T. E., Caspi, A., Belsky, J., & Silva, P. A. (1992). Childhood experience and the onset of menarche. *Child Development, 63,* 47–53.

Moffit, T. E., Caspi, A., Harrington, H., & Milne, B. J. (2002). Males on the life-course-persistent and adolescent-limited antisocial pathways: Follow-up at age 26 years. *Development and Psychopathology, 14,* 179–207.

Moffit, T. E., Caspi, A., Rutter, M., & Silva, P. A. (2001). *Sex differences in antisocial behavior.* New York: Cambridge Press.

Moffitt, T. E., & Lynam, D. R. (1994). The neuropsychology of conduct disorder and delinquency: Implications for understanding antisocial behavior. In D. C. Fowles, P. Sutker, & S. H. Goodman (Eds.), *Progress in experimental personality and psychopathology research* (pp. 233–262). New York: Springer-Verlag.

Molenberghs, P., Cunnington, R., & Mattingly, J. B. (2012). Brain regions with mirror properties: A meta-analysis of 125 human fMRI studies. *Neuroscience and Biobehavioral Reviews, 36,* 341–349.

Molfese, D. (1990). Auditory evoked responses recorded from 16-month-old human infants to words they did and did not know. *Brain and Language, 38,* 345–363.

Moll, H., & Meltzoff, A. N. (2011). How does it look? Level 2 perspective-taking at 36 months of age. *Child Development, 82,* 661–673.

Moll, H., & Tomasello, M. (2006). Level 1 perspective taking at 24 months of age. *British Journal of Developmental Psychology, 24,* 603–613.

Molock, S. D., Matlin, S., Barksdale, C., Puri, R., & Lyles, J. (2008). Developing suicide prevention programs for African American youth in African American churches. *Suicide & life-threatening behavior, 38,* 323–333.

Monaghan, K., Lee, J. M., & Steinberg, L. (2011). Revisiting the impact of part-time work on adolescent adjustment: Distinguishing between selection and socialization using propensity score matching. *Child Development, 82,* 96–112.

Money, J. (1988). *Gay, straight, and in-between: The sexology of erotic orientation.* New York: Oxford University Press.

Money, J., & Dalery, J. (1977). Hyperadrenocortical 46, XX hermaphroditism with penile urethra: Psychological studies in seven cases, three reared as boys, four as girls. In P. A. Lee, L. P. Plotnick, A. A. Kowarski, & C. J. Migeon (Eds.), *Congenital adrenal hyperplasia* (pp. 433–446). Baltimore: University Park Press.

Money, J., & Ehrhardt, A. (1972). *Man and woman, boy and girl.* Baltimore: Johns Hopkins University Press.

Money, J., & Tucker, P. (1975). *Sexual signatures: On being a man or a woman.* Boston: Little, Brown.

Montie, J. E., Xiang, Z., & Schweinhart, L. J. (2006). Preschool experience in 10 countries: Cognitive and language performance at age 7. *Early Childhood Research Quarterly, 21,* 313–331.

Montemayor, R. (1983). Parents and adolescents in conflict: All families some of the time and some families all of the time. *Journal of Early Adolescence, 3,* 83–103.

Montgomery, R. J. V., Borgatta, E. F., & Borgatta, M. L. (2000). Societal and family change in the burden of care. In Liu, W. T. and Kendig, H. (Eds.), *Who should care for the elderly: An East–West value divide* (pp. 27–54). Singapore: Singapore University Press Singapore.

Moore, K. J., & Patterson, G. R. (2003). Parent training. In W. O'Donohue, J. E. Fisher, & S. C. Hayes (Eds.), *Cognitive behavior therapy: Applying empirically supported techniques on your practice* (pp. 280–287). Hoboken, NJ: Wiley.

Moore, M. R., & Brooks-Gunn, J. (2002). Adolescent parenthood. In M. H. Bornstein (Ed.), *Handbook of parenting: Vol. 3. Status and social conditions of parenting* (2nd ed., pp. 173–214). Mahwah, NJ: Erlbaum.

Moore, W. (1982). The Measure of Intellectual Development: A brief review. Baltimore: University of Maryland Center for Application of Developmental Instruction.

Moran, S., & Gardner, H. (2006). Extraordinary achievements: A developmental and systems analysis. In W. Damon & R. M. Lerner (Series Eds.), D. Kuhn & R. S. Siegler (Vol. Eds.), *Handbook of child psychology: Vol. 2. Cognition, perception and language* (6th ed., pp. 904–952). Hoboken, NJ: Wiley.

Morelli, G. A., Rogoff, B., Oppenheim, D., & Goldsmith, D. (1992). Cultural variations in infants' sleeping arrangements. Questions of independence. *Developmental Psychology, 28,* 604–613.

Moreno, J. L. (1934). *Who shall survive? A new approach to the problem of human interrelations.* Washington, DC: Nervous and Mental Disease Publishing.

Morgan, K., & Hayne, H. (2011). Age-related changes in visual recognition memory during infancy and early childhood. *Developmental Psychobiology, 53,* 157–165.

Morley, J. E. (2011). Alzheimer's Disease: Future treatments. *Journal of the American Medical Directors Association, 12,* 1–7.

Morrow, J., & Nolen-Hoeksema, S. (1990). Effects of responses to depression on the remediation of depressive affect. *Journal of Personality and Social Psychology, 58,* 519–527.

Mortimer, J. (2005). *Working and growing up in America.* Cambridge, MA: Harvard University Press.

Mortimer, J. T., Harley, C., & Aronson, P. J. (1999). How do prior experiences in the workplace set the stage for transitions to adulthood? In A. Booth, A. C. Crouter, & M. J. Shanahan (Eds.), *Transitions to adulthood in a changing economy: No work, no family, no future?* New York: Praeger.

Moshman, D. (1998). Cognitive development beyond childhood. In W. Damon (Series Ed.), D. Kuhn & R. S. Siegler (Vol. Eds.), *Handbook of child psychology: Vol. 2. Cognition, perception, and language* (5th ed., pp. 947–978). New York: Wiley.

Moshman, D. (2008). Epistemic development and the perils of Pluto. In M. Shaughnessy, M. Vennman, & C. K. Kennedy (Eds.), *Metacognition: A recent review of research, theory and perspectives* (pp. 161–174). Hauppauge, NY: Nova.

Moskowitz, D. W., Suh, E. J., & Desaulniers, J. (1994). Situational influences on gender differences in agency and communion. *Journal of Personality and Social Psychology, 66,* 753–761.

Mounts, N. S., & Steinberg, L. (1995). An ecological analysis of peer influence on adolescent grade point average and drug use. *Developmental Psychology, 31,* 915–922.

Moyer-Mileur, L., Brubstetter, V., McNaught, T., Gill, G., & Chan, G. (2000). Daily physical activity programs increases bone mineralization and growth in very low birth weight infants. *Pediatrics, 106,* 1088–1092.

Mroczek, D. K., & Almeida, D. M. (2004). The effect of daily stress, personality, and age on daily negative affect. *Journal of Personality, 72,* 355–378.

MTV. (2010). Associated Press: MTV-AP Digital Abuse Study. http://www.athinline.org/ MTV-AP_Digital_Abuse_Study_Executive_ Summary.pdf (Accessed August 15, 2011).

Mufson, L., Moreau, D., Weissman, M. M., & Klerman, G. L. (1993). *Interpersonal psycho- therapy for depressed adolescents.* New York: Guilford Press.

Muis, K. (2007). The role of epistemic beliefs in self-regulated learning. *Educational Psychologist, 42,* 173–190.

Muller, M., Holsboer, F., & Keck, M. E. (2002). Genetic modification of corticosteroid receptor signaling: Novel insights into pathophysiology and treatment strategies of human affective disorders. *Neuropeptides, 36,* 117–131.

Murphy, D. M. (1985). Fears in preschool-age children. *Child Care Quarterly, 14,* 171–189.

Murphy, D. R., Daneman, M., & Schneider, B. A. (2006). Why do older adults have difficulty following conversations? *Psychology and Aging, 21,* 49–61.

Murphy, M. C., Steele, C. M., & Gross, J. J. (2007). Signaling threat: How situation cues affect women in math, science, and engineering settings. *Psychological Science, 18,* 879–885.

Murphy, S. A. (1997). A bereavement intervention for parents following the sudden, violent deaths of their 12–28-year-old children: Descriptions and applications to clinical practice. *Canadian Journal of Nursing Research, 29,* 51–72.

Murray, B. (1996, February). Psychology remains top college major. *APA Monitor,* p. 1.

Murray, S. L., Holmes, J. G., & Griffin, D. W. (1996). The benefits of positive illusions: Idealization and the construction of satisfaction in close relationships. *Journal of Personality and Social Psychology, 70,* 79–98.

Mussen, P. H., Honzik, M., & Eichorn, D. (1982). Early adult antecedents of life satisfaction at age 70. *Journal of Gerontology, 37,* 316–322.

Mustanski, B. S., Viken, R. J., Kaprio, J., Pulkkinen, L., & Rose, R. J. (2004). Genetic and environmental influences on pubertal development: Longitudinal data from Finnish twins at ages 11 and 14. *Developmental Psychology, 40,* 1188–1198.

Myers, S. M., Johnson, C. P., & Council on Children with Disabilities (2007). Management of children with autism spectrum disorders. *Pediatrics, 120,* 1162–1182.

Myers, D. G. (1993). *The pursuit of happiness.* New York: Avon.

Myers, D. G. (2000). The funds, friends, and faith of happy people. *American Psychologist, 55,* 56–57.

Myers, J. E., & Harper, M. C. (2004). Evidence-based effective practices with older adults. *Journal of Counseling and Development, 82,* 207–218.

Nanda, S. (2008). *The kaleidoscope of gender: Prisms, patterns, and possibilities* (2nd ed.). Thousand Oaks, CA: Pine Forge Press, Sage.

Nangle, D. W., Hecker, J. E., Grover, R. L., & Smith, M. G. (2003). Perspective-taking and adolescent sex offenders: From developmental theory to clinical practice. *Cognitive and Behavioral Practice, 10,* 73–84.

National Association for the Education of Young Children & Fred Rogers Center for Early Learning and Children's Media (2012). *Technology and interactive media as tools in early childhood programs serving children from birth through age 8.* Washington, DC: NAEYC.

National Association of Social Workers (2000). Cultural competence in the social work profession. In *Social work speaks: NASW policy statements* (pp. 59–62). Washington, DC: NASW Press.

National Campaign to Prevent Teen Pregnancy. (1999). Teenpregnancy.org. Retrieved April 5, 2002, from http://www.teenpregnancy.org

National Center for Education Statistics. (2002). *The condition of education, 2002.* Washington, DC: U.S. Department of Education.

National Center for Education Statistics (2012). *Digest of Education Statistics: 2011.* Retrieved from http://nces.ed.gov/programs/ digest/d11/

National Center for Health Statistics. (2012). *Health, United States, 2011: With Special Feature on Socioeconomic Status and Health.* Hyattsville, Maryland.

National Clearinghouse for English Language Acquisition & Language Instruction Educational Programs. (2007). *The growing numbers of Limited English Proficient students 1995/6 to 2005/6.* Washington, DC: U.S. Department of Education.

National Council of Teachers of Mathematics. (2000a). *Principles and standards for school mathematics: Grades 5–8: Standard 9-Algebra.* Retrieved from http://www .standards.nctm.org/previous/currevstds/ 5-8s9.htm

National Council of Teachers of Mathematics. (2000b). *Principles and standards for school mathematics: Grades 9–12: Standard 5-Algebra.* Retrieved from http://www.standards .nctm.org/previous/currevstdsv9-12s5.htm

National Institute of Child Health and Human Development, Early Child Care Research Network. (1997). The effects of infant child care on infant-mother attachment security: Results of the NICHD study of early child care. *Child Development, 68,* 860–879.

National Institute of Child Health and Human Development, Early Child Care Research Network. (1998). Early child care and self-control, compliance, and problem behavior at twenty-four and thirty-six months. *Child Development, 69,* 1145–1170.

National Institute of Child Health and Human Development, Early Child Care Research Network. (2004). Trajectories of physical aggression from toddlerhood to middle childhood. *Monographs of the Society for Research in Child Development, 69*(4, Serial No. 278).

National Institute of Child Health and Human Development, Early Child Care Research Network. (2006). Child-care effect sizes for the NICHD study of early child care and youth development. *American Psychologist, 61,* 99–116.

National School Boards Foundation. (2000). *Safe and smart: Research and guidelines for children's use of the Internet.* Alexandria VA: Author.

Neblett, E. W., Shelton, J. N., & Sellers, R. M. (2004). The role of racial identity in managing daily racial hassles. In G. Philogene (Ed.), *Race and identity: The legacy of Kenneth Clark* (pp. 77–90). Washington, DC: APA Press.

Neimeyer, R. A. (2000). Searching for the meaning of meaning: Grief therapy and the process of reconstruction. *Death Studies, 24,* 541–558.

Neisser, U. (1967). *Cognitive psychology.* New York: Appleton-Century-Crofts.

Neisser, U. (1993). *The perceived self: Ecological and interpersonal sources of self-knowledge.* New York: Cambridge University Press.

Nell, V. (2002). Why young men drive dangerously: Implications for injury prevention. *Current Directions in Psychological Science, 11,* 75–79.

Nelson, K. (1993). Events, narratives, memory: What develops? In C. A. Nelson (Ed.), *Minnesota Symposium on Child Psychology: Vol. 26. Memory and affect* (pp. 1–24). Hillsdale, NJ: Erlbaum.

Nelson, K. (2007). *Young minds in social worlds: Experience, meaning and memory.* Cambridge, MA: Harvard University Press.

Nelson, K., & Fivush, R. (2004). The emergence of autobiographical memory: A social cultural developmental theory. *Psychological Review, 111,* 486–511.

Nelson, L. J., & Chen, X. (2007). Emerging adulthood in China: The role of social and cultural factors. *Child Development Perspectives, 1,* 86–91.

Nelson, M. L., & Neufelt, S. A. (1998). The pedagogy of counseling: A critical examination. *Counselor Education and Supervision, 38,* 70–88.

Nelson, S. A. (1980). Factors influencing young children's use of motives and outcomes as moral criteria. *Child Development, 51,* 823–829.

Neumark, D., & Rothstein, D. (2005). Do school-to-work programs help the "forgotten half"? *National Bureau of Economic Research Working Paper Series.* Retrieved from http://www.nber.org/papers/w11636

Newcomb, A. F., & Bukowski, W. M. (1984). A longitudinal study of the utility of social preference and social impact sociometric classification schemes. *Child Development, 55,* 1434–1447.

Newcomb, A. F., Bukowski, W. M., & Pattee, L. (1993). Children's peer relations: A meta-analytic review of popular, rejected, neglected, and average sociometric status. *Psychological Bulletin, 113,* 99–128.

Newcombe, N. S. (2010). Picture this: Increasing math and science learning by improving spatial thinking. *American Educator, 34,* 29–35, 43.

Newman, P. R., & Newman, B. M. (1999). What does it take to have a positive impact on minority students' college retention? *Adolescence, 34,* 483–492.

Nezu, A. M., Nezu, C. M., & Lombardo, E. (2003). Problem-solving therapy. In W. O'Donohue, J. E. Fisher, & S. C. Hayes (Eds.), *Cognitive behavior therapy: Applying empirically supported techniques in your practice* (pp. 301–307). Hoboken, NJ: Wiley.

Ng, F. F. Y., Pomerantz, E. M., & Lam, S. F. (2007). European American and Chinese parents' responses to children's success and failure: Implications for children's responses. *Developmental Psychology, 43,* 1239–1255.

Ng, J. Y., Ntoumanis, N., Thøgersen-Ntoumani, C., Deci, E. L., Ryan, R. M., Duda, J. L., et al. (2012). Self-Determination Theory applied to health contexts: A meta-analysis. *Perspectives on Psychological Science, 7,* 325–340.

Niedenthal, P. M., & Brauer, M. (2012). Social functionality of human emotion. *Annual Review of Psychology, 63,* 259–285.

Nigg, J. T. (2006). Temperament and developmental psychopathology. *Journal of Child Psychology and Psychiatry, 47,* 395–422.

Nisbett, R. E., & Masuda, T. (2003). Culture and point of view. *Proceedings of the National Academy of Sciences of the United States of America, 100*(19), 11163–11170.

Nisbett, R. E., Peng, K., Choi, I., & Norenzayan, A. (2001). Culture and systems of thought: Holistic versus analytic cognition. *Psychological Review, 108*(2), 291–310.

Noam, G. G. (1992). Development as the aim of clinical intervention. *Development and Psychopathology, 4,* 679–696.

Noam, G. G. (1998). Clinical-developmental psychology: Toward developmentally differentiated interventions. In W. Damon (Series Ed.), I. E. Sigel, & K. A. Renninger (Vol. Eds.), *Handbook of child psychology: Vol. 4. Child psychology in practice* (5th ed., pp. 585–634). New York: Wiley.

Noam, G. G., & Fischer, K. W. (Eds.). (1996). *Development and vulnerability in close relationships.* Mahwah, NJ: Erlbaum.

Nolen-Hoeksema, S. (1987). Sex differences in unipolar depression: Evidence and theory. *Psychological Bulletin, 101,* 259–282.

Nolen-Hoeksema, S. (1991). Responses to depression and their effects on the duration of depressive episodes. *Journal of Abnormal Psychology, 100,* 569–582.

Nolen-Hoeksema, S. (2002). Gender differences in depression. In I. Gotlib & C. Hammen (Eds.), *Handbook of depression* (pp. 492–509). New York: Guilford Press.

Nolen-Hoeksema, S. (2008). It is not what you have; It is what you do with it: Support for Addis's gendered responding framework. *Clinical Psychology Science and Practice, 15,* 178–181.

Nolen-Hoeksema, S., & Girgus, J. S. (1994). The emergence of gender differences in depression during adolescence. *Psychological Bulletin, 115,* 424–443.

Nolen-Hoeksema, S., Girgus, J. S., & Seligman, M. E. P. (1992). Predictors and consequences of childhood depressive symptoms: A 5-year longitudinal study. *Journal of Abnormal Psychology, 101,* 405–422.

Nolen-Hoeksema, S., & Larson, J. (1999). *Coping with loss.* Mahwah, NJ: Erlbaum.

Nolen-Hoeksema, S., Morrow, J., & Fredrickson, B. L. (1993). Response styles and the duration of episodes of depressed moods. *Journal of Abnormal Psychology, 102,* 20–28.

Nolen-Hoeksema, S., & Watson, E. R. (2011). A heuristic for developing transdiagnostic models of psychopathology: Explaining multifinality and divergent trajectories. *Perspectives on Psychological Science, 6,* 589–609.

Nomaguchi, K. M., & Milkie, M. A. (2003). Costs and rewards of children: The effects of becoming a parent on adult lives. *Journal of Marriage and Family, 65,* 356–374.

Northcutt, R. G., & Kaas, J. H. (1995). The emergence and evolution of mammalian neocortex. *Trends in Neuroscience, 18,* 373–379.

Nozyce, M., Hittelman, J., Muenz, L., Durako, S. J., Fisher, M., & Willoughby, A. (1994). Effect of perinatally acquired human immunodeficiency virus infection on neurodevelopment during the first two years of life. *Pediatrics, 94,* 883–891.

Nurmi, J. (1991). How do adolescents see their future? A review of the development of future orientation and planning. *Developmental Review, 11,* 1–59.

Nyamongo, I. K. (1999). Burying the dead, culture, and economics: An assessment of two Kenyan cases. *International Social Science Journal, 51,* 255–262.

Nye, C. D., Su, R., Rounds, J., & Drasgow, F. (2012). Vocational interests and performance: A quantitative summary of over 60 years of research. *Perspectives on Psychological Science, 7,* 384–403.

Oakes, J. (2005). *Keeping track* (2nd ed.). New Haven, CT: Yale University Press.

Oakes, J., Quartz, K. H., Gong, J., Guiton, G., & Lipton, M. (1993). Creating middle schools: Technical, normative, and political considerations. *The Elementary School Journal, 93,* 461–480.

Oakley, A. E., Clifton, D. K., & Steiner, R. A. (2009). Kisspeptin signaling in the brain. *Endocrine Reviews, 30,* 713–743.

Oberman, L. M., & Ramachandran, V. S. (2007). The simulated social mind: The role of the mirror neuron system and simulation in the social and communicative deficits of autism spectrum disorders. *Psychological Bulletin, 133,* 310–327.

O'Brien, L. T., & Hummert, M. L. (2006). Memory performance of late middle-aged adults: Contrasting self-stereotyping and stereotype threat accounts of assimilation to age stereotypes. *Social Cognition, 24,* 338–358.

O'Connor, B. P. (1995). Identity development and perceived parental behavior as sources of adolescent egocentrism. *Journal of Youth and Adolescence, 24,* 204–227.

O'Connell, M., & Feliz, S. (2011). *Same-sex couple household statistics from the 2010 census.* Washington DC: U.S Bureau of Census. Retrieved from http://www.census.gov/hhes/samesex/

O'Connor, K. J., & Braverman, L. M. (1997). *Play therapy theory and practice: A comparative presentation.* New York: Wiley.

Odgers, C. L., Moffitt, T. E., Broadbent, J. M., Dickson, N., Hancox, R. J., Harrington, H., et al. (2008). Female and male antisocial trajectories: From childhood origins to adult outcomes. *Development and Psychopathology, 20,* 673–716.

Offer, D. (1969). *The psychological world of the teenager.* New York: Basic Books.

Ogbu, J. U. (2003). *Black American students in an affluent suburb: A study of academic disengagement.* Mahwah, NJ: Erlbaum.

Oishi, S., Diener, E., Lucas, R., & Soto, E. (1999). Cross-cultural variations in predictors of life satisfaction: Perspectives from needs and values. *Personality and Social Psychology Bulletin, 25,* 980–990.

O'Leary, D. D. M., & Stanfield, B. B. (1989). Selective elimination of axons extended by developing cortical neurons is dependent on regional locale: Experiments utilizing fetal cortical transplants. *Journal of Neuroscience, 9,* 2230–2246.

Oldehinkel, A. J., Ormel, J., Bosch, N. M., Bouma, E. M. C., VanRoon, A. M., Rosmalen, J. G. M., & Riese, H. (2010). Stressed out? Associations between perceived and psychological stress responses in adolescents: The TRAILS study. *Psychophysiology, 8,* 441–452.

Olendzki, A. (2010). *Unlimiting mind: The radical experiential psychology of Buddhism.* Boston: Wisdom Publications.

Oliner, S. P., & Oliner, P. M. (1988). *The altruistic personality: Rescuers of Jews in Nazi Europe.* New York: Free Press.

Ollikainen, M., Smith, K. R., Joo, E. J-H., Ng, H. K., Andronikos, R., Novakovic, B., et al. (2010). DNA methylation analysis of multiple tissues from newborn twins reveals both genetic and intrauterine components to variation in the human neonatal epigenome. *Human Molecular Genetics, 19,* 4176–4188.

Olweus, D. (1993). Victimization by peers: Antecedents and long-term consequences. In K. H. Rubin & J. B. Asendorf (Eds.), *Social withdrawal, inhibition, and shyness* (pp. 315–341). Hillsdale, NJ.: Erlbaum.

Olweus, D., & Limber, S. (2002). *Blueprints for violence prevention: Bullying prevention program.* Boulder: University for the Study and Prevention of Violence, University of Colorado at Boulder.

Omark, D. R., Omark, M., & Edelman, M. (1973). Formation of dominance hierarchies in young children. In T. R. Williams (Ed.), *Psychological anthropology.* The Hague, Netherlands: Mouton.

Oney, C. N., Cole, E. R., & Sellers, R. M. (2011). Racial identity and gender as moderators of the relationship between body image and self-esteem for African Americans. *Sex Roles, 65,* 619–631.

Orcutt, H. (1874). *The parent's manual or home and school training.* Boston: Thompson, Brown.

Ornstein, P. (1994). *School girls: Young women, self-esteem, and the confidence gap.* New York: Anchor Books, Doubleday.

O'Roak, B. J., & State, M. W. (2008). Autism genetics: strategies, challenges, and opportunities. *Autism Research, 1,* 4–17.

Orth, U., Robins, R. W., & Widaman, K. F. (2012). Life-span development of self-esteem and its effects on important life outcomes. *Personality processes and individual differences, 102,* 1271–1288.

Ortony, A., & Turner, T. T. (1992). Basic emotions: Can conflicting criteria converge? *Psychological Bulletin, 99,* 566–571.

Osherson, D. N., & Markman, E. M. (1975). Language and the ability to evaluate contradictions and tautologies. *Cognition, 2,* 213–226.

Otero, N. K. H., & Kelly, S. J. (2012). Sex differences in the teratogenic effects of alcohol: Findings from animal models. In M. Lewis & L. Kestler (Eds.), *Gender differences in prenatal substance exposure* (pp. 155–167). Washington, DC: American Psychological Association.

Overton, W. F. (1990). Competence and procedures: Constraints on the development of logical reasoning. In W. F. Overton (Ed.), *Reasoning, necessity, and logic: Developmental perspectives* (pp. 1–32). Hillsdale, NJ: Erlbaum.

Owen, M. T., & Cox, M. J. (1997). Marital conflict and the development of infant parent attachment relationships. *Journal of Family Psychology, 11,* 152–164.

Owsley, C. (2011). Aging and vision. *Vision Research, 51,* 1610–1622.

Oyserman, D., Coon, H. M., & Kemmelmeier, M. (2002). Rethinking individualism and collectivism: Evaluation of theoretical assumptions and meta-analyses. *Psychological Bulletin, 128,* 3–72.

Padilla-Walker, L. M., Barry, C. M., Carroll, J. S., Madsen, S. D., & Nelson, L. J. (2008). Looking on the bright side: The role of identity status and gender on positive orientations during emerging adulthood. *Journal of Adolescence, 31,* 451–467.

Padilla-Walker, L. M., Gustavo, C. Christensen, K. J., & Yorgason, J. B. (2012). Bidirectional relations between authoritative parenting and adolescents' prosocial behaviors. *Journal of Research on Adolescence, 22,* 400–408.

Pak, R., & Stronge, A. (2008). Health maintenance, older adults, and the Internet. *Psychological Science Agenda, 22,* 1–5.

Panksepp, J. (1982). Toward a general psychobiological theory of emotions. *The Behavioral and Brain Sciences, 5,* 407–467.

Panksepp, J. (2008). Cognitive conceptualism: Where have all the affects gone? Additional corrections for Barrett et al. (2007). *Perspectives on Psychological Science, 3,* 305–308.

Papastavrou, E., Kalokerinou, A., Papacostas, S. S., Tsangari, H., & Sourtzi, P. (2007). Caring for a relative with dementia: Family caregiver burden. *Journal of Advanced Nursing, 58,* 446–457.

Papez, J. W. (1937). A proposed mechanism of emotion. *Archives of Neurology and Psychiatry, 79,* 217–224.

Pargament, K. I., Smith, B. W., Koenig, H. G., & Perez, L. M. (1998). Patterns of positive and negative religious coping with major life stressors. *Journal for the Scientific Study of Religion, 37,* 710–724.

Parish-Morris, J., Hirsh-Pasek, K., & Maller, B. (2008, October). *Electronic console books: Independent effects on dialogic language in parents and children.* Paper presented at the Boston Language Conference, Boston.

Park, C. L., & Folkman, S. (1997). Meaning in the context of stress and coping. *Review of General Psychology, 1,* 115–144.

Park, D. C., & Huang, C. (2010). Culture wires the brain: A cognitive neuroscience perspective. *Perspectives in Psychological Sciences, 5,* 391–400.

Park, G., Lubinski, D., & Benbow, C. P. (2008). Ability differences among people who have commensurate degrees matter for scientific creativity. *Psychological Science, 19,* 957–961.

Parke, R. D. (2002). Fathers and families. In M. H. Bornstein (Ed.), *Handbook of parenting: Vol. 3. Being and becoming a parent* (2nd ed., pp. 27–74). Mahwah, NJ: Erlbaum.

Parke, R. D., & Buriel, R. (2006). Socialization in the family: Ethnic and ecological perspec-

tives. In W. Damon & R. M. Lerner (Series Eds.), N. Eisenberg (Vol. Ed.), *Handbook of child psychology: Vol. 3. Social, emotional, and personality development* (6th ed., pp. 429–504). Hoboken, NJ: Wiley.

Parke, R. D., & Slaby, R. G. (1983). The development of aggression. In P. Mussen (Series Ed.) & E. M. Hetherington (Vol. Ed.), *Handbook of child psychology: Vol. 4. Socialization, personality, and social development* (4th ed., pp. 547–641). New York: Wiley.

Parker, J. (1995). Age differences in source monitoring of performed and imagined actions on immediate and delayed tests. *Journal of Experimental Child Psychology, 60,* 84–101.

Parker, J. G., & Asher, S. R. (1987). Peer relations and later personal adjustment: Are low-accepted children at risk? *Psychological Bulletin, 102,* 357–389.

Parkes, C. M. (1965). Bereavement and mental illness. *British Journal of Medical Psychology, 38,* 388–397.

Parkes, C. M., & Weiss, R. S. (1983). *Recovery from bereavement.* New York: Basic Books.

Parks, E. E., Carter, R. T., & Gushue, G. V. (1996). At the crossroads: Racial and womanist identity development in Black and White women. *Journal of Counseling and Development, 74,* 624–631.

Parkhurst, J. T., & Asher, S. R. (1992). Peer rejection in middle school: Subgroup differences in behavior, loneliness, and interpersonal concerns. *Developmental Psychology, 28,* 231–241.

Parsons, C. E., Young, K. S., Murray, L., Stein, A., & Kringelbach, M. L. (2010). The functional neuroanatomy of the evolving parent–infant relationship. *Progress in Neurobiology, 91,* 220–241.

Parsons, T. (1951). Illness and the role of the physician: A sociological perspective. *American Journal of Orthopsychiatry, 21,* 452–460.

Partee, G. L. (2003). *Preparing youth for employment: Principles and characteristics of five leading United States youth development programs.* Washington, DC: American Youth Policy Forum.

Partnership for a Drug-Free America. (1998). *The boomer-rang: Baby boomers seriously underestimate the presence of drugs in their children's lives.* Retrieved March 28, 2002, from http://www.drugfreeamerica.org

Partnership for a Drug-Free America. (2006). *The Partnership attitude tracking study (PATS): Teens in grades 7 through 12, 2005.* Retrieved November 15, 2008, from http://www.drugfreeamerica.org

Pascarella, E., Bohr, L., Nora, A., & Terenzini, P. (1995). Cognitive effects of 2-year and 4-year colleges: New evidence. *Educational Evaluation and Policy Analysis, 17,* 83–96.

Pascarella, E., & Terenzini, P. (1991). *How college affects students: Findings and insights from twenty years of research.* New York: Wiley.

Pascarella, E. T., & Terenzini, P. T. (2005). *How college affects students: a third decade of research* (Vol. 2). San Francisco, CA: Jossey-Bass.

Pascual-Leone, A., & Taylor, M. J. (2011). A developmental framework of brain and cognition from infancy to old age. *Brain Topography, 24,* 183–186.

Pashler, H., McDaniel, M., Rohrer, D., & Bjork, R. (2009). Learning styles: Concepts and evidence. *Psychological Science in the Public Interest, 9,* 105–119.

Pasterski, V. L., Geffner, M. E., Brain, C., Hindmarsh, P., Brook, C., & Hines M. (2005). *Child Development, 76,* 264–278.

Pasupathi, M., Staudinger, U. M., & Baltes, P. B. (1999). *The emergence of wisdom-related knowledge and judgment during adolescence.* Berlin: Max Planck Institute for Human Development.

Pasupathi, M., Staudinger, U. M., & Baltes, P. B. (2001). Seeds of wisdom: Adolescents' knowledge and judgment about difficult problems. *Developmental Psychology, 37,* 351–369.

Patrick, M. E., & Schuleberg, J. E. (2011). How trajectories of reasons for alcohol use relate to trajectories of binge drinking: National Panel data spanning late adolescence to early adulthood. *Developmental Psychology, 47,* 311–317.

Patterson, C. J. (2004). Gay fathers. In M. E. Lamb (Ed.), *The role of the father in child development* (pp. 397–416). Hoboken, NJ: Wiley.

Patterson, C. J., Sutfin, E. L., & Fulcher, M. (2004). Division of labor among lesbian and heterosexual parenting couples: Correlates of specialized versus shared patterns. *Journal of Adult Development, 11,* 179–189.

Patterson, G. R. (1982). *Coercive family process.* Eugene, OR: Castalia Press.

Patterson, G. R., Chamberlain, P., & Reid, J. B. (1982). A comparative evaluation of parent training procedures. *Behavior Therapy, 13,* 638–651.

Paunonen, S. V., & Ashton, M. C. (2001). Big Five predictors of academic achievement. *Journal of Research in Personality, 35,* 78–90.

Paus, T., Leonard, G., Lerner, J. V., Lerner, R. M., Perron, M., Pike, G. B., et al. (2011). Positive youth development and age-related changes in cortical thickness during adolescence. In A. E. A. Warren, R. M. Lerner, & E. Phelps (Eds.), *Thriving and spirituality among youth: Research perspectives and future possibilities* (pp. 61–76). Hoboken, NJ: Wiley.

Pavot, W., Diener, E., & Fujita, F. (1990). Extraversion and happiness. *Personality and Individual Differences, 11,* 1299–1306.

Paxton, S. J., Eisenberg, M. E., & Neumark-Sztainer, D. (2006). Prospective predictors of body dissatisfaction in adolescent girls and boys: A five-year longitudinal study. *Developmental Psychology, 42,* 888–899.

Paxton, S. J., Schutz, H. K., Weitheim, E. H., & Muir, S. L. (1999). Friendship clique and peer influences on body image concerns, dietary restraint, extreme weight-loss behaviors, and binge-eating in adolescent girls. *Journal of Abnormal Psychology, 108,* 255–266.

Pecheux, M. G., & Labrell, F. (1994). Parent-infant interactions and early cognitive development. In A. Vyt, H. Bloch, & M. H. Bornstein (Eds.), *Early child development in the French tradition: Contributions from current research.* Hillsdale, NJ: Erlbaum.

Peets, K., Hodges, E. V. E., Kikas, E., & Salmivalli, C. (2007). Hostile attributions and behavioral strategies in children: Does relationship type matter? *Developmental Psychology, 43,* 889–900.

Peisner-Feinberg, E. S., Burchinal, M. P., Clifford, R. M., Culkin, M. L., Howes, C., Kagan, S. L., et al. (2001). The relation of preschool child-care quality to children's cognitive and social developmental trajectories through second grade. *Child Development, 72,* 1534–1553.

Pellegrini, A. C. (2009). *The role of play in human development.* New York: Oxford University Press.

Pennington, H. (2003). Building one system for youth development and opportunity. In A. Lewis (Ed.), *Shaping the future of American youth: Youth policy in the 21st century* (pp. 59–68). Washington, DC: American Youth Policy Forum.

Pentz, M. A., Mihalic, S. F., & Grotpeter, J. K. (2002). *Blueprints for violence prevention: Book One. The Midwestern Prevention Project.* Boulder, CO: Center for the Study and Prevention of Violence.

Pentz, M. A., Trebow, E. A., Hansen, W. B., MacKinnon, D. P., Dwyer, J. H., Johnson, C. A., et al. (1990). Effects of program implementation on adolescent drug use behavior: The Midwestern Prevention Project (MPP). *Evaluation Review, 14,* 264–289.

Peplau, L. A., & Fingerhut, A. W. (2007). The close relationships of lesbian and gay men. *Annual Review of Psychology, 58,* 405–424.

Pepler, D., Walsh, M., Yuile, A., Levene, K., Jiang, D., Vaughan, A., et al. (2010). Bridging the gender gap: Interventions with aggressive girls and their parents. *Prevention Science, 11,* 229–238.

Perez-Felkner, L., McDonald, S-K., Schneider, B., Grogan, E. (2012). Female and male adolescents' subjective orientations to mathematics and the influence of those orientations on postsecondary majors. *Developmental Psychology, 48,* 1658–1673.

Pergament, E., Todydemir, P. B., & Fiddler, M. (2002). Sex ratio: A biological perspective of "Sex and the City." *Reproductive BioMedicine Online, 5,* 43–46.

Perkins, H. W. (1991). Religious commitment, Yuppie values, and well-being in postcollegiate life. *Review of Religious Research, 32,* 244–251.

Perrone, K. M., & Worthington, E. L. (2001). Factors influencing ratings of marital quality by individuals within dual-career marriages: A conceptual model. *Journal of Counseling Psychology, 48,* 3–9.

Perry, W. G. (1970/1999). *Forms of ethical and intellectual development in the college years: A scheme.* San Francisco: Jossey-Bass.

Perry-Jenkins, M., Repetti, R. L., & Crouter, A. C. (2000). Work and family in the 1990s. *Journal of Marriage and the Family, 62,* 981–998.

Pert, C. B. (1997). *Molecules of emotion: The science behind mind-body medicine.* New York: Simon & Schuster.

Petanjek, Z., Judas, M., Simic, G., Rasin, M. R., (2011). Extraordinary neoteny of synaptic spines in the human prefrontal cortex. *PNAS Proceedings of the National Academy of Sciences of the United States of America, 108,* 13281–13286.

Petersen, A. C. (1988). Adolescent development. *Annual Review of Psychology, 39,* 583–607.

Petersen, A. C., Compas, B. E., Brooks-Gunn, J., Stemmler, M., Ey, S., & Grant, K. E. (1993). Depression in adolescence. *American Psychologist, 48,* 155–168.

Petersen, A. C., Kennedy, R. E., & Sullivan, P. (1991). Coping with adolescence. In M. E. Colten & S. Gore (Eds.), *Adolescent stress: Causes and consequences* (pp. 93–110). New York: Aldine de Gruyter.

Petersen, A. C., Sarigiani, P. A., & Kennedy, R. E. (1991). Adolescent depression: Why more girls? *Journal of Youth and Adolescence, 10,* 247–271.

Petersen, B. E., & Steward, A. J. (1996). Antecedents and contexts of generativity motivation at midlife. *Psychology and Aging, 11,* 21–33.

Peterson, C., Maier, S., & Seligman, M. (1993). *Learned helplessness.* New York: Oxford University Press.

Peterson, C. C., & Slaughter, V. (2003). Opening windows into the mind: Mothers' preferences for mental state explanations and children's theory of mind. *Cognitive Development, 18,* 399–429.

Pettit, F., Fegan, M., & Howie, P. (1990, September). *Interviewer effects on children's testimony.* Paper presented at the International Congress on Child Abuse and Neglect, Hamburg, Germany.

Pettito, L. A., Katerelos, M., Levy, B. G., Guana, K., Tetreault, K., & Ferraro, V. (2001). Bilingual signed and spoken language acquisition from birth: Implications for the mechanisms underlying early bilingual language acquisition. *Journal of Child Language, 28,* 453–496.

Pfeiffer, S. (2001). Emotional intelligence: Popular but elusive construct. *Roeper Review, 23,* 138–142.

Phillips, D., Simpson, J. A., Lanigan, L., & Rholes, S. W. (1995). *Providing social support: A study of adult attachment styles.* Paper presented at the joint meeting of the European Association of Social Psychology and the Society of Experimental Social Psychology, Washington, DC.

Phillips, D. A., Fox, N. A., & Gunnar, M. R. (2011). Same place, different experiences: Bringing individual differences to research in child care. *Child Development Perspectives, 5,* 44–49.

Phillips, M. (1997). What makes schools effective? A comparison of the relationships of communitarian climate and academic achievement and attendance during middle school. *American Educational Research Journal, 34,* 633–662.

Phinney, J. S. (1990). Ethnic identity in adolescents and adults: Review of research. *Psychological Bulletin, 108,* 499–514.

Phinney, J. S. (2000). Identity formation across cultures: The interaction of personal, societal, and historical change. *Human Development, 43,* 27–31.

Phinney, J. S. (2003). Ethnic identity and acculturation. In K. M. Chun, P. B. Organista, & G. Marin (Eds.), *Acculturation: Advances in theory, measurement and applied research* (pp. 63–82). Washington DC: APA Press.

Piaget, J. (1923/1929). *The child's conception of the world.* London: Kegan Paul, Trench & Trubner.

Piaget, J. (1926). *The language and thought of the child.* New York: Harcourt, Brace.

Piaget, J. (1928). *Judgment and reasoning in the child.* New York: Harcourt, Brace.

Piaget, J. (1932/1965). *The moral judgment of the child.* New York: Free Press.

Piaget, J. (1951). *Play, dreams, and imitation in childhood.* London: Kegan Paul, Trench, & Trubner.

Piaget, J. (1952). *The origins of intelligence in children.* New York: International Universities Press.

Piaget, J. (1954). *The construction of reality in the child.* New York: Basic Books.

Piaget, J. (1962). *Play, dreams, and imitation in childhood.* New York: Norton.

Piaget, J. (1964/1968). *Six psychological studies.* New York: Random House.

Piaget, J. (1970). *Science of education and the psychology of the child.* New York: Orion Press.

Piaget, J. (1975/1985). *The equilibration of cognitive structures.* Chicago: University of Chicago Press.

Piaget, J. (1977). *The development of thought. Equilibration of cognitive structures.* New York: Viking Press.

Piaget, J., & Inhelder, B. (1951/1976). *The origin of the idea of chance in children.* New York: Norton.

Piaget, J., & Inhelder, B. (1956). *The child's conception of space.* New York: Norton.

Piaget, J., & Inhelder, B. (1973). *Memory and intelligence.* New York: Basic Books.

Pianta, R. C., Barnett, W. S., Burchinal, M., & Thornburg, K. R. (2009). The effects of preschool education: What we know, how public policy is or is not aligned with the evidence base, and what we need to know. *Psychological Science in the Public Interest, 10,* 49–88.

Piedmont, R. L. (1999). Does spirituality represent the sixth factor of personality? Spiritual transcendence and the five-factor model. *Journal of Personality, 67,* 985–1014.

Piedmont, R. L., & Leach, M. M. (2002). Cross-cultural generalizability of the spiritual transcendence scale in India: Spirituality as a universal aspect of human experience. *American Behavioral Scientist, 45,* 1888–1901.

Pietromonaco, P. R., & Carnelley, K. B. (1994). Gender and working models of attachment: Consequences for self and romantic relationships. *Personal Relationships, 1,* 63–82.

Pinker, S. (1994). *The language instinct.* New York: Morrow.

Pintrich, P. R. (2000). Multiple goals, multiple pathways: The role of goal orientation in learning and achievement. *Journal of Educational Psychology, 92,* 544–555.

Pipher, M. (1994). *Reviving Ophelia: Saving the selves of adolescent girls.* New York: Ballantine Books.

Pipher, M. (1996). *The shelter of each other: Rebuilding our families.* New York: Ballantine Books.

Pipher, M. (1999). *Another country: Navigating the emotional terrain of our elders.* New York: Riverhead Books.

Pistole, M. C. (1989). Attachment in adult romantic relationships: Style of conflict resolution and relationship satisfaction. *Journal of Social and Personal Relationships, 6,* 505–510.

Pittman, F. (1998). *Grow up! How taking responsibility can make you a happy adult.* New York: St. Martin's Press.

Pittman, F. S. (1985). Children of the rich. *Family Process, 24,* 461–472.

Plante, E., Schmithorst, V. J., Holland, S, K., & Byars, A., W., (2006). Sex differences in the activation of language cortex during childhood, *Neuropsychologia, 44,* 1210–1221.

Plas, E., Berger, P., Hermann, M., & Pfluger, H. (2000). Effects of aging on male fertility? *Experimental Gerontology, 35,* 543–551.

Pluess, M., & Belsky, J. (2009). Differential susceptibility to rearing experience: The case of childcare. *Journal of Child Psychology and Psychiatry, 50,* 396–404.

Podd, M. H. (1972). Ego identity status and morality: The relationship between two developmental constructs. *Developmental Psychology, 6,* 497–507.

Pole, N., Gone, J. P., & Kulkarni. M. (2008) Posttraumatic Stress Disorder among ethnoracial minorities in the United States. *Clinical Psychology: Science and Practice, 15,* 35–61.

Pollack, W. (1998). *Real boys: Rescuing our sons from the myths of boyhood.* New York: Henry Holt.

Pollitt, E., Gorman, K. S., Engle, P. L., Martorell, R., & Rivera, J. (1993). Early supplementary feeding and cognition. *Monographs of the Society for Research in Child Development, 58* (Serial No. 235).

Poloma, M. M., & Pendleton, B. F. (1990). Religious domains and general well-being. *Social Indicators Research, 22,* 255–276.

Pomerantz, E. M., Qin, L., Wang, Q., & Chen, H. (2009). American and Chinese early adolescents' inclusion of their relationships with their parents in their self-construals. *Child Development, 80,* 792–807.

Pomerantz, E. M., Qin, L., Wang, Q., & Chen, H. (2011). Changes in early adolescents' sense of responsibility to their parents in the United States and China: Implications for academic functioning. *Child Development, 82,* 1136–1151.

Pong, S-l., & Landale, N. S. (2012). Academic achievement of legal immigrants' children: The roles of parents' pre- and postmigration characteristics in origin-group differences. *Child Development, 83,* 1543–1559.

Ponzo, Z. (1992). Promoting successful aging: Problems, opportunities, and counseling guidelines. *Journal of Counseling and Development, 71,* 210–213.

Poole, D. A., Bruck, M., & Pipe, M-E. (2011). Forensic interviewing aids: Do props help children answer questions about touching? *Current Directions in Psychological Science, 20,* 11–15.

Porges, S. W. (2007). The polyvagal perspective. *Biological Psychology, 74,* 116–143.

Porges, S. W., Doussard-Roosevelt, J. A., Portales, A. L., & Greenspan, S. I. (1996). Infant regulation of the vagal "brake" predicts child behavior problems: A psychobiological model of social behavior. *Developmental Psychobiology, 29,* 697–712.

Posada, G., Carbonell, O. A., Aolzate, G., & Plata, S. J. (2004). Through Colombian lenses: Ethnographic and conventional analyses of maternal care and their associations with secure base behavior. *Developmental Psychology, 40,* 508–518.

Post, R. M. (1985). Stress sensitization, kindling, and conditioning. *Behavioral and Brain Sciences, 8,* 372–373.

Post, R. M. (2007). Kindling and sensitization as models for affective episode recurrence, cyclicity, and tolerance phenomena. *Neuroscience & Biobehavioral Reviews, 31,* 858–873.

Pot, A.M., Bohlmeijer, E.T., Onrust, S., Melenhorst, A. S., Veerbeek, M., & De Vries, W. (2010). The impact of life review on depression in older adults: a randomized control trial. *International psychogeriatrics, 22,* 572–581.

Poulin-Dubois, D., & Serbin, L. A. (2006). Infants' knowledge about gender stereotypes and categories. *Enfance, 58,* 283–310.

Poulin, F., Dishion, T. J., & Burraston, B. (2001). Three year iatrogenic effects associated with aggregating high risk adolescents in cognitive behavioral preventive interventions. *Applied Developmental Science, 5,* 214–224.

Powell, G. J. (1985). Self-concepts among African-Americans in racially isolated minority schools: Some regional differences. *Journal of the American Academy of Child Psychiatry, 24,* 142–149.

Prasad, S., Sung, B., & Aggarwal, B. B. (2012). Age-associated chronic diseases require age-old medicine: Role of chronic inflammation. *Preventive Medicine, 54,* 29–37.

Pratt, J., & Pryor, K. (1995). *For real: The uncensored truth about America's teenagers.* New York: Hyperion.

Pressley, M., & Hilden, K. (2006). Cognitive strategies. In W. Damon & R. M. Lerner (Series Eds.), D. Kuhn & R. S. Siegler (Vol. Eds.), *Handbook of child psychology: Vol. 2. Cognition, perception and language* (6th ed., pp. 511–556). Hoboken, NJ: Wiley.

Pribram, K. H. (1997). The work in working memory: Implications for development. In N. A. Krasnegor, G. R. Lyon, & P. S. Goldman-Rakic (Eds.), *Development of the prefrontal cortex: Evolution, neurobiology, and behavior* (pp. 359–378). Baltimore: Brookes.

Price, C. A., & Joo, E. (2005). Exploring the relationship between marital status and women's retirement satisfaction. *International Journal of Aging and Human Development, 61,* 37–55.

Price, R. H. (1992). Psychosocial impact of job loss on individuals and families. *Current Directions in Psychological Science, 1,* 9–11.

Price, R. H., Choi, J. N., & Vinokur, A. D. (2002). Links in the chain of adversity following job loss: How financial strain and loss of personal control lead to depression, impaired functioning, and poor health. *Journal of Occupational Health Psychology, 7,* 302–312.

Price, R. H., & Vinokur, A. D. (1995). Supporting career transitions in time of organizational downsizing: The Michigan JOBS Program. In M. London (Ed.), *Employees, careers, and job creation: Developing growth-oriented human resource strategies and programs* (pp. 191–209). San Francisco: Jossey-Bass.

Price, T. S., Grosser, T., Plomin, R., & Jaffee, S. R. (2010). Fetal genotype for the xenobiotic metabolizing enzyme *NQO1* influences intrauterine growth among infants whose mothers smoked during pregnancy. *Child Development, 81,* 101–114.

Priess, H. A., Lindberg, S. M., & Hyde, J. S. (2009). Adolescent gender-role identity and mental health: Gender intensification revisited. *Child Development, 80,* 1531–1544

Prochaska, J. O., & DiClemente, C. C. (1982). Transtheoretical therapy: Toward a more integrated model of change. *Psychotherapy: Theory, Research and Practice, 19,* 276–288.

Pruett, M. K., Insabella, G. M., & Gustafson, K. (2005). The Collaborative Divorce Project: A court-based intervention for separating parents with young children. *Family Court Review, 43,* 38–51.

Pryor, J. H., Eagan, K., Palucki Blake, L., Hurtado, S., Berdan, J., & Case, M. H. (2012). *The American Freshman: National Norms Fall 2012.* Los Angeles: Higher Education Research Institute, UCLA.

Pujol, J., Soriano-Mas, C., Ortiz, H., Sebastian-Galles, N., Losilla, J. M., & Deus, J. (2006). Myelination of language-related areas in the developing brain. *Neurology, 66,* 339–343.

Putallaz, M. (1983). Predicting children's sociometric status from their behavior. *Child Development, 54,* 1417–1426.

Putallaz, M., & Wasserman, A. (1990). Children's entry behaviors. In S. P. Asher & J. D. Coie (Eds.), *Peer rejection in childhood.* New York: Cambridge University Press.

Putnam, R. D. (2000). *Bowling alone: The collapse and revival of American community.* New York: Simon & Schuster.

Pyszczynski, T., Greenberg, J., & LaPrelle, J. (1985). Social comparison after success and failure: Biased search for information consistent with a self-servicing conclusion. *Journal of Experimental Social Psychology, 21,* 129–138.

Quadrel, M. J., Fischhoff, B., & Davis, W. (1993). Adolescent (in) vulnerability. *American Psychologist, 48,* 102–116.

Quas, J. A., & Hayakawa, C. (2008). New directions in the study of children's memory for stressful events. *Psychological Science Agenda, 22,* 1–6.

Quatman, T., Sampson, K., Robinson, C., & Watson, C. M. (2001). Academic, motivational, and emotional correlates of adolescent dating. *Genetic, Social, and General Psychology Monographs, 127,* 211–234.

Quevedo, K., Benning, S. D., Gunnar, M. R., & Dahl, R. E. (2009). The onset of puberty: Effects on the psychophysiology of defensive and appetitive motivation. *Development and Psychopathology, 21,* 27–45.

Quintana, E. D. (1999). Racial and ethnic identity development in biracial people. *Dissertation Abstracts International: Section B. The Physical Sciences & Engineering, 60* (3-B), 1313.

Quinton, D., Pickles, A., Maughan, B., & Rutter, M. (1993). Partners, peers, and pathways: Assortative pairing and continuities in conduct disorder. *Development and Psychopathology, 5,* 763–783.

Rahman, Q. (2005). Fluctuating asymmetry, second to fourth finger length ratios and human sexual orientation. *Psychoneuroendocrinology, 30,* 382–391.

Raikes, H., Pan, B. A., Luze, G., Tamis-LeMonda, C. S., Brooks-Gunn, J., Constantine, J., et al. (2006). Mother-child book reading in low-income families: Correlates and outcomes during the first three years of life. *Child Development, 77,* 924–953.

Ramani, G. B., & Siegler, R. S. (2008). Promoting broad and stable improvements in low-income children's numerical knowledge through playing number board games. *Child Development, 79,* 375–394.

Ramchandani, S., Bhattacharya, S. K., Cervoni, N., & Szyf, M. (1999). DNA methylation is a reversible biological signal. *Proceedings of the National Academy of Sciences, 96,* 6107–6112.

Ramey, C. T., & Ramey, S. L. (1998). Early intervention and early experience. *American Psychologist, 53,* 109–120.

Ramsey, P. G., & Myers, L. C. (1990). Young children's responses to racial differences: Relations among cognitive, affective, and behavioral dimensions. *Journal of Applied Developmental Psychology, 11,* 49–67.

Rando, T. A. (1993). *Treatment of complicated mourning.* Champaign, IL: Research Press.

Randolph, P. D., Caldera, Y. M., Tacone, A. M., et al. (1999). The long-term combined effects of medical treatment and a mindfulness-based behavioral program for the multidisciplinary management of chronic pain in West Texas. *Pain Digest, 9,* 103–112.

Rapp, E. (2006). *Poster child: A memoir.* New York: Bloomsbury USA.

Raskauskas, J., & Stoltz, A. D. (2007). Involvement in traditional and electronic bullying among adolescents. *Developmental Psychology, 43,* 564–575.

Raths, L., Harmin, M., & Simon, S. (1966). *Values and teaching.* Columbus, OH: Merrill.

Raver, C. C. (2012). Low-income children's self-regulation in the classroom: Scientific inquiry for social change. *American Psychologist, 67,* 681–689.

Ravitch, D. (1983). *The troubled crusade: American education, 1945–1980.* New York: Basic Books.

Raz, N. (2000). Aging of the brain and its impact on cognitive performance: Integration of structural and functional findings. In Craik, F. I. M. & Salthouse, T. A. (Eds.), *The handbook of aging and cognition* (pp. 1–90) Mahwah, NJ: Erlbaum.

Reese, E., & Fivush, R. (1993). Parental styles of talking about the past. *Developmental Psychology, 29,* 596–606.

Reese, B. M., Haydon, A. A., Herring, A. H., & Halpern, C. T. (2012). The association between sequences of sexual initiation and the likelihood of teenage pregnancy *Journal of Adolescent Health.* Retrieved from www .sciencedirect.com.ezaccess.libraries.psu.edu/ science/article/pii/S1054139X1200225X

Reese, E., & Newcombe, R. (2007). Training mothers in elaborative reminiscing enhances children's autobiographical memory and narrative. *Child Development, 78,* 1153–1170.

Reich, R. B. (2000). *The future of success.* New York: Knopf.

Reid, J. B., Patterson, G. R., & Snyder, J. J. (2002). *Antisocial behavior in children and adolescents: A developmental analysis and the Oregon model for intervention.* Washington, DC: American Psychological Association.

Reik, W., Dean, W., & Walter, J. (2001). Epigenetic reprogramming in mammalian development. *Science, 293,* 1089–1092.

Reiner, W. G., & Gearhart, J. P. (2004). Discordant sexual identity in some genetic males with cloacal exstrophy assigned to female sex at birth. *New England Journal of Medicine, 350,* 333–341.

Reis, E. (2007). Divergence or disorder? The politics of naming intersex. *Perspectives in Biology and Medicine, 50,* 535–543.

Reisman, J. E. (1987). Touch, motion, and proprioception. In P. Salapatek & L. Cohen

(Eds.), *Handbook of infant perception: Vol. 1. From sensation to perception* (pp. 265–304). Orlando, FL: Academic Press.

Reitzes, D. C., & Mutran, E. J. (2004). The transition to retirement: Stages and factors that influence retirement adjustment. *International Journal of Aging and Human Development, 59,* 63–84.

Resnick, M. D., Catalano, R. F., Sawyer, S. M., Viner, R., & Patton, G. C. (2012). Seizing the opportunities of adolescent health. *The Lancet, 379,* 1564–1567.

Resta, R., Biesecker, B. B., Bennett, R. L., Blum, S., Hahn, S. E., Strecker, M. N., et al. (2006). A new definition of genetic counseling: National Society of Genetic Counselors' Task Force Report. *Journal of Genetic Counseling, 15,* 77–83.

Reul, J. M., & de Kloet, E. R., 1985. Two receptor systems for corticosterone in rat brain: Microdistribution and differential occupation. *Endocrinology 117,* 2505–2511.

Reuter-Lorenz, P. A., & Cappell, K. A. (2008). Neurocognitive aging and the compensation hypothesis. *Current Directions in Psychological Science, 17,* 177–182.

Reuter-Lorenz, P. A., & Mikels, J. (2006). The aging mind and brain: Implications of enduring plasticity for behavioral and cultural change. In P. Baltes, P. A. Reuter-Lorenz, & F. Roesler (Eds.), *Lifespan development and the brain: The perspective of biocultural co-constructivism* (pp. 255–276). Cambridge, UK: Cambridge University Press.

Reyna, V. F., & Farley, F. (2006). Risk and rationality in adolescent decision making: Implications for theory, practice, and public policy. *Psychological Science in the Public Interest, 7,* 1–44.

Reynolds, A. (2000). *Success in early intervention: The Chicago Child-Parent Centers.* Lincoln: University of Nebraska Press.

Reynolds, A. J., & Suh-Ruu, O. (2003). Promoting resilience through early childhood intervention. In S. S. Luthar (Ed.), *Resilience and vulnerability: Adaptation in the context of childhood adversities* (pp. 436–462). Cambridge, England: Cambridge University Press.

Rheingold, H. L. (1956). The modification of social responsiveness in institutional babies. *Monographs of the Society for Research in Child Development, 21*(2, Serial No. 63).

Rhoades, L., & Eisenberger, R. (2002). Perceived organizational support: A review of the literature. *Journal of Applied Psychology, 87,* 698–714.

Rholes, W. S., Simpson, J. A., & Stevens, J. G. (1998). Attachment orientations, social support, and conflict resolution in close relationships. In J. A. Simpson & W. S. Rholes (Eds.), *Attachment theory and close relationships* (pp. 166–188). New York: Guilford Press.

Ricciardelli, L., & McCabe, M. P. (2004). A biopsychosocial model of disordered eating and the pursuit of muscularity in adolescent boys. *Psychological Bulletin, 130,* 179–205.

Richards, J. M., Plate, R. C., & Ernst. M. (2012). Neural systems underlying motivated behavior in adolescence: Implications for preventive medicine. *Preventive Medicine, 55,* S7–S16.

Richards, T. A., Wrubel, J., & Folkman, S. (1999–2000). Death rites in the San Francisco gay community: Cultural developments of the AIDS epidemic. *Omega, 40,* 335–350.

Richmond, J., & Nelson, C. A. (2007). Accounting for change in declarative memory: A cognitive neuroscience perspective. *Developmental Review, 27,* 349–373.

Rideout, V., & Hamel, E. (2006). *The media family: Electronic media in the lives of infants, toddlers, preschoolers and their parents.* Menlo Park, CA: Kaiser Family Foundation.

Riley, E. P., Infante, M. A., & Warren, K. R. (2011). Fetal alcohol spectrum disorders: An overview. *Neuropsychological Review, 21,* 73–80.

Rindermann, H., & Ceci, S. J. (2009). Educational policy and country outcomes in international cognitive competence studies. *Perspectives on Psychological Science, 4,* 551–577.

Rindfuss, R. R. (1991). The young adult years: Diversity, structural change, and fertility. *Demography, 28,* 493–512.

Rivers, I., Poteat, V. P., & Noret, N. (2008). Victimization, social support, and psychosocial functioning among children of same-sex and opposite-sex couples in the United Kingdom. *Developmental Psychology, 44,* 127–134.

Rizzolatti, G., & Craighero, L. (2004). The mirror-neuron system. *Annual Review of Neuroscience, 27,* 169–192.

Rizzolatti, G., Fadiga, L., Fogassi, L., & Gallese, V. (1996). Premotor cortex and the recognition of motor actions. *Cognitive Brain Research, 3,* 131–141.

Roberts, B. W., & Mroczek, D. (2008). Personality trait change in adulthood. *Current Directions in Psychological Science, 17,* 31–35.

Roberts, B. W., Walton, K. E., & Viechtbauer, W. (2006). Patterns of mean-level change in personality traits across the life course: A meta-analysis of longitudinal studies. *Psychological Bulletin, 132,* 1–25.

Roberts, W., & Strayer, J. (1996). Empathy, emotional expressiveness, and prosocial behavior. *Child Development, 67,* 449–470.

Robertson, J., & Robertson, J. (1989). *Separation and the very young.* London: Free Association Books.

Robertson, K. F., Smeets, S., Lubinski, D., & Benbow, C. P. (2010). Beyond the threshold hypothesis: Even among the gifted and top math/science graduate students, cognitive abilities, vocational interests, and lifestyle preferences matter for career choice, performance, and persistence. *Current Directions in Psychological Science, 19,* 346–351.

Robins, L., & Pryzbeck, T. (1985). Age of onset of drug use as a factor in drug and other disorders. In C. R. Jones & R. J. Battjes (Eds.), *Etiology of drug abuse: Implications for prevention* (pp. 178–192). Washington, DC: U.S. Government Printing Office.

Robins, R. W., & Pals, J. (1998). *Implicit self-theories of ability in the academic domain: A test of Dweck's model.* Unpublished manuscript.

Robins, R. W., & Trzesniewski, K. H. (2005). Self-esteem development across the lifespan. *Current Directions in Psychological Science, 14,* 158–162.

Robinson, F. P., Mathews, H. L., & Witek-Janusek, L. (2003). Psycho-endocrine-immune response to mindfulness-based stress reduction in individuals infected with the human immunodeficiency virus: A quasi-experimental study. *Journal of Alternative and Complementary Medicine, 9,* 683–694.

Robinson, I., Ziss, K., Ganza, B., Katz, S., & Robinson, E. (1991). Twenty years of sexual revolution, 1965–1985: An update. *Journal of Marriage and the Family, 53,* 216–220.

Robinson, J. L., Zahn-Waxler, C., & Emde, R. N. (1994). Patterns of development in early empathic behavior: Environmental and child constitutional influences. *Social Development, 3,* 125–145.

Robinson, M., Mattes, E., Oddy, W. H., Pennell, C. E., Van Eekelen, A., McLean, N. J., et al. (2011). Prenatal stress and risk of behavioral morbidity from age 2 to 14 years: The influence of the number, type, and timing of stressful life events. *Development and Psychopathology 23,* 507–520.

Robles, T. F., Glaser, R., & Kiecolt-Glaser, J. K. (2005). Out of balance: A new look at chronic stress, depression, and immunity. *Current Directions in Psychological Science, 14,* 111–115.

Rogers, C. R. (1951). *Client-centered therapy.* Boston: Houghton Mifflin.

Rogers, S., & Lewis, H. (1989). An effective day treatment model for young children with pervasive developmental disorders. *Journal of the American Academy of Child & Adolescent Psychiatry, 28,* 207–214.

Rogers, S. J., Hayden, D., Hepburn, S., Charlifue-Smith, R., Hall, T., & Hayes, A. (2006). Teaching young nonverbal children with autism useful speech: A pilot study of the Denver Model and PROMPT interventions. *Journal of Autism and Developmental Disorders, 36,* 1007–1024.

Rogler, L. H. (2002). Historical generations and psychology: The case of the Great Depression and World War II. *American Psychologist, 57,* 1013–1023.

Rogoff, B. (1998). Cognition as a collaborative process. In W. Damon (Series Ed.), D. Kuhn & R. S. Siegler (Vol. Eds.), *Handbook of child psychology: Vol. 2. Cognition, perception, and language* (5th ed., pp. 679–744). New York: Wiley.

Rogoff, B. (2003). *The cultural nature of human development.* New York: Oxford University Press.

Roisman, G. I. (2007). The psychophysiology of adult attachment relationships: Autonomic reactivity in marital and premarital interactions. *Developmental Psychology, 43,* 39–53.

Roisman, G. I. (2009). Adult attachment: Toward a rapprochement of methodological cultures. *Current Directions in Psychological Science, 18,* 122–126.

Roisman, G. I., Clausell, E., Holland, A., Fortuna, K., & Elieff, C. (2008). Adult romantic relationships as contexts of human development: A multimethod comparison of same-sex couples with opposite-sex dating, engaged, and married dyads. *Developmental Psychology, 44,* 91–101.

Roisman, G. I., Fraley, R. C., & Belsky, J. (2007). A taxometric study of the Adult Attachment Interview. *Developmental Psychology, 43,* 675–686.

Roisman, G. I., Susman, E., Barnett-Walker, K., Booth-LaForce, C., Owen, M. T., Belsky, J., et al. (2009). Early family and child-care antecedents of awakening cortisol levels in adolescence. *Child Development, 80,* 907–920.

Roisman, G. I., Tsai, J. L., & Chiang K-H. S. (2004). The emotional integration of childhood experience: Physiological, facial expressive, and self-reported emotional response during the adult attachment interview. *Developmental Psychology, 40,* 776–789.

Rolf, J., Masten, A., Cicchetti, D., Neuchterlein, K., & Weintraub, S. (Eds.). (1990). *Risk and protective factors in the development of psychopathology.* New York: Cambridge University Press.

Rollins, B. C., & Feldman, H. (1970). Marital satisfaction over the family life cycle. *Journal of Marriage and the Family, 32,* 20–28.

Romeo, R. D. (2010). Adolescence: A central event in shaping stress reactivity. *Developmental Psychobiology, 52,* 244–253.

Romer, R., & Walker, E. (Eds.). (2007). *Adolescent psychopathology and the developing brain: Integrating brain and prevention science.* New York: Oxford University Press.

Rook, K. S. (2000). The evolution of social relationships in later adulthood. In S. H. Qualls &

N. Abeles (Eds.), *Psychology and the aging revolution: How we adapt to longer life* (pp. 173–191). Washington, DC: American Psychological Association.

Root, M. P. P. (1999). The biracial baby boom: Understanding ecological constructions of racial identity in the 21st century. In R. H. Sheets & E. R. Hollins (Eds.), *Racial and ethnic identity in school practices* (pp. 67–89). Mahwah, NJ: Erlbaum.

Roschelle, J. M., Pea, R. D., Hoadley, C. M., Gordin, D. N., & Means, D. N. (2000). Changing how and what children learn in school with computer-based technologies. *Children & Computer Technology, 10,* 76–101.

Rosemond, J. K. (1991). *Parent power: A common sense approach to parenting in the 90's and beyond.* Kansas City, MO: Andrews McMeel.

Rosenberg, M. (1979). *Conceiving the self.* New York: Basic Books.

Rosenblatt, P. C., Walsh, R., & Jackson, D. A. (1972). Coping with anger and aggression in mourning. *Omega, 3,* 271–284.

Rosenbaum, J. E., & Becker, K. I. (2011). The early college challenge: Navigating disadvantaged students' transition to college. *American Educator, 35,* 14–20, 39.

Rosenbaum, H. E., Stephan, J. L., & Rosenbaum, J. E. (2010). Beyond one-size-fits-all college dreams: Alternative pathways to desirable careers. *American Educator, 34,* 2–13.

Rosenthal, R. (2003). Covert communication in laboratories, classrooms, and the truly real world. *Current Directions in Psychological Science, 12,* 151–154.

Ross, H., Tesla, C., Kenyon, B., & Lollis, S. (1990). Maternal intervention in toddler peer conflict: The socialization of principles of justice. *Developmental Psychology, 26,* 994–1003.

Rosvold, H. E., Mirsky, A. F., Sarason, I., Bransome, E. D., Jr., & Beck, L. H. (1956). A continuous performance test of brain damage. *Journal of Consulting Psychology, 20,* 343–350.

Roth, S., & Cohen, L. J. (1986). Approach, avoidance, and coping with stress. *American Psychologist, 41,* 813–819.

Rothbart, M. K., Ahadi, S. A., & Evans, D. E. (2000). Temperament and personality: Origins and outcomes. *Journal of Personality and Social Psychology, 78,* 122–135.

Rothbart, M. K., & Bates, J. E. (1998). Temperament. In W. Damon (Series Ed.) & N. Eisenberg (Vol. Ed.), *Handbook of child psychology: Vol. 3. Social, emotional, and personality development* (5th ed., pp. 105–176). New York: Wiley.

Rothbart, M. K. (2011). *Becoming who we are: Temperament and personality in development.* New York: Guilford Press.

Rothbart, M. K., Derryberry, D., & Posner, M. I. (1994). A psychobiological approach to the development of temperament. In J. E. Bates & T. D. Wachs (Eds.), *Temperament: Individual differences at the interface of biology and behavior* (pp. 83–116). Washington, DC: American Psychological Association.

Rothbart, M. K., & Sheese, B. E. (2007). Temperament and emotion regulation. In J. J. Gross (Ed.), *Handbook of emotion regulation* (pp. 331–350). New York: Guilford Press.

Rothbaum, F., Weisz, J., Pott, M., Miyake, K., & Morelli, G. (2000). Attachment and culture: Security in the United States and Japan. *American Psychologist, 55,* 1093–1104.

Rothbaum, F., Weisz, J. R., & Snyder, S. (1982). Changing the world and changing the self: A two process model of perceived control. *Journal of Personality and Social Psychology, 42,* 5–37.

Rousseau, J. J. (1762/1948). *Emile, or education* (B. Foxley, Trans.). New York: Oxford University Press.

Rovee-Collier, C., & Barr, R. (2001). Infant learning and memory. In G. Bremner & A. Fogel (Eds.), *Blackwell handbook of infant development* (pp. 139–168). Malden, MA: Blackwell.

Rowe, J. W., & Kahn, R. L. (1998). *Successful aging.* New York: Pantheon Books.

Rowe, M. L., Raudenbush, S. W., & Goldin-Meadow, S. (2012). The pace of vocabulary growth helps predict later vocabulary. *Child Development, 83,* 508–525.

Rowe, R., Maughan, B., Worthman, C. M., Costello, E. J., & Angold, A. (2004). Testosterone, antisocial behavior, and social dominance in boys: Pubertal development and biosocial interaction. *Biological Psychiatry, 55,* 546–552.

Rozario, P. A., Morrow-Howell, N., & Hinterlong, J. E. (2004). Role enhancement or role strain: Assessing the impact of multiple productive roles on older caregiver well-being. *Research on Aging, 26,* 413–428.

Rubin, K. H., Bukowski, W., & Parker, J. G. (1998). Peer interactions, relationships, and groups. In W. Damon (Series Ed.) & N. Eisenberg (Vol. Ed.), *Handbook of child psychology: Vol. 3. Social, emotional, and personality development* (5th ed., pp. 619–700). New York: Wiley.

Rubin, K. H., Bukowski, W. M., & Parker, J. G. (2006). Peer interactions, relationships, and groups. In W. Damon & R. M. Lerner (Series Eds.), N. Eisenberg (Vol. Ed.), *Handbook of child psychology: Vol. 3. Social, emotional, and personality development* (6th ed., pp. 571–645). Hoboken, NJ: Wiley.

Rubin, K. H., & Coplan, R. J. (1992). Peer relationships in childhood. In M. H. Bornstein & M. E. Lamb (Eds.), *Developmental psychology: An advanced textbook* (3rd ed., pp. 519–578). Hillsdale, NJ: Erlbaum.

Rubin, K. H., Coplan, R. J., & Bowker, J. C. (2009). Social withdrawal in childhood. *Annual Review of Psychology, 60,* 141–171.

Rubin, K. H., Coplan, R., Chen, X., Bowker, J., & McDonald, K. L. (2011). Peer relationships in childhood. In M. E. Lamb & M. H. Bornstein (Eds.), *Social and personality development: An advanced textbook* (pp. 309–360). New York: Psychology Press.

Rubin, K. H., Hastings, P., Chen, X., Stewart, S., & McNichol, K. (1998). Intrapersonal and maternal correlates of aggression, conflict, and externalizing problems in toddlers. *Child Development, 69,* 1614–1629.

Rubin, S. (1981). A two-track model of bereavement: Theory and application in research. *American Journal of Orthopsychiatry, 51,* 101–109.

Ruble, D. N., Gruelich, F., Pomerantz, E. M., & Gochberg, G. (1993). The role of gender-related processes in the development of sex differences in self-evaluation and depression. *Journal of Affective Disorders, 29,* 97–128.

Ruble, D. N., Martin, C. L., & Berenbaum, S. A. (2006). Gender development. In W. Damon & R. M. Lerner (Series Eds.), N. Eisenberg (Vol. Ed.), *Handbook of child psychology: Vol. 3. Social, emotional, and personality development* (6th ed., pp. 789–857). Hoboken, NJ: Wiley.

Ruble, D. N., Taylor, L. J., Cyphers, L., Greulich, F. K., Lurye, L. E., & Shrout, P. E. (2007). The role of gender constancy in early gender development. *Child Development, 78,* 1121–1136.

Rudolph, K. D., & Flynn, M. (2007). Childhood adversity and youth depression: Influence of gender and pubertal status. *Development and Psychopathology, 19,* 497–521.

Rudy, D., & Grusec, J. E. (2006). Authoritarian parenting in individualist and collectivist groups: Associations with maternal emotion and cognition and children's self-esteem. *Journal of Family Psychology, 20,* 68–78.

Rueda, R., Rothbart, M., McCandliss, B., Saccomanno, L., & Posner, M. (2005). Training, maturation, and genetic influences on the development of executive attention. *Proceedings of the National Academy of Sciences USA, 102,* 14931–14936.

Ruffman, T., Slade, L., & Crowe, E. (2002). The relation between children's and mother's mental state language and theory-of-mind understanding. *Child Development, 73,* 734–751.

Rush, D., Stein, Z., & Susser, M. (Eds.). (1980). *Diet in pregnancy: A randomized controlled trial of nutritional supplements.* New York: Liss.

Rusk, N., & Rothbaum, F. (2010). From stress to learning: Attachment theory meets goal orientation theory. *Review of General Psychology, 14,* 31–43.

Russell, A., Hart, C. H., Robinson, C. C., & Olsen, S. F. (2003). Children's sociable and aggressive behavior with peers: A comparison of the United States and Australia, and contributions of temperament and parenting style. *International Journal of Behavioral Development, 27,* 74–86.

Rutter, M. (1986). The developmental pathology of depression: Issues and perspectives. In M. Rutter, C. E. Izard, & P. B. Read (Eds.), *Depression in young people: Developmental and clinical perspectives* (pp. 3–30). New York: Guilford Press.

Rutter, M. (2002). Nature, nurture, and development: From evangelism through science toward policy and practice. *Child Development, 73,* 1–21.

Rutter, M. (2005). Incidence of autism spectrum disorders: Changes over time and their meaning. *Acta paediatrica, 94,* 2–15.

Rutter, M., & Giller, H. (1983). *Juvenile delinquency: Trends and perspectives.* New York: Penguin.

Rutter, M., Sonuga-Barke, E. J., Colvert, E., Kreppner, J., Beckett, C., et al. (2007). Early adolescent outcomes for institutionally-deprived and non-deprived adoptees. I: Disinhibited attachment. *Journal of Child Psychology and Psychiatry, 48,* 17–30.

Rutter, M., & Sroufe, L. A. (2000). Developmental psychopathology: Concepts and challenges. *Development and Psychopathology, 12,* 265–296.

Rutter, M., Tizard, J., & Whitmore, K. *Health and behaviour.* London: Longman, 1970.

Rutter, V. (1995, January/February). Adolescence: Whose hell is it? *Psychology Today,* pp. 54–60, 62, 64, 66, 68.

Ryan, M. P. (1984). Monitoring text comprehension: Individual differences in epistemological standards. *Journal of Educational Psychology, 76,* 248–258.

Ryan, R. M., Chirkov, V. I., Little, T. D., Sheldon, K. M., Timoshina, E., & Deci, E. L. (1999). The American Dream in Russia: Extrinsic aspirations and well-being in two cultures. *Personality and Social Psychology Bulletin, 25,* 1509–1524.

Ryan, R. M., & Deci, E. L. (2000). Self-determination theory and the facilitation of intrinsic motivation, social development, and well-being. *American Psychologist, 55,* 68–78.

Ryan, R. M., & Deci, E. L. (2003). On happiness and human potentials: A review of research on hedonic and eudaimonic well-being. *Annual Review of Psychology, 52,* 141–166.

Ryan, R. M., Huta, V., & Deci, E. L. (2008). Living well: A self-determination theory perspective on eudaimonia. *Journal of Happiness Studies, 9,* 139–170.

Ryff, C. D., & Keyes, C. L. M. (1995). The structure of psychological well-being revisited. *Journal of Personality and Social Psychology, 69,* 719–727.

Ryff, C. D., Lee, Y. H., Essex, M. J., & Schmutte, P. S. (1994). My children and me: Mid-life evaluations of grown children and of self. *Psychology and Aging, 9,* 195–205.

Ryff, C. D., & Singer, B. (2000). Interpersonal flourishing: A positive health agenda for the new millennium. *Personality and Social Psychology Review, 4,* 30–44.

Ryff, C. D., & Singer, B. (2003). Flourishing under fire: Resilience as a prototype of challenged thriving. In C. L. M. Keyes & J. Haidt (Eds.), *Flourishing: Positive psychology and the life well-lived* (pp. 15–36). Washington, DC: American Psychological Association.

Ryff, C. D., & Singer, B. H. (2008). Know thyself and become what you are: A eudaimonic approach to psychological well-being. *Journal of Happiness Studies, 9,* 13–39.

Ryland, E. B., Riordan, R. J., & Brack, G. (1994). Selected characteristics of high-risk students and their enrollment persistence. *Journal of College Student Development, 35,* 54–58.

Saarni, C., Campos, J. J., Camras, L. A., & Witherington, D. (2006). Emotional development: Action, communication, and understanding. In W. Damon & R. M. Lerner (Series Eds.), N. Eisenberg (Vol. Ed.), *Handbook of child psychology: Vol. 3. Social, emotional, and personality development* (6th ed., pp. 226–299). Hoboken, NJ: Wiley.

Sabbagh, M. A., Xu, F., Carlson, S. M., Moses, L. J., & Lee, K. (2006). The development of executive functioning and theory of mind: A comparison of Chinese and U.S. preschoolers. *Psychological Science, 17,* 74–81.

Sachdeva, S., Singh, P., & Medin, D. (2011). Culture and the quest for universal principles in moral reasoning. *International Journal of Psychology, 46,* 161–176.

Sadker, M. P., & Sadker, D. M. (1991). *Teachers, schools, and society* (2nd ed.). New York: Random House.

Sadler, J. Z., & Hulgus, Y. F. (1994). Enriching the psychosocial context of a multiaxial nosology. In J. Z. Sadler, O. P. Wiggins, & M. A. Schwartz (Eds.), *Philosophical perspectives on psychiatric diagnostic classification* (pp. 261–278). Baltimore: Johns Hopkins University Press.

Sagi, A., Koren-Karie, N., Gini, Y. Z., & Tirtsa, J. (2002). Shedding further light on the effects of various types and quality of early child care on infant-mother attachment relationship: The Haifa study of early child care. *Child Development, 73,* 1166–1186.

Sagi, A., van IJzendoorn, M. H., Aviezer, O., Donnell, F., Koren-Karie, N., Joels, T., et al. (1995). Attachments in a multiple-caregiver and multiple-infant environment: The case of the Israeli kibbutzim. In E. Waters, B. E. Vaughn, G. Posada, & K. Kondo-Ikemura (Eds.), *Caregiving, cultural and cognitive perspectives on secure-base behavior and working models: New growing points in attachment theory and research. Monographs of the Society for Research in Child Development, 60* (Serial No. 244), 71–91.

Salmon, D. P., & Bondi, M. W. (2009). Neuropsychological assessment of dementia. *Annual Review of Psychology, 60,* 257–282.

Salovey, P., & Mayer, J. D. (1990). Emotional intelligence. *Imagination, Cognition, and Personality, 9,* 185–211.

Salthouse, T. A. (2006). Mental exercise and mental aging: Evaluating the validity of the "Use it or lose it" hypothesis. *Perspectives on Psychological Science, 1,* 68–87.

Salthouse, T. A. (2009). When does age-related cognitive decline begin? *Neurobiology of Aging, 30,* 507–514.

Salthouse, T. (2012). Consequences of age-related cognitive declines. *Annual Review of Psychology, 63,* 201–206.

Sameroff, A., & Chandler, M. J. (1975). Reproductive risk and the continuum of caretaking casualty. In F. D. Horowitz, M. Hetherington, S. Scarr-Salapatek, & G. Siegel (Eds.), *Review of child development research* (Vol. 4, pp. 187–244). Chicago: University of Chicago Press.

Sameroff, A. J. (2000). Dialectical processes in developmental psychopathology. In A. J. Sameroff, M. Lewis, & S. M. Miller (Eds.), *Handbook of developmental psychopathology* (2nd ed., pp. 23–40). New York: Kluwer Academic/Plenum Press.

Sameroff, A. J. (2012). Discontinuity: The hallmark of developmental science. *International Journal of Development Science, 6,* 37–39.

Sameroff, A. J., & Mackenzie, M. J. (2003). Research strategies for capturing transactional models of development: The limits of the possible. *Development and Psychopathology, 15,* 613–640.

Sampson, R. J., Morenoff, J. D., & Earls, F. (1999). Beyond social capital: Spatial dynamics of collective efficacy for children. *American Sociological Review, 64,* 633–660.

Sandmaier, M. (1996, May/June). More than love. *Family Therapy Networker,* pp. 21–33.

Sandnabba, N. K., & Ahlberg, C. (1999). Parents' attitudes and expectations about children's cross-gender behavior. *Sex Roles, 40,* 249–264.

Sanford, N. (1962). *The American college: A psychological and social interpretation of higher learning.* New York: Wiley.

Santelli, J. S., Orr, M., Lindberg, L. D., & Diaz, D. C. (2009). Changing behavioral risk for pregnancy among high school students in the United States, 1991–2007. *Journal of Adolescent Health, 45,* 25–32.

Santelli, J., Ott, M. A., Lyon, M., Rogers, J., Summers, D., & Schleifer, R. (2006). Abstinence and abstinence-only education: a review of U.S. policies and programs. *Journal of Adolescent Health. 2006,* 72–81.

Sapolsky, R. M. (1984). A mechanism for glucocorticoid toxicity in the hippocampus: Increased neuronal vulnerability to metabolic insult. *Journal of Neuroscience, 5,* 1228–1232.

Sapolsky, R. M. (1992). *Stress: The aging brain and the mechanisms of neuron death.* Cambridge, MA: MIT Press.

Sapolsky, R. M. (2004). *Why zebras don't get ulcers.* New York: Holt.

Saraglou, V. (2002). Religion and the five factors of personality: A meta-analytic review. *Personality and Individual Differences, 32,* 15–25.

Sarason, I. G., & Sarason, B. R. (1985). *Social support: Theory, research, and applications.* Boston: Martinus Nijhoff.

Sattler, J. M., & Ryan, J. J. (1998). *Assessment of children* (3rd ed.). San Diego, CA: Sattler.

Saudino, K. J. (2012). Sources of continuity and change in activity level in early childhood. *Child Development, 83,* 266–281.

Savin-Williams, R. C. (2005). *The new gay teenager.* Cambridge, MA: Harvard University Press.

Savin-Williams, R. C., & Diamond, L. M. (1999). Sexual orientation. In W. K. Silverman & T. H. Ollendick (Eds.), *Developmental issues in the clinical treatment of children* (pp. 241–258). Boston: Allyn & Bacon.

Savin-Williams, R. C., & Ream, G. L. (2007). Prevalence and stability of sexual orientation components during adolescence and young adulthood. *Archives of Sexual Behavior, 36,* 385–394.

Saxon, S. V., & Etten, M. J. (1987). *Physical change and aging: A guide for the helping professions.* New York: Tiresias Press.

Scafidi, F., Field, T., & Schanberg, S. M. (1993). Factors that predict which preterm infants benefit most from massage therapy. *Journal of Developmental and Behavioral Pediatrics, 14,* 176–180.

Scarr, S. (1993). Biological and cultural diversity: The legacy of Darwin for development. *Child Development, 64,* 1333–1353.

Scarr, S. (1997). Behavior-genetic and socialization theories of intelligence: Truce and reconciliation. In R. J. Sternberg & E. L. Girgorenko (Eds.), *Intelligence, heredity, and environment* (pp. 3–41). Cambridge, England: Cambridge University Press.

Scarr, S., & McCartney, K. (1983). How people make their own environments: A theory of genotype-environment effects. *Child Development, 54,* 424–435.

Schacter, S. (1959). *The psychology of affiliation.* Stanford, CA: Stanford University Press.

Schacter, S., & Singer, J. E. (1962). Cognitive, social, and physiological determinants of emotional state. *Psychological Review, 69,* 379–399.

Schafer, R. B., & Keith, P. M. (1980). Equity and depression among married couples. *Social Psychology Quarterly, 43,* 430–435.

Schaffer, H. R., & Emerson, P. E. (1964). The development of social attachments in infancy. *Monographs of the Society for Research in Child Development, 29*(3, Serial No. 94).

Schaie, K. W. (1977–1978). Toward a stage theory of adult cognitive development. *Journal of Aging and Human Development, 8,* 129–139.

Schaie, K. W. (1994). The course of adult intellectual development. *American Psychologist, 49,* 304–313.

Schaie, K. W. (1996). *Intellectual development in adulthood: The Seattle Longitudinal Study.* New York: Cambridge University Press.

Schaie, K. W., & Willis, S. L. (2000). A stage theory model of adult cognitive development revisited. In R. L. Rubinstein, M. Moss, & M. H. Kleban (Eds.), *The many dimensions of aging* (pp. 175–193). New York: Springer.

Scharf, M., Mayseless, O., & Kivenson-Baron, I. (2004). Adolescents' attachment representations and developmental tasks in emerging adulthood. *Developmental Psychology, 40,* 430–440.

Schauble, L. (1991). Belief revision in children: The role of prior knowledge and strategies for generating evidence. *Journal of Experimental Child Psychology, 49,* 31–57.

Schauble, L. (1996). The development of scientific reasoning in knowledge-rich contexts. *Developmental Psychology, 32,* 102–119.

Scheer, S. D., Unger, D. G., & Brown, M. (1994, February). *Adolescents becoming adults: Attributes for adulthood.* Poster presented at the biennial meeting of the Society for Research on Adolescence, San Diego, CA.

Schenkel, S., & Marcia, J. E. (1972). Attitudes toward premarital intercourse in determining ego identity status in college women. *Journal of Personality, 3,* 472–482.

Scheeringa, M. S.,Wright, M. J., Hunt, J. P., & Zeanah, C. H. (2006). Factors affecting the diagnosis and prediction of PTSD symptomatology in children and adolescents. *American Journal of Psychiatry, 163,* 644–651.

Schier, M. F., & Carver, C. S. (1985). Optimism, coping and health: Assessment and implications of generalized outcome expectancies. *Health Psychology, 4,* 219–247.

Schindler, R. (1996). Mourning and bereavement among Jewish religious families: A time for reflection and recovery. *Omega, 33,* 121–129.

Schlegel, A., & Barry, H. III. (1991). *Adolescence: An anthropological inquiry*. New York: Free Press.

Schlossberg, N. (2004). *Retire smart, retire happy: Finding your true path in life*. Washington, DC: American Psychological Association.

Schmader, T. (2010). Stereotype threat deconstructed. *Current Directions in Psychological Science, 19*, 14–18.

Schmidt, L. A., Fox, N. A., & Hamer, D. H. (2007). Evidence for a gene–gene interaction in predicting children's behavior problems: Association of serotonin transporter short and dopamine receptor D4 long genotypes with internalizing and externalizing behaviors in typically developing 7-year-olds. *Development and Psychopathology, 19*, 1105–1116.

Schmidt, M. E., Pempek, T. A., Kirkorian, H. L., Lund, A. F., & Anderson, D. R. (2008). The effects of background television on the toy play behavior of very young children. *Child Development, 79*, 1137–1151.

Schmidt, R. A., & Anderson, D. A. (2007). The impact of television on cognitive development and educational achievement. In N. O. Pecora, J. P. Murray, & E. Wartella (Eds.), *Children and television: Fifty years of research* (pp. 65–84). Mahwah NJ: Erlbaum.

Schmitt, D. P. (2008). Evolutionary perspectives on romantic attachment and culture: How ecological stressors Influence dismissing orientations across genders and geographies. *Cross-Cultural Research, 42*, 220–247.

Schmitt-Rodermund, E., & Vondracek, F. W. (1999). Breadth of interests, exploration, and identity development in adolescence. *Journal of Vocational Behavior, 55*, 298–317.

Schneider, W., & Bjorklund, B. F. (1998). Memory. In W. Damon (Series Ed.), D. Kuhn & R. S. Siegler (Vol. Eds.), *Handbook of child psychology: Vol. 2. Cognition, perception, and language* (5th ed., pp. 467–522). New York: Wiley.

Schneider, W., & Pressley, M. (1997). *Memory development between 2 and 20* (2nd ed.). New York: Springer.

Schneider-Rosen, K., & Cicchetti, D. (1984). The relationship between affect and cognition in maltreated infants: Quality of attachment and visual self-recognition. *Child Development, 55*, 648–658.

Schneider-Rosen, K., & Cicchetti, D. (1991). Early self-knowledge and emotional development: Visual self-recognition and affective reactions to mirror self-image in maltreated and non-maltreated toddlers. *Developmental Psychology, 27*, 481–488.

Schnurr, P. P., Ford, J. D., Friedman, M. J., Green, B. L., Dain, B. J., & Sengupta, A. (2000). Predictors and outcomes of posttraumatic stress disorder in World War II veterans exposed to mustard gas. *Journal of Consulting and Clinical Psychology, 68*, 258–268.

Schoenthaler, S., Doraz, W., & Wakefield, J. (1986). The impact of a low food additive and sucrose diet on academic performance in 803 New York City public schools. *The International Journal of Biosocial Research, 7*, 189–195.

Schommer, M. A. (1990). Effects of beliefs about the nature of knowledge on comprehension. *Journal of Educational Psychology, 82*, 498–504.

Schommer, M. (1993). Epistemological development and academic performance among secondary students. *Journal of Educational Psychology, 85*, 1–6.

Schommer, M., Crouse, A., & Rhodes, N. (1992). Epistemological beliefs and mathematical text comprehension: Believing it is simple does not make it so. *Journal of Educational Psychology, 84*, 435–443.

Schon, D. (1987). *Educating the reflective practitioner: Toward a new design for teaching and learning in the professions*. San Francisco: Jossey-Bass.

Schore, A. N. (1994). *Affect regulation and the origin of the self: The neurobiology of affective development*. Hillsdale, NJ: Erlbaum.

Schore, A. (2012). The *science of the art of psychotherapy*. New York: Norton.

Schouwenburg, H. C. (2004). Procrastination in academic settings: General introduction. In H. C. Schouwenburg, C. H. Lay, T. A. Pychyl, & J. R. Ferrari (Eds.), *Counseling the procrastinator in academic settings* (pp. 3–17). Washington, DC: American Psychological Association.

Schraw, G., & Moshman, D. (1995). Metacognitive theories. *Educational Psychology Review, 7*, 351–371.

Schreibman, T., & Friedland, G. (2003). Human immunodeficiency virus infection prevention: Strategies for clinicians. *Clinical Infectious Diseases, 36*, 1171–1176.

Schroder, L., Tõugu, P., Lenk, M., & De Geer, B. (2011). Cultural expressions of preschoolers' emerging self: Narrative and iconic representations. *Journal of Cognitive Education and Psychology, 10*, 77–95.

Schuengal, C., Bakermans-Kranenburg, M., & van IJzendoorn, M. (1999). Frightening maternal behavior linking unresolved loss and disorganized infant attachment. *Journal of Consulting and Clinical Psychology, 67*, 54–63.

Schulman, M. (2002). How we become moral: The sources of moral motivation. In C. R. Snyder & S. J. Lopez (Eds.), *Handbook of positive psychology* (pp. 499–512). New York: Oxford University Press.

Schulster, J. R. (1996). In my era: Evidence for the perception of a special period of the past. *Memory, 4*, 145–158.

Schultheiss, D. E. P. (2006). The interface of work and family life. *Professional Psychology: Research and Practice, 37*, 334–341.

Schultz, L. H. (1993). *Close peer relationship interview scoring manual*. Unpublished manual, Harvard University, Cambridge, MA.

Schultz, L. H., Barr, D. J., & Selman, R. L. (2001). The value of a developmental approach to evaluating character education programs: An outcome study of facing history and ourselves. *Journal of Moral Education, 30*, 3–27.

Schulz, R., & Curnow, C. (1988). Peak performance and age among superathletes: Track and field, swimming, baseball, tennis, and golf. *Journal of Gerontology, 43*, 113–120.

Schultz, R., & Heckhausen, R. (1996). The life span model of successful aging. *American Psychologist, 51*, 702–713.

Schunk, D. H., & Zimmerman, B. J. (2003). Self-regulation and learning. In I. B. Weiner (Series Ed.), W. M. Reynolds & G. E. Miller (Vol. Eds.), *Handbook of psychology: Vol. 7. Educational psychology* (pp. 59–78). New York: Wiley.

Schwartz, B. (2000). Self-determination: The tyranny of freedom. *American Psychologist, 55*, 79–88.

Schwartz, B. (2004). The tyranny of choice. *Scientific American, 290*, 70–76.

Schwartz, D., Lansford, J. E., Dodge, K. A., Pettit, G. S., & Bates, J. E. (2013). The link between harsh home environments and negative academic trajectories is exacerbated by victimization in the elementary school peer group. *Developmental Psychology, 49*, 305–316. doi: 10.1037/a0028249

Schwartz, R. M., & Garamoni, G. L. (1989). Cognitive balance and psychopathology: Evaluation of an information processing model of positive and negative states of mind. *Clinical Psychology Review, 9*, 271–294.

Schweinhart, L. J. (2003). Three types of early childhood programs in the United States. In H. J. Walberg, A. J. Reynolds, & C. Wang (Eds.), *Early childhood programs for a new century* (pp. 241–254). Washington, DC: Child Welfare League of America.

Schweinhart, L. J. (2007). Crime prevention by the High/Scope Perry Preschool Program, *Victims & Offenders, 2*, 141–160.

Schweinhart, L. J., Montie, J., Ziang, Z., Barnett, W. S., Belfield, C. R., & Nores, M. (2005). *Lifetime effects: The High/Scope Perry Preschool study through age 40*. (Monographs of the High/Scope Educational Research Foundation, 14.) Ypsilanti, MI: High/Scope Press.

Scott, C. G., Murray, G. C., Mertens, C., & Dustin, E. R. (1996). Student self-esteem and the school system: Perceptions and implications. *Journal of Educational Research, 89*, 286–293.

Searight, H. R., & Gafford, J. (2005). Cultural diversity at the end of life: Issues and guidelines for family physicians. *American Family Physician, 71*, 515–522.

Sears, R., Maccoby, E., & Levin, H. (1957). *Patterns of child rearing*. Evanston, IL: Row, Peterson.

Seavey, C. A., Katz, P. A., & Zalk, S. R. (1975). Baby X: The effect of gender labels on adult responses to infants. *Sex Roles, 1*, 103–110.

Sebastian, C., Viding, E., Williams, K. D., & Blakemore, S. J. (2010). Social brain development and the affective consequences of ostracism in adolescence. *Brain and Cognition, 72*, 134–145.

Sedikides, C., & Brewer, M. B. (2001). *Individual self, relational self, collective self*. Philadelphia: Brunner–Routledge.

Segal, Z. V., Williams, J. M. G., & Teasdale, J. D. (2002). *Mindfulness-based cognitive therapy for depression: A new approach to preventing relapse*. New York: Guilford Press.

Segrin, C., & Abramson, L. (1994). Negative reactions to depressed behaviors: A communications theory analysis. *Journal of Abnormal Psychology, 103*, 655–668.

Seligman, M. E. P. (1975). *Helplessness: On depression, development, and death*. San Francisco: Freeman.

Seligman, M. E. P. (1995). *The optimistic child*. Boston: Houghton Mifflin.

Seligman, M. E. P. (2002). *Authentic happiness*. New York: Free Press.

Selman, R. L. (1980). *The growth of interpersonal understanding: Developmental and clinical analysis*. Orlando, FL: Academic Press.

Selman, R. L. (2008). Through thick and thin: Commentary on Martin, Sokol, and Elfers. *Human Development, 51*, 318–325.

Selman, R. L., & Adalbjarnardottir, S. (2000). A developmental method to analyze the personal meaning adolescents make of risk and relationship: The case of "drinking." *Applied Developmental Science, 4*, 47–65.

Selman, R. L., Levitt, M. Z., & Schultz, L. H. (1997) The friendship framework: Tools for the assessment of psychosocial development. In R. L. Selman, C. L. Watts, & L. H. Schultz (Eds.), *Fostering friendship: Pair therapy for treatment and prevention* (pp. 31–52). New York: Aldine de Gruyter.

Selman, R. L., & Schultz, L. H. (1990). Making a friend in youth: Developmental theory and pair therapy. Chicago: University of Chicago Press.

Selman, R. L., Watts, C. L., & Schultz, L. H. (Eds.). (1997). *Fostering friendship: Pair therapy for treatment and prevention*. New York: Aldine de Gruyter.

Seltzer, V. C. (1982). *Adolescent social development: Dynamic functional interaction.* Lexington, MA: Heath.

Selye, H. (1950). Forty years of stress research: Principal remaining problems and misconceptions. *CMA Journal, 115,* 53–55.

Selye, H. (1956). *The stress of life.* New York: McGraw Hill.

Selye, H. (1980). The stress concept today. In I. L. Kutash, L. B. Schlesinger, & Associates (Eds.), *Handbook on stress and anxiety* (pp. 127–143). San Francisco: Jossey-Bass.

Senchak, M., & Leonard, K. E. (1992). Attachment styles and marital adjustment among newlywed couples. *Journal of Personality and Social Psychology, 9,* 51–64.

Senechal, M., & LeFevre, J. (2002). Parental involvement in the development of children's reading skill: A five-year longitudinal study. *Child Development, 73,* 445–460.

Serbin, L. A., & Karp, J. (2004). The intergeneration transfer of psychosocial risk mediators of vulnerability and resilience. *Annual Review of Psychology, 55,* 333–363.

Shaffer, D. R. (1994). *Social and personality development* (3rd ed.). Pacific Grove, CA: Brooks/Cole.

Shaffer, D. R. (2000). *Social and personality development.* Belmont, CA: Wadsworth/Thomson.

Shahaeian, A., Peterson, C. C., Slaughter, V., & Wellman, H. M. (2011). Culture and the sequence of steps in theory of mind development. *Developmental Psychology, 47,* 1239–1247.

Shallcross, A. J., Ford, B. Q., Floerke, V. A., & Mauss, I. B. (2013). Getting better with age: The relationship between age, acceptance, and negative affect. *Journal of Personality and Social Psychology, 104,* 734–749.

Shapiro, A. F., Gottman, J. M., & Carrere, S. (2000). The baby and the marriage: Identifying factors that buffer against decline in marital satisfaction after the first baby arrives. *Journal of Family Psychology, 14,* 59–70.

Shapiro, S. L., Bootzin, R. R., Figueredo, A. J., Lopez, A. M., & Schwartz, G. E. (2003). The efficacy of mindfulness-based stress reduction in the treatment of sleep disturbance in women with breast cancer: An exploratory study. *Journal of Psychosomatic Research, 54,* 85–91.

Shavelson, R. J., Hubner, J. J., & Stanton, G. C. (1976). Validation of construct interpretations. *Review of Educational Research, 46,* 407–441.

Shaw, P., Eckstrand, K., Sharp, W., Blumenthal, J., Lerch, J. P., Greenstein, D., et al. (2007). Attention-deficit/hyperactivity disorder is characterized by a delay in cortical maturation. *Proceedings of the National Academy of Sciences, 104,* 19649–19654.

Shaver, P. R., & Hazan, C. (1988). A biased overview of the study of love. *Journal of Personal and Social Relationships, 5,* 473–501.

Shedler, J., & Block, J. (1990). Adolescent drug use and psychological health: A longitudinal inquiry. *American Psychologist, 45,* 612–630.

Shellman, J., Granara, C., & Rosengarten, G. (2011). Barriers to depression care for black older adults. Practice and policy implication. *Journal of Gerontological Nursing, 37,* 13–17.

Sher, K. J., Bartholow, B. D., & Nanda, S. (2001). Short- and long-term effects of fraternity and sorority membership on heavy drinking: A social norms perspective. *Psychology of Addictive Behaviors, 15,* 42–51.

Shiner, R. L., Masten, A. S., & Roberts, J. M. (2003). Childhood personality foreshadows adult personality and life outcomes two decades later. *Journal of Personality, 71,* 1145–1170.

Shiplett, J. L. (1996). *A glass full of tears: Dementia day-by-day.* Aurora, Ohio: Writers World Press.

Shirk, S. R. (1988). *Cognitive development and child psychotherapy.* New York: Plenum Press.

Shrum, W., & Cheek, N. H. (1987). Social structure during the school years: Onset of the degrouping process. *American Sociological Review, 52,* 218–223.

Shure, M. B., & Spivak, G. (1988). Interpersonal cognitive problem-solving. In R. H. Price, E. L. Cowen, R. P. Lorion, & J. Ramos-McKay (Eds.), *Fourteen ounces of prevention: A casebook for practitioners* (pp. 69–82). Washington, DC: American Psychological Association.

Siegel, A. W., & Scovill, L. C. (2000). Problem behavior: The double symptom of adolescence. *Development and Psychopathology, 12,* 763–793.

Siegel, J. M., & Kuykendall, D. H. (1990). Loss, widowhood, and psychological distress among the elderly. *Journal of Consulting and Clinical Psychology, 58,* 519–524.

Siegel, M. (1987). Are sons and daughters treated more differently by fathers than mothers? *Developmental Review, 7,* 183–209.

Siegel, M., & Peterson, C. C. (1998). Preschoolers' understanding of lies and innocent and negligent mistakes. *Developmental Psychology, 34,* 332–341.

Siegler, R. S. (1987). Strategy choices in subtraction. In J. A. Sloboda & D. Rogers (Eds.), *Cognitive processes in mathematics* (pp. 81–106). Oxford, England: Clarendon.

Siegler, R. S. (1996). *Emerging minds: The process of change in children's thinking.* New York: Oxford University Press.

Siegler, R. S. (1998). *Children's thinking* (3rd ed.). Upper Saddle River, NJ: Prentice Hall.

Siegler, R. S. (2006). Microgenetic analyses of learning. In W. Damon & R. M. Lerner (Series Eds.), D. Kuhn & R. S. Siegler (Vol. Eds.), *Handbook of child psychology: Vol. 2. Cognition, perception and language* (6th ed., pp. 464–510). Hoboken, NJ: Wiley.

Siegler, R. S. (2007). Cognitive variability. *Developmental Science, 10,* 104–109.

Siegler, R. S., & Ramani, G. B. (2008). Playing board games promotes low-income children's numerical development. *Developmental Science, 11,* 655–661.

Siegler, R. S., & Svetina, M. (2006). What leads children to adopt new strategies? A microgenetic/cross-sectional study of class inclusion. *Child Development, 77,* 997–1015.

Siegrist, J. (1996). Adverse health effects of high-effort/low-reward conditions. *Journal of Occupational Health Psychology, 1,* 27–41.

Signorella, M. L., Bigler, R. S., & Liben, L. S. (1993). Developmental differences in children's gender schemata about others: A meta-analytic review. *Developmental Review, 13,* 147–183.

Signorella, M. L., & Liben, L. S. (1984). Recall and reconstruction of gender-related pictures: Effects of attitude, task difficulty, and age. *Child Development, 55,* 393–405.

Silk, J. S., Siegel, G. J., Whalen, D. J., Ostapenko, L. J., Ladoucer, C. D., & Dahl, R. E. (2009). Pubertal changes in emotional information processing: Pupillary, behavioral, and subjective evidence during emotional work identification. *Development and Psychopathology, 21,* 7–26.

Silveira, M., DiPiero, A., Gerrity, M. S., & Feudtner, C. (2000). Patients' knowledge of options at the end of life. *Journal of the American Medical Association, 284,* 2483–2488.

Silverman, P. (2000). Research, clinical practice, and the human experience: Putting the pieces together. *Death Studies, 24,* 469–478.

Sim, T., & Koh, S. (2003). A domain conceptualization of adolescent susceptibility to peer pressure. *Journal of Research on Adolescence, 13,* 57–80.

Sim, T. N., & Yeo, G. H. (2012). Peer crowds in Singapore. *Youth and Society, 44,* 201–216.

Simmons, R. G., & Blyth, D. A. (1987). *Moving into adolescence: The impact of pubertal change and school context.* Hawthorne, NY: Aldine de Gruyter.

Simpkins, S. D., Eccles, J. S., & Becnel, J. N. (2008). The mediational role of adolescents' friends in relations between and activity breadth and adjustment. *Developmental Psychology, 44,* 1081–1094.

Simpson, J. A. (1990). Influence of attachment styles on romantic relationships. *Journal of Personality and Social Psychology, 59,* 971–980.

Simpson, J. A., Collins, W. A., & Salvatore, J. E. (2011). The impact of early interpersonal experience on adult romantic relationship functioning: Recent findings from the Minnesota Longitudinal Study of Risk and Adaptation. *Current Directions in Psychological Science, 20,* 355–369.

Simpson, J. A., Collins, W. A., Tran, S., & Haydon, K. C. (2007). Attachment and the experience and expression of emotions in romantic relationships: A developmental perspective. *Journal of Personality and Social Psychology, 92,* 355–367.

Simpson, J. A., & Rholes, W. S. (1998). *Attachment theory and close relationships.* New York: Guilford Press.

Simpson, J. A., & Rholes, W. S. (2010). Attachment and relationships: Milestones and future directions. *Journal of Social and Personal Relationships, 27,* 173–180.

Simpson, J. A., Rholes, W. S., & Phillips, D. (1996). Conflict in close relationships: An attachment perspective. *Journal of Personality and Social Psychology, 71,* 899–914.

Sinardet, D., & Mortelmans, D. (2009). The feminine side to Santa Claus: Women's work of kinship in contemporary gift-giving relations. *The Social Science Journal, 46,* 124–142.

Singer, B., & Ryff, C. D. (1999). Hierarchies of life stories and associated health risks. In N. E. Adler, B. S. McEwen, & M. Marmot (Eds.), *Socioeconomic status and health in industrialized nations: Social, psychological, and biological pathways* (pp. 96–115). New York: New York Academy of Sciences.

Singer, B., Ryff, C. D., Carr, D., & Magee, W. J. (1998). Life histories and mental health: A person-centered strategy. In A. Raferty (Ed.), *Sociological methodology* (pp. 1–51). Washington, DC: American Sociological Association.

Singer, P., Martin, D., & Merrijoy, K. (1999). Quality of end-of-life care. *Journal of the American Medical Association, 281,* 163–168.

Singer, T., Verhaeghen, P., Ghisletta, P., Lindenberger, U., & Baltes, P. B. (2003). The fate of cognition in very old age: Six-year longitudinal findings in the Berlin Aging Study (BASE). *Psychology and Aging, 18,* 318–331.

Sinnott, J. D. (1984). Postformal reasoning: The relativistic stage. In M. L. Commons, F. A. Richards, & C. Armon (Eds.), *Beyond formal operations: Late adolescent and adult cognitive development* (pp. 298–325). New York: Praeger.

Sinnott, J. D. (1998). *The development of logic in adulthood: Postformal thought and its applications.* New York: Plenum Press.

Sirey, J., Bruce, M. L., Carpenter, M., Booker, D., Reid, M. C., Newell, K. A., et al. (2008). Depressive symptoms and suicidal ideation among older adults receiving home delivered meals. *International Journal of Geriatric Psychiatry, 23,* 1306–1311.

Skinner, B. F. (1938). *The behavior of organisms.* Englewood Cliffs, NJ: Prentice Hall.

Skinner, B. F., & Vaughan, M. E. (1983/1997). *Enjoy old age: A practical guide*. New York: Norton.

Skinner, E. A., Edge, K., Altman, J., & Sherwood, H. (2003). Searching for the structure of coping: A review and critique of category systems for classifying ways of coping. *Psychological Bulletin, 129*, 216–269.

Skinner, M. K. (2011). Environmental epigenetic transgenerational inheritance and somatic epigenetic mitotic stability. *Epigenetics, 6*, 838–842.

Slaby, R. G., & Frey, K. S. (1975). Development of gender constancy and selective attention to same-sex models. *Child Development, 52*, 849–856.

Slade, A. (1999). Attachment theory and research: Implications for the theory and practice of individual psychotherapy with adults. In J. Cassidy & P. R. Shaver (Eds.), *Handbook of attachment: Theory, research, and clinical applications* (pp. 575–594). New York: Guilford Press.

Slade, T., & Andrews, G. (2005). Latent structure of depression in a community sample: A taxometric analysis. *Psychological Medicine, 35*, 489–497.

Slavin, R. E. (1995). *Cooperative learning: Theory, research, and practice* (2nd ed.). Boston: Allyn & Bacon.

Sloane, S., Baillargeon, R., & Premack, D. (2012). Do infants have a sense of fairness? *Psychological Science, 23*, 196–204.

Slomkowski, C., & Dunn, J. (1996). Young children's understanding of other people's beliefs and feelings and their connected communication with friends. *Developmental Psychology, 32*, 442–447.

Slutske, W. S., Moffitt, T. E., Poulton, R., & Caspi, A. (2012). Undercontrolled temperament at age 3 predicts disordered gambling at age 32: A longitudinal study of a complete birth cohort. *Psychological Science, 23*, 510–516.

Smetana, J. G. (1988). Adolescents' and parents' conceptions of parental authority. *Child Development, 59*, 321–335.

Smetana, J. G. (1989). Toddlers' social interactions in the context of moral and conventional transgressions in the home. *Developmental Psychology, 25*, 499–508.

Smetana, J. G. (1995). Parenting styles and conceptions of parental authority during adolescence. *Child Development, 66*, 299–316.

Smetana, J. G. (1997). Parenting and the development of social knowledge reconceptualized: A social domain analysis. In J. E. Grusec & L. Kuczynski (Eds.), *Parenting and children's internalization of values: A handbook of contemporary theory* (pp. 162–192). New York: Wiley.

Smetana, J. G. (2008). "It's 10 o'clock: Do you know where your children are?" Recent advances in understanding parental monitoring and adolescents' information management. *Child Development Perspectives, 2*, 19–25.

Smetana, J. G., & Asquith, P. (1994). Adolescents' and parents' conceptions of parental authority and adolescent autonomy. *Child Development, 65*, 1147–1162.

Smetana, J. G., & Braeges, J. L. (1990). The development of toddler's moral and conventional judgments. *Merrill-Palmer Quarterly, 36*, 329–346.

Smetana, J. G., Crean, H. F., & Campione-Barr, N. (2005). Adolescents' and parents changing conceptions of parental authority. *New Directions for Child and Adolescent Development, 108*, 31–46.

Smetana, J. G., & Daddis, C. (2002). Domain-specific antecedents of parental psychological control and monitoring: The role of parenting beliefs and practices. *Child Development, 73*, 563–580.

Smetana, J. G., Schlagman, N., & Adams, P. W. (1993). Preschool children's judgments about hypothetical and actual transgressions. *Child Development, 64*, 204–214.

Smith, B. W., Shelley, B. M., Leahigh, L., & Vanleit, B. (2006). A preliminary study of the effects of a modified mindfulness intervention on binge eating. *Complementary Health Practice Review, 11*, 133–143.

Smith, C. A., Haynes, K. N., Lazarus, R. S., & Pope, L. K. (1993). In search of the "hot" cognitions: Attributions, appraisals, and their relation to emotion. *Journal of Personality and Social Psychology, 65*, 916–929.

Smith, C. L. (1979). Children's understanding of natural language hierarchies. *Journal of Experimental Child Psychology, 27*, 437–458.

Smith, J., Staudinger, U. M., & Baltes, P. B. (1994). Occupational settings facilitating wisdom-related knowledge: The sample case of clinical psychologists. *Journal of Counseling and Clinical Psychology, 62*, 989–999.

Smith, M., Rogers, S., & Dawson, G. (2008). The Early Start Denver Model: A comprehensive early intervention approach for toddlers with autism. In J. S. Handleman & S. L. Harris (Eds.), *Preschool education programs for children with autism* (3rd ed.). Austin, TX: Pro-Ed.

Smith, P. K., Mahdavi, J., Carvalho, M., Fisher, S., Russell, S., & Tippett, N. (2008). Cyberbullying: Its nature and impact in secondary school pupils. *The Journal of Child Psychology and Psychiatry, 49*, 376–385.

Smith, R. E., & Smoll, F. L. (1990). Self-esteem and children's enhancement to youth coaching behaviors: A field study of self-enhancement processes. *Developmental Psychology, 26*, 987–993.

Smith, S. M., Stinson, F. S., Dawson, D. A., Goldstein, R., Huang, B., & Grant, B. F. (2006). Race/ethnic differences in the prevalence and co-occurrence of substance use disorders and independent mood and anxiety disorders: Results from the National Epidemiologic Survey on Alcohol and Related Conditions. *Psychological Medicine, 36*, 987–998.

Smolak, L., Levine, M. P., & Thompson, J. K. (2001). The use of the Sociocultural Attitudes Towards Appearance Questionnaire with middle school boys and girls. *International Journal of Eating Disorders, 29*, 216–223.

Smyke, A. T., Dumitrescu, A., & Zeanah, C. (2002). Attachment disturbances in young children. I: The continuum of caretaking casualty. *Journal of the American Academy of Child and Adolescent Psychiatry, 41*, 972–982.

Snarey, J. (1985). The cross-cultural universality of social-moral development: A critical review of Kohlbergian research. *Psychological Bulletin, 97*, 202–232.

Snow, C. E. (March, 2007). *Socializing children for academic success: The power and the limit of language*. Paper presented at the meeting of the Society for Research in Child Development, Boston, MA.

Snow, M. S., Wolff, L., Hudspeth, E. F., & Etheridge, L. (2009). The practitioner as researcher: Qualitative case studies in play therapy. *International Journal of Play Therapy, 18*, 240–250.

Snowdon, D. A. (1997). Aging and Alzheimer's disease: Lessons from the Nun Study. *Gerontologist, 37*, 150–156.

Snyder, D., & Wills, R. (1989). Behavioral versus insight-oriented marital therapy: Effects on individual and interspousal functioning. *Journal of Consulting and Clinical Psychology, 57*, 39–46.

Snyder, D. K., Wills, R. M., & Grady-Fletcher, A. (1991). Long-term effectiveness of behavioral versus insight-oriented marital therapy: A four-year follow-up study. *Journal of Consulting and Clinical Psychology, 59*, 138–144.

Snyder, H. N., & Sickmund, M. (2006). *Juvenile offenders and victims: 2006 national report*. Washington, DC: U.S. Department of Justice, Office of Justice Programs, Office of Juvenile Justice and Delinquency Prevention.

Snyder, J. J., & Patterson, G. R. (1995). Individual differences in social aggression: A test of a reinforcement model of socialization info-processing mechanisms in children's social adjustment. *Behavior Therapy, 26*, 371–391.

Sodian, B. (2011). Theory of mind in infancy. *Child Development Perspectives, 5*, 39–43.

Soenens, B., Vansteenkiste, M., Luyckx, K., & Goossens, L. (2006). Parenting and adolescent problem behavior: An integrated model with adolescent self-disclosure and perceived parental knowledge as intervening variables. *Developmental Psychology, 42*, 305–318.

Somech, A. (2007). Strategies for coping with work-family conflict: The distinctive relationships of gender role ideology. *Journal of Occupational Health Psychology, 12*, 1–19.

Sorich, L., & Dweck, C. S. (1996). Mastery-oriented thinking. In C. R. Snyder (Ed.), *Coping*. New York: Oxford University Press.

Soto, C. J., & Luhmann, M. (2013). Who can buy happiness? Personality traits moderate the effects of stable income differences and income fluctuations on life satisfaction. *Social Psychological and Personality Science, 4*, 46–53.

Sowell, E. R., Peterson, B. S., Kan, E., Woods, R. P., Yoshii, J., Bansal, R., et al. (2007). Sex differences in cortical thickness mapped in 176 healthy individuals between 7 and 87 years of age. *Cerebral Cortex, 17*, 1550–1560.

Sowell, E. R., Peterson, B. S., Thompson, P. M., Welcome, S. E., Henkenius, A. L., & Toga, A. W. (2003). Mapping cortical change across the human life span. *Natural Neuroscience, 6*, 309–315.

Sowell, E. R., Thompson, P. M., & Toga, A. W. (2004). Mapping changes in the human cortex throughout the span of life. *The Neuroscientist, 10*, 372–392.

Sowell, E. R., Thompson, P. M., & Toga, A. W. (2007). Mapping adolescent brain maturation using structural magnetic resonance imaging. In D. Romer & E. Walker (Eds.), *Adolescent psychopathology and the developing brain: Integrating brain and prevention science* (pp. 55–84). New York: Oxford University Press.

Sowell, E. R., Thompson, P. M., Welcome, S. E., Henkenius, A. L., Toga, A. W., & Peterson, B. S. (2003). Cortical abnormalities in children and adolescents with attention-deficit hyperactivity disorder. *The Lancet, 362*, 1699–1707.

Spangler, G., & Grossmann, K. E. (1993). Biobehavioral organization in securely and insecurely attached infants. *Child Development, 64*, 1439–1450.

Sparzo, F. J. (2011). Functional behavioral assessment. In A. S. Davis (Ed.), *Handbook of pediatric psychology* (pp. 1017–1025). New York: Springer.

Spaulding, J., & Balch, P. (1983). A brief history of primary prevention in the twentieth century: 1908 to 1980. *American Journal of Community Psychology, 11*, 59–80.

Spear, L. P. (2009). Heightened stress responsivity and emotional reactivity during pubertal maturation: Implications for psychopathology. *Development and Psychopathology, 21*, 87–97.

Spear, L. P. (2010). *The behavioral neuroscience of adolescence*. New York: W.W. Norton.

Spear, L. P. (2011). Adolescent neurobehavioral characteristics, alcohol sensitivities and intake: Setting the stage for alcohol use disorder? *Child Development Perspectives, 5*(4), 231–238.

Spencer, M. B. (1982). Preschool children's social cognition and cultural cognition: A cognitive developmental interpretation of race dissonance findings. *Journal of Psychology, 112,* 275–286.

Spencer, M. B., & Markstrom-Adams, C. (1990). Identity processes among racial and ethnic minority children in America. *Child Development, 61,* 290–310.

Spenser, J. T. (1970). *The effects of systematic and token reinforcement on the modification of racial and color-concept attitudes in preschool-age children.* Unpublished master's thesis, University of Kansas.

Sperry, R. W. (1964). The great cerebral commissure. *Scientific American, 201,* 42–52.

Spieker, S. J., Campbell, S. B., Vandergrift, N., Pierce, K. M., Cauffman, E., et al. (2012). Relational aggression in middle childhood: Predictors and adolescent outcomes. *Social Development, 21,* 354–375.

Spinelli, S., Chefer, S,. Suomi, S. J., Higley, J. D., Barr, C. S., & Stein, E. (2009) Early-life stress induces longterm morphologic changes in primate brain. *Archives of General Psychiatry, 66,* 658–665.

Spokane, A. R., & Cruza-Guet, M. C. (2005). Holland's theory of vocational personalities in work environments. In S. D. Brown & R. W. Lent (Eds.), *Career development and counseling* (pp. 24–41). Hoboken, NJ: Wiley.

Springer, K. W., Pudrovska, T., & Hauser, R. M. (2011). Does psychological well-being change with age? Longitudinal tests of age variations and further exploration of the multidimensionality of Ryff's model of psychological well-being. *Social Science Research, 40,* 392–398.

Srivastava, S., McGonigal, K. M., Richards, J. M., Butler, E. A., & Gross, J. J. (2006). Optimism in close relationships: How seeing things in a positive light makes them so. *Journal of Personality and Social Psychology, 91,* 143–153.

Sroufe, L. A. (1989). Pathways to adaptation and maladaptation: Psychopathology as developmental deviation: The roots of maladaptation and competence. In D. Cicchetti (Ed.), *Rochester Symposium on Developmental Psychopathology: Vol. 1. The emergence of a discipline* (pp. 13–40). Hillsdale, NJ: Erlbaum.

Sroufe, L. A. (1996). *Emotional development: The organization of emotional life in the early years.* New York: Cambridge University Press.

Sroufe, L. A., Bennett, C., Englund, M., Urban, J., & Shulman, S. (1993). The significance of gender boundaries in preadolescence: Contemporary correlates and antecedents of boundary violation and maintenance. *Child Development, 64,* 455–466.

Sroufe, L. A., Egeland, B., Carlson, E., & Collins, W. (2005). *Minnesota Study of Risk and Adaptation from birth to maturity: The development of the person.* New York: Guilford Press.

Sroufe, L. A., Fox, N. E., & Pancake, V. R. (1983). Attachment and dependency in developmental perspective. *Child Development, 54,* 1615–1627.

Sroufe, L. A., & Waters, E. (1977). Attachment as an organizational construct. *Child Development, 48,* 1184–1199.

Stanovich, K. E. (1998). *How to think straight about psychology.* New York: Addison-Wesley/Longman.

Starkman, N., & Rajani, N. (2002). The case for comprehensive sex education. *AIDS Patient Care and STDs, 16*(7), 313–318.

Staudinger, U. M. (1999). Social cognition and a psychological approach to an art of life. In Blanchard-Fields, F. & Hess, T. (Eds.) *Social cognition, adult development, and aging* (pp. 343–375). New York: Academic Press.

Staudinger, U. M., & Baltes, P. B. (1996). Interactive minds: A facilitative setting for wisdom-related performance? *Journal of Personality and Social Psychology, 71,* 746–762.

Staudinger, U. M., & Gluck, J. (2011). Psychological wisdom research: Commonalities and differences in a growing field. *Annual Review of Psychology, 62,* 215–241.

Staudinger, U. M., Maciel, A. G., Smith, J., & Baltes, P. B. (1998). What predicts wisdom-related performance? A first look at personality, intelligence, and facilitative experiential contexts. *European Journal of Personality, 12,* 1–17.

Stein, Z., Susser, M., Saenger, G., & Marolla, F. (1975). *Famine and human development: The Dutch hunger winter of 1944/45.* New York: Oxford University Press.

Steinberg, L. (1996). *Beyond the classroom: Why school reform has failed and what parents need to do.* New York: Simon & Schuster.

Steinberg, L. (2007). Risk taking in adolescence: New perspectives from brain and behavioral science. *Current Directions in Psychological Science, 16,* 55–59.

Steinberg, L. (2010). Commentary: A behavioral scientist looks at the science of adolescent brain development. *Brain and Cognition, 72,* 160–164.

Steinberg, L., & Avenevoli, S. (2000). The role of context in the development of psychopathology: A conceptual framework and some speculative propositions. *Child Development, 71,* 66–74.

Steinberg, L., & Belsky, J. (1991). *Infancy, childhood, and adolescence: Development in context.* New York: McGraw-Hill.

Steinberg, L., & Belsky, J. (1996). A sociobiological perspective on psychopathology in adolescence. In D. Cicchetti & S. Toth (Eds.), *Rochester Symposium on Developmental Psychopathology, 7,* 93–124.

Steinberg, L., Cauffman, E., Banich, M., Graham, S., & Woolard, J. (2008). Age differences in sensation seeking and impulsivity as indexed by behavior and self-report: Evidence for a dual systems model. *Developmental Psychology, 44,* 1764–1778.

Steinberg, L., Dornbusch, S. M., & Brown, B. B. (1992). Ethnic differences in adolescent achievement: An ecological perspective. *American Psychologist, 47,* 723–729.

Steinberg, L., Fegley, S., & Dornbusch, S. M. (1993). The negative impact of part-time work on adolescent adjustment: Evidence from a longitudinal study. *Developmental Psychology, 29,* 171–180.

Steinberg, L., Grisso, T., Woolard, J., Cauffman, E., Scott, E., Graham, S., et al. (2003). Juveniles' competence to stand trial as adults. *Social Policy Report, 17,* 3–7, 11, 13–15.

Steinberg, L., Lamborn, S. D., Darling, N., Mounts, N. S., & Dornbusch, S. M. (1994). Overtime changes in adjustment and competence among adolescents from authoritative, authoritarian, indulgent and neglectful families. *Child Development, 65,* 754–770.

Steinberg, L., Lamborn, S. D., Dornbusch, S. M., & Darling, N. (1992). Impact of parenting practices on adolescent achievement: Authoritative parenting, school involvement and encouragement to succeed. *Child Development, 63,* 1266–1281.

Steinberg, L., & Monahan, K. C. (2007). Age differences in resistance to peer influence. *Developmental Psychology, 43,* 1531–1543.

Steinberg, L., & Scott, E. S. (2003). Less guilty by reason of adolescence: Developmental immaturity, diminished responsibility, and the juvenile death penalty. *American Psychologist, 58,* 1009–1018.

Steinberg, L., & Silk, J. S. (2002). Parenting adolescents. In M. H. Bornstein (Ed.), *Handbook of parenting: Vol. 1. Children and parenting* (2nd ed., pp. 103–133). Mahwah, NJ: Erlbaum.

Steinberg, L., & Silverberg, S. B. (1986). The vicissitudes of autonomy in early adolescence. *Child Development, 57,* 841–851.

Steinberg, S. J., & Davila, J. (2008). Romantic functioning and depressive symptoms among early adolescent girls: The moderating role of parental emotional availability. *Journal of Clinical Child and Adolescent Psychology, 37,* 350–362.

Steiner, H., Kwan, W., Shaffer, T. G., Walker, S., Miller, S., Sagar, A., et al. (2003). Risk and protective factors for juvenile eating disorders. *European Child & Adolescent Psychiatry, 12,* 38–46.

Steingraber, S. (2007). The falling age of puberty in US girls: What we know, what we need to know. Report by the Breast Cancer Fund available at http://pinkribbonblues.org/wp-content/uploads/2010/07/falling-age-of-puberty.pdf

Steinhauser, K. E., Christakis, N. A., Clipp, E. C., McNeilly, M., McIntyre, L., & Tulsky, J. A. (2000). Factors considered important at the end of life by patients, family, physicians, and other care providers. *Journal of the American Medical Association, 284,* 2476–2482.

Stenberg, C., & Campos, J. (1990). The development of anger expressions in infancy. In N. Stein, T. Trabasso, & B. Leventhal (Eds.), *Concepts in emotion* (pp. 75–99). Hillsdale, NJ: Erlbaum.

Stephen, J., Fraser, E., & Marcia, J. E. (1992). Moratorium-achievement (MAMA) cycles in life span identity development: Value orientations and reasoning system. *Journal of Adolescence, 15,* 283–300.

Stephenson, J. (2003). Genes and stress. *Journal of the American Medical Association, 290,* 740.

Steptoe, A., Willemsen, G., Owen, N., Flower, L., & Mohamed-Ali, V. (2001). Acute mental stress elicits delayed increases in circulating inflammatory cytokine levels. *Clinical Science, 101,* 185–192.

Sterling, C. M., & Van Horn, K. R. (1989). Identity and death anxiety. *Adolescence, 24,* 321–326.

Sterling, P., & Eyer, J. (1988). Allostasis: A new paradigm to explain arousal pathology. In S. Fisher & J. Reason (Eds.), *Handbook of life stress, cognition and health* (pp. 629–649). New York: John Wiley & Sons.

Stern, D. (1985). *The interpersonal world of the infant.* New York: Basic Books.

Sternberg, R. J. (1985). *Beyond IQ: A triarchic theory of human intelligence.* New York: Cambridge University Press.

Sternberg, R. J. (1986). A triangular theory of love. *Psychological Review, 93,* 119–135.

Sternberg, R. J. (2001). What is the common thread of creativity: Its dialectical relation to intelligence and wisdom. *American Psychologist, 56,* 360–362.

Sternberg, R. J. (2004). Culture and intelligence. *American Psychologist, 59,* 325–338.

Sternberg, R. J. (2006). A duplex theory of love. In R. J. Sternberg (Ed.), *The new psychology of love* (pp. 184–199). New Haven, CT: Yale University Press.

Sternberg, R. J., & Grigorenko, E. L. (1999). *Our labeled children.* Reading, MA: Perseus Books.

Sterns, H. L., & Huyck, M. H. (2001). The role of work in midlife. In M. E. Lachman (Ed.), *Handbook of midlife development* (pp. 447–486). New York: Wiley.

Stevens, T., & Muslow, M. (2006). There is no meaningful relationship between television exposure and symptoms of attention-deficit/hyperactivity disorder. *Pediatrics, 117,* 665–672.

Stevens-Long, J. (1973). The effect of behavioral context on some aspects of adult disciplinary practice and affect. *Child Development, 44,* 476–484.

Stevenson, H. W., Chen, C., & Lee, S. (1993). Mathematics achievement of Chinese, Japanese, and American children: Ten years later. *Science, 159,* 53–59.

Stevenson, H. W., & Stigler, J. W. (1992). *The learning gap: Why our schools are failing and what we can learn from Chinese and Japanese education.* New York: Simon & Schuster.

Stewart, A. J., & Vandewater, E. A. (1998). The course of generativity. In D. P. McAdams & E. de St. Aubin (Eds.), *Generativity and adult development: How and why we care for the next generation* (pp. 45–74). Washington, DC: American Psychological Association.

Stewart, E. B. (2007). School structural characteristics, student effort, peer associations, and parental involvement. *Education and Urban Society, 40,* 179–204.

Stewart, N., Winborn, B., Johnson, R., Burks, H., & Engelkes, J. (1978). *Systematic counseling.* Upper Saddle River, NJ: Prentice Hall.

Stice, E., (2002). Risk and maintenance factors for eating pathology: A meta-analytic review. *Psychological Bulletin, 128,* 825–848.

Stice, E., & Shaw, H. (2004). Eating disorder prevention programs: A meta-analytic review. *Psychological Bulletin, 130,* 206–227.

Stifter, C. A., Dollar, J. M., & Cipriano, E. A. (2010). Temperament and emotion regulation: The role of autonomic nervous system reactivity. *Developmental Psychobiology, 53,* 266–279.

Stiles, J. (2001). Neural plasticity and cognitive development. *Developmental Neuropsychology, 18,* 237–272.

Stiles, J. (2009). On genes, brains, and behavior: Why should developmental psychologists care about brain development? *Child Development Perspectives, 3,* 196–202.

Stipek, D., Recchia, A., & McClintic, S. (1992). Self-evaluation in young children. *Monographs of the Society for Research in Child Development, 57*(1, Serial No. 226).

Stipek, D. J., Gralinski, J. H., & Kopp, C. B. (1990). Self-concept development in the toddler years. *Developmental Psychology, 26,* 972–977.

St. Lawrence, J. S., Brasfield, T. L., Jefferson, K. W., Alleyne, E., O'Bannon, R. E., & Shirley, A. (1995). Cognitive behavioral interventions to reduce African-American adolescents risk for HIV infection. *Journal of Consulting and Clinical Psychology, 63,* 154–157.

Stoltenberg, C. D., & Delworth, U. (1987). *Supervising counselors and therapists: A developmental approach.* San Francisco: Jossey-Bass.

Stoltenborgh, M., Bakermans-Kranenburg, M. J., & van Ijzendoorn, M. H. (2013). The neglect of child neglect: A meta-analytic review of the prevalence of neglect. *Social Psychiatry and Psychiatric Epidemiology, 48* (55), 345–343.

Stonewater, B. B., & Stonewater, J. K. (1983). Developmental clues: An aid for the practitioner. *NASPA Journal, 21,* 52–59.

Stonewater, B. B., & Stonewater, J. K. (1984). Teaching problem-solving: Implications from cognitive development research. *AAHE Bulletin, 36,* 7–10. Washington, DC: American Association for Higher Education.

Strachan, T., & Read, A. P. (2000). *Human molecular genetics* (2nd ed.). New York: Wiley.

Strassberg, Z., Pettit, K. A., Gregory, S., & Bates, J. E. (1994). Spanking in the home and children's subsequent aggression toward their peers. *Development and Psychopathology, 6,* 445–462.

Strathearn, L. (2011). Maternal neglect: Oxytocin, dopamine and the neurobiology of attachment. *Journal of Neuroendocrinology, 23,* 1054–1065.

Stratton, K., Howe, C., & Battaglia, F. (1996). *Fetal alcohol syndrome: Diagnosis, epidemiology, prevention, and treatment.* Washington, DC: National Academy Press.

Straub, R. E., & Weinberger, D. R. (2006). Schizophrenia genes—famine to feast. *Biological Psychiatry, 60,* 81–83.

Straus, M. A. (1994). *Beating the devil out of them: Corporal punishment in American families.* New York: Lexington Books.

Straus, M. A., & Gelles, R. J. (1990). *Physical violence in American families: Risk factors and adaptation to violence in 841 families.* New Brunswick, NJ: Transaction Books.

Straus, M. A., Sugarman, D. B., & Giles-Sims, J. (1997). Spanking by parents and subsequent antisocial behavior of children. *Archives of Pediatric and Adolescent Medicine, 151,* 761–767.

Straus, M. A., & Yodanis, C. L. (1996). Corporal punishment in adolescence and physical assault on spouses in later life: What accounts for the link? *Journal of Marriage and the Family, 58,* 825–841.

Strauss, A., & Corbin, J. (1990). *Basics of qualitative research: Grounded theory, procedures, and techniques.* Newbury Park, CA: Sage.

Streissguth, A. P., & Dehaene, P. (1993). Fetal alcohol syndrome in twins of alcoholic mothers: Concordance of diagnosis and IQ. *American Journal of Medical Genetics, 47,* 857–861.

Strober, M., Freeman, R., Lampert, C., Diamond, J., & Kaye, W. (2000). A controlled family study of anorexia nervosa and bulimia nervosa: Evidence of shared liability and transmission of partial syndromes. *American Journal of Psychiatry, 157,* 393–401.

Strober, M., Freeman, R., & Morrell, W. (1997). The long-term course of severe anorexia nervosa in adolescents: Survival analysis of recovery, relapse, and outcome prediction over 10–15 years in a prospective study. *International Journal of Eating Disorders, 22,* 339–360.

Stroebe, M. (1992). Coping with bereavement: A review of the grief work hypothesis. *Omega, 26,* 19–42.

Stroebe, M., & Schut, H. (1999). The dual process model of coping with bereavement: Rationale and description. *Death Studies, 23,* 197–224.

Stroebe, M., & Stroebe, W. (1993). Determinants of adjustment to bereavement among younger widows and widowers. In M. Stroebe, W. Stroebe, & R. O. Hansson (Eds.), *Handbook of bereavement: Theory, research, and intervention* (pp. 208–226). New York: Cambridge University Press.

Stroud, L., Foster, E., Handwerger, K., Papandonatos, G. D., Granger, D., Kivilighan, K. T., et al. (2009). Stress response and the adolescent transition: Performance versus peer rejection stress. *Development and Psychopathology, 21,* 47–68.

Strouse, J., Goodwin, M. P., & Roscoe, B. (1994). Correlates of attitudes toward sexual harassment among early adolescents. *Sex Roles, 31,* 559–577.

Strube, M. J. (1981). Meta-analysis and cross-cultural comparison: Sex differences in child competitiveness. *Journal of Cross-Cultural Psychology, 12,* 3–20.

Strupp, H. H. (1988). What is therapeutic change? *Journal of Cognitive Psychotherapy, 2,* 75–82.

Styron, W. (1990). *Darkness visible: A memoir of madness.* New York: Random House.

Subotnik, R. F., Olszewski-Kubilius, P., & Worrell, F. C. (2011). Rethinking giftedness and gifted education: A proposed direction forward based on psychological science. *Psychological Science in the Public Interest, 12,* 3–54.

Substance Abuse and Mental Health Services Administration. (2011). Results from the 2010 *National Survey on Drug Use and Health: Summary of National Findings,* NSDUH Series H-41, HHS Publication No. (SMA) 11-4658. Rockville, MD: Substance Abuse and Mental Health Services Administration.

Subrahmanyam, K., Greenfield, P., Kraut, R., & Gross, E. (2001). The impact of computer use on children's and adolescents' development. *Applied Developmental Psychology, 22,* 7–30.

Suddendorf, T., Simcock, G., & Nielsen, M. (2007). Visual self-recognition in mirrors and live videos: Evidence for a developmental asynchrony. *Cognitive Development, 22,* 185–196.

Sue, D., Mack, W. S., & Sue, D. W. (1998). Ethnic identity. In L. C. Lee & N. W. S. Zane (Eds.), *Handbook of Asian American psychology* (pp. 289–323). Thousand Oaks, CA: Sage.

Sue, D. W., Arredondo, P., & McDavis, R. J. (1992). Multicultural counseling competencies and standards: A call to the profession. *Journal of Counseling and Development, 70,* 477–486.

Suess, G. J., Grossmann, K. E., & Sroufe, L. A. (1992). Effects of infant attachment to mother and father on quality of adaptation in preschool: From dyadic to individual organization of self. *International Journal of Behavioral Development, 15,* 43–65.

Sullivan, H. S. (1953a). *Conceptions of modern psychiatry.* New York: Norton.

Sullivan, H. S. (1953b). *The interpersonal theory of psychiatry.* New York: Norton.

Sullivan, H. S. (1965). *Personal psychopathology.* New York: Norton.

Sullivan, M. W., & Lewis, M. (2003). Contextual determinants of anger and other negative expressions in young infants. *Developmental Psychology, 39,* 693–705.

Suls, J. M., & Miller, R. L. (1977). *Social comparison processes: Theoretical and empirical perspectives.* Washington, DC: Hemisphere.

Sumter, S. R., Bokhorsta, C. L., Miersa, A. C., Van Pelt, J., & Westenberg, P. M. (2010). Age and puberty differences in stress responses during a public speaking task: Do adolescents grow more sensitive to social evaluation? *Psychoneuroendocrinology, 35,* 1510–1516.

Sun, S. S., Schubert, C. M., Chumlea, W. C., Roche, A. F., Kulin, H. E., Lee, P. A., et al. (2002). National estimates of the timing of sexual maturation and racial differences among US children. *Pediatrics, 110,* 911–919.

Super, D. E. (1972). Vocational development theory: Persons, positions, and processes. In J. M. Whiteley & A. Resnikoff (Eds.), *Perspectives on vocational development* (pp. 13–33). Washington, DC: American Personnel and Guidance Association.

Super, D. E. (1984). Career and life development. In D. Brown & L. Brooks (Eds.), *Career choice and development* (pp. 192–234). San Francisco: Jossey-Bass.

Super, D. E. (1990). A life-span, life-space approach to career development. In D. Brown & I. Brooks (Eds.), *Career choice and development: Applying contemporary theories to practice* (pp. 197–261). San Francisco: Jossey-Bass.

Super, D. E., & Overstreet, P. L. (1960). *The vocational maturity of ninth-grade boys.* New York: Teachers College, Columbia University.

Supple, A. J., Ghazarian, S. R., Frabutt, J. M., Plunkett, S. W., & Sands, T. (2006). Contextual influences on Latino adolescent ethnic identity and academic outcomes. *Child Development, 77,* 1427–1433.

Susman, E. J., Dockray, S., Schiefelbein, V. L., Werwehe, S., Heaton, J., & Dorn, L. D. (2007). Morningness/eveningness, morning-to-afternoon cortisol ratio, and antisocial behavior problems during puberty. *Developmental Psychology, 43,* 811–822.

Susman, E. J., Dorn, L. D., & Schiefelbein, V. L. (2003). Puberty, sexuality and health. In I. B. Weiner (Series Ed.), R. M. Lerner, M. A. Easterbrook, & J. Mistry (Vol. Eds.), *Handbook of psychology: Vol. 6. Developmental psychology* (pp. 295–324). Hoboken, NJ: Wiley.

Swaab, D. F. (2008). Sexual orientation and its basis in brain structure and function. *Proceedings of the National Academy of Sciences of the United States of America, 105,* 10273–10274.

Szinovacz, M. E., & Davey, A. (2005). Retirement and marital decision making: Effects on retirement satisfaction. *Journal of Marriage and Family, 67,* 387–398.

Szyf, M. (2011). DNA methylation, the early-life social environment and behavioral disorders. *Journal of Neurodevelopmental Disorders, 3,* 238–249.

Taffel, R. (1996, May/June). The second family. *Family Therapy Networker,* 36–45.

Taffel, R. (2001). *The second family: How adolescent power is challenging the American family.* New York: St. Martin's Press.

Tajfel, H. (1981). *Human groups and social categories.* Cambridge, England: Cambridge University Press.

Takahashi, K. (1986). Examining the strange-situation procedure with Japanese mothers and 12-month-old infants. *Developmental Psychology, 22,* 265–270.

Takahashi, M., & Overton, W. F. (2005). Cultural foundations of wisdom: An integrated developmental approach. In R. J. Sternberg & J. Jordan (Eds.), *A handbook of wisdom: Psychological Perspectives* (pp. 32–60). NY: Cambridge University Press.

Talamantes, M. A., Lawler, W. R., & Espino, D. V. (1995). Hispanic American elders. Care giving norms surrounding dying and the use of hospice services. *Hospital Journal, 10,* 35–49.

Tallal, P. (2004). Improving language and literacy is a matter of time. (2004). *Nature Reviews Neuroscience, 5,* 721–728.

Tamis-LeMonda, D. S., Cristofaro, T. N., Rodriguez, E. T., & Bornstein, M. H. (2006). Early language development: Social influences in the first years of life. In C. S. Tamis-LeMonda, T. N. Cristofaro, E. T. Rodriguez, & M. H. Bornstein (Eds.), *Child psychology: A Handbook of contemporary issues* (2nd ed., pp. 79–108). New York: Psychology Press.

Tanaka, H., & Seals, D. R. (2003). Dynamic exercise performance in master athletes: Insight into effects of primary human aging on physiological functional capacity. *Journal of Applied Physiology, 95,* 2152–2162.

Tangney, J. P, Stuewig, J., & Mashek, D. J. (2007). Moral emotions and moral behavior, *Annual Review of Psychology, 58,* 344–372.

Tanguay, P. E. (2000). Pervasive developmental disorders: A 10-year review. *Journal of the American Academy of Child and Adolescent Psychiatry, 39,* 1079–1095.

Tanner, J. M. (1962). *Growth at adolescence.* Oxford, England: Blackwell Scientific Publications.

Tanner, J. M. (1990). *Fetus into man: Physical growth from conception to maturity* (2nd ed.). Cambridge, MA: Harvard University Press.

Tatum, B. D. (1997). *"Why are all the Black kids sitting together in the cafeteria?" and other conversations about race.* New York: Basic Books.

Tardif, T., Shatz, M., & Naigles, L. (1997). Caregiver speech and children's use of nouns versus verbs: A comparison of English, Italian, and Mandarin. *Journal of Child Language, 24,* 535–565.

Taylor, M. B. (1983). The development of the Measure of Epistemological Reflection. *Dissertation Abstracts International, 44,* 1065A (University Microfilms No. DA83–18, 441).

Taylor, S. E. (1983). Adjustment to threatening events: A theory of cognitive adaptation. *American Psychologist, 38,* 1161–1173.

Taylor, S. E., & Brown, J. D. (1988). Illusion and well-being: A social-psychological perspective on mental health. *Psychological Bulletin, 103,* 193–210.

Teasdale, J. D., Moore, R. G., Hayhurst, H., Pope, M., Williams, J. M., & Segal, Z. V. (2002). Metacognitive awareness and prevention of relapse in depression: Empirical evidence. *Journal of Consulting and Clinical Psychology, 70,* 272–287.

Teasdale, J. D., Segal, Z. V., Williams, J. M., Ridgeway, V. A., Soulsby, J. M., & Lau, M. A. (2000). Prevention of relapse/recurrence in major depression by mindfulness-based cognitive therapy. *Journal of Consulting and Clinical Psychology, 68,* 615–623.

Tedeschi, R. G., & Calhoun, L. G. (1996). The posttraumatic growth inventory: Measuring the positive legacy of trauma. *Journal of Traumatic Stress, 9,* 455–471.

Tedeschi, R. G., & Calhoun, L. G. (2004). Posttraumatic growth: Conceptual foundations and empirical evidence. *Psychological Inquiry, 15,* 1–18.

Telch, C. F., Agras, W. S., Linehan, M. M. (2001). Dialectical behavior therapy for binge eating disorder. *Journal of Consulting and Clinical Psychology, 69,* 1061–1065.

Temple, J. A., & Reynolds, A. J. (2007). Benefits and costs of investments in preschool education: Evidence from the child-parent centers and related programs. *Economics of Education Review, 26,* 126–144.

ten Brummelhuis, L. L., & Bakker, A. B. (2012). A resource perspective on the work-home interface: The work-home resources model. *American Psychologist, 67,* 545–556.

Teresi, J., Abrams, R., Holmes, D., Ramirez, M., & Eimicke, J. (2001). Prevalence of depression and depression recognition in nursing homes. *Social Psychiatry and Psychiatric Epidemiology, 36,* 613–620.

Terracciano, A., Costa, P. T., Jr., & McCrae, R. R. (2006). Personality plasticity after age 30. *Personality and Social Psychology Bulletin, 32,* 999–1009.

Terracciano, A., McCrae, R. R., Costa, P. T., Jr. (2006). Longitudinal trajectories in Guilford-Zimmerman temperament survey data: Result from the Baltimore longitudinal study of aging. *Journals of Gerontology: Series B: Psychological Sciences and Social Sciences, 61B,* 108–116.

Tessler, M., & Nelson, K. (1994). Making memories: The influence of joint encoding on later recall by young children. *Consciousness and Cognition, 3,* 307–326.

Tesson, G., Lewko, J. H., & Bigelow, B. J. (1987). The social rules that children use in their interpersonal relations. *Contributions of Human Development, 18,* 36–57.

Teti, D. M., & Gelfand, D. M. (1991). Behavioral competence among mothers of infants in the first year: The mediational role of maternal self-efficacy. *Child Development, 62,* 918–929.

Tharp, R. G., & Gallimore, R. (1988). *Rousing minds to life: Teaching, learning, and schooling in social context.* New York: Cambridge University Press.

The Pew Center (2008). *One in 100: Behind Bars in America 2008.* Washington DC: The Pew Charitable Trusts. Retrieved from http://www.pewstates.org/uploadedFiles/PCS_Assets/2008/one%20in%20100.pdf

Thelen, E., & Smith, L. B. (1998). Dynamic systems theories. In W. Damon (Series Ed.) & R. M. Lerner (Vol. Ed.), *Handbook of child psychology: Vol. 1. Theoretical models of human development* (5th ed., pp. 563–634). New York: Wiley.

Thomaes, S., Reijntjes, A., Orobio de Castro, B., Bushman, B. J., Poorthuis, A., & Telch, M. J. (2010). I like me if you like me: On the interpersonal modulation and regulation of preadolescents' state self-esteem. *Child Development, 81,* 811–825.

Thomas, A., & Chess, S. (1977). *Temperament and development.* New York: Brunner/Mazel.

Thomas, K. M., Drevets, W. C., Whalen, P. J., Eccard, C. H., Dahl, R. E., Ryan, N. D., et al. (2001). Amygdala response to facial expressions in children and adults. *Biological Psychiatry, 49,* 309–316.

Thompson, E. M., & Morgan, E. M. (2008). "Mostly straight" young women: Variations in sexual behavior and identity development. *Developmental Psychology, 44,* 15–21.

Thompson, R. A. (1998). Early sociopersonality development. In W. Damon (Series Ed.) & N. Eisenberg (Vol. Ed.), *Handbook of child psychology: Vol. 3. Social, emotional, and personality development* (5th ed., pp. 25–104). New York: Wiley.

Thompson, R. A. (2006). The development of the person: Social understanding, relationships, conscience, self. In W. Damon & R. M. Lerner (Series Eds.), N. Eisenberg (Vol. Ed.), *Handbook of child psychology: Vol. 3. Social, emotional, and personality development* (6th ed., pp. 24–98). Hoboken, NJ: Wiley.

Thompson, R. A. (2012). Whither the preconventional child? Toward a life-span moral development theory. *Child Development Perspectives, 6,* 423–429.

Thompson, R. A., & Leger, D. W. (1999). From squalls to calls: The cry as a developing socioemotional signal. In B. Lester, J. Newman, & F. Pedersen (Eds.), *Biological and social aspects of infant crying.* New York: Plenum Press.

Thompson, R. A., Meyer, S., & McGinley, M. (2006). Understanding values in relationship: The development of conscience. In M. Killen & J. Smetana (Eds.), *Handbook of moral development* (pp. 267–297). Mahwah, NJ: Erlbaum.

Thompson, R. A., Winer, A. C., & Goodvin, R. (2011). The individual child: Temperament, emotion, self, and personality. In M. H. Bornstein & M. E. Lamb (Eds.). *Developmental science: An advanced textbook* (pp. 427–468). New York: Psychology Press.

Thompson, W. W., Price, C., Goodson, B., Shay, D. K., Benson, P., Hinrichsen, V. L., et al. (2007). Early thimerosal exposure and neuropsychological outcomes at 7 to 10 years. *New England Journal of Medicine, 357,* 1281–1292.

Thomsen, D. K., Pillemer, D. B., & Ivcevic, Z. (2011). Life story chapters, specific memories and the reminiscence bump. *Memory, 19,* 267–279.

Thorne, B. (1986). Girls and boys together, but mostly apart: Gender arrangements in elementary schools. In W. W. Jartup & Z. Rubin (Ed.), *Relationships and development.* Hillsdale, NJ: Erlbaum.

Thorne, B. (1994). *Gender play: Girls and boys in school.* New Brunswick, NJ: Rutgers University Press.

Tidwell, M. O., Reis, H. T., & Shaver, P. R. (1996). Attachment, attractiveness, and social interaction: A diary study. *Journal of Personality and Social Psychology, 71,* 729–745.

Tienda, M., & Mitchell, F. (Eds.). (2006). *Hispanics and the future of America.* Washington, DD: National Academy Press.

Tilton-Weaver, L., Kerr, M., Pakalniskeine, V., Tokic, A., Salihovic, S., & Stattin, H. (2010). Open up or close down: How do parental reactions affect youth information management? *Journal of Adolescence, 33,* 333–346.

Tims, M., Bakker, A. B., & Derks, D. (2012). Development and validation of the job crafting scale. *Journal of Vocational Behavior, 80,* 173–186.

Tisak, M. S. (1993). Preschool children's judgments of moral and personal events involving physical harm and property damage. *Merrill-Palmer Quarterly, 39,* 375–390.

Tither, J. M., & Ellis, B. J. (2008). Impact of fathers on daughters' age at menarche: A genetically and environmentally controlled sibling study. *Developmental Psychology, 44,* 1409–1420.

Tjepkema, M. (2005). Insomnia. *Health Reports, 17,* 9–25.

Tobi, E. W., Lumey, L. H., Talens, R. P., Kremer, D., Putter, H., Stein, A. D., et al. (2009). DNA methylation differences after exposure to prenatal famine are common and timing- and sex-specific. *Human Molecular Genetics, 18,* 4046–4053.

Tobin, J., Wu, D., & Davidson, D. (1989). *Preschool in three cultures: Japan, China, and the United States.* New Haven, CT: Yale University Press.

Tobler, N. S. (1992). Drug prevention programs can work: Research findings. *Journal of Addictive Diseases, 11,* 1–28.

Toga, A. W., Thompson, P. M., & Sowell, E. R. (2006). Mapping brain maturation. *Trends in Neurosciences, 29,* 148–159.

Tolin, D. F., & Foa, E. B. (2006). Sex differences in trauma and posttraumatic stress disorder: a quantitative review of 25 years of research. *Psychological Bulletin, 132,* 959–992.

Tolman, D. L., & McClelland, S. I. (2011). Normative sexuality development in adolescence: A decade in review, 2000–2009. *Journal of Research on Adolescence, 21,* 242–255.

Tomarken, A. J., Davidson, R. J., & Henriques, J. B. (1990). Resting frontal activation asymmetry predicts emotional reactivity to film clips. *Journal of Personality and Social Psychology, 59,* 791–801.

Tomasik, M. J., & Silbereisen, R. K. (2012). Beneficial effects of disengagement from futile struggles with occupational planning: A contextualist-motivational approach. *Developmental Psychology, 48,* 1785–1796.

Tomkins, S. S. (1962). *Affect, imagery, consciousness: Vol. 1. The positive affects.* New York: Springer.

Tomlin, A. M., & Viehweg, S. A. (2003). Infant mental health: Making a difference. *Professional Psychology: Research and Practice, 34,* 617–625.

Tooby, J., & Cosmides, L. (1996). Friendship and the banker's paradox: Other pathways to the evolution of adaptations for altruism. In W. G. Runciman, J. M. Smith, & R. I. M. Dunbar

(Eds.), Evolution of social behavior patterns in primates and man: A joint discussion meeting of the Royal Society and the British Academy. *Proceedings of the British Academy, 88,* 119–143.

Tottenham, N., & Sheridan, M. A. (2010). A review of adversity, the amygdala and the hippocampus: A consideration of developmental timing. *Frontiers in Human Neuroscience, 3,* 68.

Tout, K., de Haan, M., Campbell, E. K., & Gunnar, M. R. (1998). Social behavior correlates of cortisol activity in child care: Gender differences and time-of-day effects. *Child Development, 69,* 1247–1262.

Tov, W., & Diener, E. (2007). Culture and subjective-well-being. In S. Kitayama & D. Cohen (Eds.), *Handbook of cultural psychology* (pp. 691–713). New York: Guilford Press.

Triesch, J., Jasso, H., & Deak, G. O. (2007). Emergence of mirror neurons in a model of gaze following. *Adaptive Behavior, 15,* 149–165.

Trivits, L. C., & Repucci, N. D. (2002). Application of Megan's law to juveniles. *American Psychologist, 57,* 690–704.

Tronick, E. (1989). Emotions and emotional communication in infants. *American Psychologist, 44,* 112–119.

Tronick, E., & Beeghly, M. (2011). Infants' meaning-making and the development of mental health problems. *American Psychologist, 66,* 107–119.

Tronick, E., & Reck, C. (2009). Infants of depressed mothers. *Harvard Review of Psychiatry, 17,*147–156.

Tronick, E., Als, H., Adamson, L., Wise, S., & Brazelton, T. B. (1978). Infants' response to entrapment between contradictory messages in face-to-face interaction. *Journal of the American Academy of Child and Adolescent Psychiatry, 17,* 1–13.

Troseth, G. L., & DeLoache, J. S. (1996, April). *The medium can obscure the message: Understanding the relation between video and reality.* Poster presented at the biennial meeting of the International Conference on Infant Studies, Providence, RI.

Trzesniewski, K. H., & Donnellan, M. B. (2010). Rethinking "generation me": A study of cohort effects from 1976–2006. *Perspectives on Psychological Science, 5,* 58–75.

Tucker-Drob, E. M. (2011). Global and domain-specific changes in cognition throughout adulthood. *Developmental Psychology, 47,* 331–343.

Tuckman, B. W., Abry, D. A., & Smith, D. R. (2002). *Learning and motivational strategies: Your guide to success.* Upper Saddle River, NJ: Prentice Hall.

Tudge, J. R. H., Doucet, F., Odero, D., Sperb, T. M., Piccinini, C. A., & Lopes, R. S. (2006). A window into different cultural worlds: Young children's everyday activities in the United States, Brazil, and Kenya. *Child Development, 77,* 1446–1469.

Turiel, E. (1978). Social regulation and domains of social concepts. In W. Damon (Ed.), *Social cognition: New directions for child development* (pp. 45–74). San Francisco: Jossey-Bass.

Turiel, E. (2006). The development of morality. In W. Damon & R. M. Lerner (Series Eds.), N. Eisenberg (Vol. Ed.), *Handbook of child psychology: Vol. 3. Social, emotional, and personality development* (6th ed., pp. 789–857). Hoboken, NJ: Wiley.

Turner, F. J. (1986). *Social work treatment: Interlocking theoretical approaches* (3rd ed.). New York: Free Press.

Turner, R. J., & Lloyd, D. A. (1995). Lifetime traumas and mental health: The significance

of cumulative adversity. *Journal of Health and Social Behavior, 36,* 360–376.

Tversky, A., & Kahneman, D. (1974). Judgment under uncertainty: Heuristics and biases. *Science, 185,* 1124–1131.

Twenge, J. M. (2000). The age of anxiety? The birth cohort change in anxiety and neuroticism, 1952–1993. *Journal of Personality & Social Psychology, 79,* 1007–1021.

Twenge, J. M., Campbell, W. K., & Foster, C. A. (2003). Parenthood and marital satisfaction: A meta-analytic review. *Journal of Marriage & Family, 65,* 1–12.

Twenge, J. M., & Crocker, J. (2002). Race and self-esteem: Meta-analyses comparing Whites, Blacks, Hispanics, Asians, and American Indians and comment on Gray-Little and Hafdahl (2000). *Psychological Bulletin, 128,* 371–408.

Uba, L., & Huang, K. (1999). *Psychology.* New York: Longman.

Uccelli, P., Hemphill, L., Pan, B. A., & Snow, C. E. (1999). Telling two kinds of stories: Sources of narrative skill. In L. Batter & C. S. Tamis-LeMonda (Eds.), *Child psychology: A handbook of contemporary issues* (pp. 215–233). Philadelphia: Psychology Press.

Umana-Taylor, A., & Fine, M. A. (2001). Methodological implications of grouping Latino adolescents into one collective ethnic group. *Hispanic Journal of Behavioral Sciences, 23,* 347–362.

United Nations. (1989). *United Nations Convention on the Rights of the Child.* Geneva. Washington, DC: Office of the United Nations High Commissioner for Human Rights. Retrieved from http://www2.ohchr.org/english/law/crc.htm

United Nations Statistical Division. (2007). *Demographic Yearbook 2007.* New York: United Nations.

Urry, H. L., Nitschke, J. B., Dolski, I., Jackson, D. C., Dalton, K. M., Mueller, C. J., et al. (2004). Making a life worth living: Neural correlates of well-being. *Psychological Science, 15,* 367–372.

Ursache, A., Blair, C., Stifter, C., & Voegtline, K. (2013). Emotional reactivity and regulation in infancy interact to predict executive functioning in early childhood. *Developmental Psychology, 49,* 127–137.

U.S. Bureau of Justice Statistics. (2000). *Violent crime rate trends.* Washington, DC: Author.

U.S. Bureau of Justice Statistics. (2007). Correctional surveys. As presented in "Correctional Populations in the United States, Annual, Prisoners in 2007" and "Probation and Parole in the United States, 2007—Statistical Tables." Retrieved June 9, 2008, from http://www.bls.gov

U.S. Bureau of Labor Statistics. (2010). *Women in the labor force: A databook.* Retrieved from http://www.bls.gov/cps/wlf-databook-2010.pdf

U.S. Bureau of Labor Statistics. (2011). *Women at work.* Retrieved from http://www.bls.gov/spotlight/2011/women/pdf/women_bls_spotlight.pdf

U.S. Bureau of the Census. (1998). Current Population Reports, P60–200, *Money income in the United States: 1997* (with separate data on valuation of noncash benefits). Washington, DC: U.S. Government Printing Office.

U.S. Bureau of the Census. (2012a). *America's families and living arrangements: 2010, Table 57.* Retrieved from http://www.census.gov/compendia/statab/2012/tables/12s0057.pdf

U.S. Bureau of the Census. (2012b). *Licensed Drivers and Number in Accidents by Age: 2009.* Retrieved from http://www.census

.gov/compendia/statab/2012/tables/12s1114 .pdf on January 9, 2013.

U.S. Bureau of the Census. (2012c). *Statistical Abstract of the United States: 2012*. Washington DC: U.S. Government Printing Office.

U.S. Department of Education. (1990). *National goals for education*. Washington, DC: U.S. Government Printing Office.

U.S. Department of Health & Human Services. (2005). U.S. Surgeon General Releases Advisory on Alcohol Use in Pregnancy. Available at: http://www.surgeongeneral .gov/pressreleases/sg02222005.html

U.S. Department of Health and Human Services. (2005). *Health, United States, with chartbook on trends in the health of Americans*. Hyattsville, MD: National Center for Health Statistics.

U.S. Department of Transportation. (1996). Traffic Safety CD-ROM, 1975–1994 (BTS-CD-10). Washington, DC: Bureau of Transportation Statistics.

U.S. National Center for Health Statistics, Health, United States, 2010. http://www .cdc.gov/nchs/hus.htm and National Vital Statistics Reports (NVSR), *Deaths: Preliminary Data for 2008*, Vol. 59, No. 2, December 2010.

Urquiza, A. J. (2010). The future of play therapy: Elevating credibility through play therapy research. *International Journal of Play Therapy, 19*, 4–12.

Uttal, D. H, Liu, L. L., & DeLoache, J. S. (2006). Concreteness and symbolic development. In L. Balter & C. S. Tamis-LeMonda (Eds.), *Child psychology: A handbook of contemporary issues* (2nd ed.; pp. 167–187). New York: Psychology Press.

Uttal, D. H., Meadow, N. G., Tipton, E., Hand, L. L., Alden, A. R., Warren, C., & Newcombe, N. S. (2012, June 4). The Malleability of Spatial Skills: A Meta-Analysis of Training Studies. *Psychological Bulletin*. Advance online publication. doi: 10.1037/a0028446

Uttal, D. H., O'Doherty, K., Newland, R., Hand, L. L., & DeLoache, J. (2009). Dual representation and the linking of concrete and symbolic representations. *Child Development Perspectives, 3*, 156–159.

Vachon, M. L., Rogers, J., Lyall, W. A., Lancee, W. J., Sheldon, A. R., & Freeman, S. J. J. (1982). Predictors and correlates of adaptation to conjugal bereavement. *American Journal of Psychiatry, 139*, 998–1002.

Vaillant, C. O., & Vaillant, G. E. (1993). Is the U-curve of marital satisfaction an illusion? A 40-year study of marriage. *Journal of Marriage and the Family, 55*, 230–239.

Vaillant, G. E. (1977). *Adaptation to life*. Boston: Little, Brown.

Vaillant, G. E., & Koury, S. H. (1994). Late midlife development. In G. H. Pollock & S. I. Greenspan (Eds.), *The course of life*. Madison, CT: International Universities Press.

Valenzuela, M. (1990). Attachment in chronically underweight young children. *Child Development, 61*, 1984–1996.

Valenzuela, M. (1997). Maternal sensitivity in a developing society: The context of urban poverty and infant chronic undernutrition. *Developmental Psychology, 33*, 845–855.

Valiente, D., Eisenberg, N., Fabes, R. A., Shepard, S. A., Cumberland, A., & Losoya, S. H. (2004). Prediction of children's empathy-related responding from their effortful control and parents' expressivity. *Developmental Psychology, 40*, 911–926.

van den Boom, D. C. (1994). The influence of temperament and mothering on attachment and exploration: An experimental manipulation of sensitive responsiveness among lower-class mothers with irritable infants. *Child Development, 65*, 1457–1477.

Vandereycken, W., & Van Deth, R. (1994). *From fasting saints to anorexic girls: The history of self-starvation*. New York: New York University Press.

van der Veer, R. (1996). Vygotsky and Piaget: A collective monologue. *Human Development, 39*, 237–242.

van der Veer, R., & Valsiner, J. (1994). *The Vygotsky reader*. Cambridge, MA: Blackwell.

van der Waal, J. (1989–1990). The aftermath of suicide: A review of empirical evidence. *Omega, 20*, 149–171.

Vandewater, E. A., Ostrove, J. M., & Stewart, A. J. (1997). Predicting women's well-being in midlife: The importance of personality development and social role involvements. *Journal of Personality and Social Psychology, 72*, 1147–1160.

van Doorninck, W. J., Caldwell, B. M., Wright, C., & Frankenberg, W. K. (1981). The relationship between twelve-month home stimulation and school achievement. *Child Development, 52*, 1080–1083.

van Emmerik, A. P., Kamphuis, J. H., Hulsbosch, A. M., & Emmelkamp, P. M. (2002). Single session debriefing after psychological trauma: A meta-analysis. *The Lancet, 360*, 766–771.

van Essen, T., van den Heuvell, S., & Ossebaard, M. (2004). A student course on self-management for procrastinators. In H. C. Schouwenburg, C. Lay, T. Pychyl, & J. R. Ferrari (Eds.), *Counseling the procrastinator in academic settings* (pp. 59–73). Washington, DC: American Psychological Association.

van Geert, P. (1998). A dynamic systems model of basic developmental mechanisms: Piaget, Vygotsky and beyond. *Psychological Review, 105*, 634–677.

Van Hecke, A. V., Lebow, J., Bal, E., Lamb, D. Harden, E., Kramer, A., et al. (2009). EEG and heart rate regulation to familiar and unfamiliar people in children with autism spectrum disorders. *Child Development, 80*, 1118–1133.

Van Hesteren, F., & Ivey, A. E. (1990). Counseling and development: Toward a new identity for a profession in transition. *Journal of Counseling and Development, 68*, 524–528.

van IJzendoorn, M. H. (1995). Adult attachment representations, parental responsiveness, and infant attachment: A meta-analysis on the predictive validity of the Adult Attachment Interview. *Psychological Bulletin, 117*, 387–403.

van IJzendoorn, M. H., & Bakermans-Kranenburg, M. J. (1997). Intergenerational transmission of attachment: A move to the contextual level. In L. Atkinson & K. Zucker (Eds.), *Attachment and psychopathology*. New York: Guilford Press.

van IJzendoorn, M. H., & Bakermans-Kranenburg, M. J. (2003). Attachment disorders and disorganized attachment: Similar and different. *Attachment and Human Development, 5*, 313–320.

van IJzendoorn, M. H., Bakermans-Kranenburg, M. J., & Ebstein, R. P. (2011). Methylation matters in child development: Toward developmental behavioral epigenetics. *Child Development Perspectives, 4*, 305–310.

van IJzendoorn, M. H., & deWolff, M. S. (1997). In search of the absent father—meta-analysis of infant-father attachment: A rejoinder to our discussants. *Child Development, 68*, 604–609.

van IJzendorn, M. H., & Sagi, A. (1999). Cross-cultural patterns of attachment. In J. Cassidy & P. R. Shaver (Eds.), *Handbook of attachment* (pp. 713–734). New York: Guilford Press.

Van IJzendoorn, M. H., & Sagi-Schwartz, A. (2008). Cross-cultural patterns of attachment: Universal and contextual dimensions. In J. Cassidy & P. R. Shaver (Eds.), *Handbook of attachment: Theory, research, and clinical applications* (2nd ed., pp. 880–905). New York: Guilford Press.

van Zeijl, J., Mesman, J., Stolk, M. N., Alink, L. R. A., van IJzendoorn, M. H., Bakermans-Kranenburg, N. J., et al. (2007). Differential susceptibility to discipline: The moderating effect of child temperament on the association between maternal discipline and early childhood externalizing problems. *Journal of Family Psychology, 21*, 626–636.

Varela, F. J., Thompson, E., & Rosch, E. (1991). *The embodied mind: Cognitive science and human experience*. Cambridge, MA: MIT Press.

Vargas, J. S. (2009). *Behavior analysis for effective teaching*. New York: Routledge.

Vasiliadis, H., Buka, S. L., Martin, L. T., & Gilman, S. T. (2010). Fetal growth and the lifetime risk of generalized anxiety disorder. *Depression and Anxiety, 27*, 1066–1072.

Vasquez, C., & Javier, R. A. (1991). The problem with interpreters: Communicating with Spanish-speaking patients. *Hospital and Community Psychiatry, 42*, 163–165.

Vaughn, B. E., Bost, K. K., & van IJzendorn, M. H. (2008). Attachment and temperament: Additive and interactive influences on behavior, affect, and cognition during infancy and childhood. In J. Cassidy & P. R. Shaver (Eds.), *Handbook of attachment: Theory, research, and clinical applications* (2nd ed., pp. 192–216). New York: Guilford Press.

Vaughn, B. E., Egeland, B., Sroufe, L. A., & Waters, E. (1979). Individual differences in infant-mother attachment at twelve and eighteen months: Stability and change in families under stress. *Child Development, 50*, 971–975.

Vazquez, D. M., Bailey, C., Dent, G. W., Okimoto, D. K., Steffek A., López J. F., et al. (2006). Brain corticotropin-releasing hormone (CRH) circuits in the developing rat: effect of maternal deprivation. *Brain Research, 1121*, 83–94.

Veenhoven, R. (1984). *Conditions of happiness*. Dordrecht, The Netherlands: Kluwer Academic.

Veenstra, R., Lindenberg, S., Munniksma, A., & Dijkstra, J. K. (2010). The complex relation between bullying, victimization, acceptance, and rejection; Giving special attention to status, affection, and sex differences. *Child Development, 81*, 480–486.

Ventura S. J., & Hamilton B. E. (2011) U. S. teenage birth rate resumes decline. NCHS data brief no. 58. Hyattsville, MD: US Department of Health and Human Services, CDC.

Vereijken, C., Riksen-Walraven, J., & Kondo-Ikemura, K. (1997). Maternal sensitivity and infant attachment security in Japan: A longitudinal study. *International Journal of Behavioral Development, 21*, 35–49.

Verhaeghen, P. (2012). Working memory still working: Age-related differences in working-memory functioning and cognitive control. In P. Verhaeghen (Ed.) *Memory and aging: Current issues and future directions* (pp. 3–30). New York: Psychology Press.

Vermeulen, M. E., & Minor, C. W. (1998). Context of career decisions: Women reared in a rural community. *The Career Development Quarterly, 46*, 230–245.

Veroff, J., Kulka, R. A., & Douvan, E. (1981). *Mental health in America: Patterns of help-seeking from 1957 to 1976*. New York: Basic Books.

Vierck, C. J. (2006). Mechanisms underlying development of spatially distributed chronic pain (fibromyalgia). *Pain, 124,* 242–263.

Vinokur, A. D., Price, R. H., & Schul, Y. (1995). Impact of the JOBS intervention on unemployed workers varying in risk for depression. *American Journal of Community Psychology, 23,* 39–74.

Vinokur, A. D., Schul, Y., Vuori, J., & Price, R. H. (2000). Two years after a job loss: Long-term impact of the JOBS program on reemployment and mental health. *Journal of Occupational Health Psychology, 5,* 32–47.

Vispoel, W. P. (1995). Self-concept in the arts: An extension of the Shavelson, Hubner, and Stanton (1976) model. *Educational and Psychological Measurement, 53,* 1023–1033.

Vitousek, K., & Manke, F. (1994). Personality variables and disorders in anorexia nervosa and bulimia nervosa. *Journal of Abnormal Psychology, 103,* 137–147.

Vivona, J. M. (2000). Parental attachment style of late adolescents: Qualities of attachment relationships and consequences for adjustment. *Journal of Counseling Psychology, 47,* 316–329.

Volk, H. E., Hertz-Picciotto, I., Delwiche, L., Lurmann, F., & McConnell, R. (2011). Residential proximity to freeways and Autism in the CHARGE Study. *Environmental Health Perspectives, 119,* 873–877.

von Bertalanffy, L. (1968). *General systems theory: Foundations, development, applications.* New York: Braziller.

Vosniadou, S., & Brewer, W. F. (1992). Mental models of the earth: A study of conceptual change in childhood. *Cognitive Psychology, 24,* 535–585.

Vosniadou, S., & Mason, L. (2012). Conceptual change induced by instruction: A complex interplay of multiple factors. In S.Vosniadou & L. Mason (Eds.), *APA educational psychology handbook, Vol 2: Individual differences and cultural and contextual factors* (pp. 221–246). Washington, DC, US: American Psychological Association, 2012.

Vosniadou, S., Skopeliti, I., & Ikospentaki, K. (2004). Modes of knowing and ways of reasoning in elementary astronomy. *Cognitive Development, 19,* 203–222.

Vygotsky, L. S. (1934). *Thought and language.* Cambridge, MA: MIT Press.

Vygotsky, L. S. (1978). *Mind and society.* Cambridge, MA: MIT Press.

Vygotsky, L. S. (1981). Development of higher mental functions. In J. V. Wertsch (Ed.), *The concept of activity in Soviet psychology* (pp. 144–188) Armonk, NY: Sharpe. (Originally published in 1931)

Vygotsky, L. S., & Luria, A. R. (1930). The function and fate of egocentric speech. In J. M. Cattell (Ed.), *Ninth International Congress of Psychology. Proceedings and papers* (pp. 464–465). Princeton, NJ: Psychological Review Company.

Wachs, T. D. (2006). The nature, etiology and consequences of individual differences in temperament. In L. Balter & C. S. Tamis-LeMonda (Eds.), *Child psychology: A handbook of contemporary issues* (2nd ed., pp. 27–52). New York: Psychology Press.

Wager, T. D., Phan, K. L., Liberzon, I., & Taylor, S. F. (2003). Valence, gender, and lateralization of functional brain anatomy in emotion: A meta-analysis of findings from neuroimaging. *Neuroimage, 19,* 513–531.

Waite, L. J., & Joyner, K. (2001). Emotional satisfaction and physical pleasure in sexual unions: Time horizon, sexual behavior, and sexual exclusivity. *Journal of Marriage and the Family, 63,* 247–264.

Waite, L. J., Laumann, E. O., Das, A., & Schumm, L. P. (2009). Sexuality: Measures of partnerships, practices, attitudes, and problems in National Social Life, Health, and Aging Study. *The Journals of Gerontology: Series B: Psychological Sciences and Social Sciences, 64,* 156–I66.

Walker, E., & Bollini, A. M. (2002). Pubertal neurodevelopment and the emergence of psychotic symptoms. *Schizophrenia Research, 54,* 17–23.

Walker, E., & Diforio, D. (1997). Schizophrenia: A neural diathesis-stress model. *Psychological Review, 104,* 667–685.

Walker, L. J., & Hennig, K. H. (2004). Differing conceptions of moral exemplarity: Just, brave, and caring. *Journal of Personality and Social Psychology, 86*(4), 629–647.

Walker, L. J., & Pitts, R. C. (1998). Naturalistic conceptions of moral maturity. *Developmental Psychology, 34,* 403–419.

Walker, L. J., & Taylor, J. H. (1991). Family interactions and the development of moral reasoning. *Child Development, 62,* 264–283.

Walker-Barnes, C. J., & Mason, C. A. (2001). Ethnic differences in the effect of parenting on gang involvement and gang delinquency: A longitudinal, hierarchical linear modeling perspective. *Child Development, 72,* 1814–1831.

Wallace, I., & McCarton, C. (1997). Neurodevelopmental outcomes of the premature, small-for-gestational infant through age 6. *Clinical Obstetrics and Gynecology, 40,* 843–852.

Wallen, K. (2005). Hormonal influences on sexually differentiated behavior in nonhuman primates. *Frontiers in Neuroendocrinology, 26,* 7–26.

Waller, W. (1938). *The family: A dynamic interpretation.* New York: Cordon.

Wallerstein, N., & Duran, B. (2002). The conceptual, historical, practice roots of community based participatory research and related participatory traditions. In M. Minkler & N. Wallerstein (Eds.) *Community-based participatory research for health* (pp. 27–52). San Francisco, CA: Jossey-Bass.

Walmsley, R. (2007). *World prison population list* (7th ed.). Kings College, London: International Centre for Prison Studies.

Walmsley, R. (2011). *World prison population list* (9th ed.). London: International Centre for Prison Studies, University of Essex. Retrieved November 2, 2012 from http://www.idcr.org.uk/wp-content/uploads/2010/09/WPPL-9-22.pdf

Walsh, W. B. (Ed.). (2003). *Counseling psychology and optimal human functioning.* Mahwah, NJ: Erlbaum.

Wanberg, C. R. (2012). The individual experience of unemployment. *Annual Review of Psychology, 63,* 369–396.

Wang, D. (2004). Ritualistic coresidence and the weakening of filial practice in rural China. In Ikels, C. (Ed.), *Filial Piety: Practice and discourse in contemporary East Asia* (pp. 16–33). Stanford, CA: Stanford University Press.

Wang, M., & Huguley, J. P. (2012). Parental racial socialization as a moderator of the effects of racial discrimination on educational success among African American adolescents. *Child Development, 83,* 1716–1731.

Wang, Q., Pomerantz, E. M., & Chen, H. (2007). The role of parents' control in early adolescents' psychological functioning: A longitudinal investigation in the United States and China. *Child Development, 78,* 1592–1610.

Ward, B. A., Mergendoller, J. R., Tikunoff, W. J., Rounds, T. S., Dadey, G. J., & Mitman, A. L. (1982). *Junior high school transition study: Executive summary.* San Francisco: Far West Laboratory.

Ward, I. L. (1992). Sexual behavior: The product of perinatal hormonal and prepuberal social factors. In A. A. Gerall, H. Moltz, & I. L. Ward (Eds.), *Handbook of behavioral neurobiology: Vol. 11. Sexual differentiation* (pp. 157–180). New York: Plenum Press.

Ward, I. L., & Stehm, K. E. (1991). Prenatal stress feminizes juvenile play patterns in male rats. *Physiology and Behavior, 50,* 601–605.

Ward, L. M. (2002). Does television exposure affect emerging adults' attitudes and assumptions about sexual relationships? Correlational and experimental confirmation. *Journal of Youth and Adolescence, 31,* 1–15.

Warner, C. W., Santelli, J. S., Everett, S. A., Kann, L., Collins, J. L., Cassell, C., et al. (1998). Sexual behavior among U.S. high school students, 1990–1995. *Family Planning Perspectives, 30,* 170–172, 200.

Warr, P. (1999). Well-being and the workplace. In D. Kahneman, E. Diener, & N. Schwarz (Eds.), *Well-being: The foundations of hedonic psychology* (pp. 392–412). New York: Russell Sage Foundation.

Wartella, E., Caplovitz, A. G., & Lee, J. H. (2004). From Baby Einstein to Leapfrog, from Doom to The Sims, from instant messaging to Internet chat rooms: Public interest in the role of interactive media in children's lives. *Social Policy Report, 18,* 3–16.

Watamura, S. E., Coe, C. L., Laudenslager, M. L., & Robertson, S. S. (2010). Child care setting affects salivary cortisol and antibody secretion in young children. *Psychoneuroendocrinology, 35,* 1156–1166.

Watamura, S. E., Donzella, B., Alwin, J., & Gunnar, M. R. (2003). Morning-to-afternoon increases in cortisol concentrations for infants and toddlers at child care: Age differences and behavioral correlates. *Child Development, 74,* 1006–1020.

Waterman, A. S. (1993a). Developmental perspectives on identity formation. In J. E. Marcia, A. S. Waterman, D. R. Matteson, S. L. Archer, & J. L. Orlofsky (Eds.), *Ego identity: A handbook for psychosocial research* (pp. 42–68). New York: Springer-Verlag.

Waterman, A. S. (1993b). Two conceptions of happiness: Contrasts of personal expressiveness (eudaimonia) and hedonic enjoyment. *Journal of Personality and Social Psychology, 64,* 678–691.

Watson, D., & Pennebaker, J. W. (1989). Health complaints, stress, and distress: Exploring the central role of negative affectivity. *Psychological Review, 96,* 234–254.

Watson, D., Wiese, D., Vaidya, J., & Tellegen, A. (1999). The two general activation systems of affect: Structural findings, evolutionary considerations, and psychobiological evidence. *Journal of Personality and Social Psychology, 76,* 820–838.

Watson, J. B. (1913). Psychology as the behaviorist views it. *Psychological Review, 20,* 158–177.

Watts, C. L., Nakkula, M. J., & Barr, D. (1997). Person-in-pairs, pairs-in-program: Pair therapy in different institutional contexts. In R. J. Selman, C. L. Watts, & L. H. Schultz (Eds.), *Fostering friendship: Pair therapy for treatment and prevention* (pp. 167–184). New York: Aldine de Gruyter.

Way, N. (2011). *Deep secrets: Boys friendships and the crisis of connection.* Cambridge MA: Harvard University Press.

Webster-Stratton, C., & Hammond, M. (1997). Treating children with early-onset conduct problems: A comparison of child and parent training interventions. *Journal of Consulting and Clinical Psychology, 65,* 93–109.

Webster-Stratton, C., Mihalic, S., Fagan, A., Arnold, D., Taylor, T., & Tingley, C. (2001). *The Incredible Years: Parent, Teacher And Child Training Series: Blueprints for Violence Prevention, Book Eleven.* Blueprints for Violence Prevention Series (D. S. Elliott, Series Editor). Boulder: Center for the Study and Prevention of Violence, Institute of Behavioral Science, University of Colorado.

Webster-Stratton, C., & Reid, M. J. (2003). Treating conduct problems and strengthening social emotional competence in young children (ages 4 to 8 years): The Dina Dinosaur treatment program. *Journal of Emotional and Behavioral Disorders, 11,* 130–143.

Webster-Stratton, C., Reid, M. J., & Stoolmiller, M. (2008). Preventing conduct problems and improving school readiness: Evaluation of the Incredible Years Teacher and Child Training Programs in high-risk schools. *Journal of Child Psychology and Psychiatry, 49,* 471–488.

Weder, N., Yang, B. Z., Douglas-Palumberi, H., Massey, J., Krystal, J. H., Gelernter, J., et al. (2009). MAOA genotype, maltreatment, and aggressive behavior: The changing impact of genotype at varying levels of trauma. *Biological Psychiatry, 65,* 417–424.

Wei, M., Liao, K. Y-H., Chao, R. C-L., Mallinckrodt, B., Tsai, P-C., & Botello-Zamarron, R. (2010). Minority stress perceived bicultural competence, and depressive symptoms among ethnic minority college students. *Journal of Counseling Psychology, 57,* 411–422.

Weinfield, N. S., Sroufe, L. A., & Egeland, B. (2000). Attachment from infancy to early adulthood in a high-risk sample: Continuity, discontinuity and their correlates. *Child Development, 71,* 695–702.

Weinraub, M., Clemens, L. P., Sockloff, A., Ethridge, R., Gracely, E., & Myers, B. (1984). The development of sex role stereotypes in the third year: Relationships to gender labeling, gender identity, sex-typed toy preferences, and family characteristics. *Child Development, 55,* 1493–1503.

Weisgram, E. S., Bigler, R. S., & Liben, L. S. (2010). Gender, values, and occupational interests among children, adolescents, and adults. *Child Development, 81,* 778–796

Weiss, A., Bates, T. C., & Luciano, M. (2008). Happiness is a personal(ity) thing: The genetics of personality and well-being in a representative sample. *Psychological Science, 19,* 205–210.

Weiss, B., & Garber, J. (2003). Developmental differences in the phenomenology of depression. *Development and Psychopathology, 15,* 403–430.

Weiss, R. L., & Hayman, R. E. (1990). Observation of marital distress. In F. D. Findham & T. N. Bradlary (Eds.), *The psychology of marriage* (pp. 87–117). New York: Guilford Press.

Weissbecker, I., Salmon, P., Studts, J. L., Floyd, A. R., Dedert, E. A., & Sephton, S. E. (2002). Mindfulness-based stress reduction and sense of coherence among women with fibromyalgia. *Journal of Clinical Psychology in Medical Settings, 9,* 297–307.

Weissberg, R. P., Caplan, M. Z., & Bennetto, L. (1988). *The Yale-New Haven Middle School Social Problem Solving (SPS) Program.* New Haven, CT: Yale University.

Weissberg, R. P., Kumpfer, K. L., & Seligman, M. E. P. (2003). Prevention that works for children and youth: An introduction. *American Psychologist, 58,* 425–432.

Weissman, J. R., Kelley, R. I., Bauman, M.L., Cohen, B. H., Murray, K.F., Mitchell, R. L., et al. (2008). Mitochondrial disease in autism spectrum disorder patients: A cohort analysis. *PLos One, 3,* 1–6.

Weissman, M. M., Markowitz, J. C., & Klerman, G. L. (2000). *Comprehensive guide to interpersonal psychotherapy.* New York: Basic Books.

Weizman, Z. O., & Snow, C. E. (2001). Lexical input as related to children's vocabulary acquisition: Effects of sophisticated exposure and support for meaning. *Developmental Psychology, 37,* 265–279.

Welch-Carre, E. (2005). The neurodevelopmental consequences of prenatal alcohol exposure. *Advances in Neonatal Care, 5,* 217–229.

Welch-Ross, M. K., & Schmidt, E. R. (1996). Gender-schema development and children's constructive story memory: Evidence for a developmental model. *Child Development, 67,* 820–835.

Wellman, H. M. (1990). *The child's theory of mind.* Cambridge, MA: MIT Press.

Wellman, H. M., Cross, D., & Watson, J. (2001). Meta-analysis of theory of mind development: The truth about false belief. *Child Development, 72,* 655–684.

Wellman, H. M., Fang, F., & Peterson, C. C. (2011). Sequential progressions in a theory-of-mind scale: Longitudinal perspectives. *Child Development, 82,* 780–792.

Wentzel, K. (2002). Are effective teachers like good parents? Teaching styles and student adjustment in early adolescence. *Child Development, 73,* 287–301.

Wentzel, K. R. (1997). Student motivation in middle school: The role of perceived pedagogical caring. *Journal of Educational Psychology, 89,* 411–419.

Wentzel, K. R., & Asher, S. R. (1995). The academic lives of neglected, rejected, popular, and controversial children. *Child Development, 66,* 754–763.

Wertsch, J. V. (1991). *Voices of the mind: A sociocultural approach to mediated action.* Cambridge, MA: Harvard University Press.

West, J., Denton, K., & Reaney, L. M. (2001). *The kindergarten year: Findings from the Early Childhood Longitudinal Study, Kindergarten Class of 1998–99. (NCES 2001–023).* U.S. Department of Education, National Center for Education Statistics. Washington, DC: U.S. Government Printing Office.

Westlye, L. T., Walhovd, K., Dale, A. M., Bjørnerud, A., Due-Tønnesse, P., Engvig, A., et al. (2010). Life-span changes of the human brain white matter: Diffusion tensor imaging (DTI) and volumetry. *Cerebral Cortex, 20,* 2055–2068.

Wheaton, B. (1985). Models for the stress-buffering functions of coping resources. *Journal of Health and Social Behavior, 26,* 352–364.

Wheedon, A., Scafidi, F., Field, T., Ironson, G., Valdeon, C., & Bandstra, E. (1993). Massage effects on cocaine-exposed preterm neonates. *Journal of Developmental and Behavioral Pediatrics, 14,* 318–322.

Whitaker, D., & Miller, K. (2000). Parent-adolescent discussions about sex and condoms: Impact on peer influences of sexual risk behavior. *Journal of Adolescent Research, 15,* 251–273.

Whitbourne, S. K. (1989). Psychological treatment of the aging individual. *Journal of Integrative and Eclectic Psychotherapy, 8,* 161–173.

Whitbourne, S. K. (1996). *The aging individual: Physical and psychological perspectives.* New York: Springer.

Whitbourne, S. K., Sneed, J. R., & Sayer, A. (2009). Psychosocial development from college through midlife: A 34-year sequential study. *Developmental Psychology, 45,* 1328–1340.

Whitbourne, S. K., & Whitbourne, S. B. (2011). *Adult development & aging: Biopsychosocial perspectives* (4th ed.). Hoboken, NJ: Wiley.

Whitehead, B. D., & Popenoe, D. (2003). *The state of the unions. The social health of marriage in America 2003. Essay: Marriage and children: Coming together again?* The National Marriage Project, Rutgers University. Available from http://marriage.rutgers.edu/Publications/Print/PrintSOOU2003.htm

Whiting, B. B., & Whiting, J. M. W. (1975). *Children of six cultures: A psycho-cultural analysis.* Cambridge, MA: Harvard University Press.

Whiting, B. B., & Edwards, C. P. (1988). *Children of different worlds: The formation of social behavior.* Cambridge, MA: Harvard University Press.

Whyte, D. (2001). *Crossing the unknown sea: Work as a pilgrimage of identity.* New York: Riverhead Books.

Wicher, C. P., & Meeker, M. A. (2012). What influences African American end-of-life preferences? *Journal of Health Care for the Poor and Underserved, 23,* 28–58.

Wichstrom, L. (1999). The emergence of gender differences in depressed mood during adolescence: The role of intensified gender socialization. *Developmental Psychology, 35,* 232–245.

Wickrama, K. A. S., Lorenz, F. O., Wallace, L. E., Peiris, L., Conger, R. D., & Elder, G. H. (2001). Family influence on physical health during the middle years: The case of onset of hypertension. *Journal of Marriage and the Family, 63,* 527–539.

Wiesel, T. N., & Hubel, D. H. (1965). Comparison of the effects of unilateral and bilateral eye closure on cortical response in kittens. *Journal of Neurophysiology, 26,* 1029–1040.

Wilcox, B. L. (2003). Developmental research and the formulation and evaluation of legal policy. *Social Policy Report, 17,* 12.

Wilcox, T., Haslup, J. A., & Boas, D. A. (2010). Dissociation of processing of featural and spatiotemporal information in the infant cortex. *NeuroImage, 53,* 1256–1263.

Wilkinson, W. K., & Maxwell, S. (1991). The influence of college students' epistemological style on selected problem-solving processes. *Research in Higher Education, 32,* 333–350.

Willatts, P. (1989). Development of problem-solving in infancy. In A. Slater & G. Bremner (Eds.), *Infant development.* Hove, England: Erlbaum.

William T. Grant Foundation Commission on Work, Family, and Citizenship. (1988). *The forgotten half: Noncollege-bound youth in America.* New York: William T. Grant Foundation.

Williams, C. D. (1933). A nutritional disease of childhood associated with a maize diet. *Archives of Disease in Childhood, 8,* 423–433.

Williams, D. D., Yanchar, S. C., Jenson, L. C., & Lewis, C. (2003). Character education in a public high school: A multi-year inquiry into Unified Studies. *Journal of Moral Education, 32,* 3–33.

Williams, T. L., & Davidson, D. (2009). Interracial and intra-racial stereotypes and constructive memory in 7- and 9-year-old African-American children. *Journal of Applied Developmental Psychology, 30,* 366–377.

Willingham, D. T. (Winter 2009/10). Is it true that some people just can't do math? *American Educator, 33,* 14–19, 39.

Willoughby, T. (2008). A short-term longitudinal study of Internet and computer game use by adolescent boys and girls: Prevalence, frequency of use, and psychosocial predictors. *Developmental Psychology, 44,* 195–204.

Willoughby, T., Adachi, P. J. C., & Good, M. (2012). A longitudinal study of the association between violent video game play and aggression among adolescents. *Developmental Psychology, 48*, 1044–1057.

Wilson, D. R., & Warise, L. (2008). Cytokines and their role in depression. *Perspectives in Psychiatric Care, 44*, 285–289.

Wilson, G. T. (2005). Psychological treatment of eating disorders. *Annual Review of Clinical Psychology, 1*, 439–465.

Wilson, J. G. (1973). *Environment and birth defects*. New York: Academic Press.

Wilson, R. S., Mendes De Leon, C. F., Barnes, L. L., Schneider, J. A., Bienias, J. L., Evans, D. A., et al. (2002). Participation in cognitively stimulating activities and risk of incident Alzheimer disease. *Journal of American Medical Assoiation, 287*, 742–748.

Wilson, R. S., Beck, T. L., Bienias, J. L., & Bennet, D. A. (2007). Terminal cognitive decline: Accelerated loss of cognition in the last years of life. *Psychosomatic Medicine, 69*, 131–137.

Wilson, S. A., Kovach, C. R., & Stearns, S. A. (1996). Hospice concepts in the care for end-stage dementia. *Geriatric Nursing, 17*, 6–10.

Wilson, T. D., & Brekke, N. (1994). Mental contamination and mental correction: Unwanted influences on judgments and evaluations. *Psychological Bulletin, 116*, 117–142.

Wilson, W. J. (1996). *When work disappears: The world of the new urban poor*. New York: Random House.

Wimmer, H., & Perner, J. (1983). Beliefs about beliefs: Representation and constraining function of wrong beliefs in young children's understanding of deception. *Cognition, 13*, 103–128.

Winnicott, D. W. (1965). *The maturational processes and the facilitating environment*. New York: International Universities Press.

Winsler, A. (2009). Still talking to ourselves after all these years: A review of current research on private speech. In A. Winsler, C. Fernyhough, & I. Montero (Eds.), *Private speech, executive functioning and the development of verbal self-regulation* (pp. 3–41). New York: Cambridge University Press.

Winsler, A., DeLeon, J. R., Wallace, B., Carlton, M. P., & Willson-Quayle, A. (2003). Private speech in preschool children: Developmental stability and change, across-task consistency, and relations with classroom behavior. *Journal of Child Language, 30*, 583–608.

Winsler, A., Diaz, R. M., & Montero, I. (1997). The role of private speech in the transition from collaborative to independent task performance in young children. *Early Childhood Research Quarterly, 12*, 59–79.

Wittig, W. (1997). The right hemisphere and the human stress response. *Acta Physiologica Scandinavica, 640* (suppl), 55–59.

Wittling, W., & Pflüger, M. (1990). Neuroendocrine hemisphere asymmetries: Salivary cortisol secretion during lateralized viewing of emotion-related and neutral films. *Brain and Cognition, 14*, 243–265.

Witvliet, C. V., Ludwig, T. E., & Vander Laan, K. L. (2001). Granting forgiveness or harboring grudges: Implications for emotion, physiology, and health. *Psychological Science, 12*, 117–123.

Wolfe, J. L., & Fodor, I. G. (1996). The poverty of privilege: Therapy with women of the "upper classes." *Women and Therapy, 18*, 73–89.

Wolfle, J., Hopffner, W., Sippell, W. G., Bramswig, J. H., Heidemann, P., Deib, D., et al. (2002). Complete virilization in congenital adrenal hyperplasia: Clinical course, medical management and disorder-related complications. *Clinical Endocrinology, 56*, 231–238.

Wolinsky, F. D., & Johnson, R. D. (1992). Perceived health status and mortality among older men and women. *Journal of Gerontology: Social Sciences, 47*, S304–S312.

Wong, A. H. C., Caspi, A., Williams, B., Craig, I. W., Houts, R., Ambler, A., et al. (2010). A longitudinal study of epigenetic variation in twins. *Epigenetics, 5*, 516–526.

Wong, A. H. C., Gottesman, I. I., & Petronis, A. (2005). Phenotypic differences in genetically identical organisms: The epigenetic perspective. *Human Molecular Genetics, 14*, R11–R18.

Wood, D., & Middleton, D. (1975). A study of assisted problem solving. *British Journal of Educational Psychology, 66*, 181–191.

Woodward, A. L. (1998). Infants selectively encode the goal object of an actor's reach. *Cognition, 69*, 1–34.

Woolley, M. E., & Grogan-Kaylor, A. (2006). Protective family factors in the context of neighborhood: Promoting positive school outcomes. *Family Relations, 55*, 93–104.

Worden, J. W. (1982). *Grief counseling and grief therapy: A handbook for the mental health practitioner*. New York: Springer.

World Alzheimer Report 2009. Alzheimer's disease international. Retrieved October 13, 2013 from http://www.alz.co.uk/research/files/WorldAlzheimerReport.pdf

Wortman, C. B., Battle, E. S., & Lemkau, J. P. (1997). Coming to terms with sudden, traumatic death of a spouse or child. In R. C. Davis & A. J. Lurigio (Eds.), *Victims of crime* (pp. 108–133). Thousand Oaks, CA: Sage.

Wortman, C. B., & Silver, R. C. (1987). Coping with irrevocable loss. In G. R. Vanden Bos & B. K. Bryant (Eds.), *Cataclysms, crises, and catastrophes: Psychology in action* (pp. 189–235). Washington, DC: American Psychological Association.

Wortman, C. B., & Silver, R. C. (1989). The myths of coping with loss. *Journal of Consulting and Clinical Psychology, 57*, 349–357.

Wortman, C. B., & Silver, R. C. (2001). The myths of coping with loss revisited. In M. S. Stroebe, R. O. Hansson, W. Stroebe, & H. Schut (Eds.), *Handbook of bereavement research: Consequences, coping, and care* (pp. 405–429). Washington, DC: American Psychological Association.

Wright, B. A. (1983). *Physical disability: A psychosocial approach*. New York: Harper & Row.

Wright, M. O., Fopma-Loy, J., & Oberle, K. (2012). In their own words: The experience of mothering as a survivor of childhood sexual abuse. *Development and Psychopathology, 24*, 537–552.

Wrosch, C., Heckhausen, J., & Lachman, M. E. (2006). Goal management across adulthood and old age: The adaptive value of primary and secondary control. In D. K. Mroczek & T. D. Little (Eds.), *Handbook of personality development* (pp. 399–421). Mahwah, NJ: Erlbaum.

Wrosch, C., & Schulz, R. (2008). Health-engagement control strategies and 2-year changes in older adults' physical health. *Psychological Science, 19*, 537–541.

Wrzesniewski, A., & Dutton, J. E. (2001). Crafting a job: Revisoning employees as active crafters of their work. *Academy of Management Review, 26*, 179–201.

Wyden, R. (2000). Steps to improve the quality of life for people who are dying. *Psychology, Public Policy, and Law, 6*, 575–581.

Wynn, K. (1992). Addition and subtraction by human infants. *Nature, 358*, 749–750.

Yasui, M., & Dishion, T. J. (2007). The ethnic context of child and adolescent problem behavior: Implications for child and family interventions. *Clinical Child and Family Review, 10*, 137–179.

Yates, M., & Youniss, J. (1996). A developmental perspective on community service in adolescence. *Social Development, 5*, 85–111.

Yatkin, U. S., & McClaren, D. S. (1970). The behavioral development of infants recovering from severe malnutrition. *Journal of Mental Deficiency Research, 14*, 25–32.

Yeh, C. J., Inman, A. G., Kim, A. B., & Okubo, Y. (2006). Asian American families' collectivistic coping strategies in response to 9/11. *Cultural Diversity and Ethnic Minority Psychology, 12*, 134–148.

Yin, T., Zhou, Q., & Bashford, C. (2002). Burden on family members: Caring for frail elderly: A meta-analysis of interventions. *Nursing Research, 51*, 199–208.

Yip, T., Seaton, E. K., & Sellers, R. M. (2006). African American racial identity across the lifespan: Identity status, identity content, and depressive symptoms. *Child Development, 77*, 1504–1517.

Yoshikawa, H., & Kalil, A. (2011). The effects of parental undocumented status on the developmental contexts of young children in immigrant families. *Child Development Perspectives, 5*, 291–297.

Youngblade, L. M., & Belsky, J. (1992). Parent-child antecedents of 5-year-olds' close friendships: A longitudinal analysis. *Developmental Psychology, 28*, 700–713.

Younger, A. J., Gentile, C., & Burgess, K. (1993). Children's perceptions of withdrawal: Changes across age. In K. H. Rubin & J. Asendorpf (Eds.), *Social withdrawal, inhibition, and shyness in childhood* (pp. 215–236). Hillsdale, NJ: Erlbaum.

Youth Risk Behavior Surveillance System, Centers for Disease Control and Prevention. (2008). *Youth online: Comprehensive results*. Retrieved from http://apps.nccd.cdc.gov/yrbss/CategoryQuestions.asp?Cat=4&desc=Sexual%20behaviors.

Yunger, J. L., Carver, P. R., & Perry, D. G. (2004). Does gender identity influence children's psychological well-being? *Developmental Psychology, 40*, 572–582.

Zabin, L. S., Hirsch, M. B., Smith, E. A., Streett, R., & Hardy, J. B. (1986). Evaluation of a pregnancy prevention program for urban teenagers. *Family Planning Perspectives, 18*, 119–126.

Zacks, R. T., & Hasher, L. (1994). Directed ignoring: Inhibitory regulation of working memory. In D. Dagenbach & T. H. Carr (Eds.), *Inhibitory mechanisms in attention, memory, and language* (pp. 241–264). San Diego, CA: Academic Press.

Zacks, R. T., Hasher, L., & Li, K. Z. H. (2000). Human memory. In F. I. M. Craik & T. A. Salthouse (Eds.), *The handbook of aging and cognition* (2nd ed., pp. 293–357). Mahwah, NJ: Erlbaum.

Zagar, R., Arbit, J., Sylvies, R., & Busch, K. G. (1991). Homicidal adolescents: A replication. *Psychological Reports, 67*, 1235–1242.

Zahn-Waxler, C., Cole, P. M., Welsh, J. D., & Fox, N. A. (1995). Psychophysiological correlates of empathy and prosocial behaviors in preschool children with problem behaviors. *Development and Psychopathology, 7*, 27–48.

Zahn-Waxler, C., Iannotti, R. J., Cummings, E. M., & Denham, S. (1990). Antecedents of problem behaviors in children of depressed mothers. *Development and Psychopathology, 2*, 349–366.

Zahn-Waxler, C., & Kochanska, G. (1990). The origins of guilt. In R. Thompson (Ed.),

The 36th Annual Nebraska Symposium on Motivation: Socioemotional development (pp. 183–258). Lincoln: University of Nebraska Press.

Zahn-Waxler, C., & Radke-Yarrow, M. (1982). The development of altruism: Alternative research strategies. In N. Eisenberg (Ed.), *The Development of prosocial behavior* (pp. 109–137). New York: Academic Press.

Zahn-Waxler, C., Radke-Yarrow, M., Wagner, E., & Chapman, M. (1992). Development of concern for others. *Developmental Psychology, 28,* 126–136.

Zal, H. M. (1992). *The sandwich generation: Caught between growing children and aging parents.* New York: Insight Books/Plenum Press.

Zaporozhets, A. V. (1986). *Izbrannye psychologicheskie trudy* [Selected Works in Psychology]. Moscow: Pedagogika.

Zarbatany, L., Hartmann, D. P., & Rankin, D. B. (1990). The psychological functions of preadolescent peer activities. *Child Development, 61,* 1067–1080.

Zeanah, C. H. (1996). Beyond insecurity: A reconceptualization of attachment disorders of infancy. *Journal of Consulting and Clinical Psychology, 64,* 42–52.

Zeanah, C. H., & Zeanah, P. D. (2001). Towards a definition of infant mental health. *Zero to three, 22,* 13–20.

Zeanah C. H., & Smyke, A. T. (2008). Attachment disorders in family and social context. *Infant Mental Health Journal, 29,* 219–233.

Zelazo, P. D., Anderson, J. E., Richler, J., Wallner-Allen, K., Beaumont, J. L., & Weintraub, S. (2013). NIH Toolbox Cognitive Function Battery (CFB): Measuring executive function and attention. *Monographs of the Society for Research in Child Development, 78* (Serial No. 309), 1–149.

Zelazo, P. D., & Carlson, S. M. (2012). Hot and cool executive function in childhood and adolescence: Development and plasticity. *Child Development Perspectives, 6,* 354–360.

Zelazo, P. D., & Cunningham, W. (2007). Executive function: Mechanisms underlying emotion regulation. In J. Gross (Ed.), *Handbook of emotion regulation* (pp. 135–158). New York: Guilford Press.

Zelazo, P. D., Hevlwig, C. C., & Lau, A. (1996). Intention, act, and outcome in behavioral prediction and moral judgment. *Child Development, 67,* 2478–2492.

Zelazo, P. D., Muller, U., Frye, D., & Marcovitch, S. (2003). The development of executive function in early childhood. *Monographs of the Society for Research in Child Development, 68* (Serial No. 274), 1–136.

Zhou, Q., Chen, S. H., & Main, A. (2012). Commonalities and differences in the research on children's effortful control and executive function; A call for an integrated model of self-regulation. *Child Development Perspectives, 6,* 112–121.

Zhu, Y., Zhang, L., Fan, J., & Han, S. (2007). Neural basis of cultural influence on self-representation. *NeuroImage, 34,* 1310–1326.

Zimmer-Gembeck, M. J., & Helfand, M. (2008). Ten years of longitudinal research on U.S. adolescent sexual behavior: Developmental correlates of sexual intercourse, and the importance of age, gender and ethnic background. *Developmental Review, 28,* 153–224.

Zimmerman, C. (2007). The development of scientific thinking skills in elementary and middle school. *Developmental Review, 27,* 172–223.

Zimmerman, F. J., & Christakis, D. A. (2007). Associations between content types of early media exposure and subsequent attentional problems. *Pediatrics, 120,* 986–992.

Zimmerman, F. J., Christakis, D. A., & Meltzoff, A. N. (2007). Associations between media viewing and language development in children under age 2 years. *Journal of Pediatrics, 151,* 364–368.

Zinnbauer, B. J., & Pargament, K. I. (2000). Working with the sacred: Four approaches to religious and spiritual issues in counseling. *Journal of Counseling and Development, 78,* 162–171.

Zinnbauer, B. J., Pargament, K. I., & Scott, A. B. (1999). The emerging meanings of religiousness and spirituality: Problems and prospects. *Journal of Personality, 67,* 889–920.

Ziol-Guest, K. M., & Kalil, A. (2012). Health and medical care among the children of immigrants. *Child Development, 83,* 1486–1493.

Zoellner, L. A., Rothbaum, B. O., & Feeny, N. C. (2011). PTSD not an anxiety disorder? DSM committee proposal turns back the hands of time. *Depression and Anxiety, 28,* 853–856.

Zosuls, K. M., Ruble, D. N., Bornstein, M. H., & Greulich, F. K. (2009). The acquisition of gender labels in infancy: Implications for gender-typed play. *Developmental Psychology, 45,* 688–701.

Zucker, K. J. (1999). Intersexuality and gender identity differentiation. *Annual Review of Sex Research, 10,* 1–69.

Zuckerman, M. (1979). *Sensation seeking: Beyond the optimal level of arousal.* Hillsdale, NJ: Erlbaum.

Author Index

Subject Index

Photo Credits